Ground Rules

A Celebration Of Test Cricket

Edited by
Barney Spender

Contents

FOREWORD
David Gower

It is all too easy to overlook the cricket grounds of this world and the part they play in the game. Let me put it this way: all of us that have ever wandered onto a cricket field, whatever our level of achievement on that or any other field, will know exactly what it is that sends the spirit soaring in anticipation of a great day's play.

Sometimes it is the setting alone that warms the heart. There are myriad beautiful private grounds around the world in this category, such as the late Sir Paul Getty's ground at Wormsley and Dave Mackay's at Constantia Uitsig with the mountains of Cape Town providing the backdrop, to name but two. Somehow it is impossible to avoid the link between such scenic venues and superlative hospitality, Sir Paul producing legendary lunches and Uitsig being home to vineyards and fine restaurants. What more could you ask for?

Unfortunately the major international grounds seldom come with such frills, though they make up for such shortcomings with an abundance of history and above all atmosphere. What is atmosphere? It is that expectant buzz that in the biggest of stadia, Eden Gardens or the Melbourne Cricket Ground, becomes a roar. It is what makes the best players in the world puff out their chests as they prepare to take on not just the man at the other end with the ball in his hand but the full might of the crowd as well. It is what makes lesser players sweat and tremble, fearful of failure. It can bring out the best and the worst in you.

For sheer weight of numbers you cannot beat the two stadia I have just mentioned. Eden Gardens will hold well over 100,000 of the keenest cricket fans in the world. The MCG, an expanding and changing super-stadium, can manage similar attendances for Australian Rules Football but only a mere 90,000 or so for cricket. Play well there and your reputation around Australia will rocket skywards.

My two favourite grounds, though, will always be Lord's and the Sydney Cricket Ground, grounds where the history of the game just oozes out of every part of every stand and every fixture and every fitting. Despite modern refurbishment you can still sense the ghosts of former players as you enter the dressing-rooms. If I ever presented myself at the Lord's pavilion somewhat the worse for wear, never of course for a Test match, I could at least console myself that it was nothing that the great Denis Compton had not done with infinitely more panache in days gone by. When meeting in the home dressing-room at the end of a hot day at the SCG to share a beer with a Chappell, a Lillee or a Marsh, the great players of my era, one could still imagine The Don, the great Don Bradman, sitting quietly in the corner plotting another triple-century.

There was always something extra special about the walk through the Long Room and out onto the pristine turf at Lord's. Nothing can beat that feeling as you walk to the crease in an Ashes Test, dreaming of a hundred – except of course the feeling as you make the return journey several hours later having actually made that century. Likewise at the SCG, where you know that the crowd as a whole would rather you did not make that hundred, the satisfaction of heading back to the old Victorian pavilion with three figures to your name is one that lasts a lifetime. And again I have to say that they will forgive you, respect you and love you for it too.

I might add, briefly, that we also all have our least favourite grounds. Mine was always the County Ground at Northampton for the simplest of reasons: my first class career average there was the sort of figure I would have preferred for a handicap if ever I had found the will to play golf in any real sense. Forget the splinters you got in your feet as you took the stairs down to the basement for a shower in the old pavilion and the odd bounces you always got on the football field and the walk to the pub outside the ground for lunch. They were all part of the character, and anyway it has all changed now, enormously so and much for the better.

Everyone will have a favourite and every ground will have its fans. There are plenty to go round and the best are all here in Ground Rules.

INTRODUCTION
Barney Spender

All the world's a stage
And all the men and women merely players.

As You Like It, William Shakespeare

The West Indian writer CLR James said that cricket is first and foremost a dramatic spectacle. If he is right, and given the twists of fortune that occur on any cricket field he is almost certainly is, the stages on which these dramas are played deserve some attention. For in the same way that today's actors draw inspiration from the knowledge that they are following in the footsteps of Edmund Kean or Lawrence Olivier when they take to the stage at Drury Lane or the Old Vic, then so should cricketers when they play a Test match.

Every cricket ground has its own appeal and history, whether it is the imposing hulk of the Melbourne Cricket Ground or an understated village green or school ground. I grew up with the tree-ringed Bigside ground at Pangbourne College in the leafy Berkshire countryside. It was a delightful place to play and watch the game but the atmosphere was heightened by the presence of a rickety pavilion decorated with black-and-white photographs of the every College XI since 1917, when the school was founded.

There were no famous cricketers among them but there was the ghostly presence of Percy John de Paravicini, a former Middlesex cricketer and England footballer, who was the bursar and cricket coach at the school when he died in 1921. His is no longer a famous name but for us he was a direct link to WG Grace and the golden age of cricket. As a Cambridge Blue between 1882 and 1885, he would have witnessed in some form the birth of Test cricket in England and he must have played with or against some of the giants of the era. To come down the steps of the pavilion was to march in de Paravicini's footsteps – and, by imaginative extension, Grace's.

College Park in Dublin, where I frittered away four years as an undergraduate, has much the same feeling, although the link to Grace is more direct.

According to Gerard Siggins, a man who knows everything that needs to be known – and then some – about Irish cricket, WG played there seven times.

On one occasion, he was bowled first ball by RM Gwynn, brother of the more celebrated Lucius who, according to folklore, turned down the offer to play for England against the Australians at Old Trafford in 1896 because he had a conflicting appointment for tea with an aged aunt that could not be broken. A fellow called Ranjitsinhji took his place and Lucius was never asked again.

Laze under one of the trees around the College Park boundary, close off your ears to the traffic that now rushes headlong down Nassau Street and it is easy to imagine the good doctor "blocking shooters to the boundary" and cussing the umpire who dares to give him out.

Such is the legacy that minor grounds create for future generations. Test-match grounds have the capacity to do the same thing, except on a much grander scale. It is the difference between the village hall and the Royal Opera House.

Which is your favourite Test-match ground? Ask yourself the question and then, when you think you have come up with an answer, ask yourself why. Is it because you have been going there since you were a child or where you caught your first glimpse of Test cricket? Perhaps you associate it with one great game – many Englishmen of a certain age believe Headingley to be the most magical ground in the world because of the events of a single Test in 1981. Presumably there are many Indians who think of Eden Gardens with similar fondness after their famous win against Australia in 2000-01.

Is it because the banter is witty without being coarse or that the old boy on the gate of the car park always turns a blind eye to your out-of-date pass?

Maybe it is simply a question of aesthetic beauty. Steve Waugh writes in his chapter that the Adelaide Oval is his favourite ground. "I love the old grandstands, how they blend together, the grass on the hill, the wooden scoreboard, the cathedrals overlooking the field," he says. He is so right: it is a stunning place to watch cricket, although my own love for the ground stems equally as much from the fact that it is the only place I ever saw The Don, sitting just two rows

behind me in the grandstand. Palpitations do not even come close.

Adelaide is not alone in admirers. Galle in Sri Lanka gets aesthetes in a lather as does Centurion in South Africa, a charming ground, even if it is the only one I know where play had to be abandoned in the middle of a sun-kissed afternoon because the smoke from the braais on the hill was drifting across the ground and choking the players.

Newlands in Cape Town, blessed with nature's gift of a ruddy great mountain, is another special setting although there are signs that the power of the buck and the need to find more space for bigger stands and corporate boxes may soon render it just another concrete bowl. Such development, all in the name of expanding the game, is a double-edged sword. Yes, you make more money but you also kill off a part of the soul.

Layer by layer, you strip away the uniqueness of the theatre until the imagination is all you do have left to link today's actors with those of the past.

And yet, take a place like the MCG and the concrete does not seem to matter. It bears absolutely no relation to the patch of turf that staged the first Test in 1877 and yet anyone who goes to watch a Test match there, yes even the Barmy Army, is virtually guaranteed to take a moment between songs and try to imagine how it might have looked when Charles Bannerman took guard that historic March morning. Players often proclaim an ignorance and disinterest in

the history of the game and yet I suspect that they too will take a deep breath on the morning of a match at the MCG and make silent promises to emulate or better the spirits of the past whose studs still echo down the corridors and out on to the field.

The MCG, however, is fairly unique in this sense: the honour of hosting the first-ever Test match can only fall to one ground. By and large, administrators have been too short-sighted and piecemeal in the development of their grounds. They should just be thankful that the players of all nationalities are filling their roles as entertainers better than ever.

If cricket is our dramatic spectacle, then the players are the actors who take their moment in the limelight. For some, such as Grace, Bradman, Spofforth and Hobbs, it can be a lifetime and beyond under the spotlight; others enjoy a brief but blazing cameo – I like the story of Samir Dighe, who made the first of his six appearances for India at the age of 32, and guided them to a famous victory against Australia in 2000-01 with an innings of, wait for it, 22 not out. Not exactly the heroics of a Kapil Dev but enough to win a match and, with it, claim a place in cricket history.

Others, sadly, such as the Australian Roy Park, whose sole Test at the MCG in 1920-21 comprised a first-ball duck and one over for nine runs, are consigned to playing cricket's equivalent of the spear-carrier. Poor old Park. His wife apparently dropped her knitting when he came in to bat, bent down to pick it up and missed his entire Test career.

Cricket, like a play, is nothing without its audience. The crowd at a Test match are much like any audience in the theatre, sometimes held in rapt silence, at other times hissing the pantomime villain.

The ambience of a ground is set by the groundlings in the cheap seats; the men, women, boys and girls who take the tickets and sell the scorecards; the ladies who peel their potatoes or do the knitting; the dozens of would-be accountants who score each ball from start to finish; the kids who prefer throw-downs in the car park; and, of course, the self-appointed poet laureates, songmeisters and comedians who, just like the scorers, keep it going all day long.

Ground Rules could celebrate the story of Test cricket through just about any of the 90 grounds that have hosted a Test match. The criteria is a simple one: which current grounds best illustrate the story of a country's cricket? There will doubtless be plenty of people who will ask why such-and-such was left out and so-and-so included. Such is life. Just as Steve Waugh suggests Adelaide, so everyone can make a case for their favourite ground.

In the north of England, there will be those who point to Old Trafford and Headingley; Australians will make a case for the Gabba or the Adelaide Oval, and in South Africa the Vaalies in Johannesburg will shake their heads at the omission of the Wanderers. As for the West Indies, each island will doubtless have its own thoughts on the subject.

Debate will probably be at its hottest in India where Mumbai is traditionally held to be the cradle of the country's cricket. The question there, however, is which ground to select. The Brabourne Stadium is no longer in use and the Wankhede Stadium has yet to build up the bank of heroic deeds that epitomise Eden Gardens in Kolkata and the MA Chidambaram Stadium in Chennai.

Let us hope that these grounds retain the power to charm the public and to inspire the players in equal measure, and continue to provide the link with the game's past that makes cricket the most fascinating game of all.

Cricket's equivalent of the parting of the Red Sea. England regained The Ashes in 1953. Denis Compton and Bill Edrich here seen leaving the field.

AUSTRALIA

Steve Waugh

One thing that I have found during my career in international cricket is that the great venues, the ones with the most history, the ones that have an atmosphere and feel of their own, these are the grounds that tend to bring exceptional performances from the great players. Grounds such as the Sydney Cricket Ground (SCG) and the Melbourne Cricket Ground (MCG) are special places to play. The big games there are rare events, and as a consequence everyone involved is more on edge before and during the play. There is plenty of inspiration in the air. It is the best players who are, as a rule, best able to control their emotions. That is why you see so many notable – even legendary – achievements at the great cricket grounds.

That is why, as I look at the history of cricket at the SCG and MCG, I will constantly be recalling the deeds of some of the game's greatest champions. I will be giving you two perspectives: one, very much a personal view, from my earliest memories of both grounds to the international matches of today; and two, a potted history, recalling many of the famous cricket moments that have been played out in Sydney and Melbourne. I'll be concentrating very much on the cricket, but I've witnessed major events in other sports at the SCG and MCG, and where they've had an impact on me, I'll share my memories.

The MCG predates the SCG by more than 20 years. The Melbourne Cricket Club obtained the lease for the area that became the MCG in September 1853, and developed the site to the point that by March 1856, the inaugural encounter between Victoria and New South Wales was played at an enclosed venue that was clearly the best cricket ground in the country. The initial first-class match at the SCG – again, Victoria v New South Wales – was not played until February 1878. Today, the MCG is dominated by the Great Southern Stand (built in the early 1990s), which extends all the way from one end of the ground to the other – in cricket terms from the point boundary on one side to the square-leg fence on the other. When a big crowd is in, the Great Southern Stand accentuates the stadium's Coliseum effect.

Unfortunately, the way the SCG has evolved over the years, the ground is something of a mismatch, especially so over where The Hill used to be. Still, Sydney is a terrific place to play. When it is packed, the fans seem to be in on top of you

and the noise that is generated is really intense; more intense than in Melbourne, if only because at the MCG the boundary fences, and thus the crowd, are that little bit further away.

My brief is to study the history of big cricket at Australia's two oldest Test-match venues but we should not forget the other grounds in Australia which have so much in the way of history and character. Brisbane has had two grounds, the Exhibition Ground staging two Tests in the days back yonder before giving way to the Brisbane Cricket Ground – or the Gabba as it is better known. No matter what else happened here, and plenty has, the Gabba was immortalised during the famous 1960-61 series when the Test against Frank Worrell's West Indians ended in a tie, just one of two in Test history.

The WACA in Perth only came into the reckoning as a Test match venue in 1970-71 but it has proved itself as a home for some breathtaking cricket, most often coming from the fast bowlers who thrive on the fast tracks and a bit of help from the Fremantle Doctor. It is no surprise that it has produced quicks of the calibre of Graham McKenzie, Dennis Lillee, Bob Massie, Bruce Reid and Terry Alderman. The Bellerive Oval in Hobart is one of the most beautiful Test grounds in the world and only time will tell how Australia's newest venues in Darwin and Cairns will take to the staging of Test cricket.

I must reveal however that, high as I regard all ,these grounds my favourite in Australia – purely from a playing perspective – is actually in Adelaide. I love the old grandstands at the Adelaide Oval, how they blend together, the grass on the hill, the wooden scoreboard, the cathedrals overlooking the field. The outfield is like carpet, the pitch is always excellent and not only are the dressing rooms good, the viewing area is outstanding as well. And it is a bit more laid back; in a way I imagine Test cricket once was like everywhere. I am not suggesting the Adelaide faithful don't take their cricket as seriously, just that that there isn't that hype that can sometimes dominate the biggest games in Sydney and Melbourne.

But then, maybe the SCG and the MCG deserve that hype. You be the judge.

SYDNEY CRICKET GROUND

y first memory of the Sydney Cricket Ground is going out there with my team-mates from the Panania-East Hills Under-10s cricket side. Our coach was our chaperon and, after playing a match in the morning, we travelled to the ground in the back of his ute to see New South Wales play South Australia in a Sheffield Shield encounter. It was November 1973. Inevitably, my memories of that day have been clouded by time, but I do recall that we sat on The Hill and I was taken by the greenness of it all – not just where we sat, but also the playing surface and the roofs of the grandstands. At the northern end were two large modern stands, named after giants of the game, the Bradman Stand and the MA Noble Stand. Closer to our right was the Bob Stand; on the far side of the ground were the Members, Ladies and Brewongle Stands. Behind the bowler's arm at the southern end was the Sheridan Stand.

Eleven summers later, I would be the last player to hit a six into that Sheridan Stand. I hit two of them in my maiden first-class match at the SCG, against Victoria. A few weeks after that, as we walked out for the start of what proved to be a thrilling Shield final against Queensland, we heard a blast, and the grand old stand imploded in a cloud of dust. In its place they would build a taller, new-age construction, without even a touch of green, to match similar stands that had been put where the Bob Stand and old Brewongle Stand had been. Soon, The Hill would be gone as well. Instead of benches and green grass you had reserved seats, which reduced the capacity – no more days where the patrons were packed in like sardines, many standing shoulder to shoulder – but helped security-wise, and stopped the hooligan element causing problems. However, like a lot of grounds around the world, the SCG has lost some of its character and uniqueness because of the coldness of its modern grandstands.

The ground needs its history and memories to keep it sacred. Back in 1973, I recall the immediate feeling that the SCG was a special place, and how I enjoyed the barrackers who were brave enough to yell good-naturedly at the players. The ground

A full house for the opening Test in the 1901-02 Ashes series. The England captain Archie MacLaren made 116 but the revelation was Sydney Barnes who was plucked from league cricket for the tour. Barnes took five for 65 in the first innings as Australia crumbled to defeat by an innings and 124 runs. Revenge was swift, however, as they won the next four Tests to retain the Ashes.

seemed so huge. The New South Wales openers, Marshall Rosen (now a NSW selector) and Ron Crippin, made runs that day, as did Doug Walters. Dougie seemed to be everyone's favourite; he quickly became mine.

Two years on, I made my Test debut, so to speak, when dad took my twin brother Mark and me to the third day of the Test against the West Indies. A study today of the scorecard shows that the day was dominated by Greg Chappell, who made 182 not out, the second of his four Test centuries at the ground. However, my main memory is of Aussie keeper Rod Marsh hitting a pull shot smack in the middle of his bat, but being caught spectacularly, one-handed with his body parallel to the ground, by Lance Gibbs in front of square leg. We were sitting in the Sheridan Stand and I was entranced by how much more vibrant the ground was with a full house in. The green grass of The Hill was now a mass of colour, bare backs, noise, energy and – late in the day – the odd brawl or two as well.

The story goes that when the young Don Bradman was taken to the fifth Ashes Test of 1920-21 at the SCG by his father, to see Charlie Macartney make 170 as Australia completed a unique five-nil clean sweep of the series, he said flatly on the way home that he would not rest until he too played at the ground. I cannot say I had the same determination after that West Indies Test. But I knew that it would be fantastic to be out there, and I was in awe of the great players – how fast were Andy Roberts and Michael Holding, and yet Greg Chappell seemed to handle them with ease. It was the same two years later, when I saw Jeff Thomson bowling to Sunil Gavaskar. I was in the Bob Stand, side on to the pitch, and Thommo was so quick, yet the Indian master's footwork was exemplary, his evasive skills superb. Earlier that day, Kim Hughes had hit Bishan Bedi, the Indian captain, a slow, shrewd, left-arm spinner, into the clock tower above the Members Stand. It was an astonishing blow, but Bedi then bowled Hughes immediately with a well-flighted, beautifully disguised arm ball. A victory for brains over brawn.

A swish of the bat and Harold Larwood leaves the crease after making 98 as a nightwatchman in the final Test of the infamous Bodyline series in 1932-33. Larwood was the scourge of Australia's batsmen taking 33 wickets as England regained the Ashes with a four-one win. Unfortunately, he was to shoulder the blame for the strain in diplomatic relations between the two countries and never played for England again.

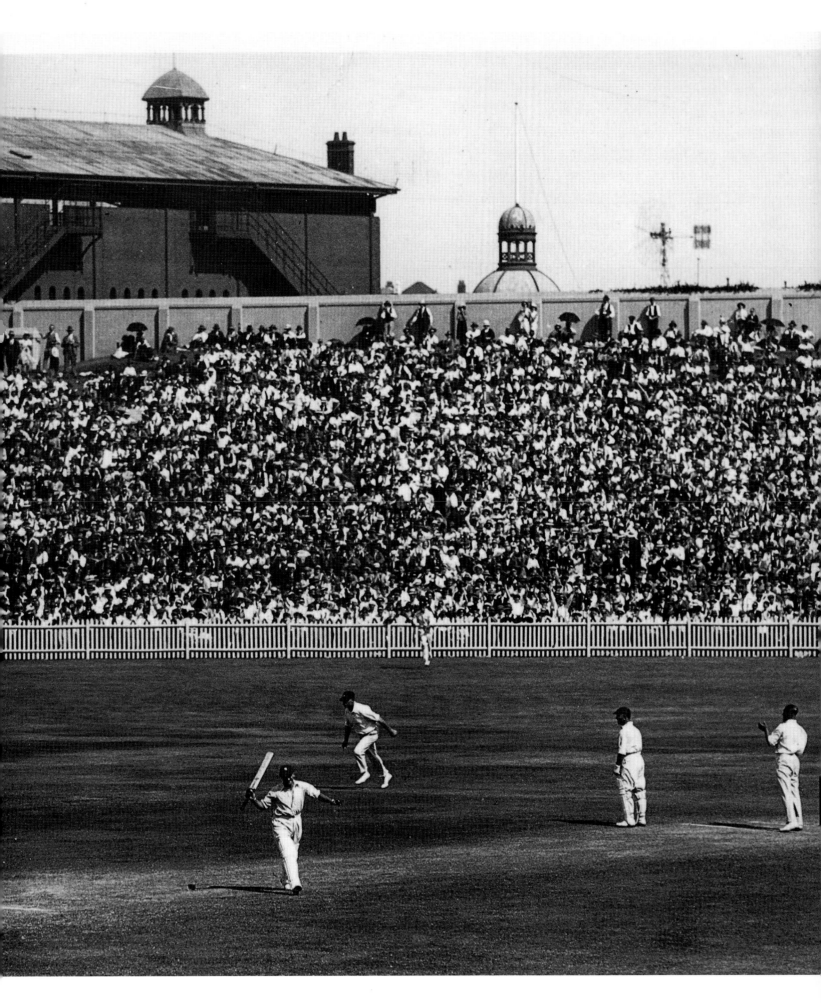

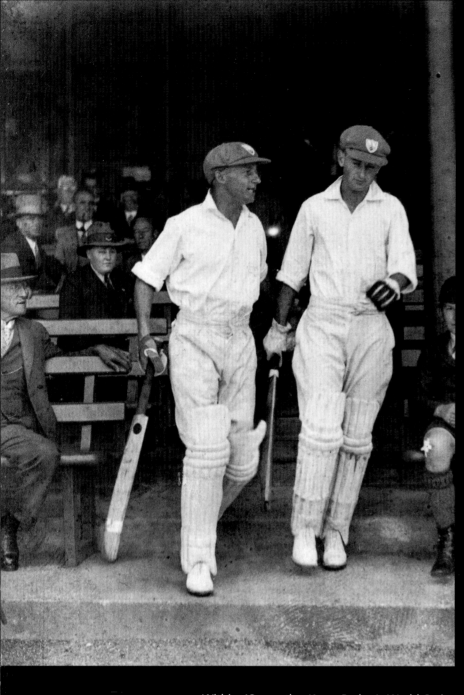

Garisto, floored the Aussie striker Ray Baartz with a karate chop. Poor Baartz never played again. The rage of the spectators around me when that disgraceful incident occurred, and the joy of these same men at the full-time whistle, will stay with me forever.

So my affinity with the great ground goes back 30 years. Of course, the history of the place goes back much further. The first cricket Test at the SCG was played in February 1882 – a five-wicket victory for the locals – and since then the ground has been host to many of cricket's most famous moments. Of all of the remarkable cricket feats that have occurred at the SCG, if I could have been at just one I would choose Stan McCabe's epic 187 not out against the English Bodyline attack in the first Test of 1932-33. The mere statistics are extraordinary – McCabe scored his runs from 233 balls and smashed 51 of a last-wicket stand of 55 in 33 minutes – but they tell nothing of the electric atmosphere, the way the little right-hander hooked and pulled Harold Larwood and Bill Voce's bouncers bravely and often, the way his Sydney crowd roared him on.

More generally, in my favourite dream, I am sitting on the grass of The Hill at a packed Sydney Cricket Ground, watching Don Bradman carve into an English attack. It is a beautiful summer's day and the operators in the old scoreboard at the back of The Hill are working overtime as The Don goes to another superb hundred. When he gets there, the spectators around me – among them the legendary "Yabba", Stephen Gascoigne, originator of lines such as "Send 'im down a piano, see if 'e can play that" – are on their feet, as hats are thrown in the air. Maybe this was the day Bradman made his 100th first-class hundred, against India, in November 1947.

Within 12 months, Kerry Packer's World Series Cricket had brought night cricket to the ground, and I had come to appreciate the SCG in all its forms – the Tests, the one-dayers and the Shield, and also its place as the headquarters for rugby league, rugby union and for major soccer internationals. One of my strongest memories is of a soccer friendly between Australia and Uruguay in 1974, played just six weeks before the two teams appeared at the World Cup Finals in West Germany. Uruguay were two-time winners of the World Cup and had reached the semi-finals in 1970 but this day they were beaten two-nil by the Socceroos and shamed themselves when their defender, Louis

Strangely, Bradman's Test record in Sydney is not, by his standards, brilliant. In eight Tests, he scored "only" two hundreds and averaged "just" 58.58. By contrast, in 11 Tests at the Melbourne Cricket Ground he made nine hundreds and averaged 128.54. Bradman's finest Test performance at the SCG was probably his 234 against Wally Hammond's England team in 1946-47. That was the Test in which Australian opening bat Sid Barnes also made 234, reputedly getting himself out on that score, same as his captain, so the innings would be better remembered. Away from the Test arena, however, Bradman certainly made his share of runs in Sydney, most notably in early January 1930.

On January 3, in a Shield match between New South Wales and Queensland, 16 wickets fell for 361 runs. In *The Sun*, the former Test captain Monty Noble wrote of the "extra lift of the pitch" the bowlers had been able to generate, while also mentioning that balls were liable to "skid through", creating uncertainty in the minds of the batsmen. One of those to fail was 21-year-old Bradman, who was the first wicket to fall, caught behind for three off a delivery from Alec Hurwood that "swung appreciably".

Day two began with Queensland needing 110 runs for a first-innings victory, with four wickets still in hand. After a brave chase, they finished eight runs short, but then came out and attacked the home team's top order. Bradman was dropped back to number three, perhaps to shield him from the new ball. Alan Fairfax, scorer of 65 on his Test debut against England 12 months before, crawled to ten in 40 minutes, as two wickets fell for 33. Hurwood, soon to be selected in the Australian team for the 1930 Ashes tour, was bowling, in the words of AG Moyes in the *Telegraph*, "plenty of good ones". The Queenslanders were like "prancing colts in the field".

What good did it do them? Bradman scored 452 not out. The innings, a new record for first-class cricket, took just 415 minutes. The slowest of his nine fifties took 58 minutes. When Alan Kippax, the NSW captain, declared, Queensland immediately collapsed to 70 for seven at stumps, all out for 84 the next day, which suggested that there might still have been something in the wicket. Of course, they were also seriously exhausted from fielding to The Don.

Left: Don Bradman (left) and Stan McCabe leave the Members' pavilion on the way out to the middle. McCabe's most famous innings was the 187 not out he made in the 1932-33 Ashes series – generally regarded as the best innings against Bodyline.

Centre: Syd Gregory was the ultimate SCG man having been born on the ground in 1870 – his father Ned, who played in the very first Test match, was the curator at the time. Gregory, only five foot tall, is recognised as the first great cover point fielder, and made 201 against England at the SCG in 1894-95.

Above: Victor Trumper: one of the early greats who made three centuries against England at the SCG, the last in 1911-12. Three years later, aged just 38, he died of Bright's disease.

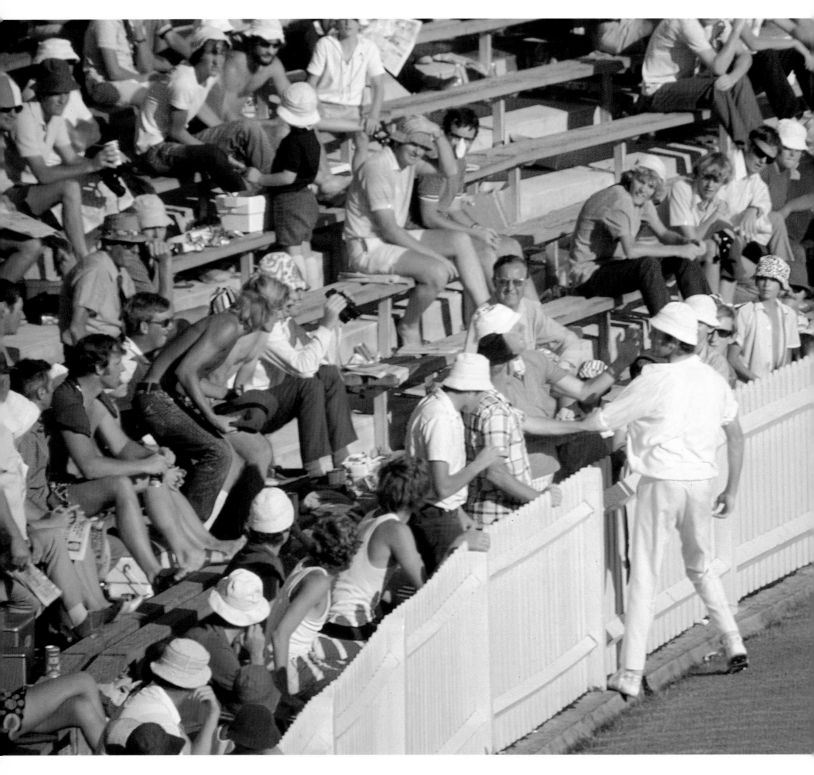

Trouble flares at the SCG in the final Test of the 1970-71 series as England fast bowler John Snow is grabbed by a member of the crowd. The incident resulted in Ray Illingworth taking his team off the field. Unfortunately for Australia, he brought them back to complete a 62-run win. England won the series two-nil with Snow taking 31 wickets.

Twelve months earlier, Bradman had been 12th man (for the only time in his Test career) when Hammond made 251 in his first Test in Sydney. The great Englishman obviously enjoyed Sydney. He belted four hundreds in Test matches there – 251 in 1928-29, then 112 and 101 in 1932-33, and 231 not out in 1936-37 – achieving an average of 256.67 in his Tests at the SCG before the Second World War. He made only one and 37 in Sydney in 1946-47, but he was 43

he was initially received as someone akin to royalty. On both tours, however, he got himself into on-field blues with umpires and opponents and was derided in some quarters. So highly regarded was the gentlemanly Hobbs that in 1928-29, his final Test in Sydney, the home crowd made a special presentation as he made a lap of honour during a break in play. In 24 minutes just before lunch in the Sydney Test in 1946-47, Hutton played one of the finest short innings in Test history – a knock of 37 made in a style that had veteran spectators recalling the days of Victor Trumper. For long periods in 1970-71, Boycott seemed undismissable; some critics thought him a little staid but, nine summers later, he was outstanding in Sydney in one-day internationals against Australia and the West Indies.

Of course, these are not the only English batsmen to play famous innings at the ground. Consider these:

In the first Test of 1903-04, RE "Tip" Foster made 287 on his debut. This score remains the highest made in a Test at the SCG, the highest made by an Englishman in a Test in Australia and the highest by anyone in their first Test. All up, Foster batted for a minute short of seven hours, but his last 127 runs were scored at better than a run a minute, an effort that gave the Poms a first-innings lead of 292. Not that the Test was over, for the immortal Trumper came out to play one of his most special innings, an unbeaten 185 – the first of his three Test centuries in Sydney – that led to a tense finish. Chasing 194, the visitors slipped to 82 for four before finally getting home by five wickets.

In the third Test of 1965-66, the unheralded Bob Barber smashed the Aussie attack for 185, made from 272 balls, dominating an opening stand of 234 with Boycott, who scored 84. This was Barber's only Test hundred and remains the highest score by an Englishman on the first day of an Ashes Test.

In 1990-91, Mike Atherton compiled the slowest hundred in the history of Ashes Tests, defending for more than seven hours, before David Gower came out and played a beautiful innings of 123. The contrast could not have been more stark, yet both innings were important; indeed, it was Atherton who was later named Man of the Match. This was Gower's only Test century in Sydney, but he still scored more Test

years old by then and by all accounts hardly the master batsman he had been between 1928 and 1938.

I sometimes wonder who was the greatest English batsman to play in Sydney. Think of the champions who have played there – WG Grace … Jack Hobbs … Hammond … Len Hutton … Geoff Boycott. Grace was the game's first superstar and when he came to Australia in 1873-74 and 1891-92

runs at the SCG than at any other ground outside England, and in this Test he batted as gracefully and stylishly as I had ever seen him.

In 2002-03, Michael Vaughan played a fantastic innings of 183 that set up England's only Test victory of the summer. This was Vaughan's third hundred of the series, made in a style that suggested he could even be the best English batsman I have opposed during my career.

For all these masterpieces, I am sure none of them represent the best innings recorded by an overseas batsman at the SCG. That honour, in my view, must go to Brian Lara, who in 1992-93 played with a surety and brilliance against Australia for 277, made from just 372 balls. Like Foster, it was Lara's maiden Test century, and only ended when he was run out; otherwise he might still be batting today. Only Hutton (364 at The Oval in 1938), Foster and VVS Laxman (281 at Kolkata in 2001) have made bigger scores against Australia. In Lara's case it wasn't so much that he

regularly beat the field but that he consistently bisected the gaps between fieldsmen. You always want to get a batsman out, but in a situation where an opponent is performing as well as Lara was in that innings, there is part of you that wants to sit back and admire the way he is playing. His placement and power were unbelievable.

Incidentally, in that same Test I scored what was probably the most important hundred of my Test career. Batting at number three, I made an even hundred, after word had reached me that if I didn't get runs then I was going to be dropped. I couldn't complain about the pressure, I needed the runs. Had I been omitted, I might not have made the 1993 Ashes tour, which is when I finally cemented my place in the Test XI. Like other Australian batsmen of the time, such as Matthew Hayden, Justin Langer and Damien Martyn, it might have taken me years to force my way back in, but for that hundred.

The other great batting performance at the SCG by a West Indian in my experience was the 143 by Desmond Haynes in 1988-89, made out of an innings total of just 256. Batting almost exclusively against the spinners, Haynes's footwork and judgment were superb as he crafted a defensive innings – five-and-a-quarter-hours in all – that both captains afterwards said was among the finest they had seen. This was the Test made famous by Allan Border's freakish bowling effort, when he took 11 for 96 (seven for 46 and four for 50). In 100 previous Test appearances AB had taken 16 wickets with his slightly round-arm left-arm finger spin, and in the preceding three Tests he had bowled two overs. But Haynes apart, the West Indies couldn't play spin bowling. The NSW duo, Bob "Dutchy" Holland and Murray Bennett, had spun them to defeat four years earlier; now AB did the same. The pitch was turning square, and our skipper landed them in the right spot. He didn't like bowling himself, but he was actually no mug with the ball. And in this Test, everything went his way.

Strangely, AB might have taken a "ten-for" in a Test in Sydney, but he never scored a Test century there, a crazy stat when you think he scored Test hundreds at 14 different venues, including all the other mainland Test grounds in Australia. Still, the SCG was the place where he scored his first Test half-century (60 not out against England in 1978-79), won his first Test as captain (1984-85 against the West Indies again) and scored his 10,000th Test run (1992-93 v the West Indies). It was also the place where he got one of his most important victories as Australian skipper, against Mike Gatting's England side in 1986-87. This was the "Peter Who" Test, when the off-spinner Peter Taylor was picked from obscurity, after just six first-class appearances and only one that summer, to take eight wickets in the match – which Australia won with the last ball of the penultimate over, bowled by our leggie Peter Sleep.

On that dramatic last day I dismissed Gatting, caught and bowled, for 96, and I remember Gatt being really cheesed off that I had got him out. It was a big breakthrough game for Australia and for me – I scored 73 in our second innings, my third half-century of the series, and secured that vital wicket, which made me feel a little more comfortable about my place in the side. And it was my first Test win, in my 13th Test (the previous 12 had yielded one tie, three losses and eight draws), at a time when the Australian team didn't believe we could win too many Tests. It was a far cry from the ultra-confident Aussie squad of more recent seasons.

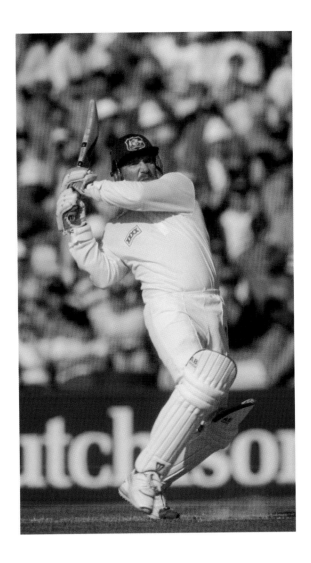

AB might never have scored a Test hundred in Sydney, but many of the game's greatest players certainly have, including legends such as KS Ranjitsinhji, Herbert Sutcliffe, George Headley, Peter May, Graeme Pollock, Gary Sobers and Sachin Tendulkar. Among Australian century-makers are names such as George Giffen, Joe Darling, Clem Hill, Warwick Armstrong, Keith Miller, Neil Harvey and Bill Lawry. And since 1985-86, from my vantage points out in the middle and in the home dressing-room, I have seen David Boon, Dean Jones, Mark Taylor, Greg Matthews, Michael Slater, Mark Waugh, Justin Langer, Ricky Ponting,

Two captains who turned Australia into the world power.
Allan Border (above) brought Australia the World Cup and led them in 93 consecutive Tests between 1984-85 and 1994, while his successor Mark Taylor (left), seen here taking Mark Ramprakash at slip to break the record for most catches, captained the team in 50 Tests before handing over to Steve Waugh.

Matthew Hayden, Damien Martyn and Adam Gilchrist all make hundreds in Sydney.

Of them all, maybe Slats's effort against England in January 1999 was the pick of them: he dominated our second innings at a time when his team-mates were falling around him. His score of 123 represented 66.84 per cent of the innings total, the second best of all time behind Charles Bannerman's 67.34 per cent; he made 165 retired hurt out of 251 in cricket's very first Test. It was a spectacular innings to watch, but more importantly it was an individual performance that determined the outcome of the match. The innings that do that are the truly great ones.

Two of the best innings ever seen at the SCG.

Above: Michael Vaughan made three fine hundreds during the 2002-03 Ashes series including 183 in Sydney.

Right: Michael Slater's muscular 123 against England in 1998-99 represented 66.84 per cent of the Australian total.

I must write a few more words about another of the Sydney century-makers – Dougie Walters – a personal favourite, of course, but also the only man to score three Test hundreds on the ground in one season (versus the West Indies in 1968-69) and also the only man to score a double-century and a century in the same Sydney Test (242 and 103 in the fifth Test of that 1968-69 summer). By 1974-75, as Ian Chappell's great team – featuring Lillee and Thommo, Marsh, Greg Chappell, et al – began to dominate England, Dougie was just about the most popular cricketer to play for Australia since the days of Miller, maybe even since Bradman. He never played to the crowd, and had a technique that was somewhat fallible, but he was always the entertainer, and seemed to be a very normal, very humble kind of guy, the sort of bloke you would like to have a beer with, or play backyard cricket with. And every so often he would produce an innings of rare genius that justified our loyal support for him. Twice in Test cricket and once against Gary Sobers' Rest of the World XI in Melbourne in 1971-72, he scored a century in a

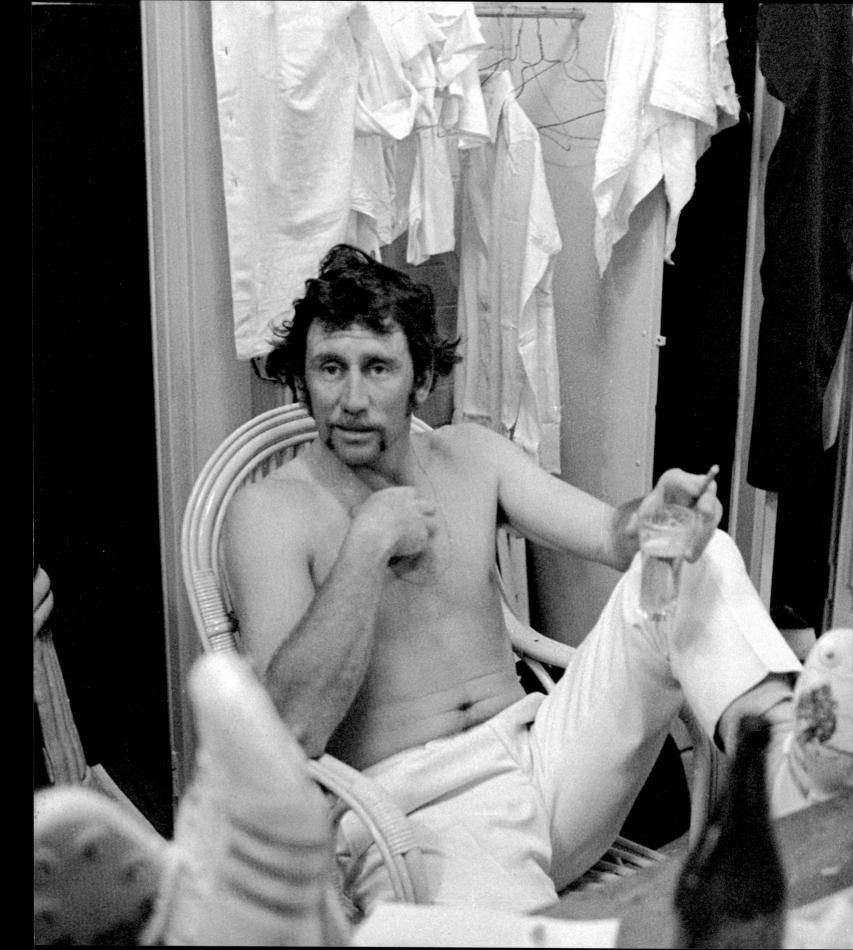

session. Every Australian cricket fan born before 1966 remembers where they were when he hit Bob Willis for six to reach his hundred at the WACA Ground in Perth in 1974-75. During that series, in Sydney (the epicentre of his acclaim), the lads in the outer renamed The Hill "The Doug Walters Stand". To me, a very impressionable eight-year-old, that was the ultimate honour.

The Sydney crowd has not always been in such good humour. Way back in February 1880, in a match between New South Wales and Lord Harris' England XI, they rioted after the local champion Billy Murdoch, was given out, run out, by the Victorian umpire George Coulthard. The fact that the ump was from Melbourne, that he had been invited to Sydney by Lord Harris, that there was heavy betting taking place, that the New South Wales captain Dave Gregory refused to send out a new batsman, and that the good Lord's attempts to placate the angry crowd were perceived by some to be a little patronising, led to a crowd invasion. An estimated 2,000 of the 10,000 crowd poured onto the field, and some of the players including Harris, were physically attacked. Coulthard seemed lucky to make it off the pitch alive, and eventually play was abandoned for the day, with the angry mob still on both sides of the fence. The other umpire that day was Edmund Barton, later Australia's first Prime Minister.

Twenty-five years later, in the same Test that RE Foster made his 287, there was an angry demonstration after the crack left-hander Clem Hill was run out in Australia's second innings. At the time Hill and Victor Trumper were mounting a brave fightback – Trumper was on his way to a century in just 94 minutes – until Hill was run out attempting a fifth run on an overthrow. Three glorious Trumper square-cuts, a peerless off-drive and four byes through the keeper had already raised 20 runs from the over so you can imagine the crowd's mood swing, from ecstasy at all the runs to devastation at the fall of wicket ... to anger when they realised that Hill was very unhappy with the decision. Umpire Crockett, a Victorian like Coulthard, was roundly hooted, and bottles and other rubbish were lobbed onto the field, to the point that the England captain Pelham Warner, was reluctant to continue.

The sweet taste of success. Ian Chappell savours the moment after his 1974-75 Australian team has just beaten England by 171 runs to win the Ashes.

Unlike the Lord Harris riot, no spectators jumped the fence. Likewise, there was no crowd invasion in the seventh Ashes Test of 1970-71. But this time there was an altercation on the boundary fence between a drunken spectator and a player. The shrewd England captain, Ray Illingworth, had quickly recognised that in his fast bowler, John Snow, he had easily the most lethal strike weapon in either side, and he backed the great but temperamental fast bowler through the series to the point that Snow took 31 wickets. In the seventh Test, when umpire Lou Rowan warned Snow about bowling bouncers, Illingworth very publicly supported his fast man, and then took his team from the field when Snow was grabbed by a fan who had stumbled down to the boundary from the old "Paddo" Hill (the site of the Bradman Stand, opened three years later). Spectators threw bottles onto the field. When the ground was cleared of debris, the Englishmen came back to win the Test and the series, and Illingworth was chaired from the field by his grateful team-mates.

Snow's efforts in this Test series were as magnificent as had been the performances of two previous English fast bowlers – Larwood in the Bodyline series and Frank Tyson in 1954-55. In the Test that McCabe made famous with his epic 187 not out, Larwood took ten wickets (five for 96 and five for 28) on a pitch that was too benign for an Australian attack that included Bill O'Reilly. In the fifth Test, also in Sydney, he took another five wickets (making it 33 for the series) before breaking down with a foot injury. And he also scored 98 as a nightwatchman. Footage of Larwood bowling during the Bodyline series gives a guide to how quick and nasty he was – you can see that the keeper is going back with the ball as he takes it, and that he has little time to adjust as the bouncers fly through.

Astonishingly, though Tyson is still regarded as one of the fastest bowlers of all time, the 1954-55 series is the only one in which he had any impact at all. And ironically, his effort came after the Englishmen were humiliated in the opening Test, when Len Hutton chose an all-pace attack at the Gabba, sent the home side in, and watched Neil

"Ashes to Ashes, Dust to dust
If Lillee don't get him, Thommo must"

This time it is Dennis Lillee who "gets" England's Keith Fletcher during the 1974-75 Ashes series.

Harvey and Arthur Morris score big hundreds as Australia made 601 for eight declared on their way to an innings victory. Tyson came back in the second Test to take ten wickets, including six for 85 in the second innings. Only Harvey, who made a heroic unbeaten 92 on the final day, stood up to him. Then in the third Test, in Melbourne, he took another nine wickets, including seven for 27 on the final day, as England went two-one up (that was the Test where the pitch was secretly and illegally watered by groundstaff on the rest day, to stop it from breaking up). Another victory in Adelaide – Tyson three for 85 and three for 47 – and the Ashes were retained.

The SCG pitch has changed its character in my lifetime. One of my great regrets is that I didn't see "live" Lillee and Thomson terrorising the Englishmen in 1974-75. But the TV coverage was enjoyable enough, as are the photographs of batsmen such as Tony Greig, Keith Fletcher and John Edrich ducking and jumping as they tried to stand up to the flyers. This couldn't have happened at the SCG when I started playing first-class cricket on it, because by then the soil was very crumbly, there was no grass on it, and the pitch was a spinner's paradise. This was not so good for quicks, especially for the great West Indian fast bowlers of that decade, who were dominant almost everywhere else in the cricket world but vulnerable in Sydney. The one member of their troupe who remained a threat whatever the conditions was Malcolm Marshall, a great professional and a great bloke, too.

In more recent times, the SCG deck has got back to how it was in the mid-1970s, quicker and with more bounce. Yet it remains a haven for the quality spinners, as our leg-spinners Shane Warne and Stuart MacGill have demonstrated in recent years. A study of the records shows that five bowlers have taken 12 wickets in a Test at the SCG.

CTB Turner, 12 for 87 v England, 1887-88

Charles Turner was nicknamed "The Terror", but today he would be described as a medium-pacer at best, bowling as he did off-cutters and off-spinners that would zip through and sometimes cut back severely on the pitches of the day. During his final Test, the fourth Test of the 1894-95 Ashes series, in Sydney, Turner became the first Australian to take 100 Test wickets. He finished with 101 at 16.53. Earlier in that same Test England's Johnny Briggs had become the first bowler to reach the 100 Test wickets milestone. Three years earlier, Briggs had taken a Test hat trick on the SCG.

HV Hordern, 12 for 175 v England, 1911-12

Herbert "Ranji" Hordern was Australia's first great leg-spinner. He only played seven Tests, but took 46 wickets in those matches, including 28 in three Tests at the SCG, before withdrawing from big-time cricket to concentrate on his profession as a dentist. Like Warne, one of Hordern's great strengths was his superb control – from a long run he rarely bowled a loose ball. "A master of his craft," the great cricket commentator AG "Johnnie" Moyes wrote in 1959. "Many who saw him and Mailey and Grimmett reckoned that he was the best."

Imran Khan, 12 for 165 for Pakistan, 1976-77

Eight years after this Test, Imran was a team-mate of mine in the Sheffield Shield final we won by one wicket over Queensland. A great all-rounder and an excellent captain, Imran stunned Greg Chappell's Australian team back in January 1977 with a dynamic spell of fast bowling, six wickets in each innings, in a performance that marked a change in the world cricket order. I don't think we in Australia really rated Pakistani cricket as being top class until this Test. Sure, they had some outstanding cricketers, but they couldn't match us as a team. But when Imran spearheaded Pakistan to a decisive eight-wicket win, we knew we could no longer underrate teams and cricketers from the sub-continent any longer.

SK Warne, 12 for 128 v South Africa, 1993-94

By the time South Africa arrived in Australia for their first post-apartheid tour, everyone knew Warney was the next big thing. The previous winter he had been fantastic in England, starting the series with the famous delivery that knocked Mike Gatting over at Old Trafford. At times against South Africa in Sydney, both in 1993-94 and four years later – when he took 11-109, including his 300th Test wicket – he was almost unplayable. He hardly bowled a bad ball, while putting a massive amount of spin on the ball and offering plenty of variations through leggies, flippers and top-spinners. His control was such that we were able to constantly put the batsmen under pressure with attacking fields. I remember thinking during the Test he reached 300 (my 100th Test) that he couldn't bowl any better; Warney at his top must be close to the greatest bowler, slow or fast, to ever play the game. Unfortunately our batting let us down in this match and Warney ended up on the losing side.

SCG MacGill, 12 for 107 v England, 1998-99

How must England have felt before the start of this series when they learnt that Warney, one of their chief bogeymen for the previous three Ashes series, was out for the first few Tests because of shoulder surgery? It must have given them a boost but we were able to bring in as his replacement a leggie who wasn't far behind Shane at all. Stuey didn't play in the second Test in Perth, but he still had 15 wickets after three games, before dominating the final match of the series. Warney was back for this match, but even he had to take a backseat as Magilla took five for 57 in the first innings, seven for 50 in the second.

Also among the bowlers to take ten wickets in a Test at the SCG are such famous names as the "Demon" Fred Spofforth, George Lohmann, George Giffen, Maurice Tate, Clarrie Grimmett and Glenn McGrath. And let's not forget the South African workhorse, Fanie de Villiers, who in spite of Warne's magnificent bowling, led his team to a famous five-run victory in the second Test of 1993-94. That Test was a thriller but probably not quite as dramatic as the Ashes Test played a mere 99 years earlier. What a spectacle that game must have been. It ended in an England victory, after Australia had led on the first innings by 261 runs and enforced the follow-on. Syd Gregory (201) had made the first Test double-century in Australia and Giffen hit 161 after Aussie captain Jack Blackham won the toss, but England's fightback on days four and five left Blackham's men needing 177 to win. At stumps on day five they were 113 for two, Giffen and Joe Darling at the crease, and some of the Poms went out on the grog that night, sure that the game was lost. But a fierce rainstorm overnight saturated the pitch, and after his captain sobered him up under a cold shower in the morning, Yorkshire's Bobby Peel came out and took five wickets as Australia lost their last eight wickets on a sticky for just 36.

What Peel might have made of one-day cricket and night cricket we can only imagine. Being a pragmatic Yorkshireman, he would definitely have adapted to it; being a great bowler he would almost certainly have been successful in it. The thing for me about the shorter form of the game is that it has opened cricket up to a lot of people who otherwise might not have become interested in the sport. Now, many more women follow the sport. Night cricket is a different game, more of a social event, there for the spectators and the treasurers who have to balance the books. The lights add to the theatre. Even now, 25 years on from the first day/night game at the SCG, a World Series Cricket one-dayer between the Australians and the West Indians which was played out in front of a full house, there is still a novelty value. And you are guaranteed a result.

For the players, day/night games are terrific value. You start at a different time, stop at a different time. It is exciting as a player to walk out under the lights at night. In my first season of one-day international cricket, 1985-86, the SCG lights were rated as good as any ground in Australia. Nowadays, they are just adequate, because you get a bit of a shadow whereas at other venues the lights are as bright as sunshine. Melbourne, for one, is superior. In what we call the twilight time in Sydney, until around 8pm when the lights take full effect, it can be difficult to bat.

I remember seeing Bruce Laird, the opening bat from Western Australia, make a sensational hundred in a day-nighter at the SCG against the West Indies in 1981-82. This was a time when we all thought they were nigh-on invincible; a now almost-forgotten innings (such can be the way with the multitude of one-day internationals on the cricket calendar), but a great one. Watching Laird, I couldn't help thinking: I'd like to be out there, batting out under those lights. The SCG that night felt like a different ground to the one I had been at for the Shield games and Test matches.

The crowds were different too; after dark The Hill wasn't a pleasant place to be. Sitting there one night during a one-day international in the early 1980s I was struck on the back of the head by a pie. Night cricket – and night football – hastened the demise of The Hill. The extra hours

Hollywood comes to the SCG
The emergence of Shane Warne in the 1990s transformed cricket and the art of leg-spin bowling. the bleach-blond with the glamour image is now the highest wicket-taker at the SCG.

gave too many people too much time to get on the drink and the recurring headlines about the drunks behaving badly forced the authorities to concrete the landmark, and put the plastic seats in. It's a shame The Hill is gone, and there is no doubt some of the character of the ground departed with its demise, but I understand why it had to go.

There have been many highlights in the one-dayers that have been played at the SCG over the years, but here are three that stand out for me. One was a catch by England's Derek Randall in a game against the West Indies in 1979-80. This was the game made notorious by the decision of the English captain Mike Brearley to put all ten of his fieldsmen, even the keeper David Bairstow, on the fence for the final ball when the West Indies needed three to win. Randall's catch of Andy Roberts – running backwards at full pace from mid-wicket, he jumped, dived and grabbed the ball one-handed – left the West Indies at 177 for seven in the 44th over, chasing 199 in 47. To that point, it seemed the experienced Roberts would get them home.

Seven seasons later, during a season in which we were too often on the receiving end against Mike Gatting's Englishmen, it seemed we had their measure in a game at the SCG. With Bruce Reid preparing to bowl the final over, England needed 18 to win. Allan Lamb was on strike, and the first ball went for two, the second for four and the third for six, pulled up into where the Hill had been. Six needed in three became four in two, and then it was over when Lamb hit a pitched-up ball on leg stump to the vacant square-leg fence.

That was the worst of times. One of the best of times came on New Year's Day 1996, when Michael Bevan won Australia a one-dayer against the West Indies we had no right to win. I missed this game through injury, but afterwards – probably because of the day on which it was played – it seemed as if everyone in the country had seen it. At one stage the Aussies were 74 for seven chasing 173, but Bevo won the night, ending the game in amazing fashion by hitting the last possible delivery, bowled by Roger Harper, absolutely straight for four.

In January 2003, I had my own moment of last-ball excitement on the ground when I scored a century in the fifth Ashes Test. The runs came after a spell where my place in the side came under fierce scrutiny, with many writers and commentators and even some ex-players suggesting that it was time for

me to retire. I found that at a time like this some people like to put the boot in, but many more – family, friends and fans – offer strong support, so it was that on the second afternoon I walked out to applause and adulation. Three hours later, I hit a four from the final ball of the day to reach my hundred and 40,000 people went crazy, clapping and cheering, roaring out my name. I never imagined that this would happen and when it did it was very emotional for me. In terms of personal performance, can it get better than this? A ton off the last ball of the day in front of my home crowd, after all the stress and media debate about my future in the days and weeks that preceded it. This was one of those occasions as a sportsperson when you are in that special place called "the zone", something that happens only once or twice in a career.

A few weeks later, in a Pura Cup (formerly Sheffield Shield) match in Sydney, I was fielding in the covers on the eastern side of the ground, in front of the Bill O'Reilly Stand, the grandstand that grew out of where the old Bob Stand once stood. From my vantage point, I could look past the batsman over to the Members Stand and the Ladies Stand. And I was thinking, "Jeez, how lucky am I? There's a lot of people who'd give a great deal to be where I am right now, playing cricket on this ground." There may even have been one or two boys in the crowd preparing to write the next chapter in this great ground's history.

A rare moment of English pleasure in Australia during the 1998-99 Ashes campaign.
Darren Gough dismisses Ian Healy, caught behind by Warren Hegg, Stuart MacGill and Colin Miller to register England's first hat-trick against Australia since Jack Hearne removed Clem Hill, Syd Gregory and Monty Noble at Headingley in 1899.

Overleaf
January 2003: Steve Waugh, playng in his record-equalling 156th Test, reaches his century off the last ball of the second day of the fifth Test against England. It was his 29th Test century bringing him level with Sir Donald Bradman.

Following in the footsteps of Trumper, Bradman and McCabe, Steve Waugh marches back to a standing ovation after his Ashes century. This game brought Australia to a standstill and delayed the nightly news.

SCG Ground Records

Result Summary

	Played	Won	Lost	Drawn
Australia	89	46	27	16
England	52	21	24	7
India	7	1	3	3
Pakistan	5	2	2	1
New Zealand	2	0	1	1
South Africa	9	1	6	2
West Indies	14	2	10	2

Sri Lanka, Bangladesh and Zimbabwe
have yet to play at the SCG

Highest Totals

659-8	Australia v England 1946-47
636	England v Australia 1928-29
619	Australia v West Indies 1968-69
606	All out West Indies v Australia 1st Innings 1992-93
600 for 4	India v Australia 1st Innings 1985-86

Lowest Completed Innings Totals

42	Australia v England 1887-88
45	England v Australia 1886-87
65	England v Australia 1894-95

Highest Match Aggregates

Runs	Wkts	
1644	38	Australia v West Indies 1968-69
1611	40	Australia v England 1924-25
1541	35	Australia v England 1903-04

Lowest Match Aggregates (Result oriented matches)

Runs	Wkts	
374	40	Australia v England 1887-88

Highest Scores

287	RE Foster England v Australia 1903-04
277	BC Lara West Indies v Australia 1992-93
251	WR Hammond England v Australia 1928-29
242	KD Walters Australia v West Indies 1968-69
234	DG Bradman Australia v England 1946-47

Highest Run Aggregates

Runs	Matches	Hundreds	
1177	17	0	AR Border
1150	12	4	GS Chappell
1127	11	4	DC Boon

Partnership Records

234 for 1st	RW Barber and G Boycott	England v Australia	1965-66
224 for 2nd	W Bardsley and C Hill	Australia v South Africa	1910-11
224 for 2nd	M Amarnath and SM Gavaskar	India v Australia	1985-86
293 for 3rd	BC Lara and RB Richardson	West Indies v Australia	1992-93
336 for 4th	WM Lawry and KD Walters	Australia v West Indies	1968-69
405 for 5th	SG Barnes and DG Bradman	Australia v England	1946-47
187 for 6th	WW Armstrong and C Kelleway	Australia v England	1920-21
160 for 7th	R Benaud and GD McKenzie	Australia v South Africa	1963-64
154 for 8th	GJ Bonnor and SP Jones	Australia v England	1884-85
154 for 9th	JM Blackham and ES Gregory	Australia v England	1894-95
130 for 10th	RE Foster and W Rhodes	England v Australia	1903-04

Best Bowling in an Innings.

8 for 35	GA Lohmann	England v Australia	1886-87
8 for 58	GA Lohmann	England v Australia	1891-92
8 for 94	T Richardson	Engand v Australia	1897-98
7 for 40	RG Barlow	Engand v Australia	1882-83
7 for 40	JA Snow	Engand v Australia	1970-71

Best Bowling in a Match

12 for 87 (5-44, 7-43)	CTB Turner	Australia v England
12 for 107 (5-57, 7-50)	SCG MacGill	Australia v England
12 for 128 (7-56, 5-72)	SK Warne	Australia v South Africa
12 for 165 (6-102, 6-63)	Imran Khan	Pakistan v Australia
12 for 175 (5-85, 7-90)	HV Hordern	Australia v England

Hat-tricks

J Briggs	England v Australia	1891-92
D Gough	England v Australia	1998-99

Highest Wicket Aggregates

Wkts	Matches	5WI	
49	10	4	SK Warne
45	6	4	CTB Turner
43	8	0	DK Lillee
42	8	2	RR Lindwall

Most Catches by Fielder

Catches	Matches	
19	12	GS Chappell
18	17	AR Border
18	11	MA Taylor
18	11	ME Waugh
18	5	IT Botham

Most Dismissals by Wicketkeeper

Dismissals	Matches	
48	12	RW Marsh
43	11	IA Healy
32	7	ATW Grout

THE MELBOURNE
CRICKET GROUND

The MCG bears little resemblance to the ramshackle ground that staged the first Test in 1877 but with its four-tier stands, it is the epitome of a modern-day cricket stadium.

The second Test of 1911-12, at the Melbourne Cricket Ground, featured a stirring battle between two of the true champions of the game. In the English corner was the great bowler, SF (Sydney) Barnes, whom the famous batsman Jack Hobbs believed to be "undoubtedly the greatest bowler of my time". Batting for Australia was Victor Trumper, a batsman rated by Herbie "Horseshoe" Collins, an Australian captain of the 1920s, as even more gifted than Don Bradman.

Throughout this series, Trumper was the key batsman, Barnes the bowler most likely to dismiss him. Barnes was a tall, wiry, often moody Englishman, who brought the ball down from his full height and could spin or cut it from leg or off. During his 27-match Test career, he took 189 wickets at an average of just 16.43. His most dangerous delivery was the leg-cutter, bowled at genuine medium pace, even quicker at times; his greatest asset was his relentless accuracy. Because he could move the ball away off the pitch, most observers put Barnes in front of the greatest bowler of the 19th century, "The Demon" Spofforth.

Trumper had scored a magnificent 113 in Sydney in the first Test of 1911-12. It was his eighth Test century, and sixth against England, both records. Tall, thin and immaculate at the crease, he was always ready to hit the first ball for four, never prepared simply to defend. Australian critics contend that he changed cricket with his aggressive outlook.

Here at the MCG, Barnes produced one of Test cricket's most famous bowling spells. After Clem Hill, the Aussie captain, decided to bat, Barnes bowled five overs for one run and the wickets of Bardsley, Hill, Kelleway and Armstrong. Trumper, in with just eight runs on the board and three men down, led a brief fightback, but relaxing against the considerable left-arm skills of Frank Foster, he was bowled. Barnes came back to get Minnett, at which point he had taken five wickets for just six runs from 11 overs. The home team never recovered, and England won the final four Tests, with Barnes dismissing Trumper four times in the series.

The history of the MCG is full of such famous confrontations. One of the first involved WG Grace, the world's greatest batsman, who had to face 18 Victorians when he made his debut at the ground, in 1873-74. He responded in style, taking ten for 58 in the Victorian XVIII's only innings and scoring 51 not out. WG's visit seriously boosted interest in the game and also revealed to the local cricketers that they were not bad at all. Indeed, so much was the Australians' confidence boosted that within three years of Grace's departure, they were taking on and beating an All-England team on level terms, 11 men per side, at the MCG. This was to become recognised as the first Test match.

The English team that played in this clash was on a privately-backed tour, the fourth such venture to come out from the Mother Country, 15 years after the first. It was not truly representative of the best of English cricket – WG for one was missing – but it was still a good team. The Melbourne Cricket Club built a new grandstand at the MCG especially for the tour, but only 1,000 people were at the ground at the start of play on day one, March 15, a Thursday, apparently because most Melburnians believed their team would be outclassed. They would be proved very wrong, thanks mainly to the efforts of one man. By later in the day, as word spread of Charlie Bannerman's grand performance, the attendance grew to more than 4,000. On day two, 12,000 people came to cheer.

The first ball in England-Australia international cricket was bowled by England's Alfred Shaw to Bannerman. By late on this inaugural day of Test cricket, Bannerman had scored the game's first Test century; at stumps he was 126 not out, and on the following day he would go all the way to 165. At that score he was struck a painful blow on the finger and had to retire hurt. But for his injury he might have gone on to 200. No other Australian batsman in the match scored more than 20 and Australia's first innings ended at 245

"We should not grudge him a jot of the honours won, even if he did come from Sydney," wrote the *Melbourne Argus's* correspondent of Bannerman. Still, by early on day four the visitors needed only 154 to win, and few thought they would not get them. That they didn't was due largely to the efforts of left-arm spinner Tom

The Centenary Test in 1977 was a wonderful game of cricket that featured a classic confrontation between Dennis Lillee and Derek Randall, seen here acknowledging another bouncer from the Western Australian. Randall made a memorable 174 but Lillee, with 11 wickets in the match, came out on top as Australia won by 45 runs – by coincidence the same margin of victory as the first Test match 100 years earlier.

Kendall, who took seven for 55 to set up a stunning 45-run victory.

In the seasons since 1877, the MCG has established itself as one of the most important venues in international cricket. It has hosted a World Cup final, the first one-day international and the Centenary Test. I remember parts of the Centenary Test so vividly ... I was 11, watching on TV, hooked by the way the history of the game was so celebrated and amazed that the winning margin was 45 runs, exactly the same as the first-ever Test. For me, the memories of this game are snapshots, such as the moment when Derek Randall was struck on the head by a Dennis Lillee bouncer but jumped back up to make 174. Most clearly of all, I recall Rick McCosker, his head seemingly held together by bandages, coming out to bat with a broken jaw, to help Rod Marsh to his century, a moment in time that has become a famous image of Australian cricket. I remember thinking how brave and gutsy that was. I sensed then and know now that this is what Test cricket is all about – testing out your courage.

The MCG has seen Test cricket's first hat-trick by Spofforth in 1879-80, and Bradman's first Test

century – against England in the third Test of 1928-29. It also witnessed Trevor Chappell's Underarm – that infamous delivery that denied New Zealand vctory in a one-day game and had prime ministers debating the game across the world. The MCG was the venue for the first instance of an umpire no-balling a bowler for throwing in a Test – Australia's Ernie Jones called by Jim Phillips in the second Ashes Test of 1897-98 – an incident mirrored 98 years later when umpire Darrell Hair called the Sri Lankan Muttiah Muralitharan. In 1907-08, the MCG would have seen Test cricket's first tie, if only Australia's Gerry Hazlitt's throw from cover had been accurate instead of wild. It was the venue for one-day international cricket's first tie – a World Series Cup finals match between Australia and the West Indies in February 1984, after Carl Rackemann was run out off the final ball, going for a desperate bye.

In 1960-61, when two captains – Australia's Richie Benaud and the West Indies' Frank Worrell – and two marvellous teams combined to produce one of the great Test series, the ground might have seen the second tied Test of that summer had the umpires given Australian keeper Wally Grout out bowled instead of awarding two crucial

byes near the end of the pulsating fifth Test. A bail had been dislodged as the ball spun through Grout, but the umps couldn't explain how that happened and gave the batsman the benefit of the doubt. That game, which drew an amazing 90,800 people on the opening day, ended in a two-wicket win to the Aussies.

I have been fortunate to play in Melbourne in front of a huge crowd, and also when the big stands have been all but empty. Without a crowd, I feel that the stadium comes over as a little unfriendly, even soulless, but when there are more than 50,000 or 60,000 people in, the experience is quite unforgettable. In such circumstances, it becomes like the Coliseum, and Australian players take on the roles of gladiators. I can imagine that some opposition cricketers in their time have felt as if they are being fed to the lions.

There have been many instances in the MCG's history when this gladiatorial element has come to the fore. Imagine how Bradman must have felt when he walked out to face the Bodyline attack in the second Ashes Test of 1932-33. He had made a first-ball duck in the first innings, hooking wildly

The origins of Test match cricket.

Left: A far cry from the concrete stadium that now exists, this was how the MCG looked at the time of the first Test match in March 1877.

Centre: Charles Bannerman claimed the first slot in the history books by scoring the first century.
His achievement of making a hundred in his country's first Test has since been equalled by Zimbabwe's Dave Houghton and Aminul Islam of Bangladesh.

Above: Arthur Mailey took the 1920-21 Ashes series by storm when he took 36 English wickets. At the MCG, he produced a return of nine for 121 which is still

depended on him. Harold Larwood was waiting for him. Bradman's heart must have been pumping so hard, but he controlled his nervous energy and responded with what is recognised as his bravest hundred, an unconquered 103 out of an innings total of 191, as the Aussies won their only victory of the series. The crowd that day was a then ground record 69,724, with many turned away after the "House Full" signs went up, and so fervent was their support for The Don that when he reached his century the play was held up for several minutes as they cheered and cheered.

Bradman's Test record in Melbourne is remarkable. During his Test career, which ran from 1928 to 1948, there were only seven Australian summers in which Test matches were played – 1928-29, 1932-33, 1936-37 and 1946-47 (all v England), 1930-31 (v West Indies), 1931-32 (v South Africa) and 1947-48 (v India). In all but the final Ashes series, Bradman scored a ton at the MCG. In three of those seven series, he made two hundreds at the MCG.

If the innings against the Bodyline attack was Bradman's most dramatic at the MCG, arguably his most important there was made four years later. This knock was compiled during The Don's first series as Australian captain, and came when he and his men were two-nil down in the series with three Tests to play. At stumps on a rain-affected day one, Australia were 181 for six. On day two, after Australia declared at 200 for nine, Wally Hammond somehow managed an innings of 32 on a treacherous deck on which 13 wickets would fall for 98 runs during the day. By making the wicket seem playable, Hammond not only produced what might have been his greatest Test innings, he also conned his captain, Gubby Allen, into postponing a declaration. After Hammond's dismissal put England at 68 for four, they lost another five

Above right: so which was Donald Bradman's favourite ground? From a purely run-scoring angle, there can be few to challenge the MCG where he scored the little matter of nine hundreds and a total of 1,671 runs.

Right: Harold Larwood was the one bowler to unsettle Bradman but even he could not stop him at Melbourne in 1932-33 when The Don made 103 and Australia won their only Test of the series.

Far right: A clash of cultures? England captain Ted Dexter pours a glass of champagne to celebrate his team's seven-wicket win in the 1962-63 series. But his opposite number, Richie Benaud, is clutching a glass of what looks suspiciously like beer.

wickets for eight meaningless runs even though Bradman told his bowlers not to get anyone out. After Allen finally closed, Australia survived to stumps just one wicket down. With the wicket much tamer the next day, Bradman scored 270, Jack Fingleton 136, and the momentum of the series was reversed. Had Allen not procrastinated, who knows how many wickets Australia might have lost on that awful second-day pitch.

Experts between the two world wars reckoned a Melbourne wet wicket was the most lethal in world cricket. In 1928-29, when England were leading the series two-nil, they were trapped on a diabolical sticky. Set 332 to win, no one gave them a chance. The Melbourne Cricket Club secretary, former Australian captain Hugh Trumble, reckoned that 70 would be a good innings total. Instead England went on to win by three wickets, principally because Australia couldn't dismiss the legendary English openers, Jack Hobbs and Herbert Sutcliffe.

So wet was the wicket that play was delayed into the early afternoon, and it quickly became apparent that the now-blazing sun was drying the pitch in patches, so that there were spots from which the ball jumped viciously, while other parts behaved more routinely. It was at its most dangerous just before tea, when the home side attacked with an army of fieldsmen around the bat. But Hobbs and Sutcliffe used dead bats when they had to, their pads when they could, and their extraordinary skill and judgment to avoid as many deliveries as they could. This battle of will and courage went for an over, 20 minutes, an hour, until the tea interval, when the score was 78 without loss. In fact, the partnership went on until 5pm, when Hobbs was out for 49 but England still scraped home.

Three years later, South Africa were trapped on a Melbourne sticky and were dismissed for just 36 and 45. Umpire George Hele, who witnessed both Tests at close quarters, had no doubt the deck that Hobbs and Sutcliffe conquered in 1928-29 was tougher.

The MCG must have been the great Hobbs's favourite Australian ground. In ten Tests in Melbourne, he made four half-centuries and five hundreds. Perhaps his most famous century in Melbourne came in the fourth Test of 1911-12, when he and Wilfred Rhodes added

323 for the first wicket. Hobbs made 178, Rhodes a single more. This was the same Wilfred Rhodes who had batted number 11 (and scored 40 out of a stand of 130) the day RE Foster made 287 in Sydney, the same all-rounder who took 15 for 124 in the second Test at the MCG in 1903-04, despite having eight catches dropped off his bowling.

Ashes contests have been pretty one-sided since Australia regained them in 1989 but there have been a few moments of English joy. Darren Gough and Mark Butcher claim their souvenirs after a narrow win at the MCG in 1998-99. In his joy, Butcher has failed to notice that he has pulled out the stumpcam.

For all the class of Hobbs and the other champion batsmen I have mentioned and admire so much, and the vagaries of the Melbourne pitches on which they made their runs, the honour of the greatest ever innings played on the MCG probably belongs with Gary Sobers, who in 1971-72 produced a knock for his Rest of the World XI against Australia that Bradman later called "the greatest exhibition of batting ever seen in Australia". Sobers made 254 against an attack led by Dennis Lillee at his fastest, and did it quite magnificently. Seeing video of this knock, it seems to me that Sobers batted something like Brian Lara – a loud flourish of a backswing, every shot in the book and more than any other batsman I have seen live or on film he treated every bowler the same, with a dash of arrogance as if his opponents were just bit players in his show.

Two other great innings played at the ground were that of the Yorkshireman JT Brown in 1894-95 and by the West Australian Kim Hughes against the West Indies in 1981-82.

In 1894-95, England and Australia played out the first five-Test Ashes series, a rubber that by my reading stands with the amazing "Botham's Ashes" English summer of 1981 as the most exciting Ashes series of them all. I have already mentioned how England won the first Test in Sydney despite having to follow on. They won again in Melbourne despite being bowled out for 75 after Australian captain George Giffen sent them in, but then lost the next two Tests when Albert Trott was brought into the Australian XI. The young Victorian began his Test career by scoring 38 not out and 72 not out and taking nought for nine and eight for 43 in Australia's 382-run win at Adelaide and then following up with 86 not out in Sydney as the Aussies won by an innings and 147 runs. After my first two Tests, I'd scored 26 runs in four innings, and taken two wickets.

The deciding Test at the MCG generated unprecedented interest. Even Queen Victoria asked for regular score updates. Thousands flocked to Melbourne for the game, and on the final day, March 6, 1895, they witnessed one of Ashes cricket's finest attacking innings. This was Jack Brown's greatest day. In at 28 for two chasing

An iconic image for all Australians. Rick McCosker, head bandaged after having his jaw broken by Bob Willis, returns to the fray in the 1977 Centenary Test.

297, he square-drove his first ball for four, hooked the next for another boundary, and raced to his 50, Adam Gilchrist-like, in 28 minutes, his century in 95. His stand with Albert Ward reached 210 before Brown was out for 140. Ward was out for 92 four runs later, but by then the Ashes were won. Trott, meanwhile, finished the series with a batting average of 102.50 but never played for Australia again. He enjoyed some more days in the sun playing for Middlesex and even played twice for England against South Africa in 1898. He also had one parting shot against his countrymen in 1899 when, playing for the Marylebone Cricket Club against the touring Australians, he became the only batsman ever to strike a ball over the Lord's pavilion. Sadly, suffering from bad health and depression, he shot himself in 1914. He was 42.

Kim Hughes's effort nearly 87 years later was a highlight of a famous Test match. Against one of the most fearsome and skilful pace attacks of all time, and after Australia had been reduced to eight for three, 26 for four and 59 for five, Hughes scored an even, unbeaten 100 while no other Aussie batsman could make more than 21. He went from 71 to his century with last man Terry Alderman at the other end. And after the innings ended, all out 198, he stood back and watched Lillee dramatically take three wickets before stumps, including, last ball of the day, Viv Richards, bowled off an inside edge for two, to leave the West Indies on ten for four. Legend has it that the crowd was still packed inside, chanting the great fast bowler's name, half an hour after stumps. The next day Lillee came back to take his 310th Test wicket, Larry Gomes caught at first slip by Greg Chappell, to break Lance Gibbs's Test wicket-taking record.

How much do you think DK Lillee liked the MCG? In 1980-81, he broke Richie Benaud's Australian record of 248 Test wickets there when he dismissed Sunil Gavaskar leg-before. Three times he took ten wickets in a Melbourne Test: 11 for 165 in the 1977 Centenary Test; 11 for 138 v England in 1979-80; ten for 127 v the West Indies in 1981-82. Bruce Reid (twice) is the only other bowler to do this more than once. Other notables to take ten or more wickets in an MCG Test include Billy Bates – 14 for 102 in 1882-83 including the first Test hat-trick by an Englishman

Dennis the Menace.
Four times Lillee took ten wickets in a match at the MCG.

being bowled. Despite the fact that 46,000 people turned up – more than the total attendance at the first Test, at the Gabba in Brisbane – the game made so little impact with the cricket authorities that the next one-day international in Australia was not played until 1974-75. On February 17, 1985, Australia's Robbie Kerr was Man of the Match in the first night game played at the MCG, in the opening clash of the World Championship of Cricket. This tournament was something of a mini-World Cup, involving the seven nations playing Test cricket at the time, staged to commemorate the 150th anniversary of the birth of Melbourne and won eventually by India. In contrast to the early 1970s, in 1984-85 there were 31 one-day internationals played in Australia between January 6 and March 10, 13 of them at the MCG. That's a lot.

A feature of India's triumph in that competition was the bowling of a teenage leggie named Laxman Sivaramakrishnan, who showed that there could be a place for good spinners in the one-day game. Mushtaq Ahmed, the Pakistani wrist-spinner, did likewise in the 1992 World Cup final, when he embarrassed England's Graeme Hick with a glorious wrong 'un. And, of course, Shane Warne, along with Muralitharan, Anil Kumble and Saqlain Mushtaq, has confirmed time and again in the last decade that spinners can play have a crucial role in one-day cricket. Warney's popularity at the MCG knows no bounds; I have read of the acclaim for locals such as Warwick Armstrong and Bill Ponsford at the MCG in earlier times, but I cannot imagine them being consistently cheered more loudly than Shane has been.

This said, back in 1920-21 Armstrong was so well respected that during a Victoria v England match at the MCG – when a meeting was staged outside the ground, to protest at Armstrong's omission from the state side because of a dispute with Victorian Cricket Association officials – many fans walked out of the ground, preferring the speeches to the cricket. This was in spite of the fact that the VCA had ruled that once out, the fans would not be allowed back in. When Armstrong, the Australian captain, scored 123 not out in the fourth Ashes Test of the summer a week later, he received an ovation, to quote the former Victorian and Australian batsman (and prominent Australian Rules football coach) Jack Worrall, "the like of which had never been seen on the famous old ground". Armstrong was then

– SF Barnes, Alec Bedser, Monty Noble, Fred Spofforth, Bill O'Reilly, Graham McKenzie, Hugh Tayfield, Michael Holding and Wasim Akram. The list of Test century-makers at the MCG is just as impressive, including Ken Barrington, David Boon, Ian Botham, Greg Chappell, Ian Chappell, Colin Cowdrey, Sunil Gavaskar, David Gower, Wally Hammond, Hanif Mohammad, Neil Harvey, Lindsay Hassett, Matthew Hayden, Clem Hill, Conrad Hunte, Jacques Kallis, Justin Langer, Clive Lloyd, Majid Khan, Vinoo Mankad, Peter May, Arthur Morris, Bill Ponsford, Viv Richards, Richie Richardson, Bob Simpson, Herbert Sutcliffe, Mark Taylor, Sachin Tendulkar, Victor Trumper, Doug Walters, Mark Waugh and Frank Worrell. Again I make the point – the great players rise to the occasion at the great grounds.

What of one-day cricket at the MCG? Did you know that England's John Edrich, another Melbourne Test century-maker, won the first ever one-day international Man of the Match award on January 5, 1971, for scoring 82 in a game won by Australia by five wickets? The match was staged at the MCG only because the third Ashes Test of that summer had been washed out without a ball

41 years old, and close on 20 stone (130 kilogrammes), but as well as leading Australia to eight straight Test victories at home and in England in 1920-21 and 1921, he also scored three centuries and took 17 wickets.

Bill Ponsford became famous for his colossal runscoring in first-class cricket through the 1920s, usually at home in Melbourne. Ponsford became the first man to score 400 in a first-class innings twice. Both scores were made at the MCG, 429 against Tasmania in 1922-23 and 437 against Queensland five seasons later. In between, he scored 352 against New South Wales – part of a world-record innings score of 1,107 – and complained about how unlucky he was when he was finally dismissed. During this innings, the New South Wales captain Alan Kippax sauntered up to his strike bowler, the leggie Arthur Mailey (who took four for 362) and said, "Are you ever going to get anyone out?" To which Mailey replied, "I'd have had 'em out days ago if that chap in the brown derby hat at the back of the grandstand had held his catches."

Another famous big innings played at the MCG in this era was scored by Kippax for New South Wales. On Christmas Day and Boxing Day 1928, he made 260 not out and added 307 for the 10th wicket with Halford Hooker after NSW had slumped to 113 for nine. Hooker made 62 but the game ended in a draw.

After the Second World War, the MCG became more bowler-friendly, but it was the venue where the Victorian left-hander Bob Cowper hit the only Test triple-century ever made in Australia – 307 against England in 1965-66. And in the 1990s, the two highest scores made by Australians in one-day international cricket were both made at the MCG. In 1998-99, Adam Gilchrist scored 154 from only 129 balls against Sri Lanka and two seasons later Mark Waugh went all the way to 173 against the West Indies, scoring his runs from 148 deliveries. Perhaps the best fightback innings I have seen in a one-day international was scored in Melbourne by Michael Bevan against New Zealand in January 2002. Chasing 246 we had collapsed to 82 for six but Bevan's 102 not out saw us through to a win we had no right to expect. The most explosive one-day innings at the MCG might have been Lance Cairns's 52 in the second World Series Cup final of 1982-83 after the Kiwis has crashed to 44 for six. Cairns hit six sixes that afternoon and reached his 50 from just 21 deliveries.

Twelve months after Chris Cairns's dad took to Dennis Lillee and company, I had my first live experience of the Melbourne Cricket Ground when I played in an Under-19 Test against Sri Lanka. Our team also included my brother Mark and Mark Taylor. For me, this was a seriously unbelievable experience. Like my first sighting of the SCG only more so, the arena was so massive. I couldn't help thinking, over and over, how big is this ground? That is the first thing that strikes you when you walk out on to the playing surface – the enormity of the ground and the stands. The Great Southern Stand was still eight years away, but the big stands that were there then were so all-

Two fast bowlers separated by a common moustache Ernie Jones (left) and Merv Hughes.

On his death in 1943, Jones, a South Australian whose Test career ran from 1894 to 1902, was described by Wisden as the fastest bowler Australia had ever produced – he once put a ball through WG Grace's beard. He was also the first man to be called for chucking in a Test

Hughes, with 212 wickets in 53 Tests between 1985 and 1993, is the most successful fast bowler to emerge from Victoria.

Awating the verdict
The Indian fielders wait on one side of the divide while the Australian batsmen
hold their brath on the other. On thi s occasion, the batsman got the benefit.

encompassing. I tried to soak it all in, and when I was out there making a few runs I kept thinking … maybe one day I will be able to do this in a Test.

Less than two years later and I was walking out there to bat on the first day of a Test match. The ground seemed even bigger, and I was nervous as any cricketer has ever been. It was surreal, as if it was someone else walking out there. Suddenly,

Back to the keeper's end, and I was trying to survive on a damp, grassy wicket. Ravi Shastri was bowling from one end, Kapil Dev from the other, and I did not know where I was going to score a run. And that was all I wanted … one run. When it came, through the covers off Kapil Dev, I whispered to myself, "Bewdy, they can't take that away from me. At least, I haven't made a duck in my first Test."

That is how I was thinking. With the big crowd in, the big stands, great bowlers operating, a posse of experienced Test players – Gavaskar, Vengsarkar, Amarnath, Shastri and Kapil Dev – around the bat, I felt completely out of place.

In the years since, I have come to the view that the MCG needs a big crowd to bring it to life. I can only imagine what it would have been like for the 1956 Olympics – how I would have liked to be a spectator when Australia's Betty Cuthbert won her three gold medals in the 100 metres, 200 metres and 4x100m relay, or when the great Russian Vladimir Kuts broke the heart of Britain's Gordon Pirie in the 5,000 metres and 10,000 metres. One MCG event I did see was the thrilling 1989 VFL Grand Final.

The MCG is the venue for the VFL/AFL premiership decider every year; I was lucky to be there for one of the great ones. The Australian squad, fresh from our 4-0 Ashes win in England, were honoured with a pre-match lap of honour and naturally we stayed to see the game. And what a contest it was. Hawthorn were the defending premiers, and a fantastic side, but early doors they were smashed by Geelong. The Hawks' champion centre half-forward Dermot Brereton suffered broken ribs in the first minute, their little rover John Platten was knocked senseless and Robert Dipierdomenico, better known as Dipper, punctured a lung. Still, they won by a goal, despite the efforts of Geelong's champion, Gary Ablett, who kicked nine goals, most of them in the last quarter. It was classic, gripping action, and the crowd never stopped, always roaring and clapping. In contrast, when there is a big attendance at the cricket, there is always that break between balls. However, when a wicket falls or an important four is struck, there is a more intense noise than you get at the footy. Or maybe it just seems that way.

The fanaticism of the Melbourne sports fan is phenomenal, whether it be cricket, Australian

now that I was a player rather than an observer, I wasn't used to big crowds at all – the noise, the colour, the intensity. This, my Test debut, had come about so quickly, so much so that when I joined the squad the day before the match I was meeting some of my new comrades for the first time in my life. The next minute, and I was having a mid-pitch chat with Geoff Marsh, a team-mate who I had never had a long conversation with.

football, tennis, Formula One, just about anything sporting. This was never better reflected that in the Boxing Day Test of 1982-83, when Australia went to stumps on day four needing another 37 to win, with the game's last partnership, Allan Border and Jeff Thomson, at the wicket. AB and Thommo had already added 37. The Test might have been over in one ball on the fifth morning, but an estimated 18,000 people turned up to see the score move to within a boundary of an amazing Australian victory. Then Thommo edged Ian Botham to Chris Tavare at second slip, who dropped the chance, but it spooned up behind him for first slip Geoff Miller to complete the dismissal. England home by three runs.

Melbourne sports fans are passionate, devoted and very parochial. They can also be rough on those they are not keen on. The old Bay 13, which was located behind the slip cordon for a right-handed bat at the southern end of the ground, used to be a nightmare place for opposition fieldsmen. I have seen players from some countries who were very reluctant to go down there. Yet these same rough diamonds beyond the boundary were the same lot who, to everyone's great amusement, mimicked Merv Hughes's stretches while the big man prepared for another bowling spell during the 1988-89 World Series Cup one-dayers.

It was down that end of the ground that I took my best catch in international cricket. During a day-nighter in that same season, the West Indies were six wickets down and needed 27 to win from the final three overs. Roger Harper swung at Craig McDermott and lofted the ball high back over the bowler's head. I spun around and sprinted, fast as I could, and managed to haul it in before running behind the sightscreen. We eventually won the game by eight runs. Another catch that springs to mind was taken by Geoff Marsh at point, one-handed, diving full length, on the final day of a Test against Pakistan in 1989-90. We had been expected to bowl them out this day but were struggling until Geoff conjured up a way to dismiss Ijaz Ahmed, who was well past his hundred and looking well set. From there, we got a roll on and won the match. And I will never forget David Boon's catch at short leg in 1994-95 – a full-length diving effort that dismissed Devon Malcolm and gave Shane Warne a Test-match hat-trick on his home turf.

David Boon holds the ball aloft after taking the catch to dismiss Devon Malcolm and give Shane Warne a hat-trick against England in 1994-95.

I will always associate the MCG with the Boxing Day Test, and the Christmas celebrations with family and team-mates. I will also think of Bruce Reid, a superb fast bowler who was very unlucky with injury, twice demolishing opponents there – 13 for 148 against England in 1990-91, 12 for 126 against India 12 months later. And two bowling spells by Warney – his seven for 53 on the last day of the second Test against the West Indies in 1992-93, and his hat-trick there against the Poms. That earlier effort was a big game for Shane, his first great performance in Tests. Most notable was the flipper that knocked over the West Indian captain Richie Richardson. Most important was that we now had a spin bowler who could take advantage of great batting performances such as the crucial stand between Allan Border and Mark Waugh, who both scored hundreds and added 204 for the fourth wicket to give us a 162-run first-innings lead.

That was a big victory for us, because for more than a decade Australian teams had found it so hard to counter the West Indies at the MCG. I know that in the late 1980s and early 1990s the pitch was a bit up and down, which made it very difficult to score against their fast bowlers. For the Boxing Day Test in 1988-89, there were actually corrugations in the wicket. This was hardly the type of deck we would have preferred to face up to Malcolm Marshall, Curtly Ambrose, Courtney Walsh and Patrick Patterson. And it was probably not the best place for us to decide that we were sick of the quicks bouncing us, that we had to give some cheek back to them, to stick it up them if you like.

After stumps on the fourth day, Patrick Patterson pushed into our dressing-room to announce his lethal intentions for the following day. I must take some responsibility for this happening. Revved up by the fact that I had already taken four wickets in the innings, I bounced Patterson who batted number 11, a few times and then, next over, when he looked around to square leg where I was fielding, I waved to him. Merv Hughes was sledging him as well, and then Allan Border got involved. After play, Patterson said to AB, "I'm going to come out tomorrow and I'm going to kill you." That was something to look forward to and he was good as his word, bowling one of the quickest spells we had ever seen. We lost that Test, but won the next in Sydney and had the better of a draw in the fifth, in Adelaide. Maybe a little of the aura of the West Indies had been broken.

As hard as it was to break that hold they had over us – and we didn't do it completely until 1995 – it was an easier process than would be the task of anyone trying to diminish the tradition and status in world cricket that both the Melbourne and Sydney Cricket Grounds possess. I spoke earlier of how, during a Pura Cup match at the SCG, I suddenly had this thought: how lucky am I …?

At the same time, I thought back 18 years to my first season of first-class cricket. Back then I simply thought that it was amazing that I was going out to play on the ground where I had spent a lot of time watching big-time cricket and football. The dressing-rooms were different in those days, the old green lockers and the urinals out the back of the SCG home dressing-room are gone now, though we have still got the same benches inside that were there in 1985, were probably there in 1935, maybe even in 1895. First game, I was just happy to be there, worried that I might not be sitting in the right place. I kept quiet and listened. Nowadays, I do stop to think that I might be sitting in the same place as Dougie or The Don, that when I walk out onto the ground I am following in the footsteps of legends such as McCabe and Trumper. The more you play at such a ground, the more you become aware of the history of the venue and its value and importance.

Great history, great traditions, great places to play cricket. The SCG and the MCG are very different grounds, but in this they are as one. Occasionally in recent years, just for a moment – because they have been part of my life for so long and part of cricket for so much longer – I might have taken them for granted. We never should.

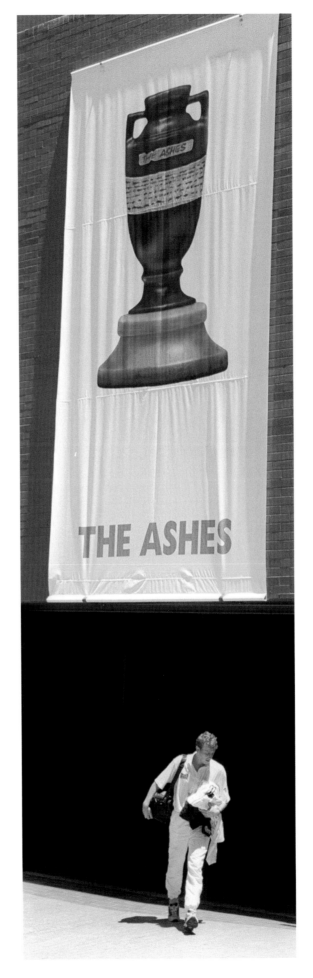

Left: Glenn McGrath celebrates yet another wicket.

Right: Another Ashes series defeat and the burden of history hangs over the head of Michael Atherton as he leaves the MCG.

MCG Ground Records

Result Summary

	Played	Won	Lost	Drawn
Australia	95	52	28	15
England	52	19	26	7
India	8	2	5	1
Pakistan	7	2	3	2
New Zealand	3	0	1	2
South Africa	10	2	6	2
Sri Lanka	1	0	1	0
West Indies	14	3	10	1

Bangladesh and Zimbabwe have yet to play at the MCG

Highest Totals

604	Australia v England 1936-37
600	Australia v England 1924-25
589	England v Australia 1911-12

Lowest Completed Innings Totals

36	South Africa v Australia 1931-32
45	South Africa v Australia 1931-32
61	England v Australia 1901-02
61	England v Australia 1903-04

Highest Match Aggregates

Runs	Wkts	
1640	33	Australia v Pakistan 1972-73
1619	40	Australia v England 1924-25
1562	37	Australia v England 1946-47

Lowest Match Aggregates (Result oriented matches)

Runs	Wkts	
234	29	Australia v South Africa 1931-32

Highest Scores

307	RM Cowper	Australia v England 1965-66
270	DG Bradman	Australia v England 1936-37
268	GN Yallop	Australia v Pakistan 1983-84
250	JL Langer	Australia v England 2002-03
208	IVA Richards	West Indies v Australia 1984-85

Highest Run Aggregates

Runs	Matches	Hundreds	
1671	11	9	DG Bradman
1271	20	4	AR Border
1265	16	3	SR Waugh
1257	17	4	GS Chappell
1178	10	5	JB Hobbs

Partnership Records

323 for 1st	JB Hobbs and W Rhodes England v Australia 1911-12
298 for 2nd	IM Chappell and WM Lawry Australia v West Indies 1968-69
249 for 3rd	DG Bradman and SJ McCabe Australia v England 1936-37
192 for 4th	MH Denness and KWR Fletcher England v Australia 1974-75
223* for 5th	DG Bradman and AR Morris Australia v India 1947-48
346 for 6th	DG Bradman and JHW Fingleton Australia v England 1936-37
185 for 7th	GRJ Matthews and GN Yallop Australia v Pakistan 1983-84
173 for 8th	JM Gregory and CE Pellew Australia v England 1920-21
100 for 9th	AEV Hartkopf and WAS Oldfield Australia v England 1924-25
120 for 10th	WW Armstrong and RA Duff Australia v England 1901-02

Best Bowling in an Innings.

9 for 86	Sarfraz Nawaz Pakistan v Australia 1978-79
9 for 121	AA Mailey Australia v England 1920-21
8 for 68	W Rhodes England v Australia 1903-04
8 for 71	GD McKenzie Australia v West Indies 1968-69
8 for 81	LC Braund England v Australia 1903-04
8 for 143	MHN Walker Australia v England 1974-75

Best Bowling in a Match

15 for 124 (7-56, 8-68)	W Rhodes England v Australia 1903-04
14 for 102 (7-28, 7-74)	W Bates England v Australia 1882-83
13 for 77 (7-17, 6-60)	MA Noble Australia v England 1901-02
13 for 110 (6-48, 7-62)	FR Spofforth Australia v England 1878-79,
13 for 148 (6-97, 7-51)	BA Reid Australia v England 1990-91

Hat Tricks

FR Spofforth	Australia v England 1878-79
W Bates	England v Australia 1882-83
H Trumble	Australia v England 1901-02
H Trumble	Australia v England 1903-04
SK Warne	Australia v England 1994-95

Highest Wicket Aggregates

Wkts	Matches	5WI	
82	14	7	DK Lillee
46	7	3	H Trumble
45	7	3	GD McKenzie
41	10	2	CJ McDermott

Most Catches by Fielder

Catches	Matches	
24	17	GS Chappell
22	10	MA Taylor
20	12	IM Chappell

Most Dismissals by Wicketkeeper

Dismissals	Matches	
62	17	RW Marsh
43	11	IA Healy
32	7	ATW Grout

ENGLAND

Christopher Martin-Jenkins

Ian Botham. Arguably, the most important English cricketer since WG Grace.

For most of my lifetime, until what you might call the age of corporate sports watching, there was a distinct and delightful contrast between Lord's and The Oval. One was all smart white paint and green perfection, peopled by deferential, long-serving, salt-of-the-earth staff and spectators in suits and ties; the other was brown and dusty, the pitch a batsman's dream, the outfield flat as an ice rink but in places mottled like a drunkard's cheek, the pavilion peopled by staff who were no less long-serving but more down to earth than salt of it; and by spectators who encompassed all sorts and conditions of man. It was as much a contrast as the cargoes in Masefield's famous poem.

Lord's was the opulent one:

Quinquereme of Nineveh from distant Ophir
Rowing down to haven from sunny Palestine
With a cargo of ivory and apes and peacocks
Cedarwood, sandalwood and sweet white wine

The Oval was the:

Dirty British coaster with a salt-caked smokestack
Butting through the channel on the mad March days
With a cargo of Tyne coal, road rail, pig lead
Firewood, ironware and cheap tin trays

Put more prosaically, perhaps, the grounds have until recent times signalled the class distinctions of the English. Lord's was the place for toffs and aristocrats. The smutty old Oval was where your working-class bloke felt completely at home.

Clear distinctions remain although, materially, the great difference is that The Oval is owned by the Duchy of Cornwall and has to beg and scratch for income when it comes to modernisation. Lord's is owned and run, from every blade of grass to Father Time's sickle, by MCC. Despite an often uneasy relationship with the England and Wales Cricket Board, the governing body of the game, the old club is firmly in control of all the developments at Lord's.

A remarkable innovator it has proved to be, too, in the field of cricket ground architecture in recent years. There is no more handsome stand anywhere in the world than the new Grand Stand and none more avant garde than the aluminium spaceship that landed a few years ago at the Nursery End and called itself the NatWest Media Centre. Nothing at Lord's, however, can compare with the pavilion. Inside and out it is a building of unrivalled majesty, perfectly proportioned and looking through its red sandstone to the sloping ground below where all the great players of the Test era have strutted their stuff.

Whereas The Oval has always been associated with big scores, Lord's in its early days was notorious for the opposite. Spinners always used to enjoy it as matches wore on, from the days of little Johnny Briggs, who took 11 Australian wickets for 74 in 1886, to those of the prodigious Fred Titmus, who spent so many hours bowling along the famous slope – six foot ten inches or "about the height of a tall man in a top hat" according to Plum Warner – that he seemed by the end of his long career to have one leg shorter than the other.

Pitches are less accommodating at Lord's now but you would still rather bowl there than at The Oval, where batting on a sunny day is heaven for a man in form. In 1938, with Len Hutton to the fore, England racked up an astonishing 903 for seven against the Australians, a record for Test cricket that stood until 1997-98 when Sri Lanka took advantage of another batsman's pitch in Colombo to make 952 for six.

It is, of course, the long history of matches at the two great cricket grounds of London that make them what they are.

They are not necessarily better than Old Trafford, which beat Lord's by ten days in 1884 to being England's second Test venue, or Trent Bridge and Edgbaston, grounds that joined the party in 1899 and 1902 respectively. Bramall Lane, Sheffield staged its only Test in the same year, 1902. In years to come perhaps Chester-le-Street, which became the first new English Test ground since then when it hosted the second Test against Zimbabwe in 2003, will enjoy the same aura and inspire the world's great players.

It is simply that every Test match played at the two London grounds adds to their allure, for players and spectators alike. If Lord's is, in the old cliché, the home of cricket, The Oval can boast the staging of the first Test in England. Between them they have been the scenes of deeds that would fill a decent-sized library. It is time to recall some of them.

LORD'S

No ground has staged more Test matches than Lord's, nor was one more appropriately named, but that is nothing but chance. Marylebone Cricket Club, born out of the White Conduit Club when its aristocratic members began to tire of playing matches in public fields at Islington, was founded in 1787, the year that one of their paid players, Thomas Lord, opened the first of the three grounds that bore his name. He did so at the request of two of the prominent White Conduit Club members, the Earl of Winchelsea and the future Duke of Richmond, Charles Lennox. Funds were provided for Lord to lease a private ground, which he did, at Dorset Fields, site of the present Dorset Square.

Being a proper Yorkshireman, Lord erected a fence round the new ground and charged sixpence for entry to the big matches that began to be played there, starting on May 31, 1787, with a game between Middlesex and Essex. No doubt he worked on the Josiah Wedgwood principle of charging customers a pretty penny and making them believe thereby that they were getting something special. Grand Opera operates on the same basis to this day.

The plan worked and his ground quickly became a focus for important matches, growing in reputation with the club whose home it was. After 21 years the lease expired, the rent went up on what was seen in a rapidly expanding city as an excellent place for new houses, and although MCC continued to play some games in Dorset Fields until 1811, Lord negotiated successfully for a second ground on another field, across Regent's Park and close to the present ground, beside the St John's Wood Road. He got this one for a song, only £54 a year, free of land tax and tithe for 80 years.

The turf from the first Lord's was moved "so that the noblemen and gentlemen of the MCC should be able to play on the same footing as before" but only two years later the Act of Parliament ordering the building of the Regent's Canal decreed a route straight across the middle of the ground. He and the members had to move again, to the present 20-acre area that has become the most hallowed in the cricket world.

Today, buses, cars and lorries race around the ground's perimeter but there are still trees between the main ground and the Nursery. I have a print of a painting by Gerry Wright of Denis Compton and Bill Edrich walking out to bat at Lord's on just such a morning. If it had a title it might borrow one from Laurie Lee: *As I walked out one sunny morning*.

It captures perfectly the air of purpose, expectation and contentment of the two batsmen, presumably in their annus mirabilis of 1947. Behind them in their flowing cream flannels, spectators air in warm comfort on the white benches, taking in the timeless serenity of the old ground on one of its quieter days.

It is the noisy ones that have generally gone down in the annals in the years between the genteel days and those like those of the first World Cup final in 1975, when Clive Lloyd's West Indies lifted the Prudential Cup after an epic battle with Ian Chappell's Australia; or the thrilling, helter-skelter chase for 326 runs by Sourav Ganguly's India in 2002. Lord's has been, after all, at the centre of the one-day revolution that started in England in the early 1960s, staging four of the eight World Cup finals to date and every one of the one-day finals played by the counties.

The prestige of Lord's is the product both of this unique accumulated history and of the loving stewardship of MCC. The years of the club's wanderings around north London had occupied the period between the French Revolution and the battle of Waterloo. Once settled for good in St John's Wood, however, they had to survive another crisis in 1825 created by, of all people, the acquisitive Lord himself. The scenario has echoed down the years. He obtained a building lease from the Eyre Estate and proposed to build new houses that would have drastically reduced the playing area and altered the character of the ground. Rescue came in the form of the substantial figure in all senses of William Ward who, five years previously, had scored what for a hundred seasons was to remain the highest score on the ground, 278 for MCC against Norfolk.

Compton and Edrich.
A legendary pair who played together for Middlesex and England. Their annus mirabilis was 1947 when they made hay against the South Africans. Compton (right) finished that series with 753 runs while Edrich made 552 and together they shared a third wicket partnership of 370 in the Lord's Test.

This great pair are now celebrated at Lord's in the Compton and Edrich Stands at the Nursery End of the ground.

That sort of immortal feat might inspire any man to dig far into his financial reserves in order to preserve the scene of its accomplishment. Ward bought the lease for what was then the huge sum of £5,000, whereupon Lord retired to West Meon in Hampshire and the cricket continued.

It is strange that as the supreme Test ground, in England at least, the first Test match that Lord's staged was the 15th played between England and Australia. On that momentous occasion, in July 1884, Lord Harris, the greatest of the patriarchs of English cricket, led his country against Billy Murdoch's Australians and the home side won by an innings and five runs. They were inspired by the first Test hundred at Lord's, by AG Steel of Marlborough, Cambridge and Lancashire; and by the bowling of the Yorkshiremen, Ted Peate and "Happy Jack" Ulyett.

Conditions suited them no doubt but Lord's was a much happier hunting-ground for batsmen by now. In its early days its surfaces resembled a billiard table, it was acidly remarked, only in the pockets. Sheep were brought in to graze the outfield in the days before a big game, and there was no mower when the local entrepreneur James Dark bought the ground from Ward in 1835 and began to turn it into something less like a rural field - complete, even then, with two ponds, one of them deep enough for Stevie Slatter, one of the ground staff, to learn to swim. It was not until 1864 that MCC employed a full- time groundsman. A year later they finally bought the freehold and immediately agreed to the construction of the first of the three Grand Stands that have occupied the higher side of the ground ever since.

If ever there was a deceptive start this was it. England had more success in the years that followed, winning four and drawing one of the seven Tests against Australia before the 19th century was done, but in the 100 years that followed, incredibly, they beat their greatest rivals only once.

The record at Lord's of the home country against Australia is by some distance the worst of all the home grounds, but the reasons have less to do with English failings than with Australian inspiration. The same would be true of all the visiting countries. This has from the very outset been the ground where they all want to do well and invariably, over the years, the finest of players have risen to the occasion of a Lord's Test.

It is, I suppose, the antiquity of Lord's and the MCC, guardians and early leaders of the world game, that explains the aura that began to surround the ground for everyone who played cricket in the colonies of the old British Empire. When Queen Victoria ascended the throne in 1837, after all, it was already celebrating its jubilee; and by the time the new century dawned Lord's was the most famous sporting venue in the world, let alone merely cricketing.

In 1890, England celebrated the building of the new pavilion – the one which still stands - by beating Australia by seven wickets and they won by six wickets half-a-dozen years later when

Rising star.
Michael Vaughan crowned a glorious 2002 by taking centuries off both India and Sri Lanka at Lord's. He went on to hit three more in England's Ashes defeat in Australia and in 2003 took over the captaincy from Nasser Hussain.

George Lohmann, whose bowling record of 110 wickets at ten runs each still staggers the eye, joined forces with the lion-hearted Tom Richardson to rattle out the old enemy for 53 on what was reputedly a perfect pitch. But there must have been some pace in it, for this was the celebrated occasion when Ernie Jones, the rough-hewn South Australian, sent a rising ball whistling through WG Grace's beard and followed the heresy with the famous apology: "Sorry doctor, she slipped."

Grace was still going strong then, having in the previous season become, at the age of 45, the first man to score 1,000 runs before the end of May.

Alas, England's bowling heroes in that match in 1896 both came to sad ends. Lohmann died of tuberculosis at the age of only 36 in South Africa while Richardson, the man who never spared his lithe frame when he bowled – at home and abroad he took 809 wickets in three years – was found dead during a walking holiday in France. He was 42.

WG and little Bobby Abel from Surrey shared in the stand that pressed home England's advantage but there was a valuable 44 at number six from FS (Stanley) Jackson who, nine summers later, was to enjoy one of the few seasons of almost unalloyed triumph among England captains against Australia. Although England won that series, however, they could only draw at Lord's where their powerful opponents had set their stall out for the century to come by winning the 1899 game easily on the back of glorious centuries by Clem Hill and Victor Trumper.

The side they beat did not include the 51-year-old WG but it did have CB Fry, AC MacLaren, KS Ranjitsinhji, Tom Hayward, Johnny Tyldesley, Gilbert Jessop and Wilfred Rhodes. Every one of them was a titan, so what did that make their opponents? Even with no doctor to discomfort, Ernie Jones took ten wickets in the match, starting it with seven for 88.

For a long time England could at least expect to win Lord's Test matches against opponents other than Australia. Despite seven wickets for one of the four leg-spinners in the South Africa side in their first Test in England, the home team would have won comfortably in 1907 had rain not come to their rescue on the third – and in those days final – day, and they duly won by an innings during the pioneering triangular tournament of 1912. Where MCC went in that year, the Aussies followed some 70 years later, with considerably greater commercial success.

Frank Woolley, arguably the greatest and certainly the most prolific of left-handed all-rounders before Gary Sobers, excelled himself against Australia in 1921 with two dazzling nineties, and Lionel Tennyson hit with great spirit for 74 not out in the second innings. It mattered not, however, that Warwick Armstrong, Australia's haughty captain and a man with "an eye like Mars to threaten and command", was bowled first ball for a duck. England supporters in those first few

In the queue.
Left: Waiting for the gates to open for the Lord's Test of 1938. Those lucky enough to watch all five days had to settle for a draw but at least they might have seen Wally Hammond's 240, Bill Brown's 206 or Don Bradman's 102.

Above: Another view of a 1930's crowd waiting patiently to get in. Notice the chap towards the top left of the picture in his cricket gear. Do people still do that?

Overleaf:
Trying to get parking at Lord's in 1930 was as difficult then as it is today.

years after the First World War had a foretaste of the hopeless nature of the cause felt by all who have followed the old country against a succession of powerful Australian teams in recent years.

Ted McDonald and Jack Gregory, one of the most hostile opening pairs of all, added 13 wickets between them at Lord's to the 16 they had taken in the first Test. An aerial photograph taken during the 1921 match shows one of the pair bowling to Woolley with four slips and a field much like the one used with the new ball by Glenn McGrath and Jason Gillespie against England 80 years later.

In that earlier period, however, things began to look up quite quickly. By 1924 Maurice Tate had been unearthed as a fast-medium bowler of the highest class and Jack Hobbs, already 41 but with many of his best years still to come, had been joined by a powerful group of batsmen of whom only Woolley had survived the consequences of the defeats three seasons before. At Lord's against South Africa, Hobbs made 211, Herbert Sutcliffe, his new opening partner, 122, Woolley 134 and Patsy Hendren 50 not out.

Percy Chapman did not get a bat but he and the other four all scored heavily against the old enemy in 1926, the year Chapman was destined to enjoy his finest hour two months later across the river. He had the pleasure of leading his country in the first Test played by the West Indies, at Lord's of course, in 1928, when Tich Freeman, enjoying his captain's confidence, took six for 77 in the game with those tantalising leg-breaks; and then of defending the Ashes gloriously in Australia. He and his colleagues had to make the most of it, too, because the Bradman era was about to begin.

The little genius from Bowral started with a taste of defeat in his first home Test against England in Brisbane, but by the time of his first visit to Lord's in 1930 he was already a phenomenon. He marked the occasion with what he himself always said was his greatest innings. What is more, although England were to lose in the end by seven wickets, he played it in the context of one of the most exhilarating games of cricket ever played. At least three sages of my acquaintance, Gubby Allen, who opened the bowling, Brian Johnston and EW Swanton, who also witnessed each of the four days, believed it to have been the finest of all the Lord's Tests.

Seldom was scoring so fast in those days as it was in this match, and generally is in Test cricket today, especially when Australia are involved. Such was the rate that England made totals of 425 and 375 yet still lost on the fourth afternoon. It proves to my mind that at many venues four days would be sufficient to get a finish to most games in the 21st century. There would need to be an improvement in the over-rate too, perhaps, but whereas Australia these days score at four an over as often as not, they got their 729 for six at Lord's in 1930 at a rate of only 3.1.

England went along at an even faster lick than that on the first day, making 405 for nine thanks largely to Ranji's nephew, Duleepsinhji, who drove beautifully in making 173 before getting out to a wild stroke. "The boy was always careless," said Ranji. But Duleep was neither the first nor the last to fall to Clarrie Grimmett, the wizened little leg-spinner of New Zealand origins who practised his variations in his garden with the help of a little terrier who returned balls from the net. He had a gift for luring batsmen into indiscretions.

England's last-wicket pair, George Duckworth and Farmer White, added another 20 runs before Australia's formidable batsmen got their chance.

Billy Woodfull and Bill Ponsford prepared the way for the boy wonder or, as the 1931 *Wisden* relates it: "They steadily wore down the bowling for Bradman later on to flog it...He seized his opportunity in rare style and, hitting all round the wicket with power and accuracy, he scored in two hours and 40 minutes 155 runs and was not out at the close."

Ponsford made 81, Woodfull, with the intense concentration for which he was famous, 155, and Australia were only 21 behind by the end of two days with eight wickets left.

Bradman's display continued on the following morning. He was finally caught by Chapman but his 254 was the record score for an overseas player at Lord's. It stood for 73 years until August 2, 2003 when South Africa's 22-year-old captain Graeme Smith struck a muscular 259 – his second double-century in successive Tests – to put his team on the path to a crushing innings victory.

Alan Kippax and Stan McCabe scored both made 83 before Woodfull declared at 729 for six, then the highest Test score.

Needing 304 to avoid an innings defeat, England lost Hobbs at 45, Woolley at 58. Wally Hammond and Duleep then took the score to 129 but Hammond's fall triggered a collapse before Chapman came in to score a timely first Test hundred, hitting Grimmett into the stand at long-on four times in what Plum Warner called "a glorious innings after a shaky start." In the end his 121 and England's 375 were insufficient – they were roundly criticised at the time for continuing to attack instead of consolidating when they had come close to parity with only five wickets down – but they took three Australian second innings wickets for 22 to bring the crowd (110,000 over four days) to what Warner called "a tiptoe of excitement".

Bradman was quite brilliantly caught at backward point, inches from the ground, off Tate, and Walter Robins got two wickets before losing his length for a couple of overs and with it, in effect, the match.

New Zealand surprised England by their talent and fighting qualities when they, in turn, made their first appearance in a Test in England the following year. England were rescued by an eighth - wicket partnership in which both Allen and Les Ames made centuries. In Ames's case it was one of more than a hundred hundreds scored by arguably the best of all England's batsmen/wicket-keepers.

The Dominions were joining the party thick and fast now. India – or All India as they were known 15 years before Partition and Independence – played their very first Test match at Lord's in 1932 and again they rose admirably to the occasion against an England team now led by Douglas Jardine. Muslims and Hindus may have played more or less happily together in the meantime but there were always social factors militating against India in the early days.

There was internal dispute when the Maharajah of Porbandar chose, with notable realism, to withdraw from the side for the Test but chose CK Nayudu to lead in his stead. Still, Amar Singh and Mohammad Nissar bowled so well with the new ball that England were 19 for three after a sensational start to a game they were supposed to win easily. The patrician Jardine top-scored in both innings of a game in which no one scored a hundred and his side duly won in the end by 158

Casualties of war.
Colin Blythe (left) and Hedley Verity were two left-arm spinners who perished in the world wars of the 20th century.

Blythe, who died in France during the First World War, only played one Test at Lord's against South Africa in 1907 but still took 100 wickets in his 19-Test career.

Verity, who died of his wounds in Italy in 1943, enjoyed one memorable outing at Lord's when he took 15 wickets against Australia in 1934. In his tribute, Don Bradman described Verity as: "One of the greatest, if not the greatest left-hand bowler of all time."

runs. Not untypically in that inter-war period England played two wrist-spinners, Robins and Freddie Brown.

Robins took six for 32 in the first innings against the West Indies the following season but it was another spinner who, in 1934, produced one of the great bowling feats of all time and the one that led to the elusive England victory over Australia in a Lord's Test. These were still the days of uncovered pitches, when finger-spinners could become unplayable if it rained during a game and the surface then began to dry under the sun.

Australians had always tended to struggle against English left-arm orthodox spinners on the soft pitches of their homeland. Johnny Briggs had had some notable successes in the early encounters, Wilfred Rhodes and his contemporary, Colin Blythe, took on the baton and now Hedley Verity enjoyed a day that made him immortal. Not literally so, alas, because, as Blythe was a tragic casualty of the First World War, so was Verity of the second; but in cricket circles the name, utterly appropriate for a man of clearest integrity, is forever in lights for the 4 wickets he took in a single day.

England had scored 440, with hundreds from Ames and Maurice Leyland, but Australia, Bradman and Bill Brown to the fore, had replied with customary confidence before rain fell on the unprotected middle during the rest day, Sunday. From 141 for one Australia collapsed to 284 before Verity bowled them out a second time for 118. Tall and unfailingly accurate, varying pace and trajectory in the classical manner, he took seven for 61 and eight for 43.

The Australia match of 1938 produced the biggest crowd ever seen at Lord's. On the Saturday 33,800 packed in uncomfortably before the gates were closed not very long after breakfast. Hammond made a majestic 240 and Brown, as courteous a man as you could wish to meet, responded with 206 not out but the bowling was not strong enough for the game to be won by either side in four days.

As with all the great players, Don Bradman relished playing at Lord's. He scored 102 there in 1938 but that was small fry compared with the 254 he made in 1930. It was the highest Test score at Lord's and stood for 60 years until Graham Gooch bettered it with his 333 against India.

That was notable for being Denis Compton's first Test at Lord's. He made a century there against the West Indies in the year the war broke out. Len Hutton, too, scored his maiden Test hundred at headquarters but in the unique atmosphere of the immediate post-war seasons it was the happy-go-lucky Compton who become perhaps the most popular cricketer the ground has known. How he, in turn, must have loved every inch of Lord's. Already before the all-conquering year of 1947, 13 of his 26 hundreds in his first five home seasons as a first-class cricketer had been scored here.

Crowds in the seasons of immense national relief that followed the years of fear and loss were larger than they have ever been, before or since, and for those who experienced it 1947, a hot summer after a bitter, snow-bound winter, was the season of seasons. Compton scored 18 hundreds, including eight more at Lord's. Bill Edrich scored 12 hundreds, four of them on the same ground and together in the Lord's Test they added 370 for the third wicket against South Africa. The cricket writer Raymond Robertson-Glasgow called them: "Champions in the fight against dullness and the commercial standard...the mirror of hope and freedom and gaiety; heroes in the manner of school heroes...They do not outgrow the habit, the ideals, the very mistakes of youth."

Both these terrific cricketers and amiably flawed characters enjoyed a lasting friendship with the most glamorous of their Australian opponents of the time, the dashing Keith Ross Miller. Batting for the Dominions at Lord's at the end of the war he had signalled his all-round greatness with a magnificent piece of batting that earned him more than a hundred in an hour and a quarter before lunch, and there was more to come on his tours of 1953 and 1956.

Two more gifted overseas cricketers, Martin Donnelly, with 206 in 1949 and Vinoo Mankad, with 184 and five for 196 in 1952, emphasised the growing tendency for great cricketers to excel especially on the most illustrious cricketing stage, but the point was never better made than by the West Indies in 1950.

Hitherto, although they had had their great individual players like George Headley, there had been no real sign that the natural talent for the

game of the men from the Caribbean would consistently be translated into effective team performances. Now their stunning and joyous performance in the Lord's Test pointed the way to the period of invincibility a single generation later. In the 1980s the strength lay in batting and ferocious fast bowling. In 1950 it was batting plus "those two little pals of mine, Ramadhin and Valentine".

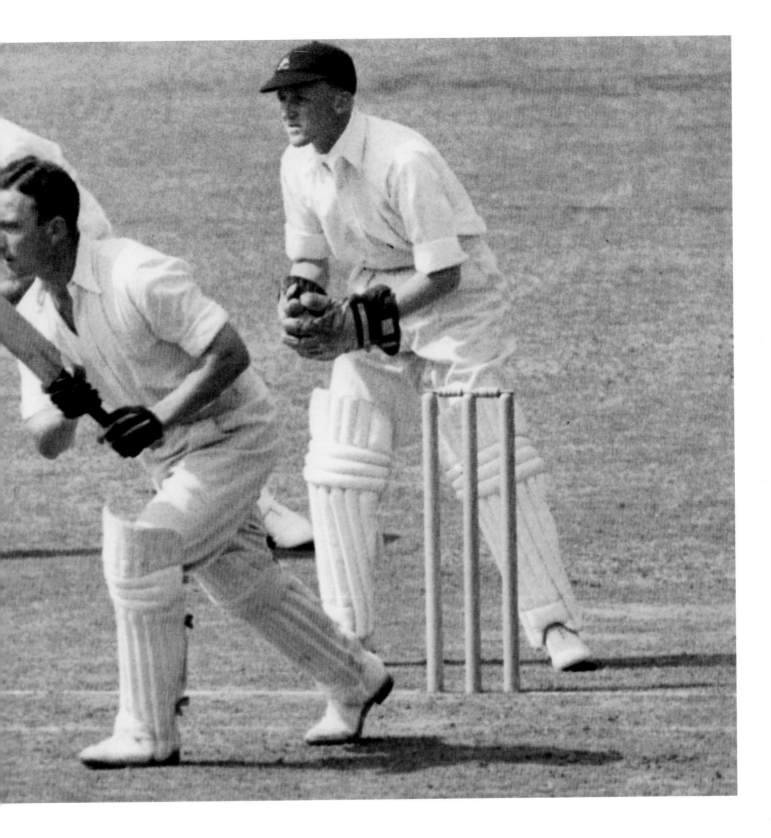

Brylcream Boy.
Long before David Beckham was a twinkle in his father's eye, Denis Compton was wowing the crowds with his cover drives and the girls with his brilliantine good looks.

Here, Compton drives through the covers during his innings of 208 against South Africa in 1947.

Their fame was born in that Lord's match: the tall bespectacled Jamaican left-arm spinner, Alf Valentine, took four for 48 and three for 79; the mysterious little wrist-spinner from Trinidad, the distinctly unorthodox Sonny Ramadhin, five for 66 and six for 86. Rae, Stollmeyer, Worrell, Weekes and Walcott did the rest.

I enter now the years of my first-hand experience of Lord's Test, starting with the dreadful anxiety of impending defeat in the year of the Coronation before Trevor Bailey and Willie Watson produced their epic fifth-wicket stand on the last day: 163 in 345 minutes after Miller, Ray Lindwall and Bill Johnston, each of them a hero of Bradman's unbeaten 1948 side, had all had prominent roles in setting up the probable victory.

In the 1950s, first under Len Hutton, then Peter May, England enjoyed, for a few years, superiority against all comers. It was based on the best group of bowlers they ever possessed: Alec Bedser, Fred Trueman, Brian Statham, Trevor Bailey, Johnny Wardle, Jim Laker and Tony Lock.

Five of this group could not prevent a win against the head for Australia in 1956 when Richie Benaud snared Colin Cowdrey in the gully with

one of the most astonishing catches ever seen and Miller took five wickets in each innings. But the West Indies and New Zealand were beaten by an innings in successive years and India by eight wickets in 1959 when Ken Barrington was embarked upon his years of wonderfully staunch batting at home and abroad in the middle-order. Less spectacular than May, Cowdrey, Tom Graveney or Ted Dexter, his great batting contemporaries, he was, nonetheless, the crag on which many a sweating bowler foundered.

Dexter had one of his finest hours in the never-to-be-forgotten game of 1963. It was a low-scoring affair that reached its desperate climax with all four results – draw, tie or win for either side – still possible as Wes Hall ran in, his shirt hanging out after a day of leonine effort, to bowl the final ball. The whole country, and no doubt the entire population of the Caribbean too, seemed to be watching or listening on that grey, rather chilly June afternoon.

From the start it was a colourful, closely contested, tense but honourable game. Conrad Hunte hit fours off each of the first three balls of the match from Trueman, but at least one of them came off the edge of an outswinging ball and

Trueman finished with six for 100 in the West Indies total of 301. England, with Barrington making 80 and Fred Titmus 52, managed only four runs fewer but the innings that had turned the tide, given that the West Indies had won the first Test at Old Trafford with ease, was Dexter's thrilling 70. On a rain affected pitch he took on the fast bowling of Hall, Charlie Griffith and Sobers with bold, classical driving, cutting and hooking.

West Indies lost their opening pair to slip catches by Cowdrey off the unlikely opening pair of Trueman and the 38-year-old Derek Shackleton, recalled after 11 years without a Test cap. Trueman, at his best, finished with 11 wickets in the match and Shackleton, as accurate as his reputation, with seven. The pride of Hampshire wheeled smoothly away at medium-pace for a total in the game of 80.4 overs, conceding only two runs an over against great strikers such as Worrell, Sobers and Rohan Kanhai. That the West Indies set England a stiff fourth-innings task in the conditions was due primarily to Basil Butcher, who played brilliantly for 133 out of 229, the innings of his life.

The target for England was 234, with five sessions to play, but in murky weather. Edrich and Stewart were quickly out to Hall, and Dexter to

Welcome to the 1970s.
Left: John Snow and Sunil Gavaskar tangle in an ugly altercation in 1971 when India recorded their first series win in England. Snow was alleged to have barged into Gavaskar and was dropped for the next Test as punishment.

Above: "It's a freaker," cried radio commentator John Arlott when this intruder hurdled the stumps in 1975. It was the start of a trend that still exists although it appears to be a peculiarly English fixation. Michael Angelow is the "freaker" watched by Alan Knott, Alan Turner and umpire Tom Spencer.

Lance Gibbs, hero of the previous Test, cleverly brought on early by Worrell to account for a batsman happier against pace. But Barrington and Cowdrey withstood some fierce stuff from Hall until one of many lifting balls struck Cowdrey above his left wrist, breaking a bone. Brian Close took his place and in the best-remembered innings of his long career he kept the fight going to 116 for three when rain and bad light brought an early end to the fourth day.

The climax was further delayed by the weather until 2.20 pm, whereupon a desperate struggle resumed. The first hour brought only 18 more runs. Griffith had Barrington caught behind by the teenage Deryck Murray but Jim Parks and Fred Titmus kept the fight going with Close until tea at 171 for five. Time was a factor now and Close changed from courageous defence to outrageous attack, advancing on Hall in the dim light, connecting with a few but then getting a nick to a big swing. He had made 70 in not far short of four hours.

Shackleton, not much of a batsman, joined David Allen with 15 left in 19 minutes. Hall bowled for the whole of the last day. Tired and running in a long way from the Pavilion End, his overs were taking a long time. When his last over started, eight runs were still needed. Singles came from the second and third balls, but Shackleton was run out by the supremely calm Worrell off the fourth, leaving Allen to face as Cowdrey returned with his arm in plaster, preparing to bat left-handed if necessary. It was not. Allen eschewed any risky attempt to hit a boundary. England finished six runs, and West Indies one wicket, short of victory.

There was a match almost to equal this one only two years later when South Africa came to Lord's with the makings of what was briefly to be the best side in the world. Barely had they flexed their muscles than they were forced out by the consequences of their government's racial policies, but the 1965 team captured the public imagination. Like most South Africa teams they fielded superbly and I do not believe even the India-rubber Jonty Rhodes caused such consternation in enemy ranks as Colin Bland, the panther in the covers whose throwing was as deadly as speed to the ball, cloaked though it was in a languid grace.

He batted beautifully too, at five in an order that also included the combative Eddie Barlow,

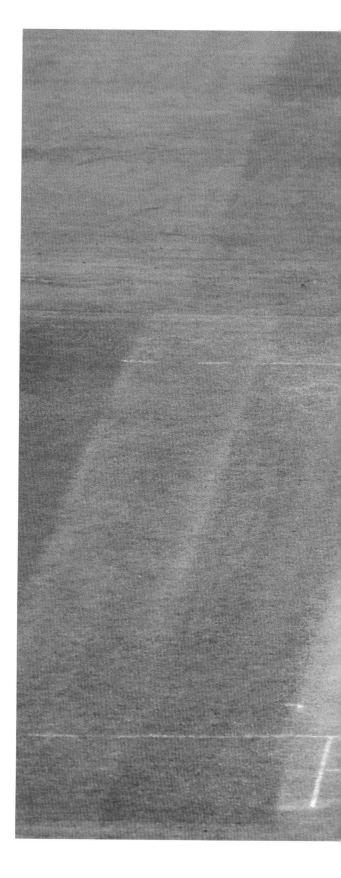

There can be few feelings worse than being run out for 99 but to do it at Lord's against the old enemy Australia must be as bad as it can get. Contemplating a third run in the 1993 Ashes Test to bring up his hundred, Michael Atherton slipped as he tried to scramble back to safety. Merv Hughes sent the throw in, Ian Healy took off the bails and England crashed to an innings defeat. Unfortunately, Atherton would never make a Test century at Lord's.

Denis Lindsay, a wicket-keeper good enough to bat at three and score heavily, and the incomparable Graeme Pollock. Luckily for England, in this year neither Barry Richards nor Mike Procter had yet graduated to the Test side, but with Peter Pollock leading an otherwise moderate bowling attack they provided an opening Test to remember. England got a first - innings lead despite the fact that Barrington and Parks were both run out by Bland, but although they needed only 191 to win in the second, they were lucky in the end to escape with a draw after John Edrich, in pre-helmet days, had been hit on the head by a bouncer from Pollock.

There was a very different sort of draw the following summer when England seemed so certain to win against the West Indies that Billy Griffith, most charming of MCC secretaries, rang Buckingham Palace to see if the Queen could come earlier than usual to meet the teams. She arrived at tea-time as usual, however, and no one needed to worry except Cowdrey and his team. Gary Sobers, later to be knighted by Her Majesty on the racecourse at Bridgetown, made 163 not out, sharing a saving partnership with his cousin David Holford.

He ended up declaring in time for Colin Milburn to make a rumbustious maiden Test century in a match that had started with a masterly second-wicket stand between the youthful Geoff Boycott and old Mr Elegance, Tom Graveney, who made 96 at the age of 39. The following year he did even better against India, scoring the 113th century of his prolific career. Later that year he made 81 against Pakistan for whom Hanif Mohammad, inspired by his surroundings, trumped Barrington's 148 with 187 not out.

Ray Illingworth made a Lord's hundred against the West Indies in 1969, four years before his captaincy ended in a crushing defeat at the hands of the same opponents, for whom Sobers made his last Test hundred in 1973.

Bowlers still had their day at this period, however. In 1972 the modest Western Australian, Bob Massie, swung the ball sensationally either way in a one-off performance of marvellous skill, taking eight wickets in each England innings. Two summers later, Arnold and Chris Old (five for 21) skittled India for 42 in 17 overs in their second innings.

Facing England's 629 – centuries for Dennis Amiss, Mike Denness and Greig – India had started their first innings well through Gavaskar, Engineer and Viswanath, only to collapse.

In 1975, Lord's had a new hero when the silver-haired, bespectacled figure of David Steele made a late entry into Test cricket. Steele was an instant hit, making a late appearance in the middle after going down one flight of stairs too many on his journey from the dressing room and locating not the Long Room but the Gents. When he appeared at last he looked, said John Arlott, like "the bank clerk going to war".

England regained the Ashes two years later but they still could not win at Lord's despite Bob Willis's seven for 78 and Bob Woolmer's 120. They were as strong as any team around at the time, however, partly because of the movement of so many of the world's best players to Kerry Packer's World Series Cricket and partly because of the emergence of their finest all-rounder since WG.

Ian Botham produced the first of many inspired performances at Lord's in 1978 against an unfortunate Pakistan, hitting 108, already his third Test century, then taking eight for 34 in Pakistan's second innings with fast swing bowling

The darkest day of Ian Botham's career.
Bowled by the Australian Ray Bright, he retreated to the pavilion with a pair to his name. The members barely acknowledged his return and he resigned the captaincy just a few hours later. A couple of weeks later, however, the whole of Britain was toasting Botham the hero as he single-handedly won the Ashes. This, of course, was 1981.

of the most irresistible kind. In the second game that summer on the ground where he had served as a member of the ground staff only a short while before he took 11 wickets against New Zealand.

One by one through the 1980s many of the finest players of the time added their names to the dressing-room board that records the hundreds scored in Tests on the ground: Haynes, Greenidge and Richards; Dilip Vengsarkar, Mohsin Khan and Martin Crowe; Sidath Wettimuny and Duleep Mendis of the newly-elevated Sri Lanka; and of the Australians, three very special innings from Kim Hughes, Allan Border and Steve Waugh.

For Englishmen, the most significant was perhaps Graham Gooch who, in 1980 scored 123 out of 269 against a West Indian attack led by Andy Roberts, Michael Holding, Joel Garner and Colin Croft. One needs only to know that of Gooch to appreciate how good he was.

Ten years later, Gooch, by now a confident captain, exceeded all expectations and all previous efforts at the great ground when he made 333 in the first innings against India and followed that with another century in the second. This was one of the great games, whatever the bowlers concerned may have thought about it at the time.

It should really be written in the lightest ink that India's captain, Mohammad Azharuddin, put England into bat on a sunny first morning. Gooch, a battleship at full speed on a flat sea, made the highest score ever seen at Lord's and Allan Lamb and Robin Smith, destroyers in his wake, added centuries of their own. Undaunted, Ravi Shastri responded with a staunch 100 and Azharuddin with an absolutely scintillating 121 on a golden Saturday afternoon. Time and again steely wrists sent good-length balls buzzing to the boundary, many of them taken off the line of the stumps to end up, badly bruised, on the mid-wicket boundary.

India were still faced with the probability of a follow-on when Kapil Dev, accompanied by a hopeless number eleven, solved the problem of knocking off the 24 required to avoid it by hitting four sixes in succession off Eddie Hemmings's off-spin. All it did was to give Gooch the chance to extend his aggregate for the game to a record 456 (many are pleased with that in a whole season) before England eventually hunted down their victory through the efforts of Devon Malcolm,

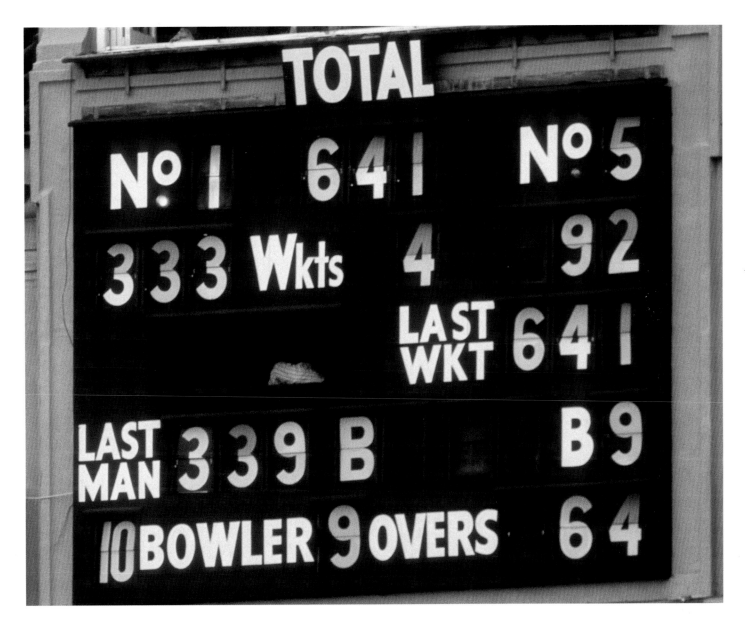

Angus Fraser and Chris Lewis. In a match so full of good things, however, another Indian also produced something out of this world: the 17-year-old Sachin Tendulkar sprinted 30 yards along the Nursery boundary to catch Lamb in the second innings in one outstretched hand.

Since that five-day feast, only two games have matched it; the nail-biting contests of 1992 and 2000, memorable less for individual deeds than the wonderful tension that only a long-drawn out Test match can produce.

Both games were difficult for batsmen and no one scored a century in either. In the first, played in sunny mid-June weather at the traditional, and ideal, time for the Lord's Test, England won the toss and started with a confident opening stand of 123 by Gooch and Alec Stewart but they were

With 2,015 runs to his name there, more than anyone else, Lord's was a happy hunting ground for Graham Gooch. He made six Test centuries there starting with his maiden ton against the West Indies in 1980. He also hit 183 against New Zealand in 1986 and 174 against Sri Lanka in 1991 but he showed a particular taste for the Indian bowlers. In 1986 he warmed up with 114 and then, in 1990, he struck a blistering 333, the ground record for Lord's, and followed up with 123 in the second innings.

undone by magical swing bowling with an old ball by Waqar Younis and Wasim Akram. Fifties by Aamir Sohail, Asif Mujtaba and Salim Malik – but not for Javed Miandad, one of the few great batsman who never made a Test hundred at Lord's – helped Pakistan to a first-innings lead of 38.

Mushtaq Ahmed helped the great opening pair to bowl England out cheaply a second time, despite Stewart's achievement in becoming the first Englishman to carry his bat through a Test innings at Lord's. Pakistan needed only 138 to win, but although Ian Botham, in his 102nd and last Test, and Phillip DeFreitas were injured, Pakistan were reduced to 95 for eight by the three remaining bowlers, Devon Malcolm, Chris Lewis and, in his first Test match, Ian Salisbury. The response of Wasim and Waqar was to attack with the bat as they always had with the ball. They won the match by two wickets late on the fourth day.

The match in 2000 produced even more drama in a shorter time span, including the first instance in any Test of at least one ball of all four innings of the game being bowled in a single day, the second. On the first, Stewart, cheerfully taking over the captaincy from his successor, the injured

they reached 170 for two by tea. A collapse followed against Darren Gough and Dominic Cork but it was Andrew Caddick who sparked the second-day mayhem by taking his only wicket of the innings with the first ball of the day.

Facing a total of 267, the highest of the match England were bowled out for 134 by Curtly Ambrose and Courtney Walsh. The touring team went in, reasonably expecting a 50th anniversary celebration of the first West Indies win at Lord's, especially as Brian Lara was there to lead the batting. In the event, on a bouncy pitch, they were bowled out for 54 in two hours and 26.4 overs, torn apart by furious fast bowling amidst a frenzied atmosphere, Caddick producing perhaps his best performance for England with five for 16 in 13 overs.

The mood was very different, one of palm-sweating tension, when England resumed on Saturday morning at nought for nought, needing 188 on a bouncing, seaming pitch. Frequently beaten by Ambrose and Walsh, giants in both senses, the tenacious Michaels, Atherton and Vaughan, added 92 for the second wicket by gritty, excellent batting. But a long struggle ebbed

lost their seventh wicket at 149 and their eighth at 160. Then Cork, with Lord's yet again bringing out the very best in him, attacked much as Wasim had done eight years before. Fortune duly favoured the bold and England won by two wickets.

It was a magnificent game of cricket played at a ground that, even up to 2003 when Graeme Smith's South African team romped to an impressive innings victory, has been inspiring players from all corners of the earth for well over a century. Lord's is that kind of place and, for as long as the game is played, it will always be seen from any corner of the earth as the home of cricket.

Kapil Dev found a special place in Lord's history in 1990 when, with India needing 24 runs to avoid the follow-on, he hit off-spinner Eddie Hemmings for four successive sixes.

Graeme Smith's 259 in 2003 is the highest score by an overseas player at Lord's.

LORD's Ground Records

Result Summary

	Played	Won	Lost	Drawn
England	104	39	25	40
Australia	33	14	5	14
India	14	1	10	3
Pakistan	11	3	3	5
New Zealand	13	1	5	7
South Africa	13	3	7	3
Sri Lanka	4	0	2	2
West Indies	16	4	6	6
Zimbabwe	2	0	2	0

Bangladesh have yet to play at Lord's

Highest Totals

729-6	Australia v England 1930
682-6	South Africa v England 2003
653-4	by England v India 1990
652-8	by West Indies v England 1973

Lowest Completed Innings Totals

42	India v England 1974
47	New Zealand v England 1958
53	England v Australia 1888
53	Australia v England 1896
54	West Indies v England 2000

Highest Match Aggregates

Runs	Wkts	
1603	28	England v India 1990
1601	29	England v Australia 1930
1406	36	England v India 2002

Lowest Match Aggregates (Result oriented matches)

Runs	Wkts	
291	40	England v Australia 1888

Highest Scores

333	GA Gooch England v India 1990
259	GA Smith South Africa v England 2003
254	DG Bradman Australia v England 1930
240	WR Hammond England v Australia 1938
214*	CG Greenidge West Indies v England 1984

Highest Run Aggregates

Runs	Matches	Hundreds	
2015	21	6	GA Gooch
1476	20	3	AJ Stewart
1241	17	2	DI Gower
1189	16	3	G Boycott
959	13	4	AJ Lamb

Partnership Records

268 for 1st	JB Hobbs and H Sutcliffe	England v South Africa 1924
287 for 2nd	HA Gomes and CG Greenidge	West Indies v England 1984
370 for 3rd	DCS Compton and JH Edrich	England v South Africa 1947
248 for 4th	DCS Compton and L Hutton	England v West Indies 1939
216 for 5th	AR Border and GM Ritchie	Australia v England 1985
274* for 6th	DAJ Holford and GStA Sobers	West Indies v England 1966
174 for 7th	MC Cowdrey and TG Evans	England v West Indies 1957
246 for 8th	GOB Allen and LEG Ames	England v New Zealand 1931
130 for 9th	GF Lawson and SR Waugh	Australia v England 1989
83 for 10th	R Illingworth (R) and JA Snow	England v West Indies 1969

Best Bowling in an Innings.

8 for 34	IT Botham	England v Pakistan 1978
8 for 38	GD McGrath	Australia v England 1997
8 for 43	H Verity	England v Australia 1934
8 for 51	DL Underwood	England v Pakistan 1974
8 for 53	RAL Massie	Australia v England 1972

Best Bowling in a Match

16 for 137 (8-84, 8-53)	RAL Massie	Australia v England 1972
15 for 104 (7-61, 8-43)	H Verity	England v Australia 1934
13 for 71 (5-20, 8-51)	DL Underwood	England v Pakistan 1974
12 for 101 (7-52, 5-49)	R Tattersall	England v South Africa 1951
11 for 70 (4-38, 7-32)	DL Underwood	England v New Zealand 1969

Hat Trick

GM Griffin South Africa v England 1960

Highest Wicket Aggregates

Wkts	Matches	5WI	
69	15	8	IT Botham
63	12	5	FS Trueman
47	9	3	RGD Willis
45	9	3	JB Statham

Most Catches by Fielder

Catches	Matches	
20	12	WR Hammond
20	13	MC Cowdrey
18	21	GA Gooch

Most Dismissals by Wicketkeeper

Dismissals	Matches	
37	13	TG Evans
37	12	AJ Stewart
33	14	APE Knott

THE OVAL

in 1844 another MCC, the Montpelier Cricket Club from Walworth, bought the lease on a market garden in Kennington from the Duchy of Cornwall, who, much to Surrey's whispered dismay, hold the freehold to this day. The first of 10,000 turfs from Tooting Common was laid on the oval-shaped ground the following March and in August Surrey County Cricket Club was formed at the Horns Tavern, Kennington. The meeting was chaired by the same William Ward who had baled out Lord's 20 years before.

The Oval has always been the home of Surrey, the heartland of the club's many triumphs, including 20 County Championship titles between 1890 and 2002 and three more in the years immediately preceding what is generally recognised as the first formally constituted championship. It was through the enterprise of Surrey's secretary, Charles William Alcock, that the ground staged the first two Tests in England, in 1880 and 1882, not to mention all but one of the FA Cup Finals between 1871 and 1882. As Keith Booth's biography of Alcock has detailed, The Oval of that period was a veritable sports centre, also staging rugby football, athletics, baseball, cycling, lacrosse and lawn tennis.

Cricket quickly became the main event. The first Test was played late in the Australians' tour of 1880 by equally late arrangement, thereby unwittingly setting a trend for the tradition that the Oval Test marked the big-match climax to a English season. It is this position in the calendar which has led to The Oval being the stage at which many of the world's greatest cricketers have made their farewells to the game. The most famous instance is the great Don Bradman in the summer of 1948: cheered all the way to the wicket and given three cheers by the England team, the Don, who needed just four to give himself a Test average of exactly 100, was bowled second ball by an Eric Hollies googly for nought. A final average of 99.94 still stands testament to the best we have yet seen.

Veterans from the First World War enjoy a privileged view of the 1934 Ashes Test. If they are not looking too happy it may be because they are watching Don Bradman (244) and Bill Ponsford (266) add 451 for the second Australian wicket. England went on to lose by the emphatic margin of 562 runs.

WG Grace, the best of his era, marked the 1880 Test match with a lordly 152 on the first day, September 5, and it proved the foundation of a five-wicket victory gained despite the fact that his great friend Billy Murdoch made one run more in Australia's second innings.

WG was joined in the England team by his brothers Fred and Edward. In what was destined to be the last big match of his life – he died of a chill after sleeping in a damp bed at Basingstoke just two weeks after the Test – Fred took one of the most famous of all catches far away at the Vauxhall End off an enormous skyer from George Bonnor, holding the ball fast after the two batsmen had turned for a third run. This was the first of only two occasions in Test cricket that three brothers have played in the same team – 90 years later, the Pakistan brethren of Hanif, Mushtaq and Sadiq Mohammad became the second set.

The greatest bowler of the early years of international cricket, Fred Spofforth, the original "Demon", took seven for 46 and seven for 44 in the second Oval Test, the one that gave rise to the Ashes and sparked the greatest of all the long-running sporting rivalries. I have a precious little book by JN Pentelow that describes the first 43 Tests between England and Australia between 1877 and 1895. This game, he says, has been so often described that "I shall content myself with a summary of the events in which they occurred." They thrill the reader to this day, starting with Murdoch winning the toss and batting on a pitch "slow and heavy, from heavy rains".

Australia were bowled out for 63, primarily due to Richard Barlow's taking five for 19 with his left-arm medium-pace, but despite a "plucky" stand of 38 for the third wicket by George Ulyett and AP Lucas, England gained a lead of only 38. Then, recalls Pentelow: "Thirty up in less than half an hour and the balance worked off by 12.45...Steel bowled Massie, who had scored

Sheer class.
Left: Nothing less than the best ever did for Douglas Jardine, the Surrey man who masterminded England's victory in Australia in 1932-33 through the use of Bodyline - or leg theory as Jardine insisted on calling it.

Right: Jack Hobbs remains a legend of Surrey and England. Having made his Test debut during the 1907-08 tour of Australia, Hobbs carried on batting for England until 1930 by which time he had played 61 Tests and was 48 years old. Two of his 15 Test centuries were compiled under the gaze of the gasholder: 100 against Australia in 1926 and 159 against the West Indies in 1928.

55...Bonnor's middle stump again sent down...two for 70...Bannerman was caught at extra mid-off, having batted 70 minutes for 13...three for 70..Horan caught at point off Peate...four for 79...Giffen out in the same way...five for 79...Blackham and Murdoch took the score to five for 99 before luncheon...And so on to 122 all out."

England needed only 85 to win, but George Giffen recalled later how during the tense ten-minute interval between innings on the second afternoon, Spofforth declared: "This thing can be done." One can feel the pressure mount in England's second innings. Grace and "Monkey" Hornby, the captain, put on 15 before Spofforth knocks back Hornby's off stump and follows up by bowling Barlow first ball. "Oh, my Hornby and my Barlow long ago."

But Grace and Ulyett add 36, leaving only 34 to get when Spofforth, switched to take over from Tom Garrett at the Pavilion End, bowls his "extra fast one" and Blackham takes the snick behind. Two balls later Grace is caught at mid-off off Harry Boyle, bringing together the amateurs Lucas and Lyttelton. Lucas plays the stonewall game; Lyttelton makes a hit or two but there are 12, yes 12, successive maiden overs before Bannerman misfields on purpose and Lyttelton is exposed to Spofforth. "Ruse succeeded after four more maidens: five for 66." Lucas hits a four. Steel caught and bowled. Six for 70. Maurice Read clean bowled second ball. Barnes hits a two...Blackham lets three byes...Lucas plays on...eight for 75...Blackham catches Barnes off his glove...Peate joins Mr Studd, hits a two to square-leg, tries to do it again and is bowled...ten for 77.

Tom Horan, one of the first player-writers, recalled how an English batsman's lips were ashen grey as he passed him on his way to bat; how the scorer's trembling hand wrote "Peate" like "Geese". There was a moment of silence when he was bowled, then the crowd broke over the ground and Spofforth was carried off, shoulder-high, having in his last 11 overs taken four for two.

At the end of the week *The Sporting Times* carried the obituary notice:

In loving memory of English Cricket which died at the Oval on 29th August, 1882, deeply lamented by a large circle of sorrowing friends and acquaintances

RIP

NB. The body will be cremated, and the Ashes taken to Australia.

It may seem to many who have experienced their Test cricket only in the last 15 years that the sorrowing friends have been lamenting ever since, but in fact The Oval has been the scene of much

Reservoir dogs.
Alan Melville leads out the South Afriicans for the final Test of 1947.

Overleaf: David Gower evades a bouncer from Malcolm Marshall during the 1984 Test. England, captained by Gower, lost by 172 runs, the final chapter in a five-nil "blackwash".

English rejoicing in the years since that colossal match and not least against Australia. Here it was that in 1902 Gilbert Jessop and George Hirst were chiefly responsible for the equally breathless finish to the fifth Test when, this time, England managed to get the runs in the fourth innings, albeit only with a wicket in hand and by dint of a last-wicket partnership of 15 by Hirst and his intrepid Yorkshire colleague, Wilfred Rhodes. Jessop, the mighty "Croucher", had turned the game with an astonishing and heroic hundred in 75 minutes after England had been 48 for five chasing 263 to win.

"Jaunty" was how the playwright, Ben Travers, recalled Jessop's approach that day as he watched the game, an excited 15-year-old schoolboy. In his

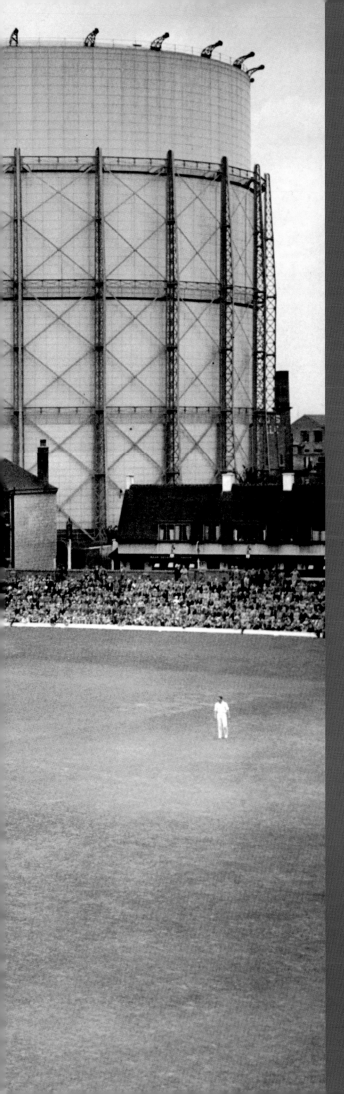

cricket reminiscences he remembered that when he got home that night his father opened the front door and greeted him with arms outstretched in mutual rejoicing. "I felt a bit of a hero at having actually been there on Jessop's Day," he wrote.

A decade later an even greater cricketer had one of his many golden days at South Africa's expense. With his huge hands, immaculate length and effortless power of swerve, cut and spin, the peerless SF Barnes took 13 wickets for 57 in the match, England winning by ten wickets on a wet pitch in a game in which the batting of one of The Oval's legendary figures, Jack Hobbs, scored the only fifty.

Amazing to relate, he was still there, aged 43, opening the batting with cool mastery, when England won back the Ashes for the first time after the war, in 1926. The series was level going into the game so this was a timeless match, and England had changed captains, from Arthur Carr to Percy Chapman, as well as recalling Rhodes at the age of 48. This time it was Australia's turn to chase the runs on the last day. There was little to choose between the two first innings but Hobbs made 100 and Herbert Sutcliffe 161 in England's second before the leg-breaks of Clarrie Grimmett and Arthur Mailey had their rewards.

After the great pace of Harold Larwood had made the early incisions, Rhodes took four for 44 with left-arm spin of wonderful control and subtlety, and the long period of Australia's domination ended. Ponsford, with 110, Bradman with 232, and the graceful and much-loved Archie Jackson, with 73, made sure the boot was on the other foot in 1930; and four years later Bradman scored another double-hundred as Australia followed up this innings victory with another, by the fairly decisive margin of 562 runs, in 1934.

This page: Len Hutton in the early stages of his world record 364 against Australia in 1938. Maurice Leyland, who made 187, is at the non-striker's end.

Overleaf: Fred Trueman leaves the field after becoming the first man to reach 300 Test wickets in the 1963 Test against Australia. "How do you feel?" he was asked. "Bloody tired," came the reply.

This time they were to keep them for 19 years despite the crushing England victory of 1938 when Len Hutton made his immortal 364, beating Wally Hammond's highest Test score and setting the target for the later record-holders, Sobers and Lara. England won this Test by the massive margin of an innings and 579 runs after making the small matter of 903 for seven declared. Hutton shared a second-wicket partnership of 382 with his fellow Yorkshireman Maurice Leyland who made 187, but the manner of their batting did not draw applause from all quarters.

At the end of the first day when Hutton was 160 not out, Douglas Jardine, a man who, just a few years before, had been ruthless in his hunting down of the Australian batsmen through the use of Bodyline, wrote: "However satisfactory a great score may be, it scarcely produces sufficient incidents to make up an enlivening day's cricket unless the rate of scoring be phenomenal. There was nothing phenomenal in the pace at which Hutton and Leyland made their runs, their great stand – and 'great' accurately describes it – paved the way for England's mastery. Throughout there was a heartening sense of mastery about the batting – workmanlike mastery." If that sounds harsh, it should be noted that 131 overs were bowled that day.

As "Young" Joe Hardstaff also made a century, Denis Compton turned to his team-mate Eddie Paynter in the pavilion and said: "Eddie, ten bob says we don't make a dozen between us." History does not relate whether Paynter took up the bet but the scorecard shows that he made a duck and Compton only managed a single.

Another Yorkshireman, Arthur Wood, celebrated his first Test cap just a few days before his 40th birthday by coming in with 500 already on the board, and knocking up a breezy 53. "I was always good in a crisis," he quipped.

It was the same Wood who offered some helpful encouragement to Hedley Verity in Sheffield in 1935 when the South African Horace Cameron hit him for 30 in one over. "You've got him in two minds," he said. "He doesn't know whether to hit you for six or four."

The Ashes did not come home until 1953, Coronation year, when their return seemed somehow in keeping with the year in which the

shackles of a costly world war were finally broken. Everest was conquered, the new Queen crowned and, at The Oval on August 19, the urn regained under Hutton when Jim Laker and Tony Lock bowled Australia out in the third innings and Bill Edrich and Denis Compton knocked off the runs in the fourth.

A youthful Fred Trueman, later to become the first bowler to 300 Test wickets when he had Neil Hawke caught by Cowdrey in the 1964 Oval Test, joined forces with the mighty Bedser in that 1953 game. Fast bowlers and spinners were linked by the fast-medium of Trevor Bailey, who also made a typically useful 64 at number six. This against an attack starting formidably with Lindwall, Miller, Johnston and Davidson but lacking Benaud. The future captain was playing, however, in the drawn game at the end of Laker's all-conquering season in 1956, and in 1961 when Norman O'Neill and Peter Burge celebrated with centuries the winning of the Ashes in the previous game at Old Trafford.

When Brian Statham, and later Frank Tyson arrived to share the fast-bowling load with Trueman, Bedser was put out to grass by the England selectors, a decision that greatly helped Surrey to their glorious years of seven successive County Championship titles in the 1950s under Stuart Surridge and Peter May. With Laker, Lock and Peter Loader, plus the Bedser twins, success was based on a superb attack, brilliant fielding, aggressive captaincy and the sheer class of May's batting. They were virtually unbeatable at The Oval on Bert Lock's sometimes dusty pitches but no less dominating everywhere else.

As Surrey's star waned, so, to some extent, did England's. The West Indies completed their series win at the Oval in 1963 with a century by Conrad Hunte; India gained their first rubber in England in 1971 when Bhagwat Chandrasekhar took six for 38 with his quick leg-breaks, and almost won again when Sunil Gavaskar, with a technique close to perfection, made 221 in 1979 as India came tantalisingly close to an improbable victory. Set 438 to win, the Indians dared to believe the impossible and with Gavaskar and Chetan Chauhan sharing an opening partnership of 213 so increasingly did The Oval crowd.

Chauhan went for 80 but Gavaskar and Dilip Vengsarkar took the score to 366 before the latter was out for 52. As the match appeared to be heading India's way, up stepped Ian Botham

with three quick wickets including that of Gavaskar who had batted just over eight hours. With three balls remaining, all four results were still possible but the game ended in a draw with India on 429 for eight – just nine runs short of a famous win.

Gavaskar's 221 remains the highest score by an Indian in England although Rahul Dravid came within a boundary of equalling it when he made 217 in the corresponding drawn Test in 2002.

The Chappell brothers, Ian and Greg, both scored hundreds in a memorable display of batting in 1972 while Viv Richards and Michael Holding dominated the match on a ground parched white by the remorseless sunshine of 1976, Richards scoring 291 before Holding took eight for 92 and six for 57. Eleven years later the Pakistani genius Javed Miandad scored 260, and their gloriously gifted captain, Imran Khan, 118 to seal Pakistan's first series win in England.

England also had their moments, of course, notably in 1985 when David Gower and Graham Gooch played some elegiac strokes in a partnership of 351 for the second wicket against Australia before Botham and Richard Ellison took most of the wickets that won the Ashes.

Neither, however, could match the performance of Devon Malcolm, like Holding originally from Jamaica, when he bowled South Africa to defeat by irresistible fast bowling in1994.

On a fast and bouncy Oval pitch, Malcolm was a handful from the start although he only took one wicket in South Africa's 332. He did, however, send Jonty Rhodes to hospital after hitting him on the helmet – although Rhodes ducked so low that Malcolm considered appealing for a leg-before.

"You guys are history."
Devon Malcolm looks on as South African batsman Jonty Rhodes comes to his senses after being hit on the head during the first innings of the 1994 Test. When Malcolm was himself hit by Fanie de Villiers, he vowed to get even – with nine for 57 he kept his word.

South Africa took a 28-run lead on the first innings although one delivery from Fanie de Villiers might have sealed their fate. It hit Malcolm on the helmet, square between the eyes. Malcolm was incensed.

Just as Hirst and Rhodes never actually said "we'll get 'em in singles", so Malcolm never actually said: "You guys are history." However, even if he did not say it, he certainly thought it and the South Africans duly found themselves on the end of a fierce spell of fast bowling that brought him nine for 57 in 99 balls. Only Daryll Cullinan held out, making 94, before being the eighth man out, caught off Darren Gough.

As England went on to win and square the series, Malcolm could look back on the sixth-best analysis in the history of Test cricket. Since then the spinners Anil Kumble and Muttiah Muralitharan have improved on it in Delhi and Kandy respectively, and the Sri Lankan off-spinner produced another extraordinary performance at The Oval in 1998.

Sri Lanka defied expectations by winning through his extraordinary bowling and the devastating speed of their scoring in response to an England first innings of 445 in which Graeme Hick and John Crawley scored centuries. They responded with 591 off 156.5 overs, mainly by means of Sanath Jarasuriya's cutting blade and Aravinda de Silva's wristy genius. Jayasuriya scored 213 from 278 balls, and de Silva 152, becoming the first Sri Lanka batsman to pass 5,000 Test runs.

Murali, a one-man attack, spun rings around the English batsmen following his seven wickets in the first innings with nine for 65 in the second as England spiralled to defeat. In what was one of the most phenomenal bowling performances in Test history, he bowled 113.5 overs in the game for a return of 16 wickets for 220, the fifth-best ever.

Another spinner, Phil Tufnell, is more generally associated with Lord's because of his association with Middlesex but this othodox left-armer enjoyed some memorable match-winning days on the bouncy pitches in SE11. The first of these came in 1991 when his six for 25 on a hot and steamy Saturday afternoon led to the West Indies' following on for the first time in England for 22 years.

Apart from being Viv Richards's last Test, this was also the game that produced one of those golden

moments of radio. Ian Botham had been dismissed in England's first innings when he tried to hook Ambrose, lost balance and knocked a bail off with his inner thigh. "He didn't quite get his leg over," observed Jonathan Agnew, a comment that led both he and Brian Johnston to collapse in giggles and the nation's drivers to pull on to the hard shoulder for fear of losing control of their cars amid the laughter.

Tufnell only took one wicket in the second innings, but David Lawrence had his day in the sun with a five-wicket return and England levelled the series.

Underwood's finest hour.
And extraordinary photograph of all 11 England fielders crowded around the bat as umpire Charlie Elliot gives Australia's John Inverarity out leg-before to Derek Underwood, so ending the fifth Test in 1968.

The England fielders from left to right: Ray Illingworth, Tom Graveney, John Edrich, Ted Dexter, Colin Cowdrey, Derek Underwood, Alan Knott, John Snow, David Brown, Colin Milburn and Basil D'Oliveira.

Three cheers for Bradman.
The England team, led by Norman Yardley, give the Don a rousing send-off when he emerged for his final Test innings in 1948. Needing just four to retire with a Test average of 100, he was bowled second ball by Eric Hollies for nought, so having to settle for an average of 99.94.

When Australia returned to The Oval for the final Test in 2001, the Ashes safely locked away, it was the turn of another spinner to enjoy himself. Under the father and son groundsmen, Harry Brind and his successor, Paul, faithfully backed up by their long-time deputy, Bill Gordon, pitches at The Oval have generally continued to be every bit as good as they were in the days of Bosser Martin and Australia totalled 641 for four declared at well over four runs an over.

Justin Langer made a courageous century on the first day and on the second the England bowlers began to wonder if they would ever separate the Waugh twins. Steve had defied medical expectation by playing in the game having ripped a calf muscle in two places just three weeks before at Trent Bridge, making his hundred all the greater. The Waughs emulated the Chappells in 1972 by each making a century of high class and buying time for Shane Warne to win the match by tireless bowling on the last three days.

Going past 400 wickets when he had Alec Stewart caught behind, Warne once more demonstrated his marvellous skill to vary pace, angle and trajectory but, above all, to rip leg-breaks past the best batsmen without bowling full-tosses or long-hops like ordinary wrist-spinners. The most prolific of all the wrist-spinners took seven for 165 and, after England had fallen ten runs short of saving the follow-on, four for 64. His great henchman, Glenn McGrath, claimed five for 43 to round off Australia's 20th win in their previous 23 games.

How Test cricket has changed since George Bonnor lifted that stratospheric drive into the Kennington sky and the world stood still as Fred Grace waited beneath it with his hands in an attitude of prayer. It is a more complicated game now, beset by international politics and recurring controversies, but it is still a joy for the most part and one must beware too much nostalgia, especially in relation to such an earthy place as The Oval.

That peerless pricker of pomposity, Bob Dylan, got it right:

Ah, but I was so much older then
I'm younger than that now.

Six years later, Tufnell was at the heart of England's 19-run win over Australia. The Ashes had already been lost but he produced another fine display of controlled spin bowling to take seven for 66 in the first innings. Then, with Australia needing just 124 to seal a four-one series win, Tufnell picked up another four wickets and, in tandem with Andrew Caddick, bowled England to victory.

Remember this.
David Gower, the England captain in 1985, celebrates a crushing win in the Ashes series. He is joined on The Oval balcony by Ian Botham and Paul Downton.

England have not won the Ashes on home soil since.

THE OVAL Ground Records

Result Summary

	Played	Won	Lost	Drawn
England	85	33	18	34
Australia	33	6	15	12
India	9	1	2	6
Pakistan	7	3	2	2
New Zealand	9	1	4	4
South Africa	11	0	4	7
Sri Lanka	1	1	0	0
West Indies	15	6	6	0

Bangladesh and Zimbabwe have yet to play at The Oval

Highest Totals

903-7	England v Australia	1938
708	Pakistan v England	1987
701	Ausralia v England	1934

Lowest Completed Innings Totals

44	Australia v England	1896
52	England v Australia	1948
63	Australia v England	1882

Highest Match Aggregates

Runs	Wkts	
1507	28	England v West Indies 1976
1494	37	England v Australia 1934
1477	33	England v South Africa 1947

Lowest Match Aggregates (Result oriented matches)

Runs	Wkts	
363	40	England v Australia 1882

Highest Scores

364	L Hutton England v Australia	1938
291	IVA Richards West Indies v England	1976
266	WH Ponsford Australia v England	1934
260	Javed Miandad Pakistan v England	1987
244	DG Bradman Australia v England	1934

Highest Run Aggregates

Runs	Matches	Hundreds	
1521	12	4	L Hutton
1097	12	1	GA Gooch
930	12	4	WR Hammond

Partnership Records

290 for 1st	MC Cowdrey and G Pullar England v South Africa	1960
451 for 2nd	DG Bradman and WH Ponsford Australia v England	1934
264 for 3rd	WR Hammond and L Hutton England v West Indies	1939
266 for 4th	WR Hammond and TS Worthington England v India	1936
191 for 5th	Imran Khan and Javed Miandad Pakistan v England	1987
215 for 6th	J Hardstaff Jr and L Hutton England v Australia	1938
142 for 7th	KL Hutchings and J Sharp England v Australia	1909
217 for 8th	TW Graveney and JT Murray England v West Indies	1966
190 for 9th	Asif Iqbal and Intikhab Alam Pakistan v England	1967
128 for 10th	K Higgs and JA Snow England v West Indies	1966

Best Bowling in an Innings

9 for 57 DE Malcolm	England v South Africa 1994
9 for 65 M Muralitharan	Sri Lanka v England 1998
8 for 29 SF Barnes	England v South Africa 1912
8 for 65 H Trumble	Australia v England 1902
8 for 92 MA Holding	England v West Indies 1976

Best Bowling in a Match

16 for 220 (7-155, 9-65)	M Muralitharan Sri Lanka v England 1998
14 for 90 (7-46, 7-44)	R Spofforth Australia v England 1882
14 for 149 (8-92, 6-57)	MA Holding West Indies v England 1976
13 for 57 (5-28, 8-29)	SF Barnes England v South Africa 1912
12 for 89 (6-59, 6-30)	H Trumble Australia v England 1896

Highest Wicket Aggregates

Wkts	Matches	5WI	
52	11	2	IT Botham
45	10	3	DL Underwood
40	8	2	JC Laker

Most Catches by Fielder

Catches	Matches	
19	11	IT Botham
14	11	MC Cowdrey
14	12	GA Gooch

Most Dismissals by Wicketkeeper

Dismissals	Matches	
31	12	APE Knott
26	10	AJ Stewart
24	10	TG Evans

SOUTH AFRICA

Peter Robinson

As the third nation, after Australia and England, to take to international cricket, South Africa enjoys a rich if occasionally chequered history on and off the field. The politics of race may have been a dominating factor virtually since South Africa first took the field but the players that have performed and the matches that have taken place have been little else but fascinating. Likewise the grounds.

South Africa can claim 11 Test grounds although two of these – the Old Wanderers and Lord's, Durban – have long since ceased to exist while Ellis Park in Johannesburg, which hosted six Tests between the exit and entrance of the Old and the New Wanderers, has returned to its rightful place as one of the world's great rugby stadia.

Of the older grounds, St George's in Port Elizabeth, with its resident band, can still claim one of the best atmospheres around while the newer of the two Wanderers, which first saw action on Christmas Eve 1956 and was more recently the scene of the 2003 World Cup final, is like a bullring, the stands tucked in tightly around an almost perfect circle of green field, giving a real sense of confrontation.

Kingsmead, which took over from Lord's in Durban in 1923, can also claim its place in history as the venue for the Timeless Test in 1938-39 when England's bid to reach 696 for victory was finally halted at 654 for five. It was the tenth day and the England team's boat was setting sail. In South Africa's last series before isolation, against Australia in 1969-70, Kingsmead was also the setting for one of their most memorable batting displays when Barry Richards, 140, and Graeme Pollock, 274, gave a glimpse of what might have been.

Since South Africa's return to Test cricket, Centurion Park, just outside Pretoria, Springbok Park in Bloemfontein, East London and Potchefstroom have also been given Test status. Of these Centurion can already be said to have made a lasting impact on world cricket having staged the match that saw Hansie Cronje set up a daring declaration and forfeiture against England in 1999-2000. England won a thrilling chase but it was later revealed that Cronje had received payments for "fixing" the game.

However, of the 11, there is only one that would find its way on to the shortlist of the world's most stunning grounds. And that ground is Newlands.

NEWLANDS, CAPE TOWN

THE EIGHTH EDITION OF THE WORLD CUP opened at Newlands on February 9, 2003 with South Africa playing the West Indies. On the previous evening the ground had hosted a 30 million rand opening ceremony, the most spectacular of its kind for both the sport and the continent. The organisers claimed that it had been watched by a worldwide television audience of some 1.4 billion. There was little evidence to verify this figure, but so smoothly did the event go that few felt inclined to challenge the numbers.

The opening ceremony was staged on a Saturday night. On the Sunday the celebrations were expected to continue. Unfortunately for the host country and the 25,000 spectators crammed into Newlands, the West Indies had not read the script. With Brian Lara, a batsman who understands the notion of timing in every sense, making the tournament's first century, South Africa were left to chase 279 for a victory that was meant to propel them towards lifting the trophy at the Wanderers six weeks later. Unfortunately, the top order failed to get going and although a characteristically brutal 57 from Lance Klusene gave South Africa a realistic chance of winning as they went into their last over, the home team fell three runs short and their World Cup dream began to crumble. In every other respect, though, Cape Town and Newlands had given the tournament a perfect start.

Newlands is not the oldest ground in South Africa, nor even in Cape Town. Cricket, it is believed, has been played on Green Point Common since 1810 when a match was staged between the Ordnance Department and the Officers of the 87th Regiment. Neither did it host South Africa's first Test match. That distinction goes to St George's Park in Port Elizabeth where England, captained by Aubrey Smith – who later went on to become the only Test cricketer to win an Oscar – beat South Africa in 1889. It is not South Africa's biggest ground, but it is the ground most synonymous with South African cricket and the ground best loved by visiting international cricketers.

Just months after being readmitted to international cricket, South Africa found themselves at the Adelaide Oval during the 1992 World Cup. Mike Procter, the coach of the South African team, was asked how the ground compared to Newlands. "It's beautiful," he said, "But it doesn't have The Mountain."

It is The Mountain that provides Newlands with its distinct character, but it also possesses a loveliness of its own. At the beginning of 1957, on the occasion of the second Test match between South Africa and England, the late Charles Fortune, the doyen of South African commentators, described the ground thus:

"Newlands on New Year's Day, with May and McGlew out in the middle to spin for choice of innings, looked the perfect picture of a great cricket ground. The scene is best from the Kelvin Grove end, where a big temporary stand to hold 5,000 had been set up. From here you can see the pavilion and the new grandstand, and just to the left of it, the distant sightscreen. All along the left flank are the Newlands oaks. Here on ground level are the seats most sought after by the Cape's cricket followers. To the Cape, "under the Oaks" at Newlands is the equivalent in outdoor pleasure to Phyllis Court at Royal Henley or a deckchair in the Parks at Oxford. Away down the right from the Kelvin end is the Railway Stand. It is a rickety single-storey ground-level shack made tolerable only by the drooping trees that mask its shabbiness. It is the trees that make Newlands, and that old Railway Stand is a permanent reminder that Newlands belongs to club cricketers prepared occasionally to tolerate all the hubbub of a Test match. From its lofty pinnacle away beyond that Railway Stand the Devil's Peak looks down. It will have known the days when Newlands was unclaimed marshland, and perhaps still recall times when strains from the military bands that once were inseparable from cricket days at the Western Province Club came floating gently up its gorges."

The English writer Jim Swanton, penning his thoughts at the same time as Fortune, was more succinct, but equally delighted. "Newlands, with its picturesque pavilion, its row of oaks making a shady grandstand along one boundary, the great grey-green mountain opposite, rising almost from the ground itself, is a beautiful survivor among the world's great cricket grounds."

It is possible that if either man was to visit the modern Newlands he might be momentarily disconcerted. But "The Mountain" remains, still linking the past with the present and warning gently of the transience of human endeavour.

In the early 1990s, following South Africa's return to international cricket, all the major South African grounds were swept up in a frenzy of redevelopment. Newlands was no exception and between the start of the decade and 1997, when India toured, the ground was gutted and reassembled as a modern cricket stadium. The improvements were not without cost. The public areas known as The Willows and The Planes disappeared to make way for a new main grandstand and Railway Stand, and even The Oaks shrank, although the continuing popularity of the area is a reminder that sometimes trees and a patch of grass provide the best, and most comfortable, setting from which to watch cricket.

Another feature of the ground to disappear was the memorial scoreboard at the Kelvin Grove end which featured a clock and a tablet bearing the inscription in English and Afrikaans: "In memory of cricketers of Southern Africa who gave their lives for their country. They played the game."

The scoreboard, unveiled in 1948, was originally intended to honour the cricketers of the Western Cape who fell during World War II. The Transvaal Cricket Union, however, suggested that it commemorate all South African cricketers and presented Newlands with the clock and plaque. It is one of the few occasions that Cape Town has listened to, or accepted something from, Johannesburg.

With his reference to Newlands belonging to club cricketers, Fortune touched upon the sometimes uneasy relationship between the Western Province Cricket Club and the provincial union, which made Newlands its home.

To go back to the beginning, the farm Mariendal, on which were to be sited both the Newlands cricket and rugby grounds, was presented as a wedding gift to Lydia Corrina, Vicomtesse de Montmort. In 1887 the WPCC leased Lot 27 from the Vicomtesse for a fee of £50

Left: The scoreboard and clock which served as a war memorial has long since disappeared.

Right: JH Sinclair was one of South Africa's first superstars. In the 1898-99 series against England, he followed his 86 in the first Test by taking six for 26 and scoring 106 in the second Test at Newlands. It was South Africa's first Test century. In 1902-03 he hit 194 against Australia which included a century off 80 balls. It was a record that stood for 50 years but remains the quickest for any South African.

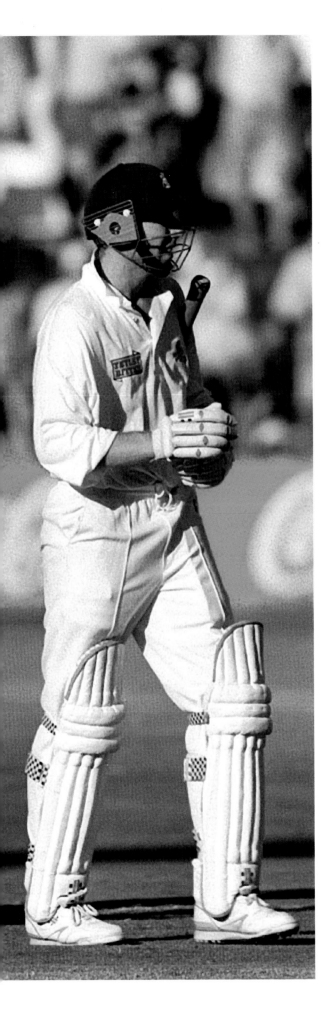

and in 1888 the ground was inaugurated with a match between teams representing the Mother Country and those Colonial Born.

The Western Province union entered the Currie Cup, previously contested by Kimberley and Transvaal, in 1892, but the visit of Joe Darling's Australian team in 1902 provided the impetus for what might be seen as the first overhaul of the ground. The cost of providing spectator facilities, however, had to be born by the WPCC, which charged the union a rental of £15 a day for the Australian games (the tourists played three times at Newlands) plus stand receipts. The arrangement whereby the WPCC owned the ground and leased it out to the Western Province union continued until 2002 when the Western Province Cricket Association finally took ownership of Newlands, with the exception of the WPCC clubhouse situated to the right of the main grandstand.

This division of ownership and responsibility was often a source of friction. As recently as 1993 a public row broke out over the preparation of the Newlands pitch, then the responsibility of the club. The New Year's Test match against India, in South Africa's first post-isolation rubber, was played on a pitch that offered neither pace nor bounce nor even spin. It seemed to have been prepared by rolling dead grass into the clay and bemused all those who inspected it. The Test duly meandered to a desperately dull draw, providing South Africa with a one-nil series victory. Within a matter of weeks, however, an entirely different type of Newlands made an appearance.

On February 25 Pakistan were bowled out at Newlands by the West Indies for what was then a one-day international record low score of 43. Not that the West Indies found the going much easier. Desmond Haynes had watched the carnage of the Pakistan innings from the field and when he was rapped on the pads off the first ball of the West Indian innings, he had turned towards the dressing-rooms even before Waqar Younis had completed his appeal. Eventually Lara slogged an unbeaten 26

South Africa's most successful bowler Allan Donald celebrates in style after dismissing England captain Michael Atherton in the first over of England's second innings in the final test at Newlands in 1995-96. His delight was based on the knowledge that Atherton was the cornerstone of England's batting. Earlier in the series the Englishman had occupied the crease for 11 hours to deny South Africa victory. With him gone, the path to victory was cleared.

Happily, by the time the 2003 World Cup arrived, Newlands could boast one of the finest pitches in the country, even if, notoriously, whatever grass left on the pitch tends to "stand up" at night, and it is always advisable to bat first upon winning the toss for a day-night match. The present groundsman, Christo Erasmus, achieved the considerable feat of preparing a near-perfect pitch for the opening match of the 2003 World Cup despite having to do so under the handicap of having to work around the dress rehearsals for the opening ceremony. These entailed the erection of a stage over the entire playing surface which had to be dismantled before Erasmus could bring his mowers and rollers to bear. Sleep, he said during the week before the opening match, was not high on his list of priorities.

The 1993 debacle aside, pitches have always played a part in Newlands' lore. Up to and into the 1920s, matting wickets were the norm in South Africa. As a result, South African teams abroad struggled when confronted by turf pitches and, following the indifferent performances of Herbie Taylor's team in England in 1924, the move to convert South African pitches to turf gained momentum. An experimental match was played on turf at Newlands at the end of the 1926-27 season providing a surface, it was reported, that tended to favour the bowlers with the ball keeping low.

By 1929, however, turf had established itself so successfully that nine days of trials were played at Newlands before the selection of the team to tour England. In 1930-31 Jack Siedle became the first man to score a turf-wicket Test-match century in South Africa when he made 141 in a 260-run opening partnership with Bruce Mitchell against England. The partnership was a record that stood until January 2003 when Herschelle Gibbs and Graeme Smith put on 368 for the first wicket against Pakistan, thereby setting a new South African record for any wicket. It was the start of a prosperous partnership as later in 2003, Gibbs and the 22-year-old Smith, who had by this time taken over the captaincy from Shaun Pollock, put on 338 for the first wicket against England at Edgbaston.

The turf and the Cape Doctor, a prevailing south-easterly wind which blows away bad weather, were to produce another characteristic for which Newlands was to become well known. The wind frequently served to dry out any early moisture in the pitch as well as offering assistance

to carry the West Indies to a seven-wicket victory. The entire match lasted fewer than 33 overs and was over well before the scheduled lunch break.

As a result, the newly formed United Cricket Board threatened to withdraw international cricket from Newlands. Recriminations were freely bandied about, many of them aimed at the hapless groundsman, an employee of the club, who, it emerged, had very little experience of preparing cricket pitches of any kind, let alone those on which international games were to be played. Indeed, his previous experience appeared to consist largely of preparing bowling greens.

to spin bowlers in the form of dip and drift. Newlands, and Western Province, became a hunting ground for South African spinners. Hugh Tayfield, an off-spinner who took 170 wickets in 37 Tests, is probably the best known of the breed, but most of his success came away from Newlands.

Of those that made their mark under the Oaks, Denys Hobson, South Africa's last great leg-spinner, is probably the most famous. Ironically, politics ensured that he never played a single Test but through the 1970s and into the '80s, in other words some years before Shane Warne made leg-spinning fashionable once more, Hobson wheeled away into the south-easter for Western Province. Hobson grew to know the ground, and the wind, intimately and his reputation was sufficient to earn him an invitation to join Kerry Packer's World Series Cricket.

Like Graeme Pollock, Hobson was eventually unable to accept Packer's offer on the somewhat complicated grounds that he was not considered a full professional because he had not played first-class cricket overseas. Nevertheless, during isolation, when South Africa's Currie Cup provided arguable the toughest competition in the world outside Test cricket, Hobson was a significant figure. If Western Province were bowling last on the third and final day, Hobson would come into his own and neither of Province's great rivals in the era, Transvaal and Natal, was ever able to overcome his threat completely.

More recently, Paul Adams, the unorthodox left-arm spinner who so bemused Michael Atherton's England team in 1995-96 with his assortment of chinamen, long-hops, googlies, and full-tosses, has become a new hero. Although he is only 26, he has already taken over 100 Test wickets, and his best years might still lie ahead of him. Like Hobson, Adams is something of a one-off, but there are signs that he may already have stamped his mark on Newlands. Among the scores of impromptu games that take place behind the Newlands stands during any big match, there are already a significant number of wannabes trying to emulate Adams's peculiar "frog-in-a-blender" action. Bowling coaches around the country view this development with some trepidation.

Even before Hobson, though, Newlands was known for its assistance to the spinners. During the 1950s and 1960s, even as South Africa began to produce strong, fiery, aggressive fast-bowling

New ball pairing.
When Allan Donald retired, the task of sharing the new ball fell to Shaun Pollock and Makhaya Ntini. Pollock, son of Peter, another fine South African fast bowler, has taken more wickets than anyone else at Newlands. Ntini, the first black man to play for South Africa, found his feet on the 2003 tour of England when he took ten wickets in the innings victory at Lord's.

combinations – Neil Adcock and Peter Heine, Peter Pollock and Mike Procter among them – it became common practice to select a pair of spinners for Newlands Test matches. If both happened to play for Western Province, as was the case with Kelly Seymour and Harry Bromfield, scarcely an eyebrow was raised.

The flip side of the coin, though, was that Newlands earned a reputation for breaking the hearts of fast bowlers. One of the theories raised to explain the perceived slowness of the pitch was that the farm Mariendal had occupied what had originally been marshland. England's Maurice Tate had said of performing at Newlands that "it was like bowling on a featherbed", and Australia's Ernie McCormick offered his view of the surface by laying a wreath upon the pitch. Digging up and relaying the pitch, it was reported, made no difference to its nature whatsoever.

The perception that Newlands possessed a low, slow wicket suitable mostly for spinners and watchful batting was fairly widely held, but not everyone agreed with this assessment. After New Zealand had beaten South Africa by 72 runs there during their 1961-62 tour, John Reid claimed that it was the "fairest wicket in the country". Then again, Reid made 1,915 runs in South Africa during the tour, so he probably said that of all the pitches.

One who dismissed Newlands' reputations as being of little concern was Eddie Barlow. Burly, bespectacled and belligerent, "Bunter" Barlow was schooled in Pretoria and played his early cricket in the Transvaal. After moving to Cape Town, however, he became synonymous with Newlands and Western Province cricket.

Through the 1960s, as South Africa gradually shrugged off an inferiority complex to become the best team in the world by the time they hammered Australia four-nil in 1969-70, Barlow provided the heartbeat of the team. He was never to captain South Africa, a fact that has always rankled with him. Barlow served under Jackie McGlew, Trevor Goddard, Peter van der Merwe and Ali Bacher

Jonty Rhodes dives for safety in the Newlands Test against the West Indies in 1998-99. One of the best fielders in the world, Rhodes also earned his corn as a dependable middle-order batsman, playing over 50 Tests and averaging 35.

Seeing is not believing.
Gary Kirsten dives to take a brilliant catch to dismiss
Alan Border during the 1993-94 Test at Newlands.
Border, however, was not out - it was a bump ball

before isolation, but there are few who would deny his influence. Louis Duffus, the greatest of all South African cricket writers, argued: "I am inclined to believe that he had more influence over South African cricket than any other player I know."

By any standards, Barlow was one of the finest batsmen to have represented his country. He scored 2,516 runs in his 30 Tests at an average of 45.74 and hit six centuries including 201 against Australia. He was an early proponent of the uppercut, the slash over the heads of the slips off anything short and wide outside off stump. It mattered not to him that that opposition teams took to placing a fly-slip for him, somewhere between the conventional slips and third man. He reasoned that if he hit the ball hard enough he would get away with the shot.

As a bowler he bustled in at medium pace, swinging the ball away from the right-hander, but his true gift was his complete faith in his own ability to take wickets. He was a partnership-breaker par excellence, and if he felt the opposition were becoming too settled, he would virtually demand to be given a bowl by

enthusiastically and ostentatiously warming up in the outfield. He took a hat-trick for the Rest of the World against England at Headingley in 1970 after the South African tour had been cancelled and went on to take four wickets in five balls and seven in the innings.

Throughout his career Barlow was scornful of players who blamed the pitch for the state of any game, and Newlands' reputation left him completely unimpressed. Of batting there he said: "The slow pitch at Newlands makes players get onto the front foot all the time. It's safer. But it cuts down a player's scoring shots because there is a wealth of runs to be made from cuts, pulls and back-foot drives."

He also believed that bowlers other than spinners could take wickets at Newlands if they were prepared to work at it. "Bowling is what you put into it," he said. "If you really make an effort you'll get your reward. Whether it's Newlands, the Wanderers or wherever."

Barlow revived Western Province cricket on and off the field. His presence helped swell the crowds at Newlands for provincial games, but

more lasting was his influence on the crop of young players who emerged, into isolation, at Newlands during the 1970s. Garth le Roux and Stephen Jefferies were as effective a new-ball pairing as any to have played in South Africa. Le Roux was big, blond, strong and aggressive, happy to get the ball up around the batsmen's noses; Jefferies, dark-haired and stocky, bent the ball disconcertingly into the right-hander from left-arm over-the-wicket. He took all ten wickets in the innings for 53 at Newlands in 1987 as Orange Free State were bowled out for 113. Indeed, he had to dismiss last man Donald twice to complete the achievement after first bowling Donald with a no-ball. As a pairing, they complemented each other perfectly. Hobson offered the spin option after the quicks had ripped through the top order. Peter Kirsten, meanwhile, was one of South African cricket's most accomplished technicians, blessed with soft hands, nimble feet and a seemingly insatiable appetite for big centuries.

Le Roux earned a call-up for the Packer circus, but Jefferies' and Hobson's achievements were mostly reserved for the provincial stage with

occasional chances to shine against rebel touring teams. Only Kirsten was able to follow Barlow into full international cricket, even though when recognition came it arrived during the autumn years of his career. After initially leaving him out of South Africa's 1992 World Cup squad, the selectors relented and he responded by ending the tournament as South Africa's leading batsman. Kirsten made only two Test appearances at Newlands, failing against India in 1993 when he made 13 in both innings before scoring 70 and three against Allan Border's Australians a year later. He finally scored a cherished Test century against England at Headingley in 1994.

As a Test-match venue, Newlands took more than a century before South African teams could approach it with any degree of confidence. In spite of some notable individual performances from players such as Augustus Tancred, who carried his bat for 26 as South Africa were bowled out for 47 by Johnny Briggs – 15 for 28 in the match – and some excellent ones from others such as Jimmy Sinclair, who made 106 against England in 1899 and then smashed ten sixes and eight fours in an 80-minute century against the Australians in 1902-03, South Africa's first Test victory only came during the 1905-06 MCC tour when Plum Warner brought a side to South Africa that was not considered to represent the full strength of England. Amid scenes of mounting excitement at the Old Wanderers, Dave Nourse carried South Africa to a thrilling one-wicket win. So delighted were the South African selectors that they named an unchanged team for the remainder of the series and South Africa duly won the next two Test matches. But when the teams travelled down to Cape Town for the last two Tests, England promptly beat South Africa by four wickets for their only victory of the series.

The teams stayed at Newlands for the fifth Test where Nourse (four for 25) and Reggie Schwarz (three for 16) bowled England out for 130 in their second innings to give South Africa victory by an innings and six runs and a four-one triumph in the series. The win ended a six-match losing streak for South Africa at Newlands.

5th Test South Africa v England Cape Town 1995-96 Atherton c Richardson b Donald.

Four years later South Africa achieved a more meaningful win at Newlands over England when a four-wicket victory in the fourth Test gave them an unbeatable three-one lead in the series. To a certain extent, England might have blamed their defeat on a rare failure by Jack Hobbs, who scored one and nought. He scored 538 runs in the other four Tests, more than a thousand runs during the tour, and he was the only batsman who would have played in an England XI of full strength at the time.

Even so, England won the fifth Test and South Africa had to wait 60 years and another 16 games before they finally won another Test at Newlands, against Australia during the four-nil whitewash in 1969-70.

There was a famous near-miss in the second Test of England's 1922-23 tour, however, with the match almost producing cricket's first tied Test. Set 173 to win, England started the fourth day on 86 for six and inched their way towards their target. With five runs needed and two wickets standing, the South African captain Herbie Taylor ran out George Brown with a direct hit on the stumps from side on. It was a brilliant piece of fielding and a precursor, perhaps, of the feats to be achieved later in the century by first Colin Bland and then Jonty Rhodes.

George Macaulay, who had taken a wicket with his first ball in Test cricket when he removed George Hearne earlier in the match, joined Alex Kennedy at the crease and a pull from Kennedy for four levelled the scores, although the stroke flew perilously close to Bob Catterall at square leg. Alfie Hall, a printer born in Lancashire, was making his debut for South Africa as a left-arm fast bowler. He had taken seven for 63 in the England first innings and was given the ball for what was to be the final over of the match. He had a confident appeal for leg-before against Macaulay turned down by umpire George Thompson, who took an age to give his decision. Then Hall shaved Macaulay's off stump as the crowd held its breath. Finally, Macaulay tapped Hall into the covers to sprint through for the single. England had won by one wicket.

Hall was carried shoulder-high from the field by spectators, having taken 11 for 112 in the match, and there were many who believed he should have finished with 12 wickets. *The Johannesburg Star's* correspondent, wrote thus: "I

know that cold-blooded statisticians will produce chapter and verse to prove that I am wrong in this statement, but they were not there, and ever since the match was over spectators behind the wicket and players alike have said that Macaulay was well and truly out when he walked in front of the ball sent down by Hall."

Up until isolation South Africa, a founding member of the Imperial Cricket Conference, played Test cricket against only three opponents, Australia, England and, as the country emerged as a Test-playing nation, New Zealand. The election of a National Party government in 1948 formalised racial segregation in South Africa with the enactment of apartheid legislation, but prior to this the colour bar had played a part in South Africa on a formal and informal basis.

As was the case in all areas of life, cricket was not unaffected by prejudice against black people, but in 1892 Newlands was to host a rare instance of play across the colour line. Only one Test match was played against WW Read's England side in 1892 with England easily winning by an innings. With time to spare, a game was arranged between England's professionals and a Malay XVIII on March 22, 1892, although the English amateurs refused to take part. Predictably, the game ended in a ten-wicket victory for the tourists, but not before L Samoodien made the highest score, 55, against England in 21 matches during the tour. As impressive was the performance of fast bowler Krom Hendricks, who took four for 50 off 25 overs.

Two years later Hendricks was nominated by Western Province, supported by Transvaal, for selection for South Africa's first tour abroad to England. He was not chosen and it seems certain now that this was as a result of pressure from the Cape government, then headed by the massively influential Cecil Rhodes. In later years Plum Warner was to recall that Rhodes told him: "They

The Frog in a Blender.
When Paul Adams made his first-class debut for Western Province in late 1995, journalists fell over themselves trying to describe his technically anarchic action. Andy Capostagno writing in the Johannesburg Sunday Times came up with the "frog in a blender". It stuck. Adams was hastily called into the South African team to play England in 1995-96, playing a major part in their win at Newlands. He has since gone on to become the third-highest wicket-taker at the ground.

to England. I would not have it. They would have expected him to throw boomerangs during the luncheon interval."

Some 80 years were to pass before black cricketers were permitted to compete with and against their white counterparts in South Africa, but in 1971 Newlands was the stage for a rare instance of cricketers publicly challenging the policies of their own government.

With the storm clouds of isolation gathering, Bill Lawry's Australians toured South Africa in 1969-70. Shortly after, however, a planned Springbok tour to England was called off and it seemed the same fate awaited the proposed tour of Australia in 1971-72. This is not the forum to discuss the merits or otherwise of opposition to South Africa's apartheid policies; suffice to say that the National Party's refusal to accept Basil D'Oliveira's selection for the MCC's proposed 1968-69 tour had served to stiffen the resolve of those opposed to sporting contact with South Africa. By 1971 it had become clear that the Australian tour was also in jeopardy. A proposal to include two black cricketers in the touring squad was dismissed by the government, a development that further dimmed the likelihood of the tour taking place.

A final trial match at Newlands to choose the touring party, between the Currie Cup champions Transvaal and a Rest of South Africa XI, was due to be played at the end of April as part of the tenth anniversary of Republic celebrations. On the eve of the game a group of players, which included the Pollock brothers, Peter and Graeme, Mike Procter, Denis Lindsay and Barry Richards, resolved to mount some form of protest. Initially they agreed that the Rest XI boycott the match, but after consultation with veteran broadcaster Charles Fortune they modified their intentions.

The first ball of the match was duly bowled by Procter to Richards, guesting for the Transvaal team, who tapped it into the covers and walked through for a single. The players then walked off the field, leaving the umpires standing bemused in the middle.

A statement was then handed to the media which read: "We cricketers feel that the time has come for an expression of our views. We fully support the South African Cricket Association's

application to include non-white players on the tour to Australia and, furthermore, subscribe to merit being the only criterion on the cricket field."

Thereupon the players returned and the match continued, and while the gesture was not enough to save the tour, it demonstrated that the country's white sportsmen were not necessarily in tune with government policies. There was, of course, a degree of self-interest in the walk-off, but there is also no doubt that it touched a nerve. It was dismissed by the then Minister of Sport, Frank Waring, as "merely a gesture for local and particularly popular overseas consumption," but Helen Suzman, the Progressive Party MP who for many years was the sole voice in Parliament opposing apartheid, said: "Good for

them. It's nice to see they are coming along so well."

The injustices of apartheid ensured that even in a city such as Cape Town where the laws of segregation were not always enforced as strictly as the authorities might have liked, Newlands was still the preserve of white cricketers only. The result was that many superbly gifted Cape Coloured and black cricketers were never given the opportunity to show just how good they were.

The 1953-54 Test series against New Zealand was a one-sided affair with South Africa triumphing four-nil. The Newlands Test provided the only respite for the Kiwis in the shape of a draw. Here, opening batsman Chapple escapes when his glide off Neil Adcock falls short of Hugh Tayfield at leg-slip.

victims of the apartheid regime, had never been allowed to play Test cricket for South Africa - Basil D'Oliveira, Frank Roro and Eric Petersen.

The talents of the Cape Town-born and bred D'Oliveira, of course, were finally given expression in the colours of England and it was his inclusion in an MCC touring team to South Africa that gave rise to the isolationist years. But Roro, regarded as the first great black African cricketer, and Petersen are less well known.

Known at home as the "Dusty Bradman", Roro played through the 1930s and 1940s and into the 1950s. He died in 1971. Although the achievements of African cricketers are poorly documented – the publication in 2003 of Andre Odendaal's book *The Story of an African Game* has gone a long way towards rectifying this – at least one tribute to his talents exists. In a tribute in the 1953-54 *South African Non-European Cricket Almanack*, Syd Reddy writes: "Barely more than five foot eight inches [1.72 metres] in height, Roro does not allow his comparatively small physique to handicap him in stroke production. What he lacks in reach he makes up for by his perfect footwork and quick eye.

"He wields his willow with grace, power and soundness. His defence tells of the long study of the game. He is not averse to going to drive the fast bowlers, he employs the hook as a safe scoring stroke and delights the onlookers by the neat skill of his glance and general placing to the leg."

Petersen, meanwhile, was another Capetonian and is regarded as the finest exponent of seam bowling to have come out of non-racial (in reality non-white) cricket. Sadly, he died in a car crash in 2002. D'Oliveira, Petersen and Roro are merely the best-known of a legion of African, Asian and mixed-blood cricketers who played the game beyond the parameters of the white establishment. In many respects, the injustices they suffered can never be corrected, but there is growing

With isolation came the rebels as South Africa bought top players from England, Australia, West Indies and Sri Lanka to play "representative" matches. They have never been recognised as Test matches but some of the cricket played was certainly Test-class. Jimmy Cook (left, facing John Lever) was one of those for whom isolation came at the wrong time. He did eventually play Test cricket, making his debut against India at the age of 38...he was out to the first ball of the match.

acknowledgement that not only could they play the game, but they could play it very well. What they might have achieved at Newlands, however, has to remain a matter for conjecture.

South Africa had won the 1970 Newlands Test against Australia, thereby breaking a sequence of 15 unsuccessful attempts to win there stretching back to 1909-10, and when Test cricket resumed in 1992-93 Newlands still refused to offer anything to the home team. In 1993 a dead surface produced a draw against India and in 1994 Allan Border's Australians won the second Test of a three-match series that ended one-all. Finally, Ken Rutherford's New Zealanders were beaten by seven wickets in the New Year Test of 1995 in a

game that produced wicketkeeper Dave Richardson's sole Test century.

Once the hoodoo had been broken, however, victories came in a rush. Of the next eight Newlands Tests, up to the beginning of 2003, South Africa won seven with only Steve Waugh's 2002 Australians interrupting the sequence.

The most significant of these matches, perhaps, was the final Test of England's 1995-96 tour. The previous four matches of the series had been drawn and after England had been bowled out for 153, South Africa were only 18 ahead when Paul Adams, the teenage unorthodox left-arm spinner, joined Richardson at the crease. Up

to that point, Adams had scored only four runs in his first-class career, but, to the delight of his home crowd, he threw his bat at everything, hitting 29 as he helped Richardson add 73 in 68 minutes for the last wicket.

The drama was not yet over as England, 91 behind, fought to save the match and the series. The conclusive moment came at 140 for six when Andrew Hudson's throw broke the wicket at the non-striker's end with England's top-scorer Graham Thorpe stretching for his ground. Umpire Dave Orchard gave Thorpe not out, but after a roar from the private boxes, where TV replays showed that Thorpe had been short, and an insistent appeal from the South African captain

Left: During the 1970s and 1980s, Basil D'Oliveira was probably the most famous South African cricketer in the world. As a Cape Coloured, he was denied the chance of playing for South Africa but went on to play 44 times for England. When the South African government opposed his inclusion in England's touring side in 1968-69, they inadvertently set sporting isolation in motion.

Above: Hansie Cronje also made world headlines when he admitted his part in match-fixing. Until then, he had been a standard bearer for South African cricket, making them one of the best two sides in the world. The highlights of his career at Newlands career were the 112 he made there against New Zealand in 1994-95 and the win against Engand the following year that gave South Africa a one-nil win. Cronje died in an aeroplane crash in 2002.

Hansie Cronje, Orchard changed his mind. He referred the decision to the third umpire. Thorpe was given out, England capitulated and South Africa won by ten wickets. Cronje was fined 50 per cent of his match fee for breaching ICC regulations, but he said that it had been worth every cent. With hindsight, perhaps he knew he could afford it.

A Saturday in January 1997 provided Newlands with perhaps the finest display of batting the ground has witnessed. Gary Kirsten and Brian McMillan had already scored centuries in the South African first innings before Lance Klusener, playing only his third Test match, crunched an unbeaten 102 off exactly 102 balls. A glorious day indeed for South African cricket but it was the response of the Indians Sachin Tendulkar and Mohammad Azharuddin that took the breath away.

India had slipped to 58 for five before Azharuddin joined Tendulkar and together the pair played comfortably through to lunch. After the interval, however, they cut loose, putting on 100 in 13 overs after the break. It was strokeplay of the highest order as the South African attack was flayed to all parts of the ground. Together they added 222 in 175 minutes off 39.2 overs before Azharuddin was run out by Hudson's throw for 115. Tendulkar went on to make 169 before he was last man out, brilliantly caught by Adam Bacher one-handed and falling backwards at square leg off a stroke that looked certain to give him his 27th four.

Another to prosper at Newlands was Daryll Cullinan, the most gifted and most enigmatic South African batsman of the modern era. After starting his career with Border, for whom he became South Africa's youngest first-class centurion, he moved to Newlands to enjoy a sometimes stormy relationship with Western Province. He had found the surroundings that were to inspire him and even after he left the province, he loved coming back.

Graeme Pollock.
South Africa's Cricketer of the [20th] Century only played 23 Tests but he still managed 2256 runs and a career average of 60.97 that is second only to Bradman. Of his seven hundreds, one of them came at Newlands, a corruscating 209 in against Australia in 1966-67.

Cullinan's first Test match was at Newlands when he made 46 against India, and he went on to rewrite the record books. In 1993-94 his innings of 337 for Transvaal against Northern Transvaal at the Wanderers set a new first-class high for South Africa while his unbeaten 275 in Auckland in 1998-99 beat by one run Graeme Pollock's previous best for South Africa in Test cricket. The following year Gary Kirsten equalled the record in Durban before Graeme Smith toppled it in 2003 with his 277 against England at Edgbaston.

Newlands, however, remains Cullinan's favourite hunting ground. The statistics alone have something to say: his average of 67.84 at Newlands in his eight matches there is substantially better than the 44.21 he averaged through his 70-Test career. "I love playing at Newlands," he said. "The ground, the crowd, the setting. It's always been good to me."

Between 1998 and 2001 Cullinan made centuries in four successive Newlands Tests: 113 against Sri Lanka, 168 against The West Indies, 120 against England and 112 against Sri Lanka again. There is no little irony in the fact that a Newlands Test probably played its part in the ending of Cullinan's international career. When South Africa hosted Steve Waugh's Australians in 2002, after suffering a three-nil beating in Australia, South Africa found themselves without a captain for the return series when injury ruled out Shaun Pollock. Vice-captain Mark Boucher took over for the first Test at the Wanderers, but South Africa suffered the worst defeat in their history, losing by an innings and 360 runs.

Cullinan had not been considered for much of the summer, having initially missed a two-Test tour of Zimbabwe after taking up a county contract with Kent and then undergoing surgery. But after the Wanderers humiliation, he was asked to captain a South African A team against the tourists and was then included in the squad for the second Test at Newlands. According to at least two of the selectors, Cullinan had been earmarked for the captaincy, but he never made it to the ground. After flying in to Cape Town airport, Cullinan became involved in a wrangle over a contract with the United Cricket Board, promptly withdrew from the team and caught the next flight back to Johannesburg. He subsequently apologised for his behaviour, but by then it was too late. History had

moved on and instead of choosing his own moment to retire, he was left to play out his career in the backwaters of provincial cricket. Not for the first time had he been his own worst enemy.

Mostly, though, Newlands stands as testimony to the great achievements of cricketers. In January 1967, Graeme Pollock batted for close on six hours to make 209 against Bobby Simpson's Australians. If the feat in itself was not sufficient, he batted virtually on one leg after pulling a hamstring.

During isolation the absence of genuine international competition raised both the profile and importance of provincial cricket. Of all the domestic rivalries, none was fiercer than that between Western Province and Transvaal. With no Test matches to intrude upon the season, the New Year clash between the provinces provided one of the highlights of every season. The Newlands crowd loved these occasions, especially those in the area known as The Willows, reserved, in the days of apartheid, for coloured spectators. And of all the visiting players, none was barracked more than Clive Rice, captain for many years of the Transvaal "Mean Machine". Rice took fearful stick at Newlands, but on at least one occasion, in 1977, he had the last laugh when he bowled Rob Drummond with the last ball of the game to give his side a four-run victory.

Today, with South Africa back on the international stage, the public interest in provincial cricket has waned. Newlands, however, still offers the biggest, best-informed and most passionate crowds. And, over the decade since readmission, they have had many of South Africa's leading players learning their trade at Newlands. Brian McMillan, Herschelle Gibbs, Craig Matthews, Jacques Kallis, Gary Kirsten, Graeme Smith, Paul Adams and Roger Telemachus are among those who have played for both Western Province and South Africa. At times, Western Province has supplied almost half the South African side even as they competed, on a regular basis, for domestic honours.

And all the while The Mountain looks down upon the passing seasons. It may be a cricket stadium these days, as opposed to a cricket ground. But even if you accept this distinction, Newlands is surely the most beautiful cricket stadium in the world.

Darryl Cullinan salutes the Newlands crowd after another century. The immensely gifted batsman scored four centuries at the ground and his total of 882 runs in eight matches is also the highest.

Overleaf: Andrew Hudson gets a mouthful from Australian fast bowler Merv Hughes after being dismissed inthe 1993-94 Test. Hudson had made 102 but merv was to have the final say as Australia won the match and squared the series.

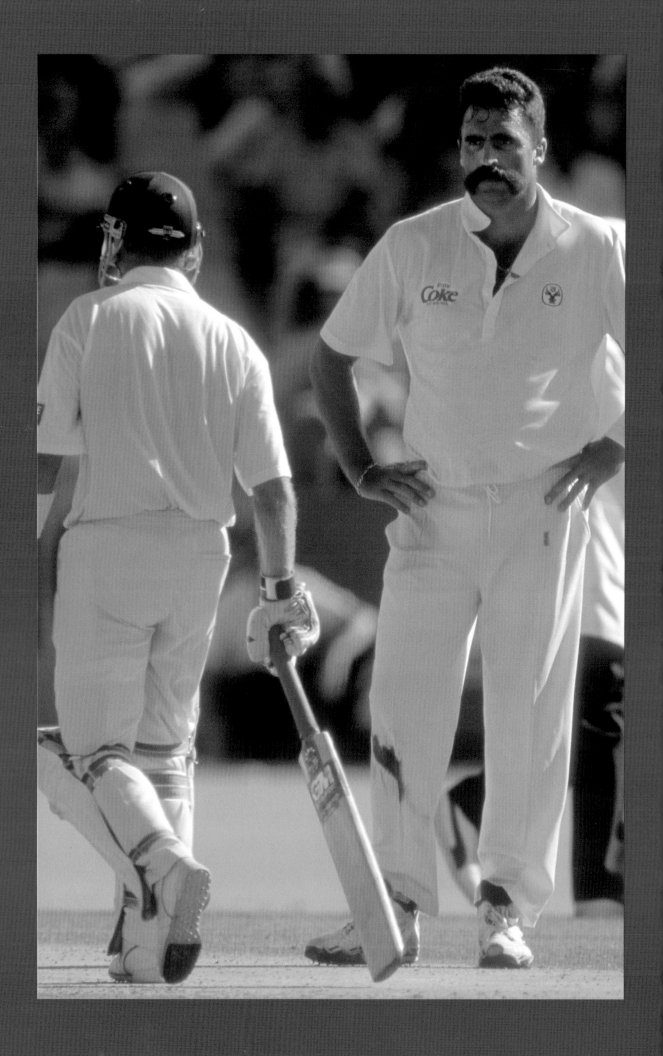

NEWLANDS Ground Records

Result Summary

	Played	Won	Lost	Drawn
South Africa	35	11	18	6
Australia	9	8	1	0
England	17	9	4	4
India	2	0	1	1
Pakistan	1	0	1	0
New Zealand	3	1	1	1
Sri Lanka	2	0	2	0
West Indies	1	0	1	0

Bangladesh and Zimbabwe have yet to play at Newlands

Highest Totals

620-7	South Africa v Pakistan 2002-03
559-9	England v South Africa 1938-39
542	Australia v South Africa 1966-67

Lowest Completed Innings Totals

35	South Africa v England 1898-99
43	South Africa v England 1888-89
47	South Africa v England 1888-89

Highest Match Aggregates

Wkts	Match
1442	34 South Africa v Australia 1966-67
1428	36 South Africa v Australia 2001-02
1304	27 South Africa v England 1964-65

Lowest Match Aggregates (Result oriented matches)

Runs	Wkts	
382	30	South Africa v England 1888-89

Highest Scores

228	HH Gibbs South	Africa v Pakistan 2002-03
209	RG Pollock South	Africa v Australia 1966-67
189	JW Burke	Australia v South Africa 1957-58
187	JB Hobbs	England v South Africa 1909-10
181	WR Hammond	England v South Africa 1938-39

Highest Run Aggregates

Runs	Matches	Hundreds	
882	8	4	DJ Cullinan
622	10	1	G Kirsten
538	7	2	JH Kallis
533	4	3	AD Nourse
462	4	2	EJ Barlow

Partnership Records

368 for 1st	HH Gibbs and GC Smith South Africa v Pakistan 2002-03
172 for 2nd	EJ Barlow and AJ Pithey South Africa v England 1964-65
235 for 3rd	DJ Cullinan and JH Kallis South Africa v West Indies 1998-99
197 for 4th	LEG Ames and WR Hammond England v South Africa 1938-39
176 for 5th	JEF Beck and JR Reid New Zealand v South Africa 1953-54
222 for 6th	M Azharuddin and SR Tendulkar India v South Africa 1996-97
132 for 7th	AC Gilchrist and SK Warne Australia v South Africa 2001-02
147* for 8th	L Klusener and BM McMillan South Africa v India 1996-97
85 for 9th	PM Pollock and RG Pollock South Africa v Australia 1996-97
94 for 10th	PW Sherwell and AEE Vogler South Africa v England 1905-06

Best Bowling in an Innings.

8 for 11 J Briggs	England v South Africa 1888-89
7 for 17 J Briggs	England v South Africa 1888-89
7 for 36 JH Wardle	England v South Africa 1956-57
7 for 37 JJ Ferris	England v South Africa 1891-92
7 for 42 GA Lohmann	England v South Africa 1895-96

Best Bowling in a Match

15 for 28 (7-17, 8-11)	J Briggs England v South Africa 1888-89
13 for 91 (6-54 7-37)	JJ Ferris England v South Africa 1891-92
12 for 89 (5-53 7-36)	JH Wardle England v South Africa 1956-57
11 for 112 (4-49 7-63)	AE Hall South Africa v England 1922-23
11 for 118 (6-68 5-50)	C Blythe England v South Africa 1905-06

Hat Trick

LF Kline Australia v South Africa 1957-58

Highest Wicket Aggregates

Wkts	Matches	5WI	
35	7	2	SM Pollock
30	7	2	AA Donald
26	6	0	PR Adams
25	4	3	C Blythe

Most Catches by Fielder

Catches	Matches	
12	10	G Kirsten
12	7	JH Kallis

Most Dismissals by Wicketkeeper

Dismissals	Matches	
25	6	MV Boucher
17	5	DJ Richardson
15	4	JHB Waite

WEST INDIES

Donna Symmonds

Brian Lara may hold the world record for his 375 made in Antigua but he has only scored one Test century to date at the Kensington Oval. It was no ordinary innings, however, as his 153 not out guided the West Indies to a nail-biting victory over Australia in 1998-99.

To watch cricket anywhere in the Caribbean is getting as close to Paradise as anything you can imagine. The weather is without fail more sunshine than rain, the grounds are colourful and laid-back, the crowds knowledgeable and enthusiastic and the cricket, well, the cricket has been known to touch the very heights.

There are eight Test grounds in the West Indies, the most recent of which are Beausejour in Gros Islet, St Lucia, which held its inaugural Test against Sri Lanka in June 2003, Queen's Park New Stadium in St George's, Grenada, which hosted a draw with New Zealand a year earlier, and Arnos Vale in St Vincent which also staged a Test against Sri Lanka in 1997.

Of the other five St John's, Antigua is the only one not to have featured in the West Indies' very first series against England in 1930. St John's made its first appearance in 1981, but has been quick to leave its mark. The home of Viv Richards saw the great man thrash the fastest century in Test cricket off just 56 balls against England's hapless bowlers in 1986. And in 1994, the English were again on the receiving end of a caning as Brian Lara stroked his way to 375, breaking Gary Sobers' long-standing world record for the highest individual score in Test cricket. Lara was again to the fore in a famous match at St John's in 2003 when he led the West Indies to an astonishing three-wicket win over Australia, his team making 418, the highest ever in the fourth innings to win a Test.

The previous record had been set at Queen's Park Oval in Port-of-Spain, the centre of cricket in Trinidad. On that occasion in 1976, it was the Indians who made 406 for four to win. Famous for its scarlet flowering tulip trees and the Northern Range Mountains, Queen's Park has proved an awkward place for batsmen over the years with three particularly embarrassing innings. In 1994, England were bowled out for just 46, while in 2000 Zimbabwe capitulated for 63. Just to show it is not always the visitors, however, the West Indies themselves were skittled by Australia in 1999 for just 51 – their lowest Test score.

Bourda in Guyana will always have a special place in West Indian hearts as it was the venue for their first Test win, over England in 1930. Their inspiration was the legendary George Headley, who made a century in each innings. His batting during that series set the tone for many a free-scoring West Indian in years to come as he made 176 in Barbados, 114 and 112 in Port-of-Spain and 223 at Sabina Park in Kingston, Jamaica, another ground with a wonderfully rich history. Set in the grandeur of the Blue Mountains, Sabina is the venue that staged Sobers's 365 not out and his second-wicket partnership of 446 with Conrad Hunte, Richie Benaud's 78-minute century, Andrew Sandham's 325 and Dennis Amiss's unbeaten 262.

On a downbeat note, it was also the ground that saw the shortest Test of all time when the first Test against England in 1998 was abandoned after just 61 deliveries, the umpires and captains having deemed the recently laid pitch to be too dangerous to continue.

Of all the grounds in the West Indies, though, the heritage and atmosphere of the Kensington Oval in Barbados is legendary.

KENSINGTON OVAL, BARBADOS

Names can carry much in the way of responsibility and expectation. As a royal palace and as gardens of international repute where the eternally youthful Peter Pan still mesmerises the children of London, Kensington is a grand name. Anyone who adopts it has chosen a great deal to live up to. Kensington Oval in Bridgetown has, undoubtedly, not let the side down. Beauty, nobility, youth; it is all there in the surroundings which have formed the stage for some of the world's greatest cricketers to strut and, occasionally, fret. The mantra of Weekes, Worrell and Walcott is almost synonymous with the ground. Throw in other names like Marshall, Garner, Greenidge, Haynes and the incomparable Sobers and you get an idea of the kind of cricket that has been inspired by the Kensington Oval.

"Thus and then it was in the latter half of the year [1882] that two elevens, chosen and captained by two gentlemen of the Civil Service and described in one of the newspapers as 22 corpulent and broken-winded fellows, met on the deserted ground of the Royal Artillery for the purpose of indulging in a stubbornly contested luncheon tournament and incidentally some cricket," wrote Bruce Hamilton in his 1947 book *Cricket in Barbados*. It is a description of the beginnings of Pickwick Cricket Club, whose home ground in due course became the Kensington Oval.

Edward Stoute's *Glimpses of Old Barbados* reports that the Pickwick Club procured an area of land at Kensington in Barbados – "a rough bit of enclosed pasture where fielders were chased by cows" – and the ground was opened on Boxing Day of 1882. He further writes that by 1891, a Barbados Cricket Committee had been established to organise inter-colonial matches with Trinidad and Guyana, and in 1898 there were eight cricket clubs vying for the Barbados Cricket Challenge Cup.

In 1914, however, a group of businessmen bought the ground for £250 at public auction for the Barbados Cricket Committee. Pickwick Cricket Club has a lease arrangement that still allows them to use the ground.

The first cricket tour occurred in early 1895 when Robert Lucas, the Middlesex amateur deputising for Lord Hawke, who was unable to lead the tour as originally planned, brought a team to the West Indies that opened its account at Kensington. That match was a thriller with Barbados scoring 517 in their first innings to secure a first-innings lead of 206 only for the Englishmen to turn things around and win by 25 runs. An indicator perhaps of some of the exciting cricket in store for the island.

Kensington was also the first venue of an official Marylebone Cricket Club side under Arthur Somerset when it toured in 1911, so it seemed quite natural that it should also stage the first official Test match in the West Indies.

On January 11, 1930 Kensington Oval became the 18th Test venue and for the next five days the batsmen made hay. Clifford Roach and the magnificent George Headley – nicknamed "the Black Bradman" – were the century-makers for the West Indies with Andrew Sandham making 152 for England in a high-scoring draw. Sandham went on to hit 325 in the Kingston Test. Given Kensington's more recent history as a pitch for the fast bowlers, it is touch quirky that the only bowler really to enjoy himself was the leg-spinner Greville Stevens, who took ten wickets in the match.

Kensington has obviously changed from the ground where entrance was three pence for the grounds between the boundary lines and the boundary on the eastern, western and part of the southern side of the ground, two shillings for the covered stand and one shilling in a stand for men only. However, with an official seating capacity of 10,500, the ground is still small by international standards, something that has raised concern over its suitability for the 2007 World Cup. Notwithstanding the influence of the bean counters, for whom cash is always more important than cricket, there is little danger of seeing Kensington Oval missing from the calendar. The Barbados Cricket Association has decided that it is the ground it will submit to the West Indies World Cup Committee and that it will, by 2007, meet all the requirements for such an event as prescribed by that committee.

In essence, it was felt that there was too much history and tradition associated with Kensington Oval to discard it in any way. So what is so special about this venue?

The power and the glory.
Only Desmond Haynes has scored more Test runs at the Kensington Oval than Viv Richards who scored 959 from 12 matches. It is unlikely, however, that anyone has batted with such disdain for the breed called bowler.

Kensington Oval borders Bridgetown, the capital city of Barbados, and is within walking distance of the city's port. It may not be the most picturesque of the grounds in the Caribbean, but it has a special character and surrounding myths all of its own. It is located near the harbour and the sage advice – from ol' timers who know the ground like their backyard – to any visiting captains that would listen was that when the tide is in, the ball is likely to swing. But always remember that, after lunch on the second day to day three, the pitch is at its sweetest for batting.

Patsy Hendren, one of the England's leading batsmen on the 1929-30 tour, could not believe his eyes when he saw the pitch at Kensington for the first time. "Does anyone ever get out on this?" he asked a team-mate and proceeded to score successive unbeaten double-centuries in the two colony games and 80 not out in the Test match.

Not that the West Indies, in the early days a collection of players from disparate islands separated by water and cultures, always prospered. They were and still are both entertaining and unpredictable but they are supported at the Kensington Oval by an adoring public that is knowledgeable on the game and its statistics. Wearing red to support the team is now a standard practice. Burgundy is the major colour for the team's standard and the colour of caps and the one-day kit. If you do not come with that gear, all sorts can be purchased from the numerous vendors who line the sides of the street leading to the entrances and sell everything from local food and drink to programmes, T-shirts and flags.

There is a Kensington Stand in the ground that prides itself on being the "happening" stand where the music, food and other things flow. It is not a stand behind the bowler so the most prevalent calls are loud shouts of no-ball even before the umpire can signal. They just want to remind all that they feel such a part of the game.

The basic stand was erected in 1944 after a fire at the ground destroyed the old wooden ones. New stands were put along with the famous wall sightscreen. There used to be a schoolboy stand as well, usually packed with rows of uniforms as schools used to have a day or half-day off specifically to allow children to go to cricket. That is an indication of its importance culturally, socially and educationally, in Barbados.

They used to love the fast bowlers especially and their use of special effects to escort the bowler to the crease became a part of the Kensington mood. As the likes of Malcolm Marshall turned at the end of his run, a slow rumble would begin to build from the schoolboy stands as they used any available object to beat out a rhythm on the wooden seats. The noise would rise as Marshall raced in, climaxing as the great fast bowler sent down another hand grenade to the unsuspecting batsman. Nowadays, drums and conch shells have taken over the production of the beat.

It is the home Test and regional ground of George Challenor, Herman Griffith, Everton Weekes, Clyde Walcott, Frank Worrell, Gary Sobers, Wesley Hall, Malcolm Marshall, Gordon Greenidge, Desmond Haynes among others so the local supporters have been privileged to see some of the world's best regularly.

Those names are ever present in memory and in fact at this oval. Over the years the cricketing authorities in Barbados have honoured its foremost players by naming a number of stands after them.

The members' stand sits at the north of the ground and is dedicated to Challenor, the great Barbadian opener of the 1930s. The life members gather next to it in the Pickwick Pavilion, which was originally male only. Interestingly, gender integration occurred in typical Barbadian fashion. There were neither organised protests nor confrontations but quiet attrition as the country acquired progressively a female Government minister and Governor-General and women moved into every sphere of activity.

There is a Garfield Sobers Pavilion where the dressing-rooms are located, and then fanning out in a ring from those stands on either side, the Three Ws, Hall and Griffith, Greenidge and Haynes Stands. To the west the popular Kensington Stand is placed alongside the Eric Innis stand, named

Bridgetown gods.
Frank Worrell (left) and Gary Sobers are two of the all-time greats of the game with the common background of a Barbados upbringing. Worrell, the first black man to captain the West Indies, made just one century at the Kensington Oval, 197 not out against England in 1959-60. During it he shared a record fourth-wicket partnership of 399 with Sobers, who made 226. Sobers duly went on to succeed Worrell as captain and become the greatest all-rounder of all time.

after a former president of the Barbados Cricket Association. Another president of the BCA, Peter Short, has had the media centre named after him.

Adjoining the media centre in the south-west corner of the ground is the Mitchie Hewitt stand. Now remodelled, it was originally built in 1969 and is named after Mitchison "Mitchie" Hewitt, who was the main founder of the Barbados Friendly Cricket Association, later to become the Barbados Cricket League. This league was absolutely crucial in developing cricket in the island as it gave opportunity to so many who, for reasons ranging from class, alma mater, lack of money or skin colour could not join the existing clubs.

Bowlers now run in from either the Malcolm Marshall End (south) or the Joel Garner End (north), while another distinguished and feisty fast bowler, Herman Griffith, who came to Test cricket comparatively late in life but still had the distinction of dismissing Don Bradman for a duck, finds his name on the gates to the entrance of the car park. At the exit you will find the name of John Goddard, who led the West Indies to their first series win against England in 1950.

Kensington Oval occupies a genuinely special place in the life of the island. It can be described as a national location whose contribution to the life of Barbadians has been marked. Kensington has been used for everything from inter-school sports and regional football matches to carnival queen and calypso shows. When it came to choosing the venue of the ceremonies to celebrate Barbados's independence from Britain, Kensington was the natural choice. These days, however, it is used less and less for anything other than cricket.

Like all landmark grounds, Kensington has witnessed some great feats on the cricket field. The fielding of the 1953 touring Indians is still spoken of in reverent tones, even though standards have risen rapidly since the arrival of one-day cricket. Two years later, Keith Miller and Ray Lindwall, a feared new-ball partnership, led the run-feast, helping themselves to centuries as Australia amassed 668, still the record score at Kensington. Ron Archer, the first change, missed

Don't look back.
Brian Lara prepares to toss up with England captain
Michael Atherton at the start of the fifth Test in 1997-98.
West Indies won the series three-one.

out with 98. The Australian bowlers then had the West Indies on the ropes at 147 for six with those four future cricketing knights Worrell, Walcott, Weekes and Sobers all back in the pavilion. Up to the plate stepped Clairmonte Depeiza, playing in only his second Test, who joined his captain Denis Atkinson in a match-saving partnership of 347. Atkinson made 219, Depeiza 122 and their stand remains the highest for the seventh wicket in Test cricket. Australia, however, were too strong and won the series three-nil.

The first Test of the 1958 series against Pakistan has also been firmly inscribed in the history books partly because Nasim-ul-Ghani made his debut at the age of 16 years and 248 – the youngest Test cricketer at the time – but more tellingly because of the batting of Hanif Mohammad. Barbadians like to tell the story of the man who was knocked unconscious in an accident while listening to Hanif's innings on the radio. When he regained consciousness he could hear someone in the ward listening to cricket and heard that the little Pakistani was still batting.

"Oh good," he said to the patient in the next bed. "At least I haven't missed much of the match."

What he didn't know was that Hanif had been batting for two days. His innings of 337, which rescued Pakistan from defeat after they had followed on, stretched across an astonishing 16 hours and ten minutes. Not a bad achievement at the best of times but, in the face of some fierce bowling from Roy Gilchrist, a supreme effort. Barbadians still swear that Gilchrist sent down the fastest ball ever bowled during this Test, a delivery that was so quick that no one in the ground saw it until it rebounded off the boundary.

If Hanif's innings turned heads towards Barbados, they were soon distracted as Sobers chose the third Test in Kingston, Jamaica to make the 365 not out which gave him the record for the highest individual innings in Test cricket. The record lasted until 1994 when Brian Lara blasted the England attack to the tune of 375 in Antigua.

But if Kensington missed out on these two records, it could claim to have witnessed another triple hundred that many believe may never be bettered in terms of elegance, technical quality and timing.

Lawrence Rowe was used to making an impact. In his first Test debut against New Zealand at Sabina Park in Kingston, he had struck 214 in the first innings and 100 not out in the second, the only time a batsman has done this on debut. His reputation was of a player of superb timing and grace, the easiest batsman of his generation to watch. His touch was reminiscent of Worrell, his appetite for runs akin to the great Bradman.

Naturally, when England, captained by the Scotsman Mike Denness, arrived for their five-Test tour in 1973-74, expectations were high and Rowe did not disappoint. The West Indies won the first Test in Port-of-Spain and in the second drawn Test, Rowe stroked his way to 120. In the third Test at Kensington, England batted first and posted a decent total of 395 thanks to a fine innings of 148 from their South African born all-rounder Tony Greig.

Greig was a competitive character and his bullish approach on the field made an impression on the West Indian players and the spectators. But Rowe was unruffled and by close of play on the second day he was 48 not out. He had delighted with the exquisite timing on his drives, particularly off the front foot but what drove the gathering ecstatic was his late-cutting. At one point, he cut so late everyone was sure Alan Knott, the wicketkeeper, had the ball until it ran fine to the third-man boundary. One sated member of the crowd left the Kensington Stand. "I'm going out to pay and come in again 'cause I just got my money's worth with that shot," he said.

The next day, the lines for those with or without tickets were miles long. The crowd was so large that some resorted to climbing through windows and over other people just to see the first and every ball. They were standing on top of stands and in coconut trees around the ground.

The reason? Lawrence Rowe. News of the majesty and manner in which he had made the first 48 drew viewers like the Pied Piper. No one was disappointed. He batted through that day and beyond until he was finally dismissed for 302, the first West Indian to score a triple-hundred against England. The match was drawn, but the crowd had the satisfaction of seeing Greig get

Perfect balance.
Gary Sobers pulls for four.

down on his knees and bow to Rowe. It was a generous gesture by Greig – especially as he had been by far England's most successful bowler with six for 162.

Greig was to have the last laugh in this series because although Rowe added yet another century in the last Test, he chipped in with 13 wickets to give England a victory that squared the series.

As a further footnote, the Barbados Test marked the debut of Andy Roberts, a moment which West Indians might pinpoint as the day that the golden years began to take shape. Not only was he the first in a stream of Antiguans such as Viv Richards and Curtly Ambrose who have contributed so much to West Indies cricket, but he also formed the first prong in the all-pace four-man attack that would terrorise opponents in various forms for some 20 years – beginning with England, now captained by Greig, in 1976.

As far as Kensington moments go there are so many that it is hard to rank them. Those who saw a young Sobers put Miller and Lindwall to all parts of the ground in the fourth Test in 1954-55 still talk about it in hushed tones. Opening the innings with JK Holt junior – not his usual position in the order – Sobers thrashed ten scintillating boundaries in an innings of 43. Not the biggest score he ever posted but one played with the panache, assurance and peerless finesse of an authentic talent in the making.

Against England a year earlier, Holt himself had produced an innings that had also touched the heights of greatness: many believe it is still the best innings under pressure to have been seen at the ground. Holt, whose father toured England with a West Indies team in 1923, was a supremely poised and elegant Jamaican batsman but, in spite of making 94 on his debut in the first Test, he was not the most popular man in Bridgetown when the teams lined up for the second Test. He was in the team in place of the injured Everton Weekes – a hometown boy – and had dropped a catch in the England first innings. In those days of capital punishment, a former Test fast bowler called Leslie Hylton had been sentenced to hang but the

Another one bites the dust.
With 52 wickets in 12 Tests at the Kensington Oval, Curtly Ambrose more than lived up to a proud tradition of West Indian fast bowling.

cricketer to be knighted), Rohan Kanhai, Sobers, Wes Hall and Lance Gibbs, the off-spinner from Guyana, winning the series five-nil. The tour, however, was overshadowed by the injury suffered by the Indian captain Nari Contractor in the first-class match against Barbados just before the third Test.

Facing an aggressive spell of bowling from Charlie Griffith, Contractor was struck on the head by a ball lifting from just short of a length, with near-tragic consequences. Contractor was rushed to hospital with a fractured skull and given emergency brain surgery. He duly recovered – with a steel plate in his head – but never played Test cricket again. India's situation might have been even worse. Soon after Contractor was hit, Vijay Manjrekar, India's best batsman at the time, was also struck between the eyes by a similarly rapid delivery from Griffith who, just to compound things, split open the boot of the Indian tailender Bapu Nadkarni with a yorker.

Contractor's absence meant the 21-year-old Nawab of Pataudi took over for the subsequent Test at Kensington, a match that was settled by an astonishing spell of bowling from Gibbs after lunch on the final day. He took eight wickets for six runs from 15.3 overs, 14 of which were maidens, as the Indian batsmen poked and prodded a series of catches to the close fielders. Gibbs's final analysis was 53.3-37-38-8, his best return in Test cricket.

Another 21-year-old Indian, Sunil Gavaskar, proved the rule that great players will capture the hearts of true cricket lovers whichever side they happen to be playing for. In 1970-71, he was nigh invincible as he scored 774 runs from eight innings with an average of 154. Who knows how the record books might have looked had he not missed the first of the five Tests.

As it was he made hundreds in three of the four Tests he played; 117 not out in India's second innings in the drawn fourth Test at Kensington, and 124 and 220 in the last Test in Port-of-Spain, another draw that clinched the series for India. Throughout the series he was "in the zone" and had crowds flocking to view and the cricket public in awe of his ability. If that was not testament enough to their adoration, he even had a calypso penned on him by a Trinidadian artiste – a true tribute.

banners at the ground the next day read: "Save Hylton, hang Holt."

After Holt's knock of 166, which included a six and 26 fours, the banners read: "Knight Holt, Knight Holt!"

This was the Test that also saw Walcott make a marvellous 220, an innings he reckoned was his best in Test cricket. West Indies won it by 181 runs but threw away a two-nil lead in the series to draw two-all.

India's tour of the Caribbean in 1961-62 was one-sided on the field with the West Indies, led by Frank Worrell and fielding a core of quality players such as Conrad Hunte (another West Indian

If you want to be picky you might say that the West Indies bowling attack was not as menacing as it might have been and certainly not in the same league as those he faced in later years. Part of West Indian folklore is the story of the last Test of India's 1975-76 tour at Sabina Park when Bishan Bedi chose to send only six batsmen out in the second innings to face the pace and bounce being extracted from the pitch by the local boy Michael Holding and Barbadian Wayne Daniel. Fast bowling did not seem to bother Gavaskar too much as he still averaged 56 for the series.

The Holding/Geoffrey Boycott over in 1981 is another legend of the ground. It was the perhaps the closest that any bowler has come to perfection in the space of six successive deliveries. Lightning fast and deadly accurate, Holding subjected Boycott to the greatest test of his career. One by one the balls flew through, each seemingly quicker than the last, until the sixth delivery

Left: George Headley, the first genuinely great West Indian batsman, announced himself to the world with a sparkling 176 in the second innings of the first Test against England in 1929-30. He followed up by scoring a century in each innings of the fourth Test in Georgetown and 223 in the fifth Test at Kingston. Headley played a total of 22 Tests, scoring 2,190 runs at an average of 60.83. In the only instance of three successive generations playing Test cricket, his son Ron played twice for the West Indies and grandson Dean 15 Tests for England.

Above: Another of the Caribbean's finest, Clive Lloyd, square cuts for four during his innings of 100 against England in 1980-1981.
David Bairstow is the wicketkeeper.

scattered the great man's stumps. Some years later when both players had retired and were doing commentary work in the Caribbean, the question of that over came up. Boycott, never one to hide the light of his talent under a bushel or anywhere else for that matter, came up with a typically deadbat response. "Ay, 'twere grand over Michael but if I 'adn't been at the crease, we would have been nought for six."

It was during this Test that Ken Barrington, the England assistant manager and a man who in his batting days would have relished the challenge of facing Holding, died of a heart attack.

The appreciation of fast bowling has never been limited to West Indian performers. In 1978, when Kerry Packer's World Series had split world cricket, Jeff Thomson toured with the Bobby Simpson-led Australians and produced another tale of Kensington. With close of play near, and the West Indian openers facing an awkward 45 minutes, Thomson produced one of the fastest and most fearsome of spells. Charging in from the pavilion end, he drew blood from the glove of Greenidge and eventually dispatched him. He also dismissed Richards and Alvin Kallicharran before Haynes and Clive Lloyd saw them through to the close.

Richards, in his typical mode of fighting fire with even more fire-power, took on the charged-up fast bowler and played his shots regardless, top-edging an attempted hook that flew over the Eric Innis Stand. Richards also drove him magnificently off the back foot but was caught by Trevor Laughlin at deep backward square trying to dispatch another quick short ball. The West Indies recovered well and won the match in three days but the memory of Thomson in full flow is the one that lingers.

The one-off Test between the West Indies and South Africa in 1991-92 must be considered more than a Kensington moment. This was a significant development in cricket history since it was the match signalling South Africa's re-entry into the Test-playing fold after 22 years of apartheid-induced cricketing isolation.

An over of sheer perfection ends with Michael Holding bowling Geoffrey Boycott for a duck. Holding, known as Whispering Death because of his almost silent approach to the wicket, must go down as one of the menacing and effective fast bowlers of all time.

This match would have been noteworthy for the socio-political reasons alone: the former white supremacists stepping back into the ring to face a team made up of black Afro-Caribbeans and Indo-Caribbeans. The implications of a win on either side could and would be interpreted to suit all agendas and there were many people around the world who were crossing their thumbs that the South Africans would not waltz back into Test cricket by beating the dominant force in world cricket.

Unfortunately, there were other factors at work within the West Indies as this Test became the first to be boycotted successfully by a Caribbean public. Ostensibly, this protest was the result of the omission of a Barbadian bowler, Anderson Cummins. Yet, there were indications of a deeper dissatisfaction.

The stands were almost empty for the five days and the silence went from eerie to oppressive. It played into the hands of the South Africans for whom opener Andrew Hudson made a superb 163, his country's first Test century since Lee Irvine's 102 against Australia in Port Elizabeth in 1969-70. By the end of the fourth day, they must have had the champagne on ice as they needed just another 79 runs for victory with eight wickets in hand. With Kepler Wessels, the captain, on 74 and Peter Kirsten, another battle-hardened veteran, on 36, they were almost home.

But when the motley crew of officials, ground staff, journalists and caterers, not to mention the South African batsmen, pitched up on the last morning and talked of an early lunch they may have forgotten one factor: Curtly. They got their early lunch but in rather different circumstances than they might have imagined as Curtly Ambrose, ably assisted by Courtney Walsh, blew away the pretenders.

From first ball to last Ambrose and Walsh bowled unchanged. Wessels was dismissed without addition, and as wickets fell, Kirsten added 16 more before he too succumbed to the relentless pressure.

At a time when the West Indies were synonymous with fast bowling, Lance Gibbs kept the spinners art well and truly alive, breaking Freddie Trueman's record of 307 Test wickets and ending his career with 309 to his name. Her he bowls during the 1972-73 Test against Australia. Greg Chappell, the non-striker, made 106.

The next highest score was 11 – the extras. The rest read five ducks, three, two, two and four. Somehow the West Indies had conjured up the old magic and South African hopes of a dream rebirth were stillborn in the face of some of the highest quality pace bowling. Ambrose took six for 34 from 24.4 overs and Walsh four for 31 from 22 overs in a display that virtually transcended sport and became art.

It was clear around this time that the West Indies, though still good, were not the seemingly impregnable outfit of the 1980s. But Kensington Oval still had the impressive distinction of being a ground at which the West Indies had not lost since 1935.

Alec Stewart and England changed all that in 1993-94 when they beat a lacklustre West Indies side which was already three-nil up in the series. Stewart, however, was a revelation, relishing the persistently short bowling and cutting and pulling his way to a century in each innings: 118 and 143.

This win was achieved despite the very visual workings of one of Kensington's most notable patrons, Mac Fingall, a trumpeter whose ritual comprised making an entrance in the most popular stand at the western side of the park with fanfare and performing thereafter. Usually accompanied by a drummer or two, he regularly mobilised a band in the Kensington stand to keep up the spirits of the crowd and the West Indian team. Occasionally, you would see him sprinkling some "dust" on the field, perhaps to give his team some particular spiritual incentive.

In contrast, King Dyal would have been elated. He was a supporter of England all his life but a citizen and resident of Barbados. He would go to most international matches at the Oval adorned in a colourful suit, be it lemon, lavender, chartreuse or some other exotic hue, with his pith helmet and walking stick to cheer especially for the motherland.

The prodigals return.
South Africa's first Test in the West indies, their first since being allowed to return from sporting isolation, was always going to be a historic event. And when play got underway on the last morning, it looked as though the newcomeers were going to turn the established world order on its head. Curtly Ambrose and Courtney Walsh, however, seen here celebrating the dismissal of the South African captain Kepler Wessels, ensured there were no fairytale returns.

interest in the promotion, propagation and enjoyment of cricket in Barbados, now comes to the game in his safari/outback-styled hat, his staff, the Barbados colours and the Barbados flag draped about his person.

This match in 1994 was also interesting from other standpoints. There was a packed crowd on all five days, which is unusual for a Test. The majority, it seems, were English visitors with money and skin to burn in the Caribbean sun. It was good for the tourist board, who estimated 8,000 visitors to the island during the Test, and good for the cricket authorities – but will it change the nature of the Kensington Oval if the trend for Barmy Army-style invasions gathers pace?

Barbadians are used to seeing celebrities at matches such as singing stars Mick Jagger and Eddy Grant, the late Sir Paul Getty, former British Prime Minister John Major, and former cricket stars either vacationing or leading a tour. Tour groups are also often in attendance since Barbados is so popular for cricket tours, but it was different on this occasion where on some days, the crowd appeared to be mostly non-West Indian. That may be an exaggeration but it did seem so and that was the point. The comment made repeatedly was "this is the kind of crowd you'd expect to see at Lord's."

Social scientists and historians posited that this change in crowd composition impacted in many ways including the result. Contrary views considered that excuses were being made.

As with everything touched by human action, there have been times when Kensington was not the best example of the cricket spirit. Missile throwing has occurred on at least two occasions and there have been some unpleasant incidents on and off field. Opening against Australia at Kensington in 1973, Roy Fredericks was given out leg-before for 98. He may have shown his surprise but, whether he did or not, all sorts of objects were thrown onto the outfield. Unfortunately, this was not an isolated incident.

He presided over the Kensington Stand and did so in 1994 celebrating in his own "regal" way. His death on May 7, 1997 has left a void in Barbados Tests. Another local character who has moved on is Gearbox, who would stand outside the ground and make the most ear-piercing noises – hence his name.

Nowadays, there is such travel between the islands that posses come from Trinidad & Tobago, Jamaica and the other islands to enjoy cricket and party in the stands. Music tends to be played in between overs (something adopted from Chicki's disco in Antigua) and there is an abundance of liquid refreshment, the flow of which does not necessarily end at close of play.

Those who blow the conch shell or play other instruments come habitually to the Oval and strut their stuff. "Blue Food" – a popular performer at Queen's Park Oval in Trinidad & Tobago - would journey to Kensington to blow the conch. Unfortunately, he too is no longer alive. Kensington, however, is not short of characters. Besides Mac Fingall, Julian Hunte, a Barbadian of European descent who has taken an active

Left: King Dyal was one of Bridgetown's most recognisable figures turning up to Test matches in his collection of bright suits. The ground is duller without him.

Right: Lawrence Rowe was one of the most elegant batsmen to grace Kensington Oval. Having made 214 and 100 not out on his debut, he produced one of the all-time great innings of 302 against England in 1973-74.

In 1988, Pakistan, under the vibrant captaincy of Imran Khan, seemed to be heading for an upset series win in Bridgetown. They had outplayed the West Indies in the first Test in Guyana where Gordon Greenidge led the team in the absence of Viv Richards while the second Test in Trinidad was drawn. The third and final Test in Bridgetown seemed headed for a Pakistani win. Needing 266 to win on the last day, the West Indies had faltered to 170 for seven and then 207 for eight when the quick bowler, Winston Benjamin, joined Jeffrey Dujon, at the crease with time and overs to spare. Benjamin survived a raucous appeal for a bat-pad catch off Benjamin which led to the Pakistani leg-spinner Abdul Qadir, apoplectic with rage, engaging in a frank exchange of words with some members of the crowd. It ended in a physical confrontation.

More recently there was trouble at a one-day international against Australia in 1999 when Sherwin Campbell was given run out, failing to make his ground at the non-striker's end after he struggled to get past the bowler on his follow-through. It appeared on first viewing and on the replays on the television screens in the stands that he had been deliberately obstructed by Brendon Julian.

As Campbell grudgingly left the arena, the bombardment began and for 45 tense minutes, outraged Barbadians again threw missiles including bottles, onto the field.

It took a plea from Gary Sobers to calm the crowd, and play resumed with Campbell being allowed to continue his innings. West Indies went on to win the game so perhaps it was a victory for the demonstrators.

It is more fitting to recall that tour in the light of the Test series, which will go down as one of the most compelling of all time. And the Bridgetown Test was especially good.

The context of the series does not make pleasant reading for West Indians. A player revolt prior to the 1998 tour to South Africa saw the once-mighty West Indies whitewashed five-nil in the Test series. With all of the racial and political import of the tour, it was humiliating stuff and the mood was grim when the team returned home to face Australia, the new world power. The first Test in

England's Graham Thorpe takes on Nixon McLean during his 103 in the 1997-98 Test.

Port-of-Spain followed the form book, disastrously so for the West Indies, who were dismissed in the second innings for just 51, their record low in Tests.

Lara, in his first stint as captain, had been put on probation after the South African debacle and appointed for the first two Tests only. After Port-of-Spain, to say his position was tenuous was something of an understatement. He responded with an unbelievably accomplished double-hundred to set up a win for the West Indies in Jamaica.

At Kensington for the third Test, the teams competed like wolves over a kill. The wits and batting skills of Steve Waugh battled with Brian Lara as captain and, more potently, the scintillating stroke-maker. Waugh just missed a double-hundred, out for199, and Ricky Ponting made 104. Together they shared a fifth wicket partnership of 281 as Australia built up a commanding first-innings total of 490. As the West Indies slipped to 98 for six in reply early on the third day, the game looked all but over. They were rescued by a century from Sherwin Campbell, who shared a seventh-wicket partnership of 153 with Ridley Jacobs.

Courtney Walsh stepped in with five for 39 as the Australians tumbled to 177 all out, but he can have had little idea that with his team chasing 308 for an unlikely victory, he would have one more act to perform.

When play began on the final day the West Indies were 85 for two with Lara on two. The crowd came hoping for rather than expecting a home win, but they were determined to enjoy it whichever way it went. On a working day, a good number came at the start and as the possibility of a win loomed the crowd swelled to near capacity.

With 223 still needed on the last day, there was enough time to get the runs but it would have to be done on a fifth-day pitch with Glenn McGrath, Jason Gillespie and the leg-spinners Shane Warne and Stuart MacGill raring to go. Everest never looked so steep. Except perhaps when Gillespie removed Adrian Griffith and Carl Hooper early on to leave the West Indies reeling on 105 for five.

Adversity is often the catalyst, however, for all great sportsmen to find a new level and Lara's response was a measured match-winning innings of 153 not out. According to *Wisden* it showed the "hand of genius" as Lara "guided his men to victory as though leading the infirm through a maze."

Lara found a useful partner in Jimmy Adams who made 38 in a sixth-wicket stand of 133 that brought out the worst and the best in McGrath, who produced a superb spell of hostile fast bowling. Hit for four by Lara, McGrath responded with a short ball that hit the West Indian on the helmet. Some snarling followed which Adams had to cool down."

His dander well and truly up, McGrath bowled Adams and followed up with the wickets of Ridley Jacobs and Nehemiah Perry in successive balls. West Indies were now 248 for eight with just the fast bowlers, Ambrose and Walsh, to come.

How many matches had these two already won for the West Indies with the ball? This time, they showed they could do their bit with the bat, Ambrose in particular lending staunch support to Lara in a ninth-wicket stand of 54. Lara, in spite of being dropped by Ian Healy with seven still needed to win, was playing quite beautifully and after Walsh came out to join him with six required, he confidently cracked Gillespie to the cover boundary for the winning runs.

Many of the players, including the two captains, described it as one of the best Test matches they had played, for its excitement and challenge. Journalists wrote that it was one of the Tests of the century, and Lara's 153 found its way into *Wisden's* list of top five Test innings. In fact it was to prove a magical series for Lara as he followed up with an 82-ball century in the final Test to finish with 586 runs in the series at an average of 91. Australia won that last match, however, to square one of the most riveting series in the history of Test cricket.

As we said at the start, it can be difficult living up to a name with such great associations but a series of West Indian teams has certainly managed that. As for the future, there is talk of structural changes at the Kensington Oval in preparation for the 2007 World Cup. The pitches have already become more batsman-friendly and it now seems that the stands and scoreboards will undergo a facelift. No matter. The soul of cricket and the spiritual presence of Walcott, Worrell and Weekes, of Sobers, Marshall and Greenidge, will ensure that anyone who is fortunate enough to witness a Test match in Barbados will be able to enjoy colour, ambience, sunshine – and some great cricket.

Malcolm Marshall.
A West Indian cricket legend, Marshall took 49 wickets at Kensington Oval including the best match return of 11 for 120 against New Zealand in 1984-85. Born and bred in Bridgetown, he also died there at the tragically young age of 41.

KENSINGTON OVAL Ground Records

Result Summary

	Played	Won	Lost	Drawn
West Indies	40	20	5	15
Australia	9	2	4	3
England	12	2	4	6
India	8	0	7	1
Pakistan	5	0	2	3
New Zealand	4	1	2	1
South Africa	2	0	1	1

Bangladesh, Sri Lanka and Zimbabwe
have yet to play at the Kensington Oval

Highest Totals

668	Australia v West Indies 1st Innings 1954-55
657-8	Pakistan v West Indies 2nd Innings 1957-58
650-6	Australia v West Indies 1st Innings 1964-65

Lowest Completed Innings Totals

81	India v West Indies 1996-97
94	New Zealand v West Indies 1984-85
97	Australia v West Indies 1983-84

Highest Match Aggregates

Runs	Wkts	
1661	36	West Indies v Australia 1954-55
1640	24	West Indies v Australia 1964-65
1398	38	West Indies v Pakistan 1976-77

Lowest Match Aggregates (Result oriented matches)

Runs	Wkts	
309	29	West Indies v England 1934-35

Highest Scores

337	Hanif Mohammad	Pakistan v West Indies 1957-58
302	LG Rowe West	Indies v England 1973-74
226	CG Greenidge	West Indies v Australia 1990-91
226	GStA Sobers	West Indies v England 1959-60
220	CL Walcott	West Indies v England 1953-54

Highest Run Aggregates

Runs	Matches	Hundreds	
1210	13	4	DL Haynes
959	12	3	IVA Richards
914	9	3	GStA Sobers
903	12	1	BC Lara
882	11	2	RB Richardson

Partnership Records

382 for 1st	WM Lawry and RB Simpson Australi v West Indies 1964-65
249 for 2nd	AI Kallicharran and LG Rowe West Indies v England 1973-74
220 for 3rd	AI Kallicharran and IVA Richards West Indies v India 1975-76
399 for 4th	GStA Sobers and FMM Worrell West Indies v England 1959-60
281 for 5th	RT Ponting and SR Waugh Australia v England 1998-99
254 for 6th	CA Davis and GStA Sobers West Indies v New Zealand 1971-72
347 for 7th	DStE Atkinson and CC Depeiza West Indies v Australia 1954-55
84 for 8th	Arshad Ayub and SV Manjrekar India v West Indies 1988-89
132 for 9th	AA Donald and SM Pollock South Africa v West Indies 2000-01
133 for 10th	Wasim Bari and Wasim Raja Pakistan v West Indies 1976-77

Best Bowling in an Innings.

8 for 38 LR Gibbs	West Indies v India 1961-62
8 for 45 CEL Ambrose	West Indies v England 1989-90
8 for 75 ARC Fraser	England v West Indies 1993-94
7 for 74 BR Taylor	New Zealand v West Indies 1971-72
7 for 80 MD Marshall	West Indies v New Zealand 1984-85

Best Bowling in a Match

11 for 120 (4-40, 7-80)	MD Marshall West Indies v New Zealand 1984-85
10 for 127 (2-82 8-45)	CEL Ambrose West Indies v England 1989-90
10 for 195 (5-105 5-90)	GTS Stevens England v West Indies 1929-30

Hat Trick

| JJC Lawson | West Indies v Australia 2002-03 |

Highest Wicket Aggregates

Wkts	Matches	5WI	
53	12	3	CA Walsh
52	13	2	CEL Ambrose
49	8	4	MD Marshall

Most Catches by Fielder

Catches	Matches	
24	12	BC Lara
14	12	IVA Richards
13	11	RB Richardson

Most Dismissals by Wicketkeeper

Dismissals	Matches	
35	8	PJL Dujon
21	6	DL Murray
15	5	RD Jacobs

NEW ZEALAND

Richard Boock

Richard Hadlee.
Eighty-six Tests, 3,124 runs, 431 wickets and a knighthood. The most successful New Zealand cricketer of all time.

In a land where the oval ball is king and where the clamour and cry is for the men in black rather than white, cricket has been both pragmatic and tenacious in stirring the imagination and support of the New Zealand public. One of the reasons for this is the widespread doubling up of rugby and cricket grounds.

Eden Park in Auckland is best known for the "Flourbomb" rugby Test against the Springboks in 1981 and for the All Blacks, victory in the inaugural Rugby World Cup in 1987. And yet along with Lancaster Park in Christchurch – another rugby ground – and the Basin Reserve in Wellington it has been staging Test matches ever since Harold Gilligan's England toured in 1929-30.

It was at Eden Park that Wally Hammond made 336 not out, 295 of them coming in one day, as he went on to average 563 for the two-Test series – he was only dismissed once – and where New Zealand crumbled to 26 all out in 1954-55, still the lowest Test score. There have been some pretty special moments for the Kiwis too. It would be hard to improve on their 190-run victory over the West Indies in March 1956, their first Test win after 26 years of trying. This was especially sweet as it came after heavy defeats in the first three Tests – by an innings and 71, an innings and 64, and nine wickets respectively. Ironically, Bert Sutcliffe, arguably New Zealand's greatest batsman, was forced to withdraw from the series for business reasons after the second Test and missed being part of the triumph. Though he returned to play again, he never did play in a Test-winning team. The Kiwis also notched up some memorable wins against Australia there in 1981-82, 1985-86 and 1992-93, while the 78-run win over England in 2001-02 was notable for the use of floodlights on the fourth day.

Nathan Astle's name is writ large in the history of Lancaster Park after destroying the England attack in 2001-02 with an innings of such strength and power that he reached his double-century in just 153 balls, a record for Test cricket. In 1983-84, New Zealand had one of their great wins there when Richard Hadlee led them to an innings victory over the English. There is now a Hadlee Stand to commemorate not just Richard's contribution but those of his father Walter, who captained New Zealand in the 1940s, and his two older brothers Dayle – 26 Tests – and Barry.

Once upon a time there was an element of cricket-ground charm to these grounds and indeed to Carisbrook in Dunedin. But today they are first and foremost rugby grounds, the stands hemming play not so much into an oval but into a rectangle. Two more recent additions to the list are McLean Park, Napier, another dual-usage ground which hosted its first Test in 1979, and Seddon Park in Hamilton. But as one of the oldest grounds in the country, one with character and history, and one that has always been and always will be dedicated primarily to the small round ball and the men in white, the Basin Reserve claims pre-eminence.

BASIN RESERVE, WELLINGTON

I n New Zealand, the locals like to say that you cannot beat Wellington on a good day, which is especially true if you happen to be spending your time at the nation's home of cricket, the Basin Reserve.

There is a degree of wryness about this, though, as the chance of finding Wellington on a good day are similar to those for winning the grand lottery; the more likely scenario involves gale-force winds, a number of airport closures, and hundreds of inverted umbrellas.

Surrounded by red-blooming pohutakawa, or native Christmas trees, the Basin not only ranks as New Zealand's most successful Test venue in the world, but for a number of reasons as one of the strangest. There is the wind for starters. No small zephyrs here; either a roaring northerly or a rasping, bone-chilling southerly, the strength of which forces pedestrians to adopt a 45-degree lean as they negotiate neighbouring Adelaide Road.

It can also be bitterly cold. The southerly swirls up from the Antarctic pack ice, intensifies as it is funneled through Cook Strait and then blasts into Wellington city, creating surreal conditions for any Test match underway.

At the Basin, heavy bails are the norm rather than the exception, groundsmen have been tossed and injured by covers acting like spinnakers and special sightscreens were invented after previous models were blown away. It blew so cold when India were touring in 1975-76 that their captain Bishan Bedi eventually had to leave the field with tonsillitis. And it was so strong for the first Test against England in 1978, that umpire Ralph Gardiner had not the faintest chance of hearing New Zealand opener John Wright edge the first ball of the match, and to the amazement of everyone downwind, gave him not out.

Cricket has not been the only casualty, either. During a Chatham Cup soccer final at the ground

The Basin Reserve is perhaps the only cricket ground in the world that doubles as a roundabout.

in 1971, one player scored an accidental goal from 80 metres, and more than 20 attempted goalkicks were blown back for corners. In 1968 the consequences were far more tragic when the steamer ferry Wahine was hit by 100-knot winds at the mouth of Wellington harbour and foundered, leading to the loss of 51 lives. No other cricket arena in the world is lashed by such ferocious storms.

Then there is the noise at the ground, effectively the hub of a giant inner-city roundabout; a junction for traffic coming and going from the airport and the south-eastern suburbs of Hataitai, Seatoun and Lyall Bay. It is, in effect, an enormous road island, surrounded by a four lanes of tarmac. When your ears are not besieged by wind, they are often assailed by squealing tyres, angry honking motorists, sirens from all sorts of emergency services, and an antique air-raid horn, which is habitually sounded from a nearby student flat.

With the wind blowing and the noise from the peak-hour traffic at its height, not to mention the faint strains of an air-raid warning, there can hardly be a more bizarre experience than watching Test cricket at the Basin.

And it is not just the players and spectators who are affected. Whatever dilemmas might confront a Test selector these days, the task of picking a combination to play at Wellington must still rate as one of the more difficult, particularly in terms of the bowling attack.

In past years, New Zealand have been reasonably well-equipped to cope, using workhorses like Lance Cairns or Ewen Chatfield to slave into the gale, while speedsters such as Richard Hadlee and Shane Bond cashed in downwind. The conditions, however, have sometimes proved too much for teams who arrive in Wellington without the necessary variation in their attack, leading to bowlers being asked to shoulder unfamiliar burdens, and more stress for the captains.

England were well equipped in 1978. They had Bob Willis looking lively and sharp, and could also call on Chris Old, Mike Hendrick and Ian Botham to share the task of bowling into the wind, which was gusting and howling on the first morning. That they failed to win had more to do

with the fragility of their batting than any problems with their bowling, but whatever the case, this was one of New Zealand's most famous games at the Basin.

New Zealand's first Test win against England, it was also the last match on the historic ground before it underwent major renovations, including new drainage, an altered pitch angle and the construction of the RA Vance stand – named after the New Zealand Cricket Council's late chairman.

It was also a match that marked a coming-of-age for the Basin spectators, who for the first time started barracking for their side like a modern-day football crowd, beating cans on cans and chanting "Hadlee, Hadlee" as the emerging star made his move in the second innings. This was the match in which Wright, on debut, edged his first ball of Test cricket straight through to wicket-keeper Bob Taylor, was given not out, and – after surviving a maelstrom of short-pitched deliveries – went on to make 55.

Later, when the wind had blown itself to a standstill, England were left requiring a mere 137 to win in two days. It looked straightforward enough until Hadlee and left-arm paceman Richard Collinge began their bid for glory. After a dressing-room pact to "make something out of nothing", the new-ball pair galvanised the crowd by making immediate inroads into the English batting line-up, at which point the number of spectators began multiplying by the minute.

Collinge, lumbering in off a long, angled run-up, started the excitement by yorking Englands captain Geoff Boycott, before sending back Geoff Miller and Derek Randall in quick succession. Hadlee then announced his arrival by knocking over the middle order, leaving England 53 for eight at stumps on the fourth day, with a sense of history and emotion hanging in the air.

The only fear for the Basin faithful at that stage was rain, and they were hardly encouraged the next morning when they awoke to drizzle and the news that the resumption had been delayed. Fortunately, the Wellington weather looked

Jeremy Coney pulls for four during his 174 not out against England in 1983-84. He went on to play 52 Tests.

kindly for once on its cricketers, enabling New Zealand to claim their long-awaited triumph over England, the final act coming at 12.30pm when Willis jabbed Hadlee to Geoff Howarth at slip. History had been made – and not for the first time, it had happened at the Basin.

That Hadlee had figured prominently was no great surprise in retrospect. He did, after all, carry on to become the first bowler to take 400 Test wickets and then the world's leading wicket-taker with 431. For all that, the man with the side-stepping start to his run-up was still a reasonably raw act in 1978, although Basin patrons had already been treated to one memorable exhibition of his talents in the summer of 1975-76, when India were in town.

This Test was also played for a time in high winds, eventually resulting in Bedi's unfortunate departure. Between the icy winds and Hadlee's fire the Indians must have felt they were at the most inhospitable venue in the world.

Bowling downwind, Hadlee found a venomous length and scythed through the Indian batsmen in the second innings, taking seven for 23 in a hostile 8.3-over spell and ending with match figures of 11 for 58. His seven-wicket bag remains the best bowling performance at the Basin. India, without injured opening batsman Sunil Gavaskar, folded for 81 as New Zealand swept to the win by an innings and 33 runs.

The match was the launchpad for a spectacular career for Hadlee who enjoyed many more great days at the Basin. Fifty-three of his 431 Test wickets were taken there, including his 300th – that of Australian skipper Allan Border.

Another compelling effort at the Basin came in 1990 when Australia, having won the toss and elected to bat, were bundled out for 110 as Hadlee built on an early breakthrough from Danny Morrison, taking five for 39.

Danny Morrison was a tearaway fast bowler who took 160 wickets in 48 Tests. He was also a stubborn tail-end batsman who had a wonderful knack of hanging around when it was most needed.
In Faisalabad in 1990-91 he occupied the crease for just over four hours in making 25.

In front of an enthralled Basin crowd, New Zealand batted solidly but not spectacularly to reply with 202, after which Australia were outfoxed by the off-spin of John Bracewell, who turned the ball sharply to take six wickets.

Needing 178 to post an upset win, the New Zealanders achieved the target at a canter courtesy of Wright, by now the captain, who led by example, hitting 17 fours and one six in his delightful unbeaten innings of 117.

It was to be one of three Test centuries scored at the Basin by Wright, whose final total of 12 centuries makes him one of the country's most successful openers. He has since gone on to make a name for himself as a coach, helping India to the 2003 World Cup final.

The Cantabrian who started out with long hair and side-burns, guitar case and selfless attitude, moulded himself into one of New Zealand's most effective batsmen, more through limiting his left-handed strokeplay than expanding it. Wright started with the complete set of clubs but gradually began reducing his shots until he gave himself the maximum chance of occupying the crease and making meaningful contributions to his team's total.

Possibly his finest innings at the Basin was his effort in the first Test against the 1986-87 West Indies side, when he defied a pace attack comprising Malcolm Marshall, Joel Garner, Courtney Walsh and Michael Holding while following his first-innings 75, which spanned five hours and five minutes, with a painstaking 138 in the second. It took him nine hours and 35 minutes and was the slowest Test century scored in New Zealand.

Wright was undoubtedly helped by the back strains that limited the contribution of Holding and Marshall in the second innings – they bowled 41 overs between them – but his record third-wicket partnership of 241 with Martin Crowe, who chalked up an impressive 119, was still a remarkable one. It would be fair to say that his innings set the scene for one of the most absorbing tussles in New Zealand Test history, as a West Indies side with batsmen such as Gordon Greenidge, Desmond Haynes, Richie Richardson and Viv Richards were forced to draw the series, after New Zealand gained a thrilling five-wicket win in the final Test.

The Basin continued to be a special ground for Wright, who scored his last Test century against England in the summer of 1991-92, and signed off with 76 and an unbeaten 42 against Australia the following year. In 82 Tests he scored 5,334 runs at 37.82 but there was a marked improvement at the Basin, where he posted 1,005 runs in 13 Tests at 47.85.

If Wright was prominent in the 1987 series against the West Indies, then so was New Zealand's premier batsman Martin Crowe, who had begun his Test career five summers earlier as a 19-year-old, thrust in against an Australian pace attack which included Jeff Thomson and Dennis Lillee.

Crowe's love affair with the Basin began in 1983-84 when scored his maiden Test century against Willis's England tourists in the first Test, making exactly 100 runs as he added 114 for the fifth wicket with Jeremy Coney – who ended with an unbeaten 174. In fact, of the five centuries Crowe scored at the Basin, each score was an improvement on the previous knock, which is really saying something considering his fourth century was 174 against Pakistan in 1988-89.

Apart from his maiden century, there was the 119 he scored against Marshall, Garner, Walsh and Holding in 1986-87 and his 143 against England in the drawn first Test of 1987-88, when New Zealand made a sound start to the series by posting 512 for six declared, with Ken Rutherford also scoring a century.

Crowe's 174 against Pakistan venue a year later was another gem in that it was scored against bowlers of the calibre of Imran Khan and Abdul Qadir, as New Zealand matched the efforts of a batting order which featured master craftsman Javed Miandad.

His finest moment, though, and arguably the most complete batting performance seen at the Basin, came in 1990-91 in the first Test against Sri Lanka when he and Andrew Jones pulled New Zealand out of the mire in the second innings with a third-wicket stand of 467 – a new world record Test partnership for any wicket.

Jones made a valuable contribution of 186 but it was Crowe's 299, the highest individual score in New Zealand Test history, that was caught in the memories of all who saw it. *Wisden*, which described Crowe as being "at the top of his bent" was suitably impressed: "Crowe is very much a stylist; Jones is not. But their combined talents shredded Sri Lanka's first-innings lead of 323 into the waste-paper basket."

Crowe's innings lasted ten minutes over ten hours before, to his and the whole country's eternal regret, he attempted to glide a single off part-time bowler Arjuna Ranatunga, and was caught at the wicket. He walked off in a daze, shaking his head at the lapse, as if he had just been bowled without scoring. "It's a bit like climbing Everest and pulling a hamstring in the last stride," he said afterwards.

The eventual total of 671 for four was the highest by any Test side in New Zealand. In the euphoria of Crowe's achievement, however, it would be foolish to overlook the consummate performance of Aravinda de Silva, whose 267 in the Sri Lanka innings was, for two days at least, the highest individual score made at the Basin Reserve.

In total, New Zealand's most prolific batsman – with 17 Test centuries – played ten of his 77 Tests at the Basin and proved a massive success, scoring 1,123 runs at 70.18 – compared with a career tally of 5,444 at 45.36.

Of New Zealand batsmen, the only player to eclipse this record was the late Stewie Dempster, a Wellingtonian who fashioned a remarkable record in Test cricket, averaging 65.42 in a brief ten-match career. A giant of a cricketer in local circles, Dempster's name is now carried on the ground's gates and he is remembered as one the country's most successful openers, especially after his deeds in New Zealand's second-ever Test, at the Basin.

The year was 1930 and history was in the making as Dempster combined with Jack Mills to put on 276 for the first wicket against England, eventually cracking 136 as his partner posted 117. It was one of two significant records set at the ground during the match. The other, which partly made up for defeat on the field, saw gate takings of £1,125, a new mark for a cricket crowd in a country where the appeal of the oval ball and black jersey has always taken precedence over the white flannels of summer.

The first Test against Australia at the Basin in 1945-46 was also New Zealand's inaugural Test against Australia. Unfortunately, New Zealand performed so poorly in this outing that their close neighbours did not bother to come again until the summer of 1973-74.

The basis of Bradman's 1948 "Invincibles" side, Australia were far too good for New Zealand, who were dismissed for 42 and 54, including a collapse of eight wickets for five runs in the second innings. The story goes that, when Australia batted, New Zealand seamer Jack Cowie found a helpful spot in the pitch and started exploiting the assistance, taking six for 40 – including scalps such as Sid Barnes, Keith Miller and Lindsay Hassett.

At 199 for eight, Australian skipper Bill Brown decided he had had enough and opted to declare, in order that his bowlers might also reap the benefits from the drying pitch, and make life difficult for their hosts. New Zealand lasted less than two hours.

The captain of the day was Walter Hadlee, the man who was to lead New Zealand's icon 49ers to England a couple of summers later, when all three Tests were drawn. An honest toiler at international level, Hadlee senior never really hit his straps at the Basin, playing only two of his 11 Tests there for a total of 33 runs at an average of 8.25. Perhaps his greatest contribution to his country's cause came in producing his son Richard, although it should not be forgotten that another son, Dayle, enjoyed a successful Test career while Barry, the eldest of the Hadlee offspring, put in some good performances for Canterbury.

Probably the most successful New Zealand captain at the ground in terms of individual performance was Auckland batsman Mark Burgess, a talented sportsman who also played for his country at soccer. Burgess, a fair-headed right-hander, played four of his 50 Tests at the Basin and averaged 56, including an initial sequence of 66, 60, 79, 21 not out and 95. The last of these setting up his side for their historic first win at the Basin – against India in 1975-76. Only in Burgess's final Test at the Basin, against England in 1978, did he fail to post double figures, although his team's first-ever win over England would have proved ample consolation.

Martin Crowe tucks Neil Foster away during his match-saving second innings of 100 in 1983-84. Crowe went on to become New Zealand's premier batsman with 5,444 runs and 17 centuries. Five of them came at the Basin Reserve including his 299 against Sri Lanka in 1990-91.

After Australia swept New Zealand aside at the end of the Second World War, it was the turn of the West Indies to dominate, with a squad in 1955-56 that included a 19-year-old Gary Sobers, Collie Smith, and the brilliant stroke-maker Everton Weekes.

Weekes was to prove irrepressible on this tour, scoring 940 runs at 104.44 in eight first-class matches and 418 at 83.60 in the four Tests, including consecutive scores of 123, 103, 156, 5 and 31. His 156 in the third Test at the Basin set the scene for a nine-wicket win, giving the tourists an impressive three-nil series lead.

The irony was that in the final Test at Auckland, New Zealand were able finally to put together something like a complete performance, and went on to claim their historic maiden win, 26 years after the quest began. Despite the celebrations, there was to be a lot more ignominy for New Zealand as they attempted to build on the success, especially through the late 1950s and early 1960s, when the team depended heavily on senior batsmen Bert Sutcliffe and John R Reid.

There was certainly little for New Zealanders to feel encouraged about in 1962-63 when England demolished them by an innings in the first two Tests and by seven wickets in the third. The most interesting showdown was the second Test at the Basin, when England amassed 428 for eight in their first innings, courtesy of a courageous 128 not out from Colin Cowdrey, batting at number eight because of a hand injury, who shared a ninth - wicket partnership – then a record for Test cricket – of 163 with AC Smith.

Although the margin of defeat was an innings and 47 runs, there was at least some cheer for the locals in January 1963, when Reid smote a world record number of sixes while playing for Wellington against Northern Districts. Reid smashed 15 sixes in his innings of 296, easily eclipsing the old record of 11 – and just for good measure lashed 35 fours. Even though the Australian Andrew Symonds improved on it by hitting 16 sixes in his 254 not out for Gloucestershire against Glamorgan in 1995, Reid's hitting that day remains a rich source of pride for the people of the Basin Reserve.

Basin patrons had to wait another six years before they had the ultimate reason to celebrate, and that

was after the 1968-69 West Indians were in town under the now world-famous Sobers.

Having been inserted on a helpful pitch, the West Indies managed to get through to 297 despite the best efforts of seamer Dick Motz, and then restricted New Zealand to 282, with Glenn Turner making 74. Up until then it had been an even contest, slightly dominated by the seamers perhaps, but certainly not to the extent suggested when West Indies collapsed for 148 in their second innings, leaving New Zealand the task of scoring 164 in a day and 72 minutes.

The win might have seemed a formality for New Zealand, but they had not reckoned on the mood of fast bowlers "Prof" Edwards and Charlie Griffith, who had just been informed of their respective axings for the looming tour of England. They proceeded to vent their fury on the New Zealand batsmen and three wickets fell for 39 during the fireworks, before Brian Hastings and Bryan Yuile ensured there would no further hiccups. New Zealand had won their first Test at the Basin.

The tour from Australia in 1973-74 was eagerly awaited in New Zealand for a couple of reasons: it was the first tour from the close rivals since 1945-46 and just the second in history, and the side was also bristling with star quality, including the Chappell brothers, Dougie Walters, Rod Marsh and Ashley Mallett.

Typically, the first Test at the Basin began in wintry conditions, with the southerly gusting and howling, and Australia would have been happy to be batting, particularly after the Chappell brothers settled into their stride.

This was the match in which Greg and Ian set a record by scoring two centuries each in the Test, the only instance of two brothers scoring centuries in each innings of a Test, and a feat only once previously recorded in first-class cricket – by Worcester brothers RE and WL Foster in 1899.

In the first innings, Ian struck 145 and Greg piled on 247 not out, as they shared in a partnership of 264 for the third wicket. Australia eventually declared at 511 for six.

New Zealand's first Test against Australia in 1945-46 was not a happy event. It was the first Test after the Second World War and Australia introduced players such as Keith Miller and Ray Lindwall who were soon to become household names. Even without Don Bradman, who was ill, they were far too strong, bowling out New Zealand for 42 in the first innings and 54 in the second. The neighbours did not play again until 1973-74.

His father's son.
Growing up with your dad as a national treasure can put the pressure on a young man but Chris Cairns (left) has managed it superbly.

His father Lance (above) played 43 times for New Zealand between 1974 and 1985, carving himself a niche as a hard-hitting batsman and a canny swing bowler.
Chris is built in the same mould but is, if anything, an improved model. He is second behind Richard Hadlee in New Zealand's list of Test wicket-takers while his batting brought a cherished century against Australia at the Basin Reserve in 1999-2000.

If New Zealand doubted that lightning would ever strike twice they were sorely mistaken. Ian scored 121 and Greg posted 133 in Australia's second innings, allowing another sizeable total to be scored, this time 460 for eight. New Zealand at least survived the onslaught, batting impressively in their only innings courtesy of 132 from skipper Bevan Congdon, 101 from Hastings and half-centuries from Turner and John Morrison.

It ended up a high-scoring draw, although the performance obviously encouraged New Zealand, who travelled to Christchurch for the second Test and completely outplayed Chappell's men, winning by five wickets.

Another popular win at the ground came in 1980-81 against India, in what was the first international match played at the Basin since the major renovation and development, a facelift which permanently changed the layout of the ground.

In the beginning, the land that eventually became the Basin Reserve had been a small inland lake, earmarked by town planners as a reserve basin, to enable ships to shelter from the frequent squalls as they unloaded their cargo. However, the best-laid plans needed to be revised after 1855, when a violent earthquake shook the region so dramatically that the floor of the lake was raised above ground level, providing municipal authorities with an unexpected opportunity for development.

At first a swamp, the land was drained and hosted its first game of cricket in 1869 between the Wellington Volunteers and the officers and men of the HMS Falcon. According to reports, the field was in an appalling condition, littered with stones and thistles and other impediments, to the extent that fielding was a risky occupation and the ball was almost immediately in a state of disrepair.

More than a century later, the ground was completely re-surfaced and top-dressed; new stands were constructed, a grass bank on the eastern side of the ground provided a natural suntrap and a new scoreboard dominated the southern skyline.

As if to celebrate, New Zealand's first game on the refurbished ground ended in a memorable 62-run win over India and it was apt perhaps that the spirit of Dempster was then in the shape of Howarth, whose 137 was the highest at the ground since Dempster's effort in the inaugural Test. Hadlee's four for 62 secured the home win.

At this stage, the Basin was proving a reasonably good batting surface, which England discovered when they visited in 1983-84, Derek Randall, with 162, and Ian Botham (138) enjoyed themselves immensely. This Test showed, however, that New Zealand were coming of age in terms of their batting and they more than matched England by posting a massive 537. Martin Crowe, needless to say, made a hundred as did Coney, whose 174 not out was his first century in 127 first-class innings.

The match ended in stalemate and the England captain Willis said he had never seen a pitch which provided less assistance to seamers or spinners. He might well have been right but his words would have been of little consolation to Rutherford's New Zealand team, who were torn apart at the Basin a few years later when Walsh's West Indians arrived in the country.

It was the second Test in 1994-95 and, coming on the back of an unsuccessful tour of South Africa which had brought with it allegations of dope-smoking and indiscipline, it almost certainly sounded the death-knell for Rutherford's tenure and several of his team-mates' international careers.

Beaten by an innings and 322 runs, the worst loss in their Test history, New Zealand were hopelessly outplayed in all facets, although most of the damage was inflicted at the start of the game as the West Indies posted 660 for five declared.

Jimmy Adams made 151, Brian Lara 147 and Junior Murray 101 not out, after which Walsh turned the blow-torch on the New Zealand batsmen, taking seven for 37 as the hosts fell over for a meagre 216. Asked to follow on, Rutherford's men fared even worse in the second innings, capitulating for just 122. Walsh took another six wickets to end the Test with remarkable figures of 13 for 55.

Ian Botham and Derek Randall produced one of the most exciting batting performances yet seen at the Basin Reserve when they added 232 for the sixth wicket during the 1983-84 Test. New Zealand saved the Test, however, and went on to record their first series win over England when they beat them by an innings and 132 runs in the second Test in Christchurch.

Within a couple of months, a new broom swept through the New Zealand team. Turner, one of the country's finest batsmen, was brought in as the coach while Rutherford and Andrew Jones were tossed on the scrapheap and wicketkeeper Adam Parore was forced to hand over the gloves to new skipper, Lee Germon. The new, disciplined approach worked well for a while, although Turner did not survive much more than a year in the job, finding himself isolated from both the players and the administrators.

England visited again in 1996-97 and in part made up for their earlier disappointments, beating New Zealand by an innings and 68 runs in the second Test at the Basin, the match which marked the debut of 18-year-old spinner Daniel Vettori.

The Basin by this stage was starting to change significantly in terms of the character of the pitch, which had been prepared in a slightly different fashion, and as a result was providing more pace and bounce for the fast bowlers. More than any other country, India probably found the adjustment at Wellington a difficult one to make, losing by four wickets after an enthralling contest in 1998-99, and being humiliated in little more than two days in their most recent tour, in 2002-03.

In terms of the modern era, the 1998 showdown at the Basin will prove hard to beat in terms of quality. India were in immediate trouble against the swing bowling of Simon Doull, who ended with seven for 65, but still managed to eke out 208 after a stubborn, counter-attacking century from their captain Mohammad Azharuddin. In reply, New Zealand's batsmen all chimed in to drag the score through to 352, after which Sachin Tendulkar made a sparkling 113 to ensure New Zealand would at least be faced with a chase of more than 200.

There were a few heart-flutters early in the innings, but the hosts were eventually able to grab the win in relative comfort, winning by four wickets after half-centuries by Chris Cairns and Craig McMillan.

However, if India were a shade downcast at that result, they would have been beside themselves after the events of the 2002-03 Test at the Basin, when they lost by ten wickets after surviving a combined total of just 96.5 overs. Laden with class players such as Sourav Ganguly, Tendulkar, Rahul Dravid and VVS Laxman, the tourists looked clueless on a Basin pitch that provided tennis-ball bounce and were bowled out for 161 and 121.

But if individual performances at the Basin were being ranked, it is a fair bet that New Zealand batsman Mathew Sinclair would find himself near the top of the list following his deeds against Lara's West Indians at the Basin in the Boxing Day Test of 1999. Called in to make his debut at the ground, Sinclair took patrons on a wild ride through the record books while making 214, setting the scene for New Zealand's emphatic win by an innings and 105 runs.

By the time he was dismissed, the 24-year-old had not only overtaken the debut efforts of great players such as Greg Chappell and Peter May, he had also marched past someone named WG Grace and the first-ever centurion in Test cricket, Charles Bannerman. Only England batsman "Tip" Foster, who played a handy debut innings of 287 against Australia 96 years before in Sydney, remained unscathed after the record innings from Sinclair, whose 214 left him in second-equal spot with West Indian Lawrence Rowe.

As some consolation, Sinclair and Rowe can now jointly claim the world record for the highest score on debut from a number three batsman.

It remains one of many outstanding performances at the Basin, to be rated alongside efforts such as Jackie McGlew's 255 not out for South Africa in 1952-53, Aravinda's special innings in 1991, and Crowe's colossal knock in the same match. And, as long as the wind blows up the Cook Straits, up through Adelaide Street and through the leaves of the pohutakawa, the Basin Reserve is sure to see many more.

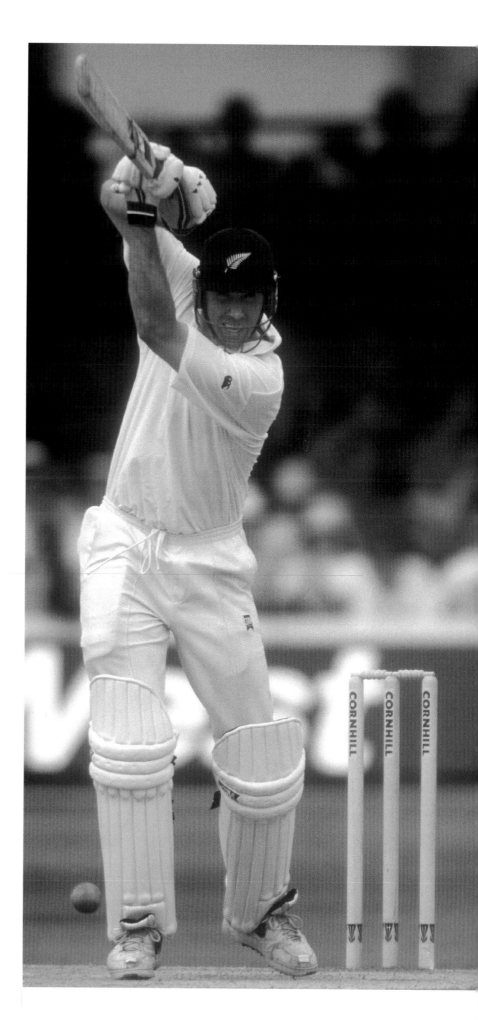

Left: Adam Parore followed in a proud tradition of New Zealand wicketkeeper-batsmen that includes Ken Wadsworth, Warren Lees and Ian Smith. Parore holds the record for dismissals at the Basin Reserve with 27 in nine Tests.

Right: Stephen Fleming is turning out to be one of New Zealand's most astute captains. He masterminded a series win in England in 1999 and came back from Australia in 2001-02 with three draws from three. In 2002-03, he led New Zealand to a ten-wicket win over India in Wellington.
He is also more than handy with a willow in his hand.

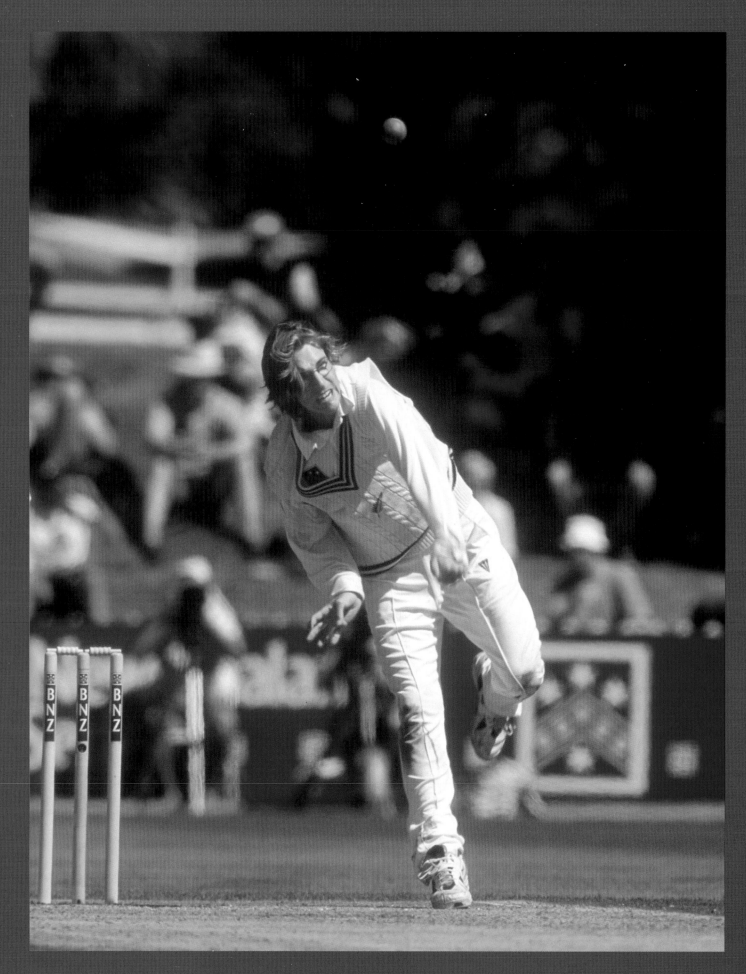

The slow-left arm spinner Daniel Vettori has become used to bowling with a Wellington gale whistling into his ear. Only Hadlee has taken more wickets there.

BASIN RESERVE Ground Records

Result Summary

	Played	Won	Lost	Drawn
New Zealand	40	11	12	17
Australia	7	2	1	4
Bangladesh	1	0	1	0
England	9	3	1	5
India	5	1	4	0
Pakistan	5	1	0	4
South Africa	4	3	0	1
Sri Lanka	2	0	1	1
West Indies	5	2	2	1
Zimbabwe	2	0	1	1

Highest Totals

671-4	New Zealand v Sri Lanka 1990-91
660-5	West Indies v New Zealand 1994-95
548-5	Pakistan v New Zealand 1993-94

Lowest Completed Innings Totals

42	New Zealand v Australia 1945-46
54	New Zealand v Australia 1945-46
64	England v New Zealand 1977-78

Highest Match Aggregates

Runs	Wkts	
1455	24	New Zealand v Australia 1973-74
1342	23	New Zealand v Sri Lanka 1990-91
1288	30	New Zealand v England 1983-84

Lowest Match Aggregates (Result oriented matches)

Runs	Wkts	
295	28	New Zealand v Australia 1945-46

Highest Scores

299	MD Crowe v Sri Lanka 1990-91
267	PA de Silva v New Zealand 1990-91
255*	DJ McGlew v New Zealand 1952-53
247*	GS Chappell v New Zealand 1973-74
214	MS Sinclair v West Indies 1999-2000

Highest Run Aggregates

Runs	Matches	Hundreds	
1123	10	5	MD Crowe
1005	13	3	JG Wright
686	7	2	AH Jones
637	9	1	NJ Astle
558	8	2	CD McMillan

Partnership Records

276 for 1st	CS Dempster and JE Mills New Zealand v England 1929-30
241 for 2nd	AH Jones and JG Wright New Zealand v England 1991-92
467 for 3rd	MD Crowe and AH Jones New Zealand v Sri Lanka 1990-91
229 for 4th	BE Congdon and BF Hastings New Zealand v Australia 1973-74
258 for 5th	Inzamam-ul-Haq and Salim Malik Pakistan v New Zealand 1993-94
232 for 6th	IT Botham and DW Randall England v New Zealand 1983-84
246 for 7th	DJ McGlew and ARA Murray South Africa v New Zealand 1952-53
137 for 8th	DJ Nash and DL Vettori New Zealand v India 1998-99
163* for 9th	MC Cowdrey and AC Smith England v New Zealand 1962-63
48 for 10th	EJ Chatfield and IDS Smith New Zealand v Pakistan 1988-89

Best Bowling in an Innings.

7 for 23	RJ Hadlee New Zealand v India 1975-56
7 for 37	CA Walsh West Indies v New Zealand 1994-95
7 for 65	SB Doull New Zealand v India 1998-99
7 for 76	FE Woolley England v New Zealand 1929-30
7 for 89	DK Morrison New Zealand v Australia 1992-93

Best Bowling in a Match

13 for 55 (7-37, 6-18)	CA Walsh West Indies v New Zealand 1994-95
11 for 58 (4-35, 7-23)	RJ Hadlee New Zealand v India 1975-76
11 for 179 (4-60, 7-119)	Wasim Akram Pakistan v New Zealand 1993-94
10 for 100 (4-74, 6-26)	RJ Hadlee New Zealand v England 1977-78

Highest Wicket Aggregates

Wkts	Matches	5WI	
53	12	3	RJ Hadlee
27	9	0	DL Vettori
25	8	2	DK Morrison

Most Catches by Fielder

Catches	Matches	
16	10	SP Fleming
10	7	BE Congdon

Most Dismissals by Wicketkeeper

Dismissals	Matches	
27	9	AC Parore
26	11	IDS Smith
11	2	WK Lees

INDIA
Sourav Ganguly

If you want one word to sum up India's relationship with cricket, try passion. Nowhere in the world will you find a population quite so obsessed with the game; the tactics, the statistics, the characters, the art of bowling the perfect arm ball, and the comparative batting techniques of Vijay Manjrekar, Sunil Gavaskar and Sachin Tendulkar are all debates to be found in the offices, streets and playgrounds of modern India.

More particularly, they will be discussed on the edge of the boundary, whether it is a schools match, a pick-up game on the maidan or a Test match at one of the great grounds. From Chandigarh to Chennai, from Mohali to Mumbai, the Indian nation loves to talk cricket.

In fairness there is much to talk about. India may only have become a Test-playing nation in 1932 but the roots were there long before. The great Ranjitsinhji, who gave his name to the first-class domestic trophy in India, the Ranji Trophy, opened up the world's eyes to the wristy style of Indian batting when he played for England at the turn of the 20th century. His nephew Duleepsinhji and Iftikhar Ali Khan, the Nawab of Pataudi senior, continued that tradition.

Since achieving Test status, India has produced many of the game's great players and has hosted some of the most memorable Test matches. It can also claim to have some of the best venues in the world. In talking about Eden Gardens, Kolkata and the Chidambaram Stadium, Chennai, we do no disservice to Mumbai, or any other centre for cricket. However this is a book about cricket grounds, not cricket centres, and not even the greatest supporter of the Wankhede Stadium in Mumbai is likely to argue that it towers over Eden Gardens or Chidambaram for romance, history or charm.

One word on the names of the grounds. Eden Gardens remains the same as when it first hosted a cricket match in 1864, but for the last few years the city in which it is situated has changed from the familiar Calcutta to Kolkata. Chennai has replaced the city name of Madras where the Chidambaram Stadium is known simply as the MAC (from MA Chidambaram, former president of the Board of Control for Cricket in India) to followers of the game.

As the names have changed so have the stadia themselves, turning from quaint old-world cricket grounds into concrete bowls with commerce pushing aside aesthetic values. But when you push the concrete far enough, art emerges. Eden Gardens is large enough to accommodate nearly 10,000 spectators, although I have little doubt there were at least 120,000 jammed in on the day in 2001 when India completed one of the most astonishing turnarounds in Test history to beat Steve Waugh's Australians. And yet there is an intimacy about the ground that the Melbourne Cricket Ground, for example, lacks. In Chennai, old-timers rue the chopping of the trees around the boundary's edge, and the necessity that forces the building of a stadium that seems to lack character. But when these stadiums are packed with shouting, cheering spectators in colourful shirts and blouses and scarves, everything seems worthwhile.

Nobody complained when Gundappa Viswanath got up on his toes to send Andy Roberts crashing to the fence, or when Javagal Srinath made use of the overcast conditions to claim 13 Pakistani wickets in Kolkata. At times such as these, the argument shifts; it is now important for as many fans as possible to see such marvellous performances.

Rudyard Kipling called Calcutta the "city of dreadful night", but the late Alan Ross, cricket writer and editor of London Magazine captured it better when he said, "Calcutta, that Brechtian city of the imagination, a metropolis beyond imagination."

Chennai is well within the imagination. Of all India's metropolitan cities it is the one which inspires the least hype. In the words of Suresh Menon, cricket writer and former editor of the New Indian Express: "The citizens find comfort in the same things happening at the same time of the year, every year. While you can set your watch by what happens daily in some of Mumbai's commercial areas, in Chennai you can only set your calendar by the various events that take place."

The two grounds somehow reflect their cities. The word that is used most often with Eden Gardens and Calcutta is "volatile". The southern people and their stadium would be happy with "secure". And yet they are both Indian, reflecting facets of the national character, most particularly that passion for bat and ball.

Eden Gardens, Kolkata

217

Sometimes in life you get so close to another person or to a place that it is hard to be objective. Such is the case for me with Eden Gardens. I have known the ground almost all my life. It is almost a part of me.

As my father was secretary of the Cricket Association, of Bengal, I was in and out of Eden Gardens from a very young age. The first Test match I went to was to see Tony Greig's 1976-77 England team. I was only four at the time so I don't actually remember anything about Greig's century and England's victory, but I still have a picture taken of me with Greig and Ken Barrington, the manager.

And I remember watching the English players like Greig and Alan Knott preparing every morning before play in the nets, the excitement as the ground began to fill up, the noise and the colour that swirled around me. In the 1980s, when I was old enough to take in fully the atmosphere of the ground, I was overwhelmed by the noise of a Kapil Dev appeal. If he passed the bat of someone like Viv Richards, it was not just Kapil who went up for the appeal – the whole ground would leap out of their seats to claim the catch.

These were delicious first tastes of a ground that already held so much history and that was to produce so many personal memories in the years to come. My first century for Bengal Under-15s against Orissa came at an empty Eden Gardens, and I played my first Ranji Trophy match there, when I replaced my injured brother in the 1990 final and scored 32 against Delhi as Bengal claimed their first title for 22 years. Shortly afterwards, I had my first taste of the international scene at Eden Gardens when I was 12th man for the one-day international against Clive Rice's South Africans as they made their comeback to the world stage.

Stangely, my main memory of that day is being heckled by my own home crowd even though I was not playing. As I took the drinks out, I was greeted by a howl of good-natured abuse along the lines of: "Get a new pair of trousers." It was in the days before sponsored kit and I had two pairs of whites which had served me well for a couple of years.

Eden Gardens has been an immense presence in my life as I have watched some of the greats of Indian cricket – Sunil Gavaskar, Dilip Vengsarkar, Kapil Dev, Gundappa Viswanath and Mohammad Azharuddin, to name just a few – produce some

thrilling cricket. Azharuddin especially will be forever linked to the ground having made five centuries in his seven Tests there; my only regret so far is that I have not yet been able to score a Test-match hundred there. On the other hand, I have been privileged enough to be at the centre of some of its most recent history.

The story of Eden Gardens, of course, begins a long time before Sourav Ganguly came to the crease. The Calcutta Cricket Club, founded in 1792, is the oldest cricket club outside the Marylebone Cricket Club, although today, in deference to Bengal's love of football – Pele is arguably the greatest sportsman ever to appear at Eden Gardens – it is called the Calcutta Cricket and Football Club.

In its edition of February 23, 1792, the *Madras Courier* reported that a cricket match was played between Englishmen residing in the districts of Barrackpore and Dum Dum. That was the start of organised cricket in India. In 1804 the club sponsored a match between Old Etonians and a team from the East India Company. The former won this match which was significant for two reasons: the first century on Indian soil was scored by Robert Vansittart, and the first bets were placed in India on a cricket match. Oh, those bookmakers...

The game did not develop among the Indians in Calcutta as quickly as it did in other parts, notably Bombay where the Parsis took to it with

Overleaf: Sachin Tendulkar has made runs just about everywhere in the world but it was not until the 2002-03 Test against the West Indies that he chalked up his first Test century at Eden Gardens. His 176 was the 31st century in his Test career.

alacrity. In Calcutta, the headquarters of the East India Company, it was very much a game for the British. Even so, it still seems strange that the third Indian member of the Calcutta Cricket Club was not elected until 1965.

It is Kolkata's maidan, the city's lungs, that has fascinated those who approach with pre-conceived notions of an overcrowded city. The maidan is a large, wide open space – "a dangerous place for anyone with a touch of agoraphobia", as one writer put it. Emily Eden, sister of Lord Auckland, a Governor General who played a significant role in the establishment of Eden Gardens, likened it to London's Regents Park, but it is twice as big as that and perhaps a third as exclusive.

The two square miles of parkland had more trees around it, but a cyclone in 1864 blew many of them away. Of the many thoroughfares that cross the maidan, the Red Road – now Indira Gandhi Road – was specially laid down so that Viceroys and their Emperors could make imperial progress towards the Government House at the top.

For the origins of Eden Gardens, we need to go back to Lord Auckland, born George Eden in 1784, whose title gives a clue to the link between this great cricket ground and one of the world's best-known rugby grounds. Auckland was the Governor General when the parkland which had originally belonged to the Maharajah of Cooch Behar came into his possession.

His two sisters Emily and Fanny nursed the huge area into a beautiful parkland. The garden was, in time, gifted to the citizens of Calcutta for "recreation and enjoyment", and appropriately enough named Eden Gardens. Besides the cricket ground, it now contains an indoor cricket stadium, two indoor sports complexes and the All India Radio building. There is also a park, a pond and a pagoda. And even the heavy roller has a name. It is called Ganga Ram, and has seen cricket for two centuries.

In New Zealand, meanwhile, Captain William Hobson, a protégé of Lord Auckland, repaid his patron by naming various places after him including, in 1840, the city of Auckland. Not content with that, he also sprinkled a fair amount of Edens about the place. Mount Eden, for example, was named after George Eden. And so was Eden Park which, apart from being a rugby ground, is one of New Zealand's senior cricket

grounds. Not a bad epitaph for man who never played the game.

Between 1932 and 2003, India played 32 Tests, the most at any centre, at Eden Gardens, winning six. As in Chennai, only one local player has made a century there – Pankaj Roy, who hit 100 against New Zealand in 1955-56. Dattu Phadkar, who made 115 here against England in 1951-52, played for Bengal but hailed from Bombay. The most successful batsman, without doubt, has to be Azharuddin, whose five centuries from seven matches give him an average of 107.5. Of the bowlers, the great left-arm spinner Bishan Bedi has claimed the most wickets, 29 from six matches, while Kapil Dev took 27 from eight.

According to the Australian writer Ray Robinson, "Calcutta's cricket enthusiasm needs no stoking to develop a full head of steam. I have placed Bengalis first among the world's most volatile cricket-watchers." Those who doubted this needed only to be present as Gary Sobers led his world champion side through India in 1966-67. Play started on New Year's Eve, but there was a sense of coming evil as more spectators than the ground could accommodate pressed forward over the boundary fence and sat on the outfield grass nine or ten deep. Overcrowding, aided by forged tickets, led to a riot on the second day. As the crowd got restless, police beat up a man called Sitesh Roy when he was actually trying to calm everybody down. "What followed was like hell being let loose and the whole of Eden Gardens was swallowed up in flames," said one writer.

The teams – who had had nothing to do with the rioting – took shelter in the dressing-room, but it was clear they would have to get away. With the riot becoming more destructive, and visibility affected by the rising smoke, West Indies opener Conrad Hunte did something that startled the younger Nawab of Pataudi, the Indian skipper. "Hunte's first reaction was to try to save the West Indian and Indian flags which were flying above the pavilion."

The players were relatively safe because, as one of the crowd told Pataudi, "It is not you, but the officials we are after." As it was, the players saved many officials from the lynch mob by smuggling them out hidden under their car seats.

Charlie Griffith the big fast bowler, overcome with emotion and disoriented, pushed aside offers

Mohammad Azharuddin cuts for four during his 182 against England in 1992-93. Of all the batsmen to have graced Eden Gardens, Azharuddin has the best record with five centuries in seven Tests.

of a lift from well-meaning people in cars and ran weeping all the way to the team hotel. Was this the man who terrified batsmen all over the world, and nearly killed an Indian captain, Nari Contractor, on the cricket field with his bowling? Calcutta does strange things to people.

The next day, the match continued after the Indian players were given a bonus as danger money, and the West Indies ultimately won by an innings, thanks to Rohan Kanhai's 90 and Sobers, who made 70 batting at number seven and took seven wickets in the match.

Less than three years later, six people were killed in a stampede outside the stadium when 7,000 tickets were being sold to the public for the match against Bill Lawry's Australians. Nearly three times that number of people jostled and pushed, and those killed were closer to the front of the queue. Again, the players were not to blame, but that did not prevent a mob from stoning the team's hotel and breaking a few windows. India's hopes in the Test, meanwhile, were smashed by Australian pacemen Eric Freeman and Alan Connolly.

Having knocked over India for 212 in the first innings, they rolled them over for just 161 in the second innings. This was too much for the crowd, who began pelting the outfield with the usual combination of bottles, stones and refuse. It was confusing at first as there did not seem to be any specific target or any particular reason but Lawry provided the crowd with both as soon as the crowd began to swarm over the edges of the field. According to the *Statesman* newspaper, "Lawry did something that, to say the least, could be termed disgraceful. A photographer who had wanted to get a close shot of Keith Stackpole and Lawry side by side brought upon himself the wrath of the Australian Pinocchio. Lawry knocked over the poor photographer and struck him with the bat. It was a horrible sight."

Stackpole, who was nearest to Lawry, defended his captain thus: "In his concern about the wicket, Lawry took exception to one of the most intrusive of the photographers. After taking a couple of sneaky photos this fellow walked away. He was still hanging around so (Lawry) went to chase him away. The chap started running, so Bill followed him, prodded him on the backside with the bat and said, 'Now Get Off!' The photographer stumbled and fell."

As someone who has been in the middle amid crowds coming on to the field, I have some sympathy for Lawry.

Australia needed to make 38 to win, and as they neared the target, the crowd turned its ire on the Indian captain Pataudi. The Australian openers escorted him into the pavilion after the match as things threatened to get out of hand. But it did not end there for the visitors. Their bus was stoned on the way to the airport.

In 1996, I saw the mayhem first-hand when match referee Clive Lloyd awarded a World Cup semi-final to Sri Lanka after poor crowd behaviour had made it difficult for the game to resume. This time, however, the reaction was much milder – plastic bottles thrown to the ground as India, falling steadily behind Sri Lanka's score of 251 for eight, threatened to fall apart. Sri Lanka would probably have won the match anyway, as India were on 120 for eight in the 35th over when the game was called off. But Vinod Kambli got it right when he said: "We might have made it. At any rate, we ought to have been given a chance to try and get to the target."

But Lloyd, who had been in the team at Calcutta during the 1966-67 riot, was determined to make an example. There was a 15-minute stoppage when the players came off the field, but the moment they returned, the rain of bottles (plastic) and fruit resumed, and Lloyd could take it no more. In retrospect, it was not a big riot at all. There was no fighting, and no one was in any danger. Yet it served to add to Calcutta's reputation as a riot-centre. As a native of the city, I can only admit to being deeply disappointed and embarrassed by the trouble.

Sri Lanka went on to win the World Cup that year, with Aravinda de Silva making a century in the final. Yet to many his 66 off 47 balls at the Eden Gardens was the innings of the tournament.

The Eden Gardens crowd is often described as inflammatory. As shown here, during the World Cup semi-final between India and Sri Lanka in 1996, that descriptiuon is not far off the literal. To the shame of the city, this game was abandoned and awarded to Sri Lanka who went on to win the tournament.

Little effort was made to look at the deeper causes of the Calcutta flare-up – the lack of amenities in the cheaper stands as well as the lack of a shade over that section under a sweltering sun, the closely packed areas that cried out trouble, and psychologically, the unrealistic expectations raised by those marketing products linked to the World Cup. An analyst in a local newspaper said, "The knowledgeable and keen spectator who came to Eden Gardens every winter has been replaced by ignorant and irresponsible hooligans. Knowledge and enjoyment of the game have been sacrificed to vulgar displays of jingoism."

Other commentators spoke of the "lumpenisation" of the Indian middle class. Mike Marqusee, the US-born cricket enthusiast, probably got closer to the nub: "This was not a riot of the dispossessed but a self-indulgent demonstration by a small and relatively privileged minority. It was

not an attempt to halt the match and save India from defeat; it was not an outburst of anger at the inoffensive Sri Lankans. It was a protest against India's defeat and elimination from the World Cup and aimed at the Indian team. It was, of course, stupid, rude and dangerous. Above all, it was futile, as all such protests must be. But it was a perversely logical response to the nationalist hype which preceded the match."

Three years later, our Test match against Pakistan in the Asian Championship ended in bizarre circumstances with the final act of the game being played out before an empty stadium. The run-out of Sachin Tendulkar on the fourth day had caused rumblings of discontent: he had made his ground before jumping out of the way to avoid a collision. Those rumblings were carried over to the final day of the match when Pakistan needed to take four wickets to win. When the crowd started

throwing stones at Yousuf Youhana on the boundary, the ground was cleared. The stands were emptied, the pavilion emptied; the only people left were the players, groundstaff and press.

It was a shameful end to the match and it did not do India any good as Pakistan won comfortably. The drama of the finale overshadowed some good cricket, especially from Saeed Anwar, the Pakistan opener, who scored a wonderful 188, and from the Indian fast bowler Srinath, who took 13 wickets and still ended up a loser.

It would be unfair, however, to characterise Eden Gardens as a hotbed of discontent. The crowds know their cricket and bring real appreciation with them. When Clive Rice led the first South African team into international following their return from exile, the streets of Calcutta were lined with cheering, flag-waving

Far left: Javagal Srinath celebrates after trapping Pakistan's Salim Malik leg-before in the inaugural match of the Asian Test Championship in 1998-99. Srinath claimed eight for 86 in the second innings.

Anil Kumble has been a consistant performer for India since he made his Test debut in 1990. He has passed the 300-wicket mark and among Indians, only Kapil Dev has taken more. His crowning achievement came at Delhi in 1998-99 against Pakistan when he became only the second man in Test history to take all ten wickets in an innings.

fans to welcome them. Eden Gardens was packed for the first one-day international, but it was clear that a mixture of emotion and sheer shock at the size of the crowd would get the South Africans long before any Indian bowling would. Sure enough, South Africa lost that match but won the hearts of the crowd.

Funnily enough for a stadium that is usually packed to capacity – and a little beyond – the first Test in Calcutta, against Douglas Jardine's Englishmen in 1933-34, saw wide-open spaces in the spectators' area. Despite the fact that a public holiday had been declared, and despite the cricket association's entreaties to the public who were asked to turn up "so that the financial guarantees of the MCC's visit to Calcutta might be met", the public largely ignored the Test. The reason? Not a single Bengali had been included. Few Bengalis have actually played Test cricket. Calcutta may have the most talked-about cricket stadium in the country, the most excitable crowd, and the most high-profile administrator in Jagmohan Dalmiya, former President of the International Cricket Council, but it has given Indian cricket precious few players.

For instance, there was no Test player from Bengal in the 1930s, although fast bowler Shute Banerjee made a trip to England in 1936 and then again in 1946. In the first instance, he might have been kept out by Baqa Jilani, who played because he curried favour with the captain, the Maharajkumar of Vizianagaram, by insulting CK Nayudu at the breakfast table.

The next important player was the wicketkeeper P Sen, who had a good tour of Australia in 1947, but it was not until Pankaj Roy entered the scene in the 1950s that Bengal had a regular in the Indian side. Two Bengal players who found favour with the selectors, the opening batsman Arun Lal and the left-arm spinner Dilip Doshi were from Delhi and Rajkot respectively. Roy was the first Bengali to captain India, in a solitary game at Lord's in 1959. It was my privilege to become the second.

That first match in Calcutta seven decades ago turned out to be the first drawn Test played by India, who, playing only their third Test, already had two stars, the captain CK Nayudu, and Lala Amarnath, who had made a century on debut in the previous Test in Bombay.

In keeping with tradition, there was enough intrigue before the Calcutta Test to take the focus off the preparations on the field. The Indian probables, staying at the Great Eastern Hotel, plotted to boycott the Test because some of them preferred to play under Wazir Ali rather than CK Nayudu. The chief instigator was Nazir Ali, Wazir's brother, but the plot came to nothing when Wazir declared he was happy to play under Nayudu.

India's hero in Calcutta was the wicketkeeper and opening batsman Dilawar Hussain, who made two half-centuries and top-scored in both innings,

A prayer of thanks.
After more than 20 years in the cricketing wilderness, South Africa were welcomed back into the fold with a series of three one-day internationals against India in 1991. Clive Rice (hands together) led the South Africans in the first of these at Eden Gardens. Although he was 12th man, it was also Sourav Ganguly's first taste of international cricket.

Cota Ramaswami has described him thus: "He was a tall and bulky person with a prominent stomach…and after batting for a while or keeping wicket for some time his shirt will be hanging out of his trousers and somebody must tuck it in now and then. He had a rather ugly and uncouth stance as he held his bat very low and bent his body forward so much that his head was practically in line with the top of the wickets. However, he had a very sound defence."

England had made 403 in the first innings and Dilawar, opening for India, was struck on the side of the head by a bouncer from Morris Nichols. He returned to bat with a bandage and made 59. When India followed on he scored 57.

The Calcutta Test was played during the holy month of Ramadan. India had four Muslims, including Hussain who showed no effects of fasting, unlike fast bowler Mohammed Nissar who could bowl only four overs in his first spell. More significantly, when India batted, skipper Jardine instructed Nobby Clark to bowl bouncers. The umpire Frank Tarrant told the England captain he would have to stop Clark from bowling. "If you do that," replied Jardine, "I will stop you from umpiring." Jardine had his way and Tarrant, unlike his colleague Bill Hitch, was not invited to officiate in the next Test in Madras.

Calcutta's next official Test was against the West Indies in 1948-49, and this time the public was exercised over the omission of Mushtaq Ali. "No Mushtaq, No Test", went the cry which has been echoed since in the shape of "No Kapil, No Test" and "No Sachin, No Test." On this occasion, India's flamboyant opening batsman – who had played the first Test as a left-arm spinner – was included in the side. Mushtaq made a century,

Legends of old:
KS Ranjitsinjhi was the first Indian to find fame in the international cricketing world. Ranji, seen here in Durbar dress, played 15 times for England between 1895 and 1902, scoring 154 not out against Australia at Old Trafford on his debut. India's domestic competition, the Ranji Trophy, is named after him.

Right: CK Nayudu captained India in their first Test match against England in 1932. A big hitting batsman, he put Indian cricket on the map when he took under two hours in making 153 against the strong MCC team, captained by Arthur Gilligan, that toured India in 1926-27.

Above: Sunil Gavaskar's relationship with the Eden Gardens crowd was always variable. They loved him when he was making opposition bowlers sweat in the sun but they were less happy when, as captain, he dropped Kapil Dev during the 1984-85 series against England. Later, when Gavaskar's wife was abused, the "Little Master" declined to play at Eden Gardens. Now in retirement, Gavaskar is as popular as ever.

Right: The 1958-59 Test against the West Indies was notable for some magnificent batting from Rohan Kanhai whose 256 was the highest Test score at Eden Gardens until VVS Laxman's 281 against the Australians in 2000-01.

and was to say years later: "That century gave me immense satisfaction because I had made it on my favourite ground and in front of my favourite spectators."

Next season, the Calcutta Cricket Club formally handed over the reins of the Eden Gardens to the Cricket Association of Bengal.

The first five Tests at the Eden Gardens were all drawn, and if one has to pick a single event that led to later crowding for tickets and long queues, it will have to be the 256 in six-and-a-half hours made by Rohan Kanhai in 1958-59. There were two other West Indian centuries in that innings, by Basil Butcher and by Sobers, making his third in a row, but 42 boundaries by Kanhai caught the imagination. India lost by an innings and 336 runs, after being dismissed for 124 and 154.

The modern-day Eden is a blend of the old and the new. The club house, named after the former Chief Minister BC Roy, houses the Cricket Association of Bengal offices, a medical unit, a sports shop, a library, the players' dressing-rooms, dining-rooms and conference halls. On the first floor is the VIP viewing gallery for 3,500 spectators. The air-conditioned sound-proof press box is suspended from the cantilever, and media men often joke about being above low-flying aircraft.

There have been many memorable moments here since the maiden first-class game in November 1917 between the Bengal Governor's XI and the Maharaja of Cooch Behar's XI. Apart from those mentioned earlier, there was Shoaib Akhtar's successive yorkers which speared into Rahul Dravid's leg stump and Tendulkar's middle stump and Salim

Malik's 72 not out off 35 balls that turned a one-dayer around for Pakistan.

India's most successful Test batsman, Sunil Gavaskar, had a love-hate relationship with Eden Gardens that ended with his refusal to play there during his final Test series.

The problem came about after Gavaskar, the captain, had chosen to drop Kapil who had played a poor shot in the previous Test. The cry of "No Kapil, No Test" went up, but he was still left out. Some of the crowd made their discontent known by flinging fruit at Gavaskar's wife in the stand, an action that prompted the great man to cut his ties with the ground. Whatever the rights and wrongs of Kapil's exclusion – he returned for the next Test and struck his first ball for six in a virtual repeat of the shot that had got him dropped in the first place – it was a

On the pull.
Sunil Gavaskar tucks into the England bowling during
the 1976-77 tour. Gavaskar made two centuries at Eden
Gardens in eight Tests.

poor way to repay Gavaskar, who had lit up Eden Gardens so often. In the 1978-79 series against the West Indies, he was awesome, making two centuries in the match and sharing an unbroken second-wicket partnership of 344 with Vengsarkar.

The relationship has mended since, to such an extent that one developer named his apartment building the Sunny Apartments in Gavaskar's honour and even gave him one of the penthouses.

Of the other great batting performances at Eden Gardens, one should mention Everton Weekes who, in 1948-49, made 162 and 101, his fifth century in successive Tests. Deepak Shodhan made a century on debut against Pakistan four years later while players of the calibre of Norm O'Neill, Bruce Taylor, John Reid, Farokh Engineer, Gordon Greenidge, Carl Hooper, Gary Kirsten – two hundreds in the 1996-97 Test – and Steve Waugh have all made runs there.

The greatest performance at Eden Gardens though, certainly in my experience, was VVS Laxman's 281 against Australia in 2000-01. It was not just a pleasure to watch, it was also an innings of incredible willpower played in adversity that turned not just that match but also the series.

Steve Waugh brought his Australia team to India knowing that although they were correctly regarded as the best Test team in the world, they had not won a series in India for 31 years. It was Waugh's greatest ambition, I think, to return to Australia as the man who laid to rest any lingering doubts about the quality of his team. He is a tough competitor and his team played cricket in his image. Hard and fast.

They hit the ground running and, with Adam Gilchrist playing a whirlwind innings, won the first Test in Mumbai in just three days. Perhaps they were inspired by the memory of Don Bradman, who died two days before the Test began; whatever it was, they had extended their run of success to 16 Test wins.

The critics rounded on us quickly but I felt there was less between the teams than the result suggested. We had a team meeting and prepared for the second Test in Kolkata with renewed belief in ourselves. The days running up to the Test were a media circus. There were calls for my removal as captain after just three Tests, with many newspaperman offering the suggestion that a Bengali was not really cut out to captain India.

Our positive outlook soon took on a more gloomy hue. Batting first on a good pitch Australia made 445 with Steve Waugh making a fine 110 and Matthew Hayden 97. Brightening up the gloom was the bowling of off-spinner Harbhajan Singh, who took seven for 123, including the first hat-trick by an Indian in Test cricket. His victims were Ricky Ponting and Gilchrist, both leg-before, and Shane Warne, caught at short leg.

We then batted poorly, skittled for 171 and conceding a first-innings lead of 274. Only Laxman batted with any fluency, making 59 batting at number six. With Dravid looking scratchy at number three, we made the decision to switch them when Waugh asked us to follow on. At that point I did not have any great hopes for the Test and when my friends in Kolkata started returning the tickets I had got for them for the fourth and fifth days, saying that there would not be much cricket to watch, I could not disagree.

But then I had no idea that I was about to watch one of the greatest innings in Test history as Laxman took the Australian attack apart. One look at Warne's figures of one for 152 from 34 overs show just how Laxman and Dravid, his partner in a record fifth-wicket partnership of 376, dominated a quality attack.

Laxman occupied the crease for ten hours, 31 minutes for his 281, India's highest individual score in Test cricket. He made his runs from 452 balls and struck 44 boundaries – and I think I saw every delivery. On the fourth day, I barely moved from my seat as he and Dravid added 335, batting through the entire day. When they came off, they were drained, their bodies so punished by the heat that they had to lie down in the dressing-room at the close of play with drips attached to their arms in a bid to rehydrate them. Rahul was aching so much he could not get up with cramping in his back and behind.

By the end of the fourth day, our lead was 315 and there were already calls for a declaration. I told Laxman, who was on 275, he had seven overs to get his 300 but he fell early to Glenn McGrath so it was left to Dravid to bat on. He was run out for a chanceless 180 which, in spite of being overshadowed by the brilliance of Laxman, was still one of the best innings I have witnessed.

I delayed the declaration until we had 657 on the board, a lead of 383. The criticism grew louder

with many people saying I had left it too late and that I was being negative. However, the reason I delayed was so that we could go on total attack for the full 75 overs that were left to play. If I had pulled out sooner there was every chance that someone like Gilchrist or Hayden would play a quickfire innings and I might have to use a defensive field. The pitch was still good and I knew that Harbhajan was the key, our only real

VVS Laxman and Rahul Dravid leave the field at the end of the fourth day's play in the 2000-01 Test against Australia. After batting through the entire day, they had lost so much body fluid that they had to be put on saline drips as soon as they came off the field. Their fifth-wicket partnership of 376 is the highest ever for India and led to a famous win.

source of attack with the ball. I wanted to be able to give him the right field to capitalise on the little edges that I knew he would find.

Australia got off to a solid start with Michael Slater and Hayden putting on 74 in 23 overs but once Slater went we were in with a chance. Just before tea when they were only three wickets down I dropped a sharp chance off Steve Waugh at backward short leg. Maybe if he had said nothing, the game would have drifted to a draw, the result that appeared to be its natural conclusion. But he could not resist the chirp: "You just dropped the Test, mate." Sometimes sledging can work against you and, on this occasion, it had the effect of geeing up the Indians.

Immediately after tea, Harbhajan got Waugh out and Dravid gave him a send-off from slip asking who had just given away the Test match now. Tendulkar, bowling leg-spin, chipped in with three wickets including the key one down the order of Gilchrist, who had followed his century in Mumbai with a king pair.

The atmosphere in the ground was electric. Every seat was taken and there were people coming in all the time from work, crammed onto the steps. It was pretty heated in the middle as well. Although we were taking wickets time was running out. When Glenn McGrath, the last man, joined Mike Kasprowicz there were seven overs to go. They defended a couple successfully before I switched the bowlers around. Harbhajan came in for his first ball after the switch, McGrath pushed forward but did not offer a shot. I will always remember that appeal; as Steve Bansal, the umpire, raised his finger, around 130,000 people just jumped and roared.

India had won a famous victory by 171 runs; only the third time in the history of Test cricket that a team has won after being asked to follow on. To cap it all Harbhajan had finished with six for 73 and match figures of 13 for 196. We flew to Chennai that night and celebrated in style. Little did we know that the third Test in the series would be equally as dramatic.

Eden Gardens has seen similar turnarounds in the fortunes of teams and individuals. In 1987, Allan Border, then leading an Australian team no one had much time for, lifted the World Cup after defeating England and putting paid to the subcontinent's hopes of an India-Pakistan final. Australia were 16-1 outsiders when the tournament began. After their victory, both Border and cricket manager Bob Simpson spoke of a mystical "special feeling", and somehow managed not to make it sound like a cliché. Border also spoke of the "love and encouragement" his team had received in India, particularly from the Bengalis. And yet it might have all turned out badly for Australia but for Border's

intervention as a bowler at a crucial point. Replying to Australia's 253, England were 135 for two when Border, a handy left-arm spinner, decided to bowl to Mike Gatting, one of the better players of spin bowling. Border pushed his first delivery too wide of the leg stump. Gatting could have easily paddled it for four but he chose, instead, to play the reverse sweep. He made an error in judgement, the ball went off his glove, bounced off his chest and into the gloves of Greg Dyer. That was the turning point as Australia won by seven runs, the closest final yet.

For Indian cricket, Eden Gardens had been the venue for another turnaround, but one which was not immediately apparent. It happened in the 1961-62 series victory against England. The seeds were sown in Calcutta by a 20-year-old Pataudi, who made 64 and 32 in the match before going on to record his first century in the next Test in Madras. Pataudi brought to the Indian team a youthful

exuberance, a positive attitude, and tried to push into the background the intrigue and stuffiness that had been so much a part of it in the previous decade. At one time, batting with Contractor, he said, "Let us hit over the fielders' heads, and see where that gets us." It got them plenty of runs.

More recently, one aberration has been set right. For all the hundreds that he has made in international cricket, Tendulkar always found runs hard to come by at Eden Gardens. It was something that worried him; that every time he came to Kolkata he left his form in Mumbai or Bangalore or Chennai. In October 2002, in the third Test against the West Indies, he put that right, giving the Bengalis something to remember with an innings of 176. It was is 31st Test century but his first at Eden Gardens. Perhaps a certain Bengali boy, who grew up with Eden Gardens, can follow suit before too long.

Victory.
Umpire Steve Bansal raises his finger to indicate that Harbhajan Singh has got Glenn McGrath leg-before and Australia are all out. Some of the Indians are already celebrating, others seem stunned that after following on 274 runs behind, they had won by 171 runs.

239

EDEN GARDENS Ground Records

Result Summary

	Played	Won	Lost	Drawn
India	32	6	8	18
Australia	7	2	2	3
England	9	1	3	5
Pakistan	5	1	0	4
New Zealand	2	0	0	2
South Africa	1	1	0	0
West Indies	8	3	1	4

Bangladesh Sri Lanka and Zimbabwe
have yet to play at Eden Gardens

Highest Totals

657-7	India v Australia 2000-01
633-5	India v Australia 1997-98
614-5	West Indies v India 1958-59

Lowest Completed Innings Totals

90	India v West Indies 1983-84
124	India v West Indies 1958-59

Highest Match Aggregates

Runs	Wkts	
1485	37	India v Australia 2000-01
1326	28	India v West Indies 2002-03
1299	32	India v West Indies 1948-49

Lowest Match Aggregates (Result oriented matches)

Runs	Wkts	
638	39	India v Australia 1956-57

Highest Scores

281	VVS Laxman India v Australia 2000-01
256	RB Kanhai West Indies v India 1958-59
188*	Saeed Anwar Pakistan v India 1998-99
182*	SM Gavaskar India v West Indies 1978-79
182	M Azharuddin India v England 1992-93

Highest Run Aggregates

Runs	Matches	Hundreds	
860	7	5	M Azharuddin
724	5	2	VVS Laxman
645	7	2	DB Vengsarkar
583	8	2	SM Gavaskar
530	7	1	ML Jaisimha

Partnership Records

236 for 1st	AC Hudson and G Kirsten South Africa v India 1996-97	
344* for 2nd	SM Gavaskar and DB Vengsarkar India v West Indies 1978-79	
206 for 3rd	KJ Hughes and GN Yallop Australia v India 1979-80	
217 for 4th	BF Butcher and RB Kanhai West Indies v India 1958-59	
376 for 5th	RS Dravid and Vv Laxman India v Australia 2000-01	
195 for 6th	S Chanderpaul and MN Samuels West Indies v India 2002-03	
163 for 7th	B Sutcliffe and BR Taylor New Zealand v India 1964-65	
161 for 8th	M Azharuddin and A Kumble India v South Africa 1996-97	
161 for 9th	CH Lloyd and AME Roberts West Indies v India 1983-84	
51 for 10th	BS Chandrasekar and RG Nadkarni India v England 1963-64	

Best Bowling in an Innings

8 for 64	L Klusener South Africa v India 1996-97
8 for 86	J Srinath India v Pakistan 1998-99
7 for 49	Ghulam Ahmed India v Australia 1956-57
7 for 98	BS Bedi India v Australia 1969-70
7 for 123	Harbhajan Singh India v Australia 2000-01

Best Bowling in a Match

13 for 132 (5 for 46, 8 for 86)	J Srintath India v Pakistan 1998-99
13 for 196 (7 for 123, 6 for 73)	Harbhajan Singh India v Australia 2000-01
11 for 105 (6 for 52, 5 for 53)	R Benaud Australia v India 1956-57
10 for 130 (7 for 49, 3 for 81)	Ghulam Ahmed India v Australia 1956-57

Hat Trick

Harbhajan Singh India v Australia 2000-01

Highest Wicket Aggregates

Wkts	Matches	5WI	
29	6	3	BS Bedi
27	8	2	Kapil Dev
22	4	2	J Srinath

Most Catches by Fielder

Catches	Matches	
9	8	SM Gavaskar
8	7	ML Jaisimha

Most Dismissals by Wicket keeper

Dismissals	Matches	
14	7	SMH Kirmani
13	4	NR Mongia

Cause to smile.
VVS Laxman holds the record for the highest individual score at Eden Gardens.

MA CHIDAMBARAM STADIUM, CHENNAI

If you could give a ground a colour, then Chennai would have to be red. It is the colour of the heat that saps every last drop of energy from your body and it is the tint of the soil that hardens and cracks, offering bounce and pace to bowlers of all persuasions. It is also the shade of the mist that occasionally descends upon the people watching.

The MA Chidambaram Stadium is also of course famous for being just one of two grounds to have hosted a tied Test. Brisbane is the other. It was a game of cricket so filled with heroics and drama that it has to go down as one of the greatest Test matches ever played. The Chepauk can claim to have seen perhaps the greatest innings from the greatest batsman India has ever produced when Sunil Gavaskar made 236 against the West Indies, although when it comes to wristy batsmanship, there may have been no better example than Gundappa's unbeaten 97 against a rampaging Andy Roberts – who took 12 for 121 – in 1974-75.

Sachin Tendulkar, the man who is snapping at Gavaskar's heels for that title, has made four Test hundreds at the Chepauk while Kapil Dev, India's greatest all-round cricketer, almost always rose to the atmosphere of there. Kapil claimed 40 wickets in 11 Tests on the ground, more than anyone else, and also played some valuable innings, notably the spectacular 119 he made in the tied Test.

It is here also that India's rich history of spin bowling has found a happy home. Led by off-spinner Erapalli Prasanna, who claimed 36 wickets in five Tests, the spinners had claimed 448 wickets overall by 2003 to the fast bowlers' 313. India have won more Tests at Chepauk – 11 out of 26 – than at any other venue, even if occasionally more energy had to be expended in overcoming domestic intrigue than in tackling the rival bowling.

Even though Test cricket has only been played at the Chepauk since February 10, 1934, the ground's history kicks off back in the 1768, the year that the Chepauk Palace and grounds, spread over 117 acres on the beautiful sea face, was completed.

The palace, built in the pioneering Indo-Saracenic style that was later followed by Robert Chisholm, was the residence of the Nawabs of the Carnatic until 1855, when the last Nawab, Ghulam Ghouse Khan Bahadur died, without leaving a son. The British decided to move in, evicting the Nawab's family and putting the palace up for

auction. They bought it themselves for 580,000 rupees and the sea-facing side of the property has housed government offices ever since.

The grounds of Chepauk once stretched from today's Bells' Road to the beach, from Pycroft's Road to the Cooum River, once navigable, but today the source of a peculiar smell that at once identifies the city. The whole area was surrounded

Sachin Tendulkar sweeps Shane Warne on his way to a brilliant 126 that led to a thrilling win over Australia in 2000-01.

by a wall with the main entrance a massive triple-arched gateway on Wallajah Road. In the days when radio commentary ruled, one end was called the Wallajah Road end.

The Chepauk Park was developed there in 1882-83, and buildings of the University of Madras were also built on the grounds. The south-west portion of the Palace ground was converted into its cricket ground in 1865 by the Madras Cricket Club which had been formed in 1846. Chisholm, the consultant architect to the government, built the pavilion for 3,700 rupees, a little "red-brick, wooden-verandahed" building in the north-west corner. But it was soon to be termed Chisholm's Folly, for it faced south and presented those watching the game from there with a sustained glare from the sun. Fortunately, it did not last long, destroyed in a cyclone in 1889-90.

The first proper pavilion was built, designed by Henry Irwin, and what remained of the old one was demolished. When the new MA Chidambaram Stadium – named after a former president of the cricket board - was completed in 1980, the older one had to make way for kitchens and badminton courts and a swimming pool.

The Madras Cricket Club inspired the city's sport. It introduced squash and tennis to Madras in 1884 and hockey in 1894, organising the South's first hockey tournament in 1901.

The Kent cricketer Conrad Johnstone is venerated as the leading spirit of Chepauk and was awarded a CBE for his work on behalf of the city's cricket. However, the first real hero was Edward Sewell, the Essex cricketer who played for the Madras Presidency, and later became a cricket writer. Sewell wrote of a six hit by Stanley Jackson, the England captain: "I have seen some sixers, including one over long leg by Learie Constantine at Lord's, but never the equal of this one for easy, effortless acquisition. The ball seemed to be persuaded over the trees, not hit." A couple of years later, Sewell himself made a "hit of 147 yards from hit to pitch." A few years later, he scored 74

India is a nation that has become synonymous with spin bowling but they have always possessed some useful pace bowlers. Amar Singh, who played seven Test matches in the 1930s, was one of their earliest and in 1933-34 he took seven for 86 against Douglas Jardine's England team.

out of 78 in the first innings and 51 out of 56 in the second in a first-class match at Chepauk.

The other famous England player to grace Chepauk at the turn of the century was CT Studd, who captained Madras against the Oxford Authentics. Studd, who remained unbeaten while the last English wicket fell chasing 85 to win in the match against Australia that gave rise to the Ashes legend, was at that stage a pastor in Ooty.

If any single person personifies Chepauk and its cricket, it is Morapakkam Gopalan, who was born on June 6, 1909 and played just a single Test against England in 1933-34. It is no coincidence that the main gates of the Chidambaram Stadium at Chepauk are named after him. A double international – he would have been in the 1936 gold-winning hockey team at the Olympics, but chose to tour England with the cricket team instead – Gopalan was the adonis of Madras cricket, an all-round sportsman who won titles in table tennis and tennis, and was proficient in the Indian game of kabaddi.

"Gopalan batted with his left toe cocked up in the air," wrote Johnstone, his captain and mentor. "Since this was the stance adopted by WG Grace, it could hardly be faulted."

It was Gopalan who bowled the first delivery in the Ranji Trophy, India's national championship. That match was played between Madras and Mysore – now Karnataka – on November 4, 1934. It finished in a day. Ram Singh, another Madras giant and patriarch of a family which produced two Test cricketers and four first-class players besides, claimed 11 for 35 on a pitch affected by overnight rain. The game was insured for 3,000 rupees, but when the only day's collection was just 800 rupees, the Commercial Union Assurance Company had to pay up the rest. That ended any insurance company's interest thereafter, and at least twice the Madras Cricket Club members had to shell out 100 rupees each to meet Ranji Trophy losses.

The early Test cricketers from Madras were Gopalan, Cota Ramaswami - who also played Davis Cup tennis for India while at Cambridge - and the fast bowler CR Rangachari, whom Don Bradman called "lion-hearted", a description that stuck like a first name. The Lionheart once broke the Black Bradman, George Headley's, stump in a Test match

Ram Singh, who also scored the first century by a Madras batsman in the Ranji Trophy, never played for India in an official Test. The senior Nawab of Pataudi had asked him to be ready with his passport for the 1946 tour of England, but during the selection game in Bombay, he suffered cramps and was forced to retire. It was rumoured that Ram Singh had a heart problem and he was not picked; he was perhaps the finest player never to have played for the country. But his value to Madras cricket was immense, as coach and father figure to more than one generation of players.

Not until Srinivas Venkataraghavan wore the

first of his many hats as India player in 1965 did Madras cricket throw up a comparable figure. But Venkat's children preferred tennis, and Venkat himself took to umpiring rather than coaching. The lone home player to make a century at Chepauk is Kris Srikkanth, who made an exciting 123 against Imran Khan's Pakistan team in 1986-87, an innings that saw him take two fours and a six off successive Imran deliveries. He decided to buy a house in the outskirts of the city that evening and continues to live there with his wife and two sons.

The city has also produced one other Test cricketer of note in Nasser Hussain, who followed the tradition of Ranji, Duleep and the senior Nawab of Pataudi by representing, and in Hussain's case captaining, England with great distinction.

The man who kept Ram Singh out of the Indian team, the all-rounder Vinoo Mankad, claimed 12 wickets against England in 1951-52 to bring about India's first Test win – by the comfortable margin of an innings and eight runs. Nearly two decades earlier, Madras hosted its first Test, against Douglas Jardine's Englishmen. It was the last match of the three-Test series, and England won by 202 runs to claim the rubber two-nil. Left-arm spinner Hedley Verity set the trend, with 11 wickets in the match for 153, while Amar Singh began a trend for fast bowlers, claiming seven for 86 in the first innings. Cyril Walters hit 102, and the India-born Jardine made his highest score of the series, 65, in what turned out to be his last Test.

Daniel Richmond, later to be knighted, but then President of the Madras Cricket Club, was responsible for organising that first Test in Chepauk. He laid down the rules and the blueprint that was faithfully followed for the next two decades at least.

The first team to be sent out by the MCC to India was the one led by Arthur Gilligan in 1926-27. Let the Madras historian S Muthiah take up the story here: "A 25-year-old bachelor planting in the High Range was included in the Presidency side for the one-day game against the visitors and top-scored with 48, earning an entry in *Wisden*, even though that venerable almanack spelt his name wrong. Right-hand bat Cowdrey was, some years later, so determined that his son should play for England that when the boy was born in Bangalore, he christened him Michael Colin, thus endowing him with the initials MCC, which the boy went on to honour."

Colin Cowdrey missed the 1963-64 Test in Madras – on a tour he should have captained – through illness but joined the England team during the trip, scoring hundreds in Calcutta and Delhi.

England enjoyed a more recent success in Madras in 1984-85 under the leadership of David Gower. With the series level at one-all, India stumbled in the face of some big-hearted pace bowling from Neil Foster, who took 11 wickets in the match, and a 241-run second-wicket partnership between Graeme Fowler and Mike Gatting, both of whom made double-centuries. India lost by nine wickets and the series with it.

Test cricket has been played at two venues in Madras, the other being the characterless Nehru Stadium, or Corporation Stadium, where the Indian opening pair of Mankad and Pankaj Roy put on 413 for the first wicket against New Zealand in 1956-57 – a world record which still stands. Corporation Stadium hosted nine matches between 1956 and 1967 while the Madras Cricket Club, who held the lease on the cricket ground, and the Madras Cricket Association who ran the

sport, tried to arrive at a working arrangement. Finally, after the club's 40-year lease ended in 1966, the club kept the area around its pavilion while the cricket association was leased the rest for a stadium. The downside of this agreement is that the quaint picturesque ground of yesteryear has gone the way of the concrete mixer.

If Mankad's finest hour in Madras is a toss-up between his world-record batting and his destruction of the England team in India's first Test victory, there is no such ambiguity about his worst hour. India played 44 Test matches in the 1950s, winning just six, all at home. The strain on the officials was probably as great as on the players as they intrigued, plotted, and planned their way into getting their favourites into the national team. When Lala Amarnath, for instance, was not made captain for the 1952-53 West Indies tour, off-spinner Ghulam Ahmed withdrew from the tour. There was as much back-scratching as back-biting, which probably explains why two talented players from Madras, Kripal Singh and CD Gopinath, played as few matches as they did.

But even for a team that sent back one of its best players, Amarnath, from the 1936 England tour, or even appointed the Maharajkumar of Vizianagram as captain on that tour, and chopped and changed national squads to suit the convenience of officialdom, what happened during the 1958-59 series with the West Indies must be considered outlandish.

Amarnath was now chief selector, and Vizianagram controlled the Board of Control for Cricket in India. In cricket, as in politics, there are no permanent friends or permanent enemies. Amarnath wanted Ghulam Ahmed, who was to finish with 68 wickets from 22 Tests, to lead India. But the first Test was in Bombay, and Ghulam did not fancy playing there, so he withdrew two days before the Test, leaving Polly Umrigar in charge.

Wes Hall and Roy Gilchrist attacked the batsmen, but India did well to hold on for a draw. Ghulam returned for the next Test in Kanpur

While his father chose to play for England, the Nawab of Pataudi junior had no such qualms about playing for India, representing them 46 times between 1961 and 1974. He made five hundreds including 103 in Madras against England in 1961-62. Later that season, when he was just 21, he took over the captaincy after Nari Contractor had been poleaxed by Charlie Griffith. He was to lead India to nine victories in his 40 Tests in charge.

which India lost – the players having to return to their hotel under police escort. When they lost again in Calcutta, where Rohan Kanhai made 256, Ghulam offered to resign but was persuaded to lead in the next Test at Madras.

Four days before the Test, Ghulam announced his retirement, and the selectors were split over his replacement. Umrigar, the new captain, was not

getting his way, and on the eve of the match made a speech at the Madras Cricket Association reception, returned to his hotel room, and resigned. At three the following morning, Subhash Gupte, the great Indian leg-spinner was awakened by sounds from the next room. Umrigar was crying.

Fifteen minutes before the start of the match, there was still no Indian captain. Then the officials

Erapalli Prassana. One of India's outstanding spin quartet, bowls during the 1976-77 3rd Test. India v England.

took Mankad aside, and very hush-hush in the toilets, made him captain of India. Today, S Annadorai, a former secretary of the Tamil Nadu Cricket Association, and a man who sees humour in most situations, will gladly take you to "the spot where Mankad was made India captain".

How India, or indeed the West Indies, managed to play a Test after such drama is a mystery. India lost by 295 runs, with GS Ramchand getting hit behind the ear as Hall and Gilchrist went round the wicket bowling to a leg-side field. The farce did not end there. The Test finished on January 26, a national holiday to mark India's Republic Day, when crowds pour out onto the streets to watch the parades. At the end of the match, the selectors in their wisdom decided that Ramchand should replace Mankad as captain for the final Test in Delhi.

An official who rushed to the hotel to bring him the glad tidings was held up by the parade, and in any case Ramchand and his Bombay boys had left for the railway station early. By the time the official got to the station, the train had left, and the selectors, probably seeing that as an omen, chose Hemu Adhikari as captain instead. Just to complete the circle, the man they wanted as captain, Ramchand, was dropped from the team altogether.

Had he been a little tardy, Ramchand might have led India in that final Test, and perhaps even led the team to England a few months later. Never mind. He was a bold captain, who, less than two years later, was at the helm when India beat Australia for the first time, in Kanpur.

The next time the West Indies played they were led by Gary Sobers in 1967. This marked the return of Test cricket to Chepauk. India's Farokh Engineer just missed scoring a century before lunch on the first day – a feat that until then had been accomplished by only three Australians, Victor Trumper, Charlie Macartney and Donald Bradman – as he tore into Hall and Griffith to remain unbeaten on 94 at the break. It was the first time the great spin trio of Bedi, Prasanna and Bhagwat Chandrasekhar played together, and it took serious pad-play from Griffith and a dogged 74 from Sobers to deny India victory.

MA Chidambaram Stadium will always be special as the venue for the second tied Test in

1986 when an Indian umpire, Vikram Raju, declared last man Maninder Singh leg-before to Australia's Greg Matthews. It was 5.18 pm on September 22, and for a while time stood still, allowing the spectators to savour history.

Maninder was to say later that he hit the ball although, having seen the replay, there is little doubt that he was out. But Raju, the umpire, appeared to give the decision even before Matthews had appealed. Perhaps it was this eagerness that was behind the decision never to appoint him in another Test. If so it was a great shame.

At least one Indian player, Srikkanth, was happy at the result. "Stop cribbing," he said the next day. "We are a part of history now," Srikkanth was to captain India three years later only to lose his job after he drew a four-Test series in Pakistan.

Even without the startling result, the tied Test would still have been memorable. It saw Kapil Dev make a century of such coruscating brilliance that despite going wicketless, he shared the Man of the Match award with Dean Jones, whose epic 210 was an innings of blood, sweat, tears, vomit and urine. At the end of that marathon, he had to be rushed to hospital.

Australia had not won a Test in India in 16 years. They had taken a decision in Madras – no alcohol and no spicy food. That might have prevented dehydration in the 35-degree heat with 84 per cent humidity on the final day. The first four days were dominated by Australia, who made an imposing 574 for seven in their first innings. There were centuries for David Boon and Allan Border but it was Jones's magnificent and brave innings which was the highlight.

Jones had not played a Test for two-and-a-half years and had been recalled to fill the troublesome number three position. He certainly did his job, reaching his century in five hours and 35 minutes. The heat was getting to him and he was losing fluid at an alarming rate. On several occasions he threw up at the wicket and he later confessed that at least twice he had dropped to his knees and bent over pretending to throw up when in fact he was urinating in his trousers.

In his book *Cricket Beyond the Bazaar*, the Australian writer Mike Coward relates how when

Jones had reached 174 he told Border, who was batting with him, that he did not feel he could go on. "I have had a gutful," said Jones.

"Okay, that's all right," came Border's reply. "I'll get someone tough out here."

Jones recomposed himself and went on to make 210, batting for eight-and-a-half hours. When he departed, he collapsed in the changing-room and was rapidly taken to the local hospital where he was put on a saline drip.

Jones has since told me that there were moments in the innings especially when he collapsed at the end when he thought he would die. Not many in the crowd realised what had gone into – or out of – that knock.

When India stumbled to 245 for seven, the Australians were already contemplating enforcing the follow-on but Kapil came in to hit 119 from 138 deliveries, moving from 50 to 100 with just 16 scoring shots. Matthews took five wickets but India reached 397, a deficit of 177. Border declared at the beginning of the fifth day leaving India the task of scoring 348 to win.

Gavaskar got things moving with 90 and India slowly closed in on the target. Going into the last 20 overs, India needed a further 118 with seven wickets in hand. The game was there for them but now it was the time for the Australian spinners, Matthews and Ray Bright, to chip away. Wickets fell and the number ten Shivlal Yadav joined Ravi Shastri at the crease with 14 needed from 19 deliveries. Yadav hit Matthews for six but then, with four needed, was bowled by Bright.

Shastri took two off the second ball of the last over and then a single to bring the scores level. Maninder, the last man, defended the fourth ball before Matthews and umpire Raju combined to have him leg-before from the fifth.

All action hero.
During his 131-Test career, Kapil Dev was never far from the action, scoring over 5,000 runs and taking 434 wickets. He particularly enjoyed himself in Madras as well, with 40 wickets and 708 runs in 11 matches. In 1979-80, he took 11 wickets in the match against Pakistan; his finest innings came in the 1986-87 tied Test when his 119 earned him a share of the Man-of-the-Match award.

In the final action picture of the match, clicked by an amateur photographer, Shastri stands at the non-striker's end, arm raised as the ball strikes Maninder on the pads. Maninder is looking towards square-leg. Border is at silly point with no thought of making an appeal. Of the seven men in the picture, three appear to think the batsman is not out. The tie-breaker was the umpire, Raju, who made that brave decision.

Was that the greatest Test to have been played in Chennai? Perhaps, although two Tests within my own experience in the last few years, against Pakistan in 1998-99 and then against Australia in 2000-01, must stand comparison.

The first of these was played amid intense security with three thousand policemen on duty after the game had been switched from Delhi. Relations on and off the cricket field between India and Pakistan are well documented but the truth is that relations between the players have always been good.

This Test match, played against the backdrop of unrest, was played in a magnificent spirit and may have done more for relations between the two countries than anything else. Disappointingly, India lost but it was a great game of cricket.

Shahid Afridi made 141 for Pakistan and Sachin led the Indian chase towards victory with a heroic 136 an innings played with a steadily deteriorating back

The fourth day was one of changing fortunes. Chasing 271 to win, we slipped to 82 for five. After scoring 52 in the first innings, made just two before falling to a dreadful decision from umpire Steve Dunne. I played a cover drive off Saqlain Mushtaq which hit silly point's shin. It then dropped in front of him and bounced again in front of the wicketkeeper Moin Khan who claimed the catch and got the verdict. How many people get given out after the ball has bounced twice?

Sachin, however, was in great form in spite of his bad back and added 136 for the sixth wicket with Nayan Mongia. Wasim Akram got Mongia for 52 and then, with just 17 needed for victory caught Sachin at mid-off as he tried to hit a ball from Saqlain out of the ground. The last three wickets fell swiftly and we had lost by 12 runs.

The Pakistani players fell to their knees in supplication and they still talk of what happened next. The Chepauk crowd stood as one and gave the Pakistanis an ovation as they did a lap of

honour. It was a great moment in sport that brought tears to many eyes, warmth to many hearts and a sense of balance to the heads of many cynics who despaired of ever witnessing sport as an instrument of bringing peoples together. For the eminent cricket writer Dicky Rutnagur, the Chepauk audience "epitomises the character of the city in which it stands – clean, cultured and genteel".

At least we had revenge in the next Test in Delhi where we squared the series with a 212-run win. This was the Test when Anil Kumble replicated Jim Laker's achievement of taking all ten wickets in an innings.

When the Australians arrived in Chennai in 2000-01, the series was on a knife edge. They had comfortably won the first Test in Mumbai only to see us reverse things in Kolkata with a memorable win. The deciding Test in Chennai was set up to be a real classic.

The fact that it started just three days after the Kolkata Test was in our favour. The Australian pace bowlers had bowled themselves into the ground trying to dislodge VVS Laxman and Rahul Dravid and, although Steve Waugh won the toss

It was a good toss to win and Matthew Hayden certainly enjoyed himself, making 203 before being last man out. His main support came from the Waugh twins although Steve's 70 came to an end in unusual circumstances when he palmed the ball away as it was bouncing towards the stumps and was given out handled ball. It was only the sixth such dismissal in Test history.

The main tormentor was again Harbhajan Singh who had taken 13 wickets in Kolkata. This time he took seven for 133 as we dismissed them for 391. In reply, we posted 501 thanks to another magnificent century from Tendulkar and 81 from Dravid. Harbhajan again got among the wickets, taking eight for 84 as Australia were bowled out a second time for 264. He took the last six wickets for

Epic ends
Left: As Maninder Singh is leg-before to Greg Matthews, amateur photographer Mala Mukherjee snaps the moment that Vikram Raju raised his finger to signal the end of the Tied Test in 1986-87.

Above: Pakistan off-spinner Saqlain Mushtaq kisses the ground at the end of his team's exciting 12-run win in 1998-99. In a show of great sporting spirit, the Pakistanis were given a standing ovation as they took a

Above: Another spinner to make his mark in Madras was Bhagwat Chandrasekhar who picked up 25 wickets in five Tests there. If his Test bowling record - 242 wickets in 58 Tests - was of the highest order, he was less successful with his batting, scoring just 167 runs at an average of 4.07. In cricketing terms he was a ferret - he went in after the rabbits.

How hot is it in Chennai?
Right: Australian opener Michael Slater walks out to the middle wearing an ice vest under his shirt in the 2000-01 Test.

just 15 runs in 17.1 overs to finish with 15 wickets in the match and 32 in the three-Test series. Not a bad return for a 20-year-old. In contrast Shane Warne, one of the all-time greats, managed just ten wickets at an average of 50 in the series.

Chasing 155 should have been a formality for us, especially as we reached the 100 mark with just two men down. However, Steve Waugh is one of cricket's toughest competitors and no side led by him will ever lie down, certainly when the fate of the series is in the balance. Jason Gillespie produced a fine delivery to remove Sachin and when Dravid and I followed quickly after we were wobbling slightly at 122 for five.

Things got worse when Mark Waugh took a stunning catch at midwicket to remove Laxman for 66. Sairaj Bahutule went for a duck and at 135 for seven, the Australians were suddenly favourites to win. Cricket is a game of personal highs and lows, however, and there is no end of fairy stories of players who seize the day to carve their name in the game's history. In this case, it was Samir Dighe, who was making his Test debut at the age of 32 in place of Mongia, our injured wicketkeeper.

With Zaheer Khan standing firm at one end and making one of the most valuable noughts of all time, Dighe slowly reeled in the target. With just four runs needed, Zaheer finally fell to McGrath, a fourth catch in the innings for Mark Waugh, but Harbhajan, fittingly, came in to hit the run that gave us a two-wicket win and a two-one win in the series. Dighe only played six Tests but this innings of 22 not out should be a guarantee of immortality in India.

Over the years the West Indies have always found themselves in interesting Test matches in Chennai. Gavaskar, a thorn in their side for so many years, made it the venue for one of his greatest acts of defiance in 1983-84 when he had asked to drop down the order to number four. Many people started asking who he thought he was to demand a particular spot in the batting order; presumably they had forgotten his 12 previous centuries against the West Indies.

Gavaskar duly delivered. Coming to the crease in the second over after Marshall had taken the first two wickets without a run on the board, the great man responded with an unbeaten 236, which until Laxman's 281 in Kolkata in 2000-01,

The Turbanator.
After taking 13 wickets, including a hat-trick, in the second Test against the Australians at Eden Gardens in 2000-01, off-spinner Harbhajan Singh returned to take 15 wickets in the next Test in Chennai as India turned a one-nil deficit into a two-one series win.

Harbhajan took seven for 133 in Australia's first innings and followed up with eight for 84 in the second. It really was a case of: "I'll be back."

was India's highest individual score. It also happened to be Gavaskar's 30th Test century which took him past Don Bradman's record of 29.

Gundappa Viswanath, to many the presiding deity at the ground, scored a century on one of the fastest tracks seen in the country, with the West Indian Sylvester Clarke ripping through the innings. Viswanath made 124 in 1978-79; the next highest Indian score in the match was 33 by wicketkeeper Syed Kirmani batting at number nine. It was enough to give India victory by three wickets.

Viswanath, one of the most stylish and pleasing batsmen to have played the game, tells a wonderfully deprecating story against himself. "'When the ball is bouncing around, play beside the line,' I told myself," he says of that incredible Chepauk innings. "I was so pleased with the result, I continued to play beside the line in the next match at Delhi – and was caught behind for nine."

He also played an innings of 222, batting through the day with Yashpal Sharma against England in 1981-82. He had been going through a lean patch then and had taken the precaution of invoking divine aid before the game. He also shaved off his beard and gave up smoking. In that Test, he helped put on 415 for the fourth wicket with two separate partners. First, he added 99 with Dilip Vengsarkar and then, when Vengsarkar retired hurt, he added a further 316 with Sharma.

The first West Indian tour in 1948-49 had brought new heroes to India. George Headley only played in the first Test but Everton Weekes became a legend. By the time the fourth Test in Madras came around, he had successive scores of 128, 194, 162 and 101 added to the century he had made in his last Test against England, a record five successive Test hundreds. The stage was set for him to make it six at but he suffered a rare failure – run out for 90.

The West Indies won that Test but they have been India's favourite opponents at Chepauk. India have won four Tests against them there, more than against any other team.

It began in 1974-75 following Viswanath's 97 and Karnataka team-mate Prasanna's five for 70 in the first innings which restricted the West Indies lead to just two runs. Marshalled by Mansur Ali

Khan, the Nawab of Pataudi, the Indian spinners then ensured a win by 100 runs in a low-scoring match. A decade after the three-wicket win in 1978-79, India won again in the only Test where Shastri captained the side. This time the hero was the debutant leg-spinner Narendra Hirwani, whose eight wickets in each innings settled the issue.

Hirwani, a bespectacled Sindhi, was by no means a classical leg-spinner. However, what he lacked in flight and deception he made up for in accuracy and on a helpful track he could be dangerous.

Although the wicket was helpful, India were aided as much by the batting technique or lack of it among the West Indies batsmen. Hirwani had troubled the team, claiming all six wickets to fall in the second innings against India's Under-25 XI. That five of the West Indies batsmen in the second innings were out stumped off Hirwani suggested the kind of panic the batsmen had got into. Hirwani finished with 16 for 136, the most spectacular debut by a bowler since Australia's

Bob Massie also took 16 wickets against England at Lord's in 1972. Interestingly, the West Indies off-spinner Clyde Butts bowled 11 overs more than Hirwani, but went wicketless.

Viv Richards, the West Indies captain, was furious. "That was a minefield of a wicket," he said. "Come to the West Indies and we will get back at you."

When India toured the West Indies later that year, Richards remembered, and led his team to victory in three of four Tests. Poor Hirwani discovered the truth behind the saying that cricket is a great leveller: he took just six wickets in that series at an average of 57.

At least, however, he had tasted success and tasted it like Harbhajan, Gavaskar, Tendulkar and others in the red heat of the Chidambaram, a stadium with a history and presence that can only inspire future generations of cricketers from every corner of the earth.

Gundappa Viswanath.
With 785 runs in Chennai and a double century against England, Viswanath is one of the most successful batsmen at Chennai.

MA CHIDAMBERAM Ground Records

Result Summary

	Played	Won	Lost	Drawn/tied
India	26	11	6	8/1
Australia	5	1	2	1/1
England	7	3	3	1/0
Pakistan	4	1	1	2/0
New Zealand	2	0	1	1/0
Sri Lanka	1	0	0	1/0
West Indies	7	1	4	2/0

Bangladesh, South Africa and Zimbabwe have
yet to play at the MA Chidamberam

Highest Totals

652-7	England v India	1984-85
582	West Indies v India	1948-49
574-7	Australia v India	1986-87
566-6	India v Sri Lanka	1982-83

Lowest Completed Innings Totals

83	India v England	1976-77
140	New Zealand v India	1976-77

Highest Match Aggregates

Runs	Wkts		
1488	32	India v Australia	1986-87
1441	33	India v Sri Lanka	1982-83
1403	37	India v West Indies	1966-67

Lowest Match Aggregates (Result oriented matches)

Runs	Wkts		
694	38	India v England	1976-77

Highest Scores

236*	SM Gavaskar	v West Indies	1983-84
222	GR Viswanath	v England	1981-82
210	DM Jones	v India	1986-87
207	MW Gatting	v India	1984-85
203	ML Hayden	v India	2000-01

Highest Run Aggregates

Runs	Matches	Hundreds	
1018	12	3	SM Gavaskar
785	10	2	GR Viswanath
714	6	4	SR Tendulkar
708	11	2	Kapil Dev

Partnership Records

239 for 1st	AF Rae and JB Stollmeyer	West Indies v India	1948-49
241 for 2nd	G Fowler and MW Gatting	England v India	1984-85
316 for 3rd	GR Viswanath and Yashpal Sharma	India v England	1981-82
190 for 4th	M Amarnath and M Azharuddin	India v England	1984-85
169 for 5th	RS Dravid and SR Tendulkar	India v Australia	2000-01
170 for 6th	SM Gavaskar and RJ Shastri	India v West Indies	1983-84
100 for 7th	AI Kallicharran and DR Parry	West Indies v India	1978-79
112 for 8th	Imran Khan and Wasim Akram	Pakistan v India	1986-87
143* for 9th	SM Gavaskar and SMH Kirmani	India v West Indies	1983-84
104 for 10th	Amir Elahi and Zulfiqar Ahmed	Pakistan v India	1952-53

Best Bowling in an Innings.

8 for 55	MH Mankad India v England	1951-52
8 for 61	ND Hirwani India v West Indies	1987-88
8 for 75	ND Hirwani India v West Indies	1987-88
8 for 84	Harbhajan Singh India v Australia	2000-01
7 for 49	H Verity England v India	1933-34

Best Bowling in a Match

16 for 136	(8-61, 8-75)	ND Hirwani India v West Indies	1987-88
15 for 217	(7-133, 8-84)	Harbhajan Singh India v Australia	2000-01
12 for 108	(8-55, 4-53)	MH Mankad India v England	1951-52
12 for 121	(7-64, 5-57)	AME Roberts West Indies v India	1974-75
11 for 146	(4-90, 7-56)	Kapil Dev India v Pakistan	1979-80

Highest Wicket Aggregates

Wkts	Matches	5WI	
40	11	2	Kapil Dev
36	5	2	EAS Prasanna
31	6	1	BS Bedi
29	5	3	A Kumble
25	5	2	BS Chandrasekar

Most Catches by Fielder

Catches	Matches	
14	3	ED Solkar
11	11	Kapil Dev
11	4	RS Dravid

Most Dismissals by Wicket keeper

Dismissals	Matches	
22	9	SMH Kirmani
10	4	FM Engineer
9	4	KS More

PAKISTAN
Qamar Ahmed

Lovers of trivia quizzes could do worse than while away the time by naming the 18 venues that have hosted Pakistan's home Test matches. It would be tough, especially as Dhaka is no longer in Pakistan and Sharjah and Colombo never have been, but it could be done.

The problem would be to take in all the grounds that have hosted just the one Test or even those with fewer than ten to their name. Of the seven one-Test wonders, the Dring Stadium in Bahwalpur is still used for first-class cricket, while the Peshawar Services Ground has been superseded by the Arbab Niaz Stadium, which hosted its first Test in 1995-96. The Pindi Club Ground in Rawalpindi, which staged a single Test against New Zealand in 1964-65, has given way to the Rawalpindi Cricket Stadium while neither of Multan's two representatives, the Ibn-e-Qasim Bagh Stadium and the Multan Cricket Stadium, has yet claimed a second Test. The Municipal Stadium in Gujranwala staged one Test against Sri Lanka in 1991-92, while the Defence Stadium in Karachi hosted Zimbabwe in 1993-94.

Because of fears over security Pakistan played the entire home series against Australia in 2002-03 away from home. After the first Test at the P Saravanamuttu Stadium in Colombo, the two teams completed the three-match series in Sharjah. Pakistan came off badly after being dismissed for 59 and 53 in the first of those.

If you include Dhaka (or Dacca as it was called in 1954-55 when it became Pakistan's first Test ground) and Sharjah, there are eight grounds that have held more than one but fewer than ten Tests. These include the Niaz Stadium in Hyderabad, Sialkot's Jinnah Stadium, the Rawalpindi Cricket Stadium, Arbab Niaz Stadium in Peshawar, where Mark Taylor famously declared when he was 334 not out so that he would sit alongside the great

Don Bradman in the record books, and the Municipal Stadium in Sheikhupura, where Wasim Akram and Saqlain Mushtaq broke the record for the eighth-wicket partnership in Test cricket, adding 313 against Zimbabwe in 1996-97.

The other one is Lawrence Gardens, Lahore, which held three Tests before giving way to the Gaddafi Stadium, which is one of just three grounds in Pakistan to have staged 20 Tests. The Gaddafi has enjoyed a major slice of cricket history including innings of contrasting tones from Zaheer Abbas, who scored a double-century against India from just 241 deliveries, and Mudassar Nazar, whose century in 557 minutes against England in 1977-78 is still the slowest in Test history. Ten years later the great leg-spinner Abdul Qadir took nine for 56, also against the English. The New Zealander Peter Petherick stole a place in history by taking a hat-trick in Lahore on his Test debut in 1976-77 although Imran Khan's 14 wickets against Sri Lanka 1981-82, Shoaib Akhtar's astonishing analysis of six for 11 in 8.2 overs against New Zealand in 2002 and Inzamam-ul-Haq's 329 in the same Test will probably live longer in the memories of the locals.

The Iqbal Stadium in Faisalabad, which has also hit the 20-Tests mark, is a regular on the circuit with more than a touch of history. It was here in 1996-97 that Hasan Raza became the youngest Test cricketer when he made his debut at the tender age of 14 years and 227 days, and where Qasim Omar (206) and Javed Miandad (203 not out) put on a mammoth 397 for the third wicket against Sri Lanka in 1985-86. More notoriously, this was the scene for Mike Gatting's famous tête-a-tête with the umpire Shakoor Rana.

Of all the grounds in Pakistan, however, none quite matches, for atmosphere and deeds, the National Stadium in Karachi.

Pakistan's greatest cricketer?
Imran Khan was an all-rounder who scored 3,807 runs and took 362 wickets. He was also a pretty good captain, turning Pakistan into a leading force in the Test arena and one-day world champions in 1991-92.

NATIONAL STADIUM, KARACHI

reat players, great deeds; an atmosphere that sometimes tips from the vibrant to the violent. A fortress for Pakistan cricket. That is the sum of the National Stadium in Karachi.

For the great players read an 'A' for Aamir Sohail to Zaheer Abbas of Pakistan's finest; Abdul Qadir, Asif Iqbal, Fazal Mahmood, Javed Miandad, Hanif Mohammad, Imran Khan, Majid Khan, Wasim Akram and Waqar Younis are just some of the names that have made a lasting impression with their performances at the National Stadium.

For the great deeds read a litany of Pakistani wins, an unbeaten run of 34 Tests that was only ended in 2000 by an England team that scampered to a narrow victory amid the worsening gloom when the fielders could barely see the ball and when the crowd needed flashlights to read the scoreboard. Plenty of players from overseas have risen to the challenge of playing at a ground where the local support can occasionally come across as hostile but the story of the National Stadium, Karachi is principally wrapped up in Pakistani colours.

Pakistan, meaning Land of the Pure, was carved out as an independent nation in 1947 as a result of the partition of India and the end of the Raj. With the exception of Kashmir, the Muslim majority areas in the north-east and north-west of the sub-continent were thus drawn out to form West and East Pakistan which were separated by a thousand miles of Indian territory.

The eastern wing of the country where cricket had yet to take root declared itself independent and became Bangladesh in 1971. However, the four provinces in the west – Sind, Baluchistan, Punjab and North-West Frontier – had rich traditions of the game and were lucky to have inherited a ready-made culture which helped the new country immensely to stand on its feet and become a Test-playing nation within five years of its existence.

Visits by West Indies, Ceylon (now Sri Lanka) and Commonwealth teams helped Pakistani cricket a lot but it was their victory by four wickets at the Karachi Gymkhana Ground against Nigel Howard's MCC tourists in 1951-52 which really opened the door internationally. India proposed and MCC seconded their application to be granted full Test-playing membership of the International Cricket Council on July 28, 1952.

The popularity and the progress of the game however owed much to the playing facilities and already existing cricket grounds in the length and breath of the country at the time of the division of India. Lawrence Gardens (now Bagh-e-Jinnah) in Lahore, and the Peshawar Services Club near the historic Khyber Pass hosted representative matches, as did the Pindi Club Ground in Rawalpindi where the grandson of the Queen Victoria, Prince Christian Victor, posted a score of 205, the first double-century in the sub-continent, while playing for the King's Rifle against the Devonshire Regiment in 1893.

On top of the Aussies.
Opening batsman Aamir Sohail on his way to 133 in
1998-99. Ian Healy and Mark Taylor look on.

In the south, the port city of Karachi had a number of grounds too – Karachi Goan Association (KGA), Karachi Parsi Institute (KPI), Muslim Gymkhana, Hindu Gymkhana and Agha Khan Gymkhana to name a few. But it was Karachi Gymkhana which staged most of the first-class games and matches against the visiting teams before and after the partition of India, including matches played by Arthur Gilligan's MCC and Lord Tennyson's XI in 1926 and 1937 respectively.

But with Pakistan gaining their Test status these grounds soon paled into insignificance with the development of new grounds in the country, including the National Stadium in Karachi, which is easily approachable and is situated about ten kilometres from the bustling city centre.

A brainchild of a cricket-loving civil engineer called Kafiluddin Ahmed, it was ready within two-and-a-half years to host its first first-class match, which was the fifth and final Test against India on February 26, 1955. With the exception of Dacca – which is now Dhaka in Bangladesh – it remains the oldest ground still used for Tests in Pakistan and held a formidable record with Pakistan unbeaten there in 34 Tests until England's six-wicket win in the gloom in December of 2000.

An unassailable fortress indeed which, with its proud record, and an excitable and, at times, raucous yet knowledgeable crowd, epitomises all that is good in Pakistan cricket.

With its redevelopment during the 1987 and 1996 World Cups, the capacity has increased from 40,000 to nearly 60,000. There is now an imposing pavilion, spacious dressing-rooms, hospitality boxes and covered stands instead of roofless concrete terraces. The wire fencing is still there to prevent pitch invasions, but the matting wickets have long since gone.

Behind the pavilion, the vast barren patch of land that used to be rented out for elite wedding receptions has given way to a cricket academy and practice wickets on lush green lawns. For the atmosphere and aura that it generates it still attracts the young and old, the rich and poor and the ladies in their colourful attire. A Test match in Karachi is like a carnival.

Religious and world leaders like the Aga Khan, Pope John Paul II and Nelson Mandela have all graced the venue – albeit not to watch cricket. And it goes without saying that most of the world's great cricketers since 1955 have trod the turf of the National Stadium. From Vinoo Mankad and Keith Miller to Gary Sobers and Richard Hadlee, they have all been there. And usually they have met with stonewall resistance from Pakistani cricketers of the highest calibre.

Strangely, all of these great players and the thousands of people who have come to watch cricket at the National Stadium can thank an American for changing the face of cricket in Pakistan. And a president at that.

When Dwight D Eisenhower allowed himself to become the first US President to watch a Test match he had little idea what he was letting himself in for. Visiting Pakistan, he was taken by Field Marshal Ayub Khan, the president of Pakistan, to the fourth day of the third Test of the 1959-60 series against Australia. It was not the most exciting Test in history: Hanif made a century and Intikhab Alam took a wicket with his first ball in Test cricket when he bowled Colin McDonald. But all Dwight got to see was a funereal day's cricket that saw just 104 runs scored, the second-slowest in Test history.

Eisenhower suffered with good grace and was introduced to the teams. Wearing a Pakistan blazer he accepted first a ribbing from Richie Benaud, the Australian captain – "I see you have joined the opposition, sir" – and then a green baggy cap. To Benaud's and almost every other cricket lover's delight Eisenhower then turned to Ayub Khan and commented: "I thought cricket was played on grass, not on mats."

To Eisenhower, it may have been a throwaway remark, but it found its target and the Field Marshal immediately instructed the cricket authorities to switch over to turf wickets. The arrival of Ted Dexter's England team in 1961-62 signalled a new era for the National Stadium.

With Pakistan and India both hell-bent on not losing the first series in 1954-55, the inaugural Test

All the President's Men: Dwight D Eisenhower is thought to be the only US President to have watched a day of Test cricket.
Perhaps the reason why the game was never taken back to the States was that the poor man had to endure a turgid day when just 104 runs
scored in the day's play. Dressed in a Pakistan blazer, he shakes hands with the Australian Les Favell on December 8, 1959.
Lindsay Kline, Wally Grout and Peter Burge are on Favell's left while Alan Davidson and Barry Jarman wait to be introduced.

Right: Hanif Mohammad, seen here batting in England, was one of Pakistan's early greats and his second-wicket partnership of of 178 with
Saeed Ahmed against the West Indies in 1958-59 is still a ground record.

second innings by the Karachi opener Alim-ud-Din, the first Test century on the ground, and 93 by Pakistan captain Abdul Hafeez Kardar. They also came up against some fine pace bowling by the tall, medium-fast bowler Fazal Mahmood and his new-ball partner Khan Mohammad, who took five wickets each in the first innings.

Even India's more experienced batsmen like Polly Umrigar and Vijay Manjrekar had no clue against the guile of Fazal's swinging deliveries and vicious leg-cutters on the mat. The Karachi-born Indian all-rounder Gulabrai Ramchand also had a flattering return of six for 49 in Pakistan's first innings.

The interest and euphoria of a match against India was such that on each day a near-capacity crowd of 30,000 turned up. Not surprisingly, however, the game and the series ended in a draw.

Only a month later on the same ground, brothers Wazir Mohammad (118), Hanif

Mohammad (109) and Raees Mohammad (110) scored a century each to help Karachi win the final of the Quaid-e-Azam Trophy, the national championship, by beating Combined Services by nine wickets.

It was in Karachi that Pakistan won its first home Test in 1954-55 when they beat the visiting New Zealanders by an innings and one run. The victory owed much to the effort of the little off-spinner Zulfiqar Ahmed, who had a haul of 11 for 79 in the match. His victims included such illustrious names as Bert Sutcliffe and John Reid. It was a victory that led to Pakistan's first home series win.

If victory over New Zealand was a tasty *hors d'oeuvres*, then Pakistan lapped up the main course when the National Stadium provided the setting for their first win over Australia in 1956-57 and the West Indies in 1958-59. In a one-off Test, their first against Australia, Pakistan achieved an imposing nine-wicket victory against Ian Johnson's team. Their hero was Fazal, whose match return of 13 for 114 included three wickets in four balls in the second innings. In the first innings Australia were bowled out for 80 as Fazal took six for 34 and by close of play Pakistan had replied with 15 for the loss of two wickets. Just 95 runs were scored during a day's play, the lowest ever in a Test. Fortunately, President Eisenhower was not there to see it.

Pakistan's first-innings lead of 119 owed much to Wazir Mohammad and Hafeez Kardar who both batted superbly against Ray Lindwall, Keith Miller, Ron Archer, Alan Davidson and Richie Benaud. Australia were out for 187 in their second innings as Fazal flattened them on the mat with seven for 80. Perhaps the only consolation for the Australians came when Lindwall claimed his 200th Test victim with the dismissal of Zulfiqar.

Fazal continued in the same vein, dominating the proceedings on matting when the West Indies visited Pakistan in 1958-59. Pakistan won the first Test by ten wickets with Fazal collecting seven for 124 in the match. When he had Sobers leg-before for the second time in the match he became the first Pakistani to reach 100 Test wickets. When it came to capitalising on Fazal's work with the ball, Pakistan were able to rely on Mr Reliable, Hanif Mohammad, 103, and Imtiaz Ahmed, who bravely defied the menacing pace of fast bowler Wes Hall and the guile of Sobers and off-spinner Lance Gibbs.

Pakistan's success at the National Stadium in its formative years in the 1950s and 1960s were a precursor to the other Tests played on the ground where Pakistan defended its unbeaten record until that fateful evening when Nasser Hussain's England got the better of them.

In the interim other players came and left an indelible mark on Karachi cricket. In the 1961-62 Test against England, Dexter struck a blistering 205, Peter Parfitt made 111 and Alim-ud-Din chimed in again with 109. Three years later, Pakistan opener Khalid Ibadulla made 166 on debut against Australia, whose captain, Bobby Simpson, replied with a century in each innings.

Memorable feats, exciting Tests, controversies and crowd disturbances, triumphs and tribulations of home as well as visiting teams have all been a part of this historic ground too.

Emulating the Graces and the Hearne brothers, the three indomitable cricketing brothers Hanif, Mushtaq and Sadiq Mohammad played here against New Zealand in first of the three Tests of 1969-70. Sadiq made 69 in his first Test and went on to play 26 times with Mushtaq but for Hanif it was the last of 55 Tests in an illustrious career.

New Zealand again in 1976-77, Pakistan arrived in Karachi aiming for a clean sweep having won in Lahore and Hyderabad. Teenage newcomer Javed

In the first Test of the 1969-70 series against New Zealand, the Mohammads became the second set of three brothers to play in the same team. Here, during the Test against England at the National Stadium in 1978, Hanif (right), Mushtaq (centre) and Sadiq (left) gather around their coach Abdul Aziz. The lad on the right is Hanif's son Shoaib who went on to play 45 times for Pakistan and scored a double-century against New Zealand in Karachi in 1990-91.

Full flight
During the 1990s Waqar Younis was one of the finest fast bowlers in the world, mastering the art of reverse swing and in-dipping yorker. With Wasim Akram at th te other end, Pakistan had a fast-bowling force to be reckoned with.

Miandad had set the pace with a magnificent 163 on debut, while Asif Iqbal, Sadiq and Mushtaq – who both made centuries in the same innings in Hyderabad – had also cashed in on the bowling.

The Test at Karachi ended in a draw but not before the New Zealand bowling was mauled again as Pakistan scored 565 for nine. Once again Miandad was the principal destroyer, striking 29 fours and two sixes in his 206. At the age of 19 years and 141 days, he was the first teenager to score a double-century in a Test. These were just the first knockings, however, of a long and distinguished career that saw Javed make 23 centuries and 8,832 runs at an average of over 52 in 124 Tests.

To add to the misery of the bowlers like Richard Collinge, Richard Hadlee and Lance Cairns, the majestic Majid Khan scored a hundred before lunch on the first day. It took just 74 deliveries. Only Victor Trumper, Charlie Macartney and Don Bradman, all Australians, had done so before him. Mushtaq weighed in with 107 and Warren Lees, the New Zealand wicketkeeper, recorded his maiden first-class hundred when making 152. In all, 1,585 runs were scored, the highest aggregate for any Test in the sub-continent.

First of the close and exciting Tests on the ground was however played against the arch-rivals India in 1978-79. For 18 years, since they had last played each other in India in 1960-61, political feuds had kept them apart. For many this was not far off George Orwell's notion of sport as "war without the shooting".

The first Test at Faisalabad had ended in a high-scoring draw but Pakistan won the second in Lahore by eight wickets with the help of the prolific Zaheer who made an unbeaten 235 and through spirited bowling by both Imran and Sarfraz.

The Test at the National Stadium therefore was a crunch match. For India, especially, it was a win-or-bust situation. The tension was palpable and the cricket of a high quality. India's master batsman Sunil Gavaskar was in particularly fine form, following his 111 in the first innings with 137 in the second. But even he could not stop Pakistan.

Taking up the challenge of scoring 164 off 35 minutes and 20 overs, Pakistan scampered home in a sensational finish, with first-innings centurion

Above: Iqbal Qasim on his way to 11 wickets in the match as Pakistan beat Australia in 1979-80.

Right: The Rawalpindi Express.
Shoaib Akhtar has already broken the 100mph barrier.
How fast can he bowl?

Javed Miandad and Asif Iqbal piling on 97 runs for the second wicket before Imran's belligerent onslaught against the Indian captain Bishan Bedi. One over went for 19 runs and Pakistan, cheered on by a crowd of around 50,000, got home by eight wickets with seven balls to spare.

Occasionally cricket throws up romantic stories of unknowns plucked from obscurity who go on to win a vital match. Exactly that happened in 1979-80 when a young off-spinner called Tauseef Ahmed was picked to play against Australia. On the eve of the match he had been down at the nets watching Pakistan practise when a friend of Mushtaq, now the coach, recommended he have a go. Into the nets he went to send down a few balls to Majid and Zaheer.

He obviously made an impression as the next day he was taking his place in the Pakistan line-up. On a spinners' pitch that saw the vastly more experienced Iqbal Qasim collect 11 wickets in the match and Australia's Ray Bright ten, Tauseef bagged seven for 126 in the match as Pakistan romped home by seven wickets. When asked about the name of his victims, he said: "I only know Chappell." He went on to take 93 Test wickets.

Another man who made the most of his debut in Karachi was Salim Malik, who made 100 not out against Sri Lanka in the first Test of the 1981-82 series. Salim, a flowing right-hander, went on to captain Pakistan in the 1990s before falling foul of the ICC investigation into match-fixing.

Two of the 1982-83 Tests of the next six-match rubber against India was played at the National Stadium on a newly-laid square. Pakistan's win in the second Test of the series by an innings and 86 runs was achieved on the fourth morning as India were bowled out twice for under 200. By this stage Imran Khan had long since developed from being an out-and-out fast bowler into one of the world's canniest operators. Still quick, he was now capable of thinking batsmen out while his own competence with the bat put him on a par with the other great all-rounders of the generation: Ian Botham, Kapil Dev, Richard Hadlee and even Malcolm Marshall.

Imran ripped through the heart of India's strong batting, taking three for 19 in the first innings and then eight for 60 in the second. When he bowled Gundappa Viswanath he became the first Pakistan bowler to reach 200 Test wickets. At

his devastating best, he took his last five wickets for three runs in 25 deliveries to finish with 11 for 79 in the match.

Kapil responded in his uniquely exciting manner, striking 73 in the first innings with his 50 coming from only 30 deliveries, three balls quicker than the half-century he made in 1978-79. As if to show that Imran was not the only bowler on show, Kapil also took five for 102, but with Zaheer and Mudassar both making hundreds, there was little he could do to prevent a comprehensive Pakistani victory. When the two teams returned to Karachi for the sixth Test, the series was already decided three-nil in favour of the home side and it ended in a draw, Ravi Shastri reaching his maiden Test hundred in the process.

Kapil was back in November 1989, playing in his 100th Test and claiming his 350th wicket in the process but it was another Indian who announced himself to the world in this match. Sachin Tendulkar did not make a hundred in his first Test, but at 16 years and 205 days he showed enough to suggest the great career that has followed, making 15 before being bowled by Waqar Younis. A week later in Faisalabad he made his first Test fifty and on the tour to England that followed in 1990, he reached his first Test century. The rest is history.

Pakistan's three-wicket win in 1983-84 set up their first-ever victory in a home series against England. David Gower's brilliance with the bat earned him a fifty in each innings but it was the spinners who held the key. Nick Cook exploited the pitch to finish with 11 for 83 in a losing cause and leg-spinner Abdul Qadir picked up seven for 133 in the match. Needing 65 to win, Pakistan struggled against Cook but the young wicketkeeper Anil Dalpat, the first Hindu to play for Pakistan, saw them home.

Later in the decade, there was a return to the slow scoring that had epitomised the ground in the matting days of the 1950s. It came in the shape of Ramiz Raja, a pretty good player on his day and now the chief executive of the Pakistan Cricket Board, who dug in heroically against the West Indies in 1986-87. Ramiz and his team-mates had had to watch a blistering 70 from Viv Richards on the first day but when wickets fell early in the Pakistan reply, Ramiz reached for the limpet's handbook. The result was a half–century in 317 minutes, the third-slowest fifty in Test history

Fiery leg-spinner Abdul Qadir celebrates the dismissal of England's Allan Lamb in the 1983-84 series. Pakistan won the Test by three wickets and with it their first home series against England. Meanwhile, Qadir went on to claim 236 wickets during a distinguished career that lasted from 1977 to 1990.

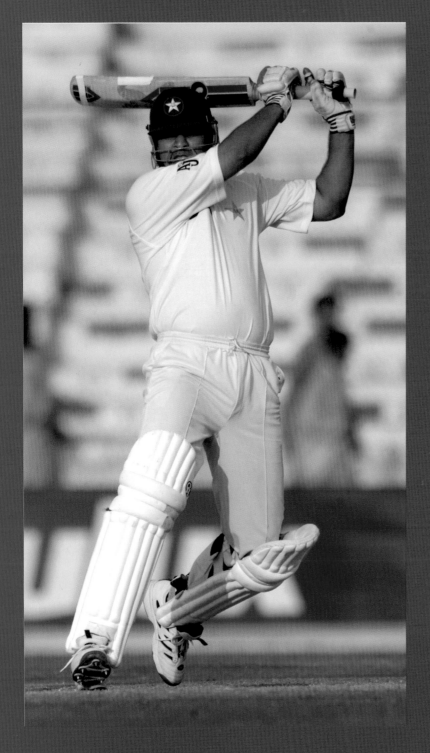

Above: Inzamam-ul-Haq, ranked second in the all-time list of Pakistan run-scorers at Test level, rings up another boundary on his way to 142 against England in 2000-01.

Right: Wasim Akram successfully dives to make his ground as England wicketkeeper Bruce French takes the bails off. The match during the 1987-88 tour was drawn but the controversy that followed the argument in the previous Test at Faisalabad between Mike Gatting and the umpire Shakoor Rana meant England did not visit Pakistan again for 13 years.

behind the two Englishmen Trevor Bailey and Chris Tavare, and his final score of 62 occupied 408 minutes and attracted a fair amount of slow hand-clapping.

In fact, it was to become rather a good Test match. Leading by one run on the first innings, the West Indies only made 211 in the their second dig with Imran taking six for 46. It would have been a lot less but for Desmond Haynes, whose unbeaten 88 was the first of the three occasions on which he carried his bat in a Test. That left Pakistan a victory target of 213 but at 25 for four early on the final day, defeat looked a more likely proposition. Ramiz dug in again, this time making 29 in 236 minutes – a match duration of 91 in 644 minutes or eight and a half runs an hour. At tea, however, the situation once again looked bad at 97 for seven. But Imran, who curbed his natural aggression by scoring 15 not out, and Tauseef Ahmed held out to ensure that the match was drawn and the three-match series ended level with one win each.

Two years later Javed Miandad made a magnificent 211 as Pakistan crushed Australia by an

innings and 188 runs but it was another Test against the Aussies in 1994-95 which can claim to have been the most exciting and closest ever at the ground.

For the locals it was all the more thrilling as Pakistan looked certain to lose their battle to score the 314 they needed for victory. Indeed, they had slumped to 258 for nine when Inzamam-ul-Haq was joined by last man Mushtaq Ahmed. Together though they took the fight to Shane Warne, who bowled beautifully throughout and, as *Wisden* reports: "To the unrestrained delight of the crowd which steadily grew in number and chanted Allah-O-Akbar (God is great), they accomplished their goal in 8.1 overs."

The match, however, will be remembered for the swings of fortune that teased both sides in the run-up to the grand finale. Mark Taylor, for example, was to go down in the history books as the first man to bag a pair in his first Test as captain. He made up for it in the future, of course, notably on Australia's next visit to Pakistan when he made 334 not out in Peshawar.

Michael Bevan, playing his first Test, gave notice of his talent with a well-crafted 82, David Boon chipped in with his 19th Test century and Saeed Anwar made 85 and 77 in his two innings. Of the bowlers, Wasim, Waqar and Warne took 23 wickets between them but it came down to the nerve of the Pakistani tail on the final day.

Rashid Latif had given the innings some momentum with a rapid 35, but few expected Mushtaq and Inzamam to make it to the finishing post. Mushtaq, the leg-spinner, responded with 20 while Inzamam, one of the game's more laid-back individuals, made an unbeaten 58. Even at the very end, though, Australia might have nicked it. The winning runs came when Inzamam gave Warne the charge. He missed the ball and, with the batsman well out of his crease, so did the Australian wicketkeeper Ian Healy and the ball went down to the boundary for four byes. Healy never forgave himself for that lapse.

The hangover from the euphoria lay several months down the road in early 1995 when the Pakistanis were on tour in Zimbabwe. An

The castle walls come tumbling down
After 34 Tests unbeaten at the National Stadium, Pakistan finally lost to England in 2000-01.

From left to right: Graham Thorpe and Moin Khan discuss the light; Thorpe and Nasser Hussain leave the field with victory secured in the gloom; Hussain reflects on England's achievement.

Australian newspaper alleged that Salim Malik, the Pakistan captain, had offered bribes to Warne, Tim May and Mark Waugh to throw the Test. It was the end for Salim and it left a bitter taste in the mouth of world cricket.

Aamir Sohail and Ijaz Ahmed were two batsmen who had a golden couple of years at the National Stadium. In the 1997-98 series against the West Indies they shared an opening partnership of 298, the highest for any wicket at the ground, Sohail making 160 and Ijaz 151. The following year they both made hundreds against the Australians.

Pakistan's proud, unbeaten record in 34 Tests at the National Stadium had to fall sometime but it was still a surprise that it should fall in the third Test in 2000-01 to an England team that had been struggling. It may have been a case of being beaten by complacency. The Pakistanis believed they had the measure of the English, especially when, bolstered by hundreds from Inzamam and Yousuf Youhana, they registered

405 in their first innings. Mike Atherton's 125 followed in the Karachi tradition of slow scoring, spanning as it did 578 minutes, but it ensured that England conceded just 17 on the first innings. Then, led by Ashley Giles and Darren Gough, they shocked Pakistan by dismissing them for a meagre 158, the last six wickets falling for just 30 runs.

Suddenly, a game that appeared to be drifting towards a draw had opened up. With England needing 176 to win from 44 overs on the final afternoon, both sides had a chance – but it was the visitors who grabbed the opportunity.

The Pakistan captain Moin Khan adopted delaying tactics that ensured that only seven overs went down in the first 40 minutes and the game came to a conclusion in virtual darkness. A partnership of 91 for the fourth wicket between Graeme Hick and Graham Thorpe took England to the cusp of victory and, with the fielders struggling to locate the ball in the gloom, an

inside edge from Thorpe settled the game. England had won by six wickets and took the series one-nil.

Over the years the ground also had its full share of crowd trouble. Most of the disturbances have been politically motivated with some resulting in stoppages and even abandonment of play. In a precursor to his infamous confrontation with Mike Gatting, the umpire Shakoor Rana was at the centre of a row in 1984-85 when he declined an appeal for a catch at the wicket off Mianded. Jeremy Coney, the New Zealand captain, was so outraged that he led his players to the edge of the field, only agreeing to return to the action after some soothing words from other members of the touring party.

Against England in 1972-73 an hour's play was lost because of four crowd invasions on the first day of the third Test after a ground steward had assaulted a student spectator. On a quirkier note, this match also gained a foothold in history by

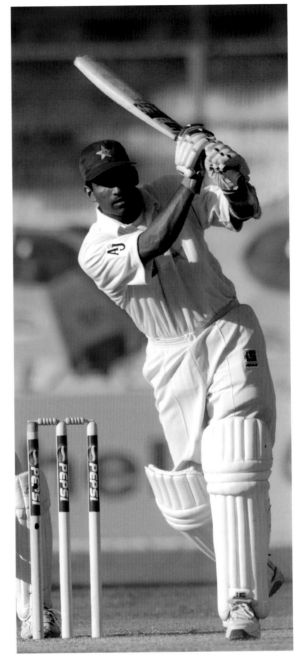

featuring three batsmen, Majid Khan, Mushtaq Mohammad and Dennis Amiss, to be dismissed for 99. And following his altercation with Shakoor Rana in the previous Test in Faisalabad in 1987-88, Gatting was once again in conflict with the umpires, showing dissent at his own dismissal as well as those of Chris Broad and Bill Athey.

The West Indies were denied a victory in 1975 when a pitch invasion cost 150 minutes of play. In the 1982 Test against India, the fourth day's play had to be abandoned after a group of students invaded the pitch protesting on the imprisonment of their colleagues belonging to the right-wing organisation of Jamaet-e-Islami.

They jumped over the fence and a group of them uprooted the stumps to dig up the pitch, while threatening the Pakistan captain Imran Khan. The commotion was such that the authorities had no alternative but to abandon the match for the day.

The 1989-90 Indian tourists were also met with a similar protest. A bearded young man – described as a "zealot" by *Wisden* – invaded the field after lunch on the opening day, making a stand against the desecration of the 400-year-old Babri Mosque at Ayodhya in India by Hindu fundamentalists, He taunted the Indian fielders Manoj Prabhakar and Kapil Dev

The worst disruption came against England in 1968-69 when Colin Cowdrey's team visited the country. Before lunch on the third day of the third Test England were 502 for seven. Colin Milburn and Tom Graveney had already scored hundreds and, when the trouble began, wicketkeeper Alan Knott was just four runs away from his maiden Test century. A group of students protesting against the appointment of Saeed Ahmed as the captain of Pakistan instead of the home hero Hanif Mohammad had been noisy all through the game before finally losing their cool by setting fire to the shamianas, the fabric covers over the stand. The Test had to be abandoned, the first instance of a Test being called off because of crowd trouble.

In the domestic arena, the National Stadium has also had its share of highlights. Left-arm spinner Shahid Mahmood bagged all ten wickets in an innings for Sind against Khairpur for 58 runs in a Quaid-e-Azam Trophy match in 1969-70. And in another national championship match in 1974, Sind posted a national record as their batsmen carved up the Baluchistan attack to the tune of 951 for seven declared. The Karachi batsman Aftab Baloch, who played two Tests for Pakistan, made the small matter of 428 as Sind won by an innings and 575 runs.

For all that, it is as Fortress Karachi that the National Stadium will be remembered by anyone who has had the chance to taste the unique flavour of a Test match there.

and then headed towards Kris Srikkanth, the Indian captain, with what can only be described as aggressive intent. Having had his shirt torn, Srikkanth reacted by hitting the intruder who was finally and belatedly apprehended. A shaken Srikkanth remarked: "What would have happened if the man had been carrying a knife? Security is non-existent."

There was further trouble on that tour when the third one-day international was abandoned after the crowd pelted the Indians with stones. A full-scale battle between the police and students ensued with tear gas and gunshots livening up the Karachi air.

Action men.
Left to right: Javed Miandad, Karachi's highest run-scorer with 1393 in 17 Tests there; Yousuf Youhana on his way to a century against England in 2000-01; Wasim Akram, 41 wicket in eight Tests at the National Stadium.

Overleaf:
Just good friends.
Abdul Qadir and Mike Gatting get to grips with each other.

NATIONAL STADIUM, KARACHI Ground Records

Result Summary

	Played	Won	Lost	Drawn
Pakistan	35	17	1	17
Australia	8	0	5	3
England	7	1	1	5
India	5	0	2	3
New Zealand	6	0	3	3
Sri Lanka	3	0	3	0
West Indies	6	0	3	3

Bangladesh, South Africa and Zimbabwe have
yet to play at the National Stadium

Highest Totals

565-9	Pakistan v New Zealand 1976-77
507	England v Pakistan 1961-61
502-7	England v Pakistan 1968-69

Lowest Completed Innings Totals

80	Australia v Pakistan 1956-57
116	Australia v Pakistan 1988-89
124	New Zealand v Pakistan 1955-56

Highest Match Aggregates

Runs	Wkts	
1585	31	Pakistan v New Zealand 1976-77
1289	31	Pakistan v India 1978-79
1279	28	Pakistan v India 1989-90

Lowest Match Aggregates (Result oriented matches)

Runs	Wkts	
531	31	Pakistan v Australia 1956-57

Highest Scores

211	Javed Miandad Pakistan v Australia 1988-89
206	Javed Miandad Pakistan v New Zealand 1976-77
205	ER Dexter England v Pakistan 1961-62
203*	Shoaib Mohammad Pakistan v New Zealand 1990-91
186	Zaheer Abbas Pakistan v India 1982-83

Highest Run Aggregates

Runs	Matches	Hundreds	
1393	17	3	Javed Miandad
855	13	4	Salim Malik
642	5	1	Shoaib Mohammad
615	11	2	Mudassar Nazar
579	9	2	Majid Khan

Partnership Records

298 for 1st	Aamir Sohail and Ijaz Ahmed Pakistan v West Indies 1997-98	
178 for 2nd	Hanif Mohammad and Saeed Ahmed Pakistan v West Indies 1958-59	
196 for 3rd	Javed Miandad and Shoaib Mohammad Pakistan v Australia 1988-89	
259 for 4th	Inzamam-ul-Haq and Yousuf Youhana Pakistan v England 2000-01	
213 for 5th	Mudassar Nazar and Zaheer Abbas Pakistan v India 1982-83	
178* for 6th	Salim Malik and Wasim Raja Pakistan v New Zealand 1984-85	
186 for 7th	RJ Hadlee and WK Lees New Zealand v Pakistan 1976-77	
100 for 8th	DR Hadlee and BW Yuile New Zealand v Pakistan 1969-70	
127 for 9th	Haroon Rashid and Rashid Khan Pakistan v Sri Lanka 1981-82	
63 for 10th	FJ Cameron and BE Congdon New Zealand v Pakistan 1964-65	

Best Bowling in an Innings.

8 for 60	Imran Khan	Pakistan v India 1982-83
7 for 49	Iqbal Qasim	Pakistan v Australia 1979-80
7 for 66	PH Edmonds	England v Pakistan 1977-78
7 for 80	Fazal Mahmood	Pakistan v Australia 1956-57
7 for 87	RJ Bright	Australia v Pakistan 1979-80

Best Bowling in a Match

13 for 114 (6-34, 7-80)	Fazal Mahmood Pakistan v Australia
11 for 79 (5-37, 6-42)	Zulfiqar Ahmed Pakistan v New Zealand
11 for 79 (3-19, 8-60)	Imran Khan Pakistan v India
11 for 83 (6-65, 5-18)	NGB Cook England v Pakistan
11 for 118 (4-69, 7-49)	Iqbal Qasim Pakistan v Australia

Highest Wicket Aggregates

Wkts	Matches	5WI	
59	13	5	Abdul Qadir
51	11	2	Imran Khan
44	9	2	Iqbal Qasim
41	8	1	Wasim Akram

Most Catches by Fielder

Catches	Matches	
17	17	Javed Miandad
16	9	Majid Khan

Most Dismissals by Wicketkeeper

Dismissals	Matches	
30	7	Salim Yousuf
21	10	Wasim Bari
20	6	Imtiaz Ahmed

SRI LANKA
Kumar Sangakkara

Since joining the league of Test-playing nations back in 1982, Sri Lankan cricket has rapidly become a serious, winning business. Once the epitome of happy-go-lucky cricketers, whose raison d'etre was not the winning but the taking part, Sri Lanka now has a team that can compete on any playing field and win. The most striking example of this was the now famous World Cup win in 1996, when Sanath Jayasuriya and Aravinda de Silva, to name but two, gave evidence, if it was needed, that Sri Lankans had the capacity to beat the best in the world.

In the Test arena also there have been some major successes both at home and overseas. What Sri Lankan can forget Muttiah Muralitharan spinning England to defeat at The Oval in 1998? In 2001-02 we whitewashed the West Indies three-nil at home and then repeated the result against Zimbabwe.

During this time seven grounds have hosted Test matches in Sri Lanka, with Colombo claiming four of them. Out of town, you will find two beautiful grounds at Kandy and at Galle while Moratuwa has the Tyronne Fernando Stadium.

The capital Colombo can claim four Test-match venues. The inaugural Test against England in February 1982 was held at the P Saravanamuttu Stadium. England won it comfortably enough although a half-century from a schoolboy called Arjuna Ranatunga served notice of what was to come.

The Colombo Cricket Club ground has hosted just three Tests while the R Premadasa Stadium achieved worldwide renown as the setting in 1997-98 for the world-record Test score. Facing an Indian first innings of 537 for eight, the Sri Lankan batsmen made the most of the pitch to compile a massive 952 for six. It was the third-highest total in first-class cricket and the highest in Test cricket, eclipsing England's 903 for seven at The Oval in 1938.

During the course of the innings, Sanath Jayasuriya and Roshan Mahanama shared a partnership of 576 – the highest for any wicket at Test level. Mahanama made 225 while Jayasuriya looked sure to overtake Brian Lara's record of 375 when he fell to the off-spinner Rajesh Chauhan for 340.

The last of Colombo's grounds and the one that has staged by far the most Test matches in Sri Lanka is the Sinhalese Sports Club ground.

SINHALESE SPORTS CLUB

England has Lord's, Australia has the MCG and Sri Lanka has the Sinhalese Sports Club, the SSC. The history is not as long and the names that figure in the annals of the ground's history are fewer but for Sri Lankans, the SSC is the home of cricket.

The setting at the SSC is not as picturesque as some other Test grounds in Sri Lanka. Asgiriya, overlooking the hills in Kandy, and the International Stadium by the sea in Galle can claim that accolade as high-rise concrete buildings have come up to spoil the vistas of the SSC.

It is, however, where the game was nurtured through schools matches and through club games and, although it cannot claim to be the first Test ground in Sri Lanka, it can claim seniority by dint of having staged more Tests than any other ground. Like Lord's and the MCG it houses the administrative headquarters of the national game; it is the spiritual home of Sri Lankan cricket.

My own association with the ground began as an 18-year-old when I turned up to play for Kandy against Colombo in the Under-19 district final. Apart from a few friends and some loyal family members, the ground was pretty deserted but it was still impressive. To walk out to the middle was

to imagine what it would be like to play in a Test match there; to take strike was to imagine how it would feel to make a hundred.

Like many other young Sri Lankans with a mad passion for cricket, I had been brought up on tales of the SSC. Bertie Wijesinghe, my cricket coach at school from Under-15 to Under-19 level, was an SSC stalwart and he used to talk about it a lot. He would also bring friends down to the Asgiriya Cricket Club. One of these was Sidath Wettimuny, something of a legend in Sri Lankan cricket after he thrashed the England bowlers around Lord's in 1984, making the small matter of 190. He was an inspiration.

Since that day, I have been fortunate enough both to play Test cricket at the SSC and to make a Test hundred there. The feeling on both occasions was better than anything I could imagine as an 18-year-old.

The cricket history of the stadium goes back over a century to the days when Sri Lanka was Ceylon, and is a saga of grit and determination of an association of very wealthy, influential and highly-educated people to display the best.

In 1899 a cricket match between a Combined Schools XI, drawn from three schools – Royal, St Thomas' and Wesley – and belonging exclusively

to the majority Sinhala community of Ceylon, and Colts CC, a leading club, resulted in an unexpected one-run win in the first innings for the Schools.

During the British occupation, which lasted from 1796 to 1948, the English expatriates tried to impress upon the natives that the game of cricket they indulged in was a part of their great upper-class cultural heritage. The Anglican missionaries, who accompanied the British rulers, introduced the game into their educational curriculum as a serious discipline containing many moral virtues and dubbed it "the king of sports". The missionaries provided ample facilities, good playing fields, equipment and coaches to impart basic coaching to the students of their two leading schools in Colombo, Royal and St Thomas' Mt Lavinia, establishments that lured the cream of the emerging native classes who could afford to pay high school fees. However, the keen and talented Sinhalese school leavers had no organised facilities to continue with the game.

This single-run victory for the Combined Schools XI created a sensation as school cricket was the centre of attraction at the time; it was to remain so in the entire pre-Test era with newspapers constantly carrying lavish praises of schoolboy achievements. Thus, the leading

newspaper, *Ceylon Independent*, wrote: "This splendid performance of the eleven members of the all-Sinhalese team brought them into the discussion on the formation of a Sinhalese club."

A club establishing itself in 1899 as the Sinhalese Sports Club acquired a lease of land with sandy soil covered with cinnamon trees at Victoria Park in 1900. The club was not short of development funds as it began to be patronised by the wealthiest of the Sinhalese, and the club duly unveiled its first turf wicket in 1917. Club membership was limited to Sinhalese men and, as in all Ceylonese clubs, the members imitated the British in every way from their mode of dress to the grammatical correctness – with a bit of slang thrown in–of their spoken English. They organised regular ballroom dancing, drank scotch and took great pride in their secondary education at leading Anglican missionary schools. They were also most particular in their use of fork and spoon instead of the fingers when eating the staple rice

Left: Cricket in Sri Lanka developed largely through the schools and the annual Battle of the Blues between the Royals and the Thomians at the SSC remains one of the big social events of the year.

Right: The SSC hosted its first Test on March 16, 1984 when Sri Lanka took on New Zealand. Since then it has become the "elder statesman" of Sri Lanka's grounds.

and curry. Arjuna Ranatunga, a man from a typical Sinhala background who went on to captain Sri Lanka in 56 Tests, once remarked in a television interview how uncomfortable he felt at the start of his career with the alien table manners of the SSC.

The club played its first match on July 14, 1900 at Galle Face against the Colombo Sports Club, which had ten Englishmen. It was an ominous beginning. *Ceylon Independent* reported: "SSC began its first match in style. Their performance has taken the cricket world by storm. Their first essay entitles them to an undisputed place among the first-class clubs." SSC fielded eight players groomed at St Thomas's and three from Royal. Five of them were schoolboys. This pattern continued during the pre-Test era. Royalists and Thomians had a stranglehold on the SSC team and consequently on the All Ceylon team, although just occasionally they recruited the best talent from outside Colombo, men like H Abeywardena who, was brought in from Galle in 1941.

In the earlier years the matches were friendly social events with even the British Governor gracing the occasion. SSC became the first Sri Lankan team to sponsor a foreign team when in, 1909, they invited the Australian team returning home from England. Thereafter the club invited many teams from India and acted as a regular stopover for Australian and English teams enroute to fight for the Ashes. The All Ceylon team, featuring the likes of Stanley Jayasinghe, FC de Saram and Gamini Goonesena who made the grade in county cricket, never beat either of these teams, although since the arrival of Test status, Sri Lanka has won against both.

In 1952, four years after independence, the club acquired another Crown lease of about 20 acres and shifted to the present venue, Maitland Place, which had been used as an aerodrome by the Allied forces during the Second World War. The first match on the new grounds was played on October 4, 1955 and a substantial pavilion was built the following year with Donovan Andree, Ceylon's biggest nightclub entrepreneur, contributing 300,000 rupees, a colossal sum of money in the 1950s.

In 1946 the club membership was opened to non-Sinhalese and ladies and, 20 years later, under the guidance of Colonel Derick de Saram, its livewire honorary cricket secretary who played for

Oxford University and Middlesex, scoring a century against the visiting Australians in 1934, the club converting the ground into a stadium with a capacity of 12,000.

Originally half a dozen workers attended to the duties on the grounds and the surrounding areas. The numbers have now trebled with much more care being taken to maintain the playing areas up to international standards and manicuring the lawns and flowerbeds to give the premises the look of quality. Ranil Abeynaike, its curator, tells a story about the inherent dangers for the ground staff:

"The eastern side of the field was once not used for cricket and was neglected. It was a breeding place for the creeping, crawling and flying types, from vicious vipers to cobras, water monitors, iguanas and tortoises and many species of feathered birds. There was only one incident of a human being falling victim to these creatures - a labourer sitting on a curled-up viper."

And you wonder why I became a wicketkeeper.

On February 17, 1982, Test cricket came to Sri Lanka. It was the dawn of an exciting new era and, after a slow start that saw just two Tests played there in the first six years, the SSC has emerged as the leading ground on the island.

In its relatively short history, it has certainly staged some memorable matches. Some of them Sri Lanka won; others we lost. One of our victories, against Bangladesh in the Asian Test championship in September 2001, gave the SSC a special place in the history books, as the Bangladeshi batsman Mohammad Ashraful became the youngest man to score a Test hundred. Perhaps that should be boy because he was one day short of his 17th birthday when he made his 114.

One of the defeats, however, came in August 1992 in a match against Australia that may be said to have changed the course of cricket history.

Sri Lanka dominated the game, bowling the Australians out for 256 and then piling up a massive 547 for eight declared. There were hundreds for Asanka Gurusinha, Romesh Kaluwitharana and Ranatunga; the only surprise was that Aravinda de Silva, who had shown a

Long before Sri Lanka gained Test status, their cricketers were making their mark across the world.
Gamini Goonesena was one such pilgrim. He not only played with Ceylon but represented Cambridge University, Nottinghamshire and New South Wales.

distinct liking for Australian bowling during the series Down Under three years before, made just six. Aravinda was a great player – as good a batsman as Sachin Tendulkar or Brian Lara – who came to relish playing at the SSC. He made five centuries there, including two in the same match against Pakistan in 1996-97, and is the only person to have made more than 1,000 Test runs at the ground. He was also one of the best off-spinners we had, although he did not often get the chance to show what he could do.

The Australians batted better in their second innings, with everyone getting into double figures, but the target for Sri Lanka in the fourth innings was only 181. The pitch was taking spin but it was still very gettable.

At 127 for two, with Aravinda batting beautifully, Sri Lanka looked home and dry. Then

Determined and inspirational.

Sri Lankan vice captain and man of the match Aravinda de Silva on his way to scoring 143 not out to pull the home to victory in the second and final tet against Zimbabwe by five wickets 18 January.

De Silva inspired skipper Arjuna Ranatunga to hit an unbeaten 87 that contributed to the Sri Lankan success.

Aravinda fell to Craig McDermott for 37. Ranatunga followed soon after and panic set in with wickets tumbling at regular intervals. Only Gurusinha held firm but he could do nothing when Allan Border tossed the ball to a chunky bleach-blonde leg-spinner. Having been caned all around the SSC in the first innings for a return of nought for 107 in 22 overs, the leg-spinner responded by taking the last three wickets for no runs in just 13 balls. Australia won by 16 runs and the legend of Shane Warne was born.

As a schoolboy watching on the television, it was a crushing experience. One minute we were all excited at the prospect of beating Australia, the next we were down and out in Colombo and Kandy.

Losing from that position was a harsh lesson in Test cricket but it was one that held Sri Lanka in good stead seven months later when England came to the SSC for a one-off Test. This time, Sri Lanka had a young spinner in their side called Muttiah Muralitharan who was to become every bit as influential as Warne over the next decade.

The English arrived in disarray having just lost three-nil in India, and Sri Lanka duly completed their misery with a five-wicket win. England started the game in positive fashion with Robin Smith making 128. But with Murali, playing his second Test, taking four wickets, they were restricted to 380.

The home batsmen responded with relish, five of the top six passing 50. Only Gurusinha with 43 missed out but de Silva, all wristy elegance, and Hashan Tillekeratne ensured a healthy first-innings lead as they took Sri Lanka to 469. The English batsmen faltered as the off-spinner Jayanantha Warnaweera spun his own web and Sri Lanka were left with the task of scoring 140 for an historic first win over the old colonial masters.

I was only 15 at the time but we followed Sri Lanka's progress on the television with our hearts in our mouths as John Emburey and Phil Tufnell started to pick up the wickets. At 61 for four, we had that sinking feeling we experienced against the Australians but then Ranatunga and Tillekeratne showed that they had learnt their lesson well, taking Sri Lanka to within four runs of the target before Ranatunga fell to Tufnell. Victory, however, was ours and, as David Hopps, one of the English journalists covering the Test wrote in *The Guardian*,

the celebrations were long and noisy. "Sri Lanka's fourth win in 43 Tests - and their second in succession - was richly deserved. It was celebrated by 7,000 spectators, at least half of whom had been given free admission at lunchtime, and by a man flinging firecrackers which made such a racket that it would have been no surprise, bearing in mind the country's recent civil disorder, if the army had not mistakenly declared another state of emergency."

It was a party to remember and one that everyone connected with the long history of the SSC enjoyed. The atmosphere at the ground has always been good although attendances for Test matches have dwindled. Sri Lankans seem to prefer watching the one-day game but you still get an array of men and women in colourful outfits, young and old and from all walks of life, baila singing, dancing and papare bands creating a carnival atmosphere. The crowd can be vociferous but they are not offensive; in many ways they are like a crowd in the West Indies. They genuinely appreciate good cricket, whoever plays it – especially Percy, the self-styled poet of Sri Lankan cricket. Percy sits up in the stands, leading the chanting and offering instant verse: he is not Byron but some of it is quite good.

We had a less happy experience when England came back in 2000-01. This time Graham Thorpe made 113 and we slipped to 81 all out in our second innings. England only needed 74 to win but we almost did an Australia on them, as we took six wickets before Thorpe took them past the winning line. Maybe if we had another 30 runs we would have won that one too.

Since that game the SSC has been good to us, as we have won five on the trot there, three of them by an innings. Murali has had a lot to do with this success. He is easily the highest wicket-taker at the ground with 96 and has taken five wickets in an innings seven times there, with a best of eight for 87 against India. With Murali, however, it is not just that he takes so many wickets; it is the aura that he brings with him to the team. We know going into a Test match that the opposition are scared of him; many of the world's top batsmen do not have a clue how to play him. It seems to be only the left-handers who get to grips with him. Thorpe is one example but Andy Flower and Lara are others who tamed him at the SSC.

As a Tamil within Sri Lanka he is also a unifying force, doing more for the peace process than any politician ever will. When Murali bowls, he bowls for the whole of Sri Lanka and people from every corner of society, never mind their political beliefs, are behind him. As for questions about his action, I have no doubt that he is absolutely legal. To me he is a clean bowler and a great one. With all due respect to Warne, I believe Murali is the greatest spinner in the world. His figures speak for themselves but they are doubly impressive when you consider that he has not had the back-up firepower that Warne has had with Glenn McGrath, Jason Gillespie, Brett Lee and so on.

The eyes have it.

Ask any Sri Lankan who is the best spin bowler in the world and there is no doubt who they will say: "Murali!"

Muttiah Muralitharan has overcome suspicions about his action to become the most successful off-spinner in the world. At the SSC he reigns supreme with 96 wickets from 15 Tests.

Asanka Gurusinha is stumped by England captain Alec Stewart off Phil Tufnell for 43 during the one-off Test in 1992-93. Sri Lanka's five-wicket win was their first against England and proved a cornerstone in their advance as a Test nation.

Murali's finest achievement at the SSC may have been the eight for 87 he took during a memorable Test against India in 2001. Murali's bowling on the first day dismissed India for 234 and we then sat back to enjoy a batting feast. I made 47 which, in the context of the innings, was a relative failure as four of my team-mates made centuries: Marvan Atapattu, Mahela Jayawardene, Tillekeratne and Thilan Samaraweera. Harbhajan Singh, fresh from his heroics against Australia, managed just two for 185. Murali picked up another three wickets in the second innings and we dismissed them for 299 to win by an innings and 77 runs.

Another bowler who has enjoyed himself at the SSC is Chaminda Vaas, a much underrated left-arm swing bowler, who earned a place in the history books with a match return of 14 for 191 in our ten-wicket defeat of the West Indies in 2001-02.

Although we won easily enough in the end, this was a great Test match that featured two truly great performances. It was pretty much a duel between Vaas and Lara, whose battles with Murali in the first two Tests were the stuff of legend. That is not to belittle the contribution of Hashan Tillekeratne, who weighed in with an, excellent 204 not out; it is just that Lara and Vaas were on a different level.

To stand behind the wicket when Lara is batting is a double-edged sword. On the one hand you want to get rid of him as soon as possible to prevent him running riot and yet on the other you don't mind him staying a while. To watch him at such close quarters is a privilege. His balance and timing is exquisite.

In the first innings he held the West Indies together, posting his fourth Test double-century and passing 7,000 runs in the process of making 221. Even then, Lara was never convinced himself that he had the better of Murali. I remember one occasion during his innings when he played down the wrong line. He turned around to me and laughed. "I just can't read this guy," he said. That did not stop him from using his feet and hitting him through midwicket, the kind of shot that makes you wonder, how does he do that?

The only other contributions came from Ramnaresh Sarwan and Carl Hooper as they made 390. Chaminda blew the rest of them away in

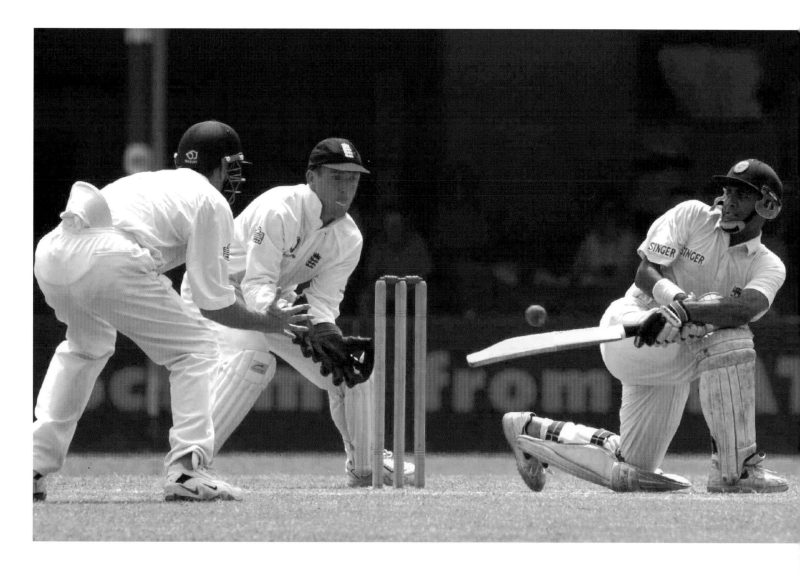

taking seven for 120 including the wicket of Lara, bowled off an inside edge.

Our innings centred around Hashan's patient double-century and for the first time since 1978-79, the West Indies conceded over 600. Chaminda was soon among the wickets again, swinging the ball awkwardly, but Lara once more stood in our path. At the start of the fifth day they were 92 behind with eight wickets in hand as Sarwan offered Lara some support. In the seventh over, however, he followed a wide one from Vaas and edged it to me. I have never been so happy to hold on to a nick. It exposed the West Indies middle order and Chaminda ran through them again, this time taking seven for 71 and finishing off the innings with four wickets in nine balls.

Lara made 130 before being bowled by Nuwan Zoysa to finish the three-Test series with 688 runs. His 351 runs in this Test were the most by a

Left: Roshan Mahanama scored 2,576 runs in his 52 Tests including 109 against new Zealand in 1992-93. Five years later, he shared in the world record partnership of 576 for the second wicket with Sanath Jayasuriya at the Premadasa Stadium in Colombo.

Above: Hashan Tillekeratne sweeps against England in 2000-01. Tillekeratne is one of Sri Lanka's heaviest run-scorers with 1,003 at the SSC. he has hit three hundreds there including an unbeaten 204 against the West indies in 2001-02.

batsman on the losing side in a match. He did not deserve to be beaten that day any more than he deserved to be a part of a team beaten three-nil.

Chaminda enjoyed another great day at the SSC in 2000-01 when he took eight for 19 against Zimbabwe, the best return ever in a one-day international.

Vaas is unusual in that the SSC seems to be more of a hunting ground for spin bowlers. Apart from Murali, Nicky Boje, Anil Kumble and the New Zealander Daniel Vettori have all had profitable experiences there. Incidentally, another Kiwi, Martin Crowe has the distinction of being the snail of the SSC – in 1983-84 he managed just 19 in 217 minutes. I know he was a fine player but I am not sure I would have enjoyed standing behind the stumps for that one.

Of the quick bowlers, Ravi Ratnayeke, Chris Cairns and Wasim Akram have all had days to remember while Brett Schultz, the South African left-armer, sent down arguably the quickest spell when he took nine wickets in their win there in 1993.

On a personal note, the SSC has been good to me. My first Test there was against South Africa in 2000. It happened to coincide with Arjuna Ranatunga's last Test so it was a very special occasion. I did not make many runs but after batting at number six during the first two Tests, I was promoted to number three in the second innings. It was the real start of my run in the team. And yet, amid all that, my abiding memory will be of Arjuna tucking into pork chops for his lunch.

A tale of two left-handers.
Left: A fine 113 from Graham Thorpe in the 2001-02 Test led to England scoring a surprise victory at the SSC. Kumar Sangakkara is the wicketkeeper.

Above: Arjuna Ranatunga was not just a robust, free-scoring batsman but a captain who took Sri Lankan cricket by the scruff of the neck and shook it vigorously. His confrontational methods did not always win him friends around the world but he turned Sri Lanka into a force to be reckoned with.

Usually we had rice, lentils, salad, what you might call healthy food for our lunch but Arjuna had requested pork chops and Chinese food and, because it was his final Test, the team physio, Alex Kountouri, complied. I am not sure I ever saw Arjuna quite so happy.

He was, of course, a massively influential player who dragged Sri Lanka out of the cosseted, forelock-tugging mindset that we were in when we first joined the Test scene. Under Arjuna, we became a Test nation that stood up to the old world and demanded respect. Some people did not like it – Warne once remarked that it would be good for international cricket if Arjuna quit – but for Sri Lanka he was a vital element in our development. He did much the same for the SSC, turning it from a club dominated by the elite public schools of Colombo to one which is now more open and forward-thinking.

Having achieved one schoolboy ambition by playing for Sri Lanka, I was fortunate enough to fulfil another when, on December 28, 2001, I completed my first and, as I write, only Test century at the SSC. It came at the expense of Zimbabwe and the best thing about it was that it led to an innings victory and ultimately a three-nil series win. I made 128 and loved every moment of it. Sometimes, as a batsman, you have days when you know it is going to be your day and this was one of those as I dropped into a rhythm right from the start. Conditions were perfect; the outfield was like glass.

When I reached three figures I did not really take in the achievement. I was too involved in the game at hand and going on to make enough runs to put Zimbabwe under pressure. It was only when I was back in the pavilion and then, when the game was over and I was able to have a few days away from the cricket that I was able to think about it.

Sri Lankan glory.

Left: The looks on the faces of England's Robin Smith and Phil Tufnell tells it all - Sri Lanka have beaten the old colonial masters for the first time in Test cricket.
Above: For all the advances Sri Lanka have made in the Test arena, their greatest achievement remains winning the one-day World Cup in 1996. For that they had to thank Arjuna Ranatunga, their wily captain, and the graceful batting skills of Aravinda de Silva.

I thought about this game and my part in it and then began to think about some of the others who have made Test hundreds at the SSC. It made me realise how privileged I am to have been a small part in the wonderful jigsaw that makes up the history of this great ground.

Above: Chaminda Vaas is undoubtedly Sri Lanka's best fast bowler ever. His tally of 52 wickets at the SSC is second only to the phenomenal Muttiah Muralitharan and in 2001-02 destroyed the West Indies by taking seven wickets in each innings.

SSC Ground Records

Result Summary

	Played	Won	Lost	Drawn
Sri Lanka	22	10	5	7
Australia	2	1	0	1
Bangladesh	2	0	2	0
England	2	1	1	0
India	5	1	1	3
Pakistan	2	1	0	1
New Zealand	3	0	2	1
South Africa	2	1	0	1
West Indies	1	0	1	0
Zimbabwe	3	0	3	0

Highest Totals

627-9	Sri Lanka v West Indies 2001-02
610-6	Sri Lanka v India 2001-02
586-6	Sri Lanka v Zimbabwe 2001-02

Lowest Completed Innings Totals

| 81 | Sri Lanka v England 2000-01 |
| 90 | Bangladesh v Sri Lanka 2001-02 |

Highest Match Aggregates

Runs	Wkts	
1438	38	Sri Lanka v Australia 1992-93
1403	32	Sri Lanka v India 1997-98
1309	22	Sri Lanka v India 1998-99

Lowest Match Aggregates (Result oriented matches)

Runs	Wkts	
645	36	Sri Lanka v England 2000-01

Highest Scores

242	DPMD Jayawardene Sri Lanka v India 1998-99
221	BC Lara 221 West Indies v Sri Lanka 2001-02
204*	HP Tillekaratne 204* Sri Lanka v West Indies 2001-02
201	MS Atapattu 201 Sri Lanka v Bangladesh 2001-02

Highest Run Aggregates

Runs	Matches	Hundreds	
1257	16	5	PA de Silva
1232	16	2	ST Jayasuriya
1003	14	3	HP Tillekaratne
988	16	2	A Ranatunga
954	11	4	DPMD Jayawardene

Partnership Records

171 for 1st	M Prabhakar and NS Sidhu India v Sri Lanka 1993-94
232 for 2nd	RS Dravid and S Ramesh India v Sri Lanka 1998-99
218 for 3rd	PA de Silva and ST Jayasuriya Sri Lanka v India 1997-98
230 for 4th	AP Gurusinha and A Ranatunga Sri Lanka v Australia 1992-93
150 for 5th	SC Ganguly and SR Tendulkar India v Sri Lanka 1997-98
189* for 6th	PA de Silva and A Ranatunga Sri Lanka v Zimbabwe 1997-98
194* for 7th	TT Samaraweera and HP Tillakaratne Sri Lanka v India 2001-02
80 for 8th	DW Fleming and RT Ponting Australia v Sri Lanka 1999-2000
83 for 9th	M Muralitharan and HP Tillakaratne Sri Lanka v England 1992-93
90 for 10th	Arshad Khan and Wasim Akram Pakistan v Sri Lanka 1999-2000

Best Bowling in an Innings

8 for 87	M Muralitharan Sri Lanka v India 2001-02
7 for 71	WPUJC Vaas Sri Lanka v West Indies 2001-02
7 for 120	WPUJC Vaas Sri Lanka v West Indies 2001-02

Best Bowling in a Match

14 for 191 (7-120, 7-71)	WPUJC Vaas Sri Lanka v West Indies
11 for 196 (8-87, 3-109)	M Muralitharan Sri Lanka v India
10 for 111 (5-13, 5-98)	M Muralitharan Sri Lanka v Bangladesh

Highest Wicket Aggregates

Wkts	Matches	5WI	
96	15	7	M Muralitharan
52	13	3	WPUJC Vaas

Most Catches by Fielder

Catches	Matches	
29	14	HP Tillakaratne
19	11	DPMD Jayawardene
14	14	MS Atapattu

Most Dismissals by Wicketkeeper

Dismissals	Matches	
27	9	RS Kaluwitharana
18	6	KC Sangakkara
11	3	A Flower

ZIMBABWE

Andy Flower

In a country where consistency and reliability are notoriously lacking these days, it is good to know that when a Test tour to Zimbabwe is announced, everyone knows exactly where the matches will be played. There are effectively only two centres capable of sustaining a Test match, Harare and Bulawayo, and each one has a single ground currently in use.

That said, Bulawayo can actually claim two of Zimbabwe's three Test grounds. The first Test to be played there in November 1992 against New Zealand took place at the Bulawayo Athletic Club Ground. The match ended in a draw but not before the Kiwi opener Rod Latham and Zimbabwe's Kevin Arnott had claimed the distinction of being the only men to score Test centuries there. Dipak Patel, an off-spinner who opened the bowling for New Zealand, took the honours with the ball claiming six for 113 in the Zimbabwe first innings.

That was it though for the Athletic Club which gave way to Queen's Sports Club in 1994 when Zimbabwe hosted Sri Lanka.

Queen's has witnessed its share of great moments, the most notable perhaps being the "we flippin' murdered 'em" Test against England in 1996-97. The comment came from David Lloyd, the England coach, who was incensed at Zimbabwe's bowling tactics as England chased 205 from 37 overs to win the match. Nick Knight hit a superb 96 but, with the Zimbabweans firing the ball down the leg side and the umpires refusing to call wides, the English just failed in their bid. In spite of what Lloyd thought, the match ended in a nail-biting draw with the scores dead level.

Dave Houghton made the highest individual score at Queen's when he hit 266 against Sri Lanka in 1994-95, although Marvan Atapattu got some measure of revenge five years later with an innings of 216. Guy Whittall's 203 not out against New Zealand in 1997-98 is the other double-century scored there. Two leg-spinners, Adam Huckle and Paul Strang, have both taken ten wickets in a match at Queen's, but perhaps the finest spell of hostile fast bowling came from Wasim Akram in 1994-95 when his second-innings five for 43 on a difficult pitch set Pakistan up for a win that helped them to take the series.

For all that, in terms of seniority of Test grounds in Zimbabwe and the depth of history, there can be little argument with the Harare Sports Club.

HARARE SPORTS CLUB

"Cricket? It civilises people and creates good gentlemen. I want everyone to play cricket in Zimbabwe. I want ours to be a nation of gentlemen."
Robert Mugabe

It seems a long time since Robert Mugabe waxed so positively about cricket. Over a decade in fact. A decade that has seen his own stock dip significantly in the world arena, a decade that has seen Zimbabwe take its place at the high table of Test cricket and a decade in which the Harare Sports Club has established itself as one of the top cricket venues in the world.

Since Dave Houghton tossed up with India's Mohammad Azharuddin at the start of Zimbabwe's inaugural Test match on October 18, 1992, the HSC has witnessed almost every major moment in the country's cricket history: Houghton's feat of becoming the first man since the Australian Charles Bannerman to score a century in his country's first Test; a first win in January 1995 against Pakistan that included a record partnership between brothers in Test cricket and the arrival of Henry Olonga, the first black man to play for Zimbabwe; "chicken farmer" Eddo Brandes humbling England with a one-day hat-trick; and a couple of World Cup matches in 2003 where politics momentarily eclipsed cricket.

I have been fortunate enough to have seen the vast majority of it, either from the pavilion or from the middle; Fortunate enough to have watched as a youngster the founding fathers of Zimbabwe cricket, Duncan Fletcher, Andy Pycroft, Peter Rawson, Jackie du Preez and even Dave Houghton, ply their trade. Fortunate enough to have played with and against many of the great names of international cricket at the HSC: Houghton's name pops up again alongside Sachin Tendulkar, Kapil Dev, Steve Waugh, Shane Warne, Glenn McGrath, Alec Stewart, Graeme Hick, Allan Donald, Wasim Akram and Heath Streak to name just a few. Not a bad roll call for what amounts to a picturesque, unpretentious little cricket ground.

During the 2003 World Cup, protests against Mugabe's government, the on/off/cancelled nature of the England match and increased security measures, lent the HSC a temporary cloak of unease. For Henry Olonga and myself there was a definite atmosphere of malice, not from the Namibian or Indian players, nor from the regular lovable hoodlums in Castle Corner. It came more

October 18, 1992.
Test cricket comes to the HSC as Zimbabwe openers
Grant Flower (left) and Kevin Arnott march out at the
start of their inaugural Test against India.

from not knowing how the government and the security guards, armed with their AK47s, might react to our black-armband protest and to the possible crowd reaction. As it happened, we should have feared the Indian bowlers more, but it did peel away briefly the laid-back charm of the ground.

The HSC's traditional cucumber sandwich-style tranquillity gives no hint of the fierce sunshine and storms that are a feature of this part of Africa. By and large the ground has a clientele that is old-school cricket lover, the deckchair brigade who appreciate a fine shot or a sharp catch with a ripple of polite applause and a second glass of Pimm's.

That is not to say the HSC does not get its share of noise, and the players in the middle catch just about every word of the heckling. This is usually at its loudest in the late afternoon, when the bar at Castle Corner, a miniature version of Bay 13 at the Melbourne Cricket Ground, is beginning to run dry. Or when either South Africa or England are in town. The South Africans bring a derby atmosphere to the HSC which has tended to inspire them more than the Zimbabweans. Indeed, Gary Kirsten, who made 220 for them in the Test in 2001-02 and Allan Donald who took eight for 71, and 11 wickets in the match, against us in 1995-96, hold the ground records.

When the English arrive so does the Barmy Army, and that changes the atmosphere completely. The songs may get a bit repetitive but they certainly bring something extra to the HSC.

The English, of course, like the South Africans have a traditional affinity with Zimbabwe from the days when it was Rhodesia, and with Harare, originally named Fort Salisbury in Victorian times in honour of the British Prime Minister, Lord Salisbury. By 1902 Salisbury was the capital of southern Rhodesia, and by 1909 the settlers were playing cricket at the Salisbury Sports Club. In 1956, a crowd of 26,000 crammed into the ground to watch Rhodesia play the MCC, still the highest attendance for any match at the HSC. Peter May marked the occasion with a fluent 206.

Many of Rhodesia's Currie Cup matches were played here although some of the most famous exploits of Mike Procter, their greatest import, in the early 1970s were played out at the Police Ground. It was there that he took five wickets for eight runs against Border and where he scored

two of the centuries that took him to a Bradman-equalling run of six successive centuries.

There have been numerous developments at the HSC, most notably in the run-up to the World Cup when the Zimbabwe Cricket Union, whose own administrative offices have been substantially upgraded from the weather-beaten wooden offices of the 1990s, built a new western stand and extensively upgraded seating arrangements. These developments, however, have not taken anything away from the homespun character of the ground.

The colonial gables of the HSC, beneath which is situated the fairly recent addition of a modern

pub, the Keg and Maiden, just across the boundary rope of the Club House End of the ground, are a reminder of how far back cricket goes. Another pub, the Red Lion, is situated closer to the nets and this is where some of the HSC's resident supporters hang out. When I say resident, I mean it. One of them, Brian Wishart, whose son Craig has played for Zimbabwe, gives the Red Lion number as his office telephone while he quaffs a couple of cold ones.

Brian is a local legend because of his drinking capacity and he is often to be found shooting the breeze with similar-minded folk, men like Horace Kinsey and Gerry Blair. They used to operate the

Behind bars.
Grant Flower, Zimbabwe's most-capped player, has saved some of his best performances for the HSC notably the unbeaten 201 he made against Pakistan in 1995 and the two hundreds in the same match against New Zealand two years later.

scoreboard on a semi-professional basis; they did not actually get paid for it, they just used to get free beer – as much as they needed during the day. On a hot day, it was never wise to trust the scoreboard. During one-day internationals they even had their own challenge going on as each of them would mark up their beer tallies on the board.

Long before the arrival of Test cricket, the HSC was hosting quality cricket and cricketers who either were already a household name or were about to become one. A quick glance at some of the Young West Indian, Australian or England A teams that toured reveals some great names: Mark Taylor, Brian Lara, Courtney Walsh, Michael Atherton, Graham Thorpe. And there was some pretty good home grown talent as well. Kevin Curran was always a consistent performer against these teams and would have flourished if he had chosen to play Test cricket rather than pursue a career in county cricket in England.

Another who lit up the HSC in the pre-Test days was Hick; a local boy, he was perhaps the most talented batsman to come out of Zimbabwe. I remember batting with him in a match against Ireland at the HSC when he made 309 in no time at all. His timing and his power were beyond anything I had seen. However, he chose to play for England, with whom he enjoyed a reasonably successful career, although I cannot help thinking that with the added pressure of expectation that followed him in the British press that he never quite did himself justice. Hick had the talent to be up there with Graeme Pollock and Barry Richards.

For Zimbabwean cricketers, October 18, 1992 was the day the circus finally came to town, the moment when Test cricket set up its tent on the HSC. The purple jacarandas were in full bloom that Sunday morning when our opening batsmen, Kevin Arnott and Grant Flower, walked out to the middle after Houghton had won the toss and chosen to bat. There was only a small crowd but that did not detract from the occasion. For the players, it was a leap into the unknown against an Indian team that contained players of the calibre of Kapil Dev, Mohammed Azharuddin, Anil Kumble, Ravi Shastri as well as a young Tendulkar.

For us the enormity of the occasion really only sank in the day before when we were swarmed by journalists, mainly Indian, after our nets session. And then there was the pre-match dinner instituted by John Hampshire, our coach. More than anyone, he prepared us for the task of Test cricket, although it helped that we had two old-stagers in the team, 35-year-old Houghton and John Traicos, who at 45 was making his own history. Traicos, a conventional off-spinner with a drifting arm ball and nagging accuracy, had played three Tests for South Africa against Australia in 1969-70 before isolation closed the door on them. Twenty-two years and 222 days later he was making his second Test debut. As it turned out both of the oldies had memorable games, with Houghton scoring Zimbabwe's first Test century and Traicos collecting our first five-wicket haul.

In some respects Houghton was fortunate to land the milestone. It should have gone to my brother Grant, who batted superbly to reach 82 before being given out caught behind by Kiran More off Javagal Srinath. He was nowhere near it. Nothing should be taken away from the way Houghton batted, though. He controlled the bowling from the moment he went in, never looking flustered against the pace of Kapil, Srinath and Manoj Prabhakar as he adopted his back-and-across shuffle, and then he attacked the spinners Shastri and Kumble with a variety of slog-sweeps and forays down the pitch to hit over the top. It was a great moment for Houghton when he reached his hundred.

On a personal level I enjoyed my first experience of Test cricket, making 59 and adding 165 with Dave for the sixth wicket. Our score of 456 was not only the highest ever made by a country in its first Test but also gave us a great chance of winning our debut match, something that only Australia had done in the very first contest against England.

Three wickets from Traicos, including Azharuddin and Tendulkar, had the Indians on the ropes at 105 for five and struggling to avoid the follow-on, but Sanjay Manjrakar and Kapil pulled them out of the mire in their contrasting styles. Manjrekar dropped anchor, scoring the fourth-slowest hundred in Test cricket, while Kapil struck a rapid 60 that only ended when he was bowled by Traicos. The old man finished with five for 86 but the Test ended in a draw.

Heath Streak burst on to the international scene with 22 wickets in the three-Test series with Pakistan in 1995. He remains by some distance Zimbabwe's finest-ever Test bowler and has taken 67 wickets in 15 matches at the HSC.

Harare Sports Club.
On the occasion of the inaugural test match played between Zimbabwe and South Africa, 1996.

The purple jacarandas were in full bloom.
Beyond the pavilion lies Harare's championship golf course, and to the right behind
the row of cypresses or pines lie the grounds of State House, residence of President Robert Mugabe.

Our first victory came in what proved to be a surreal series against Pakistan in early 1995. It started with a mix-up over the toss and ended amid allegations of match-fixing. In the light of allegations coming out of Australia, there were suggestions that Pakistan threw the first Test, but all I can say is that while their batsmen played very loosely outside off stump in all three Tests, we bowled, batted and caught like demons in that first encounter at the HSC.

It was also significant for another reason; it marked the debut of 18-year-old Henry Olonga, a fast bowler whose immense promise was undermined by an action that led to him being called for chucking. For all that, Olonga was the real McCoy whose presence in the side opened up cricket to a new generation of young black Zimbabweans.

The portents for a famous victory were hardly good when Salim Malik and I had to toss up twice. As I flipped a Zimbabwean dollar coin, which has a bird on one side and a ruin on the other, I heard a mumble from Salim, along the lines of "Brrrin." I looked at match referee Jackie Hendriks and explained that I had not understood the call. He concurred and he called for a re-toss which I won. With Zimbabwe struggling at 42 for three, I did momentarily regret questioning it.

Fortunately, Grant had dug in with that no-frills toughness that made him one of the world's leading openers and I joined him to stabilise the innings. Then we started to play pretty well in our differing styles. Grant was solidity personified; I played a few more shots. The partnership crept up to 100, moved more confidently on to 200 and by close of play we had taken it to 247.

By then we both had our hundreds. On the second morning we took it to 269 before I carelessly uppercut a short ball from Kabir Khan to backward point where Wasim took the catch. Out for 156, with the Flower partnership entering the record books as the highest between brothers in Test cricket, eclipsing Ian and Greg Chappell's third wicket stand of 264 against New Zealand in 1973-74.

My departure left the way open for Guy Whittall to take up the attack with 113 not out as he and Grant added an unbroken 233 for the fourth wicket. When the declaration came, Grant was still unbeaten with 201 to his name. Back in the changing room, another record of sorts had been set as Stuart Carlisle, making his debut, had been sitting padded up for 11 hours without batting.

The next milestone was Henry's, taking the ball at the end of the second day. His third ball claimed the wicket of Saeed Anwar but the following day saw Henry's fortunes change. First he was called for chucking and then he had to leave the field with a side strain that ruled him out of the rest of the series. But he would return with a better action and to enjoy greater success.

Without Olonga, it fell to Streak to unsettle the Pakistani batsmen. Still only 20, he bowled through the extreme heat and the pain of an infected big toe, to take six for 90 as we bowled them out for 322. Following on, they collapsed to 35 for five as David Brain, whose accuracy was once described as that of a "demented spraypainter", found his radar to claim three early wickets. Inzamam-ul-Haq resisted with 65 but, with Streak claiming another three wickets to make it nine in the match, we closed out victory on the fourth afternoon.

We had won our 11th Test by an innings and 64 runs, the most crushing victory for a first win by any Test-playing country, against one of the most powerful teams in the world. New Zealand had taken 26 years to achieve that milestone; India had needed 19 years.

The celebrations started straight after the match when Wasim led the Pakistan players into our changing-room to congratulate us. That was followed by a long night in downtown Harare. The hangovers, however, both actual and metaphorical, took a long time to clear. We lost the second Test in Bulawayo and, when we returned to the HSC, the third as well.

That was a closely contested game in which Inzamam was again to prove our stumbling block, scoring 101 not out and 83. Needing 239 to win, we batted badly in the second innings and lost by 99 runs. After the high of the first Test it was a desperate anti-climax to lose the series. That said, Streak had established himself with another eight wickets to finish with 22 in three Tests.

Zimbabwe suffered a lull when the South Africans came to visit late in 1995. Andrew Hudson made a good 135 and Donald made use of a rapid pitch and blew us away with 11 wickets.

With Donald and company gone the next big test was the arrival of England in 1996-97. Ray Illingworth, their former manager, had cranked up the rancour level when he stated: "If we cannot beat Zimbabwe, we really are in trouble." What he had not realised was that with Alastair Campbell now installed as captain and Houghton back in the frame as coach, Zimbabwe were playing some good cricket

By the time they came to the HSC they were already flustered. The first Test in Bulawayo ended with the scores level and their coach David Lloyd close to apoplexy. His mood was hardly improved when we beat them three-nil in the one-day series with Brandes taking a hat-trick, only the tenth in one-day internationals and the first against England. In between times the Test, however, ended in a draw when Alec Stewart got them out of trouble with his first Test century as a wicketkeeper.

The Test against Stephen Fleming's New Zealand team in September 1997 was notable for being the first time in the history of Test cricket that three sets of brothers were playing for the same team: Gavin and John Rennie, Paul and Bryan Strang and Grant and Andy Flower. The family connections would have had an added twist had Guy Whittall's cousin Andy also been selected. Instead, he was 12th man. Grant duly became the first Zimbabwean to score centuries in each innings when he made 104 and 151 while Fleming, an impressive close catcher, took seven catches in the Test – five in the first innings – equalling the all-time record.

Wisden described our 61-run win over India in 1998-99 as "enthralling" but noted: "Until the final moments on the fourth day, the crowd never numbered more than a few hundred."

It was a shame because it was a cracking game of cricket that we won in spite of missing Grant and Guy with injuries. Neil Johnson had just returned to Zimbabwe and made his debut, joining what must be a tiny elite of bowlers who have removed Tendulkar in both innings of a Test. Olonga was also back in the side and celebrated by taking

Herschelle Gibbs is just one of several South Africans to have enjoyed themselves at the HSC. Gibbs scored a fine 147 in 2001-02, sharing a first wicket-record partnership for the ground of 256 with Gary Kirsten.

The one that got away.
The Zimbabwe fielders realise that their chance of beating England in 1996-97 had gone following Alistair Campbell's failure to hold on to a chance from Alec Stewart.
The England wicketkeeper went on to make 101 not out.

five wickets in the first innings and earning himself the Man-of-the-Match award.

India led by 59 runs on the first innings thanks to a typically solid 118 from Rahul Dravid. However, Gavin Rennie, with 84, and Wishart put on 138 for the first wicket and suddenly we were calling the shots. When the fourth day began we were leading by 160 with eight wickets in hand but by lunchtime we had crumbled for just another 74 runs. This left India 235 to win.

Olonga, Streak and Johnson ripped into the top order to leave them teetering precariously on 37 for four. Then Dravid and Sourav Ganguly rebuilt the innings, adding 67 in a manner that changed the mood of the match. However, Adam Huckle got Ganguly leg-before and the Indians collapsed, losing five wickets for 29 runs. At 133 for nine, the game was over, wasn't it? Their last pair of Srinath and Harbhajan Singh were not so sure, putting on 40 before Srinath was run out. Relief was not the word.

At the end of the century, the top two teams in the world were Australia and South Africa and, in

the space of four weeks at the end of 1999, we suffered heavy defeats at the hands of both.

In October, Australia arrived fresh from defeat in Sri Lanka and were in no mood to allow another David to spit in Goliath's eye. Batting first on one of groundsman Charlie Wallace's fast and bouncy pitches, we were quickly dismissed for 194 whereupon we had to watch the Waugh show as Mark made 90 and Steve 151. With Murray Goodwin making 91, we saved the innings defeat but they only needed four balls to knock off the five runs they needed for a ten-wicket victory. McGrath and Warne took six wickets each in the match and it also proved to be the last hurrah of Ian Healy's career; it was an honour of sorts to be the 395th and final victim of his 119 Tests.

The following month we were outclassed by South Africa, defeated by an innings and 219 runs; it was our worst defeat since we had started playing Test cricket. The omens were bad as the players were in the midst of a pay dispute with the Zimbabwe Cricket Union and Campbell resigned as captain 48 hours before the game. We were also without the injured Streak and Paul Strang while Johnson was unfit to bowl.

All out for 102 in 46.5 overs, we were put in our place by Jacques Kallis and Mark Boucher who both made hundreds. We needed 360 to avoid the innings defeat but we collapsed for a second time for a defeat that deeply hurt.

It was September 2001, just under two years later, when we hosted the old enemy again. Zimbabwe still lost, by nine wickets this time, but from a purely selfish point of view, this was the match that reinforced my own love affair with the HSC.

The South Africans batted first, posting a huge first-innings score. Kirsten and Herschelle Gibbs put on 256 for the first wicket and when Gibbs was bowled by Travis Friend for 147, Kirsten added 199 with Kallis. By close of play on the first day South Africa were 414 for one: heartbreaking stuff. Kirsten eventually went for 220 and Kallis had 157 not out when Shaun Pollock declared at 600 for three. For our response, it may be best to turn to *Wisden*:

"(Dion) Ebrahim showed no fear of Pollock and scored a fine 71 before making a gift of his wicket. After that it was (Andy) Flower all the way; a giant among pygmies. His tenth Test century came, as so often, with all about him falling. On the way, he

passed 4,000 Test runs. Apart from Ebrahim, only Friend supported him, in a valuable ninth-wicket stand of 75, before Flower was last out, adjudged lbw (for 142) despite being hit outside off while playing a stroke.

"Three quick wickets in the follow-on meant that he was soon in again. This time Flower found the 18-year-old Masakadza able and willing to put his head down. They added 186, and Hamilton Masakadza failed by only 15 runs to join the elite few with centuries in their first two Tests. Shortly afterwards, Flower became the first wicketkeeper to make two hundreds in the same Test and he would surely have turned this one into a double had he not run out of partners...stranded on 199 after batting ten minutes short of ten hours. He was only the second player after South Africa's Jimmy Sinclair against England in 1898-99 to score more than half his team's aggregate over two innings in a Test."

Pollock's men quickly knocked off the required 79 runs to post a nine-wicket win but it was bizarre walking off the field on that last day, September 11, only to hear about events at the Twin Towers in New York. Everyone will remember where they were that day and it seems odd to think of a small band of cricketers sipping beer at the HSC keeping in touch with the outside world via the occasional cellphone update. Losing a Test match suddenly did not seem so important.

In between those two South Africa Tests, the HSC saw an array of teams stepping out from the gabled pavilion. In late 1999-2000 there was a feisty encounter with the Sri Lankans. The low point was the dismissal of Goodwin in the second Test, given out when Tillakaratne Dilshan unsportingly threw down the stumps as Murray went out to do some "gardening" at the end of an over. It was a critical moment as it ended a fighting backs-to-the-wall partnership and led to Sri Lanka's win.

However, there were some real cricket highlights as well, notably Nuwan Zoysa's hat-trick in that Test with his first three deliveries – the first three balls of the second over of our first innings that left Zimbabwe reeling at nought for three. We never fully recovered.

In June 2001, India arrived and, after losing the first Test in Bulawayo, Zimbabwe battled well to

win the second Test by four wickets, Stuart Carlisle's staunch 62 seeing us home as we chased 157 for victory. The win, however, was tinged with sadness as Trevor Madondo, who had already played three Tests and showed the potential to play a few more, died just four days before the game of cerebral malaria. He was 24.

Madondo was the first black Zimbabwean to emerge as a batsman – the others had by and large been bowlers – but the following month when the West Indies came to town, Harare saw another young black Zimbabwean stamp his mark on Test cricket when Masakadza, a schoolboy 11 days short of his 18th birthday, became the youngest player to score a century on his Test debut.

Zimbabwe, having lost the first Test in Bulawayo, were in real trouble, bowled out for 131 and then conceding a first innings lead of 216 as the West Indians cantered to 347. But Masakadza, with a wonderfully confident 119, turned the tables and with great support from Wishart, Streak and Andy Blignaut helped Zimbabwe to pile up an astonishing 563 for nine declared. Sadly rain spoiled their chances of levelling the series but the sight of Masakadza batting at number three and cheered on by hundreds of schoolkids, swatting the likes of Reon King, Marlon Black, Neil McGarrell and Stuart around the HSC was a sign of hope for Zimbabwe's future.

Masakadza's record did not last long as the Bangladeshi batsman Mohammad Ashraful, aged just 16 years and 364 days, took 114 off Sri Lanka in Colombo a couple of months later.

The next big event for Zimbabwe at the HSC came with the 2003 World Cup when politics overtook cricket. England stayed away while Henry Olonga and I marched into international retirement after our black-armband protest against the death of democracy in Zimbabwe.

To think of the HSC is to think of an old world of timelessness and gentility. And yet for those

two games against Namibia and India, the ground was tinged with something a little more threatening. How would the security guards react to any sign of sympathetic protest from the crowd? What instructions, if any, would come from Mugabe, patron of the Zimbabwe Cricket Union and the man who once said that cricket was a civilising influence?

Ultimately the repercussions were limited but walking out to bat for the India game was a particularly nervous moment. There was a tension about the place. There were about ten or 12 policemen with AK47s dotted about the perimeter and nobody was allowed to get too close. There were some thumbs up from some members of the crowd and others wore black armbands and carried placards of support.

It was a tense time but there is no doubt that the cloak of menace draped around the shoulders of the HSC is only temporary. If you put contemporary politics to one side, the HSC remains a ground of charm and history; an arena where dreams and reputations will be made and broken for many years to come.

Above: Away from the politics, the HSC is still the kind of ground where you can hear the rustle of the butterflies amid the tranquillity .

Overleaf: Alistair Campbell captained Zimbabwe with distinction and was a leading runscorer at the HSC.

Harare Sports Club Ground Records

Result Summary

	Played	Won	Lost	Drawn
Zimbabwe	21	4	10	7
Australia	1	1	0	0
Bangladesh	1	0	1	0
England	1	0	0	1
India	3	0	2	1
Pakistan	4	3	1	0
New Zealand	3	2	0	1
South Africa	3	3	0	0
Sri Lanka	4	1	0	3
West Indies	1	0	0	1

Highest Totals

600-3	South Africa v Zimbabwe 2001-02
563-9	Zimbabwe v West Indies 2001
544-4	Zimbabwe v Pakistan 1994-95

Lowest Completed Innings Totals

102 All out	Zimbabwe v South Africa 1999-2000
131 All out	Zimbabwe v West Indies 2001
137 All out	Zimbabwe v New Zealand 1992-93

Highest Match Aggregates

Runs	Wkts	
1356	24	Zimbabwe v South Africa 2001-02
1189	40	Zimbabwe v Pakistan 2002-03
1139	30	Zimbabwe v West Indies 2001-02

Lowest Match Aggregates (Result oriented matches)

Runs	Wkts	
705	29	South Africa v Zimbabwe 1999-2000

Highest Scores

220	G Kirsten South Africa v Zimbabwe 2001-02
201*	GW Flower Zimbabwe v Pakistan 1994-95
199*	A Flower Zimbabwe v South Africa 2001-02
192	Mohammad Wasim Pakistan v Zimbabwe 1997-98
188*	GJ Whittall Zimbabwe v New Zealand 2000-01

Highest Run Aggregates

Runs	Matches	Hundreds	
1535	20	4	A Flower
1210	20	3	GW Flower
954	18	2	GJ Whittall
803	21	0	ADR Campbell
520	9	2	DL Houghton

Partnership Records

256 for 1stHH	Gibbs and G Kirsten South Africa v Zimbabwe 2001-02
217 for 2nd	AP Gurusinha and S Ranatunga Sri Lanka v Zimbabwe 1994-95
194 for 3rd	ADR Campbell and DL Houghton Zimbabwe v Sri Lanka 1994-95
269 for 4th	A Flower and GW Flower Zimbabwe v Pakistan 1994-95
233* for 5th	GW Flower and GJ Whittall Zimbabwe v Pakistan 1994-95
165 for 6th	A Flower and DL Houghton Zimbabwe v India 1992-93
154 for 7th	AM Blignaut and HH Streak Zimbabwe v West Indies 2001
148 for 8th	MV Boucher and SM Pollock South Africa v Zimbabwe 1999-2000
147 for 9th	Mohammad Wasim and Mushtaq Ahmed Pakistan v Zimbabwe 1997-98
47 for 10th	A Flower and DT Hondo Zimbabwe v South Africa 2001-02

Best Bowling in an Innings.

8 for 71	AA Donald South Africa v Zimbabwe 1995-96
7 for 116	KR Pushpakumara Sri Lanka v Zimbabwe 1994-95

Best Bowling in a Match

11 for 113 (3-42, 8-71)	AA Donald South Africa v Zimbabwe 1995-96
9 for 105 (6-90, 3-15)	HH Streak Zimbabwe v Pakistan 1994-95

Hat Trick

DNT Zoysa Sri Lanka v Zimbabwe 1999-2000

Highest Wicket Aggregates

Wkts	Matches	5WI	
67	15	2	HH Streak

Most Catches by Fielder

Catches	Matches	
28	21	ADR Campbell
22	20	GW Flower

Most Dismissals by Wicket keeper

Dismissals	Matches	
58	17	A Flower
10	3	AC Parore

BANGLADESH

Richard Hobson

THE BANGABANDHU
NATIONAL STADIUM

343

The Bangabandhu National Stadium in Dhaka is unique in cricket. No other ground happens to also house administrative offices for wrestling or bridge, or has a shopping centre forming part of its outer rim. And, while a few stadia have hosted neutral Tests, only the Bangabandhu has been a genuine home to a pair of Test-playing countries. It used to house Pakistan but now provides the headquarters for Bangladesh. In between it survived a bloody civil war. Peer closely, and you can even see the bullet holes to prove it.

Even now the future of the place is open to question. The conflicting interests of football and cricket are still to be resolved and those who watched the ICC Knockout in 1998 believe that the ground carried a shabbier appearance two years later when Bangladesh made their emotional and, some observers felt, premature entry into Test cricket. The game against India represented a new, hopeful start for the still-young country, but merely the latest, eventful chapter for the ground.

People of a certain age would have remembered the original "first". That arrived on New Year's Day, 1955, when Pakistan played their initial home Test, against India, at the same ground. It was the 33rd venue ever to stage a Test match and was then known simply as Dacca Stadium. In those days the land formed the eastern part of Bengal, and had been given to Pakistan as part of the 1947 partition.

This, the first of a five-match series, would inevitably be an occasion for celebration. Yet it was a drab affair that set the tone for later games. Between them India and Pakistan could muster only 710 runs in four days at the rate of 1.83 per over. Caution remains the watchword where cricket between the countries is concerned. Perceived humiliation in defeat outweighs the glory of success.

The stadium was in use for Test cricket again ten months later. New Zealand had lost the first two games of a three-match series and would doubtless have lost the third but for wretched weather.

Play finally began on the third day in treacherous conditions for batting. As if a wet, coir-matting pitch laid on grass was not enough to contend with, a humid atmosphere added to the difficulties. Khan Mohammad generated enough swing to be close to unplayable, claiming six for 21 as New Zealand collapsed to 70 all out. Hanif Mohammad then

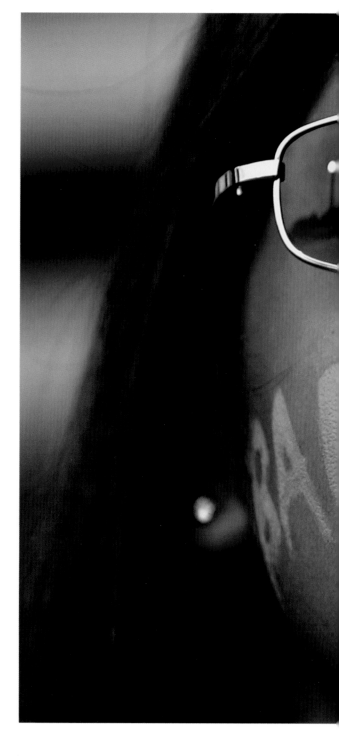

scored 103 before Pakistan declared on 195 for six. New Zealand batted through 90 overs in their second innings to finish on 69 for six in one of the most dogged, self-disciplined performances in the annals of Test cricket.

Pakistan secured their first victory at the ground on their next visit in 1959, beating a West Indies side which included Gary Sobers, Rohan Kanhai, Sonny Ramadhin and Wes Hall by 41 runs despite having been 22 for five in their first

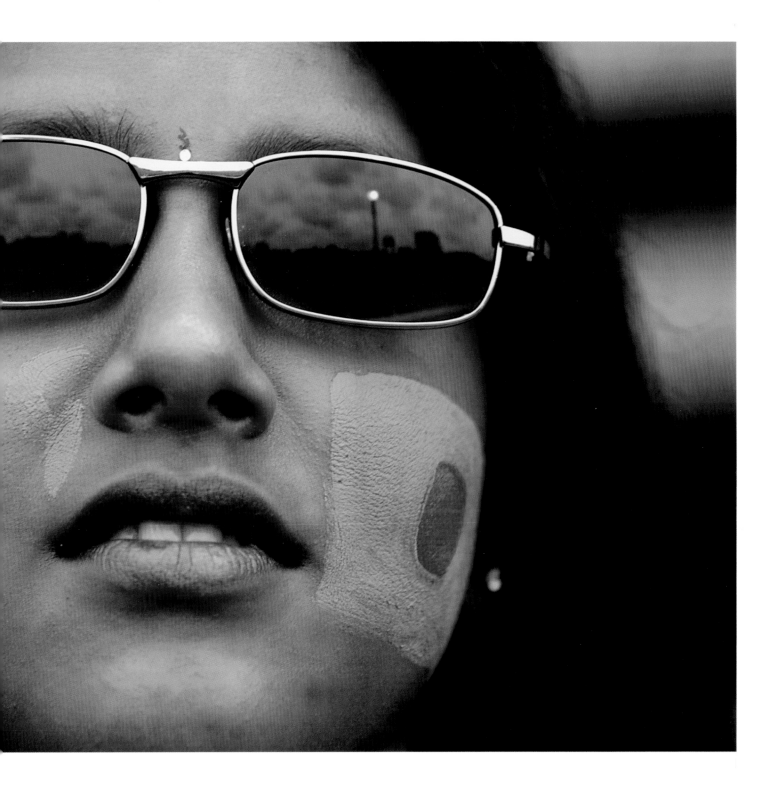

innings. Fazal Mahmood, the captain, claimed six wickets in each West Indies innings as he cut the ball both ways. The match aggregate of 537 runs for 40 wickets underlined how conditions were again substantially weighted towards the bowlers.

A new grass pitch had been laid by the following winter. Heavy rain, however, made it impossible to use for the visit of Australia, who gained their first win in Pakistan by eight wickets on matting, with Ken "Slasher" Mackay switching

Birth of a Nation.
Aminul Islam raises his hands to the heavens to celebrate his century against India in Bangladesh's inaugural Test. He became the third man to score a hundred in his country's first Test, following Dave Houghton of Zimbabwe in 1992-93 and Charles Bannerman of Australia in the very first Test match in 1876-77.

from medium-pace to off-spin to return the best figures of his Test career, six for 42.

Batsmen prevailed for England's first full visit in 1961-62, though not with any great flamboyance. Hanif became the first Pakistani to score a hundred in each innings and spent nearly 15 hours at the crease in all. Geoff Pullar's seven-hour 165 came at a quicker rate and represented a courageous effort as he was suffering from dysentery.

When England returned in 1968-69, Dhaka staged the only match of the rubber to emerge free from riot. A potentially volatile crowd was controlled not by the police or the military but by left-wing students with a nebulous grasp of order.

Politically, the relationship between East and West Pakistan had become increasingly fraught by the late 1960s and there was an inevitability about the rioting and pitch invasion which contributed towards an early finish to the final Test of this phase in the history of the ground. Pakistan needed 184 to beat New Zealand in two-and-a-half hours and were 51 for four when a combination of bad light and bad behaviour sentenced the game to a draw.

And that, for a time, was that. The push for independence grew until Pakistani forces finally withdrew and the new Bangladesh declared victory on December 16, 1971. War cost an estimated three million lives with around ten million people seeking refugee status across the Indian border. Cricket was no longer important and the ground, untended, fell into disrepair. The square sank three inches through disuse and the outer walls were pock-marked by bullet shells. This was to be the nadir for cricket in the region.

A new, military regime decided to restore cricket as an acceptable pastime, perhaps hoping that it would prove a distraction from the grimmer realities of life. Around 90,000 people watched over three days when an MCC team including John Barclay played a representative Bangladesh XI captained by Shamim Kabir in January 1977. To many this marks the start of the country's journey towards recognition. A second tour met with even greater enthusiasm two years later. By now they had become associate members of the ICC, competing in the ICC Trophy in 1979.

After a lengthy absence, top-flight cricket returned with the Asia Cup in 1988, a one-day series won by India which also involved Pakistan and Sri Lanka as well as Bangladesh, who lost all three of their games heavily.

In 1993 David Richards, the ICC chief executive, was amazed to see a league game attract 15,000 spectators and Bangladesh gave notice of their potential by winning the ICC Trophy in Kuala Lumpur in 1997.

Back home, the ground hosted a tournament christened the Silver Jubilee Independence Cup in January 1998, supposedly to mark 25 years of freedom. A three-way event that also involved India and Pakistan, it was a little belated and unsuccessful, with five of the six matches having to be shortened because of fog. Greater triumph – and favourable exposure – lay only months away, though, when the first mini-World Cup came to the city.

With its new floodlights and electronic scoreboard, the Bangabandhu - renamed after the nickname which translates as "friend of Bangladesh" given to the father of the nation, Sheikh Mujibur Rahman - provided a sound base for a tournament that raised £10 million for development. South Africa, skippered by Hansie Cronje, yet to be disgraced in the match-fixing scandal, beat West Indies by four wickets in the final.

More international cricket arrived early the following year. Nearly three full decades on from the disgraceful scenes which brought down the curtain on the ground as a five-day, international venue, Test cricket returned to the Bangabandhu. Fittingly, perhaps, Pakistan were involved, contesting the final of the Asian Test Championship – a three-nation event – with Sri Lanka.

Relatively poor crowds were attributed to India's failure to reach the final but the contest became increasingly one-sided after Pakistan restricted Sri Lanka, without Muttiah Muralitharan, to 231 in the first innings. Ijaz Ahmed and Inzamam-ul-Haq struck 211 and 200 not out respectively, Wasim Akram took his second Test hat-trick, and Pakistan eventually won by a crushing innings and 175 runs.

Clearly the Bangabandhu was capable of playing host. But how soon before the home dressing-room became exactly that? Victory in the final of the 1997 ICC Trophy in Kuala Lumpur

The pain and the glory.
Bangladesh found a new national hero when Mohammad Ashraful scored 114 on his Test debut in Colombo against Sri Lanka. Aged 16 years and 364 days, he was the youngest player ever to score a Test century. But as he discovered while playing the Australians in 2003, reputations do not count for much in the hard world of Test cricket.

showed that Bangladesh were the best of the associate members, those ranked immediately below Test standard, and the case for full recognition gained fresh impetus with victory over Pakistan at Northampton in the 1999 World Cup.

Three months after a second visit by an ICC inspection team, the events of April 2000 proved to be crucial. The Bangabandhu hosted a star-studded one-day representative match between Asia and the Rest of the World, which is still remembered for an astonishing innings of 185 not out by Michael Bevan. It was the highlight of the ICC Cricket Week and a crowd estimated at 50,000 - way over official capacity - served to remind of the growing enthusiasm for the sport.

More pertinently as far as the national side was concerned, their South African coach Eddie Barlow, who had gained widespread respect as a driving force at all levels, suffered a stroke which confined him to a wheelchair. It was an emotional moment for Barlow when, on June 26, the ICC granted Test status, with England and Australia deciding to approve the application having voted against just a year before.

Atmosphere can play havoc with emotions and some of the statements issued as the news broke might best be attributed to excitement. Addressing a rally in Dhaka, Sheikh Hasina, the Prime Minister, and a daughter of Mujibur Rahman, told the Bangladesh Cricket Board (BCB) to prepare, one day, to lift the World Cup. Syed Ashraful Huq, the BCB secretary, made a more conservative prediction – that his country would take a maximum of two years to score a Test victory.

Come the glorious day, though, Bangladesh were still without a single first-class victory, and had won just three out of 41 limited-overs internationals. Only South Africa had gone in to their inaugural Test with less preparation, and that was back in 1888-89. This did not seem to be the issue for supporters. Rabeed Imam wrote in the Dhaka-based *Daily Star* newspaper: "It hardly matters if Tendulkar creates a world record. We couldn't care less if India win the match in a thumping fashion. The message today is – Bangladesh is here to stay."

If the ground was slightly grubbier than before the ICC event two years earlier, the state of the pitch was even more worrying. Groundstaff

dropped a fine mix of soil and sand in to cracks only three days before the game. On top they sprinkled grass shavings, which were bound in to the surface with water. Such are the consequences of having to share a ground with football. As events transpired the pitch lived up to expectations. It offered slow turn and, as the game wore on, erratic bounce.

By a fitting coincidence both captains were Bengalis. Indian captain Sourav Ganguly, probably the best player to have emerged from the region, called incorrectly when his opposite number, Naimur Rahman, tossed the specially-minted gold coin and spent the whole first day in the field as a capacity crowd approaching 40,000 watched the home side make rather a better fist of Test cricket than many feared.

It was one of those occasions that could only foster optimism. Flags waved, firecrackers popped and by the time the home side passed 200, small bonfires were alight in the stands.

Barlow had begun to walk slowly with the aid of a stick but for most of the time he sat proud as his charges grafted away. His message, to avoid unnecessary risk, had clearly been absorbed by Aminul Islam, who had played club cricket in Portsmouth a few months earlier. He faced 213 balls to finish unbeaten on 70 by the close. The following day he became only the third batsman to score a hundred in his country's inaugural Test. Meanwhile, Habibul Bashar – later to become the first Bangladeshi to notch up 1,000 Test runs – made 71 from 112 balls.

The game began to go against the home side in the final session of the third day. India resumed after tea with four wickets in hand, still 139 in arrears. In the next couple of hours they lost Ganguly for a dogged 84, but added 105 against some tiring bowlers. Sunil Joshi, who should have been run out early on, continued to reach 92, the highest score of his Test career. Rahman, a slight off-spinner, was the pick of the attack and could dine out for life in his homeland after capturing the prize wicket of Sachin Tendulkar.

For two-thirds of the game it seemed that Bangladesh could pull off one of the most improbable of all Test victories. Rahman suggested afterwards that his side did not have the temperament or concentration to be able to finish the job. Part of the explanation might be

found in Ganguly's response before the contest when asked whether he felt confident that India could end a run of seven years without a Test win abroad. "Bangladesh is not abroad," he replied.

At least they had made their neighbours bat for a second time and, most important to the watching dignitaries, suggested that they might be able to hold their own at this new level.

Progress since then has been slow, however. When they lost to the West Indies in Dhaka late in 2002 – Jermaine Lawson recording the extraordinary figures of six wickets for three runs – it represented an 11th innings defeat in 16 Tests. And they only managed to secure a draw against Zimbabwe at the Bangabandhu because of heavy rain after trailing by 324 on first innings. Two more heavy defeats at the hands of South Africa in early 2003, one at Chittagong, the other in Dhaka, further compounded the problems.

It could be pointed out that New Zealand took 26 years and 45 Tests to record a first win. So, too, might the fact that the selectors have been courageous in giving young players an early opportunity. The brightest is perhaps Mohammad

Another tough lesson.
Bangladesh had another harsh dose of reality when South Africa toured in May 2003, losing both Tests with something to spare.

Ashraful, who became the youngest player to score a Test century when he struck 114 on debut against Sri Lanka in Colombo in September 2001 aged 16 years and 364 days.

Five months earlier, Mohammad Sharif made his debut at 15 years and 128 days against Zimbabwe. Even at that age, and at five foot six inches tall, he was regarded as the fastest bowler in the country. Another pace-bowling prospect is Talha Jubair, who was 16 when he made his first appearance against Sri Lanka in July 2002. Underlining his potential, he bowled Marvan Atapattu and then Mahela Jayawardene for a duck.

Without doubt, the arrival of Test cricket has aroused mass interest and, whatever recent results suggest, there is more chance of unearthing a Tendulkar than a Beckham. Whether the Bangabandhu Stadium will be cricket's biggest stage in Bangladesh when that player emerges remains to be seen.

Naimur Rahman.
Bangladesh's first captain who took six for 132 against India in the inaugural Test in November 2000.

THE BANGABANDHU
NATIONAL STADIUM Ground Records

Result Summary

	Played	Won	Lost	Drawn
Bangladesh	5	0	4	1
Australia	1	1	0	0
England	2	0	0	2
India	2	1	0	1
Pakistan	9	3	1	5
New Zealand	2	0	0	2
South Africa	1	1	0	0
Sri Lanka	1	0	1	0
West Indies	2	1	1	0
Zimbabwe	1	0	0	1

Highest Totals

594	Pakistan v Sri Lanka	1998-99
536	West Indies v Bangladesh	2002-03
490-9	Pakistan v Bangladesh	2001-02

Lowest Completed Innings Totals

70	New Zealand v Pakistan	1955-56
76	West Indies v Pakistan	1958-59
87	Bangladesh v West Indies	2002-03

Highest Match Aggregates

Runs	Wkts		
1086	27	Pakistan v England	1961-62
1013	30	Sri Lanka v Pakistan	1998-99
984	31	Bangladesh v India	2000-01

Lowest Match Aggregate (Result oriented matches)

Runs	Wkts		
537	40	Pakistan v West Indies	1958-59

Highest Scores

211	Ijaz Ahmed	Pakistan v Sri Lanka	1998-99
200*	Inzamam-ul-Haq	Pakistan v Sri Lanka	1998-99
165	G Pullar	England v Pakistan	1961-62
145	Aminul Islam	Bangladesh v India	2000-01
140	Javed Burki	Pakistan v England	1961-62

Highest Run Aggregates

Runs	Matches	Hundreds	
474	5	3	Hanif Mohammad
312	5	0	Habibul Bashar
243	2	1	Inzamam-ul-Haq
222	4	1	Aminul Islam
214	4	0	Saeed Ahmed

Partnership Records

198 for 1st	RW Barber and G Pullar England v Pakistan	1961-62
147 for 2nd	KF Barrington and G Pullar England v Pakistan	1961-62
352* for 3rd	Ijaz Ahmed and Inzamam-ul-Haq Pakistan v Sri Lanka	1998-99
176 for 4th	MN Samuels and RR Sarwan West Indies v Bangladesh	2002-03
107 for 5th	MV Boucher and JA Rudolph South Africa v Bangladesh	2002-03
175 for 6th	Abdur Razzaq and Rashid Latif Pakistan v Bangladesh	2001-02
121 for 7th	SC Ganguly and SB Joshi India v Bangladesh	2000-01
108 for 8th	TJ Friend and HH Streak Zimbabwe v Bangladesh	2001-02
96 for 9th	MG Burgess and RS Cunis New Zealand v Pakistan	1969-70
73 for 10th	KSC de Silva and HP Tillekaratne Sri Lanka v Pakistan	1998-99

Best Bowling in an Innings

7 for 77	D Kaneria Pakistan v Bangladesh	2001-02

Best Bowling in a Match

12 for 100 (6 for 34, 6 for 66)	Fazal Mahmood Pakistan v West Indies	1958-59
10 for 182 (5 for 91, 5 for 91)	Intikhab Alam Pakistan v New Zealand	1969-70

Hat Trick

Wasim Akram	Pakistan v Sri Lanka 1998-99

Highest Wicket Aggregates

Wkts	Matches	5WI	
22	4	3	Fazal Mahmood

Most Catches by Fielder

Most		
6	3	Al Sahariar Rokon
6	5	Hanif Mohammad

Most Dismissals by Wicketkeeper

Dismissals	Matches	
15	5	Imtiaz Ahmed
6	4	Khaled Mahmud

SCORECARDS

Sydney Cricket Ground

Australia v England
17,18,20,21 February 1882

Result: Australia won by 5 wickets

England Innings
G Ulyett	c Murdoch b Evans	25	lbw b Palmer	67
RG Barlow	b Palmer	31	c Blackham b Garrett	62
J Selby	c & b Evans	6	c Blackham b Palmer	2
W Bates	c Murdoch b Palmer	4	b Palmer	5
A Shrewsbury	b Palmer	7	c McDonnell b Garrett	22
WE Midwinter	c Blackham b Palmer	4	b Palmer	8
WH Scotton	b Palmer	30	lbw b Palmer	12
T Emmett	b Evans	10	c McDonnell b Garrett	9
*A Shaw	c Massie b Palmer	11	b Evans	30
+R Pilling	b Palmer	3	b Jones	9
E Peate	not out	1	not out	1
	(lb 1)	1	(b 3, lb 2)	5
	(all out)	133	(all out)	232

Bowling: Palmer 58-36-68-7 Evans 57-32-64-3
Palmer 66-29-97-4 Evans 40.1-19-49-1 Garrett 36-12-62-4 Jones 11-4-19-1

Australia Innings
HH Massie	c Shrewsbury b Bates	49	b Ulyett	22
JM Blackham	c Shaw b Midwinter	40	c & b Bates	4
E Evans	run out	11		
*+WL Murdoch	c Emmett b Bates	10	c Barlow b Midwinter	49
TP Horan	run out	4	b Ulyett	21
PS McDonnell	b Bates	14	b Shaw	25
SP Jones	c Emmett b Ulyett	37	not out	13
TW Garrett	c Shrewsbury b Peate	4	not out	31
GE Palmer	b Bates	16		
HF Boyle	c Shrewsbury b Ulyett	0		
G Coulthard	not out	6		
	(b 1, lb 2, w 2, nb 1)	6	(b 3, lb 1)	4
	(all out)	197	(5 wickets)	169

Bowling: Peate 52-28-53-1 Midwinter 34-16-43-1 Emmett 6-2-24-0 Ulyett 22.2-16-11-2 Bates 72-43-52-4 Barlow 8-4-8-0
Peate 20-12-22-0 Midwinter 18-8-23-1 Emmett 6-3-17-0 Ulyett 15-4-48-2 Bates 24-11-37-1 Barlow 4-1-6-0 Shaw 20.1-15-12-1

Umpires: James Lillywhite jnr (Eng) and JS Swift

Australia v England
3,4,6,7 March 1882

Result: Australia won by 6 wickets

England Innings
G Ulyett	b Palmer	0	b Garrett	23
RG Barlow	c Blackham b Garrett	4	c & b Garrett	8
J Selby	c Massie b Palmer	13	b Palmer	1
W Bates	c & b Palmer	1	c Bannerman b Garrett	2
A Shrewsbury	c & b Boyle	82	c Boyle b Garrett	47
WE Midwinter	b Palmer	12	b Palmer	10
WH Scotton	c Jones b Garrett	18	b Palmer	1
T Emmett	b Garrett	4	b Garrett	2
*A Shaw	b Boyle	3	b Garrett	6
+R Pilling	b Palmer	12	b Palmer	23
E Peate	not out	11	not out	8
	(b 22, lb 6)	28	(b 2, nb 1)	3
	(all out)	188	(all out)	134

Bowling: Palmer 45.2-23-46-5 Garrett 60-24-85-3 Jones 8-5-11-0 Boyle 27-18-18-2
Palmer 40-19-44-4 Garrett 36.1-10-78-6 Boyle 4-1-9-0

Australia Innings
AC Bannerman	b Midwinter	70	c Pilling b Peate	14
HH Massie	b Bates	0	c Midwinter b Peate	9
*WL Murdoch	c Ulyett b Bates	6	c Midwinter b Bates	4
TP Horan	c & b Bates	1	not out	16
PS McDonnell	c Midwinter b Peate	147	c Emmett b Peate	9
G Giffen	c Pilling b Peate	2		
+JM Blackham	b Peate	4		
SP Jones	not out	7	not out	6
TW Garrett	b Peate	0		
GE Palmer	b Midwinter	6		
HF Boyle	c Pilling b Peate	3		
	(b 6, lb 8, w 2)	16	(b 2, lb 3, w 1)	6
	(all out)	262	(4 wickets)	64

Bowling: Peate 45-24-43-5 Bates 38-17-67-3 Ulyett 3-1-10-0 Midwinter 62-25-75-2 Shaw 8-4-14-0 Emmett 16-6-37-0
Peate 25-18-15-3 Bates 24.3-13-43-1

Umpires: James Lillywhite jnr (Eng) and JS Swift

Australia v England
26,27,29,30 January 1883

Result: England won by 69 runs

England Innings
RG Barlow	c Murdoch b Spofforth	28	c Palmer b Horan	24
CT Studd	c Blackham b Garrett	21	b Spofforth	25
CFH Leslie	b Spofforth	0	b Spofforth	8
AG Steel	b Garrett	17	lbw b Spofforth	6
WW Read	c Massie b Bannerman	66	b Horan	21
W Bates	c Blackham b Spofforth	2	lbw b Spofforth	3
+EFS Tylecote	run out	66	c Bonnor b Spofforth	0
W Bates	c McDonnell b Spofforth	17	c Murdoch b Horan	4
GB Studd	b Spofforth	3	c Garrett b Spofforth	8
*Hon.IFW Bligh	b Palmer	13	not out	17
F Morley	not out	2	b Spofforth	0
	(b 8, lb 3, nb 1)	12	(b 5, lb 2)	7
	(all out)	247	(all out)	123

Bowling: Giffen 12-3-37-0 Palmer 38-21-38-2 Spofforth 51-19-73-4 Garrett 27-8-54-2 Bannerman 11-2-17-1 McDonnell 4-0-16-0
Spofforth 41.1-23-44-7 Garrett 13-3-31-0 Palmer 9-3-19-0 Horan 17-10-22-3

Australia Innings
G Giffen	st Tylecote b Bates	41	b Barlow	7
AC Bannerman	c Bates b Morley	94	c Bligh b Barlow	5
*WL Murdoch	lbw b Steel	19	c GB Studd b Morley	0
PS McDonnell	b Steel	0	c Bligh b Morley	0
TP Horan	c Steel b Morley	19	c CT Studd b Barlow	8
HH Massie	c Bligh b Steel	1	c Murdoch b Barlow	11
GB Studd	c GB Studd b Morley	8		
+JM Blackham	b Barlow	27	b Barlow	26
TW Garrett	c Barlow b Morley	0	b Barlow	0
GE Palmer	c GB Studd b Barnes	7	not out	2
FR Spofforth	not out	0	c Steel b Barlow	7
	(b 6, lb 2, w 1, nb 1)	10	(b 6, lb 2, w 1)	9
	(all out)	218	(all out)	83

Bowling: Morley 34-16-47-4 Barlow 47.1-31-52-1 Bates 45-20-55-1 Barnes 13-6-22-1 CT Studd 14-11-5-0 Steel 26-14-27-3
Morley 35-19-34-2 Barlow 34.2-20-40-7

Umpires: EH Elliott and JS Swift

Australia v England
17,19,20,21 February 1883

Result: Australia won by 4 wickets

England Innings
RG Barlow	c Murdoch b Midwinter	2	c Bonnor b Midwinter	20
CT Studd	run out	48	c Murdoch b Midwinter	31
CFH Leslie	c Bonnor b Boyle	17	b Horan	19
AG Steel	not out	135	b Spofforth	21
WW Read	c Bonnor b Boyle	11	b Spofforth	7
+EFS Tylecote	b Boyle	5	b Palmer	1
W Barnes	b Spofforth	2	c & b Boyle	20
W Bates	c Bonnor b Midwinter	9	not out	48
*Hon.IFW Bligh	b Palmer	19	c Murdoch b Horan	10
GB Studd	run out	3	c Murdoch b Boyle	9
F Morley	b Palmer	0	c Blackham b Palmer	2
	(b 4, lb 7, nb 1)	12	(b 8, lb 1, nb 1)	10
	(all out)	263	(all out)	197

Bowling: Palmer 24-9-52-2 Midwinter 47-24-50-2 Spofforth 21-8-56-1 Boyle 40-19-52-3 Horan 12-4-26-0 Evans 11-3-15-0
Palmer 43.3-19-59-2 Midwinter 23-13-21-2 Spofforth 28-6-57-2 Boyle 23-6-35-2 Horan 9-2-15-2

Australia Innings
AC Bannerman	c Barlow b Morley	10	c Bligh b CT Studd	63
GJ Bonnor	c Barlow b Steel	87	c GB Studd b Steel	3
*WL Murdoch	b Barlow	0	c Barlow b Bates	17
TP Horan	c GB Studd b Morley	4	c & b Bates	2
G Giffen	c GB Studd b Leslie	27	c Tylecote b Steel	32
WE Midwinter	b Barlow	10	not out	8
+JM Blackham	b Bates	57	not out	58
GE Palmer	c Bligh b Steel	0		
E Evans	not out	22	c Leslie b Steel	0
FR Spofforth	c Bates b Steel	1		
HF Boyle	c GB Studd b Barlow	29		
	(b 10, lb 3, w 2)	15	(b 10, lb 4, w 4)	18
	(all out)	262	(6 wickets)	199

Bowling: Barlow 48-21-88-3 Morley 44-25-45-2 Barnes 10-2-33-0 Bates 15-6-24-1 Leslie 5-2-11-1 Steel 18-6-34-3 CT Studd 6-2-12-0
Barlow 37.1-20-44-0 Morley 12-9-4-0 Barnes 16-5-22-0 Bates 39-19-52-2 Leslie 8-7-2-0 Steel 43-9-49-3 CT Studd 8-4-8-1

Umpires: EH Elliott and JS Swift

Australia v England
20,21,23,24 February 1885

Result: Australia won by 6 runs

Australia Innings
AC Bannerman	c Peel b Flowers	13	c Shrewsbury b Ulyett	16
SP Jones	st Hunter b Flowers	28	b Attewell	22
TP Horan	c Hunter b Attewell	7	b Bates	36
HJH Scott	c Ulyett b Attewell	5	c Barnes b Attewell	4
GJ Bonnor	c Barnes b Flowers	18	b Ulyett	29
JW Trumble	c Read b Attewell	13	c Ulyett b Bates	32
*HH Massie	c Scotton b Flowers	2	b Barnes	21
+AH Jarvis	b Attewell	9	c & b Peel	2
FR Spofforth	st Hunter b Flowers	3	c Attewell b Bates	0
TW Garrett	not out	51	not out	0
E Evans	c Hunter b Ulyett	33	b Bates	1
	(b 3, lb 5)	8	(b 1, lb 1)	2
	(all out)	181	(all out)	165

Bowling: Peel 32-13-51-0 Attewell 71-47-53-4 Ulyett 12.2-8-17-1 Flowers 46-24-46-5 Bates 6-2-6-0
Peel 20-10-24-1 Attewell 58-36-54-2 Ulyett 39-25-42-2 Flowers 20-14-19-0 Bates 20-10-24-5

England Innings
WH Scotton	c Jarvis b Horan	22	b Spofforth	2
*A Shrewsbury	c & b Spofforth	18	b Spofforth	24
G Ulyett	b Spofforth	2	run out	4
W Barnes	st Jarvis b Spofforth	0	c Jarvis b Trumble	5
W Bates	c Evans b Horan	12	c Jarvis b Spofforth	31
J Briggs	c Scott b Horan	3	b Spofforth	1
W Flowers	c Jarvis b Spofforth	24	c Evans b Spofforth	56
JM Read	c Evans b Horan	4	b Spofforth	56
W Attewell	b Horan	14	run out	0
R Peel	not out	8	c Jarvis b Trumble	3
+J Hunter	b Horan	13	not out	5
	(b 8, lb 3, nb 2)	13	(b 7, lb 9, w 3, nb 1)	20
	(all out)	133	(all out)	207

Bowling: Spofforth 48-23-54-4 Garrett 6-2-17-0 Horan 37.1-22-40-6 Evans 4-1-9-0
Spofforth 48.1-22-90-6 Garrett 21-8-31-0 Horan 9-4-23-0 Evans 4-1-8-0 Trumble 26-13-26-2 Jones 3-0-9-0

Umpires: EH Elliott and JW Payne

Australia v England
14,16,17 March 1885

Result: Australia won by 8 wickets

England Innings
G Ulyett	b Giffen	10	c Garrett b Palmer	2
*A Shrewsbury	b Giffen	40	c Bonnor b Spofforth	16
WH Scotton	c Blackham b Giffen	4	c Jones b Spofforth	0
W Barnes	b Giffen	50	c Bannerman b Spofforth	20
W Bates	c & b Jones	64	c Blackham b Palmer	1
JM Read	b Giffen	47	c Bannerman b Spofforth	6
W Flowers	c Giffen	14	c Jones b Palmer	7
J Briggs	c Palmer b Spofforth	3	run out	5
W Attewell	b Giffen	1	not out	1
R Peel	not out	17	c & b Spofforth	4
+J Hunter	b Spofforth	13	b Palmer	15
	(b 5, nb 1)	6	(b 14, nb 1)	15
	(all out)	269	(all out)	77

Bowling: Giffen 52-14-117-7 Palmer 16-5-35-0 Spofforth 29-10-61-2 Garrett 2-1-5-0 Trumble 12-5-16-0 Horan 5-2-12-0 Jones 10-5-17-1
Palmer 19.1-7-32-4 Spofforth 20-8-30-5

Australia Innings
GE Palmer	b Ulyett	0		
TW Garrett	b Barnes	32		
JW Trumble	b Peel	5		
PS McDonnell	c Attewell b Ulyett	20	c Ulyett b Peel	3
AC Bannerman	c Shrewsbury b Flowers	51	b Barnes	8
G Giffen	c Attewell b Barnes	1		
TP Horan	c Barnes b Ulyett	9	not out	12
GJ Bonnor	c Bates b Barnes	128		
SP Jones	run out	40	not out	15
*+JM Blackham	not out	11		
FR Spofforth	c Read b Barnes	1		
	(b 5, lb 1, w 2, nb 3)	11	()	0
	(all out)	309	(2 wickets)	38

Bowling: Ulyett 54-25-91-3 Peel 31-12-53-1 Attewell 18-13-22-0 Bates 17-5-44-0 Barnes 35.3-17-61-4 Flowers 14-5-27-1
Peel 9-4-16-1 Attewell 3-1-4-0 Barnes 9-3-15-1 Flowers 3.3-2-3-0

Umpires: EH Elliott and PG McShane

Australia v England
28,29,31 January 1887

Result: England won by 13 runs

England Innings

Batsman	1st innings		2nd innings	
W Bates	c Midwinter b Ferris	8	b Ferris	24
*A Shrewsbury	c McShane b Ferris	2	b Ferris	29
W Barnes	c Spofforth b Turner	0	b Moses b Garrett	32
RG Barlow	b Turner	2	c Jones b Ferris	4
JM Read	c Spofforth b Ferris	5	b Ferris	0
W Gunn	b Turner	0	b Turner	4
WH Scotton	c Jones b Turner	1	c Spofforth b Garrett	6
J Briggs	c Midwinter b Turner	5	b Spofforth	33
GA Lohmann	c Garrett b Ferris	17	lbw b Ferris	3
W Flowers	b Turner	2	c McDonnell b Turner	14
+M Sherwin	not out	0	not out	21
	(b 2, lb 1)	3	(b 9, lb 5)	14
	(all out)	45	(all out)	184

Bowling: Turner 18-11-15-6 Ferris 17.3-7-27-4
Turner 44.2-22-53-2 Ferris 61-30-76-5 Spofforth 12-3-17-1 Midwinter 4-1-10-0 Garrett 12-7-8-2 McShane 3-0-6-0

Australia Innings

Batsman	1st innings		2nd innings	
+JM Blackham	c Sherwin b Lohmann	4	b Barnes	5
*PS McDonnell	b Barnes	14	lbw b Barnes	0
H Moses	b Barlow	31	c Shrewsbury b Barnes	24
SP Jones	c Shrewsbury b Bates	31	c Read b Barnes	18
CTB Turner	b Barlow	0	c & b Barnes	7
AC Bannerman	not out	15	b Lohmann	4
PG McShane	lbw b Briggs	5	b Briggs	5
WE Midwinter	c Shrewsbury b Barlow	0	lbw b Barnes	10
TW Garrett	b Lohmann	12	c Gunn b Lohmann	10
FR Spofforth	b Lohmann	2	b Lohmann	5
JJ Ferris	c Barlow b Barnes	1	not out	0
	(b 1)	1	(b 12, lb 2)	14
	(all out)	119	(all out)	97

Bowling: Barnes 22.1-16-19-2 Lohmann 21-12-30-3 Briggs 14-5-25-1 Barlow 35-23-25-3 Bates 21-9-19-1
Barnes 46-29-28-6 Lohmann 24-11-20-3 Briggs 7-5-7-1 Barlow 13-6-20-0 Bates 17-11-8-0

Umpires: C Bannerman and H Rawlinson

Australia v England
25,26,28 February, 1 March 1887

Result: England won by 71 runs

England Innings

Batsman	1st innings		2nd innings	
*A Shrewsbury	b Turner	9	b Turner	6
W Bates	c Ferris b Turner	8	b Turner	30
JM Read	b Turner	11	st Burton b Ferris	2
W Gunn	b Turner	9	c Cottam b Ferris	10
RG Barlow	c Allen b Ferris	34	not out	42
GA Lohmann	b Ferris	2	b Ferris	6
WH Scotton	b Turner	0	b Ferris	2
J Briggs	b Ferris	17	b Garrett	16
W Flowers	c Allen b Ferris	37	b Turner	18
R Wood	lbw b Ferris	6	b Midwinter	0
+M Sherwin	not out	4	b Turner	5
	(b 9, lb 3, nb 2)	14	(b 12, lb 5)	17
	(all out)	151	(all out)	154

Bowling: Ferris 45-16-71-5 Turner 53-29-41-5 Garrett 6-2-12-0 Midwinter 3-1-2-0 Lyons 2-0-11-0
Ferris 60-33-69-4 Turner 64.1-33-52-4 Garrett 10-6-7-1 Midwinter 6-3-9-1

Australia Innings

Batsman	1st innings		2nd innings	
JJ Lyons	b Lohmann	11	c Gunn b Bates	0
WF Giffen	b Lohmann	2	b Briggs	0
RC Allen	b Lohmann	14	c sub (CTB Turner) b Bates	30
H Moses	b Flowers	28	st Sherwin b Bates	33
*PS McDonnell	c Gunn b Lohmann	10	c Gunn b Lohmann	35
WE Midwinter	b Lohmann	1	c Sherwin b Lohmann	4
JT Cottam	b Lohmann	1	st Sherwin b Briggs	3
CTB Turner	c & b Flowers	9	c Briggs b Bates	9
TW Garrett	b Lohmann	1	c Sherwin b Briggs	20
JJ Ferris	b Lohmann	1	run out	2
+FJ Burton	not out	0	not out	2
	(b 5, lb 1)	6	(b 9, lb 3)	12
	(all out)	84	(all out)	150

Bowling: Lohmann 27.1-12-35-8 Briggs 20-6-34-0 Flowers 8-3-9-2
Lohmann 40-16-52-2 Briggs 22-9-31-3 Flowers 13-5-17-0 Bates 26-13-26-4 Barlow 9-2-12-0

Umpires: C Bannerman and JS Swift

Australia v England
10,11,13,14,15 February 1888

Result: England won by 126 runs

England Innings

Batsman	1st innings		2nd innings	
A Shrewsbury	c Turner b Ferris	44	b Ferris	1
AE Stoddart	c McShane b Turner	16	c Blackham b Turner	17
G Ulyett	c Burton b Turner	5	b Ferris	5
*WW Read	b Turner	10	b Turner	8
JM Read	c & b Turner	0	c Bannerman b Turner	39
R Peel	hit wicket b Ferris	3	st Blackham b Turner	9
W Newham	c Worrall b Ferris	9	lbw b Turner	17
GA Lohmann	c Jones b Ferris	12	c Blackham b Turner	0
J Briggs	b Turner	0	c Worrall b McShane	14
W Attewell	not out	7	not out	10
+R Pilling	run out	3	b Turner	5
	(b 4)	4	(b 7, lb 5)	12
	(all out)	113	(all out)	137

Bowling: Turner 50-27-44-5 Ferris 47-25-60-4 Garrett 3-1-5-0
Turner 38-23-43-7 Ferris 16-4-43-2 McShane 21-7-39-1

Australia Innings

Batsman	1st innings		2nd innings	
AC Bannerman	c Ulyett b Lohmann	2	c Attewell b Lohmann	2
SP Jones	c Shrewsbury b Peel	0	c Shrewsbury b Lohmann	15
H Moses	c WW Read b Lohmann	3	c Briggs b Lohmann	11
FJ Burton	c Stoddart b Lohmann	1	c Pilling b Peel	1
J Worrall	st Pilling b Peel	6	b Lohmann	1
PG McShane	c Shrewsbury b Peel	0	b Peel	0
*PS McDonnell	b Lohmann	3	b Peel	6
+JM Blackham	c Shrewsbury b Peel	2	not out	25
TW Garrett	c Pilling b Lohmann	10	c Shrewsbury b Peel	1
CTB Turner	b Peel	8	lbw b Attewell	12
JJ Ferris	c WW Read b Peel	0	c Shrewsbury b Attewell	5
	(b 6, w 1)	7	(b 2, lb 1)	3
	(all out)	42	(all out)	82

Bowling: Lohmann 19-13-17-5 Peel 18.3-9-18-5
Lohmann 32-18-35-4 Peel 33-14-40-4 Attewell 4.2-2-4-2

Umpires: C Bannerman and J Phillips

Australia v England
29,30 January, 1,2,3 February 1892

Result: Australia won by 72 runs

Australia Innings

Batsman	1st innings		2nd innings	
AC Bannerman	c Abel b Lohmann	12	c Grace b Briggs	91
JJ Lyons	c Grace b Lohmann	41	c Grace b Lohmann	134
G Giffen	c Abel b Lohmann	6	lbw b Attewell	49
H Moses	c Grace b Lohmann	29	absent hurt	0
CTB Turner	c MacGregor b Lohmann	15	not out	14
W Bruce	c Bean b Attewell	15	c Briggs b Sharpe	72
GHS Trott	b Lohmann	2	c Sharpe b Lohmann	1
RW McLeod	c Attewell b Lohmann	13	c Read b Peel	18
WF Giffen	c & b Lohmann	1	b Briggs	3
ST Callaway	run out	1	c Grace b Briggs	0
*+JM Blackham	not out	3	lbw b Briggs	9
	(b 3, lb 3)	6	(b 6, lb 2, w 1)	9
	(all out)	144	(all out)	391

Bowling: Lohmann 43.2-18-58-8 Attewell 31-20-25-1 Briggs 10-2-24-0 Sharpe 10-1-31-0
Lohmann 51-14-84-2 Attewell 46-24-43-1 Briggs 32.4-8-69-4 Sharpe 35-7-91-1 Peel 35-13-49-1 Grace 16-2-34-0 Stoddart 4-1-12-0

England Innings

Batsman	1st innings		2nd innings	
*WG Grace	b Turner	26	c Blackham b Turner	5
R Abel	not out	132	c WF Giffen b G Giffen	1
G Bean	b G Giffen	19	c Lyons b Turner	4
AE Stoddart	c Blackham b McLeod	27	b Turner	69
JM Read	c Turner b G Giffen	3	c & b G Giffen	22
R Peel	c G Giffen b Turner	20	st Blackham b G Giffen	6
GA Lohmann	b G Giffen	10	c Bruce b G Giffen	15
+G MacGregor	lbw b McLeod	3	c & b G Giffen	12
J Briggs	lbw b Trott	28	c Trott b Turner	12
W Attewell	b Trott	0	c & b G Giffen	0
JW Sharpe	c Bannerman b G Giffen	26	not out	4
	(b 10, lb 2, w 1)	13	(b 4, lb 2)	6
	(all out)	307	(all out)	156

Bowling: Turner 37-11-90-2 McLeod 18-6-55-2 G Giffen 28.2-5-88-4 Trott 14-3-42-2 Callaway 17-10-19-0
Turner 23.2-7-46-4 G Giffen 28-10-72-6 Trott 5-0-11-0 Callaway 10-6-21-0

Umpires: T Flynn and JA Tooher

Australia v England
14,15,17,18,19,20 December 1894

Result: England won by 10 runs

Australia Innings

Batsman	1st innings		2nd innings	
JJ Lyons	b Richardson	1	b Richardson	25
GHS Trott	b Richardson	12	c Gay b Peel	8
G Giffen	c Ford b Brockwell	161	lbw b Briggs	41
J Darling	b Richardson	0	c Brockwell b Peel	53
FA Iredale	c Stoddart b Ford	81	c & b Briggs	5
SE Gregory	c Peel b Stoddart	201	c Gay b Peel	16
JC Reedman	c Ford b Peel	17	st Gay b Peel	4
CE McLeod	c Richardson	15	not out	2
CTB Turner	c Gay b Peel	1	c Briggs b Peel	2
*+JM Blackham	b Richardson	74	c & b Peel	2
E Jones	not out	11	c MacLaren b Briggs	1
	(b 8, lb 3, w 1)	12	(b 2, lb 1, nb 4)	7
	(all out)	586	(all out)	166

Bowling: Richardson 55.3-13-181-5 Peel 53-14-140-2 Briggs 25-4-96-0 Brockwell 22-7-78-1 Ford 11-2-47-1 Stoddart 3-0-31-1 Lockwood 3-2-1-0
Richardson 11-3-27-1 Peel 30-9-67-6 Lockwood 16-3-40-0 Briggs 11-2-25-3

England Innings

Batsman	1st innings		2nd innings	
AC MacLaren	c Reedman b Turner	4	b Giffen	20
A Ward	c Iredale b Turner	75	b Turner	117
*AE Stoddart	c Jones b Giffen	12	c Giffen b Turner	36
JT Brown	run out	22	c Jones b Giffen	53
W Brockwell	c Blackham b Jones	49	b Jones	37
R Peel	c Gregory b Giffen	4	b Turner	17
FGJ Ford	st Blackham b Giffen	30	c & b McLeod	48
J Briggs	b Giffen	57	b McLeod	42
WH Lockwood	c Giffen b Trott	18	b Trott	29
+LH Gay	c Gregory b Reedman	33	b Trott	4
T Richardson	not out	0	not out	12
	(b 17, lb 3, w 1)	21	(b 14, lb 8)	22
	(all out)	325	(all out)	437

Bowling: Jones 19-7-44-1 Turner 44-16-89-2 Giffen 43-17-75-4 Trott 15-4-59-1 McLeod 14-2-25-0 Reedman 3.3-1-12-1 Lyons 2-2-0-0
Jones 19-0-57-1 Turner 35-14-78-1 Giffen 75-25-164-4 Trott 12.4-2-22-2 McLeod 30-6-67-2 Reedman 6-1-12-0 Lyons 2-0-12-0 Iredale 2-1-3-0

Umpires: C Bannerman and J Phillips

Australia v England
1,2,4 February 1895

Result: Australia won by an innings and 147 runs

Australia Innings

GHS Trott	c Brown b Peel	1
W Bruce	c Brockwell b Peel	15
*G Giffen	b Peel	8
H Moses	b Richardson	1
H Graham	st Philipson b Briggs	105
SE Gregory	st Philipson b Briggs	5
FA Iredale	c & b Briggs	0
J Darling	b Richardson	31
AE Trott	not out	85
+AH Jarvis	c Philipson b Briggs	9
CTB Turner	c Richardson b Lockwood	22
	(b 3, lb 1, w 1, nb 1)	6
	(all out)	284

Bowling: Peel 24-5-74-3 Richardson 22-5-78-2 Briggs 22-4-65-4 Brockwell 5-1-25-0 Ford 2-0-14-0 Lockwood 8.5-3-22-1

England Innings

Batsman	1st innings		2nd innings	
AC MacLaren	st Jarvis b GHS Trott	1	c Bruce b Giffen	0
A Ward	c & b Turner	7	b Darling b Giffen	6
J Briggs	b GHS Trott	11	c Bruce b Giffen	6
*AE Stoddart	st Jarvis b GHS Trott	7	c Iredale b Turner	0
JT Brown	not out	20	b Giffen	0
W Brockwell	c Darling b Turner	1	c Bruce b Turner	17
FGJ Ford	c GHS Trott b Giffen	0	c Darling b Giffen	11
R Peel	st Jarvis b Turner	0	st Jarvis b Turner	0
+H Philipson	c Graham b Giffen	0	c & b Turner	9
T Richardson	c & b Giffen	2	not out	10
WH Lockwood	absent hurt	0	absent hurt	0
	(b 7, lb 3, nb 2)	12	(b 5, lb 7, nb 1)	13
	(all out)	65	(all out)	72

Bowling: GHS Trott 14-5-21-3 Turner 19-10-18-3 Giffen 5.5-1-14-3
Giffen 15-7-26-5 Turner 14.1-6-33-4

Umpires: C Bannerman and J Phillips

Sydney Cricket Ground

Australia v England
13,14,15,16,17 December 1897

Result: England won by 9 wickets

England Innings

JR Mason	b Jones	6	b McKibbin	32
*AC MacLaren	c Kelly b McLeod	109	not out	50
TW Hayward	c Trott b Trumble	72		
+W Storer	c & b Trott	43		
NF Druce	c Gregory b McLeod	20		
GH Hirst	b Jones	62		
KS Ranjitsinhji	c Gregory b McKibbin	175	not out	8
E Wainwright	b Jones	10		
JT Hearne	c & b McLeod	17		
J Briggs	run out	1		
T Richardson	not out	24		
	(lb 11, w 1)	12	(b 5, nb 1)	6
	(all out)	551	(1 wicket)	96

Bowling: McKibbin 34-5-113-1 Jones 50-8-130-3 McLeod 28-12-80-3 Trumble 40-7-138-1 Trott 23-2-78-1
Trumble 14-4-40-0 McKibbin 5-1-22-1 Jones 9-1-28-0

Australia Innings

J Darling	c Druce b Richardson	7	c Druce b Briggs	101
JJ Lyons	b Richardson	3	c Hayward b Hearne	25
FA Iredale	c Druce b Hearne	25	b Briggs	18
C Hill	b Hearne	19	b Hearne	96
SE Gregory	c Mason b Hearne	46	run out	31
*GHS Trott	b Briggs	10	b Richardson	27
+JJ Kelly	b Richardson	1	not out	46
H Trumble	c Storer b Mason	70	c Druce b Hearne	2
CE McLeod	not out	50	run out	26
TR McKibbin	b Hearne	0	b Hearne	6
E Jones	c Richardson b Hearne	0	lbw b Richardson	3
	(b 1, lb 1, nb 4)	6	(b 12, lb 1, w 4, nb 10)	27
	(all out)	237	(all out)	408

Bowling: Richardson 27-8-71-3 Hirst 28-7-57-0 Hearne 20.1-7-42-5 Briggs 20-7-42-1 Hayward 3-1-11-0 Mason 2-1-8-1
Richardson 41-9-121-2 Hirst 13-3-49-0 Hearne 38-8-99-4 Briggs 22-3-86-2 Hayward 5-1-16-0 Mason 2-0-10-0

Umpires: C Bannerman and J Phillips

Australia v England
26,28 February, 1,2 March 1898

Result: Australia won by 6 wickets

England Innings

*AC MacLaren	b Trott	65	c Darling b Jones	0
E Wainwright	c Hill b Trumble	49	b Noble	6
KS Ranjitsinhji	c Gregory b Trott	2	lbw b Jones	12
TW Hayward	b Jones	47	c Worrall b Trumble	43
+W Storer	b Jones	44	c Gregory b Trumble	31
NF Druce	lbw b Noble	64	c Howell b Trumble	18
GH Hirst	b Jones	44	c Trott b Jones	7
JR Mason	c Howell b Jones	7	b Trumble	11
J Briggs	b Jones	0	b Howell	29
JT Hearne	not out	2	not out	3
T Richardson	b Jones	1	b Howell	6
	(b 2, lb 5, w 2, nb 1)	10	(lb 12)	12
	(all out)	335	(all out)	178

Bowling: Noble 26-6-57-1 Howell 17-6-40-0 Trumble 26-4-67-1 Jones 26.2-3-82-6 Trott 23-6-56-2 McLeod 11-4-23-0
Noble 15-4-34-1 Howell 6.1-0-22-2 Trumble 24-7-37-4 Jones 26-3-61-3 Trott 7-1-12-0

Australia Innings

CE McLeod	b Richardson	64	b Hearne	4
J Darling	c Mason b Briggs	14	c Wainwright b Richardson	160
C Hill	b Richardson	8	b Richardson	2
J Worrall	c Ranjitsinhji b Richardson	26	c Hirst b Hayward	62
SE Gregory	c Storer b Richardson	21	not out	22
MA Noble	c Storer b Richardson	31	not out	15
*GHS Trott	c Ranjitsinhji b Hearne	18		
H Trumble	b Richardson	12		
+JJ Kelly	not out	27		
WP Howell	c MacLaren b Richardson	10		
E Jones	c Storer b Richardson	1		
	(b 5, w 1, nb 1)	7	(b 6, w 1, nb 4)	11
	(all out)	239	(4 wickets)	276

Bowling: Richardson 36.1-7-94-8 Briggs 17-4-39-1 Hearne 21-9-40-1 Storer 5-1-13-0 Mason 13-7-20-0 Hayward 4-0-12-0
Hirst 4-1-14-0
Richardson 21.4-1-110-2 Briggs 11-1-25-0 Hearne 15-5-52-1 Mason 11-1-27-0 Hayward 3-0-18-1 Hirst 7-0-33-0

Umpires: C Bannerman and J Phillips

Australia v England
13,14,16 December 1901

Result: England won by an innings and 124 runs

England Innings

*AC MacLaren	lbw b McLeod	116
TW Hayward	c Hill b Trumble	69
JT Tyldesley	c McLeod b Laver	1
WG Quaife	b Howell	21
GL Jessop	b McLeod	24
AO Jones	c Kelly b Noble	9
+AFA Lilley	c Laver b McLeod	84
LC Braund	c Jones b McLeod	58
JR Gunn	c & b Jones	21
SF Barnes	not out	26
C Blythe	c Trumble b Laver	20
	(b 6, lb 7, w 1, nb 1)	15
	(all out)	464

Bowling: Jones 36-8-98-1 Noble 33-17-91-1 McLeod 44-17-84-4 Howell 21-8-52-1 Trumble 34-12-85-1 Laver 17-6-39-2
Trumper 1-1-0-0

Australia Innings

SE Gregory	c Braund b Blythe	48	c MacLaren b Braund	43
VT Trumper	c & b Barnes	2	c Lilley b Blythe	34
C Hill	b Barnes	46	b Braund	0
MA Noble	st Lilley b Braund	2	c Lilley b Blythe	14
WP Howell	c Braund b Blythe	9	not out	31
CE McLeod	c Barnes	0	b Blythe	0
+JJ Kelly	c Blythe	12	c Jessop b Braund	12
*J Darling	c Quaife b Barnes	39	c Jessop b Braund	3
FJ Laver	c Quaife b Braund	6	st Lilley b Braund	0
H Trumble	not out	5	c Lilley b Barnes	26
E Jones	c Jessop b Barnes	5	c Jones b Braund	2
	(b 1, lb 3, nb 2)	6	(b 5, lb 2)	7
	(all out)	168	(all out)	172

Bowling: Barnes 35.1-9-65-5 Braund 15-4-40-2 Gunn 5-0-27-0 Blythe 16-8-26-3 Jessop 1-0-4-0
Barnes 16-2-74-1 Braund 28.4-8-61-5 Blythe 13-5-30-4

Umpires: R Callaway and RM Crockett

Australia v England
14,15,17,18 February 1902

Result: Australia won by 7 wickets

England Innings

*AC MacLaren	c Duff b Saunders	92	c Kelly b Noble	5
TW Hayward	b Saunders	41	b Noble	12
JT Tyldesley	c Kelly b Noble	79	c Trumble b Saunders	10
WG Quaife	c Kelly b Saunders	4	lbw b Noble	15
GL Jessop	c Noble b Saunders	0	b Saunders	15
LC Braund	lbw b Trumble	17	b Saunders	0
CP McGahey	b Trumble	18	c Kelly b Saunders	13
+AFA Lilley	c Kelly b Noble	40	c Trumble b Saunders	0
AO Jones	c Kelly b Trumble	15	c Kelly b Noble	6
JR Gunn	not out	0	not out	13
C Blythe	b Noble	4	c Kelly b Saunders	8
	(b 5, nb 2)	7	(lb 2)	2
	(all out)	317	(all out)	99

Bowling: Noble 33.2-12-78-3 Saunders 43-11-119-4 Howell 22-10-40-0 Trumble 38-18-65-3 Armstrong 2-1-8-0
Saunders 24.1-8-43-5 Noble 24-7-54-5

Australia Innings

*H Trumble	c MacLaren b Jessop	6		
VT Trumper	c Braund b Jessop	7	lbw b Blythe	25
C Hill	c Jones b Jessop	21	c Lilley b Gunn	30
SE Gregory	c Braund b Jessop	5	b Jessop	12
MA Noble	lbw b Braund	56		
RA Duff	c Lilley b Blythe	39	not out	51
WW Armstrong	b Braund	55		
AJY Hopkins	c Lilley b Braund	43		
+JJ Kelly	not out	24		
WP Howell	c MacLaren b Gunn	35	c sub b Gunn	0
JV Saunders	b Braund	0		
	(b 7, nb 1)	8	(b 1, nb 2)	3
	(all out)	299	(3 wickets)	121

Bowling: Braund 60-25-118-4 Gunn 16-5-48-1 Jessop 26-5-68-4 Blythe 37-17-57-1
Braund 15-2-55-0 Gunn 8.3-1-17-2 Jessop 7-0-23-0 Blythe 6-0-23-1

Umpires: C Bannerman and R Callaway

Australia v England
11,12,14,15,16,17 December 1903

Result: England won by 5 wickets

Australia Innings

RA Duff	c Lilley b Arnold	3	c Relf b Rhodes	84
VT Trumper	c Foster b Arnold	1	not out	185
C Hill	c Lilley b Hirst	51		
*MA Noble	c Foster b Arnold	133	st Lilley b Bosanquet	22
WW Armstrong	b Bosanquet	48	c Bosanquet b Rhodes	27
AJY Hopkins	b Hirst	39	c Arnold b Rhodes	20
WP Howell	c Relf b Arnold	4	c Lilley b Arnold	4
SE Gregory	b Bosanquet	23	c Lilley b Rhodes	43
FJ Laver	lbw b Rhodes	4	c Relf b Rhodes	6
+JJ Kelly	c Braund b Rhodes	10	b Arnold	13
JV Saunders	not out	11	run out	2
	(nb 3)	3	(b 10, lb 15, w 2, nb 1)	28
	(all out)	285	(all out)	485

Bowling: Hirst 24-8-47-2 Arnold 32-7-76-4 Braund 26-9-39-0 Bosanquet 13-0-52-2 Rhodes 17.2-3-41-2 Relf 6-1-27-0
Hirst 29-1-79-0 Arnold 28-2-93-2 Braund 12-2-56-0 Bosanquet 23-1-100-1 Rhodes 40.2-10-94-5 Relf 13-5-35-0

England Innings

TW Hayward	b Howell	15	st Kelly b Saunders	91
*PF Warner	c Kelly b Laver	0	b Howell	8
JT Tyldesley	b Noble	53	b Saunders	9
EG Arnold	c Laver b Armstrong	27		
RE Foster	c Noble b Saunders	287	st Kelly b Armstrong	19
LC Braund	b Howell	102	c Noble b Howell	0
GH Hirst	b Howell	0	not out	60
BJT Bosanquet	c Howell b Noble	4	not out	1
+AFA Lilley	c Hill b Noble	4		
AE Relf	c Armstrong b Saunders	31		
W Rhodes	not out	40		
	(b 6, lb 7, w 1, nb 2)	16	(b 3, lb 1, w 2)	6
	(all out)	577	(5 wickets)	194

Bowling: Saunders 36.2-8-125-2 Laver 37-12-119-1 Howell 31-7-111-3 Noble 34-8-99-3 Armstrong 23-3-47-1 Hopkins 11-1-40-0 Trumper 7-2-12-0 Gregory 2-0-8-0
Saunders 18.5-3-51-2 Laver 16-4-37-0 Howell 31-18-35-2 Noble 12-2-37-0 Armstrong 18-6-28-1

Umpires: RM Crockett and AC Jones

Australia v England
26,27,29 February, 1,2,3 March 1904

Result: England won by 157 runs

England Innings

TW Hayward	c McAlister b Trumble	18	lbw b Trumble	52
*PF Warner	b Noble	0	not out	31
JT Tyldesley	c Gregory b Noble	16	b Cotter	5
RE Foster	c McAlister b Noble	19	c Noble b Hopkins	27
AE Knight	not out	70	c McAlister b Cotter	9
LC Braund	c Trumble b Noble	39	c Noble b McLeod	19
GH Hirst	b Noble	25	c Kelly b McLeod	18
BJT Bosanquet	b Hopkins	12	c Hill b McLeod	7
EG Arnold	lbw b Noble	0	c Noble b McLeod	6
+AFA Lilley	c Hopkins b Trumble	24	b McLeod	6
W Rhodes	st Kelly b Noble	10	c McAlister b Cotter	29
	(b 6, lb 7, w 2, nb 1)	16	(b 1, lb 6)	7
	(all out)	249	(all out)	210

Bowling: Cotter 14-1-44-0 Noble 41.1-10-100-7 Trumble 43-20-58-2 Hopkins 8-3-22-1 McLeod 8-5-9-0
Cotter 18.3-3-41-3 Noble 19-8-40-1 Trumble 28-10-49-1 Hopkins 14-5-31-2 McLeod 20-5-42-3

Australia Innings

RA Duff	b Arnold	47	b Arnold	19
VT Trumper	b Braund	7	lbw b Arnold	12
C Hill	c Braund b Arnold	33	st Lilley b Bosanquet	26
PA McAlister	c Arnold b Rhodes	2	b Hirst	1
AJY Hopkins	b Arnold	9	st Lilley b Bosanquet	0
CE McLeod	b Rhodes	18	c Foster b Bosanquet	6
+JJ Kelly	c Foster b Arnold	5	c Foster b Bosanquet	10
*MA Noble	not out	6	lbw b Bosanquet	53
SE Gregory	c Foster b Rhodes	2	lbw b Bosanquet	0
H Trumble	c Lilley b Rhodes	0	st Lilley b Bosanquet	0
A Cotter	c Tyldesley b Arnold	0	b Hirst	34
	(b 1, w 1)	2	(b 10)	10
	(all out)	131	(all out)	171

Bowling: Hirst 13-1-36-0 Braund 11-2-27-2 Rhodes 11-3-33-4 Arnold 14.3-5-28-4 Bosanquet 2-1-5-0
Hirst 18.5-2-32-2 Braund 16-3-24-0 Rhodes 11-7-12-0 Arnold 12-3-42-2 Bosanquet 15-1-51-6

Umpires: P Argall and RM Crockett

Australia v England
13,14,16,17,18,19 December 1907

Result: Australia won by 2 wickets

England Innings

*FL Fane	c Trumper b Cotter	2	c Noble b Saunders	33
+RA Young	c Carter b Cotter	13	b Noble	3
G Gunn	c Hazlitt b Cotter	119	c Noble b Cotter	74
KL Hutchings	c & b Armstrong	42	c Armstrong b Saunders	17
LC Braund	b Cotter	30	not out	32
J Hardstaff snr	b Armstrong	12	b Noble	63
W Rhodes	run out	1	c McAlister b Macartney	29
JN Crawford	b Armstrong	31	c Hazlitt b Cotter	5
SF Barnes	b Cotter	1	b Saunders	11
C Blythe	b Cotter	5	c Noble b Saunders	15
A Fielder	not out	1	lbw b Armstrong	6
	(b 7, lb 6, w 1, nb 2)	16	(b 2, w 3, nb 7)	12
	(all out)	273	(all out)	300

Bowling: Cotter 21.5-0-101-6 Saunders 11-0-42-0 Hazlitt 9-2-32-0 Armstrong 26-10-63-3 Macartney 3-0-5-0 Noble 6-1-14-0
Cotter 26-1-101-2 Saunders 23-6-68-4 Hazlitt 4-2-24-0 Armstrong 27-14-33-1 Macartney 14-2-39-1 Noble 15-5-23-2

Australia Innings

VT Trumper	b Fielder	43	b Barnes	3
PA McAlister	c Hutchings b Barnes	3	b Crawford	41
C Hill	c Gunn b Fielder	87	b Fielder	1
*MA Noble	c Braund b Fielder	37	b Barnes	27
WW Armstrong	c Braund b Fielder	7	b Crawford	44
VS Ransford	c Braund b Rhodes	24	c & b Blythe	13
CG Macartney	c Young b Fielder	35	c Crawford b Fielder	9
+H Carter	b Braund	25	c Young b Fielder	61
GR Hazlitt	not out	18	not out	34
A Cotter	b Braund	2	not out	33
JV Saunders	c Braund b Fielder	9		
	(b 4, lb 2, w 2, nb 2)	10	(b 6, nb 3)	9
	(all out)	300	(8 wickets)	275

Bowling: Fielder 30.2-4-82-6 Barnes 22-3-74-1 Blythe 12-1-33-0 Braund 17-2-74-2 Crawford 5-1-14-0 Rhodes 5-2-13-1
Fielder 27.3-4-88-3 Barnes 30-7-63-2 Blythe 19-5-55-1 Braund 7-2-14-0 Crawford 8-2-33-2 Rhodes 7-3-13-0

Umpires: RM Crockett and W Hannah

Australia v England
21,22,24,25,26,27 February 1908

Result: Australia won by 49 runs

Australia Innings

*MA Noble	b Barnes	35	lbw b Rhodes	34
CG Macartney	c Crawford b Barnes	1	c Jones b Crawford	12
JDA O'Connor	c Young b Crawford	9	b Barnes	6
SE Gregory	c & b Barnes	44	b Crawford	56
C Hill	c Hutchings b Barnes	12	c Young b Crawford	44
WW Armstrong	c & b Crawford	3	c Gunn b Crawford	32
VT Trumper	c Braund b Barnes	10	c Gunn b Rhodes	166
VS Ransford	c Gunn b Barnes	11	not out	21
MJ Hartigan	c & b Crawford	1	b Crawford	5
+H Carter	not out	1	c Hobbs b Rhodes	22
JV Saunders	c Young b Barnes	0	c Young b Rhodes	0
	(b 9, lb 1)	10	(b 21, lb 3)	24
	(all out)	137	(all out)	422

Bowling: Barnes 22.4-6-60-7 Rhodes 10-5-15-0 Crawford 18-4-52-3
Barnes 27-6-78-1 Rhodes 37.4-7-102-4 Crawford 36-10-141-5 Braund 20-3-64-0 Hobbs 7-3-13-0

England Innings

JB Hobbs	b Saunders	72	c Gregory b Saunders	13
FL Fane	b Noble	0	b Noble	46
G Gunn	not out	122	b Macartney	0
KL Hutchings	run out	13	b Macartney	2
J Hardstaff snr	c O'Connor b Saunders	17	b Saunders	8
JN Crawford	c Hill b Saunders	6	not out	24
LC Braund	st Carter b Macartney	31	c Noble b Saunders	0
W Rhodes	c Noble b Armstrong	10	b Noble	69
+RA Young	st Carter b Macartney	0	c O'Connor b Saunders	11
*AO Jones	b Macartney	0	b Armstrong	34
SF Barnes	run out	1	b Saunders	11
	(b 6, lb 3)	9	(b 5, lb 6)	11
	(all out)	281	(all out)	229

Bowling: Noble 28-9-62-1 Saunders 35-5-114-3 O'Connor 6-0-23-0 Macartney 15.1-3-44-3 Armstrong 12-2-29-1
Noble 24-6-56-2 Saunders 35.1-5-82-5 O'Connor 13-3-29-0 Macartney 15-4-24-2 Armstrong 18-7-27-1

Umpires: W Hannah and AC Jones

Australia v South Africa
9,10,12,13,14 December 1910

Result: Australia won by an innings and 114 runs

Australia Innings

VT Trumper	run out	27
W Bardsley	b Pearse	132
*C Hill	b Pearse	191
DRA Gehrs	b Pearse	67
WW Armstrong	b Schwarz	48
VS Ransford	b Schwarz	11
CG Macartney	b Schwarz	1
C Kelleway	not out	14
+H Carter	st Sherwell b Schwarz	5
A Cotter	st Sherwell b Schwarz	0
WJ Whitty	c Snooke b Sinclair	15
	(b 12, lb 4, nb 1)	17
	(all out)	528

Bowling: Llewellyn 14-0-54-0 Sinclair 19.4-0-80-1 Schwarz 25-6-102-5 Nourse 12-0-61-0 Vogler 15-0-87-0 Faulkner 12-0-71-0 Pearse 12-0-56-3

South Africa Innings

LA Stricker	b Cotter	2	lbw b Whitty	4
JW Zulch	b Cotter	4	run out	1
COC Pearse	c Trumper b Cotter	16	run out	31
AW Nourse	c Kelleway b Cotter	5	not out	64
GA Faulkner	c Kelleway b Whitty	62	c Bardsley b Whitty	43
CB Llewellyn	b Cotter	0	c Macartney b Whitty	19
SJ Snooke	b Whitty	3	b Cotter	4
JH Sinclair	b Cotter	1	b Cotter	6
RO Schwarz	c Trumper b Whitty	61	c Carter b Whitty	0
*+PW Sherwell	not out	8	c Whitty b Kelleway	60
AEE Vogler	b Whitty	0	b Kelleway	0
	(lb 7, nb 5)	12	(lb 1, nb 7)	8
	(all out)	174	(all out)	240

Bowling: Cotter 20-2-69-6 Whitty 24-11-33-4 Armstrong 8-3-16-0 Kelleway 9-1-33-0 Macartney 7-4-11-0
Cotter 17-2-73-2 Whitty 21-4-75-4 Armstrong 9-1-35-0 Kelleway 15.1-4-37-2 Macartney 5-1-12-0

Umpires: RM Crockett and WG Curran

Australia v South Africa
3,4,6,7 March 1911

Result: Australia won by 7 wickets

Australia Innings

C Kelleway	c Snooke b Llewellyn	2	not out	24
CG Macartney	lbw b Schwarz	137	c Nourse b Schwarz	56
HV Hordern	lbw b Sinclair	50		
W Bardsley	c & b Sinclair	94	b Nourse	39
WJ Whitty	c Nourse b Llewellyn	13		
VT Trumper	b Schwarz	31	not out	74
*C Hill	st Sherwell b Schwarz	13		
WW Armstrong	c Pearse b Schwarz	0		
VS Ransford	st Sherwell b Schwarz	6	b Nourse	0
A Cotter	st Sherwell b Schwarz	8		
+H Carter	not out	1		
	(b 7, lb 2)	9	(b 1, lb 3, w 1)	5
	(all out)	364	(3 wickets)	198

Bowling: Llewellyn 25-0-92-2 Faulkner 12-2-38-0 Sinclair 27-6-83-2 Pegler 6-1-31-0 Schwarz 11.4-0-47-6 Nourse 5-1-26-0 Pearse 9-0-36-0 Zulch 1-0-2-0
Llewellyn 8-1-43-0 Faulkner 5-0-18-0 Sinclair 6-1-22-0 Pegler 4-0-22-0 Schwarz 9-0-42-1 Nourse 8.1-0-32-2 Pearse 3-0-14-0

South Africa Innings

COC Pearse	b Whitty	0	lbw b Hordern	2
JW Zulch	st Carter b Hordern	15	b Ransford	150
GA Faulkner	b Armstrong	52	b Cotter	92
AW Nourse	b Armstrong	3	c Cotter b Whitty	28
LA Stricker	c Macartney b Hordern	19	b Cotter	42
JH Sinclair	c Ransford b Hordern	1	c & b Whitty	12
SJ Snooke	b Hordern	18	c Carter b Whitty	12
CB Llewellyn	c Carter b Kelleway	24	b Whitty	3
RO Schwarz	run out	13	not out	6
*+PW Sherwell	c Bardsley b Whitty	5	b Armstrong	14
SJ Pegler	not out	0	c Cotter b Hordern	26
	(b 1, lb 9)	10	(b 3, lb 4, w 2, nb 5)	14
	(all out)	160	(all out)	401

Bowling: Cotter 8-2-24-0 Whitty 11.1-3-32-2 Hordern 21-3-73-4 Kelleway 4-1-4-1 Armstrong 6-1-17-2
Cotter 18-1-60-2 Whitty 27-5-66-4 Hordern 30.1-1-117-2 Kelleway 7-1-46-0 Armstrong 26-4-68-1 Macartney 10-0-21-0 Ransford 4-2-9-1

Umpires: RM Crockett and AC Jones

Australia v England
15,16,18,19,20,21 December 1911

Result: Australia won by 146 runs

Australia Innings

W Bardsley	c Strudwick b Douglas	30	b Foster	12
C Kelleway	c & b Woolley	20	b Douglas	70
*C Hill	run out	46	b Foster	65
WW Armstrong	st Strudwick b Hearne	60	b Foster	28
VT Trumper	c Hobbs b Woolley	113	c & b Douglas	14
VS Ransford	c Hearne b Barnes	26	c Rhodes b Barnes	34
RB Minnett	c Foster b Barnes	90	b Douglas	17
HV Hordern	not out	17	b Foster	18
A Cotter	c & b Barnes	6	lbw b Douglas	2
+H Carter	b Foster	13	c Gunn b Foster	15
WJ Whitty	b Foster	0	not out	9
	(b 9, lb 15, nb 2)	26	(b 16, lb 7, nb 1)	24
	(all out)	447	(all out)	308

Bowling: Foster 29-6-105-2 Douglas 24-5-62-1 Barnes 35-5-107-3 Hearne 10-1-44-1 Woolley 21-2-77-2 Rhodes 8-0-26-0
Foster 31.3-5-92-5 Douglas 21-3-50-4 Barnes 30-8-72-1 Hearne 13-2-51-0 Woolley 6-1-15-0 Rhodes 3-1-4-0

England Innings

JB Hobbs	c Hill b Whitty	63	c Carter b Cotter	22
SP Kinneir	b Kelleway	22	c Trumper b Hordern	30
G Gunn	b Cotter	4	c Whitty b Hordern	62
W Rhodes	c Hill b Hordern	41	c Trumper b Hordern	0
CP Mead	c & b Hordern	0	run out	25
JW Hearne	c Trumper b Kelleway	76	b Hordern	43
FR Foster	b Hordern	56	c Ransford b Hordern	21
FE Woolley	b Hordern	39	c Armstrong b Cotter	7
*JWHT Douglas	c Trumper b Hordern	0	b Hordern	32
SF Barnes	b Kelleway	9	b Hordern	14
+H Strudwick	not out	0	not out	12
	(b 3, lb 3, w 1, nb 1)	8	(b 14, lb 8, nb 1)	23
	(all out)	318	(all out)	291

Bowling: Cotter 19-0-88-1 Whitty 28-13-60-1 Kelleway 16.5-3-46-3 Hordern 27-4-85-5 Armstrong 9-3-28-0 Minnett 2-1-3-0
Cotter 27-3-71-2 Whitty 20-8-41-0 Kelleway 19-6-27-0 Hordern 42.2-11-90-7 Armstrong 15-3-39-0

Umpires: RM Crockett and WG Curran

Australia v England
23,24,26,27,28,29 February, 1 March 1912

Result: England won by 70 runs

England Innings

JB Hobbs	c Ransford b Hordern	32	c Hazlitt b Hordern	45
W Rhodes	b Macartney	8	lbw b Armstrong	30
G Gunn	st Carter b Hordern	52	b Hordern	61
JW Hearne	c Macartney b Armstrong	4	b Hordern	18
FR Foster	st Carter b Hazlitt	15	b McLaren	4
*JWHT Douglas	c Ransford b Hordern	18	b Armstrong	8
FE Woolley	not out	133	c Armstrong b Hazlitt	11
J Vine	b Hordern	36	not out	6
+EJ Smith	b Hordern	0	b Hordern	13
SF Barnes	c Hordern b Hazlitt	5	b Hordern	4
JW Hitch	c Hill b Hazlitt	4	c Ransford b Armstrong	4
	(b 10, lb 4, w 1, nb 2)	17	(b 8, nb 2)	10
	(all out)	324	(all out)	214

Bowling: McLaren 16-2-47-0 Macartney 12-3-26-1 Hordern 37-8-95-5 Hazlitt 31-6-75-3 Armstrong 25-8-42-1 Minnett 8-1-22-0
McLaren 8-1-23-1 Macartney 7-0-28-0 Hordern 25-5-66-5 Hazlitt 12-2-52-1 Armstrong 17.3-7-35-3 Minnett 1-1-0-0

Australia Innings

VT Trumper	c Woolley b Barnes	5	c Woolley b Barnes	50
SE Gregory	c Gunn b Douglas	32	c Smith b Barnes	40
*C Hill	c Smith b Hitch	20	b Foster	8
WW Armstrong	lbw b Barnes	33	b Barnes	33
RB Minnett	c Douglas b Hitch	0	c Woolley b Barnes	61
VS Ransford	c Hitch b Foster	29	b Woolley	9
+H Carter	c sub b Barnes	11	c Woolley b Foster	23
CG Macartney	c & b Woolley	26	c Woolley b Foster	27
HV Hordern	b Woolley	0	run out	4
GR Hazlitt	run out	1	c Rhodes b Foster	4
JW McLaren	not out	0	not out	0
	(b 14, lb 2, w 2, nb 1)	19	(b 22, lb 8, w 1, nb 2)	33
	(all out)	176	(all out)	292

Bowling: Foster 16-0-55-1 Barnes 19-2-56-3 Hitch 9-0-31-2 Douglas 7-0-14-1 Woolley 2-1-1-2
Foster 30.1-7-43-4 Barnes 39-12-106-4 Hitch 6-1-23-0 Douglas 9-0-34-0 Woolley 16-5-36-1 Rhodes 2-0-17-0

Umpires: RM Crockett and AC Jones

Sydney Cricket Ground

Australia v England
17,18,20,21,22 December 1920

Result: Australia won by 377 runs

Australia Innings

CG Macartney	b Waddington	19	b Douglas	69
HL Collins	run out	70	c Waddington b Douglas	104
W Bardsley	c Strudwick b Hearne	22	b Hearne	57
C Kelleway	run out	33	c Russell b Woolley	78
*WW Armstrong	st Strudwick b Woolley	12	b Parkin	158
JM Gregory	c Strudwick b Woolley	8	run out	0
JM Taylor	lbw b Hearne	34	c Woolley b Parkin	51
CE Pellew	c Hendren b Hearne	36	lbw b Woolley	16
J Ryder	run out	5	run out	6
+WAS Oldfield	c Hobbs b Parkin	7	c Strudwick b Parkin	16
AA Mailey	not out	10	not out	0
	(b 4, lb 6, nb 1)	11	(b 17, lb 7, nb 2)	26
	(all out)	267	(all out)	581

Bowling: Hitch 10-0-37-0 Waddington 18-3-35-1 Parkin 26.5-5-58-1 Hearne 34-8-77-3 Woolley 23-7-35-2 Douglas 3-0-14-0
Hitch 8-0-40-0 Waddington 23-4-53-0 Parkin 35.3-5-102-3 Hearne 42-7-124-1 Douglas 26-3-79-2 Woolley 36-11-90-2 Rhodes 22-2-67-0

England Innings

CAG Russell	b Kelleway	0	c Oldfield b Gregory	5
JB Hobbs	b Gregory	49	lbw b Armstrong	59
JW Hearne	c Gregory b Mailey	14	b Gregory	57
EH Hendren	c Gregory b Ryder	28	b Kelleway	56
FE Woolley	c Mailey b Ryder	52	st Oldfield b Mailey	16
*JWHT Douglas	st Oldfield b Mailey	21	c Armstrong b Mailey	7
W Rhodes	c Gregory b Mailey	3	c Ryder b Mailey	45
JW Hitch	c Kelleway b Gregory	3	c Taylor b Gregory	19
A Waddington	run out	7	c Strudwick b Gregory	3
CH Parkin	not out	4	b Kelleway	4
+H Strudwick	lbw b Gregory	2	not out	1
	(b 3, lb 4)	7	(b 6, lb 3)	9
	(all out)	190	(all out)	281

Bowling: Kelleway 6-2-10-1 Gregory 23.1-3-56-3 Mailey 23-4-95-3 Ryder 6-1-20-2 Armstrong 1-0-2-0
Kelleway 15.5-3-45-3 Gregory 33-6-70-3 Mailey 24.2-1-105-3 Ryder 17-6-24-0 Armstrong 10-0-21-1 Macartney 3-0-7-0

Umpires: RM Crockett and AC Jones

Australia v England
25,26,28 February, 1 March 1921

Result: Australia won by 9 wickets

England Innings

JB Hobbs	lbw b Gregory	40	c Taylor b Mailey	34
W Rhodes	c Carter b Kelleway	26	run out	25
JWH Makepeace	c Gregory b Mailey	3	c Gregory b Kelleway	7
EH Hendren	c Carter b Gregory	5	st Carter b Mailey	13
FE Woolley	b McDonald	53	c & b Kelleway	1
CAG Russell	c Gregory b Mailey	19	c Gregory b Armstrong	35
*JWHT Douglas	not out	32	c & b Mailey	68
PGH Fender	c Gregory b Kelleway	2	c Kelleway b McDonald	40
ER Wilson	c Carter b Kelleway	5	st Carter b Mailey	5
CH Parkin	c Taylor b Kelleway	9	c Gregory b Mailey	36
+H Strudwick	b Gregory	2	not out	5
	(b 3, lb 2, w 1, nb 2)	8	(b 3, lb 5, nb 3)	11
	(all out)	204	(all out)	280

Bowling: Gregory 16.1-4-42-3 McDonald 11-2-38-1 Kelleway 20-6-27-4 Mailey 23-1-89-2
Gregory 16-3-37-0 McDonald 25-3-58-1 Kelleway 14-3-29-2 Mailey 36.2-5-119-5 Ryder 2-2-0-0 Armstrong 8-2-26-1

Australia Innings

HL Collins	c Fender b Parkin	5	c Strudwick b Wilson	37
W Bardsley	c Fender b Douglas	7	not out	50
CG Macartney	c Hobbs b Fender	170	not out	2
JM Taylor	c Hendren b Douglas	32		
JM Gregory	c Strudwick b Fender	93		
*WW Armstrong	c Woolley b Fender	0		
J Ryder	b Fender	2		
C Kelleway	c Strudwick b Wilson	32		
+H Carter	c Woolley b Fender	17		
AA Mailey	b Wilson	5		
EA McDonald	not out	3		
	(b 18, lb 6, nb 2)	26	(b 3, nb 1)	4
	(all out)	392	(1 wicket)	93

Bowling: Douglas 16-0-84-2 Parkin 19-1-83-1 Woolley 15-1-58-0 Wilson 14.3-4-28-2 Fender 20-1-90-5 Rhodes 7-0-23-0
Parkin 9-1-32-0 Woolley 11-3-27-0 Wilson 6-1-8-1 Fender 1-0-2-0 Rhodes 7.2-1-20-0

Umpires: RM Crockett and DA Elder

Australia v England
19,20,22,23,24,26,27 December 1924

Result: Australia won by 193 runs

Australia Innings

*HL Collins	c Hendren b Tate	114	c Chapman b Tate	60
W Bardsley	c Woolley b Freeman	21	b Tate	22
WH Ponsford	b Gilligan	110	c Woolley b Freeman	27
AJ Richardson	b Hearne	22	c & b Freeman	98
JM Taylor	c Strudwick b Tate	43	b Tate	108
VY Richardson	b Freeman	42	c Hendren b Tate	18
C Kelleway	c Woolley b Tate	17	b Gilligan	23
HSTL Hendry	c Strudwick b Tate	3	c Strudwick b Tate	22
JM Gregory	c Strudwick b Tate	0	c Woolley b Freeman	2
+WAS Oldfield	not out	39	c Strudwick b Gilligan	18
AA Mailey	b Tate	21	not out	46
	(b 10, lb 8)	18	(b 2, lb 5, w 1)	8
	(all out)	450	(all out)	452

Bowling: Tate 55.1-11-130-6 Gilligan 23-0-92-1 Freeman 49-11-124-2 Hearne 12.1-3-28-1 Woolley 9-0-35-0 Hobbs 2-0-13-0 Chapman 2-0-10-0
Tate 33.7-8-98-5 Gilligan 27-6-114-2 Freeman 37-4-134-3 Hearne 25-2-88-0 Chapman 3-1-10-0

England Innings

JB Hobbs	c Kelleway b Gregory	115	c Hendry b Mailey	57
H Sutcliffe	c VY Richardson b Mailey	59	c Gregory b Mailey	115
JW Hearne	c sub b Mailey	7	b Gregory	0
FE Woolley	b Gregory	0	c Mailey b Gregory	123
EH Hendren	not out	74	c Gregory b Hendry	9
A Sandham	b Mailey	7	c Oldfield b Mailey	2
APF Chapman	run out	13	c Oldfield b Hendry	44
MW Tate	c sub b Mailey	7	c Ponsford b Kelleway	0
*AER Gilligan	b Gregory	1	b Kelleway	1
AP Freeman	b Gregory	0	not out	50
+H Strudwick	lbw b Gregory	6	c Oldfield b Hendry	2
	(b 1, lb 5, nb 3)	9	(b 4, lb 3, nb 1)	8
	(all out)	298	(all out)	411

Bowling: Gregory 28.7-2-111-5 Kelleway 14-3-44-0 Mailey 31-2-129-4 Hendry 5-1-5-0 AJ Richardson 1-1-0-0
Gregory 28-2-115-2 Kelleway 21-5-60-2 Mailey 32-0-179-3 Hendry 10.7-2-36-3 AJ Richardson 5-0-13-0

Umpires: AC Jones and AP Williams

Australia v England
27,28 February, 2,3,4 March 1925

Result: Australia won by 307 runs

Australia Innings

*HL Collins	c Strudwick b Gilligan	1	lbw b Tate	28
J Ryder	b Kilner	29	b Gilligan	7
JM Gregory	run out	29	lbw b Hearne	22
TJE Andrews	c Whysall b Kilner	26	c Woolley b Hearne	80
JM Taylor	c Whysall b Tate	15	st Strudwick b Tate	25
WH Ponsford	c Woolley b Kilner	80	run out	5
AF Kippax	b Kilner	42	c Whysall b Woolley	8
C Kelleway	lbw b Tate	9	c Whysall b Tate	73
+WAS Oldfield	c Strudwick b Tate	29	not out	65
AA Mailey	b Tate	14	b Tate	0
CV Grimmett	not out	12	b Tate	0
	(b 2, lb 5, nb 2)	9	(b 6, lb 4, w 1, nb 1)	12
	(all out)	295	(all out)	325

Bowling: Tate 39.5-6-92-4 Gilligan 13-1-46-1 Kilner 38-4-97-4 Hearne 7-0-33-0 Woolley 5-0-18-0
Tate 39.3-6-115-5 Gilligan 15-2-46-1 Kilner 34-13-54-0 Hearne 22-0-84-2 Woolley 8-1-14-1

England Innings

JB Hobbs	c Oldfield b Gregory	0	st Oldfield b Grimmett	13
H Sutcliffe	c Mailey b Kelleway	22	b Gregory	0
A Sandham	run out	4	lbw b Grimmett	15
FE Woolley	b Grimmett	47	c Andrews b Kelleway	28
EH Hendren	c Ponsford b Gregory	10	c Oldfield b Grimmett	10
JW Hearne	lbw b Grimmett	16	b Grimmett	24
WW Whysall	lbw b Grimmett	8	st Oldfield b Grimmett	18
R Kilner	st Oldfield b Grimmett	24	c Ponsford b Collins	1
MW Tate	b Ryder	25	c Mailey b Kelleway	33
*AER Gilligan	st Oldfield b Grimmett	5	not out	0
+H Strudwick	not out	1	c Mailey b Grimmett	0
	(lb 4, nb 1)	5	(b 1, lb 3)	4
	(all out)	167	(all out)	146

Bowling: Gregory 9-1-42-2 Kelleway 15-1-38-1 Mailey 5-0-13-0 Ryder 7-0-24-1 Grimmett 11.7-2-45-5
Gregory 10-0-53-1 Kelleway 7-1-16-2 Grimmett 19.4-3-37-6 Collins 8-2-36-1

Umpires: RM Crockett and DA Elder

Australia v England
14,15,17,18,19,20 December 1928

Result: England won by 8 wickets

Australia Innings

WM Woodfull	lbw b Geary	68	run out	111
VY Richardson	b Larwood	27	c Hendren b Tate	0
AF Kippax	b Geary	9	lbw b Tate	10
WH Ponsford	retired hurt	5	absent hurt	0
HSTL Hendry	b Geary	37	lbw b Tate	112
*J Ryder	lbw b Geary	25	c Chapman b Larwood	79
OE Nothling	b Larwood	8	not out	44
+WAS Oldfield	not out	41	lbw b Tate	0
CV Grimmett	run out	9	c Chapman b Geary	18
DD Blackie	b Geary	8	not out	11
H Ironmonger	c Duckworth b Larwood	1	b Geary	0
	(b 4, lb 9, w 2)	15	(b 5, lb 6, w 1)	12
	(all out)	253	(all out)	397

Bowling: Larwood 26.2-4-77-3 Tate 21-9-29-0 White 38-10-79-0 Geary 18-5-35-5 Hammond 5-0-18-0
Larwood 35-5-105-1 Tate 46-14-99-4 White 30-5-83-0 Geary 31.4-11-55-2 Hammond 9-0-43-0

England Innings

JB Hobbs	c Oldfield b Grimmett	40		
H Sutcliffe	c Hendry b Ironmonger	11		
WR Hammond	b Ironmonger	251		
DR Jardine	run out	28		
EH Hendren	c Richardson b Blackie	74		
*APF Chapman	c Ryder b Blackie	20		
H Larwood	c Ryder b Grimmett	43		
G Geary	lbw b Blackie	66	b Hendry	8
MW Tate	lbw b Blackie	25	c sub b Hendry	4
+G Duckworth	not out	39	not out	2
JC White	st Oldfield b Hendry	29	not out	2
	(b 2, lb 3, w 4, nb 1)	10		0
	(all out)	636	(2 wickets)	16

Bowling: Nothling 42-15-60-0 Grimmett 64-14-191-2 Ironmonger 68-21-142-2 Blackie 59-10-148-4 Hendry 23.1-4-52-1 Ryder 11-3-22-0 Kippax 5-3-11-0
Nothling 4-0-12-0 Hendry 3-2-4-2

Umpires: DA Elder and GA Hele

Australia v West Indies
1,2,3,5 January 1931

Result: Australia won by an innings and 172 runs

Australia Innings

WH Ponsford	b Scott	183	
A Jackson	c Francis b Griffith	8	
DG Bradman	c Barrow b Francis	25	
AF Kippax	c Bartlett b Griffith	10	
SJ McCabe	lbw b Scott	31	
*WM Woodfull	c Barrow b Constantine	58	
AG Fairfax	c Constantine b Francis	15	
+WAS Oldfield	run out	9	
CV Grimmett	b Scott	12	
A Hurwood	c Martin b Scott	5	
H Ironmonger	not out	3	
	(b 6, lb 5, nb 3)	19	
	(all out)	369	

Bowling: Griffith 28-4-57-2 Constantine 18-2-56-1 Francis 27-3-70-2 Scott 15.4-0-66-4 Martin 18-1-60-0 Birkett 10-1-41-0

West Indies Innings

CA Roach	run out	7	c Kippax b McCabe	25
LS Birkett	c Hurwood b Fairfax	3	c McCabe b Hurwood	8
GA Headley	b Fairfax	14	c Jackson b Hurwood	2
FR Martin	lbw b Grimmett	10	c McCabe b Hurwood	0
*GC Grant	c Hurwood b Ironmonger	6	not out	15
LN Constantine	c Bradman b Grimmett	12	b Hurwood	8
+IM Barrow	c Jackson b Fairfax	17	c McCabe b Ironmonger	10
GN Francis	b Grimmett	8	c Oldfield b Ironmonger	0
OC Scott	not out	15	c Woodfull b Grimmett	17
HC Griffith	c Kippax b Grimmett	8	lbw b Grimmett	0
EL Bartlett	absent hurt	0	absent hurt	0
	(b 6, nb 1)	7	(b 1, lb 2, w 1, nb 1)	5
	(all out)	107	(all out)	90

Bowling: Fairfax 13-4-19-3 Hurwood 5-1-7-0 Grimmett 19.1-3-54-4 Ironmonger 13-3-20-1
Fairfax 5-1-21-0 Hurwood 11-2-22-4 Grimmett 3.3-1-9-1 Ironmonger 4-1-13-3 McCabe 7-0-20-1

Umpires: GE Borwick and WG French

Australia v West Indies
27,28 February, 2,3,4 March 1931

Result: West Indies won by 30 runs

West Indies Innings

FR Martin	not out	123	c McCabe b Grimmett	20
CA Roach	lbw b Grimmett	31	c Oldfield b Ironmonger	34
GA Headley	lbw b McCabe	105	b Oxenham	30
*GC Grant	c McCabe b Ironmonger	62	not out	27
JED Sealy	c Kippax b Grimmett	4	run out	7
LN Constantine	c McCabe b Ironmonger	4	c Bradman b Ironmonger	4
EL Bartlett	b Grimmett	0	not out	0
+IM Barrow	not out	7		
OC Scott				
GN Francis				
HC Griffith				
	(b 6, lb 5, w 1, nb 6)	18	(b 1, lb 1)	2
	(6 wickets declared)	350	(5 wickets declared)	124

Bowling: Fairfax 21-2-60-0 Oxenham 24-10-51-0 Ironmonger 42-16-95-2 Grimmett 33-7-100-3 McCabe 15-5-26-1
Oxenham 10-4-14-1 Ironmonger 16-7-44-2 Grimmett 18-4-47-1 McCabe 7-2-17-0

Australia Innings

*WM Woodfull	c Constantine b Martin	22	c Constantine b Griffith	18
WH Ponsford	c Bartlett b Francis	7	c Constantine b Martin	28
DG Bradman	c Francis b Martin	43	b Griffith	0
AF Kippax	c Sealy b Constantine	3	c Roach b Constantine	10
KE Rigg	c Barrow b Francis	14	c Barrow b Francis	16
SJ McCabe	c Headley b Francis	21	c Grant b Martin	44
AG Fairfax	st Barrow b Scott	54	not out	60
RK Oxenham	c Barrow b Francis	0	lbw b Scott	14
+WAS Oldfield	run out	36	lbw b Griffith	0
CV Grimmett	not out	15	c Constantine b Griffith	12
H Ironmonger	b Griffith	1	not out	4
	(b 1, lb 7)	8	(b 3, lb 7, w 2, nb 2)	14
	(all out)	224	(all out)	220

Bowling: Francis 19-6-48-4 Griffith 13.2-3-31-1 Martin 27-3-67-2 Constantine 10-2-28-1 Scott 10-1-42-1
Francis 16-2-32-0 Griffith 13.3-3-50-4 Martin 18-4-44-2 Constantine 17-2-50-2 Scott 11-0-30-1

Umpires: H Armstrong and WG French

Australia v South Africa
18,19,21 December 1931

Result: Australia won by an innings and 155 runs

South Africa Innings

JAJ Christy	c Nitschke b Grimmett	14	c Woodfull b Ironmonger	41
B Mitchell	b McCabe	1	c Oldfield b Wall	24
DPB Morkel	st Oldfield b Grimmett	20	lbw b Grimmett	17
*+HB Cameron	b Wall	11	b Wall	0
HW Taylor	c Lee b Grimmett	7	c Grimmett b Ironmonger	6
KG Viljoen	b Ironmonger	37	b Grimmett	0
EL Dalton	b Grimmett	21	c Bradman b Ironmonger	14
CL Vincent	not out	31	c Ponsford b Grimmett	35
LS Brown	b McCabe	5	c Wall b Lee	8
NA Quinn	lbw b McCabe	5	st Oldfield b Grimmett	1
AJ Bell	b McCabe	0	not out	1
	(lb 3, w 1)	4	(b 5, lb 8, nb 1)	14
	(all out)	153	(all out)	161

Bowling: Wall 18-4-46-1 McCabe 12-5-13-4 Grimmett 24-12-28-4 Ironmonger 12-1-38-1 Lee 7-1-24-0
Wall 18-5-31-2 McCabe 3-0-25-0 Grimmett 20.3-7-44-4 Ironmonger 19-10-22-3 Lee 13-4-25-1

Australia Innings

*WM Woodfull	c Mitchell b Vincent	58
WH Ponsford	b Quinn	9
KE Rigg	b Bell	127
DG Bradman	c Viljoen b Morkel	112
SJ McCabe	c Christy b Vincent	79
HC Nitschke	b Bell	47
PK Lee	c Cameron b Brown	0
+WAS Oldfield	c Cameron b Bell	8
CV Grimmett	not out	9
TW Wall	c Morkel b Bell	6
H Ironmonger	c Cameron b Bell	0
	(b 5, lb 12, w 1)	18
	(all out)	469

Bowling: Bell 46.5-6-140-5 Quinn 42-10-95-1 Brown 29-3-100-1 Vincent 24-5-75-2 Morkel 12-2-33-1 Mitchell 1-0-8-0

Umpires: GE Borwick and GA Hele

Australia v England
2,3,5,6,7 December 1932

Result: England won by 10 wickets

Australia Innings

*WM Woodfull	c Ames b Voce	7	b Larwood	0
WH Ponsford	b Larwood	32	b Voce	2
JHW Fingleton	c Allen b Larwood	26	c Voce b Larwood	40
AF Kippax	lbw b Larwood	8	b Larwood	19
SJ McCabe	not out	187	lbw b Hammond	32
VY Richardson	c Hammond b Voce	49	c Voce b Hammond	0
+WAS Oldfield	c Ames b Larwood	4	c Leyland b Larwood	1
CV Grimmett	c Ames b Voce	19	c Allen b Larwood	5
LE Nagel	b Larwood	0	not out	21
WJ O'Reilly	b Voce	4	b Voce	7
TW Wall	c Allen b Hammond	4	c Ames b Allen	20
	(b 12, lb 4, nb 4)	20	(b 12, lb 2, w 1, nb 2)	17
	(all out)	360	(all out)	164

Bowling: Larwood 31-5-96-5 Voce 29-4-110-4 Allen 15-1-65-0 Hammond 14.2-0-34-1 Verity 13-4-35-0
Larwood 18-4-28-5 Voce 17.3-5-54-2 Allen 9-5-13-1 Hammond 15-6-37-2 Verity 4-1-15-0

England Innings

H Sutcliffe	lbw b Wall	194	not out	1
RES Wyatt	lbw b Grimmett	38	not out	0
WR Hammond	c Grimmett b Nagel	112		
Nawab of Pataudi snr	b Nagel	102		
M Leyland	c Oldfield b Wall	0		
*DR Jardine	c Oldfield b McCabe	27		
H Verity	b Nagel	2		
GOB Allen	c & b O'Reilly	19		
+LEG Ames	c McCabe b O'Reilly	0		
H Larwood	lbw b O'Reilly	0		
W Voce	not out	0		
	(b 7, lb 17, nb 6)	30		0
	(all out)	524	(0 wickets)	1

Bowling: Wall 38-4-104-3 Nagel 43.4-9-110-2 O'Reilly 67-32-117-3 Grimmett 64-22-118-1 McCabe 15-2-42-1 Kippax 2-1-3-0
McCabe 0.1-0-1-0

Umpires: GE Borwick and GA Hele

Australia v England
23,24,25,27,28 February 1933

Result: England won by 8 wickets

Australia Innings

VY Richardson	c Jardine b Larwood	0	c Allen b Larwood	0
*WM Woodfull	b Larwood	14	b Allen	67
DG Bradman	b Larwood	48	b Verity	71
LPJ O'Brien	c Larwood b Voce	61	c Verity b Voce	5
SJ McCabe	c Hammond b Verity	73	c Jardine b Voce	4
LS Darling	b Verity	85	c Wyatt b Verity	7
+WAS Oldfield	run out	52	c Wyatt b Verity	5
PK Lee	c Jardine b Verity	42	b Allen	15
WJ O'Reilly	b Allen	19	b Verity	1
HH Alexander	not out	17	lbw b Verity	0
H Ironmonger	b Larwood	1	not out	0
	(b 13, lb 9, w 1)	23	(b 4, nb 3)	7
	(all out)	435	(all out)	182

Bowling: Larwood 32.2-10-98-4 Voce 24-4-80-1 Allen 25-1-128-1 Hammond 8-0-32-0 Verity 17-3-62-3 Wyatt 2-0-12-0
Larwood 11-0-44-1 Voce 10-0-34-2 Allen 11.4-2-54-2 Hammond 3-0-10-0 Verity 19-9-33-5

England Innings

*DR Jardine	c Oldfield b O'Reilly	18	c Richardson b Ironmonger	24
H Sutcliffe	c Richardson b O'Reilly	56		
WR Hammond	lbw b Lee	101	not out	75
H Larwood	c Ironmonger b Lee	98		
M Leyland	run out	42	b Ironmonger	0
RES Wyatt	c Ironmonger b O'Reilly	51	not out	61
+LEG Ames	run out	4		
E Paynter	b Lee	9		
GOB Allen	c Bradman b Lee	48		
H Verity	c Oldfield b Alexander	4		
W Voce	not out	7		
	(b 7, lb 7, nb 2)	16	(b 6, lb 1, nb 1)	8
	(all out)	454	(2 wickets)	168

Bowling: Alexander 35-1-129-1 McCabe 12-1-27-0 O'Reilly 45-7-100-3 Ironmonger 31-13-64-0 Lee 40.2-11-111-4 Darling 7-5-3-0 Bradman 1-0-4-0
Alexander 11-2-25-0 McCabe 5-2-10-0 O'Reilly 15-5-32-0 Ironmonger 26-12-34-2 Lee 12.2-3-52-0 Darling 2-0-7-0

Umpires: GE Borwick and GA Hele

Australia v England
18,19,21,22 December 1936

Result: England won by an innings and 22 runs

England Innings

AE Fagg	c Sievers b McCormick	11		
CJ Barnett	b Ward	57		
WR Hammond	not out	231		
M Leyland	lbw b McCabe	42		
+LEG Ames	c sub b Ward	29		
*GOB Allen	lbw b O'Reilly	9		
J Hardstaff jnr	b McCormick	26		
H Verity	not out	0		
JM Sims				
RWV Robins				
W Voce				
	(b 8, lb 8, w 1, nb 4)	21		
	(6 wickets declared)	426		

Bowling: McCormick 20-1-79-2 Sievers 16.2-4-30-0 Ward 24-8-132-2 O'Reilly 41-17-86-1 Chipperfield 13-2-47-0 McCabe 9-1-31-1

Australia Innings

JHW Fingleton	c Verity b Voce	12	b Sims	73
LPJ O'Brien	c Sims b Voce	0	c Allen b Hammond	17
*DG Bradman	c Allen b Voce	0	b Verity	82
SJ McCabe	c Sims b Voce	0	lbw b Voce	93
AG Chipperfield	c Sims b Allen	13	b Voce	21
MW Sievers	c Voce b Verity	4	run out	24
+WAS Oldfield	b Verity	1	c Ames b Voce	1
WJ O'Reilly	not out	37	b Hammond	3
EL McCormick	b Allen	10	lbw b Hammond	0
FA Ward	b Allen	0	not out	1
CL Badcock	absent hurt	0	lbw b Allen	2
	(b 1, lb 1, nb 1)	3	(lb 3, nb 4)	7
	(all out)	80	(all out)	324

Bowling: Voce 8-1-10-4 Allen 5.7-1-19-3 Verity 3-0-17-2 Hammond 4-0-6-0 Sims 2-0-20-0 Robins 1-0-5-0
Voce 19-4-66-3 Allen 19-4-61-1 Verity 19-7-55-1 Hammond 15.7-3-29-3 Sims 17-0-80-1 Robins 7-0-26-0

Umpires: GE Borwick and JD Scott

Australia v England
13,14,16,17,18,19 December 1946

Result: Australia won by an innings and 33 runs

England Innings

L Hutton	c Tallon b Johnson	39	hit wicket b Miller	37
C Washbrook	b Freer	1	c McCool b Johnson	41
WJ Edrich	lbw b McCool	71	b McCool	119
DCS Compton	c Tallon b McCool	5	c Bradman b Freer	54
*WR Hammond	c Tallon b McCool	1	c Toshack b McCool	37
JT Ikin	c Hassett b Johnson	60	b Freer	17
NWD Yardley	c Tallon b Johnson	25	b McCool	35
TPB Smith	lbw b Johnson	4	c Hassett b Johnson	2
+TG Evans	b Johnson	5	st Tallon b McCool	9
AV Bedser	b Johnson	14	not out	3
DVP Wright	not out	15	c Tallon b McCool	0
	(b 4, lb 11)	15	(b 8, lb 6, w 1, nb 2)	17
	(all out)	255	(all out)	371

Bowling: Miller 9-2-24-0 Freer 7-1-25-1 Toshack 7-2-6-0 Tribe 20-3-70-0 Johnson 30.1-12-42-6 McCool 23-2-73-3
Miller 11-3-37-1 Freer 13-2-49-2 Toshack 6-1-16-0 Tribe 12-0-40-0 Johnson 29-7-92-2 McCool 32.4-4-109-5 Barnes 3-0-11-0

Australia Innings

SG Barnes	c Ikin b Bedser	234
AR Morris	b Edrich	5
IWG Johnson	c Washbrook b Edrich	7
AL Hassett	c Compton b Edrich	34
KR Miller	c Evans b Smith	40
*DG Bradman	lbw b Yardley	234
CL McCool	c Hammond b Smith	12
+D Tallon	c & b Wright	30
FAW Freer	not out	28
GE Tribe	not out	25
ERH Toshack		
	(lb 7, w 1, nb 2)	10
	(8 wickets declared)	659

Bowling: Bedser 46-7-153-1 Edrich 26-3-79-3 Wright 46-8-169-1 Smith 37-1-172-2 Ikin 3-0-15-0 Compton 6-0-38-0 Yardley 9-0-23-1

Umpires: GE Borwick and JD Scott

Sydney Cricket Ground

Australia v England
28 February, 1,3,4,5 March 1947

Result: Australia won by 5 wickets

England Innings

L Hutton	retired hurt	122	absent hurt	0
C Washbrook	b Lindwall	0	b McCool	24
WJ Edrich	c Tallon b Lindwall	60	st Tallon b McCool	24
LB Fishlock	b McCool	14	lbw b Lindwall	0
DCS Compton	hit wicket b Lindwall	17	c Miller b Toshack	76
*NWD Yardley	c Miller b Lindwall	2	b McCool	11
JT Ikin	b Lindwall	0	b McCool	0
+TG Evans	b Lindwall	29	b Miller	20
TPB Smith	b Lindwall	2	c Tallon b Lindwall	24
AV Bedser	not out	10	st Tallon b McCool	4
DVP Wright	c Tallon b Miller	7	not out	1
	(b 7, lb 8, w 1, nb 1)	17	(b 1, lb 1)	2
	(all out)	280	(all out)	186

Bowling: Lindwall 22-3-63-7 Miller 15.3-2-31-1 Tribe 28-2-95-0 Toshack 16-4-40-0 McCool 13-0-34-1
Lindwall 12-1-46-2 Miller 6-1-11-1 Tribe 14-0-58-0 Toshack 4-1-14-1 McCool 21.4-5-44-5 Barnes 3-0-11-0

Australia Innings

SG Barnes	c Evans b Bedser	71	c Evans b Bedser	30
AR Morris	lbw b Bedser	57	run out	17
*DG Bradman	b Wright	12	c Compton b Bedser	63
AL Hassett	c Ikin b Wright	24	c Ikin b Wright	47
KR Miller	c Ikin b Wright	23	not out	34
RA Hamence	not out	30	c Edrich b Wright	1
CL McCool	c Yardley b Wright	3	not out	13
+D Tallon	c Compton b Wright	0		
RR Lindwall	b Smith b Wright	0		
GE Tribe	c Fishlock b Wright	9		
ERH Toshack	run out	5		
	(b 7, lb 6, nb 6)	19	(b 4, lb 1, nb 4)	9
	(all out)	253	(5 wickets)	214

Bowling: Bedser 27-7-49-2 Edrich 7-0-34-0 Smith 8-0-38-0 Wright 29-4-105-7 Yardley 5-2-8-0
Bedser 22-4-75-2 Edrich 2-0-14-0 Smith 2-0-8-0 Wright 22-1-93-2 Yardley 3-1-7-0 Compton 1.2-0-8-0

Umpires: GE Borwick and JD Scott

Australia v India
12,13,15,16,17,18 December 1947

Result: Match drawn

India Innings

MH Mankad	b Lindwall	5	b Lindwall	5
CT Sarwate	b Johnston	3	c Johnson b Johnston	3
Gul Mohammad	c Brown b Miller	29	c Bradman b Johnson	5
VS Hazare	b Miller	16	not out	13
*L Amarnath	b Johnson	25	c Morris b Johnson	14
G Kishenchand	b Johnson	44	c McCool b Johnston	0
HR Adhikari	lbw b Johnston	0	not out	0
DG Phadkar	c Miller b McCool	51	c Tallon b Miller	2
CS Nayudu	c & b McCool	6		
Amir Elahi	c Miller b McCool	4	c Miller b Johnston	13
+JK Irani	not out	1		
	(b 5, lb 2)	7	(b 3, lb 3)	6
	(all out)	188	(7 wickets)	61

Bowling: Lindwall 12-3-30-1 Johnston 17-4-33-2 Miller 9-3-25-2 McCool 18-2-71-3 Johnson 14-3-22-2
Lindwall 5-1-13-1 Johnston 13-5-15-3 Miller 6-2-5-1 Johnson 13-7-22-2

Australia Innings

WA Brown	run out	18
AR Morris	lbw b Amarnath	10
*DG Bradman	b Hazare	13
AL Hassett	c Adhikari b Hazare	6
KR Miller	lbw b Phadkar	17
RA Hamence	c Adhikari b Mankad	25
IWG Johnson	lbw b Phadkar	4
CL McCool	b Phadkar	9
RR Lindwall	b Hazare	0
+D Tallon	c Irani b Hazare	6
WA Johnston	not out	0
	(b 1, lb 1)	2
	(all out)	107

Bowling: Phadkar 10-2-14-3 Amarnath 14-4-31-1 Mankad 9-0-31-1 Hazare 13.2-3-29-4

Umpires: AN Barlow and GE Borwick

Australia v England
5,6,8,9 January 1951

Result: Australia won by an innings and 13 runs

England Innings

L Hutton	lbw b Miller	62	c Tallon b Iverson	9
C Washbrook	c Miller b Johnson	18	b Iverson	34
RT Simpson	c Loxton b Miller	49	c Tallon b Iverson	5
DCS Compton	b Miller	0	c Johnson b Johnston	23
WGA Parkhouse	c Morris b Johnson	25	run out	15
*FR Brown	b Lindwall	79	c Tallon b Iverson	18
TE Bailey	c Tallon b Johnson	15	not out	0
+TG Evans	not out	23	b Johnson	14
AV Bedser	b Lindwall	3	b Iverson	4
JJ Warr	b Miller	4	b Iverson	0
DVP Wright	run out	0	absent hurt	0
	(lb 10, nb 2)	12	(b 1, lb 5)	6
	(all out)	290	(all out)	123

Bowling: Lindwall 16-0-60-2 Miller 15.7-4-37-4 Johnson 31-8-94-3 Johnston 21-5-50-0 Iverson 10-1-25-0 Loxton 5-0-12-0
Lindwall 4-1-12-0 Miller 6-2-15-0 Johnson 10-2-32-1 Johnston 13-6-31-1 Iverson 19.4-8-27-6

Australia Innings

KA Archer	c Evans b Bedser	48
AR Morris	b Bedser	0
*AL Hassett	c Bedser b Brown	70
RN Harvey	b Bedser	39
KR Miller	not out	145
SJE Loxton	c Bedser b Brown	17
+D Tallon	lbw b Bedser	18
IWG Johnson	b Brown	77
RR Lindwall	lbw b Brown	1
WA Johnston	run out	1
JB Iverson	run out	1
	(b 3, lb 7)	10
	(all out)	426

Bowling: Bedser 43-4-107-4 Warr 36-4-142-0 Brown 44-4-153-4 Compton 6-1-14-0

Umpires: AN Barlow and HAR Elphinstone

Australia v West Indies
30 November, 1,3,4,5 December 1951

Result: Australia won by 7 wickets

West Indies Innings

AF Rae	c Johnson b Johnston	17	c Ring b Miller	9
JB Stollmeyer	c Johnson b Lindwall	36	b Johnson	35
FMM Worrell	b Johnson	64	c Langley b Lindwall	20
ED Weekes	b Lindwall	5	b Johnson	56
+CL Walcott	c Langley b Ring	60	st Langley b Johnson	10
RJ Christiani	b Hole	76	c Hassett b Miller	30
GE Gomez	lbw b Johnston	54	c Miller b Lindwall	41
*JDC Goddard	c Johnson b Johnston	33	not out	57
PEW Jones	lbw b Lindwall	1	c Miller b Johnston	7
S Ramadhin	b Lindwall	0	b Miller	3
AL Valentine	not out	0	b Miller	1
	(b 12, lb 3, nb 1)	16	(b 9, lb 12)	21
	(all out)	362	(all out)	290

Bowling: Lindwall 26-2-66-4 Johnston 25.4-2-80-3 Johnson 14-3-48-1 Miller 21-3-72-0 Ring 17-1-71-1 Hole 4-1-9-1
Lindwall 17-3-59-2 Johnston 24-5-61-2 Johnson 23-2-78-3 Miller 13.2-2-50-3 Ring 7-0-21-0

Australia Innings

KA Archer	c Weekes b Gomez	11	lbw b Worrell	47
AR Morris	c Walcott b Jones	11	st Walcott b Ramadhin	30
*AL Hassett	c Christiani b Jones	132	not out	46
RN Harvey	c Gomez b Goddard	39	lbw b Worrell	1
KR Miller	b Valentine	129	not out	6
GB Hole	b Valentine	1		
RR Lindwall	run out	48		
IWG Johnson	c Walcott b Jones	5		
DT Ring	c Ramadhin b Valentine	65		
+GRA Langley	not out	15		
WA Johnston	b Valentine	28		
	(b 12, lb 18, nb 3)	33	(b 6, lb 1)	7
	(all out)	517	(3 wickets)	137

Bowling: Jones 27-5-68-3 Gomez 18-2-47-1 Worrell 11-0-60-0 Valentine 30.5-3-111-4 Ramadhin 41-7-143-0 Goddard 24-6-55-1
Jones 5-1-16-0 Gomez 5-1-9-0 Worrell 2-0-7-2 Valentine 10-0-45-0 Ramadhin 12.3-1-53-1

Umpires: AN Barlow and HAR Elphinstone

Australia v West Indies
25,26,28,29 January 1952

Result: Australia won by 202 runs

Australia Innings

CC McDonald	c Worrell b Gomez	32	b Ramadhin	62
GR Thoms	b Gomez	16	hit wicket b Worrell	28
*AL Hassett	c Guillen b Gomez	2	c Worrell b Valentine	64
RN Harvey	b Gomez	18	c Guillen b Worrell	8
KR Miller	c Rae b Worrell	20	c Weekes b Valentine	69
GB Hole	c Guillen b Worrell	1	b Worrell	62
R Benaud	c Stollmeyer b Gomez	3	sub b Worrell	19
RR Lindwall	c Worrell b Gomez	0	c Walcott b Gomez	21
DT Ring	c Atkinson b Gomez	4	b Gomez	12
+GRA Langley	c Weekes b Worrell	6	b Gomez	8
WA Johnston	not out	13	not out	6
	(lb 1)	1	(b 10, lb 8)	18
	(all out)	116	(all out)	377

Bowling: Worrell 12.2-1-42-3 Gomez 18-3-55-7 Atkinson 6-2-18-0
Worrell 23-2-95-4 Gomez 18.2-3-58-3 Atkinson 8-0-25-0 Ramadhin 34-8-102-1 Valentine 30-6-79-2

West Indies Innings

AF Rae	c Langley b Johnston	11	c Harvey b Ring	25
*JB Stollmeyer	lbw b Johnston	10	lbw b Lindwall	104
CL Walcott	b Lindwall	1	c Langley b Miller	12
ED Weekes	c Langley b Lindwall	0	c Langley b Lindwall	21
RJ Christiani	c & b Miller	7	c Johnston b Lindwall	4
FMM Worrell	b Miller	6	run out	18
GE Gomez	b Miller	11	b Miller	2
DS Atkinson	b Miller	6	hit wicket b Lindwall	2
+SC Guillen	not out	13	b Lindwall	6
S Ramadhin	b Johnston	0	not out	3
AL Valentine	c Langley b Miller	6	b Benaud	0
	(b 3, lb 3, w 1)	7	(b 4, lb 11, w 1)	16
	(all out)	78	(all out)	213

Bowling: Lindwall 8-1-20-2 Johnston 14-3-25-3 Miller 7.6-1-26-5
Lindwall 21-4-52-5 Johnston 10-2-30-0 Miller 19-2-57-2 Ring 13-1-44-1 Benaud 4.3-0-14-1

Umpires: HAR Elphinstone and MJ McInnes

Australia v South Africa
9,10,12,13 January 1953

Result: Australia won by an innings and 38 runs

South Africa Innings

DJ McGlew	run out	24	c Langley b Lindwall	9
+JHB Waite	c Morris b Johnston	32	c Hole b Lindwall	0
WR Endean	b Lindwall	18	lbw b Miller	71
KJ Funston	b Ring	56	c Hole b Miller	16
RA McLean	b Lindwall	0	c Benaud b Lindwall	65
*JE Cheetham	c Johnston b Miller	5	c Morris b Lindwall	5
ARA Murray	sub b Miller	4	c Hole b Benaud	17
JC Watkins	sub b Miller	17	c Miller b Johnston	48
PNF Mansell	b Lindwall	8	c Hole b Benaud	0
HJ Tayfield	not out	3	absent hurt	0
MG Melle	c Langley b Lindwall	1	not out	0
	(b 1, lb 3, w 1)	5	(lb 1)	1
	(all out)	173	(all out)	232

Bowling: Lindwall 14.2-1-40-4 Miller 17-1-48-3 Johnston 18-5-46-1 Ring 12-4-23-1 Hole 2-0-11-0
Lindwall 20-3-72-4 Miller 18-6-33-2 Johnston 14-6-51-1 Ring 12-1-54-0 Benaud 5-1-21-2

Australia Innings

CC McDonald	c Endean b Tayfield	67
AR Morris	b Watkins	18
*AL Hassett	c Funston b Murray	2
RN Harvey	c Watkins b Murray	190
KR Miller	lbw b Tayfield	55
GB Hole	run out	5
R Benaud	lbw b Melle	0
DT Ring	b Tayfield	58
RR Lindwall	b Murray	1
+GRA Langley	c Mansell b Murray	20
WA Johnston	not out	7
	(b 3, lb 12, w 1, nb 4)	20
	(all out)	443

Bowling: Melle 23-3-98-1 Watkins 12-5-16-1 Murray 51.2-11-169-4 Tayfield 38-9-94-3 Mansell 7-0-46-0

Umpires: HAR Elphinstone and MJ McInnes

Australia v England
17,18,20,21,22 December 1954

Result: England won by 38 runs

England Innings

*L Hutton	c Davidson b Johnston	30	c Benaud b Johnston		28
TE Bailey	b Lindwall	0	c Langley b Archer		6
PBH May	c Johnston b Archer	5	b Lindwall		104
TW Graveney	c Favell b Johnston	21	c Langley b Johnston		0
MC Cowdrey	c Langley b Davidson	23	c Archer b Benaud		54
WJ Edrich	c Benaud b Archer	10	b Archer		29
FH Tyson	b Lindwall	0	b Lindwall		9
+TG Evans	c Langley b Archer	3	c Lindwall b Archer		4
JH Wardle	c Burke b Johnston	35	lbw b Lindwall		8
R Appleyard	c Hole b Davidson	8	not out		19
JB Statham	not out	14	c Langley b Johnston		25
	(lb 5)	5	(lb 6, nb 4)		10
	(all out)	154	(all out)		296

Bowling: Lindwall 17-3-47-2 Archer 12-7-12-3 Davidson 12-3-34-2 Johnston 13.3-1-56-3
Lindwall 31-10-69-3 Archer 22-9-53-3 Davidson 13-2-52-0 Johnston 19.3-2-70-3 Benaud 19-3-42-1

Australia Innings

LE Favell	c Graveney b Bailey	26	c Edrich b Tyson		16
*AR Morris	c Hutton b Bailey	12	lbw b Statham		10
JW Burke	c Graveney b Bailey	44	b Tyson		14
RN Harvey	c Cowdrey b Tyson	12	not out		92
GB Hole	b Tyson	12	b Tyson		0
R Benaud	lbw b Statham	20	c Tyson b Appleyard		12
RG Archer	c Hutton b Tyson	49	b Tyson		6
AK Davidson	b Statham	20	c Evans b Statham		5
RR Lindwall	c Evans b Tyson	19	b Tyson		8
+GRA Langley	b Bailey	5	b Statham		0
WA Johnston	not out	0	c Evans b Tyson		11
	(b 5, lb 2, nb 2)	9	(lb 7, nb 3)		10
	(all out)	228	(all out)		184

Bowling: Statham 18-1-83-2 Bailey 17.4-3-59-4 Tyson 13-2-45-4 Appleyard 7-1-32-0
Statham 19-6-45-3 Bailey 6-0-21-0 Tyson 18.4-1-85-6 Appleyard 6-1-12-1 Wardle 4-2-11-0

Umpires: MJ McInnes and RJJ Wright

Australia v England
25,26,28 February, 1,2,3 March 1955

Result: Match drawn

England Innings

*L Hutton	c Burge b Lindwall	6			
TW Graveney	c & b Johnson	111			
PBH May	c Davidson b Benaud	79			
MC Cowdrey	c Maddocks b Johnson	0			
DCS Compton	c & b Johnson	84			
TE Bailey	b Lindwall	72			
+TG Evans	c McDonald b Lindwall	10			
JH Wardle	not out	5			
FH Tyson					
R Appleyard					
JB Statham					
	(b 1, lb 3)	4			
	(7 wickets declared)	371			

Bowling: Lindwall 20.6-5-77-3 Miller 15-1-71-0 Davidson 19-3-72-0 Johnson 20-5-68-3 Benaud 20-4-79-1

Australia Innings

WJ Watson	b Wardle	18	c Graveney b Statham		3
CC McDonald	c May b Appleyard	72	c Evans b Graveney		37
LE Favell	b Tyson	1	c Graveney b Wardle		9
RN Harvey	c & b Tyson	13	c & b Wardle		1
KR Miller	run out	19	b Wardle		28
PJP Burge	c Appleyard b Wardle	17	not out		18
R Benaud	b Wardle	7	b Hutton		22
+LV Maddocks	c Appleyard b Wardle	32			
AK Davidson	c Evans b Wardle	18			
*IWG Johnson	run out	11			
RR Lindwall	not out	2			
	(b 10, lb 1)	11			0
	(all out)	221	(6 wickets)		118

Bowling: Tyson 11-1-46-2 Statham 9-1-31-0 Appleyard 16-2-54-1 Wardle 24.4-6-79-5
Tyson 5-2-20-0 Statham 5-0-11-1 Wardle 12-1-51-3 Graveney 6-0-34-1 Hutton 0.6-0-2-1

Umpires: MJ McInnes and RJJ Wright

Australia v England
9,10,12,13,14,15 January 1959

Result: Match drawn

England Innings

TE Bailey	lbw b Meckiff	8	c sub b Benaud		25
CA Milton	c Meckiff b Davidson	8	c Davidson b Benaud		8
TW Graveney	c Harvey b Benaud	33	lbw b Davidson		22
*PBH May	c Mackay b Slater	42	b Burke		92
MC Cowdrey	c Harvey b Benaud	34	not out		100
ER Dexter	lbw b Slater	1	c Grout b Benaud		11
+R Swetman	c Mackay b Benaud	41	lbw b Burke		5
GAR Lock	lbw b Mackay	21	not out		11
FS Trueman	c Burke b Benaud	18	st Grout b Benaud		0
JC Laker	c Harvey b Benaud	2			
JB Statham	not out	0			
	(b 4, lb 5, w 2)	11	(b 11, lb 1, w 1)		13
	(all out)	219	(7 wickets declared)		287

Bowling: Davidson 12-3-21-1 Meckiff 15-2-45-1 Benaud 33.4-10-83-5 Slater 14-4-40-2 Mackay 8-3-19-1
Davidson 33-11-65-1 Meckiff 3-1-7-0 Benaud 33-7-94-4 Slater 18-5-61-0 Mackay 11-2-21-0 Burke 11-3-26-2

Australia Innings

CC McDonald	c Graveney b Lock	40	b Laker		16
JW Burke	c Lock b Laker	12	b Laker		7
RN Harvey	b Laker	7	not out		18
NC O'Neill	c Swetman b Laker	77	not out		7
LE Favell	c Cowdrey b Lock	54			
KD Mackay	b Trueman	57			
*R Benaud	b Laker	6			
AK Davidson	lbw b Lock	71			
+ATW Grout	c Statham b Laker	1			
KN Slater	not out	1			
I Meckiff	b Lock	2			
	(b 5, lb 10, nb 1)	16	(b 6)		6
	(all out)	357	(2 wickets)		54

Bowling: Statham 16-2-48-0 Trueman 18-3-37-1 Lock 43.2-9-130-4 Laker 46-9-107-5 Bailey 5-0-19-0
Statham 2-0-6-0 Trueman 4-1-9-0 Lock 11-4-23-0 Laker 8-3-10-2

Umpires: C Hoy and MJ McInnes

Australia v West Indies
13,14,16,17,18 January 1961

Result: West Indies won by 222 runs

West Indies Innings

CC Hunte	c Simpson b Meckiff	34	c O'Neill b Davidson		1
CW Smith	c Simpson b Davidson	16	c Simpson b Benaud		55
RB Kanhai	c Grout b Davidson	21	c Martin b Davidson		3
GS Sobers	c & b Davidson	168	c Grout b Davidson		1
*FMM Worrell	c Davidson b Benaud	22	lbw b Benaud		82
SM Nurse	c Simpson b Benaud	43	c & b Mackay		11
JS Solomon	c Simpson b Benaud	14	c Harvey b Benaud		1
+FCM Alexander	c Harvey b Benaud	0	lbw b Mackay		108
LR Gibbs	c Grout b Davidson	0	st Grout b Benaud		18
WW Hall	c Grout b Davidson	10	b Mackay		24
AL Valentine	not out	0	not out		10
	(b 6, lb 4, w 1)	11	(b 4, lb 7, w 1)		12
	(all out)	339	(all out)		326

Bowling: Davidson 21.6-4-80-5 Meckiff 13-1-74-1 Mackay 14-1-40-0 Benaud 23-3-86-4 Martin 8-1-37-0 Simpson 2-0-11-0
Davidson 8-1-33-3 Meckiff 5-2-12-0 Mackay 31.4-5-75-3 Benaud 44-14-113-4 Martin 10-0-65-0 Simpson 4-0-16-0

Australia Innings

CC McDonald	b Valentine	34	c Alexander b Valentine		27
RB Simpson	c Kanhai b Hall	10	b Sobers		12
RN Harvey	c Sobers b Hall	9	c Sobers b Gibbs		85
NC O'Neill	b Sobers	71	c Sobers b Gibbs		70
LE Favell	c Worrell b Valentine	16	b Gibbs		2
KD Mackay	c Worrell b Valentine	39	c Nurse b Gibbs		0
AK Davidson	c Worrell b Valentine	16	b Valentine		1
*R Benaud	c & b Valentine	3	c & b Valentine		24
JW Martin	c Solomon b Gibbs	0	b Valentine		5
+ATW Grout	c Hunte b Gibbs	0	b Gibbs		0
I Meckiff	not out	0	not out		6
	(b 1, lb 2, nb 1)	4	(b 3, lb 6)		9
	(all out)	202	(all out)		241

Bowling: Hall 13-0-53-2 Worrell 9-4-18-0 Gibbs 23-6-46-3 Valentine 24.2-6-67-4 Sobers 5-2-14-1
Hall 8-0-35-0 Worrell 4-0-7-0 Gibbs 26-5-66-5 Valentine 25.2-7-86-4 Sobers 9-1-38-1

Umpires: CJ Egar and C Hoy

Australia v England
11,12,14,15 January 1963

Result: Australia won by 8 wickets

England Innings

G Pullar	c Benaud b Simpson	53	b Davidson		0
Rev.DS Sheppard	c McKenzie b Davidson	3	c Simpson b Davidson		12
*ER Dexter	c Lawry b Benaud	32	c Simpson b Davidson		11
MC Cowdrey	c Jarman b Simpson	85	c Simpson b Benaud		8
KF Barrington	lbw b Davidson	35	b McKenzie		21
PH Parfitt	c Lawry b Simpson	0	c O'Neill b McKenzie		28
FJ Titmus	b Davidson	32	c Booth b O'Neill		6
+JT Murray	lbw b Davidson	0	not out		9
FS Trueman	b Simpson	32	c Jarman b McKenzie		9
JB Statham	c Benaud b Simpson	0	b Davidson		2
LJ Coldwell	not out	2	c Shepherd b Davidson		4
	(lb 3, w 2)	5	(b 2, lb 2)		4
	(all out)	279	(all out)		104

Bowling: Davidson 24.5-7-54-4 McKenzie 15-3-52-0 Guest 16-0-51-0 Benaud 16-2-60-1 Simpson 15-3-57-5
Davidson 10.6-2-25-5 McKenzie 14-3-26-3 Guest 20-8-0 Benaud 19-10-29-1 Simpson 4-2-5-0 O'Neill 7-5-7-1

Australia Innings

WM Lawry	c Murray b Coldwell	8	b Trueman		8
RB Simpson	b Titmus	91	not out		34
RN Harvey	c Barrington b Titmus	64	lbw b Davidson		15
BC Booth	c Trueman b Titmus	16	not out		5
NC O'Neill	b Titmus	3			
BK Shepherd	not out	71			
+BN Jarman	run out	0			
AK Davidson	c Trueman b Titmus	15			
*R Benaud	c & b Titmus	15			
GD McKenzie	lbw b Titmus	4			
CEJ Guest	b Statham	11			
	(b 10, lb 11)	21	(b 5)		5
	(all out)	319	(2 wickets)		67

Bowling: Trueman 20-2-68-0 Statham 21.2-2-67-1 Coldwell 15-1-41-1 Titmus 37-14-79-7 Barrington 8-0-43-0
Trueman 6-1-20-2 Statham 3-0-15-0 Dexter 3.2-0-27-0

Umpires: LP Rowan and WJ Smyth

Australia v England
15,16,18,19,20 February 1963

Result: Match drawn

England Innings

Rev.DS Sheppard	c & b Hawke	19	c Harvey b Benaud		68
MC Cowdrey	c Harvey b Davidson	2	c Benaud b Davidson		53
KF Barrington	c Harvey b Benaud	101	c Grout b McKenzie		94
*ER Dexter	c Simpson b O'Neill	47	st Grout b Benaud		6
TW Graveney	c Harvey b McKenzie	14	c & b Davidson		3
R Illingworth	c Grout b Davidson	27	c Hawke b Benaud		18
FJ Titmus	c Grout b Hawke	34	not out		12
FS Trueman	c Harvey b Benaud	30	c Harvey b McKenzie		0
+AC Smith	b Simpson	6	c Simpson b Davidson		1
DA Allen	c Benaud b Davidson	14			
JB Statham	not out	17			
	(b 4, lb 6)	10	(b 1, lb 4)		5
	(all out)	321	(8 wickets declared)		268

Bowling: Davidson 25.6-4-43-3 McKenzie 27-4-57-1 Hawke 20-1-51-2 Benaud 34.9-71-2 Simpson 18-4-51-1 O'Neill 10-0-38-1
Davidson 28-1-80-3 McKenzie 8-0-39-2 Hawke 9-0-38-0 Benaud 30-8-71-3 Simpson 4-0-22-0 Harvey 3-0-13-0

Australia Innings

WM Lawry	c Smith b Trueman	11	not out		45
RB Simpson	c Trueman b Titmus	32	b Trueman		0
BC Booth	b Titmus	11	b Allen		0
NC O'Neill	c Graveney b Allen	73	c Smith b Allen		17
PJP Burge	lbw b Titmus	103	not out		52
RN Harvey	c sub b Statham	22	b Allen		28
AK Davidson	c Allen b Dexter	15			
*R Benaud	c Graveney b Allen	57			
GD McKenzie	c & b Titmus	14			
NJN Hawke	c Graveney b Titmus	14			
+ATW Grout	not out	0			
	(b 6, lb 5)	11	(b 4, lb 6)		10
	(all out)	349	(4 wickets)		152

Bowling: Trueman 11-0-33-1 Statham 18-1-76-1 Dexter 7-1-24-1 Allen 47.2-9-103-5 Illingworth 5-1-15-0
Trueman 3-0-6-1 Statham 4-1-8-0 Dexter 4-1-11-0 Allen 19-11-26-3 Titmus 20-7-37-0 Barrington 8-3-22-0 Graveney 4-0-24-0 Illingworth 10-5-8-0

Umpires: CJ Egar and LP Rowan

Sydney Cricket Ground

Australia v South Africa
10,11,13,14,15 January 1964

Result: Match drawn

Australia Innings

*RB Simpson	c Goddard b PM Pollock	58	lbw b Halse	31
WM Lawry	b Partridge	23	c RG Pollock b Goddard	89
NC O'Neill	c Goddard b Halse	3	c Barlow b Partridge	88
PJP Burge	b Partridge	36	c Waite b PM Pollock	13
BC Booth	b Partridge	75	b Partridge	16
BK Shepherd	c Waite b PM Pollock	0	c Waite b Partridge	11
R Benaud	c Bland b PM Pollock	43	c DB Pithey b PM Pollock	90
GD McKenzie	c Goddard b Partridge	3	c van der Merwe b Partridge	76
NJN Hawke	c Goddard b PM Pollock	2	not out	6
+ATW Grout	c Partridge b PM Pollock	1	c Bland b Partridge	8
AN Connolly	not out	3		
	(b 5, lb 6, w 1, nb 1)	13	(b 7, lb 9, w 1, nb 5)	22
	(all out)	260	(9 wickets declared)	450

Bowling: PM Pollock 18-2-83-5 Partridge 19.6-2-88-4 Goddard 10-1-24-0 Halse 11-1-36-1 Bland 2-0-7-0 Barlow 2-0-9-0
PM Pollock 24-0-129-2 Partridge 32.5-4-123-5 Goddard 11-3-20-1 Halse 15-2-58-1 Bland 1-0-7-0 Barlow 1-0-5-0 DB Pithey 16-1-86-0

South Africa Innings

*TL Goddard	c Connolly b Benaud	80	lbw b Simpson	84
EJ Barlow	c Grout b Connolly	6	c Simpson b Hawke	35
AJ Pithey	c Grout b Hawke	9	not out	53
RG Pollock	c McKenzie b Connolly	122	c Grout b Hawke	42
+JHB Waite	b McKenzie	8		
PL van der Merwe	b McKenzie	0	not out	13
KC Bland	c McKenzie b Benaud	51	c Benaud b O'Neill	85
DB Pithey	c Lawry b Benaud	10	b McKenzie	7
PM Pollock	c Grout b Hawke	1		
JT Partridge	b McKenzie	7		
CG Halse	not out	1		
	(b 3, lb 4)	7	(b 2, lb 5)	7
	(all out)	302	(5 wickets)	326

Bowling: McKenzie 19-2-70-3 Connolly 19-2-66-2 Hawke 18-1-56-2 Simpson 9-2-32-0 Benaud 24.1-4-55-3 O'Neill 3-0-16-0
McKenzie 14-2-61-1 Connolly 13-0-41-0 Hawke 19-5-43-2 Simpson 23-8-48-1 Benaud 30-8-61-0 O'Neill 16-1-59-1 Booth 1-0-3-0 Shepherd 1-0-3-0

Umpires: CJ Egar and LP Rowan

Australia v South Africa
7,8,10,11,12 February 1964

Result: Match drawn

Australia Innings

WM Lawry	b Halse	13	c Waite b PM Pollock	12
*RB Simpson	c Lindsay b Partridge	28	lbw b Partridge	31
NC O'Neill	b PM Pollock	21	b PM Pollock	6
PJP Burge	b Partridge	56	c Partridge b Seymour	39
BC Booth	not out	102	c sub b Seymour	87
BK Shepherd	lbw b Partridge	1	c Bland b Goddard	12
R Benaud	b Goddard	11	c sub b Seymour	3
TR Veivers	b Partridge	43	c Barlow b Goddard	39
GD McKenzie	b Partridge	0	c Bland b PM Pollock	0
NJN Hawke	c Lindsay b Partridge	0	not out	16
+ATW Grout	c Waite b Partridge	29	c Barlow b Partridge	14
	(lb 2, nb 5)	7	(b 5, lb 4, nb 2)	11
	(all out)	311	(all out)	270

Bowling: PM Pollock 22-5-75-1 Partridge 31.1-6-91-7 Halse 14-3-40-1 Goddard 16-1-67-1 Barlow 9-1-31-0
PM Pollock 11-1-35-3 Partridge 32-5-85-2 Halse 7-0-22-0 Goddard 24.7-10-29-2 Barlow 1-0-8-0 Seymour 38-9-80-3

South Africa Innings

*TL Goddard	c Grout b Veivers	93	not out	44
EJ Barlow	c Benaud b O'Neill	5	not out	32
AJ Pithey	c Grout b McKenzie	49		
RG Pollock	c & b Veivers	17		
KC Bland	c Booth b Benaud	126		
+JHB Waite	c Simpson b McKenzie	19		
DT Lindsay	c sub b Benaud	65		
PM Pollock	c Lawry b Benaud	6		
MA Seymour	c Benaud b McKenzie	0		
JT Partridge	lbw b Benaud	6		
CG Halse	not out	10		
	(b 4, lb 4, w 1, nb 6)	15		0
	(all out)	411	(0 wickets)	76

Bowling: McKenzie 37-4-110-3 Hawke 22-4-69-0 O'Neill 2-0-2-1 Benaud 49-10-118-4 Veivers 35-5-97-2
McKenzie 4-0-16-0 Hawke 4-0-16-0 Benaud 8-2-25-0 Veivers 8-0-19-0

Umpires: CJ Egar and LP Rowan

Australia v England
7,8,10,11 January 1966

Result: England won by an innings and 93 runs

England Innings

G Boycott	c & b Philpott	84
RW Barber	b Hawke	185
JH Edrich	c & b Philpott	103
KF Barrington	c McKenzie b Hawke	1
MC Cowdrey	c Grout b Hawke	0
*MJK Smith	c Grout b Hawke	6
DJ Brown	c Grout b Hawke	1
+JM Parks	c Grout b Hawke	13
FJ Titmus	c Grout b Walters	14
DA Allen	not out	50
IJ Jones	b Hawke	16
	(b 3, lb 8, w 2, nb 2)	15
	(all out)	488

Bowling: McKenzie 25-2-113-0 Hawke 33.7-6-105-7 Walters 10-1-38-1 Philpott 28-3-86-2 Sincock 20-1-98-0 Cowper 6-1-33-0

Australia Innings

WM Lawry	c Parks b Jones	0	c Cowdrey b Brown	33
G Thomas	c Titmus b Brown	51	c Cowdrey b Titmus	25
RM Cowper	st Parks b Allen	60	c Boycott b Titmus	0
PJP Burge	c Parks b Brown	6	run out	1
*BC Booth	c Cowdrey b Jones	8	b Allen	27
DJ Sincock	c Parks b Brown	29	c Smith b Allen	27
KD Walters	st Parks b Allen	23	not out	35
NJN Hawke	c Barber b Brown	0	c Smith b Titmus	2
+ATW Grout	b Brown	0	c Smith b Allen	3
GD McKenzie	c Cowdrey b Barber	24	c Barber b Titmus	12
PI Philpott	not out	5	lbw b Allen	5
	(b 7, lb 8)	15	(b 3, lb 1)	4
	(all out)	221	(all out)	174

Bowling: Jones 20-6-51-2 Brown 17-1-63-5 Boycott 3-1-8-0 Titmus 23-8-40-0 Barber 2.1-1-2-1 Allen 19-5-42-2
Jones 7-0-35-0 Brown 11-2-32-1 Titmus 17.3-4-40-4 Barber 5-0-16-0 Allen 20-8-47-4

Umpires: CJ Egar and LP Rowan

Australia v India
26,27,29,30,31 January 1968

Result: Australia won by 144 runs

Australia Innings

*WM Lawry	c Engineer b Prasanna	66	c sub b Nadkarni	52
RM Cowper	b Abid Ali	32	st Engineer b Prasanna	165
AP Sheahan	c & b Bedi	72	c Wadekar b Jaisimha	22
KD Walters	not out	94	run out	5
LR Joslin	c Wadekar b Prasanna	7	c Abid Ali b Bedi	2
RB Simpson	b Bedi	7	run out	20
IM Chappell	run out	0	lbw b Prasanna	2
+BN Jarman	c Engineer b Surti	4	run out	5
EW Freeman	lbw b Kulkarni	11	c sub b Prasanna	8
NJN Hawke	c Engineer b Kulkarni	1	c Abid Ali b Prasanna	4
JW Gleeson	lbw b Prasanna	14	not out	4
	(b 2, lb 4, nb 3)	9	(b 1, lb 1, nb 1)	3
	(all out)	317	(all out)	292

Bowling: Kulkarni 17-0-73-2 Surti 11-1-64-1 Abid Ali 15-1-58-1 Jaisimha 2-0-9-0 Bedi 21-4-42-2 Prasanna 20.6-5-62-3
Kulkarni 8-0-31-0 Surti 8-1-49-0 Abid Ali 2-0-7-0 Jaisimha 1-0-2-1 Bedi 21-5-66-1 Prasanna 29.3-4-96-4 Nadkarni 16-3-38-1

India Innings

+FM Engineer	c Chappell b Walters	17	c Simpson b Gleeson	37
S Abid Ali	hit wicket b Gleeson	78	c Simpson b Cowper	81
AL Wadekar	c & b Cowper	49	lbw b Cowper	18
RF Surti	b Simpson	29	c Chappell b Simpson	26
*Nawab of Pataudi jnr	c Simpson b Freeman	51	c Chappell b Simpson	6
ML Jaisimha	c Jarman b Simpson	0	c Gleeson b Cowper	13
RG Nadkarni	c Sheahan b Simpson	0	c Sheahan b Simpson	6
EAS Prasanna	c Cowper b Freeman	26	b Simpson	0
CG Borde	lbw b Freeman	0	c Simpson b Cowper	4
BS Bedi	c Simpson b Freeman	8	b Simpson	2
UN Kulkarni	not out	1	not out	1
	(b 4, lb 2, nb 3)	9	(lb 3)	3
	(all out)	268	(all out)	197

Bowling: Hawke 18-2-51-0 Freeman 18.1-2-86-4 Walters 4-0-20-1 Gleeson 12-3-40-1 Cowper 12-5-21-1 Simpson 20-10-38-3 Chappell 1-0-3-0
Hawke 6-2-22-0 Freeman 4-0-26-0 Walters 3-1-11-0 Gleeson 12-4-27-1 Cowper 25.6-12-49-4 Simpson 23-5-59-5

Umpires: CJ Egar and LP Rowan

Australia v West Indies
3,4,5,7,8 January 1969

Result: Australia won by 10 wickets

West Indies Innings

RC Fredericks	c Chappell b McKenzie	26	c Redpath b Connolly	43
MC Carew	c Jarman b McKenzie	30	c Jarman b Freeman	10
RB Kanhai	b McKenzie	17	c Chappell b McKenzie	69
BF Butcher	b Stackpole	28	c & b Gleeson	101
SM Nurse	c Redpath b Connolly	3	c Stackpole b McKenzie	17
*GS Sobers	b Freeman	49	c Chappell b Gleeson	36
CH Lloyd	c Jarman b Freeman	50	c Stackpole b Freeman	13
+JL Hendriks	c Stackpole b Freeman	4	c Connolly b Gleeson	22
RM Edwards	b Connolly	10	b Freeman	0
WW Hall	c Gleeson b McKenzie	33	st Jarman b Gleeson	5
LR Gibbs	not out	1	not out	1
	(b 2, lb 10, nb 1)	13	(lb 3, nb 4)	7
	(all out)	264	(all out)	324

Bowling: McKenzie 22.1-3-85-4 Connolly 16-1-54-2 Freeman 13-2-57-3 Walters 2-1-3-0 Gleeson 18-7-45-0 Stackpole 4-2-7-1
McKenzie 24-2-80-2 Connolly 23-7-54-1 Freeman 15-3-59-3 Gleeson 26-5-91-4 Stackpole 5-0-33-0

Australia Innings

*WM Lawry	c Carew b Edwards	29		
KR Stackpole	c Gibbs b Hall	58	not out	21
IM Chappell	c Kanhai b Gibbs	33		
IR Redpath	st Hendriks b Carew	80		
KD Walters	b Gibbs	118		
AP Sheahan	c Lloyd b Hall	47	not out	21
+BN Jarman	c Fredericks b Hall	0		
EW Freeman	b Edwards	76		
GD McKenzie	run out	10		
JW Gleeson	not out	42		
AN Connolly	run out	37		
	(b 5, lb 11, w 1)	17		0
	(all out)	547	(0 wickets)	42

Bowling: Hall 26-2-113-3 Edwards 25-1-139-2 Sobers 21-4-109-0 Gibbs 37.6-6-124-2 Carew 12-1-45-1
Hall 2-0-8-0 Edwards 1-0-7-0 Carew 2-0-9-0 Lloyd 2-0-8-0 Kanhai 1-0-10-0

Umpires: CJ Egar and LP Rowan

Australia v West Indies
14,15,16,18,19,20 February 1969

Result: Australia won by 382 runs

Australia Innings

*WM Lawry	b Griffith	151	c Fredericks b Griffith	17
KR Stackpole	b Hall	20	c Carew b Hall	6
IM Chappell	lbw b Sobers	1	c Hendriks b Hall	10
IR Redpath	c Nurse b Sobers	0	c Sobers b Gibbs	132
KD Walters	b Gibbs	242	c Fredericks b Gibbs	103
AP Sheahan	c Fredericks b Griffith	27	c Hendriks b Sobers	34
EW Freeman	c Hendriks b Griffith	56	c Carew b Sobers	15
GD McKenzie	b Gibbs	19	c Carew b Sobers	40
+HB Taber	lbw b Hall	48	not out	15
JW Gleeson	c Hendriks b Hall	45	not out	5
AN Connolly	not out	1		
	(lb 2, w 1, nb 6)	9	(b 4, lb 6, w 1, nb 6)	17
	(all out)	619	(8 wickets declared)	394

Bowling: Hall 35.7-3-157-3 Griffith 37-1-175-3 Sobers 28-4-94-2 Gibbs 40-8-133-2 Carew 10-2-44-0 Lloyd 2-1-7-0
Hall 12-0-47-2 Griffith 14-0-41-1 Sobers 26-3-117-3 Gibbs 33-2-133-2 Carew 5-0-26-0 Lloyd 2-0-13-0

West Indies Innings

RC Fredericks	c Taber b Connolly	39	c Taber b McKenzie	0
MC Carew	c Taber b Freeman	64	b Connolly	3
RB Kanhai	c Taber b Connolly	44	c Connolly b McKenzie	18
*GS Sobers	c Taber b Connolly	13	c Redpath b Gleeson	113
BF Butcher	c Sheahan b McKenzie	10	c Gleeson b Stackpole	31
CH Lloyd	b McKenzie	53	c Freeman b Stackpole	11
SM Nurse	c Stackpole b Connolly	9	b Gleeson	137
+JL Hendriks	c Taber b McKenzie	1	c Stackpole b McKenzie	16
CC Griffith	c Freeman b Gleeson	27	b Gleeson	15
WW Hall	b Gleeson	1	c Sheahan b Chappell	0
LR Gibbs	not out	4	not out	0
	(b 2, lb 4, nb 8)	14	(b 1, lb 5, nb 2)	8
	(all out)	279	(all out)	352

Bowling: McKenzie 22.6-2-90-3 Connolly 17-2-61-4 Freeman 12-2-48-1 Gleeson 19-8-53-2 Chappell 6-1-13-0
McKenzie 16-1-93-3 Connolly 18-4-72-1 Freeman 2-0-16-0 Gleeson 15.2-1-84-3 Chappell 6-0-22-1 Stackpole 7-0-57-2

Umpires: CJ Egar and LP Rowan

Australia v England
9,10,11,13,14 January 1971

Result: England won by 299 runs

England Innings

G Boycott	c Gleeson b Connolly	77	not out	142
BW Luckhurst	lbw b Gleeson	38	c IM Chappell b McKenzie	5
JH Edrich	c Gleeson b GS Chappell	55	run out	12
KWR Fletcher	c Walters b Mallett	23	c Stackpole b Mallett	8
BL D'Oliveira	c Connolly b Mallett	0	c IM Chappell b GS Chappell	56
*R Illingworth	b Gleeson	25	st Marsh b Mallett	53
+APE Knott	st Marsh b Mallett	6	not out	21
JA Snow	c Lawry b Gleeson	37		
P Lever	c Connolly b Mallett	36		
DL Underwood	c GS Chappell b Gleeson	0		
RGD Willis	not out	15		
	(b 5, lb 2, w 1, nb 12)	20	(b 9, lb 4, nb 9)	22
	(all out)	332	(5 wickets declared)	319

Bowling: McKenzie 15-3-74-0 Connolly 13-2-43-1 Gleeson 29-7-83-4 GS Chappell 11-4-30-1 Mallett 16.7-5-40-4 Walters 3-1-11-0 Stackpole 7-2-31-0
McKenzie 15-0-65-1 Connolly 14-1-38-0 Gleeson 23-4-54-0 GS Chappell 15-5-24-1 Mallett 19-1-85-2 Walters 2-0-14-0 Stackpole 6-1-17-0

Australia Innings

*WM Lawry	c Edrich b Lever	9	not out	60
IM Chappell	c Underwood b Snow	12	c D'Oliveira b Snow	0
IR Redpath	c Fletcher b D'Oliveira	64	c Edrich b Snow	6
KD Walters	c Luckhurst b Illingworth	55	c Knott b Lever	3
GS Chappell	c & b Underwood	15	b Snow	2
KR Stackpole	c Boycott b Underwood	33	c Lever b Snow	30
+RW Marsh	c D'Oliveira b Underwood	8	c Willis b Snow	0
AA Mallett	b Underwood	4	c Knott b Willis	6
GD McKenzie	not out	11	retired hurt	6
JW Gleeson	c Fletcher b D'Oliveira	0	b Snow	0
AN Connolly	b Lever	14	c Knott b Snow	0
	(nb 11)	11	(b 2, nb 1)	3
	(all out)	236	(all out)	116

Bowling: Snow 14-6-23-1 Willis 9-2-26-0 Lever 8.6-1-31-2 Underwood 22-7-66-4 Illingworth 14-3-59-1 D'Oliveira 9-2-20-2
Snow 17.5-5-40-7 Willis 3-2-1-1 Lever 11-1-24-1 Underwood 8-2-17-0 Illingworth 9-5-9-0 D'Oliveira 7-3-16-0 Fletcher 1-0-6-0

Umpires: TF Brooks and LP Rowan

Australia v England
12,13,14,16,17 February 1971

Result: England won by 62 runs

England Innings

JH Edrich	c GS Chappell b Dell	30	c IM Chappell b O'Keeffe	57
BW Luckhurst	c Redpath b Walters	0	c Lillee b O'Keeffe	59
KWR Fletcher	c Stackpole b O'Keeffe	33	c Stackpole b Eastwood	20
JH Hampshire	c Marsh b Lillee	10	c IM Chappell b O'Keeffe	24
BL D'Oliveira	b Dell	1	c IM Chappell b Lillee	47
*R Illingworth	b Jenner	42	lbw b Lillee	29
+APE Knott	c Stackpole b O'Keeffe	27	b Dell	15
JA Snow	b Jenner	7	c Stackpole b Dell	20
P Lever	c Jenner b O'Keeffe	4	c Redpath b Jenner	17
DL Underwood	not out	8	c Marsh b Dell	0
RGD Willis	b Jenner	11	not out	2
	(b 4, lb 4, w 1, nb 2)	11	(b 3, lb 3, nb 6)	12
	(all out)	184	(all out)	302

Bowling: Lillee 13-5-32-1 Dell 16-8-32-2 Walters 4-0-10-1 GS Chappell 3-0-9-0 Jenner 16-3-42-3 O'Keeffe 24-8-48-3
Lillee 14-0-43-2 Dell 26.7-3-65-3 Walters 5-0-18-0 Jenner 21-5-39-1 O'Keeffe 26-8-96-3 Eastwood 5-0-21-1 Stackpole 3-1-8-0

Australia Innings

KH Eastwood	c Knott b Lever	5	b Snow	0
KR Stackpole	b Snow	6	b Illingworth	67
+RW Marsh	c Willis b Lever	4	b Underwood	16
*IM Chappell	b Willis	25	c Knott b Lever	6
IR Redpath	c & b Underwood	59	c Hampshire b Illingworth	14
KD Walters	st Knott b Underwood	42	c D'Oliveira b Willis	1
GS Chappell	b Willis	65	st Knott b Illingworth	30
KJ O'Keeffe	c Knott b Illingworth	3	c sub b D'Oliveira	12
TJ Jenner	b Lever	30	c Fletcher b Underwood	4
DK Lillee	c Knott b Willis	6	c Hampshire b D'Oliveira	0
AR Dell	not out	3	not out	3
	(lb 5, w 1, nb 10)	16	(b 2, nb 5)	7
	(all out)	264	(all out)	160

Bowling: Snow 18-2-68-1 Lever 14.6-3-43-3 D'Oliveira 12-2-24-0 Willis 12-1-58-3 Underwood 16-3-39-2 Illingworth 11-3-16-1
Snow 2-1-7-1 Lever 12-2-23-1 D'Oliveira 5-1-15-2 Willis 9-1-32-1 Underwood 13.6-5-28-2 Illingworth 20-7-39-3 Fletcher 1-0-9-0

Umpires: TF Brooks and LP Rowan

Australia v Pakistan
6,7,8,10,11 January 1973

Result: Australia won by 52 runs

Australia Innings

KR Stackpole	c Wasim Bari b Sarfraz Nawaz	28	c Intikhab Alam b Saleem Altaf	9
IR Redpath	run out	79	c Nasim-ul-Ghani b Sarfraz Nawaz	18
*IM Chappell	lbw b Sarfraz Nawaz	43	c Wasim Bari b Sarfraz Nawaz	27
GS Chappell	b Majid Khan	30	lbw b Sarfraz Nawaz	6
R Edwards	c Wasim Bari b Saleem Altaf	69	lbw b Saleem Altaf	3
KD Walters	b Asif Iqbal	19	lbw b Saleem Altaf	6
+RW Marsh	c Wasim Bari b Saleem Altaf	15	c Zaheer Abbas b Saleem Altaf	0
MHN Walker	c Majid Khan b Sarfraz Nawaz	5	c Mushtaq Mohammad b Sarfraz Nawaz	16
JR Watkins	not out	3	c Zaheer Abbas b Intikhab Alam	36
DK Lillee	b Sarfraz Nawaz	2	not out	0
RAL Massie	b Saleem Altaf	2	c Sadiq Mohammad b Mushtaq Mohammad	42
	(b 18, lb 8, w 4, nb 9)	39	(b 10, lb 3, nb 8)	21
	(all out)	334	(all out)	184

Bowling: Asif Masood 18-1-81-0 Saleem Altaf 21.5-3-71-3 Sarfraz Nawaz 19-3-53-4 Majid Khan 18-1-66-1 Intikhab Alam 2-0-13-0 Asif Iqbal 2-0-11-1
Asif Masood 3-0-15-0 Saleem Altaf 20-5-60-4 Sarfraz Nawaz 21-7-56-4 Intikhab Alam 4-2-9-1 Asif Iqbal 2-0-10-0 Mushtaq Mohammad 3.1-0-13-1

Pakistan Innings

Sadiq Mohammad	c GS Chappell b Lillee	30	c Edwards b Massie	6
Nasim-ul-Ghani	c Redpath b GS Chappell	64	b Lillee	5
Zaheer Abbas	c Marsh b Massie	14	c Redpath b Lillee	47
Majid Khan	b Massie	0	lbw b Walker	12
Mushtaq Mohammad	c Walker b GS Chappell	121	c Marsh b Lillee	15
Asif Iqbal	c Marsh b GS Chappell	65	c Marsh b Walker	5
*Intikhab Alam	c Marsh b Massie	9	c Watkins b Walker	8
+Wasim Bari	b GS Chappell	1	c Edwards b Walker	0
Saleem Altaf	c Marsh b Walker	12	c Massie b Walker	0
Sarfraz Nawaz	b GS Chappell	12	c Redpath b Walker	1
Asif Masood	not out	1	not out	3
	(b 12, lb 10, w 6, nb 3)	31	(lb 2, w 1, nb 1)	4
	(all out)	360	(all out)	106

Bowling: Lillee 10-2-34-1 Massie 28-6-123-3 Walker 16-2-65-1 GS Chappell 18.6-5-61-5 Walters 9-3-25-0 Watkins 6-1-21-0 IM Chappell 1-1-0-0
Lillee 23-5-68-3 Massie 7-4-19-1 Walker 16-8-15-6

Umpires: TF Brooks and JR Collins

Australia v New Zealand
5,6,7,9,10 January 1974

Result: Match drawn

New Zealand Innings

JM Parker	c Marsh b Walker	108	c Marsh b GS Chappell	11
JFM Morrison	c GS Chappell b Walters	28	c Davis b IM Chappell	117
MJF Shrimpton	b Walters	0	c & b Walters	28
*BE Congdon	c Marsh b Walters	4	b Gilmour	17
BF Hastings	c Marsh b Walker	16	b GS Chappell	83
JV Coney	c Stackpole b O'Keeffe	45	c Davis b GS Chappell	11
+KJ Wadsworth	c Marsh b Walters	54	c GS Chappell b Gilmour	2
DR Hadlee	c & b GS Chappell	14	not out	18
RJ Hadlee	c IM Chappell b GS Chappell	17	run out (Sheahan/Marsh)	1
DR O'Sullivan	not out	3	lbw b Gilmour	1
B Andrews	c Marsh b Gilmour	17		
	(lb 2, nb 4)	6	(b 4, lb 11, w 1)	16
	(all out)	312	(9 wickets dec)	305

Bowling: Gilmour 18.6-3-70-1 Walker 22-2-71-2 GS Chappell 19-2-76-2 Walters 11-0-39-4 Mallett 8-0-30-0 O'Keeffe 8-2-20-1
Gilmour 21.2-1-70-3 GS Chappell 16-3-54-3 Walters 11-0-54-1 Mallett 14-1-65-0 O'Keeffe 10-0-40-0 IM Chappell 3-0-6-1

Australia Innings

AP Sheahan	c Coney b Andrews	7	not out	14
KR Stackpole	c Morrison b RJ Hadlee	8	lbw b RJ Hadlee	2
*IM Chappell	c Hastings b DR Hadlee	45	lbw b RJ Hadlee	6
GS Chappell	c Coney b Andrews	0	not out	8
KD Walters	c Coney b DR Hadlee	41		
IC Davis	c Andrews b RJ Hadlee	29		
+RW Marsh	c Wadsworth b DR Hadlee	10		
KJ O'Keeffe	c Wadsworth b RJ Hadlee	9		
GJ Gilmour	c Wadsworth b Congdon	3		
AA Mallett	lbw b RJ Hadlee	0		
MHN Walker	not out	2		
	(lb 5, nb 3)	8		0
	(all out)	162	(2 wickets)	30

Bowling: RJ Hadlee 9.4-2-33-4 Andrews 9-1-40-2 DR Hadlee 13-3-52-3 Congdon 13-2-29-1
RJ Hadlee 4.3-0-16-2 Andrews 4-0-14-0

Umpires: PR Enright and MG O'Connell

Australia v England
4,5,6,8,9 January 1975

Result: Australia won by 171 runs

Australia Innings

IR Redpath	hit wicket b Titmus	33	c sub b Underwood	105
RB McCosker	c Knott b Greig	80		
*IM Chappell	c Knott b Arnold	53	c Lloyd b Willis	5
GS Chappell	c Greig b Arnold	84	c Lloyd b Arnold	144
R Edwards	b Greig	15	not out	17
KD Walters	lbw b Arnold	1	b Underwood	5
+RW Marsh	b Greig	30	not out	7
MHN Walker	c Greig b Arnold	30		
DK Lillee	b Arnold	8		
AA Mallett	lbw b Greig	31		
JR Thomson	not out	24		
	(lb 4, w 1, nb 11)	16	(lb 2, w 1, nb 3)	6
	(all out)	405	(4 wickets declared)	289

Bowling: Willis 18-2-80-0 Arnold 29-7-86-5 Greig 22.7-2-104-4 Underwood 13-3-54-0 Titmus 16-2-65-1
Willis 11-1-52-1 Arnold 22-3-78-1 Greig 12-1-64-0 Underwood 12-1-65-2 Titmus 7.3-2-24-0

England Innings

DL Amiss	c Mallett b Walker	12	c Marsh b Lillee	37
D Lloyd	c Thomson b Lillee	19	c GS Chappell b Thomson	26
MC Cowdrey	c McCosker b Thomson	22	c IM Chappell b Walker	1
*JH Edrich	c Marsh b Walters	50	not out	33
KWR Fletcher	c Redpath b Walker	24	c Redpath b Thomson	11
AW Greig	c GS Chappell b Thomson	9	st Marsh b Mallett	54
+APE Knott	b Thomson	82	c Redpath b Mallett	10
FJ Titmus	c Marsh b Walters	22	c Thomson b Mallett	4
DL Underwood	c Walker b Lillee	27	c & b Walker	5
RGD Willis	b Thomson	2	b Lillee	12
GG Arnold	not out	3	c GS Chappell b Mallett	14
	(b 15, lb 7, w 1)	23	(b 13, lb 3, nb 5)	21
	(all out)	295	(all out)	228

Bowling: Lillee 19.1-2-66-2 Thomson 19-3-74-4 Walker 23-2-77-2 Mallett 1-0-8-0 Walters 7-2-26-2 IM Chappell 4-0-21-0
Lillee 21-5-65-2 Thomson 23-7-74-2 Walker 16-5-46-2 Mallett 16.5-9-21-4 IM Chappell 3-2-1-0

Umpires: RC Bailhache and TF Brooks

Australia v West Indies
3,4,5,7 January 1976

Result: Australia won by 7 wickets

West Indies Innings

RC Fredericks	c IM Chappell b Thomson	48	c Turner b Gilmour	24
BD Julien	not out	46	lbw b Walker	8
AI Kallicharran	c Redpath b Thomson	9	c Walker b Thomson	7
LG Rowe	b Walker	67	c Marsh b Thomson	7
IVA Richards	c IM Chappell b GS Chappell	44	c Thomson b Gilmour	2
*CH Lloyd	c Turner b Walker	51	c Marsh b Thomson	19
+DL Murray	c Thomson b Walker	32	b Thomson	50
KD Boyce	c & b Mallett	16	c Redpath b Thomson	0
MA Holding	hit wicket b Thomson	2	b Thomson	9
AME Roberts	c Marsh b Walker	4	b Walker	2
LR Gibbs	c Marsh b GS Chappell	5	not out	0
	(b 5, lb 14, w 9, nb 3)	31		0
	(all out)	355	(all out)	128

Bowling: Thomson 25-5-117-3 Gilmour 13-2-54-0 Walker 21-8-70-4 Cosier 3-1-13-0 Mallett 13-4-50-1 GS Chappell 4.2-0-10-2 IM Chappell 1-0-10-0
Thomson 15-4-50-6 Gilmour 12-4-40-2 Walker 9.3-3-31-2 Mallett 1-0-2-0 GS Chappell 2-0-5-0

Australia Innings

IR Redpath	c Murray b Holding	25	b Boyce	28
A Turner	c Lloyd b Boyce	53	c Murray b Holding	15
GN Yallop	c Murray b Julien	16	not out	16
IM Chappell	c Murray b Holding	4	c sub b Kallicharran	9
*GS Chappell	not out	182	not out	6
GJ Cosier	b Holding	28		
+RW Marsh	c Gibbs b Julien	38		
GJ Gilmour	run out	20		
MHN Walker	c Lloyd b Roberts	8		
JR Thomson	c Richards b Roberts	0		
AA Mallett	lbw b Roberts	13		
	(b 3, lb 8, w 2, nb 5)	18	(lb 4, w 4)	8
	(all out)	405	(3 wickets)	82

Bowling: Roberts 20.6-3-94-3 Holding 21-2-79-3 Boyce 16-1-75-1 Gibbs 18-3-52-0 Julien 15-2-87-2
Roberts 4-1-12-0 Holding 7-0-33-1 Boyce 4-0-14-1 Gibbs 1-0-4-0 Kallicharran 2-1-7-1 Richards 0.1-0-4-0

Umpires: TF Brooks and RR Ledwidge

Sydney Cricket Ground

Australia v Pakistan
14,15,16,18 January 1977

Result: Pakistan won by 8 wickets

Australia Innings

IC Davis	b Sarfraz Nawaz	20	c Haroon Rashid b Imran Khan	25	
A Turner	c Wasim Bari b Sarfraz Nawaz	0	c Majid Khan b Sarfraz Nawaz	11	
RB McCosker	c Mushtaq Mohammad b Imran Khan	8	c Wasim Bari b Imran Khan	8	
*GS Chappell	c Zaheer Abbas b Imran Khan	28	c Wasim Bari b Imran Khan	5	
KD Walters	c Wasim Bari b Imran Khan	2	c Wasim Bari b Imran Khan	38	
GJ Cosier	c Wasim Bari b Imran Khan	50	c Wasim Bari b Sarfraz Nawaz	4	
+RW Marsh	c & b Imran Khan	14	run out	41	
GJ Gilmour	c Javed Miandad b Sarfraz Nawaz	32	c Zaheer Abbas b Imran Khan	0	
KJ O'Keeffe	c Asif Iqbal b Imran Khan	1	c Haroon Rashid b Imran Khan	7	
DK Lillee	lbw b Javed Miandad	14	c Zaheer Abbas b Imran Khan	27	
MHN Walker	not out	34	not out	3	
	(b 5, nb 3)	8	(b 7, nb 4)	11	
	(all out)	211	(all out)	180	

Bowling: Sarfraz Nawaz 16-4-42-3 Imran Khan 26-6-102-6 Asif Iqbal 15-5-53-0 Mushtaq Mohammad 2-1-2-0 Iqbal Qasim 4-3-2-0 Javed Miandad 1.2-0-2-1
Sarfraz Nawaz 15-3-77-3 Imran Khan 19.7-3-63-6 Iqbal Qasim 2-1-2-0 Javed Miandad 5-0-27-0

Pakistan Innings

Majid Khan	c Marsh b Walker	48	not out	26	
Sadiq Mohammad	c Cosier b Walker	25	c Marsh b Lillee	0	
Zaheer Abbas	c Turner b Lillee	5	c Walters b Lillee	4	
*Mushtaq Mohammad	c Turner b Lillee	9	not out	0	
Haroon Rashid	c Marsh b Gilmour	57			
Asif Iqbal	b Gilmour	120			
Javed Miandad	c Walters b Walker	64			
Imran Khan	c Turner b Gilmour	0			
Sarfraz Nawaz	c Turner b Walker	13			
+Wasim Bari	c Walters b Lillee	5			
Iqbal Qasim	not out	0			
	(b 6, lb 6, nb 2)	14	(b 1, nb 1)	2	
	(all out)	360	(2 wickets)	32	

Bowling: Lillee 22.3-0-114-3 Gilmour 16-1-81-3 Walker 29-4-112-4 Walters 4-1-7-0 O'Keeffe 11-2-32-0
Lillee 4-0-24-2 Walker 3.2-1-6-0

Umpires: TF Brooks and RR Ledwidge

Australia v India
7,8,9,11,12 January 1978

Result: India won by an innings and 2 runs

Australia Innings

J Dyson	lbw b Chandrasekhar	26	c & b Chandrasekhar	6	
GJ Cosier	b Amarnath	17	b Bedi	68	
PM Toohey	run out	4	c sub b Ghavri	85	
CS Serjeant	c Ghavri b Bedi	4	b Prasanna	1	
*RB Simpson	c Kirmani b Chandrasekhar	38	lbw b Prasanna	33	
KJ Hughes	b Bedi	17	c Vengsarkar b Bedi	19	
AL Mann	b Bedi	0	c & b Prasanna	0	
+SJ Rixon	lbw b Chandrasekhar	17	c Viswanath b Chandrasekhar	11	
WM Clark	c Gavaskar b Chandrasekhar	0	b Prasanna	10	
JR Thomson	not out	1	b Ghavri	16	
JB Gannon	c Amarnath b Prasanna	0	not out	0	
	(lb 5, nb 2)	7	(b 5, lb 6, nb 3)	14	
	(all out)	131	(all out)	263	

Bowling: Ghavri 7-1-25-0 Amarnath 7-4-6-1 Bedi 13-3-49-3 Chandrasekhar 15-3-30-4 Prasanna 7.4-2-14-1
Ghavri 12.7-3-42-2 Amarnath 5-3-9-0 Bedi 28-8-62-2 Chandrasekhar 24-3-85-2 Prasanna 29-11-51-4

India Innings

SM Gavaskar	c Rixon b Thomson	49	
CPS Chauhan	c Mann b Clark	42	
M Amarnath	c Gannon b Clark	9	
GR Viswanath	b Thomson	79	
DB Vengsarkar	c Rixon b Cosier	48	
AV Mankad	b Thomson	16	
+SMH Kirmani	b Cosier	42	
KD Ghavri	c Serjeant b Thomson	64	
EAS Prasanna	not out	25	
*BS Bedi	not out	1	
BS Chandrasekhar			
	(lb 9, nb 12)	21	
	(8 wickets declared)	396	

Bowling: Thomson 27-8-83-4 Clark 21-3-66-2 Gannon 20-4-65-0 Mann 20-0-101-0 Simpson 4-0-34-0 Cosier 9-1-26-2

Umpires: RC Bailhache and TF Brooks

Australia v England
6,7,8,10,11 January 1979

Result: England won by 93 runs

England Innings

G Boycott	c Border b Hurst	8	lbw b Hogg	0	
*JM Brearley	b Hogg	17	b Border	53	
DW Randall	c Wood b Hurst	0	lbw b Hogg	150	
GA Gooch	c Toohey b Higgs	18	c Wood b Higgs	22	
DI Gower	c Maclean b Hurst	7	c Maclean b Hogg	34	
IT Botham	c Yallop b Hogg	59	c Wood b Higgs	6	
G Miller	c Maclean b Hurst	4	lbw b Hogg	17	
+RW Taylor	c Border b Higgs	10	not out	21	
JE Emburey	c Wood b Higgs	0	c Darling b Higgs	14	
RGD Willis	not out	7	c Toohey b Higgs	0	
M Hendrick	b Hurst	10	c Toohey b Higgs	7	
	(b 1, lb 2, w 2, nb 8)	12	(b 5, lb 3, nb 14)	22	
	(all out)	152	(all out)	346	

Bowling: Hogg 11-3-36-2 Dymock 13-1-34-0 Hurst 10.6-2-28-5 Higgs 18-4-42-3
Hogg 28-10-67-4 Dymock 17-4-35-0 Hurst 19-3-43-0 Higgs 59.6-15-148-5 Border 23-11-31-1

Australia Innings

GM Wood	b Willis	0	run out	27	
WM Darling	c Botham b Miller	91	c Gooch b Hendrick	13	
KJ Hughes	c Emburey b Willis	48	c Emburey b Miller	15	
*GN Yallop	c Botham b Hendrick	44	c & b Hendrick	1	
PM Toohey	c Gooch b Botham	1	b Miller	5	
AR Border	not out	60	not out	45	
+JA Maclean	lbw b Emburey	12	c Botham b Miller	0	
RM Hogg	run out	6	c Botham b Emburey	0	
G Dymock	b Botham	5	b Emburey	0	
JD Higgs	c Botham b Hendrick	11	lbw b Emburey	3	
AG Hurst	run out	0	b Emburey	0	
	(b 2, lb 3, nb 11)	16	(lb 1, nb 1)	2	
	(all out)	294	(all out)	111	

Bowling: Willis 9-2-33-2 Botham 28-3-87-2 Hendrick 24-4-50-2 Miller 13-2-37-1 Emburey 29-10-57-1 Gooch 5-1-14-0
Willis 2-0-8-0 Hendrick 10-3-17-2 Emburey 17.2-7-46-4 Miller 20-7-38-3

Umpires: RC Bailhache and RA French

Australia v England
10,11,12,14 February 1979

Result: England won by 9 wickets

Australia Innings

GM Wood	c Botham b Hendrick	15	c Willis b Miller	29	
AMJ Hilditch	run out	3	c Taylor b Hendrick	1	
KJ Hughes	c Botham b Willis	16	c Gooch b Emburey	7	
*GN Yallop	c Gower b Botham	121	c Taylor b Miller	17	
PM Toohey	c Taylor b Botham	8	c Gooch b Emburey	0	
PH Carlson	c Gooch b Botham	2	c Botham b Emburey	0	
B Yardley	b Emburey	7	not out	61	
+KJ Wright	st Taylor b Emburey	3	c Boycott b Miller	5	
RM Hogg	c Emburey b Miller	9	b Miller	7	
JD Higgs	not out	9	c Botham b Emburey	2	
AG Hurst	b Botham	0	c & b Miller	4	
	(lb 3, nb 2)	5	(b 3, lb 6, nb 1)	10	
	(all out)	198	(all out)	143	

Bowling: Willis 11-4-48-1 Hendrick 12-2-21-1 Botham 9.7-1-57-4 Emburey 13-8-42-2 Miller 9-3-13-1 Boycott 1-0-6-0
Willis 3-0-15-0 Hendrick 7-3-22-1 Emburey 24-4-52-4 Miller 27.1-6-44-5

England Innings

G Boycott	c Hilditch b Hurst	19	c Hughes b Higgs	13	
*JM Brearley	c Toohey b Higgs	46	not out	20	
DW Randall	lbw b Hogg	7	not out	0	
GA Gooch	st Wright b Higgs	74			
DI Gower	c Wright b Higgs	65			
IT Botham	c Carlson b Yardley	23			
G Miller	lbw b Hurst	18			
+RW Taylor	not out	36			
JE Emburey	c Hilditch b Hurst	0			
RGD Willis	b Higgs	10			
M Hendrick	c & b Yardley	0			
	(b 3, lb 5, nb 2)	10	(nb 2)	2	
	(all out)	308	(1 wicket)	35	

Bowling: Hogg 18-6-42-1 Hurst 20-4-58-3 Yardley 25-2-105-2 Carlson 10-1-24-0 Higgs 30-8-69-4
Yardley 5.2-0-21-0 Higgs 5-1-12-1

Umpires: AR Crafter and DG Weser

Australia v England
4,5,6,8 January 1980

Result: Australia won by 6 wickets

England Innings

GA Gooch	b Lillee	18	c GS Chappell b Dymock	4	
G Boycott	b Dymock	8	c McCosker b Pascoe	18	
DW Randall	c GS Chappell b Lillee	25	c Marsh b GS Chappell	25	
P Willey	c Wiener b Dymock	8	b Pascoe	3	
*JM Brearley	c Pascoe b Dymock	7	c Marsh b Pascoe	19	
DI Gower	b GS Chappell	3	not out	98	
IT Botham	c GS Chappell b Pascoe	27	c Wiener b GS Chappell	0	
+RW Taylor	c Marsh b Lillee	10	b Lillee	8	
GR Dilley	not out	22	b Dymock	43	
RGD Willis	c Wiener b Dymock	3	c GS Chappell b Lillee	1	
DL Underwood	c Border b Lillee	12	c Border b Dymock	43	
	(nb 5)	5	(b 1, lb 10, w 1, nb 2)	14	
	(all out)	123	(all out)	237	

Bowling: Lillee 13.3-4-40-4 Dymock 17-6-42-4 Pascoe 9-4-14-1 GS Chappell 4-1-19-1 Higgs 1-0-3-0
Lillee 24.3-6-63-2 Dymock 28-8-48-3 Pascoe 23-3-76-3 GS Chappell 21-10-36-2

Australia Innings

RB McCosker	c Gower b Willis	1	c Taylor b Underwood	41	
JM Wiener	run out	22	b Underwood	13	
IM Chappell	c Brearley b Gooch	42	c Botham b Underwood	9	
*GS Chappell	c Taylor b Underwood	3	not out	98	
KJ Hughes	c Taylor b Botham	18	c Dilley b Willis	47	
AR Border	c Gooch b Botham	15	not out	2	
+RW Marsh	c Underwood b Gooch	7			
DK Lillee	c Brearley b Botham	5			
G Dymock	c Taylor b Botham	4			
LS Pascoe	not out	10			
JD Higgs	b Underwood	2			
	(b 2, lb 12, w 2)	16	(lb 8, w 1)	9	
	(all out)	145	(4 wickets)	219	

Bowling: Botham 17-7-29-4 Willis 11-3-30-1 Underwood 13.2-3-39-2 Dilley 5-1-13-0 Willey 1-0-2-0 Gooch 11-4-16-2
Botham 23.3-12-43-0 Willis 22-12-26-1 Underwood 26-6-71-3 Dilley 12-0-33-0 Willey 4-0-17-0 Gooch 8-2-20-0

Umpires: RC Bailhache and WJ Copeland

Australia v India
2,3,4 January 1981

Result: Australia won by an innings and 4 runs

India Innings

*SM Gavaskar	c Marsh b Hogg	0	c Marsh b Hogg	10	
CPS Chauhan	c Border b Pascoe	20	c Walters b Pascoe	36	
DB Vengsarkar	c Marsh b Lillee	22	c Marsh b Pascoe	34	
GR Viswanath	b Hogg	26	st Marsh b Higgs	24	
Yashpal Sharma	c Marsh b Pascoe	6	c Walters b Lillee	4	
SM Patil	retired hurt	65	c Wood b Lillee	4	
N Kapil Dev	c Marsh b Pascoe	22	c sub (SF Graf) b Higgs	19	
+SMH Kirmani	c Walters b Lillee	27	not out	43	
RMH Binny	c Marsh b Pascoe	4	lbw b Lillee	0	
KD Ghavri	c Wood b Lillee	7	c Hogg b Higgs	21	
DR Doshi	not out	0	c Lillee b Higgs	0	
	(lb 1, nb 2)	3	(b 2, lb 3, w 1)	6	
	(all out)	201	(all out)	201	

Bowling: Lillee 20.2-3-86-4 Hogg 14-1-51-1 Pascoe 19-6-61-4
Lillee 18-2-79-3 Hogg 9-1-24-1 Pascoe 11-2-35-2 Higgs 18-8-45-4 Walters 6-3-12-0

Australia Innings

GM Wood	c Kirmani b Kapil Dev	9	
J Dyson	c Gavaskar b Kapil Dev	0	
*GS Chappell	c Kapil Dev b Ghavri	204	
KJ Hughes	c Kirmani b Kapil Dev	24	
AR Border	c Kirmani b Kapil Dev	31	
KD Walters	c Viswanath b Ghavri	67	
+RW Marsh	c Binny b Ghavri	12	
DK Lillee	c Doshi b Ghavri	5	
RM Hogg	not out	26	
LS Pascoe	c Doshi b Ghavri	7	
JD Higgs	b Kapil Dev	2	
	(b 4, lb 3, w 3, nb 9)	19	
	(all out)	406	

Bowling: Kapil Dev 36.1-7-97-5 Ghavri 30-7-107-5 Binny 15-1-70-0 Doshi 27-0-103-0 Chauhan 1-0-10-0

Umpires: MW Johnson and RV Whitehead

Australia v West Indies
2,3,4,5,6 January 1982

Result: Match drawn

West Indies Innings

Batsman		Runs		Runs
CG Greenidge	c Laird b Lillee	66	c Yardley b Lillee	8
DL Haynes	lbw b Thomson	15	lbw b Lillee	51
IVA Richards	c Marsh b Lillee	44	c Border b Alderman	22
HA Gomes	c Chappell b Yardley	126	c Border b Yardley	43
*CH Lloyd	c Marsh b Thomson	40	c Hughes b Yardley	57
PJL Dujon	c & b Thomson	44	c & b Yardley	48
+DA Murray	b Yardley	13	c Laird b Yardley	1
MA Holding	lbw b Lillee	9	c Dyson b Yardley	5
ST Clarke	c Yardley	14	c Dyson b Yardley	5
J Garner	c Marsh b Lillee	1	b Yardley	0
CEH Croft	not out	0	not out	4
	(lb 3, nb 9)	12	(lb 1, w 5, nb 5)	11
	(all out)	384	(all out)	255

Bowling: Lillee 39-6-119-4 Alderman 30-9-73-0 Thomson 20-1-93-3 Yardley 26.2-3-87-3 Border 1-1-0-0
Lillee 20-6-50-2 Alderman 12-2-46-1 Thomson 15-3-50-0 Yardley 31.4-6-98-7

Australia Innings

Batsman		Runs		Runs
BM Laird	c Dujon b Garner	14	c Murray b Croft	38
GM Wood	c Murray b Holding	63	not out	7
J Dyson	lbw b Holding	28	not out	127
*GS Chappell	c Dujon b Holding	12	c Murray b Croft	0
TM Alderman	b Clarke	0		
KJ Hughes	b Garner	16	lbw b Gomes	13
AR Border	not out	53	b Gomes	9
+RW Marsh	c Holding b Gomes	17		
B Yardley	b Holding	45		
DK Lillee	c Garner b Holding	4		
JR Thomson	run out	8		
	(b 1, lb 2, w 2, nb 2)	7	(b 2, lb 1, nb 3)	6
	(all out)	267	(4 wickets)	200

Bowling: Holding 29-9-64-5 Clarke 16-4-51-1 Garner 20-4-52-2 Croft 20-7-53-0 Richards 13-7-21-0 Gomes 9-1-19-1
Holding 19-6-31-0 Clarke 16-9-25-0 Garner 12-3-27-0 Croft 27-5-58-2 Richards 13-3-33-0 Gomes 15-7-20-2

Umpires: RA French and MW Johnson

Australia v England
2,3,4,6,7 January 1983

Result: Match drawn

Australia Innings

Batsman		Runs		Runs
KC Wessels	c Willis b Botham	19	lbw b Botham	53
J Dyson	c Taylor b Hemmings	79	c Gower b Willis	2
*GS Chappell	lbw b Willis	35	c Randall b Hemmings	11
KJ Hughes	c Cowans b Botham	29	c Botham b Hemmings	137
DW Hookes	b Botham b Hemmings	17	lbw b Miller	19
AR Border	c Miller b Hemmings	89	c Botham b Cowans	83
+RW Marsh	c & b Miller	3	c Taylor b Miller	41
B Yardley	b Cowans	24	c Botham b Hemmings	0
GF Lawson	c & b Botham	6	not out	13
JR Thomson	c Lamb b Botham	0	c Gower b Miller	12
RM Hogg	not out	0	run out	0
	(b 3, lb 8, w 2)	13	(lb 7, nb 4)	11
	(all out)	314	(all out)	382

Bowling: Willis 20-6-57-1 Cowans 21-3-67-1 Botham 30-8-75-4 Hemmings 27-10-68-3 Miller 17-7-34-1
Willis 10-2-33-1 Cowans 13-1-47-1 Botham 10-0-35-1 Hemmings 47-16-116-3 Miller 49.3-12-133-3 Cook 2-1-7-0

England Innings

Batsman		Runs		Runs
G Cook	c Chappell b Hogg	8	lbw b Lawson	2
CJ Tavare	b Lawson	0	lbw b Yardley	16
DI Gower	c Chappell b Lawson	70	c Hookes b Yardley	24
AJ Lamb	b Lawson	29	c & b Yardley	29
DW Randall	b Thomson	70	b Thomson	44
IT Botham	c Wessels b Thomson	5	lbw b Thomson	32
G Miller	lbw b Thomson	34	not out	21
+RW Taylor	lbw b Thomson	0	not out	28
EE Hemmings	c Border b Yardley	29	c Marsh b Yardley	95
*RGD Willis	c Border b Thomson	1		
NG Cowans	not out	0		
	(b 4, lb 4, nb 12)	20	(b 1, lb 10, w 1, nb 11)	23
	(all out)	237	(7 wickets)	314

Bowling: Lawson 20-2-70-3 Hogg 16-2-50-1 Thomson 14.5-2-50-5 Yardley 14-4-47-1
Lawson 15-1-50-1 Hogg 13-6-25-0 Thomson 12-3-30-2 Yardley 37-6-139-4 Border 16-3-36-0 Hookes 2-1-5-0 Chappell 1-0-6-0

Umpires: RA French and MW Johnson

Australia v Pakistan
2,3,4,5,6 January 1984

Result: Australia won by 10 wickets

Pakistan Innings

Batsman		Runs		Runs
Mohsin Khan	c Border b Lillee	14	c Chappell b Lawson	1
Mudassar Nazar	c Chappell b Lawson	84	b Lawson	21
Qasim Umar	c Border b Lillee	15	c Marsh b Lawson	26
Abdul Qadir	c Hughes b Lawson	4	c Marsh b Lillee	5
Javed Miandad	c Lillee b Matthews	16	c Marsh b Lawson	60
Zaheer Abbas	c Yallop b Lawson	61	c Marsh b Hogg	33
*Imran Khan	c Yallop b Lawson	5	c Marsh b Hogg	10
Saleem Malik	c Lillee b Lawson	54	c Chappell b Lillee	7
Sarfraz Nawaz	lbw b Lillee	5	c Phillips b Lillee	20
+Wasim Bari	not out	7	c Phillips b Lillee	20
Azeem Hafeez	c Marsh b Lillee	4	not out	2
	(b 2, lb 7)	9	(b 4, nb 1)	5
	(all out)	278	(all out)	210

Bowling: Lillee 31.2-10-65-4 Hogg 18-1-61-0 Chappell 8-0-25-0 Lawson 25-5-59-5 Matthews 18-4-59-1
Lillee 29.5-5-88-4 Lawson 20-7-69-3 Matthews 7-4-17-0 Hogg 14-2-53-2

Australia Innings

Batsman		Runs		Runs
KC Wessels	c Wasim Bari b Azeem Hafeez	3	not out	14
WB Phillips	c Saleem Malik b Sarfraz Nawaz	37	not out	19
GN Yallop	c Wasim Bari b Mudassar Nazar	30		
GS Chappell	lbw b Mudassar Nazar	182		
*KJ Hughes	lbw b Sarfraz Nawaz	76		
AR Border	c Wasim Bari b Mudassar Nazar	64		
GRJ Matthews	not out	22		
+RW Marsh	not out	15		
GF Lawson				
RM Hogg				
DK Lillee				
	(lb 15, w 1, nb 9)	25	(nb 2)	2
	(6 wickets declared)	454	(0 wickets)	35

Bowling: Sarfraz Nawaz 53-13-132-2 Azeem Hafeez 36-7-121-1 Mudassar Nazar 31-9-81-3 Abdul Qadir 34-9-105-0
Sarfraz Nawaz 3-1-7-0 Azeem Hafeez 2.4-0-28-0

Umpires: RA French and MW Johnson

Australia v West Indies
30,31 December 1984, 1,2 January 1985

Result: Australia won by an innings and 55 runs

Australia Innings

AMJ Hilditch	c Dujon b Holding	2
GM Wood	c Haynes b Gomes	45
KC Wessels	b Holding	173
GM Ritchie	run out	37
*AR Border	c Greenidge b Walsh	69
DC Boon	b Garner	49
+SJ Rixon	c Garner b Holding	20
MJ Bennett	c Greenidge b Garner	23
GF Lawson	not out	5
CJ McDermott	c Greenidge b Walsh	4
RG Holland		
	(b 7, lb 20, nb 17)	44
	(9 wickets declared)	471

Bowling: Marshall 37-2-111-0 Garner 31-5-101-2 Holding 31-7-74-3 Walsh 38.2-1-118-2 Gomes 12-2-29-1 Richards 7-2-11-0

West Indies Innings

Batsman		Runs		Runs
CG Greenidge	c Rixon b McDermott	18	b Holland	12
DL Haynes	c Wessels b Holland	34	lbw b McDermott	3
RB Richardson	b McDermott	2	c Wood b Bennett	26
HA Gomes	c Bennett b Holland	28	c Wood b Lawson	8
IVA Richards	c Wessels b Holland	15	b Bennett	58
*CH Lloyd	c Wood b Holland	33	c Border b McDermott	72
+PJL Dujon	c Hildtch b Bennett	22	c & b Holland	0
MD Marshall	st Rixon b Holland	0	not out	32
MA Holding	c McDermott b Bennett	0	c Rixon b Bennett	8
J Garner	c Rixon b Holland	0	c Bennett b Holland	4
CA Walsh	not out	1	not out	1
	(lb 3, nb 7)	10	(b 2, lb 12, nb 8)	22
	(all out)	163	(all out)	253

Bowling: Lawson 9-1-27-0 McDermott 9-0-34-2 Bennett 22.5-7-45-2 Holland 22-7-54-6
Lawson 6-1-14-1 McDermott 12-0-56-2 Bennett 33-9-79-3 Holland 33-8-90-4

Umpires: RC Isherwood and MW Johnson

Australia v New Zealand
22,23,24,25,26 November 1985

Result: Australia won by 4 wickets

New Zealand Innings

Batsman		Runs		Runs
JG Wright	c O'Donnell b Bright	38	c & b Matthews	43
BA Edgar	c Border b Holland	50	c & b Holland	52
JF Reid	c Kerr b Holland	19	b Matthews	19
MD Crowe	run out	8	b Holland	0
*JV Coney	c Border b Holland	8	b Holland	7
JJ Crowe	b Holland	13	c & b Holland	6
VR Brown	lbw b Holland	0	b Bright	15
+IDS Smith	c Hookes b Bright	28	c & b Bright	12
RJ Hadlee	lbw b Holland	5	lbw b Gilbert	26
JG Bracewell	not out	83	not out	2
SL Boock	lbw b Gilbert	37	c Boon b Bright	3
	(b 6, lb 8, nb 2)	16	(b 1, lb 4, nb 3)	8
	(all out)	293	(all out)	193

Bowling: Gilbert 20.3-6-41-1 O'Donnell 6-2-13-0 Bright 34-12-87-2 Matthews 17-3-32-0 Holland 47-19-106-6
Gilbert 9-2-22-1 O'Donnell 5-4-4-0 Bright 17.5-3-39-3 Matthews 30-11-55-2 Holland 41-16-68-4

Australia Innings

Batsman		Runs		Runs
+WB Phillips	b Bracewell	31	c Bracewell b Boock	63
RB Kerr	lbw b Hadlee	7	c Wright b Bracewell	7
DC Boon	lbw b Hadlee	8	c Reid b Bracewell	81
*AR Border	b Bracewell	20	st Smith b Bracewell	11
GM Ritchie	c JJ Crowe b Hadlee	89	c MD Crowe b Hadlee	13
DW Hookes	run out	0	c MD Crowe b Hadlee	38
GRJ Matthews	c Smith b Hadlee	50	lbw b Hadlee	32
SP O'Donnell	not out	20	not out	2
RJ Bright	lbw b Boock	1		
DR Gilbert	c Smith b Hadlee	0		
RG Holland	st Smith b Boock	0		
	(b 5, lb 2, nb 2)	9	(b 3, lb 9, nb 1)	13
	(all out)	227	(6 wickets)	260

Bowling: Hadlee 24-2-65-5 MD Crowe 5-2-15-0 Bracewell 25-9-51-2 Boock 29.5-14-53-2 Brown 13-3-35-0 Coney 1-0-1-0
Hadlee 27.1-10-58-2 MD Crowe 2-1-7-0 Bracewell 30-7-91-3 Boock 22-4-49-1 Brown 7-0-28-0 Coney 9-1-15-0

Umpires: MW Johnson and BE Martin

Australia v India
2,3,4,5,6 January 1986

Result: Match drawn

India Innings

SM Gavaskar	b Holland	172
K Srikkanth	b Reid	116
M Amarnath	c Bright b Gilbert	138
*N Kapil Dev	b Gilbert	42
DB Vengsarkar	not out	37
M Azharuddin	not out	59
RJ Shastri		
+SMH Kirmani		
C Sharma		
L Sivaramakrishnan		
NS Yadav		
	(b 5, lb 9, nb 22)	36
	(4 wickets declared)	600

Bowling: Gilbert 37-3-135-2 Reid 34-8-89-1 Bright 41-7-121-0 Holland 21-6-113-1 Matthews 29-2-95-0 Waugh 7-0-33-0

Australia Innings

Batsman		Runs		Runs
DC Boon	b Kapil Dev	131	run out	25
GR Marsh	c Gavaskar b Shastri	92	lbw b Yadav	28
*AR Border	c Sharma b Shastri	71	c Sivaramakrishnan b Yadav	4
GM Ritchie	c Kapil Dev b Yadav	14	not out	17
+WB Phillips	c Kapil Dev b Yadav	14	c Srikkanth b Shastri	22
GRJ Matthews	c Amarnath b Yadav	40	c Kapil Dev b Yadav	17
SR Waugh	c Sivaramakrishnan b Yadav	8	b Shastri	
RJ Bright	c Kirmani b Shastri	3	not out	
DR Gilbert	c Azharuddin b Yadav	1		
BA Reid	st Kirmani b Yadav	4		
RG Holland	not out	1		
	(lb 14, nb 3)	17	(b 3, lb 2, nb 1)	6
	(all out)	396	(6 wickets)	119

Bowling: Kapil Dev 25-8-65-1 Shastri 57-21-101-4 Yadav 62.3-21-99-5 Sivaramakrishnan 22-2-79-0 Sharma 13-2-38-0
Kapil Dev 7-3-11-0 Yadav 33-22-19-3 Sharma 3-0-11-0 Shastri 25-12-36-2 Sivaramakrishnan 9-0-37-0

Umpires: PJ McConnell and SG Randell

Sydney Cricket Ground

Australia v England
10,11,12,14,15 January 1987

Result: Australia won by 55 runs

Australia Innings

GR Marsh	c Gatting b Small	24	c Emburey b Dilley	14
GM Ritchie	lbw b Dilley	6	c Botham b Edmonds	13
DM Jones	not out	184	c Richards b Emburey	30
*AR Border	c Botham b Edmonds	34	b Edmonds	49
DM Wellham	c Richards b Small	17	c Lamb b Emburey	1
SR Waugh	c Richards b Small	0	c Athey b Emburey	73
PR Sleep	c Richards b Small	9	c Lamb b Emburey	10
+TJ Zoehrer	c Gatting b Small	12	lbw b Emburey	1
PL Taylor	c Emburey b Edmonds	11	c Lamb b Emburey	42
MG Hughes	c Botham b Edmonds	16	b Emburey	5
BA Reid	b Dilley	4	not out	1
	(b 12, lb 4, w 2, nb 8)	26	(b 5, lb 7)	12
	(all out)	343	(all out)	251

Bowling: Dilley 23.5-5-67-2 Small 33-11-75-5 Botham 23-10-42-0 Emburey 30-4-62-0 Edmonds 34-5-79-3 Gatting 1-0-2-0
Dilley 15-4-48-1 Small 8-2-17-0 Edmonds 43-16-79-2 Emburey 46-15-78-7 Botham 3-0-17-0 Gatting 2-2-0-0

England Innings

BC Broad	lbw b Hughes	6	c & b Sleep	17
CWJ Athey	c Zoehrer b Hughes	5	b Sleep	31
*MW Gatting	lbw b Reid	0	c & b Waugh	96
AJ Lamb	c Zoehrer b Taylor	24	c Waugh b Taylor	3
DI Gower	c Wellham b Taylor	72	c Marsh b Border	37
IT Botham	c Marsh b Taylor	16	c Wellham b Taylor	0
+CJ Richards	c Wellham b Reid	46	b Sleep	38
JE Emburey	b Taylor	69	b Sleep	22
PH Edmonds	c Marsh b Taylor	3	lbw b Sleep	0
GC Small	b Taylor	14	c Border b Reid	0
GR Dilley	not out	4	not out	2
	(b 9, lb 3, w 2, nb 2)	16	(b 8, lb 6, w 1, nb 3)	18
	(all out)	275	(all out)	264

Bowling: Hughes 16-3-58-2 Reid 25-7-74-2 Waugh 6-4-6-0 Taylor 26-7-78-6 Sleep 21-6-47-0
Hughes 12-3-32-0 Reid 19-8-32-1 Sleep 35-14-72-5 Taylor 29-10-76-2 Border 13-6-25-1 Waugh 6-2-13-1

Umpires: PJ McConnell and SG Randell

Australia v England
29,30,31 January, 1,2 February 1988

Result: Match drawn

England Innings

BC Broad	b Waugh	139
MD Moxon	b Sleep	40
RT Robinson	c Veletta b Dodemaide	43
*MW Gatting	c Dyer b Waugh	13
CWJ Athey	c & b Taylor	37
DJ Capel	c Sleep b Taylor	21
JE Emburey	st Dyer b Sleep	23
+BN French	st Dyer b Taylor	47
NA Foster	c Border b Taylor	19
EE Hemmings	not out	8
GR Dilley	b Waugh	13
	(b 4, lb 9, w 1, nb 8)	22
	(all out)	425

Bowling: McDermott 35-8-65-0 Dodemaide 36-10-98-1 Taylor 34-10-84-4 Waugh 22.5-5-51-3 Sleep 45-8-114-2

Australia Innings

DC Boon	c French b Foster	12	not out	184
GR Marsh	c French b Capel	5	c Athey b Emburey	56
DM Jones	c Emburey b Hemmings	56	c Moxon b Capel	24
*AR Border	c Broad b Capel	2	not out	48
MRJ Veletta	c Emburey b Hemmings	22		
SR Waugh	c French b Dilley	27		
PR Sleep	c Athey b Foster	41		
+GC Dyer	lbw b Dilley	0		
PL Taylor	c French b Hemmings	20		
AIC Dodemaide	not out	12		
CJ McDermott	c Foster b Dilley	1		
	(lb 10, w 1, nb 5)	16	(b 3, lb 7, nb 6)	16
	(all out)	214	(2 wickets)	328

Bowling: Dilley 19.1-4-54-3 Foster 19-6-27-2 Emburey 30-10-57-0 Capel 6-3-13-2 Hemmings 22-3-53-3
Dilley 13-1-48-0 Foster 15-6-27-0 Emburey 38-5-98-1 Capel 17-4-38-1 Hemmings 52-15-107-0

Umpires: AR Crafter and PJ McConnell

Australia v West Indies
26,27,28,29,30 January 1989

Result: Australia won by 7 wickets

West Indies Innings

CG Greenidge	c Waugh b PL Taylor	56	c & b Hughes	4
DL Haynes	c Boon b Hohns	75	c MA Taylor b Border	143
RB Richardson	c PL Taylor b Border	28	c Hughes b PL Taylor	22
CL Hooper	c Marsh b Border	0	c Jones b Hohns	35
*IVA Richards	c Boon b Border	11	c Jones b Hohns	4
AL Logie	b Border	0	c PL Taylor b Hohns	6
+PJL Dujon	c Hughes b Border	18	run out	9
RA Harper	c PL Taylor b Border	17	lbw b Border	12
MD Marshall	c Marsh b Border	9	c PL Taylor b Border	3
CEL Ambrose	c Jones b PL Taylor	1	c Boon b Border	5
CA Walsh	not out	4	not out	7
	(b 1, w 1, nb 3)	5	(b 1, w 1, nb 4)	6
	(all out)	224	(all out)	256

Bowling: Alderman 10-2-17-0 Hughes 10-3-28-0 PL Taylor 25.2-8-65-2 Hohns 24-8-49-1 Border 26-10-46-7 Waugh 4-0-18-0
Hughes 18-6-29-1 Alderman 2-0-6-0 Waugh 3-0-10-0 PL Taylor 29-4-91-1 Hohns 34-11-69-3 Border 18.4-3-50-4

Australia Innings

GR Marsh	c Dujon b Marshall	2	b Richards	23
MA Taylor	b Ambrose	25	c Haynes b Ambrose	3
DC Boon	c Dujon b Walsh	149	c Harper b Marshall	10
DM Jones	b Richards	29	not out	24
*AR Border	b Marshall	75	not out	16
SR Waugh	not out	55		
+IA Healy	c Logie b Marshall	11		
PL Taylor	lbw b Marshall	0		
TV Hohns	b Marshall	12		
MG Hughes	c Dujon b Walsh	12		
TM Alderman	run out	9		
	(b 6, lb 14, nb 14)	34	(b 3, lb 1, nb 2)	6
	(all out)	401	(3 wickets)	82

Bowling: Marshall 31-16-29-5 Ambrose 33.5-5-78-1 Harper 9-7-9-86-0 Walsh 22.5-5-48-2 Hooper 37-10-72-0 Richards 31-1-68-1
Marshall 8-2-17-1 Ambrose 7-1-16-1 Hooper 10.3-2-24-0 Walsh 3-0-9-0 Richards 7-2-12-1

Umpires: LJ King and TA Prue

Australia v Pakistan
3,4,5,6,7 February 1990

Result: Match drawn

Pakistan Innings

Aamer Malik	c Healy b Alderman	7
Rameez Raja	c & b Hughes	0
Shoaib Mohammad	lbw b Alderman	9
Javed Miandad	c Jones b Hughes	49
Ijaz Ahmed	c MA Taylor b Rackemann	8
*Imran Khan	not out	82
Wasim Akram	c MA Taylor b Alderman	10
+Saleem Yousuf	c Jones b Alderman	6
Tauseef Ahmed	b Alderman	0
Waqar Younis	c Veletta b Hughes	16
Nadeem Ghauri	b Alderman	0
	(b 1, lb 7, nb 4)	12
	(all out)	199

Bowling: Alderman 33.5-10-65-5 Hughes 31-16-70-3 Rackemann 22-8-33-2 PL Taylor 8-1-23-0

Australia Innings

MA Taylor	not out	101
MRJ Veletta	lbw b Waqar Younis	9
TM Moody	c Aamer Malik b Tauseef Ahmed	26
*AR Border	not out	27
DM Jones		
SR Waugh		
+IA Healy		
PL Taylor		
MG Hughes		
TM Alderman		
CG Rackemann		
	(b 4, lb 5, nb 4)	13
	(2 wickets)	176

Bowling: Wasim Akram 10-3-29-0 Imran Khan 17-2-32-0 Tauseef Ahmed 19-3-62-1 Nadeem Ghauri 8-1-20-0 Waqar Younis 9-4-21-1 Ijaz Ahmed 2-0-3-0

Umpires: AR Crafter and PJ McConnell

Australia v England
4,5,6,7,8 January 1991

Result: Match drawn

Australia Innings

GR Marsh	c Larkins b Malcolm	13	c Stewart b Malcolm	4
MA Taylor	c Russell b Malcolm	11	lbw b Hemmings	19
DC Boon	c Atherton b Gooch	97	c Gooch b Tufnell	29
*AR Border	b Hemmings	78	c Gooch b Tufnell	20
DM Jones	st Russell b Small	60	c & b Tufnell	0
SR Waugh	c Stewart b Malcolm	48	c Russell b Hemmings	14
GRJ Matthews	c Hemmings b Tufnell	128	b Hemmings	19
+IA Healy	c Small b Hemmings	35	c Smith b Tufnell	69
CG Rackemann	b Hemmings	1	b Malcolm	9
TM Alderman	not out	26	c Gower b Tufnell	1
BA Reid	c Smith b Malcolm	0	not out	5
	(b 5, lb 8, nb 8)	21	(lb 16)	16
	(all out)	518	(all out)	205

Bowling: Malcolm 45-12-128-4 Small 31-5-103-1 Hemmings 32-7-105-3 Tufnell 30-6-95-1 Gooch 14-3-46-1 Atherton 5-0-28-0
Malcolm 6-1-19-2 Small 2-1-6-0 Hemmings 41-9-94-3 Tufnell 37-18-61-5 Atherton 3-1-9-0

England Innings

*GA Gooch	c Healy b Reid	59	c Border b Matthews	54
MA Atherton	c Boon b Matthews	105	not out	3
W Larkins	run out (Border)	11	lbw b Border	0
RA Smith	c Healy b Reid	18	not out	10
DI Gower	c Marsh b Reid	123	c Taylor b Matthews	36
AJ Stewart	lbw b Alderman	91	run out (Alderman/Matthews)	7
+RC Russell	not out	30		
GC Small	lbw b Alderman	10		
EE Hemmings	b Alderman	9		
PCR Tufnell	not out	5		
DE Malcolm				
	(b 1, lb 8, nb 8)	17	(lb 1, nb 2)	3
	(8 wickets dec)	469	(4 wickets)	113

Bowling: Alderman 20.1-4-62-3 Reid 35.1-9-79-3 Rackemann 25.5-5-89-0 Matthews 58-16-145-1 Border 19-5-45-0 Waugh 14-3-40-0
Alderman 4-0-29-0 Rackemann 3-0-20-0 Matthews 9-2-26-2 Border 9-1-37-1

Umpires: AR Crafter and PJ McConnell

Australia v India
2,3,4,5,6 January 1992

Result: Match drawn

Australia Innings

GR Marsh	b Banerjee	8	c Pandit b Kapil Dev	4
MA Taylor	c Pandit b Banerjee	56	c Kapil Dev b Shastri	35
DC Boon	not out	129	c Azharuddin b Srinath	7
ME Waugh	c Prabhakar b Banerjee	5	lbw b Prabhakar	18
DM Jones	run out	35	c Pandit b Shastri	18
*AR Border	c Pandit b Kapil Dev	19	not out	53
+IA Healy	c sub (K Srikkanth) b Prabhakar	1	c Prabhakar b Shastri	7
MG Hughes	c Pandit b Prabhakar	2	c Prabhakar b Tendulkar	21
CJ McDermott	b Prabhakar	1	c Vengsarkar b Shastri	0
SK Warne	c Pandit b Kapil Dev	20	not out	1
BA Reid	c Tendulkar b Kapil Dev	0		
	(b 4, lb 14, w 1, nb 18)	37	(lb 4, w 1, nb 4)	9
	(all out)	313	(8 wickets)	173

Bowling: Kapil Dev 33-9-60-3 Prabhakar 39-12-82-3 Banerjee 18-4-47-3 Srinath 21-5-69-0 Shastri 13-1-37-0
Kapil Dev 19-5-41-1 Prabhakar 27-10-53-1 Srinath 12-0-28-1 Shastri 25-8-45-4 Tendulkar 1-0-2-1

India Innings

RJ Shastri	c Jones b Warne	206
NS Sidhu	c Waugh b McDermott	0
SV Manjrekar	c Waugh b Hughes	34
DB Vengsarkar	c Waugh b McDermott	54
*M Azharuddin	c Boon b McDermott	4
SR Tendulkar	not out	148
M Prabhakar	c Taylor b Hughes	14
N Kapil Dev	c Marsh b Hughes	9
+CS Pandit	run out	9
ST Banerjee	c Border b McDermott	3
J Srinath	run out	1
	(b 1, lb 4, nb 5)	10
	(all out)	483

Bowling: McDermott 51-12-147-4 Reid 4-0-10-0 Hughes 41.4-8-104-3 Waugh 14-5-28-0 Warne 45-7-150-1 Border 13-3-39-0

Umpires: PJ McConnell and SG Randell; Referee: PBH May (Eng)

Australia v West Indies
2,3,4,5,6 January 1993

Result: Match drawn

Australia Innings

MA Taylor	c Murray b Bishop	20	not out	46
DC Boon	c Murray b Adams	76	not out	63
SR Waugh	c Simmons b Ambrose	100		
ME Waugh	run out	57		
DR Martyn	b Ambrose	0		
*AR Border	c Murray b Hooper	74		
GRJ Matthews	c Murray b Hooper	79		
+IA Healy	not out	36		
MG Hughes	c Haynes b Bishop	17		
SK Warne	c Simmons b Hooper	14		
CJ McDermott				
	(b 2, lb 23, nb 5)	30	(b 1, lb 2, nb 5)	8
	(9 wkts decl)	503	(0 wickets)	117

Bowling: Ambrose 35-8-87-2 Bishop 36-6-87-2 Walsh 30-8-86-0 Hooper 45.4-6-137-3 Adams 15-2-56-1 Simmons 10-2-25-0
Ambrose 6-2-10-0 Bishop 4-1-9-0 Simmons 3-2-9-0 Walsh 8-3-13-0 Hooper 10-2-22-0 Adams 8-1-29-0 Arthurton 5-1-14-0
Lara 2-0-4-0 Richardson 1-0-4-0

West Indies Innings

DL Haynes	b Matthews	22
PV Simmons	c Taylor b McDermott	3
*RB Richardson	c Warne b Hughes	109
BC Lara	run out	277
KLT Arthurton	c Healy b Matthews	47
CL Hooper	b Warne	21
JC Adams	not out	77
+JR Murray	c Healy b Hughes	11
IR Bishop	run out	1
CEL Ambrose	c Martyn b ME Waugh	16
CA Walsh	c Healy b Hughes	0
	(b 4, lb 9, w 1, nb 8)	22
	(all out)	606

Bowling: McDermott 33-3-119-1 Hughes 16.4-1-76-3 Matthews 59-12-169-2 SR Waugh 11-1-43-0 Warne 41-6-116-1 Border 14-1-41-0 ME Waugh 10-1-29-1

Umpires: DB Hair and TA Prue; Referee: DB Carr (Eng)

Australia v South Africa
2,3,4,5,6 January 1994

Result: South Africa won by 5 runs

South Africa Innings

AC Hudson	lbw b McGrath	0	c Healy b McDermott	1
G Kirsten	st Healy b Warne	67	b McDermott	41
WJ Cronje	c Waugh b McDermott	41	b McDermott	38
DJ Cullinan	b Warne	9	lbw b Warne	2
JN Rhodes	lbw b Warne	4	not out	76
*KC Wessels	c & b Warne	3	b Warne	18
+DJ Richardson	c Taylor b Warne	4	lbw b McGrath	24
PL Symcox	b Warne	7	c Healy b McDermott	4
CR Matthews	c Taylor b Warne	0	c Waugh b Warne	4
PS de Villiers	c Waugh b McDermott	18	lbw b Warne	2
AA Donald	not out	0	c Healy b Warne	10
	(b 1, lb 4, nb 11)	16	(b 13, lb 1, nb 5)	19
	(all out)	169	(all out)	239

Bowling: McDermott 18.1-2-42-2 McGrath 19-5-32-1 Warne 27-8-56-7 May 10-1-34-0
McDermott 28-9-62-4 McGrath 14-3-30-1 May 22-4-53-0 Warne 42-17-72-5 Border 3-1-8-0

Australia Innings

MJ Slater	b Donald	92	b de Villiers	1
MA Taylor	c Richardson b Donald	7	c Richardson b de Villiers	27
DC Boon	b de Villiers	19	c Kirsten b de Villiers	24
ME Waugh	lbw b Symcox	7	lbw b Donald	11
*AR Border	c Richardson b de Villiers	49	b Donald	7
DR Martyn	c Richardson b de Villiers	59	c Hudson b Donald	6
+IA Healy	c Richardson b Donald	19	b de Villiers	1
SK Warne	c Rhodes b Symcox	11	run out	1
CJ McDermott	c Cronje b de Villiers	6	not out	29
TBA May	not out	8	lbw b de Villiers	0
GD McGrath	b Donald	9	c & b de Villiers	1
	(b 1, lb 2, nb 3)	6	(lb 3)	3
	(all out)	292	(all out)	111

Bowling: Donald 31.2-8-83-4 de Villiers 36-12-80-4 Matthews 28-11-44-0 Symcox 46-11-82-2
Donald 17-5-34-3 de Villiers 23.3-8-43-6 Matthews 6-5-9-0 Symcox 10-3-22-0

Umpires: SG Randell and WP Sheahan
TV Umpire: IS Thomas; Referee: JL Hendriks (WI)

Australia v England
1,2,3,4,5 January 1995

Result: Match drawn

England Innings

GA Gooch	c Healy b Fleming	1	lbw b Fleming	29
*MA Atherton	b McDermott	88	c Taylor b Fleming	67
GA Hick	b McDermott	2	not out	98
GP Thorpe	lbw b McDermott	10	not out	47
JP Crawley	c ME Waugh b Fleming	72		
MW Gatting	c Healy b McDermott	0		
ARC Fraser	c Healy b Fleming	27		
+SJ Rhodes	run out (SR Waugh/Fleming/Healy)	1		
D Gough	c Fleming b McDermott	51		
DE Malcolm	b Warne	29		
PCR Tufnell	not out	4		
	(b 8, lb 7, nb 9)	24	(lb 6, w 1, nb 7)	14
	(all out)	309	(2 wickets decl)	255

Bowling: McDermott 30-7-101-5 Fleming 26.2-12-52-3 Warne 36-10-88-1 May 17-4-35-0 ME Waugh 6-1-10-0 Bevan 4-1-8-0
McDermott 24-2-76-0 Fleming 20-3-66-2 ME Waugh 2-1-4-0 Warne 16-2-48-0 May 10-1-55-0

Australia Innings

MJ Slater	b Malcolm	11	c Tufnell b Fraser	103
*MA Taylor	c & b Gough	49	b Malcolm	113
DC Boon	b Gough	3	c Hick b Gough	17
ME Waugh	c Rhodes b Malcolm	3	lbw b Fraser	25
MG Bevan	c Thorpe b Fraser	8	c Rhodes b Fraser	7
SR Waugh	b Gough	1	c Rhodes b Fraser	0
+IA Healy	c Hick b Gough	10	c Rhodes b Fraser	5
SK Warne	c Gatting b Fraser	0	not out	36
TBA May	c Hick b Gough	0	not out	10
CJ McDermott	not out	21		
DW Fleming	b Gough	0		
	(b 6, lb 1, nb 3)	10	(b 12, lb 3, w 1, nb 12)	28
	(all out)	116	(7 wickets)	344

Bowling: Malcolm 13-4-34-2 Gough 18.5-4-49-6 Fraser 11-1-26-2
Malcolm 21-4-75-1 Gough 28-4-72-1 Fraser 25-3-73-5 Tufnell 35.4-9-61-0 Hick 5-0-21-0 Gooch 7-1-27-0

Umpires: SA Bucknor (WI) and DB Hair
TV Umpire: WA Cameron; Referee: JR Reid (NZ)

Australia v Pakistan
30 November, 1,2,3,4 December 1995

Result: Pakistan won by 74 runs

Pakistan Innings

Aamer Sohail	c ME Waugh b McDermott	4	c Boon b McDermott	9
Rameez Raja	c Slater b Warne	33	c ME Waugh b Warne	39
Ijaz Ahmed	c McGrath b Warne	137	lbw b Warne	15
Inzamam-ul-Haq	c Healy b Warne	39	c Taylor b McDermott	59
Saleem Malik	lbw b McGrath	36	lbw b ME Waugh	45
Basit Ali	c Slater b McDermott	17	b Warne	14
+Rashid Latif	c Healy b McDermott	1	lbw b Warne	3
*Wasim Akram	c & b McGrath	21	lbw b McDermott	5
Saqlain Mushtaq	run out (Boon)	0	c ME Waugh b McDermott	2
Mushtaq Ahmed	c McDermott b Warne	0	lbw b McDermott	2
Waqar Younis	not out	0	not out	1
	(lb 3, w 2, nb 6)	11	(b 1, lb 5, nb 4)	10
	(all out)	299	(all out)	204

Bowling: McDermott 21-6-62-3 McGrath 22.2-1-79-2 Reiffel 22-5-71-0 Warne 34-20-55-4 ME Waugh 10-4-23-0 Blewett 4-2-6-0
McDermott 15.3-0-49-5 McGrath 17-3-47-0 Warne 37-13-66-4 Reiffel 8.3-2-15-0 ME Waugh 14-4-21-1 Blewett 2-2-0-0

Australia Innings

MJ Slater	b Wasim Akram	1	lbw b Mushtaq Ahmed	23
*MA Taylor	c Rashid Latif b Saqlain Mushtaq	47	st Rashid Latif b Mushtaq Ahmed	59
DC Boon	c Rashid Latif b Mushtaq Ahmed	16	c sub (Moin Khan) b Saqlain Mushtaq	6
ME Waugh	c Mushtaq Ahmed b Wasim Akram	116	c Rashid Latif b Wasim Akram	34
SR Waugh	st Rashid Latif b Mushtaq Ahmed	38	b Mushtaq Ahmed	14
GS Blewett	b Mushtaq Ahmed	5	b Waqar Younis	14
+IA Healy	c Rashid Latif b Mushtaq Ahmed	6	c Rashid Latif b Wasim Akram	7
PR Reiffel	not out	10	not out	2
SK Warne	c Rashid Latif b Wasim Akram	2	c Saqlain Mushtaq b Mushtaq Ahmed	5
CJ McDermott	b Wasim Akram	0	b Waqar Younis	0
GD McGrath	c Wasim Akram b Mushtaq Ahmed	0	b Waqar Younis	0
	(lb 6, nb 10)	16	(lb 5, nb 3)	8
	(all out)	257	(all out)	172

Bowling: Wasim Akram 24-4-50-4 Waqar Younis 11-4-26-0 Mushtaq Ahmed 36.2-7-95-5 Saqlain Mushtaq 22-2-62-1 Aamer Sohail 5-0-18-0
Wasim Akram 16-5-25-2 Waqar Younis 6.1-2-15-3 Mushtaq Ahmed 30-6-91-4 Saqlain Mushtaq 13-5-35-1 Aamer Sohail 1-0-1-0

Umpires: HD Bird (Eng) and SG Randell
TV Umpire: IS Thomas; Referee: R Subba Row (Eng)

Australia v West Indies
29,30 November, 1,2,3 December 1996

Result: Australia won by 124 runs

Australia Innings

*MA Taylor	c Chanderpaul b Bishop	27	c Lara b Bishop	16
MTG Elliott	c Lara b Bishop	29	retired hurt	78
RT Ponting	c Samuels b Walsh	9	c Browne b Bishop	4
ME Waugh	c Lara b Walsh	19	c Browne b Ambrose	67
MG Bevan	c Hooper b Benjamin	16	c Browne b Benjamin	52
GS Blewett	c Adams b Walsh	69	not out	47
+IA Healy	c Lara b Walsh	44	not out	22
SK Warne	c Browne b Bishop	28		
MS Kasprowicz	c Campbell b Walsh	21		
JN Gillespie	not out	16		
GD McGrath	lbw b Adams	24		
	(lb 10, w 1, nb 18)	29	(b 4, lb 10, w 3, nb 9)	26
	(all out)	331	(4 wickets declared)	312

Bowling: Ambrose 25-5-73-0 Walsh 30-6-98-5 Benjamin 22-4-69-1 Hooper 14-6-15-0 Bishop 23-5-55-3 Adams 5.5-1-11-1
Ambrose 20-2-66-1 Walsh 19-6-36-0 Bishop 20-6-54-2 Benjamin 16-4-46-1 Adams 4-0-21-0 Hooper 27-7-75-0

West Indies Innings

SL Campbell	b Blewett	77	lbw b McGrath	15
RG Samuels	lbw b McGrath	35	b Warne	16
BC Lara	c Healy b McGrath	2	c Healy b McGrath	1
CL Hooper	lbw b Warne	27	c Taylor b Bevan	57
S Chanderpaul	c & b Warne	48	b Warne	71
JC Adams	c Bevan b McGrath	30	c Blewett b McGrath	5
+CO Browne	c Blewett b McGrath	0	not out	25
IR Bishop	c Elliott b Warne	48	run out (Ponting)	0
CEL Ambrose	b Gillespie	9	b Bevan	0
KCG Benjamin	b Gillespie	6	c Taylor b Warne	4
*CA Walsh	not out	2	c McGrath b Warne	18
	(b 4, lb 6, nb 10)	20	(lb 2, nb 1)	3
	(all out)	304	(all out)	215

Bowling: McGrath 31-9-82-4 Kasprowicz 13-2-37-0 Warne 35.2-13-65-3 Gillespie 23-5-62-2 Bevan 11-0-35-0 Blewett 4-0-13-1
McGrath 17-7-36-3 Waugh 4-0-15-0 Gillespie 7-2-27-0 Warne 27.4-5-95-4 Bevan 14-2-40-2

Umpires: DB Hair and DR Shepherd (Eng)
TV Umpire: SJA Taufel; Referee: PL van der Merwe (SA)

Australia v South Africa
2,3,4,5 January 1998

Result: Australia won by an innings and 21 runs

South Africa Innings

AM Bacher	lbw b Blewett	39	c Ponting b Reiffel	2
G Kirsten	c Taylor b McGrath	11	lbw b McGrath	0
JH Kallis	run out (Ponting)	16	b Warne	45
*WJ Cronje	c Taylor b Warne	88	c Ponting b Warne	5
HH Gibbs	c Healy b Bevan	54	c Blewett b Warne	1
BM McMillan	c Elliott b Bevan	6	b Warne	11
SM Pollock	c Taylor b Warne	18	c Taylor b Warne	4
+DJ Richardson	b Warne	6	c & b Warne	0
PL Symcox	c Healy b Warne	29	b Reiffel	38
AA Donald	not out	4	c Healy b Reiffel	2
PR Adams	c SR Waugh b Warne	0	not out	1
	(b 4, lb 4, w 1, nb 7)	16	(b 2, lb 1, nb 1)	4
	(all out)	287	(all out)	113

Bowling: McGrath 20-6-51-1 Reiffel 24-7-48-0 Warne 32.1-8-75-5 Bevan 23-3-56-2 Blewett 13-5-30-1 SR Waugh 8-4-10-0 ME Waugh 3-1-5-0 Elliott 1-0-4-0
Reiffel 12-3-14-3 McGrath 5-2-8-1 Warne 21-9-34-6 Blewett 2-1-1-0 Bevan 3-0-18-0 ME Waugh 10-2-35-0

Australia Innings

MTG Elliott	c McMillan b Symcox	32
*MA Taylor	c Richardson b Pollock	11
GS Blewett	b McMillan	28
ME Waugh	lbw b Pollock	100
SR Waugh	b Donald	85
RT Ponting	c & b Adams	62
MG Bevan	c McMillan b Symcox	12
+IA Healy	not out	46
PR Reiffel	b Donald	0
SK Warne	lbw b Pollock	12
GD McGrath	c Richardson b Donald	14
	(b 1, lb 12, nb 6)	19
	(all out)	421

Bowling: Donald 30.4-5-81-3 Pollock 33-8-71-3 Symcox 39-9-103-2 Adams 38-9-66-1 McMillan 18-5-55-1 Kallis 8-1-30-0 Cronje 1-0-2-0

Umpires: DB Hair and P Willey (Eng)
TV Umpire: SJA Taufel; Referee: RS Madugalle (SL)

Sydney Cricket Ground

Australia v England
2,3,4,5 January 1999

Result: Australia won by 98 runs

Australia Innings

*MA Taylor	c Hick b Headley	2	c Stewart b Gough	2
MJ Slater	c Hegg b Headley	18	c Hegg b Headley	123
JL Langer	c Ramprakash b Tudor	26	lbw b Headley	1
ME Waugh	c Hegg b Headley	121	c Ramprakash b Headley	24
SR Waugh	b Such	96	b Headley	8
DS Lehmann	c Hussain b Tudor	32	c Crawley b Such	0
+IA Healy	c Hegg b Gough	14	c Crawley b Such	5
SK Warne	not out	2	c Ramprakash b Such	8
SCG MacGill	b Gough	0	c Butcher b Such	6
CR Miller	b Gough	0	not out	3
GD McGrath	c Hick b Headley	0	c Stewart b Such	0
	(lb 2, nb 9)	11	(b 3, lb 1)	4
	(all out)	322	(all out)	184

Bowling: Gough 17-4-61-3 Headley 19.3-3-62-4 Tudor 12-1-64-2 Such 24-6-77-1 Ramprakash 15-0-56-0
Headley 19-7-40-4 Gough 15-3-51-1 Such 25.5-5-81-5 Tudor 5-2-8-0

Innings

*MA Taylor	c Hick b Headley	2
MJ Slater	c Hegg b Headley	18
JL Langer	c Ramprakash b Tudor	26
ME Waugh	c Hegg b Headley	121
SR Waugh	b Such	96
DS Lehmann	c Hussain b Tudor	32
+IA Healy	c Hegg b Gough	14
SK Warne	not out	2
SCG MacGill	b Gough	0
CR Miller	b Gough	0
GD McGrath	c Hick b Headley	0
	(lb 2, nb 9)	11
	(all out)	322

Bowling: Gough 17-4-61-3 Headley 19.3-3-62-4 Tudor 12-1-64-2 Such 24-6-77-1 Ramprakash 15-0-56-0

Umpires: RS Dunne (NZ) and DB Hair
TV Umpire: SJA Taufel; Referee: JR Reid (NZ)

Australia v India
2,3,4 January 2000

Result: Australia won by an innings and 141 runs

India Innings

+MSK Prasad	c ME Waugh b McGrath	5	c ME Waugh b McGrath	3
VVS Laxman	c Slater b Lee	7	c Gilchrist b Lee	167
R Dravid	c Ponting b McGrath	29	c Warne b McGrath	0
*SR Tendulkar	lbw b McGrath	45	c Langer b Fleming	4
SC Ganguly	c SR Waugh b Blewett	1	c ME Waugh b McGrath	25
HH Kanitkar	c Gilchrist b Lee	10	c Slater b Lee	8
R Vijay Bharadwaj	c Gilchrist b Lee	6	absent hurt	0
A Kumble	c Langer b McGrath	26	c Ponting b McGrath	15
AB Agarkar	c ME Waugh b Lee	0	c Gilchrist b McGrath	0
J Srinath	c Ponting b McGrath	3	not out	15
BKV Prasad	not out	1	run out (Gilchrist)	3
	(lb 12, w 1, nb 4)	17	(b 4, lb 2, w 1, nb 14)	21
	(all out)	150	(all out)	261

Bowling: McGrath 18.5-7-48-5 Fleming 13-7-24-0 Lee 21-9-39-4 Warne 12-4-22-0 Blewett 3-2-5-1
McGrath 17-1-55-5 Fleming 13-2-47-1 Lee 11-2-67-2 Blewett 2-0-16-0 Warne 13-1-60-0 Ponting 1-0-8-0 Slater 1-0-2-0

Australia Innings

GS Blewett	b BKV Prasad	19
MJ Slater	c MSK Prasad b Srinath	1
JL Langer	c BKV Prasad b Tendulkar	223
ME Waugh	b Ganguly	32
*SR Waugh	lbw b Srinath	57
RT Ponting	not out	141
+AC Gilchrist	not out	45
SK Warne		
DW Fleming		
B Lee		
GD McGrath		
	(b 2, lb 21, nb 11)	34
	(5 wickets dec)	552

Bowling: Srinath 28-4-105-2 Agarkar 19-3-95-0 BKV Prasad 28-10-86-1 Kumble 33.2-6-126-0 Ganguly 12-1-46-1 Vijay Bharadwaj 12-1-35-0 Tendulkar 7-0-34-1 Kanitkar 1-0-2-0

Umpires: DB Hair and ID Robinson (Zim)
TV Umpire: SJA Taufel; Referee: RS Madugalle (SL)

Australia v West Indies
2,3,4,5,6 January 2001

Result: Australia won by 6 wickets

West Indies Innings

SL Campbell	c & b MacGill	79	c Gilchrist b Gillespie	54
WW Hinds	b MacGill	70	b McGrath	46
*JC Adams	lbw b McGrath	10	lbw b McGrath	5
BC Lara	c ME Waugh b MacGill	35	c Gilchrist b Miller	28
MN Samuels	c Langer b MacGill	28	lbw b Gillespie	0
RR Sarwan	lbw b McGrath	0	c Gilchrist b McGrath	51
+RD Jacobs	st Gilchrist b MacGill	12	lbw b ME Waugh	62
MV Nagamootoo	c Slater b Miller	12	c Hayden b Miller	68
NAM McLean	lbw b MacGill	0	c ME Waugh b Miller	15
CEL Stuart	not out	12	lbw b Miller	4
CA Walsh	c Hayden b McGrath	4	not out	1
	(b 4, lb 4, nb 2)	10	(b 5, lb 10, nb 3)	18
	(all out)	272	(all out)	352

Bowling: McGrath 19-7-43-1 Gillespie 16-4-44-0 MacGill 37-11-104-7 Miller 30.1-8-73-2
McGrath 24-4-80-3 Miller 32.5-3-102-4 MacGill 30-7-88-0 Gillespie 21-5-57-2 ME Waugh 9-3-10-1

Australia Innings

MJ Slater	c Samuels b Nagamootoo	96	not out	86
ML Hayden	c Lara b Walsh	3	lbw b Stuart	5
JL Langer	c Jacobs b McLean	20	lbw b Walsh	10
ME Waugh	run out (Campbell/Jacobs)	22	c Adams b McLean	3
*SR Waugh	b Nagamootoo	103	lbw b Samuels	38
RT Ponting	lbw b Stuart	51	not out	14
+AC Gilchrist	c Lara b Stuart	87		
JN Gillespie	c Hinds b Nagamootoo	2		
CR Miller	not out	37		
SCG MacGill	run out (sub [KCB Jeremy]/Nagamootoo)	1		
GD McGrath	run out (Stuart/Adams)	13		
	(b 1, lb 5, nb 11)	17	(b 3, lb 7, w 1, nb 7)	18
	(all out)	452	(4 wickets)	174

Bowling: Walsh 25-4-74-1 Stuart 23-4-81-2 Nagamootoo 35-3-119-3 McLean 20-2-81-1 Adams 16.4-2-54-0 Samuels 16-5-37-0
Walsh 15-5-35-1 Stuart 7-0-40-1 McLean 8-1-35-1 Nagamootoo 9-1-28-0 Samuels 5.5-0-26-1

Umpires: DB Hair and RE Koertzen (SA)
TV Umpire: SJA Taufel; Referee: AC Smith (Eng)

Australia v South Africa
2,3,4,5 January 2002

Result: Australia won by 10 wickets

Australia Innings

JL Langer	c McKenzie b Boje	126	not out	30
ML Hayden	c Kallis b Pollock	105	not out	21
RT Ponting	run out (Ontong/Boucher)	14		
ME Waugh	c Boucher b Donald	19		
*SR Waugh	b Pollock	30		
DR Martyn	c McKenzie b Boje	117		
+AC Gilchrist	c Boucher b Kallis	34		
SK Warne	b Pollock	37		
B Lee	b Boje	29		
SCG MacGill	c Henderson b Boje	20		
GD McGrath	not out	1		
	(b 4, lb 8, w 1, nb 9)	22	(lb 2, nb 1)	3
	(all out)	554	(0 wickets)	54

Bowling: Donald 31-6-119-1 Pollock 37-11-109-3 Kallis 22-1-129-1 Henderson 27-3-112-0 Boje 25.2-6-63-4 Ontong 2-0-10-0
Donald 3-0-12-0 Pollock 3-1-11-0 Boje 2.1-0-15-0 Henderson 2-0-14-0

South Africa Innings

HH Gibbs	c ME Waugh b MacGill	32	b Lee	10
G Kirsten	c Ponting b McGrath	18	b MacGill	153
HH Dippenaar	b McGrath	3	c Ponting b MacGill	74
JH Kallis	c Gilchrist b MacGill	4	c Butcher b Warne	34
ND McKenzie	b Warne	20	c MacGill b Lee	38
JL Ontong	lbw b Warne	9	lbw b Warne	32
+MV Boucher	c Ponting b Warne	35	c Gilchrist b McGrath	27
*SM Pollock	c Martyn b McGrath	6	not out	61
N Boje	run out (Langer/McGrath)	7	b MacGill	1
CW Henderson	c McGrath b MacGill	9	b MacGill	2
AA Donald	not out	2	c Lee b Warne	2
	(lb 8, nb 1)	9	(b 8, lb 7, nb 3)	18
	(all out)	154	(all out)	452

Bowling: McGrath 17-6-35-3 Lee 6-2-13-0 MacGill 20.2-6-51-3 Warne 19-5-47-3
McGrath 28-5-95-1 Warne 42.5-8-132-3 Lee 19-5-62-2 MacGill 45-13-123-4 ME Waugh 6-1-14-0 Ponting 1-0-11-0

Umpires: DJ Harper and DR Shepherd (Eng)
TV Umpire: SJA Taufel; Referee: RS Madugalle (SL)

Australia v England
2,3,4,5,6 January 2003

Result: England won by 225 runs

England Innings

ME Trescothick	c Gilchrist b Bichel	19	b Lee	22
MP Vaughan	c Gilchrist b Lee	0	lbw b Bichel	183
MA Butcher	b Lee	124	c Hayden b MacGill	34
*N Hussain	c Gilchrist b Gillespie	75	c Gilchrist b Lee	72
RWT Key	lbw b Waugh	3	c Hayden b Lee	14
JP Crawley	not out	35	lbw b Gillespie	8
+AJ Stewart	b Bichel	71	not out	38
RKJ Dawson	c Gilchrist b Bichel	2	c & b Bichel	12
AR Caddick	b MacGill	7	c Langer b MacGill	8
MJ Hoggard	st Gilchrist b MacGill	0	b MacGill	0
SJ Harmison	run out (Langer/MacGill)	4	not out	20
	(b 6, lb 3, nb 13)	22	(b 9, lb 20, w 2, nb 10)	41
	(all out)	362	(9 wickets dec)	452

Bowling: Gillespie 27-10-62-1 Lee 31-9-97-2 Bichel 21-5-86-3 MacGill 44-8-106-2 Waugh 4-3-2-1
Gillespie 18.3-4-70-1 Lee 31.3-5-132-3 MacGill 41-8-120-3 Bichel 25.3-3-82-2 Martyn 3-1-14-0 Waugh 6-2-5-0

Australia Innings

JL Langer	c Hoggard b Caddick	25	lbw b Caddick	3
ML Hayden	lbw b Caddick	15	lbw b Hoggard	2
RT Ponting	c Stewart b Caddick	7	lbw b Caddick	11
DR Martyn	c Caddick b Harmison	26	c Stewart b Dawson	21
*SR Waugh	c Butcher b Hoggard	102	b Caddick	6
ML Love	c Trescothick b Harmison	0	b Harmison	27
+AC Gilchrist	c Stewart b Harmison	133	c Butcher b Caddick	37
AJ Bichel	c Crawley b Hoggard	4	lbw b Caddick	49
B Lee	c Stewart b Hoggard	0	c Stewart b Caddick	46
JN Gillespie	not out	31	not out	3
SCG MacGill	c Hussain b Hoggard	1	b Caddick	1
	(b 2, lb 6, w 2, nb 9)	19	(b 6, lb 8, w 3, nb 3)	20
	(all out)	363	(all out)	226

Bowling: Hoggard 21.3-4-92-4 Caddick 23-3-121-3 Harmison 20-4-70-3 Dawson 16-0-72-0
Hoggard 13-3-35-1 Caddick 22-5-94-7 Harmison 9-1-42-1 Dawson 10-2-41-1

Umpires: DL Orchard (SA) and RB Tiffin (Zim)
TV Umpire: SJA Taufel; Referee: Wasim Raja (Pak)

Australia v England
15,16,17,19 March 1877

Result: Australia won by 45 runs

Australia Innings

C Bannerman	retired hurt	165	b Ulyett		4
NFD Thomson	b Hill	1	c Emmett b Shaw		7
TP Horan	c Hill b Shaw	12	c Selby b Hill		20
*DW Gregory	run out	1	b Shaw		3
BB Cooper	b Southerton	15	b Shaw		3
WE Midwinter	c Ulyett b Southerton	5	c Southerton b Ulyett		17
EJ Gregory	c Greenwood b Lillywhite	0	c Emmett b Ulyett		11
+JM Blackham	b Southerton	17	lbw b Shaw		6
TW Garrett	not out	18	c Emmett b Shaw		0
TK Kendall	c Southerton b Shaw	3	not out		17
JR Hodges	b Shaw	0	b Lillywhite		8
	(b 4, lb 2, w 2)	8	(b 5, lb 3)		8
	(all out)	245	(all out)		104

Bowling: Shaw 55.3-34-51-3 Hill 23-10-42-1 Ulyett 25-12-36-0 Southerton 37-17-61-3 Armitage 3-0-15-0 Lillywhite 14-5-19-1 Emmett 12-7-13-0
Shaw 34-16-38-5 Ulyett 19-7-39-3 Hill 14-6-18-1 Lillywhite 1-0-1-1

England Innings

H Jupp	lbw b Garrett	63	lbw b Midwinter		4
+J Selby	c Cooper b Hodges	7	c Horan b Hodges		38
HRJ Charlwood	c Blackham b Midwinter	36	b Kendall		13
G Ulyett	lbw b Thomson	10	b Kendall		24
A Greenwood	c EJ Gregory b Midwinter	1	c Midwinter b Kendall		5
T Armitage	c Blackham b Midwinter	9	c Blackham b Kendall		3
A Shaw	b Midwinter	10	st Blackham b Kendall		2
T Emmett	b Midwinter	8	b Kendall		9
A Hill	not out	35	c Thomson b Kendall		0
*James Lillywhite jnr	c & b Kendall	10	b Hodges		4
J Southerton	c Cooper b Garrett	6	not out		1
	(lb 1)	1	(b 4, lb 1)		5
	(all out)	196	(all out)		108

Bowling: Hodges 9-0-27-1 Garrett 18.1-10-22-2 Kendall 38-16-54-1 Midwinter 54-23-78-5 Thomson 17-10-14-1 Kendall 33.1-12-55-7 Midwinter 19-7-23-1 DW Gregory 5-1-9-0 Garrett 2-0-9-0 Hodges 7-5-7-2

Umpires: CA Reid and RB Terry

Australia v England
31 March, 2,3,4 April 1877

Result: England won by 4 wickets

Australia Innings

NFD Thomson	lbw b Hill	18	b Lillywhite		41
C Bannerman	b Hill	10	c Jupp b Ulyett		30
+JM Blackham	c Lillywhite b Hill	5	lbw b Southerton		26
TW Garrett	b Hill	12	c Jupp b Lillywhite		18
TJD Kelly	b Ulyett	19	b Southerton		35
WE Midwinter	c Emmett b Lillywhite	31	c Greenwood b Lillywhite		12
FR Spofforth	b Ulyett	0	b Hill		17
WL Murdoch	run out	3	c Shaw b Southerton		8
TK Kendall	b Lillywhite	7	b Southerton		12
*DW Gregory	not out	1	c Ulyett b Lillywhite		43
JR Hodges	run out	2	not out		0
	(b 8, lb 5, w 1)	14	(b 10, lb 7)		17
	(all out)	122	(all out)		259

Bowling: Shaw 42-27-30-0 Lillywhite 29-17-36-2 Hill 27-12-27-4 Ulyett 14.1-6-15-2
Shaw 32-19-27-0 Lillywhite 41-15-70-4 Hill 21-9-43-1 Ulyett 19-9-33-1 Emmett 13-6-23-0 Southerton 28.3-13-46-4

England Innings

H Jupp	b Kendall	0	b Kendall		1
A Shaw	st Blackham b Spofforth	1	not out		0
A Greenwood	b Hodges	49	c +Murdoch b Hodges		22
HRJ Charlwood	c Kelly b Kendall	14	b Kendall		0
+J Selby	b Kendall	7	b Spofforth		2
G Ulyett	b Spofforth	52	c Spofforth b Hodges		63
T Emmett	c Kendall b Spofforth	48	b Midwinter		8
A Hill	run out	49	not out		17
T Armitage	c Thomson b Midwinter	21			
*James Lillywhite jnr	not out	2			
J Southerton	c Thomson b Kendall	0			
	(b 5, lb 12, nb 1)	18	(b 8, lb 1)		9
	(all out)	261	(6 wickets)		122

Bowling: Kendall 52.2-21-82-4 Spofforth 29-6-67-3 Midwinter 21-8-30-1 Hodges 12-2-37-1 Garrett 5-2-10-0 Thomson 11-6-17-0
Kendall 17-7-24-2 Spofforth 15-3-44-1 Midwinter 13.1-6-25-1 Hodges 6-2-13-2 Garrett 1-0-7-0

Umpires: S Cosstick and RB Terry

Australia v England
2,3,4 January 1879

Result: Australia won by 10 wickets

England Innings

G Ulyett	b Spofforth	0	b Spofforth		14
AP Lucas	b Allan	6	c Boyle b Allan		13
AJ Webbe	b Allan	4	lbw b Allan		0
AN Hornby	b Spofforth	2	b Spofforth		4
*Lord Harris	b Garrett	33	c Horan b Spofforth		36
VPFA Royle	b Spofforth	3	c Spofforth b Boyle		18
FA MacKinnon	b Spofforth	0	b Spofforth		5
T Emmett	c Horan b Spofforth	0	not out		24
CA Absolom	c AC Bannerman b Boyle	52	c & b Spofforth		6
+L Hone	c Blackham b Spofforth	7	b Spofforth		6
SS Schultz	not out	0	c & b Spofforth		20
	(b 4, lb 2)	6	(b 10, lb 4)		14
	(all out)	113	(all out)		160

Bowling: Spofforth 25-9-48-6 Allan 17-4-30-2 Garrett 5-0-18-1 Boyle 7-1-11-1
Spofforth 35-16-62-7 Allan 28-11-50-2 Garrett 10-6-18-0 Boyle 10-4-16-1

Australia Innings

C Bannerman	b Emmett	15	not out		15
WL Murdoch	c Webbe b Ulyett	4	not out		4
TP Horan	c Hone b Emmett	10			
AC Bannerman	b Schultz	73			
FR Spofforth	c Royle b Emmett	39			
TW Garrett	c Hone b Emmett	26			
FE Allan	b Hornby	5			
HF Boyle	c Royle b Emmett	28			
+JM Blackham	b Emmett	4			
TJD Kelly	c Webbe b Emmett	10			
*DW Gregory	not out	12			
	(b 19, lb 2, w 7)	28	(0 wickets)		19
	(all out)	256	(0 wickets)		19

Bowling: Emmett 59-31-68-7 Ulyett 62-24-93-1 Lucas 18-6-31-0 Schultz 6.3-3-16-1 Hornby 7-7-0-1 Royle 4-1-6-0 Harris 3-0-14-0
Ulyett 1-0-9-0 Schultz 1.3-0-10-0

Umpires: P Coady and G Coulthard

Australia v England
31 December 1881, 2,3,4 January 1882

Result: Match drawn

England Innings

RG Barlow	c Bannerman b Palmer	0	st Blackham b Palmer		33
G Ulyett	c McDonnell b Cooper	87	st Blackham b Cooper		23
J Selby	run out	55	c Boyle b Cooper		70
W Bates	c Giffen b Boyle	58	c Bannerman b Cooper		47
A Shrewsbury	c Blackham b Evans	11	b Cooper		16
WE Midwinter	b Evans	36	c Massie b Cooper		4
T Emmett	b Evans	5	b Cooper		6
WH Scotton	not out	21	not out		50
*A Shaw	c Boyle b Cooper	5	c Cooper b Boyle		40
+R Pilling	c Giffen b Cooper	5	b Palmer		3
E Peate	not out	4	run out		2
	(lb 6, nb 1)	7	(b 7, lb 2, nb 5)		14
	(all out)	294	(all out)		308

Bowling: Palmer 36-9-73-1 Evans 71-35-81-3 Cooper 32.2-8-80-3 Boyle 18-9-18-1 Giffen 3-0-12-0 Bannerman 10-3-23-0
Palmer 77-19-77-2 Evans 73-45-63-0 Cooper 61-19-120-6 Boyle 14.3-6-19-1 McDonnell 4-1-15-0

Australia Innings

HH Massie	st Pilling b Midwinter	2			
AC Bannerman	b Ulyett	38	b Ulyett		8
*WL Murdoch	b Ulyett	39	not out		22
PS McDonnell	b Midwinter	19	not out		33
TP Horan	run out	124	c Emmett b Bates		26
G Giffen	b Emmett	30			
+JM Blackham	b Emmett	2	b Bates		25
GE Palmer	c Pilling b Bates	34			
E Evans	b Bates	3			
HF Boyle	not out	4			
WH Cooper	st Pilling b Peate	7			
	(b 4, lb 11, w 3)	18	(b 9, lb 3, w 1)		13
	(all out)	320	(3 wickets)		127

Bowling: Peate 59-24-64-1 Midwinter 39-21-50-2 Bates 41-20-43-2 Emmett 35-12-61-2 Ulyett 20-5-41-2 Barlow 23-13-22-0 Shaw 20-11-21-0
Peate 11-5-22-0 Bates 13-3-43-2 Emmett 16-11-19-0 Ulyett 15-3-30-1

Umpires: James Lillywhite jnr (Eng) and JS Swift

Australia v England
10,11,13,14 March 1882

Result: Match drawn

England Innings

G Ulyett	c Blackham b Garrett	149	c Palmer b Boyle		64
RG Barlow	c Blackham b Garrett	16	run out		56
J Selby	b Spofforth	7	not out		48
W Bates	st Blackham b Garrett	23	not out		52
A Shrewsbury	lbw b Palmer	1			
WE Midwinter	c Palmer b Boyle	21			
WH Scotton	st Blackham b Giffen	26			
T Emmett	b Giffen	27			
*A Shaw	c Murdoch b Garrett	3			
+R Pilling	not out	6			
E Peate	c & b Garrett	13			
	(b 10, lb 7)	17	(b 12, lb 2)		14
	(all out)	309	(2 wickets)		234

Bowling: Garrett 54.2-23-80-5 Spofforth 51-14-92-1 Boyle 44-8-33-1 Palmer 23-5-70-1 Giffen 13-6-17-2
Garrett 27-6-62-0 Spofforth 15-3-36-0 Boyle 25-9-38-1 Palmer 20-5-47-0 Giffen 8.3-1-25-0 Bannerman 2-0-12-0

Australia Innings

*WL Murdoch	b Midwinter	85			
AC Bannerman	c & b Midwinter	37			
TP Horan	c & b Midwinter	20			
PS McDonnell	c Barlow b Ulyett	52			
HH Massie	c Emmett b Shaw	39			
G Giffen	c Scotton b Peate	14			
+JM Blackham	c Pilling b Midwinter	6			
TW Garrett	c Ulyett b Bates	10			
GE Palmer	c Ulyett b Bates	32			
HF Boyle	c Shrewsbury b Bates	6			
FR Spofforth	not out	3			
	(b 2, lb 7, w 6, nb 1)	16			
	(all out)	300			

Bowling: Bates 28.1-14-49-3 Peate 20-6-38-1 Emmett 19-14-22-0 Ulyett 24-8-40-1 Barlow 15-6-25-0 Shaw 16-6-29-1 Midwinter 41-9-81-4

Umpires: G Coulthard and James Lillywhite jnr (Eng)

Australia v England
30 December 1882, 1,2 January 1883

Result: Australia won by 9 wickets

Australia Innings

AC Bannerman	st Tylecote b Leslie	30	not out		25
HH Massie	c & b CT Studd	4	c & b Barnes		0
*WL Murdoch	b Leslie	48	not out		33
TP Horan	c Barlow b Leslie	0			
PS McDonnell	b Bates	43			
G Giffen	st Tylecote b Steel	36			
GJ Bonnor	c Barlow b Barnes	85			
+JM Blackham	c Tylecote b CT Studd	25			
FR Spofforth	c Steel b Barnes	9			
TW Garrett	c CT Studd b Steel	0			
GE Palmer	not out	0			
	(b 4, lb 2, w 2, nb 3)	11			0
	(all out)	291	(1 wicket)		58

Bowling: CT Studd 46-30-35-2 Barnes 30-11-51-2 Steel 33-16-68-2 Barlow 20-6-37-0 Bates 21-7-31-1 Read 8-2-27-0 Leslie 11-3-13-3
CT Studd 14-11-7-0 Barnes 13-8-6-1 Steel 9-4-17-0 Barlow 4-2-6-0 Bates 13.1-7-22-0

England Innings

RG Barlow	st Blackham b Palmer	10	b Spofforth		28
*Hon.IFW Bligh	b Palmer	0	b Spofforth		3
CFH Leslie	c Garrett b Palmer	4	b Giffen		4
CT Studd	b Spofforth	0	b Palmer		21
AG Steel	b Palmer	27	lbw b Giffen		29
WW Read	b Palmer	19	b Giffen		29
W Bates	c Bannerman b Garrett	28	c Massie b Palmer		11
+EFS Tylecote	b Palmer	33	b Spofforth		38
GB Studd	run out	7	c Palmer b Giffen		0
W Barnes	b Palmer	26	not out		2
GF Vernon	not out	11	lbw b Palmer		3
	(b 8, lb 1, nb 3)	12	(lb 1)		1
	(all out)	177	(all out)		169

Bowling: Spofforth 28-11-56-1 Palmer 52.2-25-65-7 Garrett 27-6-44-1
Spofforth 41-15-65-3 Palmer 36.1-11-61-3 Garrett 2-1-4-0 Giffen 20-7-38-4

Umpires: EH Elliott and JS Swift

Melbourne Cricket Ground

Australia v England
19,20,22 January 1883

Result: England won by an innings and 27 runs

England Innings
RG Barlow	b Palmer	14
CT Studd	b Palmer	14
CFH Leslie	run out	54
AG Steel	c McDonnell b Giffen	39
WW Read	c & b Palmer	75
W Barnes	b Giffen	32
+EFS Tylecote	b Giffen	0
*Hon.IFW Bligh	b Giffen	0
W Bates	c Horan b Palmer	55
GB Studd	b Palmer	1
F Morley	not out	0
	(b 3, lb 3, nb 4)	10
	(all out)	294

Bowling: Spofforth 34-11-57-0 Palmer 66.3-25-103-5 Giffen 49-13-89-4 Garrett 34-16-35-0

Australia Innings
HH Massie	b Barlow	43	c CT Studd b Barlow	10
AC Bannerman	b Bates	14	c Bligh b Bates	14
*WL Murdoch	b Bates	19	b Bates	17
TP Horan	c & b Barnes	3	c Morley b Bates	15
PS McDonnell	b Bates	3	b Bates	13
G Giffen	c & b Bates	0	c Bligh b Bates	19
GJ Bonnor	c Read b Bates	0	c Morley b Barlow	34
+JM Blackham	b Barnes	5	b Barlow	6
TW Garrett	b Bates	10	c Barnes b Bates	6
GE Palmer	b Bates	7	c GB Studd b Bates	4
FR Spofforth	b Bates	0	not out	14
	(b 6, lb 3, nb 1)	10	(b 1)	1
	(all out)	114	(all out)	153

Bowling: CT Studd 4-1-22-0 Morley 23-16-13-0 Barnes 23-7-32-2 Barlow 22-18-9-1 Bates 26.2-14-28-7
Morley 2-0-7-0 Barnes 3-1-4-0 Barlow 31-6-67-3 Bates 33-14-74-7

Umpires: EH Elliott and JS Swift

Australia v England
1,2,3,5 January 1885

Result: England won by 10 wickets

England Innings
*A Shrewsbury	c Worrall b Morris	72	not out	0
WH Scotton	b Morris	13	not out	7
W Barnes	b Morris	58		
W Bates	b Bruce	35		
W Flowers	c Worrall b Bruce	5		
JM Read	b Jones	3		
J Briggs	c Horan b Jones	121		
G Ulyett	b Jones	10		
W Attewell	c Jones b Worrall	30		
R Peel	b Jones	5		
+J Hunter	not out	39		
	(b 7, lb 12, nb 1)	20		0
	(all out)	401	(0 wickets)	7

Bowling: Bruce 55-22-88-3 Worrall 56-28-97-1 Marr 11-6-11-0 Trumble 23-9-41-0 Robertson 11-3-24-0 Morris 34-14-73-2
Jones 25.2-9-47-4 Horan 1-1-0-0
Marr 1-0-3-0 Bruce 0.1-0-4-0

Australia Innings
SP Jones	lbw b Peel	19	b Ulyett	9
S Morris	lbw b Attewell	4	not out	10
*TP Horan	c Shrewsbury b Peel	63	c Hunter b Barnes	16
JW Trumble	c & b Barnes	59	c & b Barnes	11
+AH Jarvis	c Briggs b Flowers	82	lbw b Peel	10
RJ Pope	c Flowers b Attewell	0	c Peel b Flowers	3
AP Marr	b Barnes	0	c & b Barnes	5
HA Musgrove	c Read b Barnes	4	c Bates b Peel	9
J Worrall	b Flowers	34	c & b Barnes	6
W Bruce	not out	3	c Hunter b Barnes	45
WR Robertson	c Barnes b Peel	0	b Barnes	2
	(b 3, lb 4, w 2, nb 2)	11		0
	(all out)	279	(all out)	126

Bowling: Flowers 29-12-46-2 Attewell 61-35-54-2 Barnes 50-27-50-3 Peel 102.1-56-78-3 Bates 17-11-17-0 Ulyett 15-7-23-0
Flowers 11-6-11-0 Attewell 5-2-7-0 Barnes 38.3-26-31-6 Peel 44-26-45-3 Ulyett 8-3-19-1 Briggs 8-3-13-0

Umpires: EH Elliott and James Lillywhite jnr (Eng)

Australia v England
21,23,24,25 March 1885

Result: England won by an innings and 98 runs

Australia Innings
AC Bannerman	c Peel b Ulyett	5	c sub (GF Vernon) b Ulyett	2
W Bruce	c Briggs b Peel	15	c Bates b Attewell	35
G Giffen	b Ulyett	13	c Peel b Ulyett	12
*TP Horan	lbw b Ulyett	0	b Attewell	20
SP Jones	lbw b Peel	0	b Peel	17
FH Walters	b Ulyett	7	c Attewell b Flowers	5
+AH Jarvis	c Hunter b Peel	15	c Peel b Flowers	1
JW Trumble	not out	34	lbw b Attewell	10
PG McShane	c Hunter b Barnes	9	not out	12
TW Garrett	c Briggs b Barnes	6	b Ulyett	5
FR Spofforth	b Attewell	50	c sub (AH Jarvis) b Flowers	1
	(b 5, lb 1, nb 3)	9	(b 5)	5
	(all out)	163	(all out)	125

Bowling: Peel 41-26-28-3 Ulyett 23-7-52-4 Barnes 28-12-47-2 Flowers 9-6-9-0 Attewell 5-1-18-1
Peel 30-16-37-1 Ulyett 15-7-25-3 Flowers 21-7-34-3 Attewell 36.1-22-24-3

England Innings
W Barnes	c Horan b Bruce	74
WH Scotton	b Bruce	27
JM Read	b Giffen	13
G Ulyett	b Spofforth	1
*A Shrewsbury	not out	105
W Bates	c Walters b Bruce	61
W Flowers	b Spofforth	16
J Briggs	c Walters b Trumble	43
W Attewell	c Bannerman b Trumble	0
R Peel	b Trumble	0
+J Hunter	b Giffen	18
	(b 10, lb 14, nb 4)	28
	(all out)	386

Bowling: Giffen 74.3-31-132-2 Bruce 51-13-99-3 Spofforth 49-21-71-2 Trumble 28-14-29-3 Garrett 8-6-12-0 McShane 3-2-3-0 Jones 5-2-7-0 Horan 3-0-5-0

Umpires: GJ Hodges and J Phillips

Australia v England
1,2,4,5,6 January 1892

Result: Australia won by 54 runs

Australia Innings
AC Bannerman	c Read b Sharpe	45	c Grace b Sharpe	41
JJ Lyons	c Grace b Peel	19	c Abel b Briggs	51
G Giffen	lbw b Peel	2	b Attewell	1
W Bruce	b Sharpe	57	c Lohmann b Sharpe	40
H Donnan	b Sharpe	9	c & b Lohmann	2
H Moses	c Lohmann b Sharpe	23	run out	15
GHS Trott	c MacGregor b Sharpe	6	lbw b Attewell	23
RW McLeod	b Sharpe	14	b Peel	31
ST Callaway	b Attewell	21	not out	13
CTB Turner	b Peel	29	c Peel b Lohmann	19
*+JM Blackham	not out	4	c MacGregor b Peel	0
	(b 5, lb 6)	11		0
	(all out)	240	(all out)	236

Bowling: Sharpe 51-20-84-6 Peel 43-23-54-3 Attewell 21.1-11-28-1 Lohmann 28-14-40-0 Briggs 3-1-13-0 Stoddart 5-2-10-0
Sharpe 54-25-81-2 Peel 16.5-5-25-2 Attewell 61-32-51-2 Lohmann 39-15-53-2 Briggs 21-9-26-1

England Innings
*WG Grace	b McLeod	50	c Bannerman b Turner	25
R Abel	b McLeod	32	c Blackham b Turner	28
G Bean	c Bruce b Giffen	50	c McLeod b Trott	3
AE Stoddart	c Giffen b McLeod	0	b Callaway	35
JM Read	c & b Giffen	36	b Trott	11
R Peel	b McLeod	19	b Turner	6
GA Lohmann	lbw b Giffen	3	c Bannerman b Turner	0
J Briggs	c Bruce b Turner	41	c Trott b McLeod	4
W Attewell	c Bannerman b Turner	8	c Donnan b Turner	24
+G MacGregor	not out	9	c sub (SE Gregory) b Trott	16
JW Sharpe	c Blackham b McLeod	2	not out	5
	(b 9, lb 2, nb 3)	14	(b 1)	1
	(all out)	264	(all out)	158

Bowling: Trott 10-2-25-0 Giffen 20-3-75-3 Turner 16-3-40-2 McLeod 28.4-12-53-5 Callaway 14-2-39-0 Bruce 3-0-18-0
Trott 19-2-52-3 Giffen 3-0-8-0 Turner 33.2-14-51-5 McLeod 23-8-39-1 Callaway 4-1-7-1

Umpires: T Flynn and J Phillips

Australia v England
29,31 December 1894, 1,2,3 January 1895

Result: England won by 94 runs

England Innings
AC MacLaren	c Trott b Coningham	0	b Turner	15
A Ward	c Darling b Trumble	30	b Turner	41
*AE Stoddart	b Turner	10	b Giffen	173
JT Brown	c Trumble b Turner	0	c Jarvis b Bruce	37
W Brockwell	c Iredale b Coningham	21	b Richardson	21
R Peel	c Trumble b Turner	6	st Jarvis b Giffen	53
FGJ Ford	c Giffen b Trumble	9	c Trott b Giffen	24
WH Lockwood	not out	3	not out	33
J Briggs	c Bruce b Turner	5	lbw b Giffen	31
+H Philipson	c Darling b Turner	1	b Giffen	30
T Richardson	c Iredale b Trumble	0	c Gregory b Giffen	11
	(lb 9, nb 2)	11	(b 1, lb 2, nb 3)	6
	(all out)	75	(all out)	475

Bowling: Coningham 11-5-17-2 Turner 20-9-32-5 Trumble 9.1-4-15-3
Coningham 20-4-59-0 Turner 55-21-99-3 Trumble 26-6-72-0 Giffen 78.2-21-155-6 Lyons 2-1-3-0 Trott 17-0-60-0 Bruce 4-0-21-1

Australia Innings
JJ Lyons	b Richardson	2	b Peel	14
W Bruce	c Ford b Peel	4	c Stoddart b Peel	54
*G Giffen	c Philipson b Briggs	32	c Brown b Brockwell	43
SE Gregory	c Ward b Richardson	2	b Richardson	12
J Darling	b Lockwood	32	b Brockwell	5
FA Iredale	b Richardson	10	b Peel	68
GHS Trott	run out	16	c & b Brockwell	95
A Coningham	c Philipson b Richardson	10	b Peel	9
H Trumble	b Richardson	1	run out	2
+AH Jarvis	not out	11	b Richardson	4
CTB Turner	not out	1	not out	26
	(w 2)	2	(b 5, lb 1, nb 1)	7
	(all out)	123	(all out)	333

Bowling: Richardson 23-6-57-5 Peel 14-4-21-1 Lockwood 5-0-17-1 Briggs 13.5-2-26-2
Richardson 40-10-100-2 Peel 40.1-9-77-4 Lockwood 25-5-60-0 Briggs 12-0-49-0 Ford 5-2-7-0 Brockwell 14-3-33-3

Umpires: T Flynn and J Phillips

Australia v England
1,2,4,5,6 March 1895

Result: England won by 6 wickets

Australia Innings
GHS Trott	b Briggs	42	b Peel	42
W Bruce	c MacLaren b Peel	22	c & b Peel	11
*G Giffen	b Peel	57	b Richardson	51
FA Iredale	b Richardson	8	b Richardson	18
SE Gregory	c Philipson b Richardson	70	b Richardson	30
J Darling	c Ford b Peel	74	b Peel	50
JJ Lyons	c Philipson b Lockwood	55	b Briggs	15
H Graham	b Richardson	6	lbw b Richardson	10
AE Trott	c Lockwood b Peel	10	b Richardson	0
+AH Jarvis	not out	34	not out	14
TR McKibbin	c Peel b Briggs	23	c Philipson b Richardson	13
	(b 3, lb 10)	13	(b 5, lb 6, nb 2)	13
	(all out)	414	(all out)	267

Bowling: Richardson 42-7-138-3 Peel 48-13-114-4 Lockwood 27-7-72-1 Briggs 23.4-5-46-2 Brockwell 6-1-22-0 Ford 2-0-9-0
Richardson 45.2-7-104-6 Peel 46-16-89-3 Lockwood 16-7-24-0 Briggs 16-3-37-1

England Innings
A Ward	b McKibbin	32	b GHS Trott	93
W Brockwell	st Jarvis b GHS Trott	5	c & b Giffen	5
*AE Stoddart	st Jarvis b GHS Trott	68	lbw b GHS Trott	11
JT Brown	b AE Trott	30	c Giffen b McKibbin	140
AC MacLaren	hit wicket b GHS Trott	120	not out	20
R Peel	c Gregory b Giffen	73	not out	15
WH Lockwood	c GHS Trott b Giffen	5		
FGJ Ford	c AE Trott b GHS Trott	11		
J Briggs	c GHS Trott b Giffen	0		
+H Philipson	not out	10		
T Richardson	lbw b GHS Trott	11		
	(b 8, lb 8, w 4)	20	(b 6, lb 5, w 2, nb 1)	14
	(all out)	385	(4 wickets)	298

Bowling: Giffen 45-13-130-4 GHS Trott 24-5-71-4 AE Trott 30-4-84-1 McKibbin 29-6-73-1 Bruce 5-1-7-0
Giffen 31-4-106-1 GHS Trott 20.1-1-63-2 AE Trott 19-2-56-0 McKibbin 14-2-47-1 Bruce 3-1-10-0 Lyons 1-0-2-0

Umpires: T Flynn and J Phillips

Australia v England
1,3,4,5 January 1898

Result: Australia won by an innings and 55 runs

Australia Innings

J Darling	c Hirst b Briggs	36	
CE McLeod	b Storer	112	
C Hill	c Storer b Hayward	58	
SE Gregory	b Briggs	71	
FA Iredale	c Ranjitsinhji b Hirst	89	
*GHS Trott	c Wainwright b Briggs	79	
MA Noble	b Richardson	17	
H Trumble	c Hirst b Mason	14	
+JJ Kelly	c Richardson b Hearne	19	
E Jones	run out	7	
TR McKibbin	not out	2	
	(b 14, w 1, nb 1)	16	
	(all out)	520	

Bowling: Richardson 48-12-114-1 Hirst 25-1-89-1 Briggs 40-10-96-3 Hearne 36-6-94-1 Mason 11-1-33-1 Hayward 9-4-23-1 Storer 16-4-55-1

England Innings

*AC MacLaren	c Trumble b McKibbin	35	c Trott b Trumble	38	
JR Mason	b McKibbin	3	b Trumble	3	
E Wainwright	c Jones b Noble	21	b Noble	11	
KS Ranjitsinhji	b Trumble	71	b Noble	27	
TW Hayward	c Jones b Trott	23	c Trumble b Noble	33	
+W Storer	c Kelly b Trumble	51	c Trumble b Noble	1	
GH Hirst	b Jones	0	lbw b Trumble	3	
NF Druce	lbw b Trumble	44	c McLeod b Noble	15	
JT Hearne	b Jones	1	c Jones b Noble	0	
J Briggs	not out	46	c Trott b Trumble	12	
T Richardson	b Trumble	3	not out	2	
	(b 10, lb 3, nb 4)	17	(b 3, lb 1, w 1)	5	
	(all out)	315	(all out)	150	

Bowling: McKibbin 28-7-66-2 Trumble 26.5-5-54-4 Jones 22-5-54-2 Trott 17-3-49-1 Noble 12-3-31-1 McLeod 14-2-44-0
McKibbin 4-0-13-0 Trumble 30.4-12-53-4 Trott 7-0-17-0 Noble 17-1-49-6 McLeod 7-2-13-0

Umpires: C Bannerman and J Phillips

Australia v England
29,31 January, 1,2 February 1898

Result: Australia won by 8 wickets

Australia Innings

CE McLeod	b Hearne	1	not out	64	
J Darling	c Hearne b Richardson	12	c +Druce b Hayward	29	
C Hill	c Stoddart b Hearne	188	lbw b Hayward	0	
SE Gregory	b Richardson	0	not out	21	
FA Iredale	c Storer b Hearne	4			
MA Noble	c & b Hearne	4			
*GHS Trott	c Storer b Hearne	7			
H Trumble	c Mason b Storer	46			
+JJ Kelly	c Storer b Briggs	32			
E Jones	c Hayward b Hearne	20			
WP Howell	not out	9			
	(b 3, w 1)	4	(nb 1)	1	
	(all out)	323	(2 wickets)	115	

Bowling: Richardson 26-2-102-2 Hearne 35.4-13-98-6 Hayward 10-4-24-0 Briggs 17-4-38-1 Stoddart 6-1-22-0 Storer 4-0-24-1 Wainwright 3-1-11-0
Hearne 7-3-19-0 Hayward 10-4-24-2 Briggs 6-1-31-0 Wainwright 9-2-21-0 Mason 4-1-10-0 Ranjitsinhji 3.4-1-9-0

England Innings

AC MacLaren	b Howell	8	c Iredale b Trumble	45	
E Wainwright	c Howell b Trott	6	c McLeod b Jones	2	
KS Ranjitsinhji	c Iredale b Trumble	24	b Noble	55	
TW Hayward	c Gregory b Noble	22	c & b Trumble	25	
NF Druce	lbw b Jones	24	c Howell b Trott	16	
+W Storer	c & b Trumble	2	c Darling b McLeod	26	
JR Mason	b Jones	30	b Howell	26	
*AE Stoddart	c Darling b Jones	17	b Jones	25	
J Briggs	not out	21	c Darling b Howell	23	
JT Hearne	c Trott b Jones	0	c Trumble b McLeod	4	
T Richardson	b Trott	20	c Trumble b McLeod	2	
		0	(b 1, lb 11, w 1, nb 1)	14	
	(all out)	174	(all out)	263	

Bowling: Howell 16-7-34-1 Trott 11.1-1-33-2 Noble 7-1-21-1 Trumble 15-4-50-2 Jones 12-2-56-4
Howell 30-12-58-2 Trott 12-2-39-1 Noble 16-6-31-1 Trumble 23-6-40-2 Jones 25-7-70-2 McLeod 8.2-4-11-2

Umpires: C Bannerman and J Phillips

Australia v England
1,2,3,4 January 1902

Result: Australia won by 229 runs

Australia Innings

VT Trumper	c Tyldesley b Barnes	0	c Lilley b Barnes	16	
*J Darling	c Lilley b Blythe	19	c Tyldesley b Barnes	23	
C Hill	b Barnes	15	c Jones b Barnes	99	
H Trumble	c Braund b Blythe	16	c Braund b Barnes	16	
MA Noble	b Blythe	0	lbw b Blythe	16	
SE Gregory	st Lilley b Blythe	0	c Jones b Barnes	17	
RA Duff	c Braund b Barnes	32	b Braund	104	
+JJ Kelly	c Quaife b Barnes	5	run out	3	
WW Armstrong	not out	4	not out	45	
WP Howell	b Barnes	1	c Hayward b Barnes	0	
E Jones	c MacLaren b Barnes	14	c MacLaren b Barnes	5	
	(b 6)	6	(b 7, lb 1, nb 1)	9	
	(all out)	112	(all out)	353	

Bowling: Barnes 16.1-5-42-6 Blythe 16-2-64-4
Barnes 64-17-121-7 Blythe 31-7-85-1 Braund 53.2-17-114-1 Jessop 1-0-9-0 Gunn 6-1-13-0 Jones 1-0-2-0

England Innings

*AC MacLaren	c Jones b Trumble	13	c Trumble b Noble	1	
TW Hayward	c Darling b Trumble	0	st Kelly b Trumble	12	
JT Tyldesley	c Gregory b Trumble	2	c Trumble b Noble	66	
WG Quaife	b Noble	0	b Noble	25	
GL Jessop	st Kelly b Noble	27	c Gregory b Noble	32	
JR Gunn	st Kelly b Noble	0	c Jones b Trumble	2	
+AFA Lilley	c Trumper b Noble	6	c Darling b Trumble	0	
AO Jones	c Kelly b Noble	0	c Darling b Trumble	6	
LC Braund	not out	2	c Trumble b Noble	25	
SF Barnes	c & b Noble	1	c & b Noble	0	
C Blythe	c Trumper b Noble	4	not out	0	
	(b 6)	6	(b 1, lb 1, nb 4)	6	
	(all out)	61	(all out)	175	

Bowling: Trumble 8-1-38-3 Noble 7.4-2-17-7
Trumble 22.5-10-49-4 Noble 26-5-60-6 Jones 12-2-33-0 Howell 15-6-23-0 Armstrong 2-1-3-0 Trumper 2-1-1-0

Umpires: R Callaway and RM Crockett

Australia v England
28 February, 1,3,4 March 1902

Result: Australia won by 32 runs

Australia Innings

VT Trumper	b Blythe	27	c McGahey b Braund	18	
RA Duff	b Braund	10	c & b Braund	28	
C Hill	c Jones b Gunn	28	c Lilley b Hayward	87	
SE Gregory	c Jones b Gunn	25	b Gunn	41	
MA Noble	lbw b Hayward	7	c MacLaren b Gunn	16	
*H Trumble	c Quaife b Hayward	3	b Blythe	22	
WW Armstrong	not out	17	lbw b Braund	20	
AJY Hopkins	c Lilley b Hayward	4	c MacLaren b Blythe	0	
+JJ Kelly	c Gunn b Hayward	0	not out	11	
CJ Eady	b Gunn	5	c Gunn b Braund	3	
JPF Travers	c Braund b Gunn	9	c & b Braund	1	
	(b 7, w 1, nb 1)	9	(b 3, lb 1, nb 4)	8	
	(all out)	144	(all out)	255	

Bowling: Jessop 1-0-13-0 Braund 10-2-33-1 Blythe 9-2-29-1 Hayward 16-9-22-4 Gunn 17-6-38-4
Braund 26.1-4-95-5 Blythe 13-3-36-2 Hayward 22-4-63-1 Gunn 28-11-53-2

England Innings

*AC MacLaren	c & b Trumble	25	run out	49	
GL Jessop	c Hopkins b Trumble	35	c Trumper b Trumble	16	
WG Quaife	c Trumble b Noble	3	lbw b Noble	4	
JT Tyldesley	c Kelly b Eady	13	c Eady b Trumble	36	
TW Hayward	c Trumper b Travers	19	c Travers b Trumble	15	
LC Braund	c Hopkins b Trumble	32	c Hill b Noble	25	
+AFA Lilley	c Eady b Trumble	41	c Duff b Noble	9	
CP McGahey	b Trumble	0	c Hill b Noble	7	
AO Jones	c Kelly b Eady	10	c & b Noble	28	
JR Gunn	lbw b Eady	8	c Hill b Eady	4	
C Blythe	not out	0	not out	5	
	(b 1, lb 2)	3	(lb 2, nb 1)	3	
	(all out)	189	(all out)	178	

Bowling: Noble 26-4-80-1 Trumble 25-4-62-5 Travers 8-2-1-1-0 Eady 8.3-2-30-3
Noble 33-4-98-6 Trumble 30.3-7-64-3 Eady 2-0-13-0

Umpires: C Bannerman and RM Crockett

Australia v England
1,2,4,5 January 1904

Result: England won by 185 runs

England Innings

*PF Warner	c Duff b Trumble	68	c Trumper b Saunders	3	
TW Hayward	c Gregory b Hopkins	58	c Trumper b Trumble	0	
JT Tyldesley	c Trumble b Howell	97	c Trumble b Howell	62	
RE Foster	retired hurt	49	absent hurt	0	
LC Braund	c Howell b Trumble	20	b Saunders	3	
AE Knight	b Howell	4	lbw b Howell	0	
GH Hirst	c Noble b Howell	7	c Gregory b Howell	4	
W Rhodes	lbw b Trumble	8	c Hill b Trumble	9	
+AFA Lilley	c Howell b Trumble	4	st Kelly b Trumble	0	
AE Relf	not out	3	not out	10	
A Fielder	b Howell	4	c Hill b Trumble	4	
	(lb 3, w 1)	4	(b 7, lb 1)	8	
	(all out)	315	(all out)	103	

Bowling: Trumble 50-10-107-4 Noble 6-3-4-0 Saunders 16-3-60-0 Howell 34.5-14-43-4 Armstrong 25-6-43-0 Hopkins 20-2-50-1 Trumper 1-0-4-0
Trumble 10.5-2-34-5 Saunders 8-0-33-2 Howell 8-3-25-2 Hopkins 2-1-3-0

Australia Innings

RA Duff	st Lilley b Rhodes	10	c Braund b Rhodes	8	
VT Trumper	c Tyldesley b Rhodes	74	c Relf b Rhodes	35	
C Hill	c Rhodes b Hirst	5	c Relf b Rhodes	20	
*MA Noble	c sub b Rhodes	0	not out	31	
SE Gregory	c Hirst b Rhodes	1	c Rhodes b Hirst	0	
AJY Hopkins	c sub b Relf	18	c & b Rhodes	7	
H Trumble	c sub b Rhodes	3	c Braund b Rhodes	0	
WW Armstrong	c Braund b Rhodes	1	c Hayward b Rhodes	0	
+JJ Kelly	run out	8	c Lilley b Rhodes	7	
WP Howell	c Fielder b Rhodes	5	c Hirst b Rhodes	3	
JV Saunders	not out	2	c Fielder b Hirst	0	
	(lb 1)	1		0	
	(all out)	122	(all out)	111	

Bowling: Rhodes 15.2-3-56-7 Hirst 8-1-33-1 Relf 2-0-12-1 Braund 5-0-20-0
Rhodes 15-0-68-8 Hirst 13.4-4-38-2 Relf 1-0-5-0

Umpires: P Argall and RM Crockett

Australia v England
5,7,8 March 1904

Result: Australia won by 218 runs

Australia Innings

RA Duff	b Braund	9	c Warner b Rhodes	31	
VT Trumper	c & b Braund	88	b Hirst	0	
C Hill	c Braund b Rhodes	16	c Warner b Hirst	16	
*MA Noble	c Cricket b Braund	29	st Lilley b Rhodes	19	
PA McAlister	st Lilley b Braund	36	c Foster b Arnold	9	
DRA Gehrs	c & b Braund	3	c & b Hirst	5	
AJY Hopkins	c Knight b Braund	32	not out	25	
CE McLeod	c Rhodes b Braund	6	c Bosanquet b Braund	0	
H Trumble	c Foster b Braund	6	c Arnold b Hirst	0	
+JJ Kelly	not out	16	c & b Arnold	24	
A Cotter	b Braund	6	b Hirst	0	
	(b 4, lb 4)	8	(b 1, lb 3)	4	
	(all out)	247	(all out)	133	

Bowling: Hirst 19-6-44-0 Braund 29.1-6-81-8 Rhodes 12-1-41-1 Arnold 18-4-61-1 Bosanquet 4-0-27-0
Hirst 16.5-4-48-5 Braund 4-1-6-1 Rhodes 15-2-52-2 Arnold 8-3-23-2

England Innings

TW Hayward	b Noble	0	absent hurt	0	
W Rhodes	c Gehrs b Cotter	3	not out	16	
EG Arnold	c Kelly b Noble	0	c Duff b Trumble	19	
*PF Warner	c McAlister b Cotter	1	c & b Trumble	11	
JT Tyldesley	c Gehrs b Noble	10	c Hopkins b Cotter	15	
RE Foster	b Cotter	18	c Trumper b Trumble	30	
GH Hirst	c Trumper b Cotter	0	c McAlister b Trumble	1	
LC Braund	c Hopkins b Noble	5	c McAlister b Cotter	0	
AE Knight	b Cotter	0	c Kelly b Trumble	0	
BJT Bosanquet	c Noble b Cotter	16	c Gehrs b Trumble	4	
+AFA Lilley	not out	6	lbw b Trumble	5	
	(b 1, nb 1)	2	(b 1, lb 4)	5	
	(all out)	61	(all out)	101	

Bowling: Noble 15-8-19-4 Cotter 15.2-2-40-6 McLeod 1-1-0-0
Noble 6-2-19-0 Cotter 5-0-25-2 McLeod 5-0-24-0 Trumble 6.5-0-28-7

Umpires: P Argall and RM Crockett

Melbourne Cricket Ground

England v Australia
1,2,3,4,6,7 January 1908

Result: England won by 1 wicket

Australia Innings

VT Trumper	c Humphries b Crawford	49	lbw b Crawford	63
CG Macartney	b Crawford	37	c Humphries b Barnes	54
C Hill	b Fielder	16	b Fielder	3
*MA Noble	c Braund b Rhodes	61	b Crawford	64
WW Armstrong	c Hutchings b Crawford	31	b Barnes	77
PA McAlister	run out	10	run out	15
VS Ransford	run out	27	c Hutchings b Barnes	18
A Cotter	b Crawford	17	lbw b Crawford	27
+H Carter	not out	15	c Fane b Barnes	53
GR Hazlitt	b Crawford	1	b Barnes	3
JV Saunders	b Fielder	0	not out	0
	(lb 1, w 1)	2	(b 12, lb 8)	20
	(all out)	266	(all out)	397

Bowling: Fielder 27.5-4-77-2 Barnes 17-7-30-0 Rhodes 11-0-37-1 Braund 16-5-41-0 Crawford 29-1-79-5
Fielder 27-6-74-1 Barnes 27.4-4-72-5 Rhodes 16-6-38-0 Braund 18-2-68-0 Crawford 33-6-125-3

England Innings

*FL Fane	b Armstrong	13	b Armstrong	50
JB Hobbs	b Cotter	83	b Noble	28
G Gunn	lbw b Cotter	15	lbw b Noble	0
KL Hutchings	b Cotter	126	c Cotter b Macartney	39
LC Braund	b Cotter	49	b Armstrong	30
J Hardstaff snr	b Saunders	12	c Ransford b Cotter	19
W Rhodes	b Saunders	32	run out	15
JN Crawford	c Ransford b Saunders	16	c Armstrong b Saunders	10
SF Barnes	c Hill b Armstrong	14	not out	38
+J Humphries	b Cotter	6	lbw b Armstrong	16
A Fielder	not out	6	not out	18
	(b 3, lb 3, w 1, nb 3)	10	(b 9, lb 7, w 1, nb 2)	19
	(all out)	382	(9 wickets)	282

Bowling: Cotter 33-4-142-5 Saunders 34-7-100-3 Noble 9-3-26-0 Armstrong 34.2-15-36-2 Hazlitt 13-1-34-0 Macartney 12-2-34-0
Cotter 28-3-82-1 Saunders 30-9-58-1 Noble 22-7-41-2 Armstrong 30.4-10-53-3 Hazlitt 2-1-8-0 Macartney 9-3-21-1

Umpires: P Argall and RM Crockett

England v Australia
7,8,10,11 February 1908

Result: Australia won by 308 runs

Australia Innings

*MA Noble	b Crawford	48	b Crawford	10
VT Trumper	c Crawford b Fielder	0	b Crawford	0
C Hill	b Barnes	7	run out	25
PA McAlister	c Jones b Fielder	37	c Humphries b Fielder	4
SE Gregory	c Fielder b Crawford	10	lbw b Fielder	29
WW Armstrong	b Crawford	32	not out	133
VS Ransford	c Braund b Fielder	51	c Humphries b Rhodes	54
CG Macartney	c Hardstaff b Fielder	12	c Gunn b Crawford	29
+H Carter	c & b Crawford	2	c Braund b Fielder	66
JDA O'Connor	c Fielder b Crawford	2	c Humphries b Barnes	18
JV Saunders	not out	1	c Jones b Fielder	2
	(b 1, lb 10, nb 1)	12	(b 7, lb 2, nb 6)	15
	(all out)	214	(all out)	385

Bowling: Fielder 22-3-54-4 Barnes 23-11-37-1 Braund 12-3-42-0 Crawford 23.5-3-48-5 Rhodes 5-0-21-0
Fielder 31-2-91-4 Barnes 35-13-69-1 Braund 7-0-48-0 Crawford 25-5-72-3 Rhodes 24-5-66-1 Hutchings 2-0-24-0

England Innings

JB Hobbs	b Noble	57	c & b Saunders	0
G Gunn	c & b Saunders	13	b Saunders	43
J Hardstaff snr	c Carter b O'Connor	8	c Carter b Saunders	39
KL Hutchings	b Saunders	8	b Noble	3
LC Braund	run out	4	b Macartney	10
W Rhodes	c McAlister b Saunders	0	c Carter b O'Connor	2
JN Crawford	b Saunders	1	c Carter b O'Connor	0
*AO Jones	b Noble	3	c Saunders b O'Connor	31
SF Barnes	c O'Connor b Noble	3	not out	22
+J Humphries	not out	3	c Carter b Saunders	11
A Fielder	st Carter b Saunders	1	b Armstrong	20
	(b 1, lb 2, nb 1)	4	(lb 4, nb 1)	5
	(all out)	105	(all out)	186

Bowling: O'Connor 6-1-40-1 Armstrong 1-0-4-0 Macartney 6-1-18-0 Saunders 15.2-8-28-5 Noble 6-0-11-3
O'Connor 21-3-58-3 Armstrong 3.1-0-18-1 Macartney 6-1-15-1 Saunders 26-2-76-4 Noble 12-6-14-1

Umpires: P Argall and RM Crockett

Australia v South Africa
31 December 1910, 2,3,4 January 1911

Result: Australia won by 89 runs

Australia Innings

VT Trumper	b Pegler	34	b Faulkner	159
W Bardsley	c Snooke b Sinclair	85	st Sherwell b Schwarz	14
*C Hill	b Llewellyn	39	b Schwarz	0
DRA Gehrs	b Llewellyn	4	st Sherwell b Schwarz	22
CG Macartney	run out	7	c Snooke b Llewellyn	5
VS Ransford	run out	58	c Sinclair b Schwarz	23
WW Armstrong	c Sherwell b Faulkner	75	b Llewellyn	29
C Kelleway	c Faulkner b Stricker	18	b Pegler	48
+H Carter	not out	15	c Sherwell b Llewellyn	0
A Cotter	c Stricker b Schwarz	3	c sub b Llewellyn	15
WJ Whitty	c Nourse b Faulkner	6	not out	5
	(lb 3, nb 1)	4	(lb 6, nb 1)	7
	(all out)	348	(all out)	327

Bowling: Nourse 8-3-24-0 Snooke 5-1-19-0 Pegler 10-0-43-1 Schwarz 13-0-66-1 Llewellyn 10-0-69-2 Sinclair 13-1-53-1 Stricker 10-0-36-1 Faulkner 10.4-0-34-2
Nourse 5-1-18-0 Snooke 8-1-24-0 Pegler 6.3-1-24-1 Schwarz 22-2-76-4 Llewellyn 16-0-81-4 Sinclair 8-0-32-0 Stricker 2-1-10-0 Faulkner 12-1-55-1

South Africa Innings

JW Zulch	b Cotter	42	not out	6
*+PW Sherwell	c Carter b Cotter	24	b Whitty	16
GA Faulkner	c Armstrong b Whitty	204	c Kelleway b Whitty	8
AW Nourse	b Kelleway	33	lbw b Cotter	2
LA Stricker	b Armstrong	26	lbw b Cotter	0
CB Llewellyn	b Armstrong	5	b Cotter	17
SJ Snooke	b Whitty	77	c Armstrong b Whitty	9
JH Sinclair	not out	58	lbw b Whitty	3
RO Schwarz	b Whitty	0	c Kelleway b Cotter	7
COC Pearse	b Armstrong	6	c Kelleway b Whitty	0
SJ Pegler	lbw b Armstrong	8	lbw b Whitty	0
	(b 2, lb 10, w 2, nb 9)	23	(b 6, lb 3, nb 3)	12
	(all out)	506	(all out)	80

Bowling: Cotter 43-5-158-2 Whitty 29-6-81-3 Kelleway 17-3-67-1 Armstrong 48-9-134-4 Macartney 16-5-43-0
Cotter 15-3-47-4 Whitty 16-7-17-6 Armstrong 1-0-4-0

Umpires: RM Crockett and W Hannah

Australia v South Africa
17,18,20,21 February 1911

Result: Australia won by 530 runs

Australia Innings

VT Trumper	b Faulkner	7	c Sherwell b Vogler	87
W Bardsley	c Schwarz b Pegler	82	run out	15
*C Hill	b Llewellyn	11	st Sherwell b Pegler	100
WW Armstrong	run out	48	c Sherwell b Vogler	132
DRA Gehrs	st Sherwell b Vogler	9	c Snooke b Faulkner	58
C Kelleway	run out	59	run out	18
VS Ransford	lbw b Schwarz	75	b Faulkner	95
A Cotter	b Pegler	10	c sub b Vogler	0
HV Hordern	c Vogler b Pegler	7	c sub b Schwarz	24
+H Carter	run out	5	c Snooke b Faulkner	2
WJ Whitty	not out	0	not out	39
	(b 7, lb 7, w 1)	15	(b 4, lb 3, nb 1)	8
	(all out)	328	(all out)	578

Bowling: Llewellyn 15-1-65-1 Faulkner 18-2-82-1 Schwarz 15-2-34-1 Vogler 8-2-30-1 Sinclair 14-2-40-0 Pegler 17.4-3-40-3 Stricker 5-1-18-0 Nourse 2-0-4-0
Faulkner 28.2-5-101-3 Schwarz 38-4-168-1 Vogler 15-3-59-3 Sinclair 13-1-71-0 Pegler 17-1-88-1 Stricker 3-0-14-0 Nourse 7-0-31-0 Zulch 3-0-26-0 Snooke 2-0-12-0

South Africa Innings

JW Zulch	run out	2	c Trumper b Cotter	15
LA Stricker	b Hordern	4	c Carter b Cotter	0
GA Faulkner	c Gehrs b Hordern	20	b Whitty	80
AW Nourse	not out	92	c & b Hordern	28
SJ Snooke	b Whitty	1	b Hordern	7
JH Sinclair	b Hordern	0	lbw b Hordern	19
RO Schwarz	b Whitty	18	c Carter b Whitty	1
*+PW Sherwell	c sub b Whitty	41	c Kelleway b Hordern	0
CB Llewellyn	b Whitty	7	absent hurt	0
SJ Pegler	c Hill b Cotter	15	c Gehrs b Hordern	8
AEE Vogler	b Cotter	0	not out	2
	(b 4, lb 1)	5	(b 7, lb 1, w 2, nb 1)	11
	(all out)	205	(all out)	171

Bowling: Cotter 6.5-0-16-2 Whitty 22-5-78-4 Hordern 15-1-39-3 Armstrong 8-2-25-0 Kelleway 11-1-42-0
Cotter 6-1-22-2 Whitty 9-2-32-2 Hordern 14.2-2-66-5 Armstrong 3-0-15-0 Kelleway 8-0-25-0

Umpires: RM Crockett and W Hannah

Australia v England
30 December 1911, 1,2,3 January 1912

Result: England won by 8 wickets

Australia Innings

C Kelleway	lbw b Barnes	2	c Gunn b Foster	13
W Bardsley	b Barnes	0	run out	16
*C Hill	b Barnes	4	c Gunn b Barnes	0
WW Armstrong	c Smith b Barnes	4	b Foster	90
VT Trumper	b Foster	13	b Barnes	2
VS Ransford	c Smith b Hitch	43	c Smith b Foster	32
RB Minnett	c Hobbs b Barnes	2	b Foster	34
HV Hordern	not out	49	c Mead b Foster	31
A Cotter	run out	14	c Hobbs b Foster	41
+H Carter	c Smith b Douglas	29	b Barnes	16
WJ Whitty	b Woolley	14	not out	0
	(b 5, lb 4, nb 1)	10	(b 14, lb 7, w 1, nb 2)	24
	(all out)	184	(all out)	299

Bowling: Foster 16-2-52-1 Barnes 23-9-44-5 Hitch 7-0-37-1 Douglas 15-4-33-1 Hearne 1-0-8-0 Woolley 0.1-0-0-1
Foster 38-9-91-6 Barnes 32.1-7-96-3 Hitch 5-0-21-0 Douglas 10-0-38-0 Hearne 1-0-5-0 Woolley 3-0-21-0 Rhodes 2-1-3-0

England Innings

W Rhodes	c Trumper b Cotter	61	c Carter b Cotter	28
JB Hobbs	c Carter b Cotter	6	not out	126
JW Hearne	c Carter b Cotter	114	not out	12
G Gunn	lbw b Armstrong	10	c Carter b Whitty	43
CP Mead	c Armstrong b Whitty	11		
FR Foster	c Hill b Cotter	9		
*JWHT Douglas	b Hordern	9		
FE Woolley	c Ransford b Hordern	23		
+EJ Smith	b Hordern	5		
SF Barnes	lbw b Hordern	1		
JW Hitch	not out	0		
	(b 2, lb 10, nb 4)	16	(b 5, lb 5)	10
	(all out)	265	(2 wickets)	219

Bowling: Cotter 21-2-73-4 Whitty 19-2-47-1 Hordern 23.1-1-66-4 Kelleway 15-7-27-0 Armstrong 15-6-20-1 Minnett 5-0-16-0
Cotter 14-5-45-1 Whitty 18-3-37-1 Hordern 17-0-66-0 Kelleway 7-0-15-0 Armstrong 8-1-22-0 Minnett 2-0-13-0 Ransford 1.1-0-11-0

Umpires: RM Crockett and DA Elder

Australia v England
9,10,12,13 February 1912

Result: England won by an innings and 225 runs

Australia Innings

C Kelleway	c Hearne b Woolley	29	c Smith b Barnes	5
HV Hordern	b Barnes	19	c Foster b Douglas	5
W Bardsley	b Foster	0	b Foster	3
VT Trumper	b Foster	17	b Barnes	28
*C Hill	c Hearne b Barnes	22	b Douglas	11
WW Armstrong	b Barnes	7	b Douglas	11
RB Minnett	c Rhodes b Foster	56	b Douglas	7
VS Ransford	c Rhodes b Foster	4	not out	29
TJ Matthews	c Gunn b Barnes	3	b Foster	10
A Cotter	b Barnes	15	c Mead b Foster	8
+H Carter	not out	6	c Hearne b Douglas	38
	(b 1, lb 5, nb 7)	13	(b 9, lb 2, nb 7)	18
	(all out)	191	(all out)	173

Bowling: Foster 22-2-77-4 Barnes 29.1-4-74-5 Woolley 11-3-22-1 Rhodes 2-1-1-0 Hearne 1-0-4-0
Foster 19-3-38-3 Barnes 20-6-47-2 Woolley 2-0-7-0 Hearne 3-0-17-0 Douglas 17.5-6-46-5

England Innings

JB Hobbs	c Carter b Hordern	178
W Rhodes	c Carter b Minnett	179
G Gunn	c Hill b Armstrong	75
JW Hearne	c Armstrong b Minnett	0
FR Foster	c Hordern b Armstrong	50
*JWHT Douglas	c Bardsley b Armstrong	0
FE Woolley	c Kelleway b Minnett	56
CP Mead	b Hordern	21
J Vine	not out	4
+EJ Smith	c Matthews b Kelleway	7
SF Barnes	c Hill b Hordern	0
	(b 2, lb 4, w 4, nb 9)	19
	(all out)	589

Bowling: Cotter 37-5-125-0 Kelleway 26-2-80-1 Armstrong 36-12-93-3 Matthews 22-1-68-0 Hordern 47.5-5-137-3 Minnett 20-5-59-3 Ransford 2-1-8-0

Umpires: RM Crockett and WA Young

Australia v England
31 December 1920, 1,3,4 January 1921

Result: Australia won by an innings and 91 runs

Australia Innings

HL Collins	c Hearne b Howell	64
W Bardsley	c Strudwick b Woolley	51
RL Park	b Howell	0
JM Taylor	c Woolley b Parkin	68
*WW Armstrong	lbw b Douglas	39
C Kelleway	c Strudwick b Howell	9
CE Pellew	b Parkin	116
J Ryder	c Woolley b Douglas	13
JM Gregory	c Russell b Woolley	100
+WAS Oldfield	c & b Rhodes	24
AA Mailey	not out	8
	(b 1, lb 3, w 1, nb 2)	7
	(all out)	499

Bowling: Howell 37-5-142-3 Douglas 24-1-83-2 Parkin 27-0-116-2 Hearne 14-0-38-0 Woolley 27-8-87-2 Rhodes 8.3-1-26-1

England Innings

JB Hobbs	c Ryder b Gregory	122	b Kelleway	20
W Rhodes	b Gregory	7	c Collins b Armstrong	28
JWH Makepeace	lbw b Armstrong	4	c Gregory b Armstrong	4
EH Hendren	c Taylor b Gregory	67	c & b Collins	1
CAG Russell	c Collins b Gregory	0	c Armstrong b Collins	5
FE Woolley	b Gregory	5	b Ryder	50
*JWHT Douglas	lbw b Gregory	15	b Gregory	9
CH Parkin	c Mailey b Gregory	4	c Taylor b Armstrong	9
+H Strudwick	not out	21	c Oldfield b Armstrong	24
H Howell	st Oldfield b Armstrong	5	not out	0
JW Hearne	absent hurt	0	absent hurt	0
	(nb 1)	1	(b 3, lb 3, nb 1)	7
	(all out)	251	(all out)	157

Bowling: Gregory 20-1-69-7 Kelleway 19-1-54-0 Armstrong 24.3-8-50-2 Ryder 14-2-31-0 Park 1-0-9-0 Collins 9-0-37-0
Gregory 12-0-32-1 Kelleway 12-1-25-1 Armstrong 15.2-5-26-4 Ryder 10-2-17-1 Collins 17-5-47-2 Pellew 1-0-3-0

Umpires: RM Crockett and DA Elder

Australia v England
11,12,14,15,16 February 1921

Result: Australia won by 8 wickets

England Innings

JB Hobbs	c Carter b McDonald	27	lbw b Mailey	13
W Rhodes	c Carter b Gregory	11	c Gregory b Mailey	73
JWH Makepeace	c Collins b Mailey	117	lbw b Mailey	54
EH Hendren	c Carter b Mailey	30	b Kelleway	32
FE Woolley	lbw b Kelleway	29	st Carter b Mailey	0
*JWHT Douglas	c & b Mailey	50	st Carter b Mailey	60
A Waddington	b Mailey	9	c Carter b Mailey	6
PGH Fender	c Gregory b Kelleway	3	c Collins b Mailey	59
+A Dolphin	b Kelleway	1	c Gregory b Mailey	0
CH Parkin	run out	10	c Bardsley b Mailey	4
H Howell	not out	0	not out	0
	(b 1, lb 5)	6	(b 5, lb 5, w 1, nb 3)	14
	(all out)	284	(all out)	315

Bowling: McDonald 19-2-46-1 Gregory 18-1-61-1 Mailey 29.2-1-115-4 Ryder 10-5-10-0 Armstrong 5-1-9-0 Kelleway 18-2-37-3
McDonald 23-2-77-0 Gregory 14-4-31-0 Mailey 47-8-121-9 Ryder 10-3-25-0 Kelleway 23-8-47-1

Australia Innings

HL Collins	c Rhodes b Woolley	59	c Rhodes b Parkin	32
W Bardsley	b Fender	56	run out	38
J Ryder	lbw b Woolley	7	not out	52
JM Taylor	hit wicket b Fender	2		
JM Gregory	c Dolphin b Parkin	77	not out	76
CE Pellew	b Fender	12		
*WW Armstrong	not out	123		
C Kelleway	b Fender	27		
+H Carter	b Fender	0		
AA Mailey	run out	13		
EA McDonald	b Woolley	0		
	(b 1, lb 6, w 1, nb 5)	13	(b 5, lb 5, w 2, nb 1)	13
	(all out)	389	(2 wickets)	211

Bowling: Howell 17-2-86-0 Douglas 4-0-17-0 Waddington 5-0-31-0 Parkin 22-5-64-1 Fender 32-3-122-5 Woolley 32.1-14-56-3
Howell 10-1-36-0 Douglas 5-1-13-0 Parkin 12-2-46-1 Fender 13.2-2-39-0 Woolley 14-4-39-0 Rhodes 10-2-25-0

Umpires: RM Crockett and DA Elder

Australia v England
1,2,3,5,6,7,8 January 1925

Result: Australia won by 81 runs

Australia Innings

*HL Collins	c Strudwick b Tate	9	b Hearne	30
W Bardsley	c Strudwick b Gilligan	19	lbw b Tate	2
AJ Richardson	run out	14	b Tate	9
WH Ponsford	b Tate	128	b Tate	4
JM Taylor	run out	72	b Tate	90
VY Richardson	run out	138	c Strudwick b Hearne	8
C Kelleway	c Strudwick b Gilligan	32	c & b Hearne	17
AEV Hartkopf	c Chapman b Gilligan	80	lbw b Tate	0
JM Gregory	c Gilligan b Tate	44	not out	36
+WAS Oldfield	not out	39	lbw b Hearne	39
AA Mailey	lbw b Douglas	1	b Tate	3
	(b 18, lb 5, nb 1)	24	(b 11, lb 1)	12
	(all out)	600	(all out)	250

Bowling: Tate 45-10-142-3 Douglas 19.5-0-95-1 Tyldesley 35-3-130-0 Gilligan 26-1-114-3 Hearne 13-1-69-0 Woolley 11-3-26-0
Tate 33.3-8-99-6 Douglas 4-0-9-0 Tyldesley 2-0-6-0 Gilligan 11-2-40-0 Hearne 29-5-84-4

England Innings

JB Hobbs	b Mailey	154	lbw b Mailey	22
H Sutcliffe	b Kelleway	176	c Gregory b Mailey	127
FE Woolley	b Gregory	0	lbw b AJ Richardson	50
JW Hearne	b Mailey	9	lbw b Gregory	23
EH Hendren	c Oldfield b Kelleway	32	b Gregory	18
APF Chapman	c Oldfield b Gregory	28	not out	4
JWHT Douglas	c Collins b AJ Richardson	8	b Mailey	14
RK Tyldesley	c Collins b Gregory	5	c Ponsford b Mailey	0
MW Tate	b AJ Richardson	34	b Gregory	0
*AER Gilligan	not out	17	c & b Mailey	0
+H Strudwick	b Hartkopf	4	lbw b Gregory	22
	(b 4, lb 4, nb 4)	12	(b 6, lb 2, nb 2)	10
	(all out)	479	(all out)	290

Bowling: Gregory 34-4-124-3 Kelleway 30-10-62-2 Mailey 34.5-1-141-2 Hartkopf 26-1-120-1 AJ Richardson 14-6-20-2
Gregory 27.3-6-87-4 Kelleway 18-4-32-0 Mailey 24-2-92-5 Hartkopf 4-1-14-0 AJ Richardson 22-7-35-1 Collins 11-3-10-0

Umpires: RM Crockett and C Garing

Australia v England
13,14,16,17,18 February 1925

Result: England won by an innings and 29 runs

England Innings

JB Hobbs	st Oldfield b Ryder	66
H Sutcliffe	lbw b Mailey	143
JW Hearne	c Bardsley b Richardson	44
FE Woolley	st Oldfield b Mailey	40
EH Hendren	b Ryder	65
APF Chapman	st Oldfield b Mailey	12
WW Whysall	st Oldfield b Kelleway	76
R Kilner	lbw b Kelleway	74
*AER Gilligan	c Oldfield b Kelleway	0
MW Tate	c Taylor b Mailey	8
+H Strudwick	not out	7
	(b 6, lb 2, w 3, nb 2)	13
	(all out)	548

Bowling: Gregory 22-1-102-0 Kelleway 29-5-70-3 Mailey 43.6-2-186-4 Ryder 25-3-83-2 Richardson 26-8-76-1 Collins 6-1-18-0

Australia Innings

*HL Collins	c Kilner b Tate	22	c Whysall b Kilner	1
AJ Richardson	b Hearne	19	lbw b Hearne	3
J Ryder	b Tate	0	lbw b Woolley	38
W Bardsley	run out	24	b Tate	0
WH Ponsford	c Strudwick b Hearne	21	b Tate	19
JM Taylor	c Hendren b Woolley	86	c Woolley b Gilligan	68
TJE Andrews	c Hearne b Kilner	35	c Woolley b Kilner	3
C Kelleway	lbw b Kilner	1	c Strudwick b Tate	42
JM Gregory	c Woolley b Hearne	38	c Sutcliffe b Kilner	45
+WAS Oldfield	c Chapman b Kilner	3	b Tate	8
AA Mailey	not out	4	not out	8
	(b 13, lb 2, nb 1)	16	(b 15)	15
	(all out)	269	(all out)	250

Bowling: Tate 16-2-70-2 Gilligan 6-1-24-0 Hearne 19.3-3-1-77-3 Kilner 13-1-29-3 Woolley 9-1-53-1
Tate 25.5-6-75-5 Gilligan 7-0-26-1 Hearne 20-0-76-1 Kilner 16-3-41-2 Woolley 4-0-17-1

Umpires: RM Crockett and DA Elder

Australia v England
29,31 December 1928, 1,2,3,4,5 January 1929

Result: England won by 3 wickets

Australia Innings

WM Woodfull	c Jardine b Tate	7	c Duckworth b Tate	107
VY Richardson	c Duckworth b Larwood	3	b Larwood	5
HSTL Hendry	c Jardine b Larwood	23	st Duckworth b White	12
AF Kippax	c Jardine b Larwood	100	b Tate	41
*J Ryder	c Hendren b Tate	112	b Geary	5
DG Bradman	b Hammond	79	c Duckworth b Geary	112
+WAS Oldfield	b Geary	3	b White	7
EL a'Beckett	c Duckworth b White	41	b White	6
RK Oxenham	b Geary	15	b White	39
CV Grimmett	c Duckworth b Geary	5	not out	4
DD Blackie	not out	2	b White	0
	(b 4, lb 3)	7	(b 6, lb 7)	13
	(all out)	397	(all out)	351

Bowling: Larwood 37-3-127-3 Tate 46-17-87-2 Geary 31.5-4-83-3 Hammond 8-4-19-1 White 57-30-64-1 Jardine 1-0-10-0
Larwood 16-3-37-1 Tate 47-15-70-2 Geary 30-4-94-2 Hammond 16-6-30-0 White 56.5-20-107-5

England Innings

JB Hobbs	c Oldfield b a'Beckett	20	lbw b Blackie	49
H Sutcliffe	b Blackie	58	lbw b Grimmett	135
WR Hammond	c a'Beckett b Blackie	200	run out	32
*APF Chapman	b Blackie	24	c Woodfull b Ryder	5
EH Hendren	c a'Beckett b Hendry	19	b Oxenham	45
DR Jardine	c & b Blackie	62	b Grimmett	33
H Larwood	c & b Blackie	0		
G Geary	lbw b Grimmett	1	not out	4
MW Tate	c Kippax b Grimmett	21	not out	0
+G Duckworth	b Blackie	3		
JC White	not out	8		
	(b 1)	1	(b 15, lb 14)	29
	(all out)	417	(7 wickets)	332

Bowling: a'Beckett 37-7-92-1 Hendry 20-8-35-1 Grimmett 55-14-114-2 Oxenham 35-11-67-0 Blackie 44-13-94-6 Ryder 4-0-14-0
a'Beckett 22-5-39-0 Hendry 23-5-33-0 Grimmett 42-12-96-2 Oxenham 28-10-44-1 Blackie 39-11-75-1 Ryder 5.5-1-16-1

Umpires: DA Elder and GA Hele

Australia v England
8,9,11,12,13,14,15,16 March 1929

Result: Australia won by 5 wickets

England Innings

JB Hobbs	lbw b Ryder	142	c Fairfax b Grimmett	65
DR Jardine	c Oldfield b Wall	19	c Oldfield b Wall	0
WR Hammond	c Oldfield b Wall	38	c Ryder b Fairfax	16
GE Tyldesley	c Hornibrook b Ryder	31	c Oldfield b Wall	21
+G Duckworth	c Fairfax b Hornibrook	12	lbw b Oxenham	9
EH Hendren	c Hornibrook b Fairfax	95	b Grimmett	1
M Leyland	c Fairfax b Oxenham	137	not out	53
H Larwood	b Wall	4	b Wall	11
G Geary	b Hornibrook	4	b Wall	3
MW Tate	c sub b Hornibrook	15	c Fairfax b Hornibrook	54
*JC White	not out	9	c Oxenham b Wall	4
	(b 4, lb 6, w 1, nb 2)	13	(b 19, lb 1)	20
	(all out)	519	(all out)	257

Bowling: Wall 49-8-123-3 Hornibrook 48-8-142-3 Oxenham 45.1-15-86-1 Grimmett 25-11-40-0 Fairfax 27-4-84-1 Ryder 18-5-29-2 Kippax 3-1-2-0
Wall 26-5-66-5 Hornibrook 19-5-51-1 Oxenham 10.3-1-34-1 Grimmett 24-7-66-2 Fairfax 7-0-20-1

Australia Innings

WM Woodfull	c Geary b Larwood	102	b Hammond	35
A Jackson	run out	30	b Geary	46
AF Kippax	c Duckworth b White	38	run out	28
*J Ryder	c Tate b Hammond	30	not out	57
DG Bradman	c Tate b Geary	123	not out	37
AG Fairfax	lbw b Geary	65		
RK Oxenham	c Duckworth b Geary	7		
+WAS Oldfield	c & b Geary	6	b Hammond	48
CV Grimmett	not out	38		
TW Wall	c Duckworth b Geary	9		
PM Hornibrook	lbw b White	26	b Hammond	18
	(b 6, lb 9, w 2)	17	(b 12, lb 6)	18
	(all out)	491	(5 wickets)	287

Bowling: Larwood 34-7-83-1 Tate 62-26-108-0 Geary 81-36-105-5 White 75.3-22-136-2 Hammond 16-3-31-1 Leyland 3-0-11-0
Larwood 32.1-5-81-0 Tate 38-13-76-0 Geary 20-5-31-1 White 18-8-28-0 Hammond 26-8-53-3

Umpires: GA Hele and AC Jones

Melbourne Cricket Ground

Australia v West Indies
13,14 February 1931

Result: Australia won by an innings and 122 runs

West Indies Innings

Batsman	1st dismissal		2nd dismissal	
CA Roach	c Kippax b Grimmett	20	lbw b Fairfax	7
FR Martin	lbw b Ironmonger	17	c Oldfield b Fairfax	10
GA Headley	c Jackson b Ironmonger	33	c Fairfax b Ironmonger	11
LS Birkett	c McCabe b Ironmonger	0	c Jackson b Ironmonger	13
EL Bartlett	st Oldfield b Ironmonger	9	b Fairfax	6
*GC Grant	c Oldfield b Ironmonger	0	c McCabe b Ironmonger	3
LN Constantine	c Jackson b Grimmett	7	c Kippax b Fairfax	10
+IM Barrow	c Fairfax b Ironmonger	0	c Oxenham b Ironmonger	13
OC Scott	run out	11	not out	20
GN Francis	not out	0	c Jackson b Grimmett	0
HC Griffith	c Fairfax b Ironmonger	0	b Grimmett	4
	(nb 2)	2	(b 3, lb 6, nb 1)	10
	(all out)	99	(all out)	107

Bowling: Fairfax 5-0-14-0 Oxenham 6-1-14-0 Ironmonger 20-7-23-7 Grimmett 19-7-46-2
Fairfax 14.2-1-31-4 Ironmonger 17-4-56-4 Grimmett 4.4-0-10-2

Australia Innings

*WM Woodfull	run out	83
WH Ponsford	st Barrow b Constantine	24
DG Bradman	c Roach b Martin	152
A Jackson	c Birkett b Constantine	15
SJ McCabe	run out	2
AG Fairfax	c Birkett b Martin	16
AF Kippax	b Martin	24
RK Oxenham	c Constantine b Griffith	0
+WAS Oldfield	not out	1
H Ironmonger		
CV Grimmett		
	(b 7, lb 3, nb 1)	11
	(8 wickets declared)	328

Bowling: Francis 13-0-51-0 Griffith 8-1-33-1 Scott 11-0-47-0 Constantine 25-4-83-2 Martin 30.2-3-91-3 Birkett 2-0-12-0

Umpires: AN Barlow and J Richards

Australia v South Africa
31 December 1931, 1,2,4,5,6 January 1932

Result: Australia won by 169 runs

Australia Innings

Batsman	1st dismissal		2nd dismissal	
*WM Woodfull	c Cameron b Bell	7	c Mitchell b McMillan	161
WH Ponsford	b Bell	7	c Mitchell b Bell	34
DG Bradman	c Cameron b Quinn	2	lbw b Vincent	167
AF Kippax	c Bell b Quinn	52	c Curnow b McMillan	67
SJ McCabe	c Morkel b Bell	22	c Mitchell b McMillan	71
KE Rigg	c Mitchell b Bell	68	c Mitchell b Vincent	1
EL a'Beckett	c Morkel b Bell	9	b Vincent	4
+WAS Oldfield	c Vincent b Quinn	0	lbw b McMillan	0
CV Grimmett	c Morkel b Bell	9	not out	16
TW Wall	not out	6	b Vincent	12
H Ironmonger	run out	12	b Quinn	0
	(b 1, lb 4, w 1, nb 1)	7	(b 17, lb 3, nb 1)	21
	(all out)	198	(all out)	554

Bowling: Bell 26.1-9-69-5 Quinn 31-13-42-4 Morkel 3-0-12-0 Vincent 12-1-32-0 McMillan 2-0-22-0 Christy 3-0-14-0
Bell 36-6-101-1 Quinn 36.4-6-113-4 Morkel 4-0-15-0 Vincent 55-16-154-4 McMillan 33-3-150-4

South Africa Innings

Batsman	1st dismissal		2nd dismissal	
SH Curnow	b Grimmett	47	b Grimmett	9
B Mitchell	c McCabe b Wall	17	c & b Grimmett	46
JAJ Christy	c McCabe b Ironmonger	16	c Oldfield b Ironmonger	63
HW Taylor	lbw b Grimmett	11	b Ironmonger	38
DPB Morkel	lbw b Ironmonger	33	b Ironmonger	4
*+HB Cameron	st Oldfield b Ironmonger	39	lbw b Ironmonger	13
KG Viljoen	c Wall b McCabe	111	b Ironmonger	2
CL Vincent	c Oldfield b Wall	16	c Ponsford b Grimmett	34
Q McMillan	c Oldfield b Wall	29	c Wall b Grimmett	1
NA Quinn	b McCabe	11	not out	0
AJ Bell	not out	10	b Grimmett	0
	(b 3, lb 13, nb 2)	18	(b 8, lb 6, nb 1)	15
	(all out)	358	(all out)	225

Bowling: Wall 37-5-98-3 a'Beckett 18-5-29-0 Grimmett 63-23-100-2 Ironmonger 49-26-72-3 McCabe 21.3-4-41-2
Wall 13-3-35-0 a'Beckett 3-1-6-0 Grimmett 46-14-92-6 Ironmonger 42-18-54-4 McCabe 10-1-21-0 Bradman 1-0-2-0

Umpires: GE Borwick and GA Hele

Australia v South Africa
12,13,15 February 1932

Result: Australia won by an innings and 72 runs

South Africa Innings

Batsman	1st dismissal		2nd dismissal	
B Mitchell	c Rigg b McCabe	2	c Oldfield b Ironmonger	4
SH Curnow	c Oldfield b Nash	3	c Fingleton b Ironmonger	16
JAJ Christy	c Grimmett b Nash	4	c & b Nash	0
HW Taylor	c Kippax b Nash	0	c Bradman b Ironmonger	2
KG Viljoen	c sub b Ironmonger	1	c Oldfield b O'Reilly	0
*+HB Cameron	c McCabe b Nash	11	c McCabe b O'Reilly	0
DPB Morkel	c Nash b Ironmonger	0	c Rigg b Ironmonger	0
CL Vincent	c Nash b Ironmonger	1	not out	8
Q McMillan	st Oldfield b Ironmonger	0	c Oldfield b Ironmonger	0
NA Quinn	not out	5	c Fingleton b O'Reilly	5
AJ Bell	st Oldfield b Ironmonger	0	c McCabe b O'Reilly	6
	(b 2, lb 3, nb 3)	8	(b 3, lb 1)	4
	(all out)	36	(all out)	45

Bowling: Nash 12-6-18-4 McCabe 4-1-4-1 Ironmonger 7.2-5-6-5
Nash 7-4-4-1 Ironmonger 15.3-7-18-6 O'Reilly 9-5-19-3

Australia Innings

*WM Woodfull	b Bell	0
JHW Fingleton	c Vincent b Bell	40
KE Rigg	c Vincent b Quinn	22
AF Kippax	c Curnow b McMillan	42
SJ McCabe	c Cameron b Bell	0
LJ Nash	b Quinn	13
+WAS Oldfield	c Curnow b McMillan	11
CV Grimmett	c Cameron b Quinn	9
WJ O'Reilly	c Curnow b McMillan	13
H Ironmonger	not out	0
DG Bradman	absent hurt	0
	(lb 3)	3
	(all out)	153

Bowling: Bell 16-0-52-3 Quinn 19.3-4-29-3 Vincent 11-2-40-0 McMillan 8-0-29-3

Umpires: GE Borwick and GA Hele

Australia v England
30,31 December 1932, 2,3 January 1933

Result: Australia won by 111 runs

Australia Innings

Batsman	1st dismissal		2nd dismissal	
JHW Fingleton	b Allen	83	c Ames b Allen	1
*WM Woodfull	b Allen	10	c Allen b Larwood	26
LPJ O'Brien	run out	10	b Larwood	11
DG Bradman	b Bowes	0	not out	103
SJ McCabe	c Jardine b Voce	32	b Allen	0
VY Richardson	c Hammond b Voce	34	lbw b Hammond	32
+WAS Oldfield	not out	27	b Voce	6
CV Grimmett	c Sutcliffe b Voce	2	b Voce	0
TW Wall	run out	1	lbw b Hammond	3
WJ O'Reilly	b Larwood	15	c Ames b Hammond	0
H Ironmonger	b Larwood	4	run out	0
	(b 5, lb 1, w 2, nb 2)	10	(b 3, lb 1, w 4, nb 1)	9
	(all out)	228	(all out)	191

Bowling: Larwood 20.3-2-52-2 Voce 20-3-54-3 Allen 17-3-41-2 Hammond 10-3-21-0 Bowes 19-2-50-1
Larwood 15-2-50-2 Voce 15-2-47-2 Allen 12-1-44-2 Hammond 10.5-2-21-3 Bowes 4-0-20-0

England Innings

Batsman	1st dismissal		2nd dismissal	
H Sutcliffe	c Richardson b Wall	52	b O'Reilly	33
RES Wyatt	lbw b O'Reilly	13	lbw b O'Reilly	25
WR Hammond	b Wall	8	c O'Brien b O'Reilly	23
Nawab of Pataudi snr	b O'Reilly	15	c Fingleton b Ironmonger	5
M Leyland	b O'Reilly	22	b Wall	19
*DR Jardine	c Oldfield b Wall	1	c McCabe b Ironmonger	24
+LEG Ames	b Wall	4	c Fingleton b O'Reilly	2
GOB Allen	c Richardson b O'Reilly	30	st Oldfield b Ironmonger	23
H Larwood	b O'Reilly	9	c Wall b Ironmonger	4
W Voce	c McCabe b Grimmett	6	c O'Brien b O'Reilly	0
WE Bowes	not out	4	not out	0
	(b 1, lb 2, nb 2)	5	(lb 4, nb 1)	5
	(all out)	169	(all out)	139

Bowling: Wall 21-4-52-4 O'Reilly 34.3-17-63-5 Grimmett 16-4-21-1 Ironmonger 14-4-28-0
Wall 8-2-23-1 O'Reilly 24-5-66-5 Grimmett 4-0-19-0 Ironmonger 19.1-8-26-4

Umpires: GE Borwick and GA Hele

Australia v England
1,2,4,5,6,7 January 1937

Result: Australia won by 365 runs

Australia Innings

Batsman	1st dismissal		2nd dismissal	
JHW Fingleton	c Sims b Robins	38	c Ames b Sims	136
WA Brown	c Ames b Voce	1	c Barnett b Voce	20
*DG Bradman	c Robins b Verity	13	c Allen b Verity	270
KE Rigg	c Verity b Allen	16	lbw b Sims	47
SJ McCabe	c Worthington b Voce	63	lbw b Allen	22
LS Darling	c Allen b Verity	20	b Allen	0
MW Sievers	st Ames b Robins	1	not out	25
+WAS Oldfield	not out	27	lbw b Verity	7
WJ O'Reilly	c Sims b Hammond	4	c & b Voce	0
FA Ward	st Ames b Hammond	7	c Hardstaff b Verity	18
LO Fleetwood-Smith			c Verity b Voce	0
	(b 2, lb 6, nb 2)	10	(b 6, lb 2, w 1, nb 10)	19
	(9 wickets declared)	200	(all out)	564

Bowling: Voce 18-3-49-2 Allen 12-2-35-1 Sims 9-1-35-0 Verity 14-4-24-2 Robins 7-0-31-2 Hammond 5.3-0-16-2
Voce 29-2-120-3 Allen 23-2-84-2 Sims 23-1-109-2 Verity 37.7-9-79-3 Robins 11-2-46-0 Hammond 22-3-89-0 Worthington 4-0-18-0

England Innings

Batsman	1st dismissal		2nd dismissal	
TS Worthington	c Bradman b McCabe	0	c Sievers b Ward	16
CJ Barnett	c Darling b Sievers	11	lbw b O'Reilly	23
WR Hammond	b Wall	32	b Sievers	51
M Leyland	c Darling b O'Reilly	17	not out	111
JM Sims	c Brown b Sievers	3	lbw b Fleetwood-Smith	0
+LEG Ames	b Sievers	3	b Fleetwood-Smith	19
RWV Robins	c O'Reilly b Sievers	0	b O'Reilly	61
J Hardstaff jnr	b O'Reilly	3	c Ward b Fleetwood-Smith	17
*GOB Allen	not out	0	c Sievers b Fleetwood-Smith	11
H Verity	c Brown b O'Reilly	0	c McCabe b O'Reilly	11
W Voce	not out	0	c Bradman b Fleetwood-Smith	0
	(b 5, lb 1, nb 1)	7	(lb 3)	3
	(9 wickets declared)	76	(all out)	323

Bowling: McCabe 2-1-7-1 Sievers 11.2-5-21-5 O'Reilly 12-5-28-3 Fleetwood-Smith 3-1-13-0
McCabe 8-0-32-0 Sievers 12-2-39-1 O'Reilly 21-6-65-3 Fleetwood-Smith 25.6-2-124-5 Ward 12-1-60-1

Umpires: GE Borwick and JD Scott

Australia v England
26,27 February, 1,2,3 March 1937

Result: Australia won by an innings and 200 runs

Australia Innings

JHW Fingleton	c Voce b Farnes	17
KE Rigg	c Ames b Farnes	28
*DG Bradman	b Farnes	169
SJ McCabe	c Farnes b Verity	112
CL Badcock	c Worthington b Voce	118
RG Gregory	c Verity b Farnes	80
+WAS Oldfield	c Ames b Voce	21
LJ Nash	c Ames b Farnes	17
WJ O'Reilly	b Voce	1
EL McCormick	not out	17
LO Fleetwood-Smith	b Farnes	13
	(b 1, lb 5, w 1, nb 4)	11
	(all out)	604

Bowling: Allen 17-0-99-0 Farnes 28.5-5-96-6 Voce 29-3-123-3 Hammond 16-1-62-0 Verity 41-5-127-1 Worthington 6-0-60-0 Leyland 3-0-26-0

England Innings

Batsman	1st dismissal		2nd dismissal	
CJ Barnett	c Oldfield b Nash	18	lbw b O'Reilly	41
TS Worthington	hit wicket b Fleetwood-Smith	44	c Bradman b McCormick	6
J Hardstaff jnr	c McCormick b O'Reilly	83	b Nash	1
WR Hammond	c Nash b O'Reilly	14	c Bradman b O'Reilly	56
M Leyland	b O'Reilly	7	c McCormick b Fleetwood-Smith	28
RES Wyatt	c Bradman b O'Reilly	38	run out	9
+LEG Ames	b Nash	19	c McCabe b McCormick	11
*GOB Allen	c Oldfield b Nash	0	b O'Reilly	7
H Verity	c Rigg b Nash	0	not out	2
W Voce	st Oldfield b O'Reilly	3	c Badcock b Fleetwood-Smith	1
K Farnes	not out	0	c Nash b Fleetwood-Smith	0
	(lb 12, nb 1)	13	(lb 3)	3
	(all out)	239	(all out)	165

Bowling: McCormick 13-1-54-0 Nash 17.5-1-70-4 O'Reilly 23-7-51-5 Fleetwood-Smith 18-3-51-1
McCormick 9-0-33-2 Nash 7-1-34-1 O'Reilly 19-6-58-3 Fleetwood-Smith 13.2-3-36-3 McCabe 1-0-1-0

Umpires: GE Borwick and JD Scott

Australia v England
1,2,3,4,6,7 January 1947

Result: Match drawn

Australia Innings
SG Barnes	lbw b Bedser	45	c Evans b Yardley	32
AR Morris	lbw b Bedser	21	b Bedser	155
*DG Bradman	b Yardley	79	c & b Yardley	49
AL Hassett	c Hammond b Wright	12	b Wright	9
KR Miller	c Evans b Wright	33	c Hammond b Yardley	34
IWG Johnson	lbw b Yardley	0	run out	0
CL McCool	not out	104	c Evans b Bedser	43
+D Tallon	c Evans b Edrich	35	c & b Wright	92
RR Lindwall	b Bedser	9	c Washbrook b Bedser	100
B Dooland	c Hammond b Edrich	19	c Compton b Wright	1
ERH Toshack	c Hutton b Edrich	6	not out	2
	(nb 2)	2	(b 14, lb 2, nb 3)	19
	(all out)	365	(all out)	536

Bowling: Voce 10-2-40-0 Bedser 31-4-99-3 Wright 26-2-124-2 Yardley 20-4-50-2 Edrich 10.3-2-50-3
Voce 6-1-29-0 Bedser 34.3-4-176-3 Wright 32-3-131-3 Yardley 20-0-67-3 Edrich 18-1-86-0 Hutton 3-0-28-0

England Innings
L Hutton	c McCool b Lindwall	2	c Bradman b Toshack	40
C Washbrook	c Tallon b Dooland	62	b Dooland	112
WJ Edrich	lbw b Lindwall	89	lbw b McCool	13
DCS Compton	lbw b Toshack	11	run out	14
*WR Hammond	c & b Dooland	9	b Lindwall	26
JT Ikin	c Miller b Dooland	48	c Hassett b Miller	5
NWD Yardley	b McCool	61	not out	53
+TG Evans	b McCool	17	not out	0
W Voce	lbw b Dooland	0		
AV Bedser	not out	27	lbw b Miller	25
DVP Wright	b Johnson	10		
	(b 1, lb 12, nb 2)	15	(b 15, lb 6, w 1)	22
	(all out)	351	(7 wickets)	310

Bowling: Lindwall 20-1-64-2 Miller 10-0-34-0 Toshack 26-5-88-1 McCool 19-3-53-2 Dooland 27-5-69-4 Johnson 6.5-1-28-1
Lindwall 16-2-59-1 Miller 11-0-41-2 Toshack 16-5-39-1 McCool 24-9-41-1 Dooland 21-1-84-1 Johnson 12-4-24-0

Umpires: GE Borwick and JD Scott

Australia v India
1,2,3,5 January 1948

Result: Australia won by 233 runs

Australia Innings
SG Barnes	b Mankad	12	c Sen b Amarnath	15
AR Morris	b Amarnath	45	not out	100
*DG Bradman	lbw b Phadkar	132	not out	127
AL Hassett	lbw b Mankad	80		
KR Miller	lbw b Mankad	29		
RA Hamence	st Sen b Amarnath	25		
RR Lindwall	b Amarnath	26		
+D Tallon	c Mankad b Amarnath	2		
B Dooland	not out	21	lbw b Phadkar	6
IWG Johnson	lbw b Mankad	16	c Hazare b Amarnath	0
WA Johnston	run out	5	lbw b Amarnath	3
	(b 1)	1	(b 3, nb 1)	4
	(all out)	394	(4 wickets declared)	255

Bowling: Phadkar 15-1-80-1 Amarnath 21-3-78-4 Hazare 16.1-0-62-0 Mankad 37-4-135-4 Sarwate 3-0-16-0 Nayudu 2-0-22-0
Phadkar 10-1-28-1 Amarnath 20-3-52-3 Hazare 11-1-55-0 Mankad 18-4-74-0 Sarwate 5-0-41-0 Gul Mohammad 1-0-1-0

India Innings
MH Mankad	c Tallon b Johnston	116	b Johnston	13
CT Sarwate	c Tallon b Johnston	36	b Johnston	1
Gul Mohammad	c & b Dooland	12	c Morris b Johnson	28
VS Hazare	c Tallon b Barnes	17	c Barnes b Miller	10
*L Amarnath	lbw b Barnes	0	b Lindwall	8
DG Phadkar	not out	55	c Barnes b Johnston	13
HR Adhikari	st Tallon b Johnson	26	c Lindwall b Johnson	1
K Rai Singh	c Barnes b Johnson	2	c Tallon b Johnston	24
KM Rangnekar	c & b Johnson	6	c Hamence b Johnson	18
+PK Sen	b Johnson	4	c Hassett b Johnson	2
CS Nayudu	not out	4	not out	0
	(b 9, lb 3, nb 1)	13	(b 6, lb 1)	7
	(9 wickets declared)	291	(all out)	125

Bowling: Lindwall 12-0-47-0 Miller 13-2-46-0 Johnston 12-0-33-2 Johnson 14-1-59-4 Dooland 12-0-68-1 Barnes 6-1-25-2
Lindwall 3-0-10-1 Miller 7-0-29-1 Johnston 10-1-44-4 Johnson 5.7-0-35-4

Umpires: AN Barlow and HAR Elphinstone

Australia v India
6,7,9,10 February 1948

Result: Australia won by an innings and 177 runs

Australia Innings
SG Barnes	run out	33
WA Brown	not out	99
*DG Bradman	retired hurt	57
KR Miller	c Sen b Phadkar	14
RN Harvey	c Sen b Mankad	153
SJE Loxton	c Sen b Amarnath	80
RR Lindwall	c Phadkar b Mankad	35
+D Tallon	c Sen b Sarwate	37
LJ Johnson	not out	25
DT Ring	c Kishenchand b Hazare	11
WA Johnston	not out	23
	(b 4, lb 4)	8
	(8 wickets declared)	575

Bowling: Phadkar 9-0-58-1 Amarnath 23-1-79-1 Rangachari 17-1-97-0 Hazare 14-1-63-1 Mankad 33-2-107-2 Sarwate 18-1-82-1 Nayudu 13-0-77-0 Adhikari 1-0-4-0

India Innings
MH Mankad	c Tallon b Loxton	111	c Tallon b Lindwall	0
CT Sarwate	b Lindwall	0	lbw b Johnston	10
HR Adhikari	c Tallon b Loxton	38	c Bradman b Loxton	17
VS Hazare	lbw b Lindwall	74	c & b Johnson	10
*L Amarnath	c Barnes b Ring	12	c Johnston b Ring	8
DG Phadkar	not out	56	lbw b Johnson	0
Gul Mohammad	c Lindwall b Johnson	1	c Barnes b Ring	4
G Kishenchand	b Ring	14	c Barnes b Johnson	0
CS Nayudu	c Bradman b Ring	2	c Brown b Ring	0
+PK Sen	b Johnson	13	b Johnson	10
CR Rangachari	not out	0	not out	0
	(b 6, lb 2, nb 2)	10	(b 6, lb 1, nb 1)	8
	(all out)	331	(all out)	67

Bowling: Lindwall 25-5-66-2 Johnson 30-8-66-3 Loxton 19-1-61-2 Johnston 8-4-14-0 Ring 36-8-103-3 Miller 3-0-10-0 Barnes 2-1-1-0
Lindwall 3-0-9-1 Johnson 5.2-2-8-3 Loxton 4-1-10-1 Johnston 7-0-15-2 Ring 5-1-17-3

Umpires: AN Barlow and GS Cooper

Australia v England
22,23,26,27 December 1950

Result: Australia won by 28 runs

Australia Innings
KA Archer	c Bedser b Bailey	26	c Bailey b Bedser	46
AR Morris	c Hutton b Bedser	2	lbw b Wright	18
RN Harvey	c Evans b Bedser	42	run out	31
KR Miller	lbw b Brown	18	b Bailey	14
*AL Hassett	b Bailey	52	c Bailey b Brown	19
SJE Loxton	c Evans b Close	32	c Evans b Brown	7
RR Lindwall	lbw b Bailey	8	c Evans b Brown	7
+D Tallon	not out	7	lbw b Brown	0
IWG Johnson	c Parkhouse b Bedser	0	c Close b Bedser	23
WA Johnston	c Hutton b Bedser	6	b Bailey	6
JB Iverson	b Bailey	1	not out	0
	(b 4, lb 2)	6	(b 10, lb 5)	15
	(all out)	194	(all out)	181

Bowling: Bailey 17.1-5-40-4 Bedser 19-3-37-4 Wright 8-0-63-0 Brown 9-0-28-1 Close 6-1-20-1
Bailey 15-3-47-2 Bedser 16.3-2-43-2 Wright 9-0-42-1 Brown 12-2-26-4 Close 1-0-8-0

England Innings
RT Simpson	c Johnson b Miller	4	b Lindwall	23
C Washbrook	lbw b Lindwall	21	b Iverson	8
JG Dewes	c Miller b Lindwall	8	c Harvey b Iverson	5
L Hutton	c Tallon b Iverson	12	c Lindwall b Johnston	40
WGA Parkhouse	c Hassett b Miller	9	lbw b Johnston	28
DB Close	c Loxton b Iverson	0	lbw b Johnston	1
*FR Brown	c Johnson b Iverson	62	b Lindwall	8
TE Bailey	c Lindwall	12	b Johnson	0
+TG Evans	c Johnson b Iverson	49	b Lindwall	2
AV Bedser	not out	4	not out	14
DVP Wright	lbw b Johnston	2	lbw b Johnston	2
	(b 8, lb 6)	14	(b 17, lb 2)	19
	(all out)	197	(all out)	150

Bowling: Lindwall 13-2-46-2 Miller 13-0-39-2 Johnston 9-1-28-2 Iverson 18-3-37-4 Johnson 5-1-19-0 Loxton 4-1-14-0
Lindwall 12-1-29-3 Miller 5-2-16-0 Johnston 13.7-1-26-4 Iverson 20-4-36-2 Johnson 13-3-24-1

Umpires: GS Cooper and RJJ Wright

Australia v England
23,24,26,27,28 February 1951

Result: England won by 8 wickets

Australia Innings
JW Burke	c Tattersall b Bedser	11	c Hutton b Bedser	1
AR Morris	lbw b Brown	50	lbw b Bedser	4
*AL Hassett	c Hutton b Brown	92	b Wright	48
RN Harvey	c Evans b Brown	1	lbw b Wright	52
KR Miller	c & b Brown	7	c & b Brown	0
GB Hole	b Bedser	18	b Bailey	63
IWG Johnson	lbw b Bedser	1	c Brown b Wright	0
RR Lindwall	c Compton b Bedser	21	b Bedser	14
+D Tallon	c Hutton b Bedser	1	not out	2
WA Johnston	not out	12	b Bedser	1
JB Iverson	c Washbrook b Brown	0	c Compton b Bedser	0
	(b 2, lb 1)	3	(b 2, lb 8, w 1, nb 1)	12
	(all out)	217	(all out)	197

Bowling: Bedser 22-5-46-5 Bailey 9-1-29-0 Brown 18-4-49-5 Wright 11-1-50-0 Tattersall 11-3-40-0
Bedser 20.3-4-59-5 Bailey 15-3-32-1 Brown 9-1-32-1 Wright 12-2-56-3 Tattersall 5-2-6-0

England Innings
L Hutton	b Hole	79	not out	60
C Washbrook	c Tallon b Miller	27	c Lindwall b Johnston	7
RT Simpson	not out	156	run out	15
DCS Compton	c Miller b Lindwall	11	not out	11
DS Sheppard	c Tallon b Miller	1		
*FR Brown	b Lindwall	6		
+TG Evans	b Miller	1		
AV Bedser	b Lindwall	11		
TE Bailey	c Johnson b Iverson	5		
DVP Wright	lbw b Iverson	3		
R Tattersall	b Miller	10		
	(b 9, lb 1)	10	(lb 2)	2
	(all out)	320	(2 wickets)	95

Bowling: Lindwall 21-1-77-3 Miller 21.7-5-76-4 Johnston 12-1-55-0 Iverson 20-4-52-2 Johnson 11-1-40-0 Hole 5-0-10-1
Lindwall 2-0-12-0 Miller 2-0-5-0 Johnston 11-3-36-1 Iverson 12-2-32-0 Johnson 1-0-1-0 Hole 1-0-3-0 Hassett 0.6-0-4-0

Umpires: AN Barlow and HAR Elphinstone

Australia v West Indies
31 December 1951, 1,2,3 January 1952

Result: Australia won by 1 wicket

West Indies Innings
KR Rickards	b Miller	15	lbw b Johnston	22
JB Stollmeyer	c Langley b Miller	7	lbw b Miller	54
FMM Worrell	b Lindwall	108	b Johnston	30
ED Weekes	c Johnston b Johnston	1	lbw b Johnson	2
GE Gomez	c Langley b Miller	37	b Johnston	52
RJ Christiani	run out	37	b Miller	33
*JDC Goddard	b Miller	21	lbw b Lindwall	0
+SC Guillen	not out	22	c Johnston b Lindwall	0
J Trim	run out	0	run out	0
S Ramadhin	c Langley b Johnston	1	run out	0
AL Valentine	c Lindwall b Miller	14	not out	1
	(b 2, lb 6, w 1)	9	(b 4, lb 5)	9
	(all out)	272	(all out)	203

Bowling: Lindwall 18-2-72-1 Miller 19.3-1-60-5 Johnston 20-1-59-2 Ring 9-0-43-0 Johnson 7-0-23-0 Hole 2-0-6-0
Lindwall 17-2-59-2 Miller 16-1-49-2 Johnston 14.3-2-51-3 Ring 7-1-17-0 Johnson 5-0-18-1

Australia Innings
J Moroney	lbw b Ramadhin	26	lbw b Ramadhin	5
AR Morris	b Trim	6	lbw b Valentine	12
*AL Hassett	run out	15	lbw b Valentine	102
RN Harvey	c & b Ramadhin	83	b Valentine	33
KR Miller	b Trim	47	hit wicket b Valentine	2
GB Hole	b Valentine	2	c Gomez b Worrell	13
RR Lindwall	lbw b Trim	13	c Guillen b Ramadhin	29
IWG Johnson	c Guillen b Trim	1	c Guillen b Ramadhin	6
DT Ring	b Trim	6	not out	32
+GRA Langley	not out	0	lbw b Valentine	1
WA Johnston	b Gomez	1	not out	7
	(b 12, lb 4)	16	(b 14, lb 4)	18
	(all out)	216	(9 wickets)	260

Bowling: Trim 12-2-34-5 Gomez 13.3-7-25-1 Valentine 23-8-50-1 Ramadhin 17-4-63-2 Goddard 8-0-28-0
Trim 10-3-25-0 Gomez 9-2-18-0 Valentine 30-9-88-5 Ramadhin 39-15-93-3 Worrell 9-1-18-1

Umpires: MJ McInnes and RJJ Wright

Melbourne Cricket Ground

Australia v South Africa
24,26,27,29,30 December 1952

Result: South Africa won by 82 runs

South Africa Innings

DJ McGlew	b Lindwall	46	st Langley b Ring	13
+JHB Waite	c Lindwall b Miller	0	c Hole b Miller	62
WR Endean	c Benaud b Lindwall	2	not out	162
KJ Funston	c Ring b Miller	9	run out	26
RA McLean	c Lindwall b Ring	27	lbw b Miller	42
*JE Cheetham	c Johnston b Miller	15	lbw b Johnston	6
JC Watkins	c Langley b Benaud	19	b Johnston	3
PNF Mansell	b Lindwall	24	b Miller	18
ARA Murray	c Johnston b Benaud	51	st Langley b Ring	23
HJ Tayfield	c Langley b Miller	23	lbw b Lindwall	22
MG Melle	not out	4	b Lindwall	0
	(b 4, lb 3)	7	(b 1, lb 5, w 4, nb 1)	11
	(all out)	227	(all out)	388

Bowling: Lindwall 14-2-29-3 Miller 21-3-62-4 Johnston 12-2-37-0 Ring 18-1-72-1 Benaud 6.6-1-20-2
Lindwall 31.5-4-87-2 Miller 22-5-51-3 Johnston 31-9-77-2 Ring 31-5-115-2 Benaud 6-0-23-0 Hole 7-0-24-0

Australia Innings

CC McDonald	c sub b Mansell	82	c Mansell b Murray	23
AR Morris	c & b Tayfield	43	c Watkins b Melle	1
RN Harvey	c Cheetham b Tayfield	11	c Watkins b Tayfield	60
*AL Hassett	c Melle b Mansell	18	lbw b Mansell	21
KR Miller	c Endean b Tayfield	52	b Tayfield	31
GB Hole	c Waite b Mansell	13	b Tayfield	25
R Benaud	b Tayfield	5	c Melle b Tayfield	45
RR Lindwall	run out	1	b Melle	19
DT Ring	c McGlew b Tayfield	14	c Melle b Tayfield	53
+GRA Langley	not out	2	b Tayfield	4
WA Johnston	lbw b Tayfield	0	not out	0
	(nb 2)	2	(b 1, lb 6, nb 1)	8
	(all out)	243	(all out)	290

Bowling: Melle 14-0-73-0 Watkins 6-1-15-0 Murray 3-1-11-0 Tayfield 29.4-9-84-6 Mansell 19-3-58-3
Melle 11-1-39-2 Watkins 10-2-34-0 Murray 23-7-59-1 Tayfield 37.1-13-81-7 Mansell 14-2-69-0

Umpires: HAR Elphinstone and MJ McInnes

Australia v South Africa
6,7,9,10,11,12 February 1953

Result: South Africa won by 6 wickets

Australia Innings

CC McDonald	c McLean b Mansell	41	c Watkins b Fuller	11
AR Morris	run out	99	lbw b Tayfield	44
RN Harvey	c Cheetham b Fuller	205	b Fuller	7
*AL Hassett	run out	40	c Endean b Mansell	30
ID Craig	c Keith b Fuller	53	c Endean b Tayfield	47
RG Archer	c Waite b Fuller	18	c Watkins b Tayfield	0
R Benaud	c & b Tayfield	20	c Watkins b Fuller	30
DT Ring	b Tayfield	14	c Endean b Mansell	0
+GRA Langley	b Murray	2	not out	26
WA Johnston	c Endean b Tayfield	12	c Cheetham b Fuller	5
G Noblet	not out	13	b Fuller	1
	(lb 3)	3	(b 7, lb 1)	8
	(all out)	520	(all out)	209

Bowling: Fuller 19-4-74-3 Watkins 23-3-72-0 Tayfield 35.4-4-129-3 Murray 25-3-84-1 Mansell 22-0-114-1 Keith 9-0-44-0
Fuller 30.2-4-66-5 Watkins 14-4-33-0 Tayfield 32-8-73-3 Mansell 8-3-29-2

South Africa Innings

WR Endean	c Langley b Johnston	16	b Johnston	70
+JHB Waite	run out	64	c Archer b Noblet	18
JC Watkins	b Archer	92	b Ring	50
KJ Funston	lbw b Johnston	16	b Benaud	35
HJ Keith	b Johnston	10	not out	40
RA McLean	lbw b Noblet	81	not out	76
*JE Cheetham	c McDonald b Johnston	66		
PNF Mansell	lbw b Johnston	52		
ARA Murray	c & b Johnston	17		
HJ Tayfield	c Benaud b Ring	17		
ERH Fuller	not out	0		
	(b 1, lb 3)	4	(b 2, lb 6)	8
	(all out)	435	(4 wickets)	297

Bowling: Noblet 30-6-65-1 Archer 33-4-97-1 Johnston 46-8-152-6 Ring 19-1-62-1 Benaud 15-3-55-0
Noblet 24-9-44-1 Archer 5-0-23-0 Johnston 38-7-114-1 Ring 13-2-55-1 Benaud 15-4-41-1 Hassett 0.5-0-12-0

Umpires: MJ McInnes and RJJ Wright

Australia v England
31 December 1954, 1,3,4,5 January 1955

Result: England won by 128 runs

England Innings

*L Hutton	c Hole b Miller	12	lbw b Archer	42
WJ Edrich	c Lindwall b Miller	4	b Johnston	13
PBH May	c Benaud b Lindwall	0	b Johnston	91
MC Cowdrey	b Johnson	102	b Benaud	7
DCS Compton	c Harvey b Miller	4	c Maddocks b Archer	23
TE Bailey	c Maddocks b Johnston	30	not out	24
+TG Evans	lbw b Archer	20	c Maddocks b Miller	22
JH Wardle	b Archer	0	b Johnson	38
FH Tyson	b Archer	6	c Harvey b Johnston	6
JB Statham	b Archer	3	c Favell b Johnston	0
R Appleyard	not out	1	b Johnston	6
	(b 9)	9	(b 2, lb 4, w 1)	7
	(all out)	191	(all out)	279

Bowling: Lindwall 13-0-59-1 Miller 11-8-14-3 Archer 13.6-4-33-4 Benaud 7-0-30-0 Johnston 12-6-26-1 Johnson 11-3-20-1
Lindwall 18-3-52-0 Miller 18-6-35-1 Archer 24-7-50-2 Benaud 8-2-25-1 Johnston 24.5-2-85-5 Johnson 8-2-25-1

Australia Innings

CC McDonald	lbw b Statham	25	b Appleyard	30
AR Morris	lbw b Tyson	3	c Cowdrey b Tyson	4
KR Miller	c Evans b Statham	7	c Edrich b Tyson	6
RN Harvey	b Appleyard	31	c Evans b Statham	11
GB Hole	b Tyson	11	c Evans b Statham	5
R Benaud	c sub b Appleyard	15	b Tyson	22
RG Archer	b Wardle	23	b Statham	15
+LV Maddocks	c Evans b Statham	47	b Tyson	0
RR Lindwall	b Statham	13	lbw b Tyson	0
*IWG Johnson	not out	33	not out	4
WA Johnston	b Statham	11	c Evans b Tyson	0
	(b 7, lb 3, nb 2)	12	(b 1, lb 13)	14
	(all out)	231	(all out)	111

Bowling: Tyson 21-2-68-2 Statham 16.3-0-60-5 Bailey 9-1-33-0 Appleyard 11-3-38-2 Wardle 6-0-20-1
Tyson 12.3-1-27-7 Statham 11-1-38-2 Bailey 3-0-14-0 Appleyard 4-1-17-1 Wardle 1-0-1-0

Umpires: C Hoy and MJ McInnes

Australia v England
31 December 1958, 1,2,3,5 January 1959

Result: Australia won by 8 wickets

England Innings

PE Richardson	c Grout b Davidson	3	c Harvey b Meckiff	2
TE Bailey	c Benaud b Meckiff	48	c Burke b Meckiff	14
W Watson	b Davidson	0	b Davidson	7
TW Graveney	lbw b Davidson	0	c Davidson b Meckiff	3
*PBH May	b Meckiff	113	c Davidson b Meckiff	17
MC Cowdrey	c Grout b Davidson	44	c Grout b Meckiff	12
+TG Evans	c Davidson b Meckiff	4	run out	11
GAR Lock	st Grout b Benaud	5	c & b Davidson	6
JC Laker	not out	22	c Harvey b Davidson	3
JB Statham	b Davidson	13	not out	8
PJ Loader	b Davidson	1	b Meckiff	0
	(b 1, lb 2, w 3)	6	(b 1, lb 1, nb 2)	4
	(all out)	259	(all out)	87

Bowling: Davidson 25.5-7-64-6 Meckiff 24-4-69-3 Mackay 9-2-16-0 Benaud 29-7-61-1 Kline 11-2-43-0
Davidson 15-2-41-3 Meckiff 15.2-3-38-6 Benaud 1-0-4-0

Australia Innings

CC McDonald	c Graveney b Statham	47	lbw b Statham	5
JW Burke	b Statham	3	not out	18
RN Harvey	b Loader	167	not out	7
NC O'Neill	c Evans b Statham	37		
KD Mackay	c Evans b Statham	18		
RB Simpson	lbw b Loader	0		
*R Benaud	lbw b Statham	0		
AK Davidson	b Statham	24		
+ATW Grout	c May b Loader	8	st Evans b Laker	12
I Meckiff	b Statham	1		
LF Kline	not out	1		
	(lb 3)	3		0
	(all out)	308	(2 wickets)	42

Bowling: Statham 28-6-57-7 Loader 27.2-4-97-3 Bailey 16-0-50-0 Laker 12-1-47-0 Lock 17-2-54-0
Statham 5-1-11-1 Loader 5-1-13-0 Laker 4-1-7-1 Lock 3.1-1-11-0

Umpires: MJ McInnes and RJJ Wright

Australia v England
13,14,16,17,18 February 1959

Result: Australia won by 9 wickets

England Innings

PE Richardson	c & b Benaud	68	lbw b Benaud	23
TE Bailey	c Davidson b Lindwall	0	b Lindwall	0
*PBH May	c Benaud b Meckiff	11	c Harvey b Lindwall	4
MC Cowdrey	c Lindwall b Davidson	22	run out	46
TW Graveney	c McDonald b Benaud	19	c Harvey b Davidson	54
ER Dexter	c Lindwall b Meckiff	0	c Grout b Davidson	6
+R Swetman	c Grout b Davidson	1	b Lindwall	9
JB Mortimore	not out	44	b Rorke	11
FS Trueman	c & b Benaud	21	b Rorke	36
FH Tyson	c Grout b Benaud	9	c Grout b Rorke	6
JC Laker	c Harvey b Davidson	2	not out	5
	(b 4, w 4)	8	(b 9, lb 3, w 2)	14
	(all out)	205	(all out)	214

Bowling: Davidson 12.5-2-38-3 Lindwall 14-2-36-1 Meckiff 15-2-57-2 Rorke 6-1-23-0 Benaud 17-5-43-4
Davidson 21-1-95-2 Lindwall 11-2-37-3 Meckiff 4-0-13-0 Rorke 12.4-2-41-3 Benaud 6-1-14-1

Australia Innings

CC McDonald	c Cowdrey b Laker	133	not out	51
JW Burke	c Trueman b Tyson	16	lbw b Tyson	13
RN Harvey	c Swetman b Trueman	13	not out	1
NC O'Neill	c Cowdrey b Trueman	0		
KD Mackay	c Graveney b Laker	23		
AK Davidson	b Mortimore	17		
*R Benaud	c Swetman b Laker	64		
+ATW Grout	c Trueman b Laker	74		
RR Lindwall	c Cowdrey b Trueman	2		
I Meckiff	c & b Trueman	0		
GF Rorke	not out	0		
	(b 5, lb 4)	9	(lb 4)	4
	(all out)	351	(1 wicket)	69

Bowling: Trueman 25-0-92-4 Tyson 20-1-73-1 Bailey 14-2-43-0 Laker 30.5-4-93-4 Mortimore 11-1-41-1
Trueman 6.7-0-45-0 Tyson 6-0-20-1

Umpires: LH Townsend and RJJ Wright

Australia v West Indies
30,31 December 1960, 2,3 January 1961

Result: Australia won by 7 wickets

Australia Innings

CC McDonald	c Watson b Hall	15	c Sobers b Hall	13
RB Simpson	c Alexander b Hall	49	not out	27
RN Harvey	c Sobers b Worrell	12	c Alexander b Hall	0
NC O'Neill	c Sobers b Worrell	40	lbw b Watson	0
LE Favell	c Nurse b Sobers	51	not out	24
KD Mackay	b Ramadhin	74		
AK Davidson	b Hall	35		
*R Benaud	b Hall	2		
+ATW Grout	b Watson	5		
JW Martin	b Valentine	55		
FM Misson	not out	0		
	(lb 7, w 1, nb 2)	10	(b 4, lb 1, nb 1)	6
	(all out)	348	(3 wickets)	70

Bowling: Hall 12-2-51-4 Watson 12-1-73-1 Sobers 17-1-88-1 Worrell 9-0-50-2 Valentine 11.1-1-55-1 Ramadhin 5-0-21-1
Hall 9.4-0-32-2 Watson 9-1-32-1

West Indies Innings

CC Hunte	c Simpson b Misson	1	c Grout b O'Neill	110
JS Solomon	c Grout b Davidson	0	hit wicket b Benaud	4
SM Nurse	c Grout b Davidson	70	run out	3
RB Kanhai	c Harvey b Davidson	84	c Misson b Martin	25
GS Sobers	c Simpson b Benaud	9	c Simpson b Martin	0
*FMM Worrell	b Misson	0	c Simpson b Martin	0
+FCM Alexander	c Favell b Davidson	5	c Grout b Davidson	72
S Ramadhin	b Davidson	5	st Grout b Benaud	3
WW Hall	b Davidson	5	b Davidson	4
CD Watson	c McDonald b Benaud	4	run out	5
AL Valentine	not out	1	not out	0
	(nb 2)	2	(b 2, lb 2, w 1, nb 2)	7
	(all out)	181	(all out)	233

Bowling: Davidson 22-4-53-6 Misson 11-0-36-2 Benaud 27.2-10-58-2 Martin 8-1-32-0 Simpson 1-1-0-0
Davidson 15.4-2-51-2 Misson 12-3-36-0 Benaud 20-3-49-2 Martin 20-3-56-3 Simpson 8-0-24-0 O'Neill 5-1-10-1

Umpires: CJ Egar and C Hoy

Australia v West Indies
10,11,13,14,15 February 1961

Result: Australia won by 2 wickets

West Indies Innings

CW Smith	c O'Neill b Misson	11	lbw b Davidson	37
CC Hunte	c Simpson b Davidson	31	c Grout b Davidson	52
RB Kanhai	c Harvey b Benaud	38	c Misson b Benaud	31
GS Sobers	c Grout b Simpson	64	c Grout b Simpson	21
*FMM Worrell	c Grout b Martin	10	c Grout b Davidson	7
PD Lashley	c Misson b Benaud	41	lbw b Martin	18
+FCM Alexander	c McDonald b Misson	11	c Mackay b Davidson	73
JS Solomon	run out	45	run out	36
LR Gibbs	c Burge b Misson	11	c O'Neill b Simpson	8
WW Hall	b Misson	21	c Grout b Davidson	21
AL Valentine	not out	0	not out	3
	(b 4, lb 4, w 1)	9	(b 5, lb 8, w 1)	14
	(all out)	292	(all out)	321

Bowling: Davidson 27-4-89-1 Misson 14-3-58-4 Mackay 1-0-1-0 Benaud 21.7-5-55-2 Martin 8-0-29-1 Simpson 18-3-51-1
Davidson 24.7-4-84-5 Misson 10-1-58-0 Mackay 10-2-21-0 Benaud 23-4-53-1 Martin 10-1-36-1 Simpson 18-4-55-2

Australia Innings

RB Simpson	c Gibbs b Sobers	75	b Gibbs	92
CC McDonald	lbw b Sobers	91	c Smith b Gibbs	11
NC O'Neill	b Gibbs	10	c Alexander b Worrell	48
PJP Burge	c Sobers b Gibbs	68	b Valentine	53
KD Mackay	c Alexander b Hall	19	not out	3
RN Harvey	c Alexander b Sobers	5	c Smith b Worrell	12
AK Davidson	c Alexander b Sobers	24	c Sobers b Worrell	12
*R Benaud	b Gibbs	3	b Valentine	6
JW Martin	c Kanhai b Sobers	15	not out	1
FM Misson	not out	12		
+ATW Grout	c Hunte b Gibbs	14	c Smith b Valentine	5
	(b 4, lb 8, nb 8)	20	(b 3, lb 9, nb 3)	15
	(all out)	356	(8 wickets)	258

Bowling: Hall 15-1-56-1 Worrell 11-2-44-0 Sobers 44-7-120-5 Gibbs 38.4-18-74-4 Valentine 13-3-42-0
Hall 5-0-40-0 Worrell 31-16-43-3 Sobers 13-2-32-0 Gibbs 41-19-68-2 Valentine 21.7-4-60-3

Umpires: CJ Egar and C Hoy

Australia v England
29,31 December 1962, 1,2,3 January 1963

Result: England won by 7 wickets

Australia Innings

WM Lawry	b Trueman	52	b Dexter	57
RB Simpson	c Smith b Coldwell	38	b Trueman	14
NC O'Neill	c Graveney b Statham	19	c Cowdrey b Trueman	0
RN Harvey	b Coldwell	0	run out	10
PJP Burge	lbw b Titmus	23	b Statham	14
BC Booth	c Barrington b Titmus	27	c Trueman b Statham	103
AK Davidson	c Smith b Trueman	40	c Smith b Titmus	17
KD Mackay	lbw b Titmus	49	lbw b Trueman	9
*R Benaud	c Barrington b Titmus	36	c Cowdrey b Trueman	4
GD McKenzie	b Trueman	16	b Trueman	0
+BN Jarman	not out	10	not out	11
	(b 2, lb 4)	6	(b 4, lb 5)	9
	(all out)	316	(all out)	248

Bowling: Trueman 23-1-83-3 Statham 22-2-83-1 Coldwell 17-2-58-2 Barrington 6-0-23-0 Dexter 6-1-10-0 Titmus 15-2-43-4 Graveney 3-1-10-0
Trueman 20-1-62-5 Statham 23-1-52-2 Coldwell 25-2-60-0 Barrington 5-0-22-0 Dexter 9-2-18-1 Titmus 14-4-25-1

England Innings

Rev.DS Sheppard	lbw b Davidson	0	run out	113
G Pullar	b Davidson	11	c Jarman b McKenzie	5
*ER Dexter	c Simpson b Benaud	93	run out	52
MC Cowdrey	c Burge b McKenzie	113	not out	58
KF Barrington	lbw b McKenzie	35	not out	0
TW Graveney	run out	41		
FJ Titmus	c Jarman b Davidson	15		
+AC Smith	not out	6		
FS Trueman	c O'Neill b Davidson	6		
JB Statham	b Davidson	1		
LJ Coldwell	c Benaud b Davidson	1		
	(b 4, lb 4, nb 1)	9	(b 5, lb 3, nb 1)	9
	(all out)	331	(3 wickets)	237

Bowling: Davidson 23.1-4-75-6 McKenzie 29-3-95-2 Mackay 6-2-17-0 Benaud 18-3-82-1 Simpson 7-1-34-0 O'Neill 5-1-19-0
Davidson 19-2-53-0 McKenzie 20-3-58-1 Mackay 9-0-34-0 Benaud 14-1-69-0 Simpson 2-0-10-0 Booth 0.2-0-4-0

Umpires: CJ Egar and WJ Smyth

Australia v South Africa
1,2,3,4,6 January 1964

Result: Australia won by 8 wickets

South Africa Innings

*TL Goddard	c Grout b McKenzie	17	lbw b Hawke	8
EJ Barlow	c Connolly b McKenzie	109	run out	54
AJ Pithey	lbw b Connolly	21	c Grout b Connolly	76
RG Pollock	c Simpson b McKenzie	16	c Martin b Connolly	2
+JHB Waite	c Grout b Hawke	14	b McKenzie	77
PL van der Merwe	st Grout b Martin	14	c Grout b Martin	31
KC Bland	run out	50	c & b Martin	22
DB Pithey	c Grout b McKenzie	0	c Martin b Hawke	4
PM Pollock	c Simpson b Martin	14	b Hawke	0
MA Seymour	not out	7	not out	11
JT Partridge	run out	9	b McKenzie	12
	(lb 3)	3	(b 2, lb 3, w 2, nb 2)	9
	(all out)	274	(all out)	306

Bowling: McKenzie 19-1-82-4 Hawke 20-2-77-1 Connolly 18-2-62-1 Martin 16-3-44-2 Veivers 5-1-6-0
McKenzie 25-1-81-2 Hawke 19-1-53-3 Connolly 18-2-49-2 Martin 27-4-83-2 Simpson 12-2-31-0

Australia Innings

WM Lawry	c sub b Partridge	157	b Partridge	20
IR Redpath	b Partridge	97	c van der Merwe b Barlow	25
*RB Simpson	b PM Pollock	0	not out	55
PJP Burge	c Bland b PM Pollock	23	not out	26
BK Shepherd	c DB Pithey b Barlow	96		
+ATW Grout	c Waite b PM Pollock	3		
TR Veivers	c Waite b Partridge	19		
GD McKenzie	c Partridge b Seymour	2		
NJN Hawke	b Barlow	24		
JW Martin	c DB Pithey b Partridge	17		
AN Connolly	not out	0		
	(b 1, lb 2, nb 6)	9	(b 5, lb 2, w 1, nb 2)	10
	(all out)	447	(2 wickets)	136

Bowling: PM Pollock 20.5-1-98-3 Partridge 34-4-108-4 Bland 11-2-35-0 Goddard 21-2-70-0 DB Pithey 5-1-20-0 Seymour 19-2-56-1 Barlow 7.6-0-51-2
Partridge 17-1-49-1 Bland 2-0-6-0 Goddard 1-1-0-0 DB Pithey 6-0-18-0 Barlow 11-0-49-1 van der Merwe 0.1-0-4-0

Umpires: CJ Egar and LP Rowan

Australia v Pakistan
4,5,7,8 December 1964

Result: Match drawn

Pakistan Innings

+Abdul Kadir	c Chappell b McKenzie	0	c Jarman b Hawke	35
Mohammad Ilyas	run out	6	lbw b McKenzie	3
Saeed Ahmed	c Chappell b Hawke	80	c Chappell b McKenzie	24
Javed Burki	c Simpson b McKenzie	29	b Hawke	47
*Hanif Mohammad	c McKenzie b Sincock	104	st Jarman b Veivers	93
Nasim-ul-Ghani	b McKenzie	27	b Sincock	10
Asif Iqbal	c McKenzie b Hawke	1	c Jarman b Hawke	15
Intikhab Alam	c Shepherd b Hawke	13	c Simpson b Hawke	61
Afaq Hussain	not out	8	not out	13
Arif Butt	c Chappell b Sincock	7	c Jarman b McKenzie	12
Farooq Hamid	b Sincock	0	b McKenzie	3
	(b 4, lb 4, w 3, nb 1)	12	(b 5, lb 2, w 2, nb 1)	10
	(all out)	287	(all out)	326

Bowling: McKenzie 22-5-66-3 Hawke 21-1-69-3 Sincock 17.6-0-67-3 Simpson 9-1-21-0 Chappell 15-2-49-0 Veivers 3-2-3-0
McKenzie 24.4-1-74-4 Hawke 21-2-72-4 Sincock 28-5-102-1 Chappell 11-2-31-0 Veivers 12-4-37-1

Australia Innings

*RB Simpson	b Arif Butt	47	c Hanif Mohammad b Arif Butt	1
WM Lawry	c Hanif Mohammad b Arif Butt	41	run out	19
IM Chappell	c Hanif Mohammad b Farooq Hamid	11		
BK Shepherd	c sub b Asif Iqbal	55	not out	43
BC Booth	c Hanif Mohammad b Arif Butt	57		
RM Cowper	c Intikhab Alam b Saeed Ahmed	83		
TR Veivers	c Hanif Mohammad b Arif Butt	88	not out	16
+BN Jarman	b Asif Iqbal	33		
DJ Sincock	b Arif Butt	7		
GD McKenzie	b Arif Butt	1		
NJN Hawke	not out	1		
	(b 6, lb 3, w 1, nb 14)	24	(b 2, lb 4, w 2, nb 1)	9
	(all out)	448	(2 wickets)	88

Bowling: Farooq Hamid 19-1-82-1 Asif Iqbal 19-1-90-2 Arif Butt 21.3-1-89-6 Afaq Hussain 9-1-45-0 Intikhab Alam 10-0-51-0 Saeed Ahmed 10-0-31-1 Nasim-ul-Ghani 4-0-36-0
Farooq Hamid 4-0-25-0 Arif Butt 5.5-0-29-1 Asif Iqbal 2-0-25-0

Umpires: CJ Egar and WJ Smyth

Australia v England
30,31 December 1965, 1,3,4 January 1966

Result: Match drawn

Australia Innings

*RB Simpson	c Edrich b Allen	59	c Barrington b Knight	67
WM Lawry	c Cowdrey b Allen	88	c Smith b Barber	78
PJP Burge	b Jones	5	c Edrich b Boycott	120
RM Cowper	c Titmus b Jones	99	lbw b Jones	5
BC Booth	lbw b Jones	23	b Allen	10
KD Walters	c Parks b Knight	22	c & b Barrington	115
TR Veivers	run out	19	st Parks b Boycott	3
PI Philpott	b Knight	10	b Knight	2
+ATW Grout	c Barber b Knight	11	c Allen b Barrington	16
GD McKenzie	not out	12	run out	2
AN Connolly	c Parks b Knight	0	not out	0
	(b 2, lb 7, nb 1)	10	(b 1, lb 3, w 1, nb 3)	8
	(all out)	358	(all out)	426

Bowling: Jones 24-4-92-3 Knight 26.5-2-84-4 Titmus 31-7-93-0 Allen 20-4-55-2 Barber 6-1-24-0
Jones 20-1-92-1 Knight 21-4-61-2 Titmus 22-6-43-0 Allen 18-3-48-1 Barber 17-0-87-1 Barrington 7.4-0-47-2 Boycott 9-0-32-2 Smith 2-0-8-0

England Innings

G Boycott	c McKenzie b Walters	51	not out	5
RW Barber	c Grout b McKenzie	48	not out	0
JH Edrich	c & b Veivers	109		
KF Barrington	c Burge b Veivers	63		
MC Cowdrey	c Connolly b Cowper	104		
*MJK Smith	c Grout b McKenzie	41		
+JM Parks	c Cowper b McKenzie	71		
BR Knight	c Simpson b McKenzie	1		
FJ Titmus	not out	56		
DA Allen	c Grout b Connolly	2		
IJ Jones	b McKenzie	1		
	(b 4, lb 5, w 2)	11		0
	(all out)	558	(0 wickets)	5

Bowling: McKenzie 35.2-3-134-5 Connolly 37-5-125-1 Philpott 30-2-133-0 Walters 10-2-32-1 Simpson 16-4-61-0 Veivers 12-3-46-2 Cowper 3-0-16-1
McKenzie 1-0-2-0 Connolly 1-0-3-0

Umpires: CJ Egar and WJ Smyth

Australia v England
11,12,14,15,16 February 1966

Result: Match drawn

England Innings

G Boycott	c Stackpole b McKenzie	17	lbw b McKenzie	1
RW Barber	run out	17	b McKenzie	20
JH Edrich	c McKenzie b Walters	85	b McKenzie	3
KF Barrington	c Grout b Walters	115	not out	32
MC Cowdrey	c Grout b Walters	79	not out	11
*MJK Smith	c Grout b Walters	0		
+JM Parks	run out	89		
FJ Titmus	not out	42		
BR Knight	c Grout b Hawke	13		
DJ Brown	c & b Chappell	12		
IJ Jones	not out	4		
	(b 9, lb 2, nb 1)	12	(lb 2)	2
	(9 wickets declared)	485	(3 wickets)	69

Bowling: McKenzie 26-5-100-1 Hawke 35-5-109-1 Walters 19-3-53-4 Simpson 5-1-20-0 Stackpole 10-2-43-0 Veivers 15-3-78-0 Chappell 17-4-70-1
McKenzie 6-2-17-3 Hawke 4-1-22-0 Walters 2-0-16-0 Stackpole 3-0-10-0 Chappell 2-0-2-0

Australia Innings

WM Lawry	c Edrich b Jones	108
*RB Simpson	b Brown	4
G Thomas	c Titmus b Jones	19
RM Cowper	b Knight	307
KD Walters	c & b Barber	60
IM Chappell	c Parks b Jones	19
KR Stackpole	b Knight	9
TR Veivers	b Titmus	4
NJN Hawke	not out	0
+ATW Grout		
GD McKenzie		
	(b 6, lb 5, nb 2)	13
	(8 wickets declared)	543

Bowling: Brown 31-3-134-1 Jones 29-1-145-3 Knight 36.2-4-105-2 Titmus 42-12-86-1 Barber 16-0-60-1

Umpires: CJ Egar and LP Rowan

Melbourne Cricket Ground

Australia v India
30 December 1967, 1,2,3 January 1968

Result: Australia won by an innings and 4 runs

India Innings

DN Sardesai	b McKenzie	1	b McKenzie	5
+FM Engineer	c Connolly b McKenzie	9	c Chappell b Renneberg	42
S Abid Ali	c Jarman b McKenzie	4	lbw b Cowper	21
AL Wadekar	c Connolly b McKenzie	6	c Sheahan b Simpson	99
RF Surti	lbw b Simpson	30	c Jarman b McKenzie	43
CG Borde	c Redpath b McKenzie	0	c Redpath b Renneberg	6
*Nawab of Pataudi jnr	c Jarman b Renneberg	75	c Redpath b Simpson	85
V Subramanya	b McKenzie	5	lbw b McKenzie	10
EAS Prasanna	c Chappell b Renneberg	14	c Chappell b Simpson	21
RB Desai	not out	13	c Simpson b Connolly	14
BS Chandrasekhar	c Jarman b McKenzie	0	not out	0
	(b 8, lb 2, nb 6)	16	(b 1, lb 4, nb 1)	6
	(all out)	173	(all out)	352

Bowling: McKenzie 21.4-2-66-7 Renneberg 15-4-37-2 Connolly 13-3-33-0 Gleeson 5-0-9-0 Chappell 1-0-7-0 Simpson 2-0-5-1
McKenzie 19-2-85-3 Renneberg 14-1-98-2 Connolly 11.7-2-48-1 Gleeson 14-5-37-0 Chappell 4-0-14-0 Simpson 14-3-44-3
Cowper 8-2-20-1

Australia Innings

*RB Simpson	b Surti	109
WM Lawry	st Engineer b Prasanna	100
AP Sheahan	c Engineer b Surti	24
RM Cowper	b Prasanna	12
IM Chappell	c Wadekar b Surti	151
IR Redpath	run out	26
+BN Jarman	b Prasanna	65
GD McKenzie	c sub b Prasanna	0
JW Gleeson	c Borde b Prasanna	13
AN Connolly	c sub b Prasanna	5
DA Renneberg	not out	8
	(b 3, lb 10, nb 3)	16
	(all out)	529

Bowling: Desai 12-0-63-0 Surti 29.3-4-150-3 Abid Ali 20-0-106-0 Chandrasekhar 7-0-35-0 Prasanna 34-6-141-6 Subramanya
3-0-18-0

Umpires: CJ Egar and LP Rowan

Australia v West Indies
26,27,28,30 December 1968

Result: Australia won by an innings and 30 runs

West Indies Innings

GS Camacho	c Chappell b McKenzie	0	lbw b Gleeson	11
RC Fredericks	c Redpath b McKenzie	76	c Freeman b Gleeson	47
MC Carew	c Gleeson b McKenzie	7	b Stackpole	33
SM Nurse	c Jarman b Freeman	22	c Stackpole b Gleeson	74
BF Butcher	lbw b Gleeson	42	c Jarman b McKenzie	0
*GS Sobers	b McKenzie	19	lbw b McKenzie	67
RB Kanhai	c Sheahan b McKenzie	5	c Redpath b Freeman	4
CA Davis	b McKenzie	18	c Redpath b Gleeson	10
+JL Hendriks	c Chappell b McKenzie	0	c Stackpole b Gleeson	3
RM Edwards	not out	9	run out	21
LR Gibbs	b McKenzie	0	not out	0
	(b 1, lb 1)	2	(b 7, lb 3)	10
	(all out)	200	(all out)	280

Bowling: McKenzie 25-5-71-8 Connolly 12-2-34-0 Freeman 7-0-32-1 Gleeson 25-8-49-1 Stackpole 1-0-12-0
McKenzie 20-2-88-2 Connolly 19-7-35-0 Freeman 11-1-31-1 Gleeson 26.4-9-61-5 Stackpole 13-9-19-1 Chappell 9-1-36-0

Australia Innings

IR Redpath	c Hendriks b Edwards	7
*WM Lawry	c Carew b Davis	205
IM Chappell	b Sobers	165
KD Walters	c Camacho b Sobers	76
KR Stackpole	b Gibbs	15
AP Sheahan	c & b Sobers	18
+BN Jarman	c Butcher b Gibbs	12
EW Freeman	c Carew b Gibbs	2
GD McKenzie	b Sobers	1
JW Gleeson	b Gibbs	0
AN Connolly	not out	3
	(lb 4, nb 2)	6
	(all out)	510

Bowling: Sobers 33.3-4-97-4 Edwards 26-1-128-1 Davis 24-0-94-1 Gibbs 43-8-139-4 Carew 10-2-46-0

Umpires: CJ Egar and LP Rowan

Australia v England
21,22,23,25,26 January 1971

Result: Match drawn

Australia Innings

KR Stackpole	c Lever b D'Oliveira	30	c Knott b Willis	18
*WM Lawry	c Snow b Willis	56	c sub b Snow	42
IM Chappell	c Luckhurst b Snow	111	b Underwood	30
IR Redpath	b Snow	72	c Knott b Snow	5
KD Walters	b Underwood	55	not out	39
GS Chappell	c Edrich b Willis	3	not out	20
+RW Marsh	not out	92		
KJ O'Keeffe	c Luckhurst b Illingworth	27		
JW Gleeson	c Cowdrey b Willis	5		
JRF Duncan	c Edrich b Illingworth	3		
AL Thomson	not out	0		
	(b 10, lb 17, nb 12)	39	(b 8, lb 3, nb 4)	15
	(9 wickets declared)	493	(4 wickets declared)	169

Bowling: Snow 29-6-94-2 Lever 25-6-79-0 D'Oliveira 22-6-71-1 Willis 20-5-73-3 Underwood 19-4-78-1 Illingworth 13-0-59-2
Snow 12-4-21-2 Lever 12-1-53-0 Willis 10-1-42-1 Underwood 12-0-38-1

England Innings

G Boycott	c Redpath b Thomson	12	not out	76
BW Luckhurst	b Walters	109	not out	74
JH Edrich	c Marsh b Thomson	9		
MC Cowdrey	c & b Gleeson	13		
BL D'Oliveira	c Marsh b Thomson	117		
*R Illingworth	c Redpath b Thomson	41		
+APE Knott	lbw b Stackpole	19		
JA Snow	b IM Chappell	1		
P Lever	run out	19		
DL Underwood	c & b Gleeson	5		
RGD Willis	not out	5		
	(b 17, lb 14, nb 11)	42	(b 1, lb 8, nb 2)	11
	(all out)	392	(0 wickets)	161

Bowling: Thomson 34-5-110-3 Duncan 14-4-30-0 GS Chappell 8-0-21-0 O'Keeffe 31-11-71-0 Gleeson 25-7-60-3 Stackpole
17.5-4-41-1 Walters 5-2-7-1 IM Chappell 3-0-10-1
Thomson 11-5-26-0 GS Chappell 5-0-19-0 O'Keeffe 19-3-45-0 Gleeson 3-1-18-0 Stackpole 13-2-28-0 Walters 7-1-14-0

Umpires: MG O'Connell and LP Rowan

Australia v Pakistan
29,30 December 1972, 1,2,3 January 1973

Result: Australia won by 92 runs

Australia Innings

IR Redpath	c Saeed Ahmed b Intikhab Alam	135	c Wasim Bari b Saleem Altaf	6
AP Sheahan	run out	23	c Sarfraz Nawaz b Asif Masood	127
*IM Chappell	c Wasim Bari b Majid Khan	66	st Wasim Bari b Majid Khan	9
GS Chappell	not out	116	run out	62
J Benaud	c Sarfraz Nawaz b Intikhab Alam	13	c Wasim Bari b Saleem Altaf	142
+RW Marsh	c Wasim Bari b Sarfraz Nawaz	74	c Asif Iqbal b Asif Masood	3
KJ O'Keeffe			b Sarfraz Nawaz	24
AA Mallett			c Wasim Bari b Sarfraz Nawaz	8
MHN Walker			run out	11
JR Thomson			not out	19
DK Lillee			c Mushtaq Mohammad b Intikhab Alam	2
	(b 1, lb 6, nb 7)	14	(b 3, nb 9)	12
	(5 wickets declared)	441	(all out)	425

Bowling: Asif Masood 17-0-97-0 Saleem Altaf 9-0-49-0 Sarfraz Nawaz 22.5-4-100-2 Intikhab Alam 16-0-101-2 Majid Khan
21-2-80-0
Asif Masood 12-0-100-2 Saleem Altaf 14-0-50-2 Sarfraz Nawaz 22-2-99-2 Intikhab Alam 15.6-3-70-1 Majid Khan 17-1-61-1
Mushtaq Mohammad 7-0-33-0

Pakistan Innings

Sadiq Mohammad	lbw b Lillee	137	c Marsh b Walker	5
Saeed Ahmed	c GS Chappell b Walker	50	c Mallett b Lillee	6
Zaheer Abbas	run out	51	run out	25
Majid Khan	c Marsh b Walker	158	c Marsh b Lillee	47
Mushtaq Mohammad	c Marsh b O'Keeffe	60	run out	13
Asif Iqbal	c Lillee b Mallett	7	c Redpath b Walker	37
*Intikhab Alam	c Sheahan b Mallett	68	c IM Chappell b Mallett	48
+Wasim Bari	b Mallett	7	b Walker	0
Saleem Altaf	not out	13	b O'Keeffe	10
Sarfraz Nawaz	not out	0	run out	8
Asif Masood			not out	1
	(b 12, lb 7, w 1, nb 3)	23		0
	(8 wickets declared)	574	(all out)	200

Bowling: Lillee 16.6-1-90-1 Thomson 17-1-100-0 Walker 24-1-112-2 Mallett 38-4-124-3 O'Keeffe 23-1-94-1 IM Chappell 5-
0-21-0 Mallett 0-10-0
Lillee 11-1-59-2 Thomson 2-0-10-0 Walker 14-3-39-3 Mallett 17.5-3-56-1 O'Keeffe 9-4-10-1 IM Chappell 3-0-16-0 GS
Chappell 1-0-10-0

Umpires: JR Collins and PR Enright

Australia v New Zealand
29,30 December 1973, 1,2 January 1974

Result: Australia won by an innings and 25 runs

Australia Innings

KR Stackpole	c Parker b Shrimpton	122
AP Sheahan	c Wadsworth b DR Hadlee	28
*IM Chappell	c RJ Hadlee b Shrimpton	54
GS Chappell	c Wadsworth b Congdon	60
KD Walters	c Wadsworth b DR Hadlee	79
IC Davis	c Wadsworth b DR Hadlee	15
+RW Marsh	c Parker b DR Hadlee	6
KJ O'Keeffe	not out	40
GJ Gilmour	b Congdon	52
AA Mallett		
AR Dell		
	(lb 4, w 1, nb 1)	6
	(8 wickets dec)	462

Bowling: RJ Hadlee 25-4-104-0 Andrews 19-2-100-0 DR Hadlee 20-2-102-4 O'Sullivan 22-3-80-0 Shrimpton 7-0-39-2
Congdon 8.5-1-31-2

New Zealand Innings

GM Turner	c Gilmour b Dell	6	absent hurt	0
JM Parker	c IM Chappell b O'Keeffe	27	c IM Chappell b Walters	23
MJF Shrimpton	c Marsh b Gilmour	7	b Walters	22
BF Hastings	b O'Keeffe	1	c Marsh b Mallett	22
*BE Congdon	st Marsh b Mallett	31	c Marsh b Mallett	14
JFM Morrison	c Marsh b Gilmour	44	c Marsh b Walters	16
+KJ Wadsworth	c GS Chappell b Gilmour	80	c Stackpole b Mallett	30
RJ Hadlee	c Marsh b Gilmour	9	c IM Chappell b O'Keeffe	6
DR Hadlee	run out (Mallett/Marsh)	2	c & b O'Keeffe	37
DR O'Sullivan	c Davis b Mallett	6	c & b Mallett	8
B Andrews	not out	0	not out	5
	(b 8, lb 5, nb 2)	15	(b 8, lb 9)	17
	(all out)	237	(all out)	200

Bowling: Dell 22-7-54-1 Gilmour 22-4-75-4 GS Chappell 4-2-4-0 Mallett 16.7-2-46-2 O'Keeffe 14-4-40-2 IM Chappell 1-0-3-0
Dell 5-0-9-0 Gilmour 3-0-16-0 GS Chappell 7-3-18-0 Walters 13-4-26-3 O'Keeffe 29.6-12-51-2 Mallett 24-4-63-4

Umpires: TF Brooks and JR Collins

Australia v England
26,27,28,30,31 December 1974

Result: Match drawn

England Innings

DL Amiss	c Walters b Lillee	4	c IM Chappell b Mallett	90
D Lloyd	c Mallett b Thomson	14	c & b Mallett	44
MC Cowdrey	lbw b Thomson	35	c GS Chappell b Lillee	8
JH Edrich	c Marsh b Mallett	49	c Marsh b Thomson	4
*MH Denness	c Marsh b Mallett	8	c IM Chappell b Thomson	2
AW Greig	run out	28	c GS Chappell b Lillee	60
+APE Knott	b Thomson	52	c Marsh b Thomson	4
FJ Titmus	c Mallett b Lillee	10	b Mallett	0
DL Underwood	c Marsh b Walker	9	c IM Chappell b Mallett	4
RGD Willis	c Walters b Thomson	13	b Thomson	15
M Hendrick	not out	8	not out	0
	(lb 2, w 1, nb 9)	12	(b 2, lb 9, w 2)	13
	(all out)	242	(all out)	244

Bowling: Lillee 20-2-70-2 Thomson 22.4-4-72-4 Walker 24-10-36-1 Mallett 15-3-37-2
Lillee 17-3-55-2 Thomson 17-1-71-4 Walker 10-0-45-0 Mallett 24-6-60-4

Australia Innings

IR Redpath	c Knott b Greig	55	run out	39
WJ Edwards	c Denness b Willis	29	lbw b Greig	0
GS Chappell	c Greig b Willis	2	lbw b Titmus	61
R Edwards	c Cowdrey b Titmus	5	c Lloyd b Titmus	10
KD Walters	c Lloyd b Greig	36	c Denness b Greig	32
*IM Chappell	lbw b Willis	36	lbw b Willis	0
+RW Marsh	c Knott b Titmus	44	c Knott b Greig	40
MHN Walker	c Knott b Willis	30	c Knott b Greig	23
DK Lillee	not out	2	c Denness b Greig	14
AA Mallett	run out	0	not out	0
JR Thomson	b Willis	2		
	(b 2, lb 2)	4	(b 6, lb 9, nb 4)	19
	(all out)	241	(8 wickets)	238

Bowling: Willis 21.7-4-61-5 Hendrick 2.6-1-8-0 Underwood 22-6-62-0 Greig 24-2-63-2 Titmus 22-11-43-2
Willis 14-2-56-1 Underwood 19-7-43-0 Greig 18-2-56-4 Titmus 29-10-64-2

Umpires: RC Bailhache and TF Brooks

Australia v England
8,9,10,12,13 February 1975

Result: England won by an innings and 4 runs

Australia Innings

IR Redpath	c Greig b Lever	1	c Amiss b Greig	83
RB McCosker	c Greig b Lever	0	c Cowdrey b Arnold	76
*IM Chappell	c Knott b Old	65	c Knott b Greig	50
GS Chappell	c Denness b Lever	1	b Lever	102
R Edwards	c Amiss b Lever	0	c Knott b Arnold	18
KD Walters	c Edrich b Old	12	b Arnold	3
+RW Marsh	b Old	29	c Denness b Lever	1
MHN Walker	not out	20	c & b Greig	17
DK Lillee	c Knott b Lever	12	not out	0
AA Mallett	b Lever	7	c Edrich b Greig	0
G Dymock	c Knott b Greig	0	c Knott b Lever	0
	(b 2, lb 1, nb 2)	5	(b 9, lb 5, w 4, nb 5)	23
	(all out)	152	(all out)	373

Bowling: Arnold 6-2-24-0 Lever 11-2-38-6 Old 11-0-50-3 Greig 8.7-1-35-1
Arnold 23-6-83-3 Lever 16-1-65-3 Old 18-1-75-0 Greig 31.7-7-88-4 Underwood 18-5-39-0

England Innings

DL Amiss	lbw b Lillee	0
MC Cowdrey	c Marsh b Walker	7
JH Edrich	c IM Chappell b Walker	70
*MH Denness	c & b Walker	188
KWR Fletcher	c Redpath b Walker	146
AW Greig	c sub b Walker	89
+APE Knott	c Marsh b Walker	5
CM Old	b Dymock	0
DL Underwood	b Walker	11
GG Arnold	c Marsh b Walker	0
P Lever	not out	6
	(b 4, lb 2, nb 1)	7
	(all out)	529

Bowling: Lillee 6-2-17-1 Walker 42.2-7-143-8 Dymock 39-6-130-1 Walters 23-3-86-0 Mallett 29-8-96-0 IM Chappell 12-1-50-0

Umpires: RC Bailhache and TF Brooks

Australia v West Indies
26,27,28,30 December 1975

Result: Australia won by 8 wickets

West Indies Innings

RC Fredericks	c McCosker b Thomson	59	b GS Chappell	26
CG Greenidge	c Marsh b Thomson	3	c Marsh b Walker	8
LG Rowe	c IM Chappell b Thomson	0	c Marsh b Lillee	8
AI Kallicharran	c Marsh b Thomson	20	c Marsh b Lillee	32
IVA Richards	b Lillee	41	c Marsh b Thomson	36
*CH Lloyd	c GS Chappell b Thomson	2	c Lillee b Mallett	102
+DL Murray	c Walker b Lillee	24	c Marsh b Lillee	22
BD Julien	c Mallett b Lillee	18	b Walker	27
VA Holder	b Walker	24	run out	15
AME Roberts	c Marsh b Lillee	6	c Mallett b IM Chappell	5
LR Gibbs	not out	0	not out	5
	(lb 4, w 1, nb 22)	27	(b 8, lb 4, nb 14)	26
	(all out)	224	(all out)	312

Bowling: Lillee 14-2-56-4 Thomson 11-1-62-5 Walker 13-1-46-1 Cosier 4-0-15-0 Mallett 5-1-18-0
Lillee 15-1-70-3 Walker 19-1-74-2 GS Chappell 7-1-23-1 IM Chappell 5.2-3-7-1 Thomson 9-0-51-1 Mallett 14-0-61-1

Australia Innings

IR Redpath	b Roberts	102	c sub (KD Boyce) b Julien	9
A Turner	b Roberts	21	b Roberts	7
RB McCosker	c Murray b Julien	4	not out	22
IM Chappell	c Kallicharran b Gibbs	35	not out	13
*GS Chappell	c Murray b Julien	52		
GJ Cosier	c Kallicharran b Roberts	109		
+RW Marsh	c & b Gibbs	56		
MHN Walker	c Murray b Roberts	1		
DK Lillee	c Richards b Holder	25		
JR Thomson	lbw b Julien	44		
AA Mallett	not out	3		
	(b 5, lb 6, nb 22)	33	(lb 1, nb 3)	4
	(all out)	485	(2 wickets)	55

Bowling: Roberts 32-2-126-4 Holder 27-2-123-1 Julien 28.3-5-120-3 Gibbs 30-9-81-2 Richards 1-0-2-0
Roberts 3-0-19-1 Julien 3-0-13-1 Greenidge 1-1-0-0 Rowe 1-0-6-0 Kallicharran 0.7-0-13-0

Umpires: RC Bailhache and JR Collins

Australia v West Indies
31 January, 1,2,4,5 February 1976

Result: Australia won by 165 runs

Australia Innings

IR Redpath	c Holding b Gibbs	101	c sub b Holder	70
A Turner	c Gibbs b Holder	30	lbw b Boyce	21
RB McCosker	b Boyce	21	not out	109
IM Chappell	b Holder	1	c Holder b Boyce	31
*GS Chappell	c Boyce b Fredericks	68	not out	54
GN Yallop	c Holding b Boyce	57		
+RW Marsh	b Holding	7		
GJ Gilmour	lbw b Gibbs	9		
AA Mallett	lbw b Boyce	16		
JR Thomson	lbw b Holder	0		
DK Lillee	not out	19		
	(b 4, lb 11, nb 7)	22	(b 5, lb 9, nb 1)	15
	(all out)	351	(3 wickets declared)	300

Bowling: Boyce 17.2-1-75-3 Holding 16-4-51-1 Holder 20-2-86-3 Lloyd 7-2-20-0 Fredericks 6-0-29-1 Gibbs 24-4-68-2
Boyce 19-2-74-2 Holding 1-0-2-0 Holder 18-0-81-1 Lloyd 4-1-14-0 Fredericks 3-1-14-0 Gibbs 26-3-62-0 Richards 7-0-38-0

West Indies Innings

RC Fredericks	c Thomson b Gilmour	22	b Thomson	6
IVA Richards	c Marsh b Lillee	50	c GS Chappell b Lillee	98
L Baichan	c GS Chappell b Gilmour	3	b Thomson	20
AI Kallicharran	b Gilmour	4	c McCosker b Lillee	44
*CH Lloyd	c Redpath b Lillee	37	not out	91
LG Rowe	c Marsh b Gilmour	6	c Redpath b Mallett	6
+DL Murray	c Marsh b Lillee	1	c Marsh b Lillee	5
KD Boyce	lbw b Gilmour	0	c GS Chappell b Mallett	11
MA Holding	b Lillee	9	c Gilmour b Mallett	4
VA Holder	not out	14	b Thomson	22
LR Gibbs	c Marsh b Lillee	2	c Marsh b Thomson	0
	(lb 5, w 1, nb 6)	12	(b 6, lb 10, nb 3)	19
	(all out)	160	(all out)	326

Bowling: Thomson 9-0-51-0 Lillee 11.3-0-63-5 Gilmour 10-3-34-5
Thomson 12.5-0-80-4 Lillee 18-1-112-3 Gilmour 7-1-26-0 GS Chappell 2-0-6-0 IM Chappell 2-0-10-0 Mallett 13-1-73-3

Umpires: TF Brooks and MG O'Connell

Australia v Pakistan
1,2,3,5,6 January 1977

Result: Australia won by 348 runs

Australia Innings

IC Davis	c Imran Khan b Asif Iqbal	56	c Asif Iqbal b Iqbal Qasim	88
A Turner	b Asif Iqbal	82	lbw b Imran Khan	5
RB McCosker	lbw b Asif Iqbal	0	st Wasim Bari b Iqbal Qasim	105
*GS Chappell	c Wasim Bari b Iqbal Qasim	121	c Majid Khan b Imran Khan	67
KD Walters	st Wasim Bari b Iqbal Qasim	42	b Imran Khan	0
GJ Cosier	c Asif Masood b Majid Khan	168	b Imran Khan	8
+RW Marsh	lbw b Iqbal Qasim	2	st Wasim Bari b Iqbal Qasim	13
GJ Gilmour	st Wasim Bari b Iqbal Qasim	0	not out	7
KJ O'Keeffe	not out	28		
DK Lillee			b Imran Khan	6
MHN Walker				
	(b 3, lb 7, w 1, nb 7)	18	(b 2, lb 11, nb 3)	16
	(8 wickets declared)	517	(8 wickets declared)	315

Bowling: Imran Khan 22-0-115-0 Saleem Altaf 17-2-117-0 Asif Masood 13-1-79-0 Asif Iqbal 16-3-52-3 Javed Miandad 2-0-15-0 Iqbal Qasim 21-5-111-4 Majid Khan 1.6-0-10-1
Imran Khan 25.5-2-122-5 Saleem Altaf 6-1-28-0 Iqbal Qasim 25-2-119-3 Majid Khan 2-0-12-0 Mushtaq Mohammad 3-0-18-0

Pakistan Innings

Majid Khan	c Marsh b Lillee	76	b Lillee	35
Sadiq Mohammad	c McCosker b O'Keeffe	105	c Walters b Gilmour	0
Zaheer Abbas	b Gilmour	90	lbw b Walker	58
*Mushtaq Mohammad	lbw b Lillee	9	c Chappell b Lillee	4
Javed Miandad	lbw b Lillee	5	c Turner b O'Keeffe	10
Asif Iqbal	c sub b Gilmour	35	lbw b Lillee	6
Imran Khan	c Marsh b Lillee	5	c & b O'Keeffe	28
Saleem Altaf	c Chappell b Lillee	0	b O'Keeffe	0
+Wasim Bari	lbw b Lillee	0	c Walker b O'Keeffe	2
Iqbal Qasim	run out	1	c Marsh b Lillee	1
Asif Masood	not out	0	not out	0
	(lb 2, nb 5)	7	(b 1, lb 6)	7
	(all out)	333	(all out)	151

Bowling: Lillee 23-4-82-6 Gilmour 16.1-2-78-2 Walker 22-1-93-0 O'Keeffe 21-4-63-1 Cosier 2-0-10-0
Lillee 14-1-53-4 Gilmour 3-0-19-1 Walker 9-2-34-1 O'Keeffe 18.1-5-38-4

Umpires: TF Brooks and MG O'Connell

Australia v England
12,13,14,16,17 March 1977

Result: Australia won by 45 runs

Australia Innings

IC Davis	lbw b Lever	5	c Knott b Greig	68
RB McCosker	b Willis	4	c Greig b Old	25
GJ Cosier	c Fletcher b Lever	10	c Knott b Lever	4
*GS Chappell	b Underwood	40	b Old	2
DW Hookes	c Greig b Old	17	c Fletcher b Underwood	56
KD Walters	c Greig b Willis	4	c Knott b Greig	66
+RW Marsh	c Knott b Old	28	not out	110
GJ Gilmour	c Greig b Old	4	b Lever	16
KJ O'Keeffe	c Brearley b Underwood	0	c Willis b Old	14
DK Lillee	not out	10	c Amiss b Old	25
MHN Walker	b Underwood	2	not out	8
	(b 4, lb 2, nb 8)	14	(lb 10, nb 15)	25
	(all out)	138	(9 wickets declared)	419

Bowling: Lever 12-1-36-2 Willis 8-0-33-2 Old 12-4-39-3 Underwood 11.6-2-16-3
Lever 21-1-95-2 Willis 22-0-91-0 Old 27.6-2-104-4 Greig 14-3-66-2 Underwood 12-2-38-1

England Innings

RA Woolmer	c Chappell b Lillee	9	lbw b Walker	12
JM Brearley	c Hookes b Lillee	12	lbw b Lillee	43
DL Underwood	c Chappell b Walker	7	b Lillee	7
DW Randall	c Marsh b Lillee	4	c Cosier b O'Keeffe	174
DL Amiss	c O'Keeffe b Walker	4	b Chappell	64
KWR Fletcher	c Marsh b Walker	4	c Marsh b Lillee	1
*AW Greig	b Walker	18	c Cosier b O'Keeffe	41
+APE Knott	lbw b Lillee	15	lbw b Lillee	42
CM Old	c Marsh b Lillee	3	c Chappell b Lillee	2
JK Lever	c Marsh b Lillee	11	lbw b O'Keeffe	4
RGD Willis	not out	1	not out	5
	(b 2, lb 2, w 1, nb 2)	7	(b 8, lb 4, w 3, nb 7)	22
	(all out)	95	(all out)	417

Bowling: Lillee 13.3-2-26-6 Walker 15-3-54-4 O'Keeffe 1-0-4-0 Gilmour 5-3-4-0
Lillee 34.4-7-139-5 Walker 22-4-83-1 Gilmour 4-0-29-0 Chappell 16-7-29-1 O'Keeffe 33-6-108-3 Walters 3-2-7-0

Umpires: TF Brooks and MG O'Connell

Australia v India
30,31 December 1977, 2,3,4 January 1978

Result: India won by 222 runs

India Innings

SM Gavaskar	c Rixon b Thomson	0	c Serjeant b Gannon	118
CPS Chauhan	c Mann b Clark	0	run out	20
M Amarnath	c Simpson b Clark	72	b Cosier	41
GR Viswanath	c Rixon b Thomson	59	lbw b Clark	54
DB Vengsarkar	c Simpson b Thomson	37	c Cosier b Clark	6
AV Mankad	c Clark b Gannon	44	b Clark	38
+SMH Kirmani	lbw b Simpson	29	c Thomson b Mann	29
KD Ghavri	c Rixon b Gannon	6	c Simpson b Clark	6
EAS Prasanna	b Clark	0	c Rixon b Gannon	11
*BS Bedi	not out	2	not out	12
BS Chandrasekhar	b Clark	0	lbw b Cosier	0
	(lb 3, nb 4)	7	(lb 1, nb 7)	8
	(all out)	256	(all out)	343

Bowling: Thomson 16-2-78-3 Clark 19.2-2-73-4 Gannon 14-2-47-2 Cosier 12-3-25-0 Simpson 3-1-11-1 Mann 5-1-15-0
Thomson 18-4-47-0 Clark 29-3-96-4 Gannon 22-4-88-2 Cosier 12.7-2-58-2 Simpson 3-0-22-0 Mann 4-0-24-1

Australia Innings

J Dyson	b Ghavri	0	lbw b Bedi	12
GJ Cosier	c Chauhan b Chandrasekhar	67	b Chandrasekhar	34
AD Ogilvie	lbw b Ghavri	6	c Chauhan b Bedi	0
CS Serjeant	b Chandrasekhar	85	b Chandrasekhar	17
*RB Simpson	c Mankad b Chandrasekhar	2	lbw b Chandrasekhar	4
PM Toohey	c Viswanath b Bedi	14	c Chauhan b Chandrasekhar	14
AL Mann	c Gavaskar b Bedi	11	c Gavaskar b Chandrasekhar	18
+SJ Rixon	lbw b Chandrasekhar	11	c & b Chandrasekhar	12
WM Clark	lbw b Chandrasekhar	3	c Ghavri b Bedi	33
JR Thomson	c Ghavri b Chandrasekhar	0	c & b Bedi	7
JB Gannon	not out	0	not out	3
	(b 6, lb 7, nb 1)	14	(b 6, lb 4)	10
	(all out)	213	(all out)	164

Bowling: Ghavri 9-0-37-2 Gavaskar 2-0-7-0 Bedi 15-2-71-2 Chandrasekhar 14.1-2-52-6 Prasanna 10-1-32-0
Ghavri 4-0-29-0 Bedi 16.1-5-58-4 Chandrasekhar 20-3-52-6 Prasanna 8-4-5-0 Amarnath 3-0-10-0

Umpires: RA French and MG O'Connell

Melbourne Cricket Ground

Australia v England
29,30 December 1978, 1,2,3 January 1979

Result: Australia won by 103 runs

Australia Innings

GM Wood	c Emburey b Miller	100	b Botham	34
WM Darling	run out	33	c Randall b Miller	21
KJ Hughes	c Taylor b Botham	0	c Gower b Botham	48
*GN Yallop	c Hendrick b Botham	41	c Taylor b Miller	16
PM Toohey	c Randall b Miller	32	c Botham b Emburey	20
AR Border	c Brearley b Hendrick	29	run out	0
+JA Maclean	b Botham	8	c Hendrick b Emburey	10
RM Hogg	c Randall b Miller	0	b Botham	1
G Dymock	b Hendrick	0	c Brearley b Hendrick	6
AG Hurst	b Hendrick	0	not out	0
JD Higgs	not out	1	st Taylor b Emburey	0
	(lb 8, nb 6)	14	(b 4, lb 6, nb 1)	11
	(all out)	258	(all out)	167

Bowling: Willis 13-2-47-0 Botham 20.1-4-68-3 Hendrick 23-3-50-3 Emburey 14-1-44-0 Miller 19-6-35-3
Willis 7-0-21-0 Botham 15-4-41-3 Hendrick 14-4-25-1 Miller 14-5-39-2 Emburey 21.2-12-30-3

England Innings

G Boycott	b Hogg	1	lbw b Hurst	38
*JM Brearley	lbw b Hogg	1	c Maclean b Dymock	0
DW Randall	lbw b Hurst	13	lbw b Hogg	2
GA Gooch	c Border b Dymock	25	lbw b Hogg	40
DI Gower	lbw b Dymock	29	lbw b Dymock	49
IT Botham	c Darling b Higgs	22	c Maclean b Higgs	10
G Miller	b Hogg	7	c Hughes b Higgs	1
+RW Taylor	b Hogg	1	c Maclean b Hogg	5
JE Emburey	b Hogg	0	not out	7
RGD Willis	c Darling b Dymock	19	c Yallop b Hogg	3
M Hendrick	not out	6	b Hogg	0
	(b 6, lb 4, nb 9)	19	(b 10, lb 7, w 1, nb 6)	24
	(all out)	143	(all out)	179

Bowling: Hogg 17-7-30-5 Hurst 12-2-24-1 Dymock 15.6-4-38-3 Higgs 19-9-32-1
Hogg 17-5-36-5 Dymock 18-4-37-2 Hurst 11-1-39-1 Higgs 16-2-29-2 Border 5-0-14-0

Umpires: RA French and MG O'Connell

Australia v Pakistan
10,11,12,14,15 March 1979

Result: Pakistan won by 71 runs

Pakistan Innings

Majid Khan	c Wright b Hogg	1	b Border	108
Mohsin Khan	c Hilditch b Hogg	14	c & b Hogg	14
Zaheer Abbas	b Hogg	11	b Hogg	59
Javed Miandad	b Hogg	19	c Wright b Border	16
Asif Iqbal	c Wright b Clark	9	lbw b Hogg	44
*Mushtaq Mohammad	c Wright b Hurst	36	c sub b Sleep	28
Wasim Raja	b Hurst	13	c Wright b Hurst	28
Imran Khan	c Wright b Hurst	33	c Clark b Hurst	28
Sarfraz Nawaz	c Wright b Sleep	35	lbw b Hurst	1
+Wasim Bari	run out	0	not out	8
Sikander Bakht	not out	5		
	(b 2, lb 7, w 1, nb 10)	20	(b 4, lb 6, nb 9)	19
	(all out)	196	(9 wickets declared)	353

Bowling: Hogg 17-4-49-4 Hurst 20-4-55-3 Clark 17-4-56-1 Sleep 7.7-2-16-1
Hogg 19-2-75-3 Hurst 19.5-1-115-3 Clark 21-6-47-0 Sleep 8-0-62-1 Border 14-5-35-2

Australia Innings

GM Wood	not out	5	c Wasim Bari b Sarfraz Nawaz	0
AMJ Hilditch	c Javed Miandad b Imran Khan	3	b Sarfraz Nawaz	62
AR Border	b Imran Khan	20	b Sarfraz Nawaz	105
*GN Yallop	b Imran Khan	25	run out	8
KJ Hughes	run out	19	c Mohsin Khan b Sarfraz Nawaz	84
DF Whatmore	lbw b Sarfraz Nawaz	43	b Sarfraz Nawaz	15
PR Sleep	c Wasim Bari b Imran Khan	10	b Sarfraz Nawaz	0
+KJ Wright	c Imran Khan b Wasim Raja	9	not out	1
WM Clark	c Mushtaq Mohammad b Wasim Raja	9	b Sarfraz Nawaz	0
RM Hogg	run out	9	lbw b Sarfraz Nawaz	0
AG Hurst	c & b Sarfraz Nawaz	0	c Wasim Bari b Sarfraz Nawaz	0
	(b 1, lb 5, w 2, nb 8)	16	(b 13, lb 13, nb 9)	35
	(all out)	168	(all out)	310

Bowling: Imran Khan 18-8-26-4 Sarfraz Nawaz 21.6-6-39-2 Sikander Bakht 10-1-29-0 Mushtaq Mohammad 7-0-35-0 Wasim Raja 5-0-23-2
Imran Khan 27-9-73-0 Sarfraz Nawaz 35.4-7-86-9 Sikander Bakht 7-0-29-0 Mushtaq Mohammad 11-0-42-0 Wasim Raja 3-0-11-0 Majid Khan 9-1-34-0

Umpires: RC Bailhache and CE Harvey

Australia v West Indies
29,30,31 December 1979, 1 January 1980

Result: West Indies won by 10 wickets

Australia Innings

JM Wiener	lbw b Garner	40	c Murray b Croft	24
BM Laird	c Lloyd b Holding	16	c Garner b Holding	69
AR Border	c Richards b Garner	17	lbw b Holding	15
*GS Chappell	c Murray b Garner	19	c Murray b Roberts	22
KJ Hughes	c Rowe b Holding	4	lbw b Roberts	70
PM Toohey	c Roberts b Holding	10	c Murray b Croft	7
+RW Marsh	c Kallicharran b Holding	0	b Croft	7
DK Lillee	c Lloyd b Croft	12	c & b Roberts	0
G Dymock	c Kallicharran b Croft	7	c Lloyd b Garner	17
RM Hogg	c Greenidge b Croft	14	c Holding b Garner	11
JD Higgs	not out	0	not out	0
	(b 9, lb 4, w 2, nb 2)	17	(b 2, lb 10, nb 5)	17
	(all out)	156	(all out)	259

Bowling: Roberts 14-1-39-0 Holding 14-3-40-4 Croft 13.3-4-27-3 Garner 15-7-33-3
Roberts 21-1-64-3 Holding 23-7-61-2 Croft 22-2-61-3 Garner 20.4-2-56-2

West Indies Innings

CG Greenidge	c Higgs b Dymock	48	not out	9
DL Haynes	c Hughes b Lillee	29	not out	9
IVA Richards	c Toohey b Dymock	96		
AI Kallicharran	c Laird b Higgs	39		
LG Rowe	b Lillee	26		
*CH Lloyd	c Marsh b Dymock	40		
+DL Murray	b Dymock	24		
AME Roberts	lbw b Lillee	54		
J Garner	c Dymock b Higgs	29		
MA Holding	not out	1		
CEH Croft	lbw b Higgs	0		
	(lb 4, nb 7)	11	(lb 4)	4
	(all out)	397	(0 wickets)	22

Bowling: Lillee 36-7-96-3 Hogg 6-0-59-0 Dymock 31-2-106-4 Higgs 34.4-4-122-3 Chappell 5-2-3-0
Lillee 3-0-9-0 Dymock 3-0-5-0 Hughes 1-1-0-0 Toohey 0.2-0-4-0

Umpires: AR Crafter and CE Harvey

Australia v England
1,2,3,5,6 February 1980

Result: Australia won by 8 wickets

England Innings

GA Gooch	run out	99	b Mallett	51
G Boycott	c Mallett b Dymock	44	b Lillee	7
W Larkins	c GS Chappell b Pascoe	25	lbw b Pascoe	3
DI Gower	lbw b Lillee	0	b Lillee	11
P Willey	lbw b Pascoe	1	c Marsh b Lillee	2
IT Botham	c Marsh b Lillee	8	not out	119
*JM Brearley	not out	60	c Border b Pascoe	10
+RW Taylor	b Lillee	23	c Border b Lillee	32
DL Underwood	c IM Chappell b Lillee	3	b Pascoe	0
JK Lever	b Lillee	22	c Marsh b Lillee	12
RGD Willis	c GS Chappell b Lillee	4	c GS Chappell b Pascoe	2
	(b 1, lb 2, nb 14)	17	(b 2, lb 12, nb 10)	24
	(all out)	306	(all out)	273

Bowling: Lillee 33.1-9-60-6 Dymock 28-6-54-1 Mallett 35-9-104-0 Pascoe 32-7-71-2
Lillee 33-6-78-5 Dymock 11-2-30-0 Mallett 14-1-45-1 Pascoe 29.5-3-80-4 Border 4-0-16-0

Australia Innings

RB McCosker	c Botham b Underwood	33	lbw b Botham	2
BM Laird	c Gower b Underwood	74	c Boycott b Underwood	25
IM Chappell	c & b Underwood	75	not out	26
KJ Hughes	c Underwood b Botham	15		
AR Border	c & b Lever	63		
*GS Chappell	c Larkins b Lever	114	not out	40
+RW Marsh	c Botham b Lever	17		
DK Lillee	c Willey b Lever	8		
G Dymock	b Botham	19		
AA Mallett	lbw b Botham	25		
LS Pascoe	not out	1		
	(b 13, lb 12, w 1, nb 7)	33	(lb 8, nb 2)	10
	(all out)	477	(2 wickets)	103

Bowling: Lever 53-15-111-4 Botham 39.5-15-105-3 Willis 21-4-61-0 Underwood 53-19-131-3 Willey 13-2-36-0
Lever 7.4-3-18-0 Botham 12-5-18-1 Willis 5-3-8-0 Underwood 14-2-49-1

Umpires: RC Bailhache and PM Cronin

Australia v New Zealand
26,27,28,29,30 December 1980

Result: Match drawn

Australia Innings

GM Wood	c Lees b Hadlee	0	c Lees b Hadlee	21
J Dyson	b Troup	13	lbw b Cairns	16
*GS Chappell	c Coney b Hadlee	42	b Hadlee	78
KJ Hughes	c Parker b Hadlee	51	b Hadlee	30
AR Border	c Cairns b Coney	45	c Lees b Hadlee	9
KD Walters	b Coney	107	run out	2
+RW Marsh	c Parker b Coney	1	lbw b Cairns	0
DK Lillee	b Cairns	27	c Coney b Bracewell	8
RM Hogg	run out	0	b Hadlee	12
LS Pascoe	b Cairns	0	not out	0
JD Higgs	not out	6	b Hadlee	0
	(b 7, lb 13, w 3, nb 6)	29	(b 6, lb 4, nb 2)	12
	(all out)	321	(all out)	188

Bowling: Hadlee 39-8-89-3 Troup 26-5-54-1 Cairns 35-6-83-2 Bracewell 9-0-38-0 Coney 12.3-6-28-3
Hadlee 27.2-7-57-6 Troup 11-1-31-0 Cairns 33-13-65-2 Bracewell 15-5-22-1 Coney 1-0-1-0

New Zealand Innings

JG Wright	c Chappell b Higgs	4	c Wood b Hogg	44
BA Edgar	lbw b Higgs	21	run out	25
*GP Howarth	b Hogg	65	lbw b Chappell	20
JM Parker	c Marsh b Pascoe	56	lbw b Chappell	1
MG Burgess	lbw b Pascoe	49	not out	10
JV Coney	not out	55	lbw b Hogg	3
JG Bracewell	c Chappell b Pascoe	0		
+WK Lees	lbw b Hogg	4	b Lillee	7
RJ Hadlee	c Border b Hogg	9	not out	5
BL Cairns	lbw b Higgs	18		
GB Troup	c Hughes b Hogg	1		
	(b 13, lb 12, nb 10)	35	(b 2, lb 8, w 1, nb 2)	13
	(all out)	317	(6 wickets)	128

Bowling: Lillee 21-4-49-0 Hogg 26.2-9-60-4 Higgs 29-6-87-3 Pascoe 26-6-75-3 Border 4-1-6-0 Chappell 2-0-5-0
Lillee 13-3-30-1 Hogg 8-1-14-2 Higgs 12-4-24-0 Pascoe 11-1-35-0 Border 2-1-5-0 Chappell 7-4-7-2 Hughes 1-1-0-0

Umpires: RC Bailhache and AR Crafter

Australia v India
7,8,9,10,11 February 1981

Result: India won by 59 runs

India Innings

*SM Gavaskar	c Hughes b Pascoe	10	lbw b Lillee	70
CPS Chauhan	c Yardley b Pascoe	0	c Yardley b Lillee	85
DB Vengsarkar	c Border b Lillee	12	c Marsh b Pascoe	41
GR Viswanath	c Chappell b Yardley	114	b Lillee	30
SM Patil	c Hughes b Lillee	23	c Chappell b Yardley	36
Yashpal Sharma	c Marsh b Lillee	4	b Pascoe	9
N Kapil Dev	c Hughes b Pascoe	5	b Yardley	0
+SMH Kirmani	c Marsh b Lillee	25	run out	9
KD Ghavri	run out	0	not out	11
NS Yadav	not out	20	absent hurt	0
DR Doshi	c Walters b Yardley	0	b Lillee	7
	(b 1, lb 8, w 6, nb 9)	24	(b 11, lb 8, nb 7)	26
	(all out)	237	(all out)	324

Bowling: Lillee 25-6-65-4 Pascoe 22-11-29-3 Chappell 5-2-9-0 Yardley 13-3-45-2 Higgs 19-2-65-0
Lillee 32.1-5-104-4 Pascoe 29-4-80-2 Yardley 31-11-65-2 Higgs 15-3-41-0 Border 2-0-8-0

Australia Innings

J Dyson	c Kirmani b Kapil Dev	16	c Kirmani b Ghavri	3
GM Wood	c Doshi b Ghavri	10	st Kirmani b Doshi	10
*GS Chappell	c & b Ghavri	76	b Ghavri	0
KJ Hughes	c Chauhan b Yadav	24	b Doshi	16
AR Border	b Yadav	124	c Kirmani b Kapil Dev	9
KD Walters	st Kirmani b Doshi	78	not out	18
+RW Marsh	c sub b Doshi	45	b Kapil Dev	3
B Yardley	lbw b Doshi	0	b Kapil Dev	7
DK Lillee	c & b Patil	19	b Kapil Dev	4
LS Pascoe	lbw b Patil	3	run out	6
JD Higgs	not out	1	b Kapil Dev	0
	(b 12, lb 6, nb 5)	23	(lb 5, nb 2)	7
	(all out)	419	(all out)	83

Bowling: Kapil Dev 19-7-41-1 Doshi 52-14-109-3 Ghavri 39-4-110-2 Yadav 32-6-100-2 Chauhan 2-0-8-0 Patil 12.3-4-28-2
Kapil Dev 16.4-4-28-5 Doshi 22-9-33-2 Ghavri 8-4-10-2 Patil 2-0-5-0

Umpires: MW Johnson and RV Whitehead

Australia v Pakistan
11,12,13,14,15 December 1981

Result: Pakistan won by an innings and 82 runs

Pakistan Innings

Mudassar Nazar	c Lillee b Yardley	95
Mohsin Khan	c Thomson b Yardley	17
Majid Khan	c Wood b Yardley	74
*Javed Miandad	lbw b Yardley	62
Zaheer Abbas	c & b Yardley	90
Wasim Raja	c Laird b Yardley	50
Imran Khan	not out	70
Sarfraz Nawaz	c Yardley b Chappell	0
+Wasim Bari	b Yardley	8
Iqbal Qasim	not out	16
Sikander Bakht		
	(b 1, lb 5, nb 12)	18
	(8 wickets declared)	500

Bowling: Lillee 36.3-9-104-0 Alderman 27-8-62-0 Thomson 25-2-85-0 Yardley 66-16-187-7 Border 4-1-16-0 Chappell 9-2-17-1 Hughes 3-1-12-0 Laird 1-0-9-0

Australia Innings

BM Laird	lbw b Iqbal Qasim	35	c Sarfraz Nawaz b Iqbal Qasim	52
GM Wood	c Mohsin Khan b Sarfraz Nawaz	100	c Wasim Bari b Sarfraz Nawaz	1
*GS Chappell	c Wasim Bari b Wasim Raja	22	c Javed Miandad b Sarfraz Nawaz	0
AR Border	run out	7	run out	1
KJ Hughes	c & b Iqbal Qasim	11	c Majid Khan b Iqbal Qasim	11
DM Wellham	c Mudassar Nazar b Sarfraz Nawaz	26	b Sarfraz Nawaz	13
+RW Marsh	c Mudassar Nazar b Imran Khan	31	c Mohsin Khan b Iqbal Qasim	21
B Yardley	b Iqbal Qasim	20	b Imran Khan	0
DK Lillee	lbw b Imran Khan	1	c Wasim Bari b Iqbal Qasim	4
JR Thomson	not out	3	b Imran Khan	17
TM Alderman	lbw b Imran Khan	1	not out	4
	(b 4, lb 6, nb 3)	13	(b 1)	1
	(all out)	293	(all out)	125

Bowling: Imran Khan 24.1-7-41-3 Sarfraz Nawaz 14-3-43-2 Wasim Raja 37-7-73-1 Iqbal Qasim 55-17-104-3 Sikander Bakht 2-0-9-0 Majid Khan 2-0-10-0
Imran Khan 14.1-5-21-2 Sarfraz Nawaz 15-10-11-3 Wasim Raja 13-2-34-0 Iqbal Qasim 24-11-44-4 Majid Khan 4-1-5-0 Javed Miandad 2-0-9-0

Umpires: RC Bailhache and RA French

Australia v West Indies
26,27,28,29,30 December 1981

Result: Australia won by 58 runs

Australia Innings

BM Laird	c Murray b Holding	4	lbw b Croft	64
GM Wood	c Murray b Roberts	3	c Murray b Garner	46
*GS Chappell	c Murray b Holding	0	c Murray b Garner	6
AR Border	c Murray b Holding	4	b Holding	66
KJ Hughes	not out	100	b Holding	8
DM Wellham	c sub b Croft	17	lbw b Holding	2
+RW Marsh	c Richards b Garner	21	c Murray b Holding	2
B Yardley	b Garner	21	b Garner	13
DK Lillee	c Gomes b Holding	1	c Murray b Holding	0
GF Lawson	b Holding	2	not out	0
TM Alderman	c Murray b Croft	10	b Holding	1
	(b 1, lb 6, nb 8)	15	(lb 4, w 1, nb 4)	14
	(all out)	198	(all out)	222

Bowling: Holding 17-3-45-5 Roberts 15-6-40-1 Garner 20-6-59-2 Croft 16.1-3-39-2
Holding 21.3-5-62-6 Roberts 18-4-31-0 Garner 18-5-37-3 Croft 20-2-61-1 Richards 5-0-17-0

West Indies Innings

DL Haynes	c Border b Lillee	1	c Lillee b Yardley	28
SFAF Bacchus	c Wood b Alderman	1	lbw b Alderman	0
CEH Croft	lbw b Lillee	0	not out	2
IVA Richards	b Lillee	2	b Alderman	4
*CH Lloyd	c Alderman b Yardley	29	c Border b Lawson	19
HA Gomes	c Chappell b Lillee	55	b Yardley	24
PJL Dujon	c Hughes b Lillee	41	c Marsh b Yardley	43
+DA Murray	not out	32	c Marsh b Yardley	10
AME Roberts	c Marsh b Lillee	18	lbw b Lillee	10
MA Holding	c & b Alderman	2	lbw b Lillee	7
J Garner	c Laird b Lillee	7	lbw b Lillee	0
	(b 1, lb 3, nb 9)	13	(lb 1, lb 10, nb 9)	20
	(all out)	201	(all out)	161

Bowling: Lillee 26.3-3-83-7 Alderman 18-3-54-2 Lawson 9-2-28-0 Chappell 2-2-0-0 Yardley 7-2-23-1
Lillee 27.1-8-44-3 Alderman 9-3-23-2 Lawson 17-3-36-1 Yardley 21-7-38-4

Umpires: RC Bailhache and AR Crafter

Australia v England
26,27,28,29,30 December 1982

Result: England won by 3 runs

England Innings

G Cook	c Chappell b Thomson	10	c Yardley b Thomson	26
G Fowler	c Chappell b Hogg	4	b Hogg	65
CJ Tavare	c Yardley b Thomson	89	b Hogg	0
DI Gower	c Marsh b Hogg	18	c Marsh b Lawson	3
AJ Lamb	c Dyson b Yardley	83	c Marsh b Hogg	26
IT Botham	c Wessels b Yardley	27	c Chappell b Thomson	46
G Miller	c Border b Yardley	10	lbw b Lawson	14
DR Pringle	c Wessels b Hogg	9	c Marsh b Lawson	42
+RW Taylor	c Marsh b Yardley	1	lbw b Thomson	37
*RGD Willis	not out	6	not out	8
NG Cowans	c Lawson b Hogg	3	b Lawson	10
	(b 3, lb 6, w 3, nb 12)	24	(b 2, lb 9, nb 6)	17
	(all out)	284	(all out)	294

Bowling: Lawson 17-6-48-0 Hogg 23.3-6-69-4 Yardley 27-9-89-4 Thomson 13-2-49-2 Chappell 1-0-5-0
Lawson 21.4-6-66-4 Hogg 25-5-64-3 Yardley 15-2-67-0 Thomson 21-3-74-3 Chappell 1-0-6-0

Australia Innings

KC Wessels	b Willis	47	b Cowans	14
J Dyson	lbw b Cowans	21	c Tavare b Botham	31
*GS Chappell	c Lamb b Cowans	0	c sub (IJ Gould) b Cowans	2
KJ Hughes	b Willis	66	c Taylor b Miller	48
AR Border	b Botham	2	not out	62
DW Hookes	c Taylor b Pringle	53	c Willis b Cowans	68
+RW Marsh	b Willis	53	b Cowans	13
B Yardley	b Miller	9	b Cowans	0
GF Lawson	c Fowler b Miller	0	c Cowans b Pringle	7
RM Hogg	not out	8	lbw b Cowans	4
JR Thomson	b Miller	1	c Miller b Botham	21
	(lb 8, nb 19)	27	(b 5, lb 9, w 1, nb 3)	18
	(all out)	287	(all out)	288

Bowling: Willis 15-2-38-3 Botham 18-3-69-1 Cowans 16-0-69-2 Pringle 15-2-40-1 Miller 15-5-44-3
Willis 17-0-57-0 Botham 25.1-4-80-2 Cowans 26-6-77-6 Pringle 12-4-26-1 Miller 16-6-30-1

Umpires: AR Crafter and RV Whitehead

Australia v Pakistan
26,27,28,29,30 December 1983

Result: Match drawn

Pakistan Innings

Mohsin Khan	lbw b Lillee	152	c Hughes b Lillee	3
Mudassar Nazar	c Marsh b Lawson	7	lbw b Matthews	35
Qasim Umar	b Maguire	23	b Lawson	9
Javed Miandad	c Marsh b Maguire	27	lbw b Lillee	11
Zaheer Abbas	run out	44	b Matthews	50
Saleem Malik	c Maguire b Lawson	35	b Lillee	14
*Imran Khan	c Marsh b Lillee	83	not out	72
Sarfraz Nawaz	c Hughes b Maguire	22	not out	11
Abdul Qadir	c Lawson b Matthews	45	b Lawson	12
+Wasim Bari	not out	6		
Azeem Hafeez	c Maguire b Matthews	7		
	(lb 11, nb 8)	19	(b 10, lb 9, w 2)	21
	(all out)	470	(7 wickets)	238

Bowling: Lawson 38-8-125-2 Lillee 38-11-113-2 Maguire 29-7-111-3 Matthews 28.4-7-95-2 Chappell 7-3-15-0
Lawson 21-8-47-2 Lillee 29-7-71-3 Maguire 12-3-26-0 Matthews 21-8-48-2 Border 5-3-9-0 Chappell 8-3-13-0 Marsh 2-0-3-0 Wessels 2-1-2-0

Australia Innings

KC Wessels	c Wasim Bari b Azeem Hafeez	11		
WB Phillips	lbw b Azeem Hafeez	35		
GN Yallop	c Wasim Bari b Sarfraz Nawaz	268		
*KJ Hughes	lbw b Azeem Hafeez	94		
AR Border	lbw b Abdul Qadir	32		
GS Chappell	c Saleem Malik b Abdul Qadir	5		
+RW Marsh	c Mudassar Nazar b Abdul Qadir	0		
GRJ Matthews	lbw b Sarfraz Nawaz	75		
GF Lawson	c Mudassar Nazar b Abdul Qadir	4		
JN Maguire	c Wasim Bari b Abdul Qadir	4		
DK Lillee	not out	2		
	(b 15, lb 9, w 2, nb 3)	29		
	(all out)	555		

Bowling: Sarfraz Nawaz 51-12-106-2 Azeem Hafeez 35-8-115-3 Abdul Qadir 54.3-12-166-5 Mudassar Nazar 20-0-76-0 Javed Miandad 5-0-18-0 Zaheer Abbas 22-5-42-0 Saleem Malik 2-1-10-0

Umpires: AR Crafter and PJ McConnell

Australia v West Indies
22,23,24,26,27 December 1984

Result: Match drawn

West Indies Innings

CG Greenidge	c Bennett b Lawson	10	lbw b Lawson	1
DL Haynes	c Border b Lawson	13	b McDermott	63
RB Richardson	b McDermott	51	b Lawson	3
HA Gomes	c Matthews b McDermott	68	c Bennett b McDermott	18
IVA Richards	c Hughes b Matthews	208	lbw b McDermott	0
+PJL Dujon	b McDermott	0	not out	49
*CH Lloyd	c Lawson b Matthews	19	not out	34
MD Marshall	c Rixon b Hogg	55		
RA Harper	c & b Hogg	5		
J Garner	lbw b Lawson	8		
CA Walsh	not out	18		
	(b 1, lb 11, nb 12)	24	(b 4, lb 9, nb 5)	18
	(all out)	479	(5 wickets declared)	186

Bowling: Lawson 37-9-108-3 Hogg 27-2-96-2 McDermott 27-2-118-3 Bennett 20-0-78-0 Matthews 14.3-2-67-2
Lawson 19-4-54-2 Hogg 14-3-40-0 McDermott 21-6-65-3 Bennett 3-0-12-0 Wessels 1-0-2-0

Australia Innings

AMJ Hilditch	b Harper	70	b Gomes	113
GM Wood	lbw b Garner	12	c Dujon b Garner	5
KC Wessels	c Dujon b Marshall	90	b Garner	0
KJ Hughes	c Dujon b Walsh	0	lbw b Garner	0
*AR Border	c Richards b Walsh	35	c Dujon b Richards	41
GRJ Matthews	b Marshall	5	b Harper	2
+SJ Rixon	c Richardson b Marshall	0	c Richardson b Harper	17
MJ Bennett	not out	22	not out	3
GF Lawson	c Walsh b Garner	8	b Walsh	0
CJ McDermott	b Marshall	0		
RM Hogg	lbw b Marshall	19		
	(b 5, lb 7, w 1, nb 22)	35	(b 6, lb 2, nb 9)	17
	(all out)	296	(8 wickets)	198

Bowling: Marshall 31.5-6-86-5 Garner 24-6-74-2 Walsh 25-5-57-2 Harper 14-1-58-1 Richards 1-0-9-0
Marshall 20-4-36-0 Garner 19-1-49-3 Walsh 18-4-44-1 Harper 22-4-54-2 Richards 6-2-7-1 Gomes 2-2-0-1

Umpires: PJ McConnell and SG Randell

Australia v India
26,27,28,29,30 December 1985

Result: Match drawn

Australia Innings

+WB Phillips	b Yadav	7	c Srikkanth b Yadav	13
DC Boon	lbw b Shastri	14	c & b Kapil Dev	19
GR Marsh	c Sivaramakrishnan b Yadav	30	c Sivaramakrishnan b Shastri	19
*AR Border	c & b Sivaramakrishnan	11	st Kirmani b Yadav	163
DW Hookes	c Shastri	42	c Srikkanth b Shastri	0
SR Waugh	c Kapil Dev b Sivaramakrishnan	13	b Shastri	5
GRJ Matthews	not out	100	c Azharuddin b Sivaramakrishnan	16
RJ Bright	b Shastri	28	lbw b Kapil Dev	20
CJ McDermott	c Kapil Dev b Shastri	1	c & b Shastri	2
BA Reid	c Srikkanth b Kapil Dev	1	c Sivaramakrishnan b Yadav	13
DR Gilbert	c Kirmani b Yadav	4	not out	10
	(b 5, lb 6)	11	(b 11, lb 16, nb 1)	28
	(all out)	262	(all out)	308

Bowling: Kapil Dev 23-6-38-1 Binny 3-0-11-0 Shastri 37-13-87-4 Yadav 27.5-10-64-3 Sivaramakrishnan 13-2-51-2
Kapil Dev 22-7-53-2 Amarnath 3-0-9-0 Shastri 47-13-92-4 Yadav 38.5-15-84-3 Sivaramakrishnan 13-1-43-1

India Innings

SM Gavaskar	b Gilbert	6	b Reid	8
K Srikkanth	lbw b Gilbert	86	c Bright b Reid	38
M Amarnath	c Phillips b Reid	45	not out	3
DB Vengsarkar	c & b Matthews	75	not out	1
M Azharuddin	b Matthews	37		
RJ Shastri	c Phillips b Waugh	49		
*N Kapil Dev	c Hookes b Reid	55		
RMH Binny	c Matthews b Reid	0		
+SMH Kirmani	c Phillips b Waugh	35		
L Sivaramakrishnan	c Phillips b Reid	15		
NS Yadav	not out	6		
	(b 4, lb 15, nb 17)	36	(b 4, lb 1, nb 4)	9
	(all out)	445	(2 wickets)	59

Bowling: McDermott 15-5-52-0 Gilbert 22-1-81-2 Reid 38.2-11-100-4 Bright 31-8-76-0 Matthews 31-7-81-2 Waugh 11-5-36-2
McDermott 6-1-17-0 Gilbert 4-0-9-0 Reid 8-1-23-2 Bright 7-4-5-0

Umpires: RA French and RC Isherwood

Melbourne Cricket Ground

Australia v England
26,27,28 December 1986

Result: England won by an innings and 14 runs

Australia Innings

GR Marsh	c Richards b Botham	17	run out	60
DC Boon	c Botham b Small	7	c Gatting b Small	8
DM Jones	c Gower b Small	59	c Gatting b DeFreitas	21
*AR Border	c Richards b Botham	15	c Emburey b Small	34
SR Waugh	c Botham b Small	10	b Edmonds	49
GRJ Matthews	c Botham b Small	14	b Emburey	0
PR Sleep	c Richards b Small	0	run out	6
+TJ Zoehrer	b Botham	5	c Athey b Edmonds	1
CJ McDermott	c Richards b Botham	0	b Emburey	1
MG Hughes	c Richards b Botham	2	c Small b Edmonds	8
BA Reid	not out	2	not out	0
	(b 1, lb 1, w 1, nb 7)	10	(lb 3, w 1, nb 2)	6
	(all out)	141	(all out)	194

Bowling: Small 22.4-7-48-5 DeFreitas 11-1-30-0 Emburey 4-0-16-0 Botham 16-4-41-5 Gatting 1-0-4-0
DeFreitas 12-1-44-1 Small 15-3-40-2 Botham 7-1-19-0 Edmonds 19.4-5-45-3 Emburey 20-5-43-2

England Innings

BC Broad	c Zoehrer b Hughes	112
CWJ Athey	lbw b Reid	21
*MW Gatting	c Hughes b Reid	40
AJ Lamb	c Zoehrer b Reid	43
DI Gower	c Matthews b Sleep	7
IT Botham	c Zoehrer b McDermott	29
+CJ Richards	c Marsh b Reid	3
PAJ DeFreitas	c Matthews b McDermott	7
JE Emburey	c & b McDermott	22
PH Edmonds	lbw b McDermott	19
GC Small	not out	21
	(b 6, lb 7, w 1, nb 11)	25
	(all out)	349

Bowling: McDermott 26.5-4-83-4 Hughes 30-3-94-1 Reid 28-5-78-4 Waugh 8-4-16-0 Sleep 28-4-65-1

Umpires: AR Crafter and RA French

Australia v New Zealand
26,27,28,29,30 December 1987

Result: Match drawn

New Zealand Innings

PA Horne	c Dyer b Dodemaide	7	c Boon b Dodemaide	27
JG Wright	c Dyer b McDermott	99	b Sleep	43
AH Jones	c Dyer b McDermott	40	run out (Dodemaide/Jones)	20
MD Crowe	c Veletta b McDermott	82	c Border b Dodemaide	79
*JJ Crowe	lbw b McDermott	6	c Boon b Sleep	25
DN Patel	b McDermott	0	c Dyer b Dodemaide	38
JG Bracewell	c Dyer b Whitney	9	c Veletta b Dodemaide	1
RJ Hadlee	c Dodemaide b Whitney	11	lbw b Sleep	29
+IDS Smith	c Jones b Whitney	44	c Dyer b Dodemaide	12
DK Morrison	c Border b Whitney	0	b Dodemaide	0
EJ Chatfield	not out	6	not out	1
	(b 1, lb 4, nb 8)	13	(b 2, lb 8, nb 1)	11
	(all out)	317	(all out)	286

Bowling: McDermott 35-8-97-5 Whitney 33.3-6-92-4 Dodemaide 20-4-48-1 Waugh 10-1-44-0 Sleep 12-1-31-0
McDermott 10-3-43-0 Whitney 20-5-45-0 Dodemaide 28.3-10-58-6 Sleep 26-5-107-3 Jones 8-3-23-0

Australia Innings

DC Boon	lbw b Hadlee	10	c MD Crowe b Morrison	54
GR Marsh	c sub b Hadlee	13	c Bracewell b Hadlee	23
DM Jones	c Smith b Hadlee	4	c MD Crowe b Chatfield	8
*AR Border	c JJ Crowe b Bracewell	31	lbw b Hadlee	43
MRJ Veletta	lbw b Hadlee	31	c Patel b Bracewell	39
SR Waugh	c Jones b Bracewell	55	c Patel b Chatfield	10
PR Sleep	lbw b Hadlee	90	lbw b Hadlee	20
+GC Dyer	run out (Bracewell/Smith)	21	c Smith b Hadlee	4
AIC Dodemaide	c Smith b Morrison	50	lbw b Hadlee	3
CJ McDermott	b Morrison	33	not out	10
MR Whitney	not out	0	not out	2
	(lb 8, nb 11)	19	(b 1, lb 9, nb 4)	14
	(all out)	357	(9 wickets)	230

Bowling: Hadlee 44-11-109-5 Morrison 27.4-5-93-2 Chatfield 30-10-55-0 Bracewell 32-8-69-2 Patel 12-6-23-0
Hadlee 31-9-67-5 Morrison 16-2-54-1 Chatfield 21-6-41-2 Bracewell 24-5-58-1

Umpires: AR Crafter and RA French

Australia v West Indies
24,26,27,28,29 December 1988

Result: West Indies won by 285 runs

West Indies Innings

CG Greenidge	c Healy b Alderman	49	not out	36
DL Haynes	c Boon b McDermott	17	lbw b Alderman	23
RB Richardson	c Taylor b Alderman	26	c & b Waugh	122
CL Hooper	c Border b McDermott	38	lbw b Alderman	4
*IVA Richards	c Border b Waugh	12	lbw b Waugh	63
AL Logie	lbw b Alderman	10	c Border b Waugh	17
+PJL Dujon	c Healy b Waugh	26	c Wood b Alderman	46
MD Marshall	c Jones b Waugh	7	c Alderman b Waugh	19
CEL Ambrose	lbw b McDermott	44	c Marsh b McDermott	5
CA Walsh	not out	30	c Marsh b Waugh	6
BP Patterson	lbw b Alderman	13	not out	3
	(b 1, lb 4, nb 3)	8	(lb 1, nb 16)	17
	(all out)	280	(9 wickets declared)	361

Bowling: Hughes 14-3-52-0 Alderman 32.1-9-68-4 McDermott 19-3-62-3 Waugh 21-3-77-3 Taylor 7-3-16-0
Hughes 24-8-71-0 Alderman 36-12-78-3 Waugh 24-5-92-5 McDermott 26-3-78-1 Border 1-1-0-0 Taylor 9-1-41-0

Australia Innings

DC Boon	run out	23	lbw b Marshall	20
GR Marsh	b Patterson	36	b Patterson	1
DM Jones	b Ambrose	28	c sub (RA Harper) b Ambrose	18
GM Wood	c Haynes b Patterson	12	c Ambrose b Walsh	7
*AR Border	b Ambrose	0	c Haynes b Patterson	20
SR Waugh	c Greenidge b Ambrose	42	c sub (RA Harper) b Ambrose	3
+IA Healy	lbw b Patterson	4	c Hooper b Walsh	8
PL Taylor	c Greenidge b Ambrose	14	not out	18
CJ McDermott	c Marshall b Patterson	28	c sub (KLT Arthurton) b Patterson	0
MG Hughes	not out	21	c Dujon b Patterson	4
TM Alderman	b Walsh	3	c Dujon b Patterson	0
	(b 2, lb 14, nb 15)	31	(b 4, lb 5, nb 6)	15
	(all out)	242	(all out)	114

Bowling: Marshall 30-8-68-0 Ambrose 27-7-60-4 Walsh 17.3-3-49-1 Patterson 20-2-49-4
Marshall 9-3-12-1 Patterson 15.1-3-39-5 Ambrose 13-5-21-2 Walsh 16-7-21-2 Richards 4-1-12-0

Umpires: AR Crafter and PJ McConnell

Australia v Pakistan
12,13,14,15,16 January 1990

Result: Australia won by 92 runs

Australia Innings

GR Marsh	c Saleem Yousuf b Wasim Akram	30	c Wasim Akram b Aaqib Javed	24
MA Taylor	c Aaqib Javed b Imran Khan	52	c Aamer Malik b Tauseef Ahmed	101
DC Boon	lbw b Wasim Akram	0	run out	21
*AR Border	c Javed Miandad b Wasim Akram	24	not out	62
DM Jones	c Saleem Yousuf b Imran Khan	0	lbw b Wasim Akram	10
SR Waugh	c Saleem Yousuf b Aaqib Javed	20	c Saleem Yousuf b Wasim Akram	3
PR Sleep	lbw b Wasim Akram	23	b Wasim Akram	0
+IA Healy	c Shoaib Mohammad b Aaqib Javed	48	c Ijaz Ahmed b Wasim Akram	25
MG Hughes	c Mansoor Akhtar b Wasim Akram	8	c Mansoor Akhtar b Wasim Akram	32
TM Alderman	c Aamer Malik b Wasim Akram	0	not out	1
CG Rackemann	not out	0		
	(lb 9, nb 9)	18	(b 2, lb 10, w 1, nb 20)	33
	(all out)	223	(8 wickets declared)	312

Bowling: Imran Khan 18-6-53-2 Wasim Akram 30-9-62-6 Aaqib Javed 22.1-7-47-2 Waqar Younis 12-3-27-0 Tauseef Ahmed 8-1-25-0
Imran Khan 8-2-21-0 Wasim Akram 41.4-12-98-5 Aaqib Javed 21-1-55-1 Waqar Younis 22-4-68-0 Tauseef Ahmed 16-3-58-1

Pakistan Innings

Aamer Malik	lbw b Alderman	7	c Taylor b Hughes	0
Shoaib Mohammad	c Healy b Alderman	6	c Boon b Hughes	10
Mansoor Akhtar	c Taylor b Rackemann	5	lbw b Alderman	14
Javed Miandad	c Healy b Alderman	3	lbw b Waugh	65
Ijaz Ahmed	c Taylor b Hughes	19	c Marsh b Hughes	121
*Imran Khan	c Alderman b Rackemann	3	lbw b Alderman	45
+Saleem Yousuf	c Taylor b Hughes	16	lbw b Alderman	38
Wasim Akram	c Healy b Hughes	6	c Taylor b Sleep	6
Tauseef Ahmed	not out	9	not out	14
Waqar Younis	lbw b Sleep	18	lbw b Alderman	4
Aaqib Javed	c Healy b Rackemann	0	lbw b Alderman	0
	(b 1, lb 4, nb 10)	15	(b 1, lb 7, w 2, nb 9)	19
	(all out)	107	(all out)	336

Bowling: Alderman 19-6-30-3 Rackemann 21.5-8-32-3 Hughes 17-7-34-3 Sleep 8-5-6-1
Alderman 33.5-6-105-5 Rackemann 38-13-67-0 Hughes 42-14-79-3 Sleep 21-7-64-1 Waugh 3-0-13-1

Umpires: RJ Evans and PJ McConnell

Australia v England
26,27,28,29,30 December 1990

Result: Australia won by 8 wickets

England Innings

*GA Gooch	lbw b Alderman	20	c Alderman b Reid	58
MA Atherton	c Boon b Reid	0	c Healy b Reid	4
W Larkins	c Healy b Reid	64	c Healy b Reid	54
RA Smith	c Healy b Hughes	30	c Taylor b Reid	8
DI Gower	c & b Reid	100	c Border b Matthews	0
AJ Stewart	c Healy b Reid	79	c Marsh b Reid	8
+RC Russell	c Healy b Hughes	15	c Jones b Matthews	1
PAJ DeFreitas	c Healy b Reid	3	lbw b Reid	0
ARC Fraser	c Jones b Alderman	24	c Taylor b Reid	0
DE Malcolm	c Taylor b Reid	6	lbw b Matthews	1
PCR Tufnell	not out	0	not out	0
	(lb 2, nb 9)	11	(b 7, lb 3, nb 6)	16
	(all out)	352	(all out)	150

Bowling: Alderman 30.4-7-86-2 Reid 39-8-97-6 Hughes 29-7-83-2 Matthews 27-8-65-0 Waugh 6-2-19-0
Alderman 10-2-19-0 Reid 22-12-51-7 Hughes 9-4-26-0 Matthews 25-9-40-3 Waugh 7-6-4-0

Australia Innings

GR Marsh	c Russell b DeFreitas	36	not out	79
MA Taylor	c Russell b DeFreitas	61	c Atherton b Malcolm	5
DC Boon	c Russell b Malcolm	28	not out	94
*AR Border	c Russell b Fraser	62		
DM Jones	c Russell b Fraser	44		
SR Waugh	b Fraser	19		
GRJ Matthews	lbw b Fraser	12		
+IA Healy	c Russell b Fraser	5	c Atherton b Fraser	1
MG Hughes	lbw b Malcolm	4		
TM Alderman	b Fraser	0		
BA Reid	not out	3		
	(b 4, lb 12, nb 16)	32	(b 4, lb 12, nb 2)	18
	(all out)	306	(2 wickets)	197

Bowling: Malcolm 25.5-4-74-2 Fraser 39-10-82-6 Tufnell 21-5-62-0 DeFreitas 25-5-69-2 Atherton 2-1-3-0
Malcolm 23-7-52-1 Fraser 20-4-33-1 Tufnell 24-12-36-0 DeFreitas 16-3-46-0 Atherton 3-0-14-0

Umpires: AR Crafter and PJ McConnell

Australia v India
26,27,28,29 December 1991

Result: Australia won by 8 wickets

India Innings

RJ Shastri	c Healy b Reid	23	c Healy b Reid	22
K Srikkanth	c Boon b Reid	5	lbw b Reid	6
M Prabhakar	b Reid	0	c Healy b Reid	17
SV Manjrekar	c Waugh b Reid	25	c MA Taylor b McDermott	30
DB Vengsarkar	c Reid b Hughes	23	c sub (MR Whitney) b McDermott	54
*M Azharuddin	c Jones b McDermott	22	c MA Taylor b Reid	2
SR Tendulkar	c Waugh b Reid	15	c Border b PL Taylor	40
N Kapil Dev	c Hughes b McDermott	19	c Healy b Reid	12
+KS More	not out	67	lbw b Reid	12
SLV Raju	c Border b Hughes	31	c & b McDermott	1
J Srinath	c Border b Reid	14	not out	0
	(b 1, lb 8, w 6, nb 4)	19	(b 1, lb 6, nb 10)	17
	(all out)	263	(all out)	213

Bowling: McDermott 30-6-100-2 Reid 26.2-7-66-6 Hughes 23-6-52-2 Waugh 8-1-16-0 PL Taylor 6-0-20-0
McDermott 29-8-63-3 Reid 29-9-60-6 Hughes 19-6-43-0 PL Taylor 11-3-40-1

Australia Innings

GR Marsh	c Vengsarkar b Kapil Dev	86	lbw b Prabhakar	10
MA Taylor	c Tendulkar b Prabhakar	13	st More b Raju	60
DC Boon	c Srikkanth b Kapil Dev	11	not out	44
*AR Border	b Kapil Dev	0	not out	5
DM Jones	c More b Prabhakar	59		
ME Waugh	c More b Shastri	34		
+IA Healy	lbw b Kapil Dev	60		
PL Taylor	c More b Prabhakar	11		
MG Hughes	c Tendulkar b Kapil Dev	36		
CJ McDermott	not out	16		
BA Reid	c Kapil Dev b Prabhakar	3		
	(lb 9, nb 11)	20	(lb 3, nb 6)	9
	(all out)	349	(2 wickets)	128

Bowling: Kapil Dev 35-9-97-5 Prabhakar 34-7-84-4 Srinath 25-3-71-0 Raju 17-3-52-0 Tendulkar 4-1-16-0 Shastri 7-1-20-1
Kapil Dev 12-1-30-0 Prabhakar 11-0-38-1 Srinath 8-0-28-0 Raju 6-0-17-1 Shastri 3-1-12-0

Umpires: LJ King and TA Prue; Referee: MJK Smith (Eng)

Australia v West Indies
26,27,28,29,30 December 1992

Result: Australia won by 139 runs

Australia Innings

DC Boon	c Williams b Walsh	46	b Simmons		11
MA Taylor	c Lara b Walsh	13	b Bishop		42
SR Waugh	c Lara b Ambrose	38	c Simmons b Bishop		1
ME Waugh	c Williams b Ambrose	112	c Adams b Walsh		16
DR Martyn	c Simmons b Ambrose	7	not out		67
*AR Border	c Williams b Bishop	110	b Bishop		4
+IA Healy	c Hooper b Walsh	24	c & b Walsh		8
MG Hughes	not out	9	c Williams b Ambrose		15
SK Warne	c Adams b Bishop	1	c Arthurton b Ambrose		5
CJ McDermott	b Walsh	17	c Arthurton b Simmons		4
MR Whitney	lbw b Bishop	0	run out		13
	(lb 14, w 1, nb 3)	18	(lb 1, lb 8, nb 1)		10
	(all out)	395	(all out)		196

Bowling: Ambrose 35-10-70-3 Bishop 29-2-84-3 Simmons 10-2-23-0 Walsh 39-10-91-4 Hooper 36-3-95-0 Adams 4-0-18-0 Ambrose 30-9-57-2 Bishop 20-5-45-3 Walsh 21-7-42-2 Simmons 18-6-34-2 Hooper 2.4-1-9-0

West Indies Innings

DL Haynes	b Hughes	7	c Healy b Hughes		5
PV Simmons	c Boon b Hughes	6	c Boon b Warne		110
*RB Richardson	c Healy b Hughes	15	b Warne		52
BC Lara	lbw b Whitney	52	c Boon b Whitney		4
KLT Arthurton	c Healy b McDermott	71	st Healy b Warne		13
CL Hooper	c & b SR Waugh	3	c Whitney b Warne		0
JC Adams	c Boon b McDermott	47	c Taylor b McDermott		16
+D Williams	c Healy b McDermott	0	c ME Waugh b Warne		0
IR Bishop	b McDermott	9	c Taylor b Warne		7
CEL Ambrose	c McDermott b Warne	7	not out		6
CA Walsh	not out	0	c Hughes b Warne		0
	(lb 10, nb 6)	16	(lb 3, lb 2, nb 1)		6
	(all out)	233	(all out)		219

Bowling: McDermott 25.1-8-66-4 Hughes 19-5-51-3 Whitney 13-4-27-1 Warne 24-7-65-1 SR Waugh 4-1-14-1 McDermott 17-2-66-1 Hughes 18-7-41-1 Whitney 10-2-32-1 Warne 23.2-8-52-7 ME Waugh 3-0-23-0

Umpires: SG Randell and CD Timmins; Referee: R Subba Row (Eng)

Australia v South Africa
26,27,28,29,30 December 1993

Result: Match drawn

Australia Innings

MA Taylor	b Symcox	170
MJ Slater	c Kirsten b Donald	32
SK Warne	lbw b de Villiers	5
DC Boon	b Matthews	25
ME Waugh	lbw b Matthews	84
*AR Border	c Richardson b Matthews	2
DR Martyn	b Symcox	8
+IA Healy	not out	7
PR Reiffel		
TBA May		
CJ McDermott		
	(b 2, lb 7, nb 5)	14
	(7 wickets dec)	342

Bowling: Donald 30-4-108-1 de Villiers 32-6-83-1 Matthews 24-5-68-3 Cronje 13-4-25-0 Symcox 16.5-3-49-2

South Africa Innings

AC Hudson	retired hurt	64
G Kirsten	c Taylor b Waugh	16
WJ Cronje	c Boon b Warne	71
DJ Cullinan	c Border b McDermott	0
JN Rhodes	not out	35
*KC Wessels	not out	63
+DJ Richardson		
PL Symcox		
CR Matthews		
PS de Villiers		
AA Donald		
	(lb 2, nb 7)	9
	(3 wickets)	258

Bowling: McDermott 23-5-60-1 Reiffel 21-4-55-0 Waugh 12-3-20-1 May 28-7-58-0 Warne 31-8-63-1

Umpires: DB Hair and TA Prue
TV Umpire: LJ King; Referee: JL Hendriks (WI)

Australia v England
24,26,27,28,29 December 1994

Result: Australia won by 295 runs

Australia Innings

MJ Slater	run out (DeFreitas/Gatting)	3	st Rhodes b Tufnell		44
*MA Taylor	lbw b DeFreitas	9	lbw b Gough		19
DC Boon	c Hick b Tufnell	41	lbw b DeFreitas		131
ME Waugh	c Thorpe b DeFreitas	71	c & b Gough		29
MG Bevan	c Atherton b Gough	3	c sub (JP Crawley) b Tufnell		35
SR Waugh	not out	94	not out		26
+IA Healy	c Rhodes b Tufnell	17	c Thorpe b Tufnell		17
SK Warne	c Hick b Gough	6	c DeFreitas b Gough		0
TBA May	lbw b Gough	9			
CJ McDermott	b Gough	0	not out		2
DW Fleming	c Hick b Malcolm	16			
	(lb 7, nb 3)	10	(b 1, lb 9, w 1, nb 6)		17
	(all out)	279	(7 wickets decl)		320

Bowling: Malcolm 28.3-4-78-1 DeFreitas 23-4-66-2 Gough 26-9-60-4 Tufnell 28-7-59-2 Hick 2-0-9-0 Malcolm 22-3-86-0 DeFreitas 26-2-70-1 Tufnell 48-8-90-3 Gough 25-6-59-3 Hick 3-2-5-0

England Innings

*MA Atherton	lbw b Warne	44	c Healy b McDermott		25
AJ Stewart	c & b Warne	16	not out		8
GA Hick	c Healy b McDermott	23	b Fleming		2
GP Thorpe	c ME Waugh b Warne	51	c Healy b McDermott		9
GA Gooch	c & b McDermott	15	c Healy b Fleming		2
MW Gatting	c SR Waugh b Warne	9	c Taylor b McDermott		25
D Gough	c Healy b McDermott	20	c Healy b Warne		0
+SJ Rhodes	c ME Waugh b Warne	0	c ME Waugh b McDermott		16
PAJ DeFreitas	st Healy b Warne	14	lbw b Warne		0
DE Malcolm	not out	11	c Boon b Warne		0
PCR Tufnell	run out (Taylor)	0	c Healy b McDermott		0
	(lb 7, nb 2)	9	(lb 2, nb 3)		5
	(all out)	212	(all out)		92

Bowling: McDermott 24-6-72-3 Fleming 11-5-30-0 ME Waugh 3-1-11-0 Warne 27.4-8-64-6 May 18-5-28-0 McDermott 16.5-5-42-5 Fleming 9-1-24-2 Warne 13-6-16-3 May 4-1-8-0

Umpires: SA Bucknor (WI) and SG Randell
TV Umpire: WP Sheahan; Referee: JR Reid (NZ)

Australia v Sri Lanka
26,27,28,29,30 December 1995

Result: Australia won by 10 wickets

Australia Innings

MJ Slater	c Wickramasinghe b Vaas	62	not out		13
*MA Taylor	b Wickramasinghe	7	not out		25
DC Boon	c Muralitharan b Wickramasinghe	110			
ME Waugh	b Muralitharan	61			
SR Waugh	not out	131			
RT Ponting	c Gurusinha b Silva	71			
+IA Healy	c Muralitharan b de Silva	41			
PR Reiffel	not out	4			
SK Warne					
CJ McDermott					
GD McGrath					
	(lb 8, w 2, nb 3)	13	(lb 1, nb 2)		3
	(6 wickets decl)	500	(0 wickets)		41

Bowling: Wickramasinghe 30.2-9-77-2 Vaas 40.4-11-93-1 Hathurusingha 9-0-23-0 Gurusinha 2-0-8-0 Muralitharan 38-7-124-1 Silva 35-5-120-1 de Silva 10-0-47-1 Vaas 5-0-25-0 Gurusinha 3-1-6-0 de Silva 1-0-4-0 Tillakaratne 0.4-0-5-0

Sri Lanka Innings

RS Mahanama	c Taylor b McGrath	3	c Warne b Reiffel		3
UC Hathurusingha	lbw b McGrath	23	lbw b Warne		39
AP Gurusinha	c Healy b Ponting	27	lbw b Reiffel		143
PA de Silva	c Reiffel b Warne	18	c Healy b McDermott		28
*A Ranatunga	c Warne b McDermott	51	not out		11
HP Tillakaratne	c Taylor b Warne	14	c Ponting b ME Waugh		38
+RS Kaluwitharana	c Boon b McDermott	50	st Healy b Warne		2
WPUJC Vaas	c Healy b Reiffel	0	c Boon b McGrath		6
GP Wickramasinghe	c Healy b McGrath	10	st Healy b Warne		17
M Muralitharan	c Slater b McGrath	11	c Taylor b Warne		0
KJ Silva	not out	6	b McGrath		0
	(b 6, lb 7, nb 7)	20	(b 7, lb 5, nb 8)		20
	(all out)	233	(all out)		307

Bowling: McDermott 23-8-63-2 McGrath 23.4-9-40-5 Reiffel 20-5-60-1 Ponting 4-2-8-1 Warne 18-5-49-1 McGrath 33.5-6-92-2 McDermott 17-1-54-1 Reiffel 20-7-59-2 Warne 37-10-71-4 ME Waugh 9-1-19-1

Umpires: RS Dunne (NZ) and DB Hair
TV Umpire: WP Sheahan; Referee: GT Dowling (NZ)

Australia v West Indies
26,27,28 December 1996

Result: West Indies won by 6 wickets

Australia Innings

*MA Taylor	b Ambrose	7	c Hooper b Walsh		10
ML Hayden	c Hooper b Ambrose	5	b Ambrose		0
JL Langer	run out (Adams)	12	c Hooper b Ambrose		0
ME Waugh	lbw b Ambrose	0	lbw b Walsh		19
SR Waugh	c Murray b Bishop	58	b Benjamin		37
GS Blewett	run out (sub [AFG Griffith])	62	c Murray b Walsh		7
+IA Healy	c Hooper b Ambrose	36	b Benjamin		0
PR Reiffel	c Samuels b Benjamin	0	lbw b Benjamin		8
SK Warne	c Campbell b Bishop	10	c Adams b Ambrose		18
JN Gillespie	not out	4	lbw b Ambrose		2
GD McGrath	c Hooper b Ambrose	0	not out		5
	(lb 8, nb 17)	25	(lb 4, w 1, nb 11)		16
	(all out)	219	(all out)		122

Bowling: Ambrose 24.5-7-55-5 Bishop 11-1-31-2 Benjamin 19-2-64-1 Walsh 14-0-43-0 Adams 1-0-4-0 Hooper 5-1-14-0 Ambrose 12-4-17-4 Bishop 10-2-26-0 Benjamin 12.5-5-34-3 Walsh 11-4-41-3

West Indies Innings

SL Campbell	lbw b McGrath	7	b Hayden b McGrath		0
RG Samuels	c Taylor b Warne	17	lbw b McGrath		13
S Chanderpaul	c & b McGrath	58	b Reiffel		40
BC Lara	c Warne b McGrath	2	c Hayden b McGrath		2
CL Hooper	run out (McGrath)	7	not out		27
JC Adams	not out	74	not out		1
+JR Murray	c Reiffel b McGrath	53			
IR Bishop	lbw b McGrath	8			
CEL Ambrose	b Warne	8			
KCG Benjamin	b Reiffel	11			
*CA Walsh	c ME Waugh b Warne	4			
	(b 4, lb 7, nb 3)	14	(nb 4)		4
	(all out)	255	(4 wickets)		87

Bowling: McGrath 30-11-50-5 Reiffel 29-8-76-1 Warne 28.1-3-72-3 Gillespie 3-2-5-0 Blewett 9-3-19-0 SR Waugh 10-5-22-0 McGrath 9-1-41-3 Reiffel 9-2-16-1 Warne 3-0-17-0 Blewett 2.5-0-13-0

Umpires: PD Parker and S Venkataraghavan (Ind)
TV Umpire: WP Sheahan; Referee: PL van der Merwe (SA)

Australia v South Africa
26,27,28,29,30 December 1997

Result: Match drawn

Australia Innings

MTG Elliott	c Richardson b Klusener	6	lbw b Donald		1
*MA Taylor	c Kirsten b McMillan	20	c Cullinan b Symcox		59
GS Blewett	st Richardson b Symcox	26	c McMillan b Donald		6
ME Waugh	c Richardson b Donald	0	b Donald		1
SR Waugh	c Cullinan b Donald	96	c Richardson b Pollock		17
RT Ponting	b Symcox	105	c & b Pollock		32
+IA Healy	b Donald	16	b Donald		4
PR Reiffel	b Symcox	27	not out		79
SK Warne	c & b Pollock	1	c Symcox b Donald		10
MS Kasprowicz	c Bacher b Symcox	0	c Kirsten b Donald		19
GD McGrath	not out	0	c McMillan b Pollock		18
	(b 1, lb 6, nb 5)	12	(b 4, lb 3, nb 4)		11
	(all out)	309	(all out)		257

Bowling: Donald 29-6-74-3 Pollock 28-6-76-1 Klusener 3-3-48-1 McMillan 10-3-19-1 Symcox 27.2-4-69-4 Kallis 4-2-5-0 Cronje 4-2-11-0 Donald 27-8-59-6 Pollock 21.2-5-56-3 Symcox 35-9-90-1 McMillan 2-0-6-0 Klusener 9-2-28-0 Cronje 2-0-11-0

South Africa Innings

AM Bacher	c Healy b Kasprowicz	3	c Taylor b Warne		39
G Kirsten	c Healy b ME Waugh	83	b Reiffel		101
JH Kallis	c Healy b McGrath	15	b Reiffel		0
DJ Cullinan	run out (Ponting)	5	b Warne		0
*WJ Cronje	c Blewett b Warne	0	c Taylor b SR Waugh		70
BM McMillan	c Healy b Kasprowicz	48	c Taylor b Warne		16
SM Pollock	lbw b Warne	7	not out		15
+DJ Richardson	lbw b ME Waugh	1	lbw b McGrath		11
L Klusener	lbw b Warne	11	not out		6
PL Symcox	b Kasprowicz	4			
AA Donald	not out	0			
	(lb 2, w 1, nb 6)	9	(b 5, lb 4, nb 6)		15
	(all out)	186	(7 wickets)		273

Bowling: McGrath 17-9-20-1 Kasprowicz 14-5-32-0 Warne 42-15-64-3 ME Waugh 18-8-28-2 SR Waugh 2-0-12-0 McGrath 28-11-57-1 Reiffel 18-7-24-2 Kasprowicz 14-1-45-0 Warne 44-11-97-3 ME Waugh 10-0-25-0 SR Waugh 7-2-12-1 Blewett 1-0-4-0

Umpires: SA Bucknor (WI) and SG Randell
TV Umpire: WP Sheahan; Referee: RS Madugalle (SL)

Melbourne Cricket Ground

Australia v England
26,27,28,29 December 1998

Result: England won by 12 runs

England Innings

MA Atherton	c Healy b McGrath	0	b Fleming	0
*AJ Stewart	b MacGill	107	c Slater b MacGill	52
MA Butcher	c Langer b McGrath	0	c Slater b MacGill	14
N Hussain	c Healy b Nicholson	19	c Slater b Nicholson	50
MR Ramprakash	c McGrath b SR Waugh	63	b Nicholson	14
GA Hick	c Fleming b MacGill	39	b Fleming	60
+WK Hegg	c Healy b SR Waugh	3	c MacGill b Nicholson	9
DW Headley	c Taylor b McGrath	14	b McGrath	1
D Gough	b MacGill	11	c Slater b MacGill	4
ARC Fraser	not out	0	not out	7
AD Mullally	lbw b MacGill	0	c & b McGrath	16
	(b 7, w 1, lb 4, nb 6)	14	(b 2, lb 4, nb 11)	17
	(all out)	270	(all out)	244

Bowling: McGrath 22-5-64-3 Fleming 19-3-71-0 Nicholson 10-0-59-1 MacGill 19-2-61-4 SR Waugh 6-2-8-2
McGrath 20.2-5-56-2 Fleming 17-4-45-2 Nicholson 15-4-56-3 MacGill 27-3-81-3 ME Waugh 1-1-0-0

Australia Innings

*MA Taylor	c Hick b Gough	7	c Headley b Mullally	19
MJ Slater	lbw b Gough	1	lbw b Headley	18
JL Langer	c Hussain b Gough	44	c Ramprakash b Mullally	30
ME Waugh	lbw b Fraser	36	c Hick b Headley	43
SR Waugh	not out	122	not out	30
DS Lehmann	c Hegg b Gough	13	c Hegg b Headley	4
+IA Healy	c Headley b Fraser	36	c Hegg b Headley	0
DW Fleming	c Hick b Mullally	12	lbw b Headley	0
MJ Nicholson	b Gough	5	c Hegg b Headley	9
SCG MacGill	c Hegg b Mullally	43	b Gough	0
GD McGrath	b Mullally	0	lbw b Gough	0
	(b 4, lb 6, nb 11)	21	(b 4, lb 1, nb 4)	9
	(all out)	340	(all out)	162

Bowling: Gough 28-7-96-5 Headley 25-3-86-0 Mullally 21.3-5-64-3 Ramprakash 2-0-6-0 Fraser 22-0-78-2
Gough 15.4-2-54-2 Headley 17-5-60-6 Mullally 14-0-20-2 Fraser 4-0-23-0

Umpires: SA Bucknor (WI) and DJ Harper
TV Umpire: GTD Morrow; Referee: JR Reid (NZ)

Australia v India
26,27,28,29,30 December 1999

Result: Australia won by 180 runs

Australia Innings

GS Blewett	b Srinath	2	c Ganguly b Kumble	31
MJ Slater	c Srinath b BKV Prasad	91	lbw b Agarkar	3
JL Langer	lbw b Srinath	8	c MSK Prasad b Agarkar	9
ME Waugh	lbw b Agarkar	41	not out	51
*SR Waugh	c MSK Prasad b BKV Prasad	32	lbw b Agarkar	32
RT Ponting	lbw b Srinath	67	not out	21
+AC Gilchrist	c Ganguly b Agarkar	78	c Srinath b Kumble	55
SK Warne	c MSK Prasad b Agarkar	2		
DW Fleming	not out	31		
B Lee	c & b Srinath	27		
GD McGrath	run out (Kanitkar)	25		
	(b 1, lb 9, w 1, nb 14)		(lb 2, w 1, nb 3)	6
	(all out)	405	(5 wickets dec)	208

Bowling: Srinath 33.1-7-130-4 Agarkar 28-7-76-3 BKV Prasad 26-6-101-2 Ganguly 2-0-10-0 Kumble 29-3-78-0
Srinath 14-0-45-0 Agarkar 17-3-51-3 BKV Prasad 10-0-38-0 Kumble 18-3-72-2

India Innings

VVS Laxman	c ME Waugh b McGrath	5	c McGrath b Fleming	1
S Ramesh	b Lee	4	retired hurt	26
R Dravid	c Gilchrist b Lee	9	c Gilchrist b Lee	14
*SR Tendulkar	c Langer b Fleming	116	lbw b Warne	52
SC Ganguly	c ME Waugh b McGrath	31	b Blewett	17
HH Kanitkar	lbw b Warne	11	lbw b Fleming	45
+MSK Prasad	b Lee	1	c Warne b ME Waugh	13
AB Agarkar	lbw b Lee	0	c Blewett b ME Waugh	0
J Srinath	c ME Waugh b Lee	1	c Warne b Lee	1
A Kumble	not out	28	run out (SR Waugh/Fleming)	13
BKV Prasad	c ME Waugh b McGrath	10	not out	6
	(lb 8, nb 9)	17	(lb 4, nb 3)	7
	(all out)	238	(all out)	195

Bowling: McGrath 18.1-3-39-3 Fleming 15-0-62-1 Lee 18-2-47-5 Warne 24-5-77-1 ME Waugh 1-0-5-0
McGrath 17-8-22-0 Fleming 21.3-7-46-2 Warne 26-7-63-1 Lee 19-6-31-2 Blewett 3-1-17-1 ME Waugh 3-0-12-2

Umpires: SJ Davis and DR Shepherd (Eng)
TV Umpire: WP Sheahan; Referee: RS Madugalle (SL)

Australia v West Indies
26,27,28,29 December 2000

Result: Australia won by 352 runs

Australia Innings

MJ Slater	c Jacobs b McLean	30	c Lara b Dillon	4
ML Hayden	c Jacobs b Walsh	13	c Hinds b McLean	30
JL Langer	c Jacobs b Stuart	31	c Ganga b Adams	80
ME Waugh	c Adams b Dillon	25	not out	78
*SR Waugh	not out	121	c Jacobs b Stuart	20
RT Ponting	c Hinds b McLean	23	not out	26
+AC Gilchrist	c Campbell b Stuart	37		
AJ Bichel	c Jacobs b Dillon	3		
JN Gillespie	c Jacobs b Walsh	19		
CR Miller	c Jacobs b Dillon	29	st Jacobs b Adams	11
GD McGrath	c Jacobs b Dillon	11		
	(lb 4, nb 17)	22	(b 5, lb 4, w 1, nb 3)	13
	(all out)	364	(5 wickets dec)	262

Bowling: Walsh 33-6-62-2 Dillon 21-2-76-4 McLean 27-5-95-2 Stuart 15-4-52-2 Samuels 14-0-56-0 Adams 4-0-19-0
Walsh 18-3-46-0 Dillon 17-1-68-1 McLean 9-1-30-1 Stuart 15-2-66-1 Adams 18-8-43-2

Innings

MJ Slater	c Jacobs b McLean	30
ML Hayden	c Jacobs b Walsh	13
JL Langer	c Jacobs b Stuart	31
ME Waugh	c Adams b Dillon	25
*SR Waugh	not out	121
RT Ponting	c Hinds b McLean	23
+AC Gilchrist	c Campbell b Stuart	37
AJ Bichel	c Jacobs b Dillon	3
JN Gillespie	c Jacobs b Walsh	19
CR Miller	c Jacobs b Dillon	29
GD McGrath	c Jacobs b Dillon	11
	(lb 4, nb 17)	22
	(all out)	364

Bowling: Walsh 33-6-62-2 Dillon 21-2-76-4 McLean 27-5-95-2 Stuart 15-4-52-2 Samuels 14-0-56-0 Adams 4-0-19-0

Umpires: SJA Taufel and S Venkataraghavan (Ind)
TV Umpire: RG Patterson; Referee: AC Smith (Eng)

Australia v South Africa
26,27,28,29 December 2001

Result: Australia won by 9 wickets

South Africa Innings

HH Gibbs	c Ponting b McGrath	14	c Gilchrist b Lee	21
G Kirsten	b McGrath	10	c Ponting b Lee	10
HH Dippenaar	c Hayden b Lee	26	c Hayden b Warne	23
JH Kallis	c Gilchrist b Bichel	38	run out (Martyn/Gilchrist)	99
ND McKenzie	lbw b Lee	67	c Gilchrist b Warne	12
L Klusener	c & b Bichel	0	lbw b McGrath	7
+MV Boucher	c Bichel b ME Waugh	43	c ME Waugh b Warne	0
*SM Pollock	not out	42	run out (Martyn)	18
CW Henderson	run out (Bichel)	5	c ME Waugh b McGrath	16
AA Donald	c Ponting b Lee	0	b Bichel	7
M Hayward	c ME Waugh b Bichel	14	not out	0
	(b 1, lb 10, nb 7)	18	(b 4, nb 2)	6
	(all out)	277	(all out)	219

Bowling: McGrath 26-8-70-2 Lee 31-10-77-3 Bichel 19.5-6-44-3 Warne 19-3-56-0 ME Waugh 8-1-19-1
McGrath 21-6-43-2 Lee 18-5-52-2 Warne 24-3-68-3 Bichel 12.1-0-52-1

Australia Innings

JL Langer	c Klusener b Donald	85	c Henderson b Pollock	7
ML Hayden	c Donald b Henderson	138	not out	3
RT Ponting	c Kallis b Hayward	22	not out	0
ME Waugh	b Donald	34		
*SR Waugh	run out (Gibbs)	90		
DR Martyn	c Kallis b Pollock	52		
+AC Gilchrist	not out	30		
SK Warne	c Kirsten b Donald	1		
B Lee	c McKenzie b Hayward	3		
AJ Bichel	c Boucher b Pollock	5		
GD McGrath	lbw b Pollock	0		
	(lb 17, w 1, nb 9)	27		0
	(all out)	487	(1 wicket)	10

Bowling: Donald 29-5-103-3 Pollock 31-3-84-3 Hayward 26-1-109-2 Kallis 17-3-55-0 Henderson 29-3-108-1 Klusener 7-1-11-0
Donald 2-0-4-0 Pollock 1-0-6-1

Umpires: DB Hair and EA Nicholls (WI)
TV Umpire: RL Parry; Referee: RS Madugalle (SL)

Australia v England
26,27,28,29,30 December 2002

Result: Australia won by 5 wickets

Australia Innings

JL Langer	c Caddick b Dawson	250	lbw b Caddick	24
ML Hayden	c Crawley b Caddick	102	c sub (AJ Tudor) b Caddick	1
RT Ponting	b White	21	c Foster b Harmison	30
DR Martyn	c Trescothick b White	17	c Foster b Harmison	0
*SR Waugh	c Foster b White	77	c Foster b Caddick	14
ML Love	not out	62	not out	6
+AC Gilchrist	b Dawson	1	not out	10
B Lee				
JN Gillespie				
SCG MacGill				
GD McGrath				
	(b 11, w 5, nb 5)	21	(b 8, lb 5, nb 9)	22
	(6 wickets dec)	551	(5 wickets)	107

Bowling: Caddick 36-6-126-1 Harmison 36-7-108-0 White 33-5-133-3 Dawson 28-1-121-2 Butcher 13-2-52-0
Caddick 12-1-51-3 Harmison 11.1-1-43-2

England Innings

ME Trescothick	c Gilchrist b Lee	37	lbw b MacGill	37
MP Vaughan	b McGrath	11	c Love b MacGill	145
MA Butcher	lbw b Gillespie	25	c Love b Gillespie	6
*N Hussain	c Hayden b MacGill	24	c & b McGrath	23
RKJ Dawson	c Love b MacGill	6	not out	15
RWT Key	lbw b Lee	0	c Ponting b Gillespie	52
JP Crawley	c Langer b Gillespie	17	b Lee	33
C White	not out	85	c Gilchrist b MacGill	21
+JS Foster	lbw b Waugh	19	c Love b MacGill	6
AR Caddick	b Gillespie	17	c Waugh b MacGill	10
SJ Harmison	c Gilchrist b Gillespie	2	b Gillespie	7
	(b 3, lb 10, nb 14)	27	(b 3, lb 21, w 2, nb 6)	32
	(all out)	270	(all out)	387

Bowling: McGrath 16-5-41-1 Gillespie 16.3-7-25-4 MacGill 36-10-108-2 Lee 17-4-70-2 Waugh 4-0-13-1
McGrath 19-5-44-1 Gillespie 24.4-6-71-3 MacGill 48-10-152-5 Lee 27-4-87-1 Waugh 2-0-9-0

Umpires: DL Orchard (SA) and RB Tiffin (Zim)
TV Umpire: DB Hair; Referee: Wasim Raja (Pak)

England v Australia
21,22,23 July 1884

Result: England won by an innings and 5 runs

Australia Innings

PS McDonnell	b Peate	0	b Steel	20	
AC Bannerman	b Peate	12	c & b Ulyett	27	
*WL Murdoch	lbw b Peate	10	c Shrewsbury b Ulyett	17	
G Giffen	b Peate	63	c Peate b Ulyett	5	
WE Midwinter	b Peate	3	b Ulyett	6	
GJ Bonnor	c Grace b Christopherson	25	c & b Ulyett	4	
+JM Blackham	run out	0	retired hurt	0	
HJH Scott	b sub (WL Murdoch) b Steel	75	not out	31	
GE Palmer	c Grace b Peate	7	b Ulyett	13	
FR Spofforth	c Barlow b Grace	0	c Shrewsbury b Barlow	11	
HF Boyle	not out	26	b Ulyett	10	
	(b 5, lb 3)	8	(b 1)	1	
	(all out)	229	(all out)	145	

Bowling: Peate 40-14-85-6 Barlow 20-6-44-0 Ulyett 11-3-21-0 Christopherson 26-10-52-1 Grace 7-4-13-1 Steel 1.2-0-6-1
Peate 16-4-34-0 Barlow 21-8-31-1 Ulyett 39.1-23-36-7 Christopherson 8-3-17-0 Steel 10-2-26-1

England Innings

WG Grace	c Bonnor b Palmer	14
AP Lucas	c Bonnor b Palmer	28
A Shrewsbury	st Blackham b Giffen	27
G Ulyett	b Palmer	32
AG Steel	b Palmer	148
*Lord Harris	b Spofforth	4
RG Barlow	c Palmer b Bonnor	38
WW Read	b Palmer	12
+Hon.A Lyttelton	b Palmer	31
E Peate	not out	8
S Christopherson	c Bonnor b Spofforth	17
	(b 15, lb 5)	20
	(all out)	379

Bowling: Spofforth 55.1-19-112-2 Palmer 75-26-111-6 Giffen 22-4-68-1 Boyle 11-3-16-0 Bonnor 8-1-23-1 Midwinter 13-2-29-0

Umpires: FH Farrands and CK Pullin

England v Australia
19,20,21 July 1886

Result: England won by an innings and 106 runs

England Innings

WG Grace	c Jarvis b Palmer	18
WH Scotton	b Garrett	19
A Shrewsbury	c Bonnor b Trumble	164
WW Read	c Spofforth b Giffen	22
*AG Steel	lbw b Spofforth	5
W Barnes	c Palmer b Garrett	58
RG Barlow	c Palmer b Spofforth	12
G Ulyett	b Spofforth	19
+EFS Tylecote	b Spofforth	0
J Briggs	c Jones b Trumble	0
GA Lohmann	not out	7
	(b 24, lb 4, nb 1)	29
	(all out)	353

Bowling: Garrett 72-40-77-2 Evans 36-20-37-0 Palmer 38-15-45-1 Spofforth 56-26-73-4 Trumble 14-4-27-2 Giffen 40-18-63-1 Jones 3-1-2-0

Australia Innings

SP Jones	c Grace b Briggs	25	b Briggs	17	
*HJH Scott	lbw b Briggs	30	b Briggs	2	
G Giffen	b Steel	3	b Barlow	1	
+AH Jarvis	b Briggs	3	not out	13	
GJ Bonnor	c Grace b Steel	0	b Briggs	3	
JW Trumble	c Tylecote b Briggs	0	c Tylecote b Barnes	20	
GE Palmer	c Shrewsbury b Barnes	20	c Lohmann b Barlow	48	
JM Blackham	b Briggs	23	b Briggs	5	
TW Garrett	not out	7	b Briggs	4	
FR Spofforth	b Barnes	5	c & b Briggs	0	
E Evans	c Ulyett b Barnes	0	run out	0	
	(b 4, lb 1)	5	(b 13)	13	
	(all out)	121	(all out)	126	

Bowling: Barnes 14.3-7-25-3 Lohmann 7-3-21-0 Briggs 34-22-29-5 Steel 21-8-34-2 Barlow 6-3-7-0
Barnes 10-5-18-1 Lohmann 14-9-11-0 Briggs 38.1-17-45-6 Steel 16-9-14-0 Barlow 25-20-12-2 Ulyett 8-3-13-0

Umpires: FH Farrands and CK Pullin

England v Australia
16,17 July 1888

Result: Australia won by 61 runs

Australia Innings

AC Bannerman	c Grace b Lohmann	0	b Peel	0	
*PS McDonnell	c O'Brien b Peel	22	b Lohmann	1	
GHS Trott	c Lohmann b Peel	0	b Lohmann	3	
GJ Bonnor	b Lohmann	6	c Lohmann b Peel	8	
+JM Blackham	b Briggs	22	run out	1	
SMJ Woods	c Gunn b Briggs	18	c Grace b Peel	3	
CTB Turner	c Lohmann b Peel	3	c Grace b Briggs	12	
JD Edwards	not out	21	c Sherwin b Lohmann	0	
AH Jarvis	c Lohmann b Peel	3	c Barnes b Peel	4	
J Worrall	c Abel b Briggs	2	b Lohmann	4	
JJ Ferris	c Sherwin b Steel	14	not out	20	
	(b 5)	5	(b 3, lb 1)	4	
	(all out)	116	(all out)	60	

Bowling: Lohmann 20-9-28-2 Peel 21-7-36-4 Briggs 21-8-26-3 Barnes 6-0-17-0 Steel 3.2-2-4-1
Lohmann 14-4-33-4 Peel 10.2-3-14-4 Briggs 4-1-9-1 Steel 1-1-0-0

England Innings

WG Grace	c Woods b Ferris	10	c Bannerman b Ferris	24	
R Abel	b Ferris	3	c Bannerman b Ferris	8	
W Barnes	c Jarvis b Turner	3	st Blackham b Ferris	1	
GA Lohmann	lbw b Turner	2	c Blackham b Ferris	0	
WW Read	st Blackham b Turner	4	b Turner	3	
TC O'Brien	b Turner	0	b Turner	4	
R Peel	run out	8	b Turner	4	
*AG Steel	st Blackham b Turner	3	not out	10	
W Gunn	c Blackham b Ferris	2	b Ferris	8	
J Briggs	b Woods	17	b Turner	0	
+M Sherwin	not out	0	c Ferris b Turner	0	
			(lb 1)	1	
	(all out)	53	(all out)	62	

Bowling: Turner 25-9-27-5 Ferris 21-13-19-3 Woods 4-2-6-1
Turner 24-8-36-5 Ferris 23-11-26-5

Umpires: FH Farrands and CK Pullin

England v Australia
21,22,23 July 1890

Result: England won by 7 wickets

Australia Innings

JJ Lyons	b Barnes	55	c Attewell b Peel	33	
CTB Turner	b Attewell	24	lbw b Peel	2	
*WL Murdoch	c & b Attewell	9	b Lohmann	19	
JE Barrett	c Grace b Ulyett	9	not out	67	
GHS Trott	run out	12	b Peel	0	
SE Gregory	b Attewell	0	c Lohmann b Barnes	9	
PC Charlton	st MacGregor b Peel	6	lbw b Grace	2	
+JM Blackham	b Peel	5	c Barnes b Grace	10	
JJ Ferris	b Attewell	8	lbw b Lohmann	8	
EJK Burn	st MacGregor b Peel	0	c MacGregor b Attewell	19	
H Trumble	not out	1	c Ulyett b Attewell	5	
	(lb 3)	3	(lb 2)	2	
	(all out)	132	(all out)	176	

Bowling: Lohmann 21-10-43-0 Peel 24-11-28-3 Attewell 32-15-42-4 Barnes 6-2-16-1 Ulyett 3-3-0-1
Lohmann 29-19-28-3 Peel 43-23-59-3 Attewell 42.2-22-54-1 Barnes 6-3-10-1 Ulyett 6-2-11-0 Grace 14-10-12-2

England Innings

*WG Grace	c & b Turner	0	not out	75	
A Shrewsbury	st Blackham b Ferris	4	lbw b Ferris	13	
W Gunn	run out	14	c & b Ferris	34	
WW Read	c & b Ferris	1	b Trumble	13	
JM Read	b Lyons	34	not out	2	
G Ulyett	b Lyons	74			
R Peel	c & b Trumble	16			
W Barnes	b Lyons	9			
GA Lohmann	c & b Lyons	19			
+G MacGregor	b Lyons	0			
W Attewell	not out	0			
	(lb 2)	2		0	
	(all out)	173	(3 wickets)	137	

Bowling: Turner 35-17-53-1 Ferris 40-17-55-2 Trott 3-0-16-0 Lyons 20.1-7-30-5 Trumble 12-7-17-1
Turner 22-12-31-0 Ferris 25-11-42-2 Lyons 20-6-43-0 Trumble 8-1-21-1

Umpires: A Hill and CK Pullin

England v Australia
17,18,19 July 1893

Result: Match drawn

England Innings

A Shrewsbury	c Blackham b Turner	106	b Giffen	81	
*AE Stoddart	b Turner	24	b Turner	13	
W Gunn	c Lyons b Turner	2	c Graham b Giffen	77	
FS Jackson	c Blackham b Turner	91	c Bruce b Giffen	5	
JM Read	b Bruce	6	c McLeod b Bruce	1	
R Peel	c Bruce b Trumble	12	not out	0	
W Flowers	b McLeod	35	b Turner	4	
E Wainwright	c Giffen b Turner	1	b Turner	26	
WH Lockwood	b Bruce	22	b Giffen	0	
+G MacGregor	not out	5			
AW Mold	b Turner	0			
	(b 19, lb 9, nb 2)	30	(b 16, lb 9, w 1, nb 1)	27	
	(all out)	334	(8 wickets declared)	234	

Bowling: Turner 36-16-67-6 Bruce 22-4-58-2 Trumble 19-7-42-1 Trott 9-2-38-0 McLeod 21-6-51-1 Giffen 18-3-48-0
Turner 32-15-64-2 Bruce 20-10-34-1 Trumble 11-2-33-0 Trott 2-0-5-0 McLeod 25-11-28-0 Giffen 26.4-6-43-5

Australia Innings

JJ Lyons	b Barnes	55
CTB Turner	b Attewell	24
*WL Murdoch	c & b Attewell	9
JE Barrett	c Grace b Ulyett	9
GHS Trott	run out	12
SE Gregory	b Attewell	0
PC Charlton	st MacGregor b Peel	6
+JM Blackham	b Peel	5
JJ Ferris	b Attewell	8
EJK Burn	st MacGregor b Peel	0
H Trumble	not out	1
	(lb 3)	3
	(all out)	269

Bowling: Lohmann 21-10-43-0 Peel 24-11-28-3 Attewell 32-15-42-4 Barnes 6-2-16-1 Ulyett 3-3-0-1

England v Australia
22,23,24 June 1896

Result: England won by 6 wickets

Australia Innings

H Donnan	run out	1	b Hearne	8	
J Darling	b Richardson	22	b Richardson	0	
G Giffen	c Lilley b Lohmann	0	b Richardson	32	
*GHS Trott	b Richardson	0	c Hayward b Richardson	143	
SE Gregory	b Richardson	14	c Lohmann b Hearne	103	
H Graham	b Richardson	10	b Richardson	10	
C Hill	b Lohmann	1	b Hearne	5	
CJ Eady	not out	10	c Lilley b Richardson	2	
H Trumble	b Richardson	4	c Lilley b Hearne	4	
+JJ Kelly	c Lilley b Lohmann	0	not out	24	
E Jones	b Richardson	4	c Jackson b Hearne	4	
	(b 1)	1	(b 7, lb 4, w 1)	12	
	(all out)	53	(all out)	347	

Bowling: Richardson 11.3-3-39-6 Lohmann 11-6-13-3
Richardson 47-15-134-5 Lohmann 22-6-39-0 Hayward 11-3-44-0 Hearne 36-14-76-5 Jackson 11-5-28-0 Grace 6-1-14-0

England Innings

*WG Grace	c Trumble b Giffen	66	c Hill b Trumble	7	
AE Stoddart	b Eady	17	not out	30	
R Abel	b Eady	94	c sub (FA Iredale) b Jones	4	
JT Brown	b Jones	9	c Kelly b Eady	36	
W Gunn	c Kelly b Trumble	25	not out	13	
FS Jackson	c Darling b Giffen	44			
TW Hayward	not out	12	b Jones	13	
+AFA Lilley	b Eady	0			
GA Lohmann	c sub (FA Iredale) b Giffen	1			
JT Hearne	c Giffen b Trott	11			
T Richardson	c Hill b Trott	6			
	(b 5, lb 2)	7	(b 3, lb 4, w 1)	8	
	(all out)	292	(4 wickets)	111	

Bowling: Jones 26-6-64-1 Giffen 26-5-95-3 Eady 29-12-58-3 Trott 7.4-2-13-2 Trumble 19-3-55-1
Jones 23-10-42-2 Trumble 20-10-37-1 Giffen 1-0-9-0 Eady 3-0-11-1 Trott 0.1-0-4-0

Umpires: J Phillips (Aus) and WAJ West

Lord's

England v Australia
15,16,17 June 1899

Result: Australia won by 10 wickets

England Innings

*AC MacLaren	b Jones	4	not out	88
CB Fry	c Trumble b Jones	13	b Jones	4
KS Ranjitsinhji	c & b Jones	8	c Noble b Howell	0
CL Townsend	st Kelly b Howell	5	b Jones	8
FS Jackson	b Jones	73	c & b Trumble	37
TW Hayward	b Noble	1	c Trumble b Laver	77
JT Tyldesley	c Darling b Jones	14	c Gregory b Laver	4
GL Jessop	c Trumper b Trumble	51	c Trumble b Laver	4
+AFA Lilley	not out	19	b Jones	12
W Mead	b Jones	7	lbw b Noble	0
W Rhodes	b Jones	2	c & b Noble	2
	(b 2, lb 6, w 1)	9	(b 2, lb 2)	4
	(all out)	206	(all out)	240

Bowling: Jones 36.1-11-88-7 Howell 14-4-43-1 Noble 15-7-39-1 Trumble 15-9-27-1
Jones 36-15-76-3 Howell 31-12-67-1 Noble 19.4-8-37-2 Trumble 15-6-20-1 Laver 16-4-36-3

Australia Innings

J Worrall	c Hayward b Rhodes	18	not out	11
*J Darling	c Ranjitsinhji b Rhodes	9	not out	17
C Hill	c Fry b Townsend	135		
SE Gregory	c Lilley b Jessop	15		
MA Noble	c Lilley b Rhodes	54		
VT Trumper	not out	135		
+JJ Kelly	c Lilley b Mead	9		
H Trumble	c Lilley b Jessop	24		
FJ Laver	b Townsend	0		
E Jones	c Mead b Townsend	17		
WP Howell	b Jessop	0		
	(lb 4, nb 1)	5		0
	(all out)	421	(0 wickets)	28

Bowling: Jessop 37.1-10-105-3 Mead 53-24-91-1 Rhodes 39-10-108-3 Jackson 18-6-31-0 Townsend 15-1-50-3 Ranjitsinhji
2-0-6-0 Hayward 6-0-25-0
Jessop 6-0-19-0 Rhodes 5-1-9-0

Umpires: T Mycroft and WAJ West

England v Australia
12,13,14 June 1902

Result: Match drawn

England Innings

*AC MacLaren	not out	47
CB Fry	c Hill b Hopkins	0
KS Ranjitsinhji	b Hopkins	0
Hon.FS Jackson	not out	55
JT Tyldesley		
+AFA Lilley		
GH Hirst		
GL Jessop		
LC Braund		
WH Lockwood		
W Rhodes		
		0
	(2 wickets)	102

Bowling: Jones 11-4-31-0 Hopkins 9-3-18-2 Saunders 3-0-15-0 Trumper 8-1-33-0 Armstrong 5-0-5-0 Noble 2-2-0-0

England v Australia
15,16,17 June 1905

Result: Match drawn

England Innings

AC MacLaren	b Hopkins	56	b Armstrong	79
TW Hayward	lbw b Duff	16	c Laver b McLeod	8
JT Tyldesley	c Laver b Armstrong	43	b Noble	12
CB Fry	c Kelly b Hopkins	73	not out	36
*Hon.FS Jackson	c Armstrong b Laver	29	b Armstrong	0
AO Jones	b Laver	1	c Trumper b Armstrong	5
BJT Bosanquet	c & b Armstrong	6	not out	4
W Rhodes	b Hopkins	15		
+AFA Lilley	lbw b McLeod	0		
S Haigh	b Laver	14		
EG Arnold	not out	7		
	(b 20, lb 2)	22	(b 2, lb 4, nb 1)	7
	(all out)	282	(5 wickets)	151

Bowling: McLeod 20-7-40-1 Laver 34-8-64-3 Armstrong 30-11-41-2 Noble 34-13-61-0 Duff 7-4-14-1 Hopkins 15-4-40-3
McLeod 15-5-33-1 Laver 10-4-39-0 Armstrong 10-2-30-3 Noble 13-2-31-1 Hopkins 2-0-11-0

Australia Innings

VT Trumper	b Jackson	31
RA Duff	c Lilley b Rhodes	27
C Hill	c Bosanquet b Jackson	7
MA Noble	c Fry b Jackson	7
WW Armstrong	lbw b Jackson	33
*J Darling	c Haigh b Armstrong	41
SE Gregory	c Jones b Rhodes	5
AJY Hopkins	b Haigh	16
CE McLeod	b Haigh	0
FJ Laver	not out	4
+JJ Kelly	lbw b Rhodes	2
	(b 3, lb 5)	8
	(all out)	181

Bowling: Haigh 12-3-40-2 Rhodes 16.1-1-70-3 Jackson 15-0-50-4 Arnold 7-3-13-1

Umpires: J Phillips (Aus) and W Richards

England v South Africa
1,2,3 July 1907

Result: Match drawn

England Innings

CB Fry	b Vogler	33
TW Hayward	st Sherwell b Vogler	21
JT Tyldesley	b Vogler	52
*RE Foster	st Sherwell b Vogler	8
LC Braund	c Kotze b Faulkner	104
GH Hirst	b Vogler	7
GL Jessop	c Faulkner b Vogler	93
JN Crawford	c Sherwell b Schwarz	22
EG Arnold	b Schwarz	4
+AFA Lilley	c Nourse b Vogler	48
C Blythe	not out	4
	(b 24, lb 6, w 2)	32
	(all out)	428

Bowling: Kotze 12-2-43-0 Schwarz 34-7-90-2 Vogler 47.2-12-128-7 White 15-2-52-0 Nourse 1-0-2-0 Faulkner 12-1-59-1
Sinclair 6-1-22-0

South Africa Innings

WA Shalders	c Lilley b Arnold	2	b Hirst	0
*+PW Sherwell	run out	6	b Blythe	115
CMH Hathorn	c Foster b Hirst	6	c Fry b Blythe	30
AW Nourse	b Blythe	62	not out	11
GA Faulkner	c Jessop b Braund	44	not out	12
SJ Snooke	lbw b Blythe	5		
GC White	b Arnold	0		
JH Sinclair	b Arnold	0		
RO Schwarz	not out	0		
AEE Vogler	c Lilley b Arnold	3		
JJ Kotze	b Arnold	0		
	(b 9, lb 2, w 1)	12	(b 15, lb 2)	17
	(all out)	140	(3 wickets)	185

Bowling: Hirst 18-7-35-1 Arnold 22-7-37-5 Jessop 2-0-8-0 Crawford 8-1-20-0 Blythe 8-3-18-2 Braund 7-4-10-1
Hirst 16-8-26-1 Arnold 13-2-41-0 Crawford 4-0-19-0 Blythe 21-5-56-2 Braund 4-0-26-0

Umpires: A Millward and A White

England v Australia
14,15,16 June 1909

Result: Australia won by 9 wickets

England Innings

TW Hayward	st Carter b Laver	16	run out	6
JB Hobbs	c Carter b Laver	19	c & b Armstrong	9
JT Tyldesley	lbw b Laver	46	st Carter b Armstrong	3
G Gunn	lbw b Cotter	1	b Armstrong	0
JH King	c Macartney b Cotter	60	b Armstrong	4
*AC MacLaren	c Armstrong b Noble	7	b Noble	24
GH Hirst	b Cotter	31	b Armstrong	1
AO Jones	c Cotter	8	lbw b Laver	26
AE Relf	c Armstrong b Noble	17	b Armstrong	3
+AFA Lilley	c Bardsley b Noble	47	not out	25
S Haigh	not out	1	run out	5
	(b 8, lb 3, w 3, nb 2)	16	(b 2, lb 3, nb 10)	15
	(all out)	269	(all out)	121

Bowling: Laver 32-9-75-3 Macartney 8-3-10-0 Cotter 23-1-80-4 Noble 24.2-9-42-3 Armstrong 20-6-46-0
Laver 13-4-24-1 Cotter 18-3-35-0 Noble 5-1-12-1 Armstrong 24.5-11-35-6

Australia Innings

PA McAlister	lbw b King	22	not out	19
FJ Laver	b Hirst	14		
W Bardsley	b Relf	46	c Lilley b Relf	0
WW Armstrong	c Lilley b Relf	12		
VS Ransford	not out	143		
VT Trumper	c MacLaren b Relf	28		
*MA Noble	c Lilley b Relf	32		
SE Gregory	c Lilley b Relf	5	not out	18
A Cotter	run out	0		
CG Macartney	b Hirst	5		
+H Carter	b Hirst	7		
	(b 16, lb 8, w 1, nb 2)	27	(b 4)	4
	(all out)	350	(1 wicket)	41

Bowling: Hirst 26.5-2-83-3 King 27-5-99-1 Relf 45-14-85-5 Haigh 19-5-41-0 Jones 2-0-15-0
Hirst 8-1-28-0 Relf 7.4-4-9-1

Umpires: CE Dench and J Moss

England v South Africa
10,11,12 June 1912

Result: England won by an innings and 62 runs

South Africa Innings

GPD Hartigan	c Foster b Barnes	0	b Foster	1
HW Taylor	lbw b Barnes	1	b Barnes	5
AW Nourse	b Foster	13	run out	17
CB Llewellyn	b Foster	9	c Smith b Foster	75
GA Faulkner	b Foster	7	b Barnes	15
SJ Snooke	b Barnes	2	b Foster	16
*F Mitchell	c & b Barnes	1	b Barnes	1
RO Schwarz	c Foster b Barnes	4	b Barnes	28
SJ Pegler	b Foster	4	b Barnes	10
CP Carter	b Foster	0	not out	27
+T Campbell	not out	0	c Jessop b Barnes	3
	(b 12, lb 3, nb 2)	17	(b 17, lb 1, nb 1)	19
	(all out)	58	(all out)	217

Bowling: Foster 13.1-7-16-5 Barnes 13-3-25-5
Foster 27-10-54-3 Barnes 34-9-85-6 Brearley 6-2-4-0 Woolley 4-0-19-0 Hobbs 11-2-36-0

England Innings

JB Hobbs	b Nourse	4
W Rhodes	b Nourse	36
RH Spooner	c Llewellyn b Nourse	119
*CB Fry	b Pegler	29
PF Warner	st Campbell b Pegler	39
FE Woolley	b Pegler	73
GL Jessop	b Pegler	3
FR Foster	lbw b Pegler	11
+EJ Smith	b Pegler	2
SF Barnes	not out	0
W Brearley	b Pegler	0
	(b 11, lb 9, w 1)	21
	(all out)	337

Bowling: Nourse 16-5-46-3 Pegler 31-8-65-7 Faulkner 29-6-72-0 Carter 4-0-15-0 Llewellyn 9-0-60-0 Schwarz 20-3-44-0
Hartigan 10-2-14-0

Umpires: W Richards and WAJ West

England v Australia
24,25,26 June 1912

Result: Match drawn

England Innings

JB Hobbs	b Emery	107
W Rhodes	c Carkeek b Kelleway	59
RH Spooner	c Bardsley b Kelleway	1
*CB Fry	run out	42
PF Warner	b Emery	4
FE Woolley	c Kelleway b Hazlitt	20
FR Foster	c Macartney b Whitty	20
JW Hearne	not out	21
+EJ Smith	not out	14
SF Barnes		
H Dean		
	(b 16, lb 4, nb 2)	22
	(7 wickets declared)	310

Bowling: Whitty 12-2-69-1 Hazlitt 25-6-68-1 Matthews 13-4-26-0 Kelleway 21-5-66-2 Emery 12-1-46-2 Macartney 7-1-13-0

Australia Innings

CB Jennings	c Smith b Foster	21
C Kelleway	b Rhodes	61
CG Macartney	c Smith b Foster	99
W Bardsley	lbw b Rhodes	21
*SE Gregory	c Foster b Dean	10
DBM Smith	not out	24
TJ Matthews	b Dean	0
GR Hazlitt	b Rhodes	19
SH Emery		
WJ Whitty		
+W Carkeek		
	(b 17, lb 5, w 1, nb 4)	27
	(7 wickets)	282

Bowling: Foster 36-18-42-2 Barnes 31-10-74-0 Dean 29-10-49-2 Hearne 12-1-31-0 Rhodes 19.2-5-59-3

Umpires: J Moss and AE Street

Australia v South Africa
15,16,17 July 1912

Result: Australia won by 10 wickets

South Africa Innings

GA Faulkner	b Whitty	5	c & b Matthews	6
LJ Tancred	lbw b Matthews	31	c Bardsley b Hazlitt	19
GC White	c Carkeek b Minnett	0	b Matthews	18
CB Llewellyn	c Jennings b Minnett	8	b Macartney	59
AW Nourse	b Hazlitt	11	lbw b Kelleway	10
HW Taylor	c Kelleway b Hazlitt	93	not out	10
LA Stricker	lbw b Kelleway	48	b Hazlitt	13
*F Mitchell	b Whitty	12	b Matthews	3
RO Schwarz	b Whitty	0	c Macartney b Matthews	1
SJ Pegler	c Bardsley b Whitty	25	c Kelleway b Macartney	14
+TA Ward	not out	1	b Macartney	7
	(b 12, lb 14, w 1, nb 2)	29	(b 9, lb 4)	13
	(all out)	263	(all out)	173

Bowling: Minnett 15-6-49-2 Whitty 31-9-68-4 Hazlitt 19-9-47-2 Matthews 13-5-32-1 Kelleway 11-3-38-1 Whitty 9-0-41-0 Hazlitt 13-1-39-2 Matthews 13-2-29-4 Kelleway 8-1-22-1 Macartney 14.1-5-29-3

Australia Innings

CB Jennings	b Nourse	0	not out	22
C Kelleway	lbw b Faulkner	102		
CG Macartney	b Nourse	9		
W Bardsley	lbw b Llewellyn	164		
*SE Gregory	b Llewellyn	5		
ER Mayne	st Ward b Pegler	23	not out	25
RB Minnett	b Pegler	39		
TJ Matthews	c Faulkner b Pegler	9		
GR Hazlitt	b Nourse	6		
+W Carkeek	not out	6		
WJ Whitty	lbw b Pegler	3		
	(b 24, lb 3, w 2, nb 1)	30	(b 1)	1
	(all out)	390	(0 wickets)	48

Bowling: Nourse 36-12-60-3 Pegler 29.5-7-79-4 Schwarz 11-1-44-0 Faulkner 28-3-86-1 Llewellyn 19-2-71-2 Taylor 2-0-12-0 Stricker 3-1-8-0 Nourse 6.1-2-22-0 Pegler 4-1-15-0 Faulkner 2-0-10-0

Umpires: J Moss and AE Street

England v Australia
11,13,14 June 1921

Result: Australia won by 8 wickets

England Innings

DJ Knight	c Gregory b Armstrong	7	c Carter b Gregory	1
AE Dipper	b McDonald	11	b McDonald	40
FE Woolley	st Carter b Mailey	95	c Hendry b Mailey	93
EH Hendren	b McDonald	0	c Gregory b Mailey	10
*JWHT Douglas	b McDonald	34	b Gregory	14
AJ Evans	b McDonald	4	lbw b McDonald	14
Hon.LH Tennyson	st Carter b Mailey	74		
NE Haig	c Carter b Gregory	3	b McDonald	0
CH Parkin	b Mailey	0	c Pellew b McDonald	11
+H Strudwick	c McDonald b Mailey	8	b Gregory	12
FJ Durston	not out	6	b Gregory	2
	(b 1, lb 11, w 1, nb 1)	14	(b 4, lb 3, nb 5)	12
	(all out)	187	(all out)	283

Bowling: Gregory 16-1-51-1 McDonald 20-2-58-4 Armstrong 18-12-9-1 Mailey 14.2-1-55-4 Gregory 26.2-4-76-4 McDonald 23-3-89-4 Armstrong 12-6-19-0 Mailey 25-4-72-2 Hendry 4-0-15-0

Australia Innings

W Bardsley	c Woolley b Douglas	88	not out	63
TJE Andrews	c Strudwick b Durston	9	lbw b Parkin	49
CG Macartney	c Strudwick b Durston	31	b Durston	8
CE Pellew	b Haig	43	not out	5
JM Taylor	lbw b Douglas	36		
*WW Armstrong	b Durston	0		
JM Gregory	c & b Parkin	52		
HSTL Hendry	b Haig	5		
+H Carter	b Durston	46		
AA Mailey	c & b Parkin	5		
EA McDonald	not out	17		
	(b 2, lb 5, nb 3)	10	(b 3, lb 2, nb 1)	6
	(all out)	342	(2 wickets)	131

Bowling: Durston 24.1-2-102-4 Douglas 9-1-53-2 Parkin 20-5-72-2 Haig 20-4-61-2 Woolley 11-2-44-0 Durston 9.3-0-34-1 Douglas 6-0-23-0 Parkin 9-0-31-1 Haig 3-0-27-0 Woolley 3-0-10-0

Umpires: J Moss and W Phillips

England v South Africa
28,30 June, 1 July 1924

Result: England won by an innings and 18 runs

South Africa Innings

*HW Taylor	c Wood b Gilligan	4	b Gilligan	8
JMM Commaille	b Gilligan	0	lbw b Tyldesley	37
MJ Susskind	c Tate b Hearne	64	lbw b Tyldesley	53
AW Nourse	c Woolley b Tate	4	lbw b Gilligan	11
RH Catterall	b Gilligan	120	c Gilligan b Tyldesley	45
JM Blanckenberg	b Tate	12	c Hobbs b Fender	15
HG Deane	b Tyldesley	33	c Sutcliffe b Hearne	24
GA Faulkner	b Fender	25	run out	12
+TA Ward	b Tyldesley	1	not out	3
SJ Pegler	c Fender b Tyldesley	0	b Tate	8
GM Parker	not out	1	b Tate	0
	(b 3, lb 2, nb 4)	9	(b 13, lb 8, nb 3)	24
	(all out)	273	(all out)	240

Bowling: Gilligan 31-7-70-3 Tate 34-12-62-2 Tyldesley 24-10-52-3 Hearne 18-3-35-1 Fender 9-1-45-1 Gilligan 24-6-54-2 Tate 26.4-8-43-2 Tyldesley 36-18-50-3 Hearne 19-4-35-1 Fender 14-5-25-1 Woolley 4-1-9-0

England Innings

JB Hobbs	c Taylor b Parker	211
H Sutcliffe	b Parker	122
FE Woolley	not out	134
EH Hendren	not out	50
JW Hearne		
APF Chapman		
PGH Fender		
*AER Gilligan		
+GEC Wood		
MW Tate		
RK Tyldesley		
	(b 11, lb 1, nb 2)	14
	(2 wickets declared)	531

Bowling: Parker 24-0-121-2 Blanckenberg 28-3-113-0 Pegler 31-4-120-0 Nourse 15-1-57-0 Faulkner 17-0-87-0 Catterall 3-0-19-0

Umpires: F Chester and HI Young

England v Australia
26,28,29 June 1926

Result: Match drawn

Australia Innings

*HL Collins	b Root	1	c Sutcliffe b Larwood	24
W Bardsley	not out	193		
CG Macartney	c Sutcliffe b Larwood	39	not out	133
WM Woodfull	c Strudwick b Root	13	c Root b Woolley	0
TJE Andrews	c & b Kilner	10	b Root	9
JM Gregory	b Larwood	7	c Sutcliffe b Root	0
JM Taylor	c Carr b Tate	9		
AJ Richardson	b Kilner	35		
J Ryder	c Strudwick b Tate	28	not out	0
+WAS Oldfield	c Sutcliffe b Kilner	19	c Sutcliffe b Tate	11
AA Mailey	lbw b Kilner	1		
	(b 12, lb 16)	28	(b 5, lb 12)	17
	(all out)	383	(5 wickets)	194

Bowling: Tate 50-12-111-2 Root 36-11-70-2 Kilner 34.5-11-70-4 Larwood 32-2-99-2 Woolley 2-0-5-0 Tate 25-11-38-1 Root 19-9-40-2 Kilner 22-2-49-0 Larwood 15-3-37-1 Woolley 7-1-13-1

England Innings

JB Hobbs	c Richardson b Macartney	119
H Sutcliffe	b Richardson	82
FE Woolley	lbw b Ryder	87
EH Hendren	not out	127
APF Chapman	not out	50
*AW Carr		
R Kilner		
MW Tate		
H Larwood		
CF Root		
+H Strudwick		
	(b 4, lb 4, w 1, nb 1)	10
	(3 wickets declared)	475

Bowling: Gregory 30-3-125-0 Macartney 33-8-90-1 Mailey 30-6-96-0 Richardson 48-18-73-1 Ryder 25-3-70-1 Collins 2-0-11-0

Umpires: LC Braund and AE Street

England v West Indies
23,25,26 June 1928

Result: England won by an innings and 58 runs

England Innings

H Sutcliffe	c Constantine b Francis	48
C Hallows	c Griffith b Constantine	26
GE Tyldesley	c Constantine b Francis	122
WR Hammond	b Constantine	45
DR Jardine	lbw b Griffith	22
*APF Chapman	c Constantine b Small	50
VWC Jupp	b Small	14
MW Tate	c Browne b Griffith	22
+H Smith	b Constantine	7
H Larwood	not out	17
AP Freeman	b Constantine	1
	(b 6, lb 19, nb 2)	27
	(all out)	401

Bowling: Francis 25-4-72-2 Constantine 26.4-9-82-4 Griffith 29-9-78-2 Browne 22-5-53-0 Small 15-1-67-2 Martin 8-2-22-0

West Indies Innings

G Challenor	c Smith b Larwood	29	b Tate	0
FR Martin	lbw b Tate	44	b Hammond	12
MP Fernandes	b Tate	0	c Hammond b Freeman	8
*+RK Nunes	b Jupp	37	lbw b Jupp	10
WH St Hill	c Jardine b Jupp	4	lbw b Freeman	9
CA Roach	run out	0	c Chapman b Tate	16
LN Constantine	c Larwood b Freeman	13	b Freeman	0
JA Small	lbw b Jupp	0	c Hammond b Jupp	52
CR Browne	b Jupp	10	b Freeman	44
GN Francis	not out	19	c Jardine b Jupp	0
HC Griffith	c Sutcliffe b Freeman	2	not out	0
	(b 13, lb 6)	19	(b 10, lb 5)	15
	(all out)	177	(all out)	166

Bowling: Larwood 15-4-27-1 Tate 27-8-54-2 Freeman 18.3-5-40-2 Jupp 23-9-37-4 Tate 22-10-28-2 Freeman 21.1-10-37-4 Jupp 15-4-66-3 Hammond 15-6-20-1

Umpires: LC Braund and F Chester

Lord's

England v South Africa
29 June, 1,2 July 1929

Result: Match drawn

England Innings

H Sutcliffe	c Mitchell b Bell	100	c Catterall b Morkel	10
ET Killick	b Morkel	3	c Morkel b Christy	24
WR Hammond	c Christy b Morkel	8	b Morkel	5
J O'Connor	b Morkel	0	c Cameron b Ochse	11
EH Hendren	b Morkel	43	b Morkel	11
M Leyland	b Bell	73	c Cameron b Ochse	102
MW Tate	c Cameron b Bell	15	not out	100
RWV Robins	c Mitchell b Bell	4	c Mitchell b Ochse	0
H Larwood	b Bell	35	b Ochse	9
*JC White	b Bell	8	not out	18
+G Duckworth	not out	8		
	(lb 4, w 1)	5	(b 11, lb 6, w 2, nb 3)	22
	(all out)	302	(8 wickets declared)	312

Bowling: Ochse 24-5-51-0 Morkel 31-6-93-4 Bell 30.4-7-99-6 Christy 6-2-20-0 McMillan 7-0-31-0 Owen-Smith 1-0-3-0
Ochse 20-0-99-4 Morkel 24-6-63-3 Bell 18.2-2-60-0 Christy 3-0-15-1 McMillan 13-0-34-0 Mitchell 4-0-19-0

South Africa Innings

RH Catterall	b Larwood	0	b Tate	3
B Mitchell	st Duckworth b Hammond	29	c Hendren b Robins	22
JAJ Christy	run out	70	c Hendren b Robins	41
DPB Markel	lbw b Tate	88	not out	17
*HG Deane	b Tate	1	st Duckworth b Robins	2
+HB Cameron	c Leyland b Robins	32	retired hurt	0
HGO Owen-Smith	not out	52	not out	1
EL Dalton	b Tate	6	c Killick b Larwood	1
Q McMillan	c Killick b White	17		
AL Ochse	c Duckworth b White	1		
AJ Bell	b Robins	13		
	(b 9, lb 4)	13	(b 2, lb 1)	3
	(all out)	322	(5 wickets)	90

Bowling: Larwood 20-4-65-1 Tate 39-9-108-3 Hammond 8-3-19-1 White 35-12-61-2 Robins 24-5-47-2 Leyland 5-2-9-0
Larwood 12-3-17-1 Tate 11-3-27-1 White 9-3-11-0 Robins 19-4-32-3

Umpires: W Bestwick and F Chester

England v Australia
27,28,30 June, 1 July 1930

Result: Australia won by 7 wickets

England Innings

JB Hobbs	c Oldfield b Fairfax	1	b Grimmett	19
FE Woolley	c Wall b Fairfax	41	hit wicket b Grimmett	28
WR Hammond	b Grimmett	38	c Fairfax b Grimmett	32
KS Duleepsinhji	c Bradman b Grimmett	173	c Oldfield b Hornibrook	48
EH Hendren	c McCabe b Fairfax	48	c Richardson b Grimmett	9
*APF Chapman	c Oldfield b Wall	11	c Oldfield b Fairfax	121
GOB Allen	b Fairfax	3	lbw b Grimmett	57
MW Tate	c McCabe b Wall	54	c Ponsford b Grimmett	10
RWV Robins	c Oldfield b Hornibrook	5	not out	11
JC White	not out	23	run out	10
+G Duckworth	c Oldfield b Wall	18	lbw b Fairfax	0
	(b 2, lb 7, nb 1)	10	(b 16, lb 13, w 1)	30
	(all out)	425	(all out)	375

Bowling: Wall 29.4-2-118-3 Fairfax 31-6-101-4 Grimmett 33-4-105-2 Hornibrook 26-6-62-1 McCabe 9-1-29-0
Wall 25-2-80-0 Fairfax 12.4-2-37-2 Grimmett 53-13-167-6 Hornibrook 22-6-49-1 McCabe 3-1-11-0 Bradman 1-0-1-0

Australia Innings

*WM Woodfull	st Duckworth b Robins	155	not out	26
WH Ponsford	c Hammond b White	81	b Robins	14
DG Bradman	c Chapman b White	254	c Chapman b Tate	1
AF Kippax	b White	83	c Duckworth b Robins	3
SJ McCabe	c Woolley b Hammond	44	not out	25
VY Richardson	c Hobbs b Tate	30		
+WAS Oldfield	not out	43		
AG Fairfax	not out	20		
CV Grimmett				
PM Hornibrook				
TW Wall				
	(b 6, lb 8, w 5)	19	(b 1, lb 2)	3
	(6 wickets declared)	729	(3 wickets)	72

Bowling: Allen 34-7-115-0 Tate 64-16-148-1 White 51-7-158-3 Robins 42-1-172-1 Hammond 35-8-82-1 Woolley 6-0-35-0
Tate 13-6-21-1 White 2-0-8-0 Robins 9-1-34-2 Hammond 4.2-1-6-0

Umpires: F Chester and TW Oates

England v New Zealand
27,29,30 June 1931

Result: Match drawn

New Zealand Innings

JE Mills	b Peebles	34	b Allen	0
CS Dempster	lbw b Peebles	53	b Hammond	120
GL Weir	lbw b Peebles	37	b Allen	40
JL Kerr	st Ames b Robins	2	lbw b Peebles	0
RC Blunt	c Hammond b Robins	7	b Robins	96
ML Page	b Allen	23	c & b Peebles	104
*TC Lowry	c Hammond b Robins	1	b Peebles	34
IB Cromb	c Ames b Peebles	20	c Voce b Robins	14
CFW Allcott	c Hammond b Peebles	13	not out	20
WE Merritt	c Jardine b Hammond	17	b Peebles	5
+KC James	not out	1		
	(b 2, lb 12, w 1, nb 1)	16	(b 23, lb 10, w 1, nb 2)	36
	(all out)	224	(9 wickets declared)	469

Bowling: Voce 10-1-40-0 Allen 15-2-45-1 Hammond 10.3-5-8-1 Peebles 26-3-77-5 Robins 13-3-38-3
Voce 32-11-60-0 Allen 25-8-47-2 Hammond 21-2-50-1 Peebles 42.4-6-150-4 Robins 37-5-126-2

England Innings

AH Bakewell	lbw b Cromb	9	c Blunt b Cromb	27
J Arnold	c Page b Cromb	0	c & b Blunt	34
WR Hammond	b Cromb	7	run out	46
KS Duleepsinhji	c Kerr b Merritt	25	c James b Allcott	11
*DR Jardine	c Blunt b Merritt	38	not out	0
FE Woolley	lbw b Merritt	80	b Cromb	9
+LEG Ames	c James b Weir	137	not out	17
IAR Peebles	st James b Merritt	0		
GOB Allen	c Lowry b Weir	122		
RWV Robins	c Lowry b Weir	12		
W Voce	not out	1		
	(b 15, lb 8)	23	(lb 2)	2
	(all out)	454	(5 wickets)	146

Bowling: Cromb 37-7-113-3 Weir 31-8-38-3 Blunt 46-9-124-0 Allcott 17-3-34-0 Merritt 23-2-104-4 Page 3-0-18-0
Cromb 25-5-44-2 Weir 5-1-18-0 Blunt 14-5-54-1 Allcott 10-2-26-1 Merritt 1-0-2-0

Umpires: F Chester and J Hardstaff snr

England v India
25,27,28 June 1932

Result: England won by 158 runs

England Innings

P Holmes	b Nissar	6	b Jahangir Khan	11
H Sutcliffe	b Nissar	3	c Nayudu b Amar Singh	19
FE Woolley	run out	9	c Colah b Jahangir Khan	21
WR Hammond	b Amar Singh	35	b Jahangir Khan	12
*DR Jardine	c Navle b Nayudu	79	not out	85
E Paynter	lbw b Nayudu	14	b Jahangir Khan	54
+LEG Ames	b Nissar	65	b Amar Singh	6
RWV Robins	c Lall Singh b Nissar	21	c Jahangir Khan b Nissar	30
FR Brown	c Amar Singh b Nissar	1	c Colah b Naoomal Jaoomal	29
W Voce	not out	4	not out	0
WE Bowes	c Nissar b Amar Singh	7		
	(b 3, lb 9, nb 3)	15	(b 2, lb 6)	8
	(all out)	259	(8 wickets declared)	275

Bowling: Nissar 26-3-93-5 Amar Singh 31.1-10-75-2 Jahangir Khan 17-7-26-0 Nayudu 24-8-40-2 Palia 4-3-2-0 Naoomal Jaoomal 3-0-8-0
Nissar 18-5-42-1 Amar Singh 41-13-84-2 Jahangir Khan 30-12-60-4 Nayudu 9-0-21-0 Palia 3-0-11-0 Naoomal Jaoomal 8-0-40-1 Wazir Ali 1-0-9-0

India Innings

+JG Navle	b Bowes	12	lbw b Robins	13
Naoomal Jaoomal	lbw b Robins	33	b Brown	25
S Wazir Ali	lbw b Brown	31	c Hammond b Voce	39
*CK Nayudu	c Robins b Voce	40	b Bowes	10
SHM Colah	c Robins b Bowes	22	b Brown	4
S Nazir Ali	b Bowes	13	c Jardine b Bowes	6
PE Palia	b Voce	1	not out	1
Lall Singh	c Jardine b Bowes	15	b Hammond	29
M Jahangir Khan	b Robins	1	b Voce	0
L Amar Singh	c Robins b Voce	5	c & b Hammond	51
M Nissar	not out	1	b Hammond	0
	(b 5, lb 7, w 1, nb 2)	15	(b 5, lb 2, nb 2)	9
	(all out)	189	(all out)	187

Bowling: Bowes 30-13-49-4 Voce 17-6-23-3 Brown 25-7-48-1 Robins 17-4-39-2 Hammond 4-0-15-0
Bowes 14-5-30-2 Voce 12-3-28-2 Brown 14-1-54-2 Robins 14-5-57-1 Hammond 5.3-3-9-3

Umpires: F Chester and J Hardstaff snr

England v West Indies
24,26,27 June 1933

Result: England won by an innings and 27 runs

England Innings

CF Walters	c Barrow b Martindale	51
H Sutcliffe	c Grant b Martindale	21
WR Hammond	c Headley b Griffith	29
M Leyland	c Barrow b Griffith	1
*DR Jardine	c Da Costa b Achong	21
MJL Turnbull	c Barrow b Achong	28
+LEG Ames	not out	83
GOB Allen	run out	16
RWV Robins	b Martindale	8
H Verity	c Achong b Griffith	21
GG Macaulay	lbw b Martindale	9
	(b 3, lb 5)	8
	(all out)	296

Bowling: Martindale 24-3-85-4 Francis 18-3-52-0 Griffith 20-7-48-3 Achong 35-9-88-2 Da Costa 4-0-15-0

West Indies Innings

CA Roach	b Allen	0	c Sutcliffe b Macaulay	0
+IM Barrow	c & b Verity	7	lbw b Robins	12
GA Headley	lbw b Allen	13	b Allen	50
ELG Hoad	lbw b Robins	6	c & b Verity	36
*GC Grant	hit wicket b Robins	26	lbw b Macaulay	28
OC Da Costa	b Robins	4	lbw b Verity	1
CA Merry	lbw b Macaulay	9	b Macaulay	1
EE Achong	b Robins	15	c Hammond b Verity	10
GN Francis	b Robins	4	not out	11
EA Martindale	b Robins	4	b Macaulay	4
HC Griffith	not out	1	b Verity	18
	(b 3, lb 1, nb 2)	6	(b 1)	1
	(all out)	97	(all out)	172

Bowling: Macaulay 18-7-25-1 Allen 13-6-13-2 Verity 16-8-21-1 Robins 11.5-1-32-6
Macaulay 20-6-57-4 Allen 11-2-33-1 Verity 18.1-4-45-4 Robins 12-2-36-1

Umpires: F Chester and A Dolphin

England v Australia
22,23,25 June 1934

Result: England won by an innings and 38 runs

England Innings

CF Walters	c Bromley b O'Reilly	82
H Sutcliffe	lbw b Chipperfield	20
WR Hammond	c & b Chipperfield	2
EH Hendren	c McCabe b Wall	13
*RES Wyatt	c Oldfield b Chipperfield	33
M Leyland	b Wall	109
+LEG Ames	c Oldfield b McCabe	120
G Geary	c Chipperfield b Wall	9
H Verity	st Oldfield b Grimmett	29
K Farnes	b Wall	1
WE Bowes	not out	10
	(lb 12)	12
	(all out)	440

Bowling: Wall 49-7-108-4 McCabe 18-3-38-1 Grimmett 53.3-13-102-1 O'Reilly 38-15-70-1 Chipperfield 34-10-91-3 Darling 6-2-19-0

Australia Innings

*WM Woodfull	b Bowes	22	c Hammond b Verity	43
WA Brown	c Ames b Bowes	105	c Walters b Bowes	2
DG Bradman	c & b Verity	36	c Ames b Verity	13
SJ McCabe	c Hammond b Verity	34	c Hendren b Verity	19
LS Darling	c Sutcliffe b Verity	0	b Hammond	10
AG Chipperfield	not out	37	c Geary b Verity	14
EH Bromley	c Geary b Verity	4	c & b Verity	1
+WAS Oldfield	c Sutcliffe b Verity	23	lbw b Verity	0
CV Grimmett	b Bowes	9	c Hammond b Verity	0
WJ O'Reilly	b Verity	4	not out	8
TW Wall	lbw b Verity	0	c Hendren b Verity	1
	(b 1, lb 9)	10	(b 6, nb 1)	7
	(all out)	284	(all out)	118

Bowling: Farnes 12-3-43-0 Bowes 31-5-98-3 Geary 22-4-56-0 Verity 36-15-61-7 Hammond 4-1-6-0 Leyland 4-1-10-0
Farnes 4-2-6-0 Bowes 14-4-24-1 Verity 22.3-8-43-8 Hammond 13-0-38-1

Umpires: F Chester and J Hardstaff snr

England v South Africa
29 June, 1,2 July 1935

Result: South Africa won by 157 runs

South Africa Innings

B Mitchell	lbw b Nichols	30	not out		164
IJ Siedle	b Mitchell	6	c Farrimond b Mitchell		13
EAB Rowan	c Farrimond b Verity	40	lbw b Nichols		44
AD Nourse	b Verity	3	b Verity		2
*HF Wade	c Hammond b Langridge	23	b Verity		0
+HB Cameron	b Nichols	90	c Ames b Mitchell		3
EL Dalton	c & b Langridge	19	c Wyatt b Verity		0
XC Balaskas	b Verity	4			
ACB Langton	c Holmes b Hammond	4	c & b Hammond		44
RJ Crisp	not out	4			
AJ Bell	b Hammond	0			
	(b 1, lb 1, w 1, nb 2)	5	(b 3, lb 5)		8
	(all out)	228	(7 wickets declared)		278

Bowling: Nichols 21-5-47-2 Wyatt 4-2-9-0 Hammond 5.3-3-8-2 Mitchell 20-3-71-1 Verity 28-10-61-3 Langridge 13-3-27-2
Nichols 18-4-64-1 Wyatt 4-2-2-0 Hammond 14.4-4-26-1 Mitchell 33-5-93-2 Verity 38-16-56-3 Langridge 10-4-19-0 Holmes 4-2-10-0

England Innings

*RES Wyatt	c Nourse b Dalton	53	b Balaskas		16
H Sutcliffe	lbw b Bell	3	lbw b Langton		38
M Leyland	b Balaskas	18	b Crisp		4
WR Hammond	b Dalton	27	c Cameron b Langton		27
LEG Ames	b Balaskas	5	lbw b Langton		8
ERT Holmes	c Bell b Balaskas	10	b Langton		8
James Langridge	c Mitchell b Balaskas	27	lbw b Balaskas		17
+W Farrimond	b Balaskas	13	b Crisp		13
MS Nichols	c Cameron b Langton	10	not out		7
H Verity	lbw b Langton	17	c Langton b Balaskas		8
TB Mitchell	not out	5	st Cameron b Balaskas		1
	(b 4, lb 5, w 1)	10	(lb 4)		4
	(all out)	198	(all out)		151

Bowling: Crisp 8-1-32-0 Bell 6-0-16-1 Langton 21.3-3-58-2 Balaskas 32-8-49-5 Dalton 13-1-33-2
Crisp 15-4-30-2 Bell 12-3-21-0 Langton 11-3-31-4 Balaskas 27-8-54-4 Mitchell 2-0-11-0

Umpires: EJ Smith and FI Walden

England v India
27,29,30 June 1936

Result: England won by 9 wickets

India Innings

VM Merchant	b Allen	35	c Duckworth b Allen		0
+DD Hindlekar	b Robins	26	lbw b Robins		17
S Mushtaq Ali	c Langridge b Allen	0	lbw b Allen		8
CK Nayudu	lbw b Allen	1	c Robins b Allen		3
S Wazir Ali	b Allen	11	c Verity b Allen		4
L Amar Singh	c Langridge b Robins	12	lbw b Verity		7
PE Palia	c Mitchell b Verity	11	c Leyland b Verity		16
M Jahangir Khan	b Allen	13	c Duckworth b Verity		13
*Vizianagram	not out	19	c Wyatt b Robins		6
CS Nayudu	c Wyatt b Robins	6	c Hardstaff b Allen		9
M Nissar	st Duckworth b Verity	9	not out		2
	(b 4)	4	(b 4, lb 3, nb 1)		8
	(all out)	147	(all out)		93

Bowling: Allen 17-7-35-5 Wyatt 3-2-7-0 Verity 18.1-5-42-2 Langridge 4-1-9-0 Robins 13-4-50-3
Allen 18-1-43-5 Wyatt 7-4-8-0 Verity 16-8-17-4 Robins 5-1-17-1

England Innings

A Mitchell	b Amar Singh	14	c Merchant b Nissar		0
H Gimblett	c Mushtaq Ali b Amar Singh	11	not out		67
MJL Turnbull	b Amar Singh	0	not out		37
M Leyland	lbw b Amar Singh	60			
RES Wyatt	c Jahangir Khan b Amar Singh	0			
J Hardstaff jnr	b Nissar	2			
James Langridge	c Jahangir Khan b Amar Singh	19			
*GOB Allen	c Jahangir Khan b Amar Singh	13			
+G Duckworth	c Vizianagram b Nissar	2			
RWV Robins	c CK Nayudu b Nissar	0			
H Verity	not out	2			
	(b 4, lb 4, nb 3)	11	(b 4)		4
	(all out)	134	(1 wicket)		108

Bowling: Nissar 17-5-36-3 Amar Singh 25.1-11-35-6 Jahangir Khan 9-0-27-0 CK Nayudu 7-2-17-1 CS Nayudu 3-0-8-0
Nissar 6-3-26-1 Amar Singh 16.3-6-36-0 Jahangir Khan 10-3-20-0 CK Nayudu 7-2-22-0

Umpires: A Dolphin and FI Walden

England v New Zealand
26,28,29 June 1937

Result: Match drawn

England Innings

JH Parks	b Cowie	22	b Cowie		7
L Hutton	b Cowie	0	c Vivian b Cowie		1
J Hardstaff jnr	c Moloney b Roberts	114	c Tindill b Roberts		64
WR Hammond	c Roberts b Vivian	140			
E Paynter	c Dunning b Roberts	74			
CJ Barnett	b Cowie	5	not out		83
+LEG Ames	b Vivian	5	c sub b Roberts		20
*RWV Robins	c Tindill b Roberts	18	not out		38
W Voce	c Tindill b Cowie	27			
H Verity	c Cowie b Roberts	3			
AR Gover	not out	2			
	(b 4, lb 9, w 1)	14	(b 5, lb 8)		13
	(all out)	424	(4 wickets declared)		226

Bowling: Cowie 41-10-118-4 Roberts 43.3-11-101-4 Dunning 20-3-64-0 Vivian 46-10-106-2 Moloney 2-1-9-0 Page 3-0-12-0
Cowie 15-2-49-2 Roberts 14-3-73-2 Dunning 9-0-60-0 Vivian 4-0-31-0

New Zealand Innings

JL Kerr	c Ames b Robins	31	not out		38
HG Vivian	lbw b Gover	5	c Verity b Voce		11
WA Hadlee	c Verity b Voce	34	b Voce		3
*ML Page	c Paynter b Robins	9	c & b Robins		13
WM Wallace	lbw b Parks	52	lbw b Parks		56
MP Donnelly	lbw b Parks	0	c Ames b Voce		21
DAR Moloney	c & b Verity	64	run out		0
+EWT Tindill	c Hammond b Robins	8	lbw b Verity		3
AW Roberts	not out	66	c sub b Gover		17
JA Dunning	b Gover	0			
J Cowie	lbw b Voce	2			
	(b 4, lb 18, nb 2)	24	(b 4, lb 8, w 1)		13
	(all out)	295	(8 wickets)		175

Bowling: Gover 22-8-49-2 Voce 24.2-2-74-2 Hammond 6-2-12-0 Robins 21-5-58-3 Verity 25-13-48-1 Parks 11-3-26-2 Hutton 2-1-4-0
Gover 18-7-27-1 Voce 18.5-8-41-3 Robins 13-3-51-1 Verity 14-7-33-1 Parks 10-6-10-1

Umpires: F Chester and FI Walden

England v Australia
24,25,27,28 June 1938

Result: Match drawn

England Innings

CJ Barnett	c Brown b McCormick	18	c McCabe b McCormick		12
L Hutton	c Brown b McCormick	4	c McCormick b McCormick		5
WJ Edrich	b McCormick	0	c McCabe b McCormick		10
*WR Hammond	b McCormick	240	c sub b McCabe		2
E Paynter	lbw b O'Reilly	99	run out		43
DCS Compton	lbw b O'Reilly	6	not out		76
+LEG Ames	c McCormick b Fleetwood-Smith	83	c McCabe b O'Reilly		6
H Verity	b O'Reilly	5	b McCormick		11
AW Wellard	c McCormick b O'Reilly	4	b McCabe		38
DVP Wright	b Fleetwood-Smith	6	not out		10
K Farnes	not out	5			
	(b 1, lb 12, w 1, nb 10)	24	(b 12, lb 12, w 1, nb 4)		29
	(all out)	494	(8 wickets declared)		242

Bowling: McCormick 27-1-101-4 McCabe 31-4-86-0 Fleetwood-Smith 33.5-2-139-2 O'Reilly 37-6-93-4 Chipperfield 8.4-0-51-0
McCormick 24-5-72-3 McCabe 12-1-58-2 Fleetwood-Smith 7-1-30-0 O'Reilly 29-10-53-2

Australia Innings

JHW Fingleton	c Hammond b Wright	31	c Hammond b Wellard		4
WA Brown	not out	206	b Verity		10
*DG Bradman	b Verity	18	not out		102
SJ McCabe	c Verity b Farnes	38	c Hutton b Verity		21
AL Hassett	lbw b Wellard	56	b Wright		42
CL Badcock	b Wellard	0	c Wright b Edrich		0
+BA Barnett	c Compton b Verity	8	c Paynter b Edrich		14
AG Chipperfield	lbw b Verity	1			
WJ O'Reilly	b Farnes	42			
EL McCormick	c Barnett b Farnes	0			
LO Fleetwood-Smith	c Barnett b Verity	7			
	(b 1, lb 8, nb 6)	15	(b 5, lb 3, w 2, nb 1)		11
	(all out)	422	(6 wickets)		204

Bowling: Farnes 43-6-135-3 Wellard 23-2-96-2 Wright 16-2-68-1 Verity 35.4-9-103-4 Edrich 4-2-5-0
Farnes 13-3-51-0 Wellard 9-1-30-1 Wright 8-0-56-1 Verity 13-5-29-2 Edrich 5.2-0-27-2

Umpires: EJ Smith and FI Walden

England v West Indies
24,26,27 June 1939

Result: England won by 8 wickets

West Indies Innings

*RS Grant	c Compton b Copson	22	b Bowes		23
JB Stollmeyer	b Bowes	59	c Verity b Copson		0
GA Headley	c Wood b Copson	106	c Hutton b Copson		107
JED Sealy	c Wood b Wright	13	c Wood b Copson		29
KH Weekes	c Gimblett b Copson	20	c Wood b Verity		16
LN Constantine	lbw b Copson	14	c Hammond b Verity		17
JH Cameron	c Hutton b Bowes	1	c & b Wright		0
+IM Barrow	lbw b Copson	2	not out		6
EA Martindale	lbw b Wright	22	c Bowes b Wright		3
LG Hylton	not out	2	c Hardstaff b Copson		13
CB Clarke	b Bowes	1	c & b Copson		0
	(b 3, lb 9, nb 3)	15	(b 6, lb 4, w 1)		11
	(all out)	277	(all out)		225

Bowling: Bowes 28.4-5-86-3 Copson 24-2-85-5 Wright 13-1-57-2 Verity 16-3-34-0
Bowes 19-7-44-1 Copson 16.4-2-67-4 Wright 17-0-75-3 Verity 14-4-20-2 Compton 3-0-8-0

England Innings

L Hutton	c Grant b Hylton	196	b Hylton		16
H Gimblett	b Cameron	22	b Martindale		20
E Paynter	c Barrow b Cameron	34	not out		32
*WR Hammond	c Grant b Cameron	14	not out		30
DCS Compton	c Stollmeyer b Clarke	120			
J Hardstaff jnr	not out	3			
+A Wood	not out	0			
DVP Wright					
H Verity					
WH Copson					
WE Bowes					
	(b 8, lb 6, w 1)	15	(lb 2)		2
	(5 wickets declared)	404	(2 wickets)		100

Bowling: Martindale 20-2-86-0 Hylton 24-4-98-1 Constantine 13-0-67-0 Cameron 26-6-66-3 Clarke 6-0-28-1 Sealy 3-0-21-0 Grant 3-0-23-0
Martindale 7.7-0-51-1 Hylton 7-1-36-1 Constantine 3-0-11-0

Umpires: EJ Smith and FI Walden

England v India
22,24,25 June 1946

Result: England won by 10 wickets

India Innings

VM Merchant	c Gibb b Bedser	12	lbw b Ikin		27
MH Mankad	b Wright	14	c Hammond b Smailes		63
L Amarnath	lbw b Bedser	0	b Smailes		50
VS Hazare	b Bedser	31	c Hammond b Bedser		34
RS Modi	not out	57	lbw b Smailes		21
*Nawab of Pataudi snr	c Ikin b Bedser	9	b Wright		22
Gul Mohammad	b Wright	1	lbw b Wright		9
Abdul Hafeez	b Bowes	43	b Bedser		0
+DD Hindlekar	lbw b Bedser	3	c Ikin b Bedser		17
CS Nayudu	st Gibb b Bedser	4	b Bedser		13
SG Shinde	b Bedser	10	not out		4
	(b 10, lb 6)	16	(b 10, lb 2, nb 3)		15
	(all out)	200	(all out)		275

Bowling: Bowes 25-7-64-1 Bedser 29.1-11-49-7 Smailes 5-1-18-0 Wright 17-4-53-2
Bowes 4-1-9-0 Bedser 32.1-3-96-4 Smailes 15-2-44-3 Wright 20-3-68-2 Ikin 10-1-43-1

England Innings

L Hutton	c Nayudu b Amarnath	7	not out		22
C Washbrook	c Mankad b Amarnath	27	not out		24
DCS Compton	b Amarnath	0			
*WR Hammond	b Amarnath	33			
J Hardstaff jnr	c Hazare b Mankad	205			
+PA Gibb	c Hazare b Mankad	60			
JT Ikin	c Hindlekar b Shinde	16			
TF Smailes	c Mankad b Amarnath	25			
AV Bedser	b Hazare	30			
DVP Wright	b Mankad	3			
WE Bowes	lbw b Hazare	2			
	(b 11, lb 6, nb 1)	20	(lb 1, w 1)		2
	(all out)	428	(0 wickets)		48

Bowling: Hazare 34.4-4-100-2 Amarnath 57-18-118-5 Gul Mohammad 2-0-2-0 Mankad 48-11-107-2 Shinde 23-2-66-1 Nayudu 5-1-15-0
Hazare 4-2-7-0 Amarnath 4-0-15-0 Mankad 4.5-1-11-0 Nayudu 4-0-13-0

Umpires: HG Baldwin and JA Smart

Lord's

England v South Africa
21,23,24,25 June 1947

Result: England won by 10 wickets

England Innings

L Hutton	b Rowan	18	not out		13
C Washbrook	c Tuckett b Dawson	65	not out		13
WJ Edrich	b Mann	189			
DCS Compton	c Rowan b Tuckett	208			
CJ Barnett	b Tuckett	33			
*NWD Yardley	c Rowan b Tuckett	5			
+TG Evans	b Tuckett	16			
GH Pope	not out	8			
AV Bedser	b Tuckett	0			
DVP Wright					
WE Hollies					
	(b 2, lb 10)	12			0
	(8 wickets declared)	554	(0 wickets)		26

Bowling: Tuckett 47-8-115-5 Dawson 33-11-81-1 Mann 53-16-99-1 Rowan 65-11-174-1 Smith 17-2-73-0 Tuckett 3-0-4-0 Dawson 6-2-6-0 Mann 3.1-1-16-0

South Africa Innings

B Mitchell	st Evans b Compton	46	c Edrich b Wright		80
*A Melville	c Bedser b Hollies	117	b Edrich		8
KG Viljoen	b Wright	1	b Edrich		6
AD Nourse	lbw b Wright	61	b Edrich		58
OC Dawson	c Barnett b Hollies	36	c Edrich b Compton		33
TA Harris	st Evans b Compton	30	c Yardley b Compton		3
AMB Rowan	b Wright	8	not out		38
L Tuckett	b Wright	5	lbw b Wright		9
NBF Mann	b Wright	4	b Wright		5
+JD Lindsay	not out	7	c Yardley b Wright		5
VI Smith	c Edrich b Pope	11	c Edrich b Wright		0
	(lb 1)	1	(b 3, lb 4)		7
	(all out)	327	(all out)		252

Bowling: Edrich 9-1-22-0 Bedser 26-1-76-0 Pope 19.2-5-49-1 Wright 39-10-95-5 Hollies 28-10-52-2 Compton 21-11-32-2 Edrich 13-5-31-3 Bedser 14-6-20-0 Pope 17-7-36-0 Wright 32.2-6-80-5 Hollies 20-7-32-0 Compton 31-10-46-2

Umpires: HG Baldwin and D Davies

England v Australia
24,25,26,28,29 June 1948

Result: Australia won by 409 runs

Australia Innings

SG Barnes	c Hutton b Coxon	0	c Washbrook b Yardley		141
AR Morris	c Hutton b Coxon	105	b Wright		62
*DG Bradman	c Hutton b Bedser	38	c Edrich b Bedser		89
AL Hassett	b Yardley	47	b Yardley		0
KR Miller	lbw b Bedser	4	c Bedser b Laker		74
WA Brown	lbw b Yardley	24	c Evans b Coxon		32
IWG Johnson	c Evans b Edrich	4	not out		9
+D Tallon	c Yardley b Bedser	53			
RR Lindwall	b Bedser	15	st Evans b Laker		25
WA Johnston	st Evans b Wright	29			
ERH Toshack	not out	20			
	(b 3, lb 7, nb 1)	11	(b 22, lb 5, nb 1)		28
	(all out)	350	(7 wickets declared)		460

Bowling: Bedser 43-14-100-4 Coxon 35-10-90-2 Edrich 8-0-43-1 Wright 21.3-8-54-1 Laker 7-3-17-0 Yardley 15-4-35-2 Bedser 34-6-112-1 Coxon 28-3-82-1 Edrich 2-0-11-0 Wright 19-4-69-1 Laker 31.2-6-111-2 Yardley 13-4-36-2 Compton 3-0-11-0

England Innings

L Hutton	b Johnson	20	c Johnson b Lindwall		13
C Washbrook	c Tallon b Lindwall	8	c Tallon b Toshack		37
WJ Edrich	b Lindwall	5	c Johnson b Toshack		2
DCS Compton	c Miller b Johnson	53	c Miller b Johnson		29
HE Dollery	b Lindwall	0	b Lindwall		37
*NWD Yardley	b Lindwall	44	b Toshack		11
A Coxon	c & b Johnson	19	lbw b Toshack		0
+TG Evans	c Miller b Johnson	9	not out		24
JC Laker	c Tallon b Johnson	28	b Lindwall		0
AV Bedser	b Lindwall	9	c Hassett b Johnston		9
DVP Wright	not out	13	c Lindwall b Toshack		4
	(lb 3, nb 4)	7	(b 16, lb 4)		20
	(all out)	215	(all out)		186

Bowling: Lindwall 27.4-7-70-5 Johnston 22-4-43-2 Johnson 35-13-72-3 Toshack 18-11-23-0 Lindwall 23-9-61-3 Johnston 33-15-62-2 Johnson 2-1-3-0 Toshack 20.1-6-40-5

Umpires: D Davies and CN Woolley

England v New Zealand
25,27,28 June 1949

Result: Match drawn

England Innings

L Hutton	b Burtt	23	c Cave b Rabone		66
JDB Robertson	c Mooney b Cowie	26	c Cave b Rabone		121
WJ Edrich	b Donnelly b Cowie	9	c Hadlee b Burtt		31
DCS Compton	c Sutcliffe b Burtt	116	b Burtt		6
AJ Watkins	c Wallace b Burtt	6	not out		49
*FG Mann	b Cave	18	c Donnelly b Rabone		17
TE Bailey	c Sutcliffe b Rabone	93	not out		6
+TG Evans	b Burtt	5			
C Gladwin	run out	5			
JA Young	not out	1			
WE Hollies					
	(b 9, lb 2)	11	(b 9, lb 1)		10
	(9 wickets declared)	313	(5 wickets)		306

Bowling: Cowie 26.1-5-64-2 Cave 27-2-79-1 Rabone 14-5-56-1 Burtt 35-7-102-4 Sutcliffe 1-0-1-0 Cowie 14-3-39-0 Cave 7-1-23-0 Rabone 28-6-116-3 Burtt 37-12-58-2 Sutcliffe 16-1-55-0 Wallace 1-0-5-0

New Zealand Innings

B Sutcliffe	c Compton b Gladwin	57		
VJ Scott	c Edrich b Compton	42		
*WA Hadlee	c Robertson b Hollies	43		
WM Wallace	c Evans b Hollies	2		
MP Donnelly	c Hutton b Young	206		
FB Smith	b Hollies	23		
GO Rabone	b Hollies	25		
+FLH Mooney	c Watkins b Young	33		
TB Burtt	c Edrich b Hollies	23		
HB Cave	c & b Young	6		
J Cowie	not out	1		
	(b 16, lb 3, w 3, nb 1)	23		
	(all out)	484		

Bowling: Bailey 33-3-136-0 Gladwin 28-5-67-1 Edrich 4-0-16-0 Hollies 58-18-133-5 Compton 7-0-33-1 Young 26.4-4-65-3 Watkins 3-1-11-0

Umpires: WH Ashdown and F Chester

England v West Indies
24,26,27,28,29 June 1950

Result: West Indies won by 326 runs

West Indies Innings

AF Rae	c & b Jenkins	106	b Jenkins		24
JB Stollmeyer	lbw b Wardle	20	b Jenkins		30
FMM Worrell	b Bedser	52	c Doggart b Jenkins		45
ED Weekes	b Bedser	63	run out		63
+CL Walcott	st Evans b Jenkins	14	not out		168
GE Gomez	st Evans b Jenkins	1	c Edrich b Bedser		70
RJ Christiani	b Bedser	33	not out		5
*JDC Goddard	b Wardle	14	c Evans b Jenkins		11
PEW Jones	c Evans b Jenkins	0			
S Ramadhin	not out	1			
AL Valentine	c Hutton b Jenkins	5			
	(b 10, lb 5, w 1, nb 1)	17	(lb 8, nb 1)		9
	(all out)	326	(6 wickets declared)		425

Bowling: Bedser 40-14-60-3 Edrich 16-4-30-0 Jenkins 35.2-6-116-5 Wardle 17-6-46-2 Berry 19-7-45-0 Yardley 4-1-12-0 Bedser 44-16-80-1 Edrich 13-2-37-0 Jenkins 59-13-174-4 Wardle 30-10-58-0 Berry 32-15-67-0

England Innings

L Hutton	st Walcott b Valentine	35	b Valentine		10
C Washbrook	st Walcott b Ramadhin	36	b Ramadhin		114
WJ Edrich	c Walcott b Ramadhin	8	c Jones b Ramadhin		8
GHG Doggart	lbw b Ramadhin	0	b Ramadhin		25
WGA Parkhouse	b Valentine	0	c Goddard b Valentine		48
*NWD Yardley	b Valentine	16	c Weekes b Valentine		19
+TG Evans	b Ramadhin	8	c Rae b Ramadhin		2
RO Jenkins	c Walcott b Valentine	4	b Ramadhin		4
JH Wardle	not out	33	lbw b Worrell		21
AV Bedser	b Ramadhin	5	b Ramadhin		0
R Berry	c Goddard b Jones	2	not out		0
	(b 2, lb 1, w 1)	4	(b 16, lb 7)		23
	(all out)	151	(all out)		274

Bowling: Jones 8.4-2-13-1 Worrell 10-4-20-0 Valentine 45-28-48-4 Ramadhin 43-27-66-5 Jones 7-1-22-0 Worrell 22.3-9-39-1 Valentine 71-47-79-3 Ramadhin 72-43-86-6 Gomez 13-1-25-0 Goddard 6-6-0-0

Umpires: D Davies and FS Lee

England v South Africa
21,22,23 June 1951

Result: England won by 10 wickets

England Innings

L Hutton	lbw b McCarthy	12	not out		12
JT Ikin	b Mann	51	not out		4
RT Simpson	lbw b McCarthy	26			
DCS Compton	lbw b McCarthy	79			
W Watson	c McCarthy b Chubb	79			
*FR Brown	b Chubb	0			
+TG Evans	c Fullerton b McCarthy	0			
JH Wardle	lbw b Chubb	18			
AV Bedser	not out	26			
JB Statham	b Chubb	1			
R Tattersall	b Chubb	1			
	(b 8, lb 9)	17			0
	(all out)	311	(0 wickets)		16

Bowling: McCarthy 23-2-76-4 Chubb 34.4-9-77-5 AMB Rowan 13-1-63-0 Mann 32-12-51-1 van Ryneveld 5-0-27-0 Nourse 2-0-9-0 EAB Rowan 1.5-0-7-0

South Africa Innings

EAB Rowan	c Ikin b Tattersall	24	c Ikin b Statham		10
+JHB Waite	c Hutton b Wardle	15	c Compton b Tattersall		17
DJ McGlew	c Evans b Tattersall	2	b Tattersall		2
*AD Nourse	c Watson b Tattersall	20	lbw b Wardle		3
JE Cheetham	c Hutton b Tattersall	15	b Statham		54
GM Fullerton	b Tattersall	12	lbw b Bedser		60
CB van Ryneveld	lbw b Wardle	0	c Ikin b Tattersall		18
AMB Rowan	c Ikin b Tattersall	3	c Brown b Bedser		10
NBF Mann	c Brown b Tattersall	14	c Brown b Tattersall		13
GWA Chubb	c Tattersall b Wardle	5	b Tattersall		3
CN McCarthy	not out	1	not out		2
	(lb 3)	3	(b 11, lb 8)		19
	(all out)	115	(all out)		211

Bowling: Bedser 8-5-7-0 Statham 6-3-7-0 Tattersall 28-10-52-7 Wardle 22.5-10-46-3 Bedser 24-8-53-2 Statham 18-6-33-2 Tattersall 32.2-14-49-5 Wardle 55-4-1 Compton 2-0-13-0

Umpires: H Elliott and FS Lee

England v India
19,20,21,23,24 June 1952

Result: England won by 8 wickets

India Innings

MH Mankad	c Watkins b Trueman	72	b Laker		184
P Roy	c & b Bedser	35	b Bedser		0
PR Umrigar	b Trueman	5	b Trueman		14
*VS Hazare	not out	69	c Laker b Bedser		49
VL Manjrekar	lbw b Bedser	5	b Laker		1
DG Phadkar	b Watkins	8	b Laker		16
HR Adhikari	lbw b Watkins	0	b Trueman		16
GS Ramchand	b Trueman	18	b Trueman		42
+MK Mantri	b Trueman	1	c Compton b Laker		5
SG Shinde	st Evans b Watkins	5	c Hutton b Trueman		14
Ghulam Ahmed	b Jenkins	0	not out		1
	(b 7, nb 10)	17	(b 29, lb 3, nb 4)		36
	(all out)	235	(all out)		378

Bowling: Bedser 33-8-62-2 Trueman 25-3-72-4 Jenkins 7.3-1-26-1 Laker 12-5-21-0 Watkins 17-7-37-3 Bedser 36-13-60-2 Trueman 27-4-110-4 Jenkins 10-1-40-0 Laker 39-15-102-4 Watkins 8-0-20-0 Compton 2-0-10-0

England Innings

*L Hutton	c Mantri b Hazare	150	not out		39
RT Simpson	b Mankad	53	run out		2
PBH May	c Mantri b Mankad	74	c Roy b Ghulam Ahmed		26
DCS Compton	lbw b Hazare	6	not out		4
TW Graveney	c Mantri b Ghulam Ahmed	73			
AJ Watkins	b Mankad	0			
+TG Evans	c & b Ghulam Ahmed	104			
RO Jenkins	st Mantri b Mankad	21			
JC Laker	not out	23			
AV Bedser	c Ramchand b Mankad	3			
FS Trueman	b Ghulam Ahmed	17			
	(b 8, lb 5)	13	(b 4, lb 4)		8
	(all out)	537	(2 wickets)		79

Bowling: Phadkar 27-8-44-0 Ramchand 29-8-67-0 Hazare 24.4-5-32 Mankad 73-24-196-5 Ghulam Ahmed 43.4-12-106-3 Shinde 6-0-43-0 Umrigar 4-0-15-0 Ramchand 1-0-5-0 Hazare 1-1-0-0 Mankad 24-12-35-0 Ghulam Ahmed 23.2-9-31-1

Umpires: F Chester and FS Lee

Lord's

England v Australia
25,26,27,29,30 June 1953

Result: Match drawn

Australia Innings

*AL Hassett	c Bailey b Bedser	104	c Evans b Statham	3
AR Morris	st Evans b Bedser	30	c Statham b Compton	89
RN Harvey	lbw b Bedser	59	b Bedser	21
KR Miller	b Wardle	25	b Wardle	109
GB Hole	c Compton b Wardle	13	lbw b Brown	47
R Benaud	lbw b Wardle	0	c Graveney b Bedser	5
AK Davidson	c Statham b Bedser	76	c & b Brown	15
DT Ring	lbw b Wardle	18	lbw b Brown	7
RR Lindwall	b Statham	9	b Bedser	50
+GRA Langley	c Watson b Bedser	1	b Brown	9
WA Johnston	not out	3	not out	0
	(b 4, lb 4)	8	(b 8, lb 5)	13
	(all out)	346	(all out)	368

Bowling: Bedser 42.4-8-105-5 Statham 28-7-48-1 Brown 25-7-53-0 Bailey 16-2-55-0 Wardle 29-8-77-4
Bedser 31.5-8-77-3 Statham 15-3-40-1 Brown 27-4-82-4 Bailey 10-4-24-0 Wardle 46-18-111-1 Compton 3-0-21-1

England Innings

*L Hutton	c Hole b Johnston	145	c Hole b Lindwall	5
D Kenyon	c Davidson b Lindwall	3	c Hassett b Lindwall	2
TW Graveney	b Lindwall	78	c Langley b Johnston	2
DCS Compton	c Hole b Benaud	57	lbw b Johnston	33
W Watson	st Langley b Johnston	4	c Hole b Ring	109
TE Bailey	c & b Miller	2	c Benaud b Ring	71
FR Brown	c Langley b Lindwall	22	c Hole b Benaud	28
+TG Evans	b Lindwall	0	not out	11
JH Wardle	b Davidson	23	not out	0
AV Bedser	b Lindwall	1		
JB Statham	not out	17		
	(b 11, lb 1, w 1, nb 7)	20	(b 7, lb 6, w 2, nb 6)	21
	(all out)	372	(7 wickets)	282

Bowling: Lindwall 23-4-66-5 Miller 25-6-57-1 Johnston 35-11-91-2 Ring 14-2-43-0 Benaud 19-4-70-1 Davidson 10.5-2-25-1
Lindwall 19-3-26-2 Miller 17-8-17-0 Johnston 29-10-70-2 Ring 29-5-84-2 Benaud 17-6-51-1 Davidson 14-5-13-0 Hole 1-1-0-0

Umpires: HG Baldwin and FS Lee

England v Pakistan
10,11,12,14,15 June 1954

Result: Match drawn

Pakistan Innings

Hanif Mohammad	b Tattersall	20	lbw b Laker	39
Alimuddin	c Edrich b Wardle	19	b Bailey	0
Waqar Hasan	c Compton b Wardle	9	c Statham b Compton	53
Maqsood Ahmed	st Evans b Wardle	0	not out	29
+Imtiaz Ahmed	b Laker	12		
*AH Kardar	b Statham	2		
Fazal Mahmood	b Wardle	5		
Khalid Wazir	b Statham	3		
Khan Mohammad	b Statham	0		
Zulfiqar Ahmed	b Statham	11		
Shujauddin	not out	0		
	(b 4, lb 1, nb 1)	6		0
	(all out)	87	(3 wickets)	121

Bowling: Statham 13-6-18-4 Bailey 3-2-1-0 Wardle 30.5-22-33-4 Tattersall 15-8-12-1 Laker 22-12-17-1
Statham 5-2-17-0 Bailey 6-2-13-1 Wardle 8-6-6-0 Tattersall 10-1-27-0 Laker 10.2-5-22-1 Compton 13-2-36-1

England Innings

*L Hutton	b Khan Mohammad	0	
RT Simpson	lbw b Fazal Mahmood	40	
PBH May	b Khan Mohammad	27	
DCS Compton	b Fazal Mahmood	0	
WJ Edrich	b Khan Mohammad	4	
JH Wardle	c Maqsood Ahmed b Fazal Mahmood	3	
+TG Evans	b Khan Mohammad	25	
TE Bailey	b Khan Mohammad	3	
JC Laker	not out	13	
JB Statham	b Fazal Mahmood	0	
R Tattersall			
	(b 2)	2	
	(9 wickets declared)	117	

Bowling: Fazal Mahmood 16-2-54-4 Khan Mohammad 15-3-61-5

Umpires: TJ Bartley and D Davies

England v South Africa
23,24,25,27 June 1955

Result: England won by 71 runs

England Innings

D Kenyon	b Adcock	1	lbw b Goddard	2
TW Graveney	c Waite b Heine	15	c Heine b Goddard	60
*PBH May	c Tayfield b Heine	0	hit wicket b Heine	112
DCS Compton	c Keith b Heine	20	c Mansell b Goddard	69
KF Barrington	b Heine	34	c McLean b Tayfield	18
TE Bailey	lbw b Goddard	13	c Adcock b Tayfield	22
+TG Evans	c Waite b Heine	20	c & b Tayfield	14
FJ Titmus	lbw b Goddard	4	c Waite b Adcock	16
JH Wardle	c Tayfield b Goddard	20	c Heine b Tayfield	4
JB Statham	c McLean b Goddard	0	b Tayfield	11
FS Trueman	not out	2	not out	6
	(b 2, lb 2)	4	(b 15, lb 2, nb 2)	19
	(all out)	133	(all out)	353

Bowling: Heine 25-7-60-5 Adcock 8-3-10-1 Goddard 21.2-8-59-4
Heine 29-5-87-1 Adcock 25-5-64-1 Goddard 55-23-96-3 Tayfield 38.5-12-80-5 Mansell 2-0-7-0

South Africa Innings

DJ McGlew	c Evans b Statham	0	lbw b Statham	0
TL Goddard	c Evans b Trueman	6	c Evans b Statham	10
*JE Cheetham	lbw b Bailey	13	retired hurt	3
WR Endean	lbw b Wardle	48	c Evans b Statham	28
RA McLean	b Statham	142	b Statham	8
+JHB Waite	c Evans b Trueman	8	lbw b Statham	9
HJ Keith	c Titmus b Wardle	57	c Graveney b Statham	5
PNF Mansell	c Graveney b Wardle	2	c Kenyon b Wardle	16
HJ Tayfield	b Titmus	21	c Evans b Statham	3
PS Heine	st Evans b Wardle	2	c Kenyon b Wardle	14
NAT Adcock	not out	0	not out	0
	(b 6, lb 1, nb 4)	11	(b 11, lb 3, nb 1)	15
	(all out)	304	(all out)	111

Bowling: Statham 27-9-49-2 Trueman 16-2-73-2 Bailey 16-2-56-1 Wardle 29-10-65-4 Titmus 14-3-50-1
Statham 29-12-39-7 Trueman 19-2-39-0 Wardle 9.4-4-18-2

Umpires: F Chester and LH Gray

England v Australia
21,22,23,25,26 June 1956

Result: Australia won by 185 runs

Australia Innings

CC McDonald	c Trueman b Bailey	78	c Cowdrey b Bailey	26
JW Burke	st Evans b Laker	65	c Graveney b Trueman	16
RN Harvey	c Evans b Bailey	0	c Bailey b Trueman	10
PJP Burge	b Statham	21	b Trueman	14
KR Miller	b Trueman	28	c Evans b Trueman	30
KD Mackay	c Bailey b Laker	38	c Evans b Statham	31
RG Archer	b Wardle	28	c Evans b Bailey	1
R Benaud	b Statham	5	c Evans b Trueman	97
*IWG Johnson	c Evans b Trueman	6	lbw b Bailey	17
+GRA Langley	c Bailey b Laker	14	not out	7
WPA Crawford	not out	0	lbw b Bailey	0
	(lb 2)	2	(b 2, lb 2, nb 4)	8
	(all out)	285	(all out)	257

Bowling: Statham 35-9-70-2 Trueman 28-6-54-2 Bailey 34-12-72-2 Laker 29.1-10-47-3 Wardle 20-7-40-1
Statham 26-5-59-1 Trueman 28-2-90-5 Bailey 24.5-8-64-4 Laker 7-3-17-0 Wardle 7-2-19-0

England Innings

PE Richardson	c Langley b Miller	9	c Langley b Archer	21
MC Cowdrey	c Benaud b Mackay	23	lbw b Benaud	27
TW Graveney	b Miller	5	c Langley b Miller	18
*PBH May	b Benaud	63	c Langley b Miller	53
W Watson	c Benaud b Miller	6	b Miller	18
TE Bailey	b Miller	32	c Harvey b Archer	18
+TG Evans	st Langley b Benaud	0	c Langley b Miller	20
JC Laker	b Archer	12	c Langley b Archer	4
JH Wardle	c Langley b Archer	0	b Miller	0
FS Trueman	c Langley b Miller	7	b Archer	2
JB Statham	not out	0	not out	0
	(lb 14)	14	(lb 5)	5
	(all out)	171	(all out)	186

Bowling: Miller 34.1-9-72-5 Crawford 4.5-2-4-0 Archer 23-9-47-2 Mackay 11-3-15-1 Benaud 9-2-19-2
Miller 36-12-80-5 Archer 31.2-8-71-4 Benaud 28-14-27-1 Johnson 4-2-3-0

Umpires: DE Davies and FS Lee

England v West Indies
20,21,22 June 1957

Result: England won by an innings and 36 runs

West Indies Innings

NS Asgarali	lbw b Trueman	0	c Trueman b Wardle	26
+RB Kanhai	c Cowdrey b Bailey	34	c Bailey b Statham	0
CL Walcott	lbw b Bailey	14	c Trueman b Wardle	21
GS Sobers	c May b Statham	17	c May b Bailey	66
ED Weekes	c Evans b Bailey	13	c Evans b Bailey	90
FMM Worrell	c Close b Bailey	12	c Evans b Trueman	10
OG Smith	c Graveney b Bailey	25	lbw b Statham	5
*JDC Goddard	c Cowdrey b Bailey	1	c Evans b Trueman	21
S Ramadhin	b Trueman	0	c Statham b Bailey	0
R Gilchrist	c & b Bailey	4	not out	11
AL Valentine	not out	7	b Statham	1
	(b 2, lb 1, w 4)	7	(b 4, lb 6)	10
	(all out)	127	(all out)	261

Bowling: Statham 18-3-46-1 Trueman 12.3-2-30-2 Bailey 21-8-44-7
Statham 29.1-9-71-3 Trueman 23-5-73-2 Bailey 22-6-54-4 Wardle 22-5-53-1

England Innings

PE Richardson	b Gilchrist	76
DV Smith	lbw b Worrell	8
TW Graveney	lbw b Gilchrist	0
*PBH May	c Kanhai b Gilchrist	0
MC Cowdrey	c Walcott b Sobers	152
TE Bailey	b Worrell	1
DB Close	c Kanhai b Goddard	32
+TG Evans	b Sobers	82
JH Wardle	c Sobers b Ramadhin	11
FS Trueman	not out	36
JB Statham	b Gilchrist	7
	(b 7, lb 11, w 1)	19
	(all out)	424

Bowling: Worrell 42-7-114-2 Gilchrist 36.3-7-115-4 Ramadhin 22-5-83-1 Valentine 3-0-20-0 Goddard 13-1-45-1 Sobers 7-0-28-2

Umpires: DE Davies and CS Elliott

England v New Zealand
19,20,21 June 1958

Result: England won by an innings and 148 runs

England Innings

PE Richardson	c Petrie b Hayes	36
MJK Smith	c Petrie b Hayes	47
TW Graveney	c Petrie b Alabaster	37
*PBH May	c Alabaster b MacGibbon	19
MC Cowdrey	b Hayes	65
TE Bailey	c Petrie b Reid	17
+TG Evans	c Hayes b MacGibbon	11
GAR Lock	not out	23
FS Trueman	b Hayes	8
JC Laker	c Blair b MacGibbon	4
PJ Loader	c Playle b MacGibbon	4
	(lb 1)	1
	(all out)	269

Bowling: Hayes 22-5-36-4 MacGibbon 36.4-11-86-4 Blair 25-6-57-0 Reid 24-12-41-1 Alabaster 16-6-48-1

New Zealand Innings

LSM Miller	lbw b Trueman	4	c Trueman b Loader	0
JW D'Arcy	c Trueman b Laker	14	c Bailey b Trueman	33
WR Playle	c Graveney b Laker	1	b Loader	3
NS Harford	c & b Laker	0	c May b Lock	3
*JR Reid	c Loader b Lock	6	c Cowdrey b Trueman	5
B Sutcliffe	b Lock	18	b Bailey	0
AR MacGibbon	c May b Lock	2	c May b Lock	7
JC Alabaster	c & b Lock	0	b Laker	5
+EC Petrie	c Trueman b Laker	0	not out	4
RW Blair	not out	0	b Lock	0
JA Hayes	c Cowdrey b Lock	1	c & b Lock	14
	(lb 1)	1		0
	(all out)	47	(all out)	74

Bowling: Trueman 4-1-6-1 Loader 4-2-6-0 Laker 12-6-13-4 Lock 11.3-7-17-5 Bailey 1-0-4-0
Trueman 11-6-24-2 Loader 9-6-7-2 Laker 13-8-24-1 Lock 12.3-8-12-4 Bailey 5-1-7-1

Umpires: D Davies and CS Elliott

Lord's

England v India
18,19,20 June 1959

Result: England won by 8 wickets

India Innings

Batsman		R		R
*P Roy	c Evans b Statham	15	c May b Trueman	0
NJ Contractor	b Greenhough	81	not out	11
PR Umrigar	b Statham	1	c Horton b Trueman	0
VL Manjrekar	lbw b Trueman	12	lbw b Statham	61
JM Ghorpade	lbw b Greenhough	41	c Evans b Statham	22
AG Kripal Singh	b Greenhough	0	b Statham	41
ML Jaisimha	lbw b Greenhough	1	b Moss	8
+PG Joshi	b Horton	4	b Moss	6
Surendranath	b Greenhough	0	run out	0
SP Gupte	c May b Horton	0	st Evans b Greenhough	7
RB Desai	not out	2	b Greenhough	5
	(lb 11)	11	(lb 4)	4
	(all out)	168	(all out)	165

Bowling: Trueman 16-4-40-1 Statham 16-6-27-2 Moss 14-5-31-0 Greenhough 16-4-35-5 Horton 15.4-7-24-2
Trueman 21-3-55-2 Statham 17-7-45-3 Moss 23-10-30-2 Greenhough 18.1-8-31-2

England Innings

Batsman		R		R
CA Milton	c Surendranath b Desai	14	c Joshi b Desai	3
K Taylor	c Gupte b Desai	6	c Surendranath	3
MC Cowdrey	c Joshi b Desai	34	not out	63
*PBH May	b Surendranath	9	not out	33
KF Barrington	c sub b Desai	80		
MJ Horton	b Desai	2		
+TG Evans	b Surendranath	0		
FS Trueman	lbw b Gupte	7		
JB Statham	c Surendranath b Gupte	38		
AE Moss	b Surendranath	26		
T Greenhough	not out	0		
	(b 5, lb 4, w 1)	10	(b 5, lb 1)	6
	(all out)	226	(2 wickets)	108

Bowling: Desai 31.4-8-89-5 Surendranath 30-17-46-3 Umrigar 1-1-0-0 Gupte 19-2-62-2 Kripal Singh 3-0-19-0
Desai 7-1-29-1 Surendranath 11-2-32-1 Umrigar 1-0-8-0 Gupte 6-2-21-0 Kripal Singh 1-1-0-0 Jaisimha 1-0-8-0 Roy 0.2-0-4-0

Umpires: DE Davies and CS Elliott

England v South Africa
23,24,25,27 June 1960

Result: England won by an innings and 73 runs

England Innings

*MC Cowdrey	c McLean b Griffin	4
R Subba Row	lbw b Adcock	90
ER Dexter	c McLean b Adcock	56
KF Barrington	lbw b Goddard	24
MJK Smith	c Waite b Adcock	99
+JM Parks	c Fellows-Smith b Adcock	3
PM Walker	b Griffin	52
R Illingworth	not out	0
FS Trueman	b Griffin	0
JB Statham	not out	2
AE Moss		
	(b 6, lb 14, w 1, nb 11)	32
	(8 wickets declared)	362

Bowling: Adcock 36-11-70-3 Griffin 30-7-87-4 Goddard 31-6-96-1 Tayfield 27-9-64-0 Fellows-Smith 5-0-13-0

South Africa Innings

Batsman		R		R
*DJ McGlew	lbw b Statham	15	b Statham	17
TL Goddard	b Statham	19	c Parks b Statham	24
S O'Linn	c Walker b Moss	8	lbw b Trueman	8
RA McLean	c Cowdrey b Statham	15	c Parks b Trueman	13
+JHB Waite	c Parks b Statham	3	lbw b Statham	0
PR Carlstein	c Cowdrey b Moss	12	c Parks b Moss	6
C Wesley	c Parks b Statham	11	b Dexter	35
JP Fellows-Smith	c Parks b Moss	29	not out	27
HJ Tayfield	c Smith b Moss	12	b Dexter	4
GM Griffin	b Statham	5	b Statham	0
NAT Adcock	not out	8	b Statham	2
	(lb 4, nb 1)	5	(nb 1)	1
	(all out)	152	(all out)	137

Bowling: Statham 20-5-63-6 Trueman 13-2-49-0 Moss 10.3-0-35-4
Statham 21-6-34-5 Trueman 17-5-44-2 Moss 14-1-41-1 Illingworth 1-1-0-0 Dexter 4-0-17-2

Umpires: JS Buller and FS Lee

England v Australia
22,23,24,26 June 1961

Result: Australia won by 5 wickets

England Innings

Batsman		R		R
G Pullar	b Davidson	11	c Grout b Misson	42
R Subba Row	lbw b Mackay	48	c Grout b Davidson	8
ER Dexter	c McKenzie b Misson	27	b McKenzie	17
*MC Cowdrey	c Grout b McKenzie	16	c Mackay b Misson	7
PBH May	c Grout b Davidson	17	c Grout b McKenzie	22
KF Barrington	c Mackay b Davidson	4	lbw b Davidson	66
R Illingworth	b Misson	13	c Harvey b Simpson	0
+JT Murray	lbw b Mackay	18	c Grout b McKenzie	25
GAR Lock	c Grout b Davidson	5	b McKenzie	1
FS Trueman	b Davidson	25	c Grout b McKenzie	0
JB Statham	not out	11	not out	2
	(lb 9, w 2)	11	(b 1, lb 10, w 1)	12
	(all out)	206	(all out)	202

Bowling: Davidson 24.3-6-42-5 McKenzie 26-7-81-1 Misson 16-4-48-2 Mackay 12-3-24-2
Davidson 24-8-50-2 McKenzie 29-13-37-5 Misson 17-2-66-2 Mackay 8-6-5-0 Simpson 19-10-32-1

Australia Innings

Batsman		R		R
WM Lawry	c Murray b Dexter	130	c Murray b Statham	1
CC McDonald	b Statham	4	c Illingworth b Trueman	14
RB Simpson	c Illingworth b Trueman	0	c Illingworth b Statham	15
*RN Harvey	c Barrington b Trueman	27	c Murray b Trueman	4
NC O'Neill	b Dexter	1	b Statham	0
PJP Burge	c Murray b Statham	46	not out	37
AK Davidson	lbw b Trueman	6	not out	0
KD Mackay	c Barrington b Illingworth	54		
+ATW Grout	lbw b Dexter	0		
GD McKenzie	b Trueman	34		
FM Misson	not out	25		
	(b 1, lb 12)	13		0
	(all out)	340	(5 wickets)	71

Bowling: Statham 44-10-89-2 Trueman 34-3-118-4 Dexter 24-7-56-3 Lock 26-13-48-0 Illingworth 11.3-5-16-1
Statham 10.5-3-31-3 Trueman 10-0-40-2

Umpires: CS Elliott and WE Phillipson

England v Pakistan
21,22,23 June 1962

Result: England won by 9 wickets

Pakistan Innings

Batsman		R		R
Hanif Mohammad	c Cowdrey b Trueman	13	lbw b Coldwell	24
+Imtiaz Ahmed	b Coldwell	1	c Trueman b Coldwell	33
Saeed Ahmed	b Dexter	10	b Coldwell	20
*Javed Burki	c Dexter b Trueman	5	lbw b Coldwell	101
Mushtaq Mohammad	c Cowdrey b Trueman	7	c Millman b Trueman	18
Alimuddin	b Coldwell	9	c Graveney b Allen	10
W Mathias	b Trueman	15	c Graveney b Trueman	1
Nasim-ul-Ghani	c Millman b Trueman	17	c Graveney b Coldwell	101
Mahmood Hussain	c Cowdrey b Coldwell	1	b Coldwell	20
A D'Souza	not out	6	not out	12
Mohammad Farooq	c Stewart b Trueman	13	b Trueman	1
	(b 1, lb 2)	3	(b 6, lb 4, w 4)	14
	(all out)	100	(all out)	355

Bowling: Trueman 17.4-6-31-6 Coldwell 14-2-25-3 Dexter 12-3-41-1
Trueman 33.3-6-85-3 Coldwell 41-13-85-6 Dexter 15-4-44-0 Allen 15-6-41-1 Lock 14-1-78-0 Barrington 1-0-8-0

England Innings

Batsman		R		R
MJ Stewart	c Imtiaz Ahmed b D'Souza	39	not out	34
MC Cowdrey	c D'Souza b Mohammad Farooq	41	c Imtiaz Ahmed b D'Souza	20
*ER Dexter	c Imtiaz Ahmed b Mohammad Farooq	65	not out	32
TW Graveney	b D'Souza	153		
KF Barrington	c Imtiaz Ahmed b Mohammad Farooq	0		
DA Allen	lbw b Mohammad Farooq	2		
PH Parfitt	b Mahmood Hussain	16		
+G Millman	c Hanif Mohammad b Mahmood Hussain	7		
GAR Lock	c Mathias b Saeed Ahmed	7		
FS Trueman	lbw b Saeed Ahmed	29		
LJ Coldwell	not out	0		
	(b 1, lb 5, nb 5)	11		0
	(all out)	370	(1 wicket)	86

Bowling: Mahmood Hussain 40-9-106-2 Mohammad Farooq 19-4-70-4 D'Souza 35.4-3-147-2 Nasim-ul-Ghani 2-0-15-0 Saeed Ahmed 5-1-21-2
Mohammad Farooq 7-1-37-0 D'Souza 7-0-29-1 Saeed Ahmed 2-0-12-0 Mushtaq Mohammad 1-0-8-0

Umpires: JS Buller and N Oldfield

England v West Indies
20,21,22,24,25 June 1963

Result: Match drawn

West Indies Innings

Batsman		R		R
CC Hunte	c Close b Trueman	44	c Cowdrey b Shackleton	7
EDAS McMorris	lbw b Trueman	16	c Cowdrey b Trueman	8
GS Sobers	c Cowdrey b Allen	42	c Parks b Trueman	8
RB Kanhai	c Edrich b Trueman	73	c Cowdrey b Shackleton	21
BF Butcher	c Barrington b Trueman	14	lbw b Shackleton	133
JS Solomon	lbw b Shackleton	56	c Stewart b Allen	5
*FMM Worrell	b Trueman	0	c Stewart b Trueman	33
+DL Murray	c Cowdrey b Trueman	20	c Parks b Trueman	2
WW Hall	not out	25	c Parks b Trueman	2
CC Griffith	c Cowdrey b Shackleton	0	b Shackleton	1
LR Gibbs	c Stewart b Shackleton	1	not out	1
	(b 10, lb 1)	11	(b 5, lb 2, nb 1)	8
	(all out)	301	(all out)	229

Bowling: Trueman 44-16-100-6 Shackleton 50.2-22-93-3 Dexter 20-6-41-0 Close 9-3-21-0 Allen 10-3-35-1
Trueman 26-9-52-5 Shackleton 34-14-72-4 Allen 21-7-50-1 Titmus 17-3-47-0

England Innings

Batsman		R		R
MJ Stewart	c Kanhai b Griffith	2	c Solomon b Hall	17
JH Edrich	c Murray b Griffith	0	c Murray b Hall	8
*ER Dexter	lbw b Sobers	70	b Gibbs	2
KF Barrington	c Sobers b Worrell	80	c Murray b Griffith	60
MC Cowdrey	b Gibbs	4	not out	19
DB Close	c Murray b Griffith	9	c Murray b Griffith	70
+JM Parks	b Worrell	35	lbw b Griffith	17
FJ Titmus	not out	52	c McMorris b Hall	11
FS Trueman	b Hall	10	c Murray b Hall	0
DA Allen	lbw b Griffith	0	not out	4
D Shackleton	b Griffith	8	run out	4
	(b 8, lb 8, nb 9)	25	(b 5, lb 8, nb 3)	16
	(all out)	297	(9 wickets)	228

Bowling: Hall 18-2-65-1 Griffith 26-6-91-5 Sobers 18-4-45-1 Gibbs 27-9-59-1 Worrell 13-6-12-2
Hall 40-9-93-4 Griffith 30-7-59-3 Sobers 4-1-4-0 Gibbs 17-7-56-1

Umpires: JS Buller and WE Phillipson

England v Australia
18,19,20,22,23 June 1964

Result: Match drawn

Australia Innings

Batsman		R		R
WM Lawry	b Trueman	4	c Dexter b Gifford	20
IR Redpath	c Parfitt b Coldwell	30	lbw b Titmus	36
NC O'Neill	c Titmus b Dexter	26	c Parfitt b Titmus	22
PJP Burge	lbw b Dexter	1	c Parfitt b Titmus	59
BC Booth	lbw b Trueman	14	not out	2
*RB Simpson	c Parfitt b Trueman	0	not out	15
TR Veivers	b Gifford	54		
GD McKenzie	b Trueman	10		
+ATW Grout	c Dexter b Gifford	14		
NJN Hawke	not out	5		
GE Corling	b Trueman	0		
	(b 8, lb 5, nb 5)	18	(b 8, lb 4, nb 2)	14
	(all out)	176	(4 wickets)	168

Bowling: Trueman 25-8-48-5 Coldwell 23-7-51-1 Gifford 12-6-14-2 Dexter 7-1-16-2 Titmus 17-6-29-0
Trueman 18-6-52-1 Coldwell 19-4-59-0 Gifford 17-9-17-1 Dexter 3-0-5-0 Titmus 17-7-21-2

England Innings

*ER Dexter	b McKenzie	2
JH Edrich	c Redpath b McKenzie	120
MC Cowdrey	c Burge b Hawke	10
KF Barrington	lbw b McKenzie	5
PH Parfitt	lbw b Corling	20
PJ Sharpe	lbw b Hawke	35
+JM Parks	c Simpson b Hawke	12
FJ Titmus	b Corling	15
FS Trueman	b Corling	8
N Gifford	c Hawke b Corling	5
LJ Coldwell	not out	6
	(lb 7, nb 1)	8
	(all out)	246

Bowling: McKenzie 26-8-69-3 Corling 27.3-9-60-4 Hawke 16-4-41-3 Veivers 9-4-17-0 Simpson 21-8-51-0

Umpires: JS Buller and JF Crapp

England v New Zealand
17,18,19,21,22 June 1965

Result: England won by 7 wickets

New Zealand Innings

BE Congdon	lbw b Rumsey	0	lbw b Titmus	26
GT Dowling	lbw b Rumsey	12	b Parfitt	66
BW Sinclair	b Rumsey	1	c Parks b Barber	72
*JR Reid	c Parks b Snow	21	b Titmus	22
RW Morgan	c Parfitt b Rumsey	0	lbw b Rumsey	35
V Pollard	c & b Titmus	55	run out	55
+AE Dick	b Snow	7	c Parks b Snow	3
BR Taylor	b Trueman	51	c Smith b Snow	0
RC Motz	c Parks b Titmus	11	c Snow b Barber	8
RO Collinge	b Trueman	7	c Parks b Barber	21
FJ Cameron	not out	3	not out	9
	(b 3, lb 2, nb 2)	7	(b 8, lb 12, nb 10)	30
	(all out)	175	(all out)	347

Bowling: Rumsey 13-4-25-4 Trueman 19.5-8-40-2 Dexter 8-2-27-0 Snow 11-2-27-2 Titmus 15-7-25-2 Barber 8-2-24-0
Rumsey 26-10-42-1 Trueman 26-4-69-0 Snow 24-4-53-2 Titmus 39-12-71-2 Barber 28-10-57-3 Parfitt 6-2-25-1

England Innings

G Boycott	c Dick b Motz	14	lbw b Motz	76
RW Barber	c Dick b Motz	13	b Motz	34
ER Dexter	c Dick b Taylor	62	not out	80
MC Cowdrey	c sub b Collinge	119	not out	4
PH Parfitt	c Dick b Cameron	11		
*MJK Smith	c sub b Taylor	44		
+JM Parks	b Collinge	2		
FJ Titmus	run out	13	c Dick b Motz	1
FS Trueman	b Collinge	3		
FE Rumsey	b Collinge	3		
JA Snow	not out	2		
	(b 1, lb 7, w 1, nb 12)	21	(b 9, lb 5, nb 9)	23
	(all out)	307	(3 wickets)	218

Bowling: Collinge 28.2-4-85-4 Motz 20-1-62-2 Taylor 25-4-66-2 Cameron 19-6-40-1 Morgan 8-1-33-0
Collinge 15-1-43-0 Motz 19-5-45-3 Taylor 10-0-53-0 Cameron 13-0-39-0 Morgan 3-0-11-0 Reid 0.5-0-4-0

Umpires: JS Buller and WE Phillipson

England v South Africa
22,23,24,26,27 July 1965

Result: Match drawn

South Africa Innings

EJ Barlow	c Barber b Rumsey	1	c Parks b Brown	52
HR Lance	c & b Brown	28	c Titmus b Brown	9
+DT Lindsay	c Titmus b Rumsey	40	c Parks b Larter	22
RG Pollock	c Barrington b Titmus	56	b Brown	5
KC Bland	b Brown	39	c Edrich b Barber	70
A Bacher	lbw b Titmus	4	b Titmus	37
*PL van der Merwe	c Barrington b Rumsey	17	c Barrington b Rumsey	31
R Dumbrill	b Barber	3	c Cowdrey b Rumsey	2
JT Botten	b Brown	33	b Rumsey	0
PM Pollock	st Parks b Barber	34	not out	14
HD Bromfield	not out	9	run out	0
	(lb 14, nb 2)	16	(b 4, lb 2)	6
	(all out)	280	(all out)	248

Bowling: Larter 26-10-47-0 Rumsey 30-9-84-3 Brown 24-9-44-3 Titmus 29-10-59-2 Barber 10.3-3-30-2
Larter 17-2-67-1 Rumsey 21-8-49-3 Brown 21-11-30-3 Titmus 26-13-36-1 Barber 25-5-60-1

England Innings

G Boycott	c Barlow b Botten	31	c & b Dumbrill	28
RW Barber	b Bromfield	56	c Lindsay b PM Pollock	12
JH Edrich	lbw b PM Pollock	0	retired hurt	7
KF Barrington	run out	91	lbw b Dumbrill	18
MC Cowdrey	b Dumbrill	29	lbw b PM Pollock	37
*MJK Smith	c Lindsay b Botten	26	c Lindsay b Dumbrill	13
+JM Parks	run out	32	c van der Merwe b Dumbrill	7
FJ Titmus	c PM Pollock b Bromfield	59	not out	9
DJ Brown	c Bromfield b Dumbrill	1	c Barlow b RG Pollock	5
FE Rumsey	b Dumbrill	3	not out	0
JDF Larter	not out	0		
	(b 1, lb 4, w 1, nb 4)	10	(lb 7, w 1, nb 1)	9
	(all out)	338	(7 wickets)	145

Bowling: PM Pollock 39-12-91-1 Botten 33-11-65-2 Barlow 19-6-31-0 Bromfield 25.2-5-71-2 Dumbrill 24-11-31-3 Lance 5-0-18-0 RG Pollock 5-1-21-0
PM Pollock 20-6-52-2 Botten 12-6-25-0 Barlow 9-1-25-0 Bromfield 5-4-4-0 Dumbrill 18-8-30-4 RG Pollock 4-4-0-1

Umpires: JS Buller and AEG Rhodes

England v West Indies
16,17,18,20,21 June 1966

Result: Match drawn

West Indies Innings

CC Hunte	c Parks b Higgs	18	c Milburn b Knight	13
MC Carew	c Parks b Higgs	2	c Knight b Higgs	0
RB Kanhai	c Titmus b Higgs	25	c Parks b Knight	40
BF Butcher	c Milburn b Knight	49	lbw b Higgs	3
SM Nurse	b D'Oliveira	64	c Parks b D'Oliveira	35
*GS Sobers	lbw b Knight	46	not out	163
DAJ Holford	b Jones	26	not out	105
+DW Allan	c Titmus b Higgs	13		
CC Griffith	lbw b Higgs	5		
WW Hall	not out	8		
LR Gibbs	c Parks b Higgs	4		
	(b 2, lb 7)	9	(lb 8, nb 2)	10
	(all out)	269	(5 wickets declared)	369

Bowling: Jones 21-3-64-1 Higgs 33-9-91-6 Knight 21-0-63-2 Titmus 5-0-18-0 D'Oliveira 14-5-24-1
Jones 25-2-95-0 Higgs 34-5-82-2 Knight 30-3-106-2 Titmus 19-3-30-0 D'Oliveira 25-7-46-1

England Innings

G Boycott	c Griffith b Gibbs	60	c Allan b Griffith	25
C Milburn	lbw b Hall	6	not out	126
TW Graveney	c Allan b Hall	96	not out	30
KF Barrington	b Sobers	19	b Griffith	5
*MC Cowdrey	c Gibbs b Hall	9	c Allan b Hall	5
+JM Parks	lbw b Carew	91	b Hall	0
BL D'Oliveira	run out	27		
BR Knight	b Griffith	6		
FJ Titmus	c Allan b Hall	6		
K Higgs	b Hall	13		
IJ Jones	not out	0		
	(b 7, lb 10, nb 5)	22	(b 4, lb 2)	6
	(all out)	355	(4 wickets)	197

Bowling: Sobers 39-12-89-1 Hall 33-6-106-4 Griffith 28-4-79-1 Gibbs 37.3-18-48-2 Carew 3-0-11-1
Sobers 8-4-8-0 Hall 14-1-65-2 Griffith 11-2-43-2 Gibbs 13-4-40-0 Holford 9-1-35-0

Umpires: JS Buller and WFF Price

England v India
22,23,24,26 June 1967

Result: England won by an innings and 124 runs

India Innings

DN Sardesai	c Murray b Illingworth	28	absent hurt	0
+FM Engineer	c Murray b Brown	8	c Amiss b Snow	8
AL Wadekar	c Illingworth b D'Oliveira	57	lbw b Illingworth	19
CG Borde	b Snow	0	c Snow b Close	1
*Nawab of Pataudi jnr	c Murray b Brown	5	c Graveney b Close	5
RF Surti	c Murray b D'Oliveira	6	c D'Oliveira b Illingworth	0
V Subramanya	c Murray b Brown	1	c Edrich b Illingworth	1
BK Kunderan	c Murray b Snow	20	lbw b Illingworth	47
EAS Prasanna	run out	17	c D'Oliveira b Illingworth	0
BS Bedi	c Amiss b Snow	5	b Illingworth	11
BS Chandrasekhar	not out	2	not out	3
	(b 2, lb 2)	4	(b 11, lb 4)	15
	(all out)	152	(all out)	110

Bowling: Snow 20.4-5-49-3 Brown 18-3-61-3 D'Oliveira 15-6-38-2 Illingworth 2-2-0-1
Snow 8-4-12-1 Brown 5-2-10-0 Illingworth 22.3-12-29-6 Hobbs 6-1-16-0 Close 15-5-28-2

England Innings

JH Edrich	c & b Surti	12
KF Barrington	b Chandrasekhar	97
DL Amiss	b Chandrasekhar	29
TW Graveney	st Engineer b Bedi	151
BL D'Oliveira	c & b Chandrasekhar	33
*DB Close	c Borde b Prasanna	7
+JT Murray	b Chandrasekhar	7
R Illingworth	lbw b Chandrasekhar	4
RNS Hobbs	b Bedi	7
DJ Brown	c Pataudi b Bedi	5
JA Snow	not out	8
	(b 5, lb 18, w 1, nb 2)	26
	(all out)	386

Bowling: Surti 31-10-67-1 Subramanya 7-1-20-0 Chandrasekhar 53-9-127-5 Bedi 31.2-13-68-3 Prasanna 32-5-78-1

Umpires: JS Buller and A Jepson

England v Pakistan
27,28,29,31 July, 1 August 1967

Result: Match drawn

England Innings

C Milburn	c Wasim Bari b Asif Iqbal	3	c Asif Iqbal b Majid Khan	32
WE Russell	b Intikhab Alam	43	b Majid Khan	12
KF Barrington	c Wasim Bari b Asif Iqbal	148	b Intikhab Alam	14
TW Graveney	b Saleem Altaf	81	c Khalid Ibadulla b Asif Iqbal	30
BL D'Oliveira	c Intikhab Alam b Mushtaq Mohammad	59	not out	81
*DB Close	c sub b Saleem Altaf	4	st Wasim Bari b Nasim-ul-Ghani	36
+JT Murray	b Saleem Altaf	0	c & b Nasim-ul-Ghani	0
R Illingworth	b Asif Iqbal	4	c & b Nasim-ul-Ghani	9
K Higgs	lbw b Mushtaq Mohammad	14	Hanif Mohammad b Intikhab Alam	1
JA Snow	b Mushtaq Mohammad	0	c Hanif Mohammad b Mushtaq Mohammad	7
RNS Hobbs	not out	1	not out	1
	(lb 5, nb 7)	12	(b 12, lb 5, nb 1)	18
	(all out)	369	(9 wickets declared)	241

Bowling: Saleem Altaf 33-6-74-3 Asif Iqbal 28-10-76-3 Khalid Ibadulla 3-0-5-0 Majid Khan 11-2-28-0 Nasim-ul-Ghani 12-1-36-0 Intikhab Alam 29-3-86-1 Mushtaq Mohammad 11.3-3-23-3 Saeed Ahmed 11-3-29-0
Saleem Altaf 0.3-0-4-0 Asif Iqbal 21-5-50-1 Majid Khan 10-1-32-2 Nasim-ul-Ghani 13-3-32-3 Intikhab Alam 30-7-70-2 Mushtaq Mohammad 16-4-35-1

Pakistan Innings

Khalid Ibadulla	b Higgs	10	c Close b Illingworth	32
Javed Burki	lbw b Higgs	31	c & b Barrington	13
Mushtaq Mohammad	c Murray b Higgs	4	not out	30
*Hanif Mohammad	not out	187		
Majid Khan	c & b Hobbs	5	c Close b Barrington	5
Nasim-ul-Ghani	c D'Oliveira b Snow	2		
Saeed Ahmed	c Graveney b Snow	6	not out	6
Intikhab Alam	lbw b Illingworth	17		
Asif Iqbal	c Barrington b Illingworth	76		
+Wasim Bari	c Close b Barrington	13		
Saleem Altaf	c Milburn b Snow	2		
	(b 1, lb 2)	3	(b 1, lb 1)	2
	(all out)	354	(3 wickets)	88

Bowling: Snow 45.1-11-120-3 Higgs 39-12-81-3 D'Oliveira 15-7-17-0 Illingworth 31-14-48-2 Hobbs 35-16-46-1 Barrington 11-1-29-1 Close 6-3-10-0
Snow 4-2-6-0 Higgs 6-3-6-0 Illingworth 15-11-10-1 Hobbs 16-9-28-0 Barrington 13-2-23-2 Close 8-5-13-0

Umpires: CS Elliott and A Jepson

England v Australia
20,21,22,24,25 June 1968

Result: Match drawn

England Innings

JH Edrich	c Cowper b McKenzie	7		
G Boycott	c Sheahan b McKenzie	49		
C Milburn	c Walters b McKenzie	83		
*MC Cowdrey	c Cowper b McKenzie	45		
KF Barrington	c Jarman b Connolly	75		
TW Graveney	c Jarman b Connolly	14		
BR Knight	not out	27		
+APE Knott	run out	33		
JA Snow				
DJ Brown				
DL Underwood				
	(b 7, lb 5, w 1, nb 5)	18		
	(7 wickets declared)	351		

Bowling: McKenzie 45-18-111-3 Hawke 35-7-82-0 Connolly 26.3-8-55-2 Walters 3-2-2-0 Cowper 8-2-40-0 Gleeson 27-11-43-1

Australia Innings

*WM Lawry	c Knott b Brown	0	c Brown b Snow	28
IR Redpath	c Cowdrey b Brown	4	b Underwood	53
RM Cowper	c Graveney b Snow	8	c Underwood b Barrington	32
KD Walters	c Knight b Brown	26	b Underwood	0
AP Sheahan	c Knott b Knight	6	not out	0
IM Chappell	lbw b Knight	7	not out	12
NJN Hawke	c Cowdrey b Knight	2		
GD McKenzie	b Brown	5		
JW Gleeson	c Cowdrey b Brown	14		
+BN Jarman	retired hurt	0		
AN Connolly	not out	0		
	(lb 2, nb 4)	6	(nb 2)	2
	(all out)	78	(4 wickets)	127

Bowling: Snow 9-5-14-1 Brown 14-5-42-5 Knight 10.4-5-16-3
Snow 12-5-30-1 Brown 19-9-40-0 Knight 16-9-35-0 Underwood 18-15-8-2 Barrington 2-0-12-1

Umpires: JS Buller and AE Fagg

Lord's

England v West Indies
26,27,28,30 June, 1 July 1969

Result: Match drawn

West Indies Innings

Batsman		R		R
RC Fredericks	c Hampshire b Knight	63	c Hampshire b Illingworth	60
GS Camacho	c Sharpe b Snow	67	b D'Oliveira	45
CA Davis	c Knott b Brown	103	c Illingworth b D'Oliveira	0
BF Butcher	c Hampshire b Brown	9	b Illingworth	24
*GS Sobers	run out	29	not out	50
CH Lloyd	c Illingworth b Brown	18	c Knott b Snow	70
JN Shepherd	c Edrich b Snow	32	c Sharpe b Illingworth	11
+TM Findlay	b Snow	23	c Sharpe b Knight	11
VA Holder	lbw b Snow	6	run out	7
LR Gibbs	not out	18	b Knight	5
GC Shillingford	c Knott b Snow	3		
	(b 5, lb 4)	9	(b 4, lb 7, nb 1)	12
	(all out)	380	(9 wickets declared)	295

Bowling: Snow 39-5-114-5 Brown 38-8-99-3 Knight 38-11-65-1 D'Oliveira 26-10-46-0 Illingworth 16-4-39-0 Parfitt 1-0-8-0
Snow 22-4-69-1 Brown 9-3-25-0 Knight 27.5-6-78-2 D'Oliveira 15-2-45-2 Illingworth 27-9-66-3

England Innings

Batsman		R		R
G Boycott	c Findlay b Shepherd	23	c Butcher b Shillingford	106
JH Edrich	c Fredericks b Holder	7	c Camacho b Holder	1
PH Parfitt	c Davis b Sobers	4	c Findlay b Shepherd	39
BL D'Oliveira	c Shepherd b Sobers	0	c Fredericks b Gibbs	18
PJ Sharpe	b Holder	11	c Davis b Sobers	86
JH Hampshire	lbw b Shepherd	107	run out	5
+APE Knott	b Shillingford	53	b Shillingford	11
*R Illingworth	c & b Gibbs	113	not out	9
BR Knight	lbw b Shillingford	0	not out	1
DJ Brown	c Findlay b Shepherd	1		
JA Snow	not out	9		
	(b 1, lb 5, nb 10)	16	(b 9, lb 5, nb 5)	19
	(all out)	344	(7 wickets)	295

Bowling: Sobers 26-12-57-2 Holder 38-16-83-2 Shillingford 19-4-53-2 Shepherd 43-14-74-3 Gibbs 27.4-9-53-1 Davis 1-0-2-0 Butcher 3-1-6-0
Sobers 29-8-72-1 Holder 14-4-36-1 Shillingford 13-4-30-2 Shepherd 12-3-45-1 Gibbs 41-14-93-1

Umpires: JS Buller and AE Fagg

England v New Zealand
24,25,26,28 July 1969

Result: England won by 230 runs

England Innings

Batsman		R		R
G Boycott	c Congdon b Motz	0	c Turner b Pollard	47
JH Edrich	c Motz b Taylor	16	c Wadsworth b Hadlee	115
PJ Sharpe	c Turner b Taylor	20	c Congdon b Howarth	46
KWR Fletcher	b Motz	9	b Howarth	7
BL D'Oliveira	run out	37	c Wadsworth b Taylor	12
+APE Knott	c & b Hadlee	8	lbw b Howarth	10
*R Illingworth	c Wadsworth b Howarth	53	c Wadsworth b Taylor	0
BR Knight	c Hadlee b Pollard	29	b Motz	49
DJ Brown	not out	11	c Wadsworth b Taylor	7
DL Underwood	c Pollard b Howarth	1	b Motz	4
A Ward	b Taylor	0	not out	19
	(b 1, lb 3, w 1, nb 1)	6	(b 4, lb 15, nb 5)	24
	(all out)	190	(all out)	340

Bowling: Motz 19-5-46-2 Hadlee 14-2-48-1 Taylor 13.5-4-35-3 Howarth 19-9-24-2 Pollard 9-1-31-1
Motz 39.4-17-78-2 Hadlee 16-5-43-1 Taylor 25-4-62-3 Howarth 49-20-102-3 Pollard 8-2-20-1 Burgess 3-0-11-0

New Zealand Innings

Batsman		R		R
*GT Dowling	c Illingworth b Underwood	41	c Knott b Ward	4
GM Turner	c Knott b Ward	5	not out	43
BE Congdon	c Sharpe b Ward	41	c Fletcher b Underwood	17
BF Hastings	c Ward b Illingworth	23	c Knott b Underwood	0
V Pollard	c Ward b Underwood	8	lbw b Underwood	6
MG Burgess	lbw b Illingworth	10	lbw b Underwood	6
+KJ Wadsworth	lbw b Illingworth	14	b Underwood	5
BR Taylor	c Brown b Illingworth	3	b Underwood	0
RC Motz	b Underwood	15	c Knott b Underwood	23
DR Hadlee	c Illingworth b Underwood	1	c Sharpe b D'Oliveira	19
HJ Howarth	not out	0	b Ward	4
	(b 4, lb 4)	8	(b 5, lb 4, nb 1)	10
	(all out)	169	(all out)	131

Bowling: Brown 12-5-17-0 Ward 14-2-49-2 Underwood 29.3-16-38-4 Knight 10-3-20-0 Illingworth 22-8-37-4
Brown 5-3-6-0 Ward 10.5-0-48-2 Underwood 31-18-32-7 Knight 3-1-5-0 Illingworth 18-9-24-0 D'Oliveira 8-3-6-1

Umpires: JS Buller and A Jepson

England v Pakistan
17,18,19,21,22 June 1971

Result: Match drawn

England Innings

Batsman		R		R
G Boycott	not out	121		
BW Luckhurst	c Wasim Bari b Saleem Altaf	46	not out	53
JH Edrich	c Asif Masood b Pervez Sajjad	37		
DL Amiss	not out	19		
RA Hutton			not out	58
BL D'Oliveira				
*R Illingworth				
+APE Knott				
P Lever				
N Gifford				
JSE Price				
	(b 6, lb 2, w 5, nb 5)	18	(b 1, lb 1, nb 4)	6
	(2 wickets declared)	241	(0 wickets)	117

Bowling: Asif Masood 21-3-60-0 Saleem Altaf 19.5-5-42-1 Asif Iqbal 13-2-24-0 Majid Khan 4-0-16-0 Intikhab Alam 20-2-64-0 Pervez Sajjad 6-2-17-1
Asif Masood 3-1-3-0 Saleem Altaf 5-2-11-0 Asif Iqbal 4-1-11-0 Majid Khan 6-2-7-0 Intikhab Alam 9-1-25-0 Mushtaq Mohammad 11-3-31-0 Sadiq Mohammad 5-1-17-0 Aftab Gul 1-0-4-0 Zaheer Abbas 1-0-1-0

Pakistan Innings

Aftab Gul	c Knott b Hutton	33
Sadiq Mohammad	c Knott b D'Oliveira	28
Zaheer Abbas	c Hutton b Price	40
Mushtaq Mohammad	c Amiss b Hutton	2
Asif Iqbal	c Knott b Gifford	9
Majid Khan	c Edrich b Price	9
*Intikhab Alam	c Gifford b Lever	18
+Wasim Bari	c Knott b Price	0
Saleem Altaf	not out	0
Asif Masood	b Price	0
Pervez Sajjad	absent hurt	0
	(lb 5, w 1, nb 3)	9
	(all out)	148

Bowling: Price 11.4-5-29-3 Lever 16-3-38-2 Gifford 12-6-13-1 Illingworth 7-6-1-0 Hutton 16-5-36-2 D'Oliveira 10-5-22-1

Umpires: AE Fagg and AEG Rhodes

England v India
22,23,24,26,27 July 1971

Result: Match drawn

England Innings

Batsman		R		R
G Boycott	c Engineer b Abid Ali	3	c Wadekar b Venkataraghavan	33
BW Luckhurst	c Solkar b Chandrasekhar	30	b Solkar	1
JH Edrich	c Venkataraghavan b Bedi	18	c Engineer b Bedi	62
DL Amiss	c Engineer b Bedi	9	run out	0
BL D'Oliveira	c Solkar b Venkataraghavan	30	b Bedi	30
+APE Knott	c Wadekar b Venkataraghavan	67	c Wadekar b Chandrasekhar	24
*R Illingworth	c Engineer b Bedi	33	c Wadekar b Venkataraghavan	20
RA Hutton	b Venkataraghavan	20	c Chandrasekhar b Venkataraghavan	9
JA Snow	c Abid Ali b Chandrasekhar	73	not out	9
N Gifford	b Bedi	17	not out	7
JSE Price	not out	5	c Abid Ali b Venkataraghavan	0
	(b 8, lb 12, nb 5)	25	(lb 5)	5
	(all out)	304	(all out)	191

Bowling: Abid Ali 15-3-38-1 Solkar 8-3-17-0 Venkataraghavan 28-8-44-2 Chandrasekhar 49-10-110-3 Bedi 39.3-18-70-4
Abid Ali 9-1-20-0 Solkar 6-3-13-1 Venkataraghavan 30.5-11-52-4 Chandrasekhar 23-7-60-2 Bedi 30-13-41-2

India Innings

Batsman		R		R
AV Mankad	c Gifford b Snow	1	c Knott b Snow	5
SM Gavaskar	c Amiss b Price	4	c Edrich b Gifford	53
*AL Wadekar	c Illingworth b Gifford	85	c Boycott b Price	5
DN Sardesai	c Illingworth b Gifford	25	b Illingworth	1
GR Viswanath	c Knott b Hutton	68	c Amiss b Gifford	9
+FM Engineer	c Illingworth b Hutton	28	st Knott b Gifford	35
ED Solkar	c Knott b Gifford	67	not out	6
S Abid Ali	c Luckhurst b Snow	6	c Snow b Illingworth	14
S Venkataraghavan	c Hutton b Price	11	c Hutton b Gifford	7
BS Bedi	c Price b Gifford	0	not out	2
BS Chandrasekhar	not out	0		
	(b 7, lb 9, nb 2)	18	(lb 7, nb 1)	8
	(all out)	313	(8 wickets)	145

Bowling: Price 25-9-46-2 Snow 31-9-64-2 Hutton 24-8-38-2 Gifford 45.3-14-84-4 D'Oliveira 15-7-20-0 Illingworth 25-12-43-0
Price 4-0-26-1 Snow 8-0-23-1 Hutton 3-0-12-0 Gifford 19-4-43-4 Illingworth 16-2-33-2

Umpires: DJ Constant and CS Elliott

England v Australia
22,23,24,26 June 1972

Result: Australia won by 8 wickets

England Innings

Batsman		R		R
G Boycott	b Massie	11	b Lillee	6
JH Edrich	lbw b Lillee	10	c Marsh b Massie	6
BW Luckhurst	b Lillee	1	c Marsh b Lillee	4
MJK Smith	b Massie	34	c Edwards b Massie	30
BL D'Oliveira	lbw b Massie	32	c GS Chappell b Massie	3
AW Greig	c Marsh b Massie	54	c IM Chappell b Massie	3
+APE Knott	c Colley b Massie	43	c GS Chappell b Massie	12
*R Illingworth	lbw b Massie	30	c Stackpole b Massie	12
JA Snow	b Massie	37	c Marsh b Massie	0
N Gifford	c Marsh b Massie	3	not out	16
JSE Price	not out	4	c GS Chappell b Massie	19
	(lb 6, w 1, nb 6)	13	(w 1, nb 4)	5
	(all out)	272	(all out)	116

Bowling: Lillee 28-3-90-2 Massie 32.5-7-84-8 Colley 16-2-42-0 GS Chappell 6-1-18-0 Gleeson 9-1-25-0
Lillee 21-6-50-2 Massie 27.2-9-53-8 Colley 7-1-8-0

Australia Innings

Batsman		R		R
KR Stackpole	c Gifford b Price	5	not out	57
BC Francis	b Snow	0	c Knott b Price	9
*IM Chappell	c Smith b Snow	56	c Luckhurst b D'Oliveira	6
GS Chappell	b D'Oliveira	131	not out	7
KD Walters	c Illingworth b Snow	1		
R Edwards	c Smith b Illingworth	28		
JW Gleeson	c Knott b Greig	1		
+RW Marsh	c Greig b Snow	50		
DJ Colley	c Greig b Price	25		
RAL Massie	c Knott b Snow	0		
DK Lillee	not out	2		
	(b 5, lb 2, nb 2)	9	(lb 2)	2
	(all out)	308	(2 wickets)	81

Bowling: Snow 32-13-57-5 Price 26.1-5-87-2 Greig 29-6-74-1 D'Oliveira 17-5-48-1 Gifford 11-4-20-0 Illingworth 7-2-13-1
Snow 8-2-15-0 Price 7-0-28-1 Greig 3-0-17-0 D'Oliveira 8-3-14-1 Luckhurst 0.5-0-5-0

Umpires: DJ Constant and AE Fagg

England v New Zealand
21,22,23,25,26 June 1973

Result: Match drawn

England Innings

Batsman		R		R
G Boycott	c Parker b Collinge	61	c & b Howarth	92
DL Amiss	c Howarth b Hadlee	9	c & b Howarth	53
GRJ Roope	lbw b Howarth	56	c Parker b Taylor	51
KWR Fletcher	c Hastings b Howarth	25	c Taylor b Collinge	178
AW Greig	c Howarth b Collinge	63	c Wadsworth b Hadlee	12
*R Illingworth	c Collinge b Hadlee	3	c Turner b Howarth	22
+APE Knott	b Hadlee	0	c Congdon b Howarth	0
CM Old	b Howarth	7	c Congdon b Pollard	7
JA Snow	b Taylor	2	c Hastings b Pollard	0
GG Arnold	not out	8	not out	23
N Gifford	c Wadsworth b Collinge	8	not out	2
	(lb 1, w 1, nb 9)	11	(b 8, lb 3, nb 12)	23
	(all out)	253	(9 wickets declared)	463

Bowling: Collinge 31-8-69-3 Taylor 19-1-54-1 Hadlee 26-4-70-3 Congdon 5-2-7-0 Howarth 25-6-42-3
Collinge 19-4-41-1 Taylor 34-10-90-1 Hadlee 25-2-79-1 Congdon 8-3-22-0 Howarth 70-24-144-4 Pollard 39-11-61-2 Hastings 1-0-3-0

New Zealand Innings

GM Turner	c Greig b Arnold	4
JM Parker	c Knott b Snow	3
*BE Congdon	c Knott b Old	175
BF Hastings	lbw b Snow	86
HJ Howarth	hit wicket b Old	17
MG Burgess	b Snow	105
V Pollard	not out	105
+KJ Wadsworth	c Knott b Old	27
BR Taylor	b Old	11
DR Hadlee	c Fletcher b Old	6
RO Collinge		
	(lb 5, nb 7)	12
	(9 wickets declared)	551

Bowling: Snow 38-4-109-3 Arnold 41-6-108-1 Old 41.5-7-113-5 Roope 6-1-15-0 Gifford 39-6-107-0 Illingworth 39-12-87-0

Umpires: AE Fagg and TW Spencer

England v West Indies
23,24,25,27 August 1973

Result: West Indies won by an innings and 226 runs

West Indies Innings

RC Fredericks	c Underwood b Willis	51
+DL Murray	b Willis	4
*RB Kanhai	c Greig b Willis	157
CH Lloyd	c & b Willis	63
AI Kallicharran	c Arnold b Illingworth	14
GS Sobers	not out	150
MLC Foster	c Willis b Greig	9
BD Julien	c & b Greig	121
KD Boyce	c Amiss b Greig	36
VA Holder	not out	23
LR Gibbs		
	(b 1, lb 14, w 1, nb 8)	24
	(8 wickets declared)	652

Bowling: Arnold 35-6-111-0 Willis 35-3-118-4 Greig 33-2-180-3 Underwood 34-6-105-0 Illingworth 31.4-3-114-1

England Innings

G Boycott	c Kanhai b Holder	4	c Kallicharran b Boyce	15
DL Amiss	c Sobers b Holder	35	c Sobers b Boyce	10
BW Luckhurst	c Murray b Boyce	1	c Sobers b Julien	12
FC Hayes	c Fredericks b Holder	8	c Holder b Boyce	0
KWR Fletcher	c Sobers b Gibbs	68	not out	86
AW Greig	c Sobers b Boyce	44	lbw b Julien	13
*R Illingworth	c Sobers b Gibbs	0	c Kanhai b Gibbs	13
+APE Knott	c Murray b Boyce	21	c Murray b Boyce	5
GG Arnold	c Murray b Boyce	5	c Fredericks b Gibbs	1
RGD Willis	not out	5	c Fredericks b Julien	0
DL Underwood	c Gibbs b Holder	12	b Gibbs	14
	(b 6, lb 4, w 3, nb 17)	30	(b 9, w 1, nb 14)	24
	(all out)	233	(all out)	193

Bowling: Holder 15-3-56-4 Boyce 20-7-50-4 Julien 11-4-26-0 Gibbs 18-3-39-2 Sobers 8-0-30-0 Foster 1-0-2-0
Holder 14-4-18-0 Boyce 16-5-49-4 Julien 18-2-69-3 Gibbs 13.3-3-26-3 Sobers 4-1-7-0

Umpires: HD Bird and CS Elliott

England v India
20,21,22,24 June 1974

Result: England won by an innings and 285 runs

England Innings

DL Amiss	lbw b Prasanna	188
D Lloyd	c Solkar b Prasanna	46
JH Edrich	lbw b Bedi	96
*MH Denness	c sub b Bedi	118
KWR Fletcher	c Solkar b Bedi	15
AW Greig	c & b Abid Ali	106
+APE Knott	c & b Bedi	26
CM Old	b Abid Ali	3
GG Arnold	b Bedi	5
DL Underwood	c Solkar b Bedi	9
M Hendrick	not out	1
	(b 8, lb 4, w 2, nb 2)	16
	(all out)	629

Bowling: Abid Ali 22-2-79-2 Solkar 6-2-16-0 Madan Lal 30-6-93-0 Bedi 64.2-8-226-6 Chandrasekhar 9.3-1-33-0 Prasanna 51-6-166-2

India Innings

SM Gavaskar	c Knott b Old	49	lbw b Arnold	5
+FM Engineer	c Denness b Old	86	lbw b Arnold	0
*AL Wadekar	c Underwood b Hendrick	18	b Old	3
GR Viswanath	b Underwood	52	c Knott b Arnold	5
BP Patel	c Fletcher b Greig	1	c Knott b Arnold	1
ED Solkar	c Underwood b Hendrick	43	not out	18
S Abid Ali	c Arnold b Old	14	c Knott b Old	3
S Madan Lal	c Knott b Old	0	c Hendrick b Old	2
EAS Prasanna	c Denness b Hendrick	0	b Old	5
BS Bedi	b Arnold	14	b Old	0
BS Chandrasekhar	not out	2	absent hurt	0
	(b 4, lb 7, nb 12)	23	(all out)	0
	(all out)	302	(all out)	42

Bowling: Arnold 24.5-6-81-1 Old 21-6-67-4 Hendrick 18-4-46-3 Greig 21-4-63-1 Underwood 15-10-18-1 Lloyd 2-0-4-0
Arnold 8-1-19-4 Old 8-3-21-5 Hendrick 1-0-2-0

Umpires: AE Fagg and TW Spencer

England v Pakistan
8,9,10,12,13 August 1974

Result: Match drawn

Pakistan Innings

Sadiq Mohammad	lbw b Hendrick	40	lbw b Arnold	43
Majid Khan	c Old b Greig	48	lbw b Underwood	19
Zaheer Abbas	c Hendrick b Underwood	1	c Greig b Underwood	1
Mushtaq Mohammad	c Greig b Underwood	0	c Denness b Greig	76
Wasim Raja	c Greig b Underwood	24	c Lloyd b Underwood	53
Asif Iqbal	c Amiss b Underwood	2	c Greig b Underwood	0
*Intikhab Alam	b Underwood	5	lbw b Underwood	0
Imran Khan	c Hendrick b Greig	4	c Lloyd b Underwood	0
+Wasim Bari	lbw b Greig	4	lbw b Underwood	1
Sarfraz Nawaz	not out	0	c Lloyd b Underwood	1
Asif Masood			not out	17
	(nb 2)	2	(lb 8, nb 7)	15
	(9 wickets declared)	130	(all out)	226

Bowling: Arnold 8-1-32-0 Old 5-0-17-0 Hendrick 9-2-36-1 Underwood 14-8-20-5 Greig 8.5-4-23-3
Arnold 15-3-37-1 Old 14-1-39-0 Hendrick 15-4-29-0 Underwood 34.5-17-51-8 Greig 19-6-55-1

England Innings

DL Amiss	c Sadiq Mohammad b Asif Masood	2	not out	14
D Lloyd	c Zaheer Abbas b Sarfraz Nawaz	23	not out	12
JH Edrich	c Sadiq Mohammad b Intikhab Alam	40	
*MH Denness	b Imran Khan	20	
KWR Fletcher	lbw b Imran Khan	8	
AW Greig	run out	9	
+APE Knott	c Wasim Bari b Asif Masood	83	
CM Old	c Wasim Bari b Mushtaq Mohammad	41	
GG Arnold	c Wasim Bari b Asif Masood	10	
DL Underwood	not out	12	
M Hendrick	c Imran Khan b Intikhab Alam	6	
	(lb 14, w 1, nb 1)	16	(nb 1)	1
	(all out)	270	(0 wickets)	27

Bowling: Asif Masood 25-10-47-3 Sarfraz Nawaz 22-8-42-1 Intikhab Alam 26-4-80-2 Wasim Raja 2-0-8-0 Mushtaq Mohammad 7-3-16-1 Imran Khan 18-2-48-2 Asif Iqbal 5-0-13-0
Asif Masood 4-0-9-0 Sarfraz Nawaz 3-0-7-0 Intikhab Alam 1-1-0-0 Majid Khan 2-0-10-0

Umpires: DJ Constant and CS Elliott

England v Australia
31 July, 1,2,4,5 August 1975

Result: Match drawn

England Innings

B Wood	lbw b Lillee	6	c Marsh b Thomson	52
JH Edrich	lbw b Lillee	9	c Thomson b Mallett	175
DS Steele	b Thomson	50	c & b Walters	45
DL Amiss	lbw b Lillee	0	c GS Chappell b Lillee	10
GA Gooch	c Marsh b Lillee	6	b Mallett	31
*AW Greig	c IM Chappell b Walker	96	c Walters b IM Chappell	41
+APE Knott	lbw b Thomson	69	not out	22
RA Woolmer	c Turner b Mallett	33	b Mallett	31
JA Snow	c Walker b Mallett	11	
DL Underwood	not out	0	
P Lever	lbw b Walker	4	
	(b 3, lb 1, w 4, nb 23)	31	(lb 18, w 2, nb 9)	29
	(all out)	315	(7 wickets declared)	436

Bowling: Lillee 20-4-84-4 Thomson 24-7-92-2 Walker 21.4-7-52-2 Mallett 22-4-56-2
Lillee 33-10-80-1 Thomson 29-8-73-1 Walker 37-8-95-0 Mallett 36.4-10-127-3 IM Chappell 10-2-26-1 Walters 2-0-6-1

Australia Innings

RB McCosker	c & b Lever	29	lbw b Steele	79
A Turner	lbw b Snow	9	c Gooch b Greig	21
*IM Chappell	c Knott b Snow	2	lbw b Greig	86
GS Chappell	lbw b Snow	4	not out	73
R Edwards	lbw b Woolmer	99	not out	52
KD Walters	c Greig b Lever	2	
+RW Marsh	c Amiss b Greig	3	
MHN Walker	b Snow	5	
JR Thomson	b Underwood	17	
DK Lillee	not out	73	
AA Mallett	lbw b Steele	14	
	(lb 5, nb 6)	11	(b 4, nb 14)	18
	(all out)	268	(3 wickets)	329

Bowling: Snow 21-4-66-4 Lever 15-0-83-2 Woolmer 13-5-31-1 Greig 15-5-47-1 Underwood 13-5-29-1 Steele 0.4-0-1-1
Snow 19-3-82-0 Lever 20-5-55-0 Woolmer 3-1-3-0 Greig 26-6-82-2 Underwood 31-14-64-0 Steele 9-4-19-1 Wood 1-0-6-0

Umpires: WE Alley and TW Spencer

England v West Indies
17,18,19,21,22 June 1976

Result: Match drawn

England Innings

B Wood	c Murray b Roberts	6	c Murray b Holding	30
JM Brearley	b Roberts	40	b Holding	13
DS Steele	lbw b Roberts	7	c Jumadeen b Roberts	64
DB Close	c Holder b Jumadeen	60	c & b Holder	46
RA Woolmer	c Murray b Holding	38	c Murray b Roberts	29
*AW Greig	c Lloyd b Roberts	6	c Gomes b Holder	20
+APE Knott	b Holder	17	lbw b Roberts	4
CM Old	b Holder	19	run out	13
JA Snow	b Roberts	0	not out	6
DL Underwood	b Holder	31	b Roberts	2
PI Pocock	not out	0	c Jumadeen b Roberts	3
	(b 7, lb 5, w 5, nb 9)	26	(b 7, lb 7, nb 10)	24
	(all out)	250	(all out)	254

Bowling: Roberts 23-6-60-5 Holding 19-4-52-1 Julien 6-3-6-54-0 Holder 18.4-7-35-3 Jumadeen 12-4-23-1
Roberts 29.5-10-63-5 Holding 27-10-56-2 Julien 13-5-20-0 Holder 19-2-50-2 Jumadeen 16-4-41-0

West Indies Innings

RC Fredericks	c Snow b Old	0	c Greig b Old	138
CG Greenidge	c Snow b Underwood	84	c Close b Pocock	22
HA Gomes	c Woolmer b Snow	11	b Underwood	0
AI Kallicharran	c Old b Snow	0	b Greig	34
*CH Lloyd	c Knott b Underwood	50	c Knott b Old	33
+DL Murray	b Snow	2	not out	7
BD Julien	lbw b Snow	3	b Underwood	1
MA Holding	b Underwood	0	
VA Holder	c Woolmer b Underwood	12	not out	0
AME Roberts	b Underwood	16	
RR Jumadeen	not out	0	
	(b 2, nb 2)	4	(b 3, lb 2, nb 1)	6
	(all out)	182	(6 wickets)	241

Bowling: Old 10-0-58-1 Snow 19-3-68-4 Underwood 18.4-7-39-5 Pocock 3-0-13-0
Old 14-4-46-1 Snow 7-2-22-0 Underwood 24.3-8-73-2 Pocock 27-9-52-1 Greig 14-3-42-2

Umpires: HD Bird and DJ Constant

England v Australia
16,17,18,20,21 June 1977

Result: Match drawn

England Innings

DL Amiss	b Thomson	4	b Thomson	0
*JM Brearley	c Robinson b Thomson	9	c Robinson b O'Keeffe	49
RA Woolmer	run out	79	c Chappell b Pascoe	120
DW Randall	c Chappell b Walker	53	c McCosker b Thomson	0
AW Greig	b Pascoe	5	c O'Keeffe b Pascoe	91
GD Barlow	c McCosker b Walker	1	lbw b Pascoe	5
+APE Knott	c Walters b Thomson	8	c Walters b Walker	8
CM Old	c Marsh b Walker	9	c Marsh b Walker	0
JK Lever	b Pascoe	8	c Marsh b Thomson	3
DL Underwood	not out	11	not out	12
RGD Willis	b Thomson	17	c Marsh b Thomson	0
	(b 1, lb 3, w 1, nb 7)	12	(b 5, lb 9, w 1, nb 2)	17
	(all out)	216	(all out)	305

Bowling: Thomson 20.5-5-41-4 Pascoe 23-7-53-2 Walker 30-6-66-3 O'Keeffe 10-3-32-0 Chappell 3-0-12-0
Thomson 24.4-3-86-4 Pascoe 26-2-96-3 Walker 35-13-56-2 Chappell 12-2-24-0 O'Keeffe 15-7-26-1

Australia Innings

RD Robinson	b Lever	11	c Woolmer b Old	4
RB McCosker	b Old	23	b Willis	1
*GS Chappell	c Old b Willis	66	c Lever b Old	24
CS Serjeant	c Knott b Willis	81	c Amiss b Underwood	3
KD Walters	c Brearley b Willis	53	c sub (AGE Ealham) b Underwood	10
DW Hookes	c Brearley b Old	50	c & b Willis	50
+RW Marsh	lbw b Willis	1	not out	6
KJ O'Keeffe	c sub (AGE Ealham) b Willis	12	not out	8
MHN Walker	c Knott b Willis	4	
JR Thomson	b Willis	6	
LS Pascoe	not out	3	
	(lb 7, w 1, nb 17)	25	(nb 8)	8
	(all out)	296	(6 wickets)	114

Bowling: Willis 30.1-7-78-7 Lever 19-5-61-1 Underwood 25-6-42-0 Old 35-10-70-2 Woolmer 5-1-20-0
Willis 10-1-40-2 Old 14-0-46-2 Underwood 10-3-16-2 Lever 5-2-4-0

Umpires: HD Bird and WL Budd

Lord's

England v Pakistan
15,16,17,19 June 1978

Result: England won by an innings and 120 runs

England Innings

*JM Brearley	lbw b Liaqat Ali	2		
GA Gooch	lbw b Wasim Raja	54		
CT Radley	c Mohsin Khan b Liaqat Ali	8		
DI Gower	b Iqbal Qasim	56		
GRJ Roope	c Mohsin Khan b Iqbal Qasim	69		
G Miller	c Javed Miandad b Iqbal Qasim	0		
IT Botham	b Liaqat Ali	108		
+RW Taylor	c Mudassar Nazar b Sikander Bakht	10		
CM Old	c Mohsin Khan b Sikander Bakht	0		
PH Edmonds	not out	36		
RGD Willis	b Mudassar Nazar	18		
	(lb 2, nb 1)	3		
	(all out)	364		

Bowling: Sikander Bakht 27-3-115-2 Liaqat Ali 18-1-80-3 Mudassar Nazar 4.2-0-16-1 Iqbal Qasim 30-5-101-3 Wasim Raja 12-3-49-1

Pakistan Innings

Mudassar Nazar	c Edmonds b Willis	1	c Taylor b Botham	10
Sadiq Mohammad	c Botham b Willis	11	c Taylor b Willis	0
Mohsin Khan	c Willis b Edmonds	31	c Roope b Willis	46
Haroon Rashid	b Old	15	b Botham	4
Javed Miandad	c Taylor b Willis	0	c Gooch b Botham	22
Wasim Raja	b Edmonds	28	c & b Botham	1
Talat Ali	c Radley b Edmonds	2	c Roope b Botham	40
*+Wasim Bari	c Brearley b Willis	0	c Taylor b Botham	2
Iqbal Qasim	b Willis	0	b Botham	0
Sikander Bakht	c Brearley b Edmonds	4	c Roope b Botham	1
Liaqat Ali	not out	4	not out	0
	(nb 9)	9	(b 1, lb 3, w 5, nb 4)	13
	(all out)	105	(all out)	139

Bowling: Willis 13-1-47-5 Old 10-3-26-1 Botham 5-2-17-0 Edmonds 8-6-6-4
Willis 10-2-26-2 Old 15-4-36-0 Botham 20.5-8-34-8 Edmonds 12-4-21-0 Miller 9-3-9-0

Umpires: WL Budd and DJ Constant

England v New Zealand
24,25,26,28 August 1978

Result: England won by 7 wickets

New Zealand Innings

JG Wright	c Edmonds b Botham	17	b Botham	12
+BA Edgar	c Edmonds b Emburey	39	b Botham	4
GP Howarth	not out	123	not out	14
JM Parker	lbw b Hendrick	14	c Taylor b Botham	3
*MG Burgess	lbw b Botham	68	c Hendrick b Botham	14
BE Congdon	c Emburey b Botham	2	c Taylor b Willis	3
RW Anderson	b Botham	16	c Taylor b Willis	1
RJ Hadlee	c Brearley b Botham	0	run out	5
RO Collinge	c Emburey b Willis	19	b Botham	0
SL Boock	not out	4	c Radley b Willis	0
BP Bracewell			c Hendrick b Willis	0
	(b 4, lb 18, w 4, nb 7)	33	(lb 3, nb 8)	11
	(all out)	339	(all out)	67

Bowling: Willis 29-9-79-1 Hendrick 28-14-39-1 Botham 38-13-101-6 Edmonds 12-3-19-0 Emburey 26.1-12-39-2 Gooch 10-0-29-0
Willis 16-8-16-4 Botham 18.1-4-39-5 Emburey 3-2-1-0

England Innings

GA Gooch	c Boock b Hadlee	2	not out	42
G Boycott	c Hadlee b Bracewell	24	b Hadlee	4
CT Radley	c Congdon b Hadlee	77	b Hadlee	0
DI Gower	c Wright b Boock	71	c Congdon b Bracewell	46
*JM Brearley	c Edgar b Hadlee	33	not out	8
IT Botham	c Edgar b Collinge	21		
+RW Taylor	lbw b Hadlee	1		
PH Edmonds	c Edgar b Hadlee	5		
JE Emburey	b Collinge	2		
M Hendrick	b Bracewell	12		
RGD Willis	not out	7		
	(b 7, lb 5, nb 22)	34	(lb 3, w 4, nb 11)	18
	(all out)	289	(3 wickets)	118

Bowling: Hadlee 32-9-84-5 Collinge 30-9-58-2 Bracewell 19.3-1-68-2 Boock 25-10-33-1 Congdon 6-1-12-0
Hadlee 13.5-2-31-2 Collinge 6-1-26-0 Bracewell 6-0-32-1 Boock 5-1-11-0

Umpires: HD Bird and BJ Meyer

England v India
2,3,4,6,7 August 1979

Result: Match drawn

India Innings

SM Gavaskar	c Taylor b Gooch	42	c Brearley b Botham	59
CPS Chauhan	c Randall b Botham	2	c Randall b Edmonds	31
DB Vengsarkar	c Botham b Hendrick	0	c Boycott b Edmonds	103
GR Viswanath	c Brearley b Hendrick	21	c Gower b Lever	113
AD Gaekwad	c Taylor b Botham	13	not out	1
Yashpal Sharma	c Taylor b Botham	11	not out	5
N Kapil Dev	c Miller b Botham	4		
KD Ghavri	not out	0		
+B Reddy	lbw b Botham	0		
*S Venkataraghavan	run out	0		
BS Bedi	b Lever	0		
			(b 2, lb 2, w 1, nb 1)	6
	(all out)	96	(4 wickets)	318

Bowling: Lever 9.5-3-29-1 Botham 19-9-35-5 Hendrick 15-7-15-2 Edmonds 2-1-1-0 Gooch 10-5-16-1
Botham 35-13-80-1 Hendrick 25-12-56-0 Lever 24-7-69-1 Edmonds 45-18-62-2 Miller 17-6-37-0 Gooch 2-0-8-0

England Innings

*JM Brearley	c Reddy b Kapil Dev	12		
G Boycott	c Gavaskar b Ghavri	32		
GA Gooch	b Kapil Dev	10		
DI Gower	b Ghavri	82		
DW Randall	run out	57		
IT Botham	b Venkataraghavan	36		
G Miller	st Reddy b Bedi	62		
PH Edmonds	c Reddy b Kapil Dev	20		
+RW Taylor	c Vengsarkar b Bedi	64		
JK Lever	not out	6		
M Hendrick				
	(b 11, lb 21, w 2, nb 4)	38		
	(9 wickets declared)	419		

Bowling: Kapil Dev 38-11-93-3 Ghavri 31-2-122-2 Bedi 38.5-13-87-2 Venkataraghavan 22-2-79-1

Umpires: HD Bird and KE Palmer

England v West Indies
19,20,21,23,24 June 1980

Result: Match drawn

England Innings

GA Gooch	lbw b Holding	123	b Garner	47
G Boycott	c Murray b Holding	8	not out	49
CJ Tavare	c Greenidge b Holding	42	lbw b Garner	6
RA Woolmer	c Kallicharran b Garner	15	not out	19
MW Gatting	b Holding	18		
*IT Botham	lbw b Garner	8		
DL Underwood	lbw b Garner	3		
P Willey	b Holding	4		
+APE Knott	c Garner b Holding	9		
RGD Willis	b Garner	14		
M Hendrick	not out	10		
	(b 4, lb 1, w 4, nb 6)	15	(lb 1, nb 11)	12
	(all out)	269	(2 wickets)	133

Bowling: Roberts 18-3-50-0 Holding 28-11-67-6 Garner 24.3-8-36-4 Croft 20-3-77-0 Richards 5-1-24-0
Roberts 13-3-24-0 Holding 15-5-51-0 Garner 15-6-21-2 Croft 8-2-24-0 Richards 1-0-1-0

West Indies Innings

CG Greenidge	lbw b Botham	25	
DL Haynes	lbw b Botham	184	
IVA Richards	c sub b Willey	145	
CEH Croft	run out	0	
AI Kallicharran	c Knott b Willis	15	
SFAF Bacchus	c Gooch b Willis	0	
*CH Lloyd	b Willey	56	
+DL Murray	c Tavare b Botham	34	
AME Roberts	b Underwood	24	
J Garner	c Gooch b Willis	15	
MA Holding	not out	0	
	(b 1, lb 9, w 1, nb 9)	20	
	(all out)	518	

Bowling: Willis 31-12-103-3 Botham 37-7-145-3 Underwood 29.2-7-108-1 Hendrick 11-2-32-0 Gooch 7-1-26-0 Willey 25-8-73-2 Boycott 7-2-11-0

Umpires: WE Alley and BJ Meyer

England v Australia
28,29,30 August, 1,2 September 1980

Result: Match drawn

Australia Innings

GM Wood	st Bairstow b Emburey	112	lbw b Old	8
BM Laird	c Bairstow b Old	24	c Bairstow b Old	6
*GS Chappell	c Gatting b Old	47	b Old	59
KJ Hughes	c Athey b Old	117	lbw b Botham	84
GN Yallop	lbw b Hendrick	2		
AR Border	not out	56	not out	21
+RW Marsh	not out	16		
RJ Bright				
DK Lillee				
AA Mallett				
LS Pascoe				
	(b 1, lb 8, nb 2)	11	(b 1, lb 8, nb 2)	11
	(5 wickets declared)	385	(4 wickets declared)	189

Bowling: Old 35-9-91-3 Hendrick 30-6-67-1 Botham 22-2-89-0 Emburey 38-9-104-1 Gooch 8-3-16-0 Willey 1-0-7-0
Old 20-6-47-3 Hendrick 15-4-53-0 Botham 9.2-1-43-1 Emburey 9-2-35-0

England Innings

GA Gooch	c Bright b Lillee	8	lbw b Lillee	16
G Boycott	c Marsh b Lillee	62	not out	128
CWJ Athey	c Marsh b Lillee	9	c Laird b Pascoe	1
DI Gower	b Lillee	45	b Mallett	35
MW Gatting	lbw b Pascoe	12	not out	51
*IT Botham	c Wood b Pascoe	0		
P Willey	lbw b Pascoe	5		
+DL Bairstow	lbw b Pascoe	6		
JE Emburey	lbw b Pascoe	3		
CM Old	not out	24		
M Hendrick	c Border b Mallett	5		
	(b 6, lb 8, nb 12)	26	(b 3, lb 2, nb 8)	13
	(all out)	205	(3 wickets)	244

Bowling: Lillee 15-4-43-4 Pascoe 18-5-59-5 Chappell 2-0-2-0 Bright 21-6-50-0 Mallett 7.2-3-25-1
Lillee 19-5-53-1 Pascoe 17-1-73-1 Bright 25-9-44-0 Mallett 21-2-61-1

Umpires: HD Bird and DJ Constant

England v Australia
2,3,4,6,7 July 1981

Result: Match drawn

England Innings

GA Gooch	c Yallop b Lawson	44	lbw b Lawson	20
G Boycott	c Alderman b Lawson	17	c Marsh b Lillee	60
RA Woolmer	c Marsh b Lawson	21	lbw b Alderman	9
DI Gower	c Marsh b Lawson	27	c Alderman b Lillee	89
MW Gatting	lbw b Bright	59	c Wood b Bright	16
P Willey	c Border b Alderman	82	c Chappell b Bright	12
JE Emburey	run out (Lillee/Marsh)	31		
*IT Botham	lbw b Lawson	0	b Bright	0
+RW Taylor	c Hughes b Lawson	0	b Lillee	9
GR Dilley	not out	7	not out	27
RGD Willis	c Wood b Lawson	0		
	(b 2, lb 3, w 3, nb 10)	18	(b 2, lb 8, nb 13)	23
	(all out)	311	(8 wickets declared)	265

Bowling: Lillee 35.4-7-102-0 Alderman 30.2-7-79-1 Lawson 43.1-14-81-7 Bright 15-7-31-1
Lillee 26.4-8-82-3 Alderman 17-2-42-1 Lawson 16-9-51-1 Bright 36-18-67-3

Australia Innings

GM Wood	c Taylor b Willis	44	not out	62
J Dyson	c Gower b Botham	7	lbw b Dilley	1
GN Yallop	b Dilley	1	c Botham b Willis	3
*KJ Hughes	c Willis b Emburey	42	lbw b Dilley	4
TM Chappell	c Taylor b Dilley	2	c Taylor b Botham	5
AR Border	c Gatting b Botham	64	not out	12
+RW Marsh	lbw b Dilley	47		
RJ Bright	lbw b Emburey	33		
GF Lawson	lbw b Willis	5		
DK Lillee	not out	40		
TM Alderman	c Taylor b Willis	5		
	(b 6, lb 11, w 6, nb 32)	55	(w 1, nb 2)	3
	(all out)	345	(4 wickets)	90

Bowling: Willis 27.4-9-50-3 Dilley 30-8-106-3 Botham 26-8-71-2 Gooch 10-4-28-0 Emburey 25-12-35-2
Willis 12-3-35-1 Dilley 7.5-1-18-2 Emburey 21-10-24-0 Botham 8-3-10-1

Umpires: DO Oslear and KE Palmer

England v India
10,11,12,14,15 June 1982

Result: England won by 7 wickets

England Innings
G Cook	lbw b Kapil Dev	4	lbw b Kapil Dev	10
CJ Tavare	c Viswanath b Kapil Dev	4	b Kapil Dev	3
AJ Lamb	lbw b Kapil Dev	9	not out	37
DI Gower	c Viswanath b Kapil Dev	37	not out	14
IT Botham	c Malhotra b Madan Lal	67		
DW Randall	c Parkar b Kapil Dev	126		
DR Pringle	c Gavaskar b Doshi	7		
PH Edmonds	c Kirmani b Madan Lal	64		
+RW Taylor	c Viswanath b Doshi	31	c Malhotra b Kapil Dev	1
PJW Allott	not out	41		
*RGD Willis	b Madan Lal	28		
	(b 1, lb 5, nb 9)	15	(lb 2)	2
	(all out)	433	(3 wickets)	67

Bowling: Kapil Dev 43-8-125-5 Madan Lal 28.1-6-99-3 Shastri 34-10-73-0 Doshi 40-7-120-2 Yashpal Sharma 3-2-1-0
Kapil Dev 10-1-43-3 Madan Lal 2-1-2-0 Shastri 2-0-9-0 Doshi 5-3-11-0

India Innings
*SM Gavaskar	b Botham	48	c Cook b Willis	24
GAHM Parkar	lbw b Botham	6	b Willis	1
DB Vengsarkar	lbw b Willis	2	c Allott b Willis	157
GR Viswanath	b Botham	1	c Lloyd b Small	3
Yashpal Sharma	lbw b Pringle	4	b Willis	37
AO Malhotra	lbw b Pringle	5	c Taylor b Willis	0
N Kapil Dev	c Cook b Willis	41	c Cook b Botham	89
RJ Shastri	c Cook b Willis	4	b Allott	23
+SMH Kirmani	not out	6	c Gower b Willis	3
S Madan Lal	c Tavare b Botham	6	lbw b Pringle	15
DR Doshi	c Taylor b Botham	0	not out	4
	(lb 1, nb 4)	5	(lb 2, nb 11)	13
	(all out)	128	(all out)	369

Bowling: Botham 19.4-3-46-5 Willis 16-2-41-3 Pringle 9-4-16-2 Edmonds 2-1-5-0 Allott 4-1-15-0
Botham 31.5-7-103-1 Willis 23-3-101-6 Pringle 19-4-58-2 Edmonds 15-6-39-0 Allott 17-3-51-1 Cook 1-0-4-0

Umpires: DGL Evans and BJ Meyer

England v Pakistan
12,13,14,15,16 August 1982

Result: Pakistan won by 10 wickets

Pakistan Innings
Mohsin Khan	c Tavare b Jackman	200	not out	39
Mudassar Nazar	c Taylor b Jackman	20		
Mansoor Akhtar	c Lamb b Botham	57		
Javed Miandad	run out	6	not out	26
Zaheer Abbas	b Jackman	75		
Haroon Rashid	lbw b Botham	1		
*Imran Khan	c Taylor b Botham	12		
Tahir Naqqash	c Gatting b Jackman	2		
+Wasim Bari	not out	24		
Abdul Qadir	not out	18		
Sarfraz Nawaz				
	(b 3, lb 8, nb 2)	13	(b 1, lb 10, w 1)	12
	(8 wickets declared)	428	(0 wickets)	77

Bowling: Botham 44-8-148-3 Jackman 36-5-110-4 Pringle 26-9-62-0 Greig 13-2-42-0 Hemmings 20-3-53-0
Botham 7-0-30-0 Jackman 4-0-22-0 Hemmings 2.1-0-13-0

England Innings
DW Randall	b Sarfraz Nawaz	29	b Mudassar Nazar	9
CJ Tavare	b Sarfraz Nawaz	8	c Javed Miandad b Imran Khan	82
AJ Lamb	c Haroon Rashid b Tahir Naqqash	33	lbw b Mudassar Nazar	0
*DI Gower	c Mansoor Akhtar b Imran Khan	29	c Wasim Bari b Mudassar Nazar	0
IT Botham	c Mohsin Khan b Abdul Qadir	31	c Sarfraz Nawaz b Mudassar Nazar	69
MW Gatting	not out	32	c Wasim Bari b Mudassar Nazar	7
DR Pringle	c Haroon Rashid b Abdul Qadir	5	c Javed Miandad b Abdul Qadir	14
IA Greig	lbw b Abdul Qadir	3	lbw b Mudassar Nazar	2
EE Hemmings	b Sarfraz Nawaz	6	c Wasim Bari b Imran Khan	14
+RW Taylor	lbw b Abdul Qadir	5	not out	24
RD Jackman	lbw b Imran Khan	0	c Haroon Rashid b Abdul Qadir	17
	(b 11, lb 12, w 13, nb 10)	46	(b 10, lb 19, w 5, nb 4)	38
	(all out)	227	(all out)	276

Bowling: Imran Khan 23-4-55-2 Sarfraz Nawaz 23-4-56-3 Tahir Naqqash 12-4-25-1 Abdul Qadir 24-9-39-4 Mudassar Nazar 4-1-6-0
Imran Khan 42-13-84-2 Sarfraz Nawaz 14-5-22-0 Tahir Naqqash 7-5-6-0 Abdul Qadir 37.5-15-94-2 Mudassar Nazar 19-7-32-6

Umpires: HD Bird and DJ Constant

England v New Zealand
11,12,13,15 August 1983

Result: England won by 127 runs

England Innings
CJ Tavare	b Crowe	51	c Crowe b Hadlee	16
CL Smith	lbw b Hadlee	0	c Coney b Hadlee	43
DI Gower	lbw b Crowe	108	c Crowe b Gray	34
AJ Lamb	c sub b Chatfield	17	c Hadlee b Gray	4
MW Gatting	c Wright b Hadlee	81	b Gray	15
IT Botham	c Coney b Chatfield	8	c Coney b Chatfield	61
+RW Taylor	b Hadlee	16	c & b Coney	7
NA Foster	c Smith b Hadlee	10	c Wright b Hadlee	3
NGB Cook	b Chatfield	16	c Bracewell b Chatfield	5
*RGD Willis	c Smith b Hadlee	7	not out	2
NG Cowans	not out	1	c Smith b Chatfield	1
	(b 3, lb 3, w 2, nb 3)	11	(b 5, lb 6, nb 9)	20
	(all out)	326	(all out)	211

Bowling: Hadlee 40-15-93-5 Cairns 23-8-65-1 Chatfield 36.3-8-116-2 Crowe 13-1-35-2 Coney 8-7-6-0
Hadlee 26-7-42-3 Cairns 3-0-9-0 Chatfield 13.3-4-29-3 Coney 6-4-9-1 Bracewell 14-2-9-0 Gray 30-8-73-3

New Zealand Innings
JG Wright	c Lamb b Willis	11	c Taylor b Botham	12
BA Edgar	b Willis b Cook	70	c Lamb b Cowans	27
*GP Howarth	b Cook	25	c Taylor b Willis	0
MD Crowe	b Botham	46	c Foster b Cowans	12
JV Coney	b Cook	7	c Gatting b Foster	68
EJ Gray	c Lamb b Botham	11	c Lamb b Cook	17
JG Bracewell	c Gower b Cook	0	lbw b Willis	4
RJ Hadlee	c Botham b Cook	0	b Willis	30
BL Cairns	c Lamb b Botham	5	b Cook	16
+IDS Smith	c Lamb b Botham	3	not out	17
EJ Chatfield	not out	5	c & b Cook	2
	(lb 5, nb 3)	8	(b 3, lb 4, nb 7)	14
	(all out)	191	(all out)	219

Bowling: Willis 13-6-28-1 Foster 16-5-40-0 Cowans 9-1-30-0 Botham 20.4-6-50-4 Cook 26-11-35-5
Willis 12-5-24-3 Foster 12-0-35-1 Cowans 11-1-36-2 Botham 7-2-20-1 Cook 27.2-9-90-3

Umpires: DJ Constant and DGL Evans

England v West Indies
28,29,30 June, 2,3 July 1984

Result: West Indies won by 9 wickets

England Innings
G Fowler	c Harper b Baptiste	106	lbw b Small	11
BC Broad	c Dujon b Marshall	55	c Harper b Garner	0
*DI Gower	lbw b Marshall	3	c Lloyd b Small	21
AJ Lamb	lbw b Marshall	23	c Dujon b Marshall	110
MW Gatting	lbw b Marshall	1	lbw b Marshall	29
IT Botham	c Richards b Baptiste	30	lbw b Garner	81
+PR Downton	not out	23	lbw b Small	4
G Miller	run out	0	b Harper	9
DR Pringle	lbw b Garner	2	lbw b Garner	8
NA Foster	c Harper b Marshall	6	not out	9
RGD Willis	b Marshall	2		
	(b 4, lb 14, w 2, nb 15)	35	(b 4, lb 7, w 1, nb 6)	18
	(all out)	286	(9 wickets declared)	300

Bowling: Garner 32-10-67-1 Small 9-0-38-0 Marshall 36.5-10-85-6 Baptiste 20-6-36-2 Harper 9-0-25-0
Garner 30.3-3-91-3 Small 12-2-40-3 Marshall 22-6-85-2 Baptiste 26-8-48-0 Harper 8-1-18-1

West Indies Innings
CG Greenidge	c Miller b Botham	1	not out	214
DL Haynes	lbw b Botham	12	run out	17
HA Gomes	c Gatting b Botham	10	not out	92
IVA Richards	lbw b Botham	72		
*CH Lloyd	lbw b Botham	39		
+PJL Dujon	c Fowler b Botham	8		
MD Marshall	c Pringle b Willis	29		
EAE Baptiste	c Downton b Botham	44		
RA Harper	c Gatting b Botham	8		
J Garner	c Downton b Botham	6		
MA Small	not out	3		
	(lb 5, w 1, nb 7)	13	(b 4, lb 4, nb 13)	21
	(all out)	245	(1 wicket)	344

Bowling: Willis 19.5-5-48-2 Botham 27.4-6-103-8 Pringle 11-0-54-0 Foster 6-2-13-0 Miller 2-0-14-0
Willis 15-5-48-0 Botham 20.1-2-117-0 Pringle 8-0-44-0 Foster 12-0-69-0 Miller 11-0-45-0

Umpires: DGL Evans and BJ Meyer

England v Sri Lanka
23,24,25,27,28 August 1984

Result: Match drawn

Sri Lanka Innings
S Wettimuny	c Downton b Allott	190	c Gower b Botham	13
+SAR Silva	lbw b Botham	8	not out	102
RS Madugalle	b Ellison	3	b Botham	5
RL Dias	c Lamb b Pocock	32	lbw b Botham	38
A Ranatunga	b Agnew	84	lbw b Botham	0
*LRD Mendis	c Fowler b Pocock	111	c Fowler b Botham	94
PA de Silva	c Downton b Agnew	16	c Downton b Pocock	3
ALF de Mel	not out	20	c Ellison b Botham	14
JR Ratnayeke	not out	5	not out	7
DS de Silva				
VB John				
	(b 2, lb 8, w 2, nb 8)	20	(b 5, lb 4, nb 11)	20
	(7 wickets declared)	491	(7 wickets declared)	294

Bowling: Agnew 32-3-123-2 Botham 29-6-114-1 Ellison 28-6-70-1 Pocock 41-17-75-2 Allott 36-7-89-1
Agnew 11-3-54-0 Botham 27-6-90-6 Ellison 7-0-36-0 Pocock 29-10-78-1 Allott 1-0-2-0 Lamb 1-0-6-0 Tavare 3-3-0-0 Fowler 1-0-8-0

England Innings
G Fowler	c Madugalle b John	25	
BC Broad	c Silva b de Mel	86	
CJ Tavare	c Ranatunga b DS de Silva	14	
*DI Gower	c Silva b de Mel	55	
AJ Lamb	c Dias b John	107	
IT Botham	c sub (DM Vonhagt) b John	6	
RM Ellison	c Ratnayeke b DS de Silva	41	
+PR Downton	c Dias b de Mel	10	
PJW Allott	b de Mel	0	
PI Pocock	c Silva b John	2	
JP Agnew	not out	1	
	(b 5, lb 7, w 5, nb 6)	23	
	(all out)	370	

Bowling: de Mel 37-10-110-4 John 39.1-12-98-4 Ratnayeke 22-5-50-0 DS de Silva 45-16-85-2 Ranatunga 1-1-0-0 Madugalle 3-0-4-0

Umpires: HD Bird and DGL Evans

England v Australia
27,28,29 June, 1,2 July 1985

Result: Australia won by 4 wickets

England Innings
GA Gooch	lbw b McDermott	30	c Phillips b McDermott	17
RT Robinson	lbw b McDermott	6	b Holland	12
*DI Gower	c Border b McDermott	86	c Phillips b McDermott	22
MW Gatting	lbw b Lawson	14	not out	75
AJ Lamb	c Phillips b Lawson	47	c Holland b Lawson	9
IT Botham	c Ritchie b Lawson	5	c Border b Holland	85
+PR Downton	c Wessels b McDermott	21	c Boon b Holland	0
JE Emburey	lbw b O'Donnell	33	b Lawson	20
PH Edmonds	c Border b McDermott	21	c Boon b Holland	1
NA Foster	c Wessels b McDermott	3	c Border b Holland	0
PJW Allott	not out	1	b Lawson	0
	(b 1, lb 4, w 1, nb 17)	23	(b 1, lb 12, w 4, nb 3)	20
	(all out)	290	(all out)	261

Bowling: Lawson 25-2-91-3 McDermott 29.2-5-70-6 O'Donnell 22-3-82-1 Holland 23-6-42-0
McDermott 20-2-84-2 Lawson 23-0-86-3 Holland 32-12-68-5 O'Donnell 5-0-10-0

Australia Innings
GM Wood	c Emburey b Allott	8	c Lamb b Botham	6
AMJ Hilditch	b Foster	14	c Lamb b Botham	0
KC Wessels	lbw b Botham	11	run out	28
*AR Border	c Gooch b Botham	196	not out	41
DC Boon	c Downton b Botham	4	b Edmonds	1
GM Ritchie	lbw b Botham	94	b Allott	2
+WB Phillips	c Edmonds b Emburey	21	c Edmonds b Emburey	29
SP O'Donnell	c Lamb b Edmonds	48	not out	9
GF Lawson	not out	5		
CJ McDermott	run out	9		
RG Holland	b Edmonds	0		
	(lb 10, w 1, nb 4)	15	(lb 11)	11
	(all out)	425	(6 wickets)	127

Bowling: Foster 23-1-83-1 Allott 30-4-70-1 Botham 24-2-109-5 Edmonds 25.4-5-85-2 Gooch 3-1-11-0 Emburey 19-3-57-0
Botham 15-0-49-2 Allott 7-4-8-1 Edmonds 16-5-35-1 Emburey 8-4-24-1

Umpires: HD Bird and DGL Evans

Lord's

England v India
5,6,7,9,10 June 1986

Result: India won by 5 wickets

England Innings

GA Gooch	b Sharma	114	lbw b Kapil Dev	8
RT Robinson	c Azharuddin b Maninder Singh	35	c Amarnath b Kapil Dev	11
*DI Gower	c More b Sharma	18	lbw b Kapil Dev	8
MW Gatting	b Sharma	0	b Sharma	40
AJ Lamb	c Srikkanth b Sharma	6	c More b Shastri	39
DR Pringle	b Binny	63	c More b Kapil Dev	6
JE Emburey	c Amarnath b Kapil Dev	7	c & b Maninder Singh	1
+PR Downton	lbw b Sharma	5	c Shastri b Maninder Singh	29
RM Ellison	c Kapil Dev b Binny	12	c More b Binny	19
GR Dilley	c More b Binny	4	not out	2
PH Edmonds	not out	7	c Binny b Maninder Singh	7
	(lb 15, w 1, nb 7)	23	(lb 6, w 1, nb 3)	10
	(all out)	294	(all out)	180

Bowling: Kapil Dev 31-8-67-1 Binny 18.2-4-55-3 Sharma 32-10-64-5 Maninder Singh 30-15-45-1 Amarnath 7-1-18-0 Shastri 10-3-30-0
Kapil Dev 22-7-52-4 Binny 15-3-44-1 Sharma 17-4-48-1 Maninder Singh 20.4-12-9-3 Amarnath 2-2-0-0 Shastri 20-8-21-1

India Innings

SM Gavaskar	c Emburey b Dilley	34	c Downton b Dilley	22
K Srikkanth	c Gatting b Dilley	20	c Gooch b Dilley	0
M Amarnath	c Pringle b Edmonds	69	lbw b Pringle	8
DB Vengsarkar	not out	126	b Edmonds	33
M Azharuddin	c & b Dilley	33	run out	14
RJ Shastri	c Edmonds b Dilley	1	not out	20
RMH Binny	lbw b Pringle	9		
*N Kapil Dev	c Lamb b Ellison	1	not out	23
C Sharma	b Pringle	2		
+KS More	lbw b Pringle	25		
Maninder Singh	c Lamb b Emburey	6		
	(lb 5, w 1, nb 9)	15	(b 1, lb 9, w 1, nb 5)	16
	(all out)	341	(5 wickets)	136

Bowling: Dilley 34-7-146-4 Ellison 29-11-63-1 Emburey 27-13-28-1 Edmonds 27-7-41-1 Pringle 25-7-58-3
Dilley 10-3-28-2 Ellison 6-0-17-0 Edmonds 11-2-51-1 Pringle 15-5-30-1

Umpires: KE Palmer and DR Shepherd

England v New Zealand
24,25,26,28,29 July 1986

Result: Match drawn

England Innings

GA Gooch	c Smith b Hadlee	18	c Watson b Bracewell	183
MD Moxon	lbw b Hadlee	74	lbw b Hadlee	5
CWJ Athey	c JJ Crowe b Hadlee	44	b Gray	16
DI Gower	c MD Crowe b Bracewell	62	b Gray	3
*MW Gatting	b Hadlee	2	c MD Crowe b Gray	26
P Willey	lbw b Watson	44	b Bracewell	42
PH Edmonds	c MD Crowe b Hadlee	6	not out	9
+BN French	retired hurt	0		
GR Dilley	c Smith b Hadlee	17		
NA Foster	b Watson	8		
NV Radford	not out	12		
	(b 6, lb 7, nb 7)	20	(b 6, w 1, nb 4)	11
	(all out)	307	(6 wickets declared)	295

Bowling: Hadlee 37.5-11-80-6 Watson 30-7-70-2 MD Crowe 8-1-38-0 Coney 4-0-12-0 Bracewell 26-8-65-1 Gray 13-9-29-0
Hadlee 27-3-78-1 Watson 17-2-50-0 MD Crowe 4-0-13-0 Bracewell 23.4-7-57-2 Gray 46-14-83-3 Rutherford 3-0-8-0

New Zealand Innings

JG Wright	b Dilley	0	c Gower b Dilley	0
BA Edgar	c Gatting b Gooch	83	c Gower b Foster	0
KR Rutherford	c Gooch b Dilley	0	not out	24
MD Crowe	c & b Edmonds	106	not out	11
JJ Crowe	c Gatting b Edmonds	18		
*JV Coney	c Gooch b Radford	51		
EJ Gray	c Gower b Edmonds	11		
RJ Hadlee	b Edmonds	19		
+IDS Smith	c Edmonds b Dilley	18		
JG Bracewell	not out	1		
W Watson	lbw b Dilley	1		
	(b 4, lb 9, w 6, nb 15)	34	(lb 4, nb 2)	6
	(all out)	342	(2 wickets)	41

Bowling: Dilley 35.1-9-82-4 Foster 25-6-56-0 Radford 25-4-71-1 Edmonds 42-10-97-4 Gooch 13-6-23-1
Dilley 6-3-5-1 Foster 3-1-13-1 Edmonds 5-0-18-0 Gower 1-0-1-0

Umpires: HD Bird and AGT Whitehead

England v Pakistan
18,19,20,22,23 June 1987

Result: Match drawn

England Innings

BC Broad	b Mudassar Nazar	55
RT Robinson	c Saleem Yousuf b Mohsin Kamal	7
CWJ Athey	b Imran Khan	123
DI Gower	c Saleem Yousuf b Mudassar Nazar	8
*MW Gatting	run out	43
+BN French	b Wasim Akram	42
IT Botham	c Javed Miandad b Wasim Akram	6
JE Emburey	run out	12
NA Foster	b Abdul Qadir	21
PH Edmonds	not out	17
GR Dilley	c Saleem Yousuf b Imran Khan	17
	(lb 12, w 1, nb 4)	17
	(all out)	368

Bowling: Imran Khan 34.5-7-90-2 Wasim Akram 28-1-98-2 Mohsin Kamal 9-2-42-1 Abdul Qadir 25-1-100-1 Mudassar Nazar 16-6-26-2

England v West Indies
16,17,18,20,21 June 1988

Result: West Indies won by 134 runs

West Indies Innings

CG Greenidge	c Downton b Dilley	22	c Emburey b Dilley	103
DL Haynes	c Moxon b Dilley	12	c Downton b Dilley	5
RB Richardson	c Emburey b Dilley	5	lbw b Pringle	26
*IVA Richards	c Downton b Dilley	6	b Pringle	72
CL Hooper	c Downton b Small	3	c Downton b Jarvis	11
AL Logie	c Emburey b Small	81	not out	95
+PJL Dujon	b Emburey	53	b Jarvis	52
MD Marshall	c Gooch b Dilley	11	b Jarvis	6
CEL Ambrose	c Gower b Small	0	b Dilley	0
CA Walsh	not out	9	b Dilley	0
BP Patterson	b Small	0	c Downton b Jarvis	2
	(lb 6, nb 1)	7	(lb 19, w 1, nb 5)	25
	(all out)	209	(all out)	397

Bowling: Dilley 23-6-55-5 Jarvis 13-2-47-0 Small 18.5-5-64-4 Pringle 7-3-20-0 Emburey 6-2-17-1
Dilley 27-6-73-4 Small 19-1-76-0 Jarvis 26-3-107-4 Emburey 15-1-62-0 Pringle 21-4-60-2

England Innings

GA Gooch	b Marshall	44	lbw b Marshall	16
BC Broad	lbw b Marshall	0	c Dujon b Marshall	1
MD Moxon	c Richards b Ambrose	26	run out	14
DI Gower	c sub (KLT Arthurton) b Walsh	46	c Richardson b Patterson	1
AJ Lamb	lbw b Marshall	10	run out	113
DR Pringle	c Dujon b Walsh	1	lbw b Walsh	0
+PR Downton	lbw b Marshall	11	lbw b Marshall	27
*JE Emburey	b Patterson	7	b Ambrose	30
GC Small	not out	5	c Richardson b Marshall	7
PW Jarvis	b Marshall	7	c Haynes b Marshall	29
GR Dilley	b Marshall	0	c Richardson b Patterson	28
	(lb 6, nb 2)	8	(b 5, lb 20, w 2, nb 14)	41
	(all out)	165	(all out)	307

Bowling: Marshall 18-5-32-6 Patterson 13-3-52-1 Ambrose 12-1-39-1 Walsh 16-6-36-2
Marshall 25-5-60-4 Patterson 21.5-2-100-2 Walsh 20-1-75-1 Ambrose 20-4-47-1

Umpires: KE Palmer and DR Shepherd

England v Sri Lanka
25,26,27,29,30 August 1988

Result: England won by 7 wickets

Sri Lanka Innings

DSBP Kuruppu	c Gooch b Newport	46	c Barnett b Foster	25
+SAR Silva	c Russell b Foster	1	c Russell b Newport	16
MAR Samarasekera	c Russell b Foster	4	c Russell b Foster	57
PA de Silva	c Gooch b Newport	3	lbw b Lawrence	18
*RS Madugalle	lbw b Foster	3	b Foster	20
A Ranatunga	lbw b Newport	1	b Newport	78
LRD Mendis	c Smith b Lawrence	21	lbw b Pringle	56
JR Ratnayeke	lbw b Foster	14	c Lamb b Lawrence	32
MAWR Madurasinghe	run out	4	b Newport	2
CPH Ramanayake	lbw b Pringle	0	c Gooch b Newport	2
GF Labrooy	lbw b Pringle	42	not out	9
	(b 1, lb 7, nb 2)	10	(lb 8, nb 8)	16
	(all out)	194	(all out)	331

Bowling: Foster 21-5-51-3 Lawrence 15-4-37-1 Newport 21-4-77-3 Pringle 6.5-1-17-2 Emburey 2-1-4-0
Foster 33-10-98-2 Lawrence 21-5-74-2 Newport 26.3-7-87-4 Pringle 11-2-30-1 Emburey 18-9-34-1

England Innings

*GA Gooch	lbw b Ratnayake	75	c Silva b Samarasekera	36
RT Robinson	c Samarasekera b Ratnayeke	19	not out	34
+RC Russell	c Samarasekera b Labrooy	94		
KJ Barnett	c Ranatunga b Labrooy	66	c Silva b Samarasekera	0
AJ Lamb	b Labrooy	63	c de Silva b Ranatunga	8
RA Smith	b Ranatunga	31	not out	8
DR Pringle	c Silva b Labrooy	14		
JE Emburey	c de Silva b Samarasekera	0		
PJ Newport	c de Silva b Ramanayake	26		
NA Foster	not out	14		
DV Lawrence	c Mendis b Ramanayake	4		
	(b 1, lb 3, w 2, nb 17)	23	(lb 8, w 2, nb 4)	14
	(all out)	429	(3 wickets)	100

Bowling: Ratnayeke 32-3-107-2 Labrooy 40-7-119-4 Ramanayake 27-2-3-86-2 Madurasinghe 16-4-41-0 Samarasekera 22-5-66-1 Ranatunga 6-3-6-1
Ratnayeke 7-1-16-0 Labrooy 9-0-24-0 Samarasekera 10-0-38-2 Ranatunga 8.4-4-14-1

Umpires: DJ Constant and JW Holder

England v Australia
22,23,24,26,27 June 1989

Result: Australia won by 6 wickets

England Innings

GA Gooch	c Healy b Waugh	60	lbw b Alderman	0
BC Broad	lbw b Alderman	18	b Lawson	20
KJ Barnett	c Boon b Hughes	14	c Jones b Alderman	3
MW Gatting	c Boon b Hughes	0	lbw b Alderman	22
*DI Gower	b Lawson	57	c Border b Hughes	106
RA Smith	c Hohns b Lawson	32	b Alderman	96
JE Emburey	b Alderman	0	not out	36
+RC Russell	not out	64	c Boon b Lawson	29
NA Foster	c Jones b Hughes	16	lbw b Alderman	4
PW Jarvis	c Marsh b Hughes	6	b Alderman	5
GR Dilley	c Border b Alderman	7	c Boon b Hughes	24
	(lb 9, nb 3)	12	(b 6, lb 6, nb 2)	14
	(all out)	286	(all out)	359

Bowling: Alderman 20.5-4-60-3 Lawson 27-8-88-2 Hughes 23-6-71-4 Waugh 9-3-49-1 Hohns 7-3-9-0
Alderman 38-6-128-6 Lawson 39-10-99-2 Hughes 24-8-44-2 Border 9-3-23-0 Hohns 13-6-33-0 Waugh 7-2-20-0

Australia Innings

GR Marsh	c Russell b Dilley	3	b Dilley	1
MA Taylor	lbw b Foster	62	c Gooch b Foster	27
DC Boon	c Gooch b Dilley	94	not out	58
*AR Border	c Smith b Emburey	35	c sub (RJ Sims) b Foster	1
DM Jones	lbw b Foster	27	c Russell b Foster	0
SR Waugh	not out	152	not out	21
+A Healy	c Russell b Jarvis	3		
MG Hughes	c Gooch b Foster	30		
TV Hohns	b Emburey	21		
GF Lawson	c Broad b Emburey	74		
TM Alderman	lbw b Emburey	8		
	(lb 11, nb 8)	19	(b 3, lb 4, nb 4)	11
	(all out)	528	(4 wickets)	119

Bowling: Dilley 34-3-141-2 Foster 45-7-129-3 Jarvis 31-3-150-1 Emburey 42-12-88-4 Gooch 6-2-9-0
Dilley 10-2-27-1 Foster 18-3-39-3 Emburey 3-0-8-0 Jarvis 9.2-0-38-0

Umpires: HD Bird and NT Plews

England v New Zealand
21,22,23,25,26 June 1990

Result: Match drawn

England Innings

Batsman		1st		2nd
*GA Gooch	c & b Bracewell	85	b Hadlee	37
MA Atherton	b Morrison	0	c Bracewell b Jones	54
AJ Stewart	lbw b Hadlee	54	c sub (MW Priest) b Bracewell	42
AJ Lamb	lbw b Snedden	39	not out	84
RA Smith	c Bracewell b Morrison	64	hit wicket b Bracewell	0
NH Fairbrother	c Morrison b Bracewell	2	not out	33
+RC Russell	b Hadlee	13		
PAJ DeFreitas	c Franklin b Morrison	38		
GC Small	b Morrison	3		
EE Hemmings	b Hadlee	0		
DE Malcolm	not out	0		
	(lb 13, w 1, nb 22)	36	(b 8, lb 8, nb 6)	22
	(all out)	334	(4 wickets declared)	272

Bowling: Hadlee 29-5-113-3 Morrison 18.4-4-64-4 Snedden 21-4-72-1 Bracewell 21-3-72-2
Hadlee 13-2-32-1 Morrison 16-0-81-0 Bracewell 34-13-85-2 Jones 12-3-40-1 Rutherford 3-0-18-0

New Zealand Innings

TJ Franklin	c Russell b Malcolm	101
*JG Wright	c Stewart b Small	98
AH Jones	c Stewart b Malcolm	49
MD Crowe	c Russell b Hemmings	1
MJ Greatbatch	b Malcolm	47
KR Rutherford	c Fairbrother b Malcolm	0
Sir RJ Hadlee	b Hemmings	86
JG Bracewell	run out (DeFreitas/Russell)	4
+IDS Smith	c Small b Malcolm	27
MC Snedden	not out	13
DK Morrison	not out	2
	(b 12, lb 15, w 2, nb 5)	34
	(9 wickets declared)	462

Bowling: Malcolm 43-14-94-5 Small 35-4-127-1 DeFreitas 35.4-1-122-0 Hemmings 30-13-67-2 Gooch 13-7-25-0 Atherton 1-1-0-0

Umpires: MJ Kitchen and DR Shepherd

England v India
26,27,28,30,31 July 1990

Result: England won by 247 runs

England Innings

Batsman		1st		2nd
*GA Gooch	b Prabhakar	333	c Azharuddin b Sharma	123
MA Atherton	b Kapil Dev	8	c Vengsarkar b Sharma	72
DI Gower	c Manjrekar b Hirwani	40	not out	32
AJ Lamb	c Manjrekar b Sharma	139	c Tendulkar b Hirwani	19
RA Smith	not out	100	b Prabhakar	15
JE Morris	not out	4		
+RC Russell				
CC Lewis				
EE Hemmings				
ARC Fraser				
DE Malcolm				
	(b 2, lb 21, w 2, nb 4)	29	(lb 11)	11
	(4 wickets declared)	653	(4 wickets declared)	272

Bowling: Kapil Dev 34-5-120-1 Prabhakar 43-6-187-1 Sharma 33-5-122-1 Shastri 22-0-99-0 Hirwani 30-1-102-1
Kapil Dev 10-0-53-0 Prabhakar 11.2-2-45-1 Shastri 7-0-38-0 Sharma 15-0-75-2 Hirwani 11-0-50-1

Innings

*GA Gooch	b Prabhakar	333
MA Atherton	b Kapil Dev	8
DI Gower	c Manjrekar b Hirwani	40
AJ Lamb	c Manjrekar b Sharma	139
RA Smith	not out	100
JE Morris	not out	4
+RC Russell		
CC Lewis		
EE Hemmings		
ARC Fraser		
DE Malcolm		
	(b 2, lb 21, w 2, nb 4)	29
	(4 wickets declared)	653

Bowling: Kapil Dev 34-5-120-1 Prabhakar 43-6-187-1 Sharma 33-5-122-1 Shastri 22-0-99-0 Hirwani 30-1-102-1

Umpires: HD Bird and NT Plews

England v West Indies
20,21,22,23,24 June 1991

Result: Match drawn

West Indies Innings

Batsman		1st		2nd
PV Simmons	c Lamb b Hick	33	lbw b DeFreitas	2
DL Haynes	c Russell b Pringle	60	not out	4
RB Richardson	c DeFreitas b Hick	57	c Hick b Malcolm	1
CL Hooper	c Lamb b Pringle	111	not out	1
*IVA Richards	lbw b DeFreitas	63		
AL Logie	c DeFreitas	5		
+PJL Dujon	c Lamb b Pringle	20		
MD Marshall	lbw b Pringle	25		
CEL Ambrose	c & b Malcolm	5		
CA Walsh	c Atherton b Pringle	10		
IBA Allen	not out	1		
	(b 3, lb 7, nb 19)	29	(lb 2, nb 2)	4
	(all out)	419	(2 wickets)	12

Bowling: DeFreitas 31-6-93-2 Malcolm 19-3-76-1 Watkin 15-2-60-0 Pringle 35.1-6-100-5 Hick 18-4-77-2 Gooch 2-0-3-0
DeFreitas 3-2-1-1 Malcolm 2.5-0-9-1

England Innings

*GA Gooch	b Walsh	37
MA Atherton	b Ambrose	5
GA Hick	c Richardson b Ambrose	0
AJ Lamb	c Haynes b Marshall	1
MR Ramprakash	c Richards b Allen	24
RA Smith	not out	148
+RC Russell	c Dujon b Hooper	46
DR Pringle	c Simmons b Allen	35
PAJ DeFreitas	c Dujon b Marshall	29
SL Watkin	b Ambrose	6
DE Malcolm	b Ambrose	0
	(lb 1, nb 22)	23
	(all out)	354

Bowling: Ambrose 34-10-87-4 Marshall 30-4-78-2 Walsh 26-4-90-1 Allen 23-2-88-2 Hooper 5-2-10-1

Umpires: BJ Meyer and KE Palmer

England v Sri Lanka
22,23,24,26,27 August 1991

Result: England won by 137 runs

England Innings

Batsman		1st		2nd
*GA Gooch	c & b Ramanayake	38	b Anurasiri	174
H Morris	lbw b Ratnayake	42	c Mahanama b Anurasiri	23
AJ Stewart	not out	113	c de Silva b Anurasiri	43
RA Smith	c Tillakaratne b Ratnayake	4	not out	63
MR Ramprakash	c Mahanama b Hathurusingha	0		
IT Botham	c Mahanama b Ramanayake	22		
CC Lewis	c de Silva b Anurasiri	11		
+RC Russell	b Anurasiri	17	not out	12
PAJ DeFreitas	b Ratnayake	1		
DV Lawrence	c & b Ratnayake	3		
PCR Tufnell	lbw b Ratnayake	0		
	(b 9, lb 8, nb 14)	31	(b 15, lb 23, w 1, nb 10)	49
	(all out)	282	(3 wickets declared)	364

Bowling: Ratnayake 27-4-69-5 Ramanayake 24-5-75-2 Wijegunawardene 10-1-36-0 Hathurusingha 17-6-40-1 Anurasiri 17-4-45-2
Ramanayake 20-2-86-0 Ratnayake 26-4-91-0 Wijegunawardene 2-0-13-0 Jayasuriya 1-0-1-0 Anurasiri 36.1-8-135-3

Sri Lanka Innings

Batsman		1st		2nd
DSBP Kuruppu	b DeFreitas	5	lbw b Lewis	21
UC Hathurusingha	c Tufnell b DeFreitas	66	c Morris b Tufnell	25
AP Gurusinha	lbw b DeFreitas	4	b Tufnell	34
*PA de Silva	c Lewis b DeFreitas	42	c de Silva b Anurasiri	18
RS Mahanama	c Russell b Botham	2	c Botham b Tufnell	15
ST Jayasuriya	c Smith b DeFreitas	11	c Russell b Lewis	66
+HP Tillakaratne	c Morris b Lawrence	20	b Tufnell	16
RJ Ratnayake	b DeFreitas	52	c sub b Lawrence	17
CPH Ramanayake	lbw b DeFreitas	0	not out	34
KIW Wijegunawardene	not out	6	c Botham b DeFreitas	4
SD Anurasiri	b Lawrence	1	not out	16
	(lb 15)	15	(b 1, lb 16, nb 2)	19
	(all out)	224	(all out)	285

Bowling: DeFreitas 26-8-70-7 Lawrence 15.1-3-61-2 Lewis 10-5-29-0 Botham 13-3-26-1 Tufnell 7-2-23-0
DeFreitas 22-8-45-1 Lawrence 23-7-83-2 Lewis 18-4-31-2 Botham 6-2-15-0 Tufnell 34.3-14-94-5

Umpires: HD Bird and JH Hampshire

England v Pakistan
18,19,20,21 June 1992

Result: Pakistan won by 2 wickets

England Innings

Batsman		1st		2nd
*GA Gooch	b Wasim Akram	69	lbw b Aaqib Javed	13
AJ Stewart	c Javed Miandad b Asif Mujtaba	74	not out	69
GA Hick	c Javed Miandad b Waqar Younis	13	c Moin Khan b Mushtaq Ahmed	11
RA Smith	c sub (Rashid Latif) b Wasim Akram	9	b Mushtaq Ahmed	8
AJ Lamb	b Waqar Younis	30	lbw b Mushtaq Ahmed	12
IT Botham	b Waqar Younis	2	lbw b Waqar Younis	6
CC Lewis	lbw b Waqar Younis	2	lbw b Mushtaq Ahmed	15
+RC Russell	not out	22	b Wasim Akram	1
PAJ DeFreitas	c Inzamam-ul-Haq b Waqar Younis	3	c Inzamam-ul-Haq b Wasim Akram	0
IDK Salisbury	hit wicket b Mushtaq Ahmed	4	lbw b Wasim Akram	12
DE Malcolm	lbw b Mushtaq Ahmed	0	b Wasim Akram	0
	(b 6, lb 12, nb 9)	27	(b 5, lb 8, nb 15)	28
	(all out)	255	(all out)	175

Bowling: Wasim Akram 19-5-49-2 Aaqib Javed 14-3-40-0 Waqar Younis 21-4-91-5 Mushtaq Ahmed 19.1-5-57-2 Asif Mujtaba 3-3-0-1
Wasim Akram 17.4-2-66-4 Aaqib Javed 12-3-23-1 Waqar Younis 13-3-40-2 Mushtaq Ahmed 9-1-32-3 Asif Mujtaba 1-0-1-0

Pakistan Innings

Batsman		1st		2nd
Aamer Sohail	c Russell b DeFreitas	73	b Salisbury	39
Rameez Raja	b Lewis	24	c Hick b Lewis	0
Asif Mujtaba	c Smith b Malcolm	59	c Russell b Lewis	0
*Javed Miandad	c Botham b Salisbury	9	c Russell b Lewis	0
Saleem Malik	c Smith b Malcolm	55	c Lewis b Salisbury	12
Inzamam-ul-Haq	c & b Malcolm	0	run out	8
Wasim Akram	b Salisbury	24	not out	45
+Moin Khan	c Botham b DeFreitas	12	c Smith b Salisbury	3
Mushtaq Ahmed	c Russell b DeFreitas	4	c Hick b Malcolm	5
Waqar Younis	b Malcolm	14	not out	20
Aaqib Javed	not out	5		
	(b 4, lb 3, nb 7)	14	(b 2, lb 5, w 1, nb 1)	9
	(all out)	293	(8 wickets)	141

Bowling: DeFreitas 26-8-58-3 Malcolm 15.5-1-70-4 Lewis 24-9-77-6 Salisbury 23-3-73-2 Botham 5-2-9-0
Malcolm 15-2-42-1 Lewis 16-3-43-3 Salisbury 14.1-0-49-3

Umpires: B Dudleston and JH Hampshire; Referee: RM Cowper (Aus)

England v Australia
17,18,19,20,21 June 1993

Result: Australia won by an innings and 62 runs

Australia Innings

MA Taylor	st Stewart b Tufnell	111
MJ Slater	c sub (BF Smith) b Lewis	152
DC Boon	not out	164
ME Waugh	b Tufnell	99
*AR Border	b Lewis	77
SR Waugh	not out	13
+IA Healy		
MG Hughes		
SK Warne		
TBA May		
CJ McDermott		
	(lb 1, w 1, nb 14)	16
	(4 wkts decl)	632

Bowling: Caddick 38-5-120-0 Foster 30-4-94-0 Such 36-6-90-0 Tufnell 39-3-129-2 Lewis 36-5-151-2 Gooch 9-1-26-0 Hick 8-3-21-0

England Innings

Batsman		1st		2nd
*GA Gooch	c May b Hughes	12	c Healy b Warne	29
MA Atherton	b Warne	80	run out	99
MW Gatting	b May	5	lbw b Warne	59
RA Smith	st Healy b May	22	c sub (ML Hayden) b May	5
GA Hick	c Healy b Hughes	20	c Taylor b May	64
+AJ Stewart	lbw b Hughes	3	lbw b May	62
CC Lewis	lbw b Warne	0	st Healy b May	0
NA Foster	c Border b Warne	16	c ME Waugh b Border	20
AR Caddick	c Healy b Hughes	21	not out	0
PM Such	c Taylor b Warne	7	b Warne	4
PCR Tufnell	not out	2	b Warne	0
	(lb 8, nb 9)	17	(b 10, lb 13)	23
	(all out)	205	(all out)	365

Bowling: Hughes 20-5-52-4 ME Waugh 6-1-16-0 SR Waugh 4-1-5-0 May 31-12-64-2 Warne 35-12-57-4 Border 3-1-3-0
Hughes 31-9-75-0 ME Waugh 17-4-55-0 May 51-23-81-4 SR Waugh 2-0-13-0 Warne 48.5-17-102-4 Border 16-9-16-1

Umpires: MJ Kitchen and DR Shepherd
TV Umpire: JC Balderstone; Referee: MAK Pataudi (Ind)

Lord's

England v New Zealand
16,17,18,19,20 June 1994

Result: Match drawn

New Zealand Innings

BA Young	lbw b Fraser	0	c Hick b Such	94
BA Pocock	c Smith b Such	10	lbw b DeFreitas	2
*KR Rutherford	c Stewart b DeFreitas	37	lbw b DeFreitas	0
MD Crowe	c Smith b DeFreitas	142	b DeFreitas	9
SP Fleming	lbw b Fraser	41	lbw b Taylor	39
SA Thomson	run out	69	not out	38
+AC Parore	c Rhodes b Taylor	40	not out	15
MN Hart	b Such	25		
DJ Nash	b White	56		
C Pringle	c Hick b DeFreitas	14		
MB Owens	not out	2		
	(b 3, lb 15, w 1, nb 21)	40	(lb 4, nb 10)	14
	(all out)	476	(5 wickets declared)	211

Bowling: Fraser 36-9-102-2 DeFreitas 35-8-102-3 Taylor 20-4-64-1 Such 30-8-84-2 White 21.1-4-84-1 Gooch 5-1-13-0 Hick 2-0-9-0
Fraser 15-0-50-0 DeFreitas 16-0-63-3 Taylor 6-2-18-1 Such 25-5-55-1 White 4-1-21-0 Hick 2-2-0-0

England Innings

*MA Atherton	lbw b Hart	28	c Young b Nash	33
AJ Stewart	c Parore b Nash	45	c Crowe b Nash	119
GA Gooch	lbw b Nash	13	lbw b Nash	0
RA Smith	c & b Nash	6	c Parore b Nash	23
GA Hick	c Young b Pringle	58	lbw b Pringle	37
C White	run out	51	c Thomson b Nash	9
+SJ Rhodes	not out	32	not out	24
PAJ DeFreitas	c Parore b Thomson	11	lbw b Owens	3
ARC Fraser	c & b Nash	10	lbw b Hart	2
JP Taylor	c Parore b Nash	0	not out	0
PM Such	c Parore b Nash	4		
	(b 4, lb 12, nb 7)	23	(b 2, lb 1, nb 1)	4
	(all out)	281	(8 wickets)	254

Bowling: Owens 7-0-34-0 Nash 25-6-76-6 Pringle 23-5-65-1 Hart 44-21-50-1 Thomson 22-8-40-1
Owens 10-3-35-1 Nash 29-8-93-5 Pringle 16-5-41-1 Hart 41-23-55-1 Thomson 12-4-27-0

Umpires: SA Bucknor (WI) and NT Plews
TV Umpire: R Palmer; Referee: CH Lloyd (WI)

England v South Africa
21,22,23,24 July 1994

Result: South Africa won by 356 runs

South Africa Innings

AC Hudson	c Gooch b Gough	6	lbw b Fraser	3
G Kirsten	c DeFreitas b Hick	72	st Rhodes b Hick	44
WJ Cronje	c Crawley b Fraser	7	c Fraser b Gough	32
*KC Wessels	c Rhodes b Gough	105	c Crawley b Salisbury	28
PN Kirsten	c Rhodes b Gough	8	b Gough	42
JN Rhodes	b White	32	b Gough	32
BM McMillan	c Rhodes b Fraser	29	not out	39
+DJ Richardson	lbw b Gough	26	c Rhodes b Fraser	3
CR Matthews	c White	41	b Gough	25
PS de Villiers	c Rhodes b Fraser	8		
AA Donald	not out	5		
	(lb 9, nb 9)	18	(b 8, lb 10, nb 12)	30
	(all out)	357	(8 wickets declared)	278

Bowling: DeFreitas 18-5-67-0 Gough 28-6-76-4 Salisbury 25-2-68-0 Fraser 24.5-7-72-3 Hick 10-5-22-1 White 13-2-43-2
Fraser 23-5-62-2 Gough 19.3-5-46-4 DeFreitas 14-3-43-0 Hick 24-14-38-1 Salisbury 19-4-53-1 White 3-0-18-0

England Innings

*MA Atherton	c Wessels b Donald	20	c McMillan b de Villiers	8
AJ Stewart	b Donald	12	c Richardson b Matthews	27
JP Crawley	c Hudson b de Villiers	9	c Hudson b McMillan	7
GA Hick	c Richardson b de Villiers	38	lbw b McMillan	11
GA Gooch	lbw b de Villiers	20	lbw b Donald	28
C White	c Richardson b Donald	10	c Wessels b Matthews	0
+SJ Rhodes	b McMillan	15	not out	14
IDK Salisbury	not out	6	lbw b Donald	0
PAJ DeFreitas	c Wessels b Donald	3	c G Kirsten b Matthews	1
D Gough	c & b Donald	12	retired hurt	0
ARC Fraser	run out	1	lbw b McMillan	1
	(b 2, lb 5, nb 8)	15	(b 1, lb 1)	2
	(all out)	180	(all out)	99

Bowling: Donald 19.3-5-74-5 de Villiers 16-5-28-3 Matthews 16-6-46-0 McMillan 10-1-25-1
Donald 12-5-29-2 de Villiers 12-4-26-1 Matthews 14-6-25-3 McMillan 6.5-2-16-3 Cronje 1-0-1-0

Umpires: HD Bird and SG Randell (Aus)
TV Umpire: MJ Kitchen; Referee: PJP Burge (Aus)

England v West Indies
22,23,24,25,26 June 1995

Result: England won by 72 runs

England Innings

*MA Atherton	b Ambrose	21	c Murray b Walsh	9
+AJ Stewart	c Arthurton b Gibson	34	c Murray b Walsh	36
GA Hick	c Lara b Bishop	13	b Bishop	67
GP Thorpe	c Lara b Ambrose	52	c Richardson b Ambrose	42
RA Smith	b Hooper	61	lbw b Ambrose	90
MR Ramprakash	c Campbell b Hooper	0	c sub (SC Williams) b Bishop	0
DG Cork	b Walsh	30	c Murray b Bishop	23
D Gough	c Campbell b Gibson	11	b Ambrose	20
PJ Martin	b Walsh	29	c Arthurton b Ambrose	1
RK Illingworth	not out	16	lbw b Walsh	4
ARC Fraser	lbw b Walsh	1	not out	2
	(b 1, lb 10, nb 4)	15	(b 6, lb 27, w 2, nb 7)	42
	(all out)	283	(all out)	336

Bowling: Ambrose 26-6-72-2 Walsh 22.4-6-50-3 Gibson 20-2-81-2 Bishop 17-4-33-1 Hooper 14-3-36-2
Ambrose 24.5-7-70-4 Walsh 28.1-10-91-3 Gibson 14-1-51-0 Bishop 22-5-56-3 Hooper 9-1-31-0 Adams 2-0-4-0

West Indies Innings

SL Campbell	c Stewart b Gough	5	c Stewart b Cork	93
CL Hooper	b Martin	40	c Martin b Gough	14
BC Lara	lbw b Fraser	6	c Stewart b Gough	54
JC Adams	lbw b Fraser	54	c Hick b Cork	13
*RB Richardson	c Stewart b Fraser	49	lbw b Cork	0
KLT Arthurton	c Gough b Fraser	75	c sub b Cork	0
+JR Murray	c & b Martin	16	c sub b Gough	3
OD Gibson	lbw b Gough	29	lbw b Cork	14
IR Bishop	b Cork	8	not out	10
CEL Ambrose	c Ramprakash b Fraser	12	c Illingworth b Cork	11
CA Walsh	not out	11	c Stewart b Cork	0
	(b 8, lb 11)	19	(lb 5)	5
	(all out)	324	(all out)	223

Bowling: Gough 27-2-84-2 Fraser 33-13-66-5 Cork 22-4-72-1 Martin 23.5-6-52-2 Illingworth 7-2-18-0
Gough 20-0-79-3 Fraser 25-9-57-0 Cork 19.3-5-43-7 Martin 7-0-30-0 Illingworth 7-4-9-0

Umpires: DR Shepherd and S Venkataraghavan (Ind)
TV Umpire: AGT Whitehead; Referee: JR Reid (NZ)

England v India
20,21,22,23,24 June 1996

Result: Match drawn

England Innings

*MA Atherton	lbw b Srinath	0	b Kumble	17
AJ Stewart	b Srinath	20	c Srinath	66
N Hussain	c Rathour b Ganguly	36	c Dravid b Srinath	28
GP Thorpe	b Srinath	89	c Rathour b Kumble	21
GA Hick	c Srinath b Ganguly	1	c Mongia b Prasad	6
RC Irani	b Prasad	1	b Mhambrey	41
+RC Russell	c Tendulkar b Prasad	124	lbw b Ganguly	38
CC Lewis	c Mongia b Prasad	31	not out	26
DG Cork	c Mongia b Prasad	0	c Azharuddin b Kumble	1
PJ Martin	c Tendulkar b Prasad	4	c Rathour b Prasad	23
AD Mullally	not out	0	not out	0
	(b 13, lb 11, nb 14)	38	(b 5, lb 5, nb 5)	11
	(all out)	344	(9 wickets declared)	278

Bowling: Srinath 33-9-76-3 Prasad 33.3-10-76-5 Mhambrey 19-3-58-0 Kumble 28-9-60-0 Ganguly 15-2-49-2 Tendulkar 2-1-1-0
Srinath 29-8-76-2 Prasad 24-8-54-2 Kumble 51-14-90-3 Ganguly 3-0-5-1 Mhambrey 14-3-47-1

India Innings

V Rathour	c Hussain b Cork	15
+NR Mongia	lbw b Lewis	24
SC Ganguly	b Mullally	131
SR Tendulkar	b Lewis	31
*M Azharuddin	c Russell b Mullally	16
A Jadeja	b Irani	10
R Dravid	c Russell b Lewis	95
A Kumble	lbw b Martin	14
J Srinath	b Mullally	19
PL Mhambrey	not out	15
BKV Prasad	c Stewart b Cork	4
	(b 11, lb 25, w 10, nb 9)	55
	(all out)	429

Bowling: Lewis 40-11-103-3 Cork 42.3-10-112-2 Mullally 39-14-71-3 Martin 34-10-70-1 Irani 12-3-31-1 Hick 2-0-8-0

Umpires: HD Bird and DB Hair (Aus)
TV Umpire: AGT Whitehead; Referee: CW Smith (WI)

England v Pakistan
25,26,27,28,29 July 1996

Result: Pakistan won by 164 runs

Pakistan Innings

Aamer Sohail	lbw b Brown	2		
Saeed Anwar	c Russell b Hick	74	c Russell b Mullally	88
Ijaz Ahmed	c Cork	1	lbw b Cork	76
Inzamam-ul-Haq	b Mullally	148	c Ealham b Cork	70
Saleem Malik	run out (Salisbury/Russell)	7	not out	27
Shadab Kabir	lbw b Cork	17	c Russell b Cork	33
*Wasim Akram	lbw b Ealham	10	not out	34
+Rashid Latif	c Hick b Salisbury	45		
Mushtaq Ahmed	c Russell b Mullally	11	c Thorpe b Brown	5
Waqar Younis	b Brown b Mullally	3		
Ata-ur-Rehman	not out	10		
	(b 3, lb 5, nb 3)	11	(b 4, lb 14, nb 1)	19
	(all out)	340	(5 wickets declared)	352

Bowling: Cork 28-6-100-2 Brown 17-2-78-1 Mullally 24-8-44-3 Salisbury 12.2-1-42-1 Ealham 21-4-42-1 Hick 6-0-26-1
Cork 24-4-86-3 Brown 16-2-60-1 Salisbury 20-4-63-0 Mullally 30.2-9-70-1 Hick 7-2-16-0 Ealham 16-4-37-0

England Innings

NV Knight	lbw b Waqar Younis	51	lbw b Waqar Younis	1
*MA Atherton	lbw b Wasim Akram	12	c sub (Asif Mujtaba) b Mushtaq Ahmed	64
AJ Stewart	lbw b Mushtaq Ahmed	39	c sub (Moin Khan) b Mushtaq Ahmed	89
GP Thorpe	b Ata-ur-Rehman	77	lbw b Mushtaq Ahmed	3
GA Hick	b Waqar Younis	4	b Waqar Younis	4
MA Ealham	c Rashid Latif b Ata-ur-Rehman	25	b Mushtaq Ahmed	5
+RC Russell	not out	41	c Rashid Latif b Waqar Younis	1
DG Cork	c Saeed Anwar b Ata-ur-Rehman	3	b Waqar Younis	3
IDK Salisbury	lbw b Waqar Younis	5	c Rashid Latif b Wasim Akram	40
AD Mullally	b Waqar Younis	0	c sub (Moin Khan) b Mushtaq Ahmed	6
SJE Brown	b Ata-ur-Rehman	1	not out	10
	(b 9, lb 13, w 1, nb 4)	27	(b 6, lb 7, nb 4)	17
	(all out)	285	(all out)	243

Bowling: Wasim Akram 22-6-49-1 Waqar Younis 24-6-69-4 Mushtaq Ahmed 38-5-92-1 Ata-ur-Rehman 15.4-3-50-4 Aamer Sohail 3-1-3-0
Wasim Akram 21.1-5-45-1 Waqar Younis 25-3-85-4 Mushtaq Ahmed 38-15-57-5 Ata-ur-Rehman 11-2-33-0 Saleem Malik 1-0-1-0 Shadab Kabir 1-0-9-0

Umpires: SA Bucknor (WI) and P Willey
TV Umpire: JW Holder; Referee: PL van der Merwe (SA)

England v Australia
19,20,21,22,23 June 1997

Result: Match drawn

England Innings

MA Butcher	c Blewett b McGrath	5	b Warne	87
*MA Atherton	c Taylor b McGrath	1	hit wicket b Kasprowicz	77
+AJ Stewart	b McGrath	1	c Kasprowicz b McGrath	13
N Hussain	lbw b McGrath	19	c & b Warne	0
GP Thorpe	c Blewett b Reiffel	21	not out	30
JP Crawley	c Healy b McGrath	1	not out	29
MA Ealham	c Elliott b Reiffel	7		
RDB Croft	c Healy b McGrath	2		
D Gough	c Healy b McGrath	10		
AR Caddick	lbw b McGrath	1		
DE Malcolm	not out	0		
	(b 4, nb 5)	9	(b 8, lb 14, w 1, nb 7)	30
	(all out)	77	(4 wickets declared)	266

Bowling: McGrath 20.3-8-38-8 Reiffel 15-9-17-2 Kasprowicz 5-1-9-0 Warne 2-0-9-0
McGrath 20-5-65-1 Reiffel 13-5-29-0 Kasprowicz 13-3-54-1 Warne 19-4-47-2 Bevan 8-1-29-0 SR Waugh 4-0-20-0

Australia Innings

*MA Taylor	b Gough	1
MTG Elliott	c Crawley b Caddick	112
GS Blewett	c Hussain b Croft	45
ME Waugh	c Malcolm b Caddick	33
SK Warne	c Hussain b Gough	0
SR Waugh	lbw b Caddick	0
MG Bevan	c Stewart b Caddick	0
+IA Healy	not out	13
PR Reiffel	not out	1
MS Kasprowicz		
GD McGrath		
	(b 1, lb 3)	4
	(7 wickets declared)	213

Bowling: Gough 20-4-82-2 Caddick 22-6-71-4 Malcolm 7-1-26-0 Croft 12.5-30-1

Umpires: DR Shepherd and S Venkataraghavan (Ind)
TV Umpire: DJ Constant; Referee: RS Madugalle (SL)

England v South Africa
18,19,20,21 June 1998

Result: South Africa won by 10 wickets

South Africa Innings

Batsman		1st		2nd
AM Bacher	c Stewart b Cork	22		
G Kirsten	b Cork	4	not out	9
JH Kallis	b Cork	0		
DJ Cullinan	c Stewart b Cork	16	not out	5
*WJ Cronje	c Ramprakash b Ealham	81		
JN Rhodes	c Stewart b Fraser	117		
SM Pollock	c Hussain b Cork	14		
+MV Boucher	c Stewart b Headley	35		
L Klusener	b Headley	34		
AA Donald	not out	7		
PR Adams	c Stewart b Cork	3		
	(b 1, lb 20, nb 6)	27	(nb 1)	1
	(all out)	360	(0 wickets)	15

Bowling: Fraser 31-8-78-1 Cork 31.1-5-119-6 Headley 22-2-69-2 Ealham 15-2-50-1 Croft 9-3-23-0
Fraser 1-0-10-0 Cork 0.1-0-5-0

England Innings

Batsman		1st		2nd
SP James	c Boucher b Donald	10	c Kallis b Pollock	0
MA Atherton	c Kirsten b Pollock	0	c Kallis b Adams	44
N Hussain	c Boucher b Donald	15	lbw b Klusener	105
*+AJ Stewart	lbw b Pollock	14	c Boucher b Kallis	56
DW Headley	c Boucher b Donald	2	c Cronje b Adams	1
GP Thorpe	c Bacher b Kallis	10	lbw b Kallis	0
MR Ramprakash	c Boucher b Donald	12	b Klusener	0
M A Ealham	run out (Kirsten/Bacher)	8	b Kallis	4
DG Cork	c Klusener b Pollock	12	c Boucher b Kallis	2
RDB Croft	not out	6	not out	16
ARC Fraser	c Boucher b Donald	1	c Pollock b Adams	17
	(b 8, lb 10, nb 2)	20	(b 1, lb 6, w 5, nb 7)	19
	(all out)	110	(all out)	336

Bowling: Donald 15.3-5-32-5 Pollock 18-5-42-3 Klusener 8-5-10-0 Kallis 5-3-8-1
Donald 24-6-82-0 Pollock 27-16-29-1 Klusener 23-5-54-2 Kallis 19-9-244-4 Adams 23-7-62-3 Cronje 4-2-6-0

Umpires: G Sharp and DB Hair (Aus)
TV Umpire: b Dudleston; Referee: Javed Burki (Pak)

England v New Zealand
22,23,24,25 July 1999

Result: New Zealand won by 9 wickets

England Innings

Batsman		1st		2nd
MA Butcher	c Parore b Cairns	8	c Astle b Vettori	20
AJ Stewart	c Fleming b Nash	50	b Vettori	35
*N Hussain	c Parore b Cairns	61	absent hurt	0
GP Thorpe	c Astle b Cairns	7	b Cairns	7
MR Ramprakash	lbw b Nash	4	c Parore b Astle	24
A Habib	b Nash	6	c Astle b Allott	19
+CMW Read	b Cairns	0	lbw b Nash	37
AR Caddick	run out (Horne/Astle)	18	c Fleming b Allott	45
DW Headley	lbw b Cairns	4	c Fleming b Allott	12
AD Mullally	c Astle b Cairns	0	c Twose b Cairns	10
PCR Tufnell	not out	1	not out	5
	(b 5, lb 8, nb 14)	27	(b 5, lb 3, nb 7)	15
	(all out)	186	(all out)	229

Bowling: Allott 10-1-37-0 Cairns 21.1-1-77-6 Nash 23-11-50-3 Astle 7-3-9-0
Allott 16.4-6-36-3 Cairns 25-6-67-2 Vettori 31-12-62-2 Nash 25-9-50-1 Astle 4-2-6-1

New Zealand Innings

Batsman		1st		2nd
MJ Horne	c Hussain b Headley	100	lbw b Caddick	26
MD Bell	lbw b Headley	15	not out	26
*SP Fleming	c Read b Mullally	1	not out	5
NJ Astle	c Read b Mullally	43		
RG Twose	c Caddick b Headley	52		
CD McMillan	c Read b Caddick	3		
DL Vettori	c Thorpe b Tufnell	54		
+AC Parore	b Caddick	12		
CL Cairns	c Caddick	31		
DJ Nash	c Mullally b Tufnell	6		
GI Allott	not out	1		
	(b 1, lb 24, w 2, nb 13)	40	(b 2, nb 1)	3
	(all out)	358	(1 wicket)	60

Bowling: Mullally 27-7-98-2 Caddick 34-11-92-3 Headley 27-7-74-3 Tufnell 27.1-7-61-2 Butcher 3-0-7-0 Ramprakash 1-0-1-0
Mullally 5-0-21-0 Caddick 10-4-18-1 Tufnell 8-2-19-0

Umpires: MJ Kitchen and RE Koertzen (SA)
TV Umpire: NT Plews; Referee: PL van der Merwe (SA)

England v Zimbabwe
18,19,20,21 May 2000

Result: England won by an innings and 209 runs

Zimbabwe Innings

Batsman		1st		2nd
GW Flower	b Caddick	4	lbw b Gough	2
TR Gripper	c Stewart b Caddick	1	c Knight b Gough	5
MW Goodwin	c Knight b Gough	18	lbw b Caddick	11
ADR Campbell	c Stewart b Caddick	0	lbw b Gough	4
*+A Flower	c Atherton b Giddins	24	lbw b Gough	2
NC Johnson	c Gough b Giddins	14	c Hick b Caddick	9
GJ Whittall	b Giddins	15	c Hick b Caddick	23
HH Streak	c Atherton b Giddins	4	c Knight b Giddins	0
BC Strang	c Ramprakash b Giddins	0	not out	37
BA Murphy	c Stewart b Gough	0	lbw b Giddins	14
M Mbangwa	not out	1	lbw b Giddins	8
	(lb 2)	2	(lb 1, nb 7)	8
	(all out)	83	(all out)	123

Bowling: Gough 12.3-1-36-2 Caddick 8-3-28-3 Flintoff 3-2-2-0 Giddins 7-2-15-5
Gough 15-3-57-4 Caddick 16.2-5-38-4 Giddins 7-3-27-2

England Innings

MA Atherton	lbw b Streak	55
MR Ramprakash	c Murphy b Streak	10
*N Hussain	c Murphy b Streak	10
GA Hick	lbw b Streak	101
+AJ Stewart	not out	124
NV Knight	c Johnson b Whittall	44
A Flintoff	c Streak b Whittall	1
CP Schofield	c Johnson b Whittall	0
AR Caddick	c A Flower b Streak	13
D Gough	c Campbell b Murphy	5
ESH Giddins	c Strang b Streak	7
	(b 5, lb 29, w 1, nb 5)	40
	(all out)	415

Bowling: Streak 35.5-12-87-6 Strang 27-4-86-0 Mbangwa 21-5-69-0 Johnson 20-5-55-0 Whittall 7-0-27-3 Murphy 25-6-57-1

Umpires: DL Orchard (SA) and P Willey
TV Umpire: JW Holder; Referee: GT Dowling (NZ)

England v West Indies
29,30 June, 1 July 2000

Result: England won by 2 wickets

West Indies Innings

Batsman		1st		2nd
SL Campbell	c Hoggard b Cork	82	c Gough b Caddick	4
AFG Griffith	run out (Caddick/Stewart)	27	c Stewart b Gough	1
WW Hinds	c Stewart b Cork	59	c Ramprakash b Caddick	5
BC Lara	c Stewart b Gough	6	c Cork b Caddick	5
S Chanderpaul	b Gough	22	c Ramprakash b Gough	9
*JC Adams	lbw b Gough	1	lbw b Cork	12
+RD Jacobs	c Stewart b Cork	10	c Atherton b Caddick	12
CEL Ambrose	c Ramprakash b Cork	5	c Hoggard b Caddick	3
FA Rose	lbw b Gough	29	c & b Cork	1
RD King	not out	12	lbw b Cork	7
CA Walsh	lbw b Caddick	1	not out	3
	(b 1, lb 8, w 2, nb 2)	13	(lb 8, nb 1)	9
	(all out)	267	(all out)	54

Bowling: Gough 21-5-72-4 Caddick 20.3-3-58-1 Hoggard 13-3-49-0 Cork 24-8-39-4 White 8-1-30-0 Vaughan 3-1-10-0
Gough 8-3-17-2 Caddick 13-8-16-5 Cork 5.4-2-13-3

England Innings

Batsman		1st		2nd
MA Atherton	c Lara b Walsh	1	lbw b Walsh	45
MR Ramprakash	c Lara b Ambrose	0	b Walsh	2
MP Vaughan	c Ambrose	4	c Jacobs b Walsh	41
GA Hick	b Ambrose	25	c Lara b Walsh	15
*+AJ Stewart	c Jacobs b Walsh	28	lbw b Walsh	18
NV Knight	c Campbell b King	27	c Jacobs b Rose	2
C White	run out (Adams)	27	c Jacobs b Walsh	0
DG Cork	c Jacobs b Walsh	4	not out	33
AR Caddick	c Campbell b Walsh	6	lbw b Ambrose	7
D Gough	c Lara b Ambrose	13	not out	4
MJ Hoggard	not out	12		
	(lb 5, nb 3)	8	(b 3, lb 8, w 1, nb 12)	24
	(all out)	134	(8 wickets)	191

Bowling: Ambrose 14.2-6-30-4 Walsh 17-6-43-4 Rose 7-2-32-0 King 10-3-24-1
Ambrose 22-11-22-1 Walsh 23.5-5-74-6 Rose 16-3-67-1 King 8-2-17-0

Umpires: JH Hampshire and S Venkataraghavan (Ind)
TV Umpire: R Julian; Referee: GT Dowling (NZ)

England v Pakistan
17,18,19,20 May 2001

Result: England won by an innings and 9 runs

England Innings

MA Atherton	b Azhar Mahmood	42
ME Trescothick	c Azhar Mahmood b Abdul Razzaq	36
MP Vaughan	c Rashid Latif b Azhar Mahmood	32
*N Hussain	c Rashid Latif b Azhar Mahmood	64
GP Thorpe	c Abdul Razzaq b Waqar Younis	80
RJ Sidebottom	c Inzamam-ul-Haq b Wasim Akram	4
+AJ Stewart	lbw b Shoaib Akhtar	44
IJ Ward	c Abdul Razzaq b Waqar Younis	39
DG Cork	c Younis Khan b Wasim Akram	25
AR Caddick	b Azhar Mahmood	5
D Gough	not out	5
	(b 1, lb 5, w 1, nb 8)	15
	(all out)	391

Bowling: Wasim Akram 34.9-9-92-2 Waqar Younis 25-5-77-2 Shoaib Akhtar 19-4-64-1 Abdul Razzaq 21-2-68-1 Younis Khan 5-0-27-0 Azhar Mahmood 26-12-50-4

Pakistan Innings

Batsman		1st		2nd
Saeed Anwar	c Atherton b Gough	12	c Thorpe b Caddick	8
Saleem Elahi	c Atherton b Caddick	0	c Thorpe b Caddick	0
Abdul Razzaq	c Stewart b Caddick	22	c Stewart b Cork	53
Inzamam-ul-Haq	c Stewart b Caddick	13	c Stewart b Cork	20
Yousuf Youhana	lbw b Gough	26	c Vaughan b Gough	6
Younis Khan	b Cork	58	lbw b Cork	1
Azhar Mahmood	c Trescothick b Caddick	14	c Stewart b Caddick	24
+Rashid Latif	c Stewart b Gough	18	c Stewart b Gough	20
Wasim Akram	not out	19	c Thorpe b Gough	12
*Waqar Younis	c Thorpe b Gough	0	c Stewart b Cork	21
Shoaib Akhtar	b Gough	0	not out	2
	(b 1, lb 7, nb 13)	21	(lb 6, nb 6)	12
	(all out)	203	(all out)	179

Bowling: Gough 16-5-61-5 Caddick 17-3-52-4 Sidebottom 11-0-38-0 Cork 11-3-42-1 Trescothick 2-1-2-0
Gough 16-4-40-3 Caddick 18-3-54-4 Sidebottom 9-2-26-0 Cork 15.3-3-41-3 Vaughan 1-0-12-0

Umpires: DB Hair (Aus) and P Willey
TV Umpire: B Dudleston; Referee: BF Hastings (NZ)

England v Australia
19,20,21,22 July 2001

Result: Australia won by 8 wickets

England Innings

Batsman		1st		2nd
*MA Atherton	lbw b McGrath	37	b Warne	20
ME Trescothick	c Gilchrist b Gillespie	15	c Gilchrist b Gillespie	3
MA Butcher	c ME Waugh b McGrath	21	c Gilchrist b Gillespie	83
GP Thorpe	c Gilchrist b McGrath	20	lbw b Lee	2
MR Ramprakash	b Lee	14	b Gillespie	40
+AJ Stewart	c Gilchrist b McGrath	0	lbw b McGrath	28
IJ Ward	not out	23	c Ponting b McGrath	0
C White	c Hayden b McGrath	0	not out	27
DG Cork	c Ponting b Gillespie	24	c Warne b McGrath	2
AR Caddick	b Warne	0	c Gilchrist b Warne	7
D Gough	b Warne	5	c ME Waugh b Gillespie	1
	(b 7, lb 8, w 2, nb 11)	28	(b 3, lb 2, nb 9)	14
	(all out)	187	(all out)	227

Bowling: McGrath 24-9-54-5 Gillespie 18-6-56-2 Lee 16-3-46-1 Warne 5.3-0-16-2
McGrath 19-4-60-3 Gillespie 16-4-53-5 Lee 9-1-41-1 Warne 20-4-58-1 ME Waugh 2-1-12-0

Australia Innings

Batsman		1st		2nd
MJ Slater	c Stewart b Caddick	25	c Butcher b Caddick	4
ML Hayden	c Butcher b Caddick	0	not out	6
RT Ponting	c Thorpe b Gough	14	lbw b Gough	4
ME Waugh	run out (Gough)	108	not out	0
*SR Waugh	c Stewart b Cork	45		
DR Martyn	c Stewart b Caddick	52		
+AC Gilchrist	c Stewart b Gough	90		
SK Warne	c Stewart b Caddick	5		
B Lee	b Caddick	20		
JN Gillespie	b Gough	9		
GD McGrath	not out	0		
	(lb 9, w 1, nb 23)	33		0
	(all out)	401	(2 wickets)	14

Bowling: Gough 25-3-115-3 Caddick 32.1-4-101-5 White 7-1-80-0 Cork 23-3-84-1 Butcher 3-1-12-0
Gough 2-0-5-1 Caddick 1.1-0-9-1

Umpires: SA Bucknor (WI) and JW Holder
TV Umpire: JW Lloyds; Referee: Talat Ali (Pak)

England v Sri Lanka
16,17,18,19,20 May 2002

Result: Match Drawn

Sri Lanka Innings

MS Atapattu	c Trescothick b Cork	185	c Butcher b Caddick	7
*ST Jayasuriya	run out (Vaughan/Stewart)	18		
+KC Sangakkara	c Flintoff b Hoggard	10	not out	6
DPMD Jayawardene	c Trescothick b Flintoff	107	not out	14
PA de Silva	c Stewart b Cork	88		
RP Arnold	c Trescothick b Hoggard	50		
HP Tillakaratne	not out	17		
WPUJC Vaas	c Trescothick b Cork	6		
DNT Zoysa	c Stewart b Flintoff	28		
TCB Fernando	not out	6		
PDRL Perera				
	(b 1, lb 13, w 1, nb 25)	40	(b 5, lb 2, nb 8)	15
	(8 wickets dec)	555	(1 wicket)	42

Bowling: Caddick 38.3-6-135-0 Hoggard 39-4-160-2 Cork 35.3-11-93-3 Flintoff 39-8-101-2 Butcher 3-0-17-0 Vaughan 14-2-35-0
Caddick 7-2-10-1 Flintoff 5-0-18-0 Hoggard 1-0-7-0

England Innings

ME Trescothick	c Jayasuriya b Zoysa	13	lbw b Zoysa	76
MP Vaughan	c Zoysa b Perera	64	c Sangakkara b Perera	115
MA Butcher	c Jayawardene b Fernando	17	run out (Vaas/Sangakkara)	105
*N Hussain	c Sangakkara b Zoysa	57	lbw b Perera	68
GP Thorpe	lbw b Perera	27	c Fernando b de Silva	65
JP Crawley	c Sangakkara b Vaas	31	not out	41
+AJ Stewart	run out (sub [UDU Chandana])	7	not out	26
A Flintoff	c Sangakkara b Fernando	12		
DG Cork	c Sangakkara b Fernando	0		
AR Caddick	c Sangakkara b Perera	13		
MJ Hoggard	not out	0		
	(b 4, lb 7, w 9, nb 14)	34	(b 1, lb 9, w 1, nb 22)	33
	(all out)	275	(5 wickets dec)	529

Bowling: Vaas 21.1-4-51-1 Zoysa 19-3-82-2 Fernando 22-5-83-3 Perera 11-0-48-3
Vaas 44-8-113-0 Zoysa 34-6-84-1 Perera 30-4-90-2 de Silva 27-7-63-1 Fernando 26-1-96-0 Jayasuriya 25-6-66-0 Arnold 4-1-7-0 Tillakaratne 1-1-0-0

Umpires: DJ Harper (Aus) and S Venkataraghavan (Ind)
TV Umpire: JW Lloyds; Referee: GR Viswanath (Ind)

England v India
25,26,27,28,29 July 2002

Result: England won by 170 runs

England Innings

MA Butcher	c Jaffer b Kumble	29	lbw b Kumble	18
MP Vaughan	lbw b Khan	0	c Jaffer b Nehra	100
*N Hussain	c Ratra b Agarkar	155	c Ratra b Agarkar	12
GP Thorpe	b Khan	4	c Ganguly b Kumble	1
JP Crawley	c Dravid b Sehwag	64	not out	100
+AJ Stewart	lbw b Khan	19	st Ratra b Kumble	33
A Flintoff	c Ratra b Agarkar	59	c Tendulkar b Nehra	7
C White	st Ratra b Kumble	53	not out	6
AF Giles	b Nehra	19		
SP Jones	c Dravid b Kumble	44		
MJ Hoggard	not out	10		
	(b 11, lb 11, w 2, nb 7)	31	(b 5, lb 14, nb 5)	24
	(all out)	487	(6 wickets dec)	301

Bowling: Nehra 30-4-101-1 Khan 36-13-90-3 Agarkar 21-3-98-2 Kumble 42.2-9-128-3 Ganguly 3-1-16-0 Sehwag 10-0-32-1
Nehra 14-1-80-2 Khan 11-1-41-0 Kumble 24-1-84-3 Agarkar 11.4-1-53-1 Tendulkar 2-0-14-0 Sehwag 2-0-10-0

India Innings

W Jaffer	b Hoggard	1	c Hussain b Vaughan	53
V Sehwag	b Giles	84	b Jones	27
R Dravid	c Vaughan b Hoggard	46	b Giles	63
A Nehra	lbw b Hoggard	1	c Thorpe b White	19
SR Tendulkar	c Stewart b White	16	b Hoggard	12
*SC Ganguly	c Vaughan b Flintoff	5	lbw b Hoggard	0
VVS Laxman	not out	43	c Vaughan b Jones	74
+A Ratra	c Stewart b Jones	1	c Butcher b Hoggard	1
AB Agarkar	c Flintoff b Jones	2	not out	109
A Kumble	b White	0	c & b Hoggard	15
Z Khan	c Thorpe b Hoggard	3	c Stewart b White	7
	(b 4, lb 8, nb 8)	20	(b 4, lb 3, w 2, nb 8)	17
	(all out)	221	(all out)	397

Bowling: Hoggard 16.5-4-33-3 Flintoff 19-9-22-2 Giles 9-1-47-1 Jones 21-2-61-2 White 16-3-46-2
Hoggard 24-7-87-4 Flintoff 17-2-87-0 White 16.4-2-61-2 Jones 17-1-68-2 Giles 29-7-75-1 Vaughan 6-2-12-1

Umpires: RE Koertzen (SA) and RB Tiffin (Zim)
TV Umpire: P Willey; Referee: MJ Procter (SA)

England v Zimbabwe
22,23,24 May 2003

Result: England won by an innings and 92 runs

England Innings

ME Trescothick	c Ervine b Blignaut	59
MP Vaughan	b Streak	8
MA Butcher	c Vermeulen b Price	137
*N Hussain	c Hondo b Friend	19
RWT Key	c Taibu b Streak	18
+AJ Stewart	c Taibu b Streak	26
A McGrath	b Ervine	69
AF Giles	b Blignaut	52
SJ Harmison	c Ebrahim b Ervine	0
MJ Hoggard	c Ebrahim b Blignaut	19
JM Anderson	not out	4
	(b 14, lb 27, w 3, nb 17)	61
	(all out)	472

Bowling: Streak 37-9-99-3 Blignaut 26.1-4-96-3 Hondo 14-4-45-0 Ervine 22-5-95-2 Friend 13-2-49-1 Price 20-6-44-1 Flower 1-0-3-0

Zimbabwe Innings

DD Ebrahim	c McGrath b Butcher	68	c Key b Harmison	6
MA Vermeulen	b Anderson	1	c Trescothick b Butcher	61
SV Carlisle	c Trescothick b Hoggard	11	lbw b Butcher	24
GW Flower	c Key b Hoggard	3	c Trescothick b Harmison	26
+T Taibu	c Hoggard b Harmison	25	c Butcher b McGrath	16
SM Ervine	lbw b Hoggard	4	c Trescothick b McGrath	4
*HH Streak	b Anderson	10	lbw b McGrath	11
AM Blignaut	c Butcher b Anderson	3	b Butcher	6
TJ Friend	b Anderson	0	c Giles b Butcher	43
RW Price	not out	7	c Trescothick b Giles	26
DT Hondo	not out	0	not out	0
	(b 5, lb 1, w 1, nb 8)	15	(b 1, lb 6, w 3)	10
	(all out)	147	(all out)	233

Bowling: Hoggard 18-8-24-3 Anderson 16-4-73-5 Harmison 16-5-36-1 Butcher 5-2-8-1
Anderson 15-4-65-0 Hoggard 15-5-35-0 Harmison 12-4-35-2 Giles 8-2-15-1 Butcher 12.5-0-60-4 McGrath 6-1-16-3

Umpires: SA Bucknor (WI) and DL Orchard (SA)
TV Umpire: NA Mallender; Referee: CH Lloyd (WI)

England v South Africa
31 July, 1,2,3 August 2003

Result: South Africa won by an innings and 92 runs

England Innings

ME Trescothick	b Ntini	6	c Adams b Ntini	23
*MP Vaughan	c sub b Ntini	33	c Pollock b Hall	29
MA Butcher	c Hall b Pollock	19	c Kirsten b Hall	70
N Hussain	b Hall	14	c Boucher b Ntini	61
A McGrath	c Kirsten b Hall	4	c Boucher b Pollock	13
+AJ Stewart	c Adams b Ntini	7	c Hall b Ntini	0
A Flintoff	c Adams b Ntini	11	st Boucher b Adams	142
AF Giles	c Pollock b Hall	7	c Pollock b Hall	23
D Gough	c Adams b Pollock	34	c Adams b Pollock	14
SJ Harmison	b Ntini	0	c Hall b Ntini	7
JM Anderson	not out	21	not out	4
	(b 5, lb 3, w 1, nb 3, pen 5)	17	(b 6, lb 5, w 3, nb 17)	31
	(all out)	173	(all out)	417

Bowling: Pollock 14.4-5-28-2 Ntini 17-3-75-5 Pretorius 4-0-20-0 Hall 10-4-18-3 Adams 3-0-19-0

South Africa Innings

*GC Smith	b Anderson	259
HH Gibbs	b Harmison	49
G Kirsten	b McGrath	108
HH Dippenaar	c Butcher b Giles	92
JA Rudolph	c Stewart b Flintoff	26
+MV Boucher	b Anderson	68
SM Pollock	not out	10
AJ Hall	not out	6
PR Adams		
D Pretorius		
M Ntini		
	(b 25, lb 21, w 5, nb 13)	64
	(6 wickets declared)	682

Bowling: Gough 28-3-127-0 Anderson 27-6-90-2 Harmison 22-3-103-1 Flintoff 40-10-115-1 Giles 43-5-142-1 Butcher 6-1-19-0 McGrath 11-0-40-1

Umpires: SA Bucknor (WI) and DB Hair (Aus)
TV Umpire: P Willey; Referee: RS Madugalle (SL)

England v Australia
6,7,8 September 1880

Result: England won by 5 wickets

England Innings

EM Grace	c Alexander b Bannerman	36	b Boyle	0
WG Grace	b Palmer	152	not out	9
AP Lucas	b Bannerman	55	c Blackham b Palmer	2
W Barnes	b Alexander	28	c Moule b Boyle	5
*Lord Harris	c Bonnor b Alexander	52		
F. Penn	b Bannerman	23	not out	27
AG Steel	c Boyle b Moule	42		
+Hon.A Lyttelton	not out	11	b Palmer	13
GF Grace	c Bannerman b Moule	0	b Palmer	0
A Shaw	b Moule	0		
F Morley	run out	2		
	(b 8, lb 11)	19	(nb 1)	1
	(all out)	420	(5 wickets)	57

Bowling: Boyle 44-17-71-0 Palmer 70-27-116-1 Alexander 32-10-69-2 Bannerman 50-12-111-3 McDonnell 2-0-11-0 Moule 12.3-4-23-3
Boyle 17-7-21-2 Palmer 16.3-5-35-3

Australia Innings

AC Bannerman	b Morley	32	c Lucas b Shaw	8
*WL Murdoch	c Barnes b Steel	0	not out	153
TU Groube	b Steel	11	c Shaw b Morley	0
PS McDonnell	c Barnes b Morley	27	lbw b WG Grace	43
J Slight	c GF Grace b Morley	11	c Harris b WG Grace	0
+JM Blackham	c & b Morley	0	c EM Grace b Morley	19
GJ Bonnor	c GF Grace b Shaw	2	b Steel	16
HF Boyle	not out	36	run out	3
GE Palmer	b Morley	6	c & b Steel	4
G Alexander	c WG Grace b Steel	6	c Shaw b Morley	33
WH Moule	c Morley b WG Grace	6	b Barnes	34
	(b 9, lb 3)	12	(b 7, lb 7)	14
	(all out)	149	(all out)	327

Bowling: Morley 32-9-56-5 Steel 29-9-58-3 Shaw 13-5-21-1 WG Grace 1.1-0-2-1
Morley 61-30-90-3 Steel 31-6-73-2 Shaw 33-18-42-1 WG Grace 28-10-66-2 Barnes 8.3-3-17-1 Lucas 12-7-23-0 Penn 3-1-2-0

Umpires: HH Stephenson and RA Thoms

England v Australia
28,29 August 1882

Result: Australia won by 7 runs

Australia Innings

AC Bannerman	c Grace b Peate	9	c Studd b Barnes	13
HH Massie	b Ulyett	1	b Steel	55
*WL Murdoch	b Peate	13	run out	29
GJ Bonnor	b Barlow	1	b Ulyett	2
TP Horan	b Barlow	3	c Grace b Peate	2
G Giffen	b Peate	2	c Grace b Peate	0
+JM Blackham	c Grace b Barlow	17	c Lyttelton b Peate	7
TW Garrett	c Read b Peate	10	not out	2
HF Boyle	b Barlow	2	b Steel	0
SP Jones	c Barnes b Barlow	0	run out	6
FR Spofforth	not out	4	b Peate	0
	(b 1)	1	(b 6)	6
	(all out)	63	(all out)	122

Bowling: Peate 38-24-31-4 Ulyett 9-5-11-1 Barlow 31-22-19-5 Steel 2-1-1-0
Peate 21-9-40-4 Ulyett 6-2-10-1 Barlow 13-5-27-0 Steel 7-0-15-2 Barnes 12-5-15-1 Studd 4-1-9-0

England Innings

RG Barlow	c Bannerman b Spofforth	11	b Spofforth	0
WG Grace	b Spofforth	4	c Bannerman b Boyle	32
G Ulyett	st Blackham b Spofforth	26	c Blackham b Spofforth	11
AP Lucas	c Blackham b Boyle	9	b Spofforth	5
+Hon.A Lyttelton	c Blackham b Spofforth	2	b Spofforth	12
CT Studd	b Spofforth	0	not out	0
JM Read	not out	19	b Spofforth	0
W Barnes	b Boyle	5	c Murdoch b Boyle	2
AG Steel	b Garrett	14	c & b Spofforth	0
*AN Hornby	b Spofforth	2	b Spofforth	9
E Peate	c Boyle b Spofforth	0	b Boyle	2
	(b 6, lb 2, nb 1)	9	(b 3, nb 1)	4
	(all out)	101	(all out)	77

Bowling: Spofforth 36.3-18-46-7 Garrett 16-7-22-1 Boyle 19-7-24-2
Spofforth 28-15-44-7 Garrett 7-2-10-0 Boyle 20-11-19-3

Umpires: L Greenwood and RA Thoms

England v Australia
11,12,13 August 1884

Result: Match drawn

Australia Innings

AC Bannerman	c Read b Peate	4	
PS McDonnell	c Ulyett b Peate	103	
*WL Murdoch	c Peate b Barnes	211	
HJH Scott	c Lyttelton b Barnes	102	
G Giffen	c Steel b Ulyett	32	
GJ Bonnor	c Read b Grace	8	
WE Midwinter	c +Grace b Lyttelton	30	
+JM Blackham	lbw b Lyttelton	31	
GE Palmer	not out	8	
FR Spofforth	b Lyttelton	4	
HF Boyle	c Harris b Lyttelton	1	
	(b 7, lb 10)	17	
	(all out)	551	

Bowling: Peate 63-25-99-2 Ulyett 56-24-96-1 Steel 34-7-71-0 Barnes 52-25-81-2 Barlow 50-22-72-0 Grace 24-14-23-1
Read 7-0-36-0 Scotton 5-1-20-0 Harris 5-1-15-0 Lyttelton 12-5-19-4 Shrewsbury 3-2-2-0

England Innings

WG Grace	run out	19		
WH Scotton	c Scott b Giffen	90		
W Barnes	c Midwinter b Spofforth	19		
A Shrewsbury	c Blackham b Midwinter	10	c Scott b Giffen	37
AG Steel	lbw b Palmer	31		
G Ulyett	c Bannerman b Palmer	10		
RG Barlow	c Murdoch b Palmer	0	not out	21
*Lord Harris	lbw b Palmer	14	not out	6
+Hon.A Lyttelton	b Spofforth	8	b Boyle	17
WW Read	b Boyle	117		
E Peate	not out	8		
	(b 8, lb 7, w 6, nb 3)	24	(b 3, lb 1)	4
	(all out)	346	(2 wickets)	85

Bowling: Bonnor 13-4-33-0 Palmer 54-19-90-4 Spofforth 58-31-81-2 Boyle 13-7-24-1 Midwinter 31-16-41-1 Giffen 26-13-36-1 Scott 3-0-17-0
Palmer 2-1-2-0 Spofforth 6-2-14-0 Boyle 8-1-32-1 Midwinter 3-0-15-0 Giffen 7-1-18-1

Umpires: FH Farrands and CK Pullin

England v Australia
12,13,14 August 1886

Result: England won by an innings and 217 runs

England Innings

WG Grace	c Blackham b Spofforth	170
WH Scotton	b Garrett	34
A Shrewsbury	c Jones b Trumble	44
WW Read	c Jones b Spofforth	94
W Barnes	c Evans b Trumble	3
*AG Steel	st Blackham b Trumble	9
RG Barlow	c Trumble b Garrett	3
G Ulyett	c McIlwraith b Garrett	0
J Briggs	c Trumble b Spofforth	53
+EFS Tylecote	not out	10
GA Lohmann	b Spofforth	7
	(b 3, lb 2, nb 2)	7
	(all out)	434

Bowling: Giffen 62-32-96-0 Garrett 99-55-88-3 Palmer 47-21-80-0 Bruce 6-2-9-0 Spofforth 30.1-12-65-4 Evans 13-10-6-0 Trumble 47-14-83-3

Australia Innings

SP Jones	c Grace b Lohmann	2	c Read b Lohmann	2
GE Palmer	c Barlow b Briggs	15	st Tylecote b Steel	35
G Giffen	c Shrewsbury b Briggs	5	c & b Lohmann	47
*HJH Scott	c Tylecote b Lohmann	6	c Grace b Lohmann	4
JW Trumble	c Read b Lohmann	13	c Read b Briggs	18
J McIlwraith	b Lohmann	2	c Tylecote b Briggs	7
+JM Blackham	c & b Briggs	0	c Grace b Briggs	5
TW Garrett	c Grace b Lohmann	2	c Shrewsbury b Lohmann	4
W Bruce	c Ulyett b Lohmann	9	b Lohmann	11
E Evans	not out	9	run out	3
FR Spofforth	b Lohmann	1	not out	5
	(b 4)	4	(b 7, lb 1)	8
	(all out)	68	(all out)	149

Bowling: Lohmann 30.2-17-36-7 Briggs 30-17-28-3
Lohmann 37-14-68-5 Briggs 32-19-30-3 Barlow 14-8-13-0 Barnes 7-4-10-0 Steel 7-1-20-1

Umpires: RP Carpenter and FH Farrands

England v Australia
13,14 August 1888

Result: England won by an innings and 137 runs

Australia Innings

AC Bannerman	c Lohmann b Barnes	13	b Barnes	5
*PS McDonnell	c Lohmann b Peel	0	b Peel	32
GHS Trott	b Briggs	13	st Wood b Peel	4
GJ Bonnor	b Briggs	0	c Wood b Barnes	5
JD Edwards	b Lohmann	26	c Read b Barnes	0
AH Jarvis	b Briggs	5	b Peel	8
SMJ Woods	run out	0	c Abel b Barnes	7
CTB Turner	b Briggs	0	b Peel	18
+JM Blackham	b Briggs	0	c Lohmann b Barnes	4
J Worrall	c Grace b Barnes	8	not out	0
JJ Ferris	not out	13	run out	16
	(b 1, lb 1)	2	(lb 1)	1
	(all out)	80	(all out)	100

Bowling: Lohmann 29.3-21-21-1 Peel 8-4-14-1 Briggs 37-24-25-5 Barnes 16-9-18-2
Lohmann 6-4-11-0 Peel 28.2-13-49-4 Briggs 6-3-7-0 Barnes 29-16-32-5

England Innings

*WG Grace	c Edwards b Turner	1
J Shuter	b Turner	28
G Ulyett	c Blackham b Turner	0
WW Read	b Turner	18
R Abel	run out	70
W Barnes	c Worrall b Turner	62
FH Sugg	b Turner	31
R Peel	b Woods	25
J Briggs	b Woods	0
GA Lohmann	not out	62
+H Wood	c Bannerman b Ferris	8
	(b 6, lb 4, w 2)	12
	(all out)	317

Bowling: Turner 60-24-112-6 Ferris 35.2-15-73-1 Trott 7-2-25-0 Woods 32-10-80-2 Worrall 4-1-15-0

Umpires: RP Carpenter and FH Farrands

England v Australia
11,12 August 1890

Result: England won by 2 wickets

Australia Innings

JJ Lyons	c WW Read b Martin	13	b Martin	21
CTB Turner	c Sharpe b Lohmann	12	b Martin	0
*WL Murdoch	b Martin	2	b Lohmann	6
JE Barrett	c Lohmann b Martin	0	b Martin	4
GHS Trott	c MacGregor b Martin	39	c Cranston b Martin	25
EJK Burn	c MacGregor b Lohmann	7	b Martin	15
+JM Blackham	b Martin	1	b Lohmann	1
JJ Ferris	c Lohmann b Sharpe	3	b Lohmann	1
PC Charlton	b Martin	10	b Sharpe	11
SE Gregory	b Lohmann	2	not out	4
H Trumble	not out	0	b Martin	6
		0	(b 7, lb 1)	8
	(all out)	92	(all out)	102

Bowling: Martin 27-9-50-6 Lohmann 32.2-19-34-3 Sharpe 6-3-8-1
Martin 30.2-12-52-6 Lohmann 21-8-32-3 Sharpe 9-5-10-1

England Innings

A Shrewsbury	c Trott b Turner	4	lbw b Ferris	9
*WG Grace	c Trumble b Ferris	0	c Trumble b Ferris	16
W Gunn	b Ferris	32	st Blackham b Ferris	1
WW Read	b Turner	1	b Turner	6
J Cranston	run out	16	c Trumble b Turner	15
JM Read	c Murdoch b Charlton	19	c Barrett b Turner	35
W Barnes	c Murdoch b Charlton	5	lbw b Ferris	5
GA Lohmann	c Gregory b Ferris	3	c Blackham b Ferris	2
+G MacGregor	c Turner b Ferris	1	not out	2
JW Sharpe	not out	5	not out	2
F. Martin	c Turner b Charlton	1		
	(b 9, lb 3, nb 1)	13	(lb 1, nb 1)	2
	(all out)	100	(8 wickets)	95

Bowling: Turner 22-12-37-2 Ferris 25-14-25-4 Trumble 2-0-7-0 Charlton 6-0-18-3
Turner 25-9-38-3 Ferris 23-8-49-5 Charlton 3-1-6-0

Umpires: CK Pullin and J. Street

Kennington Oval, London

England v Australia
14,15,16 August 1893

Result: England won by an innings and 43 runs

England Innings

*WG Grace	c Giffen b Trumble	68
AE Stoddart	b Turner	83
A Shrewsbury	c Graham b Giffen	66
W Gunn	b Giffen	16
A Ward	c & b Giffen	55
WW Read	b Giffen	52
FS Jackson	run out	103
J Briggs	b Giffen	0
WH Lockwood	c & b Giffen	10
+G MacGregor	lbw b Giffen	5
AW Mold	not out	0
	(b 19, lb 4, w 2)	25
	(all out)	483

Bowling: Turner 47-18-94-1 Trumble 47-16-101-1 McLeod 23-6-57-0 Giffen 54-17-128-7 Trott 6-1-33-0 Bruce 3-0-19-0 Lyons 7-1-26-0

Australia Innings

AC Bannerman	c MacGregor b Lockwood	10	c Read b Lockwood	55
JJ Lyons	b Briggs	19	c Briggs	31
GHS Trott	b Lockwood	0	c Read b Lockwood	92
SE Gregory	lbw b Briggs	9	c Shrewsbury b Briggs	6
H Graham	c MacGregor b Lockwood	0	b Briggs	42
G Giffen	c MacGregor b Lockwood	4	b Lockwood	53
W Bruce	not out	10	c Jackson b Mold	22
H Trumble	b Briggs	5	b Briggs	8
RW McLeod	c Lockwood b Briggs	2	c Jackson b Briggs	5
CTB Turner	b Briggs	7	b Briggs	0
*+JM Blackham	run out	17	not out	2
	(b 5, lb 3)	8	(b 18, lb 15)	33
	(all out)	91	(all out)	349

Bowling: Lockwood 19-9-37-4 Mold 4-0-12-0 Briggs 14.3-5-34-5
Lockwood 29-7-96-4 Mold 23-8-73-1 Briggs 35-6-114-5 Jackson 11-3-33-0

Umpires: H Draper and CK Pullin

England v Australia
10,11,12 August 1896

Result: England won by 66 runs

England Innings

*WG Grace	c Trott b Giffen	24	b Trumble	9
FS Jackson	c McKibbin b Trumble	45	b Trumble	2
KS Ranjitsinhji	b Giffen	8	st Kelly b McKibbin	11
R Abel	c & b Trumble	26	c Giffen b Trumble	21
AC MacLaren	b Trumble	20	b Jones	6
TW Hayward	b Trumble	0	c Trott b Trumble	13
EG Wynyard	c Darling b McKibbin	10	c Kelly b McKibbin	3
R Peel	b Trumble	0	b Trumble	0
+AFA Lilley	c Iredale b Trumble	2	c McKibbin b Trumble	6
JT Hearne	b McKibbin	8	b McKibbin	1
T Richardson	not out	1	not out	10
	(lb 1)	1	(lb 2)	2
	(all out)	145	(all out)	84

Bowling: Giffen 32-12-64-2 Trumble 40-10-59-6 McKibbin 9.3-0-21-2
Trumble 25-9-30-6 McKibbin 20-8-35-3 Giffen 1-0-4-0 Jones 3-0-13-1

Australia Innings

J Darling	c MacLaren b Hearne	47	b Hearne	0
FA Iredale	run out	30	c Jackson b Hearne	3
G Giffen	b Hearne	0	b Hearne	1
*GHS Trott	b Peel	5	c sub b Peel	4
SE Gregory	b Hearne	1	c Richardson b Peel	6
C Hill	run out	1	b Peel	0
H Donnan	c Hearne	10	c Hayward b Peel	4
+JJ Kelly	not out	10	lbw b Peel	3
H Trumble	b Hearne	3	not out	7
E Jones	c MacLaren b Peel	3	b Peel	3
TR McKibbin	b Hearne	0	c Abel b Hearne	16
	(b 8, lb 1)	9	(lb 2)	2
	(all out)	119	(all out)	44

Bowling: Peel 20-9-30-2 Hearne 26.1-10-41-6 Richardson 5-0-22-0 Hayward 2-0-17-0
Hearne 13-8-19-4 Peel 12-5-23-6 Richardson 1-1-0-0

Umpires: W Hearn and J Phillips (Aus)

England v Australia
14,15,16 August 1899

Result: Match drawn

England Innings

FS Jackson	b Jones	118
TW Hayward	c Iredale b McLeod	137
KS Ranjitsinhji	c Howell b Jones	54
CB Fry	c Worrall b Jones	60
*AC MacLaren	c Trumper b Trumble	49
CL Townsend	b Jones	38
WM Bradley	run out	0
WH Lockwood	b Trumble	24
AO Jones	b Noble	31
+AFA Lilley	c Iredale b Noble	37
W Rhodes	not out	8
	(b 9, lb 6, w 4, nb 1)	20
	(all out)	576

Bowling: Jones 53-12-164-4 Noble 35.4-12-96-2 Trumble 39-11-107-2 McLeod 48-15-131-1 Howell 15-3-43-0 Worrall 3-0-15-0

Australia Innings

J Worrall	c Hayward b Lockwood	55	c Lilley b Hayward	75
H Trumble	c & b Jones	24	not out	3
VT Trumper	c Lilley b Jones	6	c & b Rhodes	7
MA Noble	b Lockwood	9	not out	69
*J Darling	c Fry b Lockwood	71	run out	6
SE Gregory	c Jones b Lockwood	117	b Rhodes	2
FA Iredale	b Lockwood	0	
+JJ Kelly	lbw b Jones	4	
CE McLeod	not out	31	b Rhodes	77
E Jones	b Lockwood	0	
WP Howell	b Lockwood	4	
	(b 5, lb 10, w 1, nb 6)	22	(b 7, nb 4)	15
	(all out)	352	(5 wickets)	254

Bowling: Bradley 29-12-52-0 Rhodes 25-2-79-0 Lockwood 40.3-17-71-7 Jones 30-12-73-3 Townsend 5-0-16-0 Jackson 14-7-39-0
Bradley 17-8-32-0 Rhodes 22-8-27-3 Lockwood 15-7-33-0 Jones 12-2-43-0 Townsend 8-4-9-0 Jackson 13-2-54-0 Hayward 11-3-38-1 Fry 2-1-3-0

Umpires: W Richards and A White

England v Australia
11,12,13 August 1902

Result: England won by 1 wicket

Australia Innings

VT Trumper	b Hirst	42	run out	2
RA Duff	c Lilley b Hirst	23	b Lockwood	6
C Hill	b Hirst	11	c MacLaren b Hirst	34
*J Darling	c Lilley b Hirst	3	c MacLaren b Lockwood	15
MA Noble	c & b Jackson	52	b Braund	13
SE Gregory	b Hirst	23	b Braund	9
WW Armstrong	b Jackson	17	b Lockwood	21
AJY Hopkins	c MacLaren b Lockwood	40	c Lilley b Lockwood	3
H Trumble	not out	64	not out	7
+JJ Kelly	c Rhodes b Braund	39	b Lockwood	0
JV Saunders	lbw b Braund	0	c Tyldesley b Rhodes	2
	(b 5, lb 3, nb 2)	10	(b 7, lb 2)	9
	(all out)	324	(all out)	121

Bowling: Lockwood 24-2-85-1 Rhodes 28-9-46-0 Hirst 29-5-77-5 Braund 16.5-5-29-2 Jackson 20-4-66-2 Jessop 6-2-11-0
Lockwood 20-6-45-5 Rhodes 22-7-38-1 Hirst 5-1-7-1 Braund 9-1-15-2 Jackson 4-3-7-0

England Innings

*AC MacLaren	c Armstrong b Trumble	10	b Saunders	2
LCH Palairet	b Trumble	20	b Saunders	6
JT Tyldesley	b Trumble	33	b Saunders	0
TW Hayward	b Trumble	0	c Kelly b Saunders	7
Hon.FS Jackson	c Armstrong b Saunders	2	c Shrewsbury b Braund	49
LC Braund	b Hill b Trumble	22	c Kelly b Trumble	2
GL Jessop	b Trumble	13	c Noble b Armstrong	104
GH Hirst	c & b Trumble	43	not out	58
WH Lockwood	c Noble b Saunders	25	lbw b Trumble	2
+AFA Lilley	c Trumper b Trumble	0	c Darling b Trumble	16
W Rhodes	not out	0	not out	6
	(b 13, lb 2)	15	(b 5, lb 6)	11
	(all out)	183	(9 wickets)	263

Bowling: Trumble 31-13-65-8 Saunders 23-7-79-2 Noble 7-3-24-0
Trumble 33.5-4-108-4 Saunders 24-3-105-4 Noble 5-0-11-0 Armstrong 4-0-28-1

Umpires: CE Richardson and A White

England v Australia
14,15,16 August 1905

Result: Match drawn

England Innings

AC MacLaren	c Laver b Cotter	6	c Kelly b Armstrong	6
TW Hayward	hit wicket b Hopkins	59	lbw b Armstrong	2
JT Tyldesley	b Cotter	16	not out	112
CB Fry	b Cotter	144	c Armstrong b Noble	16
*Hon.FS Jackson	c Armstrong b Laver	76	b Cotter	31
RH Spooner	b Cotter	0	c sub b Noble	79
GH Hirst	c Noble b Laver	5	
EG Arnold	c Trumper b Cotter	40	b Cotter	0
W Rhodes	b Cotter	36	
+AFA Lilley	b Cotter	17	
W Brearley	not out	11	
	(b 11, lb 1, w 1, nb 7)	20	(b 4, lb 5, w 1, nb 5)	15
	(all out)	430	(6 wickets declared)	261

Bowling: Cotter 40-4-148-7 Noble 18-6-51-0 Armstrong 27-7-76-0 McLeod 13-2-47-0 Laver 17-3-41-2 Hopkins 11-2-32-1 Duff 4-1-15-0
Cotter 21-2-73-2 Noble 14.3-3-56-2 Armstrong 30-13-61-2 McLeod 11-2-27-0 Laver 3-0-18-0 Hopkins 1-0-11-0

Australia Innings

VT Trumper	b Brearley	4	c Spooner b Brearley	28
RA Duff	c & b Hirst	146	
C Hill	c Rhodes b Brearley	18	b Arnold	34
MA Noble	c MacLaren b Jackson	25	b Hirst	3
WW Armstrong	c sub b Hirst	18	not out	32
*J Darling	b Hirst	57	not out	12
AJY Hopkins	b Brearley	1	run out	10
CE McLeod	b Brearley	0	
+JJ Kelly	run out	42	
A Cotter	c Fry b Brearley	6	
FJ Laver	not out	14	
	(b 17, lb 9, w 1, nb 4)	31	(b 4, lb 1)	5
	(all out)	363	(4 wickets)	124

Bowling: Hirst 23-6-86-3 Brearley 31.1-8-110-5 Arnold 9-0-50-0 Rhodes 21-2-59-0 Jackson 9-1-27-1
Hirst 9-2-32-1 Brearley 11-2-41-1 Arnold 9-2-17-1 Rhodes 8-0-29-0

Umpires: J Phillips (Aus) and WAJ West

England v South Africa
19,20,21 August 1907

Result: Match drawn

England Innings

TW Hayward	lbw b Vogler	0	c Sherwell b Nourse	3
CB Fry	c & b Faulkner	129	b Vogler	3
JT Tyldesley	b Faulkner	8	c White b Nourse	11
*RE Foster	lbw b Vogler	51	c & b SJ Snooke	35
LC Braund	b Schwarz	18	c Schwarz b Vogler	34
GH Hirst	c SJ Snooke b Schwarz	4	hit wicket b Schwarz	16
GL Jessop	c SD Snooke b Sinclair	2	st Sherwell b Schwarz	11
JN Crawford	c SD Snooke b Schwarz	2	c Nourse b Vogler	2
+AFA Lilley	b Nourse	42	not out	9
C Blythe	b Nourse	10	b Schwarz	0
NA Knox	not out	8	b Vogler	3
	(b 6, lb 12, w 1, nb 2)	21	(b 3, lb 6, nb 2)	11
	(all out)	295	(all out)	138

Bowling: Vogler 31-7-86-2 Faulkner 27-2-78-2 Schwarz 27-8-45-3 White 9-2-28-0 Sinclair 14-4-27-1 Nourse 4-1-10-2
Vogler 14.3-2-49-4 Faulkner 3-1-6-0 Schwarz 14-7-21-3 Nourse 18-6-43-2 SJ Snooke 5-3-8-1

South Africa Innings

*+PW Sherwell	b Blythe	6	
GA Faulkner	c & b Hirst	2	b Hirst	42
SJ Snooke	c Jessop b Hirst	63	c Foster b Blythe	36
AW Nourse	c Lilley b Knox	34	not out	0
JH Sinclair	c Crawford b Hirst	22	b Hirst	28
WA Shalders	c Jessop b Blythe	31	not out	24
AEE Vogler	b Blythe	5	b Blythe	19
RO Schwarz	c Blythe b Hirst	2	
GC White	st Lilley b Blythe	4	b Hirst	1
CMH Hathorn	not out	3	
SD Snooke	c Foster b Blythe	6	
	(b 3, lb 1, nb 2)	6	(b 5, lb 3, nb 1)	9
	(all out)	178	(5 wickets)	159

Bowling: Blythe 20.3-5-61-5 Hirst 22-7-39-3 Crawford 11-2-33-0 Knox 10-2-39-2
Blythe 12.3-3-36-2 Hirst 13-1-42-3 Crawford 6-3-14-0 Knox 8-0-53-0 Braund 1-0-5-0

Umpires: W Richards and WAJ West

England v Australia
9,10,11 August 1909

Result: Match drawn

Australia Innings

SE Gregory	b Carr	1	run out		74
W Bardsley	b Sharp	136	lbw b Barnes		130
*MA Noble	lbw b Carr	2	c MacLaren b Barnes		55
WW Armstrong	lbw b Carr	15	c Woolley b Carr		10
VS Ransford	b Barnes	3	not out		36
VT Trumper	c Rhodes b Barnes	73	st Lilley b Carr		20
CG Macartney	c Rhodes b Sharp	50	not out		4
AJY Hopkins	c Rhodes b Sharp	21			
A Cotter	b Carr	7			
+H Carter	lbw b Carr	4			
FJ Laver	not out	8			
	(b 1, lb 3, nb 1)	5	(b 4, lb 3, w 1, nb 2)		10
	(all out)	325	(5 wickets declared)		339

Bowling: Carr 34-2-146-5 Barnes 19-3-57-2 Sharp 16.3-3-67-3 Woolley 4-1-6-0 Hayes 4-0-10-0 Rhodes 12-3-34-0
Carr 35-1-136-2 Barnes 27-7-61-2 Sharp 12-0-34-0 Woolley 6-0-31-0 Hayes 2-0-14-0 Rhodes 14-1-35-0 Hutchings 4-0-18-0

England Innings

RH Spooner	b Cotter	13	c & b Macartney	3
*AC MacLaren	lbw b Cotter	15		
W Rhodes	c Carter b Cotter	66	st Carter b Armstrong	54
CB Fry	run out	62	not out	35
J Sharp	c Gregory b Hopkins	105	not out	0
FE Woolley	b Cotter	8		
EG Hayes	lbw b Armstrong	4	c sub b Armstrong	9
KL Hutchings	c Macartney b Cotter	59		
+AFA Lilley	not out	2		
SF Barnes	c Carter b Hopkins	0		
DW Carr	b Cotter	0		
	(b 8, lb 4, nb 6)	18	(lb 2, nb 1)	3
	(all out)	352	(3 wickets)	104

Bowling: Cotter 27.4-1-95-6 Armstrong 31-7-93-1 Laver 8-1-13-0 Macartney 16-2-49-0 Hopkins 15-2-51-2 Noble 8-1-29-0 Gregory 1-0-4-0
Cotter 8-1-21-0 Armstrong 7-4-8-2 Macartney 8-2-11-1 Hopkins 8-0-40-0 Gregory 2-0-21-0

Umpires: J Moss and W Richards

England v South Africa
12,13 August 1912

Result: England won by 10 wickets

South Africa Innings

HW Taylor	c Foster b Woolley	23	lbw b Barnes	6
*LJ Tancred	b Barnes	0	st Smith b Woolley	0
AW Nourse	lbw b Woolley	8	c & b Foster	42
GA Faulkner	c Hayes b Barnes	9	b Barnes	10
LA Stricker	b Barnes	5	c Spooner b Barnes	0
CB Llewellyn	c Rhodes b Woolley	0	c Hitch b Barnes	0
GC White	b Barnes	4	c Smith b Barnes	1
SJ Snooke	c Foster b Woolley	23	c Hearne b Barnes	7
R Beaumont	c Hearne b Barnes	3	b Barnes	6
SJ Pegler	c Hitch b Woolley	3	b Barnes	0
+TA Ward	not out	6	not out	0
	(b 8, lb 3)	11	(b 18, lb 3)	21
	(all out)	95	(all out)	93

Bowling: Foster 6-2-15-0 Barnes 21-10-28-5 Woolley 15.3-1-41-5
Barnes 16.4-4-29-8 Woolley 9-2-24-1 Foster 7-2-19-1

England Innings

JB Hobbs	c & b Faulkner	68	not out	9
W Rhodes	b Faulkner	0		
RH Spooner	c Nourse b Llewellyn	26		
*CB Fry	c Snooke b Faulkner	9		
EG Hayes	b Faulkner	4		
FE Woolley	b Pegler	13		
JW Hearne	lbw b Faulkner	20	not out	5
FR Foster	st Ward b Faulkner	8		
+EJ Smith	b Faulkner	9		
SF Barnes	c Taylor b Pegler	8		
JW Hitch	not out	0		
	(b 10, lb 1)	11		0
	(all out)	176	(0 wickets)	14

Bowling: Pegler 19-3-53-2 Faulkner 27.1-4-84-7 Llewellyn 10-1-28-1
Nourse 2.3-0-10-0 Faulkner 2-0-4-0

Umpires: W Richards and A White

England v Australia
19,20,21,22 August 1912

Result: England won by 244 runs

England Innings

JB Hobbs	c Carkeek b Macartney	66	c Matthews b Whitty	32
W Rhodes	b Minnett	49	b Whitty	4
RH Spooner	c Hazlitt b Macartney	1	c Jennings b Whitty	0
*CB Fry	c Kelleway b Whitty	5	c Jennings b Hazlitt	79
FE Woolley	lbw b Minnett	62	b Hazlitt	4
JW Hearne	c Jennings b Whitty	1	c Matthews b Hazlitt	14
JWHT Douglas	lbw b Whitty	18	lbw b Hazlitt	24
FR Foster	b Minnett	19	not out	3
+EJ Smith	b Whitty	4	b Hazlitt	0
SF Barnes	c Jennings b Minnett	7	c Whitty b Hazlitt	0
H Dean	not out	0	b Hazlitt	0
	(b 2, lb 10, nb 1)	13	(b 14, nb 1)	15
	(all out)	245	(all out)	175

Bowling: Whitty 38-12-69-4 Matthews 14-5-43-0 Hazlitt 26-10-48-0 Macartney 19-6-22-2 Minnett 10.1-3-34-4 Kelleway 7-2-16-0
Whitty 33-13-71-3 Matthews 10-3-21-0 Hazlitt 21.4-8-25-7 Macartney 22-5-43-0

Australia Innings

*SE Gregory	c Rhodes b Barnes	1	c Douglas b Dean	1
C Kelleway	lbw b Woolley	43	c Douglas b Dean	0
CG Macartney	c Barnes	4	b Dean	30
W Bardsley	b Barnes	30	run out	0
CB Jennings	c & b Woolley	0	c Fry b Woolley	14
RB Minnett	c Rhodes b Woolley	0	lbw b Woolley	4
DBM Smith	c Smith b Woolley	6	c Douglas b Dean	0
TJ Matthews	c Fry b Barnes	2	c & b Woolley	1
WJ Whitty	c Foster b Barnes	0	b Woolley	3
GR Hazlitt	not out	2	c Dean b Woolley	5
+W Carkeek	c Barnes b Woolley	5	not out	0
	(b 12, lb 6)	18	(b 1, lb 5, w 1)	7
	(all out)	111	(all out)	65

Bowling: Barnes 27-15-30-5 Dean 16-7-29-0 Foster 2-0-5-0 Woolley 9.4-3-29-5
Barnes 4-1-18-0 Dean 9-2-19-4 Woolley 7.4-1-20-5 Rhodes 2-1-1-0

Umpires: J Moss and AE Street

England v Australia
13,15,16 August 1921

Result: Match drawn

England Innings

CAG Russell	c Oldfield b McDonald	13	not out	102
+G Brown	b Mailey	32	c Mailey b Taylor	84
GE Tyldesley	c Macartney b Gregory	39		
FE Woolley	run out	23		
CP Mead	not out	182		
A Sandham	b McDonald	21		
*Hon.LH Tennyson	b McDonald	51		
PGH Fender	c Armstrong b McDonald	0	c Armstrong b Mailey	6
JW Hitch	b McDonald	18	not out	51
JWHT Douglas	not out	21		
CH Parkin				
	(lb 3)	3	(b 1)	1
	(8 wickets declared)	403	(2 wickets)	244

Bowling: Gregory 38-5-128-1 McDonald 47-9-143-5 Mailey 30-4-85-1 Armstrong 12-2-44-0
Gregory 3-0-13-0 McDonald 6-0-20-0 Mailey 18-2-77-1 Pellew 9-3-25-0 Andrews 8-0-44-0 Taylor 7-1-25-1 Collins 7-0-39-0

Australia Innings

HL Collins	hit wicket b Hitch	14
W Bardsley	b Hitch	22
CG Macartney	b Douglas	61
TJE Andrews	lbw b Parkin	94
JM Taylor	c Woolley b Douglas	75
CE Pellew	c Woolley b Parkin	1
*WW Armstrong	c Brown b Douglas	19
JM Gregory	st Brown b Parkin	27
+WAS Oldfield	not out	28
EA McDonald	st Brown b Woolley	36
AA Mailey	b Woolley	0
	(b 6, lb 3, w 2, nb 1)	12
	(all out)	389

Bowling: Hitch 19-3-65-2 Douglas 30-2-117-3 Fender 19-3-82-0 Parkin 23-4-82-3 Woolley 11-2-31-2

Umpires: J Moss and W Phillips

England v South Africa
16,18,19 August 1924

Result: Match drawn

South Africa Innings

JMM Commaille	b Tate	3
GAL Hearne	run out	4
MJ Susskind	c Woolley b Hearne	65
AW Nourse	c Sutcliffe b Woolley	37
*HW Taylor	c & b Tyldesley	11
RH Catterall	sub b Tate	95
HG Deane	c Strudwick b Hearne	30
JM Blanckenberg	not out	46
+TA Ward	lbw b Tate	5
SJ Pegler	b Tyldesley	25
CP Carter	c Sandham b Hearne	4
	(b 4, lb 9, w 1, nb 3)	17
	(all out)	342

Bowling: Gilligan 16-5-44-0 Tate 29-10-64-3 Howell 20-5-69-0 Tyldesley 22-6-36-2 Hearne 23-3-90-3 Woolley 14-4-22-1

England Innings

JB Hobbs	c Ward b Pegler	30
H Sutcliffe	c Ward b Nourse	5
JW Hearne	c Susskind b Pegler	35
FE Woolley	b Carter	51
A Sandham	c Ward b Nourse	46
EH Hendren	c Nourse b Carter	142
MW Tate	b Carter	50
*AER Gilligan	c Nourse b Pegler	36
RK Tyldesley	not out	1
+H Strudwick	not out	2
H Howell		
	(b 8, lb 13, nb 2)	23
	(8 wickets)	421

Bowling: Nourse 24-3-63-2 Blanckenberg 36-2-122-0 Carter 23-2-85-3 Pegler 48-14-128-3

Umpires: HR Butt and F Chester

England v Australia
14,16,17,18 August 1926

Result: England won by 289 runs

England Innings

JB Hobbs	b Mailey	37	b Gregory	100
H Sutcliffe	b Mailey	76	b Mailey	161
FE Woolley	b Mailey	18	lbw b Richardson	27
EH Hendren	b Gregory	8	c Oldfield b Grimmett	15
*APF Chapman	st Oldfield b Mailey	49	b Richardson	19
GTS Stevens	c Andrews b Mailey	17	c Mailey b Grimmett	22
W Rhodes	c Oldfield b Mailey	28	lbw b Grimmett	14
G Geary	run out	9	c Oldfield b Gregory	1
MW Tate	b Grimmett	23	not out	33
H Larwood	b Mailey	0	b Mailey	5
+H Strudwick	not out	4	c Andrews b Mailey	2
	(b 6, lb 5)	11	(b 19, lb 18)	37
	(all out)	280	(all out)	436

Bowling: Gregory 15-4-31-1 Grimmett 33-12-74-2 Mailey 33.5-3-138-6 Macartney 7-4-16-0 Richardson 7-2-10-0
Gregory 18-1-58-2 Grimmett 55-17-108-3 Mailey 42.5-6-128-3 Macartney 26-16-24-0 Richardson 41-21-81-2

Australia Innings

WM Woodfull	b Rhodes	35	c Geary b Larwood	0
W Bardsley	c Strudwick b Larwood	2	c Woolley b Rhodes	21
CG Macartney	b Stevens	25	c Geary b Larwood	16
WH Ponsford	run out	2	c Larwood b Rhodes	12
TJE Andrews	b Larwood	3	c Tate b Larwood	15
*HL Collins	c Stevens b Larwood	61	c Woolley b Rhodes	4
AJ Richardson	c Geary b Rhodes	16	b Rhodes	4
JM Gregory	c Stevens b Tate	73	c Sutcliffe b Tate	9
+WAS Oldfield	not out	33	b Stevens	23
CV Grimmett	b Tate	35	not out	8
AA Mailey	c Strudwick b Tate	0	b Geary	6
	(b 5, lb 12)	17	(lb 7)	7
	(all out)	302	(all out)	125

Bowling: Tate 37.1-17-40-3 Larwood 34-11-82-3 Geary 27-8-43-0 Stevens 29-3-85-1 Rhodes 25-15-35-2
Tate 9-4-12-1 Larwood 14-3-34-3 Geary 6.3-2-15-1 Stevens 3-1-13-1 Rhodes 20-9-44-4

Umpires: F Chester and HI Young

Kennington Oval, London

England v West Indies
11,13,14 August 1928

Result: England won by an innings and 71 runs

West Indies Innings

G Challenor	c Hammond b Leyland	46	c Hammond b Freeman	2
CA Roach	b Larwood	53	b Larwood	12
FR Martin	c Chapman b Freeman	25	b Tate	41
*+RK Nunes	b Tate	0	c Hendren b Larwood	12
EL Bartlett	b Larwood	13	c Larwood b Freeman	8
OC Scott	c Duckworth b Tate	35	c Duckworth b Larwood	4
LN Constantine	lbw b Jupp	37	c Larwood b Tate	17
CV Wight	c Chapman b Tate	23	not out	12
JA Small	lbw b Freeman	0	c Freeman b Tate	2
HC Griffith	not out	0	c Hammond b Freeman	5
GN Francis	c Chapman b Tate	4	c Hammond b Freeman	4
	(b 2)	2	(b 6, lb 4)	10
	(all out)	238	(all out)	129

Bowling: Larwood 21-6-46-2 Tate 21-4-59-4 Freeman 27-8-85-2 Hammond 8-0-40-1 Leyland 3-0-6-1
Larwood 14-3-41-3 Tate 13-4-27-3 Freeman 21.4-4-47-4 Hammond 4-2-4-0

England Innings

JB Hobbs	c Small b Francis	159
H Sutcliffe	b Francis	63
GE Tyldesley	c Constantine b Griffith	73
WR Hammond	c Small b Griffith	3
M Leyland	b Griffith	0
EH Hendren	c Roach b Griffith	14
*APF Chapman	c Constantine b Griffith	5
MW Tate	c Griffith b Griffith	54
H Larwood	c & b Francis	32
+G Duckworth	not out	7
AP Freeman	c Francis b Griffith	19
	(b 1, lb 2, nb 6)	9
	(all out)	351

Bowling: Francis 27-4-112-4 Constantine 20-3-91-0 Griffith 25.5-4-103-6 Scott 14-1-75-0 Small 15-2-39-0 Martin 2-1-9-0

Umpires: J Hardstaff snr and TW Oates

England v South Africa
17,19,20 August 1929

Result: Match drawn

England Innings

JB Hobbs	c Quinn b McMillan	10	c Mitchell b Vincent	52
H Sutcliffe	c Owen-Smith b Vincent	104	not out	109
WR Hammond	st Cameron b Vincent	17	not out	101
FE Woolley	hit wicket b Vincent	46		
RES Wyatt	c Deane b Vincent	6		
M Leyland	b Vincent	16		
*AW Carr	c Morkel b McMillan	15		
+LEG Ames	c Mitchell b McMillan	15		
G Geary	not out	12		
AP Freeman	c Cameron b Quinn	15		
EW Clark	b Quinn	7		
	(b 9, nb 1)	10	(b 1, lb 1)	2
	(all out)	258	(1 wicket)	264

Bowling: Morkel 9-2-20-0 Quinn 15.3-4-30-2 Vincent 45-10-105-5 McMillan 28-7-78-3 Owen-Smith 4-0-15-0
Morkel 16-6-43-0 Quinn 24-3-61-0 Vincent 15-3-42-1 McMillan 10-1-39-0 Owen-Smith 8-0-42-0 Mitchell 4-0-17-0 Catterall 3-0-18-0

South Africa Innings

RH Catterall	c Carr b Clark	0
IJ Siedle	b Geary	14
B Mitchell	b Geary	2
HW Taylor	c Ames b Clark	121
*HG Deane	c Woolley b Wyatt	93
+HB Cameron	c Freeman b Geary	62
DPB Morkel	c Ames b Clark	81
HGO Owen-Smith	b Woolley	26
Q McMillan	not out	50
CL Vincent	not out	24
NA Quinn		
	(b 4, lb 12, w 2, nb 1)	19
	(8 wickets declared)	492

Bowling: Clark 36-8-79-3 Geary 49-15-121-3 Freeman 49-9-169-0 Woolley 13-4-25-1 Leyland 9-4-25-0 Wyatt 16-4-54-1

Umpires: W Bestwick and TW Oates

England v Australia
16,18,19,20,21,22 August 1930

Result: Australia won by an innings and 39 runs

England Innings

JB Hobbs	c Kippax b Wall	47	b Fairfax	9
H Sutcliffe	c Oldfield b Fairfax	161	c Fairfax b Hornibrook	54
WW Whysall	lbw b Wall	13	c Hornibrook b Grimmett	10
KS Duleepsinhji	c Fairfax b Grimmett	50	c Kippax b Hornibrook	46
WR Hammond	b McCabe	13	c Fairfax b Hornibrook	60
M Leyland	b Grimmett	3	b Hornibrook	20
*RES Wyatt	c Oldfield b Fairfax	64	b Hornibrook	7
MW Tate	st Oldfield b Grimmett	10	run out	0
H Larwood	lbw b Grimmett	19	c McCabe b Hornibrook	9
+G Duckworth	b Fairfax	3	b Hornibrook	15
IAR Peebles	not out	3	not out	0
	(lb 17, nb 2)	19	(b 16, lb 3, nb 2)	21
	(all out)	405	(all out)	251

Bowling: Wall 37-6-96-2 Fairfax 31-9-52-3 Grimmett 66.2-18-135-4 McCabe 22-4-49-1 Hornibrook 15-1-54-0
Wall 12-2-25-0 Fairfax 10-3-21-1 Grimmett 43-12-90-1 McCabe 3-1-2-0 Hornibrook 31.2-9-92-7

Australia Innings

*WM Woodfull	c Duckworth b Peebles	54
WH Ponsford	b Peebles	110
DG Bradman	c Duckworth b Larwood	232
AF Kippax	c Wyatt b Peebles	28
A Jackson	c Sutcliffe b Wyatt	73
SJ McCabe	c Duckworth b Hammond	54
AG Fairfax	not out	53
+WAS Oldfield	c Larwood b Peebles	34
CV Grimmett	lbw b Peebles	6
TW Wall	lbw b Peebles	0
PM Hornibrook	c Duckworth b Tate	7
	(b 22, lb 18, nb 4)	44
	(all out)	695

Bowling: Larwood 48-6-132-1 Tate 65.1-12-153-1 Peebles 71-8-204-6 Wyatt 14-1-58-1 Hammond 42-12-70-1 Leyland 16-7-34-0

Umpires: J Hardstaff snr and WR Parry

England v New Zealand
29,30,31 July 1931

Result: England won by an innings and 26 runs

England Innings

H Sutcliffe	st James b Vivian	117
AH Bakewell	run out	40
KS Duleepsinhji	c Weir b Allcott	109
WR Hammond	not out	100
+LEG Ames	c James b Vivian	41
*DR Jardine	not out	7
FR Brown		
GOB Allen		
MW Tate		
IAR Peebles		
H Verity		
	(b 1, lb 1)	2
	(4 wickets declared)	416

Bowling: Cromb 30-5-97-0 Allcott 44-7-108-1 Vivian 34.3-8-96-2 Weir 10-1-36-0 Merritt 12-0-75-0 Blunt 1-0-2-0

New Zealand Innings

JE Mills	b Allen	27	b Brown	30
GL Weir	b Allen	13	b Peebles	6
RC Blunt	c Ames b Allen	2	b Peebles	43
ML Page	c Peebles b Tate	12	b Tate	3
HG Vivian	c Ames b Allen	3	b Brown b Peebles	51
*TC Lowry	c Jardine b Brown	62	c Duleepsinhji b Peebles	0
JL Kerr	c Ames b Allen	34	b Tate	28
+KC James	lbw b Brown	4	c Peebles b Verity	10
IB Cromb	c Hammond b Verity	8	not out	1
WE Merritt	c Hammond b Verity	8	lbw b Tate	4
CFW Allcott	not out	5	c Allen b Verity	1
	(b 2, lb 9, nb 4)	15	(b 6, lb 10, nb 2)	18
	(all out)	193	(all out)	197

Bowling: Tate 18-9-15-1 Brown 29-12-52-2 Verity 22.1-8-52-2 Peebles 12-3-35-0 Allen 13-7-14-5 Hammond 1-0-10-0
Tate 21-6-22-3 Brown 16-6-38-1 Verity 12.3-4-33-2 Peebles 22-4-63-4 Allen 13-4-23-0

Umpires: F Chester and J Hardstaff snr

England v West Indies
12,14,15 August 1933

Result: England won by an innings and 17 runs

England Innings

CF Walters	c Merry b Martindale	2
AH Bakewell	c Headley b Sealey	107
WR Hammond	c Barrow b Valentine	11
*RES Wyatt	c Achong b Martindale	15
MJL Turnbull	b Martindale	4
James Langridge	c Barrow b Da Costa	22
+LEG Ames	c Headley b Martindale	37
CJ Barnett	run out	52
MS Nichols	b Achong	49
EW Clark	not out	8
CS Marriott	b Martindale	0
	(lb 5)	5
	(all out)	312

Bowling: Martindale 24.5-2-93-5 Griffith 20-4-44-0 Valentine 20-6-55-1 Da Costa 12-2-30-1 Achong 23-3-59-1 Headley 4-0-16-0 Sealey 5-1-10-1

West Indies Innings

CA Roach	c Bakewell b Clark	8	lbw b Marriott	56
+IM Barrow	c Ames b Clark	3	c Ames b Clark	16
GA Headley	st Ames b Marriott	9	c Ames b Clark	12
OC Da Costa	c Bakewell b Clark	8	b Marriott	35
BJ Sealey	c Ames b Nichols	29	b Marriott	12
CA Merry	b Marriott	13	c Barnett b Nichols	11
*GC Grant	b Marriott	4	c Ames b Nichols	14
EE Achong	run out	4	c Ames b Marriott	22
VA Valentine	c Langridge b Marriott	10	c Barnett b Marriott	0
EA Martindale	not out	1	not out	9
HC Griffith	st Ames b Marriott	0	c & b Marriott	0
	(b 1, lb 10)	11	(lb 7, nb 1)	8
	(all out)	100	(all out)	195

Bowling: Clark 8-3-16-3 Nichols 10-1-36-1 Marriott 11.5-2-37-5
Clark 21-10-54-2 Nichols 14-3-51-2 Marriott 29.2-6-59-6 Langridge 7-1-23-0

Umpires: F Chester and J Hardstaff snr

England v Australia
18,20,21,22 August 1934

Result: Australia won by 562 runs

Australia Innings

WA Brown	b Clark	10	c Allen b Clark	1
WH Ponsford	hit wicket b Allen	266	c Hammond b Clark	22
DG Bradman	c Ames b Bowes	244	b Bowes	77
SJ McCabe	b Allen	10	c Walters b Clark	70
*WM Woodfull	b Bowes	49	b Bowes	13
AF Kippax	lbw b Bowes	28	c Walters b Clark	8
AG Chipperfield	b Bowes	3	c Woolley b Clark	16
+WAS Oldfield	not out	42	c Hammond b Bowes	0
CV Grimmett	c Ames b Allen	7	c Hammond b Bowes	14
HI Ebeling	b Allen	2	c Allen b Bowes	41
WJ O'Reilly	b Clark	7	not out	15
	(b 4, lb 14, w 2, nb 13)	33	(b 37, lb 8, w 1, nb 4)	50
	(all out)	701	(all out)	327

Bowling: Bowes 38-2-164-4 Allen 34-5-170-4 Clark 37.2-4-110-2 Hammond 12-0-53-0 Verity 43-7-123-0 Wyatt 4-0-28-0 Leyland 3-0-20-0
Bowes 11.3-3-55-5 Allen 16-2-63-0 Clark 20-1-98-5 Hammond 7-1-18-0 Verity 14-3-43-0

England Innings

CF Walters	c Kippax b O'Reilly	64	b McCabe	1
H Sutcliffe	c Oldfield b Grimmett	38	c McCabe b Grimmett	28
FE Woolley	c McCabe b O'Reilly	4	c Ponsford b McCabe	0
WR Hammond	c Oldfield b Ebeling	15	c & b O'Reilly	43
*RES Wyatt	b Grimmett	17	c Ponsford b Grimmett	22
M Leyland	b Grimmett	110	c Brown b Grimmett	17
+LEG Ames	retired hurt	33	absent hurt	0
GOB Allen	b Ebeling	19	st Oldfield b Grimmett	26
H Verity	b Ebeling	11	c McCabe b Grimmett	1
EW Clark	not out	2	not out	2
WE Bowes	absent hurt	0	c Bradman b O'Reilly	2
	(b 4, lb 3, nb 1)	8	(lb 1, nb 2)	3
	(all out)	321	(all out)	145

Bowling: Ebeling 21-4-74-3 McCabe 6-1-21-0 Grimmett 49.3-13-103-3 O'Reilly 37-10-93-2 Chipperfield 4-0-22-0
Ebeling 10-5-15-0 McCabe 5-3-5-2 Grimmett 26.3-10-64-5 O'Reilly 22-9-58-2

Umpires: F Chester and FI Walden

England v South Africa
17,19,20 August 1935

Result: Match drawn

South Africa Innings

IJ Siedle	c Ames b Robins	35	b Bowes	36
B Mitchell	c Ames b Read	128	b Read	9
EAB Rowan	lbw b Robins	0	b Bowes	7
AD Nourse	c Wyatt b Bowes	32	b Read	34
KG Viljoen	c Clay b Read	60	c Ames b Robins	45
+HB Cameron	c Mitchell b Read	8	st Ames b Robins	42
*HF Wade	c Hammond b Bowes	0	not out	40
EL Dalton	c Robins b Read	117	not out	57
CL Vincent	b Robins	5		
ACB Langton	not out	73		
RJ Crisp	c Ames b Bowes	0		
	(b 6, lb 10, nb 2)	18	(b 6, lb 9, nb 2)	17
	(all out)	476	(6 wickets)	287

Bowling: Read 35-13-136-4 Nichols 23-3-79-0 Bowes 40.4-7-112-3 Hammond 9-2-25-0 Clay 14-1-30-0 Robins 22-3-73-3 Wyatt 2-0-3-0
Read 10-1-64-2 Nichols 5-1-20-0 Bowes 13-2-40-2 Clay 18-6-45-0 Robins 17-1-61-2 Wyatt 3-0-25-0 Leyland 7-2-15-0

England Innings

AH Bakewell	c Cameron b Langton	20
A Mitchell	b Crisp	40
*RES Wyatt	c Cameron b Vincent	37
WR Hammond	st Cameron b Vincent	65
M Leyland	st Cameron b Mitchell	161
+LEG Ames	not out	148
MS Nichols	c Siedle b Langton	30
RWV Robins	not out	10
JC Clay		
WE Bowes		
HD Read		
	(b 5, lb 16, nb 2)	23
	(6 wickets declared)	534

Bowling: Crisp 28-0-113-1 Langton 38-5-124-2 Dalton 16-1-50-0 Vincent 42-5-188-2 Mitchell 8-0-36-1

Umpires: F Chester and J Hardstaff snr

England v India
15,17,18 August 1936

Result: England won by 9 wickets

England Innings

CJ Barnett	lbw b Nayudu	43	not out	32
AE Fagg	c Dilawar Hussain b Amar Singh	8	c Amar Singh b Nissar	22
WR Hammond	b Nissar	217	not out	5
M Leyland	b Nissar	26		
TS Worthington	b Nissar	128		
LB Fishlock	not out	19		
*GOB Allen	c Dilawar Hussain b Nissar	13		
H Verity	c Dilawar Hussain b Nissar	4		
JM Sims	lbw b Amar Singh	1		
W Voce	not out	1		
+G Duckworth				
	(lb 10, nb 1)	11	(b 4, nb 1)	5
	(8 wickets declared)	471	(1 wicket)	64

Bowling: Nissar 26-2-120-5 Amar Singh 39-8-102-2 Baqa Jilani 15-4-55-0 Nayudu 24-1-82-1 Jahangir Khan 17-1-65-0 Mushtaq Ali 2-0-13-0 Merchant 6-0-23-0
Nissar 7-0-36-1 Amar Singh 6-0-23-0

India Innings

VM Merchant	b Allen	52	c Worthington b Allen	48
S Mushtaq Ali	st Duckworth b Verity	52	c Hammond b Allen	17
+Dilawar Hussain	st Duckworth b Verity	35	lbw b Sims	54
CK Nayudu	c Allen b Voce	5	b Allen	81
C Ramaswami	b Sims	29	not out	41
S Wazir Ali	lbw b Sims	2	c Duckworth b Allen	1
L Amar Singh	b Verity	5	c Sims b Verity	44
M Jahangir Khan	c Fagg b Sims	9	c Voce b Allen	1
*Vizianagram	b Sims	1	b Allen	1
M Baqa Jilani	not out	4	c Fagg b Allen	12
M Nissar	c Worthington b Sims	14	c Voce b Sims	0
	(b 8, lb 6)	14	(b 3, lb 7, nb 2)	12
	(all out)	222	(all out)	312

Bowling: Voce 20-5-46-1 Allen 12-3-37-1 Hammond 8-2-17-0 Verity 25-12-30-3 Sims 18.5-1-73-5 Leyland 2-0-5-0
Voce 20-5-40-0 Allen 20-3-80-7 Hammond 7-0-24-0 Verity 16-6-32-1 Sims 25-1-95-2 Leyland 3-0-19-0 Worthington 2-0-10-0

Umpires: F Chester and FI Walden

England v New Zealand
14,16,17 August 1937

Result: Match drawn

New Zealand Innings

HG Vivian	c Ames b Gover	13	lbw b Hammond	57
WA Hadlee	b Matthews	18	c Compton b Matthews	0
WM Wallace	run out	8	lbw b Gover	7
GL Weir	c Matthews b Gover	3	c Barnett b Goddard	8
MP Donnelly	c Hutton b Robins	58	c Ames b Hammond	0
DAR Moloney	b Hammond	23	b Goddard	38
*ML Page	c Washbrook b Robins	53	absent hurt	0
AW Roberts	c Hutton b Gover	50	lbw b Goddard	9
+EWT Tindill	b Robins	4	not out	37
JA Dunning	c Gover b Robins	0	b Compton	19
J Cowie	not out	4	c Robins b Hutton	2
	(b 2, lb 11, nb 2)	15	(b 4, lb 5, nb 1)	10
	(all out)	249	(all out)	187

Bowling: Gover 28-3-85-3 Matthews 22-6-52-1 Goddard 10-2-25-0 Hammond 7-1-25-1 Robins 14.1-2-40-4 Hutton 2-0-7-0
Gover 12-1-42-1 Matthews 8-2-13-1 Goddard 18-8-41-3 Hammond 11-3-19-2 Robins 11-2-24-0 Hutton 2.4-1-4-1 Compton 6-0-34-2

England Innings

CJ Barnett	c Hadlee b Cowie	13	c Roberts b Dunning	21
L Hutton	c & b Vivian	12		
C Washbrook	lbw b Vivian	9	not out	8
DCS Compton	run out	65		
J Hardstaff jnr	b Cowie	103		
WR Hammond	c Wallace b Cowie	31		
+LEG Ames	not out	6		
*RWV Robins	c & b Roberts	9		
ADG Matthews	not out	2		
TWJ Goddard				
AR Gover				
	(b 2, lb 1, w 1)	4	(lb 2)	2
	(7 wickets declared)	254	(1 wicket)	31

Bowling: Cowie 24-5-73-3 Roberts 15-4-26-1 Dunning 25-5-89-0 Vivian 29-5-62-2
Cowie 4-1-15-0 Roberts 4-1-9-0 Dunning 1.2-0-5-1

Umpires: A Dolphin and EJ Smith

England v Australia
20,22,23,24 August 1938

Result: England won by an innings and 579 runs

England Innings

L Hutton	c Hassett b O'Reilly	364
WJ Edrich	lbw b O'Reilly	12
M Leyland	run out	187
*WR Hammond	lbw b Fleetwood-Smith	59
E Paynter	lbw b O'Reilly	0
DCS Compton	b Waite	1
J Hardstaff jnr	not out	169
+A Wood	c & b Barnes	53
H Verity	not out	8
K Farnes		
WE Bowes		
	(b 22, lb 19, w 1, nb 8)	50
	(7 wickets declared)	903

Bowling: Waite 72-16-150-1 McCabe 38-8-85-0 O'Reilly 85-26-178-3 Fleetwood-Smith 87-11-298-1 Barnes 38-3-84-1 Hassett 13-2-52-0 Bradman 2.2-1-6-0

Australia Innings

WA Brown	c Hammond b Leyland	69	c Edrich b Farnes	15
CL Badcock	c Hardstaff b Bowes	0	b Bowes	9
SJ McCabe	c Edrich b Farnes	14	c Wood b Farnes	2
AL Hassett	c Compton b Edrich	42	lbw b Bowes	10
SG Barnes	b Bowes	41	lbw b Verity	33
+BA Barnett	c Wood b Bowes	2	b Farnes	46
MG Waite	b Bowes	8	c Edrich b Verity	0
WJ O'Reilly	c Wood b Bowes	0	not out	7
LO Fleetwood-Smith	not out	16	c Leyland b Farnes	0
*DG Bradman	absent hurt	0	absent hurt	0
JHW Fingleton	absent hurt	0	absent hurt	0
	(b 4, lb 2, nb 3)	9	(b 1)	1
	(all out)	201	(all out)	123

Bowling: Farnes 13-2-54-1 Bowes 19-3-49-5 Edrich 10-2-55-1 Verity 5-1-15-0 Leyland 3.1-0-11-1 Hammond 2-0-8-0
Farnes 12.1-1-63-4 Bowes 10-3-25-2 Verity 7-3-15-2 Leyland 5-0-19-0

Umpires: F Chester and FI Walden

England v West Indies
19,21,22 August 1939

Result: Match drawn

England Innings

L Hutton	c & b Johnson	73	not out	165
WW Keeton	b Johnson	0	b Constantine	20
N Oldfield	c Sealy b Constantine	80	c Sealy b Johnson	19
*WR Hammond	c Grant b Constantine	43	b Clarke	138
DCS Compton	c Gomez b Martindale	21	not out	10
J Hardstaff jnr	b Constantine	94		
MS Nichols	run out	24		
+A Wood	b Constantine	0		
DVP Wright	lbw b Constantine	6		
TWJ Goddard	b Clarke	0		
RTD Perks	not out	1		
	(b 4, lb 5, nb 1)	10	(b 4, lb 5, w 4, nb 1)	14
	(all out)	352	(3 wickets declared)	366

Bowling: Martindale 13-0-87-1 Johnson 16-1-53-2 Constantine 17.3-2-75-5 Clarke 21-0-96-1 Grant 6-0-31-0
Martindale 10-2-46-0 Johnson 14-2-76-1 Constantine 20-3-97-1 Clarke 17-1-78-1 Grant 11-1-38-0 Headley 4-0-17-0

West Indies Innings

*RS Grant	c Goddard b Perks	6
JB Stollmeyer	c Perks b Hutton	59
GA Headley	run out	65
VH Stollmeyer	st Wood b Goddard	96
GE Gomez	b Perks	11
KH Weekes	c Hammond b Nichols	137
+JED Sealy	c Wright b Nichols	24
LN Constantine	c Wood b Perks	79
EA Martindale	b Perks	3
CB Clarke	b Perks	2
TF Johnson	not out	9
	(lb 6, nb 1)	7
	(all out)	498

Bowling: Nichols 34-4-161-2 Perks 30.5-6-156-5 Wright 13-2-53-0 Goddard 12-1-56-1 Hutton 7-0-45-1 Compton 5-1-20-0

Umpires: F Chester and W Reeves

England v India
17,19,20 August 1946

Result: Match drawn

India Innings

VM Merchant	run out	128
S Mushtaq Ali	run out	59
*Nawab of Pataudi snr	b Edrich	9
L Amarnath	b Edrich	8
VS Hazare	c Compton b Gover	11
RS Modi	b Smith	27
Abdul Hafeez	b Edrich	1
MH Mankad	b Bedser	42
SW Sohoni	not out	29
CS Nayudu	c Washbrook b Bedser	4
+DD Hindlekar	lbw b Edrich	3
	(b 1, lb 5, nb 4)	10
	(all out)	331

Bowling: Gover 21-3-56-1 Bedser 32-6-60-2 Smith 21-4-58-1 Edrich 19.2-4-68-4 Langridge 29-9-64-0 Compton 5-0-15-0

England Innings

L Hutton	lbw b Mankad	25
C Washbrook	c Mushtaq Ali b Mankad	17
LB Fishlock	c Merchant b Nayudu	8
DCS Compton	not out	24
*WR Hammond	not out	9
WJ Edrich		
James Langridge		
TPB Smith		
+TG Evans		
AV Bedser		
AR Gover		
	(b 11, lb 1)	12
	(3 wickets)	95

Bowling: Amarnath 15-6-30-0 Sohoni 4-3-2-0 Hazare 2-1-4-0 Mankad 20-7-28-2 Nayudu 9-2-19-1

Umpires: F Chester and JA Smart

Kennington Oval, London

England v South Africa
16,18,19,20 August 1947

Result: Match drawn

England Innings

L Hutton	b Mann	83	c Tuckett b Mann		36
C Washbrook	lbw b Mann	32	c Fullerton b Rowan		43
JDB Robertson	c Melville b Smith	4	b Rowan		30
DCS Compton	c Tuckett b Rowan	53	c Nourse b Dawson		113
*NWD Yardley	b Mann	59	c sub b Mann		11
K Cranston	st Fullerton b Rowan	45	c Mitchell b Rowan		0
R Howorth	c Fullerton b Rowan	23	not out		45
+TG Evans	run out	45	not out		39
C Gladwin	not out	51			
DVP Wright	b Mann	14			
WH Copson	b Dawson	6			
	(b 4, lb 7, nb 1)	12	(b 6, w 2)		8
	(all out)	427	(6 wickets declared)		325

Bowling: Tuckett 32-6-82-0 Dawson 35-5-80-1 Mann 64-28-93-4 Rowan 38-9-92-3 Smith 21-0-68-1
Tuckett 7-0-34-0 Dawson 15-1-59-1 Mann 27-7-102-2 Rowan 25-1-95-3 Smith 3-0-27-0

South Africa Innings

B Mitchell	c Evans b Copson	120	not out		189
DV Dyer	c Gladwin b Howorth	18	lbw b Wright		4
KG Viljoen	c Evans b Wright	10	st Evans b Howorth		33
AD Nourse	c Yardley b Howorth	10	b Howorth		97
*A Melville	lbw b Cranston	39	c Evans b Cranston		6
OC Dawson	lbw b Wright	55	c Howorth b Cranston		0
+GM Fullerton	c Howorth b Cranston	6	c Evans b Howorth		14
AMB Rowan	b Howorth	0			
NBF Mann	b Copson	36	c Hutton b Wright		10
L Tuckett	not out	0	not out		40
VI Smith	lbw b Copson	0			
	(b 3, lb 2, w 1, nb 2)	8	(b 12, lb 14, w 4)		30
	(all out)	302	(7 wickets)		423

Bowling: Copson 27-13-46-3 Gladwin 16-2-39-0 Wright 29-7-89-2 Howorth 39-16-64-3 Compton 11-4-31-0 Cranston 9-2-25-2
Copson 30-11-66-0 Gladwin 16-5-33-0 Wright 30-8-103-2 Howorth 37-12-85-3 Compton 4-0-30-0 Cranston 21-3-61-2 Hutton 2-0-14-0 Yardley 1-0-1-0

Umpires: HG Baldwin and JA Smart

England v Australia
14,16,17,18 August 1948

Result: Australia won by an innings and 149 runs

England Innings

L Hutton	c Tallon b Lindwall	30	c Tallon b Miller		64
JG Dewes	b Miller	1	b Lindwall		10
WJ Edrich	c Hassett b Johnston	3	b Lindwall		28
DCS Compton	c Morris b Lindwall	4	c Lindwall b Johnston		39
JF Crapp	b Tallon b Miller	0	b Miller		9
*NWD Yardley	b Lindwall	7	c Miller b Johnston		9
AJ Watkins	lbw b Johnston	0	c Hassett b Ring		2
+TG Evans	b Lindwall	1	b Lindwall		8
AV Bedser	b Lindwall	0	b Johnston		0
JA Young	b Lindwall	0	not out		3
WE Hollies	not out	0	c Morris b Johnston		0
	(b 6)	6	(b 9, lb 4, nb 3)		16
	(all out)	52	(all out)		188

Bowling: Lindwall 16.1-5-20-6 Miller 8-5-5-2 Johnston 16-4-20-2 Loxton 2-1-1-0
Lindwall 25-3-50-3 Miller 15-6-22-2 Johnston 27.3-12-40-4 Loxton 10-2-16-0 Ring 28-13-44-1

Australia Innings

SG Barnes	c Evans b Hollies	61	
AR Morris	run out	196	
*DG Bradman	b Hollies	0	
AL Hassett	lbw b Young	37	
KR Miller	st Evans b Hollies	5	
RN Harvey	c Young b Hollies	17	
SJE Loxton	c Evans b Edrich	15	
RR Lindwall	c Edrich b Young	9	
+D Tallon	c Crapp b Hollies	31	
DT Ring	c Crapp b Bedser	9	
WA Johnston	not out	0	
	(b 4, lb 2, nb 3)	9	
	(all out)	389	

Bowling: Bedser 31.2-9-61-1 Watkins 4-1-19-0 Young 51-16-118-2 Hollies 56-14-131-5 Compton 2-0-6-0 Edrich 9-1-38-1 Yardley 5-1-7-0

Umpires: HG Baldwin and D Davies

England v New Zealand
13,15,16 August 1949

Result: Match drawn

New Zealand Innings

B Sutcliffe	c Bedser b Hollies	88	c Brown b Bedser		54
VJ Scott	c Edrich b Bedser	60	c Evans b Bedser		6
+JR Reid	lbw b Wright	5	c Wright b Laker		93
WM Wallace	c Edrich b Bedser	55	st Evans b Hollies		58
MP Donnelly	c Edrich b Bailey	27	c Brown b Bedser		10
*WA Hadlee	c Evans b Bedser	25	c Edrich b Hollies		22
GO Rabone	c Evans b Bailey	18	lbw b Laker		20
TB Burtt	c Evans b Bailey	9	c Compton b Laker		6
HB Cave	b Compton	10	not out		14
J Cowie	c Hutton b Bedser	1	c Wright b Laker		4
GF Cresswell	not out	12	not out		0
	(lb 1, w 1, nb 6)	8	(b 10, lb 5, nb 6)		21
	(all out)	345	(9 wickets declared)		308

Bowling: Bailey 26.1-7-72-3 Bedser 31-6-74-4 Edrich 3-0-16-0 Wright 22-1-93-1 Laker 3-0-11-0 Hollies 20-7-51-1 Brown 5-1-14-0 Compton 2-0-6-1
Bailey 11-1-67-0 Bedser 23-4-59-3 Wright 6-0-21-0 Laker 29-6-78-4 Hollies 17-6-30-2 Brown 10-0-29-0 Compton 1-0-3-0

England Innings

L Hutton	c Rabone b Cresswell	206	
RT Simpson	c Donnelly b Cresswell	68	
WJ Edrich	c Cave b Cresswell	100	
DCS Compton	c Scott b Cresswell	13	
TE Bailey	c Reid b Cowie	36	
*FR Brown	c Hadlee b Cresswell	21	
+TG Evans	c Donnelly b Cowie	17	
JC Laker	c Scott b Cowie	0	
AV Bedser	c Reid b Cowie	0	
WE Hollies	not out	1	
DVP Wright	lbw b Cresswell	0	
	(b 6, lb 11, nb 3)	20	
	(all out)	482	

Bowling: Cowie 28-1-123-4 Cresswell 41.2-6-168-6 Cave 24-4-78-0 Burtt 24-2-93-0

Umpires: D Davies and FS Lee

England v West Indies
12,14,15,16 August 1950

Result: West Indies won by an innings and 56 runs

West Indies Innings

AF Rae	b Bedser	109	
JB Stollmeyer	lbw b Bailey	36	
FMM Worrell	lbw b Wright	138	
ED Weekes	c Hutton b Wright	30	
+CL Walcott	b Wright	17	
GE Gomez	c McIntyre b Brown	74	
RJ Christiani	c McIntyre b Bedser	11	
*JDC Goddard	not out	58	
PEW Jones	b Wright	1	
S Ramadhin	c McIntyre b Wright	3	
AL Valentine	b Bailey	9	
	(b 5, lb 11, nb 1)	17	
	(all out)	503	

Bowling: Bailey 34.2-9-84-2 Bedser 38-9-75-2 Brown 21-4-74-1 Wright 53-16-141-5 Hilton 41-12-91-0 Compton 7-2-21-0

England Innings

L Hutton	not out	202	c Christiani b Goddard		2
RT Simpson	c Jones b Valentine	30	b Ramadhin		16
DS Sheppard	b Ramadhin	11	c Weekes b Valentine		29
DCS Compton	run out	44	c Weekes b Valentine		11
JG Dewes	c Worrell b Valentine	17	c Christiani b Valentine		3
TE Bailey	c Weekes b Goddard	18	lbw b Ramadhin		12
*FR Brown	c Weekes b Valentine	0	c Stollmeyer b Valentine		15
+AJW McIntyre	c & b Valentine	4	c sub b Goddard		0
AV Bedser	lbw b Goddard	0	c Weekes b Valentine		0
MJ Hilton	b Goddard	3	c sub b Valentine		0
DVP Wright	lbw b Goddard	4	not out		6
	(b 5, lb 6)	11	(b 6, lb 3)		9
	(all out)	344	(all out)		103

Bowling: Jones 23-4-70-0 Worrell 20-9-30-0 Ramadhin 45-23-63-1 Valentine 64-21-121-4 Gomez 10-3-24-0 Goddard 17.4-6-25-4
Ramadhin 26-11-38-3 Valentine 26.3-10-39-6 Gomez 8-4-6-0 Goddard 9-4-11-1

Umpires: WH Ashdown and FS Lee

England v South Africa
16,17,18 August 1951

Result: England won by 4 wickets

South Africa Innings

EAB Rowan	c Hutton b Brown	55	lbw b Laker		45
+WR Endean	c Brown b Laker	31	lbw b Bedser		7
CB van Ryneveld	st Brennan b Laker	10	lbw b Laker		5
*AD Nourse	lbw b Brown	4	b Laker		4
JE Cheetham	lbw b Laker	0	c Hutton b Tattersall		18
RA McLean	c May b Laker	14	c Lowson b Laker		18
PNF Mansell	b Tattersall	8	lbw b Laker		0
AMB Rowan	c Laker b Bedser	41	not out		15
GWA Chubb	b Bedser	10	c Hutton b Bedser		7
MG Melle	b Shackleton	5	b Laker		17
CN McCarthy	not out	4	b Bedser		0
	(b 11, lb 8, nb 1)	20	(b 11, lb 7)		18
	(all out)	202	(all out)		154

Bowling: Bedser 19.3-6-36-2 Shackleton 15-5-20-1 Tattersall 14-7-26-1 Laker 37-12-64-4 Brown 20-10-31-2 Compton 1-0-5-0
Bedser 19.5-6-32-3 Shackleton 10-2-19-0 Tattersall 5-1-10-1 Laker 28-8-55-6 Brown 13-5-20-0

England Innings

L Hutton	lbw b AMB Rowan	28	obstructing the field		27
FA Lowson	c Endean b Melle	0	c van Ryneveld b AMB Rowan		37
PBH May	b Chubb	33	c EAB Rowan b AMB Rowan		0
DCS Compton	b McCarthy	73	c van Ryneveld b Chubb		18
W Watson	run out	31	c Endean b Chubb		15
*FR Brown	c van Ryneveld b AMB Rowan	1	lbw b Chubb		40
JC Laker	b Chubb	6	not out		13
D Shackleton	c van Ryneveld b Melle	14	not out		5
AV Bedser	c Endean b Melle	2			
+DV Brennan	lbw b Melle	0			
R Tattersall	not out	0			
	(lb 4, nb 2)	6	(b 5, lb 3, nb 1)		9
	(all out)	194	(6 wickets)		164

Bowling: McCarthy 17-0-45-1 Melle 10-6-9-4 AMB Rowan 27-9-44-2 Chubb 30-5-70-2 van Ryneveld 3-0-20-0
McCarthy 7-0-17-0 Melle 3-0-8-0 AMB Rowan 24.1-2-77-2 Chubb 28-10-53-3

Umpires: F Chester and D Davies

England v India
14,15,16,18,19 August 1952

Result: Match drawn

England Innings

*L Hutton	c Phadkar b Ramchand	86	
DS Sheppard	lbw b Divecha	119	
JT Ikin	c Sen b Phadkar	53	
PBH May	c Manjrekar b Mankad	17	
TW Graveney	c Divecha b Ghulam Ahmed	13	
W Watson	not out	18	
+TG Evans	c Phadkar b Mankad	1	
JC Laker	not out	6	
AV Bedser			
GAR Lock			
FS Trueman			
	(b 10, lb 2, nb 1)	13	
	(6 wickets declared)	326	

Bowling: Divecha 33-9-60-1 Phadkar 32-8-61-0 Ramchand 14-2-50-1 Mankad 48-23-88-2 Ghulam Ahmed 24-1-54-1 Hazare 3-3-0-0

India Innings

MH Mankad	c Evans b Trueman	5	
P Roy	c Lock b Trueman	0	
HR Adhikari	c Trueman b Bedser	0	
*VS Hazare	c May b Trueman	38	
VL Manjrekar	c Ikin b Bedser	1	
PR Umrigar	b Bedser	0	
DG Phadkar	b Trueman	17	
RV Divecha	b Bedser	16	
GS Ramchand	c Hutton b Bedser	5	
+PK Sen	b Trueman	9	
Ghulam Ahmed	not out	2	
	(lb 3, nb 2)	5	
	(all out)	98	

Bowling: Bedser 14.5-4-41-5 Trueman 16-4-48-5 Lock 6-5-1-0 Laker 2-0-3-0

Umpires: F Chester and H Elliott

England v Australia
15,17,18,19 August 1953

Result: England won by 8 wickets

Australia Innings

*AL Hassett	c Evans b Bedser	53	lbw b Laker	10
AR Morris	lbw b Bedser	16	lbw b Lock	26
KR Miller	lbw b Bailey	1	c Trueman b Laker	0
RN Harvey	c Hutton b Trueman	36	b Lock	1
GB Hole	c Evans b Trueman	37	lbw b Laker	17
JH de Courcy	c Evans b Trueman	5	run out	4
RG Archer	c & b Bedser	10	c Edrich b Lock	49
AK Davidson	c Edrich b Laker	22	b Lock	21
RR Lindwall	c Evans b Trueman	62	c Compton b Laker	12
+GRA Langley	c Edrich b Lock	18	c Trueman b Lock	2
WA Johnston	not out	9	not out	6
	(b 4, nb 2)	6	(b 11, lb 3)	14
	(all out)	275	(all out)	162

Bowling: Bedser 29-3-88-3 Trueman 24.3-3-86-4 Bailey 14-3-42-1 Lock 9-2-19-1 Laker 5-0-34-1
Bedser 11-2-24-0 Trueman 2-1-4-0 Lock 21-9-45-5 Laker 16.5-2-75-4

England Innings

*L Hutton	b Johnston	82	run out	17
WJ Edrich	lbw b Lindwall	21	not out	55
PBH May	c Archer b Johnston	39	c Davidson b Miller	37
DCS Compton	c Langley b Lindwall	16	not out	22
TW Graveney	c Miller b Lindwall	4		
TE Bailey	b Archer	64		
+TG Evans	run out	28		
JC Laker	c Langley b Miller	1		
GAR Lock	c Davidson b Lindwall	4		
FS Trueman	b Johnston	10		
AV Bedser	not out	22		
	(b 9, lb 5, w 1)	15	(lb 1)	1
	(all out)	306	(2 wickets)	132

Bowling: Lindwall 32-7-70-4 Miller 34-12-65-1 Johnston 45-16-94-3 Davidson 10-1-26-0 Archer 10.3-2-25-1 Hole 11-6-11-0
Lindwall 21-5-46-0 Miller 11-3-24-1 Johnston 29-14-52-0 Archer 1-1-0-0 Hassett 1-0-4-0 Morris 0.5-0-5-0

Umpires: D Davies and FS Lee

England v Pakistan
12,13,14,16,17 August 1954

Result: Pakistan won by 24 runs

Pakistan Innings

Hanif Mohammad	lbw b Statham	0	c Graveney b Wardle	19
Alimuddin	b Tyson	10	lbw b Wardle	0
Waqar Hasan	b Loader	7	run out	9
Maqsood Ahmed	b Tyson	0	c Wardle b McConnon	4
+Imtiaz Ahmed	c Evans b Tyson	23	c Wardle b Tyson	12
*AH Kardar	c Evans b Statham	36	c & b Wardle	17
Wazir Mohammad	run out	0	not out	42
Fazal Mahmood	c Evans b Loader	0	b Wardle	6
Shujauddin	not out	16	c May b Wardle	12
Zulfiqar Ahmed	c Compton b Loader	16	c May b Wardle	34
Mahmood Hussain	b Tyson	23	c Statham b Wardle	6
	(nb 2)	2	(b 3)	3
	(all out)	133	(all out)	164

Bowling: Statham 11-5-26-2 Tyson 13.4-3-35-4 Loader 18-5-35-3 McConnon 9-2-35-0
Statham 18-7-37-0 Tyson 9-2-22-1 Loader 16-6-26-0 McConnon 14-5-20-1 Wardle 35-16-56-7

England Innings

*L Hutton	c Imtiaz Ahmed b Fazal Mahmood	14	c Imtiaz Ahmed b Fazal Mahmood	5
RT Simpson	c Kardar b Mahmood Hussain	2	c & b Zulfiqar Ahmed	27
PBH May	c Kardar b Fazal Mahmood	26	c Kardar b Fazal Mahmood	53
DCS Compton	c Imtiaz Ahmed b Fazal Mahmood	53	c Imtiaz Ahmed b Fazal Mahmood	29
TW Graveney	c Hanif Mohammad b Fazal Mahmood	1	lbw b Shujauddin	0
+TG Evans	c Maqsood Ahmed b Mahmood Hussain	0	b Fazal Mahmood	3
JH Wardle	c Imtiaz Ahmed b Fazal Mahmood	8	c Shujauddin b Fazal Mahmood	9
FH Tyson	c Imtiaz Ahmed b Fazal Mahmood	3	c Imtiaz Ahmed b Fazal Mahmood	3
JE McConnon	c Fazal Mahmood b Mahmood Hussain	11	run out	2
JB Statham	c Shujauddin b Mahmood Hussain	1	not out	2
PJ Loader	not out	8	c Waqar Hasan b Mahmood Hussain	5
	(lb 1, w 1, nb 1)	3	(b 2, nb 3)	5
	(all out)	130	(all out)	143

Bowling: Fazal Mahmood 30-16-53-6 Mahmood Hussain 21.3-6-58-4 Zulfiqar Ahmed 5-2-8-0 Shujauddin 3-0-8-0
Fazal Mahmood 30-11-46-6 Mahmood Hussain 14-4-32-1 Zulfiqar Ahmed 14-2-35-1 Shujauddin 10-1-25-1

Umpires: D Davies and FS Lee

England v South Africa
13,15,16,17 August 1955

Result: England won by 92 runs

England Innings

JT Ikin	c Waite b Heine	17	c Goddard b Heine	0
DB Close	c Mansell b Goddard	32	b Goddard	15
*PBH May	c Goddard b Fuller	3	not out	89
DCS Compton	c Waite b Goddard	30	c Waite b Fuller	30
W Watson	c Mansell b Tayfield	25	b Fuller	3
TW Graveney	c Fuller b Goddard	13	b Tayfield	42
TE Bailey	c Heine b Tayfield	0	lbw b Tayfield	1
+RT Spooner	b Tayfield	0	lbw b Tayfield	0
JC Lock	c & b Goddard	2	lbw b Fuller	12
GAR Lock	c McLean b Goddard	18	lbw b Heine	1
JB Statham	not out	4	lbw b Tayfield	0
	(b 2, lb 5)	7	(b 4, lb 6, nb 1)	11
	(all out)	151	(all out)	204

Bowling: Heine 21-3-43-1 Goddard 22.4-9-31-5 Fuller 27-11-33-1 Tayfield 19-7-39-3
Heine 25-6-44-2 Goddard 19-10-29-1 Fuller 20-3-36-2 Tayfield 53.4-29-60-5 Mansell 6-0-24-0

South Africa Innings

DJ McGlew	c Spooner b Statham	30	lbw b Lock	19
TL Goddard	lbw b Bailey	8	c Graveney b Lock	20
HJ Keith	b Lock	5	c May b Lock	0
WR Endean	c Ikin b Lock	0	lbw b Laker	0
RA McLean	b Lock	1	lbw b Laker	0
+JHB Waite	c Lock b Laker	28	lbw b Laker	60
*JE Cheetham	not out	12	lbw b Laker	9
PNF Mansell	lbw b Laker	6	c Watson b Lock	9
HJ Tayfield	b Statham	4	not out	10
ERH Fuller	c Spooner b Lock	5	run out	16
PS Heine	run out	5	c Graveney b Laker	7
	(b 7, nb 1)	8	(lb 1)	1
	(all out)	112	(all out)	151

Bowling: Statham 15-3-31-2 Bailey 5-1-6-1 Lock 22-11-39-4 Laker 23-13-28-2
Statham 11-4-17-0 Bailey 6-1-15-0 Lock 33-14-62-4 Laker 37.4-18-56-5

Umpires: TJ Bartley and D Davies

England v Australia
23,24,25,27,28 August 1956

Result: Match drawn

England Innings

PE Richardson	c Langley b Miller	37	c Langley b Lindwall	34
MC Cowdrey	c Langley b Lindwall	0	c Benaud b Davidson	8
Rev.DS Sheppard	c Archer b Miller	24	c Archer b Miller	62
*PBH May	not out	83	not out	37
DCS Compton	c Davidson b Archer	94	not out	35
GAR Lock	c Langley b Archer	0		
C Washbrook	lbw b Archer	0		
+TG Evans	lbw b Miller	0		
JC Laker	c Archer b Miller	4		
FH Tyson	c Davidson b Archer	3		
JB Statham	b Archer	0		
	(w 2)	2	(b 3, lb 3)	6
	(all out)	247	(3 wickets declared)	182

Bowling: Lindwall 18-5-36-1 Miller 40-7-91-4 Davidson 5-1-16-0 Archer 28.2-7-53-5 Johnson 9-2-28-0 Benaud 9-2-21-0
Lindwall 12-3-29-1 Miller 22-3-56-1 Davidson 5-0-18-1 Archer 13-3-42-0 Johnson 4-1-7-0 Benaud 1-0-10-0 Burke 4-2-14-0

Australia Innings

CC McDonald	c Lock b Tyson	3	lbw b Statham	0
JW Burke	b Laker	8	lbw b Laker	1
RN Harvey	c May b Lock	39	c May b Lock	1
ID Craig	c Statham b Lock	2	c Lock b Laker	7
*IWG Johnson	b Laker	12	c Lock b Laker	10
AK Davidson	c May b Laker	8		
KR Miller	c Washbrook b Statham	61	not out	7
RG Archer	c Tyson b Laker	9		
R Benaud	b Statham	32	not out	0
RR Lindwall	not out	22		
+GRA Langley	lbw b Statham	0		
	(b 6)	6	(b 1)	1
	(all out)	202	(5 wickets)	27

Bowling: Statham 21-8-33-3 Tyson 14-5-34-1 Laker 32-12-80-4 Lock 25-10-49-2
Statham 2-1-1-1 Laker 18-14-8-3 Lock 18.1-11-17-1

Umpires: TJ Bartley and D Davies

England v West Indies
22,23,24 August 1957

Result: England won by an innings and 237 runs

England Innings

PE Richardson	b Smith	107
Rev.DS Sheppard	c & b Goddard	40
TW Graveney	b Ramadhin	164
*PBH May	c Worrell b Smith	1
MC Cowdrey	b Ramadhin	2
TE Bailey	run out	0
+TG Evans	c Weekes b Dewdney	40
GAR Lock	c Alexander b Sobers	17
FS Trueman	b Ramadhin	22
JC Laker	not out	10
PJ Loader	lbw b Ramadhin	0
	(b 1, lb 8)	9
	(all out)	412

Bowling: Worrell 11-3-26-0 Dewdney 15-2-43-1 Ramadhin 53.3-12-107-4 Sobers 44-6-111-1 Goddard 23-10-43-1 Smith 30-4-73-2

West Indies Innings

FMM Worrell	c Lock b Loader	4	c Cowdrey b Lock	0
NS Asgarali	c Cowdrey b Lock	29	c Cowdrey b Lock	7
GS Sobers	b Lock	39	b Lock	42
CL Walcott	b Laker	5	not out	19
ED Weekes	c Trueman b Laker	0	c May b Laker	0
OG Smith	c May b Laker	7	c Sheppard b Lock	0
RB Kanhai	not out	4	c Evans b Trueman	8
+FCM Alexander	b Lock	0	b Laker	0
DT Dewdney	b Lock	0	st Evans b Lock	1
S Ramadhin	c Trueman b Lock	0	b Laker	2
*JDC Goddard	absent hurt	0	absent hurt	0
	(nb 1)	1	(b 4, lb 2, nb 1)	7
	(all out)	89	(all out)	86

Bowling: Trueman 5-1-9-0 Loader 7-4-12-1 Laker 23-12-39-3 Lock 21.4-12-28-5
Trueman 5-2-19-1 Loader 3-2-2-0 Laker 17-4-38-2 Lock 16-7-20-6

Umpires: DE Davies and FS Lee

England v New Zealand
21,22,23,25,26 August 1958

Result: Match drawn

New Zealand Innings

LSM Miller	c Lock b Laker	25	c Evans b Statham	4
JW D'Arcy	c Milton b Bailey	9	c & b Lock	10
T Meale	c Lock b Trueman	1	c Cowdrey b Laker	3
B Sutcliffe	c Watson b Trueman	11	not out	18
*JR Reid	b Lock	27	not out	51
WR Playle	b Statham	6		
AR MacGibbon	b Bailey	26		
JT Sparling	retired hurt	0		
+EC Petrie	c Milton b Lock	8		
AM Moir	not out	41		
RW Blair	run out	3		
	(lb 4)	4	(b 2, lb 3)	5
	(all out)	161	(3 wickets)	91

Bowling: Trueman 16-3-41-2 Statham 18-6-21-1 Bailey 14-3-32-2 Laker 14-3-44-1 Lock 13-6-19-2
Trueman 6-5-3-0 Statham 7-0-26-1 Laker 20-10-25-1 Lock 18-11-20-1 Milton 4-2-12-0

England Innings

PE Richardson	b Blair	28
CA Milton	lbw b MacGibbon	36
W Watson	b MacGibbon	10
*PBH May	c Petrie b Blair	9
MC Cowdrey	c Playle b Reid	25
TE Bailey	c Petrie b MacGibbon	14
+TG Evans	c Petrie b MacGibbon	12
GAR Lock	c Reid b Moir	25
JC Laker	c Blair b Reid	15
FS Trueman	not out	39
JB Statham		
	(b 2, lb 4)	6
	(9 wickets declared)	219

Bowling: Blair 26-5-85-2 MacGibbon 27-4-65-4 Reid 7.5-2-11-2 Moir 8-1-52-1

Umpires: DE Davies and FS Lee

Kennington Oval, London

England v India
20,21,22,24 August 1959

Result: England won by an innings and 27 runs

India Innings

P Roy	b Statham	3	lbw b Statham	0
NJ Contractor	c Illingworth b Dexter	22	c Trueman b Statham	25
AA Baig	c Cowdrey b Trueman	23	c Cowdrey b Statham	4
RG Nadkarni	c Swetman b Trueman	6	lbw b Illingworth	76
CG Borde	b Greenhough	0	run out	6
*DK Gaekwad	c Barrington b Dexter	11	c Swetman b Greenhough	15
JM Ghorpade	b Greenhough	5	b Greenhough	24
+NS Tamhane	c Swetman b Statham	32	b Trueman	9
Surendranath	c Illingworth b Trueman	27	not out	17
SP Gupte	b Trueman	2	c Greenhough b Trueman	5
RB Desai	not out	3	c Swetman b Trueman	3
	(b 1, lb 4, nb 1)	6	(b 4, lb 6, nb 3)	13
	(all out)	140	(all out)	194

Bowling: Trueman 17-6-24-4 Statham 16.3-6-24-2 Dexter 16-7-24-2 Greenhough 29-11-36-2 Illingworth 1-0-2-0 Barrington 6-0-24-0
Trueman 14-4-30-3 Statham 18-4-50-3 Dexter 7-1-11-0 Greenhough 27-12-47-2 Illingworth 29-10-43-1

England Innings

G Pullar	c Tamhane b Surendranath	22
R Subba Row	c Tamhane b Desai	94
*MC Cowdrey	c Borde b Surendranath	6
MJK Smith	b Desai	98
KF Barrington	c sub b Gupte	8
ER Dexter	c Tamhane b Surendranath	0
R Illingworth	c Gaekwad b Nadkarni	50
+R Swetman	c Baig b Surendranath	65
FS Trueman	st Tamhane b Nadkarni	1
JB Statham	not out	3
T Greenhough	c Contractor b Surendranath	2
	(b 3, lb 8, w 1)	12
	(all out)	361

Bowling: Desai 33-5-103-2 Surendranath 51.3-25-75-5 Gupte 38-9-119-1 Nadkarni 25-11-52-2

Umpires: DE Davies and FS Lee

England v South Africa
18,19,20,22,23 August 1960

Result: Match drawn

England Innings

G Pullar	c Goddard b Pothecary	59	st Waite b McKinnon	175
*MC Cowdrey	b Adcock	11	lbw b Goddard	155
ER Dexter	b Adcock	28	b Tayfield	16
KF Barrington	lbw b Pothecary	1	c Carlstein b McKinnon	10
MJK Smith	b Adcock	0	c Goddard b Tayfield	11
DEV Padgett	c Waite b Pothecary	13	run out	31
+JM Parks	c Waite b Adcock	23	c Waite b Adcock	17
DA Allen	lbw b Adcock	0	not out	12
FS Trueman	lbw b Adcock	0	c Pothecary b Goddard	4
JB Statham	not out	13		
T Greenhough	b Adcock	2		
	(b 3, lb 2)	5	(b 14, lb 9, w 1)	24
	(all out)	155	(9 wickets declared)	479

Bowling: Adcock 31.3-10-65-6 Pothecary 29-9-58-4 Goddard 14-6-25-0 McKinnon 2-1-2-0
Adcock 38-8-106-1 Pothecary 27-5-93-0 Goddard 27-6-69-3 McKinnon 24-7-62-2 Tayfield 37-14-108-2 Fellows-Smith 4-0-17-0

South Africa Innings

*DJ McGlew	c Smith b Greenhough	22	c Allen b Statham	16
TL Goddard	c Cowdrey b Statham	99	c Cowdrey b Statham	28
JP Fellows-Smith	c Smith b Dexter	35	c Parks b Trueman	6
RA McLean	lbw b Dexter	0	not out	32
+JHB Waite	c Trueman b Dexter	77	not out	1
S O'Linn	b Trueman	55		
PR Carlstein	b Greenhough	42	lbw b Trueman	13
JE Pothecary	run out	4		
HJ Tayfield	not out	46		
AH McKinnon	run out	22		
NAT Adcock	b Trueman	1		
	(b 6, lb 7, nb 3)	16	(w 1)	1
	(all out)	419	(4 wickets)	97

Bowling: Trueman 31.1-4-93-2 Statham 38-8-96-1 Dexter 30-5-79-3 Greenhough 44-17-99-2 Allen 28-15-36-0
Trueman 10-0-34-2 Statham 12-1-57-2 Dexter 0.2-0-0-0 Greenhough 5-2-3-0 Allen 2-1-2-0

Umpires: CS Elliott and WE Phillipson

England v Australia
17,18,19,21,22 August 1961

Result: Match drawn

England Innings

G Pullar	b Davidson	8	c Grout b Mackay	13
R Subba Row	lbw b Gaunt	12	c & b Benaud	137
MC Cowdrey	c Grout b Davidson	0	c Benaud b Mackay	3
*PBH May	c Lawry b Benaud	71	c O'Neill b Mackay	33
ER Dexter	c Grout b Gaunt	24	c Grout b Gaunt	0
KF Barrington	c Grout b Gaunt	53	c O'Neill b Benaud	83
+JT Murray	c O'Neill b Mackay	27	c Grout b Benaud	40
GAR Lock	c Grout b Mackay	3	c Benaud b Mackay	0
DA Allen	not out	22	not out	42
JB Statham	b Davidson	18	not out	9
JA Flavell	c Simpson b Davidson	14		
	(b 1, lb 2, w 1)	4	(b 6, lb 3, w 1)	10
	(all out)	256	(8 wickets)	370

Bowling: Davidson 34.1-8-83-4 Gaunt 24-3-53-3 Benaud 17-4-35-1 Mackay 39-14-75-2 Simpson 4-2-6-0
Davidson 29-7-67-0 Gaunt 22-7-33-0 Mackay 68-21-121-5 Benaud 51-18-113-3 Simpson 2-0-13-0 O'Neill 4-1-13-0 Harvey 1-1-0-0

Australia Innings

WM Lawry	c Murray b Statham	0
RB Simpson	b Allen	40
RN Harvey	lbw b Flavell	13
NC O'Neill	c sub b Allen	117
PJP Burge	b Allen	181
BC Booth	c Subba Row b Lock	71
KD Mackay	c Murray b Flavell	5
AK Davidson	lbw b Statham	17
*R Benaud	b Allen	6
+ATW Grout	not out	30
RA Gaunt	b Statham	3
	(b 10, lb 1)	11
	(all out)	494

Bowling: Statham 38.5-10-75-3 Flavell 31-5-105-2 Dexter 24-2-68-0 Allen 30-6-133-4 Lock 42-14-102-1

Umpires: CS Elliott and FS Lee

England v Pakistan
16,17,18,20 August 1962

Result: England won by 10 wickets

England Innings

Rev.DS Sheppard	c Fazal Mahmood b Nasim-ul-Ghani	57	not out	9
MC Cowdrey	c Hanif Mohammad b Fazal Mahmood	182		
*ER Dexter	b Fazal Mahmood	172		
KF Barrington	not out	50		
PH Parfitt	c Imtiaz Ahmed b D'Souza	3		
BR Knight	b D'Souza	3		
R Illingworth	not out	2		
+JT Murray			not out	14
DA Allen				
LJ Coldwell				
JDF Larter				
	(b 4, lb 5, nb 2)	11	(b 4)	4
	(5 wickets declared)	480	(0 wickets)	27

Bowling: Fazal Mahmood 49-9-192-2 D'Souza 42-9-116-2 Intikhab Alam 38-5-109-0 Javed Burki 1-0-12-0 Nasim-ul-Ghani 9-1-39-1 Saeed Ahmed 1-0-1-0
Fazal Mahmood 4-1-10-0 D'Souza 3-1-8-0 Javed Burki 1-0-2-0 Mushtaq Mohammad 0.3-0-3-0

Pakistan Innings

Ijaz Butt	c Cowdrey b Larter	10	run out	6
+Imtiaz Ahmed	c Murray b Knight	49	c Cowdrey b Larter	98
Mushtaq Mohammad	lbw b Larter	43	b Illingworth	72
*Javed Burki	c Larter	3	c Parfitt b Knight	42
Saeed Ahmed	c Parfitt b Allen	21	c Knight b Allen	4
Hanif Mohammad	b Larter	46	c Dexter b Larter	0
W Mathias	c Murray b Larter	0	run out	48
A D'Souza	c Parfitt b Coldwell	1	not out	2
Nasim-ul-Ghani	c Murray b Coldwell	5	b Coldwell	24
Intikhab Alam	not out	3	b Larter	12
Fazal Mahmood	b Coldwell	0	b Larter	5
	(nb 2)	2	(b 4, lb 5, nb 1)	10
	(all out)	183	(all out)	323

Bowling: Coldwell 28-11-53-3 Larter 25-4-57-5 Allen 22-9-33-1 Knight 9-5-11-1 Illingworth 13-5-27-0
Coldwell 23-4-60-1 Larter 21.1-0-88-4 Knight 11-3-33-1 Illingworth 21-9-54-1 Allen 27-14-52-1 Dexter 6-1-16-0 Barrington 2-0-10-0

Umpires: CS Elliott and FS Lee

England v West Indies
22,23,24,26 August 1963

Result: West Indies won by 8 wickets

England Innings

JB Bolus	c Murray b Sobers	33	c Gibbs b Sobers	15
JH Edrich	c Murray b Sobers	25	c Murray b Griffith	12
*ER Dexter	c & b Griffith	29	c Murray b Sobers	27
KF Barrington	c Sobers b Gibbs	16	b Griffith	28
DB Close	b Griffith	46	lbw b Sobers	4
PJ Sharpe	c Murray b Griffith	63	c Murray b Hall	83
+JM Parks	c Kanhai b Griffith	19	lbw b Griffith	23
FS Trueman	b Griffith	19	c Sobers b Hall	5
GAR Lock	hit wicket b Griffith	4	b Hall	14
JB Statham	b Hall	8	b Hall	14
D Shackleton	not out	0	not out	0
	(b 4, lb 2, nb 7)	13	(b 5, lb 3, nb 4)	12
	(all out)	275	(all out)	223

Bowling: Hall 22.2-2-71-1 Griffith 27-4-71-6 Sobers 21-4-44-2 Gibbs 27-7-50-1 Worrell 5-0-26-0
Hall 16-3-39-4 Griffith 23-7-66-3 Sobers 33-6-77-3 Gibbs 9-1-29-0

West Indies Innings

CC Hunte	c Parks b Shackleton	80	not out	108
WV Rodriguez	c Lock b Statham	5	c Lock b Dexter	28
RB Kanhai	b Lock	30	c Bolus b Lock	77
BF Butcher	run out	53	not out	31
GS Sobers	run out	26		
JS Solomon	c Trueman b Statham	16		
*FMM Worrell	b Statham	9		
+DL Murray	c Lock b Trueman	5		
WW Hall	b Trueman	2		
CC Griffith	not out	13		
LR Gibbs	b Trueman	4		
	(lb 3)	3	(b 4, lb 7)	11
	(all out)	246	(2 wickets)	255

Bowling: Trueman 26.1-2-65-3 Statham 23-3-68-3 Shackleton 21-5-37-1 Lock 29-6-65-1 Dexter 6-1-8-0
Trueman 1-1-0-0 Statham 22-2-54-0 Shackleton 32-7-68-0 Lock 25-8-52-1 Dexter 9-1-34-1 Close 6-0-36-0

Umpires: JS Buller and AEG Rhodes

England v Australia
13,14,15,17,18 August 1964

Result: Match drawn

England Innings

G Boycott	b Hawke	30	c Redpath b Simpson	113
RW Barber	b Hawke	24	lbw b McKenzie	29
*ER Dexter	c Booth b Hawke	23	c Simpson b McKenzie	25
MC Cowdrey	c Grout b McKenzie	20	not out	93
KF Barrington	c Simpson b Hawke	47	not out	54
PH Parfitt	b McKenzie	3		
+JM Parks	c Simpson b Corling	10		
FJ Titmus	c Grout b Hawke	8	b McKenzie	56
FS Trueman	c Redpath b Hawke	14		
TW Cartwright	c Grout b McKenzie	0		
JSE Price	not out	0		
	(lb 3)	3	(b 6, lb 4, nb 1)	11
	(all out)	182	(4 wickets)	381

Bowling: McKenzie 26-6-87-3 Corling 14-2-32-1 Hawke 25.4-8-47-6 Veivers 6-1-13-0
McKenzie 38-5-112-3 Corling 25-4-65-0 Hawke 39-8-89-0 Veivers 47-15-90-0 Simpson 14-7-14-1

Australia Innings

*RB Simpson	c Dexter b Cartwright	24
WM Lawry	c Trueman b Dexter	94
NC O'Neill	c Parfitt b Cartwright	11
PJP Burge	lbw b Titmus	25
BC Booth	c Trueman b Price	74
IR Redpath	b Trueman	45
+ATW Grout	b Cartwright	20
TR Veivers	not out	67
GD McKenzie	c Cowdrey b Trueman	0
NJN Hawke	c Cowdrey b Trueman	14
GE Corling	c Parfitt b Trueman	0
	(b 4, lb 1)	5
	(all out)	379

Bowling: Trueman 33.3-6-87-4 Price 21-2-67-1 Cartwright 62-23-110-3 Titmus 42-20-51-1 Barber 6-1-23-0 Dexter 13-1-36-1

Umpires: JF Crapp and CS Elliott

England v South Africa
26,27,28,30,31 August 1965

Result: Match drawn

South Africa Innings

EJ Barlow	lbw b Statham	18	b Statham	18
+DT Lindsay	lbw b Higgs	4	b Brown	17
A Bacher	lbw b Higgs	28	c Smith b Statham	70
RG Pollock	b Titmus	12	run out	34
KC Bland	lbw b Statham	39	c Titmus b Higgs	127
HR Lance	lbw b Statham	69	b Higgs	53
*PL van der Merwe	c Barrington b Higgs	20	b Higgs	0
R Dumbrill	c Smith b Higgs	14	c Barrington b Brown	36
JT Botten	c Cowdrey b Statham	0	b Titmus	4
PM Pollock	b Statham	3	not out	9
AH McKinnon	not out	0	b Higgs	14
	(nb 1)	1	(b 1, lb 7, nb 2)	10
	(all out)	208	(all out)	392

Bowling: Statham 24.2-11-40-5 Brown 22-4-63-0 Higgs 24-4-47-4 Titmus 26-12-57-1
Statham 29-1-105-2 Brown 23-3-63-2 Higgs 41.1-10-96-4 Titmus 27-3-74-1 Barber 13-1-44-0

England Innings

RW Barber	st Lindsay b McKinnon	40	c & b PM Pollock	22
WE Russell	lbw b PM Pollock	0	c Bacher b McKinnon	70
KF Barrington	b Botten	18	lbw b PM Pollock	73
MC Cowdrey	c Barlow b PM Pollock	58	not out	78
PH Parfitt	c & b McKinnon	24	lbw b Botten	46
*MJK Smith	lbw b PM Pollock	7	not out	10
DJ Brown	c Dumbrill b McKinnon	0		
+JM Parks	c Bland b Botten	42		
FJ Titmus	not out	2		
K Higgs	b PM Pollock	2		
JB Statham	b PM Pollock	0		
	(lb 6, w 3)	9	(lb 6, nb 3)	9
	(all out)	202	(4 wickets)	308

Bowling: PM Pollock 25.1-7-43-5 Botten 27-6-56-2 Barlow 11-1-27-0 Dumbrill 6-2-11-0 McKinnon 27-11-50-3 Lance 2-0-6-0
PM Pollock 32.2-7-93-2 Botten 24-4-73-1 Barlow 6-1-22-0 Dumbrill 9-1-30-0 McKinnon 31-7-70-1 Lance 2-0-11-0

Umpires: JS Buller and WFF Price

England v West Indies
18,19,20,22 August 1966

Result: England won by an innings and 34 runs

West Indies Innings

CC Hunte	b Higgs	1	c Murray b Snow	7
EDAS McMorris	b Snow	14	c Murray b Snow	1
RB Kanhai	c Graveney b Illingworth	104	b D'Oliveira	15
BF Butcher	c Illingworth b Close	12	c Barber b Illingworth	60
SM Nurse	c Graveney b D'Oliveira	0	c Edrich b Barber	70
*GS Sobers	c Graveney b Barber	81	c Close b Snow	0
DAJ Holford	c D'Oliveira b Illingworth	5	run out	7
+JL Hendriks	b Barber	0	b Higgs	0
CC Griffith	c Higgs b Barber	4	not out	29
WW Hall	not out	30	c D'Oliveira b Illingworth	17
LR Gibbs	c Murray b Snow	12	c & b Barber	3
	(b 1, lb 3, nb 1)	5	(b 1, lb 14, nb 1)	16
	(all out)	268	(all out)	225

Bowling: Snow 20.5-1-66-2 Higgs 17-4-52-1 D'Oliveira 21-7-35-1 Close 9-2-21-1 Barber 15-3-49-3 Illingworth 15-7-40-2
Snow 13-5-40-3 Higgs 15-6-18-1 D'Oliveira 17-4-44-1 Close 3-1-7-0 Barber 22.1-2-78-2 Illingworth 15-9-22-2

England Innings

G Boycott	b Hall	4
RW Barber	c Nurse b Sobers	36
JH Edrich	c Hendriks b Sobers	35
TW Graveney	run out	165
DL Amiss	lbw b Hall	17
BL D'Oliveira	b Hall	4
*DB Close	run out	4
R Illingworth	c Hendriks b Griffith	3
+JT Murray	lbw b Sobers	112
K Higgs	c & b Holford	63
JA Snow	not out	59
	(b 8, lb 14, nb 3)	25
	(all out)	527

Bowling: Hall 31-8-85-3 Griffith 32-7-78-1 Sobers 54-23-104-3 Holford 25.5-1-79-1 Gibbs 44-16-115-0 Hunte 13-2-41-0

Umpires: JS Buller and CS Elliott

England v Pakistan
24,25,26,28 August 1967

Result: England won by 8 wickets

Pakistan Innings

*Hanif Mohammad	b Higgs	3	c Knott b Higgs	18
Mohammad Ilyas	b Arnold	2	c Cowdrey b Higgs	1
Saeed Ahmed	b Arnold	38	c Knott b Higgs	0
Majid Khan	c Knott b Arnold	6	b Higgs	0
Mushtaq Mohammad	lbw b Higgs	66	c D'Oliveira b Underwood	17
Javed Burki	c D'Oliveira b Titmus	27	b Underwood	7
Ghulam Abbas	c Underwood b Titmus	12	c Knott b Higgs	0
Asif Iqbal	c Close b Arnold	26	st Knott b Close	146
Intikhab Alam	b Higgs	20	b Titmus	51
+Wasim Bari	c Knott b Arnold	1	b Titmus	12
Saleem Altaf	not out	7	not out	0
	(b 5, lb 2, nb 1)	8	(b 1, lb 1, nb 1)	3
	(all out)	216	(all out)	255

Bowling: Arnold 29-9-58-5 Higgs 29-10-61-3 D'Oliveira 17-6-41-0 Close 5-1-15-0 Titmus 13-6-21-2 Underwood 9-5-12-0
Arnold 17-5-49-0 Higgs 20-7-58-5 Close 1-0-4-1 Titmus 29.1-8-64-2 Underwood 26-12-48-2 Barrington 8-2-29-0

England Innings

MC Cowdrey	c Mushtaq Mohammad b Majid Khan	16	c Intikhab Alam b Asif Iqbal	9
*DB Close	c Wasim Bari b Asif Iqbal	6	b Asif Iqbal	8
KF Barrington	c Wasim Bari b Saleem Altaf	142	not out	13
TW Graveney	c Majid Khan b Intikhab Alam	77		
DL Amiss	c Saeed Ahmed b Asif Iqbal	26	not out	3
BL D'Oliveira	c Mushtaq Mohammad b Asif Iqbal	3		
FJ Titmus	c sub b Mushtaq Mohammad	65		
+APE Knott	c Mohammad Ilyas b Mushtaq Mohammad	28		
GG Arnold	c Majid Khan b Mushtaq Mohammad	59		
K Higgs	b Mushtaq Mohammad	7		
DL Underwood	not out	2		
	(lb 4, nb 5)	9	(nb 1)	1
	(all out)	440	(2 wickets)	34

Bowling: Saleem Altaf 40-14-94-1 Asif Iqbal 42-19-66-3 Majid Khan 10-0-29-1 Mushtaq Mohammad 26.4-7-80-4 Saeed Ahmed 21-5-69-0 Intikhab Alam 28-3-93-1
Saleem Altaf 2-1-8-0 Asif Iqbal 4-1-14-2 Saeed Ahmed 2-0-7-0 Hanif Mohammad 0.2-0-4-0

Umpires: WFF Price and H Yarnold

England v Australia
22,23,24,26,27 August 1968

Result: England won by 226 runs

England Innings

JH Edrich	b Chappell	164	c Lawry b Mallett	17
C Milburn	b Connolly	8	c Lawry b Connolly	18
ER Dexter	b Gleeson	21	b Connolly	28
*MC Cowdrey	lbw b Mallett	16	b Mallett	35
TW Graveney	c Redpath b McKenzie	63	run out	12
BL D'Oliveira	c Inverarity b Mallett	158	c Gleeson b Connolly	9
+APE Knott	c Jarman b Mallett	28	run out	34
R Illingworth	lbw b Connolly	8	b Gleeson	10
JA Snow	run out	4	c Sheahan b Gleeson	13
DL Underwood	not out	9	not out	1
DJ Brown	c Sheahan b Gleeson	2	b Connolly	1
	(b 1, lb 11, w 1)	13	(lb 3)	3
	(all out)	494	(all out)	181

Bowling: McKenzie 40-8-87-1 Connolly 57-12-127-2 Walters 6-2-17-0 Gleeson 41.2-8-109-2 Mallett 36-11-87-3 Chappell 21-5-54-1
McKenzie 4-0-14-0 Connolly 22.4-2-65-4 Gleeson 7-2-22-2 Mallett 25-4-77-2

Australia Innings

*WM Lawry	c Knott b Snow	135	c Milburn b Brown	4
RJ Inverarity	c Milburn b Snow	1	lbw b Underwood	56
IR Redpath	c Cowdrey b Snow	67	lbw b Underwood	8
IM Chappell	c Knott b Brown	10	lbw b Underwood	2
KD Walters	c Knott b Brown	5	c Knott b Underwood	1
AP Sheahan	b Illingworth	14	c Snow b Illingworth	24
+BN Jarman	st Knott b Illingworth	0	b D'Oliveira	21
GD McKenzie	b Brown	12	c Brown b Underwood	0
AA Mallett	not out	43	c Brown b Underwood	0
JW Gleeson	c Dexter b Underwood	19	b Underwood	5
AN Connolly	b Underwood	3	not out	0
	(b 4, lb 7, nb 4)	15	(lb 4)	4
	(all out)	324	(all out)	125

Bowling: Snow 35-12-67-3 Brown 22-5-63-3 Illingworth 48-15-87-2 Underwood 54.3-21-89-2 D'Oliveira 4-2-3-0
Snow 11-5-22-0 Brown 8-3-19-1 Illingworth 28-18-29-1 Underwood 31.3-19-50-7 D'Oliveira 5-4-1-1

Umpires: CS Elliott and AE Fagg

England v New Zealand
21,22,23,25,26 August 1969

Result: England won by 8 wickets

New Zealand Innings

BAG Murray	b Snow	2	c & b Underwood	5
GM Turner	c Sharpe b Underwood	53	b Underwood	25
BE Congdon	c Sharpe b Underwood	24	c Knott b Ward	30
*GT Dowling	c Edrich b Illingworth	14	lbw b Snow	30
BF Hastings	b Illingworth	21	c Knott b Ward	61
V Pollard	st Knott b Illingworth	13	c Denness b Underwood	9
BR Taylor	c Denness b Underwood	0	st Knott b Underwood	4
+KJ Wadsworth	c Arnold b Underwood	2	c Knott b Snow	10
RC Motz	c Arnold b Underwood	16	c Denness b Underwood	11
RS Cunis	c Illingworth b Underwood	0	lbw b Underwood	7
HJ Howarth	not out	0	not out	4
	(nb 5)	5	(b 3, lb 11, nb 19)	33
	(all out)	150	(all out)	229

Bowling: Arnold 8-2-13-0 Snow 10-4-22-1 Ward 5-0-10-0 Illingworth 32.3-13-55-3 Underwood 26-12-41-6 D'Oliveira 1-0-4-0
Arnold 10-3-17-0 Snow 21-4-52-2 Ward 18-10-28-2 Illingworth 15-9-20-0 Underwood 38.3-15-60-6 D'Oliveira 14-9-19-0

England Innings

JH Edrich	b Howarth	68	c Wadsworth b Cunis	22
G Boycott	b Cunis	46	b Cunis	8
MH Denness	c Wadsworth b Cunis	2	not out	55
PJ Sharpe	lbw b Motz	48	not out	45
BL D'Oliveira	c Cunis b Howarth	1		
+APE Knott	c Murray b Taylor	21		
*R Illingworth	c Wadsworth b Taylor	4		
GG Arnold	b Taylor	1		
DL Underwood	lbw b Taylor	3		
JA Snow	not out	21		
A Ward	c Turner b Cunis	21		
	(lb 5, nb 1)	6	(b 2, lb 4, nb 2)	8
	(all out)	242	(2 wickets)	138

Bowling: Motz 19-6-54-1 Taylor 21-9-47-4 Cunis 19-3-49-3 Howarth 34-14-66-2 Pollard 5-1-20-0
Motz 9.3-1-35-0 Taylor 4-0-11-0 Cunis 11-3-36-2 Howarth 23-10-32-0 Pollard 5-1-16-0

Umpires: AE Fagg and TW Spencer

England v India
19,20,21,23,24 August 1971

Result: India won by 4 wickets

England Innings

BW Luckhurst	c Gavaskar b Solkar	1	c Venkataraghavan b Chandrasekhar	33
JA Jameson	run out	82	run out	16
JH Edrich	c Engineer b Bedi	41	b Chandrasekhar	0
KWR Fletcher	c Gavaskar b Bedi	1	c Solkar b Chandrasekhar	0
BL D'Oliveira	c Mankad b Chandrasekhar	2	c sub b Venkataraghavan	17
+APE Knott	c & b Solkar	90	c Solkar b Venkataraghavan	1
*R Illingworth	b Chandrasekhar	11	c & b Chandrasekhar	4
RA Hutton	b Venkataraghavan	81	not out	13
JA Snow	c Engineer b Solkar	3	c & b Chandrasekhar	0
DL Underwood	c Wadekar b Venkataraghavan	22	c Mankad b Bedi	11
JSE Price	not out	1	lbw b Chandrasekhar	3
	(b 4, lb 15, w 1)	20	(lb 3)	3
	(all out)	355	(all out)	101

Bowling: Abid Ali 12-2-47-0 Solkar 15-4-28-3 Gavaskar 1-0-1-0 Bedi 36-5-120-2 Chandrasekhar 24-6-76-2 Venkataraghavan 20.4-3-63-2
Abid Ali 3-1-5-0 Solkar 3-1-10-0 Bedi 1-0-1-1 Chandrasekhar 18.1-3-38-6 Venkataraghavan 20-4-44-2

India Innings

SM Gavaskar	b Snow	6	lbw b Snow	0
AV Mankad	b Price	10	c Hutton b Underwood	11
*AL Wadekar	c Hutton b Illingworth	48	run out	45
DN Sardesai	b Illingworth	54	c Knott b Underwood	40
GR Viswanath	b Illingworth	0	c Knott b Luckhurst	33
ED Solkar	c Fletcher b D'Oliveira	44	c & b Underwood	1
+FM Engineer	c Illingworth b Snow	59	not out	28
S Abid Ali	b Illingworth	26	not out	4
S Venkataraghavan	lbw b Underwood	24		
BS Bedi	c D'Oliveira b Illingworth	2		
BS Chandrasekhar	not out	0		
	(b 6, lb 4, nb 1)	11	(b 6, lb 5, nb 1)	12
	(all out)	284	(6 wickets)	174

Bowling: Snow 24-5-68-2 Price 15-2-51-1 Hutton 12-2-30-0 D'Oliveira 7-5-5-1 Illingworth 34.3-12-70-5 Underwood 25-6-49-1
Snow 11-7-14-1 Price 5-0-10-0 D'Oliveira 9-3-17-0 Illingworth 36-15-40-0 Underwood 38-14-72-3 Luckhurst 2-0-9-1

Umpires: CS Elliott and AEG Rhodes

Kennington Oval, London

England v Australia
10,11,12,14,15,16 August 1972

Result: Australia won by 5 wickets

England Innings

B Wood	c Marsh b Watson	26	lbw b Massie	90
JH Edrich	lbw b Lillee	8	b Lillee	18
PH Parfitt	b Lillee	51	b Lillee	18
JH Hampshire	c Inverarity b Mallett	42	c IM Chappell b Watson	20
BL D'Oliveira	c GS Chappell b Mallett	4	c IM Chappell b Massie	43
AW Greig	c Stackpole b Mallett	16	c Marsh b Lillee	29
*R Illingworth	c GS Chappell b Lillee	0	lbw b Lillee	31
+APE Knott	c Marsh b Lillee	92	b Lillee	63
JA Snow	c Marsh b Lillee	3	c Stackpole b Mallett	14
GG Arnold	b Inverarity	22	lbw b Mallett	4
DL Underwood	not out	3	not out	0
	(lb 8, w 1, nb 8)	17	(b 11, lb 8, nb 7)	26
	(all out)	284	(all out)	356

Bowling: Lillee 24.2-7-58-5 Massie 27-5-69-0 Watson 12-4-23-1 Mallett 23-4-80-3 GS Chappell 2-0-18-0 Inverarity 4-0-19-1
Lillee 32.2-8-123-5 Massie 32-10-77-2 Watson 19-8-32-1 Mallett 23-7-66-2 Inverarity 15-4-32-0

Australia Innings

GD Watson	c Knott b Arnold	13	lbw b Arnold	6
KR Stackpole	b Snow	18	c Knott b Greig	79
*IM Chappell	c Snow b Arnold	118	c sub b Underwood	37
GS Chappell	c Greig b Illingworth	113	lbw b Underwood	16
R Edwards	b Underwood	79	lbw b Greig	1
AP Sheahan	c Hampshire b Underwood	5	not out	44
+RW Marsh	b Underwood	0	not out	43
RJ Inverarity	c Greig b Underwood	28		
AA Mallett	run out	5		
RAL Massie	b Arnold	4		
DK Lillee	not out	0		
	(lb 8, w 1, nb 7)	16	(lb 6, nb 10)	16
	(all out)	399	(5 wickets)	242

Bowling: Arnold 35-11-87-3 Snow 34.5-5-111-1 Greig 18-9-25-0 D'Oliveira 9-4-17-0 Underwood 38-16-90-4 Illingworth 17-4-53-1
Arnold 15-5-26-1 Snow 6-1-21-0 Greig 25.3-10-49-2 Underwood 35-11-94-2 Illingworth 8.5-2-26-0 Parfitt 2-0-10-0

Umpires: AE Fagg and AEG Rhodes

England v West Indies
26,27,28,30,31 July 1973

Result: West Indies won by 158 runs

West Indies Innings

RC Fredericks	lbw b Arnold	35	c Hayes b Arnold	3
RGA Headley	lbw b Greig	8	b Arnold	42
*RB Kanhai	b Greig	10	c Knott b Snow	0
CH Lloyd	b Arnold	132	c Greig b Snow	14
AI Kallicharran	c Knott b Arnold	80	b Illingworth	80
+DL Murray	c Roope b Arnold	28	c Roope b Underwood	5
GS Sobers	run out	10	c Underwood b Snow	51
BD Julien	lbw b Arnold	11	b Illingworth	23
KD Boyce	b Underwood	72	b Illingworth	9
Inshan Ali	c Boycott b Underwood	15	not out	5
LR Gibbs	not out	1	c Knott b Arnold	3
	(b 1, lb 2, nb 10)	13	(b 2, lb 13, nb 6)	21
	(all out)	415	(all out)	255

Bowling: Snow 31-8-71-0 Arnold 39-10-113-5 Greig 30.3-6-81-2 Roope 6-1-26-0 Underwood 23.3-8-68-2 Illingworth 15-3-43-0
Snow 18-4-62-3 Arnold 18.1-7-49-3 Greig 8-1-22-0 Underwood 19-5-51-1 Illingworth 24-8-50-3

England Innings

G Boycott	c Murray b Julien	97	c & b Gibbs	30
DL Amiss	b Boyce	29	c Kanhai b Boyce	15
GRJ Roope	b Boyce	9	c & b Gibbs	31
FC Hayes	c Lloyd b Sobers	16	not out	106
KWR Fletcher	c Lloyd b Julien	11	c Kallicharran b Gibbs	5
AW Greig	c Sobers b Boyce	38	c Gibbs b Ali	0
*R Illingworth	lbw b Sobers	27	b Boyce	40
+APE Knott	not out	4	lbw b Boyce	5
JA Snow	b Boyce	0	b Boyce	1
GG Arnold	c Kallicharran b Boyce	4	c Headley b Boyce	4
DL Underwood	c Headley b Sobers	0	lbw b Boyce	7
	(b 2, lb 7, w 2, nb 11)	22	(lb 5, w 1, nb 5)	11
	(all out)	257	(all out)	255

Bowling: Sobers 22.1-13-27-3 Boyce 22-4-70-5 Julien 20-6-49-2 Gibbs 23-8-37-0 Ali 11-3-52-0
Sobers 11-3-22-0 Boyce 21.1-4-77-6 Julien 17-4-35-0 Gibbs 33-9-61-3 Ali 23-6-49-1

Umpires: DJ Constant and TW Spencer

England v Pakistan
22,23,24,26,27 August 1974

Result: Match drawn

Pakistan Innings

Sadiq Mohammad	c Old b Willis	21	c & b Arnold	4
Majid Khan	b Underwood	98	c Denness b Old	18
Zaheer Abbas	b Underwood	240	c Knott b Arnold	15
Mushtaq Mohammad	b Arnold	76	b Underwood	8
Asif Iqbal	c & b Greig	29		
Wasim Raja	c Denness b Greig	28	not out	30
Imran Khan	c Knott b Willis	0	not out	10
*Intikhab Alam	not out	32		
Sarfraz Nawaz	not out	14		
+Wasim Bari				
Asif Masood				
	(b 6, lb 18, nb 14)	38	(b 5, nb 4)	9
	(7 wickets declared)	600	(4 wickets)	94

Bowling: Arnold 37-5-106-1 Willis 28-3-102-2 Old 29.3-3-143-0 Underwood 44-14-106-2 Greig 25-5-92-2 Lloyd 2-0-13-0
Arnold 6-0-22-2 Willis 7-1-27-0 Old 2-0-6-1 Underwood 8-2-15-1 Greig 7-1-15-0

England Innings

DL Amiss	c Majid Khan b Intikhab Alam	183	
D Lloyd	c Sadiq Mohammad b Sarfraz Nawaz	4	
DL Underwood	lbw b Wasim Raja	43	
JH Edrich	c Wasim Bari b Intikhab Alam	26	
*MH Denness	c Imran Khan b Asif Masood	18	
KWR Fletcher	run out	122	
AW Greig	b Intikhab Alam	32	
+APE Knott	b Intikhab Alam	9	
CM Old	lbw b Intikhab Alam	65	
GG Arnold	c Wasim Bari b Mushtaq Mohammad	2	
RGD Willis	not out	1	
	(b 8, lb 13, nb 20)	41	
	(all out)	545	

Bowling: Asif Masood 40-13-66-1 Sarfraz Nawaz 38-8-103-1 Intikhab Alam 51.4-14-116-5 Imran Khan 44-16-100-0
Mushtaq Mohammad 29-12-51-1 Wasim Raja 23-6-68-1

Umpires: WE Alley and HD Bird

England v Australia
28,29,30 August, 1,2,3 September 1975

Result: Match drawn

Australia Innings

RB McCosker	c Roope b Old	127	not out	25
A Turner	c Steele b Old	2	c Woolmer b Greig	8
*IM Chappell	c Greig b Woolmer	192		
GS Chappell	c Knott b Old	0	not out	4
R Edwards	c Edrich b Snow	44	c Old b Underwood	2
KD Walters	b Underwood	65		
+RW Marsh	c & b Greig	32		
MHN Walker	c Steele b Greig	13		
JR Thomson	c Old b Greig	0		
DK Lillee	not out	28		
AA Mallett	not out	5		
	(lb 5, nb 2, nb 17)	24	(lb 1)	1
	(9 wickets declared)	532	(2 wickets)	40

Bowling: Old 28-7-74-3 Snow 27-4-74-1 Woolmer 18-3-38-1 Edmonds 38-7-118-0 Underwood 44-13-96-1 Greig 24-5-107-3
Steele 2-1-1-0
Old 2-0-7-0 Snow 2-1-4-0 Edmonds 6.1-2-14-0 Underwood 2-0-5-1 Greig 5-2-9-1

England Innings

B Wood	b Walker	32	lbw b Thomson	22
JH Edrich	lbw b Walker	12	b Lillee	96
DS Steele	b Lillee	39	c Marsh b Lillee	66
GRJ Roope	c Turner b Walker	0	b Lillee	77
RA Woolmer	c Mallett b Thomson	5	lbw b Walters	149
*AW Greig	c Marsh b Lillee	17	c Marsh b Lillee	15
+APE Knott	lbw b Walker	9	c Marsh b Walters	64
PH Edmonds	c Marsh b Thomson	4	run out	7
CM Old	not out	25	c IM Chappell b Walters	0
JA Snow	c GS Chappell b Thomson	30	c & b Walters	0
DL Underwood	c GS Chappell b Thomson	0	not out	3
	(lb 3, w 3, nb 12)	18	(b 2, lb 15, w 5, nb 17)	39
	(all out)	191	(all out)	538

Bowling: Lillee 19-7-44-2 Thomson 22.1-7-50-4 Walker 25-7-63-4 Mallett 3-1-16-0
Lillee 52-18-91-4 Thomson 30-9-63-1 Walker 46-15-91-0 Mallett 64-31-95-0 IM Chappell 17-6-52-0 Walters 10.5-3-34-4 GS
Chappell 12-2-53-0 Edwards 0-2-0-20-0

Umpires: HD Bird and TW Spencer

England v West Indies
12,13,14,16,17 August 1976

Result: West Indies won by 231 runs

West Indies Innings

RC Fredericks	c Balderstone b Miller	71	not out	86
CG Greenidge	lbw b Willis	0	not out	85
IVA Richards	b Greig	291		
LG Rowe	st Knott b Underwood	70		
*CH Lloyd	c Knott b Greig	84		
CL King	c Selvey b Balderstone	63		
+DL Murray	c & b Underwood	36		
VA Holder	not out	13		
MA Holding	b Underwood	32		
AME Roberts				
WW Daniel				
	(b 1, lb 17, nb 9)	27	(b 15, lb 3, w 8)	26
	(8 wickets declared)	687	(all out)	203

Bowling: Willis 15-3-73-1 Selvey 15-0-67-0 Underwood 60.5-15-165-3 Woolmer 9-0-44-0 Miller 27-4-106-1 Balderstone 16-0-80-1 Greig 34-5-96-2 Willey 3-0-11-0 Steele 3-0-18-0
Willis 7-0-48-0 Selvey 9-1-44-0 Underwood 9-2-38-0 Woolmer 5-0-30-0 Greig 2-0-11-0

England Innings

RA Woolmer	lbw b Holding	8	c Murray b Holding	30
DL Amiss	b Holding	203	c Greenidge b Holding	16
DS Steele	lbw b Holding	44	c Murray b Holder	42
JC Balderstone	b Holding	0	b Holding	0
P Willey	c Fredericks b King	33	c Greenidge b Holder	1
*AW Greig	b Holding	12	b Holding	1
DL Underwood	b Holding	4	c Lloyd b Roberts	2
+APE Knott	b Holding	50	b Holding	57
G Miller	c sub b Holder	36	b Richards	24
MWW Selvey	b Holding	0	not out	4
RGD Willis	not out	1	lbw b Holding	0
	(b 8, lb 11, nb 21)	40	(b 15, lb 3, w 8)	26
	(all out)	435	(all out)	203

Bowling: Roberts 27-4-102-0 Holding 33-9-92-8 Holder 27.5-7-75-1 Daniel 10-1-30-0 Fredericks 11-2-36-0 Richards 14-4-30-0 King 7-3-30-1
Roberts 13-4-37-1 Holding 20.4-6-57-6 Holder 14-5-29-2 Fredericks 12-5-33-0 Richards 11-6-11-1 King 6-2-9-0 Lloyd 2-1-1-0

Umpires: WE Alley and HD Bird

England v Australia
25,26,27,29,30 August 1977

Result: Match drawn

England Innings

*JM Brearley	c Marsh b Malone	39	c Serjeant b Thomson	4
G Boycott	c McCosker b Walker	39	not out	25
RA Woolmer	lbw b Thomson	15	c Marsh b Malone	6
DW Randall	c Marsh b Malone	3	not out	20
AW Greig	c Bright b Malone	0		
GRJ Roope	b Thomson	38		
+APE Knott	c McCosker b Malone	6		
JK Lever	lbw b Malone	3		
DL Underwood	b Thomson	20		
M Hendrick	b Thomson	15		
RGD Willis	not out	24		
	(lb 6, w 1, nb 5)	12	(w 2)	2
	(all out)	214	(2 wickets)	57

Bowling: Thomson 23.2-3-87-4 Malone 47-20-63-5 Walker 28-11-51-1 Bright 3-2-1-0
Thomson 5-1-22-1 Malone 10-4-14-1 Walker 8-2-14-0 Bright 3-2-5-0

Australia Innings

CS Serjeant	lbw b Willis	0	
RB McCosker	lbw b Willis	32	
*GS Chappell	c & b Underwood	39	
KJ Hughes	c Willis b Hendrick	1	
DW Hookes	c Knott b Greig	85	
KD Walters	b Willis	4	
+RW Marsh	lbw b Hendrick	57	
RJ Bright	lbw b Willis	16	
MHN Walker	not out	78	
MF Malone	b Lever	46	
JR Thomson	b Willis	17	
	(b 1, lb 6, nb 3)	10	
	(all out)	385	

Bowling: Willis 29.3-5-102-5 Hendrick 37-5-93-2 Lever 22-6-61-1 Underwood 35-9-102-1 Greig 8-2-17-1

Umpires: DJ Constant and TW Spencer

England v New Zealand
27,28,29,31 July, 1 August 1978

Result: England won by 7 wickets

New Zealand Innings

Batsman				
JG Wright	c Radley b Willis	62	lbw b Botham	25
RW Anderson	b Old	4	c Taylor b Botham	2
GP Howarth	c Edmonds b Botham	94	b Willis	0
BA Edgar	c & b Miller	0	b Edmonds	38
*MG Burgess	lbw b Willis	34	lbw b Botham	7
BE Congdon	run out	2	b Miller	36
+GN Edwards	b Miller	6	c Brearley b Edmonds	11
RJ Hadlee	c Brearley b Willis	5	b Edmonds	7
BL Cairns	lbw b Willis	5	b Miller	27
BP Bracewell	c Taylor b Willis	0	b Miller	0
SL Boock	not out	3	not out	0
	(b 1, lb 7, nb 11)	19	(b 8, lb 10, nb 11)	29
	(all out)	234	(all out)	182

Bowling: Willis 20.2-9-42-5 Old 20-7-43-1 Botham 27-7-58-1 Miller 25-10-31-2 Edmonds 17-2-41-0
Willis 13-2-39-1 Old 5-2-13-0 Botham 19-2-46-3 Miller 34-19-35-2 Edmonds 34.1-23-20-4

England Innings

Batsman				
*JM Brearley	c Edwards b Bracewell	2	lbw b Boock	11
GA Gooch	lbw b Bracewell	0	not out	91
CT Radley	run out	49	lbw b Bracewell	2
DI Gower	run out	111	c Howarth b Cairns	11
GRJ Roope	b Boock	14	not out	10
G Miller	lbw b Cairns	0		
IT Botham	c Bracewell b Boock	22		
+RW Taylor	c Edwards b Hadlee	8		
PH Edmonds	lbw b Hadlee	28		
CM Old	c Edwards b Cairns	16		
RGD Willis	not out	3		
	(b 15, lb 8, nb 3)	26	(b 2, lb 3, nb 8)	13
	(all out)	279	(3 wickets)	138

Bowling: Hadlee 21.5-6-43-2 Bracewell 17-8-46-2 Cairns 40-16-65-2 Boock 35-18-61-2 Congdon 21-6-38-0
Hadlee 11.3-3-18-0 Bracewell 13-3-26-1 Cairns 7-0-21-1 Boock 20-6-55-1 Congdon 1-0-5-0

Umpires: DJ Constant and BJ Meyer

England v India
30,31 August, 1,3,4 September 1979

Result: Match drawn

England Innings

Batsman				
G Boycott	lbw b Kapil Dev	35	b Ghavri	125
AR Butcher	c Yajurvindra Singh b Venkataraghavan	14	c Venkataraghavan b Ghavri	20
GA Gooch	c Viswanath b Ghavri	79	lbw b Kapil Dev	31
DI Gower	lbw b Kapil Dev	7	c Reddy b Bedi	7
P Willey	c Yajurvindra Singh b Bedi	52	c Reddy b Ghavri	31
IT Botham	st Reddy b Venkataraghavan	38	not out	0
*JM Brearley	b Ghavri	34	b Venkataraghavan	11
+DL Bairstow	c Reddy b Kapil Dev	9	c Gavaskar b Kapil Dev	59
PH Edmonds	c Kapil Dev b Venkataraghavan	16	not out	27
RGD Willis	not out	10		
M Hendrick	c Gavaskar b Bedi	0		
	(lb 9, w 4, nb 5)	18	(lb 14, w 2, nb 7)	23
	(all out)	305	(8 wickets declared)	334

Bowling: Kapil Dev 32-12-83-3 Ghavri 26-8-61-2 Bedi 29.5-4-69-2 Yajurvindra Singh 8-2-15-0 Venkataraghavan 29-9-59-3
Kapil Dev 28.5-4-89-2 Ghavri 34-11-76-3 Venkataraghavan 26-4-75-1 Bedi 26-4-67-1 Yajurvindra Singh 2-0-4-0

India Innings

Batsman				
SM Gavaskar	c Bairstow b Botham	13	c Gower b Botham	221
CPS Chauhan	c Botham b Willis	6	c Botham b Willis	80
DB Vengsarkar	c Botham b Willis	0	c Botham b Edmonds	52
GR Viswanath	c Brearley b Botham	62	c Brearley b Willey	15
Yashpal Sharma	lbw b Willis	27	lbw b Botham	19
Yajurvindra Singh	not out	43	lbw b Botham	1
N Kapil Dev	b Hendrick	16	c Gooch b Willey	0
KD Ghavri	c Bairstow b Botham	7	not out	3
+B Reddy	c Bairstow b Botham	12	not out	5
*S Venkataraghavan	c & b Hendrick	2	run out	6
BS Bedi	c Brearley b Hendrick	1		
	(b 2, lb 3, w 5, nb 3)	13	(b 11, lb 15, w 1)	27
	(all out)	202	(8 wickets)	429

Bowling: Willis 18-2-53-3 Botham 28-7-65-4 Hendrick 22.3-7-38-3 Willey 4-1-10-0 Gooch 2-0-6-0 Edmonds 5-1-17-0
Willis 28-4-89-1 Botham 29-5-97-3 Hendrick 8-2-15-0 Edmonds 38-11-87-1 Willey 43.5-15-96-2 Gooch 2-0-9-0 Butcher 2-0-9-0

Umpires: DJ Constant and KE Palmer

England v West Indies
24,25,26,28,29 July 1980

Result: Match drawn

England Innings

Batsman				
GA Gooch	lbw b Holding	83	lbw b Holding	0
G Boycott	run out	53	c Murray b Croft	5
BC Rose	b Croft	50	lbw b Garner	41
W Larkins	lbw b Garner	0	b Holding	0
MW Gatting	b Croft	48	c Murray b Garner	15
P Willey	c Lloyd b Holding	34	not out	100
+APE Knott	c Lloyd b Marshall	3	lbw b Holding	3
*IT Botham	lbw b Croft	9	c Greenidge b Garner	4
JE Emburey	c Holding b Marshall	24	c sub b Croft	2
GR Dilley	b Garner	1	c sub b Holding	1
RGD Willis	not out	1	not out	24
	(b 7, lb 21, w 10, nb 19)	57	(lb 6, w 1, nb 7)	14
	(all out)	370	(9 wickets declared)	209

Bowling: Holding 28-5-67-2 Croft 35-9-97-3 Marshall 29.3-6-77-2 Garner 33-8-67-2 Richards 3-1-5-0
Holding 29-7-79-4 Croft 10-6-8-2 Marshall 23-7-47-0 Garner 17-5-24-3 Richards 9-3-15-0 Kallicharran 6-1-22-0

West Indies Innings

Batsman		
CG Greenidge	lbw b Willis	6
DL Haynes	c Gooch b Dilley	7
IVA Richards	c Willey b Botham	26
SFAF Bacchus	c Knott b Emburey	61
AI Kallicharran	c Rose b Dilley	11
*CH Murray	hit wicket b Dilley	0
MD Marshall	c Rose b Emburey	45
J Garner	c Gatting b Botham	46
MA Holding	lbw b Dilley	22
CEH Croft	not out	0
*CH Lloyd	absent hurt	0
	(lb 12, w 1, nb 28)	41
	(all out)	265

Bowling: Willis 19-5-58-1 Dilley 23-6-57-4 Botham 18.2-8-47-2 Emburey 23-12-38-2 Gooch 1-0-2-0 Willey 11-5-22-0

Umpires: BJ Meyer and DO Oslear

England v Australia
27,28,29,31 August, 1 September 1981

Result: Match drawn

Australia Innings

Batsman				
GM Wood	c Brearley b Botham	66	c Knott b Hendrick	21
MF Kent	c Gatting b Botham	54	c Brearley b Botham	7
*KJ Hughes	hit wicket b Botham	31	lbw b Hendrick	6
GN Yallop	c Botham b Willis	26	b Hendrick	35
AR Border	not out	106	c Tavare b Emburey	84
DM Wellham	b Willis	24	lbw b Botham	103
+RW Marsh	c Botham b Willis	12	c Gatting b Botham	52
RJ Bright	c Brearley b Botham	3	b Botham	11
DK Lillee	b Willis	11	not out	8
TM Alderman	b Botham	0		
MR Whitney	b Botham	4	c Botham b Hendrick	0
	(b 4, lb 6, w 1, nb 4)	15	(lb 8, w 1, nb 7)	17
	(all out)	352	(9 wickets declared)	344

Bowling: Willis 31-6-91-4 Hendrick 31-8-63-0 Botham 47-13-125-6 Emburey 23-2-58-0
Willis 10-0-41-0 Hendrick 29.2-6-82-4 Botham 42-9-128-4 Emburey 23-3-76-1

England Innings

Batsman				
G Boycott	c Yallop b Lillee	137	lbw b Lillee	0
W Larkins	c Alderman b Lillee	34	c Alderman b Lillee	24
CJ Tavare	c Marsh b Lillee	24	c Kent b Whitney	8
MW Gatting	b Lillee	53	c Kent b Lillee	56
*JM Brearley	c Bright b Alderman	51	c Marsh b Lillee	51
PWG Parker	c Kent b Alderman	0	c Kent b Alderman	13
IT Botham	c Yallop b Lillee	3	lbw b Alderman	16
+APE Knott	b Lillee	36	not out	70
JE Emburey	lbw b Lillee	0	not out	5
RGD Willis	b Alderman	3		
M Hendrick	not out	0		
	(lb 9, w 3, nb 12)	24	(b 2, lb 5, w 2, nb 9)	18
	(all out)	314	(7 wickets)	261

Bowling: Lillee 31.4-4-89-7 Alderman 35-4-84-3 Whitney 23-3-76-0 Bright 21-6-41-0
Lillee 30-10-70-4 Alderman 19-6-60-2 Whitney 11-4-46-1 Bright 27-12-50-0 Yallop 8-2-17-0

Umpires: HD Bird and BJ Meyer

England v India
8,9,10,12,13 July 1982

Result: Match drawn

England Innings

Batsman				
G Cook	c Shastri b Patil	50	c Yashpal Sharma b Kapil Dev	8
CJ Tavare	b Kapil Dev	39	not out	75
AJ Lamb	run out	107	b Doshi	45
DI Gower	c Kirmani b Shastri	47	c & b Nayak	45
IT Botham	c Viswanath b Doshi	208		
DW Randall	st Kirmani b Shastri	95		
DR Pringle	st Kirmani b Doshi	9		
PH Edmonds	c sub b Doshi	14		
+RW Taylor	lbw b Shastri	3		
PJW Allott	c Yashpal Sharma b Doshi	3		
*RGD Willis	not out	1		
	(b 3, lb 5, nb 10)	18	(b 6, lb 8, nb 4)	18
	(all out)	594	(3 wickets declared)	191

Bowling: Kapil Dev 25-4-109-1 Madan Lal 26-8-69-0 Nayak 21-5-66-0 Patil 14-1-48-1 Doshi 46-6-175-4 Shastri 41.3-8-109-3
Kapil Dev 19-3-53-1 Madan Lal 16-1-70-0 Nayak 5.3-0-16-1 Doshi 19-5-47-1 Shastri 16-3-40-0

India Innings

Batsman				
RJ Shastri	c Botham b Willis	66	c Taylor b Willis	0
DB Vengsarkar	c Edmonds b Botham	6	c Taylor b Pringle	16
GR Viswanath	lbw b Willis	56	not out	75
Yashpal Sharma	c Gower b Willis	38	not out	9
SM Patil	c sub b Botham	62		
+SMH Kirmani	b Allott	43		
N Kapil Dev	c Allott b Edmonds	97		
S Madan Lal	c Taylor b Edmonds	5		
SV Nayak	b Edmonds	11	c Taylor b Pringle	6
DR Doshi	not out	5		
*SM Gavaskar	absent hurt	0		
	(b 3, lb 5, nb 13)	21	(lb 3, nb 2)	5
	(all out)	410	(3 wickets)	111

Bowling: Willis 23-4-78-3 Botham 19-2-73-2 Allott 24-4-69-1 Pringle 28-5-80-0 Edmonds 35.2-11-89-3
Willis 4-0-16-1 Botham 4-0-12-0 Allott 4-1-12-0 Pringle 11-5-32-2 Edmonds 13-5-34-0

Umpires: HD Bird and AGT Whitehead

England v New Zealand
14,15,16,17,18 July 1983

Result: England won by 189 runs

England Innings

Batsman				
G Fowler	lbw b Hadlee	1	run out	105
CJ Tavare	run out	45	c Howarth b Bracewell	109
DI Gower	b Hadlee	11	c Howarth b Hadlee	25
AJ Lamb	b Cairns	24	not out	102
IT Botham	b Hadlee	15	run out	26
DW Randall	not out	75	c Coney b Hadlee	3
VJ Marks	c Lees b Hadlee	4	c MD Crowe b Bracewell	2
PH Edmonds	c & b Bracewell	12	not out	43
+RW Taylor	lbw b Hadlee	0		
*RGD Willis	c JJ Crowe b Bracewell	4		
NG Cowans	b Hadlee	3		
	(b 6, lb 6, nb 3)	15	(b 8, lb 23)	31
	(all out)	209	(6 wickets declared)	446

Bowling: Hadlee 23.4-6-53-6 Chatfield 17-3-48-0 Cairns 17-3-63-1 Bracewell 8-4-16-2 MD Crowe 5-0-14-0
Hadlee 37.2-7-99-2 Chatfield 35-9-85-0 Cairns 30-7-67-0 Bracewell 54-13-115-2 MD Crowe 3-0-9-0 Coney 27-11-39-0 Howarth 3-2-1-0

New Zealand Innings

Batsman				
JG Wright	c Gower b Willis	0	run out	88
BA Edgar	c Taylor b Willis	12	c Taylor b Willis	3
JJ Crowe	c Randall b Willis	0	c Lamb b Willis	9
*GP Howarth	b Cowans	4	c Taylor b Edmonds	67
MD Crowe	b Willis	44	c Taylor b Edmonds	33
JV Coney	run out	44	lbw b Marks	2
RJ Hadlee	c & b Botham	84	c Taylor b Marks	11
JG Bracewell	c & b Botham	7	c Gower b Marks	0
+WK Lees	not out	31	not out	8
BL Cairns	c Lamb b Botham	2	c Willis b Edmonds	32
EJ Chatfield	c Willis b Botham	0	not out	10
	(lb 6, nb 6)	12	(b 3, lb 1, nb 3)	7
	(all out)	196	(all out)	270

Bowling: Willis 20-8-43-4 Cowans 19-3-60-1 Botham 16-2-62-4 Edmonds 2-0-19-0
Willis 12-3-26-2 Cowans 11-2-41-0 Botham 4-0-17-0 Edmonds 40.1-16-101-3 Marks 43-20-78-3

Umpires: HD Bird and DGL Evans

Kennington Oval, London

England v West Indies
9,10,11,13,14 August 1984

Result: West Indies won by 172 runs

West Indies Innings

CG Greenidge	lbw b Botham	22	c Botham b Agnew	34
DL Haynes	b Allott	10	b Botham	125
HA Gomes	c Botham b Ellison	18	c Tavare b Ellison	1
IVA Richards	c Allott b Botham	8	lbw b Agnew	15
+PJL Dujon	c Tavare b Botham	3	c Lamb b Ellison	49
*CH Lloyd	not out	60	c Downton b Marshall	36
MD Marshall	c Gower b Ellison	0	c Lamb b Botham	12
EAE Baptiste	c Fowler b Allott	32	c Downton b Allott	5
RA Harper	b Botham	18	c Downton b Allott	17
MA Holding	lbw b Botham	0	lbw b Botham	30
J Garner	c Downton b Allott	6	not out	10
	(b 1, lb 4, w 7, nb 1)	13	(lb 12)	12
	(all out)	190	(all out)	346

Bowling: Agnew 12-3-46-0 Allott 17-7-25-3 Botham 23-8-72-5 Ellison 18-3-34-2
Agnew 14-1-51-2 Allott 26-1-96-2 Botham 22.3-2-103-3 Ellison 26-7-60-3 Pocock 8-3-24-0

England Innings

G Fowler	c Richards b Baptiste	31	c Richards b Marshall	7
BC Broad	b Garner	4	c Greenidge b Holding	39
PI Pocock	c Greenidge b Marshall	0	c & b Holding	0
CJ Tavare	c Dujon b Holding	16	c Richards b Garner	49
*DI Gower	c Dujon b Holding	12	lbw b Holding	7
AJ Lamb	lbw b Marshall	12	c Haynes b Holding	1
IT Botham	c Dujon b Marshall	14	c Marshall b Garner	54
+PR Downton	c Lloyd b Garner	16	b Garner	10
RM Ellison	not out	20	c Holding b Garner	13
PJW Allott	b Marshall	16	c Lloyd b Holding	4
JP Agnew	b Marshall	5	not out	2
	(b 2, lb 4, nb 10)	16	(b 2, w 1, nb 13)	16
	(all out)	162	(all out)	202

Bowling: Garner 18-6-37-2 Marshall 17.5-5-35-5 Holding 13-2-55-2 Baptiste 12-4-19-1 Harper 1-1-0-0
Garner 18.4-3-51-4 Marshall 22-5-71-1 Holding 13-2-43-5 Baptiste 8-3-11-0 Harper 8-5-10-0

Umpires: DJ Constant and BJ Meyer

England v Australia
29,30,31 August, 2 September 1985

Result: England won by an innings and 94 runs

England Innings

GA Gooch	c & b McDermott	196
RT Robinson	b McDermott	3
*DI Gower	c Bennett b McDermott	157
MW Gatting	c Border b Bennett	4
JE Emburey	c Wellham b Lawson	9
AJ Lamb	c McDermott b Lawson	1
IT Botham	c Phillips b Lawson	12
+PR Downton	b McDermott	16
RM Ellison	c Phillips b Gilbert	3
PH Edmonds	lbw b Lawson	12
LB Taylor	not out	1
	(b 13, lb 11, nb 26)	50
	(all out)	464

Bowling: Lawson 29.2-6-101-4 McDermott 31-2-108-4 Gilbert 21-2-96-1 Bennett 32-8-111-1 Border 2-0-8-0 Wessels 3-0-16-0

Australia Innings

GM Wood	lbw b Botham	22	b Botham	6
AMJ Hilditch	c Gooch b Botham	17	c Gower b Taylor	9
KC Wessels	b Emburey	12	c Downton b Botham	7
*AR Border	c Edmonds	38	c Botham b Ellison	58
DM Wellham	c Downton b Ellison	13	lbw b Ellison	5
GM Ritchie	not out	64	c Downton b Ellison	6
+WB Phillips	b Edmonds	18	c Downton b Botham	10
MJ Bennett	c Robinson b Ellison	12	c & b Taylor	11
GF Lawson	c Botham b Taylor	14	c Downton b Ellison	7
CJ McDermott	run out	25	c Botham b Ellison	2
DR Gilbert	b Botham	1	not out	0
	(lb 3, w 2)	5	(b 4, nb 4)	8
	(all out)	241	(all out)	129

Bowling: Botham 20-3-64-3 Taylor 13-1-39-1 Ellison 18-5-35-2 Emburey 19-7-48-1 Edmonds 14-2-52-2
Botham 17-3-44-3 Taylor 11.3-1-34-2 Ellison 17-3-46-5 Emburey 1-0-1-0

Umpires: HD Bird and KE Palmer

England v New Zealand
21,22,23,25,26 August 1986

Result: Match drawn

New Zealand Innings

JG Wright	b Edmonds	119	not out	7
BA Edgar	c Gooch b Botham	1	not out	0
JJ Crowe	lbw b Botham	8		
MD Crowe	lbw b Dilley	13		
*JV Coney	c Gooch b Botham	38		
EJ Gray	b Dilley	30		
RJ Hadlee	c French b Edmonds	6		
JG Bracewell	c Athey b Emburey	3		
+TE Blain	c Gooch b Dilley	37		
DA Stirling	not out	18		
EJ Chatfield	c French b Dilley	5		
	(b 1, w 1, nb 7)	9		0
	(all out)	287	(0 wickets)	7

Bowling: Dilley 28.2-4-92-4 Small 18-5-36-0 Botham 25-4-75-3 Emburey 31-15-39-1 Edmonds 22-10-29-2 Gooch 4-1-15-0
Botham 1-0-7-0

England Innings

GA Gooch	c Stirling b Hadlee	32
CWJ Athey	lbw b Hadlee	17
DI Gower	b Chatfield	131
AJ Lamb	b Chatfield	0
*MW Gatting	c Chatfield	121
IT Botham	not out	59
JE Emburey	not out	9
+BN French		
PH Edmonds		
GR Dilley		
GC Small		
	(lb 9, w 5, nb 5)	19
	(5 wickets declared)	388

Bowling: Hadlee 23.5-6-92-2 Stirling 9-0-71-0 Chatfield 21-7-73-3 Gray 21-4-74-0 Bracewell 11-1-51-0 Coney 5-0-18-0

Umpires: HD Bird and DR Shepherd

England v Pakistan
6,7,8,10,11 August 1987

Result: Match drawn

Pakistan Innings

Mudassar Nazar	c Moxon b Botham	73
Rameez Raja	b Botham	14
Mansoor Akhtar	c French b Dilley	5
Javed Miandad	c & b Dilley	260
Saleem Malik	c Gower b Botham	102
*Imran Khan	run out	118
Ijaz Ahmed	c Moxon b Dilley	69
+Saleem Yousuf	c & b Dilley	42
Wasim Akram	c Botham b Dilley	5
Abdul Qadir	c Moxon b Dilley	0
Tauseef Ahmed	not out	0
	(b 2, lb 18)	20
	(all out)	708

Bowling: Dilley 47.3-10-154-6 Foster 12-3-32-0 Botham 52-7-217-3 Emburey 61-10-143-0 Edmonds 32-8-97-0 Gatting 10-2-18-0 Moxon 6-2-27-0

England Innings

BC Broad	c Saleem Yousuf b Imran Khan	0	c Ijaz Ahmed b Abdul Qadir	42
MD Moxon	c Javed Miandad b Abdul Qadir	8	c Saleem Yousuf b Tauseef Ahmed	15
RT Robinson	b Abdul Qadir	30	c Wasim Akram b Abdul Qadir	10
DI Gower	b Tauseef Ahmed	28	c Mudassar Nazar b Abdul Qadir	34
*MW Gatting	c Imran Khan b Abdul Qadir	61	not out	150
IT Botham	b Abdul Qadir	34	not out	51
JE Emburey	c Saleem Malik b Abdul Qadir	53		
+BN French	c Saleem Malik b Abdul Qadir	1		
NA Foster	c Ijaz Ahmed b Tauseef Ahmed	4		
PH Edmonds	lbw b Abdul Qadir	2		
GR Dilley	not out	0		
	(b 4, lb 3, w 1, nb 3)	11	(b 4, lb 5, w 1, nb 3)	13
	(all out)	232	(4 wickets)	315

Bowling: Imran Khan 18-2-39-1 Wasim Akram 14-2-37-0 Abdul Qadir 44.4-15-96-7 Tauseef Ahmed 23-9-53-2
Imran Khan 26.3-8-59-0 Wasim Akram 6-3-3-0 Abdul Qadir 53-21-115-3 Tauseef Ahmed 46.3-15-98-1 Mudassar Nazar 6-0-21-0 Javed Miandad 4-2-10-0

Umpires: DJ Constant and KE Palmer

England v West Indies
4,5,6,8 August 1988

Result: West Indies won by 8 wickets

England Innings

*GA Gooch	c Logie b Ambrose	9	c Greenidge b Ambrose	84
TS Curtis	c Dujon b Benjamin	30	lbw b Marshall	15
RJ Bailey	c Dujon b Ambrose	43	b Benjamin	3
RA Smith	c Harper b Marshall	57	lbw b Benjamin	0
MP Maynard	c Dujon b Ambrose	3	c & b Benjamin	10
DJ Capel	c Marshall b Harper	16	lbw b Walsh	12
+CJ Richards	c Logie b Harper	0	c Dujon b Walsh	3
DR Pringle	c Dujon b Marshall	1	b Harper	8
PAJ DeFreitas	c Haynes b Harper	18	c Haynes b Harper	0
NA Foster	c sub (KLT Arthurton) b Marshall	34	c Logie b Benjamin	34
JH Childs	not out	0	not out	0
	(lb 6, nb 15)	21	(b 3, lb 15, nb 15)	33
	(all out)	205	(all out)	202

Bowling: Marshall 24.3-3-64-3 Ambrose 20-6-31-3 Walsh 10-1-21-0 Benjamin 14-2-33-1 Harper 21-7-50-3 Hooper 1-1-0-0
Marshall 25-6-52-1 Ambrose 24.1-10-50-1 Benjamin 22-4-52-4 Walsh 15-2-21-2 Harper 6-3-9-2

West Indies Innings

CG Greenidge	c DeFreitas b Foster	10	c Richards b Childs	77
DL Haynes	c Richards b Foster	2	not out	77
CL Hooper	c Gooch b Foster	11	b Foster	23
*IVA Richards	c Curtis b Foster	47	not out	38
AL Logie	c Gooch b Foster	47		
+PJL Dujon	lbw b Pringle	64		
RA Harper	run out	17		
MD Marshall	c & b Childs	0		
CEL Ambrose	not out	17		
WKM Benjamin	b Pringle	0		
CA Walsh	c DeFreitas b Pringle	5		
	(lb 7, w 1, nb 2)	10	(b 2, lb 3, nb 6)	11
	(all out)	183	(2 wickets)	226

Bowling: Foster 16-2-64-5 DeFreitas 13-4-33-0 Pringle 17-4-45-3 Capel 7-0-21-0 Childs 6-1-13-1
Foster 18-3-52-1 DeFreitas 17-2-46-0 Childs 40-16-79-1 Pringle 13-4-24-0 Capel 3-0-20-0

Umpires: HD Bird and KE Palmer

England v Australia
24,25,26,28,29 August 1989

Result: Match drawn

Australia Innings

GR Marsh	c Igglesden b Small	17	lbw b Igglesden	4
MA Taylor	c Russell b Igglesden	71	c Russell b Small	48
DC Boon	c Atherton b Small	46	run out	37
*AR Border	c Russell b Capel	76	not out	51
DM Jones	c Gower b Small	122	b Capel	50
SR Waugh	b Igglesden	14	not out	7
+IA Healy	c Russell b Pringle	44		
TV Hohns	c Russell b Pringle	30		
MG Hughes	lbw b Pringle	21		
GF Lawson	b Pringle	2		
TM Alderman	not out	6		
	(b 1, lb 7, nb 9)	17	(b 2, lb 7, nb 13)	22
	(all out)	468	(4 wickets declared)	219

Bowling: Small 40-8-141-3 Igglesden 24-2-91-2 Pringle 24.3-6-70-4 Capel 16-2-66-1 Cook 25-5-78-0 Atherton 1-0-10-0 Gooch 2-1-2-0
Small 20-4-57-1 Igglesden 13-1-55-1 Capel 8-0-35-1 Pringle 16-0-53-0 Cook 6-2-10-0

England Innings

GA Gooch	lbw b Alderman	0	c & b Alderman	10
JP Stephenson	c Waugh b Alderman	25	lbw b Alderman	11
MA Atherton	c Healy b Hughes	12	b Lawson	14
RA Smith	b Lawson	11	not out	77
*DI Gower	c Healy b Alderman	79	c Waugh b Lawson	7
DJ Capel	c Healy b Alderman	4	c Taylor b Hohns	17
+RC Russell	c Healy b Alderman	12	not out	0
DR Pringle	c Taylor b Hohns	27		
GC Small	c Jones b Lawson	59		
NGB Cook	c Jones b Lawson	31		
AP Igglesden	not out	2		
	(b 2, lb 7, w 1, nb 13)	23	(lb 1, w 1, nb 5)	7
	(all out)	285	(5 wickets)	143

Bowling: Alderman 27-7-66-5 Lawson 29.1-9-85-3 Hughes 23-3-84-1 Hohns 10-1-30-1 Waugh 3-0-11-0
Alderman 13-3-30-2 Lawson 15.1-2-41-2 Hughes 8-2-34-0 Hohns 10-2-37-1

Umpires: HD Bird and KE Palmer

England v India
23,24,25,27,28 August 1990

Result: Match drawn

India Innings

RJ Shastri	c Lamb b Malcolm	187			
NS Sidhu	c Russell b Fraser	12			
SV Manjrekar	c Russell b Malcolm	22			
DB Vengsarkar	c & b Atherton	33			
*M Azharuddin	c Russell b Williams	78			
M Prabhakar	lbw b Fraser	28			
SR Tendulkar	c Lamb b Williams	21			
N Kapil Dev	st Russell b Hemmings	110			
+KS More	not out	61			
AS Wassan	b Hemmings	15			
ND Hirwani	not out	2			
	(b 7, lb 8, w 6, nb 16)	37			
	(9 wickets declared)	606			

Bowling: Malcolm 35-7-110-2 Fraser 42-17-112-2 Williams 41-5-148-2 Gooch 12-1-44-0 Hemmings 36-3-117-2 Atherton 7-0-60-1

England Innings

*GA Gooch	c Shastri b Hirwani	85	c Vengsarkar b Hirwani	88
MA Atherton	c More b Prabhakar	7	lbw b Kapil Dev	86
NF Williams	lbw b Prabhakar	38		
DI Gower	lbw b Wassan	8	not out	157
JE Morris	c More b Wassan	7	c More b Wassan	32
AJ Lamb	b Kapil Dev	7	c Shastri b Kapil Dev	52
RA Smith	c Manjrekar b Shastri	57	not out	7
+RC Russell	run out	35		
EE Hemmings	c Vengsarkar b Prabhakar	51		
ARC Fraser	c More b Prabhakar	0		
DE Malcolm	not out	15		
	(b 8, lb 9, w 4, nb 9)	30	(b 16, lb 22, w 5, nb 12)	55
	(all out)	340	(4 wickets declared)	477

Bowling: Kapil Dev 25-7-70-1 Prabhakar 32.4-9-74-4 Wassan 19-3-79-2 Hirwani 35-12-71-1 Shastri 12-2-29-1
Kapil Dev 24-5-66-2 Prabhakar 25-8-56-0 Wassan 18-2-94-1 Hirwani 59-18-137-1 Shastri 28-2-86-0

Umpires: NT Plews and DR Shepherd

England v West Indies
8,9,10,11,12 August 1991

Result: England won by 5 wickets

England Innings

*GA Gooch	lbw b Ambrose	60	lbw b Marshall	29
H Morris	c Lambert b Ambrose	44	c Dujon b Patterson	2
MA Atherton	c Hooper b Walsh	0	c Hooper b Patterson	13
RA Smith	lbw b Marshall	109	c Patterson b Walsh	26
MR Ramprakash	c Lambert b Hooper	25	lbw b Lambert	19
+AJ Stewart	c Richardson b Patterson	31	not out	38
IT Botham	hit wicket b Ambrose	31	not out	4
CC Lewis	not out	47		
PAJ DeFreitas	c Dujon b Walsh	7		
DV Lawrence	c Richards b Walsh	9		
PCR Tufnell	c Haynes b Patterson	2		
	(b 8, lb 10, w 1, nb 35)	54	(b 4, w 1, nb 10)	15
	(all out)	419	(5 wickets)	146

Bowling: Ambrose 36-8-83-3 Patterson 25.1-3-87-2 Walsh 32-5-91-3 Marshall 24-5-62-1 Hooper 34-1-78-1
Ambrose 8-0-48-0 Marshall 5-3-9-1 Walsh 9-3-18-1 Patterson 9-0-63-2 Lambert 0.4-0-4-1

West Indies Innings

PV Simmons	lbw b Lawrence	15	c Lewis b Botham	36
DL Haynes	not out	75	lbw b Lawrence	43
RB Richardson	c Stewart b Botham	20	c Gooch b Lawrence	121
CL Hooper	c Stewart b DeFreitas	3	c Gooch b Tufnell	54
CB Lambert	c Ramprakash b Tufnell	39	lbw b Botham	14
+PJL Dujon	lbw b Lawrence	0	c Stewart b Lawrence	5
MD Marshall	c Botham b Tufnell	0	b DeFreitas	17
*IVA Richards	c Stewart b Tufnell	2	c Morris b Lawrence	60
CEL Ambrose	c Botham b Tufnell	0	lbw b DeFreitas	0
CA Walsh	c Gooch b Tufnell	0	lbw b Lawrence	14
BP Patterson	c Botham b Tufnell	2	not out	1
	(lb 9, nb 11)	20	(b 7, lb 5, w 2, nb 6)	20
	(all out)	176	(all out)	385

Bowling: DeFreitas 13-6-38-1 Lawrence 16-1-67-2 Tufnell 14.3-3-25-6 Botham 11-4-27-1 Lewis 3-1-10-0
DeFreitas 20-9-42-2 Lawrence 25.5-4-106-5 Botham 16-4-40-2 Lewis 25-12-35-0 Tufnell 46-6-150-1

Umpires: JW Holder and MJ Kitchen

England v Pakistan
6,7,8,9 August 1992

Result: Pakistan won by 10 wickets

England Innings

*GA Gooch	c Asif Mujtaba b Aaqib Javed	20	c Aamer Sohail b Waqar Younis	24
+AJ Stewart	c Rameez Raja b Wasim Akram	31	lbw b Waqar Younis	8
MA Atherton	c Rashid Latif b Waqar Younis	60	c Rashid Latif b Waqar Younis	4
RA Smith	b Mushtaq Ahmed	33	not out	84
DI Gower	b Aaqib Javed	27	b Waqar Younis	1
MR Ramprakash	lbw b Wasim Akram	2	c Asif Mujtaba b Mushtaq Ahmed	17
CC Lewis	lbw b Wasim Akram	4	st Rashid Latif b Mushtaq Ahmed	14
DR Pringle	b Wasim Akram	1	b Wasim Akram	1
NA Mallender	b Wasim Akram	4	c Mushtaq Ahmed b Wasim Akram	3
PCR Tufnell	not out	0	b Wasim Akram	0
DE Malcolm	b Wasim Akram	2	b Waqar Younis	0
	(b 4, lb 8, w 1, nb 10)	23	(b 1, lb 8, nb 9)	18
	(all out)	207	(all out)	174

Bowling: Wasim Akram 22.1-3-67-6 Waqar Younis 16-4-37-1 Aaqib Javed 16-6-44-2 Mushtaq Ahmed 24-7-47-1
Wasim Akram 21-6-36-3 Aaqib Javed 9-2-25-0 Waqar Younis 18-5-52-5 Mushtaq Ahmed 23-6-46-2 Aamer Sohail 1-0-6-0

Pakistan Innings

Aamer Sohail	c Stewart b Malcolm	49	not out	4
Rameez Raja	b Malcolm	19	not out	0
Shoaib Mohammad	c & b Tufnell	55		
*Javed Miandad	c & b Lewis	59		
Saleem Malik	b Malcolm	40		
Asif Mujtaba	run out	50		
Wasim Akram	c Stewart b Malcolm	7		
+Rashid Latif	c Smith b Mallender	50		
Waqar Younis	c Gooch b Malcolm	6		
Mushtaq Ahmed	c Lewis b Mallender	9		
Aaqib Javed	not out	0		
	(b 2, lb 6, w 4, nb 24)	36	(w 1)	1
	(all out)	380	(0 wickets)	5

Bowling: Mallender 28.5-6-93-2 Malcolm 29-6-94-5 Lewis 30-8-70-1 Tufnell 34-9-87-1 Pringle 6-0-28-0
Ramprakash 0.1-0-5-0

Umpires: HD Bird and DR Shepherd; Referee: CL Walcott (WI)

England v Australia
19,20,21,22,23 August 1993

Result: England won by 161 runs

England Innings

GA Gooch	c Border b SR Waugh	56	c Healy b Warne	79
*MA Atherton	lbw b SR Waugh	50	c Warne b Reiffel	42
GA Hick	c Warne b May	80	c Healy b Warne	36
MP Maynard	b Warne	20	c Reiffel b Hughes	9
N Hussain	c Taylor b Warne	30	c ME Waugh b Hughes	0
+AJ Stewart	c Healy b Hughes	76	c ME Waugh b Reiffel	35
MR Ramprakash	c Healy b Hughes	6	c Slater b Hughes	64
ARC Fraser	b Reiffel	28	c Healy b Reiffel	13
SL Watkin	c SR Waugh b Reiffel	13	lbw b Warne	4
PM Such	c ME Waugh b Hughes	4	lbw b Warne	10
DE Malcolm	not out	0	not out	0
	(lb 7, w 1, nb 9)	17	(b 5, lb 12, w 1, nb 3)	21
	(all out)	380	(all out)	313

Bowling: Hughes 30-7-121-3 Reiffel 28.5-4-88-2 SR Waugh 12-2-45-2 Warne 20-5-70-2 ME Waugh 1-0-17-0 May 10-3-32-1
Hughes 31.2-9-110-3 Reiffel 24-8-55-3 Warne 40-15-78-3 May 24-6-53-1

Australia Innings

MA Taylor	c Hussain b Malcolm	70	b Watkin	8
MJ Slater	c Gooch b Malcolm	4	c Stewart b Watkin	12
DC Boon	c Gooch b Malcolm	13	lbw b Watkin	0
ME Waugh	c Stewart b Fraser	10	c Ramprakash b Malcolm	49
*AR Border	c Stewart b Fraser	48	c Stewart b Fraser	17
SR Waugh	b Fraser	20	lbw b Malcolm	26
+IA Healy	not out	83	c Maynard b Watkin	5
MG Hughes	c Ramprakash b Watkin	7	c Watkin b Fraser	12
PR Reiffel	c & b Fraser	0	c Maynard b Watkin	42
SK Warne	c Stewart b Fraser	16	lbw b Fraser	37
TBA May	c Stewart b Fraser	15	not out	4
	(b 5, lb 6, w 2, nb 4)	17	(b 2, lb 6, w 2, nb 7)	17
	(all out)	303	(all out)	229

Bowling: Malcolm 26-5-86-3 Watkin 28-4-87-2 Fraser 26.4-4-87-5 Such 14-4-32-0
Malcolm 20-3-84-3 Watkin 25-9-65-4 Fraser 19.1-5-44-3 Such 9-4-17-0 Hick 8-3-11-0

Umpires: MJ Kitchen and BJ Meyer
TV Umpire: AA Jones; Referee: CH Lloyd (WI)

England v South Africa
18,19,20,21 August 1994

Result: England won by 8 wickets

South Africa Innings

G Kirsten	c Rhodes b DeFreitas	2	c & b Malcolm	0
PN Kirsten	b Malcolm	16	c DeFreitas b Malcolm	1
WJ Cronje	lbw b Benjamin	38	b Malcolm	0
*KC Wessels	lbw b Benjamin	45	c Rhodes b Malcolm	28
DJ Cullinan	c Rhodes b DeFreitas	7	c Thorpe b Gough	94
JN Rhodes	retired hurt	8	c Rhodes b Malcolm	10
BM McMillan	c Hick b DeFreitas	93	c Thorpe b Malcolm	25
+DJ Richardson	c Rhodes b Benjamin	58	lbw b Malcolm	3
CR Matthews	c Hick b Benjamin	0	c Rhodes b Malcolm	0
PS de Villiers	c Stewart b DeFreitas	14	not out	0
AA Donald	not out	14	b Malcolm	0
	(b 8, lb 10, w 1, nb 18)	37	(lb 5, nb 9)	14
	(all out)	332	(all out)	175

Bowling: DeFreitas 26.2-5-93-4 Malcolm 25-5-81-1 Gough 19-1-85-0 Benjamin 27-2-42-4 Hick 5-1-13-0
DeFreitas 12-3-25-0 Malcolm 16.3-2-57-9 Gough 9-1-39-1 Benjamin 11-1-38-0 Hick 2-0-11-0

England Innings

GA Gooch	c Richardson b Donald	8	b Matthews	33
*MA Atherton	lbw b de Villiers	63	c Richardson b Donald	63
GA Hick	b Donald	39	not out	81
GP Thorpe	b Matthews	79	not out	15
AJ Stewart	b de Villiers	62		
JP Crawley	c Richardson b Donald	5		
+SJ Rhodes	lbw b de Villiers	11		
PAJ DeFreitas	run out	37		
D Gough	not out	42		
JE Benjamin	lbw b de Villiers	0		
DE Malcolm	c sub (TG Shaw) b Matthews	4		
	(b 1, w 1, nb 15)	17	(lb 6, nb 7)	13
	(all out)	304	(2 wickets)	205

Bowling: Donald 17-2-76-3 de Villiers 19-3-62-4 Matthews 21-4-82-2 McMillan 12-1-67-0 Cronje 8-3-16-0
Donald 12-1-96-1 de Villiers 12-0-66-0 Matthews 11.3-4-37-1

Umpires: RS Dunne (NZ) and KE Palmer
TV Umpire: AGT Whitehead; Referee: PJP Burge (Aus)

England v West Indies
24,25,26,27,28 August 1995

Result: Match drawn

England Innings

*MA Atherton	c Williams b Benjamin	36	c Browne b Bishop	95
JER Gallian	c Hooper b Ambrose	0	c Williams b Ambrose	25
JP Crawley	c Richardson b Hooper	50	c Browne b Ambrose	2
GP Thorpe	c Browne b Ambrose	74	c Williams b Walsh	38
GA Hick	c Williams b Benjamin	96	not out	51
AP Wells	c Campbell b Ambrose	0	not out	3
+RC Russell	b Ambrose	91		
M Watkinson	c Browne b Walsh	13		
DG Cork	b Ambrose	33		
ARC Fraser	not out	10		
DE Malcolm	c Lara b Benjamin	10		
	(b 15, lb 11, nb 15)	41	(lb 4, nb 5)	9
	(all out)	454	(4 wickets)	223

Bowling: Ambrose 42-10-96-5 Walsh 32-6-84-1 Benjamin 27-6-81-3 Bishop 35-5-111-0 Hooper 23-7-56-1
Ambrose 19-8-35-2 Walsh 28-7-80-1 Bishop 22-4-56-1 Hooper 22-11-26-0 Chanderpaul 6-0-22-0 Lara 1-1-0-0

West Indies Innings

SC Williams	c Russell b Malcolm	30		
SL Campbell	c Russell b Fraser	89		
KCG Benjamin	c Atherton b Cork	20		
BC Lara	c Fraser b Malcolm	179		
*RB Richardson	c Hick b Cork	93		
CL Hooper	c Russell b Malcolm	127		
S Chanderpaul	c Gallian b Cork	80		
+CO Browne	not out	27		
IR Bishop	run out	10		
CEL Ambrose	not out	5		
CA Walsh				
	(b 5, lb 20, w 5, nb 2)	32		
	(8 wickets declared)	692		

Bowling: Malcolm 39-7-160-3 Fraser 40-6-155-1 Watkinson 26-3-113-0 Cork 36-3-145-3 Gallian 12-1-56-0 Hick 10-3-38-0

Umpires: VK Ramaswamy (Ind) and DR Shepherd
TV Umpire: JH Hampshire; Referee: JR Reid (NZ)

Kennington Oval, London

England v Pakistan
22,23,24,25,26 August 1996

Result: Pakistan won by 9 wickets

England Innings

*MA Atherton	b Waqar Younis	31	c Inzamam-ul-Haq b Mushtaq Ahmed	43
+AJ Stewart	b Mushtaq Ahmed	44	c Asif Mujtaba b Mushtaq Ahmed	54
N Hussain	c Saeed Anwar b Waqar Younis	12	lbw b Mushtaq Ahmed	51
GP Thorpe	lbw b Mohammad Akram	54	c Wasim Akram b Mushtaq Ahmed	9
JP Crawley	b Waqar Younis	106	c Aamer Sohail b Wasim Akram	19
NV Knight	b Mushtaq Ahmed	17	c & b Mushtaq Ahmed	8
CC Lewis	b Wasim Akram	5	lbw b Waqar Younis	4
IDK Salisbury	c Inzamam-ul-Haq b Wasim Akram	5	not out	0
DG Cork	c Moin Khan b Waqar Younis	0	b Mushtaq Ahmed	26
RDB Croft	not out	5	c Ijaz Ahmed b Wasim Akram	6
AD Mullally	b Wasim Akram	24	b Wasim Akram	0
	(lb 12, w 1, nb 10)	23	(b 6, lb 2, w 1, nb 13)	22
	(all out)	326	(all out)	242

Bowling: Wasim Akram 29.2-9-83-3 Waqar Younis 25-6-95-4 Mohammad Akram 12-1-41-1 Mushtaq Ahmed 27-5-78-2 Aamer Sohail 6-1-17-0
Wasim Akram 15.4-1-67-3 Waqar Younis 18-3-55-1 Mushtaq Ahmed 37-10-78-6 Aamer Sohail 2-1-4-0 Mohammad Akram 10-3-30-0

Pakistan Innings

Saeed Anwar	c Croft b Cork	176	c Knight b Mullally	1
Aamer Sohail	c Cork b Croft	46	not out	29
Ijaz Ahmed	c Stewart b Mullally	61	not out	13
Inzamam-ul-Haq	c Hussain b Mullally	35		
Saleem Malik	not out	100		
Asif Mujtaba	run out (Lewis)	13		
*Wasim Akram	st Stewart b Croft	40		
+Moin Khan	b Salisbury	23		
Mushtaq Ahmed	c Crawley b Mullally	2		
Waqar Younis	not out	0		
Mohammad Akram				
	(b 4, lb 5, nb 16)	25	(nb 5)	5
	(8 wickets declared)	521	(1 wicket)	48

Bowling: Lewis 23-3-112-0 Mullally 37.1-7-97-3 Croft 47-10-116-2 Cork 23-5-71-1 Salisbury 29-3-116-1
Cork 3-0-15-0 Mullally 3-0-24-1 Croft 0.4-0-9-0

Umpires: BC Cooray (SL) and MJ Kitchen
TV Umpire: JC Balderstone; Referee: PL van der Merwe (SA)

England v Australia
21,22,23 August 1997

Result: England won by 19 runs

England Innings

MA Butcher	b McGrath	5	lbw b ME Waugh	13
*MA Atherton	c Healy b McGrath	8	c SR Waugh b Kasprowicz	8
+AJ Stewart	lbw b McGrath	36	lbw b Kasprowicz	3
N Hussain	c Elliott b McGrath	35	c Elliott b Warne	2
GP Thorpe	b McGrath	27	c Taylor b Kasprowicz	62
MR Ramprakash	c Blewett b McGrath	4	st Healy b Warne	48
AJ Hollioake	b Warne	0	lbw b Kasprowicz	4
AR Caddick	not out	26	not out	0
PJ Martin	b McGrath	20	c & b Kasprowicz	3
PCR Tufnell	c Blewett b Warne	1	c Healy b Kasprowicz	0
DE Malcolm	lbw b Kasprowicz	0	b Kasprowicz	0
	(b 2, lb 6, nb 10)	18	(b 6, lb 10, nb 4)	20
	(all out)	180	(all out)	163

Bowling: McGrath 21-4-76-7 Kasprowicz 11.4-2-56-1 Warne 17-8-32-2 Young 7-3-8-0
McGrath 17-5-33-0 Kasprowicz 15.5-5-36-7 Warne 26-9-57-2 ME Waugh 7-3-16-1 Young 1-0-5-0

Australia Innings

MTG Elliott	b Tufnell	12	lbw b Malcolm	4
*MA Taylor	c Hollioake b Tufnell	38	lbw b Caddick	18
GS Blewett	c Stewart b Tufnell	47	c Stewart b Caddick	19
ME Waugh	c Butcher b Tufnell	19	c Hussain b Tufnell	1
SR Waugh	lbw b Caddick	22	c Thorpe b Caddick	6
RT Ponting	c Hussain b Tufnell	40	lbw b Tufnell	20
+IA Healy	c Stewart b Tufnell	2	c & b Caddick	14
S Young	c Stewart b Tufnell	0	not out	4
SK Warne	b Caddick	30	c Martin b Tufnell	3
MS Kasprowicz	lbw b Caddick	0	c Hollioake b Caddick	4
GD McGrath	not out	1	c Thorpe b Tufnell	1
	(lb 3, w 1, nb 5)	9	(b 3, lb 4, w 1, nb 2)	10
	(all out)	220	(all out)	104

Bowling: Malcolm 11-2-37-0 Martin 15-5-38-0 Caddick 19-4-76-3 Tufnell 34.3-16-66-7
Malcolm 3-0-15-1 Martin 4-0-13-0 Tufnell 13.1-6-27-4 Caddick 12-2-42-5

Umpires: LH Barker (WI) and P Willey
TV Umpire: KE Palmer; Referee: CW Smith (WI)

England v Sri Lanka
27,28,29,30,31 August 1998

Result: Sri Lanka won by 10 wickets

England Innings

MA Butcher	c Jayasuriya b Wickramasinghe	10	st Kaluwitharana b Muralitharan	15
SP James	c & b Muralitharan	36	c Jayawardene b Muralitharan	25
GA Hick	c Kaluwitharana b Wickramasinghe	107	lbw b Muralitharan	0
*+AJ Stewart	c Tillakaratne b Perera	2	run out (sub [UDU Chandana])	32
MR Ramprakash	c Jayawardene b Muralitharan	53	c Tillakaratne b Muralitharan	42
JP Crawley	not out	156	b Muralitharan	14
BC Hollioake	c Atapattu b Muralitharan	14	lbw b Muralitharan	0
DG Cork	b Muralitharan	6	c Kaluwitharana b Muralitharan	8
IDK Salisbury	b Muralitharan	2	lbw b Muralitharan	0
D Gough	c Kaluwitharana b Muralitharan	4	b Muralitharan	15
ARC Fraser	b Muralitharan	32	not out	0
	(b 1, lb 11, w 2, nb 9)	23	(b 7, lb 8, w 1, nb 14)	30
	(all out)	445	(all out)	181

Bowling: Wickramasinghe 30-4-81-2 Perera 40-10-104-1 Dharmasena 18-3-55-0 Muralitharan 59.3-14-155-7 Jayasuriya 11-0-38-0
Wickramasinghe 4-0-16-0 Perera 11-2-22-0 Muralitharan 54.2-27-65-9 Dharmasena 19.3-13-12-0 Jayasuriya 28-14-30-0 de Silva 10.3-3-16-0 Jayawardene 2-0-5-0

Innings

MA Butcher	c Jayasuriya b Wickramasinghe	10
SP James	c & b Muralitharan	36
GA Hick	c Kaluwitharana b Wickramasinghe	107
*+AJ Stewart	c Tillakaratne b Perera	2
MR Ramprakash	c Jayawardene b Muralitharan	53
JP Crawley	not out	156
BC Hollioake	c Atapattu b Muralitharan	14
DG Cork	b Muralitharan	6
IDK Salisbury	b Muralitharan	2
D Gough	c Kaluwitharana b Muralitharan	4
ARC Fraser	b Muralitharan	32
	(b 1, lb 11, w 2, nb 9)	23
	(all out)	445

Bowling: Wickramasinghe 30-4-81-2 Perera 40-10-104-1 Dharmasena 18-3-55-0 Muralitharan 59.3-14-155-7 Jayasuriya 11-0-38-0

Umpires: EA Nicholls (WI) and DR Shepherd
TV Umpire: JW Holder; Referee: AM Ebrahim (Zim)

England v New Zealand
19,20,21,22 August 1999

Result: New Zealand won by 83 runs

New Zealand Innings

MJ Horne	c Caddick b Irani	15	lbw b Giddins	10
MD Bell	c Stewart b Mullally	23	c Irani b Caddick	4
*SP Fleming	not out	66	c Thorpe b Caddick	4
NJ Astle	c Stewart b Caddick	9	c Irani b Giddins	5
RG Twose	c Maddy b Giddins	1	c Stewart b Giddins	0
CD McMillan	b Tufnell	19	lbw b Mullally	26
+AC Parore	c Ramprakash b Tufnell	0	b Caddick	1
CL Cairns	b Mullally	11	c & b Mullally	80
DJ Nash	c Ramprakash b Caddick	18	not out	10
DL Vettori	lbw b Tufnell	51	c Ramprakash b Tufnell	6
SB O'Connor	lbw b Caddick	1	b Tufnell	6
	(b 9, lb 9, w 2, nb 2)	22	(lb 4, w 1, nb 5)	10
	(all out)	236	(all out)	162

Bowling: Caddick 33.1-17-66-3 Mullally 26-12-34-2 Giddins 16-4-41-1 Tufnell 16-3-39-3 Irani 11-3-38-1
Caddick 17-4-35-3 Mullally 11-1-27-2 Giddins 10-3-38-3 Tufnell 16-3-58-2

England Innings

MA Atherton	c Fleming b Nash	10	c Parore b Nash	64
DL Maddy	b Vettori	14	c Fleming b Nash	5
*N Hussain	c Bell b Cairns	40	c Parore b O'Connor	9
GP Thorpe	c Fleming b Cairns	10	c Fleming b O'Connor	44
+AJ Stewart	b Vettori	11	c Bell b Nash	12
MR Ramprakash	c Parore b Cairns	30	c Parore b Nash	0
RC Irani	lbw b Cairns	1	c Parore b Vettori	9
AR Caddick	b O'Connor	15	c Bell b Vettori	3
AD Mullally	c Bell b Vettori	5	c Twose b Cairns	3
PCR Tufnell	not out	0	run out (Nash)	1
ESH Giddins	lbw b Cairns	0	not out	0
	(b 1, lb 5, w 5, nb 6)	17	(b 2, lb 3, nb 7)	12
	(all out)	153	(all out)	162

Bowling: Cairns 19-8-31-5 Nash 14-5-40-1 O'Connor 13-3-30-1 Vettori 33-12-46-3 Astle 1-1-0-0
Cairns 15.1-4-50-1 Nash 14-3-39-4 Vettori 16-6-36-2 O'Connor 11-2-32-2

Umpires: G Sharp and S Venkataraghavan (Ind)
TV Umpire: JH Hampshire; Referee: PL van der Merwe (SA)

England v West Indies
31 August, 1,2,3,4 September 2000

Result: England won by 158 runs

England Innings

MA Atherton	b McLean	83	c Jacobs b Walsh	108
ME Trescothick	c Campbell b Nagamootoo	78	c Lara b Ambrose	7
*N Hussain	c Jacobs b Nagamootoo	0	lbw b McLean	0
GP Thorpe	lbw b Walsh	40	c Griffith b Walsh	10
+AJ Stewart	lbw b McLean	0	c Campbell b Nagamootoo	25
MP Vaughan	lbw b Ambrose	10	lbw b Walsh	9
GA Hick	lbw b Ambrose	17	c Campbell b Walsh	0
C White	not out	11	run out (Griffith)	18
DG Cork	lbw b McLean	0	lbw b McLean	26
AR Caddick	c Hinds b Walsh	4	c Jacobs b McLean	0
D Gough	b Walsh	8	not out	1
	(b 4, lb 15, w 1, nb 10)	30	(b 1, lb 7, nb 5)	13
	(all out)	281	(all out)	217

Bowling: Ambrose 31-8-38-2 Walsh 35.4-16-68-3 McLean 29-6-80-3 Nagamootoo 24-7-63-2 Adams 4-0-13-0
Ambrose 22-8-36-1 Walsh 38-17-73-4 McLean 22-5-60-3 Nagamootoo 19-7-29-1 Adams 7-3-11-0

West Indies Innings

SL Campbell	b Cork	20	c Hick b Gough	28
AFG Griffith	c Hick b White	6	c Stewart b Caddick	20
WW Hinds	lbw b Cork	2	lbw b Caddick	7
BC Lara	b White	0	lbw b Gough	47
*JC Adams	c Hick b Cork	5	c White b Caddick	15
RR Sarwan	c Trescothick b White	5	run out (Thorpe)	27
+RD Jacobs	not out	26	c Hick b Caddick	1
MV Nagamootoo	c Trescothick b Gough	18	lbw b Gough	13
CEL Ambrose	lbw b Caddick	0	c Atherton b Cork	28
NAM McLean	b White	29	not out	23
CA Walsh	b White	5	lbw b Cork	0
	(lb 3, nb 6)	9	(lb 3, w 1, nb 2)	6
	(all out)	125	(all out)	215

Bowling: Gough 13-3-25-1 Caddick 18-7-42-1 White 11.5-1-32-5 Cork 8-3-23-3
Gough 20-3-64-3 Caddick 21-7-54-4 White 11-2-32-0 Cork 15-1-50-2 Vaughan 3-1-12-0

Umpires: DJ Harper (Aus) and DR Shepherd
TV Umpire: B Leadbeater; Referee: RS Madugalle (SL)

England v Australia
23,24,25,26,27 August 2001

Result: Australia won by an innings and 25 runs

Australia Innings

ML Hayden	c Trescothick b Tufnell	68
JL Langer	retired hurt	102
RT Ponting	c Atherton b Ormond	62
ME Waugh	b Gough	120
*SR Waugh	not out	157
+AC Gilchrist	c Ramprakash b Afzaal	25
DR Martyn	not out	64
B Lee		
SK Warne		
JN Gillespie		
GD McGrath		
	(b 10, lb 13, w 1, nb 19)	43
	(4 wickets dec)	641

Bowling: Gough 29-4-113-1 Caddick 36-9-146-0 Ormond 34-4-115-1 Tufnell 39-2-174-1 Butcher 1-0-2-0 Ramprakash 4-0-19-0 Afzaal 9-0-49-1

England Innings

MA Atherton	b Warne	13	c Warne b McGrath	9
ME Trescothick	b Warne	55	c & b McGrath	24
MA Butcher	c Langer b Warne	25	c SR Waugh b Warne	14
*N Hussain	b ME Waugh	52	lbw b Warne	2
MR Ramprakash	c Gilchrist b McGrath	133	c Hayden b Warne	19
U Afzaal	c Gillespie b McGrath	54	c Ponting b McGrath	5
+AJ Stewart	c Gilchrist b Warne	29	b Warne	34
AR Caddick	lbw b Warne	0	b Lee	17
J Ormond	b Warne	18	c Gilchrist b McGrath	17
D Gough	st Gilchrist b Warne	24	not out	39
PCR Tufnell	not out	7	c Warne b McGrath	0
	(b 3, lb 13, w 1, nb 5)	22	(lb 2, nb 2)	4
	(all out)	432	(all out)	184

Bowling: McGrath 30-11-67-2 Gillespie 20-3-96-0 Warne 44.2-7-165-7 Lee 14-1-43-0 Ponting 2-0-5-0 ME Waugh 8-0-40-1
Lee 10-3-30-1 McGrath 15.3-6-43-5 Warne 28-8-64-4 Ponting 2-0-3-0 Gillespie 12-5-38-0 ME Waugh 1-0-4-0

Umpires: RE Koertzen (SA) and P Willey
TV Umpire: MJ Kitchen; Referee: Talat Ali (Pak)

England v India
5,6,7,8,9 September 2002

Result: Match Drawn

England Innings
ME Trescothick	c Bangar b Khan	57	not out	58
MP Vaughan	c Ratra b Khan	195	not out	47
MA Butcher	c Dravid b Harbhajan Singh	54		
JP Crawley	lbw b Bangar	26		
*N Hussain	c Laxman b Bangar	10		
+AJ Stewart	c Ratra b Harbhajan Singh	23		
DG Cork	lbw b Harbhajan Singh	52		
AJ Tudor	c Dravid b Harbhajan Singh	2		
AF Giles	c Dravid b Kumble	31		
AR Caddick	not out	14		
MJ Hoggard	lbw b Harbhajan Singh	0		
	(b 12, lb 31, w 1, nb 7)	51	(b 4, nb 5)	9
	(all out)	515	(0 wickets)	114

Bowling: Khan 28-4-83-2 Agarkar 24-4-111-0 Bangar 24-8-48-2 Harbhajan Singh 38.4-6-115-5 Kumble 35-11-105-1 Ganguly 4-1-6-0 Tendulkar 2-0-4-0
Khan 5-0-37-0 Bangar 2-0-6-0 Kumble 10-2-28-0 Harbhajan Singh 7-1-24-0 Agarkar 4-0-15-0

India Innings
SB Bangar	c Butcher b Hoggard	21
V Sehwag	c Cork b Caddick	12
R Dravid	run out (Giles/Stewart)	217
SR Tendulkar	lbw b Caddick	54
*SC Ganguly	c Stewart b Cork	51
VVS Laxman	c Giles b Caddick	40
AB Agarkar	b Vaughan	31
+A Ratra	c Butcher b Caddick	8
A Kumble	c Hussain b Giles	7
Harbhajan Singh	b Giles	17
Z Khan	not out	6
	(b 10, lb 6, nb 28)	44
	(all out)	508

Bowling: Hoggard 25-2-97-1 Caddick 43-11-114-4 Giles 49-12-98-2 Tudor 19-2-80-0 Cork 22-5-67-1 Vaughan 12-1-36-1

Umpires: EAR de Silva (SL) and DL Orchard (SA)
TV Umpire: NA Mallender; Referee: CH Lloyd (WI)

Newlands, Cape Town

South Africa v England
25,26 March 1889

Result: England won by an innings and 202 runs

England Innings

R Abel	b Ashley	120
G Ulyett	b Ashley	22
J Briggs	b Vintcent	6
JM Read	c Hutchinson b Ashley	12
F Hearne	b Vintcent	20
+H Wood	c Rose-Innes b Vintcent	59
*MP Bowden	c Hutchinson b Ashley	25
BAF Grieve	c Tancred b Ashley	14
JEP McMaster	c Rose-Innes b Ashley	0
Hon.CJ Coventry	not out	1
AJ Fothergill	b Ashley	1
	(b 12)	12
	(all out)	292

Bowling: Theunissen 20-5-51-0 Rose-Innes 12-3-30-0 Ashley 43.1-18-95-7 Vintcent 42-9-88-3 Milton 6-2-16-0

South Africa Innings

AB Tancred	not out	26	b Briggs		3
A Rose-Innes	lbw b Fothergill	1	run out		0
AE Ochse	run out	1	b Briggs		3
P Hutchinson	b Briggs	3	b Briggs		5
OR Dunell	b Briggs	0	b Fothergill		5
*WH Milton	b Briggs	7	b Briggs		4
WHM Richards	c Abel b Fothergill	0	b Briggs		4
CH Vintcent	b Briggs	4	b Briggs		9
+FW Smith	b Briggs	0	b Briggs		11
NHCD Theunissen	lbw b Briggs	0	not out		2
WH Ashley	b Briggs	1	b Briggs		0
	(b 2, nb 2)	4	(b 2)		2
	(all out)	47	(all out)		43

Bowling: Fothergill 24-12-26-2 Ulyett 4-4-0-0 Briggs 19.1-11-17-7
Fothergill 14-4-30-1 Briggs 14.2-5-11-8

Umpires: JAE Hickson (ENG) and RG Warton (ENG)

South Africa v England
19,21,22 March 1892

Result: England won by an innings and 189 runs

South Africa Innings

TW Routledge	b Ferris	5	c Pougher b Ferris		1
F Hearne	b Pougher	24	b Ferris		23
CG Fichardt	c & b Pougher	0	run out		10
CH Mills	b Ferris	4	b Ferris		21
+EA Halliwell	c JT Hearne b Ferris	8	b Ferris		0
CS Wimble	c Wood b Pougher	0	st Murdoch b Martin		0
G Cripps	b JT Hearne	3	b Ferris		3
*WH Milton	c Martin b Ferris	21	c A Hearne b Ferris		16
CH Vintcent	lbw b Ferris	6	b Ferris		0
DC Parkin	b Ferris	0	c & b Martin		0
JF du Toit	not out	0	not out		2
	(b 5)	5	(b 7)		7
	(all out)	97	(all out)		83

Bowling: Ferris 29.2-11-54-6 Pougher 21-8-26-3 JT Hearne 8-2-12-1
Ferris 25-16-37-7 Martin 24.3-9-39-2

England Innings

W Chatterton	c du Toit b Mills	48
A Hearne	lbw b Parkin	9
WL Murdoch	c & b Parkin	12
GG Hearne	c Mills b Parkin	0
VA Barton	c Vintcent b Mills	23
*WW Read	b du Toit	40
AD Pougher	b Hearne	17
+H Wood	not out	134
JJ Ferris	run out	16
JT Hearne	c Fichardt b Milton	40
F Martin	c Mills b Hearne	13
	(b 13, nb 4)	17
	(all out)	369

Bowling: Vintcent 24-8-50-0 Parkin 26-4-82-3 Mills 28-7-83-2 Hearne 12.2-0-40-2 du Toit 17.5-5-47-1 Milton 9-2-27-1 Cripps 3-0-23-0

Umpires: J Leaney (ENG) and CN Thomas

South Africa v England
21,23 March 1896

Result: England won by an innings and 33 runs

South Africa Innings

TW Routledge	b Lohmann	24	b Woods		4
F Hearne	c & b Lohmann	0	c Hayward b Tyler		30
RM Poore	c Woods b Lohmann	17	b Woods		8
JH Sinclair	c Woods b Tyler	2	c Hawke b Bromley-Davenport		28
*AR Richards	c Woods b Lohmann	6	b Woods		0
+EA Halliwell	c Heselmne b Tyler	23	b Hill		11
AW Seccull	c & b Lohmann	6	not out		17
GK Glover	not out	18	c Woods b Lohmann		3
J Middleton	c Hayward b Tyler	2	c Hawke b Hill		6
JT Willoughby	b Lohmann	5	st Butt b Hill		3
GA Rowe	b Lohmann	5	b Hill		3
	(b 5, w 1, nb 1)	7	(b 2, nb 2)		4
	(all out)	115	(all out)		117

Bowling: Lohmann 24-9-42-7 Tyler 18-3-49-3 Heseltine 6-0-17-0
Lohmann 23-8-45-1 Tyler 11-3-16-1 Woods 13-5-28-3 Bromley-Davenport 9-3-16-1 Hill 8-4-8-4

England Innings

CW Wright	c Seccull b Willoughby	2
AJL Hill	c Poore b Middleton	124
TW Hayward	b Seccull	31
HR Bromley-Davenport	b Seccull	7
SMJ Woods	b Rowe	30
Sir TC O'Brien	c sub (JH Anderson) b Glover	2
GA Lohmann	b Willoughby	8
C Heseltine	c Hearne b Rowe	18
*Lord Hawke	not out	12
EJ Tyler	b Middleton	0
+HR Butt	c Sinclair b Middleton	13
	(b 12, lb 4, nb 2)	18
	(all out)	265

Bowling: Willoughby 14-2-37-2 Rowe 32-9-72-2 Seccull 12-2-37-2 Sinclair 7-1-23-0 Middleton 23.4-6-50-3 Glover 13-4-28-1

Umpires: G Beves and AM Miller (Eng)

South Africa v England
1,3,4 April 1899

Result: England won by 210 runs

England Innings

F Mitchell	c Rowe b Middleton	18	lbw b Rowe		41
PF Warner	c Halliwell b Sinclair	31	b Rowe		23
JT Tyldesley	b Sinclair	13	c Shalders b Kuys		112
CEM Wilson	not out	10	b Powell		6
WR Cuttell	b Sinclair	7	b Kuys		18
AE Trott	c Powell b Sinclair	1	b Rowe		16
S Haigh	c Halliwell b Middleton	0	c Francis b Sinclair		25
FW Milligan	b Sinclair	1	b Sinclair		38
+JH Board	b Sinclair	0	b Graham		6
AG Archer	c Powell b Middleton	7	not out		24
*Lord Hawke	b Middleton	1	c & b Sinclair		3
	(lb 3)	3	(b 6, lb 10, w 1, nb 1)		18
	(all out)	92	(all out)		330

Bowling: Graham 5-0-26-0 Rowe 12-4-19-0 Middleton 19.9-18-4 Sinclair 12-4-26-6
Graham 16-4-41-1 Rowe 41-8-93-3 Middleton 28-7-74-0 Sinclair 31.2-8-63-3 Powell 4-1-10-1 Kuys 12-4-31-2

South Africa Innings

WA Shalders	b Haigh	9	lbw b Haigh		8
HH Francis	b Trott	1	c Haigh b Trott		2
*M Bisset	b Haigh	15	b Trott		1
JH Sinclair	c Tyldesley b Trott	106	c Milligan b Haigh		4
AW Powell	c Haigh b Trott	5	b Haigh		11
+EA Halliwell	st Board b Haigh	0	b Haigh		9
F Kuys	b Cuttell	26	b Trott		0
CFH Prince	run out	5	b Haigh		1
R Graham	b Trott	0	b Trott		2
J Middleton	run out	3	not out		0
GA Rowe	not out	1	c Mitchell b Haigh		0
	(b 4, w 1, nb 1)	6	(b 5)		5
	(all out)	177	(all out)		35

Bowling: Trott 20.2-5-69-4 Haigh 27-4-88-3 Cuttell 8-3-14-1 Milligan 2-2-0-0
Haigh 11.4-6-11-6 Trott 11-5-19-4

Umpires: F Hearne and A White (Eng)

South Africa v Australia
8,10,11 November 1902

Result: Australia won by 10 wickets

Australia Innings

RA Duff	c Tancred b Kotze	34	not out		20
VT Trumper	b Llewellyn	70	not out		38
C Hill	not out	91			
WW Armstrong	b Llewellyn	3			
MA Noble	c Smith b Sinclair	9			
AJY Hopkins	b Llewellyn	16			
SE Gregory	c Smith b Llewellyn	11			
*J Darling	b Llewellyn	1			
+JJ Kelly	b Kotze	1			
WP Howell	b Llewellyn	2			
JV Saunders	run out	1			
	(b 6, lb 4)	10	(nb 1)		1
	(all out)	252	(0 wickets)		59

Bowling: Llewellyn 30.5-4-97-6 Kotze 17-1-49-2 Sinclair 12-0-55-1 Middleton 8-1-28-0 Nourse 3-0-13-0
Llewellyn 4-1-19-0 Kotze 2.5-1-16-0 Sinclair 2-0-22-0 Middleton 1-0-1-0

South Africa Innings

LJ Tancred	b Howell	0	c & b Howell		2
WA Shalders	c Darling b Saunders	11	c Darling b Hopkins		40
CJE Smith	b Saunders	16	c & b Trumper		45
JH Sinclair	b Howell	0	st Kelly b Saunders		104
PS Twentyman-Jones	b Howell	0	b Hopkins		0
CB Llewellyn	b Howell	1	st Kelly b Howell		8
CMH Hathorn	run out	19	st Kelly b Saunders		18
AW Nourse	b Saunders	15	b Howell		5
*+EA Halliwell	run out	13	b Howell		1
JJ Kotze	b Saunders	1	b Howell		0
J Middleton	not out	1	not out		0
	(b 4, lb 3)	7	(lb 1, nb 1)		2
	(all out)	85	(all out)		225

Bowling: Howell 17-6-18-4 Saunders 12.2-2-37-4 Noble 4-0-23-0
Howell 26-6-81-5 Saunders 17.1-3-73-2 Noble 6-3-6-0 Trumper 6-1-26-1 Hopkins 8-0-37-2

Umpires: WH Creese and F Hearne

South Africa v England
24,26,27 March 1906

Result: England won by 4 wickets

South Africa Innings

LJ Tancred	lbw b Blythe	11	c Haigh b Blythe		10
WA Shalders	lbw b Blythe	16	c Blythe b Crawford		0
GC White	c Board b Lees	41	b Lees		73
AW Nourse	c Hayes b Blythe	2	c Crawford b Blythe		3
CMH Hathorn	b Blythe	3	b Lees		10
JH Sinclair	c Board b Blythe	0	b Lees		1
GA Faulkner	b Blythe	34	b Blythe		4
SJ Snooke	b Crawford	44	b Blythe		5
RO Schwarz	c Moon b Relf	33	c Haigh b Lees		8
AEE Vogler	b Haigh	9	not out		12
*+PW Sherwell	not out	0	b Blythe		9
	(b 20, lb 3, w 2)	25	(lb 3)		3
	(all out)	218	(all out)		138

Bowling: Lees 27-12-42-1 Blythe 32-13-68-6 Crawford 13.3-3-28-1 Haigh 19-8-38-1 Relf 6-2-17-1
Lees 14-5-27-4 Blythe 28.5-10-50-5 Crawford 15-5-46-1 Haigh 2-0-12-0

England Innings

+JH Board	b Snooke	0	not out		14
AE Relf	lbw b Faulkner	28	b Vogler		18
C Blythe	b Faulkner	27			
FL Fane	b Sinclair	9	not out		66
D Denton	c Vogler b Snooke	34	b Snooke		20
*PF Warner	c Snooke b Faulkner	1	b Sinclair		4
JN Crawford	not out	36	b Sinclair		4
LJ Moon	b Sinclair	33	lbw b Faulkner		28
EG Hayes	lbw b Sinclair	0	b Sinclair		0
S Haigh	c Nourse b Sinclair	5			
WS Lees	c Hathorn b Faulkner	5			
	(b 14, lb 6, w 1, nb 4)	25	(b 3, lb 2, nb 1)		6
	(all out)	198	(6 wickets)		160

Bowling: Snooke 18-5-41-2 Schwarz 12-2-34-0 Sinclair 27-10-41-4 Faulkner 25.5-11-49-4 Vogler 5-3-7-0 Nourse 2-1-1-0
Snooke 19-6-41-1 Schwarz 2-0-6-0 Sinclair 26.1-5-67-3 Faulkner 5-0-21-1 Vogler 6-1-13-1 Nourse 1-0-6-0

Umpires: F Hearne and J Phillips (Aus)

South Africa v England
30,31 March, 2 April 1906

Result: South Africa won by an innings and 16 runs

England Innings

JN Crawford	b Sinclair	74	b Snooke		13
*PF Warner	b Schwarz	0	c Snooke b Schwarz		4
D Denton	b Snooke	4	b Vogler		10
FL Fane	b Vogler	30	b Vogler		10
LJ Moon	lbw b Vogler	7	lbw b Sinclair		33
AE Relf	c Faulkner b Sinclair	25	b Nourse		21
+JH Board	c Nourse b Snooke	20	b Nourse		4
JC Hartley	run out	6	c Vogler b Schwarz		0
WS Lees	not out	9	b Nourse		2
S Haigh	c Tancred b Sinclair	1	c Nourse b Schwarz		2
C Blythe	b Sinclair	1	not out		11
	(b 6, nb 4)	10	(b 14, lb 2, w 2, nb 2)		20
	(all out)	187	(all out)		130

Bowling: Snooke 12-4-41-2 Schwarz 7-2-14-1 Sinclair 21.2-8-45-4 Vogler 19-6-63-2 Faulkner 4-1-11-0 Nourse 2-1-3-0
Snooke 9-3-26-1 Schwarz 8.2-2-16-3 Sinclair 11-4-20-1 Vogler 8-3-17-1 Faulkner 3-1-6-0 Nourse 10-3-25-4

South Africa Innings

LJ Tancred	c Moon b Crawford	26
WA Shalders	c & b Crawford	21
GC White	c Crawford b Lees	11
AW Nourse	c Relf b Crawford	36
CMH Hathorn	c Board b Blythe	1
JH Sinclair	b Blythe	12
GA Faulkner	c Moon b Relf	45
SJ Snooke	lbw b Relf	60
RO Schwarz	c Crawford b Relf	15
*+PW Sherwell	c Blythe b Lees	30
AEE Vogler	not out	62
	(b 12, lb 1, nb 1)	14
	(all out)	333

Bowling: Lees 24.4-6-64-2 Blythe 35-11-106-2 Crawford 18-3-69-3 Haigh 6-1-18-0 Hartley 6-0-22-0 Relf 21-6-40-3

Umpires: F Hearne and J Phillips (Aus)

South Africa v England
7,8,9 March 1910

Result: South Africa won by 4 wickets

England Innings

JB Hobbs	c Faulkner b Vogler	1	c Campbell b Snooke		0
W Rhodes	c Faulkner b Snooke	0	b Snooke		5
D Denton	c Commaille b Snooke	0	c Faulkner b Vogler		10
*FL Fane	c Campbell b Sinclair	14	c Snooke b Faulkner		37
FE Woolley	c Zulch b Sinclair	69	b Vogler		64
GJ Thompson	run out	16	c Snooke b Faulkner		6
MC Bird	c Campbell b White	57	c Schwarz b Vogler		11
GHT Simpson-Hayward	b Faulkner	13	c Faulkner b Vogler		9
CP Buckenham	b Vogler	5	c Faulkner b Vogler		17
+H Strudwick	c & b White	7	c Nourse b Faulkner		3
C Blythe	not out	1	not out		4
	(b 13, lb 5, nb 2)	20	(b 4, lb 8)		12
	(all out)	203	(all out)		178

Bowling: Snooke 8-1-35-2 Vogler 11-3-28-2 Faulkner 15-1-61-1 Sinclair 15-3-41-2 Nourse 30-13-0 White 1-0-5-2
Snooke 8-0-23-2 Vogler 21.3-3-72-5 Faulkner 14-6-40-3 Sinclair 4-1-15-0 White 4-1-15-0

South Africa Innings

JW Zulch	b Simpson-Hayward	30	c Strudwick b Thompson		13
JMM Commaille	c & b Buckenham	42	b Buckenham		3
GC White	b Bird	15	c Woolley b Thompson		31
AW Nourse	b Thompson	27	c Rhodes b Blythe		24
GA Faulkner	c Fane b Buckenham	10	not out		49
*SJ Snooke	b Woolley	9	lbw b Woolley		7
JH Sinclair	b Thompson	10	b Thompson		19
LA Stricker	lbw b Thompson		b Thompson		
RO Schwarz	c Rhodes b Thompson	27	not out		9
AEE Vogler	b Buckenham	23			
+T Campbell	not out	3			
	(b 10, nb 1)	11	(b 15, lb 3, nb 2)		20
	(all out)	207	(6 wickets)		175

Bowling: Buckenham 20-3-61-3 Blythe 15-7-26-0 Simpson-Hayward 9-1-33-1 Thompson 16-3-50-4 Bird 1-0-3-1 Woolley 6-2-23-1
Buckenham 7-2-12-1 Blythe 20-7-38-2 Simpson-Hayward 5-0-12-0 Thompson 20.3-2-62-3 Bird 1-0-5-0 Woolley 3-0-24-0 Rhodes 3-2-2-0

Umpires: AJ Atfield and SL Harris

South Africa v England
11,12,14 March 1910

Result: England won by 9 wickets

England Innings

JB Hobbs	hit wicket b Norton	187			
W Rhodes	b Nourse	77	not out		0
D Denton	c Samuelson b Nourse	26	not out		16
*FL Fane	b Norton	6			
FE Woolley	b Norton	0			
GJ Thompson	c Sinclair b Faulkner	51			
MC Bird	b Norton	0	c Bisset b Vogler		
GHT Simpson-Hayward	c Snooke b Faulkner	19			
+NC Tufnell	c & b Vogler	14			
H Strudwick	c Zulch b Faulkner	2			
C Blythe	not out	2			
	(b 30, lb 3)	33	(1 wicket)		16
	(all out)	417			0

Bowling: Snooke 5-0-17-0 Vogler 26-2-103-1 Faulkner 25.2-6-72-3 Samuelson 18-2-64-0 Norton 15-4-47-4 Sinclair 8-1-36-0
Nourse 8-1-35-2 Schwarz 3-0-10-0
Vogler 2.1-1-16-1 Snooke 2-2-0-0

South Africa Innings

JW Zulch	not out	43	b Woolley		14
JMM Commaille	b Blythe	4	lbw b Thompson		5
*SJ Snooke	b Blythe	0	b Woolley		47
AW Nourse	lbw b Thompson	8	c Simpson-Hayward b Woolley		0
GA Faulkner	c Rhodes b Blythe	10	c Woolley b Thompson		99
JH Sinclair	c Denton b Thompson	0	st Tufnell b Blythe		37
+M Bisset	c Rhodes b Blythe	4	not out		27
AEE Vogler	b Blythe	0	b Thompson		2
RO Schwarz	c Denton b Blythe	13	c Bird b Blythe		44
NO Norton	b Blythe	7	c Fane b Blythe		7
SV Samuelson	b Simpson-Hayward	15	b Blythe		7
	(lb 2, nb 1)	3	(b 25, lb 5, nb 8)		38
	(all out)	103	(all out)		327

Bowling: Hobbs 4-0-11-0 Blythe 18-5-46-7 Thompson 12-6-28-2 Simpson-Hayward 4.5-0-15-1
Hobbs 8-3-19-1 Blythe 30-13-58-3 Thompson 30-5-96-3 Simpson-Hayward 8-1-35-0 Woolley 13-3-47-3 Bird 3-0-12-0 Rhodes 7-0-22-0

Umpires: AJ Atfield and SL Harris

South Africa v Australia
26,28,29 November 1921

Result: Australia won by 10 wickets

South Africa Innings

CN Frank	b Ryder	21	b Macartney		23
JW Zulch	c Ryder b Macartney	50	c & b Macartney		40
PAM Hands	c Gregory b Ryder	0	c Andrews b Macartney		19
*HW Taylor	c Andrews b McDonald	26	run out		17
AW Nourse	c Mayne b Mailey	11	st Carter b Mailey		31
WVS Ling	b McDonald	0	b McDonald		35
WFE Marx	st Carter b Mailey	11	run out		16
JM Blanckenberg	c Carter b Mailey	25	c Carter b Mailey		20
+TA Ward	b McDonald	2	b McDonald		4
CP Carter	not out	19	not out		1
N Reid	c Mayne b Mailey	11	b Macartney		6
	(lb 2, nb 2)	4	(b 1, lb 2, nb 1)		4
	(all out)	180	(all out)		216

Bowling: Gregory 15-9-11-0 McDonald 19-3-53-3 Macartney 24-10-47-1 Ryder 16-7-25-2 Mailey 14-1-40-4
Gregory 9-1-29-0 McDonald 13-2-35-1 Macartney 24.3-10-44-5 Ryder 7-0-15-0 Mailey 26-0-89-2 Collins 1-1-0-0

Australia Innings

*HL Collins	b Blanckenberg	54			
W Bardsley	lbw b Blanckenberg	30			
CG Macartney	c Nourse b Blanckenberg	44			
J Ryder	c Taylor b Carter	142			
JM Gregory	c Hands b Blanckenberg	29			
ER Mayne	lbw b Reid	15			
TJE Andrews	c Hands b Carter	10			
CE Pellew	c Nourse b Reid	6			
+H Carter	not out	31	not out		0
EA McDonald	c Ward b Carter	4			
AA Mailey	c Taylor b Nourse	14	not out		1
	(b 9, lb 5, nb 3)	17			0
	(all out)	396	(0 wickets)		1

Bowling: Marx 7-1-29-0 Nourse 30-5-89-1 Blanckenberg 31-5-82-4 Carter 26-5-104-3 Reid 21-3-63-2 Taylor 5-2-12-0
Hands 0.1-0-1-0

Umpires: HV Adams and AG Laver

South Africa v England
1,2,3,4 January 1923

Result: England won by 1 wicket

South Africa Innings

RH Catterall	c Brown b Fender	10	b Macaulay		76
GAL Hearne	c Fender b Macaulay	0	b Kennedy		0
*HW Taylor	b Fender	9	c Jupp b Macaulay		68
AW Nourse	lbw b Fender	16	b Fender		19
WVS Ling	c Mann b Fender	13	c Fender b Macaulay		2
WH Brann	b Kennedy	0	lbw b Macaulay		4
JM Blanckenberg	c Carr b Jupp	6	c Carr b Jupp		5
CM Francois	run out	28	c & b Macaulay		19
+TA Ward	b Jupp	4	not out		15
EP Nupen	c & b Macaulay	0	b Kennedy		6
AE Hall	not out	0	b Kennedy		5
	(b 14, lb 6, nb 2)	22	(b 15, lb 6, nb 2)		23
	(all out)	113	(all out)		242

Bowling: Kennedy 18-10-24-1 Macaulay 13.5-5-19-2 Fender 14-4-29-4 Woolley 2-1-1-0 Jupp 9-3-18-2
Kennedy 35.2-13-58-4 Macaulay 37-11-64-5 Fender 20-3-52-1 Woolley 11-3-22-0 Jupp 11-3-23-0

England Innings

CAG Russell	c Catterall b Hall	39	lbw b Blanckenberg		8
A Sandham	c Francois b Blanckenberg	19	lbw b Hall		17
FE Woolley	c Francois b Hall	0	b Hall		5
CP Mead	c Francois b Blanckenberg	21	lbw b Hall		31
AW Carr	c Ward b Hall	42	c Brann b Hall		6
*FT Mann	lbw b Blanckenberg	4	c Blanckenberg b Hall		45
PGH Fender	c Hearne b Hall	3	c Nourse b Hall		2
VWC Jupp	c Hearne b Blanckenberg	12	st Ward b Hall		38
AS Kennedy	c Hearne b Nupen	2	run out		11
+G Brown	not out	10	run out		0
GG Macaulay	b Blanckenberg	19	not out		1
	(b 5, lb 4, w 1, nb 2)	12	(b 4, lb 5)		9
	(all out)	183	(9 wickets)		173

Bowling: Nupen 15-2-48-1 Hall 25-8-49-4 Blanckenberg 24.1-5-61-5 Francois 4-1-13-0
Nupen 24-8-41-0 Hall 37.3-12-63-7 Blanckenberg 24-7-56-1 Francois 3-0-4-0

Umpires: AG Laver and GJ Thompson (Eng)

South Africa v England
31 December 1927, 2,3,4 January 1928

Result: England won by 87 runs

England Innings

P Holmes	b Bissett	9	c Vincent b Nupen		88
H Sutcliffe	c Nupen b Bissett	29	b Bissett		99
GE Tyldesley	b Bissett	0	lbw b Promnitz		87
WR Hammond	lbw b Morkel	43	c Palm b Promnitz		14
GTS Stevens	c Cameron b Bissett	0	c Morkel b Bissett		2
RES Wyatt	lbw b Bissett	2	c Promnitz b Bissett		91
WE Astill	lbw b Vincent	25	c Cameron b Vincent		9
*+RT Stanyforth	b Vincent	4	b Vincent		1
G Geary	lbw b Vincent	0	b Vincent		1
IAR Peebles	not out	3	c Vincent b Promnitz		6
AP Freeman	st Cameron b Vincent	7	not out		0
	(b 5, lb 1, nb 5)	11	(b 19, lb 5, nb 6)		30
	(all out)	133	(all out)		428

Bowling: Bissett 17-5-37-5 Morkel 9-3-20-1 Vincent 15.1-4-22-4 Nupen 3-0-10-0 Promnitz 15-5-33-0
Bissett 31.5-5-99-3 Morkel 21-4-60-0 Vincent 40-10-93-3 Nupen 36-8-90-1 Promnitz 30-10-56-3

South Africa Innings

HW Taylor	hit wicket b Freeman	68	run out		71
JMM Commaille	lbw b Freeman	13	c Astill b Hammond		47
+HB Cameron	c Geary b Stevens	19	b Hammond		19
RH Catterall	b Hammond	9	lbw b Astill		10
DPB Morkel	b Freeman	36	c Holmes b Astill		23
AW Palm	c Stevens b Freeman	2	c Hammond b Freeman		13
*HG Deane	c Stanyforth b Hammond	41	c Hammond b Freeman		4
CL Vincent	b Astill	13	c Hammond b Freeman		11
EP Nupen	not out	39	b Astill		1
GF Bissett	b Hammond	3	not out		11
HLE Promnitz	run out	3	b Peebles		2
	(b 2, lb 2)	4	(b 6, lb 4, nb 2)		12
	(all out)	250	(all out)		224

Bowling: Geary 23-2-50-0 Hammond 17-4-53-3 Freeman 29-12-58-4 Peebles 14-3-27-0 Stevens 10-1-26-1 Astill 8-0-32-1
Hammond 30-13-50-2 Freeman 22-7-66-3 Peebles 12.1-4-26-1 Stevens 5-0-17-0 Astill 29-11-48-3 Wyatt 3-0-5-0

Umpires: HV Adams and GB Treadwell

Newlands, Cape Town

South Africa v England
1,2,3,5 January 1931

Result: Match drawn

South Africa Innings

B Mitchell	b Tate	123
IJ Siedle	c Chapman b White	141
EP Nupen	b Tate	12
HW Taylor	c White b Leyland	117
RH Catterall	b Tate	56
+HB Cameron	c Peebles b White	26
XC Balaskas	c Turnbull b Leyland	0
*HG Deane	b Leyland	7
Q McMillan	not out	7
CL Vincent	not out	3
AJ Bell		
	(b 8, lb 12, nb 1)	21
	(8 wickets declared)	513

Bowling: Tate 43-13-79-3 Hammond 10-2-27-0 Voce 33-11-95-0 Peebles 28-2-95-0 White 46-15-101-2 Leyland 30-6-91-3 Wyatt 2-0-4-0

England Innings

RES Wyatt	b McMillan	40	b Bell	29
WR Hammond	c & b McMillan	57	c Deane b Vincent	65
M Leyland	b Bell	52	c Mitchell b McMillan	28
EH Hendren	b Balaskas	93	b Vincent	86
MJL Turnbull	b Bell	7	b McMillan	14
*APF Chapman	b Bell	0	b Catterall	4
JC White	lbw b Balaskas	23	lbw b Catterall	8
MW Tate	c Taylor b McMillan	15	b Nupen	0
W Voce	c & b Vincent	30	not out	1
IAR Peebles	not out	7	b Catterall	0
+G Duckworth	lbw b Vincent	0	absent hurt	0
	(b 9, lb 16, nb 1)	26	(b 9, lb 4, nb 1)	14
	(all out)	350	(all out)	252

Bowling: Bell 27-9-53-3 Catterall 5-3-2-0 Nupen 22-7-43-0 Balaskas 16-0-75-2 Vincent 17.4-4-40-2 McMillan 33-6-111-3 Bell 29-8-58-1 Catterall 12-2-15-3 Nupen 17-2-26-1 Balaskas 9-1-29-0 Vincent 17-6-26-2 McMillan 32-7-64-2 Mitchell 8-0-20-0

Umpires: JC Collings and WB Ryan

South Africa v Australia
1,2,3,4 January 1936

Result: Australia won by an innings and 78 runs

Australia Innings

WA Brown	c & b Robertson	121
JHW Fingleton	c Wade b Balaskas	112
SJ McCabe	c & b Balaskas	0
LS Darling	lbw b Balaskas	12
*VY Richardson	lbw b Crisp	14
AG Chipperfield	b Langton	30
+WAS Oldfield	b Robertson	8
CV Grimmett	not out	30
WJ O'Reilly	b Balaskas	17
EL McCormick	not out	0
LO Fleetwood-Smith		
	(b 14, lb 4)	18
	(8 wickets declared)	362

Bowling: Crisp 14-2-30-1 Langton 30-2-94-1 Robertson 29-8-75-2 Balaskas 38-1-126-4 Mitchell 4-0-19-0

South Africa Innings

IJ Siedle	lbw b Grimmett	1	b Grimmett	59
*HF Wade	c & b McCabe	0	lbw b Fleetwood-Smith	31
EAB Rowan	b Grimmett	12	c Richardson b O'Reilly	19
B Mitchell	c Fingleton b O'Reilly	14	b Grimmett	0
KG Viljoen	st Oldfield b Fleetwood-Smith	14	c O'Reilly b Grimmett	23
AD Nourse	not out	44	c & b Grimmett	25
+F Nicholson	b Fleetwood-Smith	0	c & b O'Reilly	4
ACB Langton	b Grimmett	3	b O'Reilly	4
RJ Crisp	b Grimmett	0	c Richardson b O'Reilly	0
XC Balaskas	b Grimmett	0	b Grimmett	2
JB Robertson	run out	1	not out	12
	(lb 13)	13	(b 1, lb 2)	3
	(all out)	102	(all out)	182

Bowling: McCormick 2-1-3-0 McCabe 2-1-9-1 O'Reilly 11-4-24-1 Grimmett 17.4-32-5 Fleetwood-Smith 6.2-0-21-2 McCormick 2-0-8-0 O'Reilly 25-15-35-4 Grimmett 36.4-17-56-5 Fleetwood-Smith 24-4-80-1

Umpires: RGA Ashman and JC Collings

South Africa v England
31 December 1938, 2,3,4 January 1939

Result: Match drawn

England Innings

L Hutton	b Gordon	17
PA Gibb	c Wade b Gordon	58
E Paynter	lbw b Langton	1
*WR Hammond	b Davies	181
+LEG Ames	b Gordon	115
WJ Edrich	b Gordon	0
BH Valentine	lbw b Gordon	112
H Verity	b Langton	29
DVP Wright	c Nourse b Langton	33
K Farnes	not out	1
TWJ Goddard		
	(lb 9, nb 3)	12
	(9 wickets declared)	559

Bowling: Davies 16-1-77-1 Langton 30.7-3-117-3 Gordon 40-3-157-5 Balaskas 24-0-115-0 Mitchell 20-0-81-0

South Africa Innings

B Mitchell	b Wright	42	c Ames b Farnes	1
PGV van der Bijl	c Valentine b Verity	37	hit wicket b Goddard	87
EAB Rowan	b Wright	6	not out	89
AD Nourse	lbw b Verity	120	not out	19
AW Briscoe	b Verity	2		
+WW Wade	c Edrich b Verity	10		
ACB Langton	lbw b Goddard	0		
XC Balaskas	c Paynter b Verity	29		
*A Melville	b Verity	23		
N Gordon	st Ames b Goddard	0		
EQ Davies	not out	0		
	(b 2, lb 7, nb 8)	17	(b 1, lb 3, nb 1)	5
	(all out)	286	(2 wickets)	201

Bowling: Farnes 13-3-37-0 Edrich 5-1-15-0 Goddard 38-15-64-3 Wright 26-3-83-2 Verity 36.6-13-70-5 Farnes 8-1-23-1 Edrich 3-1-5-0 Goddard 11-1-68-1 Wright 12-0-62-0 Verity 10-5-13-0 Hammond 9-0-25-0

Umpires: RGA Ashman and GL Sickler

South Africa v England
1,3,4,5 January 1949

Result: Match drawn

England Innings

L Hutton	run out	41	b Rowan	87
C Washbrook	b Rowan	74	c Mitchell b McCarthy	9
JF Crapp	c Wynne b Mitchell	35	c Wade b McCarthy	54
DCS Compton	b Rowan	1	not out	51
AJ Watkins	c Melville b Dawson	27	not out	64
*FG Mann	c Mitchell b Hanley	44		
+TG Evans	b Rowan	27		
RO Jenkins	c Wynne b Rowan	1		
AV Bedser	b McCarthy	16		
C Gladwin	not out	17		
DVP Wright	c Dawson b Rowan	11		
	(b 7, lb 7)	14	(b 8, lb 3)	11
	(all out)	308	(3 wickets declared)	276

Bowling: McCarthy 26-2-95-1 Dawson 7-2-35-1 Rowan 31.2-3-80-5 Mann 3-0-18-0 Hanley 18-4-57-1 Mitchell 6-0-9-1 McCarthy 20-2-75-2 Dawson 13-3-33-0 Rowan 30-5-65-1 Mann 15-5-27-0 Hanley 11-3-31-0 Mitchell 7-1-34-0

South Africa Innings

OE Wynne	c Crapp b Watkins	50	c Bedser b Jenkins	46
A Melville	b Jenkins	15	st Evans b Jenkins	24
B Mitchell	b Compton	120	not out	20
*AD Nourse	c & b Compton	112	st Evans b Jenkins	34
+WW Wade	c Watkins b Compton	0	c Evans b Jenkins	11
DW Begbie	run out	18		
OC Dawson	c Mann b Compton	25	not out	5
AMB Rowan	c Hutton b Gladwin	2		
NBF Mann	not out	10		
MA Hanley	run out	0		
CN McCarthy	st Evans b Compton	1		
	(b 1, nb 2)	3	(lb 1, nb 1)	2
	(all out)	356	(4 wickets)	142

Bowling: Bedser 34-5-92-0 Gladwin 30-7-51-1 Wright 9-0-58-0 Jenkins 11-1-46-1 Watkins 10-0-36-1 Compton 25.2-3-70-5 Bedser 7-0-40-0 Gladwin 10-2-27-0 Wright 2-0-18-0 Jenkins 9-0-48-4 Compton 3-1-7-0

Umpires: RGA Ashman and JV Hart-Davis

South Africa v Australia
31 December 1949, 2,3,4 January 1950

Result: Australia won by 8 wickets

Australia Innings

AR Morris	c Watkins b Tayfield	42	c & b Mann	24
J Moroney	c Cheetham b Mann	87	lbw b Mann	19
KR Miller	b Watkins	58	not out	16
*AL Hassett	c & b Mann	57		
RN Harvey	c Wade b Mann	178	not out	23
SJE Loxton	b Tayfield	35		
CL McCool	not out	49		
IWG Johnson	c Watkins b Mann	0		
RR Lindwall	not out	8		
+RA Saggers				
WA Johnston				
	(b 8, lb 4)	12	(b 5)	5
	(7 wickets declared)	526	(2 wickets)	87

Bowling: McCarthy 24-2-98-0 Watkins 12-2-59-1 Mann 28-3-105-4 Tayfield 37-4-141-2 Smith 25-0-111-0 McCarthy 4-1-18-0 Watkins 2-0-10-0 Mann 8-1-23-2 Tayfield 6-1-31-0

South Africa Innings

EAB Rowan	lbw b McCool	67	c Harvey b Johnston	3
OE Wynne	c Johnson b Miller	13	c Saggers b Johnston	10
JD Nel	lbw b Johnson	38	c McCool b Johnston	19
*AD Nourse	c Johnston b Miller	65	lbw b McCool	114
+WW Wade	c Saggers b Loxton	4	b Johnston	11
JE Cheetham	c McCool b Miller	3	c Saggers b Lindwall	27
JC Watkins	st Saggers b McCool	35	c Saggers b Lindwall	9
HJ Tayfield	st Saggers b McCool	15	b Lindwall	75
NBF Mann	b McCool	16	b Lindwall	46
VI Smith	not out	11	lbw b Lindwall	4
CN McCarthy	st Saggers b McCool	0	not out	0
	(b 2, lb 8, w 1)	11	(b 3, lb 10, nb 2)	15
	(all out)	278	(all out)	333

Bowling: Lindwall 12-2-53-0 Johnston 17-3-53-0 Johnson 12-1-61-1 Miller 17-3-54-3 McCool 11.4-1-41-5 Loxton 6-0-25-1 Lindwall 15.4-2-32-5 Johnston 24-2-70-3 Johnson 24-5-91-1 Miller 11-0-43-0 McCool 21-3-71-1 Loxton 4-1-6-0 Harvey 3-1-5-0

Umpires: RGA Ashman and D Collins

South Africa v New Zealand
1,2,4,5 January 1954

Result: Match drawn

New Zealand Innings

*GO Rabone	lbw b van Ryneveld	56
ME Chapple	c Waite b van Ryneveld	76
MB Poore	c McGlew b Adcock	44
B Sutcliffe	c Waite b Ironside	66
JR Reid	b Murray	135
JEF Beck	run out	99
+FLH Mooney	b Ironside	4
AR MacGibbon	c McGlew b Ironside	8
EW Dempster	c Endean b Ironside	0
IB Leggat	c McGlew b Tayfield	0
W Bell	not out	0
	(b 14, lb 3)	17
	(all out)	505

Bowling: Adcock 29-3-105-1 Ironside 46.3-16-117-4 Murray 34-8-93-1 Tayfield 33-10-80-1 van Ryneveld 23-1-93-2

South Africa Innings

DJ McGlew	c Sutcliffe b MacGibbon	86	c Chapple b Poore	28
+JHB Waite	lbw b MacGibbon	8	st Mooney b Rabone	16
RJ Westcott	c Leggat b MacGibbon	2	b Dempster	62
WR Endean	c Sutcliffe b MacGibbon	33	not out	34
RA McLean	c Mooney b Rabone	9	not out	18
CB van Ryneveld	c Mooney b Rabone	23		
*JE Cheetham	b Rabone	89		
ARA Murray	lbw b Rabone	6		
HJ Tayfield	c Leggat b Rabone	34		
DEJ Ironside	c MacGibbon b Rabone	10		
NAT Adcock	not out	8		
	(b 6, lb 6, nb 6)	18	(b 1)	1
	(all out)	326	(3 wickets)	159

Bowling: MacGibbon 33-13-71-4 Reid 20-7-48-0 Leggat 3-0-6-0 Bell 18-5-77-0 Rabone 38.7-10-68-6 Dempster 8-3-19-0 Sutcliffe 5-1-13-0 Poore 2-0-6-0 MacGibbon 8-4-15-0 Reid 4-1-8-0 Bell 6-2-22-0 Rabone 10-6-16-1 Dempster 6-0-24-1 Sutcliffe 7-0-33-0 Poore 12-1-39-1 Chapple 1-0-1-0

Umpires: D Collins and S Collins

South Africa v England
1,2,3,4,5 January 1957

Result: England won by 312 runs

England Innings

PE Richardson	lbw b Heine	45	c Endean b Goddard	44
TE Bailey	c Waite b Tayfield	34	b Heine	28
DCS Compton	c McLean b Tayfield	58	c & b Goddard	64
*PBH May	c Waite b Tayfield	8	lbw b Tayfield	15
MC Cowdrey	lbw b Adcock	101	c Waite b Tayfield	61
DJ Insole	c Goddard b Adcock	29	not out	3
+TG Evans	c McGlew b Goddard	62	c Endean b Goddard	1
JH Wardle	st Waite b Tayfield	3		
JC Laker	b Adcock	0		
PJ Loader	c Keith b Tayfield	10		
JB Statham	not out	2		
	(b 6, lb 6, nb 5)	17	(lb 2, nb 2)	4
	(all out)	369	(6 wickets declared)	220

Bowling: Heine 19-0-78-1 Adcock 22.2-2-54-3 Tayfield 53-21-130-5 Goddard 38-12-74-1 van Ryneveld 3-0-16-0 Heine 21-1-67-2 Adcock 3-0-8-0 Tayfield 12-4-33-1 Goddard 17.5-1-62-3 Watkins 10-2-46-0

South Africa Innings

*DJ McGlew	c Cowdrey b Laker	14	b Wardle	7
TL Goddard	c Evans b Loader	18	c Bailey b Wardle	26
HJ Keith	c Evans b Loader	14	c May b Wardle	4
CB van Ryneveld	b Wardle	25	not out	0
HJ Tayfield	run out	5	c Evans b Wardle	4
RA McLean	c May b Statham	42	lbw b Laker	22
+JHB Waite	c Evans b Wardle	49	c Cowdrey b Wardle	2
WR Endean	b Wardle	17	handled the ball	3
JC Watkins	not out	7	c & b Wardle	0
PS Heine	b Wardle	0	b Wardle	0
NAT Adcock	c Evans b Wardle	11	b Laker	1
	(b 1, lb 1, nb 1)	3	(lb 2, nb 1)	3
	(all out)	205	(all out)	72

Bowling: Statham 16-0-38-1 Loader 21-5-33-2 Laker 28-8-65-1 Bailey 11-5-13-0 Wardle 23.6-9-53-5 Statham 8-2-12-0 Loader 7-2-11-0 Laker 14.1-9-7-2 Wardle 19-3-36-7 Compton 2-1-3-0

Umpires: D Collins and VJ Costello

South Africa v Australia
31 December 1957, 1,2,3 January 1958

Result: Australia won by an innings and 141 runs

Australia Innings

CC McDonald	c Waite b Fuller	99	
JW Burke	b Tayfield	189	
RN Harvey	c Goddard b Adcock	15	
*ID Craig	b Goddard	0	
KD Mackay	lbw b Tayfield	63	
R Benaud	c McGlew b Tayfield	33	
AK Davidson	c & b Tayfield	21	
RB Simpson	c Funston b Tayfield	3	
+ATW Grout	run out	0	
I Meckiff	not out	11	
LF Kline	lbw b Fuller	5	
	(b 1, lb 6, nb 3)	10	
	(all out)	449	

Bowling: Adcock 27-5-80-1 Goddard 29-9-57-1 Fuller 34.2-3-125-2 Tayfield 51-18-120-5 Westcott 4-0-22-0 van Ryneveld 7-0-35-0

South Africa Innings

DJ McGlew	c Mackay b Davidson	30	c McDonald b Davidson	0
TL Goddard	lbw b Benaud	29	not out	56
RJ Westcott	c Simpson b Davidson	0	c Davidson b Benaud	18
+JHB Waite	c Simpson b Kline	7	c Benaud b Davidson	8
RA McLean	c Harvey b Kline	38	c Burke b Benaud	2
WR Endean	c Davidson b Burke	21	b Benaud	5
KJ Funston	c & b Benaud	2	b Benaud	8
*CB van Ryneveld	b Benaud	43	c Burke b Benaud	1
ERH Fuller	c Harvey b Benaud	5	c Benaud b Kline	0
HJ Tayfield	c Benaud b Kline	21	lbw b Kline	0
NAT Adcock	not out	0	c Simpson b Kline	0
	(b 6, lb 5, w 1, nb 1)	13	(lb 1)	1
	(all out)	209	(all out)	99

Bowling: Meckiff 5.4-1-18-0 Davidson 18-5-31-2 Benaud 35-6-95-4 Kline 19.1-5-29-3 Burke 9-2-23-1 Davidson 15-6-18-2 Benaud 21-6-49-5 Kline 10.4-2-18-3 Burke 6-4-7-0 Mackay 5-3-6-0

Umpires: D Collins and VJ Costello

South Africa v New Zealand
1,2,3,4 January 1962

Result: New Zealand won by 72 runs

New Zealand Innings

SN McGregor	b Burke	68	run out	20
GT Dowling	lbw b Lawrence	0	c Barlow b Burke	12
JT Sparling	c Elgie b Burke	19	c Waite b Burke	9
*JR Reid	c Bromfield b McKinnon	92	c Bromfield b Burke	14
PGZ Harris	st Waite b Bromfield	101	c Bland b Burke	30
ME Chapple	c Waite b Burke	69	b Burke	33
+AE Dick	c Waite b Burke	4	not out	50
GA Bartlett	c Waite b Burke	12	st Waite b McKinnon	29
RC Motz	b Burke	0	st Waite b McKinnon	0
JC Alabaster	c Farrer b Bromfield	1	st Waite b McKinnon	4
FJ Cameron	not out	2	not out	10
	(lb 8, nb 9)	17	(lb 1)	1
	(all out)	385	(9 wickets declared)	212

Bowling: Burke 53.5-19-128-6 Lawrence 23-7-46-1 McKinnon 19-6-42-1 Barlow 9-0-40-0 Bromfield 46-11-94-2 Elgie 7-2-18-0 Burke 27.1-10-68-5 McKinnon 17-7-32-2 Barlow 20-2-53-0 Bromfield 24-3-58-1

Innings

SN McGregor	b Burke	68
GT Dowling	lbw b Lawrence	0
JT Sparling	c Elgie b Burke	19
*JR Reid	c Bromfield b McKinnon	92
PGZ Harris	st Waite b Bromfield	101
ME Chapple	c Waite b Burke	69
+AE Dick	c Waite b Burke	4
GA Bartlett	c Waite b Burke	12
RC Motz	b Burke	0
JC Alabaster	c Farrer b Bromfield	1
FJ Cameron	not out	2
	(lb 8, nb 9)	17
	(all out)	385

Bowling: Burke 53.5-19-128-6 Lawrence 23-7-46-1 McKinnon 19-6-42-1 Barlow 9-0-40-0 Bromfield 46-11-94-2 Elgie 7-2-18-0

Umpires: D Collins and JE Warner

South Africa v England
1,2,4,5,6 January 1965

Result: Match drawn

South Africa Innings

*TL Goddard	b Titmus	40	c Parfitt b Price	6
EJ Barlow	c Parks b Thomson	138	c Parks b Thomson	78
AJ Pithey	c Barber b Allen	154	c Parks b Thomson	2
RG Pollock	c Parks b Allen	31	b Boycott	73
KC Bland	run out	78	b Boycott	64
+DT Lindsay	lbw b Thomson	2	b Barrington	50
GD Varnals	c Smith b Titmus	19	c Smith b Parfitt	20
SF Burke	not out	10	c Barber b Boycott	20
PM Pollock			lbw b Barrington	7
HD Bromfield			not out	12
GG Hall			b Barrington	0
	(b 5, lb 11, w 1, nb 12)	29	(b 1, lb 9, w 1, nb 3)	14
	(7 wickets declared)	501	(all out)	346

Bowling: Price 34-6-133-0 Thomson 45-19-89-2 Titmus 50.2-11-133-2 Dexter 2-0-10-0 Allen 40-14-79-2 Parfitt 8-0-28-0 Price 11-4-19-1 Thomson 14-4-31-1 Allen 17-6-27-0 Barber 1-0-2-0 Titmus 6-2-21-0 Parfitt 19-4-74-1 Dexter 17-3-64-1 Boycott 20-5-47-3 Smith 11-1-43-0 Barrington 3.1-1-4-3

England Innings

G Boycott	c Barlow b Bromfield	15	not out	1
RW Barber	lbw b Goddard	58		
ER Dexter	c & b Bromfield	61		
KF Barrington	c Lindsay b PM Pollock	49	not out	14
PH Parfitt	b Hall	44		
*MJK Smith	c Goddard b Bromfield	121		
+JM Parks	c Lindsay b Barlow	59		
FJ Titmus	c Lindsay b PM Pollock	4		
DA Allen	c Barlow b Bromfield	22		
NI Thomson	c RG Pollock b Bromfield	0		
JSE Price	not out	0		
	(b 2, lb 5, nb 2)	9		0
	(all out)	442	(0 wickets)	15

Bowling: PM Pollock 39-14-89-2 Burke 29-8-61-0 Bromfield 57.2-26-88-5 Hall 31-7-94-1 Goddard 37-13-64-1 Barlow 12-3-37-1 Bland 2-0-3-0 RG Pollock 2-1-5-0 Pithey 2-0-5-0 Varnals 2-1-2-0

Umpires: VJ Costello and JE Warner

South Africa v Australia
31 December 1966, 2,3,4,5 January 1967

Result: Australia won by 6 wickets

Australia Innings

*RB Simpson	c Lance b Barlow	153	c Goddard b PM Pollock	18
WM Lawry	lbw b PM Pollock	10	c PM Pollock b Goddard	39
IR Redpath	lbw b McKinnon	54	not out	69
RM Cowper	c van der Merwe b Lance	36	c Lindsay b Goddard	4
IM Chappell	c Lindsay b Goddard	49	b McKinnon	7
TR Veivers	lbw b PM Pollock	30	not out	35
KR Stackpole	c Lindsay b Barlow	134		
GD Watson	c Lance b Barlow	50		
GD McKenzie	c & b Barlow	11		
+HB Taber	not out	2		
DA Renneberg	b Barlow	2		
	(b 2, lb 7, w 2)	11	(lb 5, nb 3)	8
	(all out)	542	(4 wickets)	180

Bowling: PM Pollock 22-4-84-2 Dumbrill 11-2-36-0 Goddard 42-15-79-1 Barlow 33.3-9-85-5 Pithey 22-5-59-0 McKinnon 38-16-93-1 Lance 20-1-95-1 PM Pollock 12-2-42-1 Goddard 29.1-10-67-2 Barlow 2-1-1-0 McKinnon 22-5-62-1

South Africa Innings

TL Goddard	c Stackpole b McKenzie	7	lbw b Simpson	37
EJ Barlow	c Redpath b McKenzie	19	run out	17
A Bacher	b McKenzie	0	c Simpson b McKenzie	4
RG Pollock	c Taber b Simpson	209	b Simpson	4
HR Lance	c Simpson b Chappell	2	run out	53
+DT Lindsay	c & b Renneberg	5	c Simpson b Cowper	81
*PL van der Merwe	c Cowper b Simpson	50	lbw b Chappell	18
DB Pithey	c Taber b McKenzie	4	c Redpath b Renneberg	55
R Dumbrill	c Chappell b McKenzie	6	b McKenzie	1
PM Pollock	c Stackpole b Veivers	41	not out	75
AH McKinnon	not out	6	b McKenzie	8
	(lb 4)	4	(b 5, lb 9)	14
	(all out)	353	(all out)	367

Bowling: McKenzie 33-10-65-5 Renneberg 18-6-51-1 Watson 11-2-27-0 Chappell 13-4-51-1 Simpson 24-9-59-2 Veivers 8.1-2-32-1 Cowper 6-0-28-0 Stackpole 14-2-36-0 McKenzie 39.3-11-67-3 Renneberg 24-2-63-1 Chappell 39-17-71-1 Simpson 39-12-99-2 Veivers 7-2-21-0 Cowper 10-2-21-1 Stackpole 8-4-11-0

Umpires: G Goldman and HC Kidson

South Africa v Australia
22,23,24,26,27 January 1970

Result: South Africa won by 170 runs

South Africa Innings

BA Richards	b Connolly	29	c Taber b Connolly	32
TL Goddard	c Taber b Walters	16	c Lawry b Mallett	17
*A Bacher	lbw b Connolly	57	lbw b Gleeson	16
RG Pollock	c Chappell b Walters	49	c Walters b Connolly	50
EJ Barlow	c Chappell b Gleeson	127	c Taber b Gleeson	16
BL Irvine	c Gleeson b Mallett	42	c Walters b Connolly	19
MJ Procter	b Mallett	22	c Taber b Gleeson	48
+D Gamsy	not out	30	c Taber b Gleeson	2
PM Pollock	lbw b Mallett	1	b Gleeson	25
MA Seymour	c Lawry b Mallett	0	c Lawry b Connolly	0
GA Chevalier	c Chappell b Mallett	0	not out	0
	(b 2, lb 5, nb 2)	9	(b 1, lb 4, nb 2)	7
	(all out)	382	(all out)	232

Bowling: McKenzie 30-8-74-0 Connolly 29-12-62-2 Walters 8-1-19-2 Gleeson 45-17-92-1 Mallett 55.1-16-126-5 McKenzie 8-0-29-0 Connolly 26-10-47-5 Gleeson 30-11-70-4 Mallett 32-10-79-1

Australia Innings

KR Stackpole	c Barlow b Procter	19	c Barlow b Goddard	29
*WM Lawry	b PM Pollock	2	lbw b Procter	83
IM Chappell	c Chevalier b PM Pollock	0	b Chevalier	13
KD Walters	c Irvine b PM Pollock	73	c Irvine b Procter	4
IR Redpath	c Barlow b Procter	0	not out	47
AP Sheahan	c Barlow b Chevalier	8	b Seymour	16
+HB Taber	lbw b Seymour	11	lbw b Procter	15
GD McKenzie	c RG Pollock b PM Pollock	5	c RG Pollock b Chevalier	19
AA Mallett	c Goddard b Chevalier	19	c PM Pollock b Procter	5
JW Gleeson	b Goddard	17	b Richards	10
AN Connolly	not out	0	b Chevalier	25
	(b 1, nb 9)	10	(b 7, lb 2, nb 5)	14
	(all out)	164	(all out)	280

Bowling: Procter 12-4-30-2 PM Pollock 12-4-20-4 Goddard 19.4-9-29-1 Chevalier 11-2-32-2 Seymour 11-2-28-1 Barlow 1-0-15-0 Procter 17-4-47-4 PM Pollock 18-12-19-0 Goddard 32-12-66-1 Chevalier 31.1-9-68-3 Seymour 19-6-40-1 Barlow 6-2-14-0 Richards 6-1-12-1

Umpires: G Goldman and WW Wade

Newlands, Cape Town

South Africa v India
2,3,4,5,6 January 1993

Result: Match drawn

South Africa Innings

AC Hudson	c & b Srinath	19	c More b Srinath	11
*KC Wessels	b Prabhakar	0	c & b Srinath	34
WJ Cronje	c Manjrekar b Kumble	33	c More b Srinath	0
PN Kirsten	c More b Kapil Dev	13	c Manjrekar b Kapil Dev	13
DJ Cullinan	c Prabhakar b Raju	46	c More b Srinath	28
JN Rhodes	c More b Srinath	86	c Srinath b Kumble	16
BM McMillan	c sub (V Yadav) b Kumble	52	not out	11
+DJ Richardson	c Tendulkar b Kumble	21	not out	10
O Henry	run out	34		
CR Matthews	not out	28		
AA Donald	not out	1		
	(b 2, lb 22, w 2, nb 1)	27	(lb 4, nb 3)	7
	(9 wickets declared)	360	(6 wickets declared)	130

Bowling: Kapil Dev 29-8-42-1 Prabhakar 23-6-48-1 Raju 47-15-94-1 Srinath 25-6-51-2 Kumble 47-13-101-3
Kapil Dev 17-4-29-1 Prabhakar 10-4-19-0 Srinath 27-10-33-4 Kumble 23-11-20-1 Raju 20-8-25-0

India Innings

A Jadeja	c Kirsten b McMillan	19	not out	20
M Prabhakar	c Wessels b Henry	62	c Richardson b Matthews	7
SV Manjrekar	c Hudson b Donald	46	not out	2
PK Amre	c McMillan b Donald	6		
SR Tendulkar	c Hudson b Cronje	73		
*M Azharuddin	c Richardson b McMillan	7		
SLV Raju	c Cullinan b Matthews	18		
N Kapil Dev	c Hudson b Cronje	34		
+KS More	lbw b Matthews	0		
A Kumble	c Hudson b Matthews	0		
J Srinath	not out	0		
	(lb 7, w 3, nb 1)	11		0
	(all out)	276	(1 wicket)	29

Bowling: Donald 36-13-58-2 McMillan 36-9-76-2 Matthews 28-12-32-3 Cronje 18.4-8-17-2 Henry 33-8-86-1
Donald 4-0-7-0 Matthews 6-1-17-1 Cronje 3-3-0-0 Rhodes 1-0-5-0

Umpires: SB Lambson, KE Liebenberg and DR Shepherd (Eng)
TV Umpire: KE Liebenberg and SB Lambson; Referee: MJK Smith (Eng)

South Africa v Australia
17,18,19,20,21 March 1994

Result: Australia won by 9 wickets

South Africa Innings

AC Hudson	run out	102	lbw b SR Waugh	49
G Kirsten	run out	29	lbw b Warne	10
WJ Cronje	b McGrath	2	c & b SR Waugh	19
*KC Wessels	c ME Waugh b McDermott	11	run out	9
PN Kirsten	lbw b Warne	70	c Taylor b Warne	3
JN Rhodes	lbw b McGrath	5	c Border b SR Waugh	27
BM McMillan	b Warne	74	lbw b SR Waugh	3
+DJ Richardson	lbw b McDermott	34	c Healy b McGrath	31
CR Matthews	not out	7	not out	0
PS de Villiers	c Taylor b Warne	7	lbw b Warne	0
AA Donald	c Healy b McGrath	7	b SR Waugh	0
	(lb 6, nb 7)	13	(b 4, lb 6, nb 3)	13
	(all out)	361	(all out)	164

Bowling: McDermott 27-6-80-2 Hughes 20-1-80-0 McGrath 26.1-4-65-3 SR Waugh 9-3-20-0 Warne 47-18-78-3 ME Waugh 10-3-23-0 Border 5-2-9-0
McDermott 13-3-39-0 Hughes 5-1-12-0 Warne 30-13-38-3 McGrath 16-6-26-1 SR Waugh 22.3-9-28-5 Border 1-1-0-0 ME Waugh 3-1-11-0

Australia Innings

MJ Slater	c PN Kirsten b de Villiers	26	not out	43
MA Taylor	c Richardson b de Villiers	70	b Donald	14
DC Boon	c Richardson b de Villiers	96	not out	32
ME Waugh	c PN Kirsten b McMillan	7		
*AR Border	c Richardson b Matthews	45		
SR Waugh	b Matthews	86		
+IA Healy	c de Villiers b Matthews	61		
MG Hughes	lbw b Matthews	0		
SK Warne	c McMillan b de Villiers	11		
CJ McDermott	c PN Kirsten b Matthews	1		
GD McGrath	not out	1		
	(b 6, lb 17, w 1, nb 7)	31	(b 1, nb 2)	3
	(all out)	435	(1 wicket)	92

Bowling: Donald 35-10-111-0 de Villiers 44.4-11-117-4 Matthews 36-12-80-5 McMillan 29-8-82-1 G Kirsten 4-0-13-0 Cronje 11-4-9-0
Matthews 6-1-14-0 de Villiers 6-0-20-0 Donald 5-0-20-1 McMillan 5-0-23-0 Cronje 2-0-4-0 G Kirsten 1.1-0-10-0

Umpires: KE Liebenberg and DR Shepherd (Eng)
TV Umpire: SB Lambson; Referee: DB Carr (Eng)

South Africa v New Zealand
2,3,4,5,6 January 1995

Result: South Africa won by 7 wickets

New Zealand Innings

BA Young	lbw b McMillan	45	c Kirsten b McMillan	51
DJ Murray	c Kirsten b McMillan	5	lbw b de Villiers	3
+AC Parore	run out	2	c Eksteen b de Villiers	34
MD Crowe	c Richardson b Jack	18	c Richardson b McMillan	5
*KR Rutherford	c Kirsten b McMillan	56	lbw b McMillan	26
SA Thomson	b McMillan	0	run out	16
SP Fleming	b Jack	79	c Richardson b de Villiers	53
MN Hart	c Richardson b Jack	24	c de Villiers b Jack	7
SB Doull	c Cronje b Jack	6	c Rhodes b de Villiers	25
DK Morrison	not out	0	lbw b de Villiers	1
C Pringle	b de Villiers	30	not out	0
	(lb 13, nb 10)	23	(b 5, lb 6, w 1, nb 6)	18
	(all out)	288	(all out)	239

Bowling: de Villiers 28.5-7-90-1 Jack 27-7-69-4 McMillan 26-5-65-4 Cronje 5-3-8-0 Eksteen 26-10-36-0 Kirsten 2-0-7-0
de Villiers 28.1-9-61-5 Jack 19-7-50-1 McMillan 25-9-52-3 Cronje 7-3-15-0 Eksteen 31-16-46-0 Kirsten 1-0-4-0

South Africa Innings

G Kirsten	b Thomson	64	lbw b Hart	25
PJR Steyn	lbw b Thomson	38	c Doull b Thomson	12
JB Commins	c Rutherford b Hart	27	not out	10
DJ Cullinan	c Young b Thomson	5	hit wicket b Hart	28
*WJ Cronje	c Pringle b Hart	112	not out	14
JN Rhodes	b Doull	18		
BM McMillan	lbw b Pringle	18		
+DJ Richardson	c Crowe b Doull	109		
CE Eksteen	b Hart	22		
SD Jack	c Murray b Morrison	7		
PS de Villiers	not out	1		
	(b 7, lb 3, w 1, nb 8)	19		0
	(all out)	440	(3 wickets)	89

Bowling: Morrison 34-7-100-1 Doull 34.2-12-55-2 Pringle 28-5-69-1 Hart 54-8-141-3 Thomson 31-7-65-3
Morrison 4-1-5-0 Hart 15.2-2-51-2 Thomson 12-3-33-1

Umpires: KT Francis (SL) and SB Lambson; Referee: PJP Burge (Aus)

South Africa v England
2,3,4 January 1996

Result: South Africa won by 10 wickets

England Innings

*MA Atherton	c Hudson b Donald	0	c Richardson b Donald	10
AJ Stewart	b McMillan	13	c Cullinan b Pollock	7
RA Smith	b Adams	66	c Richardson b Adams	13
GP Thorpe	c McMillan b Donald	20	run out	59
GA Hick	c McMillan b Donald	2	lbw b Pollock	36
+RC Russell	c McMillan b Pollock	9	c Hudson b Pollock	2
M Watkinson	lbw b Pollock	11	lbw b Adams	0
DG Cork	b Donald	16	c Kallis b Pollock	8
PJ Martin	c Hudson b Donald	0	c Adams b Pollock	9
ARC Fraser	not out	5	c Adams b Donald	1
DE Malcolm	b Adams	1	not out	0
	(b 4, lb 1, w 1, nb 4)	10	(b 2, lb 5, nb 5)	12
	(all out)	153	(all out)	157

Bowling: Donald 16-5-46-5 Pollock 14-6-26-2 McMillan 10-2-22-1 Adams 20.1-5-52-2 Kallis 4-2-2-0 Cronje 4-4-0-0
Donald 18-6-49-2 Pollock 15.5-4-32-5 Adams 22-6-53-2 McMillan 7-3-16-0

South Africa Innings

G Kirsten	c Atherton b Watkinson	23	not out	41
AC Hudson	lbw b Cork	0	not out	27
*WJ Cronje	c Russell b Cork	12		
DJ Cullinan	c Russell b Martin	62		
JN Rhodes	c Russell b Fraser	16		
BM McMillan	run out	11		
JH Kallis	lbw b Martin	7		
+DJ Richardson	not out	54		
SM Pollock	c Smith b Watkinson	4		
AA Donald	c Russell b Cork	3		
PR Adams	c Hick b Martin	29		
	(lb 22, nb 1)	23	(lb 1, nb 1)	2
	(all out)	244	(0 wickets)	70

Bowling: Cork 25-6-60-3 Malcolm 20-6-56-0 Martin 24-9-37-3 Fraser 17-10-34-1 Watkinson 15-3-35-2
Cork 4-0-23-0 Malcolm 2-0-12-0 Martin 4-2-3-0 Watkinson 4-0-24-0 Hick 1.4-0-7-0

Umpires: DL Orchard and SG Randell (Aus)
TV Umpire: KE Liebenberg; Referee: CH Lloyd (WI)

South Africa v India
2,3,4,5,6 January 1997

Result: South Africa won by 282 runs

South Africa Innings

AC Hudson	c Mongia b Prasad	16	b Srinath	55
G Kirsten	run out (Azharuddin/Ganguly)	103	lbw b Ganesh	0
AM Bacher	c Mongia b Srinath	25	lbw b Srinath	0
DJ Cullinan	c Mongia b Prasad	77	b Kumble	55
*WJ Cronje	c Mongia b Srinath	41	c Dravid b Kumble	18
BM McMillan	not out	103	not out	59
SM Pollock	c Tendulkar b Prasad	1	not out	40
+DJ Richardson	c Dravid b Srinath	39		
L Klusener	not out	102	c Dravid b Srinath	12
AA Donald				
PR Adams				
	(b 5, lb 9, nb 8)	22	(b 4, lb 12, w 1)	17
	(7 wickets declared)	529	(6 wickets declared)	256

Bowling: Srinath 38-8-130-3 Prasad 36-1-114-3 Ganesh 23.5-6-93-0 Kumble 51-7-136-0 Ganguly 9-1-24-0 Raman 5-1-18-0
Srinath 18-5-78-3 Ganesh 10-3-38-1 Prasad 7-1-16-0 Kumble 25-4-58-2 Ganguly 2-0-5-0 Raman 10-0-45-0

India Innings

WV Raman	run out (Klusener)	5	c Richardson b Pollock	16
R Dravid	b Klusener	2	c Richardson b Adams	12
SC Ganguly	c McMillan b Donald	23	c McMillan b Pollock	30
BKV Prasad	b Adams	0	st Richardson b Adams	15
*SR Tendulkar	c Bacher b McMillan	169	c Klusener b McMillan	9
VVS Laxman	c Richardson b Pollock	5	not out	35
M Azharuddin	run out (Hudson)	115	c Hudson b Donald	2
+NR Mongia	lbw b Adams	5	b Donald	2
A Kumble	c Richardson b Donald	2	c Richardson b Adams	14
J Srinath	b Pollock	11	absent ill	0
D Ganesh	not out	2	b Donald	1
	(lb 9, nb 11)	20	(lb 1, w 2, nb 5)	8
	(all out)	359	(all out)	144

Bowling: Donald 24-3-99-2 Pollock 23-2-76-2 Adams 18-5-49-2 Klusener 12-1-88-1 McMillan 6.2-0-22-1 Cronje 9-5-16-0
Donald 18-5-40-3 Pollock 12-2-29-2 Klusener 9-3-13-0 McMillan 11-4-16-1 Adams 16.2-4-45-3

Umpires: DB Hair (Aus) and RE Koertzen
TV Umpire: CJ Mitchley; Referee: BN Jarman (Aus)

South Africa v Sri Lanka
19,20,21,22,23 March 1998

Result: South Africa won by 70 runs

South Africa Innings

AM Bacher	c Mahanama b Wickramasinghe	6	c Kaluwitharana b Vaas	0
G Kirsten	lbw b Vaas	62	c Mahanama b Vaas	15
HD Ackerman	c & b Muralitharan	23	lbw b Muralitharan	8
DJ Cullinan	b Wickramasinghe	113	c Tillakaratne b Muralitharan	68
*WJ Cronje	c Mahanama b Vaas	49	c Muralitharan b Jayasuriya	74
JH Kallis	c Ranatunga b Muralitharan	3	st Kaluwitharana b Jayasuriya	49
SM Pollock	lbw b Wickramasinghe	92	st Kaluwitharana b Jayasuriya	6
+MV Boucher	run out (Mahanama)	33	c Jayasuriya b Muralitharan	10
AA Donald	b Muralitharan	12	c Pushpakumara b Jayasuriya	18
PR Adams	st Kaluwitharana b Muralitharan	2	c Kaluwitharana b Muralitharan	3
M Ntini	not out	3	not out	0
	(lb 8, nb 12)	20	(b 4, lb 3, w 1, nb 5)	13
	(all out)	418	(all out)	264

Bowling: Vaas 21-2-75-2 Pushpakumara 20-3-81-0 Wickramasinghe 28.4-7-75-3 Muralitharan 45-8-135-4 Jayasuriya 6-1-29-0 de Silva 4-0-15-0
Vaas 11-3-41-2 Pushpakumara 8-0-24-0 Wickramasinghe 8-1-24-0 Muralitharan 41-10-108-4 de Silva 1-1-0-0 Jayasuriya 33-7-53-4 Atapattu 1-0-7-0

Sri Lanka Innings

ST Jayasuriya	c Boucher b Donald	17	lbw b Donald	0
MS Atapattu	c Cullinan b Adams	60	c & b Adams	71
RS Mahanama	c Boucher b Donald	9	c Kallis b Pollock	11
PA de Silva	c Boucher b Ntini	77	c Kallis b Adams	37
*A Ranatunga	c Ackerman b Adams	20	c Kirsten b Kallis	43
HP Tillakaratne	c Boucher b Pollock	22	lbw b Donald	13
+RS Kaluwitharana	lbw b Pollock	13	b Pollock	45
WPUJC Vaas	c Boucher b Pollock	30	c Boucher b Donald	0
GP Wickramasinghe	c sub (L Klusener) b Pollock	11	b Ntini	51
M Muralitharan	not out	15	run out (Cullinan)	10
KR Pushpakumara	c Boucher b Donald	4	not out	9
	(b 8, lb 7, w 1, nb 12)	28	(b 5, lb 3, nb 8)	16
	(all out)	306	(all out)	306

Bowling: Donald 21.3-7-66-3 Pollock 26-5-83-4 Ntini 10-1-57-1 Kallis 7-1-23-0 Adams 20-2-62-2
Donald 20-4-64-3 Pollock 23-3-77-2 Kallis 15-5-45-1 Ntini 5.3-0-17-1 Adams 27-3-90-2 Cronje 5-3-5-0

Umpires: RS Dunne (NZ) and DL Orchard
TV Umpire: RE Koertzen; Referee: JR Reid (NZ)

South Africa v West Indies
2,3,4,5,6 January 1999

Result: South Africa won by 149 runs

South Africa Innings

G Kirsten	c Jacobs b Ambrose	0	c Murray b McLean	5
HH Gibbs	c Wallace b Dillon	42	c Jacobs b Dillon	25
JH Kallis	c Jacobs b Gibson	110	not out	88
DJ Cullinan	c Jacobs b McLean	168	lbw b McLean	0
*WJ Cronje	c Jacobs b McLean	0	c Hooper b Dillon	54
JN Rhodes	b Hooper	34	lbw b Hooper	23
SM Pollock	c Lara b Dillon	9	c Lara b Hooper	3
+MV Boucher	not out	15	c & b McLean	22
AA Donald	c Wallace b Dillon	0	not out	0
DJ Terbrugge	not out	4		
PR Adams				
	(lb 3, w 1, nb 20)	24	(lb 4, w 1, nb 1)	6
	(8 wickets declared)	406	(7 wickets declared)	226

Bowling: Ambrose 24.1-7-49-1 McLean 25.5-7-76-2 Gibson 30-4-92-1 Dillon 33.5-6-99-3 Hooper 27-6-60-1 Chanderpaul 6-0-27-0
McLean 16-1-53-2 Gibson 14.4-2-51-0 Dillon 17-2-37-2 Hooper 28-8-52-2 Chanderpaul 12-1-29-0

West Indies Innings

PA Wallace	c Cullinan b Donald	8	c Gibbs b Pollock	0
JR Murray	c Boucher b Donald	0	lbw b Kallis	7
S Chanderpaul	c Rhodes b Terbrugge	6	c Cullinan b Kallis	5
*BC Lara	hit wicket b Donald	4	c & b Adams	33
CL Hooper	run out (Cronje)	86	b Kallis	20
D Ganga	c Kirsten b Pollock	17	lbw b Pollock	16
+RD Jacobs	c Kallis b Pollock	29	not out	69
OD Gibson	c Kirsten b Kallis	37	run out (Rhodes)	13
NAM McLean	c Cronje b Adams	14	c Adams b Kallis	39
CEL Ambrose	not out	4	c Kirsten b Adams	19
M Dillon	c Boucher b Kallis	0	c Cronje b Kallis	36
	(lb 2, w 2, nb 3)	7	(lb 2, nb 12)	14
	(all out)	212	(all out)	271

Bowling: Donald 6-1-20-3 Pollock 22-9-35-2 Terbrugge 20-8-37-1 Kallis 15-5-34-2 Adams 16-2-61-1 Cronje 6-1-23-0
Pollock 25-3-49-2 Kallis 27.4-4-90-5 Cronje 1-1-0-0 Terbrugge 11-4-40-0 Adams 23-5-80-2 Cullinan 4-1-10-0

Umpires: DL Orchard and S Venkataraghavan (Ind)
TV Umpire: CJ Mitchley; Referee: RS Madugalle (SL)

South Africa v England
2,3,4,5 January 2000

Result: South Africa won by an innings and 37 runs

England Innings

MA Butcher	c Kirsten b Donald	40	c Boucher b Pollock	4
MA Atherton	c Kirsten b Donald	71	c Cullinan b Pollock	35
*N Hussain	c Boucher b Adams	15	lbw b Klusener	16
MP Vaughan	c Kirsten b Donald	42	c Boucher b Klusener	5
+AJ Stewart	c Kirsten b Donald	40	b Adams	5
AR Caddick	c Cullinan b Donald	5	c Gibbs b Donald	14
CJ Adams	c Pollock b Kallis	10	b Adams	31
A Flintoff	c Rhodes b Klusener	22	absent hurt	0
D Gough	c Boucher b Klusener	4	c Donald b Kallis	8
CEW Silverwood	not out	1	not out	5
PCR Tufnell	b Kallis	2	c Cullinan b Adams	0
	(lb 6, w 2, nb 3)	11	(lb 3)	3
	(all out)	258	(all out)	126

Bowling: Donald 26-13-47-5 Pollock 27-8-59-0 Kallis 20-4-61-2 Klusener 16-5-42-2 Cronje 3-2-5-0 Adams 21-9-38-1
Adams 19.3-5-42-3 Donald 10.4-2-35-1 Pollock 14-8-19-2 Kallis 9.2-2-19-1 Klusener 7-4-8-2

South Africa Innings

G Kirsten	c Stewart b Silverwood	80
HH Gibbs	c Vaughan b Silverwood	29
JH Kallis	c Atherton b Gough	105
DJ Cullinan	c Vaughan b Tufnell	120
*WJ Cronje	c Vaughan b Caddick	0
JN Rhodes	c Adams b Silverwood	16
L Klusener	b Gough	3
SM Pollock	c Adams b Caddick	4
+MV Boucher	lbw b Silverwood	36
AA Donald	c Adams b Silverwood	7
PR Adams	not out	3
	(b 1, lb 7, nb 10)	18
	(all out)	421

Bowling: Gough 37-6-88-2 Caddick 31-6-95-2 Silverwood 32-6-91-5 Flintoff 4-0-16-0 Tufnell 39.4-10-97-1 Butcher 3-0-9-0
Adams 7-2-17-0

Umpires: BC Cooray (SL) and CJ Mitchley
TV Umpire: IL Howell; Referee: BN Jarman (Aus)

South Africa v Sri Lanka
2,3,4 January 2001

Result: South Africa won by an innings and 229 runs

Sri Lanka Innings

MS Atapattu	c Kallis b Pollock	5	lbw b Pollock	13
*ST Jayasuriya	c Boucher b Pollock	8	c Pollock b Ngam	0
+KC Sangakkara	c Cullinan b Ngam	32	c Boucher b Ngam	11
DPMD Jayawardene	c Kallis b Pollock	0	lbw b Boje	45
RP Arnold	c Kirsten b Pollock	0	c Gibbs b Boje	26
TM Dilshan	c Pollock b Kallis	5	c Boucher b Boje	17
DA Gunawardene	c Kallis b Ngam	24	b Ntini	13
WPUJC Vaas	c Pollock b Ngam	7	c & b Boje	38
DNT Zoysa	c & b Pollock	10	c Kusener b Ntini	0
CRD Fernando	not out	0	c Boucher b Ngam	5
M Muralitharan	c Ntini b Pollock	0	not out	1
	(w 1, nb 3)	4	(lb 6, w 1, nb 4)	11
	(all out)	95	(all out)	180

Bowling: Pollock 13.4-6-30-6 Ngam 13-3-26-3 Kallis 6-2-19-1 Ntini 6-2-20-0
Pollock 9-3-29-1 Ngam 8.2-1-36-3 Kallis 7-1-29-0 Ntini 11-2-52-2 Boje 10-3-28-4

South Africa Innings

G Kirsten	c Dilshan b Muralitharan	52
HH Gibbs	c Sangakkara b Vaas	0
JH Kallis	c Jayawardene b Fernando	49
DJ Cullinan	run out b Arnold	112
ND McKenzie	c & b Arnold	47
+MV Boucher	c Jayawardene b Arnold	92
L Klusener	c Jayasuriya b Arnold	97
N Boje	not out	31
*SM Pollock		
M Ntini		
M Ngam		
	(lb 5, w 1, nb 18)	24
	(7 wickets dec)	504

Bowling: Vaas 32-6-109-1 Zoysa 26-6-80-0 Fernando 25-2-105-1 Muralitharan 43-11-99-1 Jayasuriya 7-1-28-0 Arnold 24.2-4-76-3 Jayawardene 1-0-2-0

Umpires: IL Howell and EA Nicholls (WI)
TV Umpire: WA Diedricks; Referee: R Subba Row (Eng)

South Africa v Australia
8,9,10,11,12 March 2002

Result: Australia won by 4 wickets

South Africa Innings

HH Gibbs	c ME Waugh b Gillespie	12	c Ponting b Warne	39
G Kirsten	c ME Waugh b Lee	7	lbw b Lee	87
GC Smith	c Ponting b McGrath	3	c Gilchrist b Warne	68
JH Kallis	c Gilchrist b McGrath	23	lbw b Warne	73
ND McKenzie	b Warne	20	run out (Martyn)	99
AG Prince	c Gilchrist b McGrath	10	c Ponting b Warne	20
*+MV Boucher	c Gilchrist b Lee	26	lbw b Gillespie	37
AJ Hall	c Gilchrist b Gillespie	70	run out (Lee/Gillespie)	0
PR Adams	c Warne b Gillespie	35	not out	23
M Ntini	c ME Waugh b Warne	14	c Langer b Warne	11
D Pretorius	not out	5	c ME Waugh b Warne	0
	(b 4, lb 5, nb 5)	14	(b 8, lb 3, w 2, nb 3)	16
	(all out)	239	(all out)	473

Bowling: McGrath 20-4-42-3 Gillespie 15-4-52-3 Lee 16-1-65-2 Warne 28-10-70-2 ME Waugh 1-0-1-0
McGrath 25-7-56-0 Gillespie 29-10-81-1 Warne 70-15-161-6 Lee 22-3-99-1 ME Waugh 9-3-34-0 Martyn 4-0-15-0 SR Waugh 3-0-16-0

Australia Innings

JL Langer	b Ntini	37	b Pretorius	58
ML Hayden	c Hall b Kallis	63	c Boucher b Kallis	96
RT Ponting	c Boucher b Adams	47	not out	100
ME Waugh	c Gibbs b Ntini	25	c Boucher b Ntini	16
*SR Waugh	b Adams	0	b Adams	14
DR Martyn	c Boucher b Ntini	2	lbw b Adams	0
+AC Gilchrist	not out	138	c McKenzie b Kallis	24
SK Warne	c Kallis b Adams	63	not out	15
B Lee	c Prince b Kallis	0		
JN Gillespie	c Kallis b Adams	0		
GD McGrath	lbw b Ntini	2		
	(b 2, lb 1, w 2)	5	(lb 6, nb 5)	11
	(all out)	382	(6 wickets)	334

Bowling: Ntini 22.5-5-93-4 Pretorius 11-1-72-0 Kallis 16-1-65-2 Hall 11-1-47-0 Adams 20-1-102-4
Ntini 24-4-90-1 Pretorius 14-5-60-1 Adams 21.1-0-104-2 Hall 3-0-6-0 Kallis 17-2-68-2

Umpires: SA Bucknor (WI) and RE Koertzen
TV Umpire: DL Orchard; Referee: CW Smith (WI)

South Africa v Pakistan
2,3,4,5 January 2003

Result: South Africa won by an innings and 142 runs

South Africa Innings

GC Smith	b Mohammad Zahid	151
HH Gibbs	c Younis Khan b Saqlain Mushtaq	228
G Kirsten	c Younis Khan b Waqar Younis	19
JH Kallis	lbw b Mohammad Sami	31
HH Dippenaar	c Kamran Akmal b Saqlain Mushtaq	62
ND McKenzie	c Kamran Akmal b Mohammad Zahid	51
+MV Boucher	b Saqlain Mushtaq	7
*SM Pollock	not out	36
N Boje	not out	7
M Ntini		
M Hayward		
	(b 1, lb 5, w 1, nb 21)	28
	(7 wickets dec)	620

Bowling: Waqar Younis 28-4-121-1 Mohammad Sami 28-2-124-1 Mohammad Zahid 25-3-108-2 Saqlain Mushtaq 50-3-237-3
Younis Khan 4-0-24-0

Pakistan Innings

Taufeeq Umar	c Kallis b Ntini	135	c Boucher b Pollock	67
Saleem Elahi	c Smith b Pollock	10	c Dippenaar b Ntini	0
Younis Khan	lbw b Pollock	46	c McKenzie b Kallis	2
Inzamam-ul-Haq	c Dippenaar b Hayward	32	st Boucher b Boje	60
Yousuf Youhana	c Boucher b Hayward	0	c Kallis b Boje	50
Faisal Iqbal	b Ntini	24	c Pollock b Ntini	11
+Kamran Akmal	lbw b Pollock	0	lbw b Ntini	4
Saqlain Mushtaq	c Boucher b Ntini	1	run out (Kirsten/Boucher/Ntini)	9
*Waqar Younis	c Kallis b Pollock	0	lbw b Hayward	9
Mohammad Sami	not out	0	not out	9
Mohammad Zahid	c Smith b Ntini	0	c Pollock b Ntini	0
	(lb 1, nb 3)	4	(lb 1, w 1, nb 3)	5
	(all out)	252	(all out)	226

Bowling: Pollock 23-6-45-4 Ntini 20.4-7-62-4 Kallis 12-2-35-0 Hayward 15-2-56-2 Boje 17-2-53-0
Pollock 12-5-32-1 Ntini 15.1-2-33-4 Kallis 6-1-34-1 Hayward 11-3-44-1 Boje 15-0-82-2

Umpires: SA Bucknor (WI) and S Venkataraghavan (Ind)
TV Umpire: BG Jerling; Referee: GR Viswanath (Ind)

Kensington Oval, Bridgetown, Barbados

West Indies v England
11,13,14,15,16 January 1930

Result: Match drawn

West Indies Innings				
CA Roach	c Hendren b Astill	122	c Rhodes b Haig	77
*ELG Hoad	c Rhodes b Voce	24	c Astill b Calthorpe	0
GA Headley	b O'Connor	21	c O'Connor b Rhodes	176
FI de Caires	c Sandham b Voce	80	c & b Stevens	70
JED Sealy	c Haig b Stevens	58	b Rhodes	15
LN Constantine	lbw b Stevens	13	c sub b Stevens	6
CR Browne	b Stevens	0	c Hendren b Rhodes	0
LA Walcott	run out	24	not out	16
EL St Hill	c Calthorpe b Stevens	0	c Ames b Stevens	12
HC Griffith	lbw b Stevens	8	c O'Connor b Stevens	0
+EAC Hunte	not out	10	lbw b Stevens	1
	(b 6, lb 3)	9	(b 4, lb 6, w 1)	11
	(all out)	369	(all out)	384

Bowling: Voce 27-1-120-2 Haig 10-4-27-0 Rhodes 27.1-9-44-0 Stevens 27-5-105-5 O'Connor 10-0-31-1 Astill 9-1-19-1 Calthorpe 4-0-14-0
Voce 3-0-15-0 Haig 20-4-40-1 Rhodes 51-10-110-3 Stevens 26.4-1-90-5 Astill 30-10-72-0 Calthorpe 20-7-38-1 Gunn 2-0-8-0

England Innings				
G Gunn	lbw b St Hill	35	b Walcott	29
A Sandham	lbw b Constantine	152	b Griffith	51
GTS Stevens	run out	9	c Constantine b Griffith	5
EH Hendren	c Constantine b St Hill	80	not out	36
J O'Connor	c Constantine b Griffith	37		
+LEG Ames	b Constantine	16	not out	44
NE Haig	c Hunte b Browne	47		
WE Astill	c Constantine b Griffith	1		
*Hon.FSG Calthorpe	b Constantine	40		
W Rhodes	not out	14		
W Voce	c Hoad b Browne	10		
	(b 20, lb 3, nb 3)	26	(w 2)	2
	(all out)	467	(3 wickets)	167

Bowling: Constantine 39-9-121-3 Griffith 36-11-102-2 St Hill 35-7-110-2 Browne 37-8-83-2 Headley 3-0-10-0 Walcott 3-0-15-0
Constantine 12-3-47-0 Griffith 15-4-37-2 St Hill 11-3-24-0 Browne 13-6-19-0 Headley 2-0-6-0 Walcott 5-1-17-1 Roach 5-1-6-0 de Caires 2-0-9-0

Umpires: W Badley and J Hardstaff snr (Eng)

West Indies v England
8,9,10 January 1935

Result: England won by 4 wickets

West Indies Innings				
CA Roach	c Paine b Farnes	9	not out	10
GM Carew	c Holmes b Farnes	0		
GA Headley	run out	44	c Paine b Farnes	0
CEL Jones	c Leyland b Farnes	3		
JED Sealy	c Paine b Farnes	0		
*GC Grant	c Hendren b Hollies	4	not out	0
RS Grant	c Hammond b Hollies	5	c Paine b Smith	0
LG Hylton	st Ames b Paine	15	lbw b Smith	19
+CM Christiani	not out	9	b Smith	11
EE Achong	st Ames b Paine	0	b Smith	0
EA Martindale	c Leyland b Paine	9	lbw b Smith	0
	(lb 2, nb 2)	4	(b 4, lb 4, nb 3)	11
	(all out)	102	(6 wickets declared)	51

Bowling: Farnes 15-4-40-4 Smith 7-3-8-0 Hollies 16-4-36-2 Paine 9-3-14-3
Farnes 9-2-23-1 Smith 8-4-16-5 Paine 1-1-0-0 Hammond 1-0-1-0

England Innings				
*RES Wyatt	c RS Grant b Martindale	8	not out	6
M Leyland	c & b Martindale	3	c RS Grant b Martindale	2
WR Hammond	c RS Grant b Hylton	43	not out	29
EH Hendren	c RS Grant b Martindale	3	b Martindale	20
+LEG Ames	lbw b RS Grant	8		
CIJ Smith	c Jones b Hylton	0	c Christiani b Martindale	0
J Iddon	not out	14		
ERT Holmes	c Achong b Hylton	0	c GC Grant b Martindale	6
K Farnes			c GC Grant b Hylton	5
GAE Paine			c RS Grant b Martindale	2
WE Hollies				
	(b 1, nb 1)	2	(b 2, nb 3)	5
	(7 wickets declared)	81	(6 wickets)	75

Bowling: Martindale 9-0-39-3 Hylton 7.3-3-8-3 Achong 6-1-14-0 RS Grant 7-0-18-1
Martindale 8.3-1-22-5 Hylton 8-0-48-1

Umpires: CW Reece and EL Ward

West Indies v England
21,22,23,24,26 January 1948

Result: Match drawn

West Indies Innings				
JB Stollmeyer	c Robertson b Ikin	78	c Evans b Howorth	31
+CL Walcott	b Laker	8	c Ikin b Howorth	16
ED Weekes	c Evans b Tremlett	35	b Laker	25
GE Gomez	b Laker	86	st Evans b Howorth	0
*GA Headley	b Laker	29	not out	7
RJ Christiani	lbw b Laker	1	lbw b Cranston	99
JDC Goddard	b Howorth	28	c Ikin b Laker	18
EAV Williams	c Ikin b Laker	2	c Evans b Howorth	72
W Ferguson	b Laker	0	not out	56
PEW Jones	not out	10	c Robertson b Howorth	7
BBM Gaskin	c Ikin b Laker	10	c Brookes b Howorth	7
	(lb 4, w 2, nb 3)	9	(b 6, lb 4, w 1, nb 2)	13
	(all out)	296	(9 wickets declared)	351

Bowling: Tremlett 26-8-49-1 Cranston 15-4-29-0 Laker 37-9-103-7 Ikin 16-3-38-1 Howorth 30-8-68-1
Tremlett 10-0-40-0 Cranston 13-3-31-1 Laker 30-12-95-2 Ikin 12-1-48-0 Howorth 41-8-124-6

England Innings				
JDB Robertson	lbw b Williams	80	not out	51
W Place	c Gomez b Goddard	12	not out	1
D Brookes	b Jones	10	c Walcott b Goddard	7
J Hardstaff jnr	b Williams	98	c Gomez b Goddard	0
JT Ikin	c Walcott b Williams	3		
GA Smithson	c Gomez b Jones	0		
*K Cranston	run out	2	lbw b Gaskin	8
R Howorth	c Goddard b Ferguson	14	b Ferguson	16
+TG Evans	b Jones	26		
JC Laker	c Walcott b Jones	2		
MF Tremlett	not out	0		
	(b 2, lb 2, w 1, nb 1)	6	(lb 3)	3
	(all out)	253	(4 wickets)	86

Bowling: Jones 25.2-6-54-4 Gaskin 11-0-30-0 Williams 33-15-51-3 Goddard 21-6-49-1 Ferguson 14-1-52-1 Headley 6-1-11-0
Jones 9-1-29-0 Gaskin 10-4-15-1 Williams 9-3-17-0 Goddard 14-4-18-2 Ferguson 3.4-1-4-1

Umpires: CS Foster and JH Walcott

West Indies v India
7,9,10,11,12 February 1953

Result: West Indies won by 142 runs

West Indies Innings				
BH Pairaudeau	c Joshi b Hazare	43	lbw b Phadkar	0
*JB Stollmeyer	c Mankad b Gupte	32	c Gupte b Mankad	54
FMM Worrell	lbw b Mankad	24	b Phadkar	7
ED Weekes	c Joshi b Hazare	47	b Mankad	15
CL Walcott	lbw b Phadkar	98	b Phadkar	34
RJ Christiani	st Joshi b Gupte	4	st Joshi b Gupte	33
GE Gomez	c Gaekwad b Gupte	0	lbw b Phadkar	35
+RA Legall	c Ramchand b Mankad	23	b Gupte	1
FM King	lbw b Mankad	0	c Manjrekar b Ramchand	19
S Ramadhin	not out	16	b Phadkar	12
AL Valentine	b Phadkar	6	not out	0
	(lb 3)	3	(b 6, lb 11, w 1)	18
	(all out)	296	(all out)	228

Bowling: Phadkar 11.4-2-24-2 Ramchand 9-1-32-0 Gupte 41-10-99-3 Mankad 46-15-125-3 Hazare 9-2-13-2
Phadkar 29.3-4-64-5 Ramchand 4-1-9-1 Gupte 36-12-82-2 Mankad 19-3-54-2 Hazare 2-1-1-0

India Innings				
P Roy	c Worrell b King	1	c Legall b Valentine	22
ML Apte	c Worrell b Valentine	64	b King	9
VL Manjrekar	lbw b Ramadhin	25	not out	32
*VS Hazare	c Weekes b King	63	b Ramadhin	0
PR Umrigar	c Christiani b Valentine	56	b Ramadhin	6
GS Ramchand	b Ramadhin	17	b Ramadhin	34
DK Gaekwad	c & b Valentine	0	absent hurt	0
DG Phadkar	b Worrell	17	c Valentine b Ramadhin	8
+PG Joshi	c Worrell b Valentine	0	c Worrell b Valentine	0
SP Gupte	run out	2	lbw b Ramadhin	5
MH Mankad	not out	0	b Gomez	3
	(b 2, lb 5, nb 1)	8	(b 8, lb 2)	10
	(all out)	253	(all out)	129

Bowling: King 28-7-66-2 Gomez 17-9-27-0 Ramadhin 30-13-59-2 Worrell 13-4-25-1 Valentine 41-21-58-4 Stollmeyer 5-2-10-0
King 9-3-18-1 Gomez 5-2-9-1 Ramadhin 24.5-11-26-5 Worrell 6-0-13-0 Valentine 35-16-53-2

Umpires: HBD Jordan and JH Walcott

West Indies v England
6,8,9,10,11,12 February 1954

Result: West Indies won by 181 runs

West Indies Innings				
JKC Holt	c Graveney b Bailey	11	c & b Statham	166
*JB Stollmeyer	run out	0	run out	28
FMM Worrell	b Statham	0	not out	76
CL Walcott	st Evans b Laker	220	not out	17
BH Pairaudeau	c Hutton b Laker	71		
GE Gomez	lbw b Statham	7		
DS Atkinson	c Evans b Laker	53		
+CA McWatt	lbw b Lock	11		
S Ramadhin	b Statham	1		
FM King	b Laker	5		
AL Valentine	not out	0		
	(lb 2, nb 2)	4	(b 4, nb 1)	5
	(all out)	383	(2 wickets declared)	292

Bowling: Statham 27-6-90-3 Bailey 22-6-63-1 Lock 41-9-116-1 Laker 30.1-6-81-4 Compton 5-0-29-0
Statham 15-1-49-1 Bailey 12-1-48-0 Lock 33-7-100-0 Laker 30-13-62-0 Compton 1-0-13-0 Palmer 5-1-15-0

England Innings				
*L Hutton	c Ramadhin b Valentine	72	c Worrell b Ramadhin	77
W Watson	st McWatt b Ramadhin	6	c McWatt b King	0
PBH May	c King b Ramadhin	7	c Walcott b Gomez	62
DCS Compton	c King b Valentine	13	lbw b Stollmeyer	93
TW Graveney	c & b Ramadhin	15	not out	64
CH Palmer	c Walcott b Ramadhin	22	c Gomez b Atkinson	0
TE Bailey	c McWatt b Atkinson	28	c sub b Stollmeyer	4
+TG Evans	b Gomez	10	b Ramadhin	5
JC Laker	c Gomez b Atkinson	1	lbw b Ramadhin	0
GAR Lock	not out	0	b King	0
JB Statham	c Holt b Valentine	3	b Gomez	0
	(b 2, lb 1, nb 1)	4	(b 6, lb 1, w 1)	8
	(all out)	181	(all out)	313

Bowling: King 14-6-28-0 Gomez 13-8-10-1 Worrell 9-2-21-0 Atkinson 9-7-5-2 Ramadhin 53-30-50-4 Valentine 51.5-30-61-3 Stollmeyer 1-0-2-0
King 18-6-56-2 Gomez 13.4-3-28-2 Worrell 1-0-10-0 Atkinson 23-10-35-1 Ramadhin 37-17-71-3 Valentine 39-18-87-0 Stollmeyer 6-1-14-2 Walcott 2-0-4-0

Umpires: HBD Jordan and JH Walcott

West Indies v Australia
14,16,17,18,19,20 May 1955

Result: Match drawn

Australia Innings				
CC McDonald	run out	46	b Smith	17
LE Favell	c Weekes b Atkinson	72	run out	53
RN Harvey	c Smith b Worrell	74	c Valentine b Smith	27
WJ Watson	c Depeiaza b Dewdney	30	b Atkinson	0
KR Miller	c Depeiaza b Dewdney	137	lbw b Atkinson	10
R Benaud	c Walcott b Dewdney	1	b Sobers	5
RG Archer	b Worrell	98	lbw b Atkinson	28
RR Lindwall	c Valentine b Atkinson	118	b Atkinson	10
*IWG Johnson	b Dewdney	23	c Holt b Smith	57
+GRA Langley	b Sobers	53	not out	28
JC Hill	not out	8	c Weekes b Atkinson	1
	(b 1, lb 2, w 4, nb 1)	8	(b 9, lb 4)	13
	(all out)	668	(all out)	249

Bowling: Worrell 40-7-120-2 Dewdney 33-5-125-4 Walcott 26-10-57-0 Valentine 31-9-87-0 Ramadhin 24-3-84-0 Atkinson 48-14-108-2 Smith 22-8-49-0 Sobers 11.5-6-30-1
Worrell 7-0-25-0 Dewdney 10-4-23-0 Valentine 6-1-16-0 Ramadhin 2-0-10-0 Atkinson 36.2-16-56-5 Smith 34-12-71-3 Sobers 14-3-35-1

West Indies Innings				
JKC Holt	b Lindwall	22	lbw b Hill	49
GS Sobers	c Hill b Johnson	43	lbw b Archer	11
CL Walcott	c Langley b Benaud	15	b Benaud	83
ED Weekes	c Langley b Miller	44	run out	6
FMM Worrell	run out	16	c Archer b Miller	34
OG Smith	c Langley b Miller	2	b Lindwall	11
*DS Atkinson	c Archer b Johnson	219	not out	20
+CC Depeiaza	b Benaud	122	not out	11
S Ramadhin	c & b Benaud	10		
DT Dewdney	b Johnson	0		
AL Valentine	not out	2		
	(b 5, lb 4, w 2, nb 4)	15	(b 6, lb 2, w 1)	9
	(all out)	510	(6 wickets)	234

Bowling: Lindwall 25-3-96-1 Miller 22-2-113-2 Archer 15-4-44-0 Johnson 35-13-77-3 Hill 24-9-71-0 Benaud 31.1-6-73-3 Harvey 4-0-16-0 Watson 1-0-5-0
Lindwall 8-1-39-1 Miller 21-3-66-1 Archer 7-1-11-1 Johnson 14-4-30-0 Hill 11-2-44-1 Benaud 11-3-35-1

Umpires: HBD Jordan and EN Lee Kow

West Indies v Pakistan
17,18,20,21,22,23 January 1958

Result: Match drawn

West Indies Innings

CC Hunte	c Imtiaz Ahmed b Fazal Mahmood	142	not out	11
RB Kanhai	c Mathias b Fazal Mahmood	27	not out	17
GS Sobers	c Mathias b Mahmood Hussain	52		
ED Weekes	c Imtiaz Ahmed b Mahmood Hussain	197		
CL Walcott	c Mathias b Kardar	43		
OG Smith	c Mathias b Alimuddin	78		
DS Atkinson	b Mahmood Hussain	4		
ES Atkinson	b Fazal Mahmood	0		
*+FCM Alexander	b Mahmood Hussain	9		
AL Valentine	not out	5		
R Gilchrist				
	(b 9, lb 4, w 3, nb 6)	22		0
	(9 wickets declared)	579	(0 wickets)	28

Bowling: Fazal Mahmood 62-21-145-3 Mahmood Hussain 41.2-4-153-4 Kardar 32-4-107-1 Haseeb Ahsan 21-0-84-0 Nasim-ul-Ghani 14-1-51-0 Alimuddin 2-0-17-1
Fazal Mahmood 2-1-3-0 Kardar 3-1-13-0 Hanif Mohammad 3-1-10-0 Saeed Ahmed 2-2-0-0 Wazir Mohammad 1-0-2-0

Pakistan Innings

Hanif Mohammad	b ES Atkinson	17	c Alexander b DS Atkinson	337
+Imtiaz Ahmed	lbw b Gilchrist	20	lbw b Gilchrist	91
Alimuddin	c Weekes b Gilchrist	3	c Alexander b Sobers	37
Saeed Ahmed	st Alexander b Smith	13	c Alexander b Smith	65
Wazir Mohammad	lbw b Valentine	4	c Alexander b ES Atkinson	35
W Mathias	c Alexander b Smith	17	lbw b ES Atkinson	17
*AH Kardar	c DS Atkinson b Smith	4	not out	23
Fazal Mahmood	b Gilchrist	4	b Valentine	19
Nasim-ul-Ghani	run out	11	b Valentine	0
Mahmood Hussain	b Gilchrist	3	not out	0
Haseeb Ahsan	not out	1		
	(b 4, lb 5)	9	(b 19, lb 7, nb 7)	33
	(all out)	106	(8 wickets declared)	657

Bowling: Gilchrist 15-4-32-4 ES Atkinson 8-0-27-1 Smith 13-4-23-3 Valentine 6.2-1-15-1
Gilchrist 41-5-121-1 ES Atkinson 49-5-136-2 Smith 61-30-93-1 Valentine 39-8-109-2 DS Atkinson 62-35-61-1 Sobers 57-25-94-1 Walcott 10-5-10-0

Umpires: HBD Jordan and JH Walcott

West Indies v England
6,7,8,9,11,12 January 1960

Result: Match drawn

England Innings

G Pullar	run out	65	not out	46
MC Cowdrey	c Sobers b Watson	30	not out	16
KF Barrington	c Alexander b Ramadhin	128		
*PBH May	c Alexander b Hall	1		
MJK Smith	c Alexander b Scarlett	39		
ER Dexter	not out	136		
R Illingworth	b Ramadhin	5		
+R Swetman	c Alexander b Worrell	45		
FS Trueman	c Alexander b Ramadhin	3		
DA Allen	lbw b Watson	10		
AE Moss	b Watson	4		
	(b 4, lb 6, nb 6)	16	(b 7, lb 1, w 1)	9
	(all out)	482	(0 wickets)	71

Bowling: Hall 40-9-98-1 Watson 32.4-6-121-3 Worrell 15-2-39-1 Ramadhin 54-22-109-3 Scarlett 26-9-46-1 Sobers 21-3-53-0
Hall 6-2-9-0 Watson 8-1-19-0 Ramadhin 7-2-11-0 Scarlett 10-4-12-0 Hunte 7-2-9-0 Kanhai 4-3-2-0

West Indies Innings

CC Hunte	c Swetman b Barrington	42
EDAS McMorris	run out	0
RB Kanhai	b Trueman	40
GS Sobers	b Trueman	226
FMM Worrell	not out	197
BF Butcher	c Trueman b Dexter	13
WW Hall	lbw b Trueman	14
*+FCM Alexander	c Smith b Trueman	3
RO Scarlett	lbw b Dexter	7
CD Watson		
S Ramadhin		
	(b 8, lb 7, w 1, nb 5)	21
	(8 wickets declared)	563

Bowling: Trueman 47-15-93-4 Moss 47-14-116-0 Dexter 37.4-11-85-2 Illingworth 47-9-106-0 Allen 43-12-82-0 Barrington 18-3-60-1

Umpires: HBD Jordan and JHJ Roberts

West Indies v India
23,24,26,27,28 March 1962

Result: West Indies won by an innings and 30 runs

India Innings

ML Jaisimha	c Allan b Hall	41	lbw b Stayers	0
DN Sardesai	c McMorris b Gibbs	31	c Solomon b Gibbs	60
RF Surti	lbw b Worrell	7	lbw b Stayers	36
VL Manjrekar	c Worrell b Hall	8	c Worrell b Gibbs	51
PR Umrigar	c Allan b Hall	8	c Allan b Gibbs	10
*Nawab of Pataudi jnr	c & b Valentine	48	c Worrell b Gibbs	0
CG Borde	c Allan b Sobers	19	c Worrell b Gibbs	8
RG Nadkarni	b Stayers	22	not out	2
+FM Engineer	c Worrell b Sobers	12	st Allan b Gibbs	0
SA Durani	not out	48	c Hunte b Gibbs	5
RB Desai	b Worrell	12	c Sobers b Gibbs	1
	(nb 2)	2	(b 8, lb 3, w 2, nb 1)	14
	(all out)	258	(all out)	187

Bowling: Hall 22-4-64-3 Stayers 11-0-81-1 Worrell 7.1-3-12-2 Gibbs 16-7-25-1 Valentine 17-7-28-1 Sobers 16-2-46-2
Hall 10-3-17-0 Stayers 18-8-24-2 Worrell 27-18-16-0 Gibbs 53.3-37-38-8 Valentine 29-19-26-0 Sobers 17-10-14-0 Solomon 29-17-33-0 Kanhai 2-1-5-0

West Indies Innings

CC Hunte	c Engineer b Surti	59
EDAS McMorris	c Engineer b Durani	39
RB Kanhai	run out	89
GS Sobers	c Engineer b Nadkarni	42
JS Solomon	c Desai b Durani	96
LR Gibbs	b Borde	7
*FMM Worrell	b Umrigar	77
SC Stayers	c Umrigar b Nadkarni	7
WW Hall	lbw b Umrigar	3
*DW Allan	not out	40
AL Valentine	b Borde	4
	(lb 5, nb 7)	12
	(all out)	475

Bowling: Desai 19-7-25-0 Surti 29-6-80-1 Durani 45-13-123-2 Nadkarni 67-28-92-2 Borde 31.3-4-89-2 Jaisimha 1-0-6-0 Umrigar 49-27-48-2

Umpires: HBD Jordan and JHJ Roberts

West Indies v Australia
5,6,7,8,10,11 May 1965

Result: Match drawn

Australia Innings

WM Lawry	c Sobers b Solomon	210	retired hurt	58
*RB Simpson	b Hall	201	c +Nurse b Sobers	5
RM Cowper	b Sobers	102	c & b Hall	4
NC O'Neill	c Kanhai b Gibbs	51	not out	74
BC Booth	b Gibbs	5	c Sobers b Gibbs	17
G Thomas	not out	27	b Gibbs	1
BK Shepherd	lbw b Hall	4		
NJN Hawke	not out	8		
PI Philpott				
+ATW Grout				
GD McKenzie				
	(b 10, lb 12, w 2, nb 18)	42	(b 11, lb 3, w 1, nb 1)	16
	(6 wickets declared)	650	(4 wickets declared)	175

Bowling: Hall 27-3-117-2 Griffith 35-3-131-0 Sobers 37-7-143-1 Gibbs 73-17-168-2 Solomon 14-1-42-1 Hunte 3-1-7-0
Hall 8-0-31-1 Griffith 7-0-38-0 Sobers 20-11-29-1 Gibbs 18.2-3-61-2

West Indies Innings

CC Hunte	c Simpson b McKenzie	75	c Grout b McKenzie	81
BA Davis	b McKenzie	8	c sub b Philpott	68
RB Kanhai	b Hawke b McKenzie	129	lbw b McKenzie	1
BF Butcher	c Simpson b O'Neill	9	c Booth b Philpott	27
SM Nurse	c Simpson b Hawke	201	lbw b Hawke	0
*GS Sobers	c Grout b McKenzie	55	not out	34
JS Solomon	c McKenzie b Hawke	1	not out	6
+JL Hendriks	retired hurt	4		
WW Hall	c Simpson b Hawke	3		
CC Griffith	run out	54		
LR Gibbs	not out	3		
	(b 13, lb 12, w 1, nb 5)	31	(b 19, lb 3, w 2, nb 1)	25
	(all out)	573	(5 wickets)	242

Bowling: McKenzie 47-11-114-4 Hawke 49-11-135-3 Philpott 45-17-102-0 O'Neill 26-13-60-1 Simpson 15-3-44-0 Cowper 21-6-64-0 Booth 6-2-17-0 Shepherd 3-1-6-0
McKenzie 24-6-60-2 Hawke 15-4-37-1 Philpott 24-7-74-2 Simpson 9-4-15-0 Cowper 8-4-19-0 Booth 5-1-12-0

Umpires: HBD Jordan and FCP Kippins

West Indies v England
29 February, 1,2,4,5 March 1968

Result: Match drawn

West Indies Innings

SM Nurse	c Cowdrey b Brown	26	c Parks b Snow	19
GS Camacho	c Graveney b Barrington	57	lbw b Snow	18
RB Kanhai	c Parks b Snow	12	lbw b Snow	12
BF Butcher	lbw b Snow	86	run out	60
CH Lloyd	c & b Pocock	20	not out	113
*GS Sobers	c Jones b Snow	68	b Brown	19
DAJ Holford	c Graveney b Snow	0		
+DL Murray	c Parks b Brown	27	c Snow b Pocock	18
CC Griffith	not out	16	not out	8
WW Hall	c Barrington b Snow	2		
LR Gibbs	b Jones	14		
	(b 1, lb 14, nb 6)	21	(b 8, lb 3, nb 6)	17
	(all out)	349	(6 wickets)	284

Bowling: Brown 32-10-66-2 Snow 35-11-86-5 D'Oliveira 19-5-36-0 Pocock 28-11-55-1 Jones 21.1-3-56-1 Barrington 8-1-29-1
Brown 11-0-61-1 Snow 12-2-39-3 D'Oliveira 6-4-19-0 Pocock 13-0-78-1 Jones 11-3-53-0 Barrington 4-0-17-0

England Innings

JH Edrich	c Murray b Griffith	146		
G Boycott	lbw b Sobers	90		
*MC Cowdrey	c Sobers b Griffith	1		
KF Barrington	c Butcher b Hall	17		
TW Graveney	c Sobers b Gibbs	55		
+JM Parks	lbw b Gibbs	42		
BL D'Oliveira	b Hall	51		
DJ Brown	b Griffith	1		
JA Snow	c Nurse b Gibbs	37		
PI Pocock	b Sobers	6		
IJ Jones	not out	1		
	(b 16, lb 9, nb 19)	44		
	(all out)	449		

Bowling: Sobers 41-10-76-2 Hall 32-8-98-2 Griffith 24-6-71-3 Gibbs 47.5-16-98-3 Holford 32-9-52-0 Lloyd 3-0-10-0 Nurse 1-1-0-0

Umpires: HBD Jordan and D Sang Hue

West Indies v India
1,2,3,4,6 April 1971

Result: Match drawn

West Indies Innings

RC Fredericks	b Abid Ali	1	b Venkataraghavan	48
+DM Lewis	b Bedi	88	b Abid Ali	14
RB Kanhai	c Mankad b Venkataraghavan	85	c Krishnamurthy b Solkar	11
CA Davis	c Venkataraghavan b Abid Ali	79	not out	22
*GS Sobers	not out	178	not out	9
CH Lloyd	c Mankad b Bedi	19	c Venkataraghavan b Abid Ali	43
MLC Foster	not out	36	not out	24
JN Shepherd			c Solkar b Venkataraghavan	3
Inshan Ali				
VA Holder				
UG Dowe				
	(b 10, lb 4, nb 1)	15	(b 2, lb 3, nb 1)	6
	(5 wickets declared)	501	(6 wickets declared)	180

Bowling: Abid Ali 31-1-127-2 Solkar 19-4-40-0 Jaisimha 10-2-32-0 Bedi 54-15-124-2 Venkataraghavan 57-12-163-1
Abid Ali 21-3-70-3 Solkar 14-0-73-1 Bedi 1-0-6-0 Venkataraghavan 7-0-25-2

India Innings

AV Mankad	c Lewis b Holder	6	c Shepherd b Ali	8
SM Gavaskar	c Holder b Dowe	1	not out	117
+P Krishnamurthy	c Ali b Dowe	1		
*AL Wadekar	c Lewis b Sobers	28	c Lloyd b Sobers	17
GR Viswanath	c Lewis b Sobers	25	c Shepherd b Sobers	0
DN Sardesai	lbw b Holder	150	c Fredericks b Shepherd	24
ML Jaisimha	b Dowe	0	lbw b Dowe	17
ED Solkar	c Lewis b Dowe	65	not out	10
S Abid Ali	run out	9		
S Venkataraghavan	b Shepherd	12		
BS Bedi	not out	20		
	(b 6, lb 6, nb 18)	30	(b 2, lb 8, w 1, nb 17)	28
	(all out)	347	(5 wickets)	221

Bowling: Holder 25.4-7-70-2 Dowe 23-7-69-4 Shepherd 24-4-54-1 Sobers 20-9-34-2 Ali 20-4-60-0 Foster 11-3-28-0 Davis 2-0-2-0
Holder 8-4-13-0 Dowe 11-5-22-1 Shepherd 20-7-36-1 Sobers 23-8-31-2 Ali 18-1-65-1 Foster 14-7-10-0 Davis 3-2-1-0 Lloyd 4-0-13-0 Fredericks 1-0-1-0 Kanhai 1-0-1-0

Umpires: HBD Jordan and D Sang Hue

Kensington Oval, Bridgetown, Barbados

West Indies v New Zealand
23,24,25,26,28 March 1972

Result: Match drawn

West Indies Innings

RC Fredericks	c Hastings b Cunis	5	lbw b Cunis	28
MC Carew	c Morgan b Taylor	1	c Turner b Howarth	45
LG Rowe	c Wadsworth b Taylor	0	lbw b Congdon	51
CA Davis	c Jarvis b Taylor	1	run out	183
*GS Sobers	c Wadsworth b Congdon	35	c Vivian b Taylor	142
MLC Foster	c Wadsworth b Taylor	22	lbw b Taylor	4
DAJ Holford	c Wadsworth b Congdon	3	c Wadsworth b Congdon	50
+TM Findlay	not out	44	c Morgan b Howarth	9
Inshan Ali	b Taylor	3	not out	12
VA Holder	b Congdon	3	not out	16
GC Shillingford	c Morgan b Taylor	15		
	(nb 1)	1	(b 6, lb 9, w 1, nb 8)	24
	(all out)	133	(8 wickets)	564

Bowling: Cunis 10-3-26-1 Taylor 20.3-6-74-7 Congdon 16-3-26-2 Howarth 3-1-6-0
Cunis 38-8-130-1 Taylor 33-3-108-2 Congdon 31-7-66-2 Howarth 74-24-138-2 Morgan 30-8-78-0 Vivian 8-2-20-0

New Zealand Innings

GM Turner	c Holford b Holder	21
TW Jarvis	lbw b Shillingford	26
*BE Congdon	lbw b Holder	126
MG Burgess	c Fredericks b Sobers	19
BF Hastings	lbw b Sobers	105
RW Morgan	c Fredericks b Ali	2
GE Vivian	b Sobers	38
+KJ Wadsworth	not out	15
BR Taylor	lbw b Sobers	0
RS Cunis	c Findlay b Holder	27
HJ Howarth	b Shillingford	8
	(lb 13, nb 22)	35
	(all out)	422

Bowling: Holder 40-13-91-3 Sobers 29-6-64-4 Shillingford 24.2-7-65-2 Davis 10-3-19-0 Ali 35-11-81-1 Holford 9-0-20-0
Foster 14-2-40-0 Fredericks 2-0-7-0

Umpires: HBD Jordan and FCP Kippins

West Indies v Australia
9,10,11,13,14 March 1973

Result: Match drawn

Australia Innings

KR Stackpole	c Kanhai b Holder	1	b Foster	53
IR Redpath	c Kanhai b Boyce	6	c Greenidge b Gibbs	20
*IM Chappell	run out	72	not out	106
GS Chappell	c Murray b Holder	106		
R Edwards	c Murray b Boyce	15		
KD Walters	c Kanhai b Gibbs	1	not out	102
+RW Marsh	c Rowe b Willett	78		
KJ O'Keeffe	b Willett	21		
JR Hammond	lbw b Boyce	0		
TJ Jenner	not out	10		
MHN Walker	b Gibbs	8		
	(nb 14)	14	(b 1, lb 6, nb 12)	19
	(all out)	324	(2 wickets declared)	300

Bowling: Holder 21-5-49-2 Boyce 22-5-68-3 Foster 15-4-35-0 Willett 37-11-79-2 Gibbs 36-9-79-2
Holder 21-5-52-0 Boyce 18-4-54-0 Foster 13-4-29-1 Willett 28-15-45-0 Gibbs 25-10-55-1 Fredericks 1-0-3-0 Greenidge 7-0-24-0 Kanhai 6.1-1-19-0

West Indies Innings

RC Fredericks	lbw b Hammond	98	not out	22
GA Greenidge	lbw b Walker	9	not out	10
LG Rowe	c Stackpole b Walker	16		
AI Kallicharran	b Walker	14		
*RB Kanhai	lbw b IM Chappell	105		
MLC Foster	b Jenner	12		
+DL Murray	c Redpath b Jenner	90		
KD Boyce	lbw b Walker	10		
ET Willett	c Stackpole b Jenner	0		
VA Holder	b Walker	1		
LR Gibbs	not out	0		
	(b 13, lb 5, w 4, nb 14)	36	(lb 2, w 1, nb 1)	4
	(all out)	391	(0 wickets)	36

Bowling: Hammond 31-9-114-1 Walker 51.4-20-97-5 GS Chappell 22-11-37-0 Jenner 28-9-65-3 O'Keeffe 10-3-18-0 Walters 2-0-7-0 IM Chappell 8-3-17-1
Hammond 4-1-10-0 Walker 4-3-1-0 O'Keeffe 6-2-15-0 Stackpole 5-3-6-0

Umpires: HBD Jordan and D Sang Hue

West Indies v England
6,7,9,10,11 March 1974

Result: Match drawn

England Innings

*MH Denness	c Murray b Sobers	24	lbw b Holder	0
DL Amiss	b Julien	12	c Julien b Boyce	4
JA Jameson	c Fredericks b Julien	3	lbw b Roberts	9
G Boycott	c Murray b Julien	10	c Kanhai b Sobers	13
KWR Fletcher	c Murray b Julien	37	not out	129
AW Greig	c Sobers b Julien	148	c Roberts b Gibbs	25
+APE Knott	b Gibbs	87	lbw b Lloyd	67
CM Old	c Murray b Roberts	1	b Lloyd	0
GG Arnold	b Holder	12	not out	2
PI Pocock	c Lloyd b Gibbs	18		
RGD Willis	not out	10		
	(lb 5, nb 28)	33	(b 7, lb 5, nb 16)	28
	(all out)	395	(7 wickets)	277

Bowling: Holder 27-6-68-1 Roberts 33-8-75-1 Julien 26-9-57-5 Sobers 18-4-57-1 Gibbs 33.4-10-91-2 Lloyd 4-2-9-0 Fredericks 3-0-5-0
Holder 15-6-37-1 Roberts 17-4-49-2 Julien 11-4-21-0 Sobers 35-21-55-1 Gibbs 28.3-15-40-1 Lloyd 12-4-13-2 Fredericks 6-2-24-0 Rowe 1-0-5-0 Kallicharran 1-0-5-0

West Indies Innings

RC Fredericks	b Greig	32
LG Rowe	c Arnold b Greig	302
AI Kallicharran	b Greig	119
CH Lloyd	c Fletcher b Greig	8
VA Holder	c & b Greig	8
*RB Kanhai	b Arnold	18
GS Sobers	c Greig b Willis	0
+DL Murray	not out	53
BD Julien	c Willis b Greig	1
AME Roberts	not out	9
LR Gibbs		
	(b 3, lb 8, nb 35)	46
	(8 wickets declared)	596

Bowling: Arnold 26-5-91-1 Willis 26-4-100-1 Greig 46-2-164-6 Old 28-4-102-0 Pocock 28-4-93-0

Umpires: SE Parris and D Sang Hue

West Indies v India
10,11,13 March 1976

Result: West Indies won by an innings and 97 runs

India Innings

SM Gavaskar	lbw b Roberts	37	c Jumadeen b Roberts	1
PH Sharma	c Fredericks b Holding	6	c Murray b Holding	1
AD Gaekwad	c Murray b Julien	16	c Murray b Roberts	14
GR Viswanath	c Rowe b Holford	11	lbw b Roberts	62
S Amarnath	c Richards b Holford	0	b Jumadeen	8
M Amarnath	b Holding	26	c Rowe b Jumadeen	25
S Madan Lal	b Holford	45	not out	55
+SMH Kirmani	b Roberts	8	lbw b Holford	15
EAS Prasanna	c Richards b Holford	3	absent hurt	0
*BS Bedi	c Julien b Holford	0	c Murray b Jumadeen	10
BS Chandrasekhar	not out	1	b Holding	0
	(b 2, lb 7, nb 15)	24	(b 7, lb 3, nb 13)	23
	(all out)	177	(all out)	214

Bowling: Roberts 11-2-48-2 Holding 15-10-24-2 Julien 15-5-46-1 Holford 8.1-1-23-5 Jumadeen 5-1-12-0
Roberts 14-4-51-3 Holding 13-6-22-2 Julien 4-2-8-0 Holford 17-1-52-1 Jumadeen 24-7-57-3 Fredericks 1-0-1-0

West Indies Innings

RC Fredericks	c M Amarnath b Chandrasekhar	54
LG Rowe	lbw b Chandrasekhar	30
IVA Richards	c Kirmani b M Amarnath	142
AI Kallicharran	c Viswanath b M Amarnath	93
*CH Lloyd	st Kirmani b Bedi	102
+DL Murray	b Bedi	27
DAJ Holford	c Kirmani b Chandrasekhar	9
BD Julien	not out	13
MA Holding	lbw b Chandrasekhar	0
AME Roberts	c S Amarnath b Bedi	0
RR Jumadeen		
	(b 7, lb 7, nb 4)	18
	(9 wickets declared)	488

Bowling: Madan Lal 16-1-61-0 M Amarnath 12-2-53-2 Bedi 43.5-8-113-3 Chandrasekhar 39-5-163-4 Prasanna 24-2-66-0 Gaekwad 4-0-14-0

Umpires: SE Parris and D Sang Hue

West Indies v Pakistan
18,19,20,22,23 February 1977

Result: Match drawn

Pakistan Innings

Majid Khan	b Garner	88	c Garner b Croft	28
Sadiq Mohammad	c Croft b Garner	37	c Garner b Croft	9
Haroon Rashid	c Kallicharran b Foster	33	b Garner	39
*Mushtaq Mohammad	c Murray b Croft	0	c Murray b Roberts	6
Asif Iqbal	c Murray b Croft	36	b Croft	0
Javed Miandad	lbw b Garner	2	c Greenidge b Croft	1
Wasim Raja	not out	117	c Garner b Foster	71
Imran Khan	c Garner b Roberts	20	c Fredericks b Garner	1
Saleem Altaf	lbw b Garner	19	b Garner	6
Sarfraz Nawaz	c Kallicharran b Foster	38	c Murray b Roberts	6
+Wasim Bari	lbw b Croft	10	not out	60
	(b 5, lb 6, w 1, nb 23)	35	(b 29, lb 11, nb 28)	68
	(all out)	435	(all out)	291

Bowling: Roberts 30-3-124-1 Croft 31.4-6-85-3 Holder 4-0-13-0 Garner 27-7-130-4 Foster 27-13-41-2 Richards 3-1-3-0 Fredericks 1-0-4-0
Roberts 25-5-66-3 Croft 15-3-47-4 Garner 17-4-60-2 Foster 8-2-34-1 Richards 2-0-16-0

West Indies Innings

RC Fredericks	c & b Sarfraz Nawaz	24	b Sarfraz Nawaz	52
CG Greenidge	c Majid Khan b Imran Khan	47	c Wasim Raja b Sarfraz Nawaz	2
IVA Richards	c Saleem Altaf b Sarfraz Nawaz	32	c Sadiq Mohammad b Sarfraz Nawaz	92
AI Kallicharran	c Sarfraz Nawaz b Imran Khan	7	c Wasim Bari b Saleem Altaf	9
*CH Lloyd	c Sadiq Mohammad b Saleem Altaf	157	c Wasim Bari b Imran Khan	11
MLC Foster	b Sarfraz Nawaz	15	b Sarfraz Nawaz	4
+DL Murray	c Mushtaq Mohammad b Imran Khan	52	c Wasim Bari b Saleem Altaf	20
J Garner	b Javed Miandad	43	b Saleem Altaf	0
AME Roberts	c Wasim Bari b Saleem Altaf	4	not out	9
CEH Croft	not out	1	not out	6
VA Holder	absent hurt	0	b Imran Khan	6
	(b 2, lb 6, nb 21)	29	(b 1, lb 8, w 1, nb 31)	41
	(all out)	421	(9 wickets)	251

Bowling: Imran Khan 28-3-147-3 Sarfraz Nawaz 29-3-125-3 Saleem Altaf 21-3-70-2 Javed Miandad 10.4-3-22-1 Mushtaq Mohammad 5-0-27-0 Majid Khan 1-0-1-0
Imran Khan 32-16-58-2 Sarfraz Nawaz 34-10-79-4 Saleem Altaf 21-7-33-3 Javed Miandad 11-4-31-0 Majid Khan 1-0-1-0 Asif Iqbal 1-0-8-0

Umpires: RR Gosein and D Sang Hue

West Indies v Australia
17,18,19 March 1978

Result: West Indies won by 9 wickets

Australia Innings

WM Darling	c Richards b Croft	4	c Murray b Croft	8
GM Wood	lbw b Croft	69	run out	56
GN Yallop	c Austin b Croft	47	c Lloyd b Garner	14
CS Serjeant	c Murray b Parry	2	c Murray b Roberts	2
*RB Simpson	c Murray b Croft	9	c Kanhai b Roberts	17
GJ Cosier	c Murray b Roberts	1	c Croft b Roberts	0
+SJ Rixon	lbw b Garner	16	c Lloyd b Roberts	0
B Yardley	b Garner	74	b Garner	43
JR Thomson	b Garner	12	c Richards b Garner	11
WM Clark	b Garner	0	lbw b Garner	0
JD Higgs	not out	0	not out	0
	(b 3, lb 4, nb 3)	10	(b 1, lb 8, nb 10)	19
	(all out)	250	(all out)	178

Bowling: Roberts 18-2-79-1 Croft 18-3-47-4 Garner 16.1-2-65-4 Parry 12-4-44-1 Austin 1-0-5-0
Roberts 18-5-50-4 Croft 15-4-53-1 Garner 15-3-56-4

West Indies Innings

CG Greenidge	c Cosier b Thomson	8	not out	80
DL Haynes	c Rixon b Higgs	66	c Yardley b Higgs	55
IVA Richards	c Clark b Thomson	23		
AI Kallicharran	c Yardley b Thomson	8		
*CH Lloyd	c Serjeant b Clark	42		
RA Austin	c Serjeant b Clark	20		
+DL Murray	c Darling b Thomson	60		
DR Parry	c Serjeant b Simpson	27	not out	3
AME Roberts	lbw b Thomson	4		
J Garner	not out	5		
CEH Croft	lbw b Thomson	3		
	(lb 3, nb 19)	22	(lb 2, w 1)	3
	(all out)	288	(1 wicket)	141

Bowling: Thomson 13-1-77-6 Clark 24-3-77-2 Cosier 9-4-24-0 Higgs 16-4-46-1 Simpson 7-1-30-1 Yardley 2-0-12-0
Thomson 6-1-22-0 Clark 7-0-27-0 Higgs 13-4-34-1 Yardley 10.5-2-55-0

Umpires: RR Gosein and SE Parris

West Indies v England
13,14,15,17,18 March 1981

Result: West Indies won by 298 runs

West Indies Innings

CG Greenidge	c Gooch b Jackman	14	lbw b Dilley	0
DL Haynes	c Bairstow b Jackman	25	lbw b Botham	25
IVA Richards	c Botham b Dilley	0	not out	182
EH Mattis	lbw b Botham	16	c Butcher b Jackman	24
*CH Lloyd	c Gooch b Jackman	100	c Botham b Dilley	66
HA Gomes	c Botham b Dilley	58	run out	34
+DA Murray	c Bairstow b Dilley	9	not out	5
AME Roberts	c Bairstow b Botham	14	c Bairstow b Botham	0
J Garner	c Bairstow b Botham	15		
MA Holding	c Gatting b Botham	0		
CEH Croft	not out	0	c Boycott b Jackman	33
	(b 4, lb 6, w 2, nb 2)	14	(b 3, lb 7)	10
	(all out)	265	(7 wickets declared)	379

Bowling: Dilley 23-7-51-3 Botham 25-1-5-77-4 Jackman 22-4-65-3 Emburey 18-4-45-0 Gooch 2-0-13-0
Dilley 25-3-111-1 Botham 29-5-102-3 Jackman 25-5-76-2 Emburey 24-7-57-0 Willey 6-0-23-0

England Innings

GA Gooch	b Garner	26	c Garner b Croft	116
G Boycott	b Holding	0	c Garner b Holding	1
MW Gatting	c Greenidge b Roberts	2	b Holding	2
DI Gower	c Mattis b Croft	17	b Holding	54
RO Butcher	c Richards b Croft	17	lbw b Richards	2
*IT Botham	c Murray b Holding	26	c Lloyd b Roberts	1
P Willey	not out	19	lbw b Croft	17
+DL Bairstow	c Mattis b Holding	0	c Murray b Croft	2
JE Emburey	c Lloyd b Roberts	0	b Garner	9
RD Jackman	c Roberts b Croft	7	b Garner	7
GR Dilley	c Gomes b Croft	0	not out	7
	(b 1, lb 1, nb 6)	8	(b 1, lb 3, nb 4)	8
	(all out)	122	(all out)	224

Bowling: Roberts 11-3-29-2 Holding 11-7-16-3 Croft 13.5-2-39-4 Garner 12-5-30-1
Roberts 20-6-42-1 Holding 19-6-46-2 Croft 19-1-65-3 Garner 16.2-6-39-2 Richards 17-6-24-2

Umpires: DM Archer and D Sang Hue

West Indies v India
15,16,17,19,20 April 1983

Result: West Indies won by 10 wickets

India Innings

SM Gavaskar	c Dujon b Holding	2	c Roberts b Garner	19
AD Gaekwad	c Marshall b Roberts	3	b Holding	55
M Amarnath	c Dujon b Marshall	91	c Dujon b Roberts	80
DB Vengsarkar	c Marshall b Holding	15	lbw b Holding	6
Yashpal Sharma	c Richards b Roberts	24	c Greenidge b Roberts	12
RJ Shastri	c Richards b Roberts	29	c Lloyd b Marshall	19
*N Kapil Dev	c Lloyd b Marshall	0	c Lloyd b Marshall	26
+SMH Kirmani	c Haynes b Roberts	11	run out	33
S Madan Lal	c Holding b Garner	6	lbw b Roberts	4
BS Sandhu	not out	8	lbw b Roberts	4
S Venkataraghavan	c Dujon b Garner	5	not out	0
	(lb 1, nb 14)	15	(b 5, lb 2, nb 16)	23
	(all out)	209	(all out)	277

Bowling: Holding 14-4-46-2 Roberts 16-4-48-4 Marshall 13-1-56-2 Garner 12.2-5-41-2 Gomes 2-1-3-0
Holding 21-2-75-2 Roberts 19.2-3-31-4 Marshall 16-1-80-2 Garner 15-4-48-1 Gomes 8-3-20-0

West Indies Innings

CG Greenidge	c Gavaskar b Madan Lal	57	not out	0
DL Haynes	c Kapil Dev b Shastri	92	not out	0
IVA Richards	c Gavaskar b Venkataraghavan	80		
HA Gomes	c sub (L Sivaramakrishnan) b Venkataraghavan	6		
AL Logie	c Amarnath b Shastri	130		
*CH Lloyd	c sub (L Sivaramakrishnan) b Venkataraghavan	50		
+PJL Dujon	c Vengsarkar b Kapil Dev	25		
MD Marshall	c Venkataraghavan b Kapil Dev	8		
AME Roberts	c Kapil Dev b Madan Lal	20		
MA Holding	c Kirmani b Kapil Dev	2		
J Garner	not out	2		
	(b 1, lb 11, nb 2)	14	(nb 1)	1
	(all out)	486	(0 wickets)	1

Bowling: Kapil Dev 32.2-7-76-3 Sandhu 5-1-21-0 Madan Lal 27-2-96-2 Shastri 50-13-133-2 Venkataraghavan 43-6-146-3
Gaekwad 1-1-0-0
Kirmani 0.1-0-0-0

Umpires: DM Archer and SE Parris

West Indies v Australia
30,31 March, 1,3,4 April 1984

Result: West Indies won by 10 wickets

Australia Innings

SB Smith	c Dujon b Marshall	10	b Marshall	7
GM Wood	c Dujon b Holding	68	lbw b Garner	20
GM Ritchie	c & b Harper	57	c Haynes b Marshall	0
*KJ Hughes	c Lloyd b Holding	20	c Lloyd b Holding	25
AR Border	c Richardson b Marshall	38	c Dujon b Holding	8
DW Hookes	c Dujon b Garner	30	b Holding	9
TG Hogan	b Garner	40	c Richardson b Holding	0
+WB Phillips	c Dujon b Garner	120	b Marshall	1
GF Lawson	c Baptiste	10	c Harper b Marshall	2
RM Hogg	c Garner b Harper	3	not out	5
TM Alderman	not out	2	b Marshall	0
	(b 14, lb 8, nb 9)	31	(b 1, lb 6, nb 11)	18
	(all out)	429	(all out)	97

Bowling: Garner 33.5-6-110-3 Marshall 26-2-83-2 Holding 30-5-94-2 Baptiste 17-5-34-1 Harper 43-9-86-2
Marshall 15.5-1-42-5 Garner 8-4-9-1 Holding 15-4-24-4 Harper 2-1-1-0 Baptiste 3-0-14-0

West Indies Innings

CG Greenidge	run out	64	not out	10
DL Haynes	b Hogg	145	not out	11
RB Richardson	not out	131		
IVA Richards	b Lawson	6		
EAE Baptiste	b Lawson	11		
+PJL Dujon	b Alderman	2		
*CH Lloyd	b Hogg	76		
MD Marshall	b Hogg	10		
RA Harper	b Hogg	19		
J Garner	c Phillips b Hogg	9		
MA Holding	c Smith b Hogg	0		
	(lb 25, nb 11)	36		0
	(all out)	509	(0 wickets)	21

Bowling: Lawson 33.2-4-150-2 Alderman 42.4-6-152-1 Hogg 32.4-4-77-6 Hogan 34-8-97-0 Border 3-1-8-0
Lawson 2-1-3-0 Alderman 1.4-0-18-0

Umpires: DM Archer and LH Barker

West Indies v New Zealand
26,27,28,30 April, 1 May 1985

Result: West Indies won by 10 wickets

New Zealand Innings

*GP Howarth	c Greenidge b Garner	1	c Haynes b Marshall	5
JG Wright	c Dujon b Marshall	0	c Richardson b Davis	64
KR Rutherford	c Richards b Marshall	0	c Holding b Marshall	2
MD Crowe	hit wicket b Holding	14	c Dujon b Marshall	2
JJ Crowe	c Dujon b Davis	21	b Davis	4
JV Coney	c Richardson b Marshall	12	c Logie b Marshall	83
+IDS Smith	c Greenidge b Marshall	2	c & b Marshall	26
RJ Hadlee	c Logie b Davis	29	c Logie b Davis	3
DA Stirling	c Logie b Davis	6	b Marshall	3
SL Boock	c Dujon b Garner	1	c Haynes b Marshall	22
EJ Chatfield	not out	0	not out	4
	(nb 8)	8	(b 8, lb 1, w 2, nb 19)	30
	(all out)	94	(all out)	248

Bowling: Marshall 15-3-40-4 Garner 15-9-14-2 Holding 7-4-12-1 Davis 10.4-5-28-3
Marshall 25.3-6-80-7 Garner 19-5-56-0 Holding 1-0-2-0 Davis 18-0-66-3 Richards 13-3-25-0 Gomes 4-0-10-0

West Indies Innings

CG Greenidge	c JJ Crowe b Hadlee	2	not out	4
DL Haynes	c Smith b Hadlee	62	not out	5
RB Richardson	lbw b MD Crowe	22		
HA Gomes	c JJ Crowe b MD Crowe	0		
WW Davis	c Smith b Stirling	16		
*IVA Richards	c MD Crowe b Boock	105		
AL Logie	c JJ Crowe b Chatfield	7		
+PJL Dujon	b Hadlee	3		
MD Marshall	c JJ Crowe b Chatfield	63		
J Garner	not out	37		
MA Holding	c Smith b Stirling	1		
	(b 2, lb 8, w 6, nb 2)	18	(w 1)	1
	(all out)	336	(0 wickets)	10

Bowling: Hadlee 26-5-86-3 Chatfield 28-10-57-2 Stirling 14.1-0-82-2 MD Crowe 10-2-25-2 Boock 15-1-76-1
Boock 1-1-0-0 Rutherford 0.4-0-10-0

Umpires: DM Archer and LH Barker

West Indies v England
21,22,23,25 March 1986

Result: West Indies won by an innings and 30 runs

West Indies Innings

CG Greenidge	c Botham b Foster	21
DL Haynes	c Botham b Foster	84
RB Richardson	lbw b Emburey	160
HA Gomes	c Gower b Thomas	33
*IVA Richards	c Downton b Thomas	51
CA Best	lbw b Foster	21
+PJL Dujon	c sub (WN Slack) b Botham	5
MA Holding	b Thomas	23
MD Marshall	run out	4
J Garner	c Gooch b Thomas	0
BP Patterson	not out	0
	(b 2, lb 9, w 3, nb 2)	16
	(all out)	418

Bowling: Botham 24-3-80-1 Thomas 16.1-2-70-4 Foster 19-0-76-3 Edmonds 29-2-85-0 Emburey 38-7-96-1

England Innings

GA Gooch	c Dujon b Garner	53	b Patterson	11
RT Robinson	c Dujon b Marshall	3	b Patterson	43
*DI Gower	c Dujon b Marshall	66	c Marshall b Garner	23
P Willey	c Dujon b Marshall	5	lbw b Garner	17
AJ Lamb	c Richardson b Marshall	5	c & b Holding	6
IT Botham	c Dujon b Patterson	14	c Dujon b Garner	21
+PR Downton	lbw b Holding	11	c Dujon b Holding	26
JE Emburey	c Best b Patterson	0	not out	35
PH Edmonds	c Richardson b Patterson	4	lbw b Garner	0
NA Foster	lbw b Holding	0	c Richardson b Holding	0
JG Thomas	not out	4	b Patterson	4
	(b 4, lb 8, w 2, nb 10)	24	(lb 1, nb 12)	13
	(all out)	189	(all out)	199

Bowling: Marshall 14-1-42-4 Garner 14-4-35-1 Patterson 15-5-54-3 Holding 13-4-37-2 Richards 3-0-9-0
Marshall 13-1-47-0 Garner 17-2-69-4 Patterson 8.4-2-28-3 Holding 10-1-47-3 Richards 4-1-7-0

Umpires: DM Archer and LH Barker

West Indies v Pakistan
22,23,24,26,27 April 1988

Result: West Indies won by 2 wickets

Pakistan Innings

Mudassar Nazar	b Ambrose	18	c Greenidge b Hooper	41
Rameez Raja	c Greenidge b Benjamin	54	c Logie b Marshall	4
Shoaib Mohammad	c Greenidge b Ambrose	54	c & b Richards	64
Javed Miandad	c Richardson b Marshall	14	c Dujon b Marshall	34
Saleem Malik	b Marshall	15	lbw b Benjamin	9
Aamer Malik	c Hooper b Benjamin	32	c Logie b Marshall	2
*Imran Khan	c Dujon b Benjamin	18	not out	43
+Saleem Yousuf	retired hurt	32	c Richards b Benjamin	28
Wasim Akram	c Benjamin b Marshall	38	lbw b Marshall	0
Abdul Qadir	c Walsh b Marshall	17	c Greenidge b Marshall	2
Saleem Jaffar	not out	1	b Ambrose	4
	(lb 7, nb 9)	16	(b 3, lb 14, nb 14)	31
	(all out)	309	(all out)	262

Bowling: Marshall 18.4-3-79-4 Ambrose 14-0-64-2 Benjamin 14-3-52-3 Walsh 10-1-53-0 Richards 6-0-19-0 Hooper 12-3-35-0
Marshall 23-3-65-5 Ambrose 26.5-3-74-1 Walsh 12-1-22-0 Benjamin 15-1-37-2 Hooper 10-1-39-1 Richards 7-3-8-1

West Indies Innings

CG Greenidge	lbw b Imran Khan	10	c Shoaib Mohammad b Saleem Jaffar	35
DL Haynes	c +Aamer Malik b Mudassar Nazar	48	c Saleem Malik b Wasim Akram	4
RB Richardson	c +Aamer Malik b Wasim Akram	67	st Aamer Malik b Abdul Qadir	64
CL Hooper	b Wasim Akram	54	run out	13
*IVA Richards	c Mudassar Nazar b Wasim Akram	67	b Wasim Akram	39
AL Logie	c Javed Miandad b Mudassar Nazar	0	b Abdul Qadir	3
+PJL Dujon	run out	0	not out	29
MD Marshall	c +Aamer Malik b Imran Khan	48	lbw b Wasim Akram	15
CEL Ambrose	lbw b Imran Khan	7	c Saleem Jaffar b Wasim Akram	1
WKM Benjamin	run out	31	not out	40
CA Walsh	not out	14		
	(b 5, lb 11, nb 8)	24	(b 9, lb 6, nb 10)	25
	(all out)	306	(8 wickets)	268

Bowling: Imran Khan 25-3-108-3 Wasim Akram 27-1-88-3 Abdul Qadir 15-1-35-0 Saleem Jaffar 7-1-35-0 Mudassar Nazar 10-4-24-2
Wasim Akram 31-7-73-4 Imran Khan 6-0-34-0 Abdul Qadir 32-5-115-2 Saleem Jaffar 5-0-25-1 Shoaib Mohammad 3-1-6-0

Umpires: DM Archer and LH Barker

Kensington Oval, Bridgetown, Barbados

West Indies v India
7,8,9,11,12 April 1989

Result: West Indies won by 8 wickets

India Innings

J Arun Lal	c Dujon b Bishop	8	c Haynes b Walsh	15
NS Sidhu	c Richards b Walsh	9	c Logie b Marshall	0
RJ Shastri	c Richardson b Bishop	6	c sub b Ambrose	107
*DB Vengsarkar	run out	20	c Dujon b Bishop	6
M Azharuddin	c Ambrose b Bishop	61	c Dujon b Marshall	14
SV Manjrekar	c Greenidge b Bishop	108	c Logie b Ambrose	3
N Kapil Dev	c Richardson b Bishop	34	c Dujon b Marshall	1
+KS More	c Dujon b Marshall	1	b Marshall	50
Arshad Ayub	c Richards b Bishop	32	b Marshall	0
C Sharma	not out	12	c Dujon b Ambrose	21
ND Hirwani	c Haynes b Walsh	1	not out	1
	(b 2, lb 5, nb 22)	29	(b 16, lb 4, nb 13)	33
	(all out)	321	(all out)	251

Bowling: Marshall 22-0-56-1 Ambrose 26-5-84-0 Bishop 25-5-87-6 Walsh 23.2-5-69-2 Richards 9-3-18-0
Marshall 26-5-60-5 Ambrose 20.3-3-66-3 Bishop 24-7-55-1 Walsh 20-6-34-1 Richards 6-0-16-0 Arthurton 1-1-0-0

West Indies Innings

CG Greenidge	c Hirwani b Sharma	117	lbw b Sharma	6
DL Haynes	c Manjrekar b Shastri	27	not out	112
RB Richardson	c Sidhu b Arshad Ayub	93	b Arshad Ayub	59
KLT Arthurton	b Hirwani	0	not out	11
*IVA Richards	c sub b Hirwani	1		
AL Logie	c Manjrekar b Shastri	26		
+PJL Dujon	c Manjrekar b Shastri	33		
MD Marshall	not out	40		
CEL Ambrose	c Kapil Dev b Shastri	3		
IR Bishop	lbw b Kapil Dev	8		
CA Walsh	b Kapil Dev	0		
	(lb 7, nb 22)	29	(lb 5, nb 3)	8
	(all out)	377	(2 wickets)	196

Bowling: Kapil Dev 24.5-3-68-2 Sharma 18-1-86-1 Arshad Ayub 17-1-55-1 Hirwani 24-1-83-2 Shastri 28-7-78-4
Kapil Dev 8-0-42-0 Sharma 4-0-19-1 Arshad Ayub 14-4-26-1 Hirwani 10-0-56-0 Shastri 11-2-41-0 Manjrekar 1-0-7-0

Umpires: DM Archer and LH Barker

West Indies v England
5,6,7,8,10 April 1990

Result: West Indies won by 164 runs

West Indies Innings

CG Greenidge	c Russell b DeFreitas	41	lbw b Small	3
DL Haynes	c Stewart b Small	0	c Malcolm b Small	109
RB Richardson	c Russell b Small	45	lbw b DeFreitas	39
CA Best	c Russell b Small	164		
*IVA Richards	c Russell b Capel	70	c Small b Capel	12
AL Logie	c Russell b Capel	31	lbw b DeFreitas	48
+PJL Dujon	b Capel	31	not out	15
MD Marshall	c Lamb b Small	4	c Smith b Small	7
CEL Ambrose	not out	20	c Capel b DeFreitas	1
IR Bishop	run out	10	not out	11
EA Moseley	b DeFreitas	4	b Small	5
	(lb 8, nb 18)	26	(lb 12, w 1, nb 4)	17
	(all out)	446	(8 wickets declared)	267

Bowling: Malcolm 33-6-142-0 Small 35-5-109-4 DeFreitas 29.5-5-99-2 Capel 24-5-88-3
Malcolm 10-0-46-0 Small 20-1-74-4 DeFreitas 22-2-69-3 Capel 16-1-66-1

England Innings

AJ Stewart	c Richards b Moseley	45	c Richards b Ambrose	37
W Larkins	c Richardson b Bishop	0	c Dujon b Bishop	0
RJ Bailey	b Bishop	17	c Dujon b Ambrose	6
*AJ Lamb	lbw b Ambrose	119	c Dujon b Moseley	10
RA Smith	b Moseley	62	not out	40
N Hussain	lbw b Marshall	18	lbw b Ambrose	0
DJ Capel	c Greenidge b Marshall	2	lbw b Ambrose	6
+RC Russell	lbw b Bishop	7	b Ambrose	55
PAJ DeFreitas	c & b Ambrose	24	lbw b Ambrose	0
GC Small	not out	1	lbw b Ambrose	0
DE Malcolm	b Bishop	12	lbw b Ambrose	4
	(b 14, lb 9, w 3, nb 25)	51	(b 8, lb 9, w 1, nb 15)	33
	(all out)	358	(all out)	191

Bowling: Bishop 24.3-8-70-4 Ambrose 25-2-82-2 Moseley 28-3-114-2 Marshall 23-6-55-2 Richards 9-4-14-0
Bishop 20-7-40-1 Ambrose 22.4-10-45-8 Marshall 18-8-31-0 Moseley 19-3-44-1 Richards 10-5-11-0 Richardson 2-1-3-0

Umpires: DM Archer and LH Barker

West Indies v Australia
19,20,21,23,24 April 1991

Result: West Indies won by 343 runs

West Indies Innings

CG Greenidge	c Reid b McDermott	10	lbw b Hughes	226
DL Haynes	c ME Waugh b Hughes	28	c Healy b ME Waugh	40
RB Richardson	c Boon b McDermott	1	lbw b ME Waugh	99
CL Hooper	c Jones b Hughes	0	c Healy b ME Waugh	57
*IVA Richards	c Hughes b McDermott	32	lbw b ME Waugh	25
AL Logie	c Taylor b Reid	11	not out	33
+PJL Dujon	c Healy b Hughes	10	c ME Waugh b McDermott	4
MD Marshall	c Marsh b Reid	17	c Healy b McDermott	15
CEL Ambrose	not out	19	b Reid	2
CA Walsh	c ME Waugh b McDermott	10	c Marsh b Reid	0
BP Patterson	c ME Waugh b Hughes	1	not out	4
	(lb 3, nb 7)	10	(lb 19, nb 12)	31
	(all out)	149	(9 wickets decl)	536

Bowling: McDermott 22-6-49-4 Reid 21-8-50-2 Hughes 16.1-2-44-4 SR Waugh 2-0-3-0
McDermott 37.3-8-130-2 Reid 30-4-100-2 Hughes 36-6-125-1 SR Waugh 28-6-77-0 ME Waugh 28-6-80-4 Jones 3-1-5-0

Australia Innings

MA Taylor	lbw b Ambrose	26	lbw b Marshall	76
GR Marsh	c Logie b Ambrose	12	lbw b Ambrose	0
DC Boon	c Hooper b Marshall	0	b Ambrose	57
*AR Border	b Marshall	29	c Dujon b Ambrose	0
DM Jones	lbw b Marshall	22	b Hooper	37
ME Waugh	not out	20	b Hooper	3
SR Waugh	c Dujon b Patterson	2	not out	4
+IA Healy	c Dujon b Walsh	2	lbw b Marshall	0
MG Hughes	c Logie b Walsh	3	c Dujon b Marshall	3
CJ McDermott	b Walsh	2	c sub (RIC Holder) b Walsh	2
BA Reid	b Walsh	0	b Walsh	0
	(lb 2, nb 14)	16	(b 3, lb 5, nb 18)	26
	(all out)	134	(all out)	208

Bowling: Ambrose 16-5-36-2 Patterson 13-6-22-1 Marshall 16-1-60-3 Walsh 5.1-1-14-4
Ambrose 19-7-36-3 Patterson 15-3-56-0 Walsh 14.2-4-37-2 Marshall 17-4-35-3 Hooper 19-4-28-2 Richards 3-0-8-0

Umpires: DM Archer and LH Barker

West Indies v South Africa
18,19,20,22,23 April 1992

Result: West Indies won by 52 runs

West Indies Innings

DL Haynes	c Wessels b Snell	58	c Richardson b Snell	23
PV Simmons	c Kirsten b Snell	35	c Kirsten b Bosch	3
BC Lara	c Richardson b Bosch	17	c Richardson b Donald	64
*RB Richardson	c Richardson b Snell	44	lbw b Snell	2
KLT Arthurton	c Kuiper b Pringle	59	b Donald	22
JC Adams	b Donald	11	not out	79
+D Williams	c Hudson b Donald	1	lbw b Snell	5
CEL Ambrose	not out	6	c Richardson b Donald	6
KCG Benjamin	b Snell	1	lbw b Donald	7
CA Walsh	b Pringle	6	c Richardson b Snell	13
BP Patterson	run out	0	b Bosch	11
	(lb 7, nb 17)	24	(b 17, lb 11, nb 20)	48
	(all out)	262	(all out)	283

Bowling: Donald 20-1-67-2 Bosch 15-2-43-1 Pringle 18.4-2-62-2 Snell 18-3-83-4
Donald 25-3-77-4 Bosch 24.3-7-61-2 Pringle 16-0-43-0 Snell 16-1-74-4

South Africa Innings

MW Rushmere	c Lara b Ambrose	3	b Ambrose	3
AC Hudson	b Benjamin	163	c Lara b Ambrose	0
*KC Wessels	c Adams b Ambrose	59	c Lara b Walsh	74
PN Kirsten	c Lara b Benjamin	11	b Walsh	52
WJ Cronje	c Lara b Adams	5	c Williams b Ambrose	2
AP Kuiper	c Williams b Patterson	34	c Williams b Walsh	0
+DJ Richardson	c Ambrose b Adams	8	c Williams b Ambrose	2
RP Snell	run out	6	c Adams b Walsh	0
MW Pringle	c Walsh b Adams	15	b Ambrose	4
AA Donald	st Williams b Adams	0	b Ambrose	0
T Bosch	not out	5	not out	0
	(b 4, lb 6, w 1, nb 25)	36	(b 4, lb 3, nb 4)	11
	(all out)	345	(all out)	148

Bowling: Ambrose 36-19-47-2 Patterson 23-4-79-1 Walsh 27-7-71-0 Benjamin 25-3-87-2 Arthurton 3-0-8-0 Adams 21.5-5-43-4
Ambrose 24.4-7-34-6 Patterson 7-1-26-0 Walsh 22-10-31-4 Benjamin 9-2-21-0 Adams 5-0-16-0 Simmons 5-1-13-0

Umpires: DM Archer and SA Bucknor; Referee: R Subba Row (Eng)

West Indies v Pakistan
23,24,25,27 April 1993

Result: West Indies won by 10 wickets

West Indies Innings

DL Haynes	b Aamer Nazir	125	not out	16
PV Simmons	c Moin Khan b Ata-ur-Rehman	87	not out	8
*RB Richardson	lbw b Waqar Younis	31		
BC Lara	c Moin Khan b Ata-ur-Rehman	51		
KLT Arthurton	b Wasim Akram	56		
CL Hooper	c Moin Khan b Waqar Younis	15		
+JR Murray	st Moin Khan b Aamer Sohail	35		
IR Bishop	c Moin Khan b Aamer Nazir	11		
CEL Ambrose	not out	12		
WKM Benjamin	b Waqar Younis	0		
CA Walsh	c & b Waqar Younis	3		
	(b 1, lb 1, w 2, nb 25)	29	(w 3, nb 2)	5
	(all out)	455	(0 wickets)	29

Bowling: Wasim Akram 32-2-95-1 Waqar Younis 25.5-3-132-4 Aamer Nazir 20-1-79-2 Ata-ur-Rehman 21-1-103-2 Asif Mujtaba 3-0-30-0 Aamer Sohail 4-1-14-1
Wasim Akram 2.3-0-18-0 Aamer Nazir 2-0-11-0

Pakistan Innings

Aamer Sohail	c Murray b Ambrose	10	c Benjamin b Ambrose	4
Rameez Raja	c Haynes b Ambrose	37	lbw b Walsh	25
Asif Mujtaba	c Richardson b Walsh	13	lbw b Benjamin	41
Javed Miandad	c Richardson b Benjamin	22	c Arthurton b Hooper	43
Inzamam-ul-Haq	lbw b Bishop	7	lbw b Benjamin	26
Basit Ali	not out	92	lbw b Walsh	37
*Wasim Akram	c Simmons b Hooper	29	b Benjamin	0
+Moin Khan	c Murray b Walsh	0	c Murray b Hooper	17
Waqar Younis	c Murray b Walsh	0	c Lara b Hooper	29
Ata-ur-Rehman	c Benjamin b Walsh	0	c Simmons b Walsh	13
Aamer Nazir	c Arthurton b Benjamin	1	not out	6
	(lb 3, nb 7)	10	(b 12, lb 5, nb 4)	21
	(all out)	221	(all out)	262

Bowling: Ambrose 16-5-42-2 Bishop 16-5-43-1 Walsh 18-2-56-4 Benjamin 19-5-55-2 Hooper 7-0-22-1
Ambrose 26-10-55-1 Bishop 4-1-13-0 Walsh 24-7-51-3 Benjamin 17-7-30-3 Hooper 32.3-6-96-3

Umpires: LH Barker and HD Bird (Eng); Referee: R Subba Row (Eng)

West Indies v England
8,9,10,12,13 April 1994

Result: England won by 208 runs

England Innings

*MA Atherton	c Lara b KCG Benjamin	85	c Lara b Walsh	15
AJ Stewart	b WKM Benjamin	118	b Walsh	143
MR Ramprakash	c Murray b WKM Benjamin	20	c Chanderpaul b Walsh	3
RA Smith	c Murray b WKM Benjamin	10	lbw b KCG Benjamin	13
GA Hick	c Murray b Ambrose	34	c Lara b Walsh	59
GP Thorpe	c sub b KCG Benjamin	7	c Arthurton b Walsh	84
+RC Russell	c Chanderpaul b Ambrose	38	not out	17
CC Lewis	c Murray b Ambrose	0	c Walsh b Adams	10
AR Caddick	b Ambrose	8		
ARC Fraser	c Chanderpaul b Walsh	3		
PCR Tufnell	not out	0		
	(lb 8, nb 24)	32	(b 8, lb 6, nb 36)	50
	(all out)	355	(7 wickets declared)	394

Bowling: Ambrose 24.2-5-86-4 Walsh 24-3-88-1 WKM Benjamin 22-4-76-3 KCG Benjamin 20-5-74-2 Chanderpaul 10-4-23-0
Ambrose 22-4-75-0 Walsh 28-5-94-5 WKM Benjamin 22-3-58-0 KCG Benjamin 20-1-92-1 Chanderpaul 10-3-30-0 Adams 6.5-0-31-1

West Indies Innings

DL Haynes	c Atherton b Fraser	35	c Thorpe b Tufnell	15
*RB Richardson	c Atherton b Fraser	20	c Ramprakash b Caddick	33
BC Lara	c sub b Lewis	26	c Tufnell b Caddick	64
KLT Arthurton	c Russell b Fraser	0	b Tufnell	52
JC Adams	c Thorpe b Fraser	26	c Russell b Caddick	12
S Chanderpaul	c Ramprakash b Tufnell	77	c sub (N Hussain) b Hick	5
+JR Murray	c Thorpe b Fraser	0	c Thorpe b Caddick	5
WKM Benjamin	c Hick b Fraser	8	c Stewart b Tufnell	3
CEL Ambrose	c Hick b Fraser	44	b Lewis	12
KCG Benjamin	not out	43	c Hick b Caddick	0
CA Walsh	c Tufnell b Fraser	13	not out	18
	(lb 1, nb 11)	12	(b 1, lb 7, nb 10)	18
	(all out)	304	(all out)	237

Bowling: Fraser 28.5-7-75-8 Caddick 24-2-92-0 Lewis 17-2-60-1 Tufnell 32-12-76-1
Fraser 17-7-40-0 Caddick 17-3-63-5 Tufnell 36-12-100-3 Lewis 8.2-1-23-1 Hick 4-2-3-1

Umpires: LH Barker and DB Hair (Aus); Referee: JR Reid (NZ)

Kensington Oval, Bridgetown, Barbados

West Indies v Australia
31 March, 1,2 April 1995

Result: Australia won by 10 wickets

West Indies Innings

SC Williams	c Taylor b Julian	1	c Healy b McGrath	10
SL Campbell	c Healy b Reiffel	0	c SR Waugh b Warne	6
BC Lara	c SR Waugh b Julian	65	c Healy b McGrath	9
*RB Richardson	c Healy b Julian	0	b Reiffel	36
CL Hooper	c Taylor b Julian	60	c Reiffel b Julian	16
JC Adams	c Warne b McGrath	16	not out	39
+JR Murray	c Taylor b McGrath	21	c SR Waugh b Warne	23
WKM Benjamin	c Taylor b Warne	14	lbw b McGrath	26
CEL Ambrose	c Blewett b McGrath	7	c Blewett b McGrath	6
CA Walsh	c SR Waugh b Warne	1	b McGrath	4
KCG Benjamin	not out	0	b Warne	5
	(b 3, w 1, nb 6)	10	(lb 1, nb 8)	9
	(all out)	195	(all out)	189

Bowling: Reiffel 11-4-41-1 Julian 12-0-36-4 Warne 12-2-57-2 McGrath 12.1-1-46-3 ME Waugh 1-0-12-0
Reiffel 11-6-15-1 Julian 12-2-41-1 Warne 26.3-5-64-3 McGrath 22-6-68-5

Australia Innings

MJ Slater	c Williams b WKM Benjamin	18	not out	20
*MA Taylor	c Hooper b KCG Benjamin	55	not out	16
DC Boon	c WKM Benjamin b Walsh	20		
ME Waugh	c Murray b Ambrose	40		
SR Waugh	c Murray b KCG Benjamin	65		
GS Blewett	c Murray b Ambrose	14		
+IA Healy	not out	74		
BP Julian	c KCG Benjamin b Hooper	31		
PR Reiffel	b WKM Benjamin	1		
SK Warne	c Adams b Walsh	6		
GD McGrath	b WKM Benjamin	4		
	(lb 13, nb 5)	18	(nb 3)	3
	(all out)	346	(0 wickets)	39

Bowling: Ambrose 20-7-41-2 Walsh 25-5-78-2 KCG Benjamin 20-1-84-2 WKM Benjamin 23.2-6-71-3 Hooper 12-0-59-1
Walsh 3-0-19-0 KCG Benjamin 2.5-1-14-0 Hooper 1-0-6-0

Umpires: LH Barker and S Venkataraghavan (Ind)
TV Umpire: HA Moore; Referee: Majid Khan (Pak)

West Indies v New Zealand
19,20,21,23 April 1996

Result: West Indies won by 10 wickets

New Zealand Innings

CM Spearman	c Browne b Ambrose	0	c Lara b Thompson	20
RG Twose	c Samuels b Walsh	2	c Lara b Walsh	0
SP Fleming	c Chanderpaul b Walsh	1	c Samuels b Bishop	22
AC Parore	c Simmons b Adams	59	c Campbell b Bishop	1
NJ Astle	c Browne b Thompson	54	c Campbell b Thompson	125
CZ Harris	c Lara b Thompson	0	c Samuels b Bishop	0
JTC Vaughan	c Bishop b Adams	44	lbw b Bishop	24
*+LK Germon	c Chanderpaul b Adams	0	lbw b Walsh	23
GR Larsen	st Browne b Adams	12	lbw b Walsh	6
DK Morrison	not out	4	not out	26
RJ Kennedy	c Browne b Adams	0	c Adams b Walsh	22
	(lb 1, w 1, nb 17)	19	(lb 7, nb 29)	36
	(all out)	195	(all out)	305

Bowling: Ambrose 13-4-33-1 Walsh 17-6-30-2 Bishop 10-3-36-0 Thompson 8-0-58-2 Simmons 3-0-11-0 Adams 9-4-17-5 Chanderpaul 2-0-9-0
Ambrose 18-6-41-0 Walsh 22-3-72-4 Thompson 14-1-77-2 Bishop 19-1-67-4 Adams 6-1-32-0 Chanderpaul 3-1-9-0

West Indies Innings

SL Campbell	b Harris	208	not out	29
RG Samuels	lbw b Larsen	12	not out	0
BC Lara	c Spearman b Larsen	35		
PV Simmons	lbw b Larsen	22		
JC Adams	c Germon b Vaughan	21		
S Chanderpaul	c Harris b Morrison	82		
+CO Browne	c Astle b Kennedy	20		
IR Bishop	c Germon b Harris	31		
CEL Ambrose	c Germon b Vaughan	8		
*CA Walsh	not out	12		
PIC Thompson	lbw b Morrison	1		
	(lb 8, nb 12)	20		0
	(all out)	472	(0 wickets)	29

Bowling: Morrison 29.3-4-120-2 Kennedy 22-3-89-1 Larsen 40-15-76-3 Vaughan 34-10-81-2 Harris 34-11-75-2 Twose 4-0-20-0 Astle 1-0-3-0
Morrison 2-0-8-0 Kennedy 2-0-21-0

Umpires: SA Bucknor and P Willey (Eng)
TV Umpire: HA Moore; Referee: MH Denness (Eng)

West Indies v India
27,29,30,31 March 1997

Result: West Indies won by 38 runs

West Indies Innings

SL Campbell	c Azharuddin b Prasad	6	c Mongia b Ganesh	18
SC Williams	c Laxman b Ganesh	24	b Prasad	0
S Chanderpaul	not out	137	lbw b Kuruvilla	3
*BC Lara	c Tendulkar b Prasad	19	c Azharuddin b Prasad	45
CL Hooper	c Mongia b Ganesh	19	lbw b Ganesh	4
RIC Holder	c Azharuddin b Prasad	5	c Mongia b Prasad	13
+CO Browne	c Tendulkar b Kumble	24	c Mongia b Kuruvilla	1
IR Bishop	b Prasad	4	lbw b Kuruvilla	6
CEL Ambrose	c Tendulkar b Kuruvilla	37	not out	18
FA Rose	run out (Prasad/Mongia/Kumble)	11	c Ganguly b Kuruvilla	4
M Dillon	lbw b Prasad	0	b Kuruvilla	21
	(lb 5, nb 7)	12	(lb 5, nb 2)	7
	(all out)	298	(all out)	140

Bowling: Prasad 31.4-9-82-5 Kuruvilla 28-4-88-1 Ganesh 21-2-70-2 Kumble 16-1-44-1 Ganguly 2-1-9-0
Prasad 18-6-39-3 Kuruvilla 21-5-68-5 Ganesh 6-1-28-2

India Innings

VVS Laxman	b Ambrose	6	b Rose	19
NS Sidhu	c Browne b Rose	26	c Williams b Rose	3
R Dravid	b Bishop	78	c Browne b Rose	2
*SR Tendulkar	c Campbell b Bishop	92	c Lara b Bishop	4
SC Ganguly	c Browne b Dillon	22	b Ambrose	8
M Azharuddin	c Browne b Rose	17	b Ambrose	9
+NR Mongia	c Williams b Bishop	1	b Bishop	5
A Kumble	not out	23	c Holder b Bishop	1
A Kuruvilla	b Ambrose	0	c Holder b Ambrose	9
D Ganesh	c Browne b Rose	8	not out	6
BKV Prasad	c Holder b Rose	0	b Bishop	0
	(b 2, lb 12, w 2, nb 30)	46	(b 2, lb 2, nb 11)	15
	(all out)	319	(all out)	81

Bowling: Ambrose 29-8-74-2 Bishop 28-6-70-3 Dillon 19-5-56-1 Rose 22-4-77-4 Hooper 8-1-28-0
Ambrose 15-3-36-3 Bishop 11.5-4-22-4 Rose 9-2-19-3

Umpires: LH Barker and SG Randell (Aus)
TV Umpire: HA Moore; Referee: PL van der Merwe (SA)

West Indies v England
12,13,14,15,16 March 1998

Result: Match drawn

England Innings

*MA Atherton	c Ambrose b Walsh	11	c Williams b Bishop	64
AJ Stewart	c Williams b Walsh	12	c Lara b Bishop	48
MA Butcher	c Hooper b Ambrose	19	c Lambert b Ambrose	26
N Hussain	c Lara b McLean	5	not out	46
GP Thorpe	c Lara b Hooper	103	not out	36
MR Ramprakash	c & b McLean	154		
+RC Russell	c Wallace b Hooper	32		
DW Headley	c Holder b Hooper	31		
AR Caddick	c Chanderpaul b Hooper	3		
ARC Fraser	c Walsh b Hooper	3		
PCR Tufnell	not out	1		
	(lb 10, w 2, nb 17)	29	(b 1, lb 6, nb 6)	13
	(all out)	403	(3 wickets declared)	233

Bowling: Walsh 34-8-84-2 Ambrose 31-6-62-1 McLean 27-5-73-2 Hooper 37.5-7-80-5 Bishop 20-1-74-0 Chanderpaul 4-0-20-0
Walsh 12-1-40-0 Ambrose 12-4-48-1 Hooper 21-5-58-0 Bishop 14-1-51-2 Chanderpaul 5-3-13-0 McLean 7-0-16-0

West Indies Innings

CB Lambert	c Russell b Caddick	55	c Headley b Fraser	29
PA Wallace	lbw b Headley	45	lbw b Caddick	61
IR Bishop	c Russell b Tufnell	4		
*BC Lara	c Butcher b Headley	31	not out	13
S Chanderpaul	c Stewart b Fraser	45	not out	3
RIC Holder	b Ramprakash	10		
CL Hooper	lbw b Fraser	9		
+D Williams	c Ramprakash b Caddick	2		
NAM McLean	not out	7		
CEL Ambrose	st Russell b Tufnell	26		
CA Walsh	c & b Headley	6		
	(b 13, lb 2, nb 7)	22	(b 1, lb 5)	6
	(all out)	262	(2 wickets)	112

Bowling: Headley 17.3-2-64-3 Fraser 22-5-80-2 Caddick 17-8-28-2 Tufnell 33-15-43-2 Ramprakash 18-7-32-1
Caddick 6-1-19-1 Headley 2-0-14-0 Tufnell 16.3-3-37-0 Fraser 11-3-33-1 Ramprakash 2-1-3-0

Umpires: CJ Mitchley (SA) and EA Nicholls
TV Umpire: HA Moore; Referee: BN Jarman (Aus)

West Indies v Australia
26,27,28,29,30 March 1999

Result: West Indies won by 1 wicket

Australia Innings

MJ Slater	c Lara b Ambrose	23	run out (Campbell)	26
MTG Elliott	c Jacobs b Walsh	9	c Jacobs b Walsh	0
JL Langer	b Hooper	51	lbw b Ambrose	1
ME Waugh	b Ambrose	0	lbw b Walsh	3
*SR Waugh	lbw b Perry	199	b Collins	11
RT Ponting	c Hooper b Perry	104	c Griffith b Walsh	22
+IA Healy	lbw b Walsh	0	c Jacobs b Collins	3
SK Warne	c Lara b Perry	13	lbw b Walsh	32
JN Gillespie	not out	23	b Ambrose	14
SCG MacGill	run out (Ambrose)	17	c Campbell b Walsh	1
GD McGrath	c Joseph b Hooper	3	not out	8
	(b 4, lb 10, nb 34)	48	(lb 5, w 1, nb 19)	25
	(all out)	490	(all out)	146

Bowling: Ambrose 31.3-7-93-2 Walsh 38-8-121-2 Perry 33-5-102-3 Collins 35.3-7-110-0 Hooper 15.4-4-50-2
Walsh 17.1-3-39-5 Ambrose 20-2-60-2 Collins 9-0-31-2 Perry 4-0-11-0

West Indies Innings

SL Campbell	c SR Waugh b Gillespie	105	lbw b McGrath	33
AFG Griffith	run out (Ponting)	0	lbw b Gillespie	35
DRE Joseph	lbw b McGrath	26	lbw b MacGill	1
PT Collins	lbw b McGrath	0	lbw b McGrath	0
*BC Lara	c Healy b Gillespie	8	not out	153
CL Hooper	c Warne b McGrath	25	c Healy b Gillespie	6
JC Adams	c ME Waugh b McGrath	0	b McGrath	38
+RD Jacobs	c ME Waugh b Ponting	68	lbw b McGrath	5
NO Perry	lbw b Gillespie	24	lbw b McGrath	0
CEL Ambrose	not out	28	c Elliott b Gillespie	12
CA Walsh	c Slater b Warne	12	not out	0
	(b 10, lb 3, nb 20)	33	(b 8, lb 13, w 2, nb 5)	28
	(all out)	329	(9 wickets)	311

Bowling: McGrath 33-5-128-4 Gillespie 28-14-48-3 Warne 15.5-2-70-1 MacGill 20-5-47-0 Ponting 4-1-12-1 ME Waugh 3-0-11-0
McGrath 44-13-92-5 Gillespie 26.1-8-62-3 Warne 24-4-69-0 MacGill 21-6-48-1 SR Waugh 5-0-19-0

Umpires: EA Nicholls and DL Orchard (SA)
TV Umpire: HA Moore; Referee: R Subba Row (Eng)

West Indies v Pakistan
18,19,20,21,22 May 2000

Result: Match drawn

Pakistan Innings

Mohammad Wasim	c Adams b Walsh	4	lbw b King	82
Imran Nazir	c Campbell b Ambrose	2	c Adams b King	131
Younis Khan	c Chanderpaul b Walsh	0	c Jacobs b King	23
Inzamam-ul-Haq	c Adams b King	8	c & b Walsh	29
Yousuf Youhana	c Campbell b Walsh	115	c Adams b McLean	19
Abdul Razzaq	c Hinds b McLean	1	c sub (CH Gayle) b King	72
*+Moin Khan	c Chanderpaul b Walsh	38	b Adams	14
Wasim Akram	b Ambrose	42	c Hinds b Adams	0
Saqlain Mushtaq	c Campbell b Adams	12	b McLean	33
Waqar Younis	c Griffith b Walsh	14	not out	1
Mushtaq Ahmed	not out	2		
	(b 2, lb 9, nb 4)	15	(lb 4, w 1, nb 10)	15
	(all out)	253	(9 wickets declared)	419

Bowling: Ambrose 21-7-53-2 Walsh 13-4-22-5 King 17-1-56-1 McLean 16-3-63-1 Adams 17-1-45-1 Chanderpaul 2-0-3-0
Ambrose 37-16-54-0 Walsh 36-6-102-1 King 29-9-82-4 McLean 23.4-4-112-2 Adams 26-9-52-2 Chanderpaul 2-0-13-0

West Indies Innings

SL Campbell	b Saqlain Mushtaq	58	c sub (Shahid Afridi) b Wasim Akram	8
AFG Griffith	c Moin Khan b Waqar Younis	4	lbw b Waqar Younis	5
WW Hinds	c Inzamam-ul-Haq b Waqar Younis	165	c Moin Khan b Mushtaq Ahmed	52
S Chanderpaul	c Moin Khan b Abdul Razzaq	9	c Mohammad Wasim b Mushtaq Ahmed	16
*JC Adams	c Younis Khan b Saqlain Mushtaq	8	not out	34
RR Sarwan	not out	84	not out	11
CEL Ambrose	c Younis Khan b Wasim Akram	22		
+RD Jacobs	b Saqlain Mushtaq	10		
NAM McLean	c Yousuf Youhana b Wasim Akram	1		
RD King	c Mushtaq Ahmed b Saqlain Mushtaq	2		
CA Walsh	c Moin Khan b Saqlain Mushtaq	22		
	(lb 6, nb 7)	13	(b 1, lb 1, nb 4)	6
	(all out)	398	(4 wickets)	132

Bowling: Wasim Akram 33-9-84-2 Waqar Younis 17-2-72-2 Mushtaq Ahmed 22-2-65-0 Abdul Razzaq 16-3-50-1 Saqlain Mushtaq 51-10-121-5
Wasim Akram 7-1-24-1 Waqar Younis 4-0-14-1 Saqlain Mushtaq 21-12-28-0 Mushtaq Ahmed 20-5-64-2

Umpires: RE Koertzen (SA) and EA Nicholls
TV Umpire: HA Moore; Referee: PJP Burge (Aus)

Kensington Oval, Bridgetown, Barbados

West Indies v South Africa
29,30,31 March, 1,2 April 2001

Result: Match Drawn

South Africa Innings

G Kirsten	c Gayle b Walsh	0	c Samuels b Cuffy	0
HH Gibbs	c Hooper b Dillon	34	c Sarwan b Hooper	19
JH Kallis	c Jacobs b Dillon	11	c Sarwan b Hooper	20
DJ Cullinan	c & b Dillon	134	c Lara b Ramnarine	82
ND McKenzie	c Dillon b Hinds	72	c Cullinan b Boje	12
+MV Boucher	c Jacobs b Cuffy	3	c Jacobs b Ramnarine	0
N Boje	c Ramnarine b Dillon	34	not out	9
L Klusener	b Walsh	1	c Cuffy b Ramnarine	4
*SM Pollock	not out	106	c Hooper b Walsh	40
AA Donald	c Hooper b Walsh	37	lbw b Ramnarine	0
M Ntini	c & b Ramnarine	0		
	(b 6, lb 4, w 2, nb 10)	11	(lb 3, nb 8)	11
	(all out)	454	(9 wickets dec)	197

Bowling: Walsh 45-15-87-3 Dillon 34-1-147-4 Cuffy 30-7-71-1 Ramnarine 33.1-6-86-1 Hooper 18-5-31-0 Hinds 10-5-13-1 Samuels 2-0-6-0 Gayle 1-0-3-0
Walsh 14-3-28-1 Cuffy 10-4-28-1 Hooper 34-12-49-2 Dillon 4-2-7-0 Ramnarine 31.5-10-78-5 Samuels 2-1-4-0

West Indies Innings

WW Hinds	c Boucher b Kallis	2	c Cullinan b Boje	8
CH Gayle	c Cullinan b Ntini	40	c Boucher b Kallis	48
MN Samuels	c McKenzie b Kallis	6	c Cullinan b Boje	3
BC Lara	c Boje b Kallis	83	b Klusener	8
RR Sarwan	c Gibbs b Ntini	16	b Kallis	0
*CL Hooper	c Boucher b Kallis	74	c Boucher b Boje	5
+RD Jacobs	not out	113	c McKenzie b Boje	1
M Dillon	b Boje	14	not out	2
D Ramnarine	lbw b Boje	6	not out	0
CE Cuffy	lbw b Kallis	4		
CA Walsh	b Kallis	4		
	(b 4, lb 9, nb 12)	25	(b 8, lb 1, nb 4)	13
	(all out)	387	(7 wickets)	88

Bowling: Donald 14-7-30-0 Pollock 35-11-84-0 Kallis 36-17-67-6 Ntini 28-7-93-2 Boje 28-7-67-2 Klusener 10-3-33-0
Pollock 5-0-25-0 Kallis 8-1-34-2 Boje 16.4-10-17-4 Klusener 9-7-3-1

Umpires: SA Bucknor and DB Hair (Aus)
TV Umpire: HA Moore; Referee: MH Denness (Eng)

West Indies v India
2,3,4,5 May 2002

Result: West Indies won by 10 wickets

India Innings

SS Das	b Dillon	0	c Sarwan b Dillon	35
W Jaffer	c Jacobs b Dillon	12	run out (Chanderpaul)	51
R Dravid	run out (Chanderpaul/Cuffy)	17	c Jacobs b Sanford	14
SR Tendulkar	c Jacobs b Collins	0	lbw b Dillon	8
*SC Ganguly	c Dillon b Sanford	48	not out	60
VVS Laxman	b Cuffy	1	c Hooper b Collins	43
+A Ratra	c Jacobs b Dillon	1	lbw b Dillon	13
Harbhajan Singh	c Dillon b Sanford	13	b Cuffy	3
Z Khan	c Sarwan b Sanford	4	c Jacobs b Sarwan	46
J Srinath	lbw b Dillon	0	c Gayle b Sarwan	0
A Nehra	not out	0	c Collins b Dillon	3
	(w 2, nb 4)	6	(lb 6, nb 14)	20
	(all out)	102	(all out)	296

Bowling: Dillon 11-1-41-4 Cuffy 9-4-17-1 Collins 8-0-24-1 Sanford 5.4-0-20-3
Dillon 31.2-8-82-4 Cuffy 24-16-26-1 Collins 22-1-78-1 Sanford 15-3-78-1 Hooper 5-0-11-0 Gayle 3-0-14-0 Sarwan 1-0-1-2

West Indies Innings

SC Williams	c Jaffer b Khan	18	not out	4
CH Gayle	lbw b Khan	14	not out	1
RR Sarwan	c Jaffer b Nehra	60		
BC Lara	c & b Nehra	55		
*CL Hooper	c Tendulkar b Harbhajan Singh	115		
S Chanderpaul	not out	101		
+RD Jacobs	c Ratra b Nehra	6		
M Dillon	c Das b Nehra	6		
PT Collins	b Harbhajan Singh	0		
A Sanford	lbw b Harbhajan Singh	0		
CE Cuffy	run out (Tendulkar/Ratra/Harbhajan)	1		
	(b 3, lb 8, nb 13)	24	(nb 1)	1
	(all out)	394	(0 wickets)	5

Bowling: Srinath 32-7-85-0 Nehra 32-9-112-4 Khan 29-8-83-2 Ganguly 7-5-9-0 Harbhajan Singh 34.5-7-87-3 Tendulkar 1-0-7-0
Tendulkar 1-0-1-0 Harbhajan Singh 0.2-0-4-0

Umpires: EAR de Silva (SL) and DJ Harper (Aus)
TV Umpire: B Doctrove; Referee: RS Madugalle (SL)

West Indies v New Zealand
21,22,23,24 June 2002

Result: New Zealand won by 204 runs

New Zealand Innings

MH Richardson	b Sanford	41	c Lara b Collins	0
L Vincent	c Jacobs b Dillon	14	lbw b Collins	2
*SP Fleming	c Gayle b Hooper	130	c Hinds b Sanford	34
CZ Harris	c Lara b Collins	0	lbw b Powell	19
NJ Astle	c Lara b Dillon	2	c Lara b Collins	77
CD McMillan	lbw b Sanford	6	c Hooper b Collins	1
+RG Hart	not out	57	c Hinds b Collins	24
DL Vettori	c Hinds b Collins	39	b Sanford	11
DR Tuffey	lbw b Powell	28	c Gayle b Hooper	31
SE Bond	b Powell	5	not out	6
IG Butler	run out (Gayle)	3	c Jacobs b Collins	26
	(lb 8, nb 4)	12	(lb 8, w 1, nb 3)	12
	(all out)	337	(all out)	243

Bowling: Dillon 28-6-73-2 Collins 24-5-80-2 Powell 21-6-41-2 Sanford 28.4-7-101-2 Hooper 13-5-21-1 Gayle 10-3-12-0 Sarwan 1-0-1-0
Collins 30.4-8-76-6 Powell 20-4-61-1 Dillon 6-3-11-0 Sanford 17-5-68-2 Hooper 17-8-19-1

West Indies Innings

CH Gayle	c Vettori b Bond	3	lbw b Bond	73
WW Hinds	c McMillan b Tuffey	10	c Richardson b Vettori	37
RR Sarwan	c Butler b Bond	0	c Vettori b Bond	18
BC Lara	b Vettori	28	b Bond	73
*CL Hooper	c Tuffey b Butler	6	c Fleming b Tuffey	16
S Chanderpaul	not out	35	c Fleming b Vettori	17
+RD Jacobs	c Astle b Vettori	4	c Astle b Vettori	6
PT Collins	c Vincent b Butler	8	lbw b Bond	8
A Sanford	c Hart b Butler	1	not out	0
DB Powell	c Harris b Vettori	0	c Astle b Butler	2
M Dillon	c Fleming b Vettori	0	c Vincent b Bond	0
	(lb 4, nb 8)	12	(b 5, lb 11, w 2, nb 1)	19
	(all out)	107	(all out)	269

Bowling: Bond 12-1-34-2 Tuffey 7-3-16-1 Butler 11-2-26-3 Vettori 12.1-2-27-4
Bond 21-7-78-5 Tuffey 15-5-43-1 Butler 14-0-58-1 Vettori 19-3-53-3 Astle 5-4-4-0 Harris 9-3-17-0

Umpires: RE Koertzen (SA) and S Venkataraghavan (Ind)
TV Umpire: B Doctrove; Referee: Wasim Raja (Pak)

West Indies v Australia
1,2,3,4,5 May 2003

Result: Australia won by 9 wickets

Australia Innings

JL Langer	c Chanderpaul b Banks	78	lbw b Lawson	0
ML Hayden	c Gayle b Drakes	27	not out	2
RT Ponting	run out (Best/Baugh)	113		
DS Lehmann	lbw b Drakes	96	not out	4
*SR Waugh	b Lawson	115		
+AC Gilchrist	c Smith b Banks	65		
AJ Bichel	c Lara b Banks	71		
B Lee	b Lawson	11		
JN Gillespie	not out	18		
SCG MacGill	b Lawson	0		
GD McGrath				
	(b 3, lb 3, w 3, nb 2)	11	(b 2)	2
	(9 wickets dec)	605	(1 wicket)	8

Bowling: Lawson 32.3-2-131-3 Best 20-1-99-0 Drakes 30-2-85-2 Banks 40-2-204-3 Gayle 31-5-79-0 Sarwan 1-0-1-0
Lawson 1-0-2-1 Banks 1-0-2-0 Gayle 0.3-0-2-0

West Indies Innings

CH Gayle	b Gillespie	71	st Gilchrist b MacGill	56
DS Smith	c Gilchrist b Gillespie	59	lbw b Lee	5
D Ganga	c Bichel b Lehmann	26	lbw b Lee	6
RR Sarwan	c Gilchrist b Lee	40	lbw b MacGill	58
S Chanderpaul	c Lee b MacGill	0	c Gilchrist b Gillespie	21
OAC Banks	c Ponting b Gillespie	24	c Hayden b MacGill	32
+CS Baugh	c Ponting b MacGill	24	run out (Gillespie/Gilchrist)	18
*BC Lara	lbw b Bichel	14	lbw b Bichel	42
VC Drakes	c Lee b MacGill	11	b MacGill	0
TL Best	not out	20	c Bichel b MacGill	0
JJC Lawson	st Gilchrist b MacGill	1	not out	5
	(b 11, lb 16, nb 11)	38	(b 13, lb 25, w 1, nb 2)	41
	(all out)	328	(all out)	284

Bowling: McGrath 18-7-25-0 Gillespie 21-9-31-3 Lee 25-8-77-1 MacGill 39.5-8-107-4 Lehmann 9-2-26-1 Bichel 16-3-35-1
McGrath 18-4-39-0 Gillespie 28-11-37-1 MacGill 36-11-75-5 Lee 15-6-44-2 Bichel 12-2-35-1 Ponting 2-0-6-0 Waugh 4-1-6-0 Lehmann 1-0-4-0

Umpires: DR Shepherd (Eng) and S Venkataraghavan (Ind)
TV Umpire: EA Nicholls; Referee: MJ Procter (SA)

New Zealand v England
24,25,27 January 1930

Result: Match drawn

New Zealand Innings

CS Dempster	st Cornford b Woolley	136	not out		80
JE Mills	b Woolley	117	b Nichols		7
*TC Lowry	c Duleepsinhji b Woolley	6			
ML Page	c Cornford b Allom	67	c Bowley b Woolley		32
RC Blunt	c Duleepsinhji b Woolley	36	b Worthington		12
EG McLeod	b Woolley	16	not out		2
GL Weir	lbw b Woolley	3	c Duleepsinhji b Woolley		21
+KC James	c Cornford b Worthington	7			
GR Dickinson	c Worthington b Woolley	5			
WE Merritt	lbw b Worthington	0			
FT Badcock	not out	4			
	(b 17, lb 18, nb 8)	43	(b 1, lb 2, nb 7)		10
	(all out)	440	(4 wickets declared)		164

Bowling: Nichols 20-5-66-0 Allom 28-4-73-1 Barratt 33-4-87-0 Worthington 22-3-63-2 Bowley 5-0-32-0 Woolley 28.3-5-76-7
Nichols 9-1-22-1 Allom 6-1-21-0 Worthington 10-0-44-1 Bowley 5-0-19-0 Woolley 23-9-48-2

England Innings

EH Bowley	b Blunt	9	c Weir b Dickinson		2
EW Dawson	b Badcock	44	c Lowry b Badcock		7
KS Duleepsinhji	c Blunt b Badcock	40	not out		56
FE Woolley	c Lowry b Dickinson	6	b Merritt		23
GB Legge	c James b Dickinson	39	c Lowry b Weir		9
MS Nichols	not out	78	not out		3
TS Worthington	st James b Merritt	32			
*AHH Gilligan	b Merritt	32			
F Barratt	b Badcock	5			
+WL Cornford	c Page b Badcock	10			
MJC Allom	c Lowry b Dickinson	2			
	(b 11, lb 4, nb 8)	23	(b 4, lb 2, nb 1)		7
	(all out)	320	(4 wickets)		107

Bowling: Dickinson 19.5-3-66-3 Badcock 36-6-80-4 Blunt 14-3-44-1 Page 2-0-8-0 Merritt 34-3-94-2 McLeod 2-0-5-0
Dickinson 8-0-24-1 Badcock 17-8-22-1 Blunt 3-0-12-0 Merritt 9-1-41-1 Weir 2-1-1-1

Umpires: KH Cave and LT Cobcroft

New Zealand v South Africa
4,5,7 March 1932

Result: South Africa won by 8 wickets

New Zealand Innings

CS Dempster	c Vincent b McMillan	64	c Cameron b Quinn		20
GL Weir	b McMillan	8	b Quinn		1
RC Blunt	lbw b Quinn	25	b Brown		17
HG Vivian	c Dalton b McMillan	100	c Vincent b Balaskas		73
AW Roberts	lbw b Quinn	1	b Quinn		26
*ML Page	c Mitchell b Brown	7	c & b Balaskas		23
FT Badcock	c & b McMillan	53	run out		0
GR Dickinson	st Cameron b McMillan	2	b McMillan		5
CFW Allcott	c Dalton b Mitchell	26	b Quinn		15
IB Cromb	not out	51	c Christy b McMillan		2
+KC James	b Mitchell	11	not out		0
	(b 12, lb 4)	16	(b 4, lb 6, nb 1)		11
	(all out)	364	(all out)		193

Bowling: Bell 16-1-47-0 Quinn 28-6-51-2 Brown 14-1-59-1 McMillan 29-2-125-5 Vincent 6-1-32-0 Christy 2-0-11-0 Mitchell 4.5-0-23-2
Bell 10-0-30-0 Quinn 24-9-37-4 Brown 10-3-30-1 McMillan 21-2-71-2 Balaskas 7-2-14-2

South Africa Innings

JAJ Christy	c Dempster b Badcock	62	c Roberts b Badcock		53
B Mitchell	b Cromb	0	c James b Dickinson		53
*+HB Cameron	c Blunt b Vivian	44	not out		22
KG Viljoen	b Page	81	not out		16
EL Dalton	c James b Dickinson	42			
XC Balaskas	not out	122			
Q McMillan	c Dickinson b Allcott	1			
CL Vincent	c & b Vivian	33			
LS Brown	c Page b Vivian	7			
NA Quinn	b Vivian	8			
AJ Bell	lbw b Dickinson	2			
	(b 2, lb 2, w 1, nb 3)	8	(lb 6)		6
	(all out)	410	(2 wickets)		150

Bowling: Dickinson 26.2-7-78-2 Cromb 23-9-48-1 Badcock 24-6-70-1 Allcott 27-4-80-1 Blunt 10-0-38-0 Vivian 20-7-58-4
Page 11-3-30-1
Dickinson 8-2-33-1 Cromb 3-0-13-0 Badcock 11-2-31-1 Allcott 7-0-27-0 Blunt 2.2-0-11-0 Vivian 7-0-15-0 Page 3-0-14-0

Umpires: KH Cave and WP Page

New Zealand v Australia
29,30 March 1946

Result: Australia won by an innings and 103 runs

New Zealand Innings

*WA Hadlee	c Miller b Toshack	6	b Miller		3
WM Anderson	b Lindwall	4	b Lindwall		1
VJ Scott	c Barnes b O'Reilly	14	c Tallon b Miller		4
WM Wallace	c Barnes b Toshack	10	run out		14
+EWT Tindill	b Toshack	1	lbw b Toshack		13
CG Rowe	b O'Reilly	0	b O'Reilly		0
LA Butterfield	lbw b O'Reilly	0	lbw b O'Reilly		0
DAN McRae	c Hassett b O'Reilly	0	c Meuleman b McCool		8
C Burke	lbw b Toshack	3	b Toshack		3
J Cowie	st Tallon b O'Reilly	2	c Toshack b O'Reilly		0
DC Cleverley	not out	1	not out		1
	(b 3)	3	(b 5, nb 2)		7
	(all out)	42	(all out)		54

Bowling: Lindwall 8-1-13-1 Toshack 19-13-12-4 O'Reilly 12-5-14-5
Lindwall 9-3-16-1 Toshack 10-5-6-2 O'Reilly 7-1-19-3 Miller 6-2-6-2 McCool 0.2-0-0-1

Australia Innings

*WA Brown	c Rowe b Burke	67	
KD Meuleman	b Cowie	0	
SG Barnes	b Cowie	54	
KR Miller	c Hadlee b Burke	30	
AL Hassett	c Tindill b Cowie	19	
CL McCool	c Hadlee b Cowie	7	
IWG Johnson	not out	7	
+D Tallon	c Scott b Cowie	5	
RR Lindwall	c Anderson b Cowie	0	
WJ O'Reilly			
ERH Toshack			
	(b 5, lb 3, nb 2)	10	
	(8 wickets declared)	199	

Bowling: McRae 14-3-44-0 Cowie 21-8-40-6 Cleverley 15-1-51-0 Butterfield 13-6-24-0 Burke 11-2-30-2

Umpires: HW Gourlay and MF Pengelly

New Zealand v England
24,26,27,28 March 1951

Result: England won by 6 wickets

New Zealand Innings

B Sutcliffe	c & b Wright	20	b Tattersall		11
VJ Scott	lbw b Bailey	0	c Sheppard b Bedser		60
JR Reid	b Brown	11	b Tattersall		11
WM Wallace	b Wright	15	c Brown b Bailey		1
*WA Hadlee	lbw b Wright	15	c Bailey b Tattersall		9
AR MacGibbon	c Brown b Wright	20	lbw b Tattersall		0
+FLH Mooney	c Compton b Bailey	3	b Tattersall		31
TB Burtt	c Parkhouse b Wright	3	b Tattersall		26
AM Moir	not out	26	c Bedser b Bailey		26
JA Hayes	b Tattersall	0	b Bailey		5
GF Cresswell	run out	0	not out		0
	(b 3, lb 5, nb 4)	12	(b 30, lb 2, nb 3)		35
	(all out)	125	(all out)		189

Bowling: Bailey 11-2-18-2 Bedser 19-6-21-0 Brown 6-1-10-1 Tattersall 15-9-16-1 Wright 19-3-48-5
Bailey 14.2-1-43-3 Bedser 24-10-34-1 Brown 1-0-1-0 Tattersall 21-6-44-6 Wright 12-2-32-0

England Innings

L Hutton	c Reid b Moir	57	c Hadlee b Cresswell		29
RT Simpson	b Moir	6	b Burtt		5
WGA Parkhouse	b Burtt	2	c & b Burtt		20
DS Sheppard	b Hayes	3	not out		4
DCS Compton	b Burtt	10	b Cresswell		18
*FR Brown	b Hayes	47	not out		10
TE Bailey	st Mooney b Burtt	29			
+TG Evans	b Cresswell	13			
AV Bedser	b Cresswell	28			
DVP Wright	not out	9			
R Tattersall	b Cresswell	1			
	(b 11, lb 8, nb 3)	22	(b 1, lb 4)		5
	(all out)	227	(4 wickets)		91

Bowling: Hayes 20-2-44-2 Cresswell 15-6-18-3 Moir 28-5-65-2 Burtt 27-14-46-3 MacGibbon 7-0-32-0
Cresswell 18-8-31-2 Moir 6-0-19-0 Burtt 21.2-10-36-2

Umpires: J McLellan and MF Pengelly

New Zealand v South Africa
6,7,9,10 March 1953

Result: South Africa won by an innings and 180 runs

South Africa Innings

DJ McGlew	not out	255	
+JHB Waite	c Mooney b Blair	35	
JC Watkins	c Reid b Blair	14	
KJ Funston	b Fisher	2	
WR Endean	c Mooney b Blair	41	
RA McLean	b Blair	5	
*JE Cheetham	b Burtt	17	
ARA Murray	st Mooney b Burtt	109	
PNF Mansell	run out	10	
HJ Tayfield	not out	27	
ERH Fuller			
	(b 5, lb 4)	9	
	(8 wickets declared)	524	

Bowling: Blair 36-4-98-4 Fisher 34-6-78-1 Reid 24-8-36-0 Burtt 44-7-140-2 Moir 35-4-159-0 Sutcliffe 1-0-4-0

New Zealand Innings

B Sutcliffe	c McGlew b Watkins	62	b Murray		33
JG Leggat	c Fuller b Tayfield	22	c Endean b Watkins		47
FE Fisher	b Fuller	9	c Waite b Watkins		14
*WM Wallace	c Waite b Murray	4	b Tayfield		2
EM Meuli	c Endean b Murray	15	b Fuller		23
LSM Miller	c Endean b Tayfield	17	c Waite b Watkins		13
JR Reid	b Murray	1	c Waite b Murray		9
+FLH Mooney	not out	27	b Tayfield		9
AM Moir	run out	1	c Fuller b Watkins		0
TB Burtt	lbw b Fuller	10	b Tayfield		0
RW Blair	b Fuller	0	not out		6
	(b 3, nb 1)	4	(b 16)		16
	(all out)	172	(all out)		172

Bowling: Fuller 19 4-7-29-3 Watkins 27-17-29-1 Tayfield 38-15-53-2 Mansell 11-3-27-0 Murray 28-15-30-3
Fuller 27-8-43-1 Watkins 23.5-14-22-4 Tayfield 32-12-42-3 Mansell 13-2-30-0 Murray 23-16-19-2

Umpires: RG Currie and J McLellan

New Zealand v West Indies
3,5,6,7 March 1956

Result: West Indies won by 9 wickets

West Indies Innings

BH Pairaudeau	c MacGibbon b Cave	68	c Sinclair b MacGibbon		8
GS Sobers	c Barber b Reid	27			
JDC Goddard	c Beard b MacGibbon	16	not out		0
ED Weekes	c Guillen b Cave	156			
OG Smith	lbw b MacGibbon	1			
*DS Atkinson	run out	60			
+AP Binns	lbw b Beard	27	not out		5
S Ramadhin	c Beard b Reid	15			
FM King	not out	13			
DT Dewdney	run out	2			
AL Valentine	c McGregor b Reid	2			
	(b 9, lb 3, nb 5)	17			0
	(all out)	404	(1 wicket)		13

Bowling: MacGibbon 24-4-75-2 Cave 37-10-96-2 Beard 34-9-90-1 Reid 32.5-8-85-3 Sinclair 8-0-41-0
MacGibbon 3-1-6-1 Beard 2.2-0-7-0

New Zealand Innings

LSM Miller	c & b King	16	c Binns b Dewdney		7
SN McGregor	c Weekes b Smith	3	b Binns b Atkinson		41
AR MacGibbon	c Goddard b Valentine	3	b Atkinson		36
DD Taylor	run out	43	c Pairaudeau b Atkinson		77
*JR Reid	b Ramadhin	1	b Atkinson		5
JEF Beck	lbw b Sobers	55	b Smith		6
RT Barber	b Ramadhin	12	c Goddard b Ramadhin		5
+SC Guillen	b Smith	36	c Goddard b Dewdney		0
DD Beard	not out	17	c Binns b Ramadhin		5
HB Cave	b Atkinson	0	c & b Sobers		5
IM Sinclair	lbw b Atkinson	0	not out		18
	(b 11, lb 9)	20	(b 2, nb 1)		3
	(all out)	208	(all out)		208

Bowling: Dewdney 11-3-26-0 King 8.4-3-18-1 Smith 29-15-27-2 Ramadhin 30-11-63-2 Valentine 35-20-31-1 Atkinson 12.2-2-20-2 Sobers 14-11-3-1
Dewdney 17-3-54-2 Smith 14-7-23-1 Ramadhin 21-10-33-1 Valentine 15-9-18-0 Atkinson 31-12-66-5 Sobers 8.5-4-11-1

Umpires: LG Clark and WJC Gwynne

Basin Reserve, Wellington

New Zealand v England
1,2,4 March 1963

Result: England won by an innings and 47 runs

New Zealand Innings

GT Dowling	c Smith b Trueman	12	c Knight b Trueman	2
WR Playle	c Smith b Knight	23	c & b Illingworth	65
PT Barton	c Cowdrey b Trueman	0	c Barrington b Knight	3
*JR Reid	c Smith b Knight	0	c Barrington b Titmus	9
BW Sinclair	b Trueman	4	c & b Barrington	36
MJF Shrimpton	lbw b Knight	28	c Parfitt b Barrington	10
+AE Dick	c Sheppard b Trueman	7	not out	38
BW Yuile	c Illingworth b Titmus	13	b Titmus	0
RW Blair	not out	64	c Larter b Titmus	5
BD Morrison	run out	10	c Larter b Titmus	0
FJ Cameron	lbw b Barrington	12	lbw b Barrington	0
	(b 13, lb 5, nb 3)	21	(b 13, lb 4, nb 2)	19
	(all out)	194	(all out)	187

Bowling: Trueman 20-5-46-4 Larter 14-2-52-0 Knight 21-8-32-3 Titmus 18-3-40-1 Barrington 2.3-1-1-1 Dexter 1-0-2-0
Trueman 18-7-27-1 Larter 7-1-18-0 Knight 4-1-7-1 Titmus 31-15-50-4 Barrington 11-3-32-3 Illingworth 27-14-34-1

England Innings

Rev.DS Sheppard	b Blair	0
R Illingworth	c Morrison b Blair	46
KF Barrington	c Dick b Reid	76
*ER Dexter	b Morrison	31
PH Parfitt	c Dick b Morrison	0
BR Knight	c Dick b Cameron	31
FJ Titmus	run out	33
MC Cowdrey	not out	128
FS Trueman	b Cameron	3
+AC Smith	not out	69
JDF Larter		
	(b 3, lb 6, nb 2)	11
	(8 wickets declared)	428

Bowling: Blair 33-11-81-2 Morrison 31-5-129-2 Cameron 43-16-98-2 Reid 32-8-73-1 Yuile 10-1-36-0

Umpires: DP Dumbleton and WT Martin

New Zealand v South Africa
21,22,24,25 February 1964

Result: Match drawn

South Africa Innings

*TL Goddard	b Cameron	24	b Reid	40
EJ Barlow	b Cameron	22	c Ward b Cameron	92
AJ Pithey	c Chapple b Motz	31		
WS Farrer	b Reid	30	not out	38
KC Bland	c Ward b Blair	40	not out	46
+JHB Waite	b Blair	30		
DT Lindsay	b Cameron	27		
PL van der Merwe	b Motz	44		
DB Pithey	b Blair	7		
PM Pollock	c Dowling b Reid	24		
JT Partridge	not out	2		
	(b 9, lb 3, nb 9)	21	(b 2)	2
	(all out)	302	(2 wickets declared)	218

Bowling: Motz 25-3-68-2 Cameron 30-13-58-3 Blair 41-10-86-3 Reid 29.5-12-47-2 Sparling 6-1-22-0
Motz 15-2-53-0 Cameron 19-6-60-1 Blair 11-0-48-0 Reid 21-8-55-1

New Zealand Innings

GT Dowling	b Pollock	1	lbw b Bland	32
SG Gedye	lbw b Pollock	10	c van der Merwe b Pollock	52
BW Sinclair	lbw b DB Pithey	44	b Bland	0
*JR Reid	c Barlow b Partridge	16	b Goddard	12
SN McGregor	b DB Pithey	39	lbw b van der Merwe	24
JT Sparling	lbw b Pollock	49	c van der Merwe b Pollock	1
ME Chapple	c Goddard b Partridge	59	not out	0
RC Motz	c DB Pithey b Pollock	2	not out	0
+JT Ward	b Pollock	5		
RW Blair	b Pollock	5		
FJ Cameron	not out	1		
	(b 10, lb 5, nb 7)	22	(b 6, lb 7, w 1, nb 3)	17
	(all out)	253	(6 wickets)	138

Bowling: Pollock 31.5-9-47-6 Partridge 45-24-50-2 Goddard 38-21-42-0 Barlow 11-0-38-0 DB Pithey 24-11-53-2 Bland 3-2-1-0
Pollock 16-4-31-2 Partridge 14-8-10-0 Goddard 16-10-11-1 Barlow 2-1-13-0 DB Pithey 14-3-34-0 Bland 9-3-16-2 van der Merwe 5-4-6-1

Umpires: DP Dumbleton and WT Martin

New Zealand v Pakistan
22,23,25,26 January 1965

Result: Match drawn

New Zealand Innings

SG Gedye	b Asif Iqbal	1	b Arif Butt	26
GT Dowling	c Javed Burki b Pervez Sajjad	29	b Arif Butt	19
BW Sinclair	c Nasim-ul-Ghani b Saeed Ahmed	65	b Saeed Ahmed b Pervez Sajjad	17
BE Congdon	c Naushad Ali b Asif Iqbal	42	b Asif Iqbal	30
*JR Reid	b Arif Butt	97	c Saeed Ahmed b Pervez Sajjad	14
SN McGregor	lbw b Asif Iqbal	11	not out	37
BW Yuile	b Asif Iqbal	4	run out	7
+AE Dick	b Arif Butt	1		
RC Motz	b Asif Iqbal	0	b Arif Butt	13
RO Collinge	not out	0		
FJ Cameron	lbw b Arif Butt	0		
	(b 2, lb 14)	16	(b 12, lb 3, nb 1)	16
	(all out)	266	(7 wickets declared)	179

Bowling: Arif Butt 22.2-10-46-3 Asif Iqbal 25-11-48-5 Pervez Sajjad 24-7-48-1 Intikhab Alam 17-6-35-0 Saeed Ahmed 16-7-40-1 Nasim-ul-Ghani 3-1-5-0 Mohammad Ilyas 7-1-28-0
Arif Butt 29-10-62-3 Asif Iqbal 20.4-6-33-1 Pervez Sajjad 25-5-61-2 Intikhab Alam 5-1-7-0 Saeed Ahmed 1-1-0-0

Pakistan Innings

+Naushad Ali	run out	11	c & b Motz	3
Mohammad Ilyas	b Collinge	13	c Reid b Motz	4
Saeed Ahmed	c Congdon b Motz	11	c Yuile b Collinge	4
Javed Burki	b Motz	0	c Dick b Collinge	25
*Hanif Mohammad	b Collinge	5	b Collinge	25
Abdul Kadir	c & b Motz	46	b Motz	0
Nasim-ul-Ghani	b Cameron	16	c Dowling b Reid	23
Asif Iqbal	c Sinclair b Yuile	30	not out	52
Intikhab Alam	b Motz	28	not out	13
Arif Butt	b Yuile	20		
Pervez Sajjad	not out	1		
	(b 2, lb 4)	6	(b 8, lb 6, w 1, nb 1)	16
	(all out)	187	(7 wickets)	140

Bowling: Collinge 17-6-51-2 Cameron 19-11-33-1 Motz 20-9-45-4 Yuile 26-16-28-2 Reid 13-6-24-0
Collinge 13-3-43-3 Cameron 8-5-10-0 Motz 15-6-34-3 Yuile 8-2-21-0 Reid 8-3-16-1

Umpires: DEA Copps and WT Martin

New Zealand v India
29 February, 1,2,4 March 1968

Result: India won by 8 wickets

New Zealand Innings

*GT Dowling	c Wadekar b Surti	15	c Abid Ali b Nadkarni	14
BAG Murray	run out	10	c Pataudi b Nadkarni	22
BE Congdon	c Wadekar b Surti	4	c Jaisimha b Bedi	51
MG Burgess	c Surti b Prasanna	66	c Pataudi b Nadkarni	60
K Thomson	b Surti	25	c Wadekar b Nadkarni	0
V Pollard	c Engineer b Nadkarni	24	c Abid Ali b Nadkarni	1
BR Taylor	st Engineer b Prasanna	17	c Subramanya b Prasanna	28
RC Motz	c Surti b Prasanna	5	c Subramanya b Prasanna	9
RO Collinge	c Wadekar b Prasanna	5	c sub b Nadkarni	5
JC Alabaster	not out	3	not out	2
+RI Harford	c Engineer b Prasanna	1	c Subramanya b Prasanna	0
	(b 2, nb 9)	11	(b 5, lb 2)	7
	(all out)	186	(all out)	199

Bowling: Surti 22-6-44-3 Abid Ali 8-0-31-0 Jaisimha 22-11-34-0 Bedi 20-12-0 Nadkarni 17-8-22-1 Prasanna 18.2-6-32-5
Surti 8-1-31-0 Jaisimha 5-1-10-0 Bedi 16-5-42-1 Nadkarni 30-12-43-6 Prasanna 20.2-3-56-3 Subramanya 2-1-10-0

India Innings

S Abid Ali	c Harford b Collinge	11	c Harford b Murray	36
+FM Engineer	run out	44	c Harford b Thomson	18
AL Wadekar	c Harford b Collinge	143	not out	5
RF Surti	c Congdon b Taylor	10	not out	0
*Nawab of Pataudi jnr	c Harford b Taylor	30		
CG Borde	c Harford b Collinge	10		
ML Jaisimha	c Harford b Alabaster	20		
RG Nadkarni	c Murray b Alabaster	3		
V Subramanya	not out	32		
EAS Prasanna	b Taylor	1		
BS Bedi	run out	8		
	(lb 8, nb 7)	15		0
	(all out)	327	(2 wickets)	59

Bowling: Collinge 18-3-65-3 Motz 20-5-62-0 Taylor 27.1-9-59-3 Alabaster 18-2-64-2 Pollard 25-6-62-0
Collinge 2-0-7-0 Motz 3-0-21-0 Alabaster 1-0-8-0 Pollard 1-0-7-0 Thomson 3.3-1-9-1 Burgess 2-0-7-0 Murray 1-1-0-1

Umpires: DEA Copps and WT Martin

New Zealand v West Indies
7,8,10,11 March 1969

Result: New Zealand won by 6 wickets

West Indies Innings

RC Fredericks	c Milburn b Motz	15	c Hastings b Motz	2
MC Carew	c Taylor b Motz	17	run out	1
SM Nurse	b Motz	21	c Congdon b Cunis	16
BF Butcher	lbw b Motz	50	lbw b Yuile	59
CH Lloyd	c Milburn b Cunis	44	b Cunis	1
*GS Sobers	c Morgan b Motz	20	c Pollard b Cunis	39
DAJ Holford	lbw b Cunis	1	b Yuile	12
+JL Hendriks	not out	54	b Motz	5
CC Griffith	c Congdon b Motz	31	b Yuile	4
RM Edwards	run out	22	run out	1
LR Gibbs	c Milburn b Yuile	2	not out	1
	(b 3, lb 6, w 1, nb 10)	20	(nb 7)	7
	(all out)	297	(all out)	148

Bowling: Motz 18-2-69-6 Taylor 14-1-67-0 Cunis 18-4-76-2 Yuile 9.4-4-27-1 Pollard 2-0-19-0 Morgan 4-0-19-0
Motz 13-3-44-2 Taylor 6-0-36-0 Cunis 12-2-36-3 Yuile 6.4-0-25-3

New Zealand Innings

*GT Dowling	c Gibbs b Griffith	21	c Hendriks b Griffith	23
GM Turner	c Sobers b Edwards	74	c Griffith b Edwards	1
BE Congdon	c Sobers b Carew	52	c Griffith b Edwards	4
BF Hastings	c Hendriks b Edwards	8	not out	62
V Pollard	c Hendriks b Griffith	9		
RW Morgan	c Gibbs b Edwards	0	not out	16
BW Yuile	c Hendriks b Sobers	33	lbw b Gibbs	37
BR Taylor	c Holford b Griffith	33		
RC Motz	c Gibbs b Edwards	18		
RS Cunis	lbw b Edwards	5		
+BD Milburn	not out	4		
	(lb 7, nb 18)	25	(b 13, lb 4, w 1, nb 5)	23
	(all out)	282	(4 wickets)	166

Bowling: Griffith 26-2-92-3 Edwards 24.7-5-84-5 Sobers 9-2-22-1 Gibbs 14-3-41-0 Carew 10-3-18-1
Griffith 15-6-29-1 Edwards 11-2-42-2 Sobers 8-2-22-0 Gibbs 14.5-3-50-1

Umpires: ECA MacKintosh and RWR Shortt

New Zealand v Pakistan
2,3,4,5 February 1973

Result: Match drawn

Pakistan Innings

Sadiq Mohammad	c sub b Hadlee	166	c Congdon b Howarth	68
Talat Ali	c Turner b Collinge	6	lbw b Taylor	2
Zaheer Abbas	c Hadlee b Taylor	2	c Wadsworth b Collinge	8
Majid Khan	c Congdon b Taylor	79	c Burgess b Howarth	79
Asif Iqbal	c & b Hadlee	39	c Hastings b Howarth	23
Wasim Raja	c Congdon b Taylor	10	c sub b Howarth	41
*Intikhab Alam	run out	16	not out	53
+Wasim Bari	retired hurt			
Saleem Altaf	c Howarth b Taylor	14	not out	6
Sarfraz Nawaz	c Wadsworth b Collinge	9		
Pervez Sajjad	not out	1		
	(b 1, lb 5, nb 5)	11	(b 4, lb 2, nb 4)	10
	(all out)	357	(6 wickets declared)	290

Bowling: Hadlee 18-0-84-2 Collinge 20-1-63-2 Taylor 24.4-1-110-4 Howarth 25-6-73-0 Congdon 3-0-16-0
Hadlee 7-0-28-0 Collinge 13-1-50-1 Taylor 11-2-63-1 Howarth 31-7-99-4 Congdon 9-0-40-0

New Zealand Innings

GM Turner	c Intikhab Alam b Sarfraz Nawaz	43	not out	49
TW Jarvis	c Majid Khan b Sarfraz Nawaz	0	c Majid Khan b Saleem Altaf	0
*BE Congdon	run out	19	c & b Saleem Altaf	0
BF Hastings	c Majid Khan b Sarfraz Nawaz	72	c Wasim Bari b Saleem Altaf	0
MG Burgess	c & b Intikhab Alam	79	not out	21
BR Taylor	c Zaheer Abbas b Majid Khan	5		
+KJ Wadsworth	c Asif Iqbal b Sarfraz Nawaz	28		
RJ Hadlee	c Asif Iqbal b Saleem Altaf	46		
HJ Howarth	not out	3		
RO Collinge	b Saleem Altaf	0		
JM Parker	absent hurt	0		
	(b 9, lb 9, nb 12)	30	(lb 1, w 1, nb 6)	8
	(all out)	325	(3 wickets)	78

Bowling: Saleem Altaf 16.4-3-70-2 Sarfraz Nawaz 29.5-12-6-4 Asif Iqbal 21-6-0 Intikhab Alam 13-1-55-1 Pervez Sajjad 5-0-19-0 Majid Khan 9-2-19-1
Saleem Altaf 6-1-15-3 Sarfraz Nawaz 5-1-15-0 Intikhab Alam 3-0-11-0 Pervez Sajjad 4-1-5-0 Wasim Raja 4-0-10-0 Sadiq Mohammad 3-0-13-0 Talat Ali 1-0-1-0

Umpires: ECA MacKintosh and WT Martin

New Zealand v Australia
1,2,3,5,6 March 1974

Result: Match drawn

Australia Innings

KR Stackpole	b Webb	10	c Collinge	27
IR Redpath	c Coney b Hadlee	19	c Howarth b Congdon	93
*IM Chappell	c Wadsworth b Webb	145	c Hadlee b Howarth	121
GS Chappell	not out	247	c Wadsworth b Collinge	133
IC Davis	c Wadsworth b Hadlee	16	c Wadsworth b Howarth	8
KD Walters	c Howarth b Collinge	32	c Morrison b Hadlee	8
+RW Marsh	lbw b Congdon	22	c Collinge b Congdon	17
KJ O'Keeffe			c Howarth b Congdon	2
MHN Walker			not out	22
AA Mallett			not out	4
G Dymock				
	(b 1, lb 4, nb 15)	20	(b 4, lb 4, w 1, nb 16)	25
	(6 wickets declared)	511	(8 wickets)	460

Bowling: Webb 21-1-114-2 Collinge 24-3-103-1 Hadlee 27-7-107-2 Howarth 21-0-113-0 Congdon 12.5-0-54-1
Webb 19-0-93-0 Collinge 19-3-60-2 Hadlee 21-2-106-1 Howarth 25-3-97-2 Congdon 13-1-60-3 Coney 2-0-13-0 Hastings 2-0-6-0

New Zealand Innings

GM Turner	c Redpath b O'Keeffe	79
JM Parker	lbw b Walker	10
JFM Morrison	b Walker	66
*BE Congdon	c Davis b Mallett	132
BF Hastings	c IM Chappell b Dymock	101
JV Coney	c GS Chappell b Walker	13
+KJ Wadsworth	b Dymock	5
DR Hadlee	c Davis b O'Keeffe	9
RO Collinge	run out	2
HJ Howarth	not out	29
MG Webb	c O'Keeffe b Dymock	12
	(b 10, lb 5, nb 11)	26
	(all out)	484

Bowling: Walker 41-11-107-3 Dymock 35-7-77-3 Walters 8-1-39-0 Mallett 41-8-117-1 O'Keeffe 33-9-83-2 GS Chappell 7-0-27-0 IM Chappell 4-0-8-0

Umpires: DEA Copps and FR Goodall

New Zealand v India
13,14,15,17 February 1976

Result: New Zealand won by an innings and 33 runs

India Innings

SM Gavaskar	c Wadsworth b RJ Hadlee	22	absent hurt	0
DB Vengsarkar	c Wadsworth b RJ Hadlee	20	c Turner b Collinge	4
S Amarnath	c Roberts b RJ Hadlee	2	c Burgess b RJ Hadlee	27
GR Viswanath	c Turner b DR Hadlee	4	c Congdon b RJ Hadlee	20
BP Patel	c Congdon b Cairns	81	c Wadsworth b RJ Hadlee	3
M Amarnath	lbw b Collinge	26	c Roberts b DR Hadlee	13
S Madan Lal	b DR Hadlee	3	not out	4
+SMH Kirmani	c Wadsworth b RJ Hadlee	49	c Burgess b RJ Hadlee	1
EAS Prasanna	not out	0	b RJ Hadlee	0
*BS Bedi	run out	2	b RJ Hadlee	2
BS Chandrasekhar	b Cairns	0	b RJ Hadlee	0
	(lb 8, nb 3)	11	(b 5, lb 2, nb 2)	9
	(all out)	220	(all out)	81

Bowling: Collinge 12-1-33-1 Cairns 20.7-2-57-2 DR Hadlee 18-1-51-2 RJ Hadlee 14-1-35-4 Congdon 9-1-33-0
Collinge 5-0-21-1 Cairns 4-1-9-0 DR Hadlee 9-2-19-1 RJ Hadlee 8.3-0-23-7

New Zealand Innings

*GM Turner	st Kirmani b Bedi	64
JFM Morrison	c Kirmani b Madan Lal	12
BE Congdon	c Viswanath b Chandrasekhar	52
JM Parker	c Gavaskar b Bedi	5
MG Burgess	lbw b Madan Lal	95
ADG Roberts	c Kirmani b Chandrasekhar	0
+KJ Wadsworth	c Gavaskar b Bedi	10
BL Cairns	c sub b M Amarnath	47
RJ Hadlee	c Prasanna b Madan Lal	12
DR Hadlee	c Kirmani b Chandrasekhar	13
RO Collinge	not out	5
	(lb 15, nb 4)	19
	(all out)	334

Bowling: M Amarnath 18.2-2-60-1 Madan Lal 38-4-116-3 Bedi 27-6-63-3 Chandrasekhar 22.5-2-55-3 Prasanna 8-2-21-0

Umpires: WRC Gardiner and RL Monteith

New Zealand v England
10,11,12,14,15 February 1978

Result: New Zealand won by 72 runs

New Zealand Innings

JG Wright	lbw b Botham	55	c Roope b Willis	19
RW Anderson	c Taylor b Old	28	lbw b Old	26
GP Howarth	c Botham b Old	13	c Edmonds b Willis	21
*MG Burgess	b Willis	9	c Boycott b Botham	6
BE Congdon	c Taylor b Old	44	c Roope b Willis	0
JM Parker	c Rose b Willis	16	c Edmonds b Willis	4
+WK Lees	c Taylor b Old	1	lbw b Hendrick	11
RJ Hadlee	not out	27	c Boycott b Willis	2
DR Hadlee	c Taylor b Old	1	c Roope b Botham	2
RO Collinge	b Old	1	c Edmonds b Hendrick	6
SL Boock	b Botham	4	not out	0
	(b 12, lb 3, w 1, nb 13)	29	(b 2, lb 9, w 2, nb 13)	26
	(all out)	228	(all out)	123

Bowling: Willis 25-7-65-2 Hendrick 17-2-46-0 Old 30-11-54-6 Edmonds 3-1-7-0 Botham 12.6-2-27-2
Willis 15-2-32-5 Hendrick 10-2-16-2 Old 9-2-32-1 Edmonds 1-0-4-0 Botham 9.3-3-13-2

England Innings

BC Rose	c Lees b Collinge	21	not out	5
*G Boycott	c Congdon b Collinge	77	b Collinge	1
G Miller	b Boock	24	c Anderson b Collinge	4
+RW Taylor	c & b Collinge	8	run out	4
DW Randall	c Burgess b RJ Hadlee	4	lbw b Collinge	9
GRJ Roope	c Lees b RJ Hadlee	37	c Lees b RJ Hadlee	0
IT Botham	c Burgess b RJ Hadlee	7	c Boock b RJ Hadlee	19
CM Old	b RJ Hadlee	10	lbw b RJ Hadlee	9
PH Edmonds	lbw b Congdon	4	c Parker b RJ Hadlee	11
M Hendrick	lbw b Congdon	0	c Parker b RJ Hadlee	0
RGD Willis	not out	6	c Howarth b RJ Hadlee	3
	(lb 4, nb 13)	17	(nb 3)	3
	(all out)	215	(all out)	64

Bowling: RJ Hadlee 28-5-74-4 Collinge 18-5-42-3 DR Hadlee 21-5-47-0 Boock 10-5-21-1 Congdon 17.4-11-14-2
Collinge 13-5-35-3 RJ Hadlee 13.3-4-26-6 DR Hadlee 1-1-0-0

Umpires: WRC Gardiner and RL Monteith

New Zealand v India
21,22,23,25 February 1981

Result: New Zealand won by 62 runs

New Zealand Innings

JG Wright	c Binny b Yograj Singh	32	c Viswanath b Kapil Dev	8
BA Edgar	c Kirmani b Patil	39	c Patil b Binny	28
JF Reid	c Kirmani b Patil	46	lbw b Kapil Dev	7
*GP Howarth	not out	137	c Kirmani b Patil	7
JV Coney	c & b Shastri	4	c sub b Kapil Dev	8
GN Edwards	c Kirmani b Kapil Dev	23	c sub b Kapil Dev	6
+IDS Smith	c Vengsarkar b Kapil Dev	20	not out	15
RJ Hadlee	c Kirmani b Binny	20	c Kirmani b Binny	7
BL Cairns	c Gavaskar b Kapil Dev	13	c Vengsarkar b Shastri	0
MC Snedden	b Shastri	2	c Vengsarkar b Shastri	0
GB Troup	c Gavaskar b Shastri	0	c Vengsarkar b Shastri	0
	(b 4, lb 17, w 1, nb 17)	39	(lb 10, w 2, nb 2)	14
	(all out)	375	(all out)	100

Bowling: Kapil Dev 38-9-112-3 Yograj Singh 15-3-63-1 Binny 22-4-67-1 Shastri 28-9-54-3 Patil 16-3-40-2
Kapil Dev 16-4-34-4 Binny 12-4-26-2 Shastri 3-0-9-3 Patil 17-10-12-1 Azad 1-0-5-0

India Innings

*SM Gavaskar	b Cairns	23	b Snedden	12
CPS Chauhan	c Coney b Troup	17	b Hadlee	1
DB Vengsarkar	lbw b Cairns	39	c Smith b Hadlee	26
GR Viswanath	b Cairns	0	b Troup	9
SM Patil	c Smith b Troup	64	c Smith b Cairns	42
KBJ Azad	b Cairns	20	b Hadlee	16
N Kapil Dev	c Smith b Troup	0	c Hadlee b Troup	9
+SMH Kirmani	run out	13	b Cairns	11
RMH Binny	b Snedden	11	not out	26
RJ Shastri	not out	3	c Smith b Snedden	19
B Yograj Singh	c Smith b Cairns	4	c Smith b Hadlee	6
	(b 10, lb 13, nb 6)	29	(b 2, lb 5, nb 6)	13
	(all out)	223	(all out)	190

Bowling: Hadlee 16-4-62-0 Cairns 19.4-8-33-5 Snedden 20-7-56-1 Troup 17-5-43-3
Hadlee 22.3-7-65-4 Cairns 19-8-30-2 Snedden 17-4-39-2 Troup 13-4-34-2 Coney 4-1-9-0

Umpires: FR Goodall and SJ Woodward

New Zealand v Australia
26,27,28 February, 1,2 March 1982

Result: Match drawn

New Zealand Innings

BA Edgar	lbw b Alderman	55
JG Wright	c Chappell b Yardley	38
JFM Morrison	b Thomson	15
*GP Howarth	not out	58
JV Coney	lbw b Yardley	1
MD Crowe	run out	9
RJ Hadlee	b Thomson	21
+IDS Smith	c Chappell b Yardley	11
BL Cairns	not out	19
MC Snedden		
EJ Chatfield		
	(b 5, lb 19, w 4, nb 11)	39
	(7 wickets declared)	266

Bowling: Thomson 26-13-35-2 Alderman 44-20-93-1 Lillee 15-5-32-0 Chappell 8-2-18-0 Yardley 23-10-49-3

Australia Innings

GM Wood	b Cairns	41
BM Laird	not out	27
J Dyson	not out	12
*GS Chappell		
KJ Hughes		
AR Border		
+RW Marsh		
B Yardley		
DK Lillee		
JR Thomson		
TM Alderman		
	(lb 2, nb 3)	5
	(1 wicket)	85

Bowling: Hadlee 7-2-15-0 Snedden 8-1-24-0 Cairns 11-4-20-1 Chatfield 8-5-7-0 Crowe 4-1-14-0

Umpires: FR Goodall and SJ Woodward

New Zealand v Sri Lanka
11,12,13,14,15 March 1983

Result: New Zealand won by 6 wickets

Sri Lanka Innings

S Wettimuny	c Cairns b Hadlee	8	c Coney b Hadlee	9
MD Wettimuny	c Coney b Snedden	6	c Cairns b Snedden	0
ERNS Fernando	c Wright b Hadlee	12	c Lees b Snedden	12
Y Goonasekera	c Lees b Cairns	13	c Lees b Chatfield	23
RS Madugalle	run out	79	c Lees b Hadlee	13
*DS de Silva	lbw b Chatfield	61	c Lees b Snedden	0
+SAR Silva	c Lees b Chatfield	8	c Crowe b Hadlee	0
JR Ratnayeke	not out	29	b Hadlee	12
S Jeganathan	c Lees b Chatfield	5	c Lees b Chatfield	0
RJ Ratnayake	b Snedden	12	c sub b Chatfield	1
VB John	c Wright b Chatfield	0	not out	8
	(b 1, lb 5, nb 1)	7	(b 5, lb 10)	15
	(all out)	240	(all out)	93

Bowling: Hadlee 25-9-47-2 Snedden 24-5-56-2 Chatfield 26.5-7-66-4 Cairns 20-5-53-1 Coney 5-2-11-0
Hadlee 17-5-34-4 Snedden 17-7-21-3 Chatfield 12-5-15-3 Cairns 7-2-8-0

New Zealand Innings

GM Turner	c Goonasekera b John	10	b Ratnayeke	29
BA Edgar	c John b Ratnayake	10	not out	47
JG Wright	c de Silva b Ratnayeke	14		
*GP Howarth	c S Wettimuny b de Silva	36	c Silva b John	1
JJ Crowe	c Silva b Ratnayeke	36	b Ratnayake	11
JV Coney	c Goonasekera b John	2	c Goonasekera b de Silva	17
RJ Hadlee	c Goonasekera b John	30	not out	17
+WK Lees	c Goonasekera b John	0		
BL Cairns	c de Silva b John	45		
MC Snedden	lbw b Ratnayeke	5		
EJ Chatfield	not out	2		
	(b 4, lb 3, w 3, nb 1)	11	(lb 11, nb 1)	12
	(all out)	201	(4 wickets)	134

Bowling: Ratnayake 24-5-81-4 John 25.2-9-60-5 Ratnayeke 14-3-36-0 de Silva 9-5-13-1
Ratnayake 15-0-46-1 John 8-2-38-1 Ratnayeke 8.1-4-20-1 de Silva 6-1-18-1

Umpires: IC Higginson and SJ Woodward

New Zealand v England
20,21,22,23,24 January 1984

Result: Match drawn

New Zealand Innings

JG Wright	c Cook b Botham	17	c Foster b Cook	35
BA Edgar	c Taylor b Botham	9	c Taylor b Willis	30
*GP Howarth	c Gower b Botham	15	run out	34
MD Crowe	b Willis	13	c Botham b Gatting	100
JJ Crowe	c Taylor b Foster	52	lbw b Botham	3
JV Coney	c Gower b Cook	27	not out	174
RJ Hadlee	c Gatting b Botham	24	c Lamb b Foster	18
MC Snedden	c Taylor b Willis	11	c Taylor b Foster	16
+IDS Smith	lbw b Botham	24	b Cook	29
BL Cairns	c Gatting b Willis	3	c sub b Willis	64
EJ Chatfield	not out	4	b Cook	0
	(b 4, lb 9, nb 7)	20	(b 4, lb 14, w 2, nb 14)	34
	(all out)	219	(all out)	537

Bowling: Willis 19-7-37-3 Botham 27.4-8-59-5 Foster 24-9-60-1 Cook 23-11-43-1
Willis 37-8-102-2 Botham 36-6-137-1 Foster 37-12-91-2 Cook 66.3-26-153-3 Gatting 8-4-14-1 Smith 3-1-6-0

England Innings

CJ Tavare	b Cairns	9	not out	36
CL Smith	c Hadlee b Cairns	27	not out	30
DI Gower	c Hadlee b Cairns	33		
AJ Lamb	c MD Crowe b Cairns	13		
MW Gatting	lbw b Cairns	19		
IT Botham	c JJ Crowe b Cairns	138		
DW Randall	c MD Crowe b Hadlee	164		
+RW Taylor	run out	14		
NGB Cook	c Smith b Cairns	7		
NA Foster	c Howarth b Hadlee	10		
*RGD Willis	not out	5		
	(lb 8, nb 16)	24	(nb 3)	3
	(all out)	463	(0 wickets)	69

Bowling: Hadlee 31.5-6-97-2 Snedden 21-3-101-0 Cairns 45-10-143-7 Chatfield 28-6-68-0 MD Crowe 3-0-20-0 Coney 4-1-10-0
Snedden 7-2-28-0 Chatfield 5-0-24-0 MD Crowe 6-1-11-0 Edgar 3-1-3-0 JJ Crowe 1-1-0-0

Umpires: FR Goodall and SJ Woodward

New Zealand v Pakistan
18,19,20,21,22 January 1985

Result: Match drawn

New Zealand Innings

*GP Howarth	run out	33	c Anil Dalpat b Azeem Hafeez	17
JG Wright	c Shoaib Moh'd b Azeem Hafeez	11	lbw b Mudassar Nazar	11
JF Reid	b Azeem Hafeez	148	c Abdul Qadir b Iqbal Qasim	3
MD Crowe	c Anil Dalpat b Iqbal Qasim	37	c Abdul Qadir b Iqbal Qasim	33
JJ Crowe	c Shoaib Mohammad b Iqbal Qasim	4	not out	19
JV Coney	b Abdul Qadir	11	not out	18
RJ Hadlee	c Javed Miandad b Azeem Hafeez	89		
+IDS Smith	c & b Mudassar Nazar	65		
BL Cairns	b Azeem Hafeez	36		
SL Boock	c Anil Dalpat b Azeem Hafeez	0		
EJ Chatfield	not out	3		
	(b 5, lb 12, nb 1)	18	(lb 2)	2
	(all out)	492	(4 wickets)	103

Bowling: Mudassar Nazar 29-5-80-1 Azeem Hafeez 48-12-127-5 Abdul Qadir 51-13-142-1 Iqbal Qasim 41-5-105-2 Wasim Raja 2-0-10-0 Shoaib Mohammad 1-0-4-0 Javed Miandad 3-1-7-0
Mudassar Nazar 6-3-13-1 Azeem Hafeez 15-3-51-1 Abdul Qadir 8-1-18-0 Iqbal Qasim 16-8-19-2

Pakistan Innings

Mudassar Nazar	c & b Boock	38	
Mohsin Khan	c Wright b Boock	40	
Shoaib Mohammad	run out	7	
Qasim Umar	b Boock	8	
*Javed Miandad	c Smith b Boock	30	
Saleem Malik	c Cairns b Hadlee	66	
Wasim Raja	c MD Crowe b Boock	14	
Abdul Qadir	c Smith b Hadlee	54	
+Anil Dalpat	c Smith b Chatfield	15	
Iqbal Qasim	not out	27	
Azeem Hafeez	c Boock b Cairns	3	
	(b 9, lb 9, nb 2)	20	
	(all out)	322	

Bowling: Hadlee 32-11-70-2 Cairns 27.4-5-65-1 Chatfield 25-10-52-1 Boock 45-18-117-5

Umpires: GC Morris and SJ Woodward

New Zealand v Australia
21,22,23,24,25 February 1986

Result: Match drawn

Australia Innings

DC Boon	c Smith b Troup	70	
GR Marsh	c Coney b Chatfield	43	
WB Phillips	b Gillespie	32	
*AR Border	lbw b Hadlee	13	
GM Ritchie	b Troup	92	
GRJ Matthews	c Rutherford b Coney	130	
SR Waugh	c Smith b Coney	11	
+TJ Zoehrer	c sub b Coney	18	
CJ McDermott	b Hadlee	2	
BA Reid	not out	0	
SP Davis	c & b Hadlee	0	
	(b 2, lb 9, w 4, nb 9)	24	
	(all out)	435	

Bowling: Hadlee 37.1-5-116-3 Chatfield 36-10-96-1 Troup 28-6-86-2 Gillespie 27-2-79-1 Coney 18-7-47-3

New Zealand Innings

TJ Franklin	c Border b McDermott	0	
BA Edgar	c Waugh b Matthews	38	
JF Reid	c Phillips b Reid	32	
SR Gillespie	c Border b Reid	28	
MD Crowe	b Matthews	19	
KR Rutherford	c sub b Reid	65	
*JV Coney	not out	101	
RJ Hadlee	not out	72	
+IDS Smith			
GB Troup			
EJ Chatfield			
	(b 2, lb 6, w 1, nb 15)	24	
	(6 wickets)	379	

Bowling: McDermott 25.3-5-80-1 Davis 25-4-70-0 Reid 31-6-104-3 Matthews 37-10-107-2 Border 4-3-1-0 Waugh 4-1-9-0

Umpires: FR Goodall and SJ Woodward

New Zealand v West Indies
20,21,22,23,24 February 1987

Result: Match drawn

New Zealand Innings

JG Wright	c Garner b Richards	75	c & b Gomes	138
KR Rutherford	c Logie b Garner	6	lbw b Garner	6
*JV Coney	c Logie b Marshall	3	c Richards b Garner	4
MD Crowe	lbw b Walsh	3	c Holding b Richards	119
DN Patel	c Garner b Walsh	18	b Walsh	20
JJ Crowe	c Logie b Garner	37	not out	27
JG Bracewell	lbw b Garner	17	not out	28
RJ Hadlee	not out	35		
+IDS Smith	lbw b Garner	0		
SL Boock	c Garner b Marshall	3		
EJ Chatfield	lbw b Garner	0		
	(lb 7, nb 24)	31	(b 10, lb 10, nb 24)	44
	(all out)	228	(5 wickets declared)	386

Bowling: Marshall 22-3-57-2 Garner 27-5-51-5 Walsh 12-1-46-2 Holding 16-4-34-0 Richards 11-3-32-1 Gomes 1-0-1-0
Marshall 20-6-43-0 Garner 30-9-72-2 Walsh 34-13-59-1 Holding 21-4-65-0 Richards 47-13-86-1 Gomes 21-6-37-1 Richardson 4-1-4-0

West Indies Innings

CG Greenidge	c Rutherford b Chatfield	78	c Rutherford b Boock	25
DL Haynes	b Bracewell	121	c Hadlee b Boock	13
HA Gomes	c Smith b Hadlee	18	not out	8
RB Richardson	b Boock	37	not out	0
*IVA Richards	c Smith b Chatfield	24		
AL Logie	c Coney b Hadlee	3		
+PJL Dujon	c Smith b Chatfield	22		
MD Marshall	c & b Boock	30		
MA Holding	c sub b Chatfield	0		
J Garner	c Hadlee b Boock	0		
CA Walsh	not out	1		
	(b 1, lb 8, w 1, nb 1)	11	(b 3, lb 1)	4
	(all out)	345	(2 wickets)	50

Bowling: Hadlee 31-9-77-2 Chatfield 39-14-102-4 Coney 3-0-8-0 Bracewell 14-5-47-1 Boock 35-14-76-3 MD Crowe 3-1-13-0 Patel 3-0-13-0
Hadlee 4-0-12-0 Chatfield 4-0-13-0 Bracewell 7-2-13-0 Boock 7-4-8-2

Umpires: BL Aldridge and SJ Woodward

New Zealand v England
3,4,5,6,7 March 1988

Result: Match drawn

New Zealand Innings

*JG Wright	c Fairbrother b Capel	36	
TJ Franklin	lbw b DeFreitas	14	
RH Vance	run out	47	
MD Crowe	lbw b Gatting	143	
MJ Greatbatch	c DeFreitas b Emburey	68	
KR Rutherford	not out	107	
JG Bracewell	c Fairbrother b Capel	54	
+IDS Smith	not out	33	
DK Morrison			
SL Boock			
EJ Chatfield			
	(lb 10)	10	
	(6 wickets declared)	512	

Bowling: Dilley 11-1-36-0 DeFreitas 50.1-21-110-1 Capel 39-7-129-2 Emburey 45.5-10-99-1 Hemmings 45-15-107-0 Gatting 6-1-21-1

England Innings

BC Broad	b Boock	61	
MD Moxon	not out	81	
RT Robinson	c Smith b Chatfield	0	
*MW Gatting	not out	33	
NH Fairbrother			
DJ Capel			
JE Emburey			
+BN French			
PAJ DeFreitas			
EE Hemmings			
GR Dilley			
	(lb 6, nb 2)	8	
	(2 wickets)	183	

Bowling: Morrison 6-0-41-0 Chatfield 23-10-38-1 Bracewell 23-9-44-0 Boock 26-9-53-1 Rutherford 1-0-1-0

Umpires: BL Aldridge and SJ Woodward

New Zealand v Pakistan
10,11,12,13,14 February 1989

Result: Match drawn

New Zealand Innings

RH Vance	c Saleem Yousuf b Mudassar Nazar	5	lbw b Imran Khan	44
*JG Wright	c Saleem Yousuf b Mudassar Nazar	7	c Javed Miandad b Imran Khan	19
AH Jones	c Shoaib Mohammad b Saleem Jaffar	86	c sub (Rameez Raja) b Saleem Jaffar	39
MD Crowe	c Javed Miandad b Saleem Jaffar	174	lbw b Saleem Jaffar	0
DN Patel	lbw b Imran Khan	0	b Saleem Jaffar	8
JJ Crowe	b Abdul Qadir	39	c Saleem Jaffar	23
JG Bracewell	b Imran Khan	15	lbw b Saleem Jaffar	0
RJ Hadlee	c Rizwan-uz-Zaman b Saleem Jaffar	32	c sub (Rameez Raja) b Imran Khan	7
+IDS Smith	not out	40	not out	29
DK Morrison	lbw b Imran Khan	0	not out	1
EJ Chatfield	run out	14		
	(b 10, lb 14, nb 11)	35	(b 10, lb 6, nb 6)	22
	(all out)	447	(8 wickets)	186

Bowling: Imran Khan 46.4-18-75-3 Saleem Jaffar 34-5-94-3 Mudassar Nazar 22-5-59-2 Aaqib Javed 34-5-103-0 Abdul Qadir 29-4-83-1 Aamer Malik 4-1-9-0
Imran Khan 17-8-34-3 Aaqib Javed 13-1-57-0 Abdul Qadir 14-3-39-0 Saleem Jaffar 17-4-40-5

Pakistan Innings

Mudassar Nazar	c & b Morrison	6	
Rizwan-uz-Zaman	lbw b Hadlee	18	
Shoaib Mohammad	b Hadlee	163	
Javed Miandad	lbw b Hadlee	118	
Saleem Malik	c Smith b Bracewell	38	
*Imran Khan	b Chatfield	71	
Aamer Malik	not out	8	
+Saleem Yousuf	c Jones b Hadlee	4	
Abdul Qadir	not out	0	
Saleem Jaffar			
Aaqib Javed			
	(b 1, lb 8, nb 3)	12	
	(7 wickets declared)	438	

Bowling: Hadlee 54-14-101-4 Morrison 36-10-96-1 Chatfield 53-21-82-1 Patel 12-3-27-0 Bracewell 40-8-123-1

Umpires: RS Dunne and SJ Woodward

Basin Reserve, Wellington

New Zealand v Australia
15,16,17,18,19 March 1990

Result: New Zealand won by 9 wickets

Australia Innings

MA Taylor	lbw b Morrison	4	lbw b Hadlee	5
GR Marsh	b Morrison	4	c Rutherford b Bracewell	41
DC Boon	lbw b Hadlee	0	c Smith b Bracewell	12
*AR Border	lbw b Morrison	1	not out	78
DM Jones	c Wright b Snedden	20	lbw b Morrison	0
SR Waugh	b Hadlee	25	c Greatbatch b Hadlee	25
+IA Healy	b Snedden	0	c Rutherford b Bracewell	10
PL Taylor	c Wright b Hadlee	29	c Smith b Morrison	87
GD Campbell	lbw b Hadlee	4	b Bracewell	0
CG Rackemann	not out	6	b Bracewell	1
TM Alderman	b Hadlee	4	st Smith b Bracewell	1
	(lb 6, nb 7)	13	(lb 6, nb 3)	9
	(all out)	110	(all out)	269

Bowling: Hadlee 16.2-5-39-5 Morrison 10-4-22-3 Snedden 15-2-33-2 Rutherford 2-0-8-0 Bracewell 2-1-2-0
Hadlee 25-3-70-2 Morrison 24-8-58-2 Snedden 25-5-46-0 Bracewell 34.2-11-85-6 Jones 1-0-4-0

New Zealand Innings

TJ Franklin	c Marsh b PL Taylor	28	c Healy b Campbell	18
*JG Wright	c Healy b Alderman	36	not out	117
AH Jones	c & b Border	18	not out	33
MC Snedden	b Alderman	23		
MJ Greatbatch	c Healy b PL Taylor	16		
KR Rutherford	c Healy b PL Taylor	12		
JJ Crowe	lbw b Alderman	9		
RJ Hadlee	lbw b Campbell	18		
+IDS Smith	c MA Taylor b Campbell	1		
JG Bracewell	not out	19		
DK Morrison	c MA Taylor b Alderman	12		
	(b 2, lb 5, nb 3)	10	(b 2, lb 10, nb 1)	13
	(all out)	202	(1 wicket)	181

Bowling: Alderman 29-9-46-4 Rackemann 32-17-42-0 PL Taylor 33-19-44-3 Campbell 21-3-51-2 Border 6-3-12-1
Alderman 14-8-27-0 Rackemann 15-4-39-0 PL Taylor 11-3-39-0 Campbell 7-2-23-1 Border 10.4-5-27-0 Jones 6-3-14-0

Umpires: RS Dunne and SJ Woodward

New Zealand v Sri Lanka
31 January, 1,2,3,4 February 1991

Result: Match drawn

New Zealand Innings

TJ Franklin	c sub b Labrooy	3	lbw b Ramanayake	39
JG Wright	c Gurusinha b Labrooy	15	c Tillakaratne b Ramanayake	88
AH Jones	c Tillakaratne b Ramanayake	5	sub b Ranatunga	186
*MD Crowe	c Tillakaratne b Ramanayake	30	c Tillakaratne b Ranatunga	299
MJ Greatbatch	c Gurusinha b Labrooy	13	not out	14
KR Rutherford	c Tillakaratne b Ramanayake	25		
GE Bradburn	c Tillakaratne b Ramanayake	14		
+IDS Smith	c Senanayake b Ratnayake	28		
C Pringle	lbw b Labrooy	0		
DK Morrison	b Ratnayake	13		
W Watson	not out	10		
	(b 1, lb 7, w 1, nb 9)	18	(lb 9, w 1, nb 35)	45
	(all out)	174	(4 wickets)	671

Bowling: Ratnayake 18.2-6-45-4 Labrooy 23.5-6-84 Ramanayake 11-3-39-2 Warnaweera 6-1-14-0
Ratnayake 30-1-101-0 Labrooy 26-1-88-0 Ramanayake 40-5-122-2 Warnaweera 34-8-75-0 Ranatunga 19.3-4-60-2 EAR de Silva 56-14-141-0 PA de Silva 8-0-59-0 Gurusinha 7-0-16-0

Sri Lanka Innings

CP Senanayake	c Smith b Watson	0
+HP Tillakaratne	c Greatbatch b Morrison	21
AP Gurusinha	c Crowe b Watson	70
PA de Silva	c Bradburn b Morrison	267
*A Ranatunga	hit wicket b Watson	55
EAR de Silva	c Smith b Morrison	26
GF Labrooy	c Wright b Morrison	0
RJ Ratnayake	b Watson	26
CPH Ramanayake	not out	14
KPJ Warnaweera	b Watson	3
RS Mahanama	absent hurt	0
	(lb 7, nb 8)	15
	(all out)	497

Bowling: Morrison 44-6-153-5 Watson 46.1-10-121-4 Pringle 31-4-116-0 Bradburn 26-5-83-0 Rutherford 2-0-11-0 Jones 2-0-6-0

Umpires: BL Aldridge and SJ Woodward

New Zealand v England
6,7,8,9,10 February 1992

Result: Match drawn

England Innings

*GA Gooch	b Patel	30	c Rutherford b Cairns	11
AJ Stewart	b Morrison	107	c Smith b Patel	63
GA Hick	b Patel	43	c Smith b Su'a	22
RA Smith	c Rutherford b Patel	6	c & b Su'a	76
AJ Lamb	c Smith b Patel	30	c Latham b Patel	142
DA Reeve	c Latham b Su'a	18	b Su'a	0
DV Lawrence	c Rutherford b Cairns	6		
IT Botham	c Cairns b Su'a	1	lbw b Patel	1
+RC Russell	lbw b Morrison	18	not out	24
PAJ DeFreitas	lbw b Morrison	3		
PCR Tufnell	not out	2		
	(b 4, lb 12, nb 11)	27	(lb 13, nb 7)	20
	(all out)	305	(7 wickets declared)	359

Bowling: Morrison 22.1-6-44-3 Cairns 25-3-89-1 Su'a 36-10-62-2 Patel 34-10-87-4 Jones 1-0-7-0
Morrison 23-5-63-0 Cairns 22-4-84-1 Su'a 33-10-87-3 Patel 41.3-12-112-3

New Zealand Innings

BR Hartland	c Botham b Lawrence	2	lbw b Botham	19
JG Wright	c Reeve b Tufnell	116	c Russell b Botham	0
AH Jones	b Hick	143	lbw b Reeve	9
*MD Crowe	b Tufnell	30	not out	13
KR Rutherford	run out	8	not out	2
RT Latham	b Hick	25		
DN Patel	lbw b Hick	9		
CL Cairns	c Russell b Botham	33		
+IDS Smith	b Hick	21		
ML Su'a	not out	20		
DK Morrison	not out	0		
	(b 1, lb 15, w 1, nb 8)	25		0
	(9 wickets declared)	432	(3 wickets)	43

Bowling: DeFreitas 8-4-12-0 Lawrence 27-7-67-1 Tufnell 71-22-147-2 Hick 69-27-126-4 Botham 14-4-53-1 Reeve 3-1-11-0
Lawrence 2.1-1-4-0 Tufnell 9-5-12-0 Botham 8-1-23-2 Reeve 4.5-2-4-1

Umpires: BL Aldridge and RS Dunne; Referee: PJP Burge (Aus)

New Zealand v Australia
4,5,6,7,8 March 1993

Result: Match drawn

New Zealand Innings

MJ Greatbatch	c Taylor b Reiffel	61	b McDermott	0
JG Wright	c Healy b Hughes	72	not out	46
AH Jones	b Reiffel	4	lbw b Warne	42
*MD Crowe	b McDermott	98	lbw b McDermott	3
KR Rutherford	c Healy b Hughes	32	c Healy b Reiffel	11
+TE Blain	b Hughes	1	c Healy b Warne	51
CL Cairns	c Border b McDermott	13	lbw b McDermott	14
DN Patel	not out	13	c Healy b ME Waugh	25
DK Morrison	c Warne b McDermott	2	not out	0
W Watson	c Taylor b Warne	3		
MB Owens	b Warne	0		
	(b 7, lb 11, w 2, nb 10)	18	(b 8, lb 8, w 1, nb 1)	18
	(all out)	329	(7 wickets)	210

Bowling: McDermott 31-8-66-3 Hughes 35-9-100-3 Reiffel 23-8-55-2 SR Waugh 15-7-28-0 Warne 29-9-59-2 ME Waugh 2-1-3-0
McDermott 23-9-54-3 Hughes 11-5-22-0 Warne 40-25-49-2 Reiffel 16-7-27-1 Border 12-5-15-0 ME Waugh 8-3-12-1 Taylor 4-2-15-0 Boon 1-1-0-0

Australia Innings

MA Taylor	run out	50
DC Boon	c & b Morrison	37
JL Langer	c Blain b Watson	24
ME Waugh	c & b Owens	12
SR Waugh	c Blain b Morrison	75
*AR Border	lbw b Morrison	30
+IA Healy	c Rutherford b Morrison	8
MG Hughes	c Wright b Morrison	8
PR Reiffel	lbw b Morrison	7
SK Warne	c Greatbatch b Morrison	22
CJ McDermott	not out	7
	(lb 14, nb 4)	18
	(all out)	298

Bowling: Morrison 26.4-5-89-7 Cairns 24-3-77-0 Watson 29-12-60-1 Owens 21-3-54-1 Patel 1-0-4-0

Umpires: BL Aldridge and RS Dunne; Referee: Javed Burki (Pak)

New Zealand v Pakistan
17,18,19,20 February 1994

Result: Pakistan won by an innings and 12 runs

New Zealand Innings

BA Young	lbw b Wasim Akram	0	b Wasim Akram	4
BA Pocock	b Ata-ur-Rehman	16	b Waqar Younis	0
AH Jones	b Ata-ur-Rehman	43	b Wasim Akram	76
*KR Rutherford	c Akram Raza b Ata-ur-Rehman	7	c Akram Raza b Ata-ur-Rehman	63
MJ Greatbatch	c Rashid Latif b Waqar Younis	45	c Rashid Latif b Wasim Akram	10
SA Thomson	b Wasim Akram	7	c Ata-ur-Rehman b Wasim Akram	47
+TE Blain	c Saeed Anwar b Waqar Younis	78	c Basit Ali b Wasim Akram	78
MN Hart	not out	12	b Wasim Akram	7
DK Morrison	c Rashid Latif b Wasim Akram	5	lbw b Waqar Younis	42
SB Doull	c Basit Ali b Waqar Younis	17	c Saleem Malik b Wasim Akram	15
RP de Groen	b Wasim Akram	4	not out	1
	(lb 7, nb 4)	11	(b 1, lb 5, nb 12)	18
	(all out)	175	(all out)	361

Bowling: Wasim Akram 24-10-60-4 Waqar Younis 22-5-51-3 Ata-ur-Rehman 15-4-50-3 Akram Raza 6-4-7-0
Wasim Akram 37-7-119-7 Waqar Younis 25.2-4-111-2 Ata-ur-Rehman 18-1-86-1 Akram Raza 14-4-25-0 Aamer Sohail 1-0-1-0 Saleem Malik 2-0-13-0

Pakistan Innings

Saeed Anwar	run out	169
Aamer Sohail	lbw b Morrison	2
Akram Raza	c Blain b Morrison	0
Basit Ali	b Thomson	85
*Saleem Malik	c & b Hart	140
Inzamam-ul-Haq	not out	135
Asif Mujtaba		
+Rashid Latif		
Wasim Akram		
Waqar Younis		
Ata-ur-Rehman		
	(b 5, lb 6, nb 6)	17
	(5 wickets declared)	548

Bowling: Morrison 31-4-139-2 de Groen 31-8-104-0 Doull 27-6-112-0 Hart 31.2-9-102-1 Thomson 17-3-80-1

Umpires: BL Aldridge and HD Bird (Eng)
TV Umpire: EA Watkin (Eng); Referee: R Subba Row (Eng)

New Zealand v West Indies
10,11,12,13 February 1995

Result: West Indies won by an innings and 322 runs

West Indies Innings

SC Williams	c Parore b Doull	26
SL Campbell	c Su'a b Morrison	88
BC Lara	lbw b Morrison	147
JC Adams	c Su'a b Doull	151
KLT Arthurton	run out	70
S Chanderpaul	not out	61
+JR Murray	not out	101
CEL Ambrose		
*CA Walsh		
KCG Benjamin		
R Dhanraj		
	(lb 6, nb 10)	16
	(5 wickets declared)	660

Bowling: Morrison 29-5-82-2 Su'a 44-4-179-0 Doull 37.2-5-162-2 Hart 46-4-181-0 Jones 13-2-50-0

New Zealand Innings

BA Young	lbw b Walsh	29	b Walsh	0
DJ Murray	lbw b Ambrose	52	b Walsh	43
AH Jones	c Murray b Walsh	8	lbw b Benjamin	2
*KR Rutherford	lbw b Dhanraj	22	lbw b Ambrose	5
SP Fleming	c Lara b Walsh	47	b Walsh	30
SA Thomson	b Walsh	6	b Dhanraj	8
+AC Parore	c Adams b Walsh	32	not out	5
MN Hart	c Lara b Dhanraj	1	c Ambrose b Dhanraj	1
ML Su'a	c Murray b Walsh	6	c Arthurton b Walsh	8
SB Doull	b Walsh	0	lbw b Walsh	0
DK Morrison	not out	0	c Murray b Walsh	14
	(b 1, lb 14, nb 7)	22	(lb 2, nb 4)	6
	(all out)	216	(all out)	122

Bowling: Ambrose 19-9-32-1 Walsh 20.4-7-37-7 Dhanraj 33-6-97-2 Benjamin 12-1-35-0
Walsh 15.2-8-18-6 Benjamin 8-0-36-1 Ambrose 5-1-17-1 Dhanraj 12-2-49-2

Umpires: RS Dunne and VK Ramaswamy (Ind)
TV Umpire: EA Watkin; Referee: BN Jarman (Aus)

Basin Reserve, Wellington

New Zealand v England
6,7,8,9,10 February 1997

Result: England won by an innings and 68 runs

New Zealand Innings

BA Young	c Stewart b Gough	8	c Stewart b Tufnell		56
BA Pocock	c Cork b Caddick	6	c Knight b Gough		64
AC Parore	c Stewart b Gough	4	lbw b Croft		15
SP Fleming	c & b Caddick	1	c & b Croft		0
NJ Astle	c Croft b Gough	36	c Stewart b Gough		4
CL Cairns	c Hussain b Gough	3	c Knight b Caddick		22
*+LK German	c Stewart b Caddick	10	b Gough		11
DN Patel	c Cork b Caddick	45	lbw b Croft		0
SB Doull	c Stewart b Gough	0	c Knight b Gough		2
GI Allott	c Knight b Cork	1	b Caddick		2
DL Vettori	not out	3	not out		2
	(lb 5, nb 2)	7	(b 5, lb 4, nb 6)		15
	(all out)	124	(all out)		191

Bowling: Cork 14-4-34-1 Caddick 18.3-5-45-4 Gough 16-6-40-5
Cork 10-1-42-0 Caddick 27.2-11-40-2 Croft 20-9-19-3 Gough 23-9-52-4 Tufnell 23-9-29-1

England Innings

NV Knight	c Patel b Doull	8
*MA Atherton	lbw b Doull	30
+AJ Stewart	c Fleming b Allott	52
N Hussain	c Young b Vettori	64
GP Thorpe	st German b Patel	108
JP Crawley	c German b Doull	56
DG Cork	lbw b Astle	7
RDB Croft	c Fleming b Doull	0
D Gough	c Fleming b Doull	18
AR Caddick	c Allott b Vettori	20
PCR Tufnell	not out	6
	(b 3, lb 9, nb 2)	14
	(all out)	383

Bowling: Doull 28-10-75-5 Allott 31-6-91-1 Vettori 34.3-10-98-2 Cairns 4-2-8-0 Astle 14-5-30-1 Patel 24-6-59-1 Pocock 2-0-10-0

Umpires: SA Buckner (WI) and DB Cowie
TV Umpire: EA Watkin; Referee: PJP Burge (Aus)

New Zealand v Zimbabwe
19, 20, 21, 22 February 1998

Result: New Zealand won by 10 wickets

Zimbabwe Innings

GJ Rennie	b Doull	13	lbw b Doull		15
GW Flower	b Nash	38	c & b Vettori		4
MW Goodwin	lbw b Vettori	8	c Fleming b Cairns		72
GJ Whittall	c Parore b O'Connor	6	c Astle b Nash		22
+A Flower	c Parore b O'Connor	2	c O'Connor b Vettori		6
*ADR Campbell	run out (Nash)	37	c Horne b Cairns		56
PA Strang	c Young b Doull	1	b Cairns		0
HH Streak	lbw b O'Connor	39	not out		43
AR Whittall	c Parore b Cairns	1	run out (McMillan)		12
AG Huckle	c Parore b O'Connor	19	lbw b Vettori		0
M Mbangwa	not out	0	lbw b Cairns		0
	(lb 10, nb 6)	16	(b 6, lb 14)		20
	(all out)	180	(all out)		250

Bowling: Cairns 16-2-50-1 O'Connor 18.3-7-52-4 Doull 17-8-18-2 Nash 14-7-11-1 Vettori 20-10-39-1
Cairns 24.3-4-56-4 O'Connor 14-3-39-0 Doull 13-1-47-1 Vettori 41-18-73-3 Nash 9-6-10-1 McMillan 5-1-5-0

New Zealand Innings

BA Young	c Strang b Streak	0	not out		10
MJ Horne	c A Flower b Mbangwa	44	not out		9
+AC Parore	c A Flower b Huckle	78			
*SP Fleming	c Campbell b Huckle	36			
NJ Astle	c A Flower b Streak	42			
CD McMillan	c AR Whittall b Huckle	139			
CL Cairns	run out (sub [HK Olonga])	0			
DJ Nash	b Strang	41			
DL Vettori	b Strang	16			
SB Doull	c Goodwin b Strang	8			
SB O'Connor	not out	2			
	(b 1, lb 4)	5	(lb 1)		1
	(all out)	411	(0 wickets)		20

Bowling: Streak 22-6-74-2 Mbangwa 17-4-42-1 Strang 49.1-13-126-3 GJ Whittall 5-2-12-0 AR Whittall 12-0-50-0 Huckle 40-10-102-3
Streak 2-0-13-0 Huckle 1.5-0-6-0

Umpires: RS Dunne and SG Randell (Aus)
TV Umpire: EA Watkin; Referee: Hanuman Singh (Ind)

New Zealand v India
26,27,28,29,30 December 1998

Result: New Zealand won by 4 wickets

India Innings

NS Sidhu	c Fleming b Doull	0	lbw b Doull		34
A Jadeja	lbw b Doull	10	b Nash		22
R Dravid	lbw b Doull	0	b Wiseman		28
SC Ganguly	c Parore b Doull	5	c Bell b Wiseman		48
SR Tendulkar	c Bell b Doull	47	c Fleming b Nash		113
*M Azharuddin	not out	103	c Parore b Nash		48
+NR Mongia	c Astle b Doull	2	c Fleming b Doull		2
A Kumble	c McMillan b Doull	11	c Nash b Vettori		23
J Srinath	c Fleming b Nash	7	not out		27
BKV Prasad	c Fleming b Vettori	15	c & b Astle		0
Harbhajan Singh	c Astle b McMillan	1	c Horne b McMillan		1
	(lb 3, nb 6)	9	(b 3, lb 1, nb 5)		10
	(all out)	208	(all out)		356

Bowling: Doull 24-7-65-7 Cairns 17-3-69-0 Nash 14-1-46-1 Vettori 7-0-20-1 Astle 2-0-5-0 McMillan 1.4-1-0-1
Doull 25-10-49-2 Cairns 19-2-68-0 Nash 15-9-20-3 Vettori 20-6-92-1 McMillan 10-2-26-1 Wiseman 19-1-90-2 Astle 7-3-7-1

New Zealand Innings

MD Bell	c Mongia b Prasad	4	c Dravid b Srinath		0
MJ Horne	b Kumble	38	lbw b Kumble		31
*SP Fleming	run out (Jadeja)	42	b Kumble		17
NJ Astle	b Kumble	56	retired hurt		1
CD McMillan	c Dravid b Srinath	24	not out		74
+AC Parore	lbw b Kumble	2	run out (Dravid/Mongia)		1
CL Cairns	c Tendulkar b Prasad	3	c Jadeja b Srinath		61
DJ Nash	not out	89	not out		4
DL Vettori	b Tendulkar	57			
PJ Wiseman	b Tendulkar	0	lbw b Srinath		0
SB Doull	lbw b Kumble	0			
	(b 13, lb 19, nb 5)	37	(b 9, lb 9, nb 8)		26
	(all out)	352	(6 wickets)		215

Bowling: Srinath 36-6-89-1 Prasad 30-8-67-2 Kumble 45.4-17-83-4 Harbhajan Singh 25-6-61-0 Ganguly 6-0-13-0 Tendulkar 6-2-7-2
Srinath 19.3-1-82-3 Prasad 10-3-26-0 Kumble 23-6-70-2 Harbhajan Singh 5-1-11-0 Tendulkar 3-0-8-0

Umpires: EA Nicholls (WI) and EA Watkin
TV Umpire: RS Dunne; Referee: BN Jarman (Aus)

New Zealand v South Africa
18,19,20,21,22 March 1999

Result: South Africa won by 8 wickets

New Zealand Innings

MJ Horne	c Cullinan b Pollock	2	lbw b Elworthy		27
BA Young	c Rhodes b Kallis	18	c Boucher b Pollock		2
RG Twose	c Boucher b Elworthy	12	c Pollock b Elworthy		5
NJ Astle	b Elworthy	20	b Elworthy		62
GR Stead	c Pollock b Elworthy	68	lbw b Elworthy		33
CZ Harris	c Rhodes b Pollock	68	b Adams		41
DL Vettori	c Kallis b Elworthy	4	lbw b Elworthy		16
+AC Parore	c Cullinan b Pollock	5	c Rhodes b Adams		19
*DJ Nash	c Adams b Pollock	2	c Boucher b Adams		27
SB Doull	c Boucher b Pollock	0	not out		38
SB O'Connor	not out	2	c Rhodes b Adams		2
	(lb 18, nb 3)	21	(b 9, lb 7, nb 3)		19
	(all out)	222	(all out)		291

Bowling: Pollock 28.3-14-33-5 Elworthy 27-10-66-4 Kallis 20-5-44-1 Klusener 15-7-33-0 Adams 7-2-12-0 Cronje 5-3-16-0
Pollock 25-8-54-2 Elworthy 28-5-93-4 Kallis 19-7-50-0 Klusener 11-7-15-0 Adams 22.3-6-63-4

South Africa Innings

G Kirsten	b O'Connor	40	not out		12
HH Gibbs	c O'Connor b Vettori	120	run out (Horne/Vettori/Harris)		0
JH Kallis	c Horne b Nash	17	b Vettori		4
DJ Cullinan	c & b Astle	152	not out		0
*WJ Cronje	c Nash b Vettori	72			
JN Rhodes	c Young b Vettori	3			
SM Pollock	not out	43			
+MV Boucher	b Vettori	8			
L Klusener	c Parore b Nash	19			
S Elworthy	not out	3			
PR Adams					
	(b 10, lb 6, nb 5)	21			0
	(8 wickets dec)		(2 wickets)		16

Bowling: Doull 24-4-77-0 O'Connor 24-4-89-1 Nash 25-7-76-2 Vettori 54-16-153-4 Harris 22-0-66-0 Astle 16-8-21-1
O'Connor 4.1-0-9-0 Vettori 4-0-7-1

Umpires: RS Dunne and S Venkataraghavan (Ind)
TV Umpire: BF Bowden; Referee: AC Smith (Eng)

New Zealand v West Indies
26,27,28,29 December 1999

Result: New Zealand won by an innings and 105 runs

New Zealand Innings

CM Spearman	c Walsh b King	24
GR Stead	c Campbell b King	17
MS Sinclair	b King	214
*SP Fleming	c Adams b Chanderpaul	67
NJ Astle	run out (Rose/Walsh)	93
CD McMillan	c Jacobs b King	31
CL Cairns	c Adams b Rose	31
+AC Parore	b Rose	5
DJ Nash	not out	2
DL Vettori	c Campbell b Rose	2
SB O'Connor	not out	0
	(b 5, lb 12, w 1, nb 14)	32
	(9 wickets dec)	518

Bowling: Walsh 41-5-112-0 King 36-11-96-4 Rose 32.3-5-113-3 Perry 32-5-120-0 Adams 26-9-45-0 Chanderpaul 6-1-15-1

West Indies Innings

AFG Griffith	c Fleming b Nash	67	run out (Nash/Parore)		45
SL Campbell	lbw b Cairns	0	lbw b Cairns		3
NO Perry	c Parore b Cairns	3	lbw b Astle		0
S Chanderpaul	c Parore b Cairns	5	c Parore b Nash		70
*BC Lara	b Vettori	67	c Parore b Nash		75
JC Adams	c Stead b Vettori	8	c Parore b Nash		4
+RD Jacobs	not out	19	c Stead b Vettori		20
FA Rose	c Parore b Cairns	0	lbw b Cairns		10
RD King	run out (Vettori)	0	not out		4
CA Walsh	b Cairns	0	lbw b Nash		0
D Ganga	absent hurt		absent hurt		
	(b 4, lb 2, w 2, nb 2)	10	(b 1, lb 1, w 1)		3
	(all out)	179	(all out)		234

Bowling: Cairns 19-5-44-5 Nash 18-8-23-1 Vettori 31-10-69-2 O'Connor 19-8-25-0 Astle 4-1-12-0
O'Connor 16-3-50-0 Vettori 32-8-86-1 Nash 16-4-38-4 Cairns 12.1-4-25-2 Astle 7-0-33-1

Umpires: RB Tiffin (Zim) and EA Watkin
TV Umpire: RS Dunne; Referee: R Subba Row (Eng)

New Zealand v Australia
24,25,26,27 March 2000

Result: Australia won by 6 wickets

New Zealand Innings

MJ Horne	c Warne b Lee	4	b Lee		14
CM Spearman	c Gilchrist b Lee	4	c Langer b Miller		38
MS Sinclair	lbw b Miller	4	b Lee		0
*SP Fleming	c Miller b Warne	16	c Blewett b Miller		60
NJ Astle	c ME Waugh b Warne	61	b Warne		4
CD McMillan	c Gilchrist b Lee	1	c ME Waugh b Warne		0
CL Cairns	c Blewett b Miller	109	lbw b McGrath		69
+AC Parore	c Gilchrist b Blewett	46	run out (Blewett)		33
DL Vettori	c Langer b Warne	27	c SR Waugh b Lee		8
SB Doull	c Slater b Warne	12	c SR Waugh b Warne		40
SB O'Connor	not out	2	not out		4
	(b 1, lb 8, nb 3)	12	(b 3, lb 8, nb 3)		14
	(all out)	298	(all out)		294

Bowling: McGrath 17-4-60-0 Lee 17-2-49-3 Miller 20-2-78-2 Warne 14.5-1-68-4 Blewett 8-1-24-1 SR Waugh 4-0-10-0
McGrath 22.2-11-35-1 Lee 23-6-87-3 Miller 21-5-54-2 Warne 27-7-92-3 Blewett 3-0-15-0

Australia Innings

MJ Slater	c Parore b McMillan	143	st Parore b Vettori		12
GS Blewett	c Astle b Doull	0	b Cairns		25
SK Warne	lbw b Vettori	7			
JL Langer	c Parore b Cairns	12	c Spearman b O'Connor		57
ME Waugh	c Sinclair b Cairns	3	not out		44
*SR Waugh	not out	151	c Fleming b O'Connor		15
DR Martyn	c Parore b McMillan	78	not out		17
+AC Gilchrist	c Parore b O'Connor	0			
B Lee	lbw b O'Connor	3			
CR Miller	c & b McMillan	4			
GD McGrath	c & b Cairns	14			
	(lb 1, nb 3)	4	(b 2, lb 2, w 3)		7
	(all out)	419	(4 wickets)		177

Bowling: Cairns 26.3-2-110-3 Doull 19-3-78-1 Vettori 15-1-50-1 O'Connor 26-2-78-2 Astle 11-2-45-0 McMillan 23-10-57-3
Cairns 13-2-45-1 O'Connor 11-3-42-2 Vettori 8-1-19-1 Doull 10-2-35-0 McMillan 2-0-13-0 Astle 10.1-4-19-0

Umpires: DM Quested and Riazuddin (Pak)
TV Umpire: EA Watkin; Referee: MH Denness (Eng)

New Zealand v Zimbabwe
26,27,28,29,30 December 2000

Result: Match drawn

New Zealand Innings

MH Richardson	run out (Olonga/Flower)	75			
MJ Horne	c Flower b Streak	1	c Flower b Streak	0	
MS Sinclair	lbw b Strang	9	c Flower b Murphy	18	
*SP Fleming	run out (Whittall/Strang)	22	run out (Olonga)	55	
NJ Astle	c Carlisle b Strang	141	not out	51	
CD McMillan	b Murphy	142	c Madondo b Strang	10	
+AC Parore	not out	50	not out	3	
BGK Walker	c Olonga b Strang	27			
PJ Wiseman	not out	0			
BA Murphy					
BC Strang					
HK Olonga					
SB O'Connor					
CS Martin					
	(b 1, lb 8, w 5, nb 6)	20	(b 5, lb 5, nb 6)	16	
	(7 wickets dec)	487	(4 wickets dec)	153	

Bowling: Streak 37-10-74-1 Strang 46-16-116-3 Olonga 30-2-105-0 Murphy 46-9-128-1 Whittall 22-6-55-0
Streak 5-1-18-1 Strang 11-2-25-1 Murphy 18-0-86-1 Olonga 2-0-12-0 Whittall 4-3-2-0

Zimbabwe Innings

GJ Whittall	b Martin	9	c Parore b O'Connor	6	
GJ Rennie	c Parore b McMillan	93	c Parore b Wiseman	37	
SV Carlisle	c Horne b Martin	0	not out	16	
ADR Campbell	lbw b Martin	24	not out	0	
+A Flower	c Parore b Martin	79			
TN Madondo	not out	74			
DA Marillier	c Parore b Martin	28			
*HH Streak	not out	19			
BA Murphy					
BC Strang					
HK Olonga					
SB O'Connor					
CS Martin					
	(b 3, lb 9, nb 2)	14	(lb 1)	1	
	(6 wickets dec)	340	(2 wickets)	60	

Bowling: Martin 32.5-11-71-5 O'Connor 16-7-29-0 Wiseman 54-13-131-0 Walker 22-1-68-0 McMillan 9-4-22-1 Astle 5-2-7-0
Martin 5-2-6-0 O'Connor 8-4-8-1 Wiseman 6-2-15-1 Walker 11-1-30-0

Umpires: BC Cooray (SL) and RS Dunne
TV Umpire: AL Hill; Referee: GR Viswanath (Ind)

New Zealand v Bangladesh
26,27,28,29 December 2001

Result: New Zealand won by an innings and 74 runs

Bangladesh Innings

Javed Omar	c Vincent b Cairns	0	lbw b Bond	12	
Al Sahariar	c Bond b Vettori	18	c Horne b Bond	0	
Habibul Bashar	c Sinclair b Cairns	6	lbw b Drum	32	
Aminul Islam	c Vincent b Bond	42	c Vettori b Bond	4	
Mohammad Ashraful	c Fleming b Cairns	11	lbw b Vettori	10	
Sanwar Hossain	run out (Vincent/Vettori)	10	b Bond	7	
Khaled Mahmud	c Parore b Drum	10	run out (McMillan/Parore)	4	
*+Khaled Mashud	not out	10	not out	19	
Hasibul Hossain	c Vincent b Drum	4	c Parore b Vettori	7	
Manjural Islam	b Vettori	0	c Sinclair b Cairns	0	
Mashrafe Mortaza	run out (McMillan)	8	b Cairns	29	
	(lb 4, w 1, nb 8)	13	(lb 7, w 1, nb 3)	11	
	(all out)	132	(all out)	135	

Bowling: Cairns 15-7-24-3 Bond 13-4-21-1 Drum 11-1-26-2 Vettori 25-6-57-2
Cairns 6-1-27-2 Bond 15-5-54-4 Vettori 17-8-38-2 Drum 3-0-9-1

New Zealand Innings

MH Richardson	c Mashrafe Mortaza b Hasibul Hossain	83	
MJ Horne	c Khaled Mashud b Manjural Islam	38	
L Vincent	c Khaled Mashud b Mashrafe Mortaza	23	
*SP Fleming	c Khaled Mashud b Manjural Islam	61	
CD McMillan	run out (Mashrafe Mortaza)	70	
MS Sinclair	not out	19	
CL Cairns	c Habibul Bashar b Manjural Islam	36	
+AC Parore			
DL Vettori			
SE Bond			
CJ Drum			
	(b 1, lb 6, w 1, nb 3)	11	
	(6 wickets dec)	341	

Bowling: Mashrafe Mortaza 16-1-57-1 Manjural Islam 29-5-99-3 Hasibul Hossain 21-3-88-1 Aminul Islam 7-0-37-0 Khaled Mahmud 12-2-42-0 Mohammad Ashraful 3-0-11-0

Umpires: BF Bowden and DJ Harper (Aus)
TV Umpire: DM Quested; Referee: BN Jarman (Aus)

New Zealand v England
21,22,23,24,25 March 2002

Result: Match drawn

England Innings

ME Trescothick	c Vincent b Vettori	37	c Richardson b Vettori	88	
MP Vaughan	c Fleming b Drum	7	c Drum b Vettori	34	
MA Butcher	c Astle b Drum	47	c Martin b Drum	60	
*N Hussain	c Astle b Vettori	66	not out	13	
GP Thorpe	c Fleming b Martin	11	not out	1	
MR Ramprakash	b Butler	24			
A Flintoff	c Drum b Butler	2	c & b Vettori	75	
+JS Foster	not out	25			
AF Giles	c McMillan b Butler	10			
AR Caddick	c Richardson b Martin	10			
MJ Hoggard	c Parore b Butler	7			
	(b 4, lb 2, w 6, nb 22)	34	(b 5, lb 13, nb 4)	22	
	(all out)	280	(4 wickets dec)	293	

Bowling: Butler 18.3-2-60-4 Drum 24-6-85-2 Martin 17-3-58-2 Vettori 25-3-62-2 Astle 1-0-1-0 McMillan 3-0-8-0
Butler 6-0-32-0 Drum 16-2-78-1 Vettori 24-1-90-3 Astle 9-4-18-0 Martin 7-1-40-0 McMillan 3-0-17-0

New Zealand Innings

MH Richardson	c Giles b Caddick	60	c Thorpe b Giles	4	
MJ Horne	b Caddick	8	c Foster b Flintoff	38	
L Vincent	c Thorpe b Giles	57	lbw b Hoggard	71	
*SP Fleming	c Thorpe b Caddick	3	b Hoggard	11	
NJ Astle	c Hussain b Giles	4	not out	11	
CD McMillan	lbw b Caddick	41	not out	17	
+AC Parore	c Ramprakash b Giles	0			
DL Vettori	c Thorpe b Caddick	11			
CJ Drum	c Trescothick b Giles	2			
IG Butler	c Foster b Caddick	12			
CS Martin	not out	0			
	(b 2, lb 9, nb 9)	20	(b 3, lb 1, nb 2)	6	
	(all out)	218	(4 wickets)	158	

Bowling: Caddick 28.3-8-63-6 Hoggard 13-5-32-0 Giles 37-3-103-4 Flintoff 10-4-9-0
Caddick 17-6-31-0 Hoggard 13-4-31-2 Giles 33-11-53-1 Flintoff 16-6-24-1 Vaughan 5-1-15-0

Umpires: RS Dunne and DB Hair (Aus)
TV Umpire: EA Watkin; Referee: JL Hendriks (WI)

New Zealand v India
12,13,14 December 2002

Result: New Zealand won by 10 wickets

India Innings

SB Bangar	c Styris b Tuffey	1	lbw b Oram	12	
V Sehwag	b Tuffey	2	lbw b Bond	12	
R Dravid	b Styris	76	b Bond	7	
SR Tendulkar	lbw b Oram	8	b Bond	51	
*SC Ganguly	c Vincent b Bond	17	c Hart b Bond	2	
VVS Laxman	c Hart b Bond	0	c Fleming b Oram	0	
+PA Patel	c Vincent b Oram	8	c Fleming b Tuffey	10	
AB Agarkar	c Astle b Styris	12	c McMillan b Tuffey	9	
Harbhajan Singh	c McMillan b Styris	0	c Styris b Tuffey	1	
Z Khan	c Oram b Bond	19	c Styris b Oram	9	
A Nehra	not out	10	not out	0	
	(lb 1, w 1, nb 6)	8	(lb 1, nb 7)	8	
	(all out)	161	(all out)	121	

Bowling: Bond 18.4-4-66-3 Tuffey 16-7-25-2 Oram 15-4-31-2 Styris 6-0-28-3 Astle 3-1-10-0
Bond 13.1-5-33-4 Tuffey 9-3-35-3 Oram 11-3-28-3 Styris 5-0-24-0

New Zealand Innings

MH Richardson	lbw b Khan	89	not out	14	
L Vincent	c Patel b Bangar	12	not out	21	
*SP Fleming	b Khan	25			
CD McMillan	lbw b Bangar	9			
NJ Astle	c Harbhajan Singh b Khan	41			
SB Styris	st Patel b Harbhajan Singh	0			
JDP Oram	lbw b Harbhajan Singh	0			
+RG Hart	lbw b Khan	6			
DL Vettori	c Patel b Khan	21			
DR Tuffey	not out	9			
SE Bond	b Agarkar	2			
	(b 6, lb 12, w 2, nb 8, pen 5)	33	(w 1)	1	
	(all out)	247	(0 wickets)	36	

Bowling: Khan 25-8-53-5 Nehra 19-4-50-0 Agarkar 13.1-1-54-1 Bangar 15-4-23-2 Harbhajan Singh 17-4-33-2 Ganguly 2-0-11-0
Khan 3-0-13-0 Nehra 4.3-0-21-0 Harbhajan Singh 2-1-2-0

Umpires: EAR de Silva (SL) and DJ Harper (Aus)
TV Umpire: BF Bowden; Referee: MJ Procter (SA)

Eden Gardens, Kolkata

India v England
5,6,7,8 January 1934

Result: Match drawn

England Innings

CF Walters	c Gopalan b Amar Singh	29	not out	2
A Mitchell	c Gopalan b CK Nayudu	47		
CJ Barnett	lbw b Amar Singh	8	c Gopalan b Nissar	0
James Langridge	c Nissar b Gopalan	70		
*DR Jardine	c CS Nayudu b Mushtaq Ali	61		
BH Valentine	lbw b CK Nayudu	40	st Dilawar Hussain b Naoomal Jaoomal	3
+WHV Levett	b CK Nayudu	5	not out	2
MS Nichols	lbw b Nissar	13		
LF Townsend	c Dilawar Hussain b Amar Singh	40		
H Verity	not out	55		
EW Clark	c Merchant b Amar Singh	10		
	(b 13, lb 10, nb 2)	25		0
	(all out)	403	(2 wickets)	7

Bowling: Nissar 34-6-112-1 Amar Singh 54.5-13-106-4 Gopalan 19-7-39-1 Mushtaq Ali 19-5-45-1 Amarnath 2-0-10-0 CS Nayudu 8-1-26-0 CK Nayudu 23-7-40-3
Nissar 2-1-2-1 Amar Singh 2-1-1-0 Naoomal Jaoomal 1-0-4-1

India Innings

Naoomal Jaoomal	c Jardine b Nichols	2	c Levett b Townsend	43
+Dilawar Hussain	c Jardine b Clark	59	b Clark	57
S Wazir Ali	c Nichols b Verity	39	c Nichols b Verity	0
*CK Nayudu	b Clark	5	lbw b Verity	38
L Amarnath	c Jardine b Clark	0	c Levett b Clark	9
VM Merchant	b Verity	54	c Jardine b Verity	17
S Mushtaq Ali	lbw b Nichols	9	c Barnett b Nichols	18
CS Nayudu	c Verity b Nichols	36	lbw b Verity	15
L Amar Singh	c Nichols b Verity	10	c Jardine b Townsend	18
MJ Gopalan	not out	11	c Levett b Clark	7
M Nissar	c Walters b Verity	2	not out	0
	(b 5, lb 5, nb 10)	20	(b 10, lb 4, nb 1)	15
	(all out)	247	(all out)	237

Bowling: Clark 26-8-39-3 Nichols 28-6-78-3 Verity 28.4-13-64-4 Langridge 17-7-27-0 Townsend 8-4-19-0
Clark 19.3-4-50-3 Nichols 20-6-48-1 Verity 31-12-76-4 Langridge 10-4-19-0 Townsend 8-3-22-2 Barnett 2-0-7-0

Umpires: JW Hitch (Eng) and FA Tarrant (Eng)

India v West Indies
31 December 1948, 1,2,3,4 January 1949

Result: Match drawn

West Indies Innings

AF Rae	lbw b Banerjee	15	run out	34
DS Atkinson	b Banerjee	0	not out	5
+CL Walcott	c Banerjee b Ghulam Ahmed	54	c Amarnath b Mankad	108
ED Weekes	c & b Ghulam Ahmed	162	c & b Ghulam Ahmed	101
GE Gomez	b Mankad	26	b Ghulam Ahmed	29
GM Carew	lbw b Mankad	11	b Banerjee	9
*JDC Goddard	not out	39	c Banerjee b Amarnath	9
RJ Christiani	c & b Banerjee	23	b Amarnath	22
FJ Cameron	c Mushtaq Ali b Banerjee	23	c & b Mankad	2
W Ferguson	b Ghulam Ahmed	2	lbw b Mankad	6
PEW Jones	b Ghulam Ahmed	6		
	(b 1, lb 4)	5	(b 6, lb 1, w 1, nb 3)	11
	(all out)	366	(9 wickets declared)	336

Bowling: Banerjee 30-3-120-4 Amarnath 20-6-34-0 Hazare 5-0-33-0 Ghulam Ahmed 35.2-5-94-4 Mankad 23-5-74-2 Sarwate 2-0-6-0
Banerjee 21-0-61-1 Amarnath 23-4-75-2 Hazare 11-3-33-0 Ghulam Ahmed 25-0-87-2 Mankad 24.3-5-68-3 Sarwate 1-0-1-0

India Innings

S Mushtaq Ali	c Rae b Goddard	54	lbw b Atkinson	106
KC Ibrahim	b Gomez	1	c Atkinson b Gomez	25
RS Modi	b Jones	80	c Christiani b Goddard	87
VS Hazare	b Gomez	59	not out	58
*L Amarnath	c +Christiani b Gomez	3	not out	34
MH Mankad	c Ferguson b Goddard	29		
HR Adhikari	not out	31		
CT Sarwate	b Goddard	0		
+PK Sen	lbw b Ferguson	1		
Ghulam Ahmed	st Christiani b Ferguson	0		
SA Banerjee	st Christiani b Ferguson	0		
	(b 5, lb 6, nb 3)	14	(b 12, nb 3)	15
	(all out)	272	(3 wickets)	325

Bowling: Jones 17-3-48-1 Gomez 32-10-65-3 Ferguson 29-8-66-3 Goddard 13-3-34-3 Cameron 7-2-12-0 Atkinson 9-0-27-0 Christiani 2-0-6-0
Jones 21-5-49-0 Gomez 29-10-47-1 Ferguson 9-0-35-0 Goddard 23-11-41-1 Cameron 30-7-67-0 Atkinson 14-3-42-1 Christiani 3-0-12-0 Carew 3-2-2-0 Walcott 3-0-12-0 Weekes 1-0-3-0

Umpires: AR Joshi and BJ Mohoni

India v England
30,31 December 1951, 1,3,4 January 1952

Result: Match drawn

England Innings

JDB Robertson	c Phadkar b Divecha	13	st Sen b Mankad	22
+RT Spooner	c Sen b Mankad	71	b Mankad	92
TW Graveney	c Amarnath b Divecha	24	c Sen b Divecha	21
AJ Watkins	c Sen b Phadkar	68	b Divecha	2
D Kenyon	c Manjrekar b Mankad	3	b Phadkar	0
CJ Poole	c Divecha b Phadkar	55	not out	69
*ND Howard	c Amarnath b Mankad	23	not out	20
JB Statham	b Phadkar	1		
E Leadbeater	run out	38		
F Ridgway	st Sen b Mankad	24		
R Tattersall	not out	5		
	(b 4, lb 1, w 1, nb 11)	17	(b 13, lb 6, w 2, nb 5)	26
	(all out)	342	(5 wickets declared)	252

Bowling: Phadkar 38-11-89-3 Divecha 33-9-60-2 Amarnath 20-5-35-0 Mankad 52.5-16-89-4 Gupte 13-0-43-0 Hazare 3-0-9-0
Phadkar 20-7-27-1 Divecha 25-7-55-2 Amarnath 22-5-43-0 Mankad 35-13-64-2 Gupte 5-0-14-0 Hazare 9-4-11-0 Umrigar 4-1-12-0

India Innings

P Roy	c Spooner b Ridgway	42	not out	31
MH Mankad	c Tattersall b Leadbeater	59	not out	71
PR Umrigar	c Howard b Ridgway	10		
*VS Hazare	b Tattersall	2		
L Amarnath	b Tattersall	0		
DG Phadkar	c Leadbeater b Ridgway	115		
VL Manjrekar	b Tattersall	48		
CD Gopinath	c Robertson b Ridgway	19		
RV Divecha	c Watkins b Tattersall	26		
SP Gupte	c Leadbeater b Statham	0		
+PK Sen	not out	7		
	(b 3, lb 10, w 1, nb 2)	16	(b 1)	1
	(all out)	344	(0 wickets)	103

Bowling: Statham 27-10-46-1 Ridgway 38.1-10-83-4 Tattersall 48-13-104-4 Leadbeater 15-2-64-1 Watkins 21-9-31-0
Statham 4-0-8-0 Ridgway 2-1-8-0 Tattersall 4-2-4-0 Leadbeater 8-0-54-0 Poole 5-1-9-0 Robertson 5-1-10-0 Graveney 1-0-9-0

Umpires: AR Joshi and BJ Mohoni

India v Pakistan
12,13,14,15 December 1952

Result: Match drawn

Pakistan Innings

Nazar Mohammad	c Amarnath b Ghulam Ahmed	55	lbw b Mankad	47
Hanif Mohammad	c Ramchand b Phadkar	56	b Ramchand	12
Waqar Hasan	lbw b Phadkar	29	b Ramchand	97
+Imtiaz Ahmed	c Gaekwad b Phadkar	57	b Mankad	13
*AH Kardar	b Phadkar	7	c Ramchand b Ghulam Ahmed	1
Maqsood Ahmed	c Manjrekar b Amarnath	17	c Shodhan b Ghulam Ahmed	8
Anwar Hussain	lbw b Phadkar	9	c Mankad b Ghulam Ahmed	3
Fazal Mahmood	c Mankad b Ramchand	5	not out	28
Zulfiqar Ahmed	not out	6	not out	5
Mahmood Hussain	st Sen b Ramchand	5		
Amir Elahi	c Sen b Ramchand	4		
	(b 3, lb 3, nb 1)	7	(b 14, lb 6, nb 2)	22
	(all out)	257	(7 wickets declared)	236

Bowling: Phadkar 32-10-72-5 Ramchand 13-6-20-3 Amarnath 21-7-31-1 Mankad 28-7-78-0 Ghulam Ahmed 22-6-49-1
Phadkar 21-8-30-0 Ramchand 16-3-43-2 Amarnath 3-2-1-0 Mankad 41-18-68-2 Ghulam Ahmed 33-11-56-3 Shodhan 2-1-6-0 Roy 2-1-4-0 Manjrekar 2-0-6-0

India Innings

P Roy	c Zulfiqar Ahmed b Amir Elahi	29	not out	8
DK Gaekwad	b Mahmood Hussain	21	not out	20
MH Mankad	lbw b Fazal Mahmood	35		
VL Manjrekar	c Fazal Mahmood b Mahmood Hussain	29		
PR Umrigar	c Kardar b Fazal Mahmood	22		
DG Phadkar	c Imtiaz Ahmed b Kardar	57		
*L Amarnath	c Maqsood Ahmed b Fazal Mahmood	11		
RH Shodhan	c Imtiaz Ahmed b Fazal Mahmood	110		
GS Ramchand	b Mahmood Hussain	25		
+PK Sen	b Anwar Hussain	13		
Ghulam Ahmed	not out	20		
	(b 7, lb 16, nb 2)	25		0
	(all out)	397	(0 wickets)	28

Bowling: Mahmood Hussain 46-11-114-3 Fazal Mahmood 64-19-141-4 Maqsood Ahmed 8-2-20-0 Amir Elahi 6-0-29-1 Kardar 15-3-43-1 Anwar Hussain 5-1-25-1
Anwar Hussain 1-0-4-0 Nazar Mohammad 2-1-4-0 Hanif Mohammad 2-0-10-0 Waqar Hasan 1-0-10-0

Umpires: JR Patel and MG Vijayasarathi

India v New Zealand
28,29,31 December 1955, 1,2 January 1956

Result: Match drawn

India Innings

MH Mankad	c McMahon b Reid	25	c MacGibbon b Reid	17
NJ Contractor	b Hayes	6	b Hayes	61
P Roy	b Hayes	28	lbw b Cave	100
VL Manjrekar	c Reid b Cave	1	c MacGibbon b Reid	90
*PR Umrigar	run out	1	b MacGibbon	15
GS Ramchand	b Reid	1	not out	106
JM Ghorpade	b Alabaster	39	c Sutcliffe b Cave	4
DG Phadkar	run out	0	b Hayes	17
+CT Patankar	b Reid	13	not out	1
GR Sunderam	not out	3		
SP Gupte	b Alabaster	4		
	(b 4, lb 2, nb 5)	11	(b 9, lb 10, nb 8)	27
	(all out)	132	(7 wickets declared)	438

Bowling: Hayes 14-3-38-2 MacGibbon 13-3-27-0 Cave 14-6-29-1 Reid 16-9-19-3 Alabaster 2.3-0-8-2
Hayes 30-4-67-2 MacGibbon 43-16-92-1 Cave 57-26-85-2 Reid 45-21-87-2 Alabaster 27-7-52-0 Sutcliffe 7-0-28-0

New Zealand Innings

JG Leggat	c Patankar b Sunderam	8	c Mankad b Phadkar	7
B Sutcliffe	c Patankar b Ramchand	25	lbw b Gupte	5
JW Guy	lbw b Gupte	91	b Phadkar	0
JR Reid	b Sunderam	120	b Mankad	5
SN McGregor	b Gupte	6	b Mankad	29
AR MacGibbon	st Patankar b Gupte	23	not out	21
NS Harford	c Mankad b Ramchand	25	c Phadkar b Gupte	1
*HB Cave	c Umrigar b Gupte	5	not out	4
JC Alabaster	c Patankar b Gupte	18		
JA Hayes	b Gupte	1		
+TG McMahon	not out	1		
	(b 7, lb 3, nb 3)	13	(lb 2, nb 1)	3
	(all out)	336	(6 wickets)	75

Bowling: Phadkar 35-9-76-0 Sunderam 21-6-46-2 Gupte 33.5-7-90-6 Ramchand 37-15-64-2 Mankad 1-0-9-0 Ghorpade 1-0-17-0 Umrigar 17-7-21-0
Phadkar 4-1-11-2 Sunderam 3-1-13-0 Gupte 14-7-30-2 Ramchand 1-0-4-0 Mankad 12-8-14-2

Umpires: DD Desai and SK Ganguli

India v Australia
2,3,5,6 November 1956

Result: Australia won by 94 runs

Australia Innings

CC McDonald	b Ghulam Ahmed	3	lbw b Ramchand	0
JW Burke	c Manjrekar b Ghulam Ahmed	10	c Contractor b Ghulam Ahmed	2
RN Harvey	c Tamhane b Ghulam Ahmed	7	c Umrigar b Mankad	69
ID Craig	c Tamhane b Gupte	36	b Ghulam Ahmed	6
PJP Burge	c Ramchand b Ghulam Ahmed	58	c Ramchand b Ghulam Ahmed	22
KD Mackay	lbw b Mankad	5	hit wicket b Mankad	27
R Benaud	b Ghulam Ahmed	24	b Gupte	21
RR Lindwall	b Ghulam Ahmed	8	c Tamhane b Mankad	28
*IWG Johnson	c Ghulam Ahmed b Mankad	1	st Tamhane b Mankad	5
WPA Crawford	c Contractor b Ghulam Ahmed	18	not out	1
+GRA Langley	not out	1		
	(b 6)	6	(b 6, lb 2)	8
	(all out)	177	(9 wickets declared)	189

Bowling: Ramchand 2-1-1-0 Umrigar 16-3-30-0 Ghulam Ahmed 20.3-6-49-7 Gupte 23-11-35-1 Mankad 25-4-56-2
Ramchand 2-1-6-1 Umrigar 20-9-21-0 Ghulam Ahmed 29-5-81-3 Gupte 7-1-24-1 Mankad 9.4-1-49-4

India Innings

P Roy	b Lindwall	13	lbw b Burke	24
NJ Contractor	lbw b Benaud	22	b Johnson	20
*PR Umrigar	c Burge b Johnson	5	c Burke b Benaud	28
VL Manjrekar	c Harvey b Benaud	33	c Harvey b Benaud	22
MH Mankad	lbw b Benaud	4	c Harvey b Benaud	24
GS Ramchand	st Langley b Benaud	2	b Burke	3
AG Kripal Singh	c Mackay b Benaud	14	b Benaud	0
P Bhandari	lbw b Lindwall	17	c Harvey b Burke	2
+NS Tamhane	b Benaud	5	b Benaud	0
Ghulam Ahmed	c Mackay b Lindwall	10	b Burke	0
SP Gupte	not out	1	not out	0
	(b 7, lb 1, nb 2)	10	(b 5, lb 5, nb 3)	13
	(all out)	136	(all out)	136

Bowling: Lindwall 25.2-12-32-3 Crawford 3-3-0-0 Johnson 12-2-27-1 Benaud 29-10-52-6 Harvey 1-1-0-0 Burke 8-3-15-0
Lindwall 12-7-9-0 Crawford 2-1-1-0 Johnson 14-5-23-1 Benaud 24.2-6-53-5 Burke 17-4-37-4

Umpires: G Ayling and BJ Mohoni

India v West Indies
31 December 1958, 1,3,4 January 1959

Result: West Indies won by an innings and 336 runs

West Indies Innings

JKC Holt	c Contractor b Surendranath	5
CC Hunte	c Surendranath b Gupte	23
RB Kanhai	c Umrigar b Surendranath	256
OG Smith	b Umrigar	34
BF Butcher	lbw b Ghulam Ahmed	103
GS Sobers	not out	106
JS Solomon	not out	69
*+FCM Alexander		
S Ramadhin		
WW Hall		
R Gilchrist		
	(b 8, lb 9, nb 1)	18
	(5 wickets declared)	614

Bowling: Phadkar 43-6-173-0 Surendranath 46-8-168-2 Gupte 39-8-119-1 Ghulam Ahmed 16.1-1-52-1 Umrigar 16-1-62-1 Ghorpade 2-0-22-0

India Innings

P Roy	c Solomon b Gilchrist	11	c Alexander b Hall	0
NJ Contractor	lbw b Ramadhin	4	b Gilchrist	6
JM Ghorpade	c Alexander b Gilchrist	7	b Sobers	16
RB Kenny	c Alexander b Hall	16	b Hall	0
PR Umrigar	not out	44	c Alexander b Hall	2
VL Manjrekar	b Hall	0	b Hall	58
DG Phadkar	c Sobers b Gilchrist	3	b Gilchrist	35
+NS Tamhane	c Sobers b Hall	0	b Gilchrist	0
Surendranath	run out	8	c Alexander b Gilchrist	3
*Ghulam Ahmed	lbw b Sobers	4	b Gilchrist	0
SP Gupte	b Ramadhin	12	b Gilchrist	15
	(b 2, lb 8, w 1, nb 4)	15	(b 3, nb 16)	19
	(all out)	124	(all out)	154

Bowling: Gilchrist 23-13-18-3 Hall 15-6-31-3 Ramadhin 16.5-8-27-2 Smith 2-1-1-0 Sobers 6-0-32-1
Gilchrist 21-7-55-6 Hall 18-5-55-3 Ramadhin 8-3-14-0 Sobers 2-0-11-1

Umpires: Mohammad Yunus and ND Nagarwala

India v Australia
23,24,25,27,28 January 1960

Result: Match drawn

India Innings

+BK Kunderan	b Mackay	12	b Davidson	0
NJ Contractor	b Benaud	36	c Davidson b Benaud	30
P Roy	c Grout b Davidson	33	lbw b Benaud	39
RG Nadkarni	c Burge b Lindwall	2	c Grout b Lindwall	29
RB Kenny	c Grout b Lindwall	7	c Grout b Mackay	62
CD Gopinath	b Benaud	39	c Grout b Benaud	0
CG Borde	b Benaud	6	b Meckiff	50
*GS Ramchand	b Davidson	9	b Benaud	9
ML Jaisimha	not out	20	b Mackay	74
RB Desai	c Grout b Davidson	17	not out	17
JM Patel	run out	0	c Benaud b Davidson	12
	(b 5, lb 1, w 1, nb 3)	10	(b 11, lb 4, nb 2)	17
	(all out)	194	(all out)	339

Bowling: Davidson 16-2-37-3 Meckiff 17-5-28-0 Mackay 11-5-16-1 Lindwall 16-6-44-2 Benaud 29.3-12-59-3
Davidson 36.2-13-76-2 Meckiff 21-2-41-1 Mackay 21-7-36-2 Lindwall 20-3-66-1 Benaud 48-23-103-4

Australia Innings

LE Favell	b Desai	26	not out	62
+ATW Grout	b Patel	50		
RN Harvey	c Jaisimha b Patel	17	c & b Contractor	36
NC O'Neill	c Kunderan b Desai	113		
PJP Burge	b Desai	60		
CC McDonald	lbw b Borde	27	run out	6
KD Mackay	b Patel	18		
RR Lindwall	c Kunderan b Desai	10		
AK Davidson	b Borde	4		
*R Benaud	c & b Borde	3	not out	10
I Meckiff	not out	0		
	(lb 3)	3	(b 1, lb 5, nb 1)	7
	(all out)	331	(2 wickets)	121

Bowling: Desai 36-4-111-4 Ramchand 10-1-37-0 Patel 26-2-104-3 Nadkarni 22-10-36-0 Borde 13.1-4-23-3 Jaisimha 4-0-17-0
Desai 11-4-18-0 Ramchand 3-2-4-0 Patel 7-1-15-0 Nadkarni 7-4-10-0 Borde 13-1-45-0 Jaisimha 6-2-13-0 Contractor 5-1-9-1

Umpires: SK Ganguli and ND Sane

India v Pakistan
30,31 December 1960, 1,3,4 January 1961

Result: Match drawn

Pakistan Innings

Hanif Mohammad	c Baig b Desai	56	not out	63
+Imtiaz Ahmed	b Surendranath	9	b Desai	9
Saeed Ahmed	c Nadkarni b Surendranath	41	lbw b Surendranath	13
Javed Burki	lbw b Borde	48	run out	42
W Mathias	c Umrigar b Desai	8		
Mushtaq Mohammad	c Jaisimha b Borde	61		
Nasim-ul-Ghani	b Surendranath	0		
Intikhab Alam	c Tamhane b Surendranath	56	not out	11
*Fazal Mahmood	lbw b Borde	8		
Mahmood Hussain	b Borde	4		
Haseeb Ahsan	not out	1		
	(b 6, lb 3)	9	(b 3, lb 5)	8
	(all out)	301	(3 wickets declared)	146

Bowling: Desai 35-3-118-2 Surendranath 46-19-93-4 Umrigar 6-2-15-0 Gupte 18-5-41-0 Borde 16.2-7-21-4 Nadkarni 6-5-4-0
Desai 16-4-37-1 Surendranath 18-2-51-1 Umrigar 7-2-14-0 Gupte 1-1-0-0 Nadkarni 7-0-36-0

India Innings

*NJ Contractor	b Intikhab Alam	25	c Fazal Mahmood b Haseeb Ahsan	12
ML Jaisimha	c Mathias b Mahmood Hussain	28	c Mathias b Intikhab Alam	26
AA Baig	b Intikhab Alam	19	b Haseeb Ahsan	1
PR Umrigar	c Imtiaz Ahmed b Mahmood Hussain	1	b Intikhab Alam	4
VL Manjrekar	b Fazal Mahmood	29	not out	45
CG Borde	c Imtiaz Ahmed b Fazal Mahmood	44	not out	23
RG Nadkarni	c Imtiaz Ahmed b Fazal Mahmood	1		
RB Desai	b Haseeb Ahsan	14		
+NS Tamhane	c Intikhab Alam b Fazal Mahmood	0		
Surendranath	not out	5		
SP Gupte	b Fazal Mahmood	14	(b 3, lb 9, nb 4)	16
	(b 10, lb 3, nb 1)	14	(4 wickets)	127
	(all out)	180		

Bowling: Mahmood Hussain 31-12-56-2 Fazal Mahmood 25.3-12-26-5 Intikhab Alam 24-11-35-2 Nasim-ul-Ghani 12-5-32-0 Haseeb Ahsan 7-1-17-1
Mahmood Hussain 8-3-9-0 Fazal Mahmood 12-2-19-0 Intikhab Alam 15-2-33-2 Nasim-ul-Ghani 2-1-5-0 Haseeb Ahsan 14-6-25-2 Saeed Ahmed 1-0-2-0 Mushtaq Mohammad 3-1-9-0 Hanif Mohammad 1-0-6-0 Javed Burki 1-0-3-0

Umpires: SK Ganguli and B Satyaji Rao

India v England
30,31 December 1961, 1,3,4 January 1962

Result: India won by 187 runs

India Innings

*NJ Contractor	b Smith	4	st Millman b Allen	11
VL Mehra	c Parfitt b Lock	62	not out	7
VL Manjrekar	b Allen	24	st Millman b Lock	27
Nawab of Pataudi jnr	c Lock b Allen	64	c Millman b Lock	32
PR Umrigar	c Smith b Allen	36	b Allen	36
ML Jaisimha	c Millman b Smith	37	b Lock	36
CG Borde	run out	68	c Barrington b Allen	61
SA Durani	b Allen	43	c Parfitt b Lock	0
+FM Engineer	c Parfitt b Lock	12	c Millman b Allen	9
RB Desai	not out	13	c Parfitt b Knight	29
VB Ranjane	c Barber b Allen	7	c Lock b Knight	0
	(b 2, lb 6, nb 2)	10	(lb 3, nb 1)	4
	(all out)	380	(all out)	252

Bowling: Smith 31-10-60-2 Knight 18-3-61-0 Dexter 29-7-83-0 Allen 34-13-67-5 Lock 36-19-63-2 Barber 3-0-17-0 Russell 5-0-19-0
Smith 3-0-15-0 Knight 7-2-18-2 Allen 43.2-16-95-4 Lock 46-15-111-4 Barber 2-0-9-0

England Innings

PE Richardson	c Contractor b Borde	62	b Umrigar	42
WE Russell	b Ranjane	10	b Ranjane	9
KF Barrington	b Durani	14	c sub b Borde	3
PH Parfitt	c sub b Borde	21	lbw b Umrigar	46
*ER Dexter	b Borde	57	lbw b Durani	62
RW Barber	b Borde	12	c Jaisimha b Durani	6
BR Knight	st Engineer b Durani	12	not out	39
DA Allen	b Durani	15	c Manjrekar b Desai	7
+G Millman	c Engineer b Durani	0	b Ranjane	4
GAR Lock	not out	2	run out	1
DR Smith	b Durani	0	c Manjrekar b Durani	2
	(b 1, lb 2, nb 4)	7	(b 1, lb 11)	12
	(all out)	212	(all out)	233

Bowling: Desai 10-1-34-0 Ranjane 21-3-59-1 Durani 23.2-8-47-5 Borde 25-8-65-4
Desai 17-4-32-2 Ranjane 14-3-31-2 Durani 33.2-12-66-3 Borde 22-10-46-0 Umrigar 30-10-46-2

Umpires: HE Choudhury and SK Raghunatha Rao

India v England
29,30 January, 1,2,3 February 1964

Result: Match drawn

India Innings

ML Jaisimha	c Binks b Price	33	c Larter b Titmus	129
+BK Kunderan	c Binks b Price	23	lbw b Wilson	27
DN Sardesai	c Binks b Larter	54	c & b Parfitt	36
VL Manjrekar	c & b Price	25	b Parfitt	16
RF Surti	b Price	0		
CG Borde	c Cowdrey b Wilson	21	c Parks b Titmus	8
*Nawab of Pataudi jnr	c Binks b Wilson	2	c Smith b Larter	31
SA Durani	c Binks b Price	8	c Cowdrey b Larter	25
RG Nadkarni	not out	43	not out	10
RB Desai	lbw b Titmus	11	not out	2
BS Chandrasekhar	c Cowdrey b Knight	16		
	(lb 1, nb 4)	5	(b 7, lb 5, nb 4)	16
	(all out)	241	(7 wickets declared)	300

Bowling: Knight 13.2-5-39-1 Price 23-4-73-5 Larter 18-4-61-1 Titmus 15-4-46-1 Wilson 16-10-17-2
Knight 4-0-33-0 Price 7-0-31-0 Larter 8-0-27-2 Titmus 46-23-67-2 Wilson 21-7-55-1 Parfitt 34-16-71-2

England Innings

JB Bolus	c & b Durani	39	c Jaisimha b Borde	35
+JG Binks	c Desai b Durani	13	b Durani	10
*MJK Smith	c Jaisimha b Borde	19	not out	75
MC Cowdrey	c Pataudi b Desai	107	not out	13
JM Parks	lbw b Nadkarni	30		
PH Parfitt	c & b Desai	4		
D Wilson	st Kunderan b Chandrasekhar	1		
BR Knight	c Manjrekar b Nadkarni	13		
FJ Titmus	b Desai	26		
JSE Price	not out	1		
JDF Larter	c Manjrekar b Desai	0		
	(b 6, lb 5, nb 3)	14	(b 9)	9
	(all out)	267	(2 wickets)	145

Bowling: Desai 22.5-3-62-4 Surti 6-2-8-0 Jaisimha 4-1-10-0 Durani 22-7-59-2 Borde 31-14-40-1 Chandrasekhar 21-5-36-1 Nadkarni 42-24-38-2
Desai 5-0-12-0 Jaisimha 13-5-32-0 Durani 8-3-15-1 Borde 15-5-39-1 Chandrasekhar 8-2-20-0 Pataudi 3-1-8-0 Sardesai 3-0-10-0

Umpires: MV Nagendra and S Roy

India v Australia
17,18,20,21,22 October 1964

Result: Match drawn

Australia Innings

WM Lawry	b Durani	50	not out	47
+RB Simpson	lbw b Surti	67	c Hanumant Singh b Surti	71
RM Cowper	c Nadkarni b Durani	4	not out	14
PJP Burge	c Hanumant Singh b Durani	4		
BC Booth	b Durani	0		
IR Redpath	not out	32		
TR Veivers	c Pataudi b Durani	1		
+BN Jarman	b Durani	1		
GD McKenzie	st Indrajitsinhji b Surti	0		
RHD Sellers	b Surti	0		
AN Connolly	c Hanumant Singh b Chandrasekhar	0		
	(b 1, lb 8, nb 5)	14	(b 6, nb 5)	11
	(all out)	174	(1 wicket)	143

Bowling: Surti 21-7-38-3 Jaisimha 5-3-2-0 Durani 28-11-73-6 Chandrasekhar 28.5-15-39-1 Nadkarni 2-0-8-0
Surti 10-2-37-1 Jaisimha 2-1-4-0 Durani 18-3-59-0 Chandrasekhar 8-3-27-0 Nadkarni 8-6-5-0

India Innings

DN Sardesai	c Veivers b Booth	42
ML Jaisimha	c Booth b Simpson	57
SA Durani	c Simpson b Veivers	12
VL Manjrekar	lbw b Veivers	9
Hanumant Singh	c Veivers b Veivers	5
*Nawab of Pataudi jnr	b Simpson	2
RG Nadkarni	b McKenzie	24
CG Borde	not out	68
RF Surti	c Sellers b Simpson	9
+KS Indrajitsinhji	st Jarman b Booth	1
BS Chandrasekhar	b Simpson	1
	(b 4)	4
	(all out)	235

Bowling: McKenzie 13-1-31-1 Connolly 8-4-10-0 Veivers 52-18-81-3 Sellers 5-1-17-0 Booth 18-10-33-2 Cowper 6-0-14-0 Simpson 28-12-45-4

Umpires: SP Pan and B Satyaji Rao

Eden Gardens, Kolkata

India v New Zealand
5,6,7,8 March 1965

Result: Match drawn

New Zealand Innings
Batsman	1st innings		2nd innings	
GT Dowling	lbw b Venkataraghavan	27	c Engineer b Gupte	23
BE Congdon	b Desai	9	c Borde b Desai	0
RW Morgan	c Engineer b Desai	20	b Durani	33
*JR Reid	c Borde b Venkataraghavan	11	lbw b Venkataraghavan	11
B Sutcliffe	not out	151	c Hanumant Singh b Venkataraghavan	6
BW Yuile	b Gupte	1	lbw b Venkataraghavan	21
V Pollard	c Jaisimha b Desai	31	b Jaisimha	43
BR Taylor	c Kunderan b Nadkarni	105	not out	0
GE Vivian	b Desai	1	c Jaisimha b Nadkarni	43
RC Motz	lbw b Venkataraghavan	21	c Nadkarni b Durani	0
+JT Ward	not out	1		
	(b 10, lb 3)	13	(b 10, nb 1)	11
	(9 wickets declared)	462	(9 wickets declared)	191

Bowling: Desai 33-6-128-4 Jaisimha 20-6-73-0 Durani 15-3-49-0 Nadkarni 35-12-59-1 Gupte 16-3-54-1 Venkataraghavan 41-18-86-3
Desai 12-6-32-1 Jaisimha 15.1-12-21-1 Durani 18-10-34-2 Nadkarni 7-4-14-1 Gupte 22-7-64-1 Venkataraghavan 17-11-15-3

India Innings
Batsman	1st innings		2nd innings	
ML Jaisimha	b Motz	22	c Morgan b Congdon	0
BK Kunderan	b Congdon	36	not out	12
+FM Engineer	c Pollard b Taylor	10	c Pollard b Dowling	45
CG Borde	c Pollard b Taylor	62		
RG Nadkarni	b Taylor	0		
*Nawab of Pataudi jnr	c Ward b Taylor	153		
Hanumant Singh	c sub b Yuile	31		
SA Durani	c sub b Yuile	20	b Vivian	23
RB Desai	c Ward b Yuile	0		
S Venkataraghavan	b Taylor	7	not out	0
BP Gupte	not out	3		
	(b 23, lb 2, nb 11)	36	(b 11, lb 1)	12
	(all out)	380	(3 wickets)	92

Bowling: Motz 21-3-74-1 Taylor 23.5-2-86-5 Congdon 18-5-49-1 Pollard 15-1-50-0 Vivian 12-3-37-0 Reid 2-1-5-0 Yuile 14-3-43-3
Congdon 5-0-33-1 Vivian 3-0-14-1 Dowling 6-2-19-1 Sutcliffe 3-2-14-0

Umpires: SK Ganguli and AR Joshi

India v West Indies
31 December 1966, 1,3,4,5 January 1967

Result: West Indies won by an innings and 45 runs

West Indies Innings
CC Hunte	run out	43
MR Bynoe	run out	19
RB Kanhai	c Pataudi b Surti	90
BF Butcher	c Pataudi b Bedi	35
CH Lloyd	c Kunderan b Bedi	5
SM Nurse	c Surti b Jaisimha	56
*GS Sobers	c Jaisimha b Chandrasekhar	70
+JL Hendriks	b Surti	3
WW Hall	c Subramanya b Chandrasekhar	1
LR Gibbs	lbw b Chandrasekhar	1
CC Griffith	not out	9
	(b 7, lb 11, nb 4)	22
	(all out)	390

Bowling: Surti 30-3-106-2 Subramanya 6-1-9-0 Chandrasekhar 46-11-107-3 Bedi 36-11-92-2 Venkataraghavan 14-3-43-0 Jaisimha 6-2-11-1

India Innings
Batsman	1st innings		2nd innings	
+BK Kunderan	b Hall	39	lbw b Hall	4
ML Jaisimha	b Gibbs	37	c & b Gibbs	31
RF Surti	lbw b Sobers	16	c Griffith b Sobers	31
CG Borde	run out	10	b Lloyd	28
*Nawab of Pataudi jnr	c Griffith b Gibbs	2	c Griffith b Lloyd	2
Hanumant Singh	c Bynoe b Gibbs	4	b Sobers	37
V Subramanya	c Hendriks b Gibbs	12	run out	17
S Venkataraghavan	b Sobers	18	c Hendriks b Sobers	2
AA Baig	b Gibbs	4	b Gibbs	6
BS Bedi	st Hendriks b Sobers	5	c Bynoe b Sobers	0
BS Chandrasekhar	not out	3	not out	1
	(b 12, lb 1, nb 4)	17	(b 14, lb 2, nb 3)	19
	(all out)	167	(all out)	178

Bowling: Sobers 28.5-15-42-3 Griffith 6-3-14-0 Gibbs 37-17-51-5 Hall 6-0-32-1 Lloyd 4-2-4-0 Nurse 4-1-7-0
Sobers 20-2-56-4 Griffith 5-4-4-0 Gibbs 30.4-8-36-2 Hall 7-0-35-1 Lloyd 14-5-23-2 Hunte 1-0-5-0

Umpires: I Gopalakrishnan and SP Pan

India v Australia
12,13,14,16 December 1969

Result: Australia won by 10 wickets

India Innings
Batsman	1st innings		2nd innings	
+FM Engineer	c Stackpole b McKenzie	0	c Redpath b Freeman	10
AV Mankad	c Stackpole b McKenzie	9	c Taber b McKenzie	20
AL Wadekar	c Freeman b McKenzie	0	lbw b Freeman	62
GR Viswanath	c Taber b Mallett	54	b Freeman	5
*Nawab of Pataudi jnr	c Chappell b Mallett	15	c Connolly b Mallett	1
AK Roy	c Taber b McKenzie	18	c Sheahan b Connolly	19
ED Solkar	c Taber b McKenzie	42	lbw b Connolly	21
S Venkataraghavan	c Stackpole b Mallett	24	b Connolly	0
EAS Prasanna	run out	26	c Stackpole b Freeman	0
S Guha	b McKenzie	4	not out	1
BS Bedi	not out	9	c Chappell b Connolly	7
	(b 5, lb 1, w 1, nb 4)	11	(b 6, lb 4, nb 5)	15
	(all out)	212	(all out)	161

Bowling: McKenzie 33.4-12-67-6 Freeman 17-6-43-0 Connolly 17-5-27-0 Mallett 27-9-55-3 Stackpole 2-0-9-0
McKenzie 18-4-34-1 Freeman 26-7-54-4 Connolly 16.1-3-31-4 Mallett 17-5-27-1

Australia Innings
Batsman	1st innings		2nd innings	
*WM Lawry	c Solkar b Bedi	35	not out	17
KR Stackpole	run out	41	not out	25
IM Chappell	c Wadekar b Bedi	99		
KD Walters	st Engineer b Bedi	56		
IR Redpath	c Wadekar b Bedi	0		
AP Sheahan	run out	32		
EW Freeman	c Prasanna b Bedi	29		
+HB Taber	b Bedi	2		
GD McKenzie	c Pataudi b Bedi	0		
AA Mallett	not out	2		
AN Connolly	c Guha b Solkar	31		
	(b 4, lb 2, nb 2)	8		0
	(all out)	335	(0 wickets)	42

Bowling: Guha 19-5-55-0 Solkar 9.1-1-28-1 Prasanna 49-15-116-0 Venkataraghavan 16-6-30-0 Bedi 50-19-98-7
Guha 3-1-25-0 Wadekar 2-0-17-0

Umpires: SP Pan and J Reuben

India v England
30,31 December 1972, 1,3,4 January 1973

Result: India won by 28 runs

India Innings
Batsman	1st innings		2nd innings	
SM Gavaskar	c Old b Underwood	18	lbw b Old	2
RD Parkar	c Knott b Old	26	c Fletcher b Old	15
*AL Wadekar	run out	44	lbw b Greig	0
GR Viswanath	c Wood b Cottam	3	c Fletcher b Old	34
SA Durani	b Greig	4	c Fletcher b Greig	53
ED Solkar	b Old	19	c Knott b Greig	6
+FM Engineer	b Underwood	75	c Knott b Underwood	17
S Abid Ali	b Cottam	3	c Amiss b Old	1
EAS Prasanna	lbw b Cottam	6	b Greig	0
BS Bedi	not out	0	not out	9
BS Chandrasekhar	not out	1	b Greig	1
	(lb 3, nb 8)	11	(b 8, lb 2, nb 5)	15
	(all out)	210	(all out)	155

Bowling: Old 26-7-72-2 Cottam 23-6-45-3 Underwood 20.4-11-43-2 Pocock 19-10-26-0 Greig 9-1-13-1
Old 21-6-43-4 Cottam 5-0-18-0 Underwood 14-4-36-1 Pocock 8-1-19-0 Greig 19.5-9-24-5

England Innings
Batsman	1st innings		2nd innings	
B Wood	b Bedi	11	b Abid Ali	1
DL Amiss	c Solkar b Chandrasekhar	11	c Engineer b Bedi	1
KWR Fletcher	c Gavaskar b Prasanna	16	lbw b Bedi	5
MH Denness	c Solkar b Chandrasekhar	21	lbw b Chandrasekhar	32
*AR Lewis	lbw b Bedi	4	c Solkar b Bedi	3
AW Greig	c sub b Prasanna	29	lbw b Chandrasekhar	67
+APE Knott	st Engineer b Chandrasekhar	35	c Durani b Chandrasekhar	2
CM Old	not out	33	not out	17
PI Pocock	b Prasanna	3	c & b Bedi	5
DL Underwood	c Solkar b Chandrasekhar	0	c Wadekar b Bedi	4
RMH Cottam	lbw b Chandrasekhar	3	lbw b Chandrasekhar	13
	(lb 4, nb 4)	8	(b 6, lb 5, nb 2)	13
	(all out)	174	(all out)	163

Bowling: Abid Ali 4-1-4-0 Solkar 3-1-5-0 Bedi 26-7-59-2 Chandrasekhar 26.2-5-65-5 Prasanna 16-4-33-3
Abid Ali 8-2-12-1 Solkar 1-1-0-0 Bedi 40-12-63-5 Chandrasekhar 29-14-42-4 Prasanna 9-0-19-0 Durani 4-1-14-0

Umpires: AM Mamsa and J Reuben

India v West Indies
27,28,29,31 December 1974, 1 January 1975

Result: India won by 85 runs

India Innings
Batsman	1st innings		2nd innings	
SS Naik	c Murray b Roberts	0	c Fredericks b Roberts	6
+FM Engineer	c Lloyd b Roberts	24	c Lloyd b Willett	61
PH Sharma	b Julien	6	run out	9
GR Viswanath	lbw b Gibbs	52	b Holder	139
*Mansur Ali Khan	b Roberts	36	c Holder b Willett	8
AD Gaekwad	c Murray b Fredericks	36	c Greenidge b Gibbs	4
S Madan Lal	c Murray b Holder	48	b Roberts	15
KD Ghavri	b Holder	3	b Roberts	27
EAS Prasanna	c Greenidge b Roberts	17	lbw b Holder	2
BS Bedi	b Roberts	0	c Julien b Holder	5
BS Chandrasekhar	not out	4	not out	7
	(lb 1, nb 6)	7	(b 3, lb 13, nb 17)	33
	(all out)	233	(all out)	316

Bowling: Roberts 19.3-6-50-5 Julien 12-1-57-1 Holder 16-3-48-2 Fredericks 9-4-24-1 Gibbs 17-6-34-1 Willett 7-3-13-0
Roberts 31-6-88-3 Julien 17-8-29-0 Holder 27.2-5-61-3 Fredericks 1-0-1-0 Gibbs 37-17-53-1 Willett 30-14-51-2

West Indies Innings
Batsman	1st innings		2nd innings	
RC Fredericks	c Viswanath b Madan Lal	100	b Bedi	21
CG Greenidge	c Bedi b Madan Lal	20	lbw b Ghavri	3
AI Kallicharran	c Mansur Ali Khan b Madan Lal	0	c Viswanath b Chandrasekhar	57
IVA Richards	run out	15	b Madan Lal	47
*CH Lloyd	c Engineer b Bedi	19	b Chandrasekhar	28
+DL Murray	run out	24	lbw b Bedi	13
BD Julien	c Viswanath b Bedi	19	b Chandrasekhar	7
ET Willett	b Ghavri	13	not out	16
VA Holder	b Chandrasekhar	2	run out	0
LR Gibbs	not out	6	c Prasanna b Bedi	3
AME Roberts	lbw b Madan Lal	1	b Bedi	6
	(b 6, lb 11, nb 4)	21	(b 8, lb 10, nb 5)	23
	(all out)	240	(all out)	224

Bowling: Ghavri 7-1-28-1 Madan Lal 16.1-5-22-4 Bedi 25-8-68-2 Chandrasekhar 22-6-80-1 Prasanna 11-4-21-0
Ghavri 7-0-18-1 Madan Lal 6-1-23-1 Bedi 26.2-13-52-4 Chandrasekhar 20-3-66-3 Prasanna 25-12-42-0

Umpires: J Reuben and HP Sharma

India v England
1,2,3,5,6 January 1977

Result: England won by 10 wickets

India Innings
Batsman	1st innings		2nd innings	
SM Gavaskar	c Old b Willis	0	b Underwood	18
AD Gaekwad	b Lever	32	c Tolchard b Greig	8
PH Sharma	c Greig b Lever	9	c Knott b Willis	20
GR Viswanath	c Tolchard b Underwood	35	c Lever b Greig	3
BP Patel	hit wicket b Willis	21	lbw b Old	56
ED Solkar	c Greig b Willis	2	c Knott b Willis	3
S Madan Lal	c Knott b Old	17	c Brearley b Old	16
+SMH Kirmani	not out	25	b Old	9
EAS Prasanna	b Willis	2	c Brearley b Underwood	13
*BS Bedi	c Lever b Old	1	b Underwood	18
BS Chandrasekhar	b Willis	1	not out	4
	(lb 2, nb 8)	10	(b 2, lb 4, nb 16)	22
	(all out)	155	(all out)	181

Bowling: Willis 20-3-27-5 Lever 22-2-57-2 Underwood 13-5-24-1 Old 20-5-37-2
Willis 13-1-32-2 Lever 3-0-12-0 Underwood 32.5-18-50-3 Old 12-4-38-3 Greig 10-0-27-2

England Innings
Batsman	1st innings		2nd innings	
DL Amiss	c Kirmani b Prasanna	35	not out	7
GD Barlow	c Kirmani b Madan Lal	4	not out	7
JM Brearley	c Solkar b Bedi	5		
DW Randall	lbw b Prasanna	37		
RW Tolchard	b Bedi	67		
*AW Greig	lbw b Prasanna	103		
+APE Knott	c Gavaskar b Bedi	2		
CM Old	c Madan Lal b Prasanna	52		
JK Lever	c Gavaskar b Bedi	2		
DL Underwood	c Gavaskar b Bedi	4		
RGD Willis	not out	0		
	(b 5, lb 5)	10	(lb 1, nb 1)	2
	(all out)	321	(0 wickets)	16

Bowling: Madan Lal 17-4-25-1 Solkar 6-1-15-0 Bedi 64-25-110-5 Chandrasekhar 33-9-66-0 Prasanna 57.4-16-93-4 Sharma 1-0-2-0
Madan Lal 1-0-3-0 Bedi 1.4-0-6-0 Prasanna 1-0-5-0

Umpires: B Satyaji Rao and HP Sharma

India v West Indies
29,30,31 December 1978, 2,3 January 1979

Result: Match drawn

India Innings

*SM Gavaskar	c Bacchus b Phillip	107	not out	182
CPS Chauhan	b Clarke	11		
AD Gaekwad	c Murray b Marshall	7	b Clarke	5
GR Viswanath	b Phillip	32		
DB Vengsarkar	c Williams b Parry	42	not out	157
MV Narasimha Rao	c Gomes b Parry	1		
KD Ghavri	c Marshall b Phillip	5		
+SMH Kirmani	lbw b Phillip	0		
N Kapil Dev	b Parry	61		
S Venkataraghavan	lbw b Holder	7		
BS Bedi	not out	4		
	(b 3, lb 2, nb 18)	23	(b 1, lb 4, nb 12)	17
	(all out)	300	(1 wicket declared)	361

Bowling: Clarke 27-8-70-1 Phillip 22-6-64-4 Marshall 12-3-44-1 Holder 21-5-48-1 Gomes 1-1-0-0 Parry 20.3-7-51-3 Shivnarine 1-1-0-0
Clarke 28-4-104-1 Phillip 16-0-81-0 Marshall 14-3-45-0 Holder 20-3-59-0 Gomes 1-0-3-0 Parry 13-3-50-0 Shivnarine 1-0-2-0

West Indies Innings

AB Williams	c & b Ghavri	111	b Ghavri	11
SFAF Bacchus	b Ghavri	26	c & b Ghavri	20
HA Gomes	b Venkataraghavan	8	b Venkataraghavan	5
*AI Kallicharran	c Narasimha Rao b Venkataraghavan	55	c Viswanath b Narasimha Rao	46
VA Holder	c Narasimha Rao b Venkataraghavan	3	b Ghavri	4
+DA Murray	c Kapil Dev b Venkataraghavan	2	st Kirmani b Venkataraghavan	66
S Shivnarine	c sub b Ghavri	48	not out	36
DR Parry	b Bedi	4	c Gavaskar b Venkataraghavan	0
N Phillip	lbw b Kapil Dev	47	lbw b Ghavri	0
MD Marshall	c Kirmani b Kapil Dev	4	lbw b Bedi	1
ST Clarke	not out	4	not out	0
	(b 5, lb 9, nb 4)	18	(b 2, lb 4, nb 2)	8
	(all out)	327	(9 wickets)	197

Bowling: Kapil Dev 20.4-3-88-2 Ghavri 29-5-74-3 Bedi 24-4-59-1 Venkataraghavan 33-15-55-4 Narasimha Rao 11-0-33-0
Kapil Dev 13-6-21-0 Ghavri 23-8-46-4 Bedi 22-14-32-1 Venkataraghavan 30-13-47-3 Narasimha Rao 17.1-6-43-1

Umpires: SN Hanumantha Rao and PR Punjabi

India v Australia
26,27,28,30,31 October 1979

Result: Match drawn

Australia Innings

AMJ Hilditch	c Kirmani b Kapil Dev	0	b Ghavri	29
GN Yallop	c Gavaskar b Yadav	167	lbw b Kapil Dev	4
AR Border	lbw b Kapil Dev	54	st Kirmani b Doshi	6
*KJ Hughes	lbw b Kapil Dev	92	not out	64
DF Whatmore	b Kapil Dev	4	c Vengsarkar b Doshi	4
WM Darling	st Kirmani b Doshi	39	c Gavaskar b Yadav	7
B Yardley	not out	61	c Narasimha Rao b Yadav	12
+KJ Wright	lbw b Doshi	0	not out	12
G Dymock	lbw b Doshi	3		
RM Hogg	c Yashpal Sharma b Doshi	0		
JD Higgs	lbw b Kapil Dev	1		
	(b 7, lb 7, nb 7)	21	(b 9, lb 4)	13
	(all out)	442	(6 wickets declared)	151

Bowling: Kapil Dev 32-9-74-5 Ghavri 24-3-85-0 Yadav 42-8-135-2 Narasimha Rao 8-0-24-0 Doshi 43-10-92-4 Chauhan 4-0-11-0
Kapil Dev 11-3-33-1 Ghavri 13.3-5-39-1 Yadav 11-6-16-2 Doshi 22-6-50-2

India Innings

*SM Gavaskar	lbw b Hogg	14	c Hilditch b Dymock	25
CPS Chauhan	c Border b Higgs	39	c Wright b Dymock	50
DB Vengsarkar	c Hughes b Yardley	89	c Wright b Dymock	2
GR Viswanath	c Wright b Yardley	96	lbw b Dymock	7
Yashpal Sharma	c Wright b Hogg	22	not out	85
MV Narasimha Rao	run out	10	not out	20
N Kapil Dev	c Hughes b Dymock	30		
+SMH Kirmani	not out	13		
KD Ghavri	c Wright b Yardley	1		
NS Yadav	c Wright b Yardley	0		
DR Doshi	b Dymock	0		
	(b 12, lb 9, w 4, nb 8)	33	(b 4, lb 7)	11
	(all out)	347	(4 wickets)	200

Bowling: Dymock 26.4-8-56-2 Hogg 26-2-103-2 Yardley 42-11-91-4 Higgs 28-12-56-1 Border 2-0-8-0 Yallop 1-1-0-0
Dymock 25-7-63-4 Hogg 8-2-1-26-0 Yardley 13-1-47-0 Higgs 16-3-51-0 Yallop 1-0-2-0

Umpires: SN Hanumantha Rao and S Kishen

India v Pakistan
29,30,31 January, 2,3 February 1980

Result: Match drawn

India Innings

SM Gavaskar	c Iqbal Qasim b Imran Khan	44	c Javed Miandad b Imran Khan	15
CPS Chauhan	lbw b Ehteshamuddin	18	b Ehteshamuddin	21
RMH Binny	lbw b Imran Khan	15	c Wasim Raja b Imran Khan	0
*GR Viswanath	b Ehteshamuddin	13	b Imran Khan	13
SM Patil	b Imran Khan	62	run out	31
Yashpal Sharma	c Wasim Bari b Imran Khan	62	b Ehteshamuddin	21
N Kapil Dev	st Wasim Bari b Iqbal Qasim	16	b Iqbal Qasim	30
+SMH Kirmani	c Iqbal Qasim b Ehteshamuddin	37	c Sadiq Mohammad b Imran Khan	0
KD Ghavri	run out	16	not out	37
NS Yadav	not out	18	c & b Iqbal Qasim	3
DR Doshi	b Ehteshamuddin	3	c Asif Iqbal b Imran Khan	6
	(b 3, lb 9, nb 15)	27	(b 9, lb 3, nb 16)	28
	(all out)	331	(all out)	205

Bowling: Imran Khan 35-5-67-4 Sikander Bakht 22-5-87-0 Ehteshamuddin 35-7-87-4 Iqbal Qasim 17-3-53-1 Majid Khan 2-0-10-0
Imran Khan 23.5-3-63-5 Sikander Bakht 6-2-18-0 Ehteshamuddin 19-5-44-2 Iqbal Qasim 21-5-50-2 Wasim Raja 1-0-2-0

Pakistan Innings

Taslim Arif	c Chauhan b Kapil Dev	90	c & b Binny	46
Sadiq Mohammad	lbw b Kapil Dev	5	b Ghavri	8
Majid Khan	c Kirmani b Binny	54	b Doshi	11
Javed Miandad	lbw b Ghavri	50	c & b Doshi	46
Wasim Raja	not out	50	run out	12
*Asif Iqbal	not out	5	run out	15
Imran Khan			not out	19
+Wasim Bari			not out	0
Iqbal Qasim				
Sikander Bakht				
Ehteshamuddin				
	(b 1, lb 8, nb 9)	18	(b 12, lb 8, nb 2)	22
	(4 wickets declared)	272	(6 wickets)	179

Bowling: Kapil Dev 26-4-65-2 Ghavri 21.5-3-77-1 Doshi 25-12-38-0 Binny 17-3-35-1 Yadav 10-0-39-0
Kapil Dev 20-7-49-0 Ghavri 11-2-32-1 Doshi 20-5-46-2 Binny 8-2-20-1 Yadav 4-3-10-0

Umpires: PR Punjabi and KB Ramaswami

India v England
1,2,3,5,6 January 1982

Result: Match drawn

England Innings

GA Gooch	c Viswanath b Doshi	47	b Doshi	63
G Boycott	c Kirmani b Kapil Dev	18	lbw b Madan Lal	6
CJ Tavare	c Kirmani b Kapil Dev	7	run out	25
DI Gower	c Kirmani b Shastri	11	run out	74
*KWR Fletcher	lbw b Madan Lal	69	not out	60
IT Botham	c Gavaskar b Kapil Dev	58	c Yadav b Doshi	31
DL Underwood	c Patil b Kapil Dev	13		
MW Gatting	c Kirmani b Kapil Dev	0	not out	2
JE Emburey	lbw b Kapil Dev	1		
+RW Taylor	c Vengsarkar b Doshi	6		
RGD Willis	not out	11		
	(lb 3, nb 4)	7	(lb 4)	4
	(all out)	248	(5 wickets declared)	265

Bowling: Kapil Dev 31-6-91-6 Madan Lal 20-4-58-1 Doshi 19.2-8-28-2 Yadav 17-7-42-0 Shastri 21-10-22-1
Kapil Dev 21-3-81-0 Madan Lal 19-3-58-1 Doshi 27-5-63-2 Yadav 3-0-11-0 Shastri 17-4-35-0 Patil 3-0-13-0

India Innings

*SM Gavaskar	b Underwood	42	not out	83
K Srikkanth	b Underwood	10	c Botham b Emburey	25
DB Vengsarkar	c Taylor b Botham	70	c Tavare b Fletcher	32
GR Viswanath	c & b Emburey	15	c Gooch b Emburey	0
SM Patil	c Fletcher b Emburey	0	not out	17
N Kapil Dev	c Tavare b Underwood	22		
RJ Shastri	run out	8		
+SMH Kirmani	b Botham	10		
S Madan Lal	c Gooch b Willis	1		
NS Yadav	c Taylor b Willis	5		
DR Doshi	not out	7		
	(b 2, lb 4, w 1, nb 11)	18	(lb 2, nb 11)	13
	(all out)	208	(3 wickets)	170

Bowling: Willis 14-3-28-2 Botham 27-8-63-2 Underwood 29-13-45-3 Emburey 24-11-44-2 Gooch 6-1-10-0
Willis 6-0-21-0 Botham 11-3-26-0 Underwood 31-18-38-0 Emburey 30-11-62-2 Gooch 2-0-4-0 Fletcher 3-1-6-1

Umpires: MV Gothoskar and S Kishen

India v West Indies
10,11,12,14 December 1983

Result: West Indies won by an innings and 46 runs

India Innings

SM Gavaskar	c Dujon b Marshall	0	c Dujon b Holding	20
AD Gaekwad	b Marshall	2	b Holding	4
DB Vengsarkar	b Holding	23	lbw b Marshall	1
M Amarnath	c & b Marshall	0	b Holding	0
AO Malhotra	c Gomes b Davis	20	c Dujon b Marshall	30
RJ Shastri	b Holding	12	b Marshall	2
RMH Binny	lbw b Roberts	44	c Harper b Marshall	6
*N Kapil Dev	b Holding	69	c Dujon b Marshall	0
+SMH Kirmani	b Roberts	49	b Roberts	13
NS Yadav	c Greenidge b Roberts	10	b Marshall	4
Maninder Singh	not out	0	not out	0
	(lb 6, nb 6)	12	(b 1, lb 5, nb 4)	10
	(all out)	241	(all out)	90

Bowling: Marshall 22-7-65-3 Roberts 23.4-9-56-3 Davis 14-1-39-1 Holding 20-4-59-3 Harper 8-2-16-0
Marshall 15-4-37-6 Roberts 4-1-11-1 Davis 2-0-7-0 Holding 9-3-29-3

West Indies Innings

CG Greenidge	c Yadav b Binny	25	
DL Haynes	lbw b Kapil Dev	5	
IVA Richards	c Kirmani b Kapil Dev	9	
HA Gomes	b Yadav	18	
+PJL Dujon	c Gaekwad b Kapil Dev	0	
*CH Lloyd	not out	161	
MD Marshall	lbw b Maninder Singh	54	
MA Holding	c Shastri b Maninder Singh	17	
RA Harper	lbw b Kapil Dev	0	
AME Roberts	c Amarnath b Yadav	68	
WW Davis	lbw b Yadav	0	
	(b 8, lb 7, w 1, nb 4)	20	
	(all out)	377	

Bowling: Kapil Dev 35-5-91-4 Binny 13-2-62-1 Amarnath 7-1-19-0 Yadav 27-1-80-3 Shastri 18-2-56-0 Maninder Singh 28-7-54-2

Umpires: MV Gothoskar and S Kishen

India v England
31 December 1984, 1,3,4,5 January 1985

Result: Match drawn

India Innings

*SM Gavaskar	c Gatting b Edmonds	13		
AD Gaekwad	c Downton b Cowans	18		
DB Vengsarkar	b Edmonds	48		
M Amarnath	c Cowdrey b Edmonds	42		
M Azharuddin	c Gower b Cowans	110		
RJ Shastri	b Cowans	111	not out	7
+SMH Kirmani	c Fowler b Pocock	35		
M Prabhakar	not out	35	lbw b Lamb	21
C Sharma	not out	13		
NS Yadav			not out	0
L Sivaramakrishnan				
	(lb 8, w 1, nb 3)	12	(nb 1)	1
	(7 wickets declared)	437	(1 wicket)	29

Bowling: Cowans 41-12-103-3 Ellison 53-14-117-0 Edmonds 47-22-72-3 Pocock 52-14-108-1 Gatting 2-1-1-0 Cowdrey 2-0-15-0 Gower 3-0-13-0
Cowans 4-1-6-0 Ellison 1-0-1-0 Edmonds 4-3-2-0 Pocock 2-1-4-0 Cowdrey 4-0-10-0 Lamb 1-0-6-1 Robinson 1-1-0-0 Fowler 1-1-0-0

England Innings

G Fowler	c Vengsarkar b Sivaramakrishnan	49	
RT Robinson	b Yadav	36	
*DI Gower	c Shastri b Yadav	19	
PI Pocock	c Azharuddin b Sivaramakrishnan	5	
MW Gatting	b Yadav	48	
AJ Lamb	c Kirmani b Sharma	67	
CS Cowdrey	lbw b Yadav	27	
+PR Downton	not out	6	
PH Edmonds	c Gavaskar b Sharma	8	
RM Ellison	c & b Sharma	1	
NG Cowans	b Sharma	1	
	(lb 2, nb 7)	9	
	(all out)	276	

Bowling: Sharma 12.3-0-38-4 Prabhakar 5-1-16-0 Sivaramakrishnan 28-7-90-2 Yadav 32-10-86-4 Shastri 23-6-44-0

Umpires: B Ganguli and V Vikramraju

Eden Gardens, Kolkata

India v Pakistan
11,12,14,15,16 February 1987

Result: Match drawn

India Innings

K Srikkanth	c Saleem Malik b Wasim Akram	22	lbw b Imran Khan	21
J Arun Lal	c Tauseef Ahmed b Saleem Jaffar	52	c Wasim Akram b Imran Khan	70
M Amarnath	run out	9	b Tauseef Ahmed	31
DB Vengsarkar	c Saleem Yousuf b Wasim Akram	38	not out	41
M Azharuddin	b Wasim Akram	141		
RJ Shastri	b Abdul Qadir	5		
*N Kapil Dev	c Javed Miandad b Saleem Jaffar	66		
RMH Binny	not out	52		
+KS More	run out	0		
RR Kulkarni	lbw b Wasim Akram	0		
Maninder Singh	b Wasim Akram	3		
	(b 1, lb 8, w 1, nb 5)	15	(b 4, lb 12, nb 2)	18
	(all out)	403	(3 wickets declared)	181

Bowling: Imran Khan 27-2-93-0 Wasim Akram 31-6-96-5 Saleem Jaffar 36-2-115-2 Tauseef Ahmed 10-1-39-0 Abdul Qadir 14-3-51-1
Imran Khan 7.1-0-28-2 Wasim Akram 18-4-46-0 Saleem Jaffar 7-0-33-0 Tauseef Ahmed 18-2-50-1 Abdul Qadir 2-0-8-0

Pakistan Innings

Shoaib Mohammad	run out	24	lbw b Binny	5
Rameez Raja	c sub b Shastri	69	c More b Binny	29
Rizwan-uz-Zaman	b Kapil Dev	60	b Shastri	8
Javed Miandad	c More b Binny	17	not out	63
Saleem Malik	lbw b Binny	0	lbw b Kapil Dev	20
*Imran Khan	c Kapil Dev b Binny	1	not out	5
+Saleem Yousuf	lbw b Kapil Dev	33	b Maninder Singh	43
Wasim Akram	b Binny	1		
Abdul Qadir	b Binny	2		
Tauseef Ahmed	c Vengsarkar b Binny	0		
Saleem Jaffar	not out	0		
	(b 4, lb 4, w 1, nb 13)	22	(b 1, lb 2, w 2, nb 1)	6
	(all out)	229	(5 wickets)	179

Bowling: Kapil Dev 29-5-88-2 Binny 25.1-8-56-6 Maninder Singh 20.1-11-21-0 Shastri 20.5-10-18-1 Kulkarni 13-1-38-0
Kapil Dev 19-7-41-1 Binny 21-4-45-2 Maninder Singh 16-6-30-1 Shastri 24-6-41-1 Kulkarni 7-2-19-0

Umpires: RB Gupta and PD Reporter

India v West Indies
26,27,28,30,31 December 1987

Result: Match drawn

West Indies Innings

CG Greenidge	c More b Kapil Dev	141	c sub b Shastri	69
DL Haynes	c Srikkanth b Kapil Dev	5	c & b Shastri	47
RB Richardson	c Azharuddin b Shastri	51	not out	8
*IVA Richards	c Kapil Dev b Sharma	68		
AL Logie	c & b Maninder Singh	101	not out	20
CL Hooper	not out	100		
+PJL Dujon	not out	40		
CG Butts				
WW Davis				
CA Walsh				
BP Patterson				
	(b 2, lb 12, nb 10)	24	(b 4, lb 2, nb 7)	13
	(5 wickets declared)	530	(2 wickets)	157

Bowling: Kapil Dev 28-6-103-2 Sharma 15.1-0-80-1 Maninder Singh 36.5-5-111-1 Arshad Ayub 46-5-146-0 Shastri 22-4-60-1 Amarnath 3.5-0-16-0
Kapil Dev 10-2-19-0 Sharma 4-0-24-0 Maninder Singh 16-2-43-0 Arshad Ayub 14-5-34-0 Amarnath 4-0-11-0 Shastri 10-3-13-2 Srikkanth 3-0-7-0 Arun Lal 1-1-0-0

India Innings

K Srikkanth	c Dujon b Walsh	23
J Arun Lal	lbw b Walsh	93
M Amarnath	b Davis	43
*DB Vengsarkar	retired hurt	102
M Azharuddin	c Logie b Walsh	60
RJ Shastri	b Davis	47
N Kapil Dev	lbw b Davis	4
+KS More	c Richardson b Richards	44
Arshad Ayub	c Richardson b Patterson	57
C Sharma	b Walsh	27
Maninder Singh	not out	1
	(b 12, lb 25, nb 27)	64
	(all out)	565

Bowling: Patterson 22.2-0-107-1 Walsh 29-3-136-4 Davis 27-3-84-3 Butts 50-13-122-0 Richards 24-6-39-1 Hooper 20-5-40-0

Umpires: RB Gupta and PD Reporter

India v England
29,30,31 January, 1,2 February 1993

Result: India won by 8 wickets

India Innings

M Prabhakar	c Lewis b Salisbury	46	b Hick	13
NS Sidhu	c Hick b Taylor	13	st Stewart b Hick	37
VG Kambli	c Hick b Jarvis	16	not out	18
SR Tendulkar	c Hick b Malcolm	50	not out	9
*M Azharuddin	c Gooch b Hick	182		
PK Amre	c Hick b Jarvis	12		
N Kapil Dev	c Lewis b Hick	13		
+KS More	not out	4		
A Kumble	b Malcolm	0		
RK Chauhan	b Malcolm	2		
SLV Raju	c Salisbury b Hick	1		
	(b 6, lb 6, w 10, nb 10)	32	(lb 4, nb 1)	5
	(all out)	371	(2 wickets)	82

Bowling: Malcolm 24-3-67-3 Jarvis 27-5-72-2 Lewis 23-5-64-0 Taylor 19-2-65-1 Salisbury 17-2-72-1 Hick 12.5-5-19-3
Malcolm 6-1-16-0 Jarvis 5.2-1-23-0 Taylor 3-1-9-0 Salisbury 6-3-16-0 Lewis 3-1-5-0 Hick 6-1-9-2

England Innings

*GA Gooch	c Azharuddin b Raju	17	st More b Kumble	18
+AJ Stewart	b Prabhakar	0	c Tendulkar b Kumble	49
MW Gatting	b Chauhan	33	b Chauhan	81
RA Smith	c Amre b Kumble	1	c More b Chauhan	8
GA Hick	b Kumble	1	lbw b Raju	25
NH Fairbrother	c More b Kumble	17	c sub (WV Raman) b Kumble	25
IDK Salisbury	c More b Chauhan	28	c More b Kapil Dev	26
CC Lewis	b Raju	21	c Amre b Raju	16
PW Jarvis	c Prabhakar b Raju	4	lbw b Raju	6
JP Taylor	st More b Chauhan	17	not out	17
DE Malcolm	not out	4	lbw b Kapil Dev	0
	(b 8, lb 8, w 4)	20	(lb 13, nb 2)	15
	(all out)	163	(all out)	286

Bowling: Kapil Dev 6-1-18-0 Prabhakar 9-3-10-1 Kumble 29-8-50-3 Raju 27-14-39-3 Chauhan 29.1-15-30-3
Kapil Dev 8.2-5-12-2 Prabhakar 9-4-26-0 Kumble 40-16-76-3 Raju 35-9-80-3 Chauhan 45-17-79-2

Umpires: PD Reporter and S Venkataraghavan; Referee: CW Smith (WI)

India v South Africa
27,28,29,30 November, 1 December 1996

Result: South Africa won by 329 runs

South Africa Innings

AC Hudson	b Prasad	146	retired hurt	6
G Kirsten	b Srinath	102	run out (Joshi)	133
HH Gibbs	lbw b Prasad	31	c Dravid b Srinath	9
DJ Cullinan	lbw b Prasad	43	not out	153
*WJ Cronje	c Mongia b Srinath	4	c & b Kumble	34
BM McMillan	lbw b Prasad	0	not out	17
+DJ Richardson	not out	36		
L Klusener	b Prasad	10		
PL Symcox	b Prasad	13		
AA Donald	c Laxman b Kumble	0		
PR Adams	b Kumble	4		
	(b 6, lb 24, nb 9)	39	(b 1, lb 11, w 1, nb 2)	15
	(all out)	428	(3 wickets declared)	367

Bowling: Srinath 37-7-107-2 Prasad 35-6-104-6 Joshi 12-1-48-0 Ganguly 3-1-10-0 Kumble 20.1-1-78-2 Hirwani 14-2-51-0
Srinath 24.2-2-101-1 Prasad 15-0-63-0 Kumble 32-4-101-1 Hirwani 11-1-40-0 Joshi 11-0-50-0

India Innings

+NR Mongia	run out (Gibbs)	35	c Cullinan b Klusener	8
R Dravid	c Hudson b McMillan	31	b McMillan	23
SC Ganguly	b McMillan	6	c Richardson b Klusener	0
*SR Tendulkar	b Donald	18	c Kirsten b Symcox	2
M Azharuddin	c & b Adams	109	c McMillan b Klusener	52
VVS Laxman	b Donald	14	b Klusener	1
SB Joshi	run out (Donald)	4	c McMillan b Klusener	1
J Srinath	b Donald	11	c McMillan b Klusener	19
A Kumble	run out (Gibbs)	88	b Klusener	17
BKV Prasad	c Richardson b Adams	1	not out	3
ND Hirwani	not out	0	b Klusener	0
	(lb 5, nb 7)	12	(lb 2, nb 9)	11
	(all out)	329	(all out)	137

Bowling: Donald 21.2-4-72-3 Klusener 14-1-75-0 Adams 13-1-69-2 McMillan 16-4-52-2 Cronje 6-3-13-0 Symcox 11-1-43-0
McMillan 19-8-33-1 Klusener 21.3-4-64-8 Cronje 7-4-10-0 Symcox 6-1-28-1

Umpires: BC Cooray (SL) and VK Ramaswamy
TV Umpire: SK Porel; Referee: JR Reid (NZ)

India v Australia
18,19,20,21 March 1998

Result: India won by an innings and 219 runs

Australia Innings

MJ Slater	c Dravid b Srinath	0	b Srinath	5
*MA Taylor	c Mongia b Ganguly	3	run out (Laxman/Mongia)	45
GS Blewett	b Srinath	0	lbw b Srinath	25
ME Waugh	lbw b Srinath	10	c Laxman b Kumble	0
SR Waugh	run out (Dravid/Kumble)	80	lbw b Kumble	33
RT Ponting	b Kumble	60	c Srinath b Kumble	9
+IA Healy	c Laxman b Kumble	1	lbw b Srinath	38
SK Warne	c Azharuddin b Kumble	11	c & b Kumble	9
GR Robertson	lbw b Ganguly	29	c Azharuddin b Kumble	0
MS Kasprowicz	c Azharuddin b Ganguly	25	c Raju b Chauhan	10
P Wilson	not out	0	not out	0
	(lb 2, nb 12)	14	(b 1, lb 3, nb 3)	7
	(all out)	233	(all out)	181

Bowling: Srinath 17-0-80-3 Ganguly 13.4-5-28-3 Kumble 28-11-44-3 Tendulkar 2-0-6-0 Raju 17-2-42-0 Chauhan 11-2-30-0 Laxman 1-0-1-0
Srinath 19-6-44-3 Ganguly 4-0-9-0 Kumble 31-10-62-5 Chauhan 18.4-4-42-1 Raju 16-7-20-0

India Innings

VVS Laxman	c Healy b Robertson	95
NS Sidhu	lbw b M Waugh	97
R Dravid	c & b Blewett	86
SR Tendulkar	c Blewett b Kasprowicz	79
*M Azharuddin	not out	163
SC Ganguly	c sub b Robertson	65
+NR Mongia	not out	30
J Srinath		
RK Chauhan		
SLV Raju		
A Kumble		
	(b 2, lb 7, nb 9)	18
	(5 wickets declared)	633

Bowling: Kasprowicz 34-6-122-1 Wilson 12-2-50-0 Blewett 20-3-65-1 Warne 42-4-147-0 Robertson 33-2-163-2 M Waugh 18-1-77-1

Umpires: BC Cooray (SL) and K Parthasarathy
TV Umpire: S Choudhary; Referee: PL van der Merwe (SA)

India v Pakistan
16,17,18,19,20 February 1999

Result: Pakistan won by 46 runs

Pakistan Innings

Saeed Anwar	b Prasad	0	not out	188
Shahid Afridi	c Mongia b Srinath	8	c Laxman b Srinath	0
Ijaz Ahmed	lbw b Srinath	1	c Mongia b Srinath	11
Wajahatullah Wasti	c Mongia b Prasad	6	c Mongia b Srinath	9
Yousuf Youhana	c Azharuddin b Srinath	2	c Dravid b Srinath	56
Saleem Malik	c Mongia b Srinath	32	lbw b Srinath	9
Azhar Mahmood	b Srinath	0	lbw b Srinath	0
+Moin Khan	c Laxman b Tendulkar	70	c Mongia b Prasad	8
*Wasim Akram	c sub (HH Kanitkar) b Harbhajan Singh	38	c Mongia b Srinath	1
Shoaib Akhtar	lbw b Kumble	4	b Srinath	1
Saqlain Mushtaq	not out	4	c Mongia b Harbhajan Singh	21
	(lb 11, w 1, nb 8)	20	(lb 3, w 5, nb 4)	12
	(all out)	185	(all out)	316

Bowling: Srinath 19-4-46-5 Prasad 18-6-27-2 Ganguly 5-2-9-0 Kumble 19.2-8-48-1 Harbhajan Singh 12-2-36-1 Tendulkar 3-1-8-1
Srinath 27-6-86-8 Prasad 24-5-61-1 Kumble 27-4-91-0 Harbhajan Singh 16-1-56-1 Laxman 2-0-4-0 Ramesh 1-0-5-0 Tendulkar 2-0-10-0

India Innings

S Ramesh	lbw b Wasim Akram	79	lbw b Saqlain Mushtaq	40
VVS Laxman	b Shoaib Akhtar	5	c Yousuf Youhana b Saqlain Mushtaq	67
A Kumble	c Moin Khan b Azhar Mahmood	18	c Shahid Afridi b Shoaib Akhtar	16
R Dravid	b Shoaib Akhtar	24	c Moin Khan b Shoaib Akhtar	13
SR Tendulkar	b Shoaib Akhtar	0	run out (sub [Nadeem Khan])	9
*M Azharuddin	c Saqlain Mushtaq b Wasim Akram	23	c Yousuf Youhana b Saqlain Mushtaq	20
SC Ganguly	c Wasim Akram b Saqlain Mushtaq	17	c Azhar Mahmood b Wasim Akram	24
+NR Mongia	run out (Moin Khan)	5	lbw b Shoaib Akhtar	1
J Srinath	c Moin Khan b Wasim Akram	3	c Moin Khan b Wasim Akram	3
BKV Prasad	b Shoaib Akhtar	0	b Shoaib Akhtar	2
Harbhajan Singh	not out	8	not out	0
	(lb 9, nb 32)	41	(b 10, lb 9, nb 18)	37
	(all out)	223	(all out)	232

Bowling: Wasim Akram 24-5-65-3 Shoaib Akhtar 19.2-1-71-4 Azhar Mahmood 18-5-40-1 Saqlain Mushtaq 13-4-31-1 Shahid Afridi 2-0-7-0
Shoaib Akhtar 20.1-5-47-4 Wasim Akram 24-4-64-2 Azhar Mahmood 6-0-23-0 Saqlain Mushtaq 25-5-69-3 Shahid Afridi 4-1-10-0

Umpires: SA Bucknor (WI) and DL Orchard (SA)
TV Umpire: KT Francis (SL); Referee: CW Smith (WI)

India v Australia
11,12,13,14,15 March 2001

Result: India won by 171 runs

Australia Innings

MJ Slater	c Mongia b Khan	42	c Ganguly b Harbhajan Singh	43
ML Hayden	c sub (HK Badani) b Harbhajan Singh	97	lbw b Tendulkar	67
JL Langer	c Mongia b Khan	58	c Ramesh b Harbhajan Singh	28
ME Waugh	c Mongia b Harbhajan Singh	22	lbw b Raju	0
*SR Waugh	lbw b Harbhajan Singh	110	c sub (HK Badani) b Harbhajan Singh	24
RT Ponting	lbw b Harbhajan Singh	6	c Das b Harbhajan Singh	0
+AC Gilchrist	lbw b Harbhajan Singh	0	lbw b Tendulkar	0
SK Warne	c Ramesh b Harbhajan Singh	0	lbw b Tendulkar	0
MS Kasprowicz	lbw b Ganguly	7	not out	13
JN Gillespie	c Ramesh b Harbhajan Singh	46	c Das b Harbhajan Singh	6
GD McGrath	not out	21	lbw b Harbhajan Singh	12
	(b 19, lb 10, nb 7)	36	(b 6, nb 8, pen 5)	19
	(all out)	445	(all out)	212

Bowling: Khan 28.4-6-89-2 Prasad 30-5-95-0 Ganguly 13.2-3-44-1 Raju 20-2-58-0 Harbhajan Singh 37.5-7-123-7 Tendulkar 2-0-7-0
Khan 8-4-30-0 Prasad 3-1-7-0 Harbhajan Singh 30.3-8-73-6 Raju 15-3-58-1 Tendulkar 11-3-31-3 Ganguly 1-0-2-0

India Innings

SS Das	c Gilchrist b McGrath	20	hit wicket b Gillespie	39
S Ramesh	c Ponting b Gillespie	0	c ME Waugh b Warne	30
R Dravid	b Warne	25	run out (SR Waugh/Kasprowicz)	180
SR Tendulkar	lbw b McGrath	10	c Gilchrist b Gillespie	10
*SC Ganguly	c SR Waugh b Kasprowicz	23	c Gilchrist b McGrath	48
VVS Laxman	c Hayden b Warne	59	c Ponting b McGrath	281
+NR Mongia	c Gilchrist b Kasprowicz	2	b McGrath	4
Harbhajan Singh	c Ponting b Gillespie	4	not out	8
Z Khan	b McGrath	3	not out	23
SLV Raju	lbw b McGrath	4		
BKV Prasad	not out	7		
	(lb 2, nb 12)	14	(b 6, lb 12, w 2, nb 14)	34
	(all out)	171	(7 wickets dec)	657

Bowling: McGrath 14-8-18-4 Gillespie 11-0-47-2 Kasprowicz 13-2-39-2 Warne 20-1-3-65-2
McGrath 39-12-103-3 Gillespie 31-6-115-2 Warne 34-3-152-1 ME Waugh 18-1-58-0 Kasprowicz 35-6-139-0 Ponting 12-1-41-0 Hayden 6-0-24-0 Slater 2-1-4-0 Langer 1-0-3-0

Umpires: SK Bansal and P Willey (Eng)
TV Umpire: SN Bandekar; Referee: CW Smith (WI)

India v West Indies
30,31 October, 1,2,3 November 2002

Result: Match Drawn

India Innings

SB Bangar	c Hinds b Cuffy	77	c Chanderpaul b Dillon	0
V Sehwag	lbw b Dillon	35	c Chanderpaul b Dillon	10
R Dravid	lbw b Powell	14	lbw b Powell	17
SR Tendulkar	c Gayle b Lawson	36	c Gayle b Cuffy	176
*SC Ganguly	c Jacobs b Hooper	29	lbw b Cuffy	16
VVS Laxman	c Gayle b Dillon	48	not out	154
+PA Patel	c Chanderpaul b Lawson	47	run out (sub [GR Breese]/Jacobs)	27
Harbhajan Singh	b Cuffy	6	c Hooper b Samuels	26
J Srinath	c Hooper b Dillon	46	c Hooper b Chanderpaul	21
A Kumble	lbw b Powell	4	not out	8
A Nehra	not out	0		
	(lb 7, w 1, nb 8)	16	(b 8, lb 7, w 1)	16
	(all out)	358	(8 wickets)	471

Bowling: Dillon 22-3-82-3 Cuffy 25-4-84-2 Lawson 20-3-76-2 Powell 16.2-4-62-2 Hooper 15-5-36-1 Gayle 2-0-6-0 Sarwan 1-0-5-0
Dillon 25-6-85-2 Cuffy 17-3-52-2 Lawson 22-3-65-0 Powell 24-4-53-1 Hooper 20-1-63-0 Gayle 23-5-70-0 Sarwan 8-1-38-0 Samuels 16-3-21-1 Chanderpaul 3-0-9-1

West Indies Innings

CH Gayle	c Sehwag b Kumble	88
WW Hinds	c Ganguly b Harbhajan Singh	100
RR Sarwan	st Patel b Harbhajan Singh	2
M Dillon	b Harbhajan Singh	0
S Chanderpaul	c Harbhajan Singh b Sehwag	140
*CL Hooper	c Patel b Nehra	19
MN Samuels	c Sehwag b Harbhajan Singh	104
+RD Jacobs	not out	22
DB Powell	lbw b Kumble	0
JJC Lawson	lbw b Kumble	5
CE Cuffy	c Laxman b Harbhajan Singh	0
	(b 4, lb 7, nb 6)	17
	(all out)	497

Bowling: Srinath 19-3-62-0 Nehra 23-9-66-1 Harbhajan Singh 57.3-15-115-5 Kumble 54-9-169-3 Bangar 6-3-14-0 Tendulkar 7-0-33-0 Sehwag 5-0-27-1

Umpires: EAR de Silva (SL) and DR Shepherd (Eng)
TV Umpire: AV Jayaprakash; Referee: MJ Procter (SA)

India v England
10,11,12,13 February 1934

Result: England won by 202 runs

England Innings

AH Bakewell	c CS Nayudu b Amarnath	85	c Patiala b Amar Singh	4
CF Walters	lbw b Amar Singh	59	sub b Amarnath	102
A Mitchell	lbw b Amarnath	25	c & b Amarnath	28
James Langridge	lbw b Amar Singh	1	c Dilawar Hussain b Nazir Ali	46
*DR Jardine	c Wazir Ali b Amar Singh	65	not out	35
CJ Barnett	c Patiala b Amar Singh	4	c Dilawar Hussain b Nazir Ali	26
MS Nichols	b Amar Singh	1	c Dilawar Hussain b Nazir Ali	8
LF Townsend	b Amar Singh	10	c CK Nayudu b Nazir Ali	8
H Verity	lbw b Mushtaq Ali	42		
+H Elliott	c Mushtaq Ali b Amar Singh	14		
EW Clark	not out	4		
	(b 22, lb 2, nb 1)	25	(b 1, lb 3)	4
	(all out)	335	(7 wickets declared)	261

Bowling: Amar Singh 44.4-13-86-7 CK Nayudu 11-1-32-0 Amarnath 31-14-69-2 Mushtaq Ali 25-3-64-1 CS Nayudu 13-1-43-0 Naoomal Jaoomal 6-0-16-0 Wazir Ali 1-1-0-0
Amar Singh 23-6-55-1 CK Nayudu 9-0-38-0 Amarnath 11.5-3-32-2 Mushtaq Ali 4-0-16-0 CS Nayudu 2-0-17-0 Wazir Ali 3-0-16-0 Nazir Ali 23-1-83-4

India Innings

+Dilawar Hussain	c Barnett b Verity	13	b Langridge	36
Naoomal Jaoomal	retired hurt	5	absent hurt	0
S Wazir Ali	b Nichols	2	c Mitchell b Verity	21
*CK Nayudu	b Verity	20	st Elliott b Langridge	2
L Amarnath	c Elliott b Langridge	12	not out	26
VM Merchant	b Verity	26	c & b Verity	28
Yuvraj of Patiala	b Verity	24	c Elliott b Langridge	60
S Nazir Ali	c Mitchell b Verity	3	c Nichols b Langridge	8
CS Nayudu	c Nichols b Verity	11	st Elliott b Verity	0
S Mushtaq Ali	not out	7	c Mitchell b Verity	8
L Amar Singh	c Barnett b Verity	16	c Barnett b Langridge	48
	(b 1, lb 3, nb 2)	6	(b 10, lb 1, nb 1)	12
	(all out)	145	(all out)	249

Bowling: Clark 15-4-37-0 Nichols 12-3-33-1 Verity 23.5-10-49-7 Langridge 6-1-9-1 Townsend 3-0-14-0
Clark 8-2-27-0 Nichols 6-1-23-0 Verity 27.2-6-104-4 Langridge 24-5-63-5 Townsend 3-0-19-0 Barnett 1-0-1-0

Umpires: JB Higgins (Eng) and JW Hitch (Eng)

India v West Indies
27,28,29,31 January 1949

Result: West Indies won by an innings and 193 runs

West Indies Innings

AF Rae	c Rege b Phadkar	109
JB Stollmeyer	c Sen b Chowdhury	160
+CL Walcott	lbw b Phadkar	43
ED Weekes	run out	90
RJ Christiani	c Modi b Phadkar	18
*JDC Goddard	c Sen b Phadkar	24
GE Gomez	c Mankad b Phadkar	50
FJ Cameron	c Hazare b Phadkar	48
PEW Jones	c Ghulam Ahmed b Mankad	10
J Trim	c Sen b Phadkar	9
W Ferguson	not out	2
	(b 10, lb 7, nb 2)	19
	(all out)	582

Bowling: Phadkar 45.3-10-159-7 Hazare 12-1-44-0 Amarnath 16-4-39-0 Chowdhury 37-6-130-1 Mankad 33-4-93-1 Ghulam Ahmed 32-3-88-0 Adhikari 1-0-10-0

India Innings

S Mushtaq Ali	lbw b Trim	32	c Walcott b Jones	14
MR Rege	b Jones	15	c Walcott b Jones	0
RS Modi	b Ferguson	56	b Gomez	6
VS Hazare	c Goddard b Ferguson	27	c Stollmeyer b Trim	52
*L Amarnath	hit wicket b Trim	13	b Jones	1
HR Adhikari	c Stollmeyer b Jones	32	c Walcott b Jones	1
DG Phadkar	c Jones b Goddard	48	c Rae b Trim	10
MH Mankad	b Trim	1	b Trim	21
+PK Sen	c Stollmeyer b Gomez	2	not out	19
Ghulam Ahmed	b Trim	5	c sub b Gomez	11
NR Chowdhury	not out	3	c Rae b Gomez	0
	(b 5, lb 1, nb 5)	11	(lb 2, nb 2)	4
	(all out)	245	(all out)	144

Bowling: Jones 16-5-28-2 Gomez 28-10-60-1 Trim 27-7-48-4 Ferguson 20-2-72-2 Goddard 8-1-26-1
Jones 10-3-30-4 Gomez 20.3-12-35-3 Trim 16-5-28-3 Ferguson 11-1-39-0 Goddard 6-3-8-0

Umpires: AR Joshi and BJ Mohoni

India v England
6,8,9,10 February 1952

Result: India won by an innings and 8 runs

England Innings

FA Lowson	b Phadkar	1	c Mankad b Phadkar	7
+RT Spooner	c Phadkar b Hazare	66	lbw b Divecha	6
TW Graveney	st Sen b Mankad	39	c Divecha b Ghulam Ahmed	25
JDB Robertson	c & b Mankad	77	lbw b Ghulam Ahmed	56
AJ Watkins	c Gopinath b Mankad	9	c & b Mankad	48
CJ Poole	b Mankad	15	c Divecha b Ghulam Ahmed	3
*DB Carr	st Sen b Mankad	40	c Mankad b Ghulam Ahmed	5
MJ Hilton	st Sen b Mankad	0	st Sen b Mankad	15
JB Statham	st Sen b Mankad	6	c Gopinath b Mankad	9
F Ridgway	lbw b Mankad	0	b Mankad	0
R Tattersall	not out	2	not out	0
	(b 4, lb 4, nb 3)	11	(b 7, lb 2)	9
	(all out)	266	(all out)	183

Bowling: Phadkar 16-2-49-1 Divecha 12-2-27-0 Amarnath 27-6-56-0 Ghulam Ahmed 18-5-53-0 Mankad 38.5-15-55-8 Hazare 10-5-15-1
Phadkar 9-2-17-1 Divecha 7-1-21-1 Amarnath 3-0-6-0 Ghulam Ahmed 26-6-77-4 Mankad 30.5-9-53-4

India Innings

S Mushtaq Ali	st Spooner b Carr	22
P Roy	c Watkins b Tattersall	111
*VS Hazare	b Hilton	20
MH Mankad	c Watkins b Carr	22
L Amarnath	c Spooner b Statham	31
DG Phadkar	b Hilton	61
PR Umrigar	not out	130
CD Gopinath	b Tattersall	35
RV Divecha	c Spooner b Ridgway	12
+PK Sen	b Watkins	2
Ghulam Ahmed	not out	1
	(b 8, lb 2)	10
	(9 wickets declared)	457

Bowling: Statham 19-3-54-1 Ridgway 17-2-47-1 Tattersall 39-13-94-2 Hilton 40-9-100-2 Carr 19-2-84-2 Watkins 14-1-50-1 Robertson 5-1-18-0

Umpires: BJ Mohoni and MG Vijayasarathi

MA Chidambaram Stadium, Chennai

India v Pakistan
28,29,30 November, 1 December 1952

Result: Match drawn

Pakistan Innings		
Nazar Mohammad	run out	13
Hanif Mohammad	lbw b Divecha	22
Waqar Hasan	st Maka b Mankad	49
+Imtiaz Ahmed	c Maka b Divecha	6
*AH Kardar	b Ramchand	79
Maqsood Ahmed	c sub b Mankad	1
Anwar Hussain	run out	17
Fazal Mahmood	c Maka b Phadkar	30
Zulfiqar Ahmed	not out	63
Mahmood Hussain	b Phadkar	0
Amir Elahi	b Amarnath	47
	(b 9, lb 7, nb 1)	17
	(all out)	344

Bowling: Phadkar 19-3-61-2 Divecha 19-4-36-2 Ramchand 20-3-66-1 Amarnath 6.5-3-9-1 Mankad 35-3-113-2 Gupte 5-2-14-0 Hazare 6-0-28-0

India Innings		
MH Mankad	b Fazal Mahmood	7
ML Apte	c Maqsood Ahmed b Kardar	42
VS Hazare	c Zulfiqar Ahmed b Mahmood Hussain	1
CD Gopinath	c Nazar Moh'd b Mahmood Hussain	0
PR Umrigar	c Nazar Moh'd b Fazal Mahmood	62
*L Amarnath	c Imtiaz Ahmed b Kardar	14
DG Phadkar	not out	18
GS Ramchand	not out	25
RV Divecha		
+ES Maka		
SP Gupte		
	(b 4, nb 2)	6
	(6 wickets)	175

Bowling: Mahmood Hussain 22-4-70-2 Fazal Mahmood 27-11-52-2 Maqsood Ahmed 4-1-10-0 Kardar 21-7-37-2

Umpires: ND Nagarwala and PK Sinha

India v West Indies
13,14,15,17,18 January 1967

Result: Match drawn

India Innings				
DN Sardesai	c Hendriks b Gibbs	28	lbw b Hall	0
+FM Engineer	c Kanhai b Sobers	109	c Butcher b Hall	24
AL Wadekar	c Hendriks b Gibbs	0	c Sobers b Gibbs	67
CG Borde	c Kanhai b Hunte	125	c Lloyd b Gibbs	49
*Nawab of Pataudi jnr	b Hall	40	c Sobers b Gibbs	5
Hanumant Singh	c Kanhai b Griffith	7	b Griffith	50
V Subramanya	c Sobers b Hall	17	c Lloyd b Griffith	61
RF Surti	not out	50	c Hendriks b Griffith	8
EAS Prasanna	b Bynoe	1	c Sobers b Gibbs	24
BS Bedi	c Griffith b Gibbs	11	c Nurse b Griffith	8
BS Chandrasekhar	c Hendriks b Sobers	1	not out	10
	(b 4, lb 2, nb 9)	15	(lb 13, w 1, nb 3)	17
	(all out)	404	(all out)	323

Bowling: Hall 19-1-68-2 Griffith 23-4-96-1 Sobers 27.2-7-69-2 Gibbs 46-10-87-3 Lloyd 13-2-39-0 Hunte 10-2-25-1 Bynoe 5-4-5-1
Hall 12-2-67-2 Griffith 14-2-61-4 Sobers 27-11-58-0 Gibbs 40.4-13-96-4 Lloyd 12-3-24-0

West Indies Innings				
CC Hunte	c Subramanya b Chandrasekhar	49	c Surti b Prasanna	26
MR Bynoe	lbw b Chandrasekhar	48	c Surti b Bedi	36
RB Kanhai	c Borde b Surti	77	c Pataudi b Bedi	36
BF Butcher	b Prasanna	0	c Surti b Prasanna	24
CH Lloyd	b Surti	38	b Bedi	24
SM Nurse	b Chandrasekhar	26	lbw b Bedi	0
*GS Sobers	c Engineer b Chandrasekhar	95	not out	74
+JL Hendriks	c Engineer b Surti	0	lbw b Prasanna	9
CC Griffith	c Surti b Bedi	27	not out	40
WW Hall	b Prasanna	31		
LR Gibbs	not out	1		
	(b 5, lb 6, nb 3)	14	(nb 1)	1
	all out)	406	(7 wickets)	270

Bowling: Surti 19-2-68-3 Subramanya 7-1-21-0 Chandrasekhar 46-15-130-4 Bedi 19-3-55-1 Prasanna 41-11-118-2
Surti 9-1-27-0 Subramanya 7-3-14-0 Chandrasekhar 12-2-41-0 Bedi 28-7-81-4 Prasanna 37-9-106-3

Umpires: SK Raghunatha Rao and S Roy

India v Australia
24,25,27,28 December 1969

Result: Australia won by 77 runs

Australia Innings				
KR Stackpole	c Solkar b Venkataraghavan	37	b Amarnath	4
*WM Lawry	c Bedi b Prasanna	33	b Prasanna	2
IM Chappell	b Prasanna	4	b Amarnath	5
KD Walters	c Venkataraghavan b Bedi	102	c Solkar b Prasanna	1
AP Sheahan	c Solkar b Prasanna	1	st Engineer b Prasanna	8
IR Redpath	c Engineer b Prasanna	33	lbw b Prasanna	63
+HB Taber	lbw b Venkataraghavan	10	c Solkar b Prasanna	0
GD McKenzie	lbw b Venkataraghavan	2	lbw b Venkataraghavan	24
LC Mayne	c Chauhan b Venkataraghavan	10	c Viswanath b Prasanna	13
AA Mallett	not out	2	not out	11
AN Connolly	c & b Solkar	11	c Engineer b Venkataraghavan	8
	(b 11, lb 2)	13	(b 8, lb 5, nb 1)	14
	(all out)	258	(all out)	153

Bowling: Amarnath 7-0-21-0 Solkar 8.2-5-8-1 Bedi 26-10-45-1 Prasanna 40-13-100-4 Venkataraghavan 34-13-71-4
Amarnath 24-11-31-2 Solkar 4-2-2-0 Bedi 9-5-6-0 Prasanna 31-14-74-6 Venkataraghavan 12.5-2-26-2

India Innings				
CPS Chauhan	c Chappell b Mallett	19	c Redpath b McKenzie	1
AV Mankad	c Taber b Mayne	0	c Redpath b McKenzie	10
AL Wadekar	c Chappell b Mallett	12	c Stackpole b Mayne	55
GR Viswanath	b Mallett	6	c Redpath b Mallett	59
+FM Engineer	c Connolly b Mallett	32	c & b McKenzie	3
*Nawab of Pataudi jnr	c Sheahan b McKenzie	59	c Chappell b Mallett	4
ED Solkar	c Taber b Mallett	11	c & b Mallett	12
M Amarnath	not out	16	c Taber b Mayne	0
S Venkataraghavan	run out	2	b Mallett	13
EAS Prasanna	c Chappell b McKenzie	0	c McKenzie b Mallett	5
BS Bedi	absent hurt	0	not out	0
	(lb 5, nb 1)	6	(lb 4, nb 5)	9
	(all out)	163	(all out)	171

Bowling: McKenzie 16.4-8-19-2 Mayne 7-2-21-1 Connolly 14-5-26-0 Mallett 25-7-91-5
McKenzie 24-9-45-3 Mayne 18-8-32-2 Connolly 9-4-18-0 Mallett 29.2-12-53-5 Stackpole 5-2-14-0

Umpires: I Gopalakrishnan and B Satyaji Rao

India v England
12,13,14,16,17 January 1973

Result: India won by 4 wickets

England Innings				
B Wood	c Engineer b Bedi	20	c sub b Bedi	5
DL Amiss	c Solkar b Chandrasekhar	15	c Engineer b Chandrasekhar	8
+APE Knott	c Mansur Ali Khan b Bedi	10	c Chandrasekhar b Bedi	13
MH Denness	b Prasanna	17	c Solkar b Prasanna	76
KWR Fletcher	not out	97	c Chauhan b Bedi	21
AW Greig	lbw b Chandrasekhar	17	c Solkar b Durani	5
*AR Lewis	c Solkar b Chandrasekhar	4	c Chauhan b Bedi	11
CM Old	c Durani b Chandrasekhar	4	c Bedi b Prasanna	9
GG Arnold	c Solkar b Prasanna	17	c Wadekar b Prasanna	0
N Gifford	lbw b Chandrasekhar	19	not out	3
PI Pocock	lbw b Chandrasekhar	2	c Wadekar b Prasanna	0
	(b 8, lb 11, nb 1)	20	(b 2, lb 3, nb 3)	8
	(all out)	242	(all out)	159

Bowling: Solkar 2-0-13-0 Gavaskar 1-0-6-0 Bedi 30-9-66-2 Chandrasekhar 38.5-9-90-6 Prasanna 15-3-47-2
Solkar 2-2-0-0 Bedi 43-24-38-4 Chandrasekhar 35-9-69-1 Prasanna 10-5-16-4 Mansur Ali Khan 1-0-4-0 Durani 15-5-24-1

India Innings				
CPS Chauhan	c Knott b Arnold	0	c Knott b Pocock	11
SM Gavaskar	c Greig b Gifford	20	not out	0
*AL Wadekar	c Wood b Pocock	44	c Greig b Old	0
SA Durani	c & b Gifford	38	lbw b Pocock	38
Mansur Ali Khan	c sub b Pocock	73	not out	14
GR Viswanath	c Old b Pocock	37	b Pocock	0
+FM Engineer	c Wood b Gifford	31	lbw b Old	10
ED Solkar	b Pocock	10	c Denness b Pocock	7
EAS Prasanna	lbw b Arnold	37		
BS Bedi	b Arnold	5		
BS Chandrasekhar	not out	3		
	(b 6, lb 3, nb 9)	18	(lb 1, nb 5)	6
	(all out)	316	(6 wickets)	86

Bowling: Arnold 23.1-12-34-3 Old 20-4-51-0 Gifford 34-15-64-3 Greig 12-1-35-0 Pocock 46-15-114-4
Arnold 4-1-11-0 Old 9-3-19-2 Gifford 7.5-2-22-0 Pocock 13-3-28-4

Umpires: AM Mamsa and MV Nagendra

India v West Indies
11,12,14,15 January 1975

Result: India won by 100 runs

India Innings				
+FM Engineer	c Greenidge b Julien	14	b Holder	28
ED Solkar	c Kallicharran b Julien	4	c Kallicharran b Julien	15
AD Gaekwad	lbw b Roberts	7	run out	80
GR Viswanath	not out	97	c Murray b Roberts	46
*Mansur Ali Khan	lbw b Roberts	6	lbw b Roberts	4
AV Mankad	c Fredericks b Roberts	19	b Boyce	20
S Madan Lal	b Roberts	0	c Murray b Roberts	5
KD Ghavri	b Roberts	12	not out	35
EAS Prasanna	c Murray b Roberts	0	lbw b Boyce	0
BS Bedi	b Gibbs	14	c Murray b Roberts	0
BS Chandrasekhar	c Lloyd b Roberts	1	b Roberts	0
	(b 1, lb 6, nb 9)	16	(b 12, lb 3, nb 8)	23
	(all out)	190	(all out)	256

Bowling: Roberts 20.5-5-64-7 Julien 6-2-12-2 Boyce 11-3-40-0 Holder 9-1-26-0 Gibbs 12-1-32-1
Roberts 21.4-6-57-5 Julien 13-4-31-1 Boyce 15-4-61-2 Holder 24-8-40-1 Gibbs 26-11-36-0 Fredericks 5-2-8-0

West Indies Innings				
RC Fredericks	c Solkar b Ghavri	14	c Solkar b Prasanna	19
CG Greenidge	c Prasanna b Bedi	14	b Chandrasekhar	17
AI Kallicharran	c Viswanath b Bedi	17	run out	51
VA Holder	hit wicket b Bedi	0	c Viswanath b Bedi	4
IVA Richards	c Chandrasekhar b Prasanna	50	c Engineer b Prasanna	2
*CH Lloyd	c Viswanath b Prasanna	39	st Engineer b Prasanna	7
+DL Murray	c Engineer b Prasanna	8	c Solkar b Bedi	18
BD Julien	c & b Prasanna	2	not out	14
KD Boyce	c Bedi b Prasanna	0	lbw b Prasanna	4
LR Gibbs	not out	14	c Solkar b Chandrasekhar	3
AME Roberts	lbw b Chandrasekhar	17	lbw b Bedi	0
	(b 7, lb 10)	17	(b 14, lb 1)	15
	(all out)	192	(all out)	154

Bowling: Ghavri 6-0-25-1 Madan Lal 2-0-7-0 Prasanna 23-6-70-5 Bedi 19-7-40-3 Chandrasekhar 9.2-1-33-1
Ghavri 2-0-13-0 Madan Lal 2-0-5-0 Prasanna 24-8-41-4 Bedi 19-8-29-3 Chandrasekhar 20-6-51-2

Umpires: B Satyaji Rao and MS Sivasankariah

India v New Zealand
26,27,28,30 November, 1,2 December 1976

Result: India won by 216 runs

India Innings				
SM Gavaskar	b Cairns	2	st Lees b O'Sullivan	43
AD Gaekwad	c Parker b Cairns	0	b Hadlee	11
M Amarnath	c Petherick b Cairns	21	c Morrison b Hadlee	55
GR Viswanath	c Lees b Hadlee	87	st Lees b O'Sullivan	17
BP Patel	run out	33	not out	40
AV Mankad	b Cairns	14	c Burgess b Petherick	21
+SMH Kirmani	lbw b Petherick	44		
KD Ghavri	c Petherick b Hadlee	8		
S Venkataraghavan	c sub b Cairns	64		
*BS Bedi	c Cairns b Hadlee	5		
BS Chandrasekhar	not out	1		
	(b 7, lb 8, w 1, nb 3)	19	(b 11, lb 2, nb 1)	14
	(all out)	298	(5 wickets declared)	201

Bowling: Hadlee 21-7-37-3 Cairns 33.1-11-55-5 Roberts 17-5-32-0 O'Sullivan 34-9-69-0 Petherick 25-5-77-1 Howarth 3-1-9-0
Hadlee 17-3-52-2 Cairns 16-2-49-0 Roberts 2-0-4-0 O'Sullivan 20-3-70-2 Petherick 6.5-0-12-1

New Zealand Innings				
*GM Turner	c Kirmani b Chandrasekhar	37	c Amarnath b Chandrasekhar	5
JFM Morrison	c Kirmani b Ghavri	7	c Chandrasekhar b Ghavri	1
JM Parker	c Patel b Ghavri	9	c Kirmani b Chandrasekhar	38
MG Burgess	b Bedi	40	run out	15
ADG Roberts	c Venkataraghavan b Chandrasekhar	1	c Gavaskar b Bedi	0
GP Howarth	c Venkataraghavan b Bedi	3	c Chandrasekhar b Bedi	18
+WK Lees	c Venkataraghavan b Bedi	9	c sub b Bedi	21
RJ Hadlee	c Gaekwad b Bedi	21	c Amarnath b Bedi	5
BL Cairns	c Mankad b Bedi	5	not out	8
DR O'Sullivan	c Venkataraghavan b Chandrasekhar	0	c Patel b Chandrasekhar	21
PJ Petherick	not out	0	lbw b Venkataraghavan	1
	(b 1, lb 2, nb 5)	8	(b 7, lb 1, nb 2)	10
	(all out)	140	(all out)	143

Bowling: Ghavri 13-3-32-2 Amarnath 8-3-17-0 Bedi 16.4-4-48-5 Chandrasekhar 16-5-28-3 Venkataraghavan 2-0-7-0
Ghavri 8-4-14-1 Amarnath 3-1-6-0 Bedi 22-12-22-4 Chandrasekhar 20-3-64-3 Venkataraghavan 14-8-27-1

Umpires: Mohammad Ghouse and KB Ramaswami

India v England
14,15,16,18,19 January 1977

Result: England won by 200 runs

England Innings

DL Amiss	lbw b Madan Lal	4	c Amarnath b Chandrasekhar	46
RA Woolmer	c Gavaskar b Madan Lal	22	lbw b Prasanna	16
JM Brearley	c & b Prasanna	59	b Chandrasekhar	29
DW Randall	run out	2	c Kirmani b Chandrasekhar	0
RW Tolchard	not out	8	not out	10
*AW Greig	c Viswanath b Bedi	54	lbw b Prasanna	41
+APE Knott	c Viswanath b Bedi	45	c Patel b Prasanna	11
JK Lever	c Kirmani b Bedi	23	c Amarnath b Chandrasekhar	2
CM Old	c Amarnath b Bedi	2	c Chandrasekhar b Prasanna	4
DL Underwood	b Prasanna	23	st Kirmani b Chandrasekhar	8
RGD Willis	run out	7	not out	4
	(b 5, lb 8)	13	(b 14)	14
	(all out)	262	(9 wickets declared)	185

Bowling: Madan Lal 21-5-43-2 Amarnath 14-3-26-0 Chandrasekhar 25-4-63-0 Bedi 38.5-16-72-4 Prasanna 27-11-45-2
Madan Lal 9-2-15-0 Amarnath 7-2-18-0 Chandrasekhar 20.5-4-50-5 Bedi 13-3-33-0 Prasanna 22-5-55-4

India Innings

SM Gavaskar	c Brearley b Old	39	c Woolmer b Underwood	24
M Amarnath	b Old	0	c Woolmer b Underwood	12
GR Viswanath	c Knott b Lever	9	c Brearley b Underwood	6
AV Mankad	b Lever	0	c Old b Lever	4
BP Patel	b Underwood	32	c Old b Willis	4
DB Vengsarkar	c Randall b Lever	8	retired hurt	1
S Madan Lal	c Underwood b Willis	12	c Knott b Willis	1
+SMH Kirmani	c Brearley b Lever	27	c Brearley b Willis	1
EAS Prasanna	c & b Underwood	13	c Brearley b Underwood	0
*BS Bedi	c sub b Lever	5	not out	11
BS Chandrasekhar	not out	1	b Lever	6
	(b 1, nb 17)	18	(b 5, lb 1, nb 2)	8
	(all out)	164	(all out)	83

Bowling: Willis 19-5-46-1 Old 13-4-19-2 Lever 19.5-2-59-5 Woolmer 1-0-2-0 Greig 4-1-4-0 Underwood 17-9-16-2
Willis 13-4-18-3 Old 5-1-11-0 Lever 6.5-0-18-2 Underwood 14-7-28-4

Umpires: J Reuben and MS Sivasankariah

India v West Indies
12,13,14,16 January 1979

Result: India won by 3 wickets

West Indies Innings

SFAF Bacchus	c Vengsarkar b Kapil Dev	0	c Vengsarkar b Ghavri	4
AE Greenidge	b Venkataraghavan	13	c Kirmani b Kapil Dev	15
HA Gomes	c Narasimha Rao b Kapil Dev	14	c Gavaskar b Venkataraghavan	91
*AI Kallicharran	b Venkataraghavan	98	c sub b Venkataraghavan	4
HS Chang	c Chauhan b Kapil Dev	6	hit wicket b Ghavri	2
*DA Murray	hit wicket b Kapil Dev	0	c Narasimha Rao b Kapil Dev	15
S Shivnarine	c sub b Ghavri	5	c Vengsarkar b Ghavri	9
DR Parry	run out	12	c sub b Kapil Dev	1
N Phillip	not out	22	not out	7
VA Holder	c Kapil Dev b Parsana	20	c Narasimha Rao b Venkataraghavan	0
ST Clarke	lbw b Venkataraghavan	12	st Kirmani b Venkataraghavan	0
	(lb 9, w 1, nb 16)	26	(nb 3)	3
	(all out)	228	(all out)	151

Bowling: Kapil Dev 14-0-38-4 Ghavri 16-5-41-1 Parsana 12-3-32-1 Venkataraghavan 20.5-5-60-3 Narasimha Rao 10-1-31-0
Kapil Dev 14-3-46-3 Ghavri 13-3-52-3 Parsana 2-0-7-0 Venkataraghavan 16.5-5-43-4

India Innings

*SM Gavaskar	c Bacchus b Phillip	4	c Murray b Clarke	1
CPS Chauhan	c Murray b Holder	20	c Bacchus b Phillip	10
DB Vengsarkar	c Bacchus b Clarke	0	c Shivnarine b Clarke	0
GR Viswanath	c Shivnarine b Clarke	124	c Kallicharran b Holder	31
AD Gaekwad	b Phillip	24	c Murray b Holder	21
MV Narasimha Rao	c Greenidge b Parry	6	c Murray b Phillip	4
N Kapil Dev	c Bacchus b Clarke	0	not out	26
KD Ghavri	c Murray b Clarke	1	c Clarke b Phillip	8
+SMH Kirmani	c Shivnarine b Phillip	33	not out	4
DD Parsana	c sub b Phillip	0	
S Venkataraghavan	not out	0	
	(b 15, lb 11, nb 17)	43	(b 5, lb 1, nb 14)	20
	(all out)	255	(7 wickets)	125

Bowling: Clarke 29.1-3-75-4 Phillip 22-8-48-4 Holder 11-2-28-1 Gomes 1-0-2-0 Parry 5-2-43-1 Shivnarine 5-1-16-0
Clarke 21.2-3-46-2 Phillip 15-5-37-3 Holder 10-3-22-2

Umpires: JD Ghosh and S Kishen

India v Australia
11,12,14,15,16 September 1979

Result: Match drawn

Australia Innings

AMJ Hilditch	c Venkataraghavan b Kapil Dev	4	lbw b Doshi	55
GM Wood	lbw b Doshi	33	c Chauhan b Kapil Dev	2
AR Border	run out	162	b Venkataraghavan	50
*KJ Hughes	c Venkataraghavan b Doshi	100	lbw b Venkataraghavan	36
GN Yallop	c Yajurvindra Singh b Doshi	18	run out	2
DF Whatmore	c Venkataraghavan b Doshi	20	c Chauhan b Doshi	8
+KJ Wright	b Venkataraghavan	20	b Venkataraghavan	5
G Dymock	lbw b Kapil Dev	16	not out	28
RM Hogg	c Kapil Dev b Doshi	3	not out	8
AG Hurst	c Kirmani b Doshi	0	
JD Higgs	not out	1	
	(b 1, lb 7, w 1, nb 4)	13	(b 11, lb 4, nb 3)	18
	(all out)	390	(7 wickets)	212

Bowling: Kapil Dev 25.4-3-95-2 Ghavri 20-4-49-0 Yajurvindra Singh 9-1-29-0 Venkataraghavan 46-16-101-1 Doshi 43-10-103-6
Kapil Dev 9-3-30-1 Ghavri 17.4-8-23-0 Venkataraghavan 45-10-77-3 Doshi 42-15-64-2

India Innings

*SM Gavaskar	c Wood b Hogg	50
CPS Chauhan	c Wright b Higgs	26
+SMH Kirmani	c Border b Hogg	57
GR Viswanath	c Hughes b Higgs	17
DB Vengsarkar	c Whatmore b Higgs	65
Yashpal Sharma	lbw b Higgs	52
Yajurvindra Singh	c Wright b Yallop	15
N Kapil Dev	c Hurst b Higgs	83
KD Ghavri	not out	23
S Venkataraghavan	lbw b Higgs	4
DR Doshi	c Hogg b Higgs	3
	(b 2, lb 5, nb 23)	30
	(all out)	425

Bowling: Hogg 22-1-85-2 Hurst 23-8-51-0 Higgs 41.3-12-143-7 Dymock 24-6-65-0 Border 14-4-30-0 Yallop 6-1-21-1

Umpires: MV Gothoskar and S Kishen

India v Pakistan
15,16,17,19,20 January 1980

Result: India won by 10 wickets

Pakistan Innings

Mudassar Nazar	c Kirmani b Kapil Dev	6	c Vengsarkar b Kapil Dev	8
Sadiq Mohammad	c Kirmani b Kapil Dev	46	c Binny b Kapil Dev	0
Majid Khan	run out	56	c Patil b Ghavri	11
Zaheer Abbas	c Kirmani b Kapil Dev	0	c Chauhan b Kapil Dev	15
Javed Miandad	c Vengsarkar b Kapil Dev	45	c Kirmani b Doshi	52
*Asif Iqbal	c Kirmani b Ghavri	34	c Kirmani b Kapil Dev	5
Wasim Raja	c Kapil Dev b Doshi	15	c Viswanath b Doshi	57
Imran Khan	run out	34	c Doshi b Kapil Dev	29
+Wasim Bari	c Binny b Ghavri	13	lbw b Kapil Dev	15
Iqbal Qasim	not out	3	not out	19
Sikander Bakht	c Vengsarkar b Ghavri	1	b Kapil Dev	2
	(lb 3, nb 16)	19	(lb 3, nb 17)	20
	(all out)	272	(all out)	233

Bowling: Kapil Dev 19-5-90-4 Ghavri 18.4-3-73-3 Binny 10-1-42-0 Doshi 26-6-48-1
Kapil Dev 24.3-4-57-6 Ghavri 14-0-82-1 Binny 12-2-33-0 Doshi 16-3-42-2

India Innings

*SM Gavaskar	c Iqbal Qasim b Imran Khan	166	not out	29
CPS Chauhan	c Iqbal Qasim b Mudassar Nazar	5	not out	46
DB Vengsarkar	c Javed Miandad b Imran Khan	17	
GR Viswanath	c Mudassar Nazar b Iqbal Qasim	16	
SM Patil	c Javed Miandad b Sikander Bakht	15	
Yashpal Sharma	b Iqbal Qasim	46	
+SMH Kirmani	b Imran Khan	2	
N Kapil Dev	lbw b Imran Khan	84	
RMH Binny	not out	42	
KD Ghavri	b Iqbal Qasim	1	
DR Doshi	c Javed Miandad b Imran Khan	9	
	(b 1, lb 2, nb 24)	27	(nb 3)	3
	(all out)	430	(0 wickets)	78

Bowling: Imran Khan 38.2-6-114-5 Sikander Bakht 32.5-6-105-1 Mudassar Nazar 16-3-54-1 Iqbal Qasim 37-13-81-3 Wasim Raja 2-0-19-0 Majid Khan 9-1-30-0
Imran Khan 5-1-20-0 Sikander Bakht 6-0-37-0 Mudassar Nazar 2-0-2-0 Iqbal Qasim 4-1-12-0 Sadiq Mohammad 1-0-4-0

Umpires: MV Gothoskar and S Kishen

India v England
13,14,15,17,18 January 1982

Result: Match drawn

India Innings

*SM Gavaskar	c Taylor b Willis	25	c Botham b Willis	11
P Roy	c Taylor b Dilley	6	not out	60
DB Vengsarkar	retired hurt	71	
GR Viswanath	b Willis	222	
Yashpal Sharma	c Tavare b Botham	140	c Botham b Underwood	25
N Kapil Dev	not out	6	not out	15
AO Malhotra			run out	31
+SMH Kirmani				
RJ Shastri				
S Madan Lal				
DR Doshi				
	(lb 1, w 1, nb 9)	11	(b 12, lb 1, nb 5)	18
	(4 wickets declared)	481	(3 wickets declared)	160

Bowling: Willis 28.1-7-79-2 Botham 31-10-83-1 Dilley 31-4-87-1 Allott 31-4-135-0 Underwood 22-7-59-0 Gooch 9-2-27-0
Willis 7-2-15-1 Botham 8-1-29-0 Dilley 5-1-13-0 Underwood 15-8-30-1 Gooch 8-2-24-0 Fletcher 1-0-9-0 Taylor 2-0-6-0 Tavare 2-0-11-0 Gower 1-0-1-0 Gatting 1-0-4-0

England Innings

GA Gooch	c & b Shastri	127
CJ Tavare	c Gavaskar b Doshi	35
*KWR Fletcher	b Doshi	3
DI Gower	lbw b Shastri	64
IT Botham	c Kirmani b Shastri	52
MW Gatting	c Viswanath b Doshi	0
GR Dilley	c & b Kapil Dev	8
+RW Taylor	b Doshi	8
DL Underwood	c Kirmani b Kapil Dev	0
PJW Allott	c Roy b Kapil Dev	6
RGD Willis	not out	1
	(b 1, lb 11, nb 12)	24
	(all out)	328

Bowling: Kapil Dev 25.5-7-88-3 Madan Lal 9-1-41-0 Shastri 63-23-104-3 Doshi 57-31-69-4 Gavaskar 1-0-2-0

Umpires: B Ganguli and SN Hanumantha Rao

India v Sri Lanka
17,18,19,21,22 September 1982

Result: Match drawn

Sri Lanka Innings

*B Warnapura	c Yashpal Sharma b Madan Lal	4	c Yashpal Sharma b Kapil Dev	6
+HM Goonatilleke	c Patil b Kapil Dev	7	c sub (K Srikkanth) b Kapil Dev	0
RL Dias	c Arun Lal b Doshi	60	c Gavaskar b Shukla	97
LRD Mendis	lbw b Doshi	105	b Shukla	105
A Ranatunga	c Vengsarkar b Doshi	25	c Kirmani b Doshi	15
RS Madugalle	c Madan Lal b Doshi	46	c Patil b Doshi	4
AN Ranasinghe	c Arun Lal b Doshi	0	b Kapil Dev	77
DS de Silva	c Gavaskar b Madan Lal	49	not out	46
JR Ratnayeke	lbw b Kapil Dev	23	c Yashpal Sharma b Kapil Dev	6
ALF de Mel	not out	18	b Doshi	12
GRA de Silva	c Viswanath b Kapil Dev	0	b Doshi	14
	(b 4, lb 5)	9	(b 4, lb 5, w 1, nb 2)	12
	(all out)	346	(all out)	394

Bowling: Kapil Dev 22.5-2-97-3 Madan Lal 16-1-72-2 Doshi 30-8-85-5 Patil 2-0-13-0 Shukla 22-4-70-0
Kapil Dev 24.3-3-110-5 Madan Lal 7-1-43-0 Doshi 38-4-147-3 Shukla 27-5-82-2

India Innings

*SM Gavaskar	c de Mel b DS de Silva	155	not out	4
J Arun Lal	b de Mel	1	c Dias b de Mel	1
DB Vengsarkar	run out	90	c & b de Mel	5
GR Viswanath	c Warnapura b DS de Silva	9	lbw b de Mel	2
SM Patil	not out	114	run out	46
Yashpal Sharma	c Goonatilleke b de Mel	17	not out	31
N Kapil Dev	c Goonatilleke b Ratnayeke	31	c Goonatilleke b de Mel	30
S Madan Lal	not out	37	c & b DS de Silva	9
+SMH Kirmani			b de Mel	5
RC Shukla				
DR Doshi				
	(b 11, lb 8, w 2, nb 29)	50	(lb 2)	2
	(6 wickets declared)	566	(7 wickets)	135

Bowling: de Mel 29-2-133-2 Ratnayeke 19-1-75-1 GRA de Silva 18-2-78-0 Warnapura 9-3-27-0 DS de Silva 48-4-162-2 Ranasinghe 7-0-29-0 Ranatunga 1-0-12-0
de Mel 14-0-68-5 Ratnayeke 5-0-36-0 DS de Silva 9-1-29-1

Umpires: MV Gothoskar and S Kishen

MA Chidambaram Stadium, Chennai

India v West Indies
24,26,27,28,29 December 1983

Result: Match drawn

West Indies Innings

CG Greenidge	c Gavaskar b Shastri	34	not out	26
DL Haynes	b Maninder Singh	23	c Vengsarkar b Shastri	24
IVA Richards	c Kirmani b Maninder Singh	32		
HA Gomes	b Yadav	28	not out	10
+PJL Dujon	c Kapil Dev b Binny	62		
*CH Lloyd	lbw b Kapil Dev	32		
WW Davis	b Sidhu b Binny	12		
MD Marshall	b Kapil Dev	38		
MA Holding	lbw b Kapil Dev	34		
AME Roberts	not out	0		
RA Harper	c & b Maninder Singh	0		
	(lb 12, nb 6)	18	(lb 2, nb 2)	4
	(all out)	313	(1 wicket)	64

Bowling: Kapil Dev 15-3-44-3 Binny 12-1-48-2 Shastri 28-6-72-1 Yadav 28-4-96-1 Maninder Singh 29.3-9-41-3
Kapil Dev 6-2-11-0 Binny 2-0-14-0 Shastri 6-3-10-1 Maninder Singh 6-2-10-0 Kirmani 1-0-4-0 Vengsarkar 1-0-4-0 Sidhu 1-0-9-0

India Innings

AD Gaekwad	c Harper b Marshall	0
NS Sidhu	c Richards b Roberts	20
DB Vengsarkar	c Harper b Marshall	0
SM Gavaskar	not out	236
AO Malhotra	c sub b Harper	9
NS Yadav	c Dujon b Marshall	3
RJ Shastri	lbw b Davis	72
RMH Binny	c sub b Marshall	1
*N Kapil Dev	c sub b Marshall	26
+SMH Kirmani	not out	63
Maninder Singh		
	(b 1, lb 5, w 9, nb 6)	21
	(8 wickets declared)	451

Bowling: Marshall 26-8-72-5 Roberts 28-4-81-1 Davis 30-4-75-1 Holding 26-2-85-0 Harper 42-7-108-1 Gomes 8-0-24-0

Umpires: S Kishen and MG Subramaniam

India v England
13,14,15,17,18 January 1985

Result: England won by 9 wickets

India Innings

*SM Gavaskar	b Foster	17	c Gatting b Foster	3
K Srikkanth	c Downton b Cowans	0	c Cowdrey b Foster	16
DB Vengsarkar	c Lamb b Foster	17	c Downton b Foster	2
M Amarnath	c Downton b Foster	78	c Cowans b Foster	95
M Azharuddin	b Cowdrey	48	c Gower b Pocock	105
RJ Shastri	c Downton b Foster	2	c Cowdrey b Edmonds	33
N Kapil Dev	c Cowans b Cowdrey	53	c Gatting b Cowans	49
+SMH Kirmani	not out	30	c Lamb b Edmonds	75
NS Yadav	b Foster	5	c Downton b Cowans	5
L Sivaramakrishnan	c Cowdrey b Foster	13	lbw b Foster	5
C Sharma	c Lamb b Cowans	5	not out	17
	(lb 3, nb 4)	7	(b 1, lb 4, nb 2)	7
	(all out)	272	(all out)	412

Bowling: Cowans 12.5-3-39-2 Foster 23-2-104-6 Edmonds 6-1-33-0 Cowdrey 19-1-65-2 Pocock 7-1-28-0
Cowans 15-1-73-2 Foster 28-8-59-5 Edmonds 41.5-13-119-2 Cowdrey 5-0-26-0 Pocock 33-8-130-1

England Innings

G Fowler	c Kirmani b Kapil Dev	201	c Kirmani b Sivaramakrishnan	2
RT Robinson	c Kirmani b Sivaramakrishnan	74	not out	21
MW Gatting	c sub b Shastri	207	not out	10
AJ Lamb	b Amarnath	62		
PH Edmonds	lbw b Shastri	36		
NA Foster	b Amarnath	5		
*DI Gower	b Kapil Dev	18		
CS Cowdrey	not out	3		
+PR Downton	not out	3		
PI Pocock				
NG Cowans				
	(b 7, lb 19, nb 17)	43	(lb 1, w 1)	2
	(7 wickets declared)	652	(1 wicket)	35

Bowling: Kapil Dev 36-5-131-2 Sharma 18-0-95-0 Sivaramakrishnan 44-6-145-1 Yadav 23-4-76-0 Shastri 42-7-143-2 Amarnath 12-1-36-2
Kapil Dev 3-0-20-0 Sivaramakrishnan 4-0-12-1 Shastri 1-0-2-0

Umpires: MY Gupte and VK Ramaswamy

India v Australia
18,19,20,21,22 September 1986

Result: Match tied

Australia Innings

DC Boon	c Kapil Dev b Sharma	122	lbw b Maninder Singh	49
GR Marsh	c Kapil Dev b Yadav	22	b Shastri	11
DM Jones	b Yadav	210	c Azharuddin b Maninder Singh	24
RJ Bright	c Shastri b Yadav	30		
*AR Border	c Gavaskar b Shastri	106	b Maninder Singh	27
GM Ritchie	run out	13	c Pandit b Shastri	28
GRJ Matthews	c Pandit b Yadav	44	not out	27
SR Waugh	not out	12	not out	2
+TJ Zoehrer				
CJ McDermott				
BA Reid				
	(b 1, lb 7, w 1, nb 6)	15	(lb 1, nb 1)	2
	(7 wickets dec)	574	(5 wickets dec)	170

Bowling: Kapil Dev 18-5-52-0 Sharma 16-1-70-1 Maninder Singh 39-8-135-0 Yadav 49.5-9-142-4 Shastri 47-8-161-1 Srikkanth 1-0-6-0
Sharma 6-0-19-0 Kapil Dev 1-0-5-0 Shastri 14-2-50-2 Maninder Singh 19-2-60-3 Yadav 9-0-35-0

India Innings

SM Gavaskar	c & b Matthews	8	c Jones b Bright	90
K Srikkanth	c Ritchie b Matthews	53	c Waugh b Matthews	39
M Amarnath	run out	1	c Border b Matthews	51
M Azharuddin	c & b Bright	50	c Ritchie b Bright	42
RJ Shastri	c Zoehrer b Matthews	62	not out	48
CS Pandit	c Waugh b Matthews	35	b Matthews	39
*N Kapil Dev	c Border b Matthews	119	c Bright b Matthews	1
+KS More	c Zoehrer b Waugh	4	lbw b Bright	0
C Sharma	c Zoehrer b Reid	30	c McDermott b Bright	23
NS Yadav	c Border b Bright	19	b Bright	8
Maninder Singh	not out	0	lbw b Matthews	0
	(b 1, lb 9, nb 6)	16	(b 1, lb 3, nb 2)	6
	(all out)	397	(all out)	347

Bowling: McDermott 14-2-59-0 Reid 18-4-93-1 Matthews 28.2-3-103-5 Bright 23-3-88-2 Waugh 11-2-44-1
McDermott 5-0-27-0 Reid 10-2-48-0 Matthews 39.5-7-146-5 Bright 25-3-94-5 Border 3-0-12-0 Waugh 4-1-16-0

Umpires: DN Dotiwalla and V Vikramraju

India v Pakistan
3,4,6,7,8 February 1987

Result: Match drawn

Pakistan Innings

Rizwan-uz-Zaman	c More b Kulkarni	1	not out	54
Shoaib Mohammad	lbw b Maninder Singh	101	c Vengsarkar b Maninder Singh	45
Rameez Raja	c Srikkanth b Maninder Singh	14	c Azharuddin b Kulkarni	14
Javed Miandad	run out	94	st More b Maninder Singh	54
Saleem Malik	b Maninder Singh	19	not out	6
Ijaz Ahmed	c Vengsarkar b Maninder Singh	3		
Abdul Qadir	c Azharuddin b Shastri	21		
*Imran Khan	not out	135		
Wasim Akram	c Gavaskar b Yadav	62		
+Saleem Yousuf	c Kulkarni b Maninder Singh	1		
Tauseef Ahmed	not out	13		
	(lb 11, w 1, nb 1)	13	(lb 3, nb 6)	9
	(9 wickets declared)	487	(3 wickets)	182

Bowling: Kapil Dev 18-1-68-0 Kulkarni 7-0-41-1 Maninder Singh 59-16-135-5 Yadav 41-3-127-1 Shastri 38-8-105-1
Kapil Dev 9-1-36-0 Kulkarni 5-0-15-1 Maninder Singh 26-10-47-2 Yadav 15-4-29-0 Shastri 18-5-42-0 Srikkanth 3-0-6-0 Gavaskar 1-0-4-0

India Innings

SM Gavaskar	c Tauseef Ahmed b Abdul Qadir	91
K Srikkanth	c Wasim Akram b Tauseef Ahmed	123
M Amarnath	run out	89
DB Vengsarkar	st Saleem Yousuf b Tauseef Ahmed	96
M Azharuddin	st Saleem Yousuf b Tauseef Ahmed	20
RJ Shastri	c Saleem Yousuf b Imran Khan	41
*N Kapil Dev	c Rameez Raja b Abdul Qadir	5
+KS More	lbw b Wasim Akram	28
RR Kulkarni	c Saleem Yousuf b Imran Khan	2
NS Yadav	not out	6
Maninder Singh	not out	7
	(b 9, lb 5, nb 5)	19
	(9 wickets declared)	527

Bowling: Wasim Akram 34-10-78-1 Imran Khan 27-4-103-2 Abdul Qadir 39-4-130-2 Tauseef Ahmed 67-6-189-3 Shoaib Mohammad 3-0-13-0

Umpires: R Mehra and VK Ramaswamy

India v West Indies
11,12,14,15 January 1988

Result: India won by 255 runs

India Innings

K Srikkanth	c Davis b Walsh	23	lbw b Davis	17
J Arun Lal	c Logie b Hooper	69	lbw b Walsh	1
M Amarnath	c Dujon b Walsh	3	c Richardson b Walsh	1
WV Raman	c Dujon b Davis	9	c Dujon b Walsh	83
M Azharuddin	c Haynes b Hooper	47	c Davis b Richards	39
AK Sharma	lbw b Richards	30	lbw b Patterson	23
N Kapil Dev	c Richards b Walsh	109	lbw b Patterson	5
*RJ Shastri	b Davis	23	not out	20
+KS More	b Davis	17	c Dujon b Walsh	0
Arshad Ayub	not out	23	not out	3
ND Hirwani	c Richardson b Davis	1		
	(b 15, lb 4, nb 9)	28	(b 8, lb 7, nb 10)	25
	(all out)	382	(8 wickets declared)	217

Bowling: Patterson 15-1-62-0 Walsh 27-3-85-3 Davis 18.1-0-76-4 Butts 24-4-62-0 Richards 8-1-36-1 Hooper 12-3-42-2
Patterson 9-2-17-2 Walsh 16-5-55-4 Davis 6-0-20-1 Butts 21-1-62-0 Richards 18-4-28-1 Hooper 6-1-20-0

West Indies Innings

DL Haynes	c Kapil Dev b Shastri	13	lbw b Hirwani	6
PV Simmons	c & b Kapil Dev	8	c Amarnath b Hirwani	14
RB Richardson	c Azharuddin b Hirwani	36	c Amarnath b Arshad Ayub	7
*IVA Richards	b Hirwani	68	c Kapil Dev b Hirwani	4
AL Logie	c Azharuddin b Hirwani	12	st More b Hirwani	67
CL Hooper	lbw b Hirwani	2	st More b Hirwani	8
+PJL Dujon	st More b Hirwani	24	st More b Hirwani	2
CG Butts	c Raman b Hirwani	0	c Sharma b Hirwani	38
WW Davis	lbw b Hirwani	1	st More b Hirwani	7
CA Walsh	c More b Hirwani	8	st More b Raman	0
BP Patterson	not out	0	not out	0
	(b 8, lb 2, nb 2)	12	(b 4, lb 1, nb 2)	7
	(all out)	184	(all out)	160

Bowling: Kapil Dev 7-0-20-1 Amarnath 3-0-8-0 Shastri 13-6-29-1 Arshad Ayub 28-10-47-0 Hirwani 18.3-3-61-8 Sharma 4-0-9-0
Kapil Dev 4-3-8-0 Amarnath 2-0-7-0 Shastri 5-0-25-0 Arshad Ayub 14-5-33-1 Hirwani 15.2-3-75-8 Raman 1-0-7-1

Umpires: RB Gupta and PD Reporter

India v England
11,12,13,14,15 February 1993

Result: India won by an innings and 22 runs

India Innings

M Prabhakar	c Blakey b Lewis	27
NS Sidhu	c Hick b Jarvis	106
VG Kambli	lbw b Hick	59
SR Tendulkar	c & b Salisbury	165
*M Azharuddin	c Smith b Jarvis	6
PK Amre	c Jarvis b Salisbury	78
N Kapil Dev	not out	66
+KS More	not out	26
A Kumble		
RK Chauhan		
SLV Raju		
	(lb 10, w 2, nb 15)	27
	(6 wickets declared)	560

Bowling: Malcolm 27-7-87-0 Jarvis 28-7-72-2 Lewis 11-1-40-1 Tufnell 43-3-132-0 Hick 29-2-77-1 Salisbury 29-1-142-2

England Innings

RA Smith	lbw b Kumble	17	c Amre b Kumble	56
*AJ Stewart	c sub (WV Raman) b Raju	74	lbw b Kapil Dev	0
GA Hick	lbw b Chauhan	64	c Tendulkar b Kapil Dev	0
MW Gatting	run out (Amre/More?)	2	lbw b Raju	19
NH Fairbrother	c Kapil Dev b Chauhan	83	c Prabhakar b Kumble	9
+RJ Blakey	b Raju	0	b Kumble	6
CC Lewis	c Azharuddin b Raju	117	c & b Kumble	117
IDK Salisbury	lbw b Kumble	4	b Kumble	12
PW Jarvis	c sub (WV Raman) b Raju	8	c Tendulkar b Kumble	2
PCR Tufnell	c Azharuddin b Chauhan	2	not out	22
DE Malcolm	not out	0	c sub (WV Raman) b Raju	0
	(b 14, lb 16, nb 2)	32	(b 4, lb 5)	9
	(all out)	286	(all out)	252

Bowling: Prabhakar 3-2-7-0 Kumble 25-9-61-2 Chauhan 39.3-16-69-3 Raju 54-21-103-4 Kapil Dev 4-0-11-0 Tendulkar 2-1-5-0
Prabhakar 3-2-4-0 Kapil Dev 11-5-36-2 Raju 23.1-3-76-2 Chauhan 21-4-59-0 Kumble 21-7-64-6 Tendulkar 2-1-4-0

Umpires: VK Ramaswamy and RS Rathore; Referee: CW Smith (WI)

India v New Zealand
25,26,27,28,29 October 1995

Result: Match drawn

India Innings
M Prabhakar	not out	41
A Jadeja	b Nash	3
NS Sidhu	c Twose b Cairns	33
SR Tendulkar	not out	52
*M Azharuddin		
VG Kambli		
+NR Mongia		
A Kumble		
J Srinath		
RK Chauhan		
SLV Raju		
	(lb 1, w 1, nb 13)	15
	(2 wickets)	144

Bowling: Morrison 14-3-34-0 Cairns 16-7-18-1 Nash 15-3-22-1 Haslam 17.1-4-50-0 Thomson 9-0-19-0

India v Australia
6,7,8,9,10 March 1998

Result: India won by 179 runs

India Innings
+NR Mongia	c Healy b Kasprowicz	58	lbw b Blewett		18
NS Sidhu	run out (ME Waugh)	62	c Ponting b Robertson		64
R Dravid	c Robertson b Warne	52	c Healy b Warne		56
SR Tendulkar	c Taylor b Warne	4	not out		155
*M Azharuddin	c Reiffel b Warne	26	c SR Waugh b ME Waugh		64
SC Ganguly	lbw b Robertson	3	not out		30
A Kumble	c SR Waugh b Robertson	30			
J Srinath	c Taylor b Warne	1			
RK Chauhan	c Healy b Robertson	3			
Harvinder Singh	not out	0			
SLV Raju	b Robertson	0			
	(b 8, lb 6, nb 4)	18	(b 18, lb 6, nb 7)		31
	(all out)	257	(4 wickets dec)		418

Bowling: Kasprowicz 21-8-44-1 Reiffel 15-4-27-0 Warne 35-11-85-4 Robertson 28.2-4-72-4 ME Waugh 1-0-4-0 SR Waugh 4-1-11-0
Kasprowicz 14-6-42-0 Reiffel 9-1-32-0 Robertson 27-4-92-1 Warne 30-7-122-1 Blewett 10-2-35-1 ME Waugh 9-0-44-1 SR Waugh 8-0-27-0

Australia Innings
*MA Taylor	c Mongia b Harvinder Singh	12	c Srinath b Kumble		13
MJ Slater	c Dravid b Kumble	11	b Srinath		13
ME Waugh	c Ganguly b Raju	66	c Dravid b Kumble		18
SR Waugh	b Kumble	12	c Dravid b Raju		27
RT Ponting	c Mongia b Raju	18	lbw b Raju		2
GS Blewett	lbw b Chauhan	9	c Dravid b Kumble		5
+IA Healy	c Ganguly b Raju	90	not out		32
PR Reiffel	c Dravid b Kumble	15	c Azharuddin b Raju		8
SK Warne	c Tendulkar b Kumble	17	c Kumble b Chauhan		35
GR Robertson	c Mongia b Srinath	57	b Chauhan		0
MS Kasprowicz	not out	11	c Srinath b Kumble		4
	(b 1, lb 6, nb 3)	10	(b 4, lb 3, nb 4)		11
	(all out)	328	(all out)		168

Bowling: Srinath 17.3-3-46-1 Harvinder Singh 11-4-28-1 Kumble 45-10-103-4 Chauhan 25-3-90-1 Raju 32-8-54-3
Srinath 6-4-9-1 Harvinder Singh 2-0-9-0 Chauhan 22-7-60-2 Kumble 22.5-7-46-4 Raju 15-4-31-3

Umpires: G Sharp (Eng) and S Venkataraghavan
TV Umpire: KSB Murali; Referee: PL van der Merwe (SA)

India v Pakistan
28,29,30,31 January 1999

Result: Pakistan won by 12 runs

Pakistan Innings
Saeed Anwar	lbw b Srinath	24	lbw b Prasad		7
Shahid Afridi	c Ganguly b Srinath	11	b Prasad		141
Ijaz Ahmed	lbw b Kumble	13	c & b Kumble		11
Inzamam-ul-Haq	c & b Kumble	10	c Laxman b Tendulkar		51
Yousuf Youhana	lbw b Tendulkar	53	b Tendulkar		26
Saleem Malik	b Srinath	8	c Dravid b Joshi		32
+Moin Khan	c Ganguly b Kumble	60	c Mongia b Prasad		3
*Wasim Akram	c Laxman b Kumble	38	c Joshi b Prasad		1
Saqlain Mushtaq	lbw b Kumble	2	lbw b Prasad		0
Nadeem Khan	c Dravid b Kumble	8	not out		1
Waqar Younis	not out	0	c Ramesh b Prasad		5
	(lb 5, nb 6)	11	(b 1, lb 4, nb 3)		8
	(all out)	238	(all out)		286

Bowling: Srinath 15-3-63-3 Prasad 16-1-54-0 Kumble 24.5-7-70-6 Joshi 8-3-36-0 Tendulkar 3-0-10-1
Srinath 16-1-68-0 Prasad 10.2-5-33-6 Kumble 22-4-93-1 Joshi 14-3-42-1 Tendulkar 7-1-35-2 Laxman 2-0-10-0

India Innings
S Ramesh	lbw b Wasim Akram	43	c Inzamam-ul-Haq b Waqar Younis		5
VVS Laxman	lbw b Wasim Akram	23	lbw b Waqar Younis		0
R Dravid	lbw b Saqlain Mushtaq	53	b Wasim Akram		10
SR Tendulkar	c Saleem Malik b Saqlain Mushtaq	0	c Wasim Akram b Saqlain Mushtaq		136
*M Azharuddin	c Inzamam-ul-Haq b Saqlain Mushtaq	11	lbw b Saqlain Mushtaq		7
SC Ganguly	c Ijaz Ahmed b Saqlain Mushtaq	54	c Moin Khan b Saqlain Mushtaq		2
+NR Mongia	st Moin Khan b Saqlain Mushtaq	5	c Waqar Younis b Wasim Akram		52
A Kumble	c Yousuf Youhana b Saqlain Mushtaq	4	lbw b Wasim Akram		1
SB Joshi	not out	25	c & b Saqlain Mushtaq		8
J Srinath	c Ijaz Ahmed b Shahid Afridi	10	b Saqlain Mushtaq		1
BKV Prasad	st Moin Khan b Shahid Afridi	4	not out		0
	(b 2, lb 2, nb 18)	22	(b 8, lb 10, nb 18)		36
	(all out)	254	(all out)		258

Bowling: Wasim Akram 20-4-60-2 Waqar Younis 12-2-48-0 Saqlain Mushtaq 35-8-94-5 Shahid Afridi 7.1-0-31-3 Nadeem Khan 7-0-17-0
Wasim Akram 22-4-80-3 Waqar Younis 12-6-26-2 Shahid Afridi 16-7-23-0 Saqlain Mushtaq 32.2-8-93-5 Nadeem Khan 13-5-18-0

Umpires: RS Dunne (NZ) and VK Ramaswamy
TV Umpire: AV Jayaprakash; Referee: CW Smith (WI)

India v Australia
18,19,20,21,22 March 2001

Result: India won by 2 wickets

Australia Innings
MJ Slater	c Laxman b Khan	4	c Laxman b Harbhajan Singh		48
ML Hayden	c Ganguly b Harbhajan Singh	203	c Khan b Kulkarni		35
JL Langer	c Dravid b Harbhajan Singh	35	c Laxman b Bahutule		21
ME Waugh	c sub (HK Badani) b Bahutule	70	c Dravid b Harbhajan Singh		57
*SR Waugh	handled the ball	47	c Das b Harbhajan Singh		47
RT Ponting	st Dighe b Harbhajan Singh	0	c Dravid b Harbhajan Singh		11
+AC Gilchrist	lbw b Harbhajan Singh	1	lbw b Harbhajan Singh		1
SK Warne	c Das b Harbhajan Singh	0	lbw b Harbhajan Singh		11
JN Gillespie	c Ganguly b Harbhajan Singh	0	c Dravid b Harbhajan Singh		2
CR Miller	c Bahutule b Harbhajan Singh	0	b Harbhajan Singh		2
GD McGrath	not out	3	not out		11
	(b 8, lb 10, nb 10)	28	(b 8, lb 6, nb 4)		18
	(all out)	391	(all out)		264

Bowling: Khan 15-5-57-1 Ganguly 2-1-11-0 Harbhajan Singh 38.2-6-133-7 Kulkarni 23-5-67-0 Bahutule 21-3-70-1 Tendulkar 16-1-35-0
Khan 4-0-13-0 Ganguly 1-0-8-0 Harbhajan Singh 41.5-20-84-8 Kulkarni 30-11-70-1 Tendulkar 12-0-43-0 Bahutule 9-0-32-1

India Innings
SS Das	lbw b McGrath	84	c & b McGrath		9
S Ramesh	c Ponting b Warne	61	run out (Ponting/Gilchrist)		25
VVS Laxman	c ME Waugh b McGrath	65	c ME Waugh b Miller		66
SR Tendulkar	c Gilchrist b Gillespie	126	c ME Waugh b Gillespie		17
*SC Ganguly	c Gilchrist b McGrath	22	c ME Waugh b Gillespie		4
R Dravid	c Gilchrist b Gillespie	81	c SR Waugh b Miller		4
+SS Dighe	lbw b Warne	4	not out		22
SV Bahutule	not out	21	c Warne b Miller		0
Z Khan	c & b Miller	4	c ME Waugh b McGrath		0
Harbhajan Singh	c ME Waugh b Miller	2	not out		3
NM Kulkarni	lbw b Miller	0			
	(b 19, lb 2, w 1, nb 5)	27	(lb 3, nb 2)		5
	(all out)	501	(8 wickets)		155

Bowling: McGrath 36-15-75-3 Gillespie 35-11-88-2 Miller 46-6-160-3 Warne 42-7-140-2 Ponting 2-1-2-0 ME Waugh 3-0-8-0 Hayden 1-0-7-0
McGrath 11.1-3-21-2 Gillespie 12-2-49-2 Miller 9-1-41-3 Warne 6-0-41-0

Umpires: AV Jayaprakash and RE Koertzen (SA)
TV Umpire: CR Vijayaraghavan; Referee: CW Smith (WI)

India v West Indies
17,18,19,20 October 2002

Result: India won by 8 wickets

West Indies Innings
CH Gayle	c Tendulkar b Harbhajan Singh	23	c Kumble b Srinath		0
WW Hinds	lbw b Kumble	18	c Ganguly b Harbhajan Singh		61
RR Sarwan	b Srinath	19	lbw b Khan		78
S Chanderpaul	c Patel b Kumble	27	c Harbhajan Singh b Srinath		3
*CL Hooper	c Ganguly b Khan	35	c Patel b Kumble		46
RO Hinds	lbw b Kumble	16	c Kumble b Harbhajan Singh		7
+RD Jacobs	c Sehwag b Harbhajan Singh	9	c Patel b Khan		3
GR Breese	c Sehwag b Harbhajan Singh	5	c Ganguly b Harbhajan Singh		0
M Dillon	b Kumble	4	lbw b Harbhajan Singh		4
PT Collins	not out	1	not out		6
JJC Lawson	c Ganguly b Kumble	0	b Khan		2
	(b 8, lb 1, nb 1)	10	(b 12, lb 3, w 1, nb 3)		19
	(all out)	167	(all out)		229

Bowling: Srinath 10-5-14-1 Khan 10-3-21-1 Bangar 6-3-29-0 Harbhajan Singh 29-13-56-3 Kumble 23.3-10-30-5 Sehwag 1-0-8-0
Srinath 9-4-16-2 Khan 12.4-5-23-3 Harbhajan Singh 30-6-79-4 Kumble 26-3-87-1 Sehwag 2-0-9-0

India Innings
SB Bangar	c Hooper b Dillon	40	c Gayle b Hooper		20
V Sehwag	b Collins	61	st Jacobs b Hooper		33
R Dravid	b Lawson	11	not out		6
SR Tendulkar	b Lawson	43	not out		16
*SC Ganguly	lbw b Dillon	0			
VVS Laxman	c & b Breese	24			
+PA Patel	st Jacobs b Breese	23			
Harbhajan Singh	b Dillon	37			
J Srinath	run out (WW Hinds)	39			
A Kumble	not out	12			
Z Khan	run out (WW Hinds/Jacobs)	4			
	(b 4, lb 10, nb 7)	22	(lb 3, nb 3)		6
	(all out)	316	(2 wickets)		81

Bowling: Dillon 26-11-44-3 Collins 23-5-59-1 Lawson 20-4-63-2 Breese 26.1-3-108-2 Hooper 6-2-19-0 RO Hinds 5-1-9-0
Dillon 5-1-10-0 Collins 2-0-7-0 Lawson 2-0-2-0 Breese 5.1-0-27-0 Hooper 7-1-32-2

Umpires: EAR de Silva (SL) and DR Shepherd (Eng)
TV Umpire: K Hariharan; Referee: MJ Procter (SA)

National Stadium, Karachi

Pakistan v India
26,27,28 February, 1 March 1955

Result: Match drawn

Pakistan Innings

Hanif Mohammad	c Tamhane b Phadkar	2	c Tamhane b Umrigar	28
Alimuddin	c Tamhane b Ramchand	7	not out	103
Waqar Hasan	c Umrigar b Ramchand	12	not out	1
Maqsood Ahmed	c Tamhane b Ramchand	22	c Bhandari b Umrigar	2
+Imtiaz Ahmed	c Ramchand b Patel	37	run out	1
Wazir Mohammad	c Phadkar b Patel	23		
*AH Kardar	c Tamhane b Ramchand	14	st Tamhane b Gupte	93
Shujauddin	c Mankad b Ramchand	0	b Ramchand	8
Fazal Mahmood	lbw b Patel	3		
Khan Mohammad	not out	15		
Mahmood Hussain	c Phadkar b Ramchand	14		
	(b 10, nb 3)	13	(b 1, lb 3, nb 1)	5
	ß(all out)	162	(5 wickets declared)	241

Bowling: Phadkar 10-6-7-1 Ramchand 28-10-49-6 Patel 33-12-49-3 Gupte 15-4-24-0 Mankad 5-0-16-0 Umrigar 5-3-4-0
Phadkar 34-6-95-0 Ramchand 11-4-27-1 Patel 7-1-23-0 Gupte 6-0-24-1 Mankad 1-0-3-0 Umrigar 27-6-64-2

India Innings

P Roy	c Kardar b Khan Mohammad	37	lbw b Maqsood Ahmed	16
PH Punjabi	lbw b Khan Mohammad	12	c Imtiaz Ahmed b Fazal Mahmood	22
PR Umrigar	b Fazal Mahmood	16	not out	14
VL Manjrekar	c Kardar b Khan Mohammad	14		
*MH Mankad	c Maqsood Ahmed b Fazal Mahmood	6		
GS Ramchand	c Hanif Mohammad b Fazal Mahmood	15	not out	12
+NS Tamhane	b Fazal Mahmood	9		
P Bhandari	b Khan Mohammad	19		
DG Phadkar	not out	6		
JM Patel	lbw b Khan Mohammad	0		
SP Gupte	c Shujauddin b Fazal Mahmood	1		
	(lb 7, nb 3)	10	(b 1, lb 1, nb 3)	5
	(all out)	145	(2 wickets)	69

Bowling: Khan Mohammad 28-5-73-5 Mahmood Hussain 7-0-14-0 Fazal Mahmood 28.3-7-48-5
Khan Mohammad 7-5-4-0 Mahmood Hussain 3-0-16-0 Fazal Mahmood 11-4-21-1 Hanif Mohammad 6-1-18-0 Maqsood Ahmed 5-2-5-1

Umpires: Daud Khan and Masood Salahuddin

Pakistan v New Zealand
13,14,15,17 October 1955

Result: Pakistan won by an innings and 1 run

New Zealand Innings

JG Leggat	c Imtiaz Ahmed b Fazal Mahmood	16	lbw b Zulfiqar Ahmed	39
B Sutcliffe	c Kardar b Zulfiqar Ahmed	15	b Shujauddin	17
MB Poore	st Imtiaz Ahmed b Zulfiqar Ahmed	43	b Shujauddin	0
JR Reid	c Khan Mohammad b Kardar	10	c Waqar Hasan b Zulfiqar Ahmed	11
PGZ Harris	c Wazir Mohammad b Kardar	7	run out	21
SN McGregor	c Alimuddin b Shujauddin	10	lbw b Shujauddin	0
*HB Cave	b Kardar	0	c sub b Zulfiqar Ahmed	21
JC Alabaster	c sub b Zulfiqar Ahmed	14	b Zulfiqar Ahmed	8
AR MacGibbon	b Zulfiqar Ahmed	33	c Hanif Mohammad b Zulfiqar Ahmed	0
AM Moir	c Khan Mohammad b Zulfiqar Ahmed	10	c Alimuddin b Zulfiqar Ahmed	2
+TG McMahon	not out	0	not out	0
	(b 4, lb 2)	6	(b 1, lb 4)	5
	(all out)	164	(all out)	124

Bowling: Fazal Mahmood 31-12-46-1 Khan Mohammad 23-9-27-0 Zulfiqar Ahmed 37.2-19-37-5 Kardar 31-10-35-3 Shujauddin 11-7-13-1
Khan Mohammad 13-3-33-0 Zulfiqar Ahmed 46.3-21-42-6 Kardar 27-15-22-0 Shujauddin 22-12-22-3

Pakistan Innings

Hanif Mohammad	c McGregor b Cave	5
Alimuddin	c MacGibbon b Moir	28
Waqar Hasan	c McMahon b Cave	17
Maqsood Ahmed	b MacGibbon	2
+Imtiaz Ahmed	c McMahon b MacGibbon	64
*AH Kardar	run out	22
Wazir Mohammad	c & b Cave	43
Shujauddin	b MacGibbon	47
Zulfiqar Ahmed	b MacGibbon	10
Fazal Mahmood	not out	34
Khan Mohammad	run out	5
	(b 4, lb 1, nb 7)	12
	(all out)	289

Bowling: MacGibbon 37.1-8-98-4 Cave 24-6-56-3 Reid 30-17-34-0 Moir 37-9-87-1 Poore 2-0-2-0

Umpires: Idris Beg and Shujauddin

Pakistan v Australia
11,12,13,15,17 October 1956

Result: Pakistan won by 9 wickets

Australia Innings

CC McDonald	c Imtiaz Ahmed b Fazal Mahmood	17	b Fazal Mahmood	3
JW Burke	c Mathias b Fazal Mahmood	4	c Mathias b Fazal Mahmood	10
RN Harvey	lbw b Fazal Mahmood	2	b Fazal Mahmood	4
ID Craig	c Imtiaz Ahmed b Fazal Mahmood	0	lbw b Fazal Mahmood	18
KR Miller	c Wazir Mohammad b Fazal Mahmood	21	b Khan Mohammad	11
RG Archer	c Imtiaz Ahmed b Khan Mohammad	10	c Fazal Mahmood b Khan Mohammad	27
R Benaud	c Waqar Hasan b Fazal Mahmood	4	b Fazal Mahmood	56
AK Davidson	c Kardar b Khan Mohammad	3	c Imtiaz Ahmed b Khan Mohammad	37
RR Lindwall	c Mathias b Khan Mohammad	2	lbw b Fazal Mahmood	0
*IWG Johnson	not out	13	b Fazal Mahmood	0
+GRA Langley	c Waqar Hasan b Khan Mohammad	1	not out	13
	(lb 2, nb 1)	3	(lb 2, nb 6)	8
	(all out)	80	(all out)	187

Bowling: Fazal Mahmood 27-11-34-6 Khan Mohammad 26.1-9-43-4
Fazal Mahmood 48-17-80-7 Khan Mohammad 40.5-13-69-3 Zulfiqar Ahmed 9-1-18-0 Kardar 12-5-12-0

Pakistan Innings

Hanif Mohammad	c Langley b Miller	0	c Harvey b Davidson	5
Alimuddin	c Lindwall b Archer	10	not out	34
Gul Mohammad	b Davidson	12	not out	27
+Imtiaz Ahmed	c McDonald b Benaud	15		
Waqar Hasan	c Langley b Miller	6		
Wazir Mohammad	c & b Johnson	67		
*AH Kardar	lbw b Johnson	69		
W Mathias	b Johnson	0		
Fazal Mahmood	not out	10		
Zulfiqar Ahmed	c Langley b Lindwall	0		
Khan Mohammad	b Johnson	3		
	(b 5, lb 2)	7	(lb 1, nb 2)	3
	(all out)	199	(1 wicket)	69

Bowling: Lindwall 27-8-42-1 Miller 17-5-40-2 Archer 4-0-18-1 Davidson 6-4-6-1 Benaud 17-5-36-1 Johnson 20.3-3-50-4
Lindwall 16-8-22-0 Miller 12-4-18-0 Archer 3.5-3-1-0 Davidson 9-5-9-1 Johnson 7.5-2-16-0

Umpires: Daud Khan and Idris Beg

Pakistan v West Indies
20,21,22,24,25 February 1959

Result: Pakistan won by 10 wickets

West Indies Innings

CC Hunte	c Imtiaz Ahmed b Fazal Mahmood	0	lbw b Fazal Mahmood	21
JKC Holt	lbw b Nasim-ul-Ghani	29	c Ijaz Butt b Fazal Mahmood	2
RB Kanhai	c Hanif Mohammad b Nasim-ul-Ghani	33	c Imtiaz Ahmed b Mahmood Hussain	12
GS Sobers	lbw b Fazal Mahmood	0	lbw b Fazal Mahmood	14
OG Smith	st Imtiaz Ahmed b Nasim-ul-Ghani	0	lbw b Mahmood Hussain	11
BF Butcher	not out	45	c Imtiaz Ahmed b Nasim-ul-Ghani	61
JS Solomon	c Hanif Mohammad b D'Souza	14	run out	66
*+FCM Alexander	b D'Souza	0	lbw b Shujauddin	16
LR Gibbs	b Nasim-ul-Ghani	5	b Shujauddin	21
WW Hall	b Fazal Mahmood	7	st Imtiaz Ahmed b Shujauddin	4
JO Taylor	b Fazal Mahmood	0	not out	0
	(b 3, nb 10)	13	(lb 7, nb 10)	17
	(all out)	146	(all out)	245

Bowling: Fazal Mahmood 22-9-35-4 Mahmood Hussain 8-3-13-0 D'Souza 14-0-50-2 Nasim-ul-Ghani 16-5-35-4
Fazal Mahmood 36-9-89-3 Mahmood Hussain 26-10-59-2 D'Souza 13-5-28-0 Nasim-ul-Ghani 25-16-34-1 Shujauddin 13-7-18-3

Pakistan Innings

Hanif Mohammad	c Alexander b Smith	103	retired hurt	5
Ijaz Butt	c Alexander b Hall	14	not out	41
Saeed Ahmed	run out	78	not out	33
+Imtiaz Ahmed	lbw b Smith	31		
Wazir Mohammad	st Alexander b Gibbs	23		
W Mathias	b Hall	16		
*Fazal Mahmood	c Alexander b Hall	0		
Shujauddin	run out	1		
Nasim-ul-Ghani	b Gibbs	11		
Mahmood Hussain	b Gibbs	1		
A D'Souza	not out	3		
	(b 9, lb 3, w 1, nb 10)	23	(nb 9)	9
	(all out)	304	(0 wickets)	88

Bowling: Hall 30-7-57-3 Taylor 21-7-43-0 Gibbs 38.2-13-92-3 Sobers 40-24-45-0 Smith 27-14-36-2 Solomon 4-1-8-0
Hall 8-1-35-0 Taylor 6-2-15-0 Gibbs 7-4-8-0 Sobers 9-5-12-0 Smith 3-2-9-0 Holt 1-1-0-0

Umpires: Daud Khan and Murawwat Hussain

Pakistan v Australia
4,5,6,8,9 December 1959

Result: Match drawn

Pakistan Innings

Hanif Mohammad	lbw b Lindwall	51	not out	101
+Imtiaz Ahmed	b Davidson	18	c Harvey b Davidson	9
Saeed Ahmed	c Harvey b Lindwall	91	c Harvey b Davidson	8
Shujauddin	c O'Neill b Benaud	5	c Favell b Mackay	4
DA Sharpe	c Burge b Benaud	4	c Mackay b Lindwall	26
Ijaz Butt	c Grout b Benaud	58	run out	8
W Mathias	c Favell b Mackay	43	c Davidson b Benaud	13
Intikhab Alam	run out	0	c Burge b Mackay	6
*Fazal Mahmood	c Harvey b Benaud	7	c Benaud b Davidson	11
Mohammad Munaf	not out	4	not out	4
Munir Malik	st Grout b Benaud	0		
	(lb 3, nb 3)	6	(lb 2, nb 2)	4
	(all out)	287	(8 wickets declared)	194

Bowling: Davidson 26-5-59-1 Lindwall 25-6-72-2 Benaud 49.5-17-93-5 Mackay 27-8-53-1 O'Neill 4-1-4-0
Davidson 34-8-70-3 Lindwall 17-10-14-1 Benaud 26-13-48-1 Mackay 32.4-11-58-2

Australia Innings

CC McDonald	b Intikhab Alam	19	lbw b Munir Malik	30
GB Stevens	c Mathias b Fazal Mahmood	13	c Imtiaz Ahmed b Intikhab Alam	28
+ATW Grout	c & b Intikhab Alam	20		
KD Mackay	c Ijaz Butt b Fazal Mahmood	40		
RN Harvey	c Imtiaz Ahmed b Fazal Mahmood	54	not out	13
NC O'Neill	b Munir Malik	6	not out	7
LE Favell	c Sharpe b Fazal Mahmood	10		
PJP Burge	c Sharpe b Mohammad Munaf	12		
*R Benaud	c Imtiaz Ahmed b Munir Malik	18		
AK Davidson	not out	39		
RR Lindwall	c Imtiaz Ahmed b Fazal Mahmood	23		
	(lb 1, nb 2)	3	(lb 3, nb 2)	5
	(all out)	257	(2 wickets)	83

Bowling: Fazal Mahmood 30.2-12-74-5 Mohammad Munaf 8-0-42-1 Intikhab Alam 19-4-49-2 Munir Malik 22-5-76-2 Shujauddin 3-0-13-0
Fazal Mahmood 10-5-16-0 Mohammad Munaf 3-0-10-0 Intikhab Alam 6-1-13-1 Munir Malik 9-1-24-1 Shujauddin 2-1-9-0 Saeed Ahmed 3-0-6-0

Umpires: Munawar Hussain and KA Saeed

Pakistan v England
2,3,4,6,7 February 1962

Result: Match drawn

Pakistan Innings

Hanif Mohammad	c Dexter b Lock	67	c Dexter b Knight	89
*+Imtiaz Ahmed	b White	0	c Smith b Dexter	86
Saeed Ahmed	c Millman b Knight	16	c & b Barber	19
Javed Burki	c Millman b Dexter	3	c Millman b Dexter	44
Mushtaq Mohammad	lbw b Knight	14	b Lock	41
Alimuddin	c Lock b Knight	109	c Parfitt b Barber	53
Shujauddin	c Parfitt b Allen	15	c Lock b Barber	5
Nasim-ul-Ghani	b Barber	3	not out	41
Fazal Mahmood	b Knight	12	b Dexter	0
A D'Souza	b Dexter	3	not out	10
Haseeb Ahsan	not out	4		
	(b 2, lb 1, nb 4)	7	(b 8, lb 2, nb 6)	16
	(all out)	253	(8 wickets)	404

Bowling: Knight 19-4-66-4 White 2.4-0-12-1 Dexter 18.2-4-48-2 Allen 27-14-51-1 Barber 14-1-44-1 Lock 14-8-25-1
Knight 17-3-43-1 Dexter 32-9-86-3 Lock 37-16-86-1 Allen 35-19-42-0 Barber 41-7-117-3 Parfitt 3-2-4-0 Richardson 2-1-10-0

England Innings

PE Richardson	c Alimuddin b Nasim-ul-Ghani	26
G Pullar	c Alimuddin b Nasim-ul-Ghani	60
*ER Dexter	c Saeed Ahmed b D'Souza	205
MJK Smith	c Imtiaz Ahmed b Nasim-ul-Ghani	56
PH Parfitt	c Saeed Ahmed b D'Souza	111
RW Barber	st Imtiaz Ahmed b Haseeb Ahsan	23
BR Knight	c Imtiaz Ahmed b D'Souza	6
DA Allen	c Imtiaz Ahmed b D'Souza	1
+G Millman	c Nasim-ul-Ghani b Haseeb Ahsan	0
GAR Lock	not out	0
DW White	b D'Souza	0
	(b 7, lb 11, nb 1)	19
	(all out)	507

Bowling: Fazal Mahmood 63-23-98-0 D'Souza 57.5-16-112-5 Nasim-ul-Ghani 45-10-125-3 Haseeb Ahsan 36-7-68-2
Shujauddin 27-5-63-0 Saeed Ahmed 3-0-12-0 Mushtaq Mohammad 2-0-10-0

Umpires: Daud Khan and Shujauddin

Pakistan v Australia
24,25,27,28,29 October 1964

Result: Match drawn

Pakistan Innings

Khalid Ibadulla	c Grout b McKenzie	166	c Redpath b McKenzie	3
+Abdul Kadir	run out	95	hit wicket b Veivers	26
Saeed Ahmed	c Redpath b Martin	7	sub b Martin	35
Javed Burki	hit wicket b McKenzie	8	c Grout b Cowper	62
*Hanif Mohammad	c & b McKenzie	2	c McKenzie b Booth	40
Shafqat Rana	c Grout b McKenzie	0	lbw b McKenzie	24
Nasim-ul-Ghani	c Redpath b Hawke	15	c Grout b Veivers	22
Majid Khan	lbw b Martin	0		
Intikhab Alam	c Grout b McKenzie	53	not out	21
Asif Iqbal	c Booth b McKenzie	41	c & b Simpson	36
Pervez Sajjad	not out	3		
	(b 9, lb 12, nb 3)	24	(b 1, lb 6, nb 3)	10
	(all out)	414	(8 wickets declared)	279

Bowling: McKenzie 30-9-69-6 Hawke 20-2-84-1 Martin 36-11-106-2 Veivers 16-5-33-0 Simpson 30-8-69-0 Booth 5-2-15-0 Redpath 1-0-14-0
McKenzie 25-5-62-2 Hawke 6-2-20-0 Martin 17-4-42-1 Veivers 30-16-44-2 Simpson 20-5-47-1 Booth 13-4-18-1 Cowper 11-3-36-1

Australia Innings

WM Lawry	hit wicket b Majid Khan	7	c Khalid Ibadulla b Majid Khan	22
*RB Simpson	c Pervez Sajjad b Saeed Ahmed	153	c Khalid Ibadulla b Nasim-ul-Ghani	115
IR Redpath	lbw b Intikhab Alam	19	not out	40
PJP Burge	c Majid Khan b Pervez Sajjad	54	not out	28
BC Booth	c Asif Iqbal b Majid Khan	15		
RM Cowper	b Asif Iqbal	16		
TR Veivers	st Abdul Kadir b Saeed Ahmed	25		
JW Martin	b Asif Iqbal	26		
+ATW Grout	c Asif Iqbal b Saeed Ahmed	0		
GD McKenzie	lbw b Intikhab Alam	2		
NJN Hawke	not out	8		
	(b 12, lb 8, nb 7)	27	(lb 14, nb 8)	22
	(all out)	352	(2 wickets)	227

Bowling: Majid Khan 30-9-55-2 Asif Iqbal 23.5-5-68-2 Pervez Sajjad 22-5-52-1 Intikhab Alam 28-5-83-2 Nasim-ul-Ghani 4-0-17-0 Saeed Ahmed 19-5-41-3 Khalid Ibadulla 7-3-9-0
Majid Khan 16-3-42-1 Asif Iqbal 12-4-28-0 Pervez Sajjad 8-2-17-0 Intikhab Alam 16-3-48-0 Nasim-ul-Ghani 12-3-24-1 Saeed Ahmed 13-6-28-0 Khalid Ibadulla 2-0-14-0 Javed Burki 2-1-3-0 Shafqat Rana 1-0-1-0

Umpires: Daud Khan and Shujauddin

Pakistan v New Zealand
9,10,11,13,14 April 1965

Result: Pakistan won by 8 wickets

New Zealand Innings

TW Jarvis	lbw b Salahuddin	27	b Asif Iqbal	0
+AE Dick	c Naushad Ali b Asif Iqbal	33	b Majid Khan	2
BW Sinclair	c Majid Khan b Mohammad Farooq	24	lbw b Mohammad Farooq	14
*JR Reid	b Asif Iqbal	128	c Majid Khan b Salahuddin	76
RW Morgan	lbw b Saeed Ahmed	13	c Salahuddin b Pervez Sajjad	25
BE Congdon	c sub b Intikhab Alam	57	b Intikhab Alam	57
BR Taylor	c Pervez Sajjad b Intikhab Alam	6	c Hanif Mohammad b Intikhab Alam	3
V Pollard	b Mohammad Farooq	1	b Salahuddin	4
RC Motz	b Intikhab Alam	0	lbw b Intikhab Alam	2
B Sutcliffe	not out	13	c Majid Khan b Intikhab Alam	18
FJ Cameron	c Naushad Ali b Asif Iqbal	9	not out	10
	(lb 2, nb 12)	14	(b 1, lb 3, nb 8)	12
	(all out)	285	(all out)	223

Bowling: Asif Iqbal 11-3-35-3 Majid Khan 20-1-63-0 Mohammad Farooq 21-5-59-2 Salahuddin 6-4-3-1 Pervez Sajjad 11-4-29-0 Intikhab Alam 24-6-53-3 Saeed Ahmed 10-3-29-1
Asif Iqbal 14-7-29-1 Majid Khan 8-0-30-1 Mohammad Farooq 17-5-41-1 Salahuddin 26-5-56-2 Pervez Sajjad 8-3-16-1 Intikhab Alam 26.4-10-39-4

Pakistan Innings

Mohammad Ilyas	lbw b Motz	20	st Dick b Reid	126
+Naushad Ali	c Taylor b Motz	9	c sub (GE Vivian) b Pollard	39
Saeed Ahmed	b Cameron	172	not out	19
Javed Burki	c Morgan b Pollard	29	not out	4
*Hanif Mohammad	b Reid	1		
Majid Khan	run out	12		
Salahuddin	not out	11		
Asif Iqbal	lbw b Cameron	4		
Intikhab Alam	c Dick b Congdon	3		
Pervez Sajjad	not out	8		
Mohammad Farooq				
	(b 17, lb 12, nb 9)	38	(b 8, lb 2, w 1, nb 3)	14
	(8 wickets declared)	307	(2 wickets)	202

Bowling: Motz 22-11-35-2 Cameron 28-7-70-2 Pollard 27-13-41-1 Taylor 15-2-54-0 Morgan 13-2-31-0 Reid 10-5-28-1 Congdon 6-3-10-1
Cameron 11-3-29-0 Pollard 18-3-52-1 Taylor 14-3-43-0 Morgan 7-2-31-0 Reid 1-0-6-1 Congdon 9-2-27-0

Umpires: Daud Khan and Shujauddin

Pakistan v England
6,7,8,9,10 March 1969

Result: Match drawn

England Innings

C Milburn	c Wasim Bari b Asif Masood	139
JH Edrich	c Saeed Ahmed b Intikhab Alam	32
TW Graveney	c Asif Iqbal b Intikhab Alam	105
*MC Cowdrey	c Hanif Mohammad b Intikhab Alam	14
KWR Fletcher	b Mushtaq Mohammad	38
BL D'Oliveira	c Aftab Gul b Mushtaq Mohammad	16
+APE Knott	not out	96
JA Snow	b Asif Masood	9
DJ Brown	not out	25
DL Underwood		
RNS Hobbs		
	(b 5, lb 12, nb 11)	28
	(7 wickets)	502

Bowling: Asif Masood 28-2-94-2 Majid Khan 20-5-51-0 Sarfraz Nawaz 34-6-78-0 Intikhab Alam 48-4-129-3 Saeed Ahmed 22-5-53-0 Mushtaq Mohammad 23.1-5-69-2

Pakistan v New Zealand
24,25,26,27 October 1969

Result: Match drawn

Pakistan Innings

Hanif Mohammad	c Yuile b Howarth	22	lbw b Yuile	35
Sadiq Mohammad	b Howarth	69	run out	37
Younis Ahmed	c Dowling b Howarth	8	c Dowling b Cunis	62
Mushtaq Mohammad	b Yuile	14	c Murray b Howarth	19
Zaheer Abbas	c Murray b Yuile	12	c Burgess b Hadlee	27
Asif Iqbal	st Wadsworth b Howarth	22	c Hastings b Yuile	0
*Intikhab Alam	c Congdon b Howarth	0	c Yuile b Cunis	47
+Wasim Bari	c Murray b Hadlee	15	c Congdon b Howarth	19
Mohammad Nazir	not out	29	not out	17
Pervez Sajjad	b Hadlee	0		
Asif Masood	c Howarth b Hadlee	17		
	(b 2, lb 10)	12	(b 13, lb 7)	20
	(all out)	220	(8 wickets declared)	283

Bowling: Hadlee 17.2-5-27-3 Cunis 11-5-18-0 Congdon 8-5-14-0 Howarth 33-10-80-5 Pollard 15-5-34-0 Yuile 13-3-35-2 Hadlee 16-5-31-1 Cunis 15.4-4-38-2 Howarth 31-13-60-2 Pollard 31-11-50-0 Yuile 35-13-70-2 Burgess 6-1-14-0

New Zealand Innings

*GT Dowling	b Mohammad Nazir	40	lbw b Pervez Sajjad	3
BAG Murray	c Mohammad Nazir b Mohm'd Nazir	50	c Asif Iqbal b Pervez Sajjad	6
BE Congdon	c Sadiq Mohammad b Pervez Sajjad	20	c Sadiq Mohammad b Pervez Sajjad	2
BF Hastings	b Mohammad Nazir	22	b Pervez Sajjad	9
MG Burgess	b Mohammad Nazir	21	c Asif Iqbal b Pervez Sajjad	45
V Pollard	b Mohammad Nazir	2	not out	28
BW Yuile	b Mohammad Nazir	47	not out	5
+KJ Wadsworth	st Wasim Bari b Pervez Sajjad	0		
DR Hadlee	lbw b Mushtaq Mohammad	56		
RS Cunis	b Mohammad Nazir	5		
HJ Howarth	b Mohammad Nazir	0		
	(b 6, lb 3, nb 2)	11	(b 12, lb 2)	14
	(all out)	274	(5 wickets)	112

Bowling: Asif Masood 3-0-18-0 Asif Iqbal 3-0-12-0 Intikhab Alam 13-3-51-0 Mohammad Nazir 30.1-3-99-7 Pervez Sajjad 31-7-71-2 Mushtaq Mohammad 5-0-12-1
Asif Masood 2-1-7-0 Asif Iqbal 2-0-2-0 Intikhab Alam 5-1-18-0 Mohammad Nazir 14-5-15-0 Pervez Sajjad 24-12-33-5 Mushtaq Mohammad 12-5-20-0 Sadiq Mohammad 2-0-2-0 Hanif Mohammad 2-1-1-0

Umpires: Idris Beg and Munawar Hussain

Pakistan v England
24,25,27,28,29 March 1973

Result: Match drawn

Pakistan Innings

Sadiq Mohammad	c Denness b Gifford	89	b Gifford	1
Talat Ali	c Amiss b Gifford	33	b Gifford	39
*Majid Khan	c Amiss b Pocock	99	b Gifford	23
Mushtaq Mohammad	run out	99	c Denness b Birkenshaw	0
Asif Iqbal	c & b Pocock	6	c Fletcher b Gifford	36
Intikhab Alam	c & b Birkenshaw	61	c Greig b Birkenshaw	0
Zaheer Abbas	not out	22	c Knott b Gifford	4
+Wasim Bari	not out	17	c Denness b Birkenshaw	41
Saleem Altaf			c Knott b Birkenshaw	13
Sarfraz Nawaz			not out	33
Asif Masood			c Gifford b Birkenshaw	0
	(b 4, lb 9, nb 6)	19	(lb 4, nb 5)	9
	(6 wickets declared)	445	(all out)	199

Bowling: Arnold 19-2-69-0 Greig 20-1-76-0 Pocock 38-7-93-2 Gifford 46-12-99-2 Birkenshaw 31-5-89-1
Arnold 15-2-52-0 Greig 17-8-31-0 Gifford 29-9-55-5 Birkenshaw 18.3-5-57-5

England Innings

B Wood	c Sarfraz Nawaz b Asif Masood	3	c Asif Masood b Saleem Altaf	5
DL Amiss	c Sarfraz Nawaz b Intikhab Alam	99	not out	21
KWR Fletcher	c Talat Ali b Intikhab Alam	54	not out	1
MH Denness	lbw b Asif Masood	47		
*AR Lewis	c Asif Iqbal b Intikhab Alam	88		
PI Pocock	c Sarfraz Nawaz b Mushtaq Mohm'd	4		
AW Greig	b Majid Khan	48		
+APE Knott	b Majid Khan	2		
J Birkenshaw	c Majid Khan b Mushtaq Mohammad	21		
GG Arnold	c Mushtaq Moham'd b Intikhabb Alam	2		
N Gifford	not out	4		
	(b 3, lb 3, nb 8)	14	(nb 3)	3
	(all out)	386	(1 wicket)	30

Bowling: Saleem Altaf 15-3-38-0 Asif Masood 21-4-41-2 Intikhab Alam 39-8-105-4 Sarfraz Nawaz 25-3-64-0 Mushtaq Mohammad 34.3-9-73-2 Majid Khan 22-5-51-2
Saleem Altaf 5-1-16-1 Asif Masood 4-1-11-0 Sarfraz Nawaz 1-1-0-0

Umpires: Daud Khan and Mohammad Aslam

Pakistan v West Indies
1,2,3,5,6 March 1975

Result: Match drawn

Pakistan Innings

Majid Khan	c Baichan b Gibbs	100	run out	18
Sadiq Mohammad	c Murray b Roberts	27	not out	98
Zaheer Abbas	c Murray b Gibbs	18	c Fredericks b Roberts	2
Mushtaq Mohammad	c Murray b Holder	5	c Kallicharran b Boyce	1
Asif Iqbal	c Boyce b Holder	3	c Holder b Julien	77
Wasim Raja	not out	107	b Gibbs	1
*Intikhab Alam	c Fredericks b Julien	34	c Richards b Fredericks	6
+Wasim Bari	c Baichan b Roberts	58	run out	0
Sarfraz Nawaz	b Gibbs	0	not out	15
Asif Masood	not out	5	c Julien b Gibbs	0
Liaqat Ali			c & b Richards	12
	(b 1, lb 16, nb 32)	49	(b 6, lb 6, nb 14)	26
	(8 wickets declared)	406	(all out)	256

Bowling: Roberts 25-3-81-2 Julien 11-0-51-1 Holder 19-2-66-2 Boyce 12-1-60-0 Fredericks 1-0-10-0 Gibbs 26-4-89-3 Roberts 16-0-54-1 Julien 16-7-37-1 Holder 6-3-19-0 Boyce 3-0-15-1 Fredericks 12-3-39-1 Gibbs 37.1-19-49-2 Richards 9-2-17-1

West Indies Innings

RC Fredericks	c Liaqat Ali b Intikhab Alam	77	not out	0
L Baichan	c Wasim Bari b Intikhab Alam	36	not out	0
Al Kallicharran	c Zaheer Abbas b Sarfraz Nawaz	115		
IVA Richards	lbw b Mushtaq Mohammad	10		
*CH Lloyd	c Sadiq Mohammad b Asif Masood	73		
+DL Murray	c Majid Khan b Intikhab Alam	19		
BD Julien	b Asif Masood	101		
KD Boyce	run out	2		
VA Holder	lbw b Liaqat Ali	29		
AME Roberts	run out	6		
LR Gibbs	not out	4		
	(b 1, lb 2, nb 18)	21	(nb 1)	1
	(all out)	493	(0 wickets)	1

Bowling: Asif Masood 15.2-2-76-2 Sarfraz Nawaz 21-1-106-1 Liaqat Ali 19-1-90-1 Intikhab Alam 28-1-122-3 Mushtaq Mohammad 15-4-56-1 Wasim Raja 4.7-0-22-0
Zaheer Abbas 1-1-0-0

Umpires: Amanullah Khan and Mahboob Shah

National Stadium, Karachi

Pakistan v New Zealand
30,31 October, 1,3,4 November 1976

Result: Match drawn

Pakistan Innings

Sadiq Mohammad	c Burgess b Hadlee	34	c Lees b Collinge	31
Majid Khan	c Burgess b Collinge	112	run out	50
Zaheer Abbas	b O'Sullivan	3	c Lees b O'Sullivan	16
Javed Miandad	c Hadlee b Collinge	206	st Lees b O'Sullivan	85
*Mushtaq Mohammad	c Lees b Hadlee	107	not out	67
Asif Iqbal	c Lees b Hadlee	12	st Lees b Roberts	30
Imran Khan	c O'Sullivan b Hadlee	59	not out	4
Intikhab Alam	lbw b O'Sullivan	0		
Sarfraz Nawaz	lbw b Cairns	15		
+Shahid Israr	not out	7		
Sikander Bakht				
	(b 3, lb 5, nb 2)	10	(lb 4, nb 3)	7
	(9 wickets declared)	565	(5 wickets declared)	290

Bowling: Collinge 21-1-141-2 Hadlee 20.2-1-138-4 Cairns 28-2-142-1 O'Sullivan 35-6-131-2 Morrison 1-0-3-0
Collinge 12-0-88-1 Hadlee 12-0-75-0 O'Sullivan 17-0-96-2 Morrison 2-0-6-0 Roberts 4.4-2-18-1

New Zealand Innings

JFM Morrison	b Sarfraz Nawaz	4	c Mushtaq Mohammad b Sikander Bakht	31
NM Parker	c Shahid Israr b Sarfraz Nawaz	2	c Imran Khan b Intikhab Alam	40
*JM Parker	c Majid Khan b Imran Khan	24	c Sadiq Mohammad b Javed Miandad	16
ADG Roberts	b Imran Khan	39	b Sikander Bakht	45
MG Burgess	c Javed Miandad b Sarfraz Nawaz	44	c Majid Khan b Javed Miandad	1
RW Anderson	lbw b Imran Khan	8	lbw b Imran Khan	30
+WK Lees	b Sikander Bakht	152	c Asif Iqbal b Imran Khan	46
RJ Hadlee	c Shahid Israr b Intikhab Alam	87	not out	30
BL Cairns	not out	52	not out	9
DR O'Sullivan	c Mushtaq Mohammad b Intikhab Alam	1		
RO Collinge	b Intikhab Alam	3		
	(b 12, lb 7, nb 33)	52	(b 4, lb 5, nb 5)	14
	(all out)	468	(7 wickets)	262

Bowling: Sarfraz Nawaz 20-1-84-3 Imran Khan 24.6-4-107-3 Sikander Bakht 16-3-68-1 Intikhab Alam 20.7-5-76-3 Mushtaq Mohammad 6-2-30-0 Javed Miandad 10-3-34-0 Majid Khan 5-2-17-0 Sadiq Mohammad 1-1-0-0
Imran Khan 21.6-1-104-2 Sikander Bakht 8-2-38-2 Intikhab Alam 17-5-42-1 Mushtaq Mohammad 6-2-9-0 Javed Miandad 17-4-45-2 Majid Khan 9-4-6-0 Sadiq Mohammad 1-0-4-0

Umpires: Shakoor Rana and Shujauddin

Pakistan v England
18,19,20,22,23 January 1978

Result: Match drawn

England Innings

*G Boycott	b Iqbal Qasim	31	c Javed Miandad b Sikander Bakht	56
BC Rose	c Javed Miandad b Sarfraz Nawaz	10	c Haroon Rashid b Abdul Qadir	18
DW Randall	lbw b Iqbal Qasim	23	b Sikander Bakht	55
GRJ Roope	lbw b Sikander Bakht	56	not out	33
MW Gatting	lbw b Abdul Qadir	5	lbw b Iqbal Qasim	6
G Miller	c Mudassar Nazar b Wasim Raja	11	c Wasim Bari b Iqbal Qasim	3
+RW Taylor	lbw b Abdul Qadir	36	not out	18
PH Edmonds	lbw b Abdul Qadir	6		
GA Cope	b Iqbal Qasim	18		
JK Lever	not out	33		
RGD Willis	lbw b Abdul Qadir	5		
	(b 3, lb 21, nb 8)	32	(b 9, lb 6, w 3, nb 15)	33
	(all out)	266	(5 wickets)	222

Bowling: Sarfraz Nawaz 15-6-27-1 Sikander Bakht 15-4-39-1 Iqbal Qasim 40-20-56-3 Abdul Qadir 40.1-9-81-4 Wasim Raja 13-3-31-1
Sarfraz Nawaz 28-7-57-0 Sikander Bakht 17-4-40-2 Iqbal Qasim 29-11-51-2 Abdul Qadir 8-2-26-1 Mudassar Nazar 1-0-1-0 Javed Miandad 2-0-5-0 Shafiq Ahmed 1-0-1-0 Wasim Bari 1-0-2-0 Haroon Rashid 1-0-3-0 Mohsin Khan 1-0-3-0

Pakistan Innings

Mudassar Nazar	c sub (IT Botham) b Edmonds	76
Shafiq Ahmed	c sub (IT Botham) b Willis	10
Mohsin Khan	c Willis b Cope	44
Haroon Rashid	c Taylor b Edmonds	27
Javed Miandad	c Roope b Edmonds	23
Wasim Raja	c Gatting b Edmonds	47
Abdul Qadir	c Roope b Edmonds	21
*+Wasim Bari	lbw b Miller	6
Sarfraz Nawaz	c Gatting b Edmonds	0
Iqbal Qasim	b Edmonds	8
Sikander Bakht	not out	7
	(b 2, lb 3, nb 7)	12
	(all out)	281

Bowling: Willis 8-1-23-1 Lever 12-4-32-0 Edmonds 33-7-66-7 Cope 28-8-77-1 Miller 14-0-71-1

Umpires: Amanullah Khan and Shakoor Rana

Pakistan v India
14,15,17,18,19 November 1978

Result: Pakistan won by 8 wickets

India Innings

SM Gavaskar	c Sarfraz Nawaz b Imran Khan	111	c Wasim Bari b Sarfraz Nawaz	137
CPS Chauhan	c Iqbal Qasim b Sarfraz Nawaz	33	c Wasim Bari b Sarfraz Nawaz	0
S Amarnath	c Mushtaq Mohammad b Iqbal Qasim	30	run out	14
GR Viswanath	b Imran Khan	0	c Wasim Bari b Sarfraz Nawaz	1
DB Vengsarkar	c Majid Khan b Sikander Bakht	11	c Wasim Bari b Sikander Bakht	1
M Amarnath	lbw b Sarfraz Nawaz	14	b Imran Khan	53
+SMH Kirmani	c Mushtaq Mohmd b Sikander Bakht	14	c Iqbal Qasim b Imran Khan	4
KD Ghavri	c Majid Khan b Sarfraz Nawaz	42	c Javed Miandad b Imran Khan	35
N Kapil Dev	lbw b Sarfraz Nawaz	59	c Mushtaq Mohammad b Sarfraz Nawaz	34
*BS Bedi	c Majid Khan b Imran Khan	4	not out	0
BS Chandrasekhar	not out	0	b Sarfraz Nawaz	0
	(b 10, lb 6, w 1, nb 9)	26	(b 9, lb 4, w 1, nb 7)	21
	(all out)	344	(all out)	300

Bowling: Imran Khan 32-12-75-3 Sarfraz Nawaz 31.2-4-89-4 Sikander Bakht 22-6-76-2 Iqbal Qasim 23-6-67-1 Mudassar Nazar 4-2-5-0 Mushtaq Mohammad 3-0-6-0
Imran Khan 28-7-76-3 Sarfraz Nawaz 24-5-70-5 Sikander Bakht 10-2-42-1 Iqbal Qasim 7-1-27-0 Mudassar Nazar 2-0-13-0 Mushtaq Mohammad 9-0-36-0 Javed Miandad 2-0-15-0

Pakistan Innings

Majid Khan	b Kapil Dev	44	c Chauhan b Kapil Dev	14
Mudassar Nazar	c Chauhan b Chandrasekhar	57		
+Wasim Bari	c Kirmani b Ghavri	3		
Zaheer Abbas	c Viswanath b Bedi	42		
Asif Iqbal	lbw b Chandrasekhar	1	c Kirmani b M Amarnath	44
Javed Miandad	c Kirmani b Kapil Dev	100	not out	62
*Mushtaq Mohammad	c sub b Ghavri	78		
Imran Khan	b Chandrasekhar	32	not out	31
Sarfraz Nawaz	c sub b Kapil Dev	28		
Iqbal Qasim	not out	29		
Sikander Bakht	not out	22		
	(b 5, lb 20, w 1, nb 19)	45	(b 3, lb 9, nb 1)	13
	(9 wickets declared)	481	(2 wickets)	164

Bowling: Kapil Dev 42-4-132-3 Ghavri 24-5-66-2 M Amarnath 14-2-39-0 Chandrasekhar 25-4-97-3 Bedi 35-5-99-1 Chauhan 1-0-3-0
Kapil Dev 9-0-47-1 Ghavri 6-0-36-0 M Amarnath 5.5-0-35-1 Bedi 4-0-33-0

Umpires: Mahboob Shah and Shujauddin

Pakistan v Australia
27,28,29 February, 2 March 1980

Result: Pakistan won by 7 wickets

Australia Innings

BM Laird	lbw b Imran Khan	6	c Javed Miandad b Iqbal Qasim	23
GN Yallop	c Taslim Arif b Tauseef Ahmed	12	c Majid Khan b Iqbal Qasim	16
KJ Hughes	c Majid Khan b Tauseef Ahmed	85	st Taslim Arif b Tauseef Ahmed	8
*GS Chappell	st Taslim Arif b Iqbal Qasim	20	c Taslim Arif b Tauseef Ahmed	13
DW Hookes	c Majid Khan b Iqbal Qasim	0	lbw b Iqbal Qasim	0
AR Border	lbw b Iqbal Qasim	30	not out	58
+RW Marsh	c Haroon Rashid b Tauseef Ahmed	13	c Mudassar Nazar b Iqbal Qasim	1
GR Beard	b Imran Khan	9	b Iqbal Qasim	4
RJ Bright	c Majid Khan b Iqbal Qasim	15	c Majid Khan b Iqbal Qasim	0
DK Lillee	not out	12	lbw b Iqbal Qasim	5
G Dymock	c Wasim Raja b Tauseef Ahmed	3	b Tauseef Ahmed	0
	(b 8, lb 9, nb 3)	20	(b 4, lb 5, w 1, nb 2)	12
	(all out)	225	(all out)	140

Bowling: Imran Khan 16-4-28-2 Sarfraz Nawaz 13-4-20-0 Mudassar Nazar 2-0-6-0 Iqbal Qasim 30-12-69-4 Tauseef Ahmed 30.2-9-64-4 Majid Khan 2-0-13-0 Wasim Raja 2-0-5-0
Sarfraz Nawaz 7-2-7-0 Mudassar Nazar 2-0-4-0 Iqbal Qasim 42-22-49-7 Tauseef Ahmed 34-11-62-3 Majid Khan 1-1-0-0 Wasim Raja 4-1-6-0

Pakistan Innings

+Taslim Arif	c Marsh b Bright	58	b Bright	8
Haroon Rashid	b Bright	6	b Bright	10
Zaheer Abbas	c Lillee b Bright	8	not out	18
*Javed Miandad	c Border b Chappell	40	b Bright	21
Wasim Raja	c sub b Chappell	0	not out	12
Majid Khan	c Border b Bright	89		
Mudassar Nazar	c Border b Bright	29		
Imran Khan	c Border b Chappell	9		
Sarfraz Nawaz	c Chappell b Bright	17		
Iqbal Qasim	not out	14		
Tauseef Ahmed	b Bright	0		
	(lb 12, nb 10)	22	(lb 3, nb 4)	7
	(all out)	292	(3 wickets)	76

Bowling: Lillee 28-4-76-0 Dymock 5-2-5-0 Bright 46.5-17-87-7 Beard 17-8-39-0 Chappell 20-3-49-3 Yallop 2-0-14-0
Lillee 11-2-22-0 Dymock 2-0-9-0 Bright 11-5-24-3 Beard 1.1-0-14-0

Umpires: Mahboob Shah and Shakoor Rana

Pakistan v West Indies
22,23,24,26,27 December 1980

Result: Match drawn

Pakistan Innings

Shafiq Ahmed	lbw b Clarke	0	lbw b Garner	17
Sadiq Mohammad	lbw b Croft	0	c Bacchus b Clarke	36
Zaheer Abbas	not out	13	lbw b Croft	1
*Javed Miandad	c Lloyd b Clarke	60	c Haynes b Clarke	5
Majid Khan	c Bacchus b Croft	0	c Murray b Croft	18
Wasim Raja	c Bacchus b Croft	2	not out	77
Imran Khan	lbw b Garner	21	c Murray b Marshall	12
Ijaz Faqih	b Marshall	0	c Murray b Marshall	8
+Wasim Bari	c Murray b Clarke	23	b Garner	3
Iqbal Qasim	c Richards b Clarke	0	b Croft	2
Mohammad Nazir	b Garner	0	not out	2
	(lb 1, w 1, nb 7)	9	(b 4, lb 3, nb 16)	23
	(all out)	128	(9 wickets)	204

Bowling: Clarke 15-7-27-4 Croft 14-5-27-3 Garner 18.1-8-27-2 Marshall 14-0-38-1
Clarke 11-3-14-2 Croft 23-6-50-3 Garner 19-4-39-2 Marshall 17-1-54-2 Richards 8-2-10-0 Gomes 6-0-14-0

West Indies Innings

DL Haynes	lbw b Iqbal Qasim	1
SFAF Bacchus	b Imran Khan	16
IVA Richards	c Zaheer Abbas b Iqbal Qasim	18
AI Kallicharran	b Imran Khan	4
*CH Lloyd	c Javed Miandad b Imran Khan	1
+DA Murray	c Javed Miandad b Iqbal Qasim	42
HA Gomes	c Javed Miandad b Mohammad Nazir	61
MD Marshall	b Mohammad Nazir	0
ST Clarke	b Iqbal Qasim	17
J Garner	lbw b Imran Khan	1
CEH Croft	not out	3
	(lb 1, w 4)	5
	(all out)	169

Bowling: Imran Khan 29-5-66-4 Iqbal Qasim 34.1-11-48-4 Mohammad Nazir 9-1-21-2 Ijaz Faqih 4-1-9-0 Wasim Raja 1-0-8-0 Majid Khan 8-3-12-0

Umpires: Javed Akhtar and Shakoor Rana

Pakistan v Sri Lanka
5,6,7,9,10 March 1982

Result: Pakistan won by 204 runs

Pakistan Innings

Mansoor Akhtar	c Goonatilleke b de Mel	6	c Mendis b DS de Silva	23
Rizwan-uz-Zaman	c Goonatilleke b Ratnayeke	42	c Goonatilleke b de Mel	10
Saleem Malik	b DS de Silva	12	not out	100
*Javed Miandad	c Goonatilleke b de Mel	4	st Goonatilleke b DS de Silva	92
Wasim Raja	c Dias b de Mel	31	not out	12
Haroon Rashid	run out	153		
+Saleem Yousuf	st Goonatilleke b DS de Silva	4		
Tahir Naqqash	c Mendis b DS de Silva	57		
Iqbal Qasim	lbw b DS de Silva	1	c sub (RGCE Wijesuriya) b DS de Silva	56
Rashid Khan	c Madugalle b GRA de Silva	59		
Tauseef Ahmed	not out	5		
	(lb 9, w 4, nb 9)	22	(b 5, lb 1, w 1, nb 1)	8
	(all out)	396	(4 wickets declared)	301

Bowling: de Mel 28-2-124-3 Ratnayeke 16-6-49-1 DS de Silva 38-8-102-4 GRA de Silva 17.2-2-69-1 Warnapura 2-0-9-0 Wettimuny 2-0-21-0
de Mel 23.2-3-100-1 Ratnayeke 5.4-2-20-0 DS de Silva 26-3-99-3 GRA de Silva 35-5-74-0

Sri Lanka Innings

*B Warnapura	lbw b Tahir Naqqash	13	b Tahir Naqqash	0
S Wettimuny	c Mansoor Akhtar b Rashid Khan	71	c Saleem Yousuf b Rashid Khan	14
RL Dias	lbw b Iqbal Qasim	53	lbw b Tahir Naqqash	19
RS Madugalle	c Saleem Yousuf b Rashid Khan	29	c Tauseef Ahmed b Iqbal Qasim	18
JR Ratnayeke	c Rizwan-uz-Zaman b Iqbal Qasim	24	c Saleem Malik b Wasim Raja	0
LRD Mendis	c Rashid Khan b Tahir Naqqash	54	c Saleem Yousuf b Iqbal Qasim	15
A Ranatunga	st Saleem Yousuf b Tauseef Ahmed	13	c Saleem Yousuf b Tauseef Ahmed	33
DS de Silva	b Tauseef Ahmed	26	st Saleem Yousuf b Iqbal Qasim	12
+HM Goonatilleke	c Saleem Yousuf b Tahir Naqqash	14	c Haroon Rashid b Wasim Raja	13
ALF de Mel	run out	9	c Javed Miandad b Iqbal Qasim	2
GRA de Silva	not out	10	not out	0
	(b 1, lb 12, w 3, nb 12)	28	(b 9, lb 11, w 1, nb 2)	23
	(all out)	344	(all out)	149

Bowling: Tahir Naqqash 32-11-83-3 Rashid Khan 26-7-53-2 Iqbal Qasim 28-7-88-2 Tauseef Ahmed 21.4-6-64-2 Wasim Raja 5-1-28-0
Tahir Naqqash 9-1-34-2 Rashid Khan 8-3-25-1 Iqbal Qasim 15.1-8-27-4 Tauseef Ahmed 12-1-39-1 Wasim Raja 3-2-1-2

Umpires: Amanullah Khan and Mahboob Shah

Pakistan v Australia
22,23,24,26,27 September 1982

Result: Pakistan won by 9 wickets

Australia Innings

GM Wood	c Wasim Bari b Imran Khan	0	c sub (Saleem Malik) b Abdul Qadir	17
BM Laird	run out	32	c Mansoor Akhtar b Imran Khan	3
J Dyson	b Iqbal Qasim	87	b Abdul Qadir	6
*KJ Hughes	c Wasim Bari b Iqbal Qasim	54	c Wasim Bari b Abdul Qadir	14
AR Border	not out	55	c sub (Saleem Malik) b Abdul Qadir	8
GM Ritchie	c Haroon Rashid b Abdul Qadir	4	b Iqbal Qasim	17
+RW Marsh	b Tahir Naqqash	19	lbw b Imran Khan	32
B Yardley	c Javed Miandad b Tahir Naqqash	0	lbw b Abdul Qadir	0
RJ Bright	c Haroon Rashid b Tahir Naqqash	2	not out	32
GF Lawson	c Wasim Bari b Tahir Naqqash	0	run out	11
JR Thomson	st Wasim Bari b Abdul Qadir	14	c Wasim Bari b Iqbal Qasim	18
	(b 4, lb 10, w 1, nb 2)	17	(b 2, lb 19)	21
	(all out)	284	(all out)	179

Bowling: Imran Khan 23-3-38-1 Tahir Naqqash 16-3-61-4 Mudassar Nazar 13-0-33-0 Abdul Qadir 21.4-1-80-2 Iqbal Qasim 26-10-55-2
Imran Khan 12-5-17-2 Tahir Naqqash 7-3-17-0 Abdul Qadir 26-7-76-5 Iqbal Qasim 21.5-6-48-2

Pakistan Innings

Mohsin Khan	handled the ball	58	not out	14
Mansoor Akhtar	c Bright b Thomson	32	not out	26
Haroon Rashid	c Laird b Yardley	82		
Javed Miandad	b Lawson	32		
Zaheer Abbas	c Marsh b Lawson	91		
Mudassar Nazar	not out	52	c Border b Thomson	5
*Imran Khan	c Yardley b Bright	1		
Tahir Naqqash	st Marsh b Bright	15		
+Wasim Bari	b Bright	0		
Abdul Qadir	run out	29		
Iqbal Qasim	not out	2		
	(b 4, lb 8, w 1, nb 12)	25	(nb 2)	2
	(9 wickets declared)	419	(1 wicket)	47

Bowling: Thomson 29-5-103-1 Lawson 39-10-93-2 Bright 36-8-96-3 Yardley 23-2-98-1 Border 1-0-4-0
Thomson 3-1-16-1 Bright 5-0-14-0 Yardley 3-1-9-0 Hughes 0.1-0-6-0

Umpires: Khizer Hayat and Mahboob Shah

Pakistan v India
23,24,25,27 December 1982

Result: Pakistan won by an innings and 86 runs

India Innings

*SM Gavaskar	run out	8	b Imran Khan	42
J Arun Lal	lbw b Sarfraz Nawaz	35	lbw b Abdul Qadir	11
DB Vengsarkar	c Mohsin Khan b Imran Khan	0	c Wasim Bari b Imran Khan	79
GR Viswanath	c Wasim Bari b Abdul Qadir	24	b Imran Khan	0
M Amarnath	lbw b Imran Khan	5	lbw b Imran Khan	3
SM Patil	c Javed Miandad b Abdul Qadir	4	b Imran Khan	0
N Kapil Dev	c & b Sarfraz Nawaz	73	b Imran Khan	1
+SMH Kirmani	c Mohsin Khan b Abdul Qadir	11	c Saleem Malik b Abdul Qadir	1
S Madan Lal	not out	3	not out	52
Maninder Singh	lbw b Abdul Qadir	0	lbw b Imran Khan	0
DR Doshi	b Imran Khan	0	b Imran Khan	0
	(lb 4, nb 2)	6	(b 1, lb 3, w 1, nb 3)	8
	(all out)	169	(all out)	197

Bowling: Imran Khan 12.1-6-19-3 Jalal-ud-Din 10-2-28-0 Sarfraz Nawaz 16-2-49-2 Abdul Qadir 15-3-67-4
Imran Khan 20.1-4-60-8 Jalal-ud-Din 7-2-31-0 Sarfraz Nawaz 10-2-23-0 Abdul Qadir 23-3-75-2

Pakistan Innings

Mohsin Khan	c Amarnath b Madan Lal	12
Mansoor Akhtar	c Kirmani b Madan Lal	0
Saleem Malik	c Kirmani b Madan Lal	3
Javed Miandad	b Amarnath	39
Zaheer Abbas	lbw b Kapil Dev	186
Mudassar Nazar	c Kirmani b Kapil Dev	119
*Imran Khan	c Amarnath b Kapil Dev	33
+Wasim Bari	c Arun Lal b Doshi	30
Abdul Qadir	b Kapil Dev	0
Sarfraz Nawaz	lbw b Kapil Dev	13
Jalal-ud-Din	not out	0
	(b 2, lb 6, w 2, nb 7)	17
	(all out)	452

Bowling: Kapil Dev 28.5-3-102-5 Madan Lal 23-1-129-3 Maninder Singh 23-2-67-0 Amarnath 17-1-69-1 Doshi 18-1-68-1

Umpires: Khizer Hayat and Shakoor Rana

Pakistan v India
30,31 January, 1,3,4 February 1983

Result: Match drawn

India Innings

*SM Gavaskar	c Wasim Bari b Tahir Naqqash	5	b Imran Khan	67
RJ Shastri	st Wasim Bari b Abdul Qadir	128	c Wasim Bari b Imran Khan	17
M Amarnath	c Wasim Bari b Imran Khan	19	not out	103
Yashpal Sharma	c Wasim Bari b Imran Khan	9	not out	19
DB Vengsarkar	c & b Tahir Naqqash	89		
GR Viswanath	b Mudassar Nazar	10		
+SMH Kirmani	c Zaheer Abbas b Sarfraz Nawaz	18		
N Kapil Dev	lbw b Imran Khan	33		
BS Sandhu	not out	32		
TAP Sekhar	not out	0		
Maninder Singh				
Saleem Malik				
Tahir Naqqash				
Abdul Qadir				
	(b 13, lb 9, nb 28)	50	(b 10, w 3, nb 5)	18
	(8 wickets declared)	393	(2 wickets)	224

Bowling: Imran Khan 32-11-65-3 Sarfraz Nawaz 41-10-92-1 Tahir Naqqash 24-7-69-2 Abdul Qadir 23-3-86-1 Mudassar Nazar 15-4-30-1 Wasim Raja 1-0-1-0
Imran Khan 16-3-41-2 Sarfraz Nawaz 14-4-45-0 Tahir Naqqash 8-1-28-0 Abdul Qadir 14-2-42-0 Wasim Raja 5-2-12-0 Zaheer Abbas 8-0-24-0 Mohsin Khan 1-0-3-0 Javed Miandad 2-0-11-0

Pakistan Innings

Mohsin Khan	lbw b Kapil Dev	91
Mudassar Nazar	lbw b Kapil Dev	152
Javed Miandad	c Kirmani b Sandhu	47
Zaheer Abbas	c Amarnath b Shastri	43
Wasim Raja	run out	10
*Imran Khan	not out	32
+Wasim Bari	c Kirmani b Sandhu	12
Sarfraz Nawaz	not out	6
Maninder Singh		
Saleem Malik		
Tahir Naqqash		
Abdul Qadir		
	(b 5, lb 12, w 1, nb 9)	27
	(6 wickets declared)	420

Bowling: Kapil Dev 33-2-137-2 Sandhu 28.2-4-87-2 Sekhar 14-1-43-0 Maninder Singh 16-3-49-0 Shastri 22-1-62-1 Amarnath 4-1-15-0

Umpires: Javed Akhtar and Khizer Hayat

Pakistan v England
2,3,4,6 March 1984

Result: Pakistan won by 3 wickets

England Innings

CL Smith	c Wasim Raja b Sarfraz Nawaz	28	lbw b Sarfraz Nawaz	5
MW Gatting	b Tauseef Ahmed	26	lbw b Sarfraz Nawaz	4
DI Gower	lbw b Abdul Qadir	58	c Mohsin Khan b Tauseef Ahmed	57
AJ Lamb	c Rameez Raja b Sarfraz Nawaz	4	c Anil Dalpat b Abdul Qadir	20
DW Randall	b Abdul Qadir	8	b Abdul Qadir	16
IT Botham	c Rameez Raja b Abdul Qadir	22	b Tauseef Ahmed	10
VJ Marks	c Rameez Raja b Sarfraz Nawaz	5	b Abdul Qadir	1
+RW Taylor	lbw b Abdul Qadir	4	c Mohsin Khan b Tauseef Ahmed	19
NGB Cook	c Saleem Malik b Abdul Qadir	9	c Mohsin Khan b Wasim Raja	5
*RGD Willis	c Wasim Raja b Sarfraz Nawaz	6	c Tauseef Ahmed b Wasim Raja	2
NG Cowans	not out	1	not out	0
	(lb 6, nb 5)	11	(b 6, lb 6, nb 8)	20
	(all out)	182	(all out)	159

Bowling: Azeem Hafeez 11-3-21-0 Sarfraz Nawaz 25.5-8-42-4 Tauseef Ahmed 24-11-33-1 Wasim Raja 3-2-1-0 Abdul Qadir 31-12-74-5
Azeem Hafeez 8-3-14-0 Sarfraz Nawaz 15-1-27-2 Tauseef Ahmed 21-6-37-3 Wasim Raja 3.3-1-2-2 Abdul Qadir 31-4-59-3

Pakistan Innings

Mohsin Khan	c Botham b Cook	54	b Cook	10
Qasim Umar	lbw b Cook	29	c Botham b Cook	7
Rameez Raja	c Smith b Cook	1	c Botham b Marks	1
*Zaheer Abbas	c Lamb b Botham	0	b Cook	8
Saleem Malik	lbw b Willis	74	run out	11
Wasim Raja	c Cowans b Cook	3	c Cowans b Cook	0
+Anil Dalpat	c Taylor b Willis	12	not out	16
Abdul Qadir	c Lamb b Botham	40	b Cook	7
Sarfraz Nawaz	c Botham b Cook	8	not out	4
Tauseef Ahmed	not out	17		
Azeem Hafeez	c Willis b Cook	24		
	(lb 5, nb 10)	15	(b 1, nb 1)	2
	(all out)	277	(7 wickets)	66

Bowling: Willis 17-6-33-2 Cowans 12-3-34-0 Botham 30-5-90-2 Cook 30-12-65-6 Marks 13-4-40-0
Willis 2-0-13-0 Cowans 2.3-1-10-0 Cook 14-8-18-5 Marks 12-5-23-1

Umpires: Khizer Hayat and Shakoor Rana

Pakistan v New Zealand
10,11,12,14,15 December 1984

Result: Match drawn

Pakistan Innings

Mudassar Nazar	c Smith b Stirling	5	c McEwan b Stirling	0
Shoaib Mohammad	c Smith b Stirling	31	c McEwan b Boock	34
Qasim Umar	lbw b Boock	45	c & b MD Crowe	17
Javed Miandad	c Smith b MD Crowe	13	c JJ Crowe b Boock	58
*Zaheer Abbas	c Smith b Stirling	14	c Smith b Bracewell	3
Saleem Malik	c & b MD Crowe	50	not out	119
Wasim Raja	lbw b Stirling	51	not out	60
Abdul Qadir	c Wright b Boock	7		
+Anil Dalpat	b Boock	52		
Iqbal Qasim	not out	45		
Azeem Hafeez	lbw b Boock	0		
	(b 5, lb 6, w 1, nb 3)	15	(b 2, lb 8, nb 7)	17
	(all out)	328	(5 wickets)	308

Bowling: Stirling 29-5-88-4 MD Crowe 21-4-81-2 McEwan 4-1-6-0 Boock 41-9-83-4 Coney 5-3-5-0 Bracewell 20-5-54-0
Stirling 14-1-82-1 MD Crowe 10-3-26-1 McEwan 2-0-7-0 Boock 30-10-83-2 Bracewell 33-11-83-1 Reid 2-0-7-0 JJ Crowe 2-0-9-0 Wright 1-0-1-0

New Zealand Innings

JG Wright	c Anil Dalpat b Iqbal Qasim	107
BA Edgar	run out	15
JF Reid	c Iqbal Qasim b Azeem Hafeez	97
MD Crowe	lbw b Wasim Raja	45
JJ Crowe	c Javed Miandad b Azeem Hafeez	62
*JV Coney	c & b Iqbal Qasim	16
PE McEwan	not out	40
+IDS Smith	c Saleem Malik b Iqbal Qasim	0
DA Stirling	c Qasim Umar b Iqbal Qasim	7
JG Bracewell	c Anil Dalpat b Azeem Hafeez	30
SL Boock	c Anil Dalpat b Azeem Hafeez	0
	(b 1, lb 5, nb 1)	7
	(all out)	426

Bowling: Mudassar Nazar 15.4-2-45-0 Azeem Hafeez 46.4-9-132-4 Iqbal Qasim 57-13-133-4 Wasim Raja 33-8-97-1 Zaheer Abbas 5.2-1-13-0

Umpires: Javed Akhtar and Shakoor Rana

Pakistan v Sri Lanka
7,8,9,11 November 1985

Result: Pakistan won by 10 wickets

Sri Lanka Innings

S Wettimuny	b Wasim Akram	17	c Saleem Yousuf b Imran Khan	10
JR Ratnayeke	b Abdul Qadir	36	c Saleem Yousuf b Imran Khan	3
RS Madugalle	lbw b Wasim Akram	0	b Tauseef Ahmed	5
RL Dias	c Saleem Yousuf b Imran Khan	7	c Saleem Malik b Abdul Qadir	4
*LRD Mendis	c Javed Miandad b Abdul Qadir	15	b Imran Khan	2
A Ranatunga	c Javed Miandad b Tauseef Ahmed	12	c Saleem Yousuf b Wasim Akram	25
PA de Silva	c & b Abdul Qadir	13	c Saleem Yousuf b Tauseef Ahmed	105
+AP Gurusinha	lbw b Imran Khan	17	c Saleem Yousuf b Tauseef Ahmed	12
ALF de Mel	st Saleem Yousuf b Abdul Qadir	3	b Tauseef Ahmed	18
RJ Ratnayake	not out	21	c Qasim Umar b Tauseef Ahmed	22
RGCE Wijesuriya	lbw b Abdul Qadir	2	not out	2
	(b 5, lb 10, w 1, nb 3)	19	(b 5, lb 11, nb 6)	22
	(all out)	162	(all out)	230

Bowling: Imran Khan 20-9-36-2 Wasim Akram 14-7-17-2 Tauseef Ahmed 22-10-50-1 Abdul Qadir 20.5-5-44-5
Imran Khan 14.1-5-28-3 Wasim Akram 14-4-24-1 Tauseef Ahmed 23.2-8-54-5 Abdul Qadir 25.5-4-102-1 Mudassar Nazar 3-0-6-0

Pakistan Innings

Mudassar Nazar	c Gurusinha b de Mel	16	not out	57
Mohsin Khan	c Gurusinha b de Mel	13	not out	36
Qasim Umar	c Ranatunga b de Mel	8		
*Javed Miandad	lbw b de Mel	63		
Saleem Malik	b de Mel	4		
Rameez Raja	c & b de Mel	52		
Imran Khan	c Ratnayake b Ratnayeke	63		
+Saleem Yousuf	lbw b Ratnayake	27		
Abdul Qadir	c Wettimuny b Wijesuriya	19		
Tauseef Ahmed	b Ratnayake	1		
Wasim Akram	not out	5		
	(b 13, lb 8, w 2, nb 1)	24	(b 1, lb 3, nb 1)	5
	(all out)	295	(0 wickets)	98

Bowling: de Mel 22-1-109-6 Ratnayake 15-2-48-2 Ratnayeke 15-2-48-1 Wijesuriya 22-5-68-1 Ranatunga 1-0-1-0
de Mel 3-0-28-0 Ratnayeke 6-1-24-0 Ratnayake 4-0-33-0 Wijesuriya 3.4-2-9-0

Umpires: Khizer Hayat and Mahboob Shah

National Stadium, Karachi

Pakistan v West Indies
20,21,22,24,25 November 1986

Result: Match drawn

West Indies Innings

CG Greenidge	c Saleem Yousuf b Mudassar Nazar	27	b Abdul Qadir	8
DL Haynes	lbw b Imran Khan	3	not out	88
RB Richardson	c Asif Mujtaba b Saleem Jaffar	44	c Rameez Raja b Abdul Qadir	32
HA Gomes	lbw b Abdul Qadir	18	lbw b Abdul Qadir	5
*IVA Richards	c Rameez Raja b Tauseef Ahmed	70	c Saleem Yousuf b Imran Khan	28
+PJL Dujon	c Saleem Yousuf b Abdul Qadir	19	c Saleem Yousuf b Saleem Jaffar	6
RA Harper	lbw b Imran Khan	9	b Imran Khan	4
MD Marshall	b Tauseef Ahmed	4	lbw b Imran Khan	0
CG Butts	lbw b Abdul Qadir	17	c Mohsin Khan b Imran Khan	12
AH Gray	c Imran Khan b Abdul Qadir	0	b Imran Khan	0
CA Walsh	not out	0	b Imran Khan	0
	(b 14, lb 11, w 1, nb 3)	29	(b 7, lb 13, w 1, nb 7)	28
	(all out)	240	(all out)	211

Bowling: Imran Khan 19-4-32-2 Saleem Jaffar 15-5-34-1 Mudassar Nazar 4-0-15-1 Abdul Qadir 31.5-3-107-4 Tauseef Ahmed 17-7-27-2
Imran Khan 22.3-2-46-6 Saleem Jaffar 14-4-23-1 Tauseef Ahmed 12-2-36-0 Abdul Qadir 44-9-84-3 Asif Mujtaba 3-2-2-0

Pakistan Innings

Mudassar Nazar	b Gray	16	lbw b Butts	25
Mohsin Khan	c Richards b Marshall	1	c Greenidge b Marshall	4
Rameez Raja	c Harper b Butts	62	b Butts	29
Javed Miandad	run out	76	b Marshall	4
*Imran Khan	lbw b Butts	1	not out	15
Asif Mujtaba	c Dujon b Marshall	12	c Dujon b Walsh	6
Qasim Umar	c Richardson b Butts	5	c Dujon b Gray	1
+Saleem Yousuf	c Walsh b Butts	22	c Haynes b Marshall	10
Tauseef Ahmed	c Richardson b Gray	3	not out	7
Saleem Jaffar	b Gray	9		
Abdul Qadir	not out	8		
	(b 9, lb 12, w 1, nb 2)	24	(b 17, lb 6, w 1)	24
	(all out)	239	(7 wickets)	125

Bowling: Marshall 33-9-57-2 Gray 21.1-6-40-3 Harper 7-0-31-0 Walsh 11-2-17-0 Butts 38-15-73-4
Marshall 19-5-31-3 Gray 14-7-18-1 Walsh 22-11-30-1 Butts 22-9-22-2 Harper 1-0-1-0

Umpires: VK Ramaswamy (Ind) and PD Reporter (Ind)

Pakistan v England
16,17,18,20,21 December 1987

Result: Match drawn

England Innings

GA Gooch	c Ashraf Ali b Wasim Akram	12	b Mudassar Nazar	93
BC Broad	lbw b Wasim Akram	7	lbw b Abdul Qadir	13
CWJ Athey	b Abdul Qadir	26	c Ashraf Ali b Saleem Jaffar	12
*MW Gatting	b Abdul Qadir	18	lbw b Saleem Jaffar	0
NH Fairbrother	c sub (Asif Mujtaba) b Saleem Jaffar	3	c sub (Asif Mujtaba) b Abdul Qadir	1
DJ Capel	b Abdul Qadir	98	c Iqbal Qasim b Abdul Qadir	24
PAJ DeFreitas	b Abdul Qadir	12	lbw b Abdul Qadir	6
JE Emburey	c Abdul Qadir b Saleem Jaffar	70	not out	74
+BN French	c Javed Miandad b Saleem Malik	31	lbw b Saleem Jaffar	0
NGB Cook	lbw b Abdul Qadir	2	b Abdul Qadir	14
GR Dilley	not out	0	not out	0
	(lb 8, w 1, nb 6)	15	(b 9, lb 5, w 1, nb 6)	21
	(all out)	294	(9 wickets)	258

Bowling: Wasim Akram 24.1-3-64-2 Saleem Jaffar 23.5-6-74-2 Abdul Qadir 49.4-15-88-5 Iqbal Qasim 18-4-51-0 Mudassar Nazar 1-1-0-0 Saleem Malik 5-2-9-1
Saleem Jaffar 42-9-79-3 Aamer Malik 2-0-7-0 Abdul Qadir 55-16-98-5 Iqbal Qasim 27-10-44-0 Saleem Malik 7-2-14-0 Mudassar Nazar 4-3-2-1

Pakistan Innings

Mudassar Nazar	lbw b DeFreitas	6
Rameez Raja	c French b Cook	50
Saleem Malik	c Gatting b DeFreitas	55
*Javed Miandad	lbw b Emburey	4
Ijaz Ahmed	run out	0
Aamer Malik	not out	98
+Ashraf Ali	c French b Dilley	12
Wasim Akram	c French b DeFreitas	37
Abdul Qadir	b Capel	61
Iqbal Qasim	c French b DeFreitas	11
Saleem Jaffar	lbw b DeFreitas	0
	(lb 11, nb 8)	19
	(all out)	353

Bowling: Dilley 21-2-102-1 DeFreitas 23.5-3-86-5 Emburey 53-24-90-1 Cook 33-12-56-1 Capel 3-0-8-1

Umpires: Khizer Hayat and Mahboob Shah

Pakistan v Australia
15,16,17,19,20 September 1988

Result: Pakistan won by an innings and 188 runs

Pakistan Innings

Mudassar Nazar	b Reid	0
Rameez Raja	c Healy b Reid	9
Shoaib Mohammad	b Waugh	94
*Javed Miandad	c Boon b Reid	211
Tauseef Ahmed	c Boon b May	35
Saleem Malik	c Boon b May	45
Ijaz Ahmed	c Boon b Reid	12
Aamer Malik	not out	17
+Saleem Yousuf	c Wood b May	5
Abdul Qadir	c Marsh b May	8
Iqbal Qasim		
	(b 16, lb 12, nb 5)	33
	(9 wickets declared)	469

Bowling: Reid 41-10-109-4 Dodemaide 29-13-35-0 Waugh 26-3-94-1 May 40.5-10-97-4 Taylor 16-2-73-0 Border 17-7-33-0

Australia Innings

GR Marsh	b Iqbal Qasim	8	lbw b Tauseef Ahmed	17
DC Boon	b Abdul Qadir	14	b Iqbal Qasim	4
DM Jones	lbw b Iqbal Qasim	3	c Ijaz Ahmed b Abdul Qadir	4
GM Wood	c Iqbal Qasim b Tauseef Ahmed	23	lbw b Iqbal Qasim	15
*AR Border	c Aamer Malik b Iqbal Qasim	4	b Iqbal Qasim	18
SR Waugh	lbw b Iqbal Qasim	0	st Saleem Yousuf b Iqbal Qasim	13
PL Taylor	not out	54	c Ijaz Ahmed b Aamer Malik	2
+IA Healy	c Ijaz Ahmed b Mudassar Nazar	26	c Shoaib Mohammad b Abdul Qadir	21
AIC Dodemaide	c Ijaz Ahmed b Saleem Malik	8	st Saleem Yousuf b Tauseef Ahmed	2
TBA May	c Saleem Yousuf b Abdul Qadir	6	lbw b Abdul Qadir	0
BA Reid	lbw b Iqbal Qasim	0	not out	8
	(b 12, lb 7)	19	(b 6, lb 6)	12
	(all out)	165	(all out)	116

Bowling: Mudassar Nazar 10-3-15-1 Aamer Malik 2-0-6-0 Iqbal Qasim 39-24-35-5 Abdul Qadir 37-16-54-2 Tauseef Ahmed 26-15-28-1 Shoaib Mohammad 2-1-1-0 Saleem Malik 6-4-7-1
Mudassar Nazar 3-0-5-0 Aamer Malik 2-2-0-1 Iqbal Qasim 25-14-49-4 Abdul Qadir 13-4-34-3 Tauseef Ahmed 21.4-13-16-2

Umpires: Khizer Hayat and Mahboob Shah

Pakistan v India
15,16,17,19,20 November 1989

Result: Match drawn

Pakistan Innings

Aamer Malik	c Azharuddin b Kapil Dev	0	c Manjrekar b Kapil Dev	15
Rameez Raja	c Shastri b Prabhakar	44	b Prabhakar	2
Shoaib Mohammad	c Azharuddin b Kapil Dev	67	lbw b Kapil Dev	95
Javed Miandad	c Azharuddin b Kapil Dev	78	b Kapil Dev	36
Saleem Malik	c Azharuddin b Ankola	36	not out	102
*Imran Khan	not out	109	not out	28
Shahid Saeed	c More b Kapil Dev	12		
+Saleem Yousuf	c More b Prabhakar	36	c More b Ankola	4
Wasim Akram	c Azharuddin b Prabhakar	0		
Abdul Qadir	c More b Prabhakar	4		
Waqar Younis	c More b Prabhakar	0		
	(b 4, lb 9, w 3, nb 7)	23	(b 3, lb 11, nb 9)	23
	(all out)	409	(5 wickets declared)	305

Bowling: Kapil Dev 24-5-69-4 Prabhakar 34.5-6-104-5 Ankola 19-1-93-1 Shastri 10-1-37-0 Arshad Ayub 27-3-81-0 Srikkanth 1-0-2-0 Tendulkar 1-0-10-0
Kapil Dev 36-15-82-3 Prabhakar 30-4-107-1 Ankola 11-6-35-1 Shastri 5-0-15-0 Arshad Ayub 10-1-37-0 Tendulkar 4-0-15-0

India Innings

*K Srikkanth	lbw b Wasim Akram	4	lbw b Wasim Akram	31
NS Sidhu	b Wasim Akram	0	c Rameez Raja b Imran Khan	85
SV Manjrekar	c Saleem Yousuf b Waqar Younis	3	not out	113
M Azharuddin	lbw b Imran Khan	35	c Aamer Malik b Abdul Qadir	35
M Prabhakar	b Waqar Younis	9		
SR Tendulkar	b Waqar Younis	15		
RJ Shastri	c Imran Khan b Abdul Qadir	45	not out	22
N Kapil Dev	c Javed Miandad b Waqar Younis	55		
+KS More	not out	58		
Arshad Ayub	lbw b Wasim Akram	1		
SA Ankola	b Wasim Akram	6		
	(b 5, lb 10, w 5, nb 11)	31	(b 9, lb 4, w 1, nb 3)	17
	(all out)	262	(3 wickets)	303

Bowling: Wasim Akram 26.2-4-83-4 Waqar Younis 19-1-80-4 Imran Khan 15-4-44-1 Shahid Saeed 2-0-7-0 Abdul Qadir 10-1-33-1
Wasim Akram 25-7-68-1 Waqar Younis 2-0-11-0 Imran Khan 28-10-56-1 Shahid Saeed 13-0-36-0 Abdul Qadir 28-3-119-1

Umpires: JH Hampshire (Eng) and JW Holder (Eng)

Pakistan v New Zealand
10,11,12,14,15 October 1990

Result: Pakistan won by an innings and 43 runs

New Zealand Innings

TJ Franklin	c Saleem Yousuf b Waqar Younis	16	b Wasim Akram	0
DJ White	c Saleem Yousuf b Wasim Akram	9	b Wasim Akram	18
MJ Greatbatch	c & b Ijaz Ahmed	43	lbw b Aaqib Javed	21
*MD Crowe	c Rameez Raja b Waqar Younis	7	not out	68
KR Rutherford	b Aaqib Javed	79	lbw b Aaqib Javed	0
DN Patel	lbw b Waqar Younis	2	lbw b Wasim Akram	19
DK Morrison	lbw b Wasim Akram	4	b Wasim Akram	0
GE Bradburn	not out	11	c Saleem Yousuf b Waqar Younis	2
+IDS Smith	lbw b Wasim Akram	4	b Waqar Younis	14
C Pringle	b Waqar Younis	0	lbw b Abdul Qadir	20
W Watson	lbw b Wasim Akram	0	lbw b Waqar Younis	11
	(b 5, lb 11, w 2, nb 3)	21	(b 7, lb 9, nb 5)	21
	(all out)	196	(all out)	194

Bowling: Wasim Akram 29.5-12-44-4 Waqar Younis 22-7-40-4 Aaqib Javed 16-4-37-1 Abdul Qadir 7-1-32-0 Tauseef Ahmed 5-0-18-0 Ijaz Ahmed 5-0-9-1
Wasim Akram 24-5-60-4 Aaqib Javed 12-1-45-2 Waqar Younis 15.4-4-39-3 Abdul Qadir 10-2-32-1 Tauseef Ahmed 1-0-2-0

Pakistan Innings

Rameez Raja	c Crowe b Bradburn	78
Shoaib Mohammad	not out	203
Saleem Malik	c Rutherford b Pringle	43
*Javed Miandad	lbw b Morrison	27
Wasim Akram	run out	28
Ijaz Ahmed	b Watson	9
+Saleem Yousuf	c Crowe b Morrison	13
Abdul Qadir	not out	6
Tauseef Ahmed		
Waqar Younis		
Aaqib Javed		
	(b 3, lb 11, w 1, nb 11)	26
	(6 wickets declared)	433

Bowling: Morrison 28.3-5-86-2 Pringle 25-3-68-1 Watson 40-8-125-1 Bradburn 17-3-56-1 Patel 24-6-62-0 Crowe 6-1-22-0

Umpires: Feroze Butt and Mahboob Shah

Pakistan v West Indies
15,16,17,19,20 November 1990

Result: Pakistan won by 8 wickets

West Indies Innings

CG Greenidge	lbw b Waqar Younis	3	st Saleem Yousuf b Abdul Qadir	11
*DL Haynes	lbw b Wasim Akram	117	c Saleem Yousuf b Waqar Younis	47
RB Richardson	st Saleem Yousuf b Mushtaq Ahmed	26	lbw b Waqar Younis	11
CA Best	c Rameez Raja b Mushtaq Ahmed	1	lbw b Mushtaq Ahmed	8
CL Hooper	lbw b Waqar Younis	8	lbw b Wasim Akram	0
AL Logie	c Saleem Yousuf b Wasim Akram	25	not out	58
+PJL Dujon	c Javed Miandad b Waqar Younis	17	b Shoaib Mohammad	1
MD Marshall	b Waqar Younis	13	b Wasim Akram	21
CEL Ambrose	lbw b Waqar Younis	2	lbw b Waqar Younis	0
IR Bishop	c Saleem Yousuf b Wasim Akram	22	b Waqar Younis	0
CA Walsh	not out	6	b Wasim Akram	0
	(b 6, lb 6, nb 9)	21	(b 10, lb 8, nb 6)	24
	(all out)	261	(all out)	181

Bowling: Wasim Akram 23.3-1-61-3 Waqar Younis 22-0-76-5 Abdul Qadir 20-2-56-0 Mushtaq Ahmed 18-3-56-2
Wasim Akram 20.3-6-39-3 Waqar Younis 17-3-44-4 Abdul Qadir 8-1-22-1 Mushtaq Ahmed 15-5-38-1 Shoaib Mohammad 6-1-15-1 Saleem Malik 1-0-5-0

Pakistan Innings

Shoaib Mohammad	c Richardson b Marshall	86	not out	32
Rameez Raja	b Bishop	0	lbw b Walsh	7
Zahid Fazal	c Logie b Ambrose	7	c Richardson b Walsh	12
Javed Miandad	c Dujon b Bishop	7		
Saleem Malik	c Dujon b Marshall	102	not out	30
*Imran Khan	not out	73		
+Saleem Yousuf	b Ambrose	5		
Wasim Akram	c Richardson b Walsh	9		
Mushtaq Ahmed	c Richardson b Ambrose	3		
Abdul Qadir	c Dujon b Ambrose	0		
Waqar Younis	c Hooper b Bishop	5		
	(b 7, lb 14, w 1, nb 26)	48	(lb 8, nb 9)	17
	(all out)	345	(2 wickets)	98

Bowling: Ambrose 34-7-78-4 Bishop 27.2-3-81-3 Marshall 24-5-48-2 Walsh 19-0-50-1 Hooper 28-6-65-0 Best 1-0-2-0
Ambrose 2-0-4-0 Bishop 7-0-21-0 Marshall 5-1-8-0 Walsh 12-2-27-2 Hooper 11-2-30-0

Umpires: Khizer Hayat and Riazuddin

Pakistan v Australia
28,29,30 September, 1,2 October 1994

Result: Pakistan won by 1 wicket

Australia Innings

MJ Slater	lbw b Wasim Akram	36	lbw b Mushtaq Ahmed	23
*MA Taylor	c & b Wasim Akram	0	c Rashid Latif b Waqar Younis	0
DC Boon	b Mushtaq Ahmed	19	not out	114
ME Waugh	c Zahid Fazal b Mushtaq Ahmed	20	b Waqar Younis	61
MG Bevan	c Aamer Sohail b Mushtaq Ahmed	82	b Wasim Akram	0
SR Waugh	b Waqar Younis	73	lbw b Wasim Akram	0
+IA Healy	c Rashid Latif b Waqar Younis	57	c Rashid Latif b Wasim Akram	8
SK Warne	c Rashid Latif b Aamer Sohail	22	lbw b Waqar Younis	0
J Angel	b Wasim Akram	5	c Rashid Latif b Wasim Akram	8
TBA May	not out	1	b Wasim Akram	1
GD McGrath	b Waqar Younis	0	b Waqar Younis	1
	(b 2, lb 12, nb 8)	22	(b 7, lb 4, nb 5)	16
	(all out)	337	(all out)	232

Bowling: Wasim Akram 25-4-75-3 Waqar Younis 19.2-2-75-3 Mushtaq Ahmed 24-2-97-3 Akram Raza 14-1-50-0 Aamer Sohail 5-0-19-1 Saleem Malik 1-0-7-0
Wasim Akram 22-3-63-5 Waqar Younis 18-2-69-4 Mushtaq Ahmed 21-3-51-1 Akram Raza 10-1-19-0 Aamer Sohail 7-0-19-0

Pakistan Innings

Saeed Anwar	c ME Waugh b May	85	c & b Angel	77
Aamer Sohail	c Bevan b Warne	36	run out	34
Zahid Fazal	c Boon b May	27	c Boon b Warne	3
*Saleem Malik	lbw b Angel	26	c Taylor b Angel	43
Basit Ali	c Bevan b McGrath	0	lbw b Warne	12
Inzamam-ul-Haq	c Taylor b Warne	9	not out	58
+Rashid Latif	c Taylor b Warne	2	lbw b SR Waugh	35
Wasim Akram	c Healy b Angel	39	c & b Warne	4
Akram Raza	b McGrath	13	lbw b Warne	2
Waqar Younis	c Healy b Angel	6	c Healy b Warne	7
Mushtaq Ahmed	not out	2	not out	20
	(lb 7, nb 4)	11	(b 4, lb 13, nb 3)	20
	(all out)	256	(9 wickets)	315

Bowling: McGrath 25-6-70-2 Angel 13.1-0-54-3 May 20-5-55-2 Warne 27-10-61-3 SR Waugh 2-0-9-0
McGrath 6-2-18-0 Angel 28-10-92-2 SR Waugh 15-3-28-1 Warne 36.1-12-89-5 May 18-4-67-0 ME Waugh 3-1-4-0

Umpires: HD Bird (Eng) and Khizer Hayat
TV Umpire: Riazuddin; Referee: JR Reid (NZ)

Pakistan v West Indies
6,7,8,9 December 1997

Result: Pakistan won by 10 wickets

West Indies Innings

SL Campbell	c Aamer Sohail b Saqlain Mushtaq	50	c Inzamam-ul-Haq b Waqar Younis	5
SC Williams	run out (Mushtaq Ahmed)	33	lbw b Waqar Younis	12
BC Lara	b Saqlain Mushtaq	36	c Mohammad Wasim b Saqlain Mushtaq	37
CL Hooper	lbw b Mushtaq Ahmed	0	b Wasim Akram	106
S Chanderpaul	lbw b Wasim Akram	21	c Moin Khan b Saqlain Mushtaq	16
RIC Holder	b Saqlain Mushtaq	26	c Aamer Sohail b Saqlain Mushtaq	5
+D Williams	not out	22	b Saqlain Mushtaq	2
IR Bishop	st Moin Khan b Saqlain Mushtaq	2	not out	6
FA Rose	lbw b Wasim Akram	13	c Moin Khan b Wasim Akram	5
*CA Walsh	c Inzamam-ul-Haq b Saqlain Mushtaq	1	b Wasim Akram	0
M Dillon	b Wasim Akram	0	lbw b Wasim Akram	4
	(b 4, lb 7, nb 1)	12	(b 7, lb 2, nb 5)	14
	(all out)	216	(all out)	212

Bowling: Wasim Akram 17.1-2-76-3 Waqar Younis 9-3-21-0 Azhar Mahmood 10-3-14-0 Mushtaq Ahmed 13-2-40-1 Saqlain Mushtaq 24-6-54-5
Wasim Akram 16.4-7-42-4 Waqar Younis 6-0-31-2 Azhar Mahmood 3-0-32-0 Mushtaq Ahmed 8-0-72-0 Saqlain Mushtaq 19-9-26-4

Pakistan Innings

Aamer Sohail	lbw b Chanderpaul	160		
Ijaz Ahmed	c D Williams b Dillon	151		
Saeed Anwar	c D Williams b Dillon	15		
Inzamam-ul-Haq	lbw b Dillon	4		
Mohammad Wasim	lbw b Dillon	12	not out	0
+Moin Khan	lbw b Walsh	5		
Azhar Mahmood	not out	26	not out	13
*Wasim Akram	lbw b Walsh	0		
Saqlain Mushtaq	c Lara b Walsh	0		
Mushtaq Ahmed	b Walsh	1		
Waqar Younis	c SC Williams b Dillon	12		
	(b 3, lb 9, w 2, nb 17)	31	(nb 2)	2
	(all out)	417	(0 wickets)	15

Bowling: Walsh 23-2-74-4 Rose 12-1-44-0 Dillon 29.4-4-111-5 Bishop 15-0-68-0 Hooper 32-10-74-0 Chanderpaul 7-0-34-1
Walsh 3-0-11-0 Rose 2-0-4-0

Umpires: CJ Mitchley (SA) and Saleem Badar
TV Umpire: Riazuddin; Referee: R Subba Row (Eng)

Pakistan v Australia
22,23,24,25,26 October 1998

Result: Match drawn

Australia Innings

*MA Taylor	c Inzamam-ul-Haq b Arshad Khan	16	b Arshad Khan	68
MJ Slater	st Moin Khan b Arshad Khan	96	c Yousuf Youhana b Arshad Khan	11
JL Langer	lbw b Shoaib Akhtar	30	run out (Ijaz Ahmed)	51
ME Waugh	c Inzamam-ul-Haq b Shahid Afridi	26	st Moin Khan b Shakeel Ahmed	117
SR Waugh	lbw b Shahid Afridi	0	c Moin Khan b Shakeel Ahmed	28
DS Lehmann	b Shahid Afridi	3	c Ijaz Ahmed b Wasim Akram	26
+IA Healy	c Moin Khan b Arshad Khan	47	c Shahid Afridi b Shoaib Akhtar	3
GR Robertson	c Yousuf Youhana b Shahid Afridi	5	c Wasim Akram b Shakeel Ahmed	45
CR Miller	b Wasim Akram	0	c Shahid Afridi b Shakeel Ahmed	0
SCG MacGill	not out	23	run out (Saleem Malik)	10
GD McGrath	c Shakeel Ahmed b Shahid Afridi	6	not out	4
	(b 1, lb 17, nb 10)	28	(b 4, lb 8, nb 15)	27
	(all out)	280	(all out)	390

Bowling: Wasim Akram 22-4-51-1 Shoaib Akhtar 14.2-3-39-1 Shakeel Ahmed 24.4-9-48-0 Arshad Khan 41-14-72-3 Shahid Afridi 23.3-6-52-5
Wasim Akram 22-2-60-1 Shoaib Akhtar 17-3-37-1 Arshad Khan 56-14-141-2 Shahid Afridi 18-3-49-0 Shakeel Ahmed 29.3-3-91-4

Pakistan Innings

*Aamer Sohail	c Langer b Miller	133	lbw b Miller	25
Shahid Afridi	c Taylor b McGrath	10	c Healy b Miller	6
Ijaz Ahmed	c Healy b McGrath	5	not out	120
Inzamam-ul-Haq	c Lehmann b McGrath	9	not out	21
Saleem Malik	c McGrath b MacGill	0	lbw b Miller	0
Yousuf Youhana	b Robertson	9	c ME Waugh b MacGill	11
+Moin Khan	c Slater b McGrath	20	c MacGill b Lehmann	75
Wasim Akram	lbw b MacGill	35		
Shakeel Ahmed snr	c Langer b McGrath	1		
Arshad Khan	lbw b MacGill	7		
Shoaib Akhtar	not out	6		
	(b 6, lb 5, w 1, nb 5)	17	(b 2, nb 2)	4
	(all out)	252	(5 wickets)	262

Bowling: McGrath 25-6-66-5 Miller 14-2-53-1 MacGill 25.4-5-64-3 Robertson 22-4-46-1 Lehmann 1-0-6-0 SR Waugh 2-0-6-0
McGrath 18-11-40-0 Miller 25-5-82-3 MacGill 17-2-66-1 SR Waugh 8-5-10-0 Robertson 16-2-56-0 Lehmann 2-0-6-1

Umpires: DL Orchard (SA) and Riazuddin
TV Umpire: Feroze Butt; Referee: PL van der Merwe (SA)

Pakistan v Sri Lanka
12,13,14,15 March 2000

Result: Pakistan won by 222 runs

Pakistan Innings

Naved Ashraf	b Pushpakumara	5	lbw b Muralitharan	27
Shahid Afridi	c Wickramasinghe b Muralitharan	74	b Pushpakumara	34
Ijaz Ahmed	lbw b Vaas	7	c Dilshan b Muralitharan	3
Inzamam-ul-Haq	run out (Pushpakumara/Muralitharan)	86	c Wickramasinghe b Muralitharan	138
Yousuf Youhana	c Wickramasinghe b Muralitharan	7	c Kaluwitharana b Pushpakumara	11
Younis Khan	lbw b Vaas	7	c Kaluwitharana b Wickramasinghe	61
*+Moin Khan	c de Saram b Wickramasinghe	6	c Arnold b Pushpakumara	70
Waqar Younis	c Dilshan b Muralitharan	16	c Dilshan b Muralitharan	39
Shoaib Akhtar	c Pushpakumara b Muralitharan	26	lbw b Vaas	0
Irfan Fazil	not out	1	c Jayasuriya b Pushpakumara	3
Mohammad Akram	c Atapattu b Jayasuriya	0	not out	1
	(lb 2, nb 19)	21	(lb 16, nb 18)	34
	(all out)	256	(all out)	421

Bowling: Vaas 18-4-49-2 Pushpakumara 16-4-37-1 Wickramasinghe 13-2-64-1 Muralitharan 32-10-89-4 Jayasuriya 6.5-2-15-1
Vaas 34-8-107-1 Pushpakumara 20.5-3-66-4 Wickramasinghe 26-7-82-1 Muralitharan 40-5-107-4 Jayasuriya 9-1-28-0 Arnold 4-0-15-0

Sri Lanka Innings

MS Atapattu	lbw b Waqar Younis	3	c Moin Khan b Mohammad Akram	23
*ST Jayasuriya	c Ijaz Ahmed b Shoaib Akhtar	24	lbw b Waqar Younis	10
RP Arnold	c Younis Khan b Irfan Fazil	48	c Moin Khan b Waqar Younis	8
DPMD Jayawardene	c Moin Khan b Waqar Younis	1	b Irfan Fazil	29
TM Dilshan	c Moin Khan b Shahid Afridi	31	run out (Yousuf Youhana)	5
+RS Kaluwitharana	run out (Naved Ashraf)	42	b Shoaib Akhtar	33
SI de Saram	c Waqar Younis b Shahid Afridi	5	lbw b Shahid Afridi	18
WPUJC Vaas	not out	25	c Shoaib Akhtar b Shahid Afridi	28
KR Pushpakumara	c Moin Khan b Shoaib Akhtar	1	c Irfan Fazil b Shahid Afridi	44
GP Wickramasinghe	b Shoaib Akhtar	0	run out (sub [Imran Nazir])	0
M Muralitharan	c Irfan Fazil b Mohammad Akram	14	not out	5
	(b 10, lb 2, nb 21)	33	(b 1, lb 7, nb 17)	25
	(all out)	227	(all out)	228

Bowling: Waqar Younis 10-2-39-2 Shoaib Akhtar 18-4-52-3 Mohammad Akram 14.1-2-49-1 Irfan Fazil 4-0-35-1 Shahid Afridi 12-3-40-2
Waqar Younis 11-4-32-2 Shoaib Akhtar 13-1-64-1 Mohammad Akram 10-1-44-1 Irfan Fazil 4-0-30-1 Shahid Afridi 8-1-50-3

Umpires: Riazuddin and RB Tiffin (ZIM)
TV Umpire: Afzaal Ahmed; Referee: BF Hastings (NZ)

Pakistan v England
7,8,9,10,11 December 2000

Result: England won by 6 wickets

Pakistan Innings

Saeed Anwar	lbw b Gough	8	c Thorpe b Caddick	21
Imran Nazir	c Giles b Trescothick	20	c Stewart b Gough	4
Saleem Elahi	b Caddick	28	c Thorpe b Giles	37
Inzamam-ul-Haq	c Trescothick b White	142	b Giles	27
Yousuf Youhana	c & b Giles	117	c Stewart b White	24
Abdul Razzaq	c Hussain b Giles	21	c Atherton b Giles	1
*+Moin Khan	c Hick b Giles	13	c Hussain b White	14
Shahid Afridi	b Giles	10	not out	15
Saqlain Mushtaq	b Gough	16	lbw b Gough	4
Waqar Younis	b Gough	17	run out (Stewart)	0
Danish Kaneria	not out	0	lbw b Gough	0
	(b 3, lb 3, nb 7)	13	(b 3, lb 5, nb 3)	11
	(all out)	405	(all out)	158

Bowling: Gough 27.4-5-82-3 Caddick 23-1-76-1 Trescothick 14-1-34-1 White 22-3-64-1 Salisbury 18-3-49-0 Giles 35-7-94-4
Gough 13-4-30-3 Caddick 15-2-40-1 Giles 27-12-38-3 Salisbury 3-0-12-0 White 12-4-30-2

England Innings

MA Atherton	c Moin Khan b Abdul Razzaq	125	c Saeed Anwar b Saqlain Mushtaq	26
ME Trescothick	c Imran Nazir b Waqar Younis	13	c Inzamam-ul-Haq b Saqlain Mushtaq	24
*N Hussain	c Inzamam-ul-Haq b Shahid Afridi	51	not out	6
GP Thorpe	lbw b Waqar Younis	18	not out	64
+AJ Stewart	c Yousuf Youhana b Saqlain Mushtaq	29	c Moin Khan b Saqlain Mushtaq	5
GA Hick	c Shahid Afridi b Waqar Younis	12	b Waqar Younis	40
C White	st Moin Khan b Danish Kaneria	35		
AF Giles	b Waqar Younis	19		
IDK Salisbury	not out	20		
AR Caddick	c Moin Khan b Danish Kaneria	3		
D Gough	c Yousuf Youhana b Saqlain Mushtaq	18		
	(b 12, lb 9, nb 24)	45	(b 8, lb 2, w 1)	11
	(all out)	388	(4 wickets)	176

Bowling: Waqar Younis 36-5-88-4 Abdul Razzaq 28-7-64-1 Shahid Afridi 16-3-34-1 Saqlain Mushtaq 52.1-17-101-2 Danish Kaneria 47-17-80-2
Waqar Younis 6-0-27-1 Abdul Razzaq 4-0-17-0 Saqlain Mushtaq 17.3-1-64-3 Danish Kaneria 3-0-18-0 Shahid Afridi 11-1-40-0

Umpires: SA Bucknor (WI) and Mohammad Nazir
TV Umpire: Feroze Butt; Referee: RS Madugalle (SL)

Sinhalese Sports Club Ground, Colombo

Sri Lanka v New Zealand
16,17,18,20,21 March 1984

Result: Match drawn

Sri Lanka Innings

S Wettimuny	c Coney b Chatfield	26	c Hadlee b Chatfield	65
ERNS Fernando	b MD Crowe	8	c JJ Crowe b Hadlee	0
SMS Kaluperuma	b Boock	23	c Cairns b Hadlee	2
RL Dias	run out	16	b Cairns	108
*LRD Mendis	b Hadlee	1	b Chatfield	36
RS Madugalle	not out	44	c JJ Crowe b Chatfield	36
A Ranatunga	c Smith b Cairns	6	run out	7
JR Ratnayeke	lbw b Hadlee	22	c & b Hadlee	12
DS de Silva	c Coney b Cairns	0	not out	13
+RG de Alwis	c Smith b Cairns	2	b Chatfield	2
VB John	c Smith b Cairns	0	not out	3
	(b 5, lb 7, w 8, nb 6)	26	(lb 4, nb 1)	5
	(all out)	174	(9 wickets declared)	289

Bowling: Hadlee 22-12-27-2 Cairns 24.5-6-47-4 Chatfield 20-7-35-1 MD Crowe 13-5-21-1 Boock 11-2-18-1
Hadlee 30-14-58-3 Cairns 22-3-79-1 Chatfield 29-9-78-4 Boock 42-16-65-0 Coney 4-3-4-0

New Zealand Innings

*GP Howarth	b John	24	c Kaluperuma b John	10
JG Wright	c Dias b John	20	c de Silva b Ranatunga	48
JF Reid	c de Alwis b John	7	lbw b John	0
JJ Crowe	b Ratnayeke	50	c de Alwis b Ranatunga	16
JV Coney	c John b de Silva	30	not out	20
RJ Hadlee	b Ratnayeke	19		
SL Boock	c Madugalle b Ratnayeke	4		
MD Crowe	c Kaluperuma b Ratnayeke	0	not out	19
+IDS Smith	c Kaluperuma b Ratnayeke	7		
BL Cairns	lbw b de Silva	14		
EJ Chatfield	not out	9		
	(b 4, lb 6, w 1, nb 3)	14	(b 4, lb 4, nb 2)	10
	(all out)	198	(4 wickets)	123

Bowling: John 24-1-89-3 Ratnayeke 21-8-42-5 Kaluperuma 1-0-3-0 Ranatunga 4-1-11-0 de Silva 14.3-6-39-2
John 21-11-26-2 Ratnayeke 21-11-17-0 Kaluperuma 6-3-10-0 Ranatunga 18-7-29-2 de Silva 19-10-31-0 Madugalle 1-1-0-0

Umpires: DP Buultjens and HC Felsinger

Sri Lanka v India
30,31 August, 1,3,4 September 1985

Result: Match drawn

India Innings

LS Rajput	c Silva b Ahangama	32	c Silva b Ratnayake	61
K Srikkanth	b Ratnayake	2	c Silva b Ratnayake	9
M Azharuddin	c Silva b Ahangama	3	lbw b Ahangama	16
DB Vengsarkar	c Silva b de Mel	6	not out	98
SM Gavaskar	run out	51	c de Mel b Ratnayake	0
RJ Shastri	c Silva b de Mel	9	lbw b Ratnayake	40
*N Kapil Dev	c Silva b de Mel	36	c sub (SD Anurasiri) b Ratnayake	6
+S Viswanath	c EAR de Silva b de Mel	20	c Silva b Ratnayake	0
C Sharma	c Silva b de Mel	38	run out	4
G Sharma	not out	10	lbw b Ahangama	1
Maninder Singh	lbw b Ratnayake	0	b Ahangama	3
	(lb 5, w 1, nb 5)	11	(b 4, lb 3, nb 6)	13
	(all out)	218	(all out)	251

Bowling: de Mel 28-8-64-5 Ratnayake 24.2-7-64-2 Ahangama 23-3-60-2 EAR de Silva 12-5-18-0 Ranatunga 10-8-7-0
de Mel 30-3-84-0 Ratnayake 41-10-85-6 Ahangama 27.3-10-49-3 EAR de Silva 15-6-20-0 Ranatunga 6-2-6-0

Sri Lanka Innings

S Wettimuny	c Viswanath b C Sharma	13		
+SAR Silva	c Azharuddin b C Sharma	7	not out	1
RS Madugalle	c & b Maninder Singh	103	not out	5
RL Dias	c Azharuddin b C Sharma	4	c Srikkanth b Kapil Dev	0
*LRD Mendis	c Gavaskar b Maninder Singh	51	c Kapil Dev b C Sharma	18
A Ranatunga	b Shastri	111	run out	15
PA de Silva	c Azharuddin b Shastri	33	c Maninder Singh b Kapil Dev	21
ALF de Mel	c Viswanath b Kapil Dev	16		
RJ Ratnayake	lbw b Kapil Dev	2		
EAR de Silva	not out	1		
FS Ahangama	c Viswanath b Kapil Dev	0		
	(lb 5, nb 1)	6	(lb 1)	1
	(all out)	347	(4 wickets)	61

Bowling: Kapil Dev 30.4-8-74-3 C Sharma 25-3-81-3 Shastri 34-9-70-2 Maninder Singh 40-12-82-2 G Sharma 15-6-35-0
Kapil Dev 4-0-36-2 C Sharma 4-0-24-1

Umpires: HC Felsinger and KT Francis

Sri Lanka v Australia
17,18,19,21,22 August 1992

Result: Australia won by 16 runs

Australia Innings

MA Taylor	lbw b Wickramasinghe	42	c Gurusinha b Anurasiri	43
TM Moody	lbw b Ramanayake	1	b Ramanayake	13
DC Boon	c Ramanayake b Hathurusingha	32	c Ranatunga b Anurasiri	68
DM Jones	lbw b Hathurusingha	10	run out	57
ME Waugh	c Kaluwitharana b Hathurusingha	5	c Kaluwitharana b Wickramasinghe	56
*AR Border	b Hathurusingha	3	c Gurusinha b Anurasiri	15
GRJ Matthews	lbw b Ramanayake	6	c Kaluwitharana b Ramanayake	64
+IA Healy	not out	66	lbw b Hathurusingha	12
CJ McDermott	c Ranatunga b Ramanayake	22	lbw b Ramanayake	40
SK Warne	c & b Anurasiri	24	b Anurasiri	35
MR Whitney	c & b Wickramasinghe	13	not out	10
	(lb 10, w 3, nb 19)	32	(lb 23, w 1, nb 34)	58
	(all out)	256	(all out)	471

Bowling: Ramanayake 20-4-51-3 Wickramasinghe 18-4-69-2 Hathurusingha 22-5-66-4 Madurasinghe 10-1-21-0 Gurusinha 2-0-17-0 Anurasiri 12-2-22-1
Ramanayake 37-10-113-3 Wickramasinghe 19-0-79-1 Hathurusingha 27-7-79-1 Madurasinghe 14-1-50-0 Anurasiri 35-3-127-4

Sri Lanka Innings

RS Mahanama	c Healy b Waugh	78	c Boon b Matthews	39
UC Hathurusingha	c Taylor b Waugh	18	run out	36
AP Gurusinha	c Jones b Whitney	137	not out	31
PA de Silva	lbw b Matthews	6	c Border b McDermott	37
*A Ranatunga	c Warne b Matthews	127	c Border b McDermott	0
MS Atapattu	b Matthews	0	b Matthews	1
+RS Kaluwitharana	not out	132	b Matthews	4
CPH Ramanayake	c Healy b McDermott	0	lbw b Matthews	6
GP Wickramasinghe	c Matthews b McDermott	21	c Waugh b Warne	2
MAWR Madurasinghe	not out	5	c Matthews b Warne	0
SD Anurasiri			c Waugh b Warne	1
	(b 2, lb 7, w 1, nb 13)	23	(b 2, lb 3, nb 2)	7
	(8 wickets declared)	547	(all out)	164

Bowling: McDermott 40-9-125-2 Whitney 32-10-84-1 Moody 17-3-44-0 Waugh 17-3-77-2 Warne 22-2-107-0 Matthews 38-11-93-3 Border 4-1-8-0
McDermott 14-4-43-2 Whitney 5-2-13-0 Moody 5-0-10-0 Waugh 2-0-6-0 Matthews 20-2-76-4 Warne 5.1-3-11-3

Umpires: KT Francis and TM Samarasinghe; Referee: FJ Cameron (NZ)

Sri Lanka v New Zealand
6,7,8,9 December 1992

Result: Sri Lanka won by 9 wickets

Sri Lanka Innings

RS Mahanama	c Bradburn b Owens	109	c Parore b Owens	29
UC Hathurusingha	c Harris b Owens	27	not out	26
AP Gurusinha	st Parore b Bradburn	22	not out	14
PA de Silva	c Parore b Pringle	3		
*A Ranatunga	c Parore b Su'a	76		
HP Tillakaratne	c Parore b Bradburn	93		
+AGD Wickremasinghe	c Rutherford b Owens	2		
DK Liyanage	c Parore b Su'a	16		
SD Anurasiri	c Su'a b Owens	24		
M Muralitharan	not out	4		
KPJ Warnaweera	c Crowe b Bradburn	5		
	(b 3, lb 4, w 3, nb 3)	13	(lb 2, nb 2)	4
	(all out)	394	(1 wicket)	73

Bowling: Su'a 26-7-50-2 Owens 30-7-101-4 Pringle 32-7-85-1 Bradburn 37.3-4-134-3 Harris 3-0-17-0
Owens 6-1-36-1 Pringle 2-1-5-0 Su'a 2-0-14-0 Bradburn 3-1-8-0 Jones 1.4-1-8-0

New Zealand Innings

BR Hartland	c Gurusinha b Warnaweera	21	c Muralitharan b Gurusinha	21
JG Wright	c Wickremasinghe b Warnaweera	30	c Mahanama b Muralitharan	50
AH Jones	c Tillakaratne b Warnaweera	20	c Tillakaratne b Warnaweera	5
*MD Crowe	b Muralitharan	0	c Tillakaratne b Muralitharan	107
KR Rutherford	c Tillakaratne b Warnaweera	0	c sub (ST Jayasuriya) b Warnaweera	38
CZ Harris	run out	9	lbw b Anurasiri	19
+AC Parore	lbw b Muralitharan	5	c Tillakaratne b Muralitharan	60
GE Bradburn	c Tillakaratne b Liyanage	1	c Wickremasinghe b Anurasiri	7
ML Su'a	not out	2	b Muralitharan	0
C Pringle	b Liyanage	0	c Tillakaratne b Liyanage	23
MB Owens	c Anurasiri b Muralitharan	0	not out	8
	(lb 4, w 1, nb 9)	14	(b 2, lb 8, nb 13)	23
	(all out)	102	(all out)	361

Bowling: Liyanage 9-3-9-2 Gurusinha 4-1-15-0 Anurasiri 6-1-13-0 Hathurusingha 7-3-14-0 Warnaweera 14-3-25-4 Muralitharan 12.1-3-22-3
Liyanage 12-2-35-1 Gurusinha 8-1-19-1 Warnaweera 34-4-107-2 Muralitharan 40-6-134-4 Anurasiri 22-4-54-2 Hathurusingha 3-2-2-0

Umpires: I Anandappa and TM Samarasinghe; Referee: S Venkataraghavan (Ind)

Sri Lanka v England
13,14,15,17,18 March 1993

Result: Sri Lanka won by 5 wickets

England Innings

RA Smith	b Muralitharan	128	b Jayasuriya	35
MA Atherton	lbw b Ramanayake	13	c Tillakaratne b Gurusinha	2
MW Gatting	c Jayasuriya b Muralitharan	29	c Tillakaratne b Warnaweera	18
GA Hick	c Tillakaratne b Muralitharan	68	c Ramanayake b Warnaweera	26
*+AJ Stewart	c Tillakaratne b Warnaweera	63	c Mahanama b Warnaweera	3
NH Fairbrother	b Warnaweera	18	run out	3
CC Lewis	run out	22	c Jayasuriya b Muralitharan	45
JE Emburey	not out	1	b Gurusinha	59
PW Jarvis	lbw b Warnaweera	0	st AM de Silva b Jayasuriya	3
PCR Tufnell	lbw b Muralitharan	1	c AM de Silva b Warnaweera	1
DE Malcolm	c Gurusinha b Warnaweera	13	not out	8
	(b 5, lb 3, w 1, nb 15)	24	(b 4, lb 2, w 1, nb 18)	25
	(all out)	380	(all out)	228

Bowling: Ramanayake 17-2-66-1 Gurusinha 5-1-12-0 Warnaweera 40.1-11-90-4 Hathurusingha 8-2-22-0 Muralitharan 45-12-118-4 Jayasuriya 12-1-53-0 Ranatunga 3-0-11-0
Ramanayake 3-0-16-0 Gurusinha 6-3-7-2 Warnaweera 25-4-98-4 Muralitharan 16-3-55-1 Jayasuriya 16-3-46-2

Sri Lanka Innings

RS Mahanama	c Smith b Emburey	64	c Stewart b Lewis	6
UC Hathurusingha	c Stewart b Lewis	59	c Stewart b Tufnell	14
AP Gurusinha	st Stewart b Tufnell	43	b Emburey	29
PA de Silva	c Stewart b Jarvis	80	c Jarvis b Emburey	7
*A Ranatunga	c Stewart b Lewis	64	c Gatting b Tufnell	35
HP Tillakaratne	not out	93	not out	36
ST Jayasuriya	c Atherton b Lewis	4	not out	6
+AM de Silva	c Gatting b Emburey	9		
CPH Ramanayake	c Lewis b Jarvis	1		
M Muralitharan	b Lewis	19		
KPJ Warnaweera	b Jarvis	1		
	(b 2, lb 13, w 2, nb 15)	32	(b 1, lb 2, nb 6)	9
	(all out)	469	(5 wickets)	142

Bowling: Malcolm 25-7-60-0 Jarvis 25.5-1-76-3 Lewis 31-5-66-4 Tufnell 33-5-108-1 Emburey 34-6-117-2 Hick 8-0-27-0
Malcolm 3-1-11-0 Jarvis 8-2-14-0 Lewis 8-1-21-1 Tufnell 7.4-1-34-2 Emburey 14-2-48-2 Hick 2-0-11-0

Umpires: KT Francis and TM Samarasinghe; Referee: CW Smith (WI)

Sri Lanka v India
27,28,29,31 July, 1 August 1993

Result: India won by 235 runs

India Innings

M Prabhakar	lbw b Gurusinha	4	c Tillakaratne b Kalpage	95
NS Sidhu	c Tillakaratne b Warnaweera	82	c AM de Silva b Hathurusingha	104
VG Kambli	c Mahanama b Hathurusingha	125	c AM de Silva b Warnaweera	4
SR Tendulkar	c Tillakaratne b Kalpage	28	not out	104
*M Azharuddin	lbw b Wickramasinghe	26	c Tillakaratne b Kalpage	21
PK Amre	c Kalpage b Warnaweera	21	not out	15
N Kapil Dev	lbw b Gurusinha	35		
+KS More	c Mahanama b Warnaweera	4		
A Kumble	lbw b Wickramasinghe	1		
RK Chauhan	c AM de Silva b Wickramasinghe	2		
J Srinath	not out	0		
	(b 9, lb 3, w 10, nb 16)	38	(b 5, lb 1, w 2, nb 8)	16
	(all out)	366	(4 wickets declared)	359

Bowling: Liyanage 19-3-64-0 Wickramasinghe 27-6-83-3 Hathurusingha 17-2-48-1 Gurusinha 16-2-49-2 Warnaweera 20.1-1-76-3 Kalpage 8-1-34-1
Wickramasinghe 22-4-58-0 Liyanage 10-2-31-0 Warnaweera 20-1-86-1 Gurusinha 7-0-24-0 Hathurusingha 12-1-35-1 Kalpage 38-3-97-2 Ranatunga 2-1-5-0 PA de Silva 7-0-17-0

Sri Lanka Innings

RS Mahanama	c More b Prabhakar	22	lbw b Kapil Dev	9
UC Hathurusingha	b Kumble	37	c Azharuddin b Prabhakar	43
AP Gurusinha	lbw b Prabhakar	4	c Chauhan b Kumble	39
PA de Silva	c Azharuddin b Kumble	22	c Azharuddin b Kumble	93
*A Ranatunga	c Srinath b Kumble	88	c More b Prabhakar	14
HP Tillakaratne	c More b Srinath	28	c sub (WV Raman) b Prabhakar	2
+AM de Silva	c Amre b Kumble	0	b Kapil Dev	1
RS Kalpage	c More b Srinath	1	c Amre b Srinath	5
DK Liyanage	lbw b Kumble	2	c Azharuddin b Chauhan	8
GP Wickramasinghe	not out	11	lbw b Kumble	4
KPJ Warnaweera	b Prabhakar	20	not out	2
	(b 9, lb 5, w 4, nb 1)	19	(b 6, lb 6, w 3, nb 1)	16
	(all out)	254	(all out)	236

Bowling: Kapil Dev 11-4-26-0 Prabhakar 15.5-5-43-3 Srinath 17-5-42-2 Kumble 24-3-87-5 Chauhan 10-1-42-0
Kapil Dev 26-13-34-2 Prabhakar 18-4-49-3 Srinath 15-2-36-1 Chauhan 24-18-20-1 Kumble 38.1-14-85-3

Umpires: I Anandappa and S Ponnadurai; Referee: PJP Burge (Aus)

Sri Lanka v South Africa
6,7,8,10 September 1993

Result: South Africa won by an innings and 208 runs

Sri Lanka Innings

RS Mahanama	c Richardson b Schultz	7	b Schultz	0
UC Hathurusingha	c McMillan b Donald	34	c Cronje b Donald	0
HP Tillakaratne	c Cronje b McMillan	9	c Richardson b Snell	9
PA de Silva	c Richardson b Schultz	34	c & b Donald	24
*A Ranatunga	c Cullinan b Snell	11	c Richardson b Schultz	14
ST Jayasuriya	b Schultz	44	b Schultz	16
+PB Dassanayake	c Richardson b Donald	0	c Richardson b Snell	10
HDPK Dharmasena	c Richardson b Schultz	5	c Richardson b Schultz	2
CPH Ramanayake	not out	3	lbw b McMillan	0
GP Wickramasinghe	b Schultz	17	c Donald b Snell	21
M Muralitharan	c Rhodes b Snell	0	not out	14
	(lb 3, nb 1)	4	(lb 4, nb 5)	9
	(all out)	168	(all out)	119

Bowling: Donald 12-4-22-2 Schultz 20-8-48-5 Snell 19-3-57-2 McMillan 9-1-38-1 Symcox 2-2-0-0
Donald 10-7-6-2 Schultz 16-4-58-4 Snell 12-4-32-3 McMillan 4-0-11-1 Symcox 1-0-8-0

South Africa Innings

*KC Wessels	c Dassanayake b Muralitharan	92
AC Hudson	lbw b Wickramasinghe	58
WJ Cronje	b de Silva	122
DJ Cullinan	c & b Muralitharan	52
JN Rhodes	run out (Mahanama)	10
BM McMillan	b Muralitharan	0
+DJ Richardson	c Jayasuriya b Muralitharan	11
PL Symcox	st Dassanayake b de Silva	50
RP Snell	st Dassanayake b de Silva	48
AA Donald	not out	4
BN Schultz	st Dassanayake b Muralitharan	6
	(b 5, lb 20, w 1, nb 16)	42
	(all out)	495

Bowling: Ramanayake 20-5-63-0 Wickramasinghe 31-6-111-1 Hathurusingha 7-4-12-0 Dharmasena 45-12-91-0 Muralitharan 54-17-101-5 Jayasuriya 9-1-47-0 de Silva 13-1-39-3 Ranatunga 2-0-6-0

Umpires: BL Aldridge (NZ) and TM Samarasinghe; Referee: JR Reid (NZ)

Sri Lanka v Zimbabwe
18,19,20,21 September 1996

Result: Sri Lanka won by 10 wickets

Zimbabwe Innings

GW Flower	c Mahanama b Muralitharan	52	lbw b Silva	13
MH Dekker	c Mahanama b Muralitharan	18	lbw b Vaas	4
AH Omarshah	c Kaluwitharana b Pushpakumara	1	c Vaas b Pushpakumara	62
*ADR Campbell	st Kaluwitharana b Silva	36	c sub (MS Atapattu) b Silva	4
+A Flower	run out	3	c Gurusinha b Muralitharan	31
CB Wishart	c Kaluwitharana b Silva	2	c Kaluwitharana b Jayasuriya	25
GJ Whittall	c Silva b Muralitharan	0	c Gurusinha b Jayasuriya	3
PA Strang	not out	2	c & b Vaas	50
AR Whittall	c Gurusinha b Muralitharan	3	b Muralitharan	12
BC Strang	c de Silva b Silva	3	b Muralitharan	2
HK Olonga	c Mahanama b Silva	3	not out	3
	(b 3, lb 10, nb 5)	18	(b 2, lb 6, w 1, nb 17)	26
	(all out)	141	(all out)	235

Bowling: Vaas 10-1-31-0 Pushpakumara 11-3-34-1 Muralitharan 20-5-40-4 Silva 10.1-4-16-4 de Silva 2-0-7-0
Vaas 26.3-11-34-2 Pushpakumara 8-0-24-1 Muralitharan 41-9-94-3 Silva 26-7-49-2 de Silva 5-1-10-0 Jayasuriya 7-3-16-2

Sri Lanka Innings

RS Mahanama	c A Flower b BC Strang	3	not out	12
ST Jayasuriya	c AR Whittall b PA Strang	41	not out	18
AP Gurusinha	c Wishart b BC Strang	88		
PA de Silva	c & b PA Strang	16		
*A Ranatunga	c Wishart b BC Strang	6		
HP Tillakaratne	not out	126		
+RS Kaluwitharana	c A Flower b GJ Whittall	27		
WPUJC Vaas	st A Flower b PA Strang	8		
KR Pushpakumara	c BC Strang b PA Strang	23		
M Muralitharan	not out	1		
KJ Silva				
	(lb 4, w 3, nb 4)	11		0
	(8 wickets declared)	350	(0 wickets)	30

Bowling: Olonga 26-6-81-0 BC Strang 20-6-63-3 AR Whittall 31-7-75-0 PA Strang 38-11-66-4 GJ Whittall 16.5-4-48-1 GW Flower 2-0-13-0
Olonga 3.4-0-17-0 PA Strang 3-0-13-0

Umpires: KT Francis and CJ Mitchley (SA)
TV Umpire: BC Cooray; Referee: JR Reid (NZ)

Sri Lanka v Pakistan
26,27,28,29,30 April 1997

Result: Match drawn

Sri Lanka Innings

ST Jayasuriya	c Mushtaq Ahmed b Saqlain Mushtaq	72	c sub (Abdul Razzaq) b Saqlain Mushtaq	113
RP Arnold	run out	37	b Mushtaq Ahmed	50
MS Atapattu	c Saleem Elahi b Mushtaq Ahmed	14	run out	4
PA de Silva	not out	138	not out	103
*A Ranatunga	c Saleem Elahi b Saqlain Mushtaq	4	st Saleem Elahi b Mushtaq Ahmed	66
HP Tillakaratne	b Mohammad Zahid	10	not out	24
+RS Kaluwitharana	b Asif Mujtaba	22		
RS Kalpage	c Saleem Elahi b Saqlain Mushtaq	5		
WPUJC Vaas	c Saleem Elahi b Saqlain Mushtaq	17		
KSC de Silva	st Moin Khan b Mushtaq Ahmed	0		
KJ Silva	run out	0		
	(b 6, lb 3, nb 3)	12	(b 12, lb 6, w 1, nb 7)	26
	(all out)	331	(4 wickets declared)	386

Bowling: Mohammad Zahid 12-1-44-1 Shahid Nazir 8-1-50-0 Mushtaq Ahmed 32-6-90-2 Saqlain Mushtaq 45-12-115-4 Asif Mujtaba 15-3-23-1
Saleem Malik 9-2-33-0 Ijaz Ahmed 5-0-18-0 Saqlain Mushtaq 42.5-4-171-1 Mushtaq Ahmed 33-4-113-2 Asif Mujtaba 6-0-33-0

Pakistan Innings

Saleem Elahi	c Tillakaratne b Vaas	0	c Arnold b Vaas	14
*Rameez Raja	c Arnold b KSC de Silva	36	c Kaluwitharana b Vaas	0
Ijaz Ahmed	c Arnold b Vaas	4	c Vaas b Silva	47
Saleem Malik	c Ranatunga b KSC de Silva	24	c Kaluwitharana b Silva	155
Inzamam-ul-Haq	c Kaluwitharana b Vaas	43	not out	54
Asif Mujtaba	c PA de Silva b Vaas	49	c Ranatunga b Atapattu	6
+Moin Khan	c Atapattu b Silva	98		
Saqlain Mushtaq	b KSC de Silva	23	not out	5
Mushtaq Ahmed	c Atapattu b KSC de Silva	1		
Mohammad Zahid	c Kaluwitharana b KSC de Silva	0		
Shahid Nazir	not out	0		
	(lb 4, w 4, nb 6)	14	(lb 3, nb 1)	4
	(all out)	292	(5 wickets)	285

Bowling: Vaas 27-7-60-4 KSC de Silva 24.2-5-85-5 Silva 25-5-91-1 Kalpage 23-8-42-0 Ranatunga 4.1-1-8-0 Arnold 5-3-2-0
Vaas 16-7-40-2 KSC de Silva 19-2-73-0 Silva 28-10-71-2 Kalpage 20-6-60-0 Atapattu 4-0-9-1 Tillakaratne 2-1-3-0 Arnold 6-0-26-0

Umpires: PT Manuel and ID Robinson (Zim)
TV Umpire: I Anandappa; Referee: JR Reid (NZ)

Sri Lanka v India
9,10,11,12,13 August 1997

Result: Match drawn

Sri Lanka Innings

ST Jayasuriya	c Tendulkar b Mohanty	32	b Kuruvilla	199
MS Atapattu	c Azharuddin b Prasad	19	c Azharuddin b Kumble	29
RS Mahanama	c Azharuddin b Mohanty	37	st Mongia b Kumble	35
PA de Silva	c Mongia b Mohanty	146	c sub (VG Kambli) b Kumble	120
*A Ranatunga	c Mongia b Ganguly	14	run out (Ganguly)	1
DPMD Jayawardene	c Mongia b Prasad	16	c Mongia b Kuruvilla	7
+RS Kaluwitharana	b Kuruvilla	7	run out (Ganguly)	2
WPUJC Vaas	b Kuruvilla	10	not out	5
M Muralitharan	c Azharuddin b Kumble	39		
KR Pushpakumara	b Mohanty	0		
KSC de Silva	not out	0		
	(b 4, lb 4, nb 4)	12	(b 1, lb 4, w 1, nb 11)	17
	(all out)	332	(7 wickets declared)	415

Bowling: Prasad 26-5-104-2 Kuruvilla 20-5-68-2 Mohanty 20.4-5-78-4 Kumble 25-8-51-1 Ganguly 4-0-23-1
Mohanty 16-0-72-0 Prasad 16-1-72-0 Kuruvilla 24-3-90-2 Kumble 38.4-2-156-3 Ganguly 3-0-18-0 Dravid 1-0-2-0

Innings

ST Jayasuriya	c Tendulkar b Mohanty	32
MS Atapattu	c Azharuddin b Prasad	19
RS Mahanama	c Azharuddin b Mohanty	37
PA de Silva	c Mongia b Mohanty	146
*A Ranatunga	c Mongia b Ganguly	14
DPMD Jayawardene	c Mongia b Prasad	16
+RS Kaluwitharana	b Kuruvilla	7
WPUJC Vaas	b Kuruvilla	10
M Muralitharan	c Azharuddin b Kumble	39
KR Pushpakumara	b Mohanty	0
KSC de Silva	not out	0
	(b 4, lb 4, nb 4)	12
	(all out)	332

Bowling: Prasad 26-5-104-2 Kuruvilla 20-5-68-2 Mohanty 20.4-5-78-4 Kumble 25-8-51-1 Ganguly 4-0-23-1

Umpires: BC Cooray and RE Koertzen (SA)
TV Umpire: PT Manuel; Referee: JR Reid (NZ)

Sri Lanka v Zimbabwe
14,15,16,17,18 January 1998

Result: Sri Lanka won by 5 wickets

Zimbabwe Innings

GJ Rennie	c Kaluwitharana b Muralitharan	50	c Kaluwitharana b de Silva	12
GW Flower	b Pushpakumara	41	b Jayasuriya	52
MW Goodwin	b Anurasiri	73	b Jayasuriya	39
GJ Whittall	run out (Muralitharan)	11	c sub (DPMD Jayawardene) b Muralitharan	17
+A Flower	c & b Anurasiri	8	not out	105
*ADR Campbell	c Kaluwitharana b Vaas	44	c Kaluwitharana b Anurasiri	37
CB Wishart	lbw b Muralitharan	2	c Kaluwitharana b Pushpakumara	18
PA Strang	c Pushpakumara b Anurasiri	5	b Muralitharan	3
HH Streak	b Vaas	3	run out (Kaluwitharana)	1
AR Whittall	not out	1	c Tillakaratne b de Silva	2
M Mbangwa	lbw b Pushpakumara	0	c de Silva b Muralitharan	4
	(lb 3, w 1, nb 9)	13	(lb 6, w 1, nb 2)	9
	(all out)	251	(all out)	299

Bowling: Vaas 12-1-35-2 Pushpakumara 12.2-2-43-2 de Silva 7-1-33-0 Muralitharan 32-10-72-2 Anurasiri 27-7-65-3
Pushpakumara 17-2-54-1 de Silva 23-4-61-2 Muralitharan 37.5-9-73-3 Anurasiri 19-7-41-1 Jayasuriya 29-9-64-2

Sri Lanka Innings

ST Jayasuriya	c GJ Whittall b Streak	5	c A Flower b Streak	68
MS Atapattu	c A Flower b Strang	48	c A Flower b Streak	0
RS Mahanama	b Mbangwa	8	lbw b Mbangwa	0
PA de Silva	c & b Streak	27	not out	143
*A Ranatunga	c Streak b Strang	52	not out	87
HP Tillakaratne	c Rennie b AR Whittall	7	lbw b Streak	0
+RS Kaluwitharana	c A Flower b Strang	51	c Campbell b Streak	4
SD Anurasiri	not out	3		
M Muralitharan	c A Flower b Mbangwa	11		
KR Pushpakumara	b Strang	1		
WPUJC Vaas	absent ill	0		
	(lb 11, w 1)	12	(b 11, lb 13)	24
	(all out)	225	(5 wickets)	326

Bowling: Streak 15-5-28-2 Mbangwa 16-4-61-2 GJ Whittall 3-0-18-0 Strang 19.5-2-77-4 AR Whittall 20-6-30-1
Streak 25-6-84-4 Mbangwa 14-5-34-1 GJ Whittall 7-1-12-0 Strang 24-4-75-0 AR Whittall 43-10-93-0 Goodwin 0.5-0-4-0

Umpires: KT Francis and Saleem Badar (Pak)
TV Umpire: I Anandappa; Referee: R Subba Row (Eng)

Sri Lanka v New Zealand
10,11,12,13 June 1998

Result: Sri Lanka won by 164 runs

Sri Lanka Innings

ST Jayasuriya	c Young b Cairns	13	c Parore b Cairns	8
MS Atapattu	c Vettori b Wiseman	48	lbw b Vettori	5
DPMD Jayawardene	c Parore b Cairns	16	c Horne b Vettori	11
PA de Silva	c Spearman b Cairns	4	c Astle b Vettori	3
*A Ranatunga	run out (McMillan)	4	c Cairns b Priest	64
HP Tillakaratne	c Young b McMillan	43	b Vettori	40
+RS Kaluwitharana	b McMillan	28	lbw b Priest	88
HDPK Dharmasena	c Parore b Cairns	11	b McMillan	11
GP Wickramasinghe	not out	24	c Fleming b Vettori	0
MRCN Bandaratilleke	lbw b Vettori	5	c Fleming b Vettori	7
M Muralitharan	c Astle b Cairns	1	not out	26
	(b 1, lb 8)	9	(b 8, lb 10, nb 1)	19
	(all out)	206	(all out)	282

Bowling: Cairns 17.4-1-62-5 Vettori 25-7-52-1 Priest 24-11-35-0 Wiseman 10-4-21-1 McMillan 12-5-27-2
Cairns 17-0-75-1 Vettori 33-10-64-6 Astle 3-0-8-0 Wiseman 6-2-29-0 McMillan 14-2-46-1 Priest 11.5-0-42-2

New Zealand Innings

BA Young	c Atapattu b Bandaratilleke	2	st Kaluwitharana b Muralitharan	24
CM Spearman	c de Silva b Wickramasinghe	4	c & b Muralitharan	22
*SP Fleming	b Wickramasinghe	78	lbw b Dharmasena	3
NJ Astle	c Atapattu b Dharmasena	16	c & b Muralitharan	16
MJ Horne	c Tillakaratne b de Silva	35	c Kaluwitharana b Bandaratilleke	12
CD McMillan	st Kaluwitharana b de Silva	2	c Jayawardene b Muralitharan	1
+AC Parore	lbw b de Silva	19	b Bandaratilleke	2
CL Cairns	run out (Jayawardene)	6	b Bandaratilleke	26
MW Priest	c sub (ASA Perera) b Muralitharan	12	b Bandaratilleke	2
DL Vettori	c Jayasuriya b Muralitharan	0	b Muralitharan	3
PJ Wiseman	not out	1	not out	0
	(b 11, lb 2, nb 5)	18	(b 6, lb 10, nb 4)	20
	(all out)	193	(all out)	131

Bowling: Wickramasinghe 6.3-3-7-2 Bandaratilleke 20-6-48-1 Dharmasena 18-4-35-1 de Silva 18.5-7-30-3 Muralitharan 23.1-3-60-2
Wickramasinghe 6-2-5-0 Bandaratilleke 17-3-52-4 de Silva 3-0-14-0 Dharmasena 10-2-14-1 Muralitharan 18.3-8-30-5

Umpires: PT Manuel and VK Ramaswamy (Ind)
TV Umpire: I Anandappa; Referee: Talat Ali (Pak)

Sinhalese Sports Club Ground, Colombo

Sri Lanka v India
24,25,26,27,28 February 1999

Result: Match drawn

India Innings

S Ramesh	c Ranatunga b Jayawardene	143	c Tillakaratne b Upashantha	30
VVS Laxman	c de Silva b Perera	11	lbw b Upashantha	25
R Dravid	c Ranatunga b Hathurusingha	107		
SR Tendulkar	c Kaluwitharana b Vaas	53	not out	124
*M Azharuddin	c Hathurusingha b Arnold	87	c Arnold b de Silva	15
SC Ganguly	c sub (RS Kalpage) b Upashantha	56	st Kaluwitharana b de Silva	78
+NR Mongia	c de Silva b Arnold	25		
A Kumble	not out	10	c Vaas b Arnold	10
BKV Prasad			not out	9
Harbhajan Singh				
A Nehra				
	(b 5, lb 6, w 3, nb 12)	26	(b 1, lb 3, w 2, nb 9)	15
	(7 wickets declared)	518	(5 wickets)	306

Bowling: Vaas 31-5-108-1 Perera 30-4-125-1 Upashantha 28-3-94-1 Hathurusingha 18-3-51-1 Arnold 24.5-2-94-2 Jayawardene 11-3-35-1
Vaas 18-3-58-0 Perera 14-2-60-0 Upashantha 15-2-41-2 Arnold 23.4-4-54-1 de Silva 18.2-2-59-2 Jayawardene 14-1-30-0 Tillakaratne 1-1-0-0

Sri Lanka Innings

RP Arnold	run out (Dravid)	34
MS Atapattu	lbw b Nehra	6
DPMD Jayawardene	c & b Kumble	242
UC Hathurusingha	lbw b Prasad	14
PA de Silva	b Harbhajan Singh	23
*A Ranatunga	c sub (HH Kanitkar) b Kumble	66
HP Tillakaratne	st Mongia b Harbhajan Singh	14
+RS Kaluwitharana	b Harbhajan Singh	23
WPUJC Vaas	c Laxman b Kumble	23
KEA Upashantha	lbw b Kumble	6
PDRL Perera	not out	1
	(b 1, lb 19, w 4, nb 9)	33
	(all out)	485

Bowling: Prasad 31-6-94-1 Nehra 28-5-94-1 Kumble 54.1-10-134-4 Harbhajan Singh 40-9-127-3 Tendulkar 5-0-16-0 Ganguly 1-1-0-0

Umpires: RE Koertzen (SA) and RB Tiffin (Zim)
TV Umpire: Saleem Badar (Pak); Referee: CW Smith (WI)

Sri Lanka v Australia
30 September, 1,2,3,4 October 1999

Result: Match drawn

Australia Innings

GS Blewett	c Atapattu b Herath	70
MJ Slater	st Kaluwitharana b Arnold	59
JL Langer	c Ranatunga b Muralitharan	32
ME Waugh	c Arnold b Muralitharan	13
*SR Waugh	c Kaluwitharana b Herath	14
RT Ponting	not out	105
+IA Healy	c Jayawardene b Vaas	7
SK Warne	lbw b Vaas	0
DW Fleming	c Atapattu b Muralitharan	32
CR Miller	lbw b Vaas	0
GD McGrath	c Atapattu b Vaas	0
	(nb 10)	10
	(all out)	342

Bowling: Vaas 23.4-5-54-4 Zoysa 10-4-23-0 Herath 35-10-98-2 Muralitharan 52-5-150-3 Jayasuriya 9-2-14-0 Arnold 7-4-3-1

Sri Lanka Innings

*ST Jayasuriya	c Warne b McGrath	0
MS Atapattu	c Healy b Fleming	2
RP Arnold	lbw b Fleming	0
PA de Silva	not out	19
DPMD Jayawardene	c Healy b Fleming	21
A Ranatunga	not out	1
+RS Kaluwitharana		
WPUJC Vaas		
HMRKB Herath		
DNT Zoysa		
M Muralitharan		
	(b 8, lb 1, w 5, nb 4)	18
	(4 wickets)	61

Bowling: McGrath 10-3-25-1 Fleming 5.5-0-14-3 Warne 5-1-11-0 Miller 1-0-2-0

Umpires: KT Francis and P Willey (Eng)
TV Umpire: EAR de Silva; Referee: CW Smith (WI)

Sri Lanka v Pakistan
14,15,16,17 June 2000

Result: Pakistan won by 5 wickets

Sri Lanka Innings

MS Atapattu	c Mohammad Wasim b Arshad Khan	73	c Saeed Anwar b Arshad Khan	40
*ST Jayasuriya	c Younis Khan b Waqar Younis	26	lbw b Waqar Younis	8
RP Arnold	b Waqar Younis	4	c Mohammad Wasim b Wasim Akram	1
PA de Silva	c Wasim Akram b Arshad Khan	30	c Inzamam-ul-Haq b Abdul Razzaq	21
DPMD Jayawardene	c Moin Khan b Wasim Akram	77	c Mohammad Wasim b Arshad Khan	1
A Ranatunga	run out (Mushtaq Ahmed)	6	c Saeed Anwar b Wasim Akram	7
+RS Kaluwitharana	c Mohammad Wasim b Arshad Khan	4	c Younis Khan b Arshad Khan	6
WPUJC Vaas	b Mushtaq Ahmed	3	c & b Wasim Akram	20
DNT Zoysa	st Moin Khan b Arshad Khan	17	c Inzamam-ul-Haq b Wasim Akram	13
M Muralitharan	c Wasim Akram b Waqar Younis	18	not out	3
CRD Fernando	not out	5	b Wasim Akram	0
	(b 5, lb 1, nb 4)	10	(lb 1, w 1, nb 1)	3
	(all out)	273	(all out)	123

Bowling: Wasim Akram 20-6-55-1 Waqar Younis 14.2-0-50-3 Abdul Razzaq 18-1-58-0 Mushtaq Ahmed 14-1-42-1 Arshad Khan 31-8-62-4
Waqar Younis 9-3-21-1 Wasim Akram 15.3-1-45-5 Abdul Razzaq 14-6-23-1 Arshad Khan 22-8-30-3 Mushtaq Ahmed 1-0-3-0

Pakistan Innings

Saeed Anwar	c Ranatunga b Muralitharan	56	c Fernando b Zoysa	6
Mohammad Wasim	c Arnold b Fernando	8	lbw b Muralitharan	30
Younis Khan	c Fernando b Muralitharan	23	not out	32
Yousuf Youhana	c Jayawardene b Muralitharan	2	b Muralitharan	11
*+Moin Khan	c Fernando b Zoysa	47	lbw b Zoysa	11
Inzamam-ul-Haq	c Jayawardene b Zoysa	12	c Arnold b Muralitharan	13
Abdul Razzaq	run out (Fernando)	0		
Wasim Akram	b Fernando	78	not out	20
Waqar Younis	c Zoysa b Muralitharan	4		
Mushtaq Ahmed	c Arnold b Muralitharan	2		
Arshad Khan	not out	9		
	(lb 4, w 3, nb 18)	25	(b 4, nb 4)	8
	(all out)	266	(5 wickets)	131

Bowling: Vaas 29-7-52-0 Zoysa 19-4-30-2 de Silva 3-1-4-0 Fernando 15.5-1-53-2 Muralitharan 47-12-115-5 Jayawardene 2-1-2-0 Jayasuriya 4-3-6-0 Ranatunga 1-1-0-0
Vaas 8-3-20-0 Zoysa 13-1-38-2 Muralitharan 17-3-53-3 Fernando 3-0-14-0 Arnold 1-0-2-0

Umpires: SA Bucknor (WI) and BC Cooray
TV Umpire: PT Manuel; Referee: JR Reid (NZ)

Sri Lanka v South Africa
6,7,8,9,10 August 2000

Result: Match drawn

South Africa Innings

G Kirsten	c Ranatunga b Perera	11	lbw b Muralitharan	40
ND McKenzie	c Arnold b Perera	0	run out (Jayasuriya)	17
JH Kallis	c Sangakkara b Vaas	19	b de Silva	0
DJ Cullinan	c Atapattu b Vaas	38	c Arnold b Muralitharan	3
JN Rhodes	b Muralitharan	21	c Jayawardene b Muralitharan	54
L Klusener	not out	95	c Sangakkara b Muralitharan	35
+MV Boucher	c Chandana b Vaas	4	b Muralitharan	25
*SM Pollock	b Muralitharan	33	c Sangakkara b Jayasuriya	13
N Boje	c Sangakkara b Vaas	21	not out	29
PR Adams	lbw b Muralitharan	15	c & b Jayasuriya	3
M Hayward	c de Silva b Chandana	0	not out	3
	(b 2, lb 8, nb 12)	22	(lb 4, nb 15)	19
	(all out)	279	(9 wickets dec)	241

Bowling: Vaas 36-9-85-4 Perera 18-3-60-2 de Silva 5-2-16-0 Muralitharan 39-14-70-3 Chandana 4.2-0-26-1 Jayasuriya 3-0-9-0 Arnold 3-1-3-0
Vaas 10-2-22-0 Perera 2-0-13-0 Arnold 2.1-0-6-0 de Silva 24.5-7-49-1 Muralitharan 45.5-14-68-5 Jayasuriya 24-4-56-2 Chandana 5-0-23-0

Sri Lanka Innings

MS Atapattu	b Hayward	10	c Kirsten b Pollock	0
*ST Jayasuriya	c Kirsten b Boje	85	b Adams	17
RP Arnold	c Klusener b Boje	28		
PA de Silva	st Boucher b Boje	2	lbw b Klusener	41
DPMD Jayawardene	c Kirsten b Boje	34	not out	101
WPUJC Vaas	lbw b Pollock	5		
A Ranatunga	b Boje	14	not out	28
+KC Sangakkara	c Boucher b Hayward	25	c Rhodes b Hayward	6
UDU Chandana	c McKenzie b Pollock	32		
PDRL Perera	c Boje b Pollock	10		
M Muralitharan	not out	0		
	(b 3, lb 1, w 1, nb 8)	13	(nb 2)	2
	(all out)	258	(4 wickets)	195

Bowling: Pollock 22.2-10-40-3 Hayward 20-2-68-2 Kallis 13-3-48-0 Klusener 9-2-36-0 Boje 34-8-62-5
Pollock 6-3-13-1 Hayward 9-1-21-1 Kallis 4-2-4-0 Klusener 12.1-4-20-1 Adams 16-3-72-1 Boje 20-4-65-0

Umpires: BC Cooray and EA Nicholls (WI)
TV Umpire: TH Wijewardene; Referee: BF Hastings (NZ)

Sri Lanka v England
15,16,17 March 2001

Result: England won by 4 wickets

Sri Lanka Innings

MS Atapattu	b Caddick	0	c Croft b Gough	0
*ST Jayasuriya	c White b Croft	45	lbw b Gough	23
+KC Sangakkara	c Vaughan b Gough	45	c Stewart b Caddick	0
PA de Silva	c Vaughan b Giles	38	c Thorpe b Caddick	23
DPMD Jayawardene	c Stewart b Croft	71	lbw b Giles	11
RP Arnold	lbw b Giles	0	c Hussain b Croft	0
TM Dilshan	lbw b Croft	5	b Giles	10
WPUJC Vaas	not out	19	c Atherton b Giles	6
CRD Fernando	c Trescothick b Croft	2	c Giles b Gough	5
D Hettiarachchi	b Gough	0	not out	0
M Muralitharan	b Caddick	1	lbw b Giles	1
	(b 4, lb 4, w 1, nb 6)	15	(nb 2)	2
	(all out)	241	(all out)	81

Bowling: Gough 14-5-33-2 Caddick 11.1-1-40-2 White 10-1-45-0 Giles 34-13-59-2 Croft 32-9-56-4
Gough 6-1-23-3 Caddick 8-2-29-2 Giles 9.1-4-11-4 Croft 5-0-18-1

England Innings

MA Atherton	lbw b Vaas	21	c & b Fernando	13
ME Trescothick	c Arnold b Hettiarachchi	23	c Sangakkara b Jayasuriya	10
*N Hussain	c Jayasuriya b Hettiarachchi	8	c Arnold b Jayasuriya	0
GP Thorpe	not out	113	not out	32
+AJ Stewart	b Muralitharan	3	c Dilshan b Jayasuriya	0
MP Vaughan	c Sangakkara b Vaas	26	b Muralitharan	8
C White	c Sangakkara b Vaas	0	c Jayawardene b Jayasuriya	8
AF Giles	c Jayawardene b Vaas	0	not out	1
RDB Croft	run out (Atapattu)	16		
AR Caddick	c Jayasuriya b Vaas	0		
D Gough	c Jayawardene b Vaas	14		
	(b 10, lb 9, nb 6)	25	(lb 1, nb 1)	2
	(all out)	249	(6 wickets)	74

Bowling: Vaas 27.5-6-73-6 Fernando 5-0-26-0 de Silva 3-1-2-0 Muralitharan 41-9-73-1 Hettiarachchi 24-6-36-2 Jayasuriya 9-1-20-0
Vaas 3-0-11-0 Hettiarachchi 3-1-5-0 Muralitharan 8-1-26-1 Fernando 2-0-7-1 Jayasuriya 8.3-0-24-4

Umpires: EAR de Silva and DL Orchard (SA)
TV Umpire: BC Cooray; Referee: Hanumant Singh (Ind)

Sri Lanka v India
29,30,31 August 1,2 September 2001

Result: Sri Lanka won by an innings and 77 runs

India Innings

SS Das	b Muralitharan	59	c Tillakaratne b Muralitharan	68
S Ramesh	c Jayawardene b Muralitharan	46	b Muralitharan	55
R Dravid	c Tillakaratne b Muralitharan	36	run out (Atapattu)	36
*SC Ganguly	lbw b Muralitharan	1	c Jayawardene b Samaraweera	30
M Kaif	c Sangakkara b Vaas	14	run out (Sangakkara)	5
HK Badani	c Tillakaratne b Muralitharan	38	lbw b Vaas	11
+SS Dighe	lbw b Muralitharan	0	run out (Atapattu)	4
SV Bahutule	st Sangakkara b Muralitharan	18	b Jayasuriya	0
Harbhajan Singh	lbw b Vaas	2	c Atapattu b Vaas	17
Z Khan	c Jayawardene b Muralitharan	0	c Atapattu b Muralitharan	45
BKV Prasad	not out	10	not out	4
	(b 2, lb 3, w 2, nb 3)	10	(b 8, lb 5, w 2, nb 9)	24
	(all out)	234	(all out)	299

Bowling: Vaas 24-7-60-2 Liyanage 9-2-32-0 Fernando 12-2-38-0 Muralitharan 34.1-9-87-8 Samaraweera 2-0-12-0
Vaas 27-9-62-2 Fernando 17-3-59-0 Muralitharan 46.5-17-109-3 Jayasuriya 21-10-34-1 Liyanage 5-0-12-0 Samaraweera 8-4-10-1

Sri Lanka Innings

MS Atapattu	c Das b Harbhajan Singh	108
*ST Jayasuriya	b Prasad	30
+KC Sangakkara	c Badani b Prasad	47
DPMD Jayawardene	lbw b Bahutule	139
RP Arnold	b Prasad	31
DK Liyanage	c Dighe b Harbhajan Singh	3
HP Tillakaratne	not out	136
TT Samaraweera	not out	103
WPUJC Vaas		
CRD Fernando		
M Muralitharan		
	(lb 4, w 4, nb 5)	13
	(6 wickets dec)	610

Bowling: Khan 27-3-134-0 Prasad 34-8-101-3 Harbhajan Singh 53.3-6-185-2 Ganguly 12.3-3-44-0 Bahutule 31-5-101-1 Badani 8-2-17-0 Ramesh 5-0-24-0

Umpires: EAR de Silva and DL Orchard (SA)
TV Umpire: TH Wijewardene; Referee: CW Smith (WI)

Sri Lanka v Bangladesh
6,7,8 September 2001

Result: Sri Lanka won by an innings and 137 runs

Bangladesh Innings
Javed Omar	c Jayasuriya b Vaas	7	lbw b Muralitharan	40
Mehrab Hossain	run out (Atapattu)	23	lbw b Muralitharan	4
Habibul Bashar	b Vaas	4	c Jayawardene b Muralitharan	19
Aminul Islam	c Sangakkara b Perera	6	b Jayasuriya	56
Al Sahariar	c Sangakkara b Muralitharan	16	lbw b Samaraweera	7
*Naimur Rahman	b Muralitharan	0	c Atapattu b Perera	48
Mohammad Ashraful	c Jayasuriya b Muralitharan	26	c & b Perera	114
+Khaled Mashud	b Muralitharan	0	lbw b Muralitharan	3
Hasibul Hossain	b Muralitharan	2	c Sangakkara b Perera	0
Mohammad Sharif	c Vandort b Vaas	1	c & b Muralitharan	19
Manjural Islam	not out	3	not out	1
	(lb 1, nb 1)	2	(b 5, lb 5, nb 7)	17
	(all out)	90	(all out)	328

Bowling: Vaas 14-2-47-3 Pushpakumara 7-4-9-0 Perera 5-1-17-1 Muralitharan 9.4-4-13-5 Samaraweera 1-0-3-0
Vaas 16-2-71-0 Pushpakumara 8-5-15-0 Muralitharan 35.3-6-98-5 Perera 13-3-40-3 Samaraweera 13-2-42-1 Jayasuriya 16-2-52-1

Sri Lanka Innings
MS Atapattu	retired	201
*ST Jayasuriya	lbw b Naimur Rahman	89
+KC Sangakkara	c Aminul Islam b Hasibul Hossain	54
DPMD Jayawardene	retired	150
MG Vandort	c Manjural Islam b Naimur Rahman	36
HP Tillakaratne	not out	10
TT Samaraweera		
M Muralitharan		
KR Pushpakumara		
WPUJC Vaas		
PDRL Perera		
	(lb 5, w 2, nb 8)	15
	(5 wickets dec)	555

Bowling: Manjural Islam 18-1-94-0 Mohammad Sharif 17-0-120-0 Hasibul Hossain 23-6-122-1 Naimur Rahman 30.3-8-117-2 Mohammad Ashraful 10-0-63-0 Habibul Bashar 5-0-34-0

Umpires: RE Koertzen (SA) and Mian Mohammad Aslam (Pak)
TV Umpire: Riazuddin (Pak); Referee: JR Reid (NZ)

Sri Lanka v West Indies
29,30 November, 1,2,3 December 2001

Result: Sri Lanka won by 10 wickets

West Indies Innings
D Ganga	lbw b Vaas	6	lbw b Vaas	10
CH Gayle	c Sangakkara b Vaas	0	c Jayawardene b Vaas	0
RR Sarwan	run out (Jayawardene)	69	c Sangakkara b Vaas	66
BC Lara	b Vaas	221	b Zoysa	130
*CL Hooper	lbw b Vaas	56	st Sangakkara b Muralitharan	9
MN Samuels	lbw b Vaas	4	c Jayawardene b Muralitharan	0
+RD Jacobs	b Zoysa	2	not out	31
M Dillon	lbw b Vaas	2	c sub (UDU Chandana) b Vaas	8
D Ramnarine	c Jayawardene b Muralitharan	0	lbw b Vaas	0
PT Collins	c Samaraweera b Vaas	4	lbw b Vaas	0
MI Black	not out	0	lbw b Vaas	0
	(b 5, lb 7, nb 14)	26	(b 4, lb 1, nb 3)	8
	(all out)	390	(all out)	262

Bowling: Vaas 32.2-5-120-7 Zoysa 20-4-55-1 Samaraweera 8-0-31-0 Bandaratilleke 9-2-37-0 Muralitharan 37-6-115-1 Jayasuriya 3-0-11-0 Arnold 3-0-8-0 Tillakaratne 1-0-1-0
Vaas 25-3-71-7 Zoysa 11-1-45-1 Muralitharan 36-5-116-2 Samaraweera 8-2-23-0 Bandaratilleke 2-0-2-0

Sri Lanka Innings
MS Atapattu	c Gayle b Collins	4	not out	19
*ST Jayasuriya	c Ramnarine b Black	85	not out	8
+KC Sangakkara	c Gayle b Dillon	55		
DPMD Jayawardene	lbw b Dillon	39		
RP Arnold	c Jacobs b Hooper	65		
HP Tillakaratne	not out	204		
TT Samaraweera	run out (Black)	87		
WPUJC Vaas	c Samuels b Collins	23		
DNT Zoysa	b Hooper	10		
MRCN Bandaratilleke	c Jacobs b Collins	25		
M Muralitharan	not out	4		
	(b 5, lb 14, w 2, nb 5)	26		0
	(9 wickets dec)	627	(0 wickets)	27

Bowling: Dillon 46-9-131-2 Collins 47-4-156-3 Black 32-6-123-1 Ramnarine 17-3-51-0 Hooper 43-7-112-2 Gayle 10-1-28-0 Sarwan 2-0-7-0
Dillon 3-0-12-0 Collins 2.3-0-15-0

Umpires: EAR de Silva and RB Tiffin (Zim)
TV Umpire: MG Silva; Referee: R Subba Row (Eng)

Sri Lanka v Zimbabwe
27,28,29,31 December 2001

Result: Sri Lanka won by an innings and 166 runs

Sri Lanka Innings
MS Atapattu	c A Flower b Streak	25
*ST Jayasuriya	c A Flower b Gripper	92
+KC Sangakkara	c Wishart b Brent	128
DPMD Jayawardene	c Carlisle b Gripper	18
RP Arnold	lbw b Streak	13
HP Tillakaratne	c A Flower b Streak	96
TT Samaraweera	not out	123
WPUJC Vaas	not out	74
DNT Zoysa		
TCB Fernando		
M Muralitharan		
	(b 2, lb 4, w 3, nb 8)	17
	(6 wickets dec)	586

Bowling: Streak 34-5-113-3 Friend 27-5-102-0 Olonga 23-3-103-0 Brent 33-5-82-1 Gripper 22-3-91-2 GW Flower 22-3-89-0

Zimbabwe Innings
H Masakadza	c Tillakaratne b Zoysa	3	c Atapattu b Muralitharan	28
TR Gripper	c Jayawardene b Muralitharan	30	c Sangakkara b Muralitharan	10
*SV Carlisle	c Jayasuriya b Vaas	10	c Sangakkara b Fernando	32
GJ Rennie	lbw b Muralitharan	35	c Jayawardene b Fernando	4
+A Flower	b Samaraweera	42	lbw b Zoysa	10
GW Flower	c Tillakaratne b Muralitharan	0	c Tillakaratne b Muralitharan	18
CB Wishart	c Tillakaratne b Zoysa	21	c Tillakaratne b Samaraweera	27
HH Streak	not out	26	not out	36
TJ Friend	lbw b Vaas	6	b Muralitharan	44
GB Brent	b Muralitharan	4	c Jayasuriya b Zoysa	7
HK Olonga	lbw b Fernando	4	c Sangakkara b Vaas	0
	(lb 1, nb 6)	7	(b 4, lb 7, nb 9)	20
	(all out)	184	(all out)	236

Bowling: Vaas 24-6-63-2 Zoysa 14-6-24-2 Muralitharan 26-8-53-4 Jayasuriya 1-0-4-0 Fernando 9.5-0-32-1 Samaraweera 5-1-7-1
Vaas 21.2-6-76-1 Zoysa 15-4-34-2 Fernando 15-3-48-2 Muralitharan 36-17-35-4 Jayasuriya 7-3-22-0 Samaraweera 7-2-10-1

Umpires: PT Manuel and Riazuddin (Pak)
TV Umpire: TH Wijewardene; Referee: CW Smith (WI)

Sri Lanka v Bangladesh
28,29,30,31 July 2002

Result: Sri Lanka won by 288 runs

Sri Lanka Innings
MG Vandort	lbw b Alok Kapali	61	b Talha Jubair	140
J Mubarak	lbw b Tapash Baisya	24	run out (Tapash Baisya/Khaled Mashud)	31
MN Nawaz	c Khaled Mashud b Fahim Muntasir	21	not out	78
HP Tillakaratne	c & b Fahim Muntasir	18	not out	5
*ST Jayasuriya	c Khaled Mashud b Manjural Islam	85		
TT Samaraweera	c Habibul Bashar b Manjural Islam	58		
+HAPW Jayawardene	c Khaled Mashud b Manjural Islam	0		
UDU Chandana	c Habibul Bashar b Alok Kapali	20		
TCB Fernando	not out	29		
WRS de Silva	c Khaled Mashud b Talha Jubair	5		
MKGCP Lakshitha	c Alok Kapali b Talha Jubair	40		
	(b 1, lb 5, nb 6)	12	(b 4, lb 1, w 1, nb 3)	9
	(all out)	373	(2 wickets dec)	263

Bowling: Manjural Islam 23-4-46-3 Talha Jubair 21.4-3-74-2 Tapash Baisya 12-1-69-1 Fahim Muntasir 18-3-46-2 Alok Kapali 29-2-122-2 Habibul Bashar 3-1-10-0
Manjural Islam 9-0-28-0 Talha Jubair 14-1-52-1 Alok Kapali 11-0-54-0 Tapash Baisya 8-0-40-0 Fahim Muntasir 19-3-56-0 Habibul Bashar 5-0-28-0

Bangladesh Innings
Hannan Sarkar	lbw b Fernando	5	c Jayawardene b de Silva	30
Al Sahariar	c Jayawardene b Jayasuriya	12	b de Silva	6
Habibul Bashar	lbw b Fernando	11	c Jayawardene b Lakshitha	3
Mohammad Ashraful	b Lakshitha	1	c Mubarak b Samaraweera	75
Tushar Imran	lbw b Lakshitha	8	st Jayawardene b Chandana	28
*+Khaled Mashud	c Tillakaratne b Samaraweera	15	not out	13
Alok Kapali	lbw b Jayasuriya	39	c Mubarak b Samaraweera	23
Fahim Muntasir	c & b Samaraweera	7	lbw b de Silva	1
Tapash Baisya	not out	52	c Chandana b de Silva	3
Manjural Islam	c Jayawardene b Jayasuriya	0	c Tillakaratne b Samaraweera	0
Talha Jubair	c Jayasuriya b Chandana	0	c Mubarak b Samaraweera	0
	(lb 4, nb 10)	14	(lb 1, nb 1)	2
	(all out)	164	(all out)	184

Bowling: Fernando 15-3-36-2 de Silva 11-2-45-0 Jayasuriya 7-2-17-3 Lakshitha 12-5-33-2 Samaraweera 12-3-18-2 Chandana 5-1-11-1
Fernando 5-2-12-0 de Silva 13-5-35-4 Lakshitha 12-2-48-1 Jayasuriya 9-4-14-0 Samaraweera 11.4-1-49-4 Chandana 10-3-25-1

Umpires: SA Bucknor (WI) and DR Shepherd (Eng)
TV Umpire: PT Manuel; Referee: Wasim Raja (Pak)

Harare Sports Club

Zimbabwe v India
18,19,20,21,22 October 1992

Result: Match drawn

Zimbabwe Innings

KJ Arnott	c Raman b Kumble	40	b Prabhakar	32
GW Flower	c More b Srinath	82	c More b Kapil Dev	6
ADR Campbell	lbw b Kapil Dev	45	b Kapil Dev	0
AJ Pycroft	c Azharuddin b Prabhakar	39	lbw b Shastri	46
MG Burmester	c Azharuddin b Prabhakar	7		
*DL Houghton	c More b Srinath	121	not out	41
+A Flower	b Prabhakar	59	not out	1
GJ Crocker	not out	23		
EA Brandes	lbw b Srinath	0		
AJ Traicos	b Kumble	5		
MP Jarvis	c Raman b Kumble	0		
	(b 1, lb 19, nb 15)	35	(b 11, lb 4, nb 5)	20
	(all out)	456	(4 wickets)	146

Bowling: Kapil Dev 39-13-71-1 Prabhakar 45-15-66-3 Srinath 39-12-89-3 Raju 39-15-79-0 Kumble 35.2-11-79-3 Shastri 17-3-52-0
Kapil Dev 15-4-22-2 Prabhakar 14-4-22-1 Srinath 5-1-15-0 Raju 7-2-17-0 Kumble 9-1-15-0 Shastri 12-4-32-1 Tendulkar 4-3-8-0

India Innings

RJ Shastri	c Pycroft b Burmester	11
WV Raman	b Crocker	43
SV Manjrekar	c sub (SG Davies) b Jarvis	104
SR Tendulkar	c & b Traicos	0
*M Azharuddin	c GW Flower b Traicos	9
SLV Raju	c Arnott b Traicos	7
N Kapil Dev	b Traicos	60
M Prabhakar	c Arnott b Traicos	14
+KS More	c Traicos b Burmester	41
A Kumble	c A Flower b Burmester	0
J Srinath	not out	6
	(b 2, lb 9, nb 1)	12
	(all out)	307

Bowling: Brandes 2-0-3-0 Burmester 39.4-18-78-3 Jarvis 38-17-73-1 Crocker 35-18-41-1 Traicos 50-16-86-5 GW Flower 5-0-15-0

Umpires: HD Bird (Eng), K Kanjee and ID Robinson; Referee: PL van der Merwe (SA)

Zimbabwe v New Zealand
7,9,10,11,12 November 1992

Result: New Zealand won by 177 runs

New Zealand Innings

MJ Greatbatch	c A Flower b Brain	55	c Brandes b Brain	13
RT Latham	c A Flower b Crocker	15	c Houghton b Brandes	10
AH Jones	c Pycroft b Brandes	8	st A Flower b Traicos	28
*MD Crowe	c Burmester b Crocker	140	lbw b Traicos	61
KR Rutherford	c A Flower b Traicos	74	c Arnott b Brandes	89
DN Patel	c Campbell b Traicos	6	not out	58
+AC Parore	run out	2		
DJ Nash	not out	11		
ML Su'a	c Arnott b Brandes	1		
W Watson	b Brain	3		
MJ Haslam	c A Flower b Brain	3		
	(lb 11, nb 6)	17	(lb 2, w 1)	3
	(all out)	335	(5 wickets declared)	262

Bowling: Brandes 22-6-49-2 Brain 18-5-49-3 Crocker 15-1-65-2 Burmester 10-2-34-0 Traicos 23-1-82-2 GW Flower 6-0-45-0
Brandes 19.4-3-59-2 Brain 16-2-52-1 Crocker 7-0-24-0 Traicos 27-8-70-2 GW Flower 4-0-11-0 Burmester 9-1-44-0

Zimbabwe Innings

KJ Arnott	b Watson	68	c Watson b Nash	10
GW Flower	lbw b Su'a	5	c Latham b Su'a	1
ADR Campbell	c Su'a b Patel	52	c Greatbatch b Patel	35
AJ Pycroft	b Su'a	60	c Latham b Watson	5
*DL Houghton	c Parore b Su'a	21	c Nash b Patel	2
+A Flower	c Patel b Nash	14	c Parore b Patel	9
EA Brandes	c Parore b Su'a	0	c & b Patel	6
GJ Crocker	b Su'a	12	c Greatbatch b Haslam	33
DH Brain	c Su'a b Patel	11	c Su'a b Patel	17
MG Burmester	not out	30	not out	17
AJ Traicos			lbw b Patel	0
	(lb 7, nb 2)	9	(lb 2)	2
	(9 wickets declared)	283	(all out)	137

Bowling: Su'a 37-8-85-5 Nash 28-10-59-1 Watson 25-6-51-1 Patel 37-7-81-2
Su'a 12-3-30-1 Nash 8-3-19-1 Watson 3-2-3-1 Patel 17.3-5-50-6 Haslam 10-2-33-1

Umpires: HD Bird (Eng), K Kanjee and ID Robinson; Referee: DJ McGlew (SA)

Zimbabwe v Sri Lanka
11,12,13,15,16 October 1994

Result: Match drawn

Sri Lanka Innings

RS Mahanama	c James b Jarvis	8
AP Gurusinha	c A Flower b Whittall	128
S Ranatunga	c James b Whittall	118
PA de Silva	c & b Jarvis	19
*A Ranatunga	c sub b Streak	62
HP Tillakaratne	c James b Whittall	1
+PB Dassanayake	lbw b Whittall	0
WPUJC Vaas	lbw b Streak	3
GP Wickramasinghe	c James b Streak	15
M Muralitharan	c & b Streak	0
KR Pushpakumara	not out	6
	(lb 19, w 1, nb 3)	23
	(all out)	383

Bowling: Brain 5-2-9-0 Streak 42.5-14-79-4 Jarvis 41-18-76-2 Whittall 33-8-70-4 Peall 50-11-114-0 GW Flower 8-2-16-0

Zimbabwe Innings

GW Flower	c Dassanayake b Vaas	41
MH Dekker	c sub b Muralitharan	40
ADR Campbell	c Tillakaratne b Wickramasinghe	44
DL Houghton	c Dassanayake b Vaas	58
A Flower	c Dassanayake b Vaas	26
GJ Whittall	c Dassanayake b Pushpakumara	4
+WR James	c Dassanayake b Vaas	18
HH Streak	c Gurusinha b Muralitharan	8
SG Peall	not out	9
DH Brain	not out	6
MP Jarvis		
	(b 10, lb 18, w 1, nb 36)	65
	(8 wickets)	319

Bowling: Wickramasinghe 26-4-60-1 Vaas 37-11-74-4 Pushpakumara 20-0-68-1 de Silva 6-0-20-0 Muralitharan 32-7-60-2 A Ranatunga 2-0-9-0

Umpires: LH Barker (WI) and ID Robinson
TV Umpire: RC Strang; Referee: PL van der Merwe (SA)

Zimbabwe v Sri Lanka
26,27,28,30,31 October 1994

Result: Match drawn

Sri Lanka Innings

RS Mahanama	c Dekker b Streak	24	lbw b Brain	0
AP Gurusinha	c A Flower b Brain	54	c Whittall b Brain	13
S Ranatunga	c Whittall b Strang	43	c Whittall b Streak	8
+HP Tillakaratne	c Dekker b Strang	116		
PA de Silva	c Dekker b Streak	25	not out	41
*A Ranatunga	c Dekker b Streak	39	not out	22
ST Jayasuriya	c James b Streak	10		
RS Kalpage	c James b Brain	14		
HDPK Dharmasena	c A Flower b Strang	21		
WPUJC Vaas	not out	16		
KR Pushpakumara	c A Flower b Jarvis	8		
	(b 7, lb 11, w 4, nb 10)	32	(lb 2, nb 3)	5
	(all out)	402	(3 wickets)	89

Bowling: Brain 34-4-90-2 Streak 38-8-97-4 Jarvis 37-13-58-1 Whittall 28-5-74-0 Strang 25-6-65-3
Streak 12-4-32-1 Brain 11-1-48-2 Jarvis 1-0-7-0

Zimbabwe Innings

GW Flower	c Tillakaratne b Pushpakumara	5
MH Dekker	lbw b Pushpakumara	14
ADR Campbell	c Tillakaratne b Pushpakumara	99
DL Houghton	b Vaas	142
*A Flower	c Tillakaratne b Vaas	10
GJ Whittall	not out	61
+WR James	c Mahanama b Pushpakumara	2
HH Streak	c Tillakaratne b Pushpakumara	20
DH Brain	lbw b Pushpakumara	6
PA Strang	b Dharmasena	6
MP Jarvis	b Pushpakumara	2
	(lb 8, nb 6)	14
	(all out)	375

Bowling: Vaas 44-12-76-2 Pushpakumara 35.4-7-116-7 Dharmasena 35-9-71-1 Gurusinha 13-3-39-0 Kalpage 12-5-31-0 Jayasuriya 2-0-12-0 A Ranatunga 9-1-22-0

Umpires: K Kanjee and Mahboob Shah (Pak)
TV Umpire: RC Strang; Referee: PL van der Merwe (SA)

Zimbabwe v Pakistan
31 January, 1,2,4 February 1995

Result: Zimbabwe won by an innings and 64 runs

Zimbabwe Innings

MH Dekker	c Rashid Latif b Aaqib Javed	2
GW Flower	not out	201
ADR Campbell	lbw b Wasim Akram	1
DL Houghton	c Aamer Sohail b Aaqib Javed	23
*+A Flower	c Wasim Akram b Kabir Khan	156
GJ Whittall	not out	113
SV Carlisle		
PA Strang		
HH Streak		
DH Brain		
HK Olonga		
	(b 4, lb 19, w 3, nb 22)	48
	(4 wickets declared)	544

Bowling: Wasim Akram 39.5-12-95-1 Aaqib Javed 34.1-8-73-2 Kabir Khan 35.5-142-1 Saleem Malik 9-0-42-0 Akram Raza 34-6-112-0 Asif Mujtaba 7-0-30-0 Aamer Sohail 6-1-27-0

Pakistan Innings

Aamer Sohail	c Houghton b Brain	61	c Campbell b Brain	5
Saeed Anwar	c A Flower b Olonga	8	lbw b Whittall	7
Akram Raza	c Whittall b Streak	19	not out	4
Asif Mujtaba	c Carlisle b Streak	2	b Brain	4
*Saleem Malik	c Carlisle b Whittall	32	c A Flower b Brain	6
Ijaz Ahmed	c GW Flower b Streak	65	b Brain b Streak	8
+Rashid Latif	c Campbell b Whittall	6	c Houghton b Whittall	38
Inzamam-ul-Haq	c GW Flower b Streak	71	c A Flower b Whittall	65
Wasim Akram	c Carlisle b Streak	27	c Dekker b Strang	19
Kabir Khan	not out	2	b Streak	0
Aaqib Javed	lbw b Streak	0	b Streak	2
	(b 3, lb 4, w 9, nb 13)	29	(w 2, nb 6)	8
	(all out)	322	(all out)	158

Bowling: Streak 39-11-90-6 Brain 27-4-94-1 Olonga 10-0-27-1 Whittall 29-10-49-2 Strang 15-5-45-0 Dekker 4-1-10-0
Brain 16-4-50-3 Streak 11-5-15-3 Strang 19-3-35-1 Whittall 16-3-58-3

Umpires: MJ Kitchen (Eng) and ID Robinson
TV Umpire: QJ Goosen; Referee: JL Hendriks (WI)

Zimbabwe v Pakistan
15,16,18,19 February 1995

Result: Pakistan won by 99 runs

Pakistan Innings

Aamer Sohail	c PA Strang b Streak	21	c GW Flower b Whittall	19
Shakeel Ahmed jnr	c A Flower b Whittall	29	c A Flower b BC Strang	33
Saeed Anwar	c Butchart b Streak	4	c Carlisle b Streak	26
*Saleem Malik	c GW Flower b Streak	20	c Carlisle b Whittall	5
Ijaz Ahmed	lbw b Streak	41	c Whittall b Streak	55
Inzamam-ul-Haq	c PA Strang b Brain	101	c GW Flower b Whittall	83
+Rashid Latif	c PA Strang b BC Strang	6	c A Flower b Streak	6
Wasim Akram	b BC Strang	0	c Campbell b Brain	4
Manzoor Elahi	c Streak b BC Strang	0	c A Flower b Streak	0
Aaqib Javed	run out	0	c A Flower b Brain	3
Aamer Nazir	not out	0	not out	0
	(lb 3, w 3, nb 3)	9	(lb 3, w 3, nb 10)	16
	(all out)	231	(all out)	250

Bowling: Streak 18.4-4-53-4 Brain 12.3-1-48-1 BC Strang 32-15-43-3 Whittall 18-3-73-1 Butchart 3-0-11-0
Streak 18-5-52-4 Brain 16.1-2-61-2 Whittall 22-3-66-3 BC Strang 26-16-27-1 PA Strang 13-3-41-0

Zimbabwe Innings

GW Flower	b Aamer Nazir	6	b Aamer Nazir	2
SV Carlisle	c Saleem Malik b Aaqib Javed	31	b Aamer Nazir	0
ADR Campbell	c Manzoor Elahi b Aamer Nazir	14	c Rashid Latif b Aamer Nazir	18
DL Houghton	c Rashid Latif b Wasim Akram	19	c Rashid Latif b Aamer Nazir	5
*+A Flower	c Aaqib Javed b Manzoor Elahi	37	c Aamer Nazir b Aaqib Javed	35
GJ Whittall	b Aaqib Javed	34	c Shakeel Ahmed b Wasim Akram	2
IP Butchart	c Inzamam-ul-Haq b Wasim Akram	15	c & b Aamer Nazir	8
PA Strang	c Aamer Sohail b Aamer Nazir	28	c Ijaz Ahmed b Aaqib Javed	5
HH Streak	lbw b Aaqib Javed	0	not out	30
DH Brain	not out	22	c Inzamam-ul-Haq b Wasim Akram	4
BC Strang	c Inzamam-ul-Haq b Aaqib Javed	6	c Shakeel Ahmed b Aaqib Javed	0
	(lb 4, w 1, nb 26)	31	(b 5, lb 5, nb 16)	26
	(all out)	243	(all out)	139

Bowling: Wasim Akram 28-2-90-2 Aaqib Javed 25-5-64-4 Aamer Nazir 13-3-50-3 Manzoor Elahi 10-3-28-1 Aamer Sohail 2-0-7-0
Wasim Akram 20-1-45-2 Aamer Nazir 19-3-46-5 Aaqib Javed 17.4-3-26-2 Manzoor Elahi 3-0-12-1

Umpires: SG Randell (Aus) and ID Robinson
TV Umpire: MA Esat; Referee: JL Hendriks (WI)

Zimbabwe v South Africa
13,14,15,16 October 1995

Result: South Africa won by 7 wickets

Zimbabwe Innings

MH Dekker	c Hudson b Donald	1	c Hudson b Schultz	24
GW Flower	c Richardson b Donald	24	c McMillan b Donald	5
*+A Flower	b Schultz	7	c Richardson b Donald	63
DL Houghton	c Richardson b Schultz	5	c Matthews b Donald	30
ADR Campbell	c Richardson b Schultz	0	c Schultz b McMillan	28
GJ Whittall	c Richardson b Matthews	29	lbw b Donald	38
CB Wishart	c Kirsten b Symcox	24	b Donald	13
PA Strang	b Matthews	0	c Richardson b Donald	37
HH Streak	c McMillan b Donald	53	c Cronje b Donald	0
BC Strang	lbw b Schultz	0	not out	25
ACI Lock	not out	8	b Donald	0
	(lb 10, w 5, nb 4)	19	(lb 10, w 1, nb 9)	20
	(all out)	170	(all out)	283

Bowling: Donald 17.1-3-42-3 Schultz 21-7-54-4 Matthews 13-5-30-2 McMillan 3-0-13-0 Symcox 11-5-21-1
Donald 33-12-71-8 Schultz 24-7-72-1 Symcox 11-3-22-0 Matthews 20-7-52-0 McMillan 15-3-53-1 Cronje 1-0-3-0

South Africa Innings

AC Hudson	b BC Strang	135	c BC Strang b Lock	4
G Kirsten	lbw b Streak	1	c A Flower b Lock	13
*WJ Cronje	c Houghton b Streak	5	not out	56
DJ Cullinan	c Whittall b Lock	11		
CR Matthews	c GW Flower b BC Strang	10		
JN Rhodes	c A Flower b BC Strang	15	b Streak	6
BM McMillan	not out	98	not out	25
+DJ Richardson	c BC Strang b Lock	13		
PL Symcox	c Houghton b Lock	4		
AA Donald	b BC Strang	33		
BN Schultz	lbw b BC Strang	0		
	(b 9, lb 6, w 3, nb 3)	21	(lb 2, w 2)	4
	(all out)	346	(3 wickets)	108

Bowling: Streak 26-6-79-2 Lock 17-4-68-3 BC Strang 32-4-101-5 PA Strang 23-2-58-0 Whittall 2-0-11-0 GW Flower 3-1-14-0
Streak 9-2-24-1 Lock 13-1-37-2 BC Strang 12-6-18-0 PA Strang 4-0-27-0

Umpires: DR Shepherd (Eng) and RB Tiffin
TV Umpire: ID Robinson; Referee: BN Jarman (Aus)

Zimbabwe v England
26,27,28,29,30 December 1996

Result: Match drawn

England Innings

NV Knight	c A Flower b Olonga	15	c Campbell b Strang	30
*MA Atherton	c Campbell b Whittall	13	c Campbell b Streak	1
+AJ Stewart	c GW Flower b Streak	19	not out	101
N Hussain	c A Flower b Streak	11	c Houghton b Strang	6
GP Thorpe	c Dekker b Streak	5	not out	50
JP Crawley	not out	47		
C White	c Campbell b Whittall	9		
RDB Croft	c GW Flower b Whittall	14		
D Gough	b Strang	2		
AD Mullally	c & b Whittall	0		
PCR Tufnell	b Streak	9		
	(b 1, lb 5, w 1, nb 5)	12	(lb 5, w 1, nb 1)	7
	(all out)	156	(3 wickets)	195

Bowling: Streak 24.1-7-43-4 Brandes 16-6-35-0 Olonga 9-1-23-1 Whittall 16-5-18-4 Strang 18-7-31-1
Streak 18-5-47-1 Brandes 21-6-45-0 Olonga 7-0-31-0 Whittall 14-6-16-0 Strang 26-6-42-2 GW Flower 7-2-9-0

Zimbabwe Innings

GW Flower	c Crawley b Gough	73
MH Dekker	c Stewart b Mullally	2
*ADR Campbell	c Thorpe b White	22
DL Houghton	c Stewart b Gough	29
+A Flower	lbw b Gough	6
AC Waller	lbw b Tufnell	4
GJ Whittall	b Gough	1
PA Strang	not out	47
HH Streak	c Crawley b Croft	7
EA Brandes	c Gough b Croft	9
HK Olonga	c Hussain b Croft	0
	(lb 8, w 1, nb 6)	15
	(all out)	215

Bowling: Mullally 23-7-32-1 Gough 26-10-40-4 Croft 15-2-39-3 White 16-4-41-1 Tufnell 25-3-55-1

Umpires: KT Francis (SL) and RB Tiffin
TV Umpire: ID Robinson; Referee: Hanumant Singh (Ind)

Zimbabwe v New Zealand
18,19,20,21,22 September 1997

Result: Match drawn

Zimbabwe Innings

GJ Rennie	c Fleming b Cairns	23	c Harris b O'Connor	57
GW Flower	c Parore b Cairns	104	c Fleming b O'Connor	151
+A Flower	c Spearman b Cairns	8	c Parore b O'Connor	20
GJ Whittall	c Fleming b O'Connor	33	run out (O'Connor)	4
*ADR Campbell	c Pocock b Astle	18	c Fleming b Davis	21
DL Houghton	lbw b Davis	23	c Davis b Astle	1
PA Strang	c Fleming b Davis	42	c Horne b Davis	17
HH Streak	c Fleming b Cairns	0	run out (Harris)	0
JA Rennie	c Fleming b Davis	22	c & b Astle	16
BC Strang	lbw b Cairns	1	not out	4
AG Huckle	not out	0		
	(b 1, lb 5, w 4, nb 14)	24	(lb 12, nb 8)	20
	(all out)	298	(9 wickets declared)	311

Bowling: O'Connor 26-1-104-1 Davis 20-1-57-3 Cairns 28.1-9-50-5 Astle 23-12-40-1 Vettori 4-0-14-0 Harris 13-5-27-0
O'Connor 26-3-73-3 Davis 13-2-45-2 Cairns 9-0-44-0 Vettori 13-2-40-0 Harris 5-3-11-0 Astle 25.5-2-86-2

Innings

GJ Rennie	c Fleming b Cairns	23
GW Flower	c Parore b Cairns	104
+A Flower	c Spearman b Cairns	8
GJ Whittall	c Fleming b O'Connor	33
*ADR Campbell	c Pocock b Astle	18
DL Houghton	lbw b Davis	23
PA Strang	c Fleming b Davis	42
HH Streak	c Fleming b Cairns	0
JA Rennie	c Fleming b Davis	22
BC Strang	lbw b Cairns	1
AG Huckle	not out	0
	(b 1, lb 5, w 4, nb 14)	24
	(all out)	298

Bowling: O'Connor 26-1-104-1 Davis 20-1-57-3 Cairns 28.1-9-50-5 Astle 23-12-40-1 Vettori 4-0-14-0 Harris 13-5-27-0

Umpires: BC Cooray (SL) and ID Robinson
TV Umpire: GR Evans; Referee: S Wettimuny (SL)

Zimbabwe v Pakistan
21,22,23,24,25 March 1998

Result: Pakistan won by 3 wickets

Zimbabwe Innings

GW Flower	c Rashid Latif b Azhar Mahmood	39	lbw b Wasim Akram	6
GJ Rennie	c Rashid Latif b Azhar Mahmood	13	c Yousuf Youhana b Waqar Younis	0
MW Goodwin	c Inzamam-ul-Haq b Mushtaq Ahmed	53	c Inzamam-ul-Haq b Waqar Younis	81
*ADR Campbell	c Yousuf Youhana b Mushtaq Ahmed	23	lbw b Azhar Mahmood	14
+A Flower	lbw b Waqar Younis	1	c Inzamam-ul-Haq b Mushtaq Ahmed	49
GJ Whittall	c Inzamam-ul-Haq b Wasim Akram	62	c Rashid Latif b Azhar Mahmood	15
TN Madondo	run out (Yousuf Youhana)	0	c Rashid Latif b Azhar Mahmood	2
HH Streak	c Mohammad Wasim b Waqar Younis	6	not out	37
BC Strang	c & b Waqar Younis	53	c Yousuf Youhana b Mushtaq Ahmed	21
AG Huckle	b Waqar Younis	0	b Wasim Akram	0
M Mbangwa	not out	2	lbw b Wasim Akram	3
	(b 6, lb 14, w 1, nb 4)	25	(b 13, lb 15, nb 12)	40
	(all out)	277	(all out)	268

Bowling: Wasim Akram 20.5-6-67-1 Waqar Younis 20-8-47-4 Mushtaq Ahmed 20-2-74-2 Azhar Mahmood 22-6-69-2
Wasim Akram 33-8-70-3 Waqar Younis 25-3-60-2 Azhar Mahmood 16-7-26-3 Mushtaq Ahmed 37-6-84-2

Pakistan Innings

Saeed Anwar	lbw b Whittall	15	c sub (AR Whittall) b Whittall	65
Ali Naqvi	c A Flower b Whittall	13	c A Flower b Huckle	8
Mohammad Wasim	c Mbangwa b Whittall	192	run out (Mbangwa)	8
Inzamam-ul-Haq	c & b Strang	13	st A Flower b Huckle	10
Yousuf Youhana	c A Flower b Mbangwa	9	c Goodwin b Whittall	52
Moin Khan	b Strang	12	c Campbell b Streak	21
Azhar Mahmood	c Whittall b Mbangwa	20	c Campbell b Streak	9
Wasim Akram	c Rennie b Mbangwa	0	not out	12
*+Rashid Latif	c sub (AR Whittall) b Strang	4	not out	1
Mushtaq Ahmed	c Campbell b Streak	57		
Waqar Younis	not out	8		
	(lb 8, w 1, nb 2)	11	(b 2, lb 3, nb 1)	6
	(all out)	354	(7 wickets)	192

Bowling: Streak 31-8-83-1 Mbangwa 33-12-56-3 Strang 28-10-65-3 Whittall 32.5-4-78-3 Huckle 21-7-55-0 Goodwin 2-0-9-0
Streak 13-5-40-2 Whittall 15-4-35-2 Mbangwa 2-0-11-0 Huckle 18.5-1-81-2 Strang 5-0-20-0

Umpires: SG Randell (Aus) and RB Tiffin
TV Umpire: QJ Goosen; Referee: GT Dowling (NZ)

Zimbabwe v India
7,8,9,10 October 1998

Result: Zimbabwe won by 61 runs

Zimbabwe Innings

CB Wishart	c Harbhajan Singh b Ganguly	21	c & b Kumble	63
GJ Rennie	c sub (DS Mohanty) b Agarkar	47	c Singh b Harbhajan Singh	84
MW Goodwin	lbw b Srinath	42	c & b Kumble	44
*ADR Campbell	c Dravid b Srinath	0	c Azharuddin b Harbhajan Singh	25
+A Flower	c Singh b Srinath	30	not out	41
NC Johnson	c Singh b Kumble	4	c Singh b Kumble	1
CN Evans	c Mongia b Harbhajan Singh	11	lbw b Kumble	4
HH Streak	c Singh b Harbhajan Singh	8	c Dravid b Agarkar	3
HK Olonga	lbw b Kumble	5	c Azharuddin b Harbhajan Singh	5
AG Huckle	not out	28	lbw b Srinath	1
M Mbangwa	st Mongia b Kumble	2	b Srinath	0
	(lb 1, w 2, nb 20)	23	(b 1, lb 12, nb 9)	22
	(all out)	221	(all out)	293

Bowling: Srinath 21-3-59-3 Agarkar 16-3-40-1 Ganguly 5-1-21-1 Singh 6-2-16-0 Harbhajan Singh 15-2-42-2 Kumble 17.4-3-42-3
Srinath 23.3-7-43-2 Agarkar 18-2-60-1 Ganguly 4-1-10-0 Kumble 36-4-87-4 Harbhajan Singh 20-5-64-3 Singh 4-2-16-0

India Innings

+NR Mongia	b Olonga	1	c Wishart b Olonga	0
NS Sidhu	c Flower b Olonga	6	c Johnson b Streak	0
A Kumble	b Streak	29	c Goodwin b Johnson	12
R Dravid	c Johnson b Mbangwa	118	c Flower b Mbangwa	44
SR Tendulkar	c Campbell b Johnson	34	c Flower b Johnson	7
*M Azharuddin	c Johnson b Olonga	1	c Campbell b Streak	7
SC Ganguly	lbw b Olonga	47	lbw b Huckle	36
RR Singh	lbw b Olonga	15	lbw b Johnson	12
AB Agarkar	c Flower b Streak	4	c Olonga b Mbangwa	5
J Srinath	c sub (AR Whittall) b Streak	6	run out (Rennie/Flower)	23
Harbhajan Singh	not out	0	not out	15
	(lb 4, w 4, nb 11)	19	(lb 3, w 1, nb 8)	12
	(all out)	280	(all out)	173

Bowling: Streak 29-9-62-3 Olonga 26-7-70-5 Johnson 18-5-64-1 Huckle 15-2-39-0 Mbangwa 14.2-4-28-1 Evans 3-0-8-0 Goodwin 2-0-5-0
Olonga 10-1-40-1 Streak 14-2-49-2 Johnson 14.4-5-41-3 Mbangwa 12-6-16-2 Huckle 6-0-24-1

Umpires: RE Koertzen (SA) and ID Robinson
TV Umpire: KC Barbour; Referee: AC Smith (Eng)

Zimbabwe v Australia
14,15,16,17 October 1999

Result: Australia won by 10 wickets

Zimbabwe Innings

GJ Rennie	c Ponting b McGrath	18	c McGrath b Miller	23
GW Flower	c Ponting b Fleming	1	lbw b McGrath	32
MW Goodwin	run out (Blewett/Langer)	0	c SR Waugh b Warne	91
*ADR Campbell	c Slater b Fleming	5	run out (Slater/Healy)	1
+A Flower	c ME Waugh b McGrath	28	c Healy b McGrath	0
NC Johnson	c ME Waugh b McGrath	75	c ME Waugh b McGrath	5
TR Gripper	lbw b Warne	4	lbw b Miller	60
HH Streak	c ME Waugh b Warne	3	lbw b Warne	0
GJ Whittall	c Healy b Warne	27	c ME Waugh b Warne	2
BC Strang	run out (Blewett)	17	c Langer b Miller	0
HK Olonga	not out	0	not out	0
	(b 2, lb 4, nb 10)	16	(b 9, lb 2, w 1, nb 6)	18
	(all out)	194	(all out)	232

Bowling: McGrath 23-7-44-3 Fleming 15-6-22-2 Miller 19-6-36-0 Warne 23-2-69-3 Ponting 1-1-0-0 SR Waugh 4-1-17-0
McGrath 31-12-46-3 Fleming 21-6-31-0 Miller 34-10-66-3 Ponting 1-1-0-0 Warne 30.1-11-68-3 Blewett 5-1-10-0

Australia Innings

MJ Slater	c A Flower b Strang	4	not out	0
GS Blewett	c Campbell b Streak	1	not out	4
JL Langer	run out (Olonga)	44		
ME Waugh	c & b GW Flower	90		
*SR Waugh	not out	151		
RT Ponting	c Johnson b Streak	31		
+IA Healy	c A Flower b Strang	5		
SK Warne	c A Flower b Streak	6		
DW Fleming	lbw b Streak	65		
CR Miller	c Johnson b Streak	2		
GD McGrath	c Johnson b Whittall	13		
	(lb 5, w 4, nb 1)	10	(w 1)	1
	(all out)	422	(0 wickets)	5

Bowling: Olonga 17-1-83-0 Streak 34-8-93-5 Strang 44-14-96-2 Johnson 2-0-14-0 Whittall 21.4-3-74-1 GW Flower 18-3-38-1 Gripper 3-0-19-0
Strang 0.4-0-5-0

Umpires: ID Robinson and G Sharp (Eng)
TV Umpire: KC Barbour; Referee: GR Viswanath (Ind)

Harare Sports Club

Zimbabwe v South Africa
11,12,13,14 November 1999

Result: South Africa won by an innings and 219 runs

Zimbabwe Innings

GW Flower	c Kallis b Klusener	5	b Donald	0
TR Gripper	b Pollock	1	c Kallis b Cronje	18
MW Goodwin	c Cronje b Pollock	17	lbw b Pollock	7
NC Johnson	c Boucher b Pollock	20	c Boucher b Klusener	9
*+A Flower	c Boucher b Pollock	8	b Donald	14
ADR Campbell	c Pollock b Cronje	15	c Rhodes b Adams	25
GJ Rennie	c Cullinan b Klusener	11	c Donald b Adams	34
GJ Whittall	c Pollock b Klusener	3	c Dippenaar b Pollock	17
BC Strang	lbw b Cronje	11	lbw b Pollock	0
HK Olonga	c Boucher b Cronje	0	not out	4
M Mbangwa	not out	1	lbw b Adams	3
	(lb 7, nb 3)	10	(lb 4, w 2, nb 4)	10
	(all out)	102	(all out)	141

Bowling: Donald 10-5-10-0 Pollock 17-7-32-4 Klusener 12-3-39-3 Cronje 7.5-2-14-3
Donald 9-2-25-2 Pollock 16-9-23-3 Klusener 9-1-29-1 Cronje 6-1-20-1 Adams 10.5-0-40-3

South Africa Innings

AM Bacher	c A Flower b Strang	8
HH Dippenaar	c Johnson b Olonga	33
JH Kallis	lbw b Strang	115
DJ Cullinan	c A Flower b Strang	0
*WJ Cronje	c Rennie b Olonga	58
+MV Boucher	c Goodwin b Gripper	125
JN Rhodes	c GW Flower b Mbangwa	4
L Klusener	c Olonga b Mbangwa	25
SM Pollock	c Campbell b Olonga	61
AA Donald	not out	17
PR Adams	not out	3
	(lb 3, nb 10)	13
	(9 wickets declared)	462

Bowling: Olonga 33-7-107-3 Strang 38-10-92-3 Mbangwa 28-6-91-2 Whittall 27-8-78-0 GW Flower 18-3-52-0 Goodwin 2-0-11-0 Gripper 8-1-28-1

Umpires: DB Hair (Aus) and RB Tiffin
TV Umpire: GR Evans; Referee: JL Hendriks (WI)

Zimbabwe v Sri Lanka
26,27,28,29,30 November 1999

Result: Sri Lanka won by 6 wickets

Zimbabwe Innings

GW Flower	b Muralitharan	19	c Kaluwitharana b Muralitharan	13
TR Gripper	lbw b Zoysa	0	c Arnold b Vaas	4
MW Goodwin	c Kaluwitharana b Zoysa	0	run out (de Saram)	48
NC Johnson	lbw b Zoysa	0	c Atapattu b Zoysa	14
*+A Flower	lbw b Vaas	74	c Atapattu b Jayasuriya	129
ADR Campbell	lbw b Wickramasinghe	36	lbw b Muralitharan	5
GJ Whittall	b Muralitharan	1	not out	53
GB Brent	c Kaluwitharana b Vaas	3	lbw b Jayasuriya	0
BC Strang	c Dilshan b Vaas	4	c Jayawardene b Jayasuriya	3
HK Olonga	not out	10	lbw b Jayasuriya	0
EZ Matambanadzo	c Jayawardene b Muralitharan	6	run out (de Saram)	0
	(b 2, lb 8, nb 11)	21	(b 3, lb 15, nb 5)	23
	(all out)	174	(all out)	292

Bowling: Vaas 27-8-50-3 Zoysa 13-4-22-3 Wickramasinghe 18-7-31-1 Muralitharan 29.5-11-44-3 Jayasuriya 3-1-7-0 Arnold 5-2-10-0
Vaas 35-7-78-1 Zoysa 11-2-24-1 Wickramasinghe 28-10-51-0 Muralitharan 43-15-71-2 Jayasuriya 12.4-3-40-4 Arnold 1-0-3-0 Jayawardene 4-2-7-0

Sri Lanka Innings

MS Atapattu	run out (Johnson/Campbell)	37	run out (Goodwin)	6
*ST Jayasuriya	c A Flower b Olonga	6	c Gripper b Brent	7
RP Arnold	c Campbell b Strang	49	c A Flower b Brent	1
DPMD Jayawardene	c A Flower b Strang	91	not out	6
TM Dilshan	not out	163	lbw b Brent	0
+RS Kaluwitharana	run out (Olonga)	19	not out	14
SI de Saram	c Goodwin b Matambanadzo	17		
WPUJC Vaas	c Gripper b Matambanadzo	5		
GP Wickramasinghe	c A Flower b Whittall	7		
M Muralitharan	c GW Flower b Olonga	5		
DNT Zoysa	c Gripper b GW Flower	5		
	(b 1, lb 10, w 7, nb 10)	28	(lb 1, w 2, nb 1)	4
	(all out)	432	(4 wickets)	38

Bowling: Olonga 30-5-88-2 Brent 22-4-68-0 Matambanadzo 31-6-95-2 Strang 37-13-70-2 Gripper 1-0-6-0 Whittall 19-2-60-1 GW Flower 9.3-2-34-1
Olonga 5-1-14-0 Brent 7.2-3-21-3 Strang 3-1-2-0

Umpires: SA Bucknor (WI) and RB Tiffin
TV Umpire: ID Robinson; Referee: JL Hendriks (WI)

Zimbabwe v Sri Lanka
4,5,6,7,8 December 1999

Result: Match drawn

Zimbabwe Innings

GW Flower	c Dilshan b Pushpakumara	13	c Dilshan b Vaas	13
CB Wishart	lbw b Vaas	1	b Vaas	9
MW Goodwin	b Pushpakumara	11	c Jayawardene b Muralitharan	38
NC Johnson	lbw b Wickramasinghe	70	c Dilshan b Wickramasinghe	9
*+A Flower	c Arnold b Vaas	14	not out	70
ADR Campbell	lbw b Pushpakumara	9	c Jayawardene b Vaas	27
GJ Whittall	c Arnold b Pushpakumara	37	c Arnold b Muralitharan	9
RW Price	lbw b Pushpakumara	2	run out (Jayasuriya/Muralitharan)	4
EA Brandes	b Vaas	9	not out	1
BC Strang	c Atapattu b Vaas	28		
HK Olonga	not out	3		
	(lb 4, w 2, nb 15)	21	(b 3, lb 5, nb 9)	17
	(all out)	218	(7 wickets declared)	197

Bowling: Vaas 29.4-10-56-4 Pushpakumara 25-5-56-5 Wickramasinghe 16-6-41-1 Muralitharan 24-6-51-0 Jayasuriya 4-1-10-0
Vaas 22-5-48-3 Pushpakumara 21-5-39-0 Wickramasinghe 21-6-30-1 Jayawardene 2-0-12-0 Muralitharan 35-12-52-2 Jayasuriya 8-4-8-0

Sri Lanka Innings

MS Atapattu	c Johnson b Olonga	0	c A Flower b Brandes	6
RP Arnold	not out	104	not out	14
DPMD Jayawardene	c Goodwin b Brandes	2		
*ST Jayasuriya	c A Flower b Brandes	4	not out	16
TM Dilshan	c A Flower b Strang	37		
+RS Kaluwitharana	c A Flower b Whittall	7		
SI de Saram	c GW Flower b Whittall	38		
WPUJC Vaas	c Campbell b Brandes	0		
KR Pushpakumara	lbw b Strang	7		
GP Wickramasinghe	c A Flower b Olonga	18		
M Muralitharan	b Olonga	5		
	(lb 2, w 2, nb 5)	9		0
	(all out)	231	(1 wicket)	36

Bowling: Olonga 22.4-2-54-3 Brandes 17-5-45-3 Strang 24-8-71-2 Whittall 17-9-37-2 Price 8-3-22-0
Olonga 4-1-11-0 Brandes 4-0-20-1 Strang 1-0-5-0

Umpires: ID Robinson and S Venkataraghavan (Ind)
TV Umpire: GR Evans; Referee: JL Hendriks (WI)

Zimbabwe v New Zealand
19,20,21,22,23 September 2000

Result: New Zealand won by 8 wickets

New Zealand Innings

MH Richardson	lbw b Nkala	99		
CM Spearman	c A Flower b Olonga	2	c Rennie b Streak	2
MS Sinclair	c Carlisle b Olonga	44	not out	35
*SP Fleming	c Campbell b Mbangwa	9		
NJ Astle	run out (Mbangwa/A Flower)	86		
CD McMillan	lbw b Mbangwa	15		
CL Cairns	st A Flower b Strang	124	not out	19
+AC Parore	c A Flower b Olonga	4	c Carlisle b Streak	13
DJ Nash	c GW Flower b Strang	62		
PJ Wiseman	not out	1		
SB O'Connor	c Whittall b GW Flower	2		
	(lb 3, w 2, nb 12)	17	(lb 2, w 1, nb 2)	5
	(all out)	465	(2 wickets)	74

Bowling: Olonga 27-5-115-3 Streak 29-6-74-0 Nkala 15-0-60-1 Mbangwa 28-10-58-2 Strang 38-11-80-2 GW Flower 20.3-6-59-1 Rennie 3-0-16-0
Streak 8-2-33-2 Nkala 3-0-17-0 Mbangwa 4.2-0-22-0

Zimbabwe innings

GW Flower	c Parore b Astle	49	run out (Wiseman/Astle)	10
GJ Rennie	c Spearman b Cairns	4	c Spearman b O'Connor	1
SV Carlisle	c Sinclair b Cairns	31	c Fleming b Astle	20
ADR Campbell	c Fleming b O'Connor	0	run out (Sinclair/Parore)	10
+A Flower	lbw b McMillan	48	c Sinclair b O'Connor	65
GJ Whittall	c Parore b Astle	9	not out	188
*HH Streak	c Wiseman b O'Connor	8	lbw b Cairns	54
ML Nkala	c Parore b McMillan	0	lbw b O'Connor	0
PA Strang	c Parore b O'Connor	5	b Cairns	8
HK Olonga	c Parore b Nash	4	lbw b O'Connor	8
M Mbangwa	not out	0	run out (Nash)	5
	(b 3, lb 3, w 1, nb 1)	8	(b 4, lb 4, nb 1)	9
	(all out)	166	(all out)	370

Bowling: Cairns 17.1-7-33-2 O'Connor 28-9-43-3 Nash 17-11-25-1 McMillan 12.5-2-29-2 Astle 14-9-22-2 Wiseman 3-0-8-0
O'Connor 45-17-73-4 Nash 17.3-8-28-0 McMillan 20-4-53-0 Astle 36-16-73-1 Cairns 33-7-80-2 Wiseman 27-11-55-0

Umpires: ID Robinson and DR Shepherd
TV umpire: KC Barbour. Referee: CW Smith

Zimbabwe v Bangladesh
26,27,28,29,30 April 2001

Result: Zimbabwe won by 8 wickets

Bangladesh Innings

Javed Omar	c Blignaut b Streak	1	c GW Flower b Price	43
+Mehrab Hossain	c Carlisle b Price	71	c Blignaut b Watambwa	0
Al Sahariar	c GW Flower b Streak	11	c Streak b Watambwa	68
Aminul Islam	c Campbell b Price	12	lbw b Price	2
Habibul Bashar	st A Flower b Price	64	c A Flower b Streak	76
Akram Khan	c Campbell b Streak	44	c Campbell b Price	31
*Naimur Rahman	lbw b Price	16	run out (sub [GJ Rennie]/Watambwa)	36
Mushfiqur Rahman	c A Flower b Streak	2	not out	2
Enamul Haque	not out	20	c A Flower b Watambwa	3
Mohammad Sharif	c Carlisle b Watambwa	0	c Carlisle b Streak	0
Manjural Islam	c Campbell b Watambwa	0	c A Flower b Watambwa	0
	(lb 8, w 3, nb 2)	13	(lb 2, w 1, nb 2)	5
	(all out)	254	(all out)	266

Bowling: Blignaut 27-6-67-0 Streak 30-12-38-4 Watambwa 14.5-3-48-2 Nkala 19-11-22-0 Price 30-9-71-4
Streak 21-7-47-2 Watambwa 22-5-64-4 Blignaut 15-6-27-0 Price 30-9-94-3 GW Flower 6-0-13-0 Nkala 6-0-19-0

Zimbabwe Innings

GJ Whittall	run out (Sharif/Hossain)	59	b Enamul Haque	60
DD Ebrahim	c Akram Khan b Naimur Rahman	39	run out (Javed Omar/Mehrab Hossain)	10
SV Carlisle	c Habibul Bashar b Mohammad Sharif	21	not out	29
ADR Campbell	c Mushfiqur Rahman b Naimur Rahman	73	not out	0
+A Flower	run out (Javed Omar)	23		
GW Flower	c Mohammad Sharif b Enamul Haque	84		
*HH Streak	c Mehrab Hossain b Mohammad Sharif	87		
AM Blignaut	run out (Sharif/Hossain)	15		
ML Nkala	c Mushfiqur Rahman b Enamul Haque	7		
RW Price	not out	0		
BT Watambwa				
	(b 7, lb 6)	13	(lb 1)	1
	(9 wickets dec)	421	(2 wickets)	100

Bowling: Manjural Islam 34-9-113-0 Mohammad Sharif 28.4-6-108-2 Enamul Haque 46-15-94-2 Mushfiqur Rahman 11-1-33-0 Naimur Rahman 28-12-60-2
Manjural Islam 9-2-21-0 Mohammad Sharif 6-0-36-0 Enamul Haque 3-0-8-1 Mushfiqur Rahman 6-1-26-0 Naimur Rahman 0.3-0-8-0

Umpires: DB Cowie (NZ) and RB Tiffin
TV Umpire: GR Evans; Referee: B Warnapura (SL).

Zimbabwe v India
15,16,17,18 June 2001

Result: Zimbabwe won by 4 wickets

India Innings

SS Das	c A Flower b Blignaut	57	lbw b Streak	70
HK Badani	lbw b Watambwa	2	not out	16
VVS Laxman	c Blignaut b Streak	15	c Murphy b Friend	20
SR Tendulkar	b Streak	20	c GW Flower b Streak	69
*SC Ganguly	c Blignaut b Streak	9	lbw b Blignaut	0
R Dravid	not out	68	c A Flower b Blignaut	26
+SS Dighe	c GW Flower b Friend	20	c A Flower b Blignaut	4
AB Agarkar	c Blignaut b Friend	6	c A Flower b Streak	0
Harbhajan Singh	b Murphy	31	c Ebrahim b Blignaut	5
J Srinath	run out (Murphy)	0	c A Flower b Streak	3
A Nehra	c sub (PA Strang) b Murphy	0	b Blignaut	0
	(lb 2, w 6, nb 1)	9	(lb 9, w 12)	21
	(all out)	237	(all out)	234

Bowling: Watambwa 3.4-0-14-1 Streak 20-4-69-3 Friend 20.2-4-48-2 Blignaut 20-1-84-1 Murphy 9.2-3-17-2 GW Flower 1-0-3-0
Streak 27-12-46-4 Blignaut 31.5-14-74-5 Friend 22-4-47-1 Whittall 7-4-15-0 Murphy 10-1-42-0 GW Flower 1-0-1-0

Zimbabwe Innings

GJ Whittall	c Dravid b Nehra	0	c Dravid b Srinath	10
DD Ebrahim	lbw b Harbhajan Singh	49	c Badani b Harbhajan Singh	20
SV Carlisle	c Badani b Nehra	3	not out	62
ADR Campbell	b Nehra	8	lbw b Nehra	13
+A Flower	c Das b Harbhajan Singh	45	not out	8
GW Flower	c Laxman b Srinath	86	c Laxman b Agarkar	3
*HH Streak	b Tendulkar	40	c Dighe b Srinath	8
AM Blignaut	st Dighe b Harbhajan Singh	35	b Nehra	16
TJ Friend	b Nehra	15		
BA Murphy	b Harbhajan Singh	17		
BT Watambwa	not out	2		
	(b 4, lb 5, w 2, nb 4)	15	(b 1, lb 11, nb 5)	17
	(all out)	315	(6 wickets)	157

Bowling: Srinath 29.3-7-82-1 Nehra 24-6-72-4 Agarkar 24-7-62-0 Harbhajan Singh 26-5-71-4 Tendulkar 4-0-19-1
Nehra 13-0-45-2 Srinath 13-1-46-2 Harbhajan Singh 19-6-25-1 Agarkar 8-3-22-1 Tendulkar 1-0-7-0

Umpires: EAR de Silva (SL) and ID Robinson
TV Umpire: GR Evans; Referee: DT Lindsay (SA)

Zimbabwe v West Indies
27,28,29,30,31 July 2001

Result: Match Drawn

Zimbabwe Innings

DD Ebrahim	c Browne b King	19	c Browne b Stuart	12
ADR Campbell	lbw b Stuart	13	c Gayle b Hooper	65
H Masakadza	b Stuart	9	c Hooper b McGarrell	119
CB Wishart	lbw b McGarrell	8	run out (Browne)	93
GJ Whittall	c Ganga b Black	43	lbw b McGarrell	12
GW Flower	c Browne b McGarrell	0	c Chanderpaul b King	15
*HH Streak	lbw b McGarrell	6	not out	83
AM Blignaut	c Browne b McGarrell	0	b Stuart	92
+T Taibu	c King b Stuart	9	b Stuart	10
BC Strang	c Sarwan b Black	20	c Gayle b McGarrell	13
RW Price	not out	0		
	(lb 1, w 2, nb 1)	4	(b 11, lb 21, nb 17)	49
	(all out)	131	(9 wickets dec)	563

Bowling: King 16-6-39-1 Black 11.1-2-35-2 Stuart 13-2-33-3 McGarrell 17-7-23-4
King 27-7-80-1 Black 17-1-93-0 McGarrell 60-19-162-3 Stuart 32-9-99-3 Hooper 28-7-86-1 Samuels 3-0-11-0

West Indies Innings

D Ganga	c Taibu b Blignaut	43	c Strang b Streak	5
CH Gayle	lbw b Strang	6	not out	52
S Chanderpaul	c Taibu b Streak	74		
RR Sarwan	run out (Masakadza)	86	not out	31
*CL Hooper	c Streak b Strang	39		
MN Samuels	c Campbell b Price	39		
+CO Browne	c Taibu b Blignaut	13		
NC McGarrell	c sub (TJ Friend) b Strang	33		
CEL Stuart	lbw b Strang	1		
MI Black	b Price	6		
RD King	not out	2		
	(lb 2, w 2, nb 1)	5	(b 4, lb 5, w 1)	10
	(all out)	347	(1 wicket)	98

Bowling: Streak 22-6-75-1 Strang 32-13-83-4 Blignaut 16-2-92-2 Price 35.2-13-81-2 Flower 6-3-14-0
Streak 15.2-4-34-1 Blignaut 8-3-24-0 Strang 14-8-19-0 Price 8-3-9-0 Masakadza 1-0-3-0

Umpires: KC Barbour and AV Jayaprakash (Ind)
TV Umpire: QJ Goosen; Referee: DT Lindsay (SA)

Zimbabwe v South Africa
7,8,9,10,11 September 2001

Result: South Africa won by 9 wickets

South Africa Innings

HH Gibbs	b Friend	147		
G Kirsten	c A Flower b Hondo	220	not out	31
JH Kallis	not out	157	not out	42
ND McKenzie	c Hondo b Friend	52		
L Klusener	not out	8		
+MV Boucher				
HH Dippenaar			lbw b Friend	0
*SM Pollock				
CW Henderson				
M Ntini				
A Nel				
	(lb 2, w 6, nb 8)	16	(b 5, lb 1)	6
	(3 wickets dec)	600	(1 wicket)	79

Bowling: Streak 34-4-120-0 Friend 27-2-147-2 Hondo 18-0-87-1 Price 42-2-192-0 Whittall 12-2-34-0 GW Flower 6-0-18-0
Friend 7-0-44-1 Streak 4-2-10-0 Price 3.2-0-19-0 Hondo 1-1-0-0

Zimbabwe Innings

DD Ebrahim	st Boucher b Henderson	71	lbw b Pollock	0
ADR Campbell	c Boucher b Nel	0	b Kallis	7
H Masakadza	run out (McKenzie)	13	c Dippenaar b Henderson	85
CB Wishart	c Klusener b Kallis	0	c Klusener b Pollock	6
+A Flower	lbw b Pollock	142	not out	199
RW Price	c Kirsten b Nel	0	c McKenzie b Klusener	4
GW Flower	c Dippenaar b Nel	0	c Dippenaar b Ntini	16
GJ Whittall	b Kallis	16	lbw b Henderson	3
*HH Streak	lbw b Henderson	7	c Kallis b Pollock	19
TJ Friend	c Pollock b Nel	30	b Klusener	17
DT Hondo	not out	1	lbw b Nel	6
	(b 4, nb 2)	6	(b 10, lb 9, nb 10)	29
	(all out)	286	(all out)	391

Bowling: Pollock 22.3-5-62-1 Nel 16-6-53-4 Ntini 13-2-60-0 Kallis 12-1-39-2 Henderson 24-5-55-2 Klusener 3-0-13-0
Pollock 29-5-67-3 Nel 14.5-5-33-1 Kallis 21-5-52-1 Henderson 55-16-122-2 Ntini 23-10-48-1 Klusener 29-9-50-2

Umpires: DB Hair (Aus) and RB Tiffin
TV Umpire: QJ Goosen; Referee: Naushad Ali (Pak)

Zimbabwe v Pakistan
9,10,11,12 November 2002

Result: Pakistan won by 119 runs

Pakistan Innings

Taufeeq Umar	c A Flower b Blignaut	75	c Taibu b Blignaut	111
Saleem Elahi	c Campbell b Blignaut	2	c Campbell b Olonga	0
Younis Khan	c Ebrahim b Blignaut	40	c Campbell b Olonga	8
Inzamam-ul-Haq	c sub (MA Vermeulen) b Olonga	39	c GW Flower b Olonga	112
Yousuf Youhana	lbw b Price	63	c Taibu b Blignaut	0
Hasan Raza	c Campbell b Mahwire	46	c Blignaut b Price	11
+Kamran Akmal	b Price	0	b Price	38
Saqlain Mushtaq	c A Flower b Whittall	2	not out	29
*Waqar Younis	lbw b Blignaut	2	b Blignaut	0
Shoaib Akhtar	c GW Flower b Blignaut	1	c Taibu b Olonga	16
Mohammad Sami	not out	0	c GW Flower b Olonga	17
	(lb 2, w 4, nb 9)	15	(b 4, lb 3, w 11, nb 9)	27
	(all out)	285	(all out)	369

Bowling: Blignaut 21-4-79-5 Olonga 16-2-46-1 Mahwire 14.5-2-58-1 Price 16-4-56-2 Whittall 22-10-44-1
Blignaut 20-1-81-3 Olonga 17.5-1-93-5 Mahwire 14-4-60-0 Whittall 14-5-62-0 Price 24-5-66-2

Zimbabwe Innings

DD Ebrahim	c Inzamam-ul-Haq b Mohammad Sami	31	b Shoaib Akhtar	69
H Masakadza	c Kamran Akmal b Mohammad Sami	9	c Saleem Elahi b Shoaib Akhtar	0
*ADR Campbell	b Shoaib Akhtar	2	c Kamran Akmal b Mohammad Sami	30
GW Flower	lbw b Waqar Younis	31	c Kamran Akmal b Saqlain Mushtaq	69
A Flower	c Kamran Akmal b Mohammad Sami	29	c & b Shoaib Akhtar	67
GJ Whittall	b Shoaib Akhtar	7	c Younis Khan b Saqlain Mushtaq	2
+T Taibu	not out	51	lbw b Waqar Younis	28
AM Blignaut	c Hasan Raza b Mohammad Sami	50	c Younis Khan b Saqlain Mushtaq	12
NB Mahwire	c Younis Khan b Saqlain Mushtaq	4	lbw b Waqar Younis	3
RW Price	c Younis Khan b Saqlain Mushtaq	2	not out	5
HK Olonga	b Shoaib Akhtar	3	b Shoaib Akhtar	5
	(lb 1, w 2, nb 3)	6	(b 8, lb 6, w 1, nb 5)	20
	(all out)	225	(all out)	310

Bowling: Waqar Younis 14-3-58-1 Shoaib Akhtar 14.5-1-43-3 Mohammad Sami 19-3-53-4 Saqlain Mushtaq 19-5-70-2
Waqar Younis 16-1-73-2 Shoaib Akhtar 18.3-4-75-4 Mohammad Sami 15-3-50-1 Saqlain Mushtaq 31-5-98-3 Taufeeq Umar 1-1-0-0

Umpires: DL Orchard (SA) and S Venkataraghavan (Ind)
TV Umpire: ID Robinson; Referee: CH Lloyd (WI)

Bangabandhu National Stadium, Dhaka

Pakistan v India
1,2,3,4 January 1955

Result: Match drawn

Pakistan Innings

Hanif Mohammad	c Tamhane b Ghulam Ahmed	41	c Umrigar b Phadkar	14
Alimuddin	c Phadkar b Ghulam Ahmed	7	c sub b Gupte	51
Waqar Hasan	c & b Ghulam Ahmed	52	st Tamhane b Gupte	51
Maqsood Ahmed	c Tamhane b Ghulam Ahmed	11	c Mantri b Gupte	16
Wazir Mohammad	c Phadkar b Gupte	23	run out	0
+Imtiaz Ahmed	b Phadkar	54	c Umrigar b Gupte	5
*AH Kardar	b Ramchand	29	c Mantri b Phadkar	3
Shujauddin	st Tamhane b Mankad	25	run out	1
Fazal Mahmood	c Tamhane b Ramchand	0	not out	15
Mahmood Hussain	b Ghulam Ahmed	9	c Punjabi b Gupte	0
Khan Mohammad	not out	4	run out	0
	(lb 2)	2	(lb 2)	2
	(all out)	257	(all out)	158

Bowling: Phadkar 18-11-24-1 Ramchand 15-7-19-2 Gupte 46-14-79-1 Ghulam Ahmed 45-8-109-5 Mankad 12.2-3-24-1
Phadkar 28.2-11-57-2 Ramchand 19-10-30-0 Gupte 6-0-18-5 Mankad 18-6-34-0 Umrigar 15-8-17-0

India Innings

P Roy	b Mahmood Hussain	0	not out	67
PH Punjabi	b Khan Mohammad	26	lbw b Khan Mohammad	3
MK Mantri	b Mahmood Hussain	0	c Imtiaz Ahmed b Khan Mohammad	2
VL Manjrekar	b Khan Mohammad	18	not out	74
PR Umrigar	c Kardar b Mahmood Hussain	32		
GS Ramchand	c Imtiaz Ahmed b Mahmood Hussain	37		
DG Phadkar	c Imtiaz Ahmed b Mahmood Hussain	11		
*MH Mankad	c Imtiaz Ahmed b Mahmood Hussain	2		
+NS Tamhane	b Khan Mohammad	5		
Ghulam Ahmed	b Khan Mohammad	2		
SP Gupte	not out	1		
(b 7, lb 5, nb 2)	14 — (b 1)	1		
(all out)	148 — (2 wickets)	147		

Bowling: Fazal Mahmood 25-19-18-0 Mahmood Hussain 27-6-67-6 Khan Mohammad 26.5-12-42-4 Shujauddin 4-2-7-0
Fazal Mahmood 23-11-34-0 Mahmood Hussain 7-2-21-0 Khan Mohammad 12-5-18-2 Shujauddin 14-6-25-0 Maqsood Ahmed 3-1-4-0 Kardar 12-3-17-0 Hanif Mohammad 5-1-15-0 Alimuddin 5-0-12-0 Imtiaz Ahmed 1-1-0-0

Umpires: Daud Khan and Idris Beg

Pakistan v New Zealand
7,8,9,11,12 November 1955

Result: Match drawn

New Zealand Innings

JG Leggat	b Khan Mohammad	1	c Agha Saadat Ali b Fazal Mahmood	1
B Sutcliffe	b Fazal Mahmood	3	c Imtiaz Ahmed b Khan Mohammad	17
MB Poore	b Fazal Mahmood	0	c Agha Saadat Ali b Kardar	18
SN McGregor	b Khan Mohammad	7	c Imtiaz Ahmed b Zulfiqar Ahmed	4
JR Reid	c Imtiaz Ahmed b Khan Mohammad	9	b Kardar	12
NS Harford	c Imtiaz Ahmed b Fazal Mahmood	0	c Hanif Mohammad b Khan Mohammad	1
JW Guy	st Imtiaz Ahmed b Zulfiqar Ahmed	11	not out	8
AR MacGibbon	not out	29	not out	7
+EC Petrie	lbw b Khan Mohammad	6		
*HB Cave	c Agha Saadat Ali b Khan Mohammad	0		
AM Moir	c Shujauddin b Khan Mohammad	0		
	(lb 4)	4	(lb 1)	1
	(all out)	70	(6 wickets)	69

Bowling: Fazal Mahmood 20-7-34-3 Khan Mohammad 16.2-6-21-6 Zulfiqar Ahmed 3-1-11-1
Fazal Mahmood 6-3-12-1 Khan Mohammad 30-19-20-2 Zulfiqar Ahmed 16-8-13-1 Kardar 28-17-21-2 Shujauddin 9-8-1-0 Hanif Mohammad 1-0-1-0

Pakistan Innings

Alimuddin	b Reid	5
Hanif Mohammad	c Reid b Cave	103
Waqar Hasan	lbw b Reid	8
Shujauddin	c Guy b Cave	3
+Imtiaz Ahmed	b Cave	11
*AH Kardar	b MacGibbon	14
W Mathias	not out	41
Agha Saadat Ali	not out	8
Fazal Mahmood		
Zulfiqar Ahmed		
Khan Mohammad		
	(lb 1, nb 1)	2
	(6 wickets declared)	195

Bowling: MacGibbon 20-4-64-1 Cave 20-4-45-3 Reid 30-10-67-2 Moir 6-1-17-0

Umpires: Daud Khan and Idris Beg

Pakistan v West Indies
6,7,8 March 1959

Result: Pakistan won by 41 runs

Pakistan Innings

Ijaz Butt	b Hall	2	b Ramadhin	21
Alimuddin	c & b Hall	6	c Smith b Atkinson	0
Saeed Ahmed	c Alexander b Hall	6	lbw b Ramadhin	22
+Imtiaz Ahmed	b Ramadhin	3	c Smith b Atkinson	4
Wazir Mohammad	b Hall	1	c Alexander b Atkinson	4
W Mathias	c Atkinson b Gibbs	64	b Atkinson	45
Shujauddin	b Atkinson	26	b Hall	17
*Fazal Mahmood	c Alexander b Ramadhin	12	not out	7
Nasim-ul-Ghani	run out	7	b Hall	0
Mahmood Hussain	b Ramadhin	4	b Hall	2
Haseeb Ahsan	not out	4	b Hall	0
	(b 5, lb 2, nb 3)	10	(b 9, lb 4, w 1, nb 8)	22
	(all out)	145	(all out)	144

Bowling: Hall 13-5-28-4 Atkinson 10-2-22-1 Ramadhin 23.3-6-45-3 Gibbs 21-8-33-1 Sobers 8-4-7-0
Hall 16.5-2-49-4 Atkinson 22-9-42-4 Ramadhin 15-9-10-2 Gibbs 6-0-17-0 Sobers 3-2-4-0

West Indies Innings

JKC Holt	b Mahmood Hussain	4	c Imtiaz Ahmed b Fazal Mahmood	5
RB Kanhai	c Wazir Mohammad b Fazal Mahmood	4	lbw b Fazal Mahmood	8
GS Sobers	lbw b Fazal Mahmood	29	c Fazal Mahmood b Mahmood Hussain	45
*+FCM Alexander	st Imtiaz Ahmed b Nasim-ul-Ghani	14	c Imtiaz Ahmed b Fazal Mahmood	18
BF Butcher	c Shujauddin b Fazal Mahmood	11	b Fazal Mahmood	8
OG Smith	c Nasim-ul-Ghani b Fazal Mahmood	0	b Fazal Mahmood	39
JS Solomon	c Imtiaz Ahmed b Nasim-ul-Ghani	0	c Mahmood Hussain b Fazal Mahmood	8
ES Atkinson	c Mathias b Fazal Mahmood	0	lbw b Mahmood Hussain	20
LR Gibbs	st Imtiaz Ahmed b Nasim-ul-Ghani	0	b Mahmood Hussain	0
WW Hall	c Mathias b Fazal Mahmood	0	lbw b Mahmood Hussain	6
S Ramadhin	not out	0	not out	4
	(b 5, lb 3, nb 6)	14	(lb 5, nb 6)	11
	(all out)	76	(all out)	172

Bowling: Fazal Mahmood 18.3-9-34-6 Mahmood Hussain 10-1-21-1 Nasim-ul-Ghani 7-5-4-3 Haseeb Ahsan 1-0-3-0
Fazal Mahmood 27-10-66-6 Mahmood Hussain 19.5-1-48-4 Nasim-ul-Ghani 8-2-34-0 Shujauddin 6-2-13-0

Umpires: Munawar Hussain and KA Saeed

Bangabandhu National Stadium, Dhaka

Pakistan v Australia
13,14,15,17,18 November 1959

Result: Australia won by 8 wickets

Pakistan Innings				
Hanif Mohammad	b Mackay	66	b Benaud	19
Ijaz Butt	c Grout b Davidson	0	b Mackay	20
Saeed Ahmed	c Harvey b Davidson	37	b Mackay	15
W Mathias	c & b Benaud	4	lbw b Mackay	1
DA Sharpe	run out	56	lbw b Mackay	35
Wazir Mohammad	c Meckiff b Benaud	0	lbw b Benaud	5
+Imtiaz Ahmed	b Davidson	13	b Mackay	4
Israr Ali	st Grout b Benaud	7	b Benaud	1
Shujauddin	not out	2	not out	16
*Fazal Mahmood	b Benaud	1	c & b Mackay	4
Nasim-ul-Ghani	b Davidson	5	c McDonald b Benaud	0
	(b 5, lb 1, nb 3)	9	(b 7, lb 5, nb 2)	14
	(all out)	200	(all out)	134

Bowling: Davidson 23.5-7-42-4 Meckiff 10-2-33-0 Lindwall 15-1-31-0 Benaud 38-10-69-4 Mackay 19-12-16-1
Davidson 11-3-23-0 Meckiff 3-1-8-0 Lindwall 2-0-5-0 Benaud 39.3-26-42-4 Mackay 45-27-42-6

Australia Innings				
CC McDonald	lbw b Fazal Mahmood	19	not out	44
LE Favell	b Israr Ali	0	c & b Israr Ali	4
RN Harvey	b Fazal Mahmood	96	b Fazal Mahmood	30
NC O'Neill	b Nasim-ul-Ghani	2	not out	26
PJP Burge	c Imtiaz Ahmed b Nasim-ul-Ghani	0		
*R Benaud	lbw b Nasim-ul-Ghani	16		
KD Mackay	b Fazal Mahmood	7		
AK Davidson	lbw b Israr Ali	4		
+ATW Grout	not out	66		
RR Lindwall	lbw b Fazal Mahmood	4		
I Meckiff	b Fazal Mahmood	2		
	(lb 9)	9	(b 3, lb 3, nb 2)	8
	(all out)	225	(2 wickets)	112

Bowling: Fazal Mahmood 35.5-11-71-5 Israr Ali 23-5-85-2 Nasim-ul-Ghani 17-4-51-3 Shujauddin 3-0-9-0
Fazal Mahmood 20.1-4-52-1 Israr Ali 9-0-20-1 Nasim-ul-Ghani 10-2-16-0 Shujauddin 8-4-12-0 Saeed Ahmed 1-0-4-0

Umpires: AA Qureshi and KA Saeed

Pakistan v England
19,20,21,23,24 January 1962

Result: Match drawn

Pakistan Innings				
Hanif Mohammad	c Lock b Allen	111	b Allen	104
Alimuddin	c Smith b Lock	7	c Dexter b Richardson	50
Saeed Ahmed	b Knight	69	c Parfitt b Lock	13
Javed Burki	c & b Lock	140	c Knight b Lock	0
Intikhab Alam	c Barrington b Lock	18	b Lock	5
Mushtaq Mohammad	b Allen	26	c & b Allen	6
*+Imtiaz Ahmed	b Lock	0	hit wicket b Allen	0
Nasim-ul-Ghani	not out	15	c Richardson b Allen	12
Shujauddin			b Lock	0
Mohammad Munaf			b Allen	12
A D'Souza			not out	7
	(b 4, lb 3)	7	(b 5, lb 1, nb 1)	7
	(7 wickets declared)	393	(all out)	216

Bowling: Knight 29-13-52-1 Dexter 28-12-34-0 Lock 73-24-155-4 Allen 40.3-13-94-2 Barrington 11-1-39-0 Barber 11-8-12-0
Knight 14-6-19-0 Dexter 5-4-1-0 Lock 42-23-70-4 Barrington 21-13-17-0 Parfitt 8-3-14-0 Richardson 12-5-28-1 Pullar 9-3-30-0 Allen 23.1-11-30-5

England Innings				
G Pullar	c & b D'Souza	165	not out	8
RW Barber	lbw b Nasim-ul-Ghani	86		
KF Barrington	b D'Souza	84		
MJK Smith	lbw b D'Souza	10		
*ER Dexter	b Mohammad Munaf	12		
PE Richardson	c D'Souza b Nasim-ul-Ghani	19	not out	21
PH Parfitt	c & b Shujauddin	9		
BR Knight	b D'Souza	10		
DA Allen	b Shujauddin	0		
+G Millman	not out	3		
GAR Lock	c Hanif Mohammad b Shujauddin	4		
	(b 16, lb 15, nb 6)	37	(b 2, lb 6, nb 1)	9
	(all out)	439	(0 wickets)	38

Bowling: Mohammad Munaf 30-5-55-1 D'Souza 46-13-94-4 Shujauddin 34-10-73-3 Nasim-ul-Ghani 50-19-119-2 Intikhab Alam 9-0-43-0 Saeed Ahmed 12-3-18-0
Nasim-ul-Ghani 3-3-0-0 Javed Burki 2-1-3-0 Saeed Ahmed 4-2-2-0 Intikhab Alam 5-0-16-0 Hanif Mohammad 2-0-8-0

Umpires: Daud Khan and Shujauddin

Pakistan v England
28 February, 1,2,3 March 1969

Result: Match drawn

Pakistan Innings				
Mohammad Ilyas	c Knott b Snow	20	c Snow b Cottam	21
Salahuddin	c Brown b Snow	6	lbw b Underwood	5
*Saeed Ahmed	b Brown	19	c Knott b Underwood	33
Asif Iqbal	b Brown	44	b Underwood	16
Mushtaq Mohammad	c Cottam b Snow	52	c D'Oliveira b Underwood	31
Majid Khan	c Knott b Brown	27	not out	49
Hanif Mohammad	lbw b Snow	8	lbw b Underwood	8
Intikhab Alam	lbw b Underwood	25	not out	19
+Wasim Bari	c Knott b Cottam	14		
Niaz Ahmed	not out	16		
Pervez Sajjad	b Cottam	2		
	(b 4, lb 4, nb 5)	13	(lb 5, nb 8)	13
	(all out)	246	(6 wickets declared)	195

Bowling: Snow 25-5-70-4 Brown 23-8-51-3 Underwood 27-13-45-1 Cottam 27.1-6-52-2 D'Oliveira 8-1-15-0
Snow 12-7-15-0 Brown 6-1-18-0 Underwood 44-15-94-5 Cottam 30-17-43-1 D'Oliveira 9-2-12-0

England Innings				
JH Edrich	c Mushtaq Mohammad b Intikhab Alam	24	not out	12
RM Prideaux	c Hanif Mohammad b Pervez Sajjad	4	not out	18
TW Graveney	b Pervez Sajjad	46		
KWR Fletcher	c Hanif Mohammad b Saeed Ahmed	16		
*MC Cowdrey	lbw b Pervez Sajjad	7		
BL D'Oliveira	not out	114		
+APE Knott	c & b Pervez Sajjad	2		
DJ Brown	c Hanif Mohammad b Saeed Ahmed	4		
JA Snow	c Majid Khan b Niaz Ahmed	9		
DL Underwood	c Mohammad Ilyas b Mushtaq Mohammad	22		
RMH Cottam	c Hanif Mohammad b Saeed Ahmed	4		
	(b 14, lb 8)	22	(b 2, nb 1)	3
	(all out)	274	(0 wickets)	33

Bowling: Niaz Ahmed 10-4-20-1 Majid Khan 11-4-15-0 Pervez Sajjad 37-8-75-4 Saeed Ahmed 37.4-15-59-3 Intikhab Alam 26-7-65-1 Mushtaq Mohammad 11-3-18-1
Niaz Ahmed 2-0-2-0 Pervez Sajjad 3-2-1-0 Saeed Ahmed 3-2-4-0 Intikhab Alam 4-0-19-0 Asif Iqbal 4-2-2-0 Hanif Mohammad 3-2-1-0 Mohammad Ilyas 1-0-1-0

Umpires: Mohammad Gulzar Mir and Shujauddin

Pakistan v New Zealand
8,9,10,11 November 1969

Result: Match drawn

New Zealand Innings				
BAG Murray	b Asif Iqbal	7	c Asif Iqbal b Intikhab Alam	2
GM Turner	c Shafqat Rana b Pervez Sajjad	110	c Intikhab Alam b Pervez Sajjad	26
*GT Dowling	c Asif Iqbal b Intikhab Alam	15	c Wasim Bari b Intikhab Alam	2
BE Congdon	c Pervez Sajjad b Intikhab Alam	6	b Pervez Sajjad	0
BF Hastings	b Intikhab Alam	22	b Pervez Sajjad	3
MG Burgess	c Wasim Bari b Pervez Sajjad	59	not out	119
V Pollard	c Shafqat Rana b Intikhab Alam	2	b Intikhab Alam	11
DR Hadlee	c Javed Burki b Intikhab Alam	16	lbw b Intikhab Alam	0
+KJ Wadsworth	c Wasim Bari b Saleem Altaf	7	c Aftab Gul b Pervez Sajjad	0
RS Cunis	lbw b Saleem Altaf	0	b Shafqat Rana	23
HJ Howarth	not out	0	c Wasim Bari b Intikhab Alam	2
	(b 14, lb 11, nb 4)	29	(b 2, lb 8, nb 2)	12
	(all out)	273	(all out)	200

Bowling: Saleem Altaf 19.3-6-27-2 Asif Iqbal 13-4-22-1 Pervez Sajjad 48-20-66-2 Intikhab Alam 56-26-91-5 Mohammad Nazir 30-15-38-0
Saleem Altaf 11-4-18-0 Asif Iqbal 7-2-8-0 Pervez Sajjad 34-11-60-4 Intikhab Alam 39.4-13-91-5 Mohammad Nazir 3-1-3-0 Sadiq Mohammad 2-1-4-0 Aftab Baloch 2-0-2-0 Shafqat Rana 3-1-2-1

Pakistan Innings				
Aftab Gul	c & b Howarth	30	b Cunis	5
Sadiq Mohammad	c Turner b Pollard	21	b Cunis	3
Javed Burki	c Turner b Howarth	22	not out	17
Shafqat Rana	run out	65	c Dowling b Cunis	3
Aftab Baloch	lbw b Pollard	25		
Asif Iqbal	c Wadsworth b Howarth	92	b Cunis	16
*Intikhab Alam	b Howarth	20	not out	3
+Wasim Bari	not out	6		
Saleem Altaf				
Mohammad Nazir				
Pervez Sajjad				
	(b 6, lb 3)	9	(b 1, lb 3)	4
	(7 wickets declared)	290	(4 wickets)	51

Bowling: Hadlee 17-2-41-0 Cunis 23-5-65-0 Congdon 14-2-41-0 Howarth 33.1-8-85-4 Pollard 14-2-49-2
Hadlee 7-0-17-0 Cunis 7-0-21-4 Pollard 1-0-9-0

Umpires: Daud Khan and Shujauddin

Sri Lanka v Pakistan
12,13,14,15 March 1999

Result: Pakistan won by an innings and 175 runs

Sri Lanka Innings				
RP Arnold	b Shoaib Akhtar	10	c Wasim Akram b Arshad Khan	30
DA Gunawardene	c Wajahatullah b Wasim Akram	4	c Shahid Afridi b Wasim Akram	0
DPMD Jayawardene	lbw b Wasim Akram	0	c Wajahatullah b Wasim Akram	1
MS Atapattu	lbw b Saqlain Mushtaq	36	run out (Wasim Akram)	22
*PA de Silva	lbw b Arshad Khan	72	c Wajahatullah b Saqlain Mushtaq	6
HP Tillakaratne	c Wajahatullah b Arshad Khan	15	not out	55
+RS Kaluwitharana	c Yousuf Youhana b Arshad Khan	9	c & b Saqlain Mushtaq	0
UDU Chandana	c Moin Khan b Shoaib Akhtar	15	lbw b Shahid Afridi	28
WPUJC Vaas	not out	20	b Wasim Akram	0
GP Wickramasinghe	c Wajahatullah b Arshad Khan	2	b Shahid Afridi	7
KSC de Silva	c Moin Khan b Arshad Khan	11	b Saqlain Mushtaq	27
	(b 12, lb 9, nb 16)	37	(b 4, lb 7, nb 1)	12
	(all out)	231	(all out)	188

Bowling: Wasim Akram 14-2-45-2 Shoaib Akhtar 13-3-36-2 Saqlain Mushtaq 29-7-76-1 Shahid Afridi 2-0-15-0 Arshad Khan 20-5-38-5
Wasim Akram 7-0-33-3 Shoaib Akhtar 10.4-3-26-0 Saqlain Mushtaq 28.5-15-46-3 Arshad Khan 12-3-41-1 Shahid Afridi 7-1-31-2

Pakistan Innings		
Saeed Anwar	c & b Arnold	57
Wajahatullah Wasti	c Jayawardene b KSC de Silva	22
Ijaz Ahmed	st Tillakaratne b Chandana	211
Inzamam-ul-Haq	not out	200
Yousuf Youhana	c sub (Hathurusingha) b Chandana	19
Shahid Afridi	c & b Chandana	21
+Moin Khan	c KSC de Silva b Arnold	10
*Wasim Akram	c Vaas b Chandana	8
Saqlain Mushtaq	run out (Tillakaratne/Gunawardene)	4
Arshad Khan	c Tillakaratne b Chandana	3
Shoaib Akhtar	st Tillakaratne b Chandana	4
	(b 13, lb 14, nb 8)	35
	(all out)	594

Bowling: Vaas 32-4-101-0 Wickramasinghe 20-3-53-0 KSC de Silva 25.4-3-75-1 Chandana 47.5-7-179-6 PA de Silva 12-0-44-0 Arnold 37.2-7-80-2 Jayawardene 10-1-35-0

Umpires: DB Cowie (NZ) and DR Shepherd (Eng)
TV Umpire: VK Ramaswamy (Ind); Referee: CW Smith (WI)

Bangladesh v India
10,11,12,13 November 2000

Result: India won by 9 wickets

Bangladesh Innings				
Shahriar Hossain	c Ganguly b Joshi	12	lbw b Joshi	7
Mehrab Hossain	c Karim b Khan	4	c Kartik b Khan	2
Habibul Bashar	c Ganguly b Khan	71	c Khan b Agarkar	30
Aminul Islam	c Srinath b Agarkar	145	lbw b Agarkar	6
Akram Khan	c Dravid b Joshi	35	c Das b Joshi	2
Al Sahariar	lbw b Agarkar	12	c & b Joshi	6
*Naimur Rahman	c Das b Joshi	15	c Ganguly b Srinath	3
+Khaled Mashud	c Das b Joshi	32	not out	21
Mohammad Rafique	c Das b Tendulkar	22	c Ganguly b Srinath	4
Hasibul Hossain	not out	28	lbw b Srinath	0
Ranjan Das	c Ganguly b Joshi	2	c Das b Kartik	0
	(b 13, lb 6, nb 3)	22	(b 7, lb 1, nb 2)	10
	(all out)	400	(all out)	91

Bowling: Srinath 22-9-47-0 Khan 21-6-49-2 Agarkar 31-13-68-2 Joshi 45.3-8-142-5 Kartik 24-9-41-0 Tendulkar 10-2-34-1
Srinath 11-3-19-3 Khan 5-0-20-1 Agarkar 11-4-16-2 Joshi 18-5-27-3 Kartik 1.3-0-1-1

India Innings				
SS Das	b Naimur Rahman	29	not out	22
S Ramesh	b Ranjan Das	58	b Hasibul Hossain	1
M Kartik	c sub (Rajin Saleh) b Naimur Rahman	43		
R Dravid	c Al Sahariar b Mohammad Rafique	28	not out	41
SR Tendulkar	c sub (Rajin Saleh) b Naimur Rahman	18		
*SC Ganguly	c Al Sahariar b Naimur Rahman	84		
+SS Karim	st Shahriar Hossain b Naimur Rahman	15		
SB Joshi	c Al Sahariar b Mohammad Rafique	92		
AB Agarkar	c Ranjan Das b Naimur Rahman	34		
J Srinath	c & b Mohammad Rafique	2		
Z Khan	not out	7		
	(b 13, lb 4, w 2)	19		0
	(all out)	429	(1 wicket)	64

Bowling: Hasibul Hossain 19-2-60-0 Ranjan Das 19-3-64-1 Naimur Rahman 44.3-9-132-6 Mohammad Rafique 51-12-117-3 Habibul Bashar 8-0-39-0
Hasibul Hossain 6-0-31-1 Ranjan Das 3-0-8-0 Naimur Rahman 4-0-22-0 Mohammad Rafique 2-0-3-0

Umpires: SA Bucknor (WI) and DR Shepherd (Eng)
TV Umpire: Mahbubur Rahman; Referee: R Subba Row (Eng)

Bangladesh v Zimbabwe
8,9,10,11,12 November 2001

Result: Match drawn

Bangladesh Innings

Batsman	1st Innings		2nd Innings	
Javed Omar	b Streak	3	c Olonga b Marillier	35
Al Sahariar	lbw b Friend	4	c GW Flower b Friend	5
Habibul Bashar	c A Flower b Friend	0	c Murphy b Friend	65
Aminul Islam	lbw b Olonga	12	not out	6
Mohammad Ashraful	c Wishart b Olonga	0	not out	0
Khaled Mahmud	c Gripper b Friend	6		
*Naimur Rahman	b Friend	13		
+Khaled Mashud	c Carlisle b Friend	6		
Mashrafe Mortaza	c A Flower b Streak	8		
Enamul Haque	not out	24		
Manjural Islam	c Gripper b Olonga	9		
Extras	(b 3, lb 3, w 1, nb 15)	22	(b 3, lb 1, nb 10)	14
	(all out)	107	(3 wickets)	125

Bowling: Streak 18-8-30-2 Friend 18-7-31-5 Olonga 6.2-0-18-3 Murphy 6-1-22-0
Streak 11-4-25-0 Friend 11.4-2-26-2 Olonga 5-1-17-0 Murphy 12-4-37-0 Marillier 7-2-16-1

Zimbabwe Innings

DD Ebrahim	lbw b Manjural Islam	3
TR Gripper	c Javed Omar b Manjural Islam	0
SV Carlisle	c Khaled Mashud b Mashrafe Mortaza	33
GW Flower	c Al Sahariar b Mashrafe Mortaza	10
+A Flower	b Enamul Haque	28
CB Wishart	run out (Khaled Mashud)	94
DA Marillier	lbw b Enamul Haque	73
HH Streak	c Khaled Mashud b Mas'fe Mortaza	65
TJ Friend	b Enamul Haque	81
*BA Murphy	c Habibul Bashar b Mas'fe Mortaza	25
HK Olonga	not out	2
Extras	(b 4, lb 7, w 4, nb 2)	17
	(all out)	431

Bowling: Manjural Islam 26-5-74-2 Mashrafe Mortaza 32-8-106-4 Khaled Mahmud 15-2-59-0 Enamul Haque 43-13-74-3
Naimur Rahman 18-1-56-0 Mohammad Ashraful 15-3-49-0 Aminul Islam 1-0-2-0

Umpires: AFM Akhtaruddin and Mian Mohammad Aslam (Pak)
TV Umpire: Sailab Hossain; Referee: Hanumant Singh (Ind)

Bangladesh v Pakistan
9,10,11 January 2002

Result: Pakistan won by an innings and 178 runs

Bangladesh Innings

Batsman	1st Innings		2nd Innings	
Al Sahariar	lbw b Abdul Razzaq	18	lbw b Waqar Younis	21
Mehrab Hossain	c Shadab Kabir b Abdul Razzaq	11	c Inzamam-ul-Haq b Danish Kaneria	19
Mohammad Ashraful	c Yousuf Youhana b Danish Kaneria	27	c Younis Khan b Abdul Razzaq	22
Habibul Bashar	c Danish Kaneria b Waqar Younis	53	c Waqar Younis b Danish Kaneria	0
Aminul Islam	lbw b Danish Kaneria	25	lbw b Abdul Razzaq	11
Sanwar Hossain	c Inzamam-ul-Haq b Waqar Younis	3	c Shadab Kabir b Danish Kaneria	1
*+Khaled Mashud	lbw b Waqar Younis	0	c Waqar Younis b Danish Kaneria	5
Enamul Haque	c Inzamam-ul-Haq b Waqar Younis	12	b Danish Kaneria	19
Fahim Muntasir	b Waqar Younis	0	c sub (Mohammad Sami) b Danish Kaneria	33
Mohammad Sharif	b Waqar Younis	0	c Waqar Younis b Danish Kaneria	11
Manjural Islam	not out	0	not out	2
Extras	(lb 8, w 1, nb 2)	11	(lb 5, nb 3)	8
	(all out)	160	(all out)	152

Bowling: Wasim Akram 2.4-1-5-0 Waqar Younis 16.2-2-55-6 Abdul Razzaq 8.2-2-42-2 Danish Kaneria 19-5-36-2 Saqlain Mushtaq 7-2-14-0
Waqar Younis 9-3-27-1 Abdul Razzaq 10-2-29-2 Danish Kaneria 19.4-4-77-7 Saqlain Mushtaq 5-1-14-0

Pakistan Innings

Taufeeq Umar	lbw b Mohammad Sharif	53
Shadab Kabir	b Enamul Haque	55
Younis Khan	c Khaled Mashud b Enamul Haque	0
Yousuf Youhana	run out (Mehrab Hossain)	72
Saqlain Mushtaq	lbw b Enamul Haque	9
Abdul Razzaq	c Aminul Islam b Manjural Islam	134
+Rashid Latif	c Al Sahariar b Mohammad Sharif	94
Inzamam-ul-Haq	c Mehrab Hossain b Enamul Haque	43
*Waqar Younis	c Al Sahariar b Manjural Islam	8
Danish Kaneria	not out	3
Wasim Akram		
Extras	(lb 13, w 2, nb 4)	19
	(9 wickets dec)	490

Bowling: Manjural Islam 33-4-124-2 Mohammad Sharif 35-9-95-2 Fahim Muntasir 32-6-109-0 Enamul Haque 39.4-9-136-4 Mohammad Ashraful 1-0-13-0

Umpires: AFM Akhtaruddin and JH Hampshire (Eng)
TV Umpire: Mesbahuddin Ahmed; Referee: BF Hastings (NZ)

Bangladesh v West Indies
8,9,10 December 2002

Result: West Indies won by an innings and 310 runs

Bangladesh Innings

Batsman	1st Innings		2nd Innings	
Hannan Sarkar	b Collins	0	c Ganga b Drakes	25
Anwar Hossain	c Jacobs b Drakes	2	b Drakes	12
Mohammad Ashraful	c Jacobs b Collins	6	b Drakes	0
Habibul Bashar	c Ganga b Collins	24	lbw b Collins	22
Aminul Islam	lbw b Lawson	5	lbw b Lawson	12
Alok Kapali	lbw b Drakes	52	lbw b Lawson	0
*+Khaled Mashud	b Drakes	22	lbw b Lawson	0
Naimur Rahman	c Gayle b Collins	1	not out	5
Enamul Haque	b Collins	6	c Jacobs b Lawson	0
Tapash Baisya	c Jacobs b Drakes	7	b Lawson	0
Talha Jubair	not out	4	b Lawson	0
Extras	(lb 6, w 1, nb 3)	10	(b 4, lb 3, nb 4)	11
	(all out)	139	(all out)	87

Bowling: Collins 17.1-7-26-5 Drakes 18-2-61-4 Lawson 9-2-24-1 Powell 10-2-22-0
Collins 9-2-30-1 Drakes 9-3-19-3 Powell 7-1-28-0 Lawson 6.5-4-3-6

West Indies Innings

CH Gayle	c Khaled Mashud b Tapash Baisya	51
WW Hinds	c Naimur Rahman b Tapash Baisya	75
RR Sarwan	c Naimur Rahman b Talha Jubair	119
S Chanderpaul	c Khaled Mashud b Enamul Haque	4
MN Samuels	lbw b Talha Jubair	91
D Ganga	run out (Hannan Sarkar)	40
*+RD Jacobs	not out	91
VC Drakes	c sub (Al Sahariar) b Naimur Rahman	15
DB Powell	st Khaled Mashud b Mohmd Ashraful	16
PT Collins	c Habibul Bashar b Mohmd Ashraful	13
JJC Lawson	lbw b Talha Jubair	1
Extras	(lb 8, w 3, nb 9)	20
	(all out)	536

Bowling: Tapash Baisya 34-3-117-2 Talha Jubair 31-3-135-3 Naimur Rahman 36-5-118-1 Enamul Haque 46-13-101-1 Mohammad Ashraful 13-0-57-2

Umpires: DL Orchard (SA) and DR Shepherd (Eng)
TV Umpire: AFM Akhtaruddin; Referee: RS Madugalle (SL)

Bangladesh v South Africa
1,2,3,4 May 2003

Result: South Africa won by an innings and 18 runs

South Africa Innings

*GC Smith	c Mohammad Ashraful b Tapash Baisya	15
HH Gibbs	c Tapash Baisya b Mohammad Rafique	21
JA Rudolph	st Mohammad Salim b Mohammad Ashraful	71
HH Dippenaar	c Mehrab Hossain b Mohammad Rafique	1
ND McKenzie	lbw b Mohammad Rafique	7
+MV Boucher	b Mohammad Rafique	71
SM Pollock	lbw b Mashrafe Mortaza	41
RJ Peterson	c Akram Khan b Mohammad Ashraful	61
AC Dawson	c Mohammad Salim b Mohammad Rafique	10
PR Adams	b Mohammad Rafique	9
M Ntini	not out	0
Extras	(b 6, lb 6, w 1, nb 5, pen 5)	23
	(all out)	330

Bowling: Tapash Baisya 19-5-67-1 Mashrafe Mortaza 20-3-53-1 Khaled Mahmud 14-6-36-0 Mohammad Rafique 37.2-7-77-6
Alok Kapali 11-2-33-0 Mohammad Ashraful 10-0-42-2 Mehrab Hossain 2-0-5-0

Bangladesh Innings

Batsman	1st Innings		2nd Innings	
Javed Omar	c sub (AJ Hall) b Ntini	11	c Pollock b Adams	27
Mehrab Hossain	c Smith b Pollock	8	run out (Dippenaar/Boucher)	14
Habibul Bashar	lbw b Pollock	14	c Boucher b Peterson	33
Mohammad Ashraful	c Pollock b Ntini	15	c Boucher b Peterson	23
Akram Khan	c Boucher b Ntini	13	c Rudolph b Ntini	23
Alok Kapali	run out (Adams/Ntini)	1	c Ntini b Dawson	23
*Khaled Mahmud	not out	20	c sub (AJ Hall) b Peterson	0
+Mohammad Salim	c Boucher b Peterson	7	c Smith b Pollock	26
Mohammad Rafique	c Pollock b Dawson	0	c Boucher b Adams	18
Tapash Baisya	b Dawson	4	not out	8
Mashrafe Mortaza	c Dippenaar b Peterson	1	b Pollock	4
Extras	(lb 4, w 1, nb 3)	8	(b 5, w 1, nb 5)	11
	(all out)	102	(all out)	210

Bowling: Pollock 8-3-21-2 Ntini 11-4-32-3 Dawson 7-2-20-2 Peterson 8.5-1-22-2 Adams 1-0-3-0
Pollock 8-1-21-2 Ntini 12-2-37-1 Peterson 27-13-46-3 Dawson 10-5-12-1 Adams 19-3-70-2 Smith 7-0-19-0

Umpires: BF Bowden (NZ) and SA Bucknor (WI)
TV Umpire: AFM Akhtaruddin; Referee: CH Lloyd (WI)

First published 2003 Dakini Books Limited

211-212 Piccadilly
London W1J 9HG
T (44) 020 7830 9692
F (44) 020 7830 9693

www.dakinibooks.com

Publisher Lucky Dissanayake
Associate publishers Dolly Thakore, Carolyn Barripp

Editorial advisor Steven Lynch
Picture selection Rashmika Patel
Proof reader Rob Smyth
Design mrm@mrmcreative.com
Scorecard design Alexander Knight
All statistics and scorecards supplied by Wisden Cricinfo
Printed and bound in Italy

A CIP catalogue record for this book is available from the British Library

Library of Congress Cataloguing in Publication Data available

ISBN 0953 70 32 66
ISBN 0953 70 32 58 - leather edition

With special thanks to Suresh Menon, Kshema Sangakkara, Keith Meadow, Geoff Armstrong, Rick Mayston, Matt Eades, Alex Balfour, Dav Whatmore Diana Morris, Peter Milne and Jacqueline Spender.

Pictures courtesy of Patrick Eagar, Graham Morris, Giles Ridley, Don Neely, Getty Images, Empics, Trace Images, Touchline Photo. NPB Photographics, Marylebone Cricket Ground, Surrey CCC, Sydney Cricket & Sports Ground Trust, Melbourne Cricket Ground.